COMPUTER ARCHITECTURE

Concepts and Evolution

Gerrit A. Blaauw

Universiteit Twente

Frederick P. Brooks, Jr.

University of North Carolina at Chapel Hill

ADDISON-WESLEY

An imprint of Addison Wesley Longman, Inc.

Reading, Massachusetts   Harlow, England   Menlo Park, California
Berkeley, California   Don Mills, Ontario   Sydney
Bonn   Amsterdam   Tokyo   Mexico City

Reproduced by Addison-Wesley from camera-ready files supplied by the authors.

The publisher offers discounts on this book when ordered in quantity for special sales. For more information, please contact:

> Corporate & Professional Publishing Group
> Addison Wesley Longman, Inc.
> One Jacob Way
> Reading, Massachusetts 01867

Library of Congress Cataloging-in-Publication Data
Blaauw, Gerrit A., 1924–
  Computer architecture / Gerrit A. Blaauw, Frederick P. Brooks, Jr.
    p. cm.
  Includes bibliographical references and index.
  ISBN 0-201-10557-8
    1. Computer architecture. I. Brooks, Frederick P. (Frederick Phillips) II. Title.
QA76.9.A73B57   1997
004.2'2—DC20   89-6697
                                                                            CIP

Text printed on recycled and acid-free paper

ISBN 0-201-10557-8
1 2 3 4 5 6 7 8 9-DOC-00999897
First printing, February 1997

To Paula and Nancy

Preface

Our aim in this book is to give a thorough treatment of the art of computer architecture. This work is not intended primarily as a textbook, but rather as a guide and reference for the practicing architect and as a research monograph setting forth a new conceptual framework for computer architecture. We have given enough of the historical evolution that one can see not only what present practice is, but how it came to be so, as well as what has been already tried and discarded. Our goal is to display unfamiliar design alternatives, and to analyze and systematize familiar ones.

It seems useful to provide a compendium of the issues arising in the design of computer architecture, and to discuss the factors pro and con on the various known solutions to design problems. Each architect will then be able to provide his own set of weightings to these factors, as dictated by his application, his technology, and his taste and ingenuity.

Since any technical matter must be read pen-in-hand, we have provided exercises that will guide one's study, focus attention on critical points, or explore interesting byways.

Scope. We distinguish *architecture, implementation,* and *realization* as three separable concerns in the construction of anything, including computer systems. This book is about architecture—the property of a system that determines what programs run, and what results they produce. This is the aspect of a system as perceived by the user. Matters of implementation will be touched upon where they interact strongly with architecture, but implementation is not generally covered. Realization is not treated at all.

We are concerned with entire computer systems, but in a detail that diminishes as one goes outward from the central processing unit. That is, we have aimed for completeness in our coverage of central processing unit (CPU) architecture, and of input/output (I/O) subsystems. We have not covered the architecture of I/O devices, except as to their role in overall system architecture. The whole large topic of communications and terminals is similarly discussed only as it affects I/O subsystem design.

New results. Considering computer architecture as a separate concern yields many consequences that are not piecemeal publishable. Hence this book contains many results of our original research not previously published at all or not widely available:

In Chapter 1, we demonstrate the use of APL for formal description of architectures (after Falkoff, Iverson, and Sussenguth). This yields a descriptive language which is executable, usable separately to describe the implementation level, allows verification that an implementation and its architecture are consistent, and allows a denotational, rather than operational, semantics.

Chapter 1 also explores the opposing esthetic principles characterizing *good* architecture, and introduces *decision trees* as a formal tool for representing architectural choices. All the trees in Part I are components of one unified architecture decision tree.

Chapter 2 introduces the concept of architecture as programming language design and presents a new treatment of the old issue of the optimal level of such languages (for example, RISC vs. object-oriented). Iverson's dual concepts of *interpretation* and *representation* are incorporated into a general paradigm.

Chapter 3 treats the issues of machine addressing under a unified concept of naming and progressive name-binding, a concept suggested by F. Don Smith.

Chapter 4 follows Bell and Newell in treating data representation in terms of abstract datatypes.

Chapter 5 provides a unified view of invalid results in terms of the domains and ranges of representation transformations.

Chapter 6 recognizes machine-language Branch operations as *sub-primitives* and treats all sequencing operations in terms of high-level control structures.

Chapter 7 unifies the treatment of supervisory functions in terms of communicating asynchronous processes.

Chapter 8 similarly treats I/O operations in terms of concurrent asynchronous processes and their processors. The system corollaries of I/O's inherent (1) asynchrony and (2) slowness are set forth.

Overall, the least visible of the new results may prove to be the most useful:

- The attempting in Part II of exact descriptions of many architectures in a consistent language, enabling correction and criticism
- The tabulation, and comparison, of many specific features over some fifty architectures. Many of the tables in Part I are columns of one unified architectural property table.

Relationships with other works. Since we were participants in Buchholz's *Planning a Computer System* [1962], that book and this one reflect the same philosophy. This one is more general, emphasizing comparative studies of techniques across machines from many generations, designers, and manufacturers. It also reflects lessons learned and viewpoints changed since that book.

Bell and Newell's *Computer Structures* [1971], on the other hand, reflects an independent viewpoint and a different machine-designing tradition. Their treatment is masterful on many points, and they provide the first conceptual framework for computer architecture.

Bell and Newell, and its 1980 successor by Siewiorek, Bell, and Newell, provide a library of machine descriptions to which we often refer for illustration. For a selected sample of machines, we give in the Computer Zoo short sketches in a common format, plus evaluative comment. Some of our sketches cover machines they treat; most cover different and more recent machines. We have rigorously limited our discussions to real machines actually built; this provides a first screening for the utility of innovations.

Hennessy and Patterson's *Computer Architecture: A Quantitative Approach* [1990] provides a superb discussion of the "converged architecture" whose evolution and convergence is one of our themes. They document four specific instances of the converged architecture, as well as discussing architectural and implementation issues in depth, furnishing much useful data. Their book is an excellent complement to this book.

Each of us has published a related book since we began this joint work. Blaauw's *Digital System Implementation* [1976] complements this book on the hardware side, treating implementation just as this one treats architecture. Brooks's *The Mythical Man-Month* [1975, 1995] lies on the software side of this one. Chapters 4-7 of that book deal with the organization and philosophy of the architectural function in a development project. Those chapters treat the *process* of architecture design. They supplement this book, which treats the *content* of computer architecture.

Illustrative designs.   What should the architect read and study? Applications and machines. Applications as varied as possible, as innovative as possible. These are the raw materials from which he will form his own visions of usefulness.

Why machines?   To understand problems, design alternatives, and philosophies. It is sometimes fashionable to scorn all past design, seeking only the original, the radical. Experience does not prove this attitude fruitful.

J.S. Bach trained himself by hand-copying the works of his predecessors. As Tovey [1950] says, "There is no branch of music, from Palestrina onwards, conceivably accessible in Bach's time, of which we do not find specimens carefully copied in his own handwriting." Humbling his mind to this detailed study equipped him with technique and furnished his mind with hundreds of ideas. So it is with creative computer design. The most important study of the designer is other people's designs.

We have illustrated the concepts with early computers as well as recent ones. Many parts of the design space were explored in early machines, and not later. It is important for the designer to know what concepts were explored and found unfruitful, and why.

We have described the decisions and attempted to reconstruct the arguments of our predecessors and contemporaries. Since we have lived and practiced through the first two (human) generations of computer architects, we have attempted to collect, summarize, and evaluate all the experiences from 1937 to 1985. This is our legacy to architects now active and those who shall come later.

When reading the professional paper describing the architecture of a new machine, it is often difficult to discern the real design dilemmas, compromises, and struggles behind the smooth, after-the-fact description. It is sometimes possible, though risky, to guess the motives and reasoning of designers. We have occasionally made here such guesses and marked them as such.

We have participated together in the design of three computer architectures, and we have each participated separately in several more. About the motives and reasoning of these we can speak first hand, and we believe it more useful to do so than to hide behind the mask of impersonal professionalism.

So we use these experiences to illustrate the general themes and principles of design. The IBM System/360 was the first family of computers in which the architecture was clearly distinguished from the implementations; it figures prominently here. The amount of space used for such systems, especially the 360, is not intended to reflect their relative importance in the history of computer architecture; they are merely the systems we know best.

The examples of the DEC PDP11 and the IBM System/360 illustrate once more the intertwined nature of computer architecture. Just knowing the right solutions is half the problem. The other half is making all the right solutions fit with each other.

Prerequisites.   We assume familiarity with certain elements of computer science including:

- Logical design, number systems, and coding systems
- Elementary computer organization, implementation technique, and I/O technology
- Computer programming in some machine language
- Programming systems, including some knowledge of how assemblers and compilers work
- An acquaintance with a modern version of Iverson's APL language (An Appendix summarizes APL.)

Order.   The order of topics is designed for the practitioner of computer architecture. Hence the first chapter gives a certain overview and viewpoint of the subject as a whole, addressing the difficult question: What is *good* computer architecture? Students without design experience will find this viewpoint too general to have much content. We recommend that they read the first chapter lightly, then study the detailed material in Chapters 2–8, and finally return to Chapter 1 for a closer view of the general issues.

The plates.   The chapter frontispieces, evocative rather than illustrative, are from Palladio's work, *The Four Books of Architecture*. In his introduction to the Dover edition (1964), Adolf K. Placzek says:

> Andrea Palladio was . . . the spokesman for the belief in valid rules, in immutable canons, for the belief that there is a correct, a right way to design. . . . Palladianism is the conviction, first of all, that a universally applicable vocabulary of architectural forms is both desirable and possible; secondly, that such a vocabulary had been developed by the ancient Romans . . . and, thirdly, that a careful and judicious use of these forms will result in Beauty. This beauty, according to the Palladians, is therefore not only derived from ideal forms and their harmony; . . . it includes the most practical, reasonable solution of the specific problem on hand.

Computers have evolved, over fifty years, a robust "classical" architecture, whose elements produce both an esthetic delight and the most practical solutions to the design problems.

Acknowledgements   We appreciate the contribution of the Guggenheim Foundation, which generously supported Brooks for the book's crucial initial period.

The work has been mightily advanced by our secretaries and editorial assistants,

Rebekah Bierly, Victoria Baker, Steven Bellovin, Mary Mayfield, Helga Thorvaldsdottir, Larry Margolese-Malin, Scott Lane,

and especially,

Alice W. Hoogvliet-Haverkate
Sara Elizabeth Moore Jones.

Mark Smotherman, Pierre Delesalle, Jan Raatgerink, Judy Popelas, Ryutarou Ohbuchi, and Amos Omondi made substantial contributions to the scholarly work as research assistants. Gordon Hill, Richard P. Case, Harvey Cragon Richard Sites, and F. Don Smith helped by meticulous reviews and the teaching of drafts. Joey Tuttle provided the APL font. Kim Blakeley Herring helped design the figures. We are indebted also for many suggestions from the students in our annual class tests since 1977.

David Lines typeset and laid out the book, producing camera-ready copy. As important, he has played a major role in the literary and visual styling, working closely with us and with Addison-Wesley.

We thank our Lord for enabling us to do this work. "And establish thou the work of our hands upon us; yes, the work of our hands, establish thou it" (Psalm 90:17).

Enschede   1996   Chapel Hill

Table of Contents

Part I. Design Decisions

Part II. A Computer Zoo

List of Illustrations

Part I
Design Decisions

THE FIRST BOOK

OF

Andrea Palladio's
ARCHITECTURE.

CHAPTER I.

Of the several particulars that ought to be consider'd and prepar'd before we begin to build.

GREAT care ought to be taken, before a building is begun, of the several parts of the plan and elevation of the whole edifice intended to be raised : For three things, according to VITRUVIUS, ought to be considered in every fabrick, without which no edifice will deserve to be commended; and these are utility or convenience, duration and beauty. That work therefore cannot be called perfect, which should be useful and not durable, or durable and not useful, or having both these should be without beauty.

AN edifice may be esteemed commodious, when every part or member stands in its due place and fit situation, neither above or below its dignity and use; or when the *loggia's*, halls, chambers, cellars and granaries are conveniently disposed, and in their proper places.

THE strength, or duration, depends upon the walls being carried directly upright, thicker below than above, and their foundations strong and solid: observing to place the upper columns directly perpendicular over those that are underneath, and the openings of the doors and windows exactly over one another; so that the solid be upon the solid, and the void over the void.

BEAUTY will result from the form and correspondence of the whole, with respect to the several parts, of the parts with regard to each other, and of these again to the whole; that the structure may appear an entire and compleat body, wherein each member agrees with the other, and all necessary to compose what you intend to form.

WHEN those several particulars have been duly examined upon the model or draught, then an exact calculation ought to be made of the whole expence, and a timely provision made of the money, and of those materials that shall seem most necessary, to the end that nothing may be wanting, or prevent the compleating of the work. In so doing, the builder will not only be commended; but it will also be of the utmost advantage to the whole structure, if the walls are equally and expeditiously carried up : for being thus dispatch'd, they will settle proportionably, every where alike, and not be subject to those clefts so commonly found in buildings that have been finish'd at divers times.

THEREFORE, having made choice of the most skilful artists that can be had, by whose advice the work may the more judiciously be carried on, you must then provide a sufficient quantity of timber, stone, sand, lime and metals; concerning which provision I intend to lay down some very useful directions. There must also be a sufficient number of joysts, to frame the floors of the halls and chambers; which ought to be disposed and placed in such a manner, that the distance betwixt each joyst may be the width of one joyst and an half when they are framed together.

1

Introduction

1.1
What Is Computer Architecture?

The *architecture* of a computer system we define as *the minimal set of properties that determine what programs will run and what results they will produce.* The architecture is thus the system's functional appearance to its immediate user, its conceptual structure and functional behavior as seen by one who programs in machine language.

A computer's architecture is by this definition distinguished from other domains of computer design:

- The logical organization of its dataflow and controls, which we call the *implementation*
- The physical structure embodying the implementation, which we call the *realization*

Architecture concerns the specification of the *function* that is provided to the programmer, such as addressing, addition, interruption, and input/output (I/O). Implementation concerns the *method* that is used to achieve this function, such as a parallel datapath and a microprogrammed control. Realization concerns the *means* used to materialize this method, such as electrical, magnetic, mechanical, and optical devices and the powering and packaging for them. The realization also includes the visual appearance—the industrial design—of the computer.

Limiting the definition of *architecture* to a computer's functional specifications focuses attention on exactly the set of properties that enables program portability from one machine to another. Because programs are labor-intensive and modern computers have large programming systems, program compatibility is, together with speed, cost, and reliability, one of the crucial parameters of a computer.

Table 1-1 summarizes the distinctions among architecture, implementation, and realization. We shall use each term primarily to describe the *product* of that design domain, but also, at times, to denote the design *process*, and again, the design *discipline*. The distinction will be clear from the context.

Design domains	Questions	Concerns

Architecture
    Functional appearance
        (to the systems programmer)
	What?	Function

Implementation
    Logical structure
        (performs the architecture)
	How?	Method

Realization
    Physical structure
        (embodies the implementation)
	Which?
	Where?
	When?
		Means

TABLE 1-1   Domains of computer design.

1.1.1

The Domain of Architecture

Architecture as a General Design Concept

We can clarify concepts by distinguishing among the architecture, the implementation, and the realization aspects of all kinds of designs: those for buildings, bridges, airplanes, appliances, cars, computer programs, operating systems, and computers themselves. To appreciate these distinctions, let us consider clocks.

The architecture of a clock.   When children are taught to tell time, they are taught the architecture of the analog clock: the dial divided into twelfths and sixtieths, the short hand that goes around twice a day, and the long hand that goes twelve times as fast. They learn first to distinguish the hands from each other and then to relate the hands' positions to the hours and minutes. Equally important, they learn to ignore all aspects of the hands other than their lengths and angular positions. They learn that the minutes may or may not be marked, and that the hours may be labeled with Arabic or Roman numerals, or may not be numbered at all, but merely marked. Figure 1-2 shows three clock faces that conform to the essential architecture while displaying variations in industrial design.

Once children learn to distinguish the architecture from the accidents of visual appearance, they can tell time as easily from a wristwatch as from the clock on the church tower. Even a Mickey Mouse watch embodies the essential architecture. A digital clock does not; its architecture is fundamentally different.

The architecture of the clock, then, specifies the conceptual structure and functional behavior as perceived by the user. The inner structure is not at all specified by the architecture; one does not need to know what makes the clock tick to know what time it is.

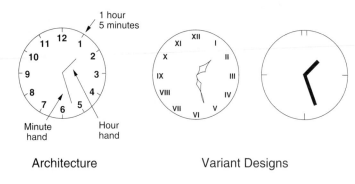

FIGURE 1-2   Architecture of the analog clock.

The implementation of a clock.   Whereas architecture tells us *what* happens, implementation tells us *how* it is made to happen. The implementation of a clock requires two major designs: how the clock is powered and how its time-keeping precision is achieved.

The standard clock architecture has seen hundreds of different implementations; for example:

- A weight, driving a pendulum
- A spring, driving a balance wheel
- A battery, driving a quartz oscillator
- A remote electrical generator, driving a synchronous motor

Any one of these implementations involves many design decisions. What period shall the pendulum have? How many gears, of how many teeth, how connected? How shall the escapement deliver power to the pendulum? How shall the weights be wound?

The implementation, then, is the logical organization of the inner structure of a designed object.

The realization of a clock.   Below the implementation lies the level of realization. Given the period of the pendulum and the number of teeth of the gears, *where* are they placed in relation to each other and *which* materials are to be used? With what geometries, strengths, tolerances, and finishes? If the clock is to be hand-made, these realization decisions are often left to the craftsman. If it is to be mass-produced, they are specified in dozens of detailed engineering drawings.

Clearly, any one implementation may have many different realizations.

Architecture as Applied to Computers

The architecture of a computer is a minimal behavioral specification— *behavioral* so that software can be written, *minimal* so that the widest possible range of excellence criteria can be chosen for implementations.

Computer architecture is like the first phase of building architecture in that it focuses on the intended *uses* and *functions* of the design. As the building architect allocates floor space and arranges the floor plan, so the computer architect allocates bits and arranges formats, to match the patterns of the user.

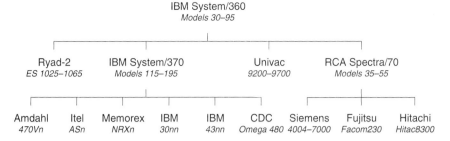

TREE 1-3   Computers with IBM System/360 architecture.

How to implement the structure comes later; the first thing is to determine what the structure is to *do*.

We believe that the term *computer architecture* was first introduced in our description of the IBM Stretch (1961) computer [Buchholz, 1962], with the same concept as set forth here but with a less precise definition. The definition was sharpened to exclude implementation and realization in our 1964 paper with G. M. Amdahl [Amdahl et al., 1964]. The three-way distinction among architecture, implementation, and realization was subsequently developed [Blaauw, 1965; 1970; 1972]. It has been followed by other authors [Fuller and Burr, 1977c; Bell et al., 1978].

The term *architecture* has been alternatively used by some authors to refer to the union of architecture and implementation. Such usage merely adds to the professional vocabulary another glamorous but ambiguous term. We find that the narrow definition and sharp distinctions of the original usage of *computer architecture* aid clarity of thought. We argue strongly for preserving these distinctions. We have no quarrel with those authors who recognize the same distinctions but use different terms—such as *behavior, structure,* and *realization*—for the domains.

Different implementations of a common architecture.   The IBM System/360 (1965) illustrates the possibility of having one architecture—as specified in the *IBM System/360 Principles of Operation* manual [IBM, 1964]—and multiple distinct implementations, originally the five Models 30, 40, 50, 65, and 75.

Because the architecture of the 360 was defined precisely and was allowed a wide range of implementation, it could readily be adopted by other manufacturers, each using its own methods of implementation. Tree 1-3 illustrates the various machines that adhere to the architecture of the 360, or to that of its successor, the IBM System/370 (1971), which (almost exactly) includes the 360's architecture.

Compatibility.   Implementations of the same architecture are called *compatible*. An upright and a grand piano are compatible, insofar as they have the same keyboard and sustain pedal.

If computer A's machine language is a perfect subset of computer B's, B is *upward compatible* from A.

Any program that runs on one of two compatible computers will run on the other, producing identical outputs for any inputs. Such program portability is what makes compatibility a fruitful concept.

Manufacturer	Machine	Date		Manufacturer	Machine	Date
Univac	1103	1953		CDC	6600	1964
	1103A	1956			6400	1966
	1105	1959			6500	1967
	1107	1962			7600	1969
	1108	1966			Cyber70	1970
	1110	1970			Cyber170	1973
IBM	702	1954		DEC	PDP11/20	1970
	705	1956			PDP11/05	1972
	705-III	1958			PDP11/45	1972
	7080	1961			PDP11/40	1973
					LSI-11	1975
IBM	701	1953			PDP11/70	1975
	704	1955			PDP11/60	1977
	709	1959			PDP11/34	1978
	7090	1959				
	7094	1963		Intel	8008	1972
	7094-II	1964			8080	1974
					8085	1976
Burroughs	B5500	1964			8086	1978
	B5700	1964			80186	1981
	B6500	1968			80286	1983
	B6700	1969			80386	1985
	B7700	1972			80486	1989

TABLE 1-4   Some computer families with similar architectures.

The desire for compatibility has encouraged the explicit, intentional defini-tion of computer architectures. With early computers, the way they turned out to work—when they worked properly—*was* the architecture. The architecture was implicitly defined by the implementation. The years proved that even an ad hoc computer architecture had a remarkably long life through successive implementations, as illustrated in Table 1-4.

As programming became a major factor in computer cost, the need for standard architectures grew: Architecture common across successive imple-mentations saves reprogramming; architecture common across models of various speeds and sizes allows wider sharing of programming costs.

Configuration.   Compatible computers are not required to have the same configuration of memory capacity and I/O devices. The configuration of a particular machine is not part of that machine's architecture, by convention. The convention is useful because configurations change frequently, and usually upward, such that the new one includes the old one or its equivalent as a subset.   Program portability requires architectural compatibility plus a sufficient configuration on the target computer.

Speed.   By universal convention, running speed, even though visible to the user, is not considered a part of computer architecture.   Programs that are to run on any realization must not be implicitly time-dependent. They may explicitly depend on values from a timer or time-of-day clock.

Validity of inputs.   Absolutely compatible computers will allow identical behavior, not only for valid inputs, but also for invalid ones. A weaker, but

still useful, *valid compatibility* requires only that the machines behave alike for valid inputs. Each version of such architectures will require its own debugging tools.

Enforcement of the specified architecture.   In most computer projects, there comes a day when it is discovered that the machine and the manual do not agree. In the confrontation that follows, the manual usually loses, for it can be changed far more quickly and cheaply than can the machine. Not so when there are compatibility constraints, whether to some ancestral machine or to other contemporary implementations. When multiple machines are being designed concurrently, the delays and costs associated with fixing an errant machine are overmatched by delays and costs in revising the machines that faithfully follow the manual. In the 360, the central processing unit (CPU) architecture, which was implemented in five different ways by five independent teams, was more successfully controlled than were the peripheral device architectures, which often had only single implementations.

This notion can be fruitfully applied whenever a language is being defined. Several interpreters or machines will surely be built sooner or later to meet various objectives. The definition will be cleaner and the discipline tighter if at least two implementations are built initially.

1.1.2

The Domain of Implementation

The implementation of a computer is a distinct design effort with its own objective, product, documentation, and quality criteria.

Objective and quality of implementation.   The objective of the implementation is a minimal *cost/performance* ratio for a given application and performance range. An indication of the quality of the design is the *scope* to which the cost/performance ratio applies. The designer must consider, at an early stage, all ramifications of cost and performance, as opposed to optimizing only against a given program benchmark or instruction mix. The overall costs include maintenance, software, and user education; they directly affect design decisions, such as whether to ignore, detect, or correct temporary malfunctions.

Designing to a given architecture is not a limitation to the implementer's creativity. The watchmaker does not feel frustrated by the conventions of the dial. On the contrary, the domain of his design contains many degrees of freedom. So it is for the designer of a computer implementation.

Different architectures with common implementation.   Model 30 of the 360 illustrates how several distinct architectures can, to a major degree, share a single implementation. A single dataflow and microcode structure implements, at various times during its operation, the architectures of a 360 CPU, a selector channel, a burst-mode multiplexor channel, a byte-mode multiplexor channel, and even an IBM 1401 (1960) computer [Brooks and Iverson, 1969, Chapter 5]!

Each architecture's implementation has a distinct microcode, although the microcode-interpreting mechanism is common. In a strict sense, therefore,

⍝ *Original implementation description:*

JKRO   Type E7

1. K out (β2320)	βout'; 7	βH3'; 4	βT12'; 5	βU0' 6
2. J out (β3002)	βout'; 20	βH0'; 16	βT10'; 17	βU12' 18
3. IJ out (β3003)	βout'; 8	βH0'; 10	βT10'; 11	βU13' 9

⍝ *Equivalent APL description:*

```
out←IJKRO;Kout;Jout;Iout
⍝ I,J,K-register readout signal
Kout←Bout∧BH3∧BT12∧BU0 ⍝ opcode B2320
Jout←Bout∧BH0∧BT10∧BU12 ⍝ opcode B3002
Iout←Bout∧BH0∧BT11∧BU12 ⍝ opcode B3003
out←Kout∨Jout∨Iout
```

PROGRAM 1-5   Implementation description of the Harvard Mark IV.

each of the four architectures has its own distinct implementation, the union of which is the IBM 2030 box. Still, it is intriguing to think of the Model 30 as a computer chameleon, taking on each architectural color in turn.

Product and documentation of implementation.   The tangible product of the implementation process is the documentation of the logical structure. Two different methods of documenting implementations were used even with the earliest computers. One was diagrams, showing components in a symbolic way and representing interconnections by lines. This representation had its origin in electrical wiring diagrams, most notably those used in electromechanical tabulating machines and electronic circuits. It eventually developed into diagrams consisting of blocks, each representing a series of statements.

The second method of representation is algebraic and was introduced by Shannon [Shannon, 1938]. It basically consists of logical statements representing the circuits. Names are used to indicate signals, and their occurrences imply the interconnections.

An early example of an algebraic description is the classical 1957 paper on the Librascope LGP30 (1957); the whole implementation was described in half a page [Frankel, 1957]. As early as 1951, however, logical statements were used to document the machine design of the Harvard Mark IV (1952; Program 1-5). The formal language describing the implementation is sometimes called a *register-transfer language*. The direct presentation of the statements is more suitable and, although originally less familiar to the electrical engineer, more easily understood.

The design process of an implementation can be viewed as a reworking of the formal-language statements of the given architecture into the formal-language statements of an implementation. Of course, the process entails many design decisions; much information is added. One can verify that a

design in fact implements the given architecture by step-by-step comparison of the two formal representations [Blaauw, 1976].

Virtual system.   A *virtual system* is one whose architectural simplicity is preserved in spite of realization limitations by means of indirectness in implementation. The automatic gear shift is such a virtual system. It presents to the driver a car without a gear shift even though the engine still requires this function.

The computers' implementations have come to resemble their architectures less and less. With faster and cheaper components, the implementer can more effectively hide the extraneous implementation characteristics.

A familiar example of a virtual function is cache memory [Wilkes, 1965]. Here, the implementation pretends to offer a large amount of information with uniform high speed, whereas actually the information resides on devices with radically different access times.

Because the virtual system is an artifice, under pressure it usually will reveal its true limitations. Thus, a car stuck in the snow may spin its wheels even though the accelerator is only slightly depressed. Such an occurrence reveals that the car really does have a hidden gear shift—one that indeed needs special control for such occasions.

In computers, as in cars, a simple virtual system may be easier to use than a complex system with a more direct implementation, but, as in cars, there is the danger that the simple architecture will not remain simple under all circumstances. For instance, a particular program may have its addresses distributed so as to miss cached information. It will then, by its slow speed, show the underlying structure, and one may need to rework it to take that structure into account.

Borderline cases.   The virtual system suggests that there are borderline cases between architecture and implementation. An example is the behavior of a system in the presence of a component malfunction. The source of the malfunction is the realization. The implementation may or may not hide the resulting errors—by error-correcting circuits, for example. The user may nevertheless need to be told of the fault via the architecture—through a program interruption, for example. Further, he may need to act via special diagnostic operations specified in the machine language but directed to the implementation, as though it were an external device.

Debating exactly how much is architecture in such a case is bootless. Even so, the architectural documentation must state clearly where the boundaries are drawn. The operation Diagnose of the 360, for example, was defined to have the same syntax for all the 360's implementations, whereas its semantics were explicitly declared to be implementation-dependent.

1.1.3

The Domain of Realization

Objective and quality of realization.   Computer realization has as its objective the economical manufacture and maintenance of computer hardware of

specified performance. The quality of a realization of a given implementation is determined by the realization's reliability and serviceability.

The design of a realization is closely tied to the evolution of components, and therefore, in contrast to the implementation, changes sharply with advancing technologies. The so-called *computer generations* are defined by their realization technologies: zeroth, relays and other electromechanical parts; first, vacuum tubes; second, discrete transistors; third, integrated transistor circuits; and fourth, large-scale integrated circuits.

Sequence versus time.   Realization concerns the *which* of component selection, such as transistor technology, and the *where* of component placement and interconnection routing. It also deals with the *when* of absolute time: the speed of components and the delays of transmission. Implementation, on the other hand, establishes relative times: the number and order of sequential logical actions. Architecture deals only with logical sequence: what must happen in succession and what may progress concurrently. In the DEC PDP11 (1970), for instance, the Instruction Address can also be used as an operand or as a data address. The user must know whether the Instruction Address is updated before or after execution of the instruction it specifies; no other timing knowledge is needed to predict the results.

Serial-number differences.   If hundreds or thousands of copies of a particular model of a computer are made, the last usually has a realization substantially different from that of the first, although the two copies embody the same architecture and implementation.   The insides of the chips and cabinets look different even to the untrained eye.   Engineering and technological improvements occur throughout the manufacturing process.   Yet not only will the same programs run unchanged (same architecture), but also the same diagnostic programs will run unchanged (same implementation).   The machines have the same logical components and connectivity; their physical components, however, may be of different types, differently placed.

Different realizations of a common implementation.   In 1959, an urgent requirement from the U.S. Department of Defense for computers for the Ballistic Missile Early Warning System radar network imposed an almost-impossible schedule on the engineers of the IBM 7090 (1959), a second-generation transistorized scientific computer. To meet this schedule, they adopted essentially without change the architecture of the IBM 709 (1959), a first-generation vacuum-tube computer.   Moreover, they adopted the 709's implementation essentially unchanged.   The entire logical organization—dataflow, control sequences, timing-pulse structures—was carried over wholesale into a totally new realization, one whose technology was in turn adopted wholesale from the Stretch computer.   The 7090 had Stretch memories, transistors, circuits, cards, frames, power supplies; it realized a 709 implementation with a clock frequency exactly six times that of the 709.

Although the 7090 implementation and the Stretch implementation shared a common realization *technology*, they did not share a common realization; each realization embodied a different implementation.

In summary, one architecture may have many implementations, and one implementation may have many realizations.   Conversely, one realization

technology may be used to realize many implementations, and one logical organization may be used to implement several architectures.

Product and documentation of realization.   The product of the realization design is the drawings and lists for the production process.

1.1.4
Why Distinguish Design Domains?

The characteristics of each of the three design domains are summarized in Table 1-6.

Setting up precisely defined fences among architecture, implementation, and realization does not prevent designers from looking across them. The genius of Seymour Cray's work lies precisely in his total personal control of all three design domains and his consequent freedom in making trades across the fences. Yet, stating precisely when and how one domain affects another allows greater freedom of design in each domain, even if all are in one mind. It also avoids many errors.

Division of Labor

The need to make distinctions among architecture, implementation, and realization arises first from the need somehow to divide the labor of design. No one person can possibly do *all* the work of designing a computer so quickly that a product conceivable when begun will still be competitive when finished.

Horizontal subdivision.   Given the necessity of dividing the task of design, the question becomes how to make the division. A standard division is the horizontal one, shown in Figure 1-7, in which someone partitions the system into parts, and a designer is responsible for each part. Such a subdivision is called *horizontal subdivision.*

	Architecture	Implementation	Realization
Purpose	function	cost and performance	build and maintain
Product	*Principles of Operation*	logical design	release documents for manufacturing
Language	natural and formal	block diagrams and expressions	lists and drawings
Quality	consistency	broad scope	speed, reliability

TABLE 1-6   Characteristics of design domains.

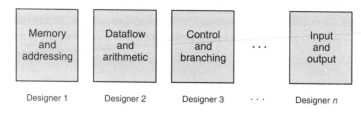

Memory and addressing	Dataflow and arithmetic	Control and branching	· · ·	Input and output
Designer 1	Designer 2	Designer 3	· · ·	Designer n

FIGURE 1-7   Horizontal subdivision of the design task.

This method has four drawbacks. First, the most fundamental task is the determination of the partitions, and this must be undertaken without much knowledge of what one will encounter in the design process. Melvin Conway [1968] says that any system design will therefore reflect the structure of the organization that designs it. In short, although one theoretically builds the team structure to reflect the desired design, the converse more often happens.

Second, when one first partitions a computer system, the parts may be quite disproportionate. In particular, the CPU is so massive in its logical detail that its design must in turn be partitioned—a partitioning that is very difficult.

Third, the horizontal division leaves the designer of each piece concerned with all design domains: the functions of the piece and the language by which they are invoked, the organization of elements for implementing these functions, and the arrangement of elements for realizing that implementation. Each domain involves separate technologies, and the designer must be a master of each.

The final and most serious drawback of horizontal division is that the *user*—the one on whose behalf the design is being undertaken—sees only one part of the design of each piece: the language by which its function is invoked. But he sees the language parts of all the pieces, and horizontal division ensures that the language concepts of the parts will be different. The ensemble is sure to be hard to use.

Vertical subdivision.   The obvious alternative to dividing the task horizontally is to divide it vertically (Figure 1-8).

Here the design of function and of language for invoking function is separated from the design of the logical organization; in turn, the latter is separated from the design of the components and of their placements in phys-

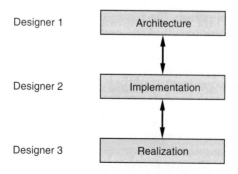

FIGURE 1-8   Vertical subdivision of the design task.

ical assemblies. The opportunities for misunderstanding and inefficiency are now quite different: A function and its implementation may be mismatched, or the implementation may be peculiarly awkward to realize with available technology. Each designer needs a working knowledge of the domain below his own, as well as of that above.

Conceptual Integrity

The inherent and fundamental advantage of vertical subdivision is that the architecture, the implementation, and the realization each capture the conceptual integrity of a single unified design approach. Most important, the outermost unit across which conceptual integrity is preserved—the function and the language for invoking it—is the unit that must be comprehended by the single mind of the user. By dividing so that its design is done by a single mind, one best ensures that the result will be readily comprehensible to the user's single mind. The result is a *consistent*—that is, conceptually integrated—design *as perceived by the user*.

That good design demands conceptual unity has long been recognized. Descartes, in his *Discourse on Method*, observes:

> ... there is frequently less perfection in a work ... produced by several persons than in one produced by a single hand. Thus we notice that buildings conceived and completed by a single architect are usually more beautiful and better planned than those remodeled by several persons .... [Descartes, 1637]

Consistency of concept demands, we think, that an architecture specification be written by a single person, or by two operating as a coauthoring team for the entire work. Each paragraph of a manual embodies microdecisions too small ever to claim attention or debate by any reviewer. Yet it is the consistency of these hundreds of microdecisions that gives unity to a design.

Too big?   But, some may object, this labor is too vast to be performed by one person. The pressures that led to the separation of architecture from implementation likewise demand the partitioning of the architectural task.

Two rejoinders are in order. First, there are indeed techniques available by which one person can be so supported by a team that his productivity is greatly enhanced. The span of conceptual unity can thus be broadened beyond normal reach. The same techniques support a surgeon in the busy loneliness of the operating room, or a trial lawyer in an intricate and subtle case. Their application to computer programming has been detailed by H. Mills [1971] and elaborated elsewhere in the literature [Baker, 1972; Brooks, 1975]. The key notion is that all tasks not involving design decisions are lifted off the architect, so that his complete attention can be given to design. Conversely, all the tasks of the team that do involve design decisions are concentrated in his hands.

The more radical answer to the "too big" objection is that if, after all techniques to make the task manageable by a single mind have been applied, the architectural task is still so large and complex that it cannot be done in that way, *the product conceived is too complex to be usable and should not be built*. In other words, the mind of a single user must comprehend a computer

architecture. If a planned architecture cannot be designed by a single mind, it cannot be comprehended by one.

We have in our own experience seen one such computer system designed. Its complexity was indeed fatal; it was never built.

Too slow?   Another objection concerns timing and phasing. Will the many implementers not have to sit idle while the specifications come through the narrow funnel that is the architecture team? A quick solution is to refrain from engaging implementers until the specifications are complete. This is what is done when a building is constructed.

In the computer-systems business, however, the pace is quicker, and one wants to compress the schedule as much as possible. How much can specification and building be overlapped? It turns out that architecture, implementation, and realization can in fact begin in parallel and proceed simultaneously.

For example, the implementers can start as soon as they have even vague assumptions about the manual, somewhat clearer ideas about the technology, and well-defined cost and performance objectives. They can begin selecting arithmetic algorithms, designing dataflows, control sequences, and so on. They devise or adapt the tools they will need, especially the record-keeping system, including the design-automation system.

Meanwhile, at the realization level, circuits, cards, cables, frames, power supplies, and memories must each be designed, refined, and documented. This work proceeds in parallel with architecture and implementation.

Conceptual integrity does require that a system reflect a single philosophy and that the specification as seen by the user flow from few minds. Yet, the real division of labor into architecture, implementation, and realization does not imply that a system so designed will take longer to build. Experience shows the opposite—the integral system goes together faster and takes less time to test. In effect, a wide horizontal division of labor has been sharply reduced by a vertical division of labor, and the result is radically simplified communications and improved conceptual integrity.

1.1.5

The Nature of Computer Architecture

The Level and Scope of Computer Architecture

We stated earlier that the term *architecture* can be applied to all kinds of designs—for example, to the designs of an application language, an operating system, a programming language, a machine language, a microcode language, or the specification of a storage unit (Figure 1-9).

Level.   In those cases where an architecture is implemented in another architecture, as for a compiler implemented in an assembly language, we can speak of *vertical recursion*. Thus, one or two levels of microcoding are often found below the machine-language level. Each of these levels has an architecture and an implementation. Only the lowest has a realization.

Vertical recursion is widely recognized in computer science and is referred to under various names, such as *levels of abstraction*, or *layers*. Since it implies

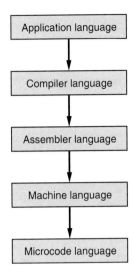

FIGURE 1-9   Vertical recursion of architecture.

that the detail of the implementation is not part of the architecture, it is also called *information hiding* [Parnas, 1972].

Scope.   A design that is partitioned horizontally consists of memory, processors, and peripheral units (Tree 1-10). Each has an architecture, an implementation, and a realization. In talking about an architecture, then, one must be clear about what is included. There is considerable difference between a microprocessor and a microcomputer.

Unless explicitly stated otherwise, we use the term *architecture* in this text to refer only to the machine-language level of a complete computer system.

Computer Architecture as Language

Computer programmers have a somewhat Platonic view of reality with respect to computers. To them the "real" computer is that entity described in the *Principles of Operation*, just as to Plato the "real" table is an ideal existing somewhere in "heaven." The machine models purring busily, but occasionally errantly, on the computer-room floor are but the imperfect images, Plato's shadows, of the real thing [Plato, *Republic* Book VI]. Programmers use, in implementing their own logical constructions, only the architecture of the computer—its machine language.

Machine language.   Every computer is an interpreter of its machine language.

We define *machine language* to be that representation of programs that resides in memory and is interpreted (executed) directly by the hardware. It usually consists of a string of bits. From this point of view, the design of a computer's architecture is the design of that computer's machine language. Because language design is a major subject of computer science, this viewpoint is unifying and fruitful.

If, however, we consider the machine language to be just one of the many programming languages related to a computer, as sketched in the vertical

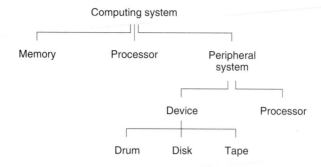

TREE 1-10   Horizontal partitioning of computer architecture.

recursion of Figure 1-9, we must answer the questions of how and why machine languages differ from other programming languages.

Costliness.   Although machine languages are often simpler and more constrained than many other programming languages, there is only one essential difference: In machine language the *expressions are costly*.

Conciseness.   The criterion of costliness is measured in *space* (the number of components of logic and memory that are used) and *time* (the delay caused by the components that are traversed).   Each operator and variable in the vocabulary must be implemented and realized by the interpreting mechanism. Each bit in a machine-language program occupies a costly memory cell and must be obtained from that cell at the expense of costly time.   So costliness urges *conciseness*—economy of expression.

Conciseness is a central consideration in design.   It manifests itself in compactness of representation, sparsity and simplicity of constructs, and independence of interpretation.

Bit budget.   Whereas the implementer counts logical elements, and the realizer counts components, square microns of silicon, microns or millimeters of connection, and watts, the architect counts bits of representation in his first-instance budget, the *bit budget*.

Bit traffic.   Furthermore, computer technologies from the very beginning have been of such a nature that the critical factor limiting the performance of a computer is the *memory bandwidth*, the number of bits per second the memory subsystem can deliver.   When memory bandwidth is limiting, each additional bit in a machine-language program slows its execution.   The architect therefore wants to reduce the *bit traffic* between the memory and the processor.

Few constructs.   The number of types of utterances affects cost, because each type requires some interpretation activity unique to it.   Specifying a type costs also according to (the logarithm of) the number from which selection is made. So sparsity of operations, of addressing modes, and of possible addresses all contribute to conciseness.

Simple constructs.   Not only the number, but also the complexity of constructs affect costs.   Complex constructs require costlier implementations of their semantics.   Moreover, one can often reduce both gain costs and power by decomposing them into simpler but more general constructs.

Independent interpretability.   The cost of executing machine-language state-ments is sharply reduced if each statement can be interpreted independently. Compilation, which requires scanning of the program as a whole, violates this criterion. Interpretation of languages such as APL or Basic also violates it, in that it requires symbol tables to be built and maintained.

Summary.   The design process of computer architecture is the *design of a programming language when expressions are costly.*

The costliness constraint has the nature of an economic, not a physical, law. One can violate it, but competition from within the design environment or from the marketplace is a strong enforcer.

The corollaries are developed in Chapter 2.

1.1.6
Bibliography

Amdahl et al. [1964], Baker [1972], Bell et al. [1978], Blaauw [1965; 1970; 1972; 1976], Brooks and Iverson [1969], Brooks [1975], Buchholz [1962], Conway [1968], Descartes [1637], Frankel [1957], Fuller and Burr [1977c], IBM [1964], Mills [1971], Parnas [1972], Piepho and Wu [1989], Shannon [1938], Wilkes [1965].

1.2
The Design of Computer Architecture

Computer architecture is not just a matter of judgment and taste. On the contrary, design decisions can usually be based on quantitative analysis of the applications for which a machine is intended and of the technology in which it will be built. So architectural arguments become, in the final analysis, frequency arguments: How shall the bit budget best be used? How shall the bit traffic be utilized most effectively?

Still, computer architecture has not become a cut-and-dried mechanical application of formulas, nor does it threaten to become so soon. The fre-quencies that determine design decisions are those frequencies *expected* to be experienced in an *estimated* application mix within some *particular vision* of the future. So there is still abundant scope for judgment and for argument.

Matching Needs and Means

We consider first the role of the computer architect in matching the needs of the user and the means of the realization. We then identify the key design steps that constitute the task.

The user's agent.   The architect's chief role is to serve as the *user's agent*, applying his training and experience to the design as the user would himself, if he could.

Those people associated with designing a computer system naturally reflect diverse interests that have inherent conflicts. The market-requirements specialist, with sales orientation, perceives most clearly the new functions

and features that a system should have to distinguish it from its known competitors. He feels equally strongly the necessity for the price to be low. But differentials of function become apparent long before differentials of cost, much less differentials of price, so his pressure is usually for more function.

Similarly, the system programmer brings unique perceptions—those pertaining to ease of use under his special and restrictive circumstances. The implementing engineer likewise has very clear cost, speed, and schedule targets against which to measure his success.

Someone must balance these conflicting interests. The result is best if this person is especially and solely charged with giving the best overall value to the user, if his focus on that interest is not clouded by any competing interests.

We see the architect as the balancer. He must be familiar with users' applications, with programming languages, with implementing techniques, and with available technologies. He must be a skilled estimator of the marginal usefulness of proposed functions, a probing asker of technological questions, and an inventor of new approaches.

A vision of usefulness.   Besides, beyond, and more important than possessing all these skills, the architect must bring to the design his own unique *vision of usefulness* for the computer. Whereas most buildings are each built for one client, each computer is built for a *set of users*. The architect must characterize the set of intended users and must project their applications.

Since computer designs must begin 2 to 5 years before product shipment, and since architectures endure at least 10 years after first shipment, the vision of usefulness is always largely a vision of the future; it is never a mere measurement of today's perceived needs and means. Users, and the marketers who serve them, will readily see today's need, and next year's. The architect must listen carefully to what they see, but he must not stop with that. From the most imaginative users he will get sparklike glimpses of the 5-year need; by careful questioning he must fan these to little flames of insight into the 10-year need. Similarly, the architect must develop a sound feel for the evolution of realization technology. He must consider not only the technology for the first models to be built, but also that for successor machines.

Developing a vision of the future is a special function of the architect. No one else can do it for him; everyone else must contribute. Whether explicit or not, his vision of usefulness will guide every decision, every detail of design.

Design steps.   Since computer-architecture design is language design, it can be characterized as the selection of language primitives and the syntax for combining them. The various design possibilities from which a selection is made we call   *architectural alternatives*.   The alternatives may concern a function's presence or absence (as for a square-root operation), or its form (such as the manner of recording and absorbing the carry in an extended-precision addition).

How to choose among possible designs? The center of Figure 1-11 shows a set of architectural alternatives. Above them are the desiderata of the user, represented by their *application set*, from which the user functions, identified as *programming primitives*, are derived; below are the potentialities of the builder,

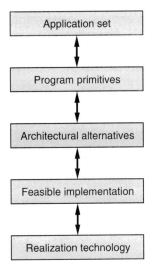

FIGURE 1-11   A design paradigm.

embodied in a *feasible implementation*, which is based on the resources of the *realization technology*.

An application set might be engineering computing, and a program primitive might be a square root, which might be executed either as a subroutine or as a single operation. The feasible implementation might be a square-root algorithm, giving a rough cost and performance indication of a square-root operation. From this information one can assess the differences between a separate operation and a subroutine in equipment cost, program space, and execution speed.

The paradigm indicated by Figure 1-11 is applied universally. What else can a designer do than to see how well his design suits the needs of the user and what demands it makes on the means of the builder? But the question is: How shall the method be applied systematically? Since this book uses this design paradigm extensively, let us briefly consider each of its constituent parts.

1.2.1
Application Set

Probably the hardest part of the design of an architecture is the definition of the product to be designed. As we have seen, the architect serves as agent for the set of intended users. He must assess and extrapolate their present needs, and envision modes of operation they do not yet imagine.

Before he can do that, however, he must identify clearly and precisely whom the user set is intended to include. This task is central not only to product coherence, but also to product success, so the architect will usually have a great deal of help from marketers and managers.

Dimensions of the User Set

The intended user set can be conceived as a subspace within the space of all computer users. These spaces can be described within five dimensions:

- **Industry.** One dimension is the intended industries of use. Examples are petroleum; paper; automotive; airlines; retail; and education.
- **Application.** Applications have much in common across industry lines. General purpose computers are more often characterized by sets of applications than by industries of applicability. Examples of applications are payroll, general ledger, inventory control, mailing-list maintenance, solving partial differential equations, and database management.
- **System model.** A few system strategies can each address many applications. Examples of system models are batch, inquiry, interactive updating, mixed on-line and batch, and interactive program building.
- **System power.** Power includes many parameters, such as processor speed, auxiliary-store speed, memory size, and auxiliary-store size. The required power of a system will be dominated by different subdimensions for different applications [Bell and Newell, 1971].
- **System dedication.** Will the system be dedicated to one application, switched from application to application while doing only one at a time, or time-shared among many tasks?

Within this five-dimensional user space, particular uses are points:

- A dedicated airlines-reservation (interactive-inventory) system capable of handling 25,000 transactions per hour
- A dedicated educational time-sharing system supporting 32 Basic users
- A batch-sequenced, uniprogrammed business computer for payroll with file-passing requirements of 250,000 records per month
- An aerospace, batch-sequenced, uniprogrammed computer for partial differential equations, operating at 500 million floating-point instructions per second and holding 32 megabytes (MB) in main memory
- A personal dedicated text-processing system, fast enough for one user and equipped with at least 80 MB of on-line file

Current, Extended, and Future Applications

Current set.   The intended user set determines the current application set. From this set the performance and cost targets follow—one can readily establish what a design must do to be more useful than today's designs on today's tasks.

Extended set.   Next, the architect must extrapolate these applications over the lifetime of the design. Weather problems for North America have been calculated on meshes that have been steadily refined from thousands of miles per grid point to 250 miles per grid point. The models have moved from strict two-dimensional grids to two-and-one-half–dimensional models with seven or more layers. Extrapolation tells that the models of tomorrow will have more layers, and grid points only scores of miles apart.

Future set.   Extrapolation is not enough. The vision of usefulness must stretch beyond the current and extended application set. Totally new application techniques have always awaited more power or cheaper computing. The finite-element method of structural analysis is an example. So is interactive program building.

The 360, for example, included communication-based systems, of a kind and extent not then current, as a new application. The handling of substantial amounts of natural-language text was another new application. From a close look at such a set, specific technical requirements can be formulated. For the 360 text-processing set, we derived specific needs; they were for:

- A character set of at least 96, preferably 128, characters
- An easy-to-manipulate representation of these characters in the computer memory (we chose the 8-bit byte)
- New tape drives, disks, and so on, for this byte size
- Variable-length character-string data and operations
- Special operations for editing and searching character strings (Translate, Translate And Test)
- A high-speed printer adaptable to use of large character sets (the 1403 changeable-chain printer)
- A keyboard-entry system for the larger character set (the 2260 terminal, the 029 keypunch)
- A high-level language capability for large character sets and for character strings (PL/I features)

If a new application is to be realized, *all* the identified needs must be met, and its users must be specifically courted when the product is marketed.

1.2.2

Program Primitives

The elementary actions or resources that machine-language programmers desire to have available are called *program primitives*. The total set must allow them to express themselves completely and efficiently. The primitives are *elementary* in the sense that each is an atomic function; when one needs a primitive, one needs all its action, not some part thereof.

The programmer's wishes may not be economically realizable. Still, it is useful to know what he desires. Otherwise, the architect's perception of hardware limitations will restrain his demands, and limited hardware will then seem to be justified.

Some designers of the Manchester MU3, which later became the Ferranti Atlas (1962), saw the need for the one-level store. The function appeared to them to be too expensive to implement, but they proposed it anyway. They found that technology and invention had progressed to the point of making such a function feasible.

Ranking.   When, on the other hand, a desired primitive has been requested and rejected, the system programmers must express their next-best primitive for the same function. It would be ideal if the mathematical concept of a real

number were available as a program primitive. Since this primitive implies an unlimited representation range, it can hardly be implemented. So the question must be addressed again, with lowered sights. The programmer might request a variable representation range with constant relative precision (floating point), or, if this is also too expensive, some machine aids for programmed scaling.

As this discussion shows, there is a ranking among alternative primitives for any function. Some primitive is ideal, but if it is too costly there are second and third alternative formulations, progressively harder to use but easier to implement.

Source.   The builders of operating systems and compilers, even though they work in a high-level language, produce code that ultimately translates into the new machine language for interpretation. Since they are the first users to do so, they are the most obvious source of the set of programming primitives that will be needed by any user of the machine language; the system programmer becomes a rich source of feedback before it is too late to amend the architecture.

The programming primitives derived from the source language of operating systems and compilers want direct analogs in the machine language; the correspondence between the two should be free from minor exceptions and side effects. Since the more subtle effects will not show up until the system software is built, interaction between the architect and the system programmers must be continuous and prolonged.

Specification.   Each program primitive proposed must be specified completely and precisely, when proposed, to avoid discrepant conceptions about its actual functioning. Such misconceptions have resulted in classic mistakes. Architects have built functions that did roughly what the programmers wanted, but failed just enough to miss real usefulness. Edit For Print on the IBM 705 (1956, Program 12-44) is a good example.

Devising a formal statement of each program primitive is in itself very useful. Once a formal description is available, an equivalent program can be obtained that is constructed from any particular set of proposed machine functions.

Frequency.   Current experiences in computer use furnish frequency data on programming primitives that help predict what frequencies will be seen in the future. The prudent architect will build a lifetime file of all such frequency data he can find.

Published data give operation-code dynamic frequencies for several computers, the exponent differences of floating-point operands, the frequency of recomplementation for algebraic sums, and the lengths of decimal numbers in business files. These data illuminate design decisions; we quote them at appropriate places. Hennessy and Patterson [1990] give lots of data.

A discipline that will open an architect's eyes is to assign to each little function an estimated value before implementation begins: Primitive x is worth not more than m bytes of microcode and n microseconds per invocation. These values will direct initial decisions and will serve during implementation as a guide and warning to all.

1.2.3

Feasible Implementation

A *feasible* or *initial implementation* is an algorithm that adheres to the given architecture, but is expressed in terms whose implementation with dataflow, controls, and logical operators is straightforward [Blaauw, 1976]. Its purpose is to show that there exists a way to implement the specified architecture.

Implementation Design

Computer implementation is a well-established design discipline, so most architectures are readily implemented, and the implementer usually needs no suggestions from the architect.

Occasionally, however, an architect must supplement his specification by a feasible implementation, because there is no known art or because the straightforward solution is inefficient. The concept of lookaside tables was furnished as a feasible implementation for the architecture of the address translation of the 360's Model 67, because a more direct implementation would have been far too slow.

Similarly, if one specifies the Least Recently Used (LRU) algorithm as part of some architectural specification, it might be useful to furnish a feasible implementation. The name LRU, and the architecture of Program 1-12, suggest implementing with a list of identifiers (lrul) ordered according to the time elapsed since the corresponding resource was last used. When a resource is used, its identifier must be moved to the head of the list. Such an implementation can be built, but it is so awkward that the implementer might properly consider specification of the LRU function to be extravagant. In such

```
A Architecture

archru in                               lrul
A recently used input          3 4 6 1 0 5 7 2
lrul←(2⊥in),(lrul≠2⊥in)/lrul


out←archlru
A least-recently used output
out←,(3ρ2)⊤¯1↑lrul

A Implementation

impru in                                lrum
A recently used input          0 0 1 0 0 0 1 0 1
lrum[2⊥in;]←1                  1 0 1 0 0 1 0 1
lrum[;2⊥in]←0                  0 0 0 0 0 0 0 0 0
                              1 1 1 0 1 1 1 1
                              1 1 1 0 0 1 1 1
out←implru                     0 0 1 0 0 0 0 1
A least-recently used output   1 1 1 0 0 1 0 1
out←encode8~∨/lrum             0 0 1 0 0 0 0 0
```

Legend: encode8 = one-out-of-eight to binary encoder.

PROGRAM 1-12   An efficient feasible implementation of LRU algorithm.

a case, the architect has an obligation to furnish a feasible implementation that is plausibly efficient.

An efficient, feasible implementation for n resources uses an $n \times n$ square matrix of 1-bit registers `lrum` (Program 1-12). As a resource is used, the corresponding row in `lrum` is made 1 and the corresponding column is made 0. An all-zeros row now indicates the least-recently-used resource. As a further refinement, only a triangle of registers below or above the main diagonal need be built. Since such an implementation is not immediately obvious, the architect should furnish it.

When to quit.   Only the principle of the feasible implementation need be given. The architect does not necessarily know the details, interfaces, and constraints of the particular implementation context; the implementer will usually improve the design as well.

Implementation Cost

The computer architect is a designer, and the design process is basically the same for him as for any other designer.

Design is the process of synthesizing new form to satisfy a set of desiderata, subject to a cost function [Alexander, 1964]. Usually there are minimum standards set for some desiderata and maximum limits for some cost components—for example, "Total power requirements may not exceed 5 KVA."

For computer architecture, the desiderata are the program primitives, weighted by their estimated frequencies, and the cost function is the long-run, overall cost of implementation for a given realization technology.

Cost estimate.   The architect of a building works against a budget, using estimating techniques that are later confirmed or corrected by the contractors' bids. It often happens that all the bids exceed the budget. The architect then revises his estimating technique upward and his design downward for another iteration. He may suggest to the contractors ways to implement his design more cheaply than they had devised. The implementer, in turn, may counter by suggesting changes to the architecture. Often the implementer is right—some minor feature may have unexpectedly large costs when the implementation is worked out.

An analogous process governs the design of a computer or programming system. In this case, though, the architect has the advantage of getting bids from the contractor at many early points in the design, almost any time he asks for them. The architect usually has the disadvantage of working with only one contractor, who can raise or lower his estimates to reflect his pleasure with the design. In practice, early and continuous communication can give the architect good cost readings and the builder confidence in the design without blurring the clear division of responsibilities [Brooks, 1975, Chapter 5].

Technological ratios.   The *absolute* costs and performances of a computer's technologies do not determine that computer's architecture. That is, if the cost of all components falls *by the same proportion* for each, the fall will not influence any architectural decision. Likewise, if the speeds of all components increase proportionately, no architectural decision will be influenced.

In practice, this exactly proportionate decrease or increase never happens. But observe that it is *technological ratios* that influence architectural decisions. As the ratio

$$\frac{cost\ per\ bit\ of\ internal\ memory}{cost\ per\ bit\ of\ backing\ store}$$

drops, the optimal size of internal memories becomes larger, and more address bits must be provided.

The other especially significant cost ratios are memory to logic, electronics to mechanical I/O, development cost to manufacturing cost, and hardware cost to software cost.

Performance ratios are also crucial: memory access to backing-store access, memory speed to logic speed, and memory access time to memory data rate.

Case's ratio.   Some application characteristics appear to be invariant over a broad spectrum of applications and performances, leading to some heuristic rules. Case, for example, finds an invariant ratio between memory size and CPU speed in well-balanced systems:

$$\frac{instructions\ per\ second}{bytes\ of\ memory} = 1$$

By this rule, a 16-million-instructions-per-second (MIPS) computer needs a 16-MB memory to be balanced [Case, 1970].

Amdahl 's rule.   Similarly, Amdahl finds an invariant ratio between internal processing and I/O traffic:

$$\frac{bits\ of\ input/output\ per\ second}{instructions\ executed\ per\ second} = 1$$

Amdahl also observes that housekeeping operations—those used for controlling I/O and for calculating addresses—occupied some 40 percent of all instruction executions, a ratio holding constant for at least a decade [Amdahl, 1970].

1.2.4

Architectural Alternatives

Much of this book is a discussion of architectural alternatives. We attempt a comprehensive representation of historic and current solutions to many architectural questions.

Classifying Alternatives

Most computer-architecture designs evolved from several alternative proposals. Such was the case for the 360 and for the DEC VAX11 (1978) [Strecker, 1978]. Not only the overall design structure, but also the various design details are decided by evaluation of competing alternatives. This suggests that the architectural alternatives can be classified hierarchically.

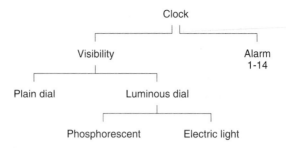

TREE 1-13   Partial design choices for an analog alarm clock.

Design tree.   In Section 2.1 we shall develop the generic principle of classification that we apply throughout this book. We represent this classification with *design trees*.

Branch types.   Tree 1-13 gives an example of a design tree. In it and in Tree 1-14 we observe two types of branches, indicated by open and closed roots. The first type, as shown for Alarm (Tree 1-14), shows a subdivision; each leaf is a different design attribute that must be specified. This is called an *attribute branch*. The second type of branch, as shown for Sound, enumerates alternatives; one or more can be chosen. We call this an *alternative branch*.

In Tree 1-13 the main hierarchy is that of the attributes; a minor hierarchy may appear within a domain, as for Visibility.

Tree structure.   Some trees are broken into two or more fragments. The bottom part expands the concept of the leaf in the top part that is labeled with the same term. All computer-architecture trees are parts of one gigantic tree. For ease of representation, they are divided into segments that reflect conceptual chunks and fit the page. The interconnection of trees is indicated by figure numbers set under a term that is expanded later, and over a term that links to the parent tree. This practice also allows the parts of a design tree to be placed with the corresponding discussion.

Emphasis.   In all design trees the choices that are common—although not necessarily preferred—are set in boldface. In Tree 1-14, for example, Buzzer has been emboldened, since it is more common than Melody or Radio. The computer-architecture design trees also give a typical machine example, usually an early or especially prominent one.

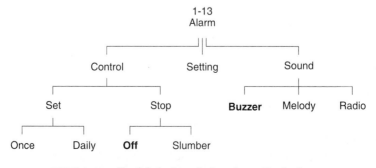

TREE 1-14   Partial design choices for a clock alarm.

	Announced/ paper	Delivered/ operational	Family	Architect/ author	Z
Difference Engine	1833	1843		Babbage	Z
Harvard Mark I	1938	1944		Aiken	Z
Zuse Z4	1941	1945	Z3	Zuse	Z
Cambridge EDSAC	1948	1949	IAS	Wilkes	Z
Ferranti Mark 1	1948	1951	MU1	Kilburn	Z
Univac I	1945	1951	Binac	Eckert	Z
Princeton IAS	1946	1952		Burks	Z
Harvard Mark IV	1949	1952		Aiken	
IBM 701	1952	1953	IAS	Rochester	Z
IBM 650	1953	1954		Hughes	Z
IBM 702	1953	1954		Phelps	
IBM NORC	1954	1954		Havens	
IBM 704	1954	1955	IBM 701	Amdahl	Z
IBM 705	1954	1956	IBM 702	Buchholz	Z
Univac 1103A	1953	1956	Univac 1103	Cohen	Z
Librascope LGP30	1956	1957		Frankel	
STC ZEBRA	1956	1959		Van der Poel	Z
Lincoln Lab TX2	1957	1959	TX0	Forgie	
Bull Gamma 60	1957	1960		Dreyfus	Z
IBM 1401	1959	1960		Underwood	Z
IBM 1620	1959	1960		Jones	
IBM 7070	1958	1960	IBM 650	Morley	
CDC 1604		1960		Cray	

Legend: Z = Detailed in the Computer Zoo; only first author listed.

TABLE 1-15   Origins of various machines (up to 1960).

Parameter table.   Besides the typical example, we give a separate *parameter table* to show the variety of choices that have been made for a selected set of computers. The table indicates the frequency and historic trend for each choice.

Sample computers.   Understanding the whys of present-day computer architecture requires a knowledge of the historical evolution of concepts. We use many earlier machines to illustrate this evolution, as well as concepts that, although not present in current computers, appear to be still viable.

Historical Tables 1-15 and 1-16 jointly show the computers used as examples in the parameter tables. Those that appear in all applicable tables are marked by a Z; the others occur only incidentally. Many other machines are mentioned in the text but do not appear in the tables. The parameter table for any particular function omits computers not containing that function in any form.

The Computer Zoo.   The machines marked Z in the historical tables are residents of the Computer Zoo, the second part of this book. The Zoo serves here the same purpose as an ordinary zoological collection serves. Exemplars of all the major species are exposed to the gaze of the students. They can see how each is designed and specialized for its own environment and function, how each works as an integrated whole. Likewise, they can study comparatively how common functions and needs are met in similar and different ways.

Each specimen is presented in a short sketch that summarizes the architectural decisions and noteworthy features, good and bad.

	Announced/ paper	Delivered/ operational	Family	Architect/ author	Z
Bendix G20		1961		Huskey	
Honeywell 800		1961			
IBM Stretch	1959	1961		Buchholz	Z
IBM 7080	1960	1961	IBM 702	Bradshaw	
Chicago Maniac III	1958	1961		Metropolis	
Ferranti Atlas	1960	1962	MU3	Kilburn	
English Electric KDF9	1960	1963		Davis	
IBM 7094	1962	1963	IBM 704	Sweeney	
CDC 6600	1963	1964		Cray	Z
CDC 6600 PPU	1963	1964	CDC 160	Cray	Z
Burroughs B5500	1961	1964	B5000	Barton	Z
IBM System/360	1964	1965		Amdahl	Z
RCA Spectra 70	1964	1965	System/360		
Electrologica X8	1963	1965	X1	Scholten	
GE 645		1965		Wild	
DEC PDP8	1965	1965	DEC PDP5	Bell	Z
Honeywell H8200		1967	Series 200		
DEC PDP10		1968	DEC PDP6	Bell	
Burroughs B6500	1968	1968	B5500	Barton	
DEC PDP11	1970	1970		Bell	Z
IBM System/370	1970	1971	System/360	Case	
Burroughs B1700	1972	1972		Wilner	
CDC Star100		1973		Thornton	
Intel 8080A		1974	Intel 8008	Faggin	Z
Cray 1	1975	1975		Cray	Z
Motorola M6800		1975			Z
MOS 6502	1976	1976	M6800		Z
DEC VAX11	1977	1978	DEC PDP11	Strecker	Z
Motorola MC68000	1979	1980	M6800	Gunter	Z
IBM System/38		1980			
IBM 6150	1983	1986	IBM 801	Cocke	Z

Legend: Z = Detailed in the Computer Zoo; only first author listed.

TABLE 1-16   Origins of various machines (after 1960).

Dates.   The historical tables are ordered by date of completion.   For commercial products, we use the date of first delivery; for the early laboratory machines, the date on which the system was declared to be operational. Since the concepts in some machines, such as von Neumann's IAS computer (1952), were made known long before completion, we also list the date of publication.

Later is dirtier.   Usually the later members of a computer family have architectural function added while designers attempt to stay within formats not originally planned for such function. Consequently, the later members of any family are not so clean and systematic as are earlier members. The student of architecture will usually do best, except when examining the process of architectural evolution, to study the ancestral member of each family. We usually identify a concept with the first machine of a family to embody it, not the everchanging latest or necessarily even the most familiar. We identify subtractive indexing with the IBM 704 (1955), not with the IBM 7094 (1963); family compatibility with the 360, not with the 370 or the IBM 4300s and 3000s.

Family membership implies strong resemblance, but not necessarily compatibility. Tables 1-15 and 1-16 list the earliest ancestors of descendant machines.

Evaluating Alternatives

The task of design consists of postulating designs that appear to meet the requirements, inventing alternatives, and selecting the best. This process requires a methodology for evaluating designs—what is *satisfactory*, what is *better*. In any design field, evaluating designs is difficult.

Evaluation methodology.   Evaluating the cost/performance ratio of complete computers is hard enough, although measurement technology has made great strides in the past two decades [Drummond, 1973; Hellerman and Smith, 1970; Ferrari et al., 1983]. Evaluating the excellence of a computer's architecture, independently of its implementations and realizations, is much harder. One needs implementation-independent measures of cost, of performance, and of ease of use—measures that are invariant under changes in technology.

Research has been done on this problem. Fundamentally, such work rests upon measuring the power and conciseness of the computer language—how many bits are required for the programs for typical applications?

The most elementary method—one that can be applied in a few minutes—is to have some standard benchmark task set. From this, one derives frequency weightings for operations, distribution of addresses over spaces of various sizes, frequency of address modification, and other such distributions. With such elementary models of "normal use," one can quickly evaluate the effects of a proposed architectural decision on instruction-storage efficiency and memory-bandwidth use.

Fuller and his coworkers [Fuller et al., 1977a, 1977b, 1977c] developed this methodology and applied it carefully to the evaluation of candidate architectures for a standard military computer family. Their three 1977 papers represent a high-water mark in published work on implementation-independent evaluation of architecture.

One can argue with their list of mandatory features. Such lists are dangerous because they arbitrarily rule out new techniques that accomplish the same function as a mandatory feature does, without having the same form. And, of course, each evaluator would have his own weightings to be applied to the component measures to yield a single index of merit. Nevertheless, the work is a model of architectural evaluation.

Another attack is to develop realization-independent measures for implementations, using such technology-invariant units as clock beats or logic levels to characterize performance, or register bits and logic gates to characterize cost. Then one can compare two architectures by sketching appropriate implementations of each. Such a technique is clearly less direct, but may be capable of more precision. J. Sneeringer showed that the technique can be used to assess the cost/performance effects of even rather small architectural changes [J. Sneeringer, 1975].

Strecker [1971] pioneered this idea by modeling realization-independent implementations by unit instructions, each occasioning one memory reference and one datapath action. J. Sneeringer [1975] went on to model costs in terms of register bits.

1.2.5
Bibliography

Akela and Siewiorek [1991], Alexander [1964], Amdahl [1970], Barbacci and Siewiorek [1982], Bell and Newell [1971], Blaauw [1976], Brooks [1975], Case [1970], Chen and Patterson [1994], Drummond [1973], Ferrari et al. [1983], Fuller et al. [1977a, 1977b, 1977c], Gustafson [1988], Hellerman and Smith [1970], Iliffe [1982], Kain [1996], R.E. Smith [1989], J. Sneeringer [1975], Strecker [1971, 1978], Swartzlander [1976].

1.3
The Description of Computer Architecture

1.3.1
The Completeness of Description

A computer always *has* an architecture, whether it is defined in advance, as with modern computers, or found out after the fact, as with many early machines. A machine's *architecture* must not be understood as a vague overall idea of how the machine is organized. Rather, it is the set of precise concepts that specify the functional behavior of the computer.

The need for completeness.   The product of the computer architect, the *Principles of Operation* manual, should contain all the detail that the users can know; sooner or later they will discover and use it all.

The manual must not only describe everything the user does see; it must also refrain from describing what the user cannot see. That is the implementer's business, and there his design freedom must be unconstrained. For example, the Burroughs B5500 manual [Burroughs, 1964] states that the top levels of its stack are kept in two registers, called A and B. Only extensive and careful reading assures us that this information is gratuitous and that the user can ignore these registers.

A specification must also be precise as to what is *not* specified. Consider the Appendix to *IBM System/360 Principles of Operation* [IBM, 1964]. It describes with precision the limits of the 360's compatibility. It enumerates those areas of external appearance where the architecture is intentionally silent: where results from one model may differ from those of another, where one copy of a given model may differ from another copy, or where a copy may differ even from itself after an engineering change. One must define what is not prescribed as carefully as what is.

The style must be precise, fully detailed, and accurate. A user will often look up just one definition, so each one must repeat all the essentials, yet all must agree. This requirement makes manuals dull reading, but precision is more important than liveliness.

An early Soviet proposal describes a plan to build several machines to be "compatible with the IBM System/360 or the RCA Spectra 70." Already the knowing reader senses trouble, for these two machine families differ from each

other in certain vital ways. He reads on, attempting to see which family the Russians are matching, and it becomes evident that the author is not sensitive to such differences. He is describing a concept not yet detailed, rather than an architecture that has been developed.

The preservation of completeness.   The 1401 manual mentioned only the permissible operations, those specified by the architects. The machine did more, however, and the unmentioned functions, such as the actions that resulted from the spare operation codes, were soon found out. Some proved to be useful. As a consequence, when we emulated the 1401 on the 360 Model 30, an addendum to the manual of about a hundred items had to be included in the design, since these had by widespread use become de facto parts of the architecture.

In the 360 this problem was recognized in advance [Amdahl et al., 1964]. A mere admonition against using spare codes was known to be insufficient, so the architecture specified a program interruption upon the use of these spares. Such *policing* is an effective means of safeguarding the architectural intention. It was first proposed by von Neumann [Burks et al., 1946]. It was a lifesaver when the 370 was designed.

The cost of incompleteness.   The implementer, as well as the user, must know how every detail is to be treated. Seemingly nitty architectural requirements may greatly influence the form of the implementation—as they do the programming. Ignoring these details early in the design may occasion disproportionately large costs when they are finally specified as the design nears completion. In the 360, an early specification called for I/O devices to be separately switchable off-power. When the I/O architecture was designed, this specification was overlooked; in the implementation, the last device on a channel was required to be powered to make the channel work. The fix, necessitated by field conditions, cost millions to retrofit.

1.3.2
The Manner of Description

There are two fundamentally different ways to give a specification. One may specify a place by saying, "Take the third left, then the second right, and proceed to the first traffic light." Or one may say that the place is "at the corner of Main and Market Streets." The first description is *generative*; it specifies the place by telling one how to get there. It does not mean one actually must follow this route; there may be other routes better suited to one's purpose. The second description is verifying or *assertive*; it tells when one has arrived. One need only look at the street signs to know that he is at the right place. One is not told how to get there; in fact, there may not be a way to get there at all.

Generative Description

A generative description prescribes constructively how each output of a system can be produced from the inputs.

Executing the architecture.   When a generative description of a computer is given in an executable language, it can be operated by feeding the outputs from one function into the next as inputs.   One can thus demonstrate an entire architecture.   The user can see whether he got what he asked for, whether he asked what he intended, and whether he really wants what he originally intended.   This exercise makes it possible to refine the desired function an entire level beyond what would otherwise be possible: At the architectural-definition level, changes can still be readily made.

A demonstration is all the more important because an architecture cannot be proven or verified to be correct; it is the starting point of a machine design. If one demonstrates that an operation called Add behaves very much like a subtraction, one cannot say that the specification is wrong; one can only question the intention of the designer and the choice of the name Add.

A complete and executable generative architecture is in essence a *prototype*. It can be used by the designers of the system software to execute programs and to verify their operation. Furthermore, the results of such an architecture can be compared with those of an implementation to verify the latter's correctness.

Need for high-level language.   Is it a disadvantage that the generative description suggests an implementation?   The problem arises only when the description language is not of sufficiently high level and is therefore incapable of expressing the required function directly, so the architect must use a construct to provide that function. For instance, in a language that cannot express vector addition directly, the architect may describe this function by a loop controlled by an index and count. The reader must now reconstruct the concept of vector addition from indexing, incrementation, and counting. Furthermore, he must realize that the element-execution order implied by the loop was not inherently part of the architecture, but was necessitated only by the limitation of the description language.

Therefore, a generative description must use a suitable high-level language and a clear convention to distinguish the essential from the accidental. A sufficiently abstract description of an architecture shows directly the relation of the architecture to the program primitives and usually does not suggest an implementation. For instance, when the operation Add is specified in terms of the arithmetic concept of addition, the relation to the program primitive is obvious, and there is not the slightest hint that the implementer should use a ripple-carry adder or a carry-predict adder.

Assertive Description

The assertive description of an architecture gives the relation that holds between the inputs and outputs of the system. The right part of Figure 1-17 illustrates that the description generates an output True, which indicates whether a set of inputs and outputs adheres to the architecture. An example of assertive definition is that for floating-point normalization of non-zero numbers: Output value is equal to input value, and output coefficient has its leftmost bit set to 1.

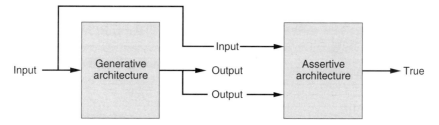

FIGURE 1-17   Generative and assertive architecture.

Verifying the implementation.   When the input and output of a generative description are applied to an equivalent assertive description, the signal True must be generated (Figure 1-17). The same must be the case when the inputs and outputs of an implementation are supplied to the assertive description. The assertive description proves convenient for verifying the validity of an implementation.

Unpredictable results.   There are cases in which the architect wants to specify arbitrary outputs, also known as *unpredictable* or *don't-care* outputs. Such an architecture gives freedom to the implementer. Division by zero, for instance, may be specified to give an error indication and arbitrary values for quotient and remainder. The assertive description of the division architecture now states that either the error signal is false and the quotient, remainder, divisor, and dividend have the proper relations, or the error signal is true and the divisor is zero.

The *don't-care* outputs of an architecture are not describable through an executable generative description. This fact was noted during the description of the 360 in APL [Falkoff et al., 1964]. The random operator, denoted by the question mark, was introduced to specify the *don't-care* output. As long as the description is read but not executed, this solution is satisfactory. But when the description is executed, the result that the random operator produces appears to be unique; it certainly cannot be used to verify an implementation.

The assertive description cannot be used to simulate or demonstrate the architecture. Games such as chess or nim are usually specified assertively because the freedom within the rules is best described that way. Since the assertive definition does not appeal to the imagination, the explanation of a game is usually supplemented by generative examples: "Let's start a game; then you can see how it goes."

Generative and assertive descriptions can be combined without difficulty. In arithmetic, the add operation is defined generatively by counting, subtraction assertively from addition, multiplication generatively by addition, and division assertively from multiplication, as illustrated in Table 1-18.

The generative specifications of addition and multiplication are not followed in the usual implementations of manual and machine arithmetic; the use of positional representation gives remarkably faster algorithms. Also observe that the assertively defined subtraction and division are not always possible; the number system must first be extended to negative numbers to close subtraction, then to fractions for division; even then, division by zero is not defined.

Operation	Defined from	Result	Manner
Addition	counting	cardinal numbers	generative
Subtraction	addition	integers	assertive
Multiplication	addition	integers	generative
Division	multiplication	fractions	assertive

TABLE 1-18   Generative and assertive definitions in arithmetic.

Because the generative description can be used to demonstrate and simulate, and because it appeals to the imagination, it is the one used more frequently. In this text, almost all architectures are described in this fashion. Most generative descriptions do not prescribe an implementation; those that do need not be followed—as any mature implementer knows.

Generative implementation of assertions.   In those cases where the assertive architecture is used to indicate unpredictable outputs, a generative equivalent may be used to obtain an executable description. The assertive architecture, however, is the normative (and surely the simplest) definition. In that case, the generative equivalent should protect the unpredictability of the results by giving a suitable warning. Otherwise, a de facto definition arises when the prototype is run.

Such de facto definitions sometimes give unexpected answers when sharp questions are asked, and are often found to be inelegant in these particulars precisely because they have never received any thought. This inelegance normally turns out to be slow or costly to duplicate in a compatible implementation. For example, some machines may leave trash in the multiplicand register after a multiplication. When the register is not properly policed, the precise nature of this trash becomes part of the de facto definition, yet duplicating it may preclude the use of a faster multiplication algorithm.

1.3.3
The Form of Description

How shall so precise a specification as a computer architecture be expressed?

Natural language.   The use of written English or some other natural language has been conventional and is indispensable. The main advantage of written natural language is its ready comprehensibility and the large audience that it consequently reaches. This audience includes, besides the immediately involved systems programmer and implementer, the less immediately but no less vitally involved people in education, maintenance, and sales.

Written English, however, is not naturally a precision instrument for such definitions. It is more apt for convincing than for specifying. It must be redundant to be understood and, in fact, to be believed. If, for instance, the architecture specifies that "the sign of a product is determined by the signs of multiplier and multiplicand," the experienced manual reader immediately raises the question of the sign of the product of zero and a negative number. The manual writer must therefore strain himself and his language to achieve the precision needed. To forestall such ambiguities, manuals are written not

order digit of the product field is zero.
All operands and results are treated as
signed integers, right-aligned in their field.

*The sign of the of the product is determined
by the rules of algebra from the multiplier
and multiplicand signs, even if one or both
operands are zero.*

The multiplier and product fields may
overlap only if their low-order bytes coincide.

Condition Code:

The code remains unchanged.

FIGURE 1-19   Excerpts from *IBM System/360 Principles of Operation.*

in standard English, but in a highly restricted and stylized sublanguage—abundant in words, repetitive in constructs, and using terms in carefully defined senses. This sublanguage comes to resemble the stylized language of guarantees, contracts, and laws. The italics we have added in Figure 1-19 illustrate this characteristic from the *IBM System/360 Principles of Operation* manual [IBM, 1964].

Formal language.   Because of the difficulties inherent in the use of natural language, an attractive alternative is to use a formal notation for architectural definition. After all, precision is the stock in trade of formal notations.

A language is called *formal* when explicit rules define the possible forms and their semantics. From the explicitness of the rules flows the power of the formality. The rules may allow one to test descriptions for contradictions, by formal manipulations. They may, in some cases, allow one to test a description for completeness; even if they do not, gaps show more conspicuously. Formality makes it easier to avoid ambiguity in definition and prescription.

Side-by-side use.   What formal languages lack is comprehensibility. With English prose one can show principles, delineate structure in stages or levels, and give examples. One can mark exceptions and emphasize contrasts. Most important, one can explain *why* something is so. The formal definitions put forward so far have inspired wonder at their elegance and confidence in their precision. But they have demanded prose explanations to make their content easy to learn and teach. Moreover, they are subject to catastrophic alteration by even a single-symbol error. The solution is to use both formal- and natural-language descriptions side by side, with each description complete in itself. Possible misconceptions in the informal text can be eliminated by the formal expressions, whereas the expressions in turn are explained by the text. The process of making a formal description poses many useful questions to the architect.

Normative description.   "Never go to sea with two chronometers; take one or three." This ancient warning clearly applies to prose and formal definitions. If both are used, one must be the standard, and the other must be a derivative description, clearly labeled as such. The architect can choose either as the primary standard. ALGOL68 has its formal definition as standard and a prose

Year	Name	Author	Use	Domain
1952	RTL	Reed		i
1962	APL	Iverson	IBM System/360	a and i
1964	Register transfer	Schorr		i
1964	Lotis	Schlaeppi		a
1965	CDL	Chu		i
1966	Cassandre	Anceau and Mermet		i
1967	DDL	Duley and Dietmeyer		i
1968	AHPL	Hill and Peterson		i
1969	Hargol	Giese		i
1969	APDL	Darringer		i
1969	Alert	Friedman		a and i
1970	PMS and ISP	Bell and Newell	DEC PDP11	a
1976	ISPS	Barbacci et al.		a
1980	Conlan	Piloty		a and i
1987	VHDL	IEEE standard comm.		a and i

Legend: a = architecture; i = implementation.

TABLE 1-20   Computer-description languages.

description as derivative. PL/I and the 360's machine language have the prose as standard and a formal description as derivative.

A formal description is, in contrast to words and illustrations, unambiguous. Moreover, it is easier to test by execution. The best practice is to define it to be normative in all cases where the descriptions seem to be in conflict.

Illustrations and examples.   Besides using formal- and natural-language descriptions, one can illustrate an architecture by figures and tables. These may indeed be worth a thousand words, but they replace words, not formal descriptions.

Examples are also useful, since they too indicate typical usage and reveal the intention of the designer. Examples can only add to the description; they cannot replace it. Yet system interfaces are often specified by an elaborate set of timing sequences. Since the possible event sequences are far too numerous to specify, such a definition is inevitably incomplete [Vissers, 1977].

1.3.4
Architectural-Description Languages

A classical example of a formal machine description is the APL description of the 360 [Falkoff et al., 1964]. The description was completed concurrently with the system development and was not actually used as a means of description by the designers. Nonetheless, it shows that a programming language can describe a complex system in all its details. Also, the formal description process raised questions that were used to clarify the written description.

The original version of the APL language was considerably improved when APL was implemented as a terminal language. A part of the original APL description of the 360 is shown in Program 1-21; the same portion in current APL is shown in Program 1-22 [Pakin, 1972]. To make the two programs match line by line, we have placed multiple expressions (separated by ◊) and comments on one line in Program 1-22. We do not use multiple expressions elsewhere in this work.

PROGRAM 1-21   Fragment of IBM System/360 description in early APL.

Table 1-20 shows some of the computer-description languages that have been proposed. As indicated in the table, the intended use for some of these languages was implementation rather than architecture. Only a few of these proposals were used in the design of a real computer, produced and used in quantity.

Bell and Newell [1971] have proposed the PMS and the ISP notations for describing configurations and machine architectures, and they have illustrated these notations with several machines, including the DEC PDP8 (1965), the 7090, and the 360.

Requirements

The requirements for a formal architectural-description language follow from the preceding discussion. We summarize them by stating that the language must be high level, general purpose, and well-structured. Moreover, it is most desirable that the language be executable with a conversational implementation and be established with a user community.

High level.   An architectural-description language should express each desired function directly. Such a direct presentation avoids auxiliary constructions, avoids involved idiomatic constructs that draw attention to the mode of expression instead of the object of description, and reduces the danger of suggesting implementations.

Since the operands that appear in an architecture are usually multidimensional arrays, the language must contain that datatype. All logical, arithmetic, and relational operations must apply to arrays. Operators that modify the dimensions of arrays, and those that decode and encode numbers, must both be available.

Executable.   An architectural design language must be executable if it is to allow demonstration and simulation. Since it is a design language, however, its users benefit from the fast turnaround of an interactive implementation. Such celerity considerably reduces errors, since expressions can be checked for syntactic correctness when written and since the number of transcriptions is reduced. Moreover, one wants a shared database, so that the description can readily be accessed and used by all members of a design team.

```
fragment360;count;status;value;increment;comparand
ⴰ equivalent description of Program 1-20
b8:count←(magni reg[fld R1;])-1 ⴰ BCT BCTR
b9:→(b12,b15)[0=count]
b10:status←psw[Ilc,Cc,Programmask,Iadr] ◊ →b12 ⴰ BAL BALR
b11:→(0=fld Mask[magni psw[Cc]])/0 ⴰ BC BCR
b12:→n[4]/b14 ⴰ n identifies the instruction format
b13:→(0=fld R2)/b15 ◊ psw[Iadr]←reg[fld R2;Address] ◊ →b15 ⴰBCR BALR BCTR
b14:psw[Iadr]←adrsize magnr adr360bxd ⴰ BC BAL BCT
b15:→(˜n[5])/0 ⴰ BC BCR BCT BCTR
b16:reg[fld R1;]←status ◊ →0 ⴰ BAL BALR
b17:value←radixcompi reg[fld R1;] ⴰ BXH BXLE
b18:increment←radixcompi reg[fld R2;]
b19:comparand←radixcompi reg[odd R2;]
b20:reg[fld R1;]←word radixcompr value+increment
```

PROGRAM 1-22   Fragment of IBM System/360 description in current APL.

General purpose.   The argument in favor of a general purpose language is pragmatic: An architectural-description language is not used in isolation but as part of a total design environment.

A general purpose language can cover all levels of the design, from architecture to realization. One also needs design tools for the gathering of statistics, the evaluation of performance, and the generation of test cases. If all the descriptions and tools are expressed in the same language, unity of thought is preserved. The designer turns always to the same interactive system; he develops skill and stays in practice. Even though a general purpose language may not be as ideal as a language that is specially designed for one purpose, it is better than a set of languages for the set of different needs encountered in design. The widely used ISP is not executable; its executable descendant, ISPS, is not general purpose.

Established.   Using a special-purpose architectural-description language often (but not necessarily) involves designing a new language or extending an old one. If the architect decides to use a general purpose language, though, an established language can be chosen—one that is already tested and debugged. An established language furthermore allows the designer to share the expression techniques and inventions of a large community of language users. We believe that the known disadvantages of each established language are easily offset by the advantages of establishment.

Structured.   The language structure must allow and encourage a clear design structure. The several functions must be independently, directly, and generally expressible. Furthermore, it must be possible to delegate detail to subordinate functions. A gradual, hierarchical development of the design is thus possible.

Such a design procedure is often referred to as *top-down design* or *stepwise refinement*. Top-down design in a strictly unidirectional sense is not really possible. In practice, the various levels are modified in a series of iterations so that the total design is optimal. But what *is* possible is to design in such a manner that a top-down description results. This final description need not reflect the perturbations, backtrackings, and upheavals that are part of a design process. Rather, the clarity of its top-down structure reflects the aim of the designers throughout the entire design process.

APL as an Architecture-Description Language

Since APL is an established high-level general purpose language that is conversationally executable, it is a ready candidate for an architecture design language. It is the only language on the list in Table 1-20 that meets all our criteria. We think that the modular function mechanism of APL gives the language good structuring abilities, although the current restriction to two operands is a limitation. The absence of control structures is also a great disadvantage. We therefore introduce APL functions for the familiar control structures If, Case, While, and Repeat [Blaauw and Duijvestijn, 1980].

Symbolism.   APL represents each of its high-level operators by a single symbol. The language is unique in using a character set with a rich set of symbols that places special requirements on keyboards, printers, and displays, rather than conforming to the normal limitations of these devices. But the symbols are desirable because they directly represent natural units of thought. The argument that Leibniz used when he introduced and standardized the now-familiar mathematical symbols (such as the equal-to sign and the parentheses) is still valid: Through proper symbolism, "indeed the labour of thought is wonderfully diminished" [Cajori, 1929]. Whitehead and Russell [1910–13] state even more strongly, "The symbolic form of our work has been forced upon us by necessity; without its help we must have been unable to perform the requisite reasoning."

1.3.5
Introduction to the Computer Descriptions

Knowing a language—its grammar and vocabulary—and having something to say do not of themselves make a person a good writer. What is true for natural languages is also true for formal languages. Good descriptions do not come naturally; they take effort and experience.

We have tried to give good descriptions of various machines and their parts. Sometimes the object was in the way—a clear description of an obscure function is hard to formulate. At other times we failed, and others will improve upon our attempts. Nevertheless, we intend that these descriptions contribute not only to an understanding of their objects, but also to the development of a good style of description.

The Purpose of Descriptions

Clarity versus efficiency.   The prime purpose of our APL descriptions is to describe, although the descriptions are executable and hence can be used to simulate and demonstrate. Clarity is favored over efficiency. We do not shrink from computing a value twice if this repetition makes the meaning of the description clearer.

Reading versus writing.   Although the APL descriptions are intended to be read by many people, they should also be convenient to write and use. A description should be a design tool. As soon as one must make a separate

effort to derive a description from a design, the description almost inevitably becomes out of date as the design changes.

The desiderata for reading and writing sometimes conflict. Unabridged names are easier to comprehend than abbreviations, but are also more tedious to write correctly. We have struck a balance. For frequently recurring concepts we use abbreviations. The abbreviations are clarified by legends and comments; a glossary of abbreviations is given in the introduction to the Zoo (Chapter 9).

Single use versus comparison.   A description may present the architecture of just one computer. In this case the mode of expression can be tailored to the special concepts of that machine. Our purpose is different, however. Although we want to exhibit what is special in a given design, we also want to be clear about what is common in many designs. So we try to use the same manner of expression for common features. Such descriptions differ slightly from descriptions tailored to individual machines, especially in nomenclature. We use the same name for the same function across machines, even when such names deviate from the language subcultures peculiar to particular manufacturers.

Sample Description

In this section we preview the APL descriptions used in this book, emphasizing the method of description rather than the objects described. We take the IBM 650 (1954) as our example. The order of presentation roughly matches that of Chapters 2 through 6. Except as noted, the description refers to the basic machine without optional features. The aggregate 650 description in this book is executable and essentially complete—one can use it to run 650 programs.

We assume that the reader is familiar with APL. The Appendix gives a brief introduction to the subset of APL that is used in this book.

Space

The programs that describe a machine are executable as a whole or in part: The whole operation of a machine can be simulated, or just a specific instruction or addressing mode can be executed. In either case some objects must be available to the program.

Declaration.   Because APL needs no prior declaration for the objects that are generated in a program, only the global environment need be declared, and can be limited to the spaces and overall parameters that characterize the machine at hand.

Initiation.   Program 1-23 shows the function `initiate650` that initiates the format and space declarations for the 650. The suffix `650` reflects our intention of presenting many machines. Where there is little chance of confusion, we omit suffixes for brevity.

`initiate650` indicates that the declaration uses the defined functions `format650`, `configure650`, `space650`, `name650`, `control650`, and

```
initiate650
∧ initiation of the IBM 650
format650
configure650
space650
name650
control650
data650
```

PROGRAM 1-23   Initiation of the IBM 650.

data650, in that order. initiate650 both declares and initializes; it need be executed only once to create the proper environment for the other description programs of the 650.

Reference. The functions that initiate650 uses are not shown in Program 1-23. Some follow immediately, others later in this section. All these functions are listed systematically in Chapter 9 for easy reference.

Some machines that are used as illustration are not described in the Zoo. For such machines the function name indicates the kind of function that is intended, omitting further detail.

Format. The basic parameters of the 650 are given in format650 (Program 1-24). We observe that the 650 is a decimal machine with a word size of 11 decimal digits. Two digits form a byte that can represent a character. The address capacity of memory is 2000 words.

```
format650
∧ IBM 650 information units
∧ representation radix
radix←10
∧ information units
word←11
accsize←21
adrsize←4
byte←2
∧ address capacity
adrcap←2000
```

PROGRAM 1-24   Parameters of the IBM 650.

Configuration.   configure650 (Program 1-25) gives the configuration of the 650 that is assumed to be installed.

```
configure650
∧ configuration for the IBM 650
∧ memory capacity
memcap←adrcap
```

PROGRAM 1-25   Configuration of the IBM 650.

Space. space650 (Program 1-26) shows that the basic 650 has a memory, a double-length accumulator, acc, an accessible memory-data register called the Distributor, dist, a remainder sign, and several control registers and switches.

```
    space650
  ⍝ IBM 650 spaces                ⍝ control store
  ⍝ memory                        ⍝ - instruction address
    memory←?(memcap,word)⍴radix     iadr←?memcap
  ⍝ working store                 ⍝ - indicators
  ⍝ - accumulator                   ind←?4⍴2
    acc←?accsize⍴radix            ⍝ - manual entry
  ⍝ - distributor                   switch←?word⍴radix
    dist←?word⍴radix             ⍝ - stop enable switches
  ⍝ - remainder sign                mask←?3⍴2
    rmsign←?radix                ⍝ input/output
                                   cardin←(10,word)⍴radix
                                   cardout←(10,word)⍴radix
```

PROGRAM 1-26   Spaces of the IBM 650.

Dimensions.   Memory is initiated as a matrix of dimension 2000 11. `space650` indicates that each element is decimal and is initially unspecified by use of a random selection from digits 0 through 9. The function further indicates that the dimension 11 is not arbitrary, but rather matches the word size, called `word`, whereas the high-order dimension is the installed capacity.

Embedding.   `name650` (Program 1-27) shows that the two parts of the accumulator, the distributor, and the switches have a memory address and as such are embedded in the memory address space.

```
    name650
  ⍝ IBM 650 space names
  ⍝ memory embedding
  ⍝ - lower accumulator   ⍝ - switches
    Accl←8002                Switch←8000
  ⍝ - upper accumulator   ⍝ - input/output transfer
    Accu←8003                Input←1+⍳10
  ⍝ - distributor           Output←27+⍳10
    Dist←8001
```

PROGRAM 1-27   Embedding of spaces in memory in the IBM 650.

Cycle

The hierarchy of the functions describing the execution is more complex than that of the declaration functions. `cycle650` (Program 1-28) presents the top of the execution hierarchy. It states that, for the 650, the execution cycle consists of fetching an instruction, executing it, and repeating the cycle until the computer is stopped.

```
    cycle650
  ⍝ basic cycle of the IBM 650
    REPEAT:execute ifetch650
           interrupt650
    →UNTIL stop650
```

PROGRAM 1-28   Execution cycle of the IBM 650.

Deferred detail.   The description method attempts to focus the attention of the reader on the subject under discussion. For example, `cycle650` tells us that the 650 is a simple machine. There is a (primitive) interrupt in this basic

version of the machine, and some means of stopping the machine is available through `stop650`. The reader can pursue any particular subject further by looking in the Zoo. Deferring detail to lower levels of the hierarchy is a key principle of the description method.

Control structures.   `cycle650` contains an iteration. Depending upon the value returned by `stop650`, the body of the Repeat-Until structure is or is not executed. When it is not executed, the program continues beyond the structure. The general expression →`UNTIL` `condition` is one of the control structures used in the description. `condition` should be a Boolean value. Other control structures are If, Case, and While. The control structures are explained in Chapter 9; they occur only occasionally in the descriptions.

Control

Program 1-29 details the allocation of the control formats: the instructions and the indicators.

```
control650
ᴀ IBM 650 control allocation
   instruction650
   indicator650
```

PROGRAM 1-29   Control allocation in the IBM 650.

Allocation.   `instruction650` (Program 1-30) gives the allocation of the distinct instruction fields by means of global variables, such as `Next`. The leftmost digit (the sign position) of the word is not used, as indicated by an asterisk in the diagram and by the name `Unused` in the function. The names of the allocation index-vectors have their first letter capitalized. This convention aids in recognizing the purpose of these vectors, which is to serve as an index of an information unit.

Diagram.   The diagram of Program 1-30 is similar to the diagrams found in most manuals of machine operation. Such diagrams show very quickly the allocation of information units. We preserve, where possible, the relative sizes of format subfields.

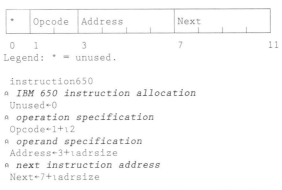

```
instruction650
ᴀ IBM 650 instruction allocation
   Unused←0
ᴀ operation specification
   Opcode←1+ι2
ᴀ operand specification
   Address←3+ιadrsize
ᴀ next instruction address
   Next←7+ιadrsize
```

PROGRAM 1-30   Instruction of the IBM 650.

Field demarcation.   We indicate the allocation of the subfields in Program 1-30 by giving the index of the leftmost digit of each field as well as the index of the digit to the right of the entire format. This last number shows the length of the information unit, so the 650 instruction consists of 11 decimal digits.

Zero-origin indexing.   In all diagrams, indexing starts with zero (*zero origin*) and proceeds from left to right, even if a manufacturer uses a different convention, as was the case for the 650. Zero-origin indexing has a slight advantage over one-origin indexing in matching the names of digits, which also start with zero.

All descriptions assume zero-origin indexing. Except for the allocation functions, the reader need not be aware of this convention.

Left-to-right indexing.   We always index fields from left to right. This convention has the major advantage that it matches the normal writing direction. Some writers have used a right-to-left numbering when representing a number, since such a progression follows the weight of the digits. In an architecture, however, the individual digits of a number are not that prominent, and even for an implementation this practice is questionable [Blaauw, 1976]. Right-to-left numbering within an information unit conflicts directly with placing the units in a memory that is numbered left to right. The PDP11 and the Intel 8080A (1974) have encountered conceptual problems here, as will be shown in Section 2.3.

Highest possible level.   The decimal digits of the 650 each require four bits. Actually, the 650 used five bits for the 2-out-of-5 code of the drum memory and seven bits for the bi-quinary code of the capacitor register used as an accumulator. Program 1-30 suggests—and a careful inspection of the 650 architecture confirms—that the 650 architecture can be described entirely in terms of decimal digits.

We attempt to use the highest level of description possible. This practice not only simplifies the description, but also asserts that the underlying details are a free implementation choice and can be ignored by the user of the architecture.

Error detection and correction.   As a direct consequence of describing only the architecture, we do not mention in the description the bits that are used in the implementation for error detection and correction.

Addressing

The 650 instruction contains a data-address field, `Address`, and an instruction-address field, `Next`, which are interpreted as unsigned numbers.

Magnitude interpretation and representation.   We so commonly use a construct such as 365 to represent a value that we forget that it is also a vector of individual symbols, decimal digits. In a computer, such a construct is usually just a vector of symbols, and we must specify explicitly when and how it is treated as a value. The *interpretation* of a vector of digits as a single value, a positive number, is called that vector's *magnitude*; it is obtained by `magni`. The inverse action, supplied by `magnr`, *represents* a positive number

```
value←magni rep              rep←size magnr value
ᴀ magnitude interpretation   ᴀ magnitude representation
value←radix⊥⍉rep             rep←⍉(size⍴radix)⊤value
```

PROGRAM 1-31   Magnitude interpretation and representation.

by a vector of digits. Program 1-31 shows both functions. The suffixes i and r stand for *interpretation* and *representation*; they occur often. (These concepts are defined in Section 2.2.)

In the 650 the digits are decimal, but in most machines the digits are binary. magni is kept general by use of the parameter radix.

We further generalize magni by allowing it to apply to arrays of rank 0, 1, and 2—that is, to scalars, vectors, and matrices. A common use is the interpretation of a matrix of bits as a vector of digits, where each row of the matrix represents a digit. The APL decode operator (⊥) serves this purpose. Unfortunately, it eliminates the high-order dimension of a matrix instead of the low-order dimension. It treats columns, not rows, as representing digits.

We think that the APL language definition is wrong at this point, but the price for using an established language is living with its shortcomings. Here this price is the transpose operator, ⍉, which interchanges rows and columns in magni and magnr.

General functions.   The magnitude functions have no suffix 650 since they apply to many machines. We use them wherever appropriate to denote the magnitude concept. The general functions are also given in Section 9.3 as part of the introduction to the Zoo.

Field.   Because instruction fields are frequently interpreted as numbers, a simple general function fld (Program 1-32) is defined for this purpose. fld field is just an abbreviation for magni inst[field].

```
value←fld field
ᴀ instruction field decoding
value←magni inst[field]
```

PROGRAM 1-32   Instruction field decoding.

Data address.   The data addresses of the 650 are obtained by adr650 (Program 1-33). This function is also very simple, and if we were describing only the 650 we might not have bothered with it. In most computers, however, addressing is more complex and deserves a separate function. Compared to such functions, this one emphasizes the simplicity of the 650.

```
address←adr650
ᴀ IBM 650 addressing
address←fld Address
```

PROGRAM 1-33   Addressing in the IBM 650.

Reading

An actual machine is usually just slightly more complex than a hypothetical one. As simple as the 650 is, it contains several complications, the first of which we must face here.

```
data←read650 address
ᴀ IBM 650 read from store
→CASE(Switch,Dist,Accl,Accu)ιaddress
C0:data←switch
   →ENDCASE
C1:data←dist
   →ENDCASE
C2:data←acc[Sign,Lower]
   →ENDCASE
C3:data←acc[Sign,Upper]
   →ENDCASE
C4:data←memory[memcap|address;]
   Invadr report address≥adrcap
ENDCASE:
```

PROGRAM 1-34   Read from store in the IBM 650.

Although four decimal digits are available for an address, only the addresses 0 through 1999 and 8000 through 8003 are valid. Moreover, in the locations 8000 through 8003, some other spaces are embedded. read650 (Program 1-34) distinguishes the various spaces with a Case structure. The value of address is successively compared with Switch, Dist, Accl, and Accu. The first equality that is found causes a jump to the corresponding case C0 through C3; no equality gives a jump to C4. The function also deals in C4 with invalid addresses—another complication.

Indicators.   The allocation of the indicators of the 650 is given in indica-tor650 (Program 1-35). The invalid-address indication used in read650 is allocated to indicator 2. Invalid operations and machine errors also set this indicator—the 650 does not distinguish these in its processing.

```
indicator650
ᴀ IBM 650 indicator allocation
ᴀ programmed stop            ᴀ invalid operation code
 Progr←0                      Invop←2
ᴀ overflow                   ᴀ invalid address
 Oflo←1                       Invadr←2
ᴀ machine malfunction        ᴀ absolute stop
 Mach←2                       Stop←3
```

PROGRAM 1-35   Indicator allocation in the IBM 650.

Error reports.   The general function report shown in Program 1-36 is used in read650 to report invalid addresses. The left operand of report gives the name of an indicator to be set; the right operand gives the condition for which the indicator is set to one.

The function i, also shown in Program 1-36, reports invalid operations. For machines that notice unused operation codes (as is the case for the 650), the function i is used to set the invalid-operation indicator.

```
which report condition                         i
ᴀ set identified indicator if condition true  ᴀ invalid operation
 ind[which]←v/ind[which],condition             Invop report 1
```

PROGRAM 1-36   Error report using indicators.

Numbers

Program 1-37 shows the number representation of the 650. The allocation of sign and digits is given for a memory word and for the accumulator in data650. The encoding of the sign is also given.

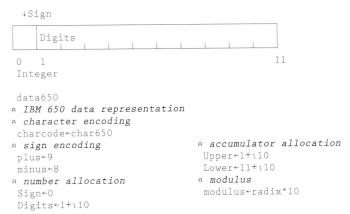

```
data650
A IBM 650 data representation
A character encoding
charcode←char650
A sign encoding              A accumulator allocation
plus←9                        Upper←1+ι10
minus←8                       Lower←11+ι10
A number allocation           A modulus
Sign←0                        modulus←radix*10
Digits←1+ι10
```

PROGRAM 1-37   Data representation in the IBM 650.

Synonyms. An inspection of data650 shows that Digits and Upper are identical. They can be used interchangeably. The only justification for the two names is that they increase clarity. Upper distinguishes the high-order 10 digits of the accumulator from the low-order 10 digits, identified by Lower. Digits identifies the digit portion (as opposed to the sign) of any memory word. It would be confusing to use Upper for a memory word.

Characters

Program 1-38 gives a general format and an algorithmic description of character strings. The format diagram shows the allocation of the data. The number of characters is kept general, as indicated by the break in the diagram. The encoding of the data cannot be seen in a diagram; a table is necessary. The algorithm embodying the table also contains the allocation information, of course.

Observe the complementary nature of index generation (ι) and index use ([ ]). Also note that index use requires two symbols, not one as is otherwise the case in APL.

Char	Char	Char	Char		Char	Char

Legend: Char = character.

```
string←alphai rep            rep←size alphar string
A character string interpretation  A character string representation
string←charcode[magni rep]    rep←size magnr charcodeιstring
```

PROGRAM 1-38   Character-string interpretation and representation.

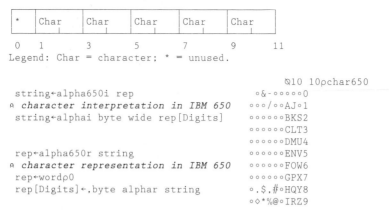

*	Char	Char	Char	Char	Char

```
0   1       3       5       7       9       11
Legend: Char = character; * = unused.
```

```
                                        ⍳10 10⍴char650
string←alpha650i rep                    ∘&-∘∘∘∘∘0
⍝ character interpretation in IBM 650   ∘∘∘/∘∘AJ∘1
string←alphai byte wide rep[Digits]     ∘∘∘∘∘∘BKS2
                                        ∘∘∘∘∘∘CLT3
                                        ∘∘∘∘∘∘DMU4
rep←alpha650r string                    ∘∘∘∘∘∘ENV5
⍝ character representation in IBM 650   ∘∘∘∘∘∘FOW6
rep←word⍴0                              ∘∘∘∘∘∘GPX7
rep[Digits]←,byte alphar string         ∘.$.#∘HQY8
                                        ∘◊*%@∘IRZ9
```

PROGRAM 1-39   Fixed-length character string in the IBM 650.

Character interpretation.   The character-string format of the 650 is shown in Program 1-39. Since two decimal digits represent one alphabetic character, the 10 digits of the 650 word accommodate five characters. `alpha650i` first shapes the 10 digits into a 5×2 matrix by the general function `wide` (Program 1-40). The 5 digit pairs are decoded in `alphai` as five integers. The resulting vector of five elements is used as an index for the code table `charcode`, which has obtained the value of `char650` in `format650`. The result is a vector of five characters, called `string`.

Character representation.   The five-element character vector of the 650 is represented by `alpha650r`. First, `string` is encoded in `alphar` as a vector of five numbers using the index generator (`⍳`) with the code table `charcode`. Next, the numbers are each encoded as two-digit decimal codes using the function `magnr`, resulting in a 5×2 -digit decimal representation. Finally, this matrix is raveled (`,`) in `alpha650r` to a 10-element decimal vector. The sign digit of the 650 is not used in character representation.

Width adjustment.   The general function `wide` shapes a given input to a matrix with a specified lower dimension. When necessary, zero elements are used to complete the matrix.

```
out←size wide in;dimension
⍝ width adjustment
dimension←(⌈(⍴,in)÷size),size
⍝ extend with zero as needed
out←dimension⍴(-×/dimension)↑,in
```

PROGRAM 1-40   General width function.

Operation

As an example of an operation description, we show in Program 1-41 the instruction Add Lower, which adds a number obtained from memory to the accumulator. The function `AL` shows that the entire accumulator participates in the add operation, although the name might suggest otherwise.

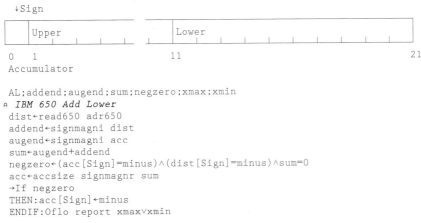

```
AL;addend;augend;sum;negzero;xmax;xmin
ѧ IBM 650 Add Lower
dist←read650 adr650
addend←signmagni dist
augend←signmagni acc
sum←augend+addend
negzero←(acc[Sign]=minus)∧(dist[Sign]=minus)∧sum=0
acc←accsize signmagnr sum
→If negzero
THEN:acc[Sign]←minus
ENDIF:Oflo report xmax∨xmin
```

PROGRAM 1-41   Add Lower in the IBM 650.

The 650 uses signed-magnitude notation, as expressed by the general signed-magnitude interpretation and representation functions `signmagni` and `signmagnr` of Program 4-38.

Paradigm. The basic addition paradigm given by the function `add` (Program 1-42) is not part of the 650 description. Its purpose is to establish a basic pattern and nomenclature that applies to many machines.

Comparison of any machine's addition function with the `add` paradigm highlights that machine's peculiarities. In AL (Program 1-41), for example, the operands `augend`, `addend`, and `sum` are standard concepts of addition, but the distributor `dist` sticks out as a 650 peculiarity. This register is definitely part of the architecture, although in AL it serves no direct purpose. AL also shows that a zero sum has a negative sign, if and only if both operands are negative zeros. This exceptional result is described with an If–THEN structure.

Generic function name. The pattern established by `add` (Program 1-42) is independent of various design choices. The pattern is as true for the radix-complement notation of the PDP11 as for the signed-magnitude notation of the 650. Consequently, the generic function names `interpret` and `represent` are used. There are no functions corresponding to these names; a designer can make his own functions by substituting an appropriate design choice.

Appeal to higher-level concepts.   AL operates upon two representations (strings of decimal digits in the 650) to yield a new representation. We describe this operation through higher-level concepts, such as numbers and addition.

```
add;ad;au;addend;augend;sum;sm
ѧ basic addition
ad←size1 read adr1
au←size2 read adr2
addend←interpret ad
augend←interpret au
sum←augend+addend
sm←size3 represent sum
adr3 write sm
```

PROGRAM 1-42   Basic addition.

Such an appeal to higher-level concepts is a major theme of this book. For the description of architecture, it is essential.

When we cannot use the higher-level concepts, as in the implementation (not to mention the realization), the description becomes very complex. There are digit encodings, carries, complements, and recomplements, all of which are not our concern in the architecture and obscure what we really want to know: Does AL adhere to the well-established mathematical concept of addition? The answer shown in Program 1-41 is "almost": The negative zero is an implementation quirk that has protruded into the architecture. We might have overlooked it had we been presented with all the implementation detail.

Local variables. The variables addend, augend, sum, and negzero appear in the architecture of AL only to describe the operation; they do not change the state of the machine, as does the accumulator acc. The implementer need not make a signal called sum (in fact, he could not if he wanted to), nor can the programmer use this value. So that the private nature of these variables is made clear and secure, they are declared as local variables in the function header. This important convention is followed in all descriptions. It is therefore significant that dist is a global, not a local, variable. The value it attains as part of the operand fetch remains available for subsequent use.

Simplification. Sometimes the explicit steps of the general function add become trivial. In AL, for example, fetching the operand from the accumulator is trivial. In such a case we simplify the description by combining two steps.

Sequencing

The sequencing of instructions is indicated by cycle650 (Program 1-28); it includes the instruction fetch and the stop condition.

Instruction fetch. The next instruction to be executed is obtained by ifetch650, shown in Program 1-43. The 650 obtains the address of the next instruction from the Next field of the current instruction. The merits of this method are evaluated in Section 2.6. Here we only note how this action is described.

```
inst←ifetch650
ɑ IBM 650 instruction fetch
ind[Progr,Mach,Stop]←0
inst←read650 iadr
iadr←fld Next
```

PROGRAM 1-43   Instruction fetch in the IBM 650.

As a new instruction is obtained, three of the four indicators (identified in Program 1-35) are reset.

ifetch650 can be kept simple because read650 (Program 1-34) contains the necessary detail. The fetching of data and the fetching of instructions are thus presented as a unified action whose precise definition is detailed only once.

Stop. The sequencing of instructions in the 650 is stopped by stop650 (Program 1-44). This function inspects the indicators after applying the enable switches mask to three of them.

```
yes←stop650
ꟼ IBM 650 stop condition
yes←v/ind[Stop].mask∧ind[Progr.Oflo.Mach]
```

PROGRAM 1-44   Stop condition in the IBM 650.

Execution

After an instruction is fetched, it is performed as indicated by `cycle650`; the general function `execute` (Program 1-45) is used for this purpose.

```
execute inst
ꟼ instruction execution
⍕oplist[decode inst;]
```

PROGRAM 1-45   General execute function.

Mnemonics.   The operations of a computer are normally represented in the assembly language by a short character string. We have adopted that mnemonic name as the name of the function that executes the corresponding operation. The name is capitalized to make it more distinct. The operation Add Lower, for example, has the mnemonic AL and is described by the function `AL` discussed earlier.

Opcode list.   For descriptive clarity, we gather the mnemonics of all operations of a computer into a character matrix called `oplist`. Each row of `oplist` contains one mnemonic, extended if necessary by blanks. The number of the row matches the numeric value of the operation code. For the 650 the operation code occupies two decimal digits, which gives 100 possible codes. For the 650, `oplist` is shown in Program 1-46 folded into columns of 20 entries, to compress the figure. The second column continues the first. `oplist` has 100 rows, and `decode` selects the row in `oplist` that matches the instruction field `Opcode`. For example, the operation code for AL is 15, and AL is the corresponding entry of `oplist`. The character string obtained

```
a→NOOP      STL       i       RAU       i
    STOP    STU       i       RSU       i
    i       STDA      i       i         i
    i       STIA      i       i         i
    i       STD       BRNZU   DIVRU     TLU
    i       i         BRNZ    RAL       i
    i       i         BRMIN   RSL       i
    i       i         BROV    RAABL     i
    i       i         i       RSABL     i
    i       i         i       LD        i
    AU      SRT       i       RD        BRD10
    SU      SRD       i       PCH       BRD1
    i       i         i       i         BRD2
    i       i         i       i         BRD3
    DIV     i         i       i         BRD4
    AL      SLT       i       i         BRD5
    SL      SCT       i       i         BRD6
    AABL    i         i       i         BRD7
    SABL    i         i       i         BRD8
    MULT    i         i       i         BRD9
```

PROGRAM 1-46   Operation-code list of the IBM 650.

```
          syntax650
     a Unused,Opcode,Address,Next
```

PROGRAM 1-47   Instruction syntax of the IBM 650.

from `oplist` is then decoded using the execute operator (ϕ); as a result, the function `AL` is performed.

Syntax.   The simplicity of the opcode structure of the 650 is apparent from the instruction syntax. Program 1-47 shows that there is only one syntactic pattern, identified by `a`, that applies to all instructions. Such simplicity is rarely found in other computers. More typically, various digits all over the format are used for subclasses of operations. As a consequence, the structure of an operation list is complicated, as explained in Chapter 9.

Not all the description elements given here are of interest for each machine, and some will get only passing mention in the following chapters. For instance, the decoding of the opcode requires less discussion than does the choice between floating-point notations or the action of an interrupt mechanism. Nevertheless, this section and the illustrations in the Zoo indicate how a complete description can be obtained.

1.3.6
Bibliography

Amdahl et al. [1964], Barbacci [1981], Bell and Newell [1971], Blaauw [1976], Blaauw and Duijvestijn [1980], Burks et al. [1946], Burroughs [1964], Cajori [1929], Falkoff et al. [1964], Hoffnagle [1991], IBM [1964], Pakin [1972], Vissers [1977], Whitehead and Russell [1910–13].

1.4
What Is Good Computer Architecture?

An architecture that does not include needed functions is erroneous. But even if the needed functions are present, they may still be awkward. Or the whole may be so complex that it is hard to learn and remember the functions and their rules. An architecture that is straightforward to use is often called *clean*.

1.4.1
The Principles of Quality

In this subsection we set forth general principles that we believe characterize good architectural designs. These are fundamentally esthetic principles, describing the nature of beauty in computer architecture. As is always true with lists of esthetic principles, clean design is a matter of balance, of taste.

Consistency

A good architecture is *consistent* in the sense that, given a partial knowledge of the system, one can predict the remainder. We believe that consistency underlies all principles of quality [Blaauw, 1965; 1970].

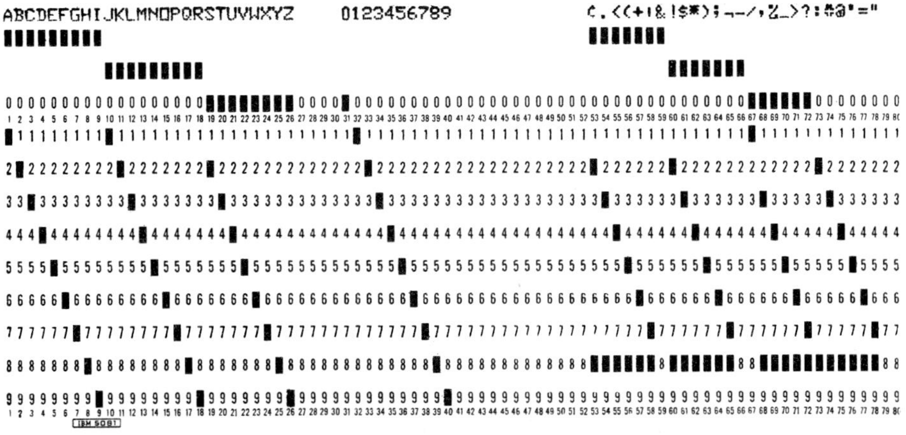

FIGURE 1-48   Punched card with the Binary Coded Decimal code.

For example, the mere decision to incorporate a square-root operation in an operation set should almost fully define the operation. The data and instruction formats should be the same as those for other arithmetic operations. Precision, range, rounding, and significance should be handled as with other results. Even taking the square root of a negative number should have an exception treatment similar, for example, to that of division by zero.

An example of lack of consistency can be found in the Hollerith punched-card code. Here a study of the codes for the letters A through R leads one to expect an S where the slash (/) is found, as illustrated in Figure 1-48.

The floating-point operation Halve was added to the 360 late in the design. Because of implementation problems, the postnormalization was omitted. This lack of consistency with the other floating-point operations made the function almost useless. Soon after the machine was in production, the design had to be corrected.

Consistency is reinforcing and self-teaching, because it encourages and confirms our expectations. It also solves the conflict between ease of use and ease of learning. Ease of learning requires a simple architecture, as with fixed-point arithmetic; ease of use requires a more complex one, as with floating-point arithmetic. When the designer makes fixed point a subset of floating point and makes both part of a consistent design, the user's comprehension of the architecture can grow naturally.

Still, the truly consistent solution can be hard to identify. For computer architecture, some touchstones are: brevity of description, freedom in implementation, and simplicity of code generation.

Derived principles.   People often appeal to consistency in their thinking, although not always consciously. We say, "Let's not confuse the issues," "That has nothing to do with the case," and "If this, why not that?" We are warning not to link what is independent, not to introduce what is immaterial, and not to restrict what is inherent—we are appealing to the principles of *orthogonality*, *propriety*, and *generality*. From these three main design principles, still others follow (Tree 1-49).

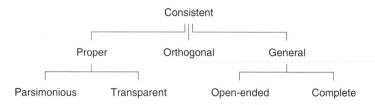

TREE 1-49   Relation of quality principles.

Orthogonality

The principle of keeping independent functions separate in their specification is called *orthogonality*. This term has several meanings in mathematics. Originally it described the property of a set of coordinates that are so related that a change in position along any one of them has no components along any other. It has been metaphorically extended to sets of mathematical functions; here it is further extended to computer functions. A change of one orthogonal computer function has no observable effect on any other function in the set.

For a clock, a set of optional functions might be:

- Visibility of the time in the dark—the luminous dial
- Signaling at a preset time—the alarm

Clearly, these functions are independent of each other, and the principle of orthogonality would be violated if the alarm could operate only with a lighted dial. Wishing to know the hour at night has nothing to do with wanting to be roused at a preset time.

Constructing a design tree, such as Tree 1-13 for the alarm clock, can help one recognize orthogonal functions.

Orthogonality does not concern the presence or absence of a function. A manufacturer may reasonably offer a package deal that consists of a clock with luminous dial and alarm. What is required by orthogonality is that independent functions, if provided, be independently invoked in use.

For example, the amount of shift in the 650's shift operations is determined by the low-order address digit; the other address digits are not used. Yet, if the address exceeds addressable memory, the machine stops and gives an error indication. Orthogonality is violated—the other digits should always be ignored.

The 705 uses a special character, the group mark (code 111111), to stop data transfer in a Write operation. The control of transmission of a message is tied to the content of the message. As a result, the machine cannot handle binary information.

The IBM 7030, the Stretch computer [Buchholz, 1962], includes three flag bits in the floating-point format (Figure 1-50). These bits are logical variables attached to numbers. Such mixing of purposes proves unsatisfactory.

FIGURE 1-50   Floating-point format in the IBM Stretch.

Arithmetic operations are complicated with concern about flags; for example, loading an operand from memory requires the provision of two operations, Load With Flags and plain Load. Moreover, the flag logic can be performed much more effectively by the regular logical operations, acting on bits in separate arrays.

Propriety

A function's meeting an essential requirement is called *propriety*. For a car, functions such as steering, lights, and windshield wipers are proper to its purposes.

The opposite of propriety is *extraneousness*, the introduction of something alien to the purpose to be served. A typical example is the automotive gear shift, which also illustrates the main source of extraneousness: the implementation. Shifting gears is not proper to driving. It is required because of the limited effective speed range of the piston engine.

An example of propriety in computers is the unique representation of zero in 2's-complement notation. In contrast, signed-magnitude and 1's-complement notation each attach a sign to zero, yielding inherently distinct positive and negative zeros. The distinction is extraneous; a mathematical zero has no sign. The introduction of this sign results in a set of rules that do not help the user solve his problems. Explicit architectural prescriptions, such as "all zero results are positive" or "plus zero is equal to minus zero," are required to prevent behavior contrary to mathematical convention. And these rules may have unexpected effects in use.

Parsimony.   A principle that follows from propriety is that "improper" functions must not be present. This principle is called *parsimony*. Mies van der Rohe said, "Less is more"; a popular phrasing is, "When in doubt, leave it out." A useful touchstone is, "Even if the function were free, would it be proper to the concepts of this computer?"

At some point in each technological-development cycle, designers tend to add bells and whistles. Such design is typical when the art is developed to the point where the options can be afforded, but designers lack enough use experience to know the options' true usefulness.

The Stretch computer, for example, introduced the concept of variable byte size, which allowed characters of 1 through 8 bits to participate in arithmetic and logical operations. In the 360 this concept was dropped. Variable byte size passes the choice of the byte size to the user, who does not really care what the size is, as long as it is large enough. The introduction of such a concept poses a series of strange and extraneous questions to the user: How must bytes of unequal size be matched? If extended, what bits are supplied? On which side? If truncated, is the deletion of significant bits signaled?

Parsimony also prescribes that a function must not be provided in two competing ways. Otherwise, redundant knowledge and an unnecessary choice are forced upon the user. Since a machine has to have only one operation [Van der Poel, 1956], a new operation is justified only when it gives such efficiency of expression that it obviously surpasses constructs composed of the existing operations. A typical example is floating-point arithmetic, which is justified because it obviates cumbersome scaling procedures.

Parsimony usually advances economy. Moreover, it aids comprehensibility by concentrating the user's attention. Surprisingly, it even aids open-endedness—by not prescribing for partly understood needs, one avoids foreclosing the future.

Transparency.   Another concept that results from propriety is transparency. An architectural function is *transparent* if its implementation does not produce any architecturally visible side effects. Just as window glass, whose functions are to admit light but obstruct air, should ideally not even be visible, so the side effects of implementation must not be architecturally visible.

In dialing a long-distance telephone call, a subscriber should not have to choose the channels and exchanges through which his call is routed. All he inherently needs to specify is the telephone number of the person he wants to call. Similarly, limitations on the number of calls that can be made simultaneously should be invisible to him.

Likewise, in a computer, the implementation of the datapath—say, with a pipelined organization—should not affect the handling of an interruption. Model 91 of the 360 illustrates the kind of exceptions often made at this point [S.F. Anderson et al., 1967].

Generality

Generality is the ability to use a function for many ends. It expresses the professional humility of the designer, his conviction that users will be inventive beyond his imagination and that needs may change beyond his capacity to forecast. The designer must not limit a function by his own notions about its use unless these have become widely accepted through experience. In the absence of knowledge, freedom must be safeguarded.

Some clocks cannot be set by turning the hands back. Such lack of generality is due to the implementation of the clock and is of no benefit to the user. In fact, most modern clocks can be set in either direction.

Babbage's first computer was the special-purpose Difference Engine (ca. 1832). During its development, Babbage realized that by generalizing his design he could make its application much wider than just computing tables with the use of differences. This consideration led him to design a second machine, the Analytical Engine (ca. 1867). Generality has thus proved to be a powerful architectural principle from the start. The success of the modern computer has been mostly due to its general purpose character.

The 8080A has an operation called Restart. This operation was indeed intended as a restart after interruption, but it was designed with enough generality that its most frequent use is a return from a subroutine.

Generality is lost when the implementation exerts too much influence over the architecture. This is true not only for implementation-derived restrictions; even implementation-offered gifts must be viewed with skepticism.

A certain function of marginal utility may appear to be "free." If it is not general, however, it requires extra tests for the compilers to handle the exceptions. These tests may entail such inefficiencies that it is better for the code generator not to use the function at all. Furthermore, since architectures last for many generations of implementations, the function may not be at all "free" for some of them.

Three major ways in which generality can be achieved are open-endedness, completeness, and decomposition.

Open-endedness.   Provision for future expansion is called *open-endedness*. To provide for future developments, the designer is wise to leave spares in the spaces his design has created, such as format bits and codes. One reason why the successful IBM 701-7094II family (1953–1964) could not be extended any further was that the address space of its instruction format was limited. In the 360 this space was expanded 100-fold, with intentional provision for straightforward extension by another factor of 256 [Brooks, 1965]. Within a few years, serious demands for this added space were made in the Model 67 (1966).

Completeness.   The requirements of generality are met by *completeness* when all functions of a given class are provided.

For example, if a computer incorporates division, one might expect it to include multiplication. If it has floating-point addition, multiplication, and division, as well as fixed-point addition, one would expect fixed-point multiplication and division, too—and is surprised not to find these functions in the CDC 6600 (1964). In general, completeness prescribes that the Cartesian product sets of combined orthogonal properties be furnished entirely or not at all.

An important special case of completeness is *symmetry*, the property of an operation set wherein the inverse or converse is provided for each operation.

The Stretch computer, which, as the name indicates, deliberately tried to stretch computer technology, provided all 16 connective functions of two binary variables. The symmetry is apparent.

In a program, the criterion of a branching decision is independent of the arrangement of the program into mainroutines and subroutines. Symmetry is therefore violated if Branch On Not-Plus is furnished, but Branch On Plus is not provided, as in the MIT Whirlwind (1953) and the 1401.

As with all principles, completeness must not be taken as the sole good. Completeness may introduce the problem of *proliferation*: The full range of choices may result in a superabundance of specification, demanding excess format space. For example, a variable-field-length instruction in the Stretch computer required 64 bits, even though the byte address was only 21 bits long. Thirty-three bits were required by bit addressing, field length, sign and radix control, indexing, index mode control, byte size selection, and a relative shift, called `Offset` (Figure 1-51).

Decomposition.   One can diminish proliferation by localizing the options through *decomposition* into orthogonal operations. The screwdriver set that includes several handles and bits that can fit all of the handles is such a solution. It requires far fewer parts than a full set of complete screwdrivers.

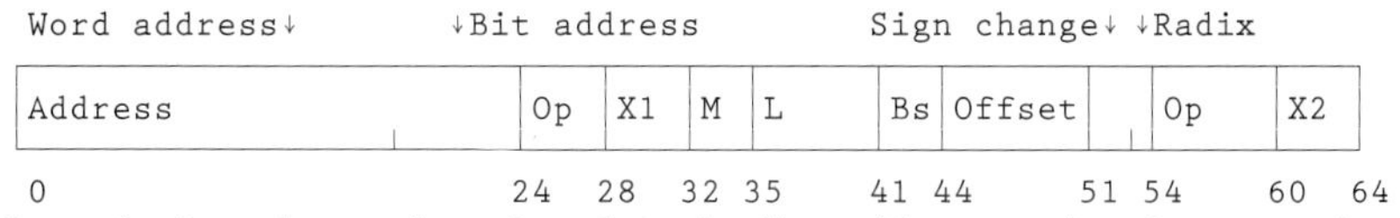

```
Word address↓        ↓Bit address         Sign change↓ ↓Radix

Address              Op  X1  M  L      Bs Offset      Op   X2

0                    24  28 32 35      41 44     51 54    60  64
Legend: Bs = byte size; L = length; M = address mode; Op = opcode;
        X = index.
```

FIGURE 1-51   Variable-length specification in the IBM Stretch.

The symmetry of branching is secured in most modern computers by decomposing that operation in the evaluation of a branch criterion as part of arithmetic or logic and by specifying the branch targets as part of a branch instruction.

Instead of multiplying all instructions by a given set of options, one may expand only one basic function. In contrast to the Stretch, which provides sign-control options on all arithmetic operations, the 360 delegates control of operand sign to a set of four sign-modifying Load operations. Similarly, immediate and indirect addressing are provided by separate operations appropriately loading index registers, instead of including these options with each address. These decisions improve the bit efficiency of the instructions.

Summary of Quality Principles

The architect of a system creates a world in which other people can be creative in turn. Steinway and his predecessors made possible the compositions of Chopin, which in turn allow pianists such as Rubinstein to be creative. In the world created by the computer architect, programmers and implementers must be able to work creatively. If the architecture is well-designed, they will be free to do so.

The principles that lead to a clean design are not peculiar to computers, as shown by examples drawn from other fields of engineering. An even wider scope could have been taken. The underlying principle of consistency also applies to other areas of creative endeavor, as illustrated in drama by the unities of time, place, and person, and in philosophy by Ockham's famous razor, the canon of parsimony.

1.4.2

The Value of Quality

The design principles presented are essentially esthetic. This concern with esthetics seems at once strange and unjustifiable. The computer architect is, after all, hired to design a machine, not a piece of art. Moreover, most users will never see the architecture, for they will use the machine through a high-level programming language. It seems therefore utterly unjustifiable to sacrifice a jot of cost or a tittle of performance to satisfy some abstract principle of esthetics, to achieve some vaguely felt cleanliness.

Good Esthetics Yields Good Economics

Our own experience with computer architecture, however, has brought us to conclude that adherence to good esthetic principles yields computers with the best overall economics.

We shall support our conclusion with historical examples and logical arguments. The examples are scattered throughout this work. The logical arguments we present here: They rest on the objective of minimizing the *overall long-run* cost of using a computer.

Overall cost.   The overall costs include a major cost for programming and lower, but substantial, costs for running compilers and for educating users. All these costs are reduced by clean architecture.

The software costs of using computers quite outweigh the hardware costs, so savings in the first can easily outweigh savings in hardware. This principle has always been true [Wilkes and Renwick, 1949b], but in the early days users were abundant and machines scarce. Programming therefore appeared free, or at least cheap in comparison with machine costs. This perception has endured hardily. But machine cost/performance ratios have improved 1000-fold in 25 years; programming cost/performance ratios have improved only about 10-fold. Such developments have strongly enhanced the economic value of clean computer architecture.

Long-run cost.   The long-run costs of using a computer architecture are deeply affected by the long lifetimes experienced by architectures. Because of heavy software investments, architectures typically live through several generations of implementations. During these lives many aspects of applications change, and many technological ratios shift. If an architecture is esthetically sound at its start, changes can be accommodated more simply and systematically, and long-run costs will be lower.

For example, we remarked that the slash in the Hollerith punch-card code was inconsistently placed between the letters R and S, an inconsistency that has been costly to implement for about 60 years. How did it come about? First, a hole was left in the alphabet because the current electromechanical realization could not reliably distinguish the adjacent punchings in rows 0 and 1. Next, the hole was used for the slash even though a more consistent three-punch code, only slightly more expensive than this two-punch code, was available. Hindsight teaches that the long-run cost of this ugliness was orders of magnitude greater than the initial savings. But, at the moment of decision, an architect must have foresight and conviction to withstand the short-run pressures of schedules and estimates.

Consider a second example. As remarked, the universal mistake of computer architects has been providing too little addressing capacity. Not only has this mistake been widespread, but also it has been iterated in turn for minicomputers and then for microcomputers [Bell, Mudge, and McNamara, 1978].

Part of good architectural design is enough long-run vision to leave room for future growth—as much room as possible, but not so much as to cost-kill the ancestral product. This balancing act is a prime challenge to every architect.

1.4.3
Bibliography

S.F. Anderson et al. [1967], Bell, Mudge, and McNamara [1978], Blaauw [1965, 1970], Brooks [1965], Buchholz [1962], Cornyn et al. [1977], Cragon [1979], Flynn [1980], Huck and Flynn [1983], Lunde [1977], MacDougall [1984], Van der Poel [1956], Wilkes and Renwick [1949b].

1.5
Rules of Good Practice

The rules of good practice for architectural design that have been derived in this chapter are summarized here. They are necessarily oversimplified, but they illustrate how a unified architectural philosophy works out into specifics:

1. Describe the architecture in natural language and in a formal language, using the formal language as normative.
2. Enhance the natural-language description with illustrations and examples of use.
3. Give a feasible implementation of those architectural functions whose efficient implementation is not well-known or easily derived.
4. Use an executable, high-level, formal description to demonstrate the architecture and to verify the implementation.
5. Prohibit the use of bit patterns that are deliberately left undefined, and enforce the prohibition by policing.
6. Test the design for consistency—hence for orthogonality, propriety, and generality.

1.6
Exercises

1-1 State whether each of the following machine concepts belongs primarily to the architecture, the implementation, or the realization of a system:

   a. Carry prediction in an adder

   b. Double-precision addition

   c. Core storage

   d. Tape-control unit

   e. Pipelined memory access

   f. Cache memory

   g. Sign of zero

   h. Floating-point underflow

   i. Representation of decimal digits

   j. I/O channel

   k. Interleaved memory

   l. 2's-complement notation

1-2 Make a list of inconsistencies you discern in your favorite computer machine language. Characterize each as a lack of orthogonality, propriety, generality, or otherwise. To what can you trace the source of each inconsistency? What difference do these inconsistencies make to you as a user?

1-3 Give an architectural definition, in words, of a machine to play nim, or an elevator system that you use frequently.

   a. Did you describe the machine generatively or assertively?

   b. Does the architectural definition imply an initial implementation?

   c. Does the definition require additional notes to the user?

1-4 Choose a branch of the historical family tree shown in Table 1-4 and show how the architectures of the members of that tree:

    a. Have converged toward the esthetic principles of Section 1.4

    b. Have diverged from the esthetic principles of Section 1.4

    c. Illustrate arguments for or against the statement, "Good esthetics is good economics"

1-5 Analyze the Institute for Advanced Studies (IAS) computer [von Neumann, 1946; see also Section 11.1] in terms of the esthetic principles set forth in this chapter, then answer these questions:

    a. Where are these principles clearly violated?

    b. Where are these principles too vague?

    c. Is this set of principles inherently self-contradictory? Can the set be true if self-contradictory? How, or why not?

1-6 Make a design tree for the major architectural functions of a car, a telephone, a washing machine, or a slide projector.

1-7 Suppose you are designing a medium-scale computer that will be sold or leased to business data-processing service bureaus that now provide batch-processing services for small businesses, now tailor a basic set of programs to the needs of their customers, but want interactive capabilities for in-shop use that can be expanded to provide interactive service to their customers. Define the demands on the system in terms of the following parameters (and any other parameters that you think are relevant):

    a. Operation mix

    b. Job balance (CPU bound or I/O bound)

    c. Types of I/O (high-speed input versus low-speed input, non-recoverable input versus recoverable input, short message exchanges on long input streams followed by long output streams)

How would the parameter values that you determined in parts a through c constrain the architecture of the following?

    d. Data formats

    e. Instruction formats

    f. I/O processing

    g. Interrupt system

    h. Instruction sequencing

    i. What other information about the applications can be parameterized in a way that is meaningful to the architect?

1-8 Answer the questions of Exercise 1-7 for a medium-scale computer to be sold or leased to large scientific laboratories that want a computer that can monitor very many experiments, collect data, and reduce them to forms that can be handled by a big batch-processing computer. The laboratories also want to support several terminals with an interactive language such as APL or Basic.

1-9 "There is less fundamental architectural difference among third-generation minicomputers ('superminis') than among first-generation computers."

    a. Present arguments for or against this statement.

    b. Is there a relation between the development of the esthetics of architecture and the breadth of current architectural design?

    c. What are the economic constraints on architectural innovation?

    d. What changes in the computer markets can you envision that would stimulate architectural innovation?

1-10 A simple but fully general computer is to be specified to perform the 360 I/O operations and only three other operations.

    a. Select a set of three operations that will give the most flexibility and generality.

    b. Show how you would use your selected set to accomplish the principal result of (A) Add, (L) Load, (ST) Store, (SLA) Arithmetic Left Shift, (SRA) Arithmetic Right Shift, and (M) Move.

1-11 The 650 is described in this chapter with the decimal digit as the unit of information; the description hides the encoding of the digits in bits.

    a. What prevents a description with the full-word number as the unit of information, the encoding of the number being hidden?

    b. What would be an advantage if such a description could be given?

    c. Ignoring the problems mentioned under part a, describe Add in terms of numbers, as opposed to digits.

1-12 Give a feasible implementation for a hypothetical Add operation in the 650, in which the minus-zero appears naturally, not requiring special tests.

1-13 Design a Square Root operation for the 650.

    a. Give its formal description, using where applicable the functions shown in Sections 1.3 and 12.1.

    b. Comment on your design decisions in handling the following:

       • Negative operands

       • Approximate results

       • The fact that the operation needs only one operand

1-14 "A vital criterion to be able to generate efficient object code ... is an over-all simplicity of the instruction set and the entire architecture. The more facilities, such as different sets of registers available, the more complex will be the compilation process making good use of them. A truly good architecture should make so-called optimizations largely unnecessary (or impossible)" [Wirth, 1976].

    a. Compare Wirth's view with specific views presented in this chapter.

    b. Give a counterargument to the claim of the second sentence of the quotation.

1-15 Using the criteria developed in Section 1.4 and the information supplied in the Zoo, comment on the following statements:

    a. "The STAR100 is the Stretch of CDC."

    b. "The VAX11 is the Stretch of DEC."

1-16 Suppose *Computing Reviews* has started a new classification, "Computer Architecture Reviews," to contain critiques of computer architectures. Write or outline a review and critique of the PDP11, the Motorola MC68000, the Cray 1, or the IBM 6150.

    a. Describe briefly the architectural concepts that distinguish your machine from other computers in general and from direct competitors in particular.

    b. Balance the strengths and weaknesses of each of the concepts that you gave in part a.

    c. Critique the consistency of the architecture, with examples.

FIRST BOOK.

WALLS may be seen, built with squared stones, at *Rome*, where stood the piazza and the temple of AUGUSTUS, in which the lesser stones are key'd in with some courses of the larger.

V

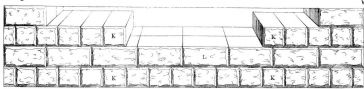

K, *courses of the lesser stones.*
L, *courses of the larger stones.*

THE method the antients made use of to build the walls called *riempiuta*, or coffer-work, was by placing two rows of planks edgeways, distant the one from the other according to the thickness they intended to give the walls, and then filled the void with cement, mix'd with all kinds of stones, and continued it in this manner from course to course. Walls of this kind may be seen at *Sirmion*, upon the lake of *Garda.*

VI

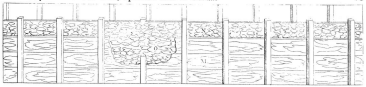

M, *planks laid edgeway.*
N, *inward part of the wall.*
O, *face of the wall, the planks being taken away.*

THE walls of *Naples*, that is, the antient ones, may be said to be after this manner; which have two walls of squared stones, four foot thick, and six foot distant the one from the other, bound together with others that run cross them. The coffers that remain between the traverse and out-walls are six foot square, which are filled up with stones and earth.

VII

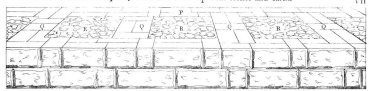

P, *the outward stone walls.*
Q, *the traverse stone walls to bind them together.*
R, *the coffers, filled with stones and earth.*

THESE, in fine, are the different sorts of walls the antients made use of, footsteps of which still remain: From which we may conclude, that all walls, let them be of what kind soever, ought to have some cross courses, as so many ligaments to bind all the other parts together. This must particularly be observed in brick walls, that, should the middle of the walls, through length of time, sink or decay, the rest may not be subject to ruin; as we see happens in many walls, particularly on the side facing the north.

2

Machine Language

Overview of the Chapter

The design of computer architecture is the design of the complete machine language of a computer system—that is, the language of the program stored in memory and interpreted by the machine.

The fundamental difference between machine languages and other programming and natural languages is that machine-language expressions are *costly*. So machine languages are lean and concise. As a consequence,

1. Cost with respect to space and time requires compactness of representation as expressed in the *bit budget* of the representation and the *bit traffic* of the use of this representation.
2. Machine languages are rigidly constrained, using *few and simple constructs*, so that interpretation can be swift and the interpreter simple.
3. Fundamental technological reasons make it simplest to represent information by two-state devices, so most machine languages employ only *two symbols*, 0 and 1.
4. To simplify interpretation, statements are constrained to be parsable *without dependence on context*, and even semantic interpretation has at most a limited context-dependence.

Subordinate and more specific properties of machine languages follow from these basic differences:

1. Words and statements are usually *delimited implicitly* by bit count in machine languages, whereas they are delimited explicitly by reserved symbols in programming and natural languages.
2. Statements, called *instructions* in machine languages, are therefore limited to a *few specific lengths*.
3. Words, called *fields* in machine languages, are of *fixed length and order* within statements; statements adhere to a few rigid syntactic patterns, called *formats*.
4. Machine languages are *phrase-structured* within statements, so that phrases can be interpreted concurrently and independently.
5. Verbs are *imperative*, so statements have no subject. In this respect, machine languages are like other programming languages but unlike

natural languages. Instructions consist of a verb phrase with a few (or no) object phrases. These are called the *operation* and *operand* phrases.

6. Computers are information manipulators, so the *universe of discourse* of machine languages consists of only
   - Units of information entities that have names and values
   - Actions to be taken on such units
   - The program itself, which is also composed of units of information
   - I/O devices, which are used for sending information to and receiving information from the outside world
   - The state of the interpreter—information that governs how the machine language is interpreted

7. The entities that can be named are fixed, few in kind, and many in number, so arbitrary names can be permanently assigned to them. These names and the properties of the entities constitute the *storage spaces*, the major structures within the universe of discourse.

8. As is true of programming languages but not of natural languages, a machine language is *unambiguous* in syntax and semantics.

What is the proper level for a machine language? Section 2.1 addresses this fundamental issue. We argue that there is indeed a proper level for machine language: the level between language constructs that can be translated during compilation and those whose translation must wait until execution.

Section 2.2 details and explains the properties of machine language. Section 2.3 examines the structure of the storage spaces that constitute so large a part of the universe of discourse. It also discusses the design decisions for storage-space architecture. Sections 2.4 and 2.5 deal with operand and operation specification, respectively. Section 2.6 treats the design of machine-language syntax, as embodied in the instruction and status formats.

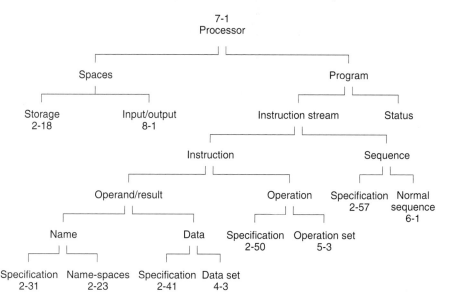

TREE 2-1   Design choices for a processor.

Whereas this chapter treats the syntax of machine languages, the later chapters treat machine-language semantics, part by part. Tree 2-1 shows the relation between these subjects as treated in this chapter and in the remainder of the book. The reference numbers point to other trees; the top reference shows that the processor is part of a computing system, as shown in Tree 7-1.

2.1

Language Level

What is the proper level for machine language?

This question was not germane in the early days of computers. The machine-language level was the only language level. Applications were programmed in machine language only; hardware decoded it directly in terms of datapaths and control.

Today, matters are different. Most applications are built in a language whose level is much higher than that of machine language—FORTRAN, COBOL, C, Pascal, APL. Conversely, many machines do not decode machine language directly; they interpret it via lower-level microcode sequences, whose language structure corresponds closely to hardware datapaths and gates.

The machine language of today is often neither an application language nor a pure hardware language, but something in between. So, why have it at all? Why not interpret one or more application languages directly, rather than requiring them to be compiled into this intermediate language? Or why not give the programmer direct access to the hardware, via the microcode, rather than restrict him to the machine language?

These three alternatives are diagrammed in Figure 2-2. We first consider the forces that push the level of machine language upward, then the downward forces, then a principle for choosing the best level.

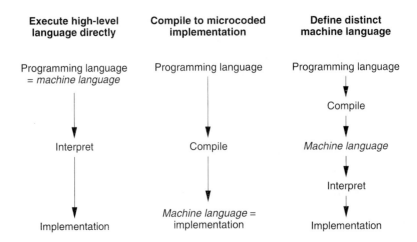

FIGURE 2-2   Alternatives for machine-language level.

Quite apart from microcode's candidacy to be the machine language, its use as an implementation technique has influenced architecture. We examine how at the end of this section.

2.1.1

High-Level Machine Language

Why have assembly-level machine language? Is it not the outworn relic of outmoded thinking? Since most applications are programmed in FORTRAN, C, COBOL, why not implement these languages directly in microcode?

The Upward Urge

Surprisingly, the motivation for raising the level of machine language is not so much ease of use as performance—reducing bit traffic and exploiting concurrency.

Bit traffic.   The classical way to reduce the bit traffic is to have the machine architecture do *more* with each instruction fetched, to abandon the low-level architecture and go as high as the software allows. Every instruction fetch that can be eliminated is a gain. So a floating-point Add wins over a corresponding subroutine, and a 32-bit fixed-point Add beats two 16-bit additions with carry.

The upward urge is clearly evident in the development of minicomputer and microcomputer architectures, as the tables throughout this book show.

Implementation concurrency.   If an implementation knows more about what is to be done, it can often perform several actions simultaneously, since the datapath of the implementation is inherently concurrent. Thus, the exponent can be evaluated concurrently with the coefficient in floating point; in a vector addition, several elements can be added at once. Once the architecture is defined, for each action of the architecture that allows concurrency, the implementer has a rich repertoire of techniques (such as parallelism, lookahead, lookaside, guess and correct, and special-casing) to improve performance, so he can use his resources to their best advantage.

This reasoning raises the question, When is enough enough? When does the upward movement of the machine language stop? To answer this question, we consider high-level machine language. High-level programming languages are themselves the source of a downward discipline that counteracts the upward urge.

The Downward Discipline

Even if all applications were written in high-level languages, there would still be strong reasons for defining a computer architecture at a lower level.

Independent interpretability.   The strongest reason is an inherent conflict between the needs of the user and those of the implementer. The user wants the ease and economy of expression of a language that makes rich use of context; the implementer wants each instruction to be interpretable independently.

Compilation.   Another compelling reason arises from the properties of the high-level languages themselves. For most such languages, translation ideally involves two steps, one at compile time and one at execute time.

An alphanumeric mnemonic name, for example, can become a compactly represented name at compile time. This name in turn can be related to a memory address (itself a compact name) at load time. Such early, one-time compilation vastly reduces the work the interpreter must do iteratively. Some interpretive action, however, must be deferred until execute time; it is data-dependent—chain-pointer following, for example.

Ideally, a machine language should stand precisely between compilation and interpretation.

Number of translators—sum versus product.   There are many high-level programming languages; as early as 1969, Sammet enumerated 120 of them [Sammet, 1976]. Each of these has its users; each has an application set for which it is considered the best language.

Similarly, there are many best computer implementations at any point in time, each optimized for performance at a different cost level or for a different application set.

The set of direct implementations of each language on each hardware dataflow is the Cartesian product of the two sets; its number is the product of their two sizes. A machine-language intermediate reduces the number of translations to the sum of the number of languages and the number of computer structures, as sketched in Figure 2-3.

The suitability of machine language is precisely that it separates the translations at a natural point, between the early-binding compilation and the late-binding interpretation.

Decoupling of instabilities.   The definitions of high-level languages change with time. Similarly, advances in technology make changes in computer realizations fruitful. These in turn urge changes in implementations. The relative stability of a certain machine language means that the instabilities of programming languages and implementations can be decoupled from each other. Translator changes can then be made piecewise.

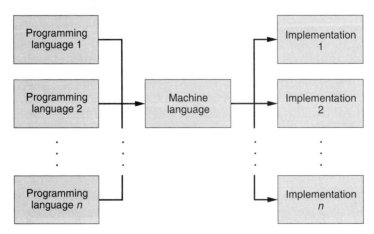

FIGURE 2-3   Intermediate language as a nexus.

Greatest common factor. A study of language concepts, such as control structures, shows that these differ among languages, often in critical detail. Therefore, incorporating exactly a complex concept from one of these languages in a machine language can make that machine language unsuitable for other higher-level languages. Myers [1977b, 1978] notes that his high-level SWARD proposal cannot possibly execute FORTRAN programs. Less extreme cases occur in machines that were actually built. A good machine language should contain those parts of a higher-level concept that can be used in practically all higher-level languages. The diversity of higher-level languages therefore lowers the proper level of the machine language.

The compiler knows better. Interpretation of a high-level language is split into two parts by the machine language. The compiler takes care of one part— for instance, from FORTRAN to machine language. The implementation takes care of the second part—for instance, via microcode. The implementation can optimize more effectively when it gets a larger part of the interpretation process, because it can know run-time information. The compiler, on the other hand, can know global information about the entire program. It can exploit its knowledge of the algorithm and of the operands in the optimization (for example, substituting a shift for multiplication by a constant power of 2). So a low-level architecture is more attractive as the target of compilation than is a higher-level architecture.

Semantic gap. The semantics of the high-level language and of the machine language are basically different. The first assumes global knowledge of the program; the second assumes only local knowledge, or at most knowledge only of the part already executed. This difference in knowledge available has been called the *semantic gap* [Gogliardi, 1973].

Many have proposed reducing, if not eliminating, the semantic gap. The foregoing considerations, however, show that it is inherent—such a gap *must* occur in the language hierarchy. We believe that it is not only proper, but indeed natural and perhaps optimal, for the semantic gap to serve as the upper bound of the machine-language level. The experience with machines that drastically raised the machine-language level and at the same time tried to preserve generality with respect to user languages seems to confirm this (for example, the IBM System/38, the Burroughs B5500 (1964), the Intel i432). For the opposite view, see Myers [1982], powerfully argued.

2.1.2
Reduced-Instruction-Set Computers

When does the downward discipline stop? How far down toward implementation should machine language go? Consider the level of the reduced-instruction-set computers.

An architecture in which most, if not all, operations can be implemented in a single datapath action and that has few constructs is called a *reduced-instruction-set computer* (RISC). Early examples are Van der Poel's STC ZEBRA (1959), the DEC PDP8 (1965), and first-generation microprocessors such as the

Intel 8008 (1972) and the Motorola 6800 (1975). More recent examples are the IBM 801 (1982), the Berkeley RISC (1982), and the IBM 6150 (1986).

The absence of operations requiring subcycles—such as multiply, divide, and multiple-bit shifts—creates a programming inconvenience; a RISC architecture explicitly assumes a compiler or macroassembler that can eliminate that burden. The instruction set is furthermore designed to be a suitable target for an optimizing compiler. At the same time, the single-cycle operation set allows a fast implementation [Radin, 1983]. The operation set facilitates realization on a single chip with the majority of the circuits serving the data flow rather than the control.

Bit traffic.   The low-level instructions should not only have the proper atomic function, but should also generate a low level of bit traffic in fetching these instructions. The ZEBRA achieves this goal for multiplications with a Repeat function. An instruction buffer—as in the ZEBRA and the CDC 6600 (1964)—or, more generally, a cache, can also help reduce the bit traffic.

Nevertheless, when all such implementation devices have been exploited, bit traffic for a RISC architecture may still be higher than that for a standard one. This drawback trades against the faster implementation.

2.1.3

Microcoding

Why not carry the downward urge still further, and push machine language down to the microcoding level?

Microcoding as an Implementation Method

The two basic parts in processor implementation are datapath and control. The datapath is made up of the components holding and transforming data. The control specifies the use of these components in time. This specification is done by *gate signals* that originate in the control and activate the gates of the datapath; conversely, the outcome of the datapath action, such as a positive or negative sign, may be used as a *test signal* to affect the sequence generated by the control.

Hardwired control.   Since each early design aimed to minimize the number of components, the control used a great variety of encodings in which little structure could be recognized. This approach was called *hardwired control*.

Microcoded control.   In 1951 Wilkes pointed out that the task of the control is similar to the task of a computer: Specific actions are to be performed in a proper sequence. The actions are simply the opening and closing of gates; the sequence includes frequent, but simple, decision making based upon the test signals. The gate signals and decision specifications are combined as a *microinstruction*; the microinstructions necessary for the proper computer action constitute a *microprogram*; the microprogram is placed in a storage, the *microstore*. This method of control is called *microcoding* [Wilkes, 1951].

Pros and cons of microcode.   Microcode increases the flexibility of an implementation. Machine debugging and later "hardware" modification can

often be reduced to changes in the microcode. This method is considerably simpler than redesigning hardwired controls.

Many complex functions can be reduced to a combination of fewer, simpler operations by microcode. So a complex machine language can have simpler hardware, which is cheaper and is easier to debug.

Microprogramming also has its disadvantages. The microstore and decoder cost money. For machines with only a few simple functions, hardwiring may be cheaper, and the microcode interpreter may slow processor operation. Finally, the concurrency of the machine is limited by the number of microcode controls that operate simultaneously. These last two factors can be decisive arguments against microcoding in fast machines.

Microcoding Architecture

The design of microinstruction syntax and semantics involves the same kinds of decisions as does design of any other machine architecture. This fact is a good example of the vertical recursion of architecture.

The criteria for design at this implementation level, however, differ somewhat from those for general purpose computers, and the resulting designs are quite different:

- Microcode structures are usually designed with a knowledge of the machine language to be interpreted, and the datapaths and primitive operations can be specialized for that language.
- Since microprogramming is done relatively rarely, ease of programming is not an important criterion.
- Program speed is crucial, since it determines computer performance.
- Microprogram size is of importance second only to speed, since the speed requirements normally preclude the use of backing store, and all the microprogram must be held in a relatively expensive microstore.
- As a rule, microinstruction operations have no further sequential substructure; they are primitives.
- Since microcode store is costly, common parts of microprograms are shared. The frequency of branching is therefore much higher than in ordinary machine language. It is common for every microinstruction to include at least one test and branch among its actions.

Since microcoding architecture has peculiar desiderata, and since it is properly an implementation concern, we shall not treat it further. Husson [1970] and Hennessy and Patterson [1990] do so at length.

User Access to Microcoding

Why conceal the microcoding structure from the user? Access to it may enable him to design special-purpose operations and to incorporate them in the operation set. The DEC PDP11/60 (1977) provides such access to its underlying microcoding structure. What are the pros and cons of such access?

Performance.   A real improvement in performance can be achieved in applications where a machine runs most of the time in one program and much of the time on a few subroutines.

Fun.   Microcoding is fun; everyone can be his own machine designer.

Difficulty.   The user now faces two languages: the machine language and the microcoding language. Microprogramming is inherently tedious because the microcode steps are primitive. It is inherently complex and error-prone, because the microcode architecture must use a datapath in which non-straightforward time-saving techniques have been used. In the PDP11/60, for example, a wrong instruction can even result in a circuit failure. Furthermore, microprogramming is the programming of concurrency—so it is inherently complex to build and maintain.

Uniformity.   Since the microcode architecture must be tied closely to the implementation, the manufacturer customarily ensures neither its uniformity from model to model or from copy to copy nor its stability from field-upgrade level to field-upgrade level in a given copy.

User community.   The lack of uniformity radically shrinks the community of users of a microcode architecture, sharply reducing opportunities for shared projects, exchanges, and back-up operation.

Microcode as the Only Machine Language

Suppose now that all programmer access to a computer is at the level of microcode; that is, the machine-language level is the microprogramming.

Uniformity.   The machine language is the interface offered to the user and maintained with stability by the manufacturer. Since microcode is by definition implementation-derived, language stability at this level implies constraints on implementations much more serious than those that apply today.   Original costs will therefore be higher, and cost savings due to implementation changes in the midst of a production run must be foregone.

User community.   By far the most serious drawback is the effect on the size of the user community.   The major conceptual advance made by the IBM System/360 (1965) was the establishment of a single machine architecture against which a variety of implementations of different performances were built. All these implementations constituted a single user base for software support.

Software costs are a substantial part of both manufacturer and user costs for computers. Since microcoding is implementation-dependent, microcode as the only user language tends to limit the size of user community across which software costs can be shared.

The Effects of Microcoding on Architecture

Fixed and marginal cost of function.   Hardwired controls have low fixed cost and are therefore appropriate for limited-function machines, whereas microcoding has low marginal cost for added function (Figure 2-4).

The use of microcoded subsequencing in the 360 made downward compatibility economically feasible: Floating-point arithmetic, for example, added relatively little to the cost of a Model 30—only more microcode memory.

The marginal cost of more elaborate function, however, is not limited to hardware cost. There are software, documentation, and comprehensibility costs that can be substantial. Microprogramming has sometimes tempted architects to gratuitous and foolish functional elaboration.

Emulation.   One architecture can be implemented using a variety of data-paths, and one datapath can be used to implement a variety of architectures. A microcoded implementation lends itself especially well to implementing various architectures. First, its structure encourages systematization, and this leads toward generality in the design of both datapath and microinstruction. Second, microcode is more easily assembled, tested, and changed than are hardware controls. Not surprisingly, the use of one datapath for multiple architectures did not happen historically until microcoded control structures came into common use.

When a datapath is used to execute some architecture for which it was not principally designed, the implementation is said to *emulate* that architecture.

Foreign architectures.   Emulation facilitates a user's transition from an old machine to a new one. It allows him to convert high-duty applications for efficient operation on his new machine, and to convert his new machine into an old one to execute an unconverted library of low-use applications.

Because a datapath is designed for a particular architecture, an emulation of another, unplanned architecture is inherently a misfit and will suffer inefficiencies. Even so, when the technology has so advanced that the new implementation is inherently much faster than the old one, the emulated machine may be faster and may even give a better cost/performance ratio than the old one, despite the inefficiences of emulation [Tucker, 1967].

Concurrent emulation.   Ordinarily, the user wants to run applications both in his new machine's own language and in the emulated machine language. He wants to mix these indiscriminately in his job stream, and may even want to do both "concurrently" in a time-shared fashion. This capability requires either enough microcode for both architectures, or a backing store that can quickly replace the microstore's contents. The machine state must also remember which architecture to execute upon return from an interruption [Bagley, 1976].

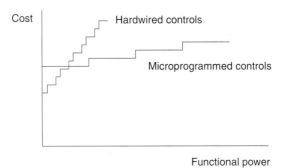

FIGURE 2-4   Cost/function relationships for implementations.

2.1.4
Bibliography

Andrews [1980], Bagley [1976], Bashkow, et al. [1967], Bose and Davidson [1984], Brooker [1970], Chesley [1971], Chu [1975], Cowart et al. [1971], Dally and Kajiya [1985], Davies [1972], Flynn [1975], Gogliardi [1973], Hayashi et al. [1983], Hennessy and Patterson [1990], Husson [1970], Lilja and Bird [1994], Melbourne and Pugmire [1965], Minter [1980], Myers [1977b, 1978, 1982], Radin [1983], Rice [1971], Sammet [1969; 1976], Smith et al. [1971], Tucker [1967], Weber [1967], Wilkes [1951, 1969, 1992], Wilkes and Stringer [1953], Wilner [1972], Zaks [1978].

2.2
Language Properties

Given that there should be a defined and controlled machine language between high-level programming languages and computer implementations, where between the two should it fall? The machine language must balance the requirements of the user against those of the builder of the machine. The key requirement of the user is ease of use; that of the builder is ease of implementation.

Positioning

The detailed positioning of a machine's architecture can be pictured schematically, as in Figure 2-5. When the architecture is close to the user language, transforming software from the user representation to the architectural representation is relatively simple. The hardware transformation (implementation) will be more complex, however. The B5500 and its successors are examples of this design choice.

Conversely, when the architectural representation is close to the realization requirements, changing software from the user representation to the architectural representation requires a larger software transformation. The implementation is less complex; this advantage may be used to make it less costly or to improve its performance. The 6600 and its successors follow this approach, as do minicomputers such as the PDP8.

The 360 exemplifies a middle-of-the-road positioning. The positioning of a machine language is non-trivial. Its consequences show up throughout the book.

Evolution. Whereas machine languages were originally required to be easy for machines to interpret, and only secondarily easy for programmers to write,

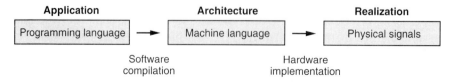

FIGURE 2-5   Positioning of machine language.

this priority has changed over the years. As hardware became cheaper and programmers more expensive, ease of use at the assembly-language level became much more important, reaching its peak importance with the IBM 1401 (1960).

Then, as high-level programming languages became standard, the priority shifted back. Only a small fraction of programs—less than 1 percent for general purpose computers—are now written directly in assembler language. Raw machine language—that is, the bit patterns themselves (or their octal or hexadecimal equivalents)—is almost never produced by users.

Minicomputers and then microcomputers followed the same evolution of language use as mainframes. Originally, many programs were written in raw machine language; then, assembly language became standard; now, high-level language has become normal for such machines.

It has therefore become much less important for machine languages to be easy for human users to write, but it has become ever more important for compilers to generate efficient machine-language code easily.

2.2.1

Semantics

The *semantics* of a language specifies the meaning of each element and how the meaning of a sentence is derived from the meanings and syntax of its components. The meaning of a language element or of a sentence as perceived in the mind is called a *concept.*

Natural languages have complex semantics. Programming-language semantics are simpler, and machine-language semantics are simpler yet.

Representation and Interpretation

A computer is essentially a concept manipulator. Concepts that are meaningful to the user can be manipulated by physical equipment via a complex sequence of representation and interpretation processes, shown schematically in Figure 2-6.

To *represent* a concept is to associate with it some sign that is henceforth perceived as a symbol for the concept. To *interpret* a sign is conversely to substitute for it the concept of which it is the symbol. We cannot talk or write, or perhaps even think, about concepts without some representation.

The farther the removal from the concept, the greater the amount of detail: A programmer may convey the concept of addition with the five symbols A ← B + C, but the machine language typically requires three instructions of some 30 bits each. The number of signals involved in the implementation of this addition is easily a few thousand, and the realization's semiconductor patterns require 10,000 to 100,000 coordinates.

Machine language is twice removed from the concepts involved in a program. Its digits, characters, operations, and locations represent the numbers and names of the higher-level programming languages, which in turn represent the concepts the user has in mind. Step A in Figure 2-6 summarizes this relation.

The machine-language level, on the other hand, is much higher than that of the concepts manipulated directly by machine hardware: The machine

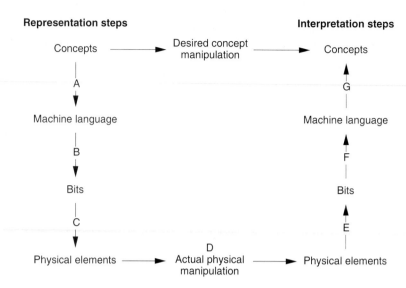

FIGURE 2-6   How a computer manipulates concepts.

language is represented (Figure 2-6) by bits (B), which are represented by physical elements such as voltage or current levels or magnetization states (C). The physical representations are manipulated electrically to produce the representations of new concepts (D), which may then in turn be interpreted as bits (E), then as language elements (F), and finally as concepts (G).

Since representation and interpretation occur at so many levels, we shall restrict these terms, unless qualified, to refer only to architectural representation, the representation of machine-language elements into the uniform minimum element (usually the bit), and the converse interpretation.

Definition of semantics.   One can define the semantics of a machine by following either of two methods.

First, one can trace the computer's interpretation of the language. Schematically, one enters the diagram of Figure 2-6 at the left on the level of the machine language, goes down to the physical elements and their manipulation, and then goes up again to the machine-language result.

One can alternatively define the meaning of the machine language by appealing to the higher-level concepts that it represents. Entering Figure 2-6 at the level of machine language, one goes up to the concepts that it represents, follows their manipulation, and then descends to the representation of the resulting concepts.

The former method defines the architecture of a computer as that machine's functional behavior; the semantics is defined *operationally*. The trouble with this method, however, is that it forces us to understand the architecture from the implementation, if not from the realization.

The top-down method, in contrast, appeals to the concepts the designer has in mind when specifying the machine language. The semantics is defined by known concepts of logic and mathematics; it is defined *denotationally*. This is the method we shall follow. Two hindrances must be overcome.

First, because the machine language must be suitable for implementation, the high-level concepts are not so pure and simple as we might assume: Numbers are restricted in domain; addition is modular or approximate.

Second, the specification must use a precisely and consistently defined set of logical and mathematical concepts—that is, a language. We use the known semantics of a higher-level language, APL, to specify the semantics of the machine language. One must always be careful, however, that the inevitable shortcomings of any particular higher-level language do not obscure the meaning of the concepts represented.

Specification of Concepts

Each machine-language element specifies a semantic concept. This specification, as Tree 2-7 shows, involves two designations: *which* concept out of *what set* of possible concepts [Delesalle, 1981]. This generic design of specifications is used again and again in defining a complete semantics.

Domain.   The set of concepts from which a language element specifies one is called a *domain*. In a microprocessor, the concept *integer* may thus have the domain 0 ... 255. Similarly, *operation* may have the domain: Add, Subtract, Load, Store. The domain set may be specified by enumeration, as "operation" is here, or by some other formal characterization, including an algorithm that generates it. The "integer" domain is usually specified by an algorithm; in this case, counting, such as ⍳256 in APL.

Specification.   The choice of a language element from its domain may be specified either explicitly or implicitly, as shown in Tree 2-7.

Implied specification.   If the specification is implied, there must be an algorithm whose result yields the specification. The most frequent algorithm is the trivial one: The concept is unique; only one choice is allowed in the language. So the radix of a number system needs no further specification in a machine language if it is always 10. A slightly less trivial algorithm is counting. When the instruction located at n is followed by the instruction at location $n + 1$, that location can be implied. Usually, the specification algorithm is about this simple. In principle, however, any algorithm yielding a unique result can be used for implicit specification.

Explicit specification.   When a concept's specification is explicit, it must be represented in more primitive concepts (Tree 2-8).

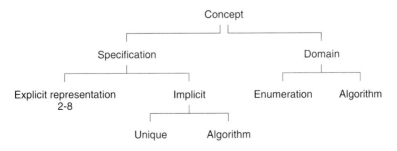

TREE 2-7   Specification of a concept.

Encoding. A *code* gives the correspondence between a concept and a combination of more primitive concepts. This correspondence is expressed by an algorithm or a table. The lower concepts must in turn be specified. This recursion stops when the lower concept is the minimal element.

Thus, a number represented in ordinary positional representation is encoded by a radix, a sign, and some digits. Each of these needs further specification, unless, as perhaps the radix, it is unique. The digits will need further encoding. Typically, the encoding stops at the bit level.

Allocation. The correspondence between a concept and a field in a format is called *allocation*. Allocation involves a place (*where* is the concept specified?) and an index (*which* elements of that place are used?):

- *Place of allocation.* The *place* is one of the spaces of the universe of discourse of the machine language, such as an addressed part of memory or an accumulator. This choice of space needs specification; it is usually implied.

  Recursive specification leads to recursive allocation: A number as a whole needs allocation, and its sign and the digits in turn need allocation within the number's format.

- *Index of allocation.* The positions occupied within a place are specified by an *index*. This term should be understood in a broad sense to denote any method of indicating specific positions. The index is in itself a concept and can be specified according to the options contained within Tree 2-7.

Recursion. Recursion in allocation and encoding is a familiar phenomenon. The word *house*, for example, is encoded with the letters of the Latin alphabet; the letters are allocated in left-to-right order. The Latin letters are recursively encoded as bit strings, and these bits are again allocated. Such recursion continues until the specification is entirely in terms of primitives. Table 2-9 illustrates this process.

The lowest-level encoding, which uses the primitive elements, corresponds to the design of the lexicography of the machine language; the allocations amount to the design of the syntax of the machine language.

Application. The general design tree (Tree 2-7) is the basis of all specifications encountered in machine languages. As it is used throughout this book, two variations occur.

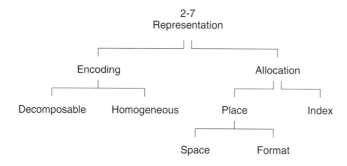

TREE 2-8 Representation as encoding and allocation.

Term: Concept	Example: Fixed structure for human habitation
Representation of concept by character string	House
Encoding	Latin alphabet
Allocation	Five characters, left to right
Representation of characters by code	1001000 1001111 1010101 1010011 1000101
Encoding	ASCII
Allocation	Seven bits, left to right

TABLE 2-9   Recursive allocation and encoding.

First, we substitute specific names for generic ones when applicable: We use *number system* instead of *encoding* in discussing number representation.

Second, some design options are either impossible or highly inefficient in a given context. We omit them even though a rigorous application of the design tree might suggest a novel design. Conversely, some design options are trivial; we omit them. We do not note all uses of allocation and encoding.

Taxonomy.   The general design tree provides the basis for a taxonomy of computer architecture [Delesalle, 1981]. This taxonomy is reflected in the trees presented in this book.

2.2.2

Syntax

The *syntax* of a language specifies how that language's primitive elements may be combined into larger patterns.

Viewed constructively, syntax specifies that some of the conceivable combinations of words are *valid*, or *well-formed*, and that others may not occur in the language—they are *invalid*, or *ill-formed*. English syntax, for example, specifies *I am* as valid, *she am* as invalid; *I am not* as valid, *I not am* as invalid.

Lexicography.   In the usual classification of linguistics, syntax contains only the combining rules for words and larger elements. *Lexicography* specifies which combinations of letters are valid words.

Machine language has the same levels. Instruction formats specify the valid sequences of primitive elements such as operation codes and addresses. Separate encoding tables specify that some bit combinations constitute valid operation codes or addresses, whereas others do not.

Parsing

People use the rules of syntax both in forming their own utterances and in interpreting those of other people. Recognizing the syntactic class and function of each word of a sentence is called *parsing*. A syntactic interpretation of a sentence is called a *parse*.

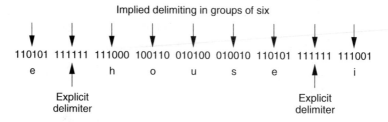

FIGURE 2-10   Explicit and implicit delimiting in the IBM 705.

Segmentation.   Interpreting utterances involves an activity not required in generating them: segmenting them into the elements of the language. Segmenting spoken English is very difficult; in contrast, the segments of written English are clearly signed by blanks and punctuation marks.

Fields and phrases.   A machine-language program is stored as a string of bits; its interpreter must segment it during parsing. The task is two-fold. The string is first parsed into distinct *instructions* and *data*; then, these are each parsed into separate elements commonly called *fields*. Such fields may be further recursively parsed into subfields; these are called *fields*, as well. So an address field may contain a displacement field, a base-address field, and an index field. For precision, we shall use *field* to refer to only the smallest aggregates of bits interpreted as entities, the language primitives. Groupings of fields that do not constitute instructions or data elements we call *phrases*.

Delimiters.   Natural and programming languages each use large numbers of distinct symbols, so they set aside blanks and punctuation symbols as *delimiters* to aid segmentation. Machine languages use only 0 and 1, so delimiting cannot be done with distinct symbols. Two extreme delimiting techniques define a spectrum.

At one extreme is *fully explicit delimiting*, in which one or more bit patterns, such as 111111, are reserved as delimiters and are not allowed to have any other significance. This technique, strictly analogous to the punctuation marks used in natural language, is used commonly in data communications but only rarely in computers. Figure 2-10 shows an example found in the IBM 705 (1956).

At the other extreme, one may adopt *fully implicit delimiting*, in which, for instance, all entities are made up of the same number n of bits. Segmentation is then done merely by uniform interpretation of n bits at a time. Figure 2-10 shows this concept also.

Syntactic classes.   The rules of syntax are constructed in terms of *syntactic classes*, such as nouns, verbs, and adjectives. These classes are sets of words that serve the same function in sentences, such that one member of a class may be substituted for another without changing the syntactic validity of the sentence. (Such substitution usually changes the sentence's sense.)

Some words are members of two or more classes: *Station*, for example, is a noun and a verb. Worse yet, some letter combinations constitute two distinct words: *Bear* is both a verb for carrying and a quite unrelated large furry noun.

Machine languages also have syntactic classes, such as the operation codes and names of operands, which correspond to verbs and objects. A set of objects specifiable in one field constitutes one syntactic class, commonly known by the field name.

Since machine languages must be highly efficient, it is the rule rather than the exception for a single bit combination to represent several different primitive language elements. In the 360, for example, "00111111" may represent the operation Floating Subtract Short Unnormalized; it may represent the field length of 64 bytes; it may specify two field lengths of 4 and 16 bytes; it may specify two registers named "3" and "15."

Whereas, in English, one can often interpret a word's semantics without parsing the enclosing sentence, conciseness in machine languages disallows this possibility.

Phrase structure.   Machine-language sentences usually exhibit a property that language theorists call *phrase structure*. That is, each instruction can be parsed into an operation phrase, some operand phrases, and perhaps a result phrase. Each of these phrases can in turn be independently parsed into components. Figure 2-11 shows an IBM 360 operand phrase consisting of a base-register specification, an index-register specification, and a displacement.   These components can be interpreted and used to generate an address specifying an operand.

Formats.   In both parsing and generating sentences, we use a set of syntactic patterns of valid sentence structures, such as

subject phrase—verb phrase	John eats.
subject phrase—verb phrase—object phrase	John eats an apple.
imperative phrase—object phrase	Eat an apple.
conditional clause—independent clause	If hungry, eat an apple.

Machine languages typically have far fewer syntactic patterns.   These *formats* specify how a string of bits is to be segmented into fields and parsed. Each expression in a machine language fits into one or another format. Some formats specify the syntax of instructions; others specify the syntax of the data objects about which the instructions speak, and of status variables that govern the whole interpretation process.

Program 1-47 gives the syntax for the IBM 650 (1954) instructions, shown in Program 1-30. More complex examples are found in the Zoo.

Context freedom.   The *state* of a computer is the contents of the spaces. The *context* of a computer is the content of the working store and control registers. The *status* of a computer is the content of just the control registers. Memory and working stores are not part of the status, unless they contain control information.

Most sentences in machine languages are *context-free*. That is, syntactic parsing and semantic interpretation of each instruction can be done without consideration of the status information.   In the 360 this is true of most of the instructions.   It is definitely not true of the Unpack instruction, whose interpretation depends on the EBCDIC-ASCII mode bit in the Program Status

```
    X   B   D
    0   4   8           20
    Legend: B = base; D = displacement; X = index.
```

FIGURE 2-11   An operand phrase of the IBM System/360.

Word (PSW). Similarly, in the Intel 8080A (1974) all instructions are context-free. But in the DEC PDP11 (1970), a mode bit tells whether an operation code should be interpreted as a Floating-Point Add Long or Add Double. These examples are cases of context-dependent semantics with a context-free syntax.

2.2.3

Information-Unit Sizes in Formats

An overall allocation decision the computer architect must make is what the sizes of data and instruction representations are to be. This decision, involving intricate interrelations, imposes basic constraints on all data and instruction formats. Therefore, the decision on information-unit sizes is perhaps the most far-reaching in design of machine-language syntax.

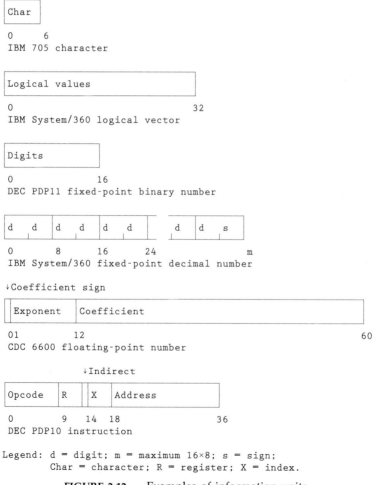

Legend: d = digit; m = maximum 16×8; s = sign;
         Char = character; R = register; X = index.

FIGURE 2-12   Examples of information units.

Information Unit

An *information unit* is the information that an operation handles as a single entity. It includes characters, groups of logical information, numbers, and instructions.

Information-unit systems.   Most general purpose computer designs have used one of two systems of information units. These will be called the *four* and *six* systems, since each unit contains multiples of 4 or 6 bits. In the *four* system, the multiples tend to be powers of 2; in the *six* system, various multiples are used. For the phrases and fields that occur within an information unit, the *four* and *six* systems, respectively, use lengths that are multiples of 4 and 6. Table 2-13 shows the sizes from which the designer is likely to select within each system. Figure 2-12 shows the formats of some information units of various machines.

Four system		*Six* system	
Units	Fields	Units	Fields
8	4	6	3
16	8	12	6
32	12	18	12
64	16	24	18
128	20	36	24
	28	72	36
	32	96	42
		144	48

TABLE 2-13   Unit and field sizes under *four* and *six* systems.

Source of unit systems.   A main source of these unit systems derives from character size, which was 6 bits in early systems, and 8 or 7 bits in later systems. The 48-character set of tabulators influenced the *six* system; the 4-bit size of a decimal digit favors the *four* system.

Interrelation

Table 2-14 shows the entire spectrum of choices for typical representatives of each unit system. The entries preceded by arrows show the sizes we would prefer for each unit if the choices could be made independently.

But the choices *cannot* be made independently. The basic reason for adopting either the *four* or *six* system consistently is that any given datum is used under several guises during program execution.

Multiple uses of data.   Suppose one traces a typical scientific program to see which classes of operations address each datum. One observes the following: A floating-point number will often be accessed by floating-point arithmetic instructions. If it were accessed only by the floating-point instructions, it could have the preferred size for this information unit, such as 48 bits. But if the sizes for integers and floating-point numbers are made to match, one set of loading and storing operations will serve both. Also, the floating-point format may be accessed in parts: Its sign may be accessed separately when a logarithm

| | *Four* system | | *Six* system | |
	IBM 360	DEC PDP11	CDC 1604	IBM 704
Data				
Characters				
Characters per word	4	2	4	6
Character size	→8	→8	6	6
Maximum set size	→256	→256	64	64
Binary fixed point				
Digits per number				
Minimum	16	8	12	→18
Normal	→32	16	24	36
Extreme			48	
Decimal fixed point				
Digits per number	1-31			
Bits per digit	→4			
Floating point				
Coefficient				
Minimum	24	24	→26	
Normal	56	56	→38	27
Extreme	112		→75	54
Exponent	7	→8	9	→8
Control				
Instruction	→16/→32/48	→16/→32/48	24	36
Operation code	→8	4/10/16	6	→9
Address phrase	→24	16	15	15
Index field	→4	3	2	3
Number of indices	→16	8	3	3
Status word	→64	16	24	
Input/output media				
Magnetic-tape width	8	8	6	6

Legend: / = or; - = through; → = preferred choice.

TABLE 2-14   *Four* and *six* systems of information unit sizes.

is taken, or its exponent may be accessed separately for exponentiation. The datum will be fetched byte by byte in I/O.

Similarly, an instruction is interpreted as an entity during program execution. But address, operation code, and index fields are accessed separately during assembly, and instructions may be transmitted as a sequence of bytes by the I/O operations.

For efficiency of bit utilization, one wants the data units to be commensurate, so that no padding is needed. For power, one wants the operations that extract subunits of a word to be applicable to most subfields.

Conflicts.   Some information units may not fit the system that has been selected. Moreover, bit-efficiency considerations often lead to conflicting ideals for the size of the various information units: One may decide that instructions are to be 32 bits long, but bit efficiency and other design considerations may suggest an operation code field of 8 bits, an index field of 4 bits, and an address field of 24 bits (Table 2-14). The resulting 36-bit instruction is 4 bits too long. So choices that can be justified independently, and hence are orthogonal, must be modified because of allocation constraints. This is a basic obstacle to the goal of orthogonality.

2.2.4

Language Efficiency

In what sense are machine languages concise? How can the information content of a language expression be defined and measured?

Information Measure

The concept of an *information measure* h was defined by Shannon in a study of communication systems [Shannon and Weaver, 1949].

The definition follows from simple desiderata. The amount of information in a message should be a function of the number of possible messages from which the particular message is chosen. An alphabetic symbol should therefore contain more information than does a decimal digit symbol, for it distinguishes one out of 26 cases rather than one out of 10. The measure should also be *additive*, so that two messages of m and n units when concatenated have a content of $m + n$ units. Such an additive measure requires using a logarithm of the number of (equiprobable) cases for each message; by convention, base 2 is used, and $h = \log_2 m$ for m equiprobable messages. So the information content of two concatenated messages is the sum of the information of each individual message; the total number of cases distinguished is the product of the cases for each message.

The foregoing definition applies only when the n cases are equiprobable. More generally, each case may occur with a different probability (as does each letter of printed English). The average information content of a sequence of symbols chosen from a set of b symbols having a priori probabilities $p_1, p_2, \ldots, p_b$ can then be derived from the fundamental defining relation.

Let each p_j be expressed as a rational fraction whose denominator m is the least common denominator of all the p_j, that is, $p_1 = c_1/m, p_2 = c_2/m, \ldots, p_b = c_b/m$. The symbols can now be considered as drawn with equal probability from a collection of m symbols, which collection contains b classes of $c_1, c_2, \ldots, c_b$ indistinguishable symbols each.

If the symbols were all distinct, the information content of each would be $h = \log_2 m$ by the defining relation. The indistinguishability from other members of its class diminishes the information content of a symbol by exactly that amount of information which would be required to distinguish the members of that class, that is, $h = \log_2 c_j$.

The average information content is then the weighted sum of the information contents of the individual symbols. Symbols belonging to the class j occur with probability c_j/m, and each carries $h_j = (\log_2 m - \log_2 c_j)$ bits. Thus the average is

$$
\begin{aligned}
h_{\text{av.}} &= \sum_{j=1}^{b} \frac{c_j}{m}(\log_2 m - \log_2 c_j) \\
&= \sum_{j=1}^{b} \frac{c_j}{m}\left(-\log_2 \frac{c_j}{m}\right). \\
&= -\sum_{j=1}^{b} p_j \log_2 p_j
\end{aligned}
$$

Unit of information.   The unit of information is called the *bit*, because the ceiling of the information content is the number of binary digits needed to represent the information. A decimal digit, for example, contains only

$\log_2 10 = 3.32$ bits of information, whereas $4 = \lceil 3.32$ binary digits are needed for its representation.

The use of *bit* both as the two-valued representor and as the unit of information represented unfortunately leads to confusion. Therefore, we uniformly use *bit* as the representor and say *bits of information* when the unit-of-information measure is intended.

Efficiency. The conciseness of a language can now be measured in terms of the *efficiency* of that language's representation, the amount of information used per bit.

If the number of equiprobable messages is a power of 2, the amount of information the message contains is equal to the number of binary digits required to represent it straightforwardly. If the number is not an exact power of 2, or if the cases are not equiprobable, the amount of information, h, is less than the number of bits required for representation, q. The ratio $h \div q$ is called the *efficiency* of the representation. The unused capacity of the representation is called the *redundancy* and is the complement of the efficiency. Thus, an 8421 code for the decimal digits has an efficiency of $0.83 = 3.32 \div 4.00$ and a redundancy of 0.17.

Unlike machine languages, most programming languages have intentional redundancy. They undergo translation before they are stored for execution. This translation can remove redundancy, so programming languages use redundancy freely to make the language easier to write and read.

2.2.5

Machine Interpretation

Execution cycle. A computer interprets the machine language by a process called the *execution cycle*. Figure 2-15 shows the steps of the execution cycle, and Programs 1-28 and 2-16 show the execution cycles for the 650 and PDP11.

Instructions are selected in turn under control of the *instruction fetch* action, ifetch, shown in the execution-cycle programs. Almost invariably, memory

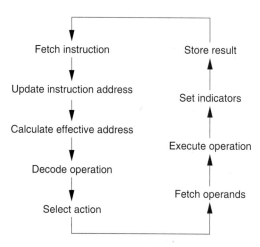

FIGURE 2-15   Diagram of execution cycle.

```
cycle11
A basic cycle of the DEC PDP11
REPEAT:interrupt11
    execute ifetch11
→UNTIL stop
```

PROGRAM 2-16   Execution cycle of the DEC PDP11.

is addressed by a variable called *instruction address*, and this address is updated as the instruction is obtained from memory.

When the instruction is fetched, it is parsed to identify the operation code and operand phrases. The latter are interpreted, including explicit or implicit specification, to fetch the operand.

When the operands are available, the operation is performed. Subsequently, the result of the operation is stored as specified, explicitly or implicitly, in the instruction. The three steps—*operand fetch*, *operation*, and *result store*—are shown in the general function `operation` (Program 5-2).

The execution cycle normally iterates using the instruction address that was updated during the instruction fetch. The iteration of the execution cycle depends, however, on the operation just performed or on some outside event. These conditions may cause the machine to branch to a new instruction address, interrupt, or stop.

Implementation of Machine Language

Even though one does not want to define machine language operationally, in terms of an implementation, it is instructive to see how an elementary CPU implementation in fact interprets its machine language.

The implementation of Figure 2-17 uses a memory that contains many data locations. Any location is selected when the number that identifies that location is sent to memory. On one memory cycle, the memory will read out or store information at one location.

The arithmetic and logic unit (ALU) consists of an adder, which may be controlled to add or subtract, and two registers for holding intermediate results—an Accumulator and a Multiplier-Quotient Register. These registers are connected such that data can be shifted laterally from one to the other.

Two registers control the sequence of operations: an Instruction Register, where the instruction to be executed is held and interpreted, and an Instruction Address Register, which is incremented when an instruction is executed and whose contents are used to address the next instruction.

In this simple hypothetical computer, each instruction consists merely of an operation code and a single unmodified address, which specifies the memory location whose content is to be used as the operand or result.

Internal cycle.   The action of such an implementation is divided into two steps, which are cycled:

1. The Instruction Address Register's content is sent to the Memory Address Register by the closing of gate IAC, and memory is controlled to read out. The incremented instruction address is read into IAR under control of gate IAI. The instruction is read out into the Memory Data Register MDR. IRI causes the Instruction Register to read from MDR.

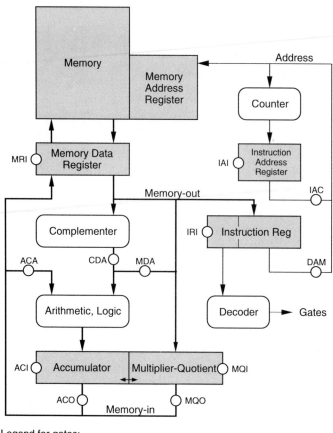

Legend for gates:

ACA = Accumulator Add	IAI = Instruction Address In
ACI = Accumulator In	IRI = Instruction Register In
ACO = Accumulator Out	MDA = Memory Data Add
CDA = Complemented Data Add	MQI = Multiplier-Quotient In
DAM = Data Address to Memory	MQO = Multiplier-Quotient Out
IAC = Instruction Address Counter	MRI = Memory Register In

FIGURE 2-17   A typical implementation of a computer.

There the operation code is decoded to select the gates to be opened during the second step.

2. If the operation is an addition, the address is sent to the Memory Address Register, via gate DAM, and the operand is fetched out into the Memory Data Register. Gates MDA, ACO, and ACA are opened to cause the sum to be generated in the adder. Then, ACI causes the sum to replace the addend in the Accumulator. For other operations, other combinations of gates are opened.

If the operation code specifies that the Accumulator should be loaded with the old content ignored, only gates MDA and ACI will be opened on the second step of the cycle. An instruction calling for a branch in the instruction sequence will be executed by opening gates DAM and IAI.

2.2.6
Bibliography

Delesalle [1981], Flynn et al. [1985], Mitchell and Flynn [1990], Norton and Abraham [1983], Shannon and Weaver [1949].

2.3
Spaces

Instructions and their operands must be obtained from a storage space or an input source; the results are placed in a storage space or an output sink. So a computing system consists of storage, processing units, and I/O.

The subject of I/O is non-trivial, and the cost and size of I/O can easily dominate an installation. Nevertheless, from a machine-language view, I/O can be treated as a specialized type of storage—read-only or write-only. So one can picture a computer system as consisting of a storage space surrounded by one or more processing units.

For architectural and for implementation reasons, storage is almost always divided into multiple spaces that have different access properties.

Design tree.   The design choices for the storage space can be derived with the basic steps of Tree 2-7 and are shown in Trees 2-18 and 2-24.

2.3.1
Nature of Storage Spaces

The spaces of a computer system follow from the program primitives. Machine language speaks in instructions about data, in the context of the machine status. So one would expect an instruction store, a data store, and a control (status) store. These three elements are indeed present in early machines, such as the Harvard Mark I (1944) and the Zuse Z4 (1945).

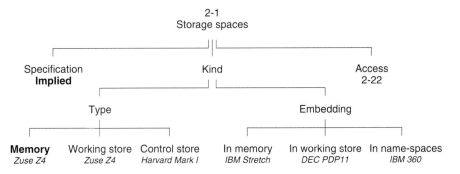

TREE 2-18   Design choices for storage spaces.

Types of Storage Spaces

Two pressures have changed this simple structure. On the one hand, generality has favored combining the data and the instruction store into a single memory. On the other hand, conciseness has almost mandated establishing a working store as a separate entity.

Three types of storage spaces must be distinguished: memory, working store, and control store. The dimensions of these stores are described in space declarations, such as space650 for the 650 (Program 1-26).

Memory.   The storage space from which programs are directly executed is called *memory*. The architecture usually presents memory as a single homogeneous space. In contrast, the implementation of the memory space need not be homogeneous. Memory is usually supplemented via I/O with *auxiliary store*, also called *secondary store*. Auxiliary store is often made to appear jointly with memory as one space.

Working store.   The *working store* is the set of concisely specifiable locations that temporarily contain operands or results of the operations. Such locations, whether in working store or control store, are often called *registers*.

An early example of a working store is the *accumulator*, found in von Neumann–family computers such as the Manchester MU1 (1949) and the Cambridge EDSAC (1949).

The working store usually has more than just a single register. The Z4, for example, has two registers organized as a stack (Section 10.3). The MU1 has two (later eight) registers for addressing, besides the double-length accumulator (Program 2-38). The IBM 704 (1955) has two arithmetic registers known as the accumulator and the MQ, as well as three index registers (Program 2-19).

Later computers usually have more working locations. The 360 includes 16 registers of 32 bits, used for integer arithmetic, logic, indexing, and addressing,

```
space704                              configure704
A IBM 704 spaces                      A configuration for the IBM 704
A memory                              A memory capacity
  memory←?(memcap,word)ρradix           memcap←2*15
A working store
A - accumulator
  acc←?accsizeρradix                  format704
A - multiplier/quotient               A IBM 704 information units
  mq←?wordρradix                      A representation radix
A - indices                             radix←2
  reg←?(3,adrsize)ρradix              A information units
A control store                         byte←6
A - instruction address                word←36
  iadr←?memcap                          adrsize←radix⊛memcap
A - indicators and lights               accsize←38
  ind←?4ρradix
A - manual entry
  switch←?6ρradix
A - stop condition
  stop←?radix
A - trapping mode
  trap←?radix
```

PROGRAM 2-19   Spaces and parameters of the IBM 704.

```
space360                          format360
ᴀ IBM 360 spaces                  ᴀ IBM 360 information units
ᴀ memory                          ᴀ principal radix
memory←?(memcap,byte)ρradix       radix←2
ᴀ working store                   ᴀ information units
ᴀ - general registers             digit←4
reg←?(16,word)ρradix              byte←8
ᴀ - floating-point registers      half←16
flreg←?(4,double)ρradix           adrsize←24
ᴀ control store                   word←32
ᴀ - indicators                    double←64
ind←?25ρradix                     block←2048
ᴀ - status word                   ᴀ address capacity
psw←?doubleρradix                 adrcap←radix*adrsize
ᴀ - stopped state
stop←?radix
→If protopt
THEN: ᴀ - protection key
   keys←?((⌈memcap÷block),4)ρradix
ENDIF:
```

PROGRAM 2-20   Spaces and parameters of the IBM System/360.

and four floating-point registers of 64 bits (Program 2-20). The Cray 1 (1976) contains 658 working-store registers (Section 14.4)! Table 2-21 shows the working and control spaces in various computers.

Control store.   The *control store* contains the status of a computer, the information to control the syntactic and semantic interpretation process. (In contrast, the working-store contents govern the result, but not the process, of interpretation.) The most important control register is the Instruction Address register. The control registers can be grouped in many ways; the 360 has most control information combined into one 64-bit word called the Program Status Word.

Specialization

Control registers are by definition specialized to contain machine status; each register has its own purpose. In contrast, memory (and working store) contain a variety of data and instructions. One can subdivide and specialize memory, or pool it as one resource.

Data specialization.   Since the incidence of the various datatypes differs among and even within programs, it is attractive to share one memory and one working store among these various types. But architectural and implementation considerations may dictate otherwise; thus, the 360 uses a separate working store for floating-point data. The architectural purpose of this specialization is to allow two chunks of working store to be distinguished implicitly, by the operation code, rather than explicitly, by addresses. The implementation purpose is to allow the floating-point working store to be accessed while address computation is accessing the fixed-point working store.

Address specialization.   In early machines, such as the MU1, addresses were much smaller than normal integer values. As address capacities grew, this

	Working store	Control store
Harvard Mark I	3	(1)
Zuse Z4	2×32s	5 (2)
Cambridge EDSAC	70 35	10* (1)
Ferranti Mark 1	80 40 8×20	10* 1 (1)
Univac I	4×12d 2×12d 10×12d	3d* 2
Princeton IAS	2×40	13* (1)
IBM 701	38 36	13* 4 1 (1)
IBM 650	21d 11d 1d	4
IBM 704	38 36 3×15	15* 4 (2)
IBM 705	2×256d 8 2 2 3,4d	3,4d* 9 4d (1)
Univac 1103A	72 36	15* 5 1
STC ZEBRA	15×33	2×33*
Bull Gamma 60	96 2×24 4×15	15* 24 4 2×15
IBM 1401	2×16	16* 9 (8)
IBM Stretch	7 128 16×64	19* 64 (2)
Ferranti Atlas	96 125×24	3×24*
CDC 6600	8×60 8×18 8×18	18* 2×18 2×21 3 1
CDC 6600 PPU	18	12* (1)
Burroughs B5500	2×48s	15* 62 7 15 2×21 5 (3)
IBM System/360	16×32 4×64	64* (26)
DEC PDP8	12 12 5 1	12* 1 (2)
DEC PDP11	(8+8)×16* 6×64	11 16 4 (2)
Intel 8080A	10×8	16* 8 1
Cray 1	8×64×64 73×64 72×24 9	22* 18 18 8 5 9 3
Motorola M6800	2×8 2×16	16* 6 4 (1)
MOS 6502	8 2×8 8	16* 7 3 (1)
DEC VAX11	16×32*	32 14 (4)
Motorola MC68000	8×32 9×32	32* 16 48 (2)
IBM 6150	16×32	16×32* (2)

Legend: d = decimal; s = stack; w = embedded in working store;
  * = contains instruction address; () = implied.

TABLE 2-21   Working and control spaces in various machines.

difference vanished; the result was the general purpose registers of the 360 and PDP11.

The 6600, which has long data words, has extreme address specialization. Besides eight 60-bit operand registers, the working store contains eight 18-bit address registers and eight 18-bit index registers (Section 14.2).

When data are fetched or stored in the 6600, the storage address is indicated by the address in the designated address register. Five of those address registers may be used for fetching, two (Registers 6 and 7) for storing, and one (Register 0) for intermediate values—a violation of generality inspired by the implementation.

Instruction specialization.   The use of memory for instructions as well as for data was a marked advance in the development of the modern computer. Babbage's Difference Engine (1833) and Analytical Engine (1867), Zuse's Z4, and Aiken's Mark I used a specialized input device for instructions. A sequence of instructions was stored on punched cards (Jacquard loom cards), film, and wide paper tape, respectively. Such devices acted as read-only memories with sequential access. These machines were able to execute sequences of instructions and to make decisions: They were computers, not calculators. The Mark I used three paper-tape readers to allow subroutine calls; the tapes were pasted into loops to give iteration.

Eckert and Mauchly's ENIAC (1946) used random-access specialized read-only memory for its instructions—a plugboard. The Harvard Mark IV (1952) also used random-access read-only memory. Its medium was a magnetic drum. The program was written on the drum from magnetic tape with a manually controlled action, not unlike the loading of a modern programmable read-only memory (PROM).

In 1944, Eckert and Mauchly proposed sharing read/write random-access memory for their EDVAC (1952). Von Neumann participated in the design of the EDVAC and published the idea of shared instruction and data memory in his report on the EDVAC [Burks, 1946]. Contrary to popular belief, however, he did not actually invent the principle [Metropolis and Worlton, 1980].

Program execution requires merely a read-only memory for instructions. Such a specialized memory can be faster, more permanent, or more economical than a read/write memory. It is frequently found in microprocessors for operating systems, language interpreters, or I/O controller functions.

The initial practice of modifying instructions in the read/write memory has been replaced by indexing. Modifying instructions, in particular the instruction to be fetched next, poses serious implementation problems and is bad programming practice as well. The sharing of memory between instructions and data is still a major advantage in storage allocation and in compiling programs for immediate execution.

Embedding

Spaces that are separately addressed are normally disjoint. So the parse of an instruction identifies one field as a memory address and another field as a working store address. The architect can, however, specify that one space is a subset of another. In that case, the subset is addressable in two syntactically distinct ways, a concept called *embedding*. name650 illustrates the embedding of the 650's working store in memory (Program 1-27).

Advantages. Embedding saves operation codes in three ways: One does not need to duplicate operations for different spaces, one avoids operations that move data from one space to another, and one can endow special locations with implicit operating functions.

The IBM Stretch (1961) embeds the entire working and control store in memory. The purpose is to allow a fast status switch by a programmed memory-to-memory Move. A secondary advantage is that the control registers need no separate address space.

The PDP11 has control store embedded in memory. The instruction address, however, is embedded in working store. This embedding is fully exploited to give relative and immediate addressing of data.

Disadvantages. Embedding destroys the homogeneity of a storage space, since some locations have extra functions. More seriously, the syntax for operations becomes obscure and idiomatic—moving data to a certain address implies, for example, a disk write. Such inhomogeneity works against easy compilability, as can be clearly seen in the DEC VAX11 (1978). Embedding obviously makes the constructs more complex; that adds cost.

Our preference is to avoid embedding. Doing so may require extra operations—the 360 used no embedding and therefore needed a fast Move to and from the working registers.

2.3.2

Storage Access

We describe storage space as a two-dimensional array of bits, whose rows are the addressable units and whose columns are the bits within each. We consider first the address sets that name locations in storage.

Address Space

The one-dimensional vector of addresses possible in a storage space is its *address space* or *name-space*. Trees 2-22 and 2-23 show the design choices.

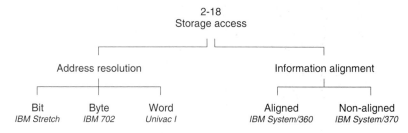

TREE 2-22   Design choices for storage access.

Name. The Oxford English Dictionary says a *name* is "the mere appellation in contrast or in opposition to the actual person or thing" [*Oxford English Dictionary*, 1989].

In machine language, the objects designated are storage elements. These objects can take on different values and therefore correspond to the variables of algebra. For these objects to be specified, each storage element must have a unique name, commonly called its *address*. The principal design questions are what sets of names to allow, and how these name sets shall be structured.

Context dependence. In an ideally simple language, each object of discourse would have a unique name. In natural human languages, however, this unique naming rarely occurs. Instead, we customarily use short polyvalent names for objects and depend on context to limit the name to one object.

So it is in machine languages. Since utterances are costly, and since unique names would require lengthy specification, machine languages use abbreviated names that are not prima facie distinct, but that are disambiguated by context.

Distinction. The *name-spaces* of a language are the disjoint sets into which the names of objects are grouped. Each object has a distinct name within its name-space, and various syntactic devices allow the interpreter to identify the active name-space. Two names are defined to be in the same name-space

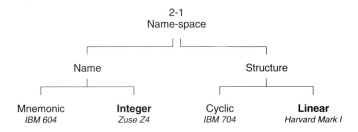

TREE 2-23   Design choices for name-spaces.

if either can be substituted for the other in any machine-language statement without altering that statement's syntactic correctness.

Most computers have many name-spaces. The memory addresses may be one, the unit addresses of I/O devices another, locations on a disk yet another, and so on. From the format or the context, the machine can determine which name-space is implied.

Properties of Name-Spaces

Names must have representations in machine languages. The encodings and allocation used to represent the set of possible names define the properties of the name-space.

Dense.   Assume a particular n bits are allocated for representing a name. If each of the possible 2^n values of those bits encodes a valid name, we say that the name-space of that representation is *dense*.

Ordered.   If a comparison operation is defined on the name representations, such that each name is either less than or greater than each other, the name-space is *ordered*. Each name but one then has a *successor*.

Dense incomplete.   If an ordered name-space is not dense, but each of the valid names is less than any of the invalid names, such a space is called *densely incomplete*. This property is the one common in computers, where the installed memory capacity may be less than the addressable maximum and the memory densely occupies the lower addresses in the space.

Measured.   The name-space has a *measure* if one can calculate the successor of a name by addition. All dense name-spaces can have measures defined; many non-dense ones have measures.

Measured name-spaces are useful because arrays of data can be simply mapped into them, such that one can find a specific element by calculation.

Address Types

Assigning a set of successive integers as addresses is so common a practice that one may easily overlook other possibilities.

Mnemonic addresses.   Consider, for example, the IBM 604 (1952). Its storage consists of 10 variables:

Counter MQ GS-1, GS-2, GS-3, GS-4, FS-1, FS-2, FS-3, FS-4

GS stands for "General Storage"; FS stands for "Factor Storage."   Each instruction specifies one of these 10 names as a *from* address and another as a *to* address. The 10 names are each encoded as a separate hub on a plugboard that contains the program.

These names are mnemonic, but are otherwise arbitrary and poorly related to one another. They describe non-uniform storage locations whose capacities vary from three to eight digits. The names could have been Jack, James, John, Bill, Bob, and so on, without any other part of the machine's architecture being changed. The name set is non-dense, unordered, and unmeasured.

Integer addresses.   The set of all possible n-bit names is isomorphic with the binary integers from 0 to $2^n - 1$. Since comparison and addition are defined on the integers, such a subset of them constitutes a dense, ordered, measured set. The same mechanisms used for operations on data can do the comparisons and additions desirable for names. Consequently, since Zuse's and Aiken's designs, name-spaces have been almost universally arranged according to the subsets of the integers.

Address-Set Structure

Choosing a dense incomplete set of integers as addresses leads to a *vectorial* structure of the name-space. Given such a name-space, shall it be considered a ring or a line segment?

Cyclic structure.   The cyclic structure has two advantages:

- Address exceptions are impossible, since address arithmetic is modular and has no overflow.
- The name-space is homogeneous, and memory allocation is much simpler. If one needs a contiguous block of size n, and there are vacant pieces totaling n at the top and bottom of memory, these pieces can be allocated. Relocation of programs is also simpler, since no memory boundary need be considered; a constant can be added to all relocatable addresses.

The first of these advantages is trivial.   The second is substantial— homogeneity is a fundamental property that gives elegance and economy to machine architecture.

Problems with the cyclic structure.   Unfortunately, the homogeneity of a cyclic memory is illusory in practice:

- One usually finds some inhomogeneity in the structure for other reasons. For example, some memory addresses may be permanently assigned to the embedding of other spaces or may for other reasons be given preferential treatment. The cycle is broken and the advantages of cyclic homogeneity cannot be realized.
- The memory capacity of a given copy of a computer often changes with time. This changes the circumference of the cycle, and programs that use the cyclic property no longer run correctly.   Furthermore, the circumference is different from copy to copy—it is no longer a fixed property of the architecture—and programs using it cannot be

```
data←read704 address
ᴀ IBM 704 read from memory
data←memory[memcap|address;]
```

PROGRAM 2-24   Cyclic address structure in the IBM 704.

transferred from one size machine to another. These disastrous effects were first experienced on a large scale with the 704, which had a cyclic structure for the installed memory capacity. `read704` (Program 2-24) shows this cyclic structure, using `memcap` as defined in Program 2-19.

Linear structure. The use of a line-segment structure, with proper detection of addresses beyond the ends of the segment, ensures that an increase of memory will not affect correct execution of programs. For this reason, we recommend linear structure and consider use of cyclic structure bad practice.

Address Resolution

Tree 2-22 gives the design choices for the addressable unit of storage and the placement of information with respect to these units.

The principal address-resolution decision concerns memory, since all formats appear there. The other stores do not necessarily have the same resolution as memory: Control store may have finer resolution; working store usually has coarser resolution, to the register word.

Resolution may be to the bit, to the byte, or to the word.

Bit resolution. The finest resolution addresses each bit of storage; memory therefore collapses from a two-dimensional array to a vector. All format sizes are acceptable with bit resolution. No padding is necessary. The earliest computer with bit resolution is the Stretch. The Burroughs B1700 (1972) and the CDC STAR100 (1973) are later examples.

Bit resolution is costly in format space, since it uses a maximum number of bits for address and length specification. Sharpening resolution from the byte to the bit costs the same as increasing address-space size eight-fold.

Since almost all storage realizations are organized as matrices, bit resolution is also expensive in time or equipment.

Byte resolution. Arbitrary bit-length fields are nowhere near so frequent as fields of an arbitrary number of characters. *Byte resolution* provides that addressing freedom. A group of bits sufficient to represent one character is called a *byte*—a term coined in 1958 by Werner Buchholz [Brooks et al., 1959]. The storage-space model is a matrix whose row dimension is the byte size of 6 or 8 bits, as shown for the 360 in Program 2-20.

Byte resolution was introduced by the IBM 702 (1954) series and continued in the 1401 and the 360. A minicomputer example is the PDP11. Microprocessors, such as the 8080A, also typically have the byte as the address resolution.

Word resolution. A group of bits sufficient to represent the most-used numbers is the addressable unit in *word resolution*. Characters or bits cannot be addressed individually, but numbers, which occupy a word, are addressed

simply. Instructions are commonly one-halfword or one-word long in word-resolution machines, so their addressing is relatively simple. Word resolution is cheaper to implement, but harder to use, than is byte resolution.

Not surprisingly, word resolution characterizes the early scientific machines such as the Z4, the Princeton IAS (1952), the MU1, and the IBM 701 (1953). This tradition is continued in the 6600, the Cray 1, and the Cray Y-MP (1988).

Bit- and Byte-Numbering Conventions

Early computers have only one address resolution, whether word or byte. Later machines, beginning with the Stretch, allow words, bytes, and even bits to be addressed. Unfortunately, there are two conventions for numbering bits and bytes within words. Cohen [1981] has unforgettably christened these the *Big Endian* tradition and the *Little Endian* tradition, after the pointless controversy in Swift's *Gulliver's Travels*.

The more logical convention, the Big Endian, considers the whole storage space as one stream of bits. Bits, bytes, and words are numbered from left to right, following the convention of writing in Western culture. Figure 2-25 shows the scheme for 32-bit words and 8-bit bytes.

A	B	C	D	E	F	G	H

Word address			0			1	
Byte address	0	1	2	3	4	5	6	7
Bit address	0 ... 7			...				63

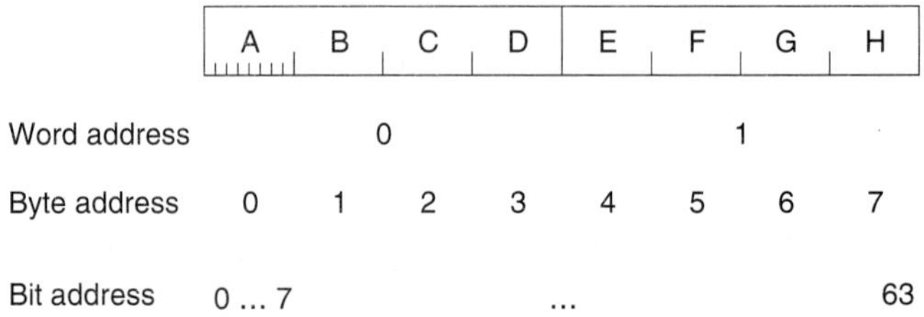

FIGURE 2-25   Big Endian space numbering.

The more venerable tradition, the Little Endian, numbers bits—and hence bytes within a word—from right to left, that is, from low order to high. In early machines this order was natural—one reads the values of binary numbers from console lights by adding the numbers of the "on" bits. That is, the bit-numbering order matches the weights in positional representation. This weight, however, is less fundamental than the writing and speaking order, and is inherently opposed to it. Figure 2-26 shows the scheme for 32-bit words and 8-bit bytes. Memory is conceived not at all as a continuous string of bits or bytes, but rather as a collection of words.

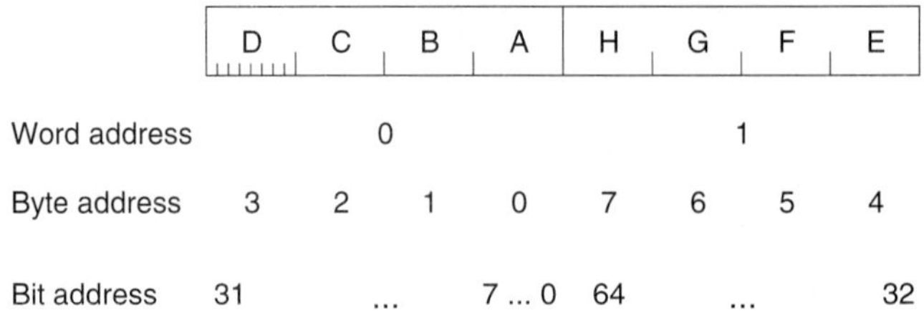

D	C	B	A	H	G	F	E

Word address			0			1	
Byte address	3	2	1	0	7	6	5	4
Bit address	31	...	7 ... 0	64	...			32

FIGURE 2-26   Little Endian space numbering.

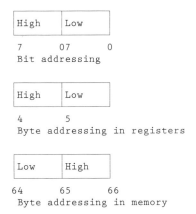

FIGURE 2-27   Bit numbering in the DEC PDP11.

Big Endian.   The Stretch design first provided multilevel resolution, and was the first to face this issue explicitly. It abandoned Little Endian bit numbering for the string-of-bits memory model. Later machines that followed the Big Endian convention include the 360, the Motorola 68000, the MIPS, and the Sun SPARC.

Little Endian.   The PDP11 (Figure 2-27) was the first machine to allow two levels of address resolution while holding to the Little Endian numbering. The bits of its 8-bit bytes are numbered 0 to 7 from right to left. Since two adjacent bytes are often combined to form a 16-bit number, such as an address, one might expect the memory address of the high-order part to be one higher than that of the low-order part, as is indeed the case. Since character strings are placed in ascending memory locations, when those locations are printed left to right, the high-order part of the number appears to the right of the low-order part. This arrangement is jocularly known as the "backwards byte." In working store, however, the high-order part is placed in a register to the left of the low-order part, as is essential for operations such as addition. Detailed complications are illustrated by the permutation function `adrperm11` given in the PDP11 description (Section 15.2).

The DEC VAX, with 32-bit words, continues the Little Endian tradition (but differs from the PDP11), as does the Intel 8080 family. In 32-bit word computers, the PDP11's "backwards byte" becomes a more elaborate permutation. Figure 2-26 shows how bytes of the alphabet successively read from disk are allocated into the words of a 32-bit Little Endian computer.

The difference shows up whenever one accesses the same data as words and as bytes, or when one attempts to port data or convert programs between machines of different character allocation.

Unlike Swift's, the computer Endian controversy is not pointless. The Little Endian design has many complications in use; we much prefer the Big Endian. Having two active conventions is very painful. Several recent Big Endian RISC computers, including the MIPS, the Motorola 88000, and the Intel i860 provide a data-movement operation that can perform the Big Endian–Little Endian permutation [Hennessy and Patterson, 1990]. We predict that Little Endian addressing will die out, just as decimal addressing did.

		Radix	Resolution Type	Size	Address size	Capacity in bytes Full	Initial
Harvard Mark I	1944	10	word	24d	8	852×2d	852×2d
Zuse Z4	1945	2	word	32	6	320×6	320×6
Cambridge EDSAC	1949	2	word	18	10	3k×6	3k×6
Ferranti Mark 1	1951	2	word	20	10	3k×6	2k×6
Univac I	1951	10	word	12d	3d	12k×6	12k×6
Princeton IAS	1952	2	word	40	12	24k×6	
IBM 701	1953	2	word	18	12,1	24k×6	12k×6
IBM 650	1954	10	word	s,10d	4d	50k×2d	10k×2d
IBM 702	1954	10	byte	6	4d	10k×6	10k×6
IBM NORC	1954	10	word	16d	4d	128k×2d	30k×2d
IBM 704	1955	2	word	36	15	192k×6	48k×6
IBM 705	1956	10	byte	6	3,4d	80k×6	20k×6
Univac 1103A	1956	2	word	36	15	192k×6	72k×6
Librascope LGP30	1957	2	word	32	12	20k×6	20k×6
STC ZEBRA	1959	2	word	33	13	40k×6	40k×6
Bull Gamma 60	1959	2	word	24	15	128k×6	16k×6
IBM 1401	1960	10	byte	1,6	4,3d	16k×6	1400×6
IBM Stretch	1961	2	bit	1	24	2m×8	512k×8
IBM 7080	1961	10	byte	6	4d,4	160k×6	160k×6
Ferranti Atlas	1962	2	byte	6	24	16m×6	8m×6
CDC 6600	1964	2	word	60	18	2.56m×6	960k×6
CDC 6600 PPU	1964	2	word	12	12	8k×6	8k×6
Burroughs B5500	1964	2	word	48	15	256k×6	256k×6
IBM System/360	1965	2	byte	8	24	16m×8	2m×8
DEC PDP8	1965	2	word	12	12	8k×6	8k×6
DEC PDP11	1970	2	bytE	8	16	64k×8	64k×8
Intel 8080A	1974	2	bytE	8	16	64k×8	64k×8
Cray 1	1975	2	word	64	24	128m×8	2m×8
Motorola M6800	1975	2	byte	8	16	64k×8	64k×8
MOS 6502	1976	2	bytE	8	16	64k×8	64k×8
DEC VAX11	1977	2	bytE	8	32	(2*32)×8	2m×8
Motorola MC68000	1980	2	byte	8	32	4096m×8	1m×8
IBM 6150	1986	2	byte	8	32	4096m×8	8m×8

Legend: d = decimal; k = 10*3 or 2*10; m = 10*6 or 2*20; s = sign;
bytE = Little Endian byte addressing.

TABLE 2-28   Address and memory sizes of various computers.

Table 2-28 shows for various machines the choices in address size and resolution made in various machines set out in Tree 2-22.

Implementation Considerations

The memory may be implemented as many physical modules, each with its own address register, decoder, data register, read and write amplifiers, and so on. Modular construction gives a wide choice of memory sizes and allows manufacturing of substantial quantities of the same module.

So far, so good—the user need not be aware of this implementation. But if a memory is made up of distinct, complete modules, these can be operated simultaneously but not independently. Such an overlap has profound consequences for the rest of the implementation; it may even affect the architecture.

Let us consider three ways of combining modules into an architecturally single store.

Parallel modules.   When the modules are operated in *parallel*, each module supplies part of a storage word. The modules now always operate at one time but not independently. Architecturally, this arrangement is not different from a single module.

Juxtaposed modules.   When the modules are *juxtaposed*, the installed addressing capacity is divided among the modules, each module being associated with a contiguous set of addresses. If the modules can be operated concurrently, the user can improve the performance by placing, say, his data at the bottom range of addresses and his procedures at the top, so that instructions and operands are fetched from separate modules. The Univac 1107 (1962) provides two such juxtaposed banks of modules.

Interleaved modules.   Performance also improves if the addresses of memory words are *interleaved* so that successive addresses are cyclically distributed among two, four, eight, or *n* modules. The 6600 may have 8-, 16-, or 32-way interleaving. Experiments, simulations, and analyses show that two-way interleaving increases utilized memory bandwidth about 1.4 times; four-way interleaving, about 2 times [Hellerman, 1972; Knuth and Rao, 1975; Hennessy and Patterson, 1990].

   None of the three methods—parallel, juxtaposed, or interleaved—formally concerns the architecture: All three are just implementation techniques to deal with an implementation concern—performance. Nevertheless, the juxtaposed method so clearly disrupts the homogeneity of memory that it dictates a particular use of the architecture. This is an example of a borderline case, where the implementation becomes in practice part of the architecture.

Memory physical-word size.   Economical implementation usually dictates that a memory fetch many bits, bytes, or words on one access. The economical unit of fetch, sometimes called a *memory word*, is governed by technological factors, and it changes every few years.

   Memory word size has several architectural consequences.   The most important is that small memory word sizes mandate some format placements; for example, they require placing the sign of a number next to the number's low-order digits. The operation code would similarly be placed leftmost in a multiword instruction.

   Optimum memory word size is a false and shifting guide in designing a lasting architecture. Because the optimum is always broad, it gives no guidance in choosing, for example, between *four* and *six* information-unit systems.

Information-Unit Alignment

   If the lengths and locations of information units can be made commensurate with the physical-memory word boundaries, such fields are said to be *aligned*. Figure 2-29 illustrates that aligned data require fewer memory accesses than unaligned data.

Need for alignment.   In the Stretch architecture, no alignment constraints are imposed. Fixed-point numbers, for instance, can begin at any bit address and

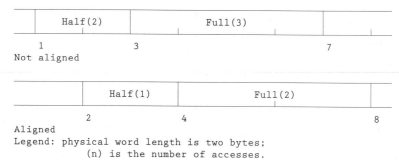

Legend: physical word length is two bytes;
          (n) is the number of accesses.

FIGURE 2-29   Examples of alignment.

can end at any. The costs of implementing this freedom were high, and the speed was slower than it needed to be.

In the 360 design we were careful about alignment. Fixed-point numbers, floating-point numbers, and halfword instruction syllables are constrained to begin on multiples of their lengths (Program 2-30). This rule guarantees alignment for any memory word size that is a power of 2 times that of the data-unit system—in this case, the *four* system. Many later machines, such as the VAX11, follow such a rule.

```
data←size read360a address
a IBM 360 read aligned from memory
  Spec report 0≠(size÷byte)|address
  data←,size read360 address
```

PROGRAM 2-30   Boundary alignment in the IBM System/360.

Obstacles to alignment.   The evolution of higher-level languages—of FORTRAN, in particular—led the language designers to define implementation-independent logical data structures. These definitions forbid alignment. For example, FORTRAN's COMMON definition makes machine-language representations visible on the high-language level and constrains them. So, when the IBM System/370 (1971) was defined, the alignment rule was removed.

The costs of non-alignment in the 370, however, are no lower than they would have been in the 360. The 370 architects have allowed the user to pay those costs whenever he wishes, and require him to pay some of them all the time so that the needed function is available. The 370 system software designer is still well-advised to follow the 360 alignment rule whenever possible. Experience shows that the software cost of obeying this rule is small.

2.3.3
Bibliography

Brooks et al. [1959], Buchholz [1981], Burks [1946], Cohen [1981], Hellerman [1972], Hennessy and Patterson [1990], Knuth and Rao [1975], Metropolis and Worlton [1980], *Oxford English Dictionary* [1989].

2.4

Operand Specification

A computer instruction consists fundamentally of an operation specification, some operand specification, and a result specification. For simplicity, we use the term *operand specification* to include the result.

Since operands and results are usually variables, one specifies their names (addresses of their locations), not their values. The format normally implies the storage space, such as memory or working store. The *location* within these spaces may be either implied or specified by an address, so there is a choice about the number of explicit addresses even though the number of operands is established by the operation. Explicit addresses are usually given by address phrases, which must be encoded and allocated. Finally, the datatype and length of each operand need specification, either explicit or implicit.

2.4.1

Number of Addresses

Most elementary arithmetic and logical operations are *dyadic*; that is, they take two operands and produce one result. Some, including arithmetic negation and the logical NOT, are *monadic*, taking one operand and producing one result. Then there are exceptions, such as integer division (taking two operands but producing both a quotient and a remainder) and cumulative multiplication (taking three operands and producing one summed product).

Classification. The relevant space is usually implied by format or operation code. The address within the space may be explicit or implied.

Instruction types are often classified according to the number of addresses that are explicitly specified: One speaks of *three-address* down to *zero-address instructions*. These terms apply to memory addresses and to working-store addresses.

Implied methods of address specification. Tree 2-31 shows that an address may be implied in three basic ways. First, a recently specified address is used

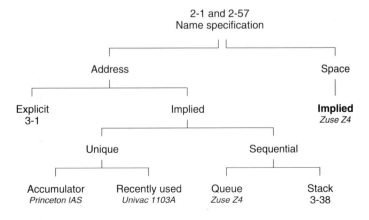

TREE 2-31 Design choices for name specification.

Result	Operand 2	Operand 1	Operand fields	Memory addresses	Machine example
Memory 3	Memory 2	Memory 1	3	3	IBM NORC
Acc	Memory 2	Memory 1	2	2	Univac 1103A
Register 1	Memory 2	Memory 1	3	2	none
Register 2	Register 1	Memory 1	3	1	CDC 6600
Register 3	Register 2	Register 1	3	0	CDC 6600
Memory 2	Memory 2	Memory 1	2	2	IBM System/360
Acc	Acc	Memory 1	1	1	Univac I
Memory 1	Memory 1	Acc	1	1	IBM Stretch
Register 1	Register 1	Memory 1	2	1	IBM 705
Memory 1	Memory 1	Register 1	2	1	IBM 705
Register 2	Register 2	Register 1	2	0	DEC PDP11
Stack	Stack	Memory 1	1	1	Manchester MU5
Stack	Stack	Stack	0	0	Zuse Z4

Legend: Acc = accumulator; dyadic operations only.

TABLE 2-32   Feasible combinations of design choices for operand specification.

again: One address identifies both an operand and the result. Second, the space has but one location, such as a single accumulator. Third, from a former address a new one is determined according to some algorithm—usually the stack, sometimes the queue.

Use of taxonomy.   Throughout this text we tacitly order our discussion by the design trees. The choices for operand specification will show the explicit use of the design tree as an aid in enumerating possibilities.

Of the three spaces in Tree 2-18, only memory and working store are suitable for operands. Tree 2-31 shows how each of these can be specified. For memory, only explicit addressing and reference to a recently used address apply. For the working store, more options apply: explicit addressing and implied use of an accumulator, a stack, or a recently used address.

From these choices we can tabulate all combinations we consider sensible for a dyadic operation (Table 2-32). We omit the combination in which the accumulator is implied for both operands and the result, even though it might be useful to double, square, or clear the accumulator content. Still, an architect might want to explore combinations that are suggested by the taxonomy but excluded from our list. The 1401, for example, implies the use of a queue for each operand (Section 12.3).

Many reasonable choices are available (Table 2-32). Almost all these choices have been explored in machines that were produced commercially. Different choices from the taxonomy may be combined in one design. Different choices may even be combined in one operand specification: The Univac 1103A (1956) combines two options by replacing a memory operand with the result and also placing this result in its accumulator.

Three-Address Format

Since most operations are dyadic, it is natural for an instruction to specify the two operands and the result explicitly. Some early computers and many languages use this *three-address* format. The IBM NORC (1954) illustrates this approach (Program 2-33).

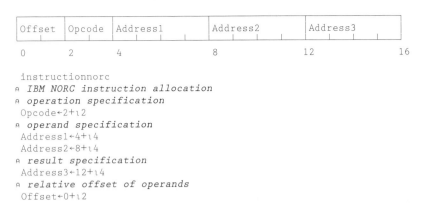

```
instructionnorc
ค IBM NORC instruction allocation
ค operation specification
 Opcode←2+ι2
ค operand specification
 Address1←4+ι4
 Address2←8+ι4
ค result specification
 Address3←12+ι4
ค relative offset of operands
 Offset←0+ι2
```

PROGRAM 2-33   Three-address instruction of the IBM NORC.

The three full memory addresses are costly in bits. The use of a working store alleviates this problem and gives a major performance improvement as well. The 6600 uses one format with three register addresses and one with two register and one memory address (Program 2-34).

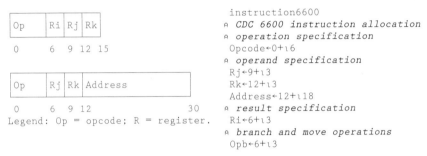

```
instruction6600
ค CDC 6600 instruction allocation
ค operation specification
 Opcode←0+ι6
ค operand specification
 Rj←9+ι3
 Rk←12+ι3
 Address←12+ι18
ค result specification
 Ri←6+ι3
ค branch and move operations
 Opb←6+ι3
```

PROGRAM 2-34   Instruction formats of the CDC 6600.

Two-Address Format

The result of an operation often replaces one of the operands, as when one increments a loop count, or adds a term to a partial sum. Designers as early as Babbage and Aiken adopted the *two-address* format. The Univac 1103A, shown in Program 2-35, and the 360 SS format (Program 2-36) specify two memory addresses.

The bit efficiency of the two-address format can be improved by a working store. Overall machine performance benefits as well. The 705, which had 16 registers, pioneered the use of the two-address format, with one a register address; the 360 RX format (Program 2-36) is another example. Going a step further, both addresses may designate registers. These formats are used frequently. They are found in the 360 RR format (Program 2-36), in minicomputers such as the PDP11 (Program 2-37), and in microprocessors such as the 8080A (Program 2-62).

Two- to three-address breakeven.   The two-address instruction is an advantage if indeed one operand can be replaced by the result; otherwise, an extra Move instruction is required.

```
Op    Addressu         Addressv

0     6                21             36
Legend: Op = opcode.

instruction1103
ρ Univac 1103A instruction allocation
ρ operation specification
Opcode←0+ι6
ρ operand specification
Addressu←6+ι15
Addressv←21+ι15
ρ increment specification
Control←6+ι3
ρ count
Count←9+ι12
```

PROGRAM 2-35   Two-address instruction of the Univac 1103A.

Consider the mathematics of the tradeoff. Let t be the length of a two-address instruction and $t + a$ the length of a three-address instruction, a being the length of an address phrase. If a program of n three-address instructions

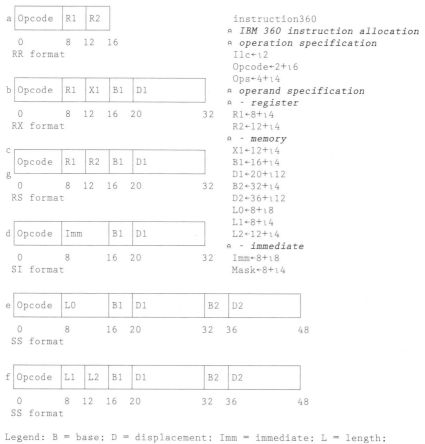

```
a Opcode  R1  R2

  0       8   12  16
  RR format


b Opcode  R1  X1  B1  D1

  0       8   12  16  20         32
  RX format


c
  Opcode  R1  R2  B1  D1
g
  0       8   12  16  20         32
  RS format


d Opcode  Imm     B1  D1

  0       8       16  20         32
  SI format


e Opcode  L0      B1  D1     B2  D2

  0       8       16  20     32  36     48
  SS format


f Opcode  L1  L2  B1  D1     B2  D2

  0       8   12  16  20     32  36     48
  SS format
```

```
instruction360
ρ IBM 360 instruction allocation
ρ operation specification
Ilc←ι2
Opcode←2+ι6
Ops←4+ι4
ρ operand specification
ρ - register
R1←8+ι4
R2←12+ι4
ρ - memory
X1←12+ι4
B1←16+ι4
D1←20+ι12
B2←32+ι4
D2←36+ι12
L0←8+ι8
L1←8+ι4
L2←12+ι4
ρ - immediate
Imm←8+ι8
Mask←8+ι4
```

Legend: B = base; D = displacement; Imm = immediate; L = length;
        R = register; X = index.

PROGRAM 2-36   Instruction formats of the IBM System/360.

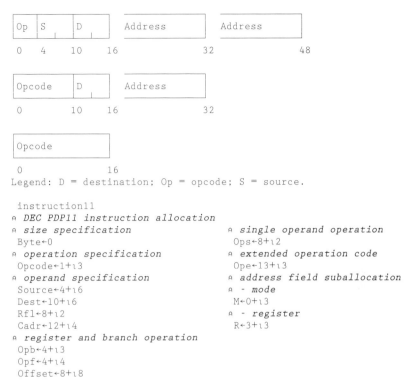

Legend: D = destination; Op = opcode; S = source.

```
instruction11
A DEC PDP11 instruction allocation
A size specification                    A single operand operation
  Byte←0                                  Ops←8+ι2
A operation specification               A extended operation code
  Opcode←1+ι3                             Ope←13+ι3
A operand specification                 A address field suballocation
  Source←4+ι6                            A - mode
  Dest←10+ι6                               M←0+ι3
  Rf1←8+ι2                               A - register
  Cadr←12+ι4                               R←3+ι3
A register and branch operation
  Opb←4+ι3
  Opf←4+ι4
  Offset←8+ι8
```

PROGRAM 2-37   Instruction formats of the DEC PDP11.

requires $n + m$ two-address instructions, the breakeven is achieved when

$$n \times (t + a) = (n + m) \times t$$

$$(n \times a) = (m \times t)$$

The fraction that an extra Move instruction is required, $m \div n$, is therefore $a \div t$. For the 1103A, this value is $15 \div 36$, or 0.42; the 1103A format is more efficient than a three-address format if the fraction is less than 0.42, which is almost always the case.

One-Address Format

Because operations often occur in multioperation expressions, the result of one instruction often serves as operand for the next. In the expression $a \leftarrow b \times (c + d)$, the result of $c + d$ serves as operand of the multiplication.

Accumulator.   The use of a previous result as operand can be exploited by implying a fixed address, called an *accumulator*, for one operand and the result. Von Neumann and his colleagues introduced this *one-address* format in 1946. The one-address format assumes a working store with one location. Program 2-38 shows the Ferranti Mark 1 (1951) format; Program 2-60 shows that of the Univac I (1951).

```
┌─────┬───┬────┬─────────┐
│ Op  │ * │ X0 │ Address │
└─────┴───┴────┴─────────┘
0      5  7 10           20
Legend: Op = opcode;
         X = index;
         * = unused.
```

PROGRAM 2-38   Instruction format of the Ferranti Mark 1.

Stack. The single accumulator does not give the performance advantage of a larger working store; hence the use of a stack with a one-address format in the Manchester MU5 (1974), the ICL 2900 (1974), and the Intel 8087 floating-point processor (1980).

One- to two-address breakeven. In a sequence of one-address instructions an extra load is required whenever an operation does not use the result of a preceding instruction, and an extra store is required when a result must be placed in memory. When a two-address operation must preserve its operands, however, it needs an extra Move. One-address instructions turn out to be less efficient than two-address instructions with one address abbreviated.

Zero-Address Format

The ultimate step in eliminating redundancy in address specifications is to do away with addresses as far as is logically possible. In the *zero-address* format, all addresses are eliminated by implying a working store exclusively as source of operands and destination of results. This format is practical only when the working store is addressed as a stack.

The first example of a computer using the zero address with a stack is the Z4. Others are the English Electric KDF9 (1963), shown in Figure 2-39, and the B5500 (Section 13.4).

Zero- to one-address breakeven. The zero-address format must be used in combination with at least a one-address format to enable memory access. We call the combination where each operation can have either the one- or the zero-address format the *extended zero address*. This combination, used in the MU5, is always equal to or better than just the one-address format.

FIGURE 2-39   Instructions of the English Electric KDF9.

Address type	il	a←a+b	a←b+c	a←b×(c+d)	a←(b+c)×(d+e)	a←f
			Sample expressions			
Three address						
m m m	56	56	56	112	168	392
r r r/r r m	20/32	96	96	128	180	300
Two address						
m m	40	40	80	120	200	440
r r/r m	16/28	84	84	112	156	264
One address						
(acc) m	24	72	72	96	168	360
Zero address						
pure	8/24	80	80	104	144	272
extended	8/24	72	72	96	128	240

Legend: $f = ((b+c)×(d+e))÷((b+d)×(c+e))$;
        m = 16-bit memory address; r = 4-bit register address;
        (acc) = implied accumulator; opcode uses 8 bits;
        il = instruction length in bits.

TABLE 2-40   Instruction bits used for various address types.

The Z4, KDF9, and B5500, however, use one-address instructions only for Load and Store, which we call the *pure zero address*. This combination spends the zero-address format length of z bits for each operation that is performed; it gains $z + a$ bits for each load and for each store that is avoided by use of a stack instead of an accumulator. We obtain the formula

$$z × p = l × (z + a)$$

for breakeven, where p is the number of operations, and l is the number of loads and stores that are avoided by using a stack. For the Z4, the ratio $l ÷ p$ must exceed 0.5 if the addressing is to be most efficient.

Table 2-40 illustrates the instruction space required by a few expressions for the various instruction types, assuming the field lengths of a *four* unit system. Observe that no one type is best for the whole range. Nevertheless, register-speed advantages have caused two-address formats with general purpose registers to become the dominant choice [Hennessy and Patterson, 1990].

2.4.2

Datatype

Each instruction must specify the type of its operands. Tree 2-41 gives the corresponding design choices.

Definition.   A *datatype* is a set of possible operand values and a set of operations defined for that set of operands [Bell and Newell, 1971]. An expression remains syntactically correct if an operand is replaced by another operand from the same set and/or if the operation is replaced by an operation of the same set. One data type may be a subset of another if the corresponding representands are a subset of the other and/or if the corresponding operation set is a subset of the other. Typical datatypes are character strings, integers, and floating-point numbers. How to specify the type of an operation?

Operation-defined.   Since each operation is defined for a datatype, the straightforward solution is to have the operation specification determine the

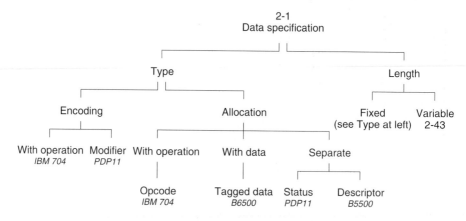

TREE 2-41   Design choices for data specification.

interpretation of the operands during the operation. So there is one operation code for fixed-point addition and another for floating-point addition if both types occur. Most machines use this approach.

Tagged data.   An alternative that has been much discussed in the literature [for example, Iliffe, 1972; Feustel, 1972, 1973; Myers, 1978], but rarely implemented in actual machines, is the use of self-defining objects. Here each information unit contains a code, the *tag*, which identifies its type. The operation is now *generic*: It needs only to be specified as Add; the operands themselves tell whether the operation is fixed point or floating point (or even mixes these types). The tags can alternatively serve for type checking; an addition with character strings as operands then signals an error.

The B5500 uses tagged data (Program 2-42). The first three bits of a word are tag bits. The tags distinguish floating-point data, control words, and descriptors.

The main disadvantage of tags is bit efficiency. Since programs iterate through multiple data instances, it usually takes more space to replicate the type with data than to give the type with the operations.

Data descriptors.   Data often appear in arrays of one type. For such an array, the type needs to be given only once. The type specification can be placed in a *data-descriptor* format that specifies other array properties (Program 2-42). The descriptor saves space, but it requires an extra fetch (from memory or register) each time a datum is used. The bit budget is improved at the expense of increased bit traffic.

Mixed types.   Any self-defining operand type invites operations on mixed types. Such operations are mathematically improper; they violate the very coherence of the datatype concept. In practice, this impropriety shows itself in difficulty in defining the operation semantics.

The cleanest solution is what the ALGOL68 specification calls *coercion*. The datatypes are ranked in generality. This ranking is possible because of type subsetting. An operation on mixed types implies that operands of less general types are converted to the more general type, whereupon a pure operation is performed, yielding a more-general-type result.

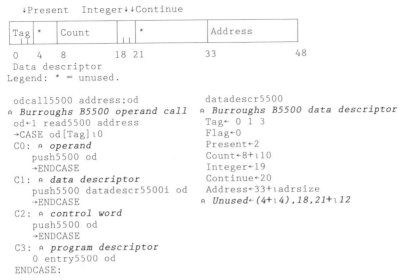

PROGRAM 2-42   Tagged information in the Burroughs B5500.

We prefer the simpler solution: to insist that all operands of an instruction be of one type, and to provide conversion operations.

Fixed-Length Data

If there are several different lengths of fixed-length data, one can consider each as a separate datatype. All the foregoing discussion applies, except that operations on mixed lengths are more necessary and are easier to define than are those for mixed-type operations in general. In the Burroughs B6500 (1968), for example, length is specified as part of the data's descriptor. Single- and double-length floating-point numbers are distinguished by the tag field.

The length is combined with the operation code in the 360 and in the 8080. The PDP11 specifies the length by a distinct operation-modifier bit for fixed-point and logical operations and by a mode bit for floating-point arithmetic.

Variable-Length Data

An operand specification has *variable length* if the operand length may be n times a unit length; if n is restricted to a few powers of 2, however, one usually speaks of a collection of fixed-length datatypes.

The term *variable length* is used in two distinct ways in computer literature. The length in question may be variable in the sense that one data item may be program-specified to have one length, and a second item to have a different length. In a tape record, for example, characters 10 and 11 may be allocated for *age*, character 12 for *sex*, and characters 15 through 20 for *salary*. The field lengths are not all the same, but each is specified and does not change.

In contrast, in communication systems, field lengths are often allowed to vary with the content at the moment; fields are separated by delimiters. *Age* might use one character or two; *salary* might use four, five, or six.

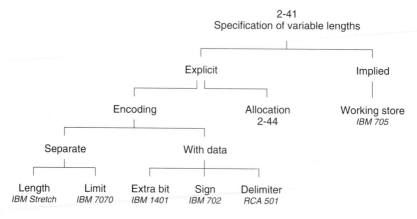

TREE 2-43   Design choices for specification of variable length.

We shall follow computer terminology, using *fixed length* to mean fixed in the design, *variable length* to mean specified in the program, and *content-dependent length* to mean specified in the data.

Length specification.   A variable length is not easily implied or encoded with other specifications and is therefore usually stated explicitly. There are surprisingly many ways of specifying this length; Trees 2-43 and 2-44 give the design choices. We can obtain these choices from Tree 2-7 by considering which bits are allocated to specify the length, and how the length is encoded.

Length specified in instruction.   The length is in practice part of the operand specification, to allow variability independently of the operation. The data length may be specified in an instruction through a length field or a limit. If specified in the instruction, operand length should be part of each operand's specification, rather than part of the operation code, to allow orthogonal construction of instructions, and simpler interpretation.

The 360 (Program 2-36) uses a length field in the SS format of its instructions. Its interpretation (Program 2-45) is not entirely trivial: Should one allow a zero length or a maximum length that is a power of 2? An efficient encoding cannot do both. For I/O, the 360 allows a zero length; for data, a power of 2. In the 360 this power of 2 is specified by adding 1 to the length field value; in the Stretch the length field is interpreted normally, except that zero signifies the power of 2.

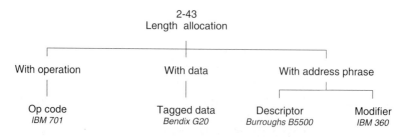

TREE 2-44   Design choices for length allocation.

```
          length←size360 field
        ⌐ IBM 360 variable size
          length←byte×(1+fld field)
```

PROGRAM 2-45   Specification of variable length in the IBM System/360.

The IBM 7070 (1960) specifies data length by pointing at both ends. This requires two addresses per datum, but the one that points at the end of the data, the *limit,* can be much abbreviated by truncation. The limit has the severe disadvantage that its value depends on the data location, a violation of orthogonality.

Length specified in data.   If length is specified in the data itself, a length value can be used, as is often done in communication. This is rarely done in computers; a delimiter is easier to update and is often more efficient.

The 1401 delimits data units by appending an extra *word-mark* bit to each 6-bit character (Section 12.3). The cost is linear with data length, whereas a length field grows logarithmically with the maximum data length.

A slightly more efficient method is used in the 705, where a plus or minus sign also delimits the end of a decimal field (Section 12.2). The redundant space in the 6-bit code is used instead of an extra bit.

The 705 has to delimit not just decimal fields, but also general 6-bit character fields. Since it uses only 48 of the 64 character codes, a special code (111111) delimits the character strings (Figure 2-10). The designers compromised the orthogonality of data length and data content, a decision they regretted when they later needed to accommodate binary data. The cost of the delimiting character is the same for each field.

Independently specified length.   Data length can be specified separately from either the instruction or the data through a descriptor as in the B6500. Another example of independent length specification is the Move Long instruction of the 370, which uses a register for the length.

	Data type	Where addressed	Extent specification Place	Extent specification Encoding
IBM 705	d	right	data	sign
IBM 705	c	left	data	delimiter
IBM 1401	c d	right	data	extra bit
IBM 1620	d f	right	data	zone bit
IBM 1620	c	left	data	delimiter
IBM Stretch	c l b d	left	instruction	length0
English Electric KDF9	b	left	descriptor	limit
English Electric KDF9	c	left	data	delimiter
Burroughs B5500	c d	left	instruction	length
IBM System/360	c l d	left	instruction	length+1
Burroughs B6500	c d	left	instruction	length
Burroughs B6500	f	left	descriptor	tag
Cray 1	v	left	instruction	length+1
DEC VAX11	l d	left	instruction	length

Legend: b = binary number; c = character string; d = decimal number;
       f = floating-point number; l = logical data; v = vector;
       length0 = maximum length encoded as zero.

TABLE 2-46   Specification of variable-length data in various machines.

Working-store size.   How should variable-length operands be placed in a working-store location? A common solution is to allot a liberal fixed length to the working-store location and to extend the operand to fill the location. The Stretch used a 128-bit accumulator for operands varying up to 64 bits.

A variable working-store length is an alternate solution, as the 705 shows. The 705 working store consists of 256 characters, which can be allocated among an accumulator and 15 registers. The accumulator can be 1 through 128 characters long; each register can be 1 to 16 characters long. Shorten and Lengthen operations move the boundaries between the registers. A Load operation will fill a register until its boundary is reached, or until a delimiter is found in memory earlier. Store copies a register into memory, stopped by the register boundary. It sets a memory delimiter.

Table 2-46 gives the parameters for specification of variable length in the same machines as those listed in Table 2-21. In such tables, we always omit machines that do not have the function under discussion; the short list shows that variable data length is infrequent.

Address Phrase

An *address phrase* consists of all the address components pertaining to a single operand. Typical components are a specification of a base register, specifications of one or more index registers, and a full or truncated explicit address field (Table 2-47). The *base* specifies the origin of a data structure, the *index* selects one out of many similar elements within that structure, and the address field, also called *displacement*, points to a component of that element or to one of the element's neighbors. The address phrase furthermore may include an *address mode* field.

Address mode.   Direct, indexed, indirect, and immediate addressing are all different addressing modes. These specify how the address components act to produce the address.

Format of the Address Phrase

How should the address components combine into an address phrase? There are three main design rules to facilitate programmed generation and manipulation of instructions:

- The address phrase, including all components and modifiers, should be the same in all instruction formats. A nice example is the DEC PDP10 (1968), in which the address phrase, bits 13 through 35, is the same in all formats, giving orthogonal operation and operand specification, as shown in Program 2-48.
- One address phrase should occupy a contiguous interval in the format. The PDP10 illustrates this rule also.
- The address-component field sizes and locations should be commensurate with the basic format system of the machine. For the PDP10, a *six* machine, this rule is true for the address field only.

	Number of phrases	Address field size	Index — Per phrase	Index — Field size	M	Number of phrases	Address field size
		Memory address phrase				Working store phrase	
Harvard Mark I	2	8					
Zuse Z4	1	6					s
Cambridge EDSAC	1	10			1		
Ferranti Mark 1	1	10	1	3			
Univac I	1	3d					
Princeton IAS	1	12					
IBM 701	1	12			1		
IBM 650	1	4d					
IBM NORC	3	4d					
IBM 704	1	15	3	1			
IBM 705	1	3,4d				1	4
Univac 1103A	2	15					
STC ZEBRA	1	13				1	5
Bull Gamma 60	1	15			2	0 1 3	2
IBM 1401	0 1 2	4,3d					
IBM 1620	2	5d	1	3			
CDC 1604	1	12 15		2		1	3
IBM Stretch	1 2	18 19 24	1	4	1		
Ferranti Atlas	1	24	2	7	4		
English Electric KDF9	0 1	15	1	4			s
CDC 6600	0 1	18				1 2 3	3
CDC 6600 PPU	0 1	12		6			
Burroughs B5500	0 1	10					s
IBM System/360	0 1 2	12	1 2	4		0 1 2	4
DEC PDP8	1	8			1		
DEC PDP11	0 1 2	16	1	3	3	0 1 2	3
Intel 8080A	0 1 2	16				0 1 2	3
Cray 1	0 1	22 25	1	3		0 1 2 3	3
Motorola M6800	0 1	8 16			2	0 1	1
MOS 6502	0 1	8 16			3		
DEC VAX11	0-6+	8 16 32	1	4	4	0-6+	4
Motorola MC68000	0 1 2	16 32	0 1	3	3	0 1 2	3
IBM 6150	1	16 24	1	4	0	0 2 3	4

Legend: d = decimal; M = address modifier bits;
  s = stack as working store; - = through; + = any number.

TABLE 2-47   Address phrases in various machines.

Indirect↓

Opcode	R	X	Address

0   9   14 18   36
Legend: R = register; X = index.

```
instruction10
⍺ DEC PDP10 instruction allocation
⍺ operation specification
  Opcode←0+⍳9
⍺ operand specification
  Reg←9+⍳4
  Indirect←13
  X←14+⍳4
  Address←18+⍳18
```

PROGRAM 2-48   Instruction format of the DEC PDP10.

When the rules clash, most designers choose commensurate sizes over contiguous subfields. In the 360 SS decimal format, there are no index specifiers, as there are in the RX format—a serious violation of the first rule. Omitting the index specifiers keeps the instruction length commensurate with 16-bit units.

In the SS format, the two length modifiers apply to the two addresses. We violated our own rule; they are separated from their address units, however, to allow the addresses to be aligned on 16-bit boundaries. They are also used together to provide an 8-bit length for character operations.

Address Length

Name-space size was governed by physical memory capacity in first- and second-generation architectures. In that era, and ever since, the most common mistake of computer architects was to allow too little addressing capacity [Bell and Strecker, 1976].

Memory capacity. If one traces a few computer families, the memory-capacity evolution is very clear. The 701 had 12-bit addresses, allowing 4096 words of memory. This capacity was cramped, so the 704 design had 15-bit addresses. This size in turn proved to be a fundamental limitation on growth of the 7090 series, so the 360 had 24-bit addresses, with an escape hatch to the 31-bit address finally provided in the 370 XA [Brooks, 1965; Padegs, 1983].

Similarly, the 702 provides 10,000 bytes of capacity; the 705 provides 40,000; the IBM 7080 (1961) provides 160,000.

Separation of name-spaces from physical-memory capacities has made it hard to predict upper bounds on desired address sizes. Table 2-28 shows maximum address sizes on various machines and the memory size initially provided. The dates show the progressions, with new cycles for minis and then for micros.

Full address. The full explicit address was quite satisfactory for early computers, early minicomputers, and early microcomputers, because the memories were small.

As memory sizes grew, so did the address capacity, and instruction formats became more and more cramped. After all, nothing had happened to change the natural sizes of data formats, and instruction and data formats must be commensurate. Indeed, it was the limitation of instruction-format space, more than the cost of the memory itself, that most severely constrained the growth of the 7090 (1959) and 7094 systems and forced IBM to abandon first- and second-generation architecture.

Address information. The number of bits required to address larger memories increases with the logarithm of memory size. The rise in the information content of the address, however, is not nearly so rapid. Rather, the number of distinct objects addressed in any portion of a program increases very slowly with total space required by the program. As a consequence, the larger addresses are more redundant than the earlier small ones, and the bit traffic is less efficiently used.

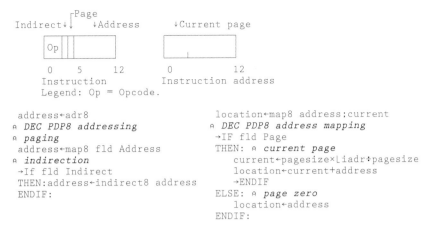

```
     address←adr8                        location←map8 address;current
   ⌐ DEC PDP8 addressing               ⌐ DEC PDP8 address mapping
   ⌐ paging                            →IF fld Page
     address←map8 fld Address          THEN: ⌐ current page
   ⌐ indirection                             current←pagesize×⌊iadr÷pagesize
   →If fld Indirect                          location←current+address
   THEN:address←indirect8 address      →ENDIF
   ENDIF:                              ELSE: ⌐ page zero
                                             location←address
                                       ENDIF:
```

PROGRAM 2-49   Truncated address of the DEC PDP8.

Truncated address.   Architects began to devise ways of improving bit-traffic efficiency for instructions by abbreviating addresses. Since, by that time, multiple address components such as indices were widely used, the basic attack was to use a truncated address in the instruction, getting the other needed bits by indirection from index or base registers. The 360 and the PDP8 (Program 2-49) are early examples.

2.4.3

Bibliography

Bell and Newell [1971], Bell and Strecker [1976], Bradlee et al. [1991], Brooks [1965], Cardelli and Wegner [1985], Feustel [1972, 1973], Gehringer and Keedy [1985], Giloi [1983], Gries [1978], Hennessy and Patterson [1990], Iliffe [1972], Myers [1978], Padegs [1983].

2.5

Operation Specification

We distinguish an *operation*, the elementary independent step carried out by a machine; an *operation code*, the encoded specification of an operation; and an *instruction*, the elementary independently reorderable unit of a program.

The term *operation code* should be understood in a broad sense: The operation code may specify not only the action to be taken, but also the datatype of the operand. It may also specify the instruction format and the format for the operation code itself.

Chapter 5 deals with the semantics of operations. Here we are concerned with specifying operations as part of the machine language. Therefore, one must decide how many operations to provide, then encode them, and then allocate them to the instruction format, as shown in Tree 2-50.

Number of Operations

How large must an operation set be? There is no inherent constraint that

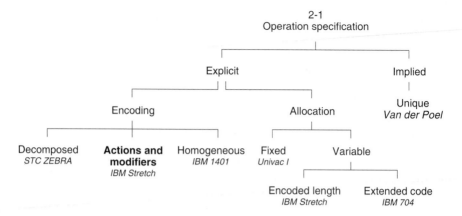

TREE 2-50   Design choices for operation specification.

limits the repertoire. The designer may choose to make the repertoire rich or lean. As with a meal, however, either extreme invokes corrective forces.

Single operation.   Van der Poel has shown that an operation set must provide for sign inversion, addition, fetching, and storing. He ingeniously combines these functions into a single operation, shown in Program 2-51, and he proves *one* to be the minimum size for an operation set. Such a machine needs no operation code at all [Van der Poel, 1956].

Lean operation repertoire.   A more practical example is the earliest version of the Manchester MU1 (1951), which has seven operations: Subtract, Load Negative, Store, Skip On Zero, Absolute and Relative unconditional indirect Branch, and Stop. One can reduce this list to three "conventional" operations—Subtract, Store, and Branch On Minus—which is again sufficient.

Lean sets quickly force the invention of idioms, sometimes called *macro-operations* or *macros*, that match the programmer's larger set of arithmetic and control concepts. Typically, these macro-operations have high redundancy in the addresses they contain. So bit-traffic efficiency improves rapidly as the lean operation set is enlarged to include these frequent macros as primitives. This is the "upward urge," the corrective force on overlean sets. Even the set of the RISCs is not lean.

Rich operation repertoire.   The oldest computers were at least as richly endowed with arithmetic operations as the modern computers. Floating point was used in the Z4 (1945), the Bell Model V relay calculator (1946), and the Harvard Mark II (1947). The Z4 and the ENIAC (1946) had square root as

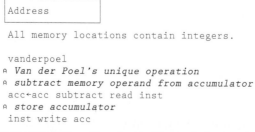

PROGRAM 2-51   Van der Poel's single instruction.

an operation. The Mark I even had operations for sine, exponentiation, and logarithm, as well as for interpolation (Section 10.2).

By 1950 these advanced operations had been removed from the Mark I. The reasons were in part peculiar to Mark I circumstances. Some operations were used infrequently and, when used, proved unreliable due to dust on the electromechanical contacts. More serious, the hardware operations were provided in full 24-decimal-digit precision, which was rarely needed, so programmed subroutines could usually outrun them.

To a surprising extent, however, the reasons are universally valid. The specialized hardware was rebuilt into generally useful registers, thus increasing the number of registers. This is an extreme example of the "downward discipline" working on a rich operation set.

Parsimony and generality, important as they were to the hand-coded Mark I, are even more vital for a modern computer that is programmed chiefly by compilers. Furthermore, the example reminds us that all such choices involve a tradeoff. Although a bodily conversion of components as in the Mark I is not likely to occur again, the designer in fact trades one function for another. The hardware that an operation requires and the software it entails can with equal total cost also be applied to improvements of the remaining functions, perhaps to greater overall advantage. An operation is never free.

Influence of compilers. The IBM 709 (1959) provides about 250 operations, yet program tracing showed that about one-half of these were hardly ever used. This result is suspect, because the most common FORTRAN compiler never generated these operations in its object code. Nevertheless, a lesson lies here. There is no point in providing operations the compilers will not generate. These operations may run faster or save instructions for special cases of more general functions, but they make hardly any contribution to the cost/performance ratio when their compiled frequencies are low.

The history of such specialized operations has been rather disappointing. The Branch On Index High of the 704, Store For Print of the 705, and the Branch On Index Low Or Equal of the 360 were not used as much as the designers had expected. Compiler writers did not do enough special-case optimization to take any substantial advantage of these operations. The compiler is most likely to use an operation repertoire that satisfies the requirements of generality, orthogonality, and parsimony.

Influence of opcode space. The size of an operation repertoire is heavily affected by the space that is available in the instruction to specify these operations. A machine that has room for a large opcode field, such as the 9-bit field of the PDP10, tends to have a richer set of operations (Program 2-48). Even so, this abundance more often expresses itself as additional variants of basic operations than as a larger set of distinct operations.

Operation count. Table 2-52 shows the operation-code count for several computers. The difficulty with such a count is finding a common basis of comparison. Because of implication, a machine may have more operations than the opcode list. On the other hand, most machines have far fewer proper operations than the table shows. The tabulated counts are inflated by code space spent on format, data length, and address-mode specification.

	Address resolution	Instruction size	Number of operations	Operation field
Harvard Mark I	24	24	62	6 8
Zuse Z4	32	8	60	2 8
Cambridge EDSAC	18	17	18	5
Ferranti Mark 1	20	20	36	5 8
Univac I	12d	6d	42	1d 2d
Princeton IAS	20	20	22	6
IBM 701	18	18	33	56
IBM 650	s,10d	10d	44	2d
IBM NORC	16d	16d	64	2d
IBM 704	36	36	86	3 12 16
IBM 705	6	30	35	6
Univac 1103A	36	36	50	6
Librascope LGP30	32	16	16	4
STC ZEBRA	33	33	1	15
Bull Gamma 60	24	24	78	5 7 8
IBM 1401	1,6	7 28 49 56	28	6 12
IBM 1620	5	12d	48	2d
CDC 1604	24	24	99	6 7
IBM Stretch	1	32 64	122	4-13
English Electric KDF9	48	8 16 24	142	8
CDC 6600	60	15 30	73	6 9
CDC 6600 PPU	12	12 24	64	6
Burroughs B5500	48	12	143	2 6 12
IBM System/360	8	16 32 48	142	8
DEC PDP8	12	12	18	3 12
DEC PDP10	36	36	403	9 12
Burroughs B6500	3,48	8 16..96	190	2 8 16
DEC PDP11	8	16 32 48	84	3 4 7..16
CDC Star100	1	32 64	231	8 16
Intel 8080A	8	8 16 24	59	2 5 6 8
Cray 1	64	16 32	104	4 7 10
Motorola M6800	8	8 16 24	72	5 6 7 8
MOS 6502	8	8 16 24	59	5 6 7 8
DEC VAX11	8	8 16..56+	244	8
Motorola MC68000	8	16 32..80	93	4-11..16
IBM 6150	8	16 32	117	4 8

Legend: d = decimal; - = through; + = any number;
.. = with increments to.

TABLE 2-52   Instruction formats of various machines.

Secondary Operations

A *secondary operation* is one implied by an explicitly specified operation; the operand and result locations are usually implied as well.

The sign test implied with arithmetic is the most common secondary operation. The Stretch implies certain bit counts with the logical operations; the 6600 uses separate operations for these counts. An extreme example is the B1700, which for a single instruction places the sum, difference, AND, and OR of the operands in specific working-store locations. Going even further, one could propose restricting the operation repertoire to Do and Move.

Side effects.   Since secondary operations create a dependence between previously independent functions, they violate orthogonality—even more so when, for lack of space to name a second result, they imply a specific storage location for it. Since secondary operations are independent primitives of

higher languages, compilers must make extra effort to cope with these side effects and to preserve through optimization the potential gain in efficiency that the secondary operations offer.

The need for efficiency is the only reason for including secondary operations in a design. They can give a savings in operation-code space, as for the B1700, or in instructions to be fetched and executed. We believe that they are better avoided.

Operation Encoding

The encoding of operations—the assignment of operations to code points—needs to be systematic in order to:

- Simplify object language generation by the compiler implementer
- Save in decoding cost, whether done by hardwired components or by microcode

Two extremes are homogeneous and fully decomposed specification.

Homogeneous encoding.   When an encoding is homogeneous, there is no internal structure to the correspondence between code points and representands—that is, no significant subsets of the representands can be discerned by examining the codes.

The 1401 illustrates the use of homogeneously encoded operations (Program 2-53 and Section 12.3). The alphabetic interpretation of the 6-bit operation code often matches the assembly mnemonic of the operation. A stands for Add and S for Subtract, and their character codes indeed specify those operations. (Move and decision operations are not homogeneously encoded; an auxiliary modifier character is used.)

Decomposed specification.   In the fully decomposed specification, each of n bits specifies a distinct action. There are n such actions. Any of the 2^n combinations of these actions can in principle be specified. The question, of course, is whether all those combinations make sense, or, even if they make sense, whether one wants them. If not, the bit efficiency suffers.

The ZEBRA of Standard Telephone and Cables (1959) has a classical example of a highly decomposed operation code (Program 2-54). The code occupies 15 bits, 12 of which have individual actions, as shown. These 12 would specify 4096 combinations of actions. The number of useful combinations is far fewer. Finding these useful combinations is an added programming burden. Most users, other than the designer Van der Poel, normally used only the software supplied by the machine.

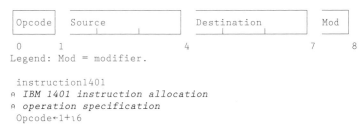

```
Legend: Mod = modifier.

    instruction1401
  A IBM 1401 instruction allocation
  A operation specification
    Opcode←1+ι6
```

PROGRAM 2-53   Operations of the IBM 1401.

Modifiers	Reg	Address

```
0                  15  20              33
```

```
instructionΔZ
ɑ STC ZEBRA instruction allocation
ɑ storage selection                    ɑ logic and arithmetic
ɑ - data/control                       ɑ - shift direction
  A←0                                    L←3
  K←1                                    R←4
ɑ - accumulator/mq                     ɑ - negate
  B←6                                    I←5
ɑ - clear                              ɑ - count in mq
  C←7                                    Q←2
ɑ read/write                           ɑ tests
ɑ - memory                               V←10
  D←8                                    Test←11+ɩ3
ɑ - register                           ɑ operand specification
  E←9                                    Reg←15+ɩ5
ɑ - no drum wait                         Address←20+ɩadrsize
  W←14
```

PROGRAM 2-54   Instruction of the Standard Telephone and Cables ZEBRA.

A partially homogeneous and partially decomposed specification is the most common choice.

Actions and modifiers.   As we have seen, operations in modern large-sized operation sets are mostly decomposable into *actions*, such as Add, and *modifiers*, usually datatype selectors. Preserving this proper distinction leads to a systematic encoding.

Table 2-55 shows the 1-byte operation-code set for the 360, as it has matured through four generations of architecture. The operation codes marked with a + are extended to a second byte, so there are more operations than this table suggests. The set was originally laid out so that the first two bits of the operation code served as a datatype selector, and the last four bits specified the same action in all codes.

Alas, not all operations are so neatly decomposed, and the misfits must be put in somewhere. When they are, they reintroduce much of the decoding complexity.

Open-endedness. Systematic encoding applies not only to those code values assigned to operations, but also to those left unassigned—the spares for future expansion. One wants these values to occur in the places where expansion is most likely to take place, but that is often not possible. So operation-set expansion during the evolution of an architecture usually has the effect of further corrupting the neatness of a systematic operation encoding (Table 2-55).

Operation-Code Allocation

The allocation of bits for the operation code is usually more complicated than the encoding. The key question is the number of sizes.

RR FORMAT

xxxx	Branching and Status Switching 0000xxxx	Fixed-Point Full Word and Logical 0001xxxx	Floating-Point Long 0010xxxx	Floating-Point Short 0011xxxx
0000	*PR* — *Program Return*	LPR — Load Positive	LPDR — Load Positive	LPER — Load Positive
0001	*UP* — *Update Tree*	LNR — Load Negative	LNDR — Load Negative	LNER — Load Negative
0010		LTR — Load And Test	LTDR — Load And Test	LTER — Load And Test
0011		LCR — Load Complement	LCDR — Load Complement	LCER — Load Complement
0100	SPM — Set Program M	NR — AND	HDR — Halve	HER — Halve
0101	BALR — Branch And Link	CLR — Compare Logical	*LRDR* — *Load Rounded (X to D)*	*RER* — *Load Rounded (D to S)*
0110	BCTR — Branch On Count	OR — OR	*MXR* — *Multiply X*	*AXR* — *Add N Extended*
0111	BCR — Branch/Condition	XR — Exclusive OR	*MSDR* — *Multiply (D to X)*	*SXR* — *Subtract N Extended*
1000	SSK* — Set Key	LR — Load	LDR — Load	LER — Load
1001	ISK* — Insert Key	CR — Compare	CDR — Compare	CER — Compare
1010	SVC — Supervisor Call	AR — Add	ADR — Add N	ALR — Add N
1011	*BSM* — *Branch And Set Mode*	SR — Subtract	SDR — Subtract N	SER — Subtract N
1100	*BASSM* — *Branch, Save, Set Mode*	MR — Multiply	MDR — Multiply	MER — Multiply
1101	*BASR* — *Branch And Save*	DR — Divide	DDR — Divide	DER — Divide
1110	MVCL — Move L	ALR — Add Logical	AWR — Add U	AUR — Add U
1111	CLCL — Compare Logical L	SLR — Subtract Logical	SWR — Subtract U	SUR — Subtract U

RX FORMAT

xxxx	Fixed-Point Halfword and Branching 0100xxxx	Fixed-Point Full Word and Logical 0101xxxx	Floating-Point Long 0110xxxx	Floating-Point Short 0111xxxx
0000	STH — Store	ST — Store	STD — Store	STE — Store
0001	LA — Load Address	LAE — Load Address X		
0010	STC — Store Character			
0011	IC — Insert Character			
0100	EX — Execute	N — AND		
0101	BAL — Branch And Link	CL — Compare Logical	*MXD* — *Multiply (D to X)*	
0110	BCT — Branch On Count	O — OR		
0111	BC — Branch/Condition	X — Exclusive OR		
1000	LH — Load	L — Load	LD — Load	LE — Load
1001	CH — Compare	C — Compare	CD — Compare	CE — Compare
1010	AH — Add	A — Add	AD — Add N	AE — Add N
1011	SH — Subtract	S — Subtract	SD — Subtract N	SE — Subtract N
1100	MH — Multiply	M — Multiply	MD — Multiply	ME — Multiply
1101	*BAS* — *Branch And Save*	D — Divide	DD — Divide	DE — Divide
1110	CVD — Convert-Decimal	AL — Add Logical	AW — Add U	AU — Add U
1111	CVB — Convert-Binary	SL — Subtract Logical	SW — Subtract U	SU — Subtract U

RS, SI FORMAT

xxxx	Branching, Status Switching and Shifting 1000xxxx	Immediate, Logical and Input/Output 1001xxxx	1010xxxx	1011xxxx
0000	SSM Set System M	STM Store Multiple		
0001		TM Test Under M		LRA Load Real Address
0010	LSPW Load PSW	MVI Move		+ Privileged Extended Ops
0011	Diagnose	TS Test And Set		
0100	WRD* Write Direct	NI AND	+ Vector Extended Ops	
0101	RDD* Read Direct	CLI Compare Logical	+ Vector Extended Ops	
0110	BXH Branch/High	OI OR	+ Vector Extended Ops	STCTL Store Control
0111	BXLE Branch/Low-Equal	XI Exclusive OR		LCTL Load Control
1000	SRL Shift Right SL	LM Load Multiple		
1001	SLL Shift Left SL	TRACE Trace		
1010	SRA Shift Right S	LAM Load Access Multiple		CS Compare And Swap
1011	SLA Shift Left S	STM Store Access Multiple		CDS Compare D And Swap
1100	SRDL Shift Right DL	SIO+* Start I/O	STNSM Store, And Systems M	
1101	SLDL Shift Left DL	TIO+* Test I/O	STOSM Store, Or Systems M	CLM Comp. Log. Char. Under M
1110	SRDA Shift Right D	HIO+* Halt I/O	SIGP Signal Processor	STCM Store Char. Under M
1111	SLDA Shift Left D	TCH+* Test Channel	MC Monitor Call	ICM Insert Char. Under M

SS FORMAT

xxxx	1100xxxx	Logical 1101xxxx	1110xxxx	Decimal 1111xxxx
0000				SRP Shift And Round
0001		MVN Move Numeric		MVO Move With Offset
0010		MVC Move		PACK Pack
0011		MVZ Move Zone		UNPK Unpack
0100		NC AND		
0101		CLC Compare Logical	+ Privileged Extended Ops	
0110		OC OR	+ Privileged Extended Ops	
0111		XC Exclusive OR		
1000			MVCIN Move Inverse	ZAP Zero And Add
1001		MVCK Move With Key		CP Compare
1010		MVCP Move To Primary		AP Add
1011		MVCS Move To Secondary		SP Subtract
1100		TR Translate		MP Multiply
1101		TRT Translate And Test		DP Divide
1110		ED Edit		
1111		EDMK Edit And Mark		

Legend: D = Double; DL = Double Logical; L = Long; M = Mask; N = Normalized; S = Single; SL = Single Logical; U = Unnormalized; X = Extended; * = Removed in later architecture; + = Extended op codes; Bold = operations originally in the 360; Boldface italic = additions of the 370; Italic = additions of the "Extended Architecture" XA; Roman = additions of the "Enterprise Architecture" ESA.

TABLE 2-55 Evolution of 1-byte operation codes in the IBM System/360 family.

Fixed-length code. The simplest allocation uses a fixed number of n bits for the operation code, which allows 2^n operations, and that's that. Most early machines had such a fixed-length operation code; many RISCs do.

Variable-length code. Since some operations require fewer bits of operand specification than do others, one can save the bits not needed for operands to specify operations. So one has a variable-length operation coding system.

Huffman [1952] describes systematic ways of constructing variable-length codes that optimize the information efficiency of the code itself. The computer architect has a different task—to optimize the bit efficiency of fixed instruction formats, given operations that require different specifications for operands; frequency of use is not the issue here.

Extended operation code. The most common variable-length operation code uses the space that becomes available when fewer operands need specification. The unused operand fields are then dedicated as *extended-operation-code* fields.

Program 2-37 illustrates the use of two levels of extended operation code in the PDP11. Here a 16-bit instruction format accommodates dyadic, monadic, and nilladic operations. Each operand consistently requires 6 bits, leaving 4, 10, and 16 bits respectively for the operation code. Some of the code values with 4-bit length indicate that the code is to be extended to 10 bits; several values of that 10-bit code specify a further extension to include the 6 low-order bits of the instruction.

Most operations are dyadic, so the operations that need the most operand specification also are most numerous. The smallest operation field is likely to be the most cramped. As a result, a single code point of the smaller fields is usually used as an *escape* to the extended code [Brooks, 1956].

Program 15-36's `syntax11` reveals that the PDP11 uses many more formats than the three actually shown. As operations such as floating point were added, a quite complex coding scheme evolved. Not surprisingly, the VAX11 made a clean break and adopted an 8-bit homogeneous operation code.

Scattered operation code. For the extended operation code, the instruction formats can be ordered such that progressively more fields are dedicated to the operation specification and remain dedicated that way. In the more general case, different fields are dedicated for different formats. Of course, some root field must always be dedicated for format selectors; other operation fields, however, come and go as space happens to be available.

The instruction formats for the Stretch show such a scattered operation code (Figure 2-56). The root is formed by bits 25, 26, 27. This field extends to the right in one format, to the left in another, and to a discontiguous field of variable size in double-length instructions. This is an extreme case among general purpose computers. Extension is carried foolishly far: It not only requires a complex decoder, but also complicates compiler design. A simpler encoding would have allowed fewer operations, but that would have been a good trade.

The Motorola MC68000 (1980) is another example of the scattered operation code. The basic format has one opcode field and two operand phrases, each with a 3-bit modifier and 3-bit working-store address. For some

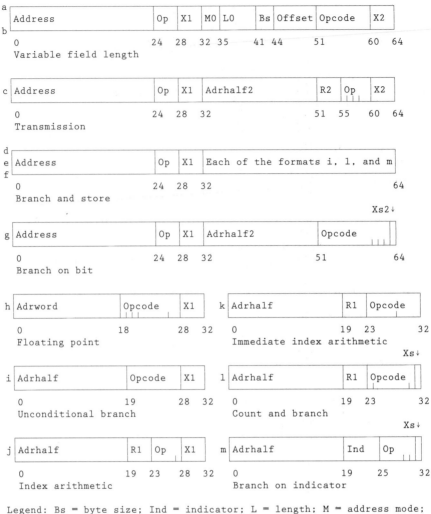

Legend: Bs = byte size; Ind = indicator; L = length; M = address mode;
        Op = opcode; R = register; X = index.

FIGURE 2-56   Instructions of the IBM Stretch.

operations, an address modification may not apply; the corresponding code pattern is then used as an extended operation code. Since this method is applied to both address phrases and iterated for the resulting formats, the outcome is a quite complex instruction syntax (Section 16.4).

The 360 appears to have a single-length operation code, the first 8 bits of the format, as shown in Program 2-36. The Supervisor Call operation, however, looks suspiciously like a 16-bit extended operation code. Indeed, the 370 Model 3033 includes implementations of some of the Supervisor Call functions previously performed entirely by software. The VAX11 similarly extends its 8-bit code to 16 bits.

If one examines almost any architecture, such cases emerge. The I/O operations are favorite candidates for such operation-code expansion. Whenever an address specifies something other than an operand, that address is likely to be an operation code.

2.5.1

Bibliography

Brooks [1956], Buchholz [1962], Huffman [1952], Van der Poel [1956].

2.6

Instructions

A language derives much of its power of expression from the word sequence, especially if its vocabulary is limited. Similarly, the computer obtains much of its processing ability by allowing a limited repertoire of instructions to be used in any desired sequence. Such a sequence of instructions is called a *procedure*. The procedure and the data to which it applies are jointly called a *program*.

We consider in this section the specification of the instruction sequence, the instruction format, and the format of status information, as summarized in Tree 2-57.

2.6.1

Sequence Specification

The status variable that indicates the location of the instruction to be fetched and executed next is the *instruction address*.

Implied sequence. Most often, instructions are stored consecutively in memory, so the instruction address is incremented each time an instruction is executed. Because of this incrementation, the instruction address is often misnamed the *instruction counter*, or even worse, the *program counter*. This variable does not count instructions or programs at all; nor is the next value of the instruction address necessarily an increment of one.

Chained sequence. One does not have to map the linearized program-sequence vector linearly into memory; any of the standard representations of a vector might be used. However, the only representation—other than the linear mapping—to have found actual use is the forward-chained representation. In this representation, each instruction contains a next-instruction address, as in the IBM 650 (Program 1-30). Instruction-sequence specification is independent of the operand specification; thus, the 650 is a one-address machine. The

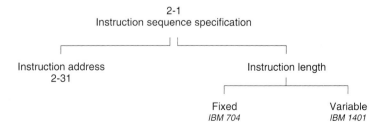

TREE 2-57 Design choices for instruction-sequence specification.

National Bureau of Standards SEAC (1951) used similar chaining in a three-address machine, to give four address fields in all.

Chaining makes it convenient to place instructions at opportune locations, if their locations matter. In a drum machine such as the 650, the instructions may be placed around the circumference of the drum in a relation to the operands such that, taking the operation time into account, minimum latency occurs. Gordon [1956] describes a program for the 650 that finds near-optimum instruction and data locations and reduces program execution time by a factor of about 2. In a machine with random-access memory, chained representation of programs has no merit.

2.6.2

Instruction Format

Whereas data representation is strongly influenced by the data to be formatted, instruction representations are constrained only by the design decisions of the computer architect. Yet the freedom to design any format that one fancies is even more severely limited for instruction formats: Almost all basic architectural-design decisions intertwine into one big allocation problem.

So CPU architecture seems to center around the design of the instruction format. Long before any hardware cost estimates are available, the architect begins to weigh cost-versus-performance tradeoffs by tentatively investing his instruction bits and exploring the consequences in data-format bits, program length, and expected hardware complexity. In this sense, the instruction format is the summary document for CPU architecture; the instruction bit budget is the first limiting resource.

We cannot, in this section, treat all the design decisions that affect or are affected by instruction-format design. Some of those, such as addressing and sequencing, are the subjects of entire chapters. Here we treat the decisions that are chiefly governed by instruction-format design, and we show how the decisions made elsewhere in the system all come to this crossroads.

Instruction Length

The length of an instruction is, of course, governed by all that it should include. On the other hand, the instruction format should match the other formats, which leads to some preliminary decisions.

Figure 2-58 shows the relation of instruction length to that of the addressable information unit for some machines.

One addressable unit per instruction.   The easiest and oldest approach equates an addressable unit, here a word, with an instruction. The 704 (Program 2-59) and the PDP10 (Program 2-48) illustrate this approach.

Variable-length instructions.   The 704's simple match of one instruction to one word is bought at the expense of unused instruction fields. Instruction content is simply not so uniform, so variable-length instructions are widely used, even for simple microprocessors.

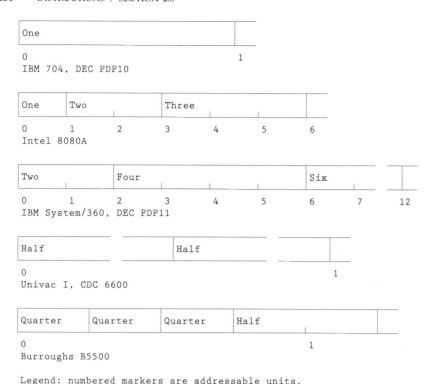

Legend: numbered markers are addressable units.

FIGURE 2-58 Instruction length related to addressable unit.

Several addressable units per instruction. The PDP8 and the 8080A use a variable instruction length of one or more addressable units.

The instructions of the 360 and PDP11 always use an even number of addressable units, in this case bytes, aligned on 2-byte boundaries. It is a minor burden for the assembler or compiler to satisfy this alignment and for the processor to check for it. The two machines differ, however, in the form of the address that points at the instruction. In the 360 the address is always uniform—including, in this case, the redundant low-order bit. In the PDP11 the low-order bit is omitted—an example of truncation.

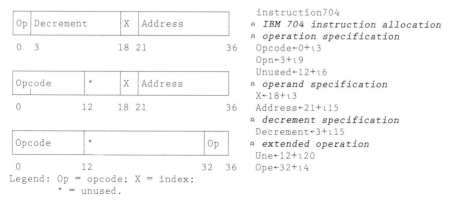

PROGRAM 2-59 Instruction formats of the IBM 704.

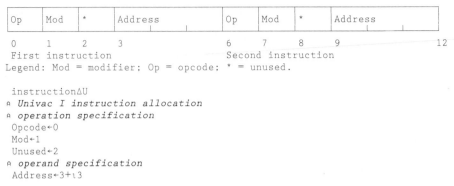

```
instruction∆U
⋀ Univac I instruction allocation
⋀ operation specification
  Opcode←0
  Mod←1
  Unused←2
⋀ operand specification
  Address←3+ι3
```

PROGRAM 2-60   Instruction format of the Univac I.

Several instructions per addressable unit.   Problems are more serious when
the addressable unit contains several instructions. The Univac I first faced this
problem (Program 2-60). Instructions are always executed in pairs, even when
the first instruction is a successful branch.

The 6600 follows this drastic approach.   An assemblage of instructions
must always fit entirely in a word, without straggling. Figure 2-61 shows the
patterns that completely fill a word. The assembler or compiler makes up any
mismatch with short empty instructions, No-ops.

The explicit address of an instruction, as specified by a branch, is always
a word address.   If one wants to branch to an instruction, the latter must
be located at a word boundary, or preceded by No-ops. This is in line with
the 6600 design philosophy of gaining speed at the expense of some added
compiler work. Unlike what happens in the Univac I, however, instructions
behind a successful branch are not executed.

As one would expect, the B5500 has a much less constrained, but more
costly, approach. Any placement is allowed, so there are no No-ops; and any

Short	Short	Short	Short
0	15	30	45 ... 60

Short	Short	Long
0	15	30 ... 60

Short	Long	Short
0	15	45 ... 60

Long	Short	Short
0	30	45 ... 60

Long	Long
0	30 ... 60

FIGURE 2-61   Instruction patterns of the CDC 6600.

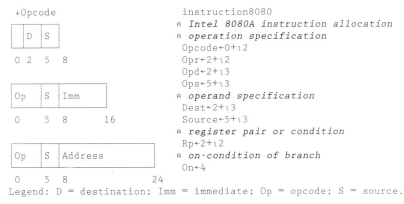

Legend: D = destination; Imm = immediate; Op = opcode; S = source.

PROGRAM 2-62   Instruction formats of the Intel 8080A.

instruction is addressable. The normal address is extended for instruction addressing at the expense of uniformity. Similarly, the IAS uses Branch Left and Branch Right (Section 11.1) [Burks et al., 1946].

Instruction-Length Specification

The length of an instruction must be either implied (if fixed) or specified in the instruction itself, so it can be parsed and the next one found.

Format selector.   The instruction-length specification is, in principle, independent of operation and operand specification; it is not independent of the number of operands. The length is therefore most often derived from a code that specifies the instruction format, the *format selector*.

The format selector may be a distinct code of fixed or variable length, or it may be encoded with operation specification and not be recognizable as a distinct entity, as in the 8080A (Program 2-62). Program 2-36 shows the format of the 360, in which the first two bits act as format selector.

Variable-length format selectors are illustrated by the Stretch (Figure 2-56). A short selector is used for short lengths and for cramped formats, as is done with variable-length operation codes.

Instruction origin.   The variable instruction length poses the problem of knowing where an instruction starts. Once one knows a valid start, one can proceed from instruction to instruction, since each instruction tells how long it is. The real problem is how to go backward—that is, to find the preceding instruction—as is often required for an interrupt handler. For this reason, the 360 provides an instruction-length code as part of the interrupt information.

2.6.3
Status Format

Status is the information that controls the interpretation process, in contrast to instructions that define this process and data that determine the result of this process. (A zero-result indication is a datum, not a status, even

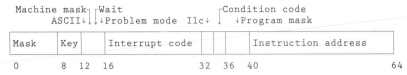

FIGURE 2-63   Program Status Word of the IBM System/360.

though it may sometimes be obtained as a secondary result and be placed in a special register. Similarly, the data descriptor encountered in Section 2.4 is an indirectly referenced instruction field.)

Status formats, like instruction formats and unlike data formats, are completely under the designer's control. There are no inherent, application-determined natural sizes for their fields. Furthermore, since the status resides in control registers and normal reference is by implication, these formats are even less constrained than instruction formats are.

Status word.   The status must be saved as part of the context saving during program switching. Similarly, part of the status is saved during subroutine call and return. The memory format for saved status is the *status format*.

Such a unit of control information is usually called a *status word* or *control word*. This nomenclature is by no means universal, and, at times, "control words" turn out to be instructions or data descriptors.

Figure 2-63 shows the PSW of the 360. All fields contain status information except for the condition code used in branching, which is a secondary result. It is convenient to store the condition code in the PSW, but that mixes status information with data. Similarly, the PSW of the PDP11 contains condition bits (Section 15.2).

2.6.4

Bibliography

Burks et al. [1946], Gordon [1956], Maurer [1966], McDaniel [1982].

2.7

Rules of Good Practice

1. A machine designed to serve more than one high-level language should have a design-controlled machine language above, and independent of, implementations, to decouple programming languages from implementations.
2. The optimum level for machine language is at the interface between what can be bound compilatively and what must be interpreted at run time because of data dependency.
3. Format fields should be encoded efficiently; format bits are precious.
4. Format encoding and allocation, such as for operations sets and characters, should leave room for future additions, taking into account rule 3.

5. Invalid or undefined operation codes and addresses in instructions should always be caught by the hardware. Otherwise, the spaces saved for the future are not really saved.
6. Each format field should be commensurate in length and alignment with the information-unit system of the machine.
7. Groups of format fields that syntactically form a phrase should be contiguous.
8. Data and control information should be separated. There should be no bit configurations whose presence as data exercises an irrepressible delimiting or control function.
9. Data aggregates should be aligned wherever possible.
10. Secondary operations and side effects should be avoided.
11. Embedding of name-spaces should be avoided.
12. Linear address spaces are superior to circular ones.
13. The binary radix is superior to others for addresses.
14. Additive expansion of truncated addresses is superior to prefixed expansion.
15. General purpose working store is superior to specialized working store.
16. The bits within a byte or word should be addressed from left to right (Big Endian).

2.8
Exercises

2-1 What modifications of the 360 instruction-format set would be required for all data specifications to have index, base, and displacement? Propose a format set.

2-2 Some machines have instructions that occupy only a fraction of a memory word: Several instructions are packed into a single word. A branch should therefore specify not only the word address of the next instruction to be executed, but also the position of this instruction within the word.

a. The 6600 and the IAS machine are two such computers. How have they solved this addressing problem? What is the disadvantage of this solution?

b. How has the Cray 1 (in many ways a descendant of the 6600) solved this problem?

2-3 Design the instruction formats for a computer having 24 address bits, 32 bit words, about 10 index registers, and 64 operations, and using extended zero address for operand specification. Give the formats for the following:

a. Arithmetic

b. Branching

c. I/O

2-4 A message-sending device has four distinguishable elements, each of which can be set high (+), low (-), or level (0).

a. How many distinct messages can be represented by one setting of the device?

b. Give an expression for the amount of information in one setting of the device.

c. Give an expression for the minimum number of two-state elements required to represent a setting of the device.

2-5 "A very-high-speed computer that executes APL directly can be made to perform faster than a machine of the same size and technology executing IBM System/360 machine language." This assertion means the APL machine executing a mix of problems coded in APL will take less time than the 360 executing the same mix coded in assembler language.

a. To what fundamental architectural principle or concept would you appeal to make a 5-minute judgment of the plausibility of this assertion?

b. Is the assertion plausible? Detail your reasoning.

2-6 Bell and Newell [1971, p. 56] say: "Only within narrow limits is word length a free design choice."

a. What do they mean?

b. What arguments do they adduce for this position? Give at least four.

c. Evaluate these arguments, indicating their strengths and weaknesses.

2-7 Define add and subtract for unpacked and packed decimal datatypes in the 360:

a. Without coercion

b. With coercion to packed decimal

2-8 Give the two- to three-address breakeven calculation for

a. The 6600

b. The NORC

2-9 Program 2-51 gives Van der Poel's single instruction. Give the corresponding space description `spacevdp`.

Names and Addresses

3

Overview of the Chapter

How does one identify the objects about which the machine language speaks, such as the data and instructions?

In programming languages, objects are identified by names. The *name* is the major program primitive of this chapter; the *address* is the corresponding machine-language element. Chapter 2 treated the syntax of address phrases; this chapter treats their semantics. Chapter 2 treated the *form* of the name of stored information; this chapter treats the interpretation of that name in the *selection* of stored information. Chapter 2 concerned formats; this chapter concerns the algorithms that map the name space onto the address space.

Binding. In the machine languages, the address space is preferably dense, measured, and linear: Addresses are integers and can usually be computed by regular arithmetic.

In programming languages, on the other hand, names may refer to single objects, but most names refer to groups of data and instructions, such as files, tables, arrays, and procedures. The programmer wants to specify such a set of objects, not the addresses of these objects in a memory. Yet, allocation of named objects to addresses must occur somehow, and the architect does his best to make it occur behind the scenes, thus concealing its complexity. (The size of named objects may change in time.) From the architect's perspective, the driving problem of addressing is the mapping of names into a linear address space—the *binding* of names to addresses, treated in Section 3.1.

Address mapping. Section 3.2 treats computer mechanisms for doing this binding. The simplest computer solution is to ignore the need and leave the task to the software. First- and second-generation computers, including minis, and early micros all did this.

The "ideal" solution is fully dynamic, fully independent mapping of program variable names directly to locations, called *associative addressing*. Its inherent implementation costs are usually prohibitive.

Intermediate solutions provide various ways of mapping blocks of the name-space to blocks of contiguous addresses, and blocks of those to memory locations.

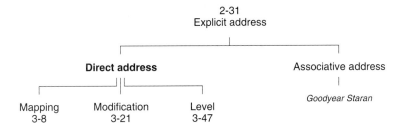

TREE 3-1   Design choices for explicit addresses.

Data structures.   Group names often refer to variables—such as matrices, stacks, and queues—called *data structures*. Occasionally, a structure of this kind can be handled as an entity both in the programming language and in the machine language. An example is the logical vector. At other times, the programming language treats the structure as an entity, but the machine language does not, as in the APL array. Quite often, however, neither the programming language nor the machine language treats the object as an entity, even though the programmer thinks of a single object; an example is a sparse matrix in a FORTRAN matrix multiplication. Furthermore, even when the programmer considers an object as a single entity, he may nevertheless be aware of its elements and want to access only some of them. He may want to select a column out of a matrix; he may want to place new elements into a queue. The names of such objects are therefore compound, consisting of the name of the whole data structure augmented by the name of the element within the structure.

We treat in Section 3.3 the naming and accessing of an element within a regular array, in Section 3.4 the naming and accessing of elements in sequential structures, such as queues and stacks, and in Section 3.5 the naming of elements in chained structures, such as trees. In each case, we first consider the appropriate program primitive, then the corresponding architectural alternatives. Tree 3-1 shows the basic design choices.

The most general address is the *direct address*, illustrated for reading and writing in Program 3-2. The direct address matches the structure of the spaces discussed in Section 2.3, and it is the means of accessing array elements by address modification. It can be conveniently used to implement sequential structures by incrementation and decrementation, and chained structures by indirect addressing.

```
data←size read address;location
⍺ read from direct-addressed memory
location←address+⍳size÷resolution
data←memory[location;]


address write data;location
⍺ write in direct-addressed memory
location←address+⍳(ρdata)÷resolution
memory[location;]←data
```

PROGRAM 3-2   Direct addressing.

3.1
Binding

The natural and proper identifier of an object such as a procedure or a data structure is its programming-language *name*. The principle of propriety forbids burdening user or machine with extraneous notions such as addresses or memory locations.

The interactive APL implementation and associatively addressed machines show that such systems can be built. The implementations, however, also show the high processing cost involved in interpreting programming-language names. The solution to this inefficiency in traditional programming languages is to compile a user-given name to a machine-language name, an *address*, which in turn is interpreted at execute time as referring to a place in memory, the memory *location* (Figure 3-3).

The names a programmer uses to specify data and instructions are mapped in machine language onto a fixed set of locations. This process of mapping, done by the compiler or assembler, the loader, and the supervisor, is called *binding*. For flexibility, some of this binding is deferred until execute time, when indexing, indirect addressing, dynamic address mapping, caches, and other mechanisms enable last-minute modifications of these bindings. The extreme solution of the *associative store* provides late binding of individual names to individual storage locations.

Late binding adds power and flexibility to program execution, but costs in equipment and execution time.

Binding times.   Why can the programming-language name of an object not have a fixed correspondence to that object's actual location in memory? For many reasons. One may want to change the set of programs whose data are simultaneously in memory without changing the names of any of them. Or

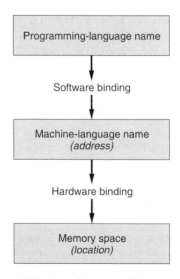

FIGURE 3-3   Relation of name, address, and location.

one may want to use a large array of data in lieu of a small one without changing the name of the array, not to mention the names of all the other variables that must be displaced.

Both programming languages and machine languages have evolved so as to offer more and more distinct *binding times*. Generally speaking, each innovation allows some class of names to be bound late, for more flexibility.

3.1.1

Software Binding

Figure 3-4 shows the binding times offered by the software of the macro-assembly program under the IBM MVS operating system. These bindings are all (except the Execute step) done by software. For each binding time, Figure 3-4 shows the name of each step, and

- On the left, new information used in the binding step and not available earlier; for example, supervisor-specified locations
- In the center boxes, the binding that occurs
- Between the boxes, the program object passed from one step to the next; for example, in-place code
- On the right, the mechanism available for communicating *outside* the bound-together chunk of program; for example, the supervisory program's passing area

Of course, each mechanism shown on the far right is also available to the user on any earlier step.

A little assembly-language program that contains some library language macro-operations (macros), such as GET and PUT, will be progressively bound as follows.

Assembler.   During the Generate part of assembly, the parameters for the macros will be combined with the macro skeletons from the library. Conditional assembly statements are evaluated then, too. The result is "generated" assembly source. The several macros, each now bound into a single routine, may nevertheless still communicate by shared memory locations (specified by global symbols in the macro language).

At assembly time, all the assembly source is translated into object code, and all mnemonic variable names are transformed into machine addresses. These are all *relocatable*, however, in that they specify positions relative to the start of a *control section*, a relocatable block of program or data. A table with each module, called a *relocation dictionary* (RLD), specifies for each address the control section to which that address belongs. Such deferral of actual address assignment until relocation at program load time is the oldest and most common deferred-binding mechanism.

Linker.   Because assembly or compilation takes time, it is common to provide a linker that combines newly assembled programs with preassembled (or precompiled) library subroutines, such as a sine routine. The already-assembled programs must have common variables with which to communicate; these

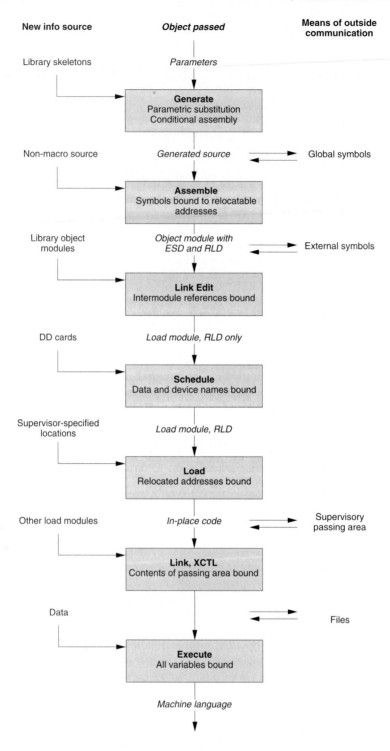

New info source	Object passed	Means of outside communication
Library skeletons	Parameters	
	Generate Parametric substitution Conditional assembly	
Non-macro source	Generated source	Global symbols
	Assemble Symbols bound to relocatable addresses	
Library object modules	Object module with ESD and RLD	External symbols
	Link Edit Intermodule references bound	
DD cards	Load module, RLD only	
	Schedule Data and device names bound	
Supervisor-specified locations	Load module, RLD	
	Load Relocated addresses bound	
Other load modules	In-place code	Supervisory passing area
	Link, XCTL Contents of passing area bound	
Data		Files
	Execute All variables bound	
	Machine language	

Legend: RLD = Relocation dictionary; ESD = External symbol dictionary; XCTL = Transfer control.

FIGURE 3-4 Binding times in a modern software system.

variables are identified by an *external symbol dictionary* (ESD) carried with each module.

Scheduler.   Most modern operating systems allow I/O data sets to be referenced in programs by symbolic names. These names are not actually bound to specific data sets on specific devices until the program is submitted for running. In MVS, this binding is specified by a *data-definition* (DD) statement in the Job Control Language (JCL) when the program is scheduled for execution.

Loader.   Prior to execution, the program is loaded into memory. The loader may put the different control sections into disjoint blocks of memory, depending upon the available space. As it does so, it binds the relocatable addresses to the locations in the machine-language name-space, the *addresses*. In modern machines these are not, in fact, final addresses: They are machine-language *address phrases*, whose components interact at execute time.

MVS and other operating systems provide for limited run-time communication among programs that have no shared variables. This communication is accomplished by calling the operating system and passing to it the information to be relayed to the other program. (The operating system knows, at run time, where the programs are.) The run-time mechanisms are called *link* (LINK) and *transfer control* (XCTL) in MVS.

Programs not otherwise bound to one another can also communicate by reading and writing shared data sets. This technique has long been the standard means for communication among programs that are not concurrently in execution.

Execute step.   At the Execute step, all the variables, now named by machine addresses, are bound by having actual values stored into them. This final binding is the purpose of all the preceding steps.

3.1.2
Hardware Binding

Figure 3-5 expands the Execute step in Figure 3-4 to show the series of further bindings of addresses done at run time by the computer hardware of the IBM System/370 (1971). The address phrases produced at load time are interpreted to effect

- The addition of a base address to the specified displacement, which is an abbreviated address
- The addition of an index value, to specify an individual element within a data structure
- A segment and page-table reference, to allow run-time flexibility in memory use
- Still another table reference to allow variables most frequently used (over any short period of time) to be placed automatically in a special fast memory, a *cache*

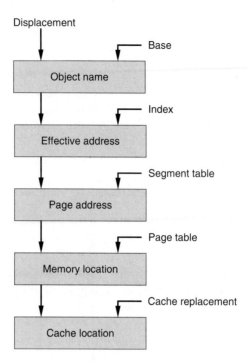

FIGURE 3-5   Hardware bindings of addresses in the IBM System/370.

3.2

Address Mapping

Dynamic mapping of an address to a memory location binds the address at the very last moment—that is, at execution time. Memory allocation can therefore be changed even in mid-execution of a program.

If the mapping system is well-designed, its effects cannot be logically discerned by the relocated program. It is said to be *transparent* for that program. Figure 3-6 gives the conceptual position of address mapping in relation to the processor and memory.

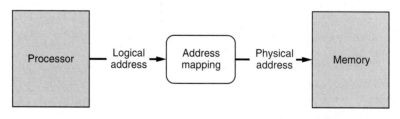

FIGURE 3-6   Position of address mapping.

3.2.1

Programmed Mapping

Name–address–location bindings have never, in fact, been kept rigid and unmodified. They have always been altered to achieve memory reuse. To understand the architectural provisions for deferred and/or dynamic binding, let us look at the software practices used when such hardware provisions are unavailable.

Static Rebinding

The most primitive way of changing the name–address–location binding in a program is for the programmer himself to modify the name–address binding—that is, to associate one address with one programming-language name at one time and with another name at another time.

Rebinding data areas.   Keeping track of the availability of individual locations for reuse (that is, rebinding to another variable name) is tedious and error-prone, but it was practiced routinely for early computers and their tiny memories. This practice quickly evolved to the systematic rebinding of whole blocks of addresses from time to time.

One universal technique in both commercial and scientific computing is to designate blocks of addresses as I/O areas and to read into them one record after another from tape or disk. In fact, most programmers do not even think of the several records as differently named variables at all.

Program overlays.   A second universal technique is overlaying one block of program with others during times when the overlaid part of the program is inactive. Operating systems provide modularization facilities and allow overlay structures to be specified; name–address binding and rebinding are deferred until separately compiled programs are linked together.

Run to completion.   In a system dedicated to one application and where the duration of all programs is known, users may be kept waiting until memory becomes free. Static relocation is possible under this system.

Programs representing jobs or job steps run till completion. Each time a program is used, memory is reallocated, and the program is loaded, rebound, and run from the beginning.

Roll in/roll out.   A time-sharing operating system divides the available time into subsecond *time slices* when the duration of a program is too long or is not known. When memory space is insufficient, the program that just finished its slice may have to give up its memory space until its next turn to execute. In this case, the procedure and data are removed to an auxiliary store. This procedure is called *rolling in and out* of memory.

The CDC 6600 (1964) uses a very fast means of rolling in and out. Here transmission from and to an Extended Core Storage (ECS) or drum takes place prior to and following program execution. Transmission is very rapid because the ECS memory is highly interleaved; 16 K words of 60 bits can be moved in 0.5 ms to or from the ECS. Execution of a program is not overlapped with

the transmission of other programs to and from this ECS. Each program can occupy most of memory when it is in at all.

Most computers provide no extra-high-speed transmission and may require 50 ms for transmission to and from auxiliary store. Therefore, the rolling in and out is overlapped with the execution of other programs.

Dynamic Software Rebinding

Under the static-binding discipline, a rolled-out program must be rolled back into its former memory locations, for the name–location bindings were established when the program was loaded and started. But the set of signed-on users active at any time keeps changing, so this rolling in to the same spot is a severe constraint on the memory-allocation strategy.

Allocation is much simpler if the program to be rolled in can be assigned memory locations different from those it formerly had. Now the addresses in the program no longer correspond to the memory locations of the relevant data. One can remedy this discrepancy by changing the address values within the program.

Rebinding a program in mid-execution is much harder than rebinding a virgin one. In the newly compiled or newly assembled program, the location-dependent address constants have been declared as such. These address constants can be operated upon as can any other data, so, after a program has begun execution, one must trace operations to identify all location-dependent variables. This tracing depends upon strong programming restrictions. W.P. Heising showed, in 1963, how programmed dynamic rebinding might be done for the IBM System/360 (1965) by a disciplined use of the base registers for all addressing. Heising's conventions were not adopted for the 360 software, so software dynamic rebinding is not practical for that system [Heising, personal communication].

3.2.2
Associative Addressing

Why not build machine hardware to accomplish run-time dynamic rebinding? Let us consider a store in which each location is independently bound to its programming-language name, and the name can be changed at any time. Since all binding is fully deferred, there is no need for a machine-language address as a compiled-to-intermediate name.

Concept

Content addressing. In such a store, each physical location is built to contain not only a datum, but a name as well. When a particular name is specified for access, the name fields of all storage locations are searched, and the datum whose stored name matches the search name is accessed. This method is sometimes called *content addressing*; it is more commonly called *associative addressing* because the data are *associated* with more or less arbitrary names.

```
data←readassociative address;location
ᴀ read from associative memory
location←(magni memory[;Address])ɩaddress
data←memory[location;Data]


address writeassociative data;location
ᴀ write in associative memory
location←(magni memory[;Address])ɩaddress
memory[location;Data]←data
```

PROGRAM 3-7   Associative addressing.

Algorithm.   Program 3-7 gives the basic algorithms for associative addressing. The program assumes that names occupy the bit locations `Address` within the memory words; the `Data` bit positions contain the data. If several cells have the same name, the first cell is used.

Many variations on the basic scheme have been proposed. In a common elaboration, each bit in a word may be taken as part of the name, under control of a mask. Those bits not used as the name carry other data. Such a memory can even be made self-sorting [Seeber, 1960]. Such elaborations have found little practical application, so we discuss only the basic scheme.

No more memory allocation.   Content addressing attacks the memory-allocation problem by concealing all physical adjacency and contiguity. The store itself consists of named objects bearing no relationship to one another. One can define relationships as one pleases by choosing the set of names to be associated with objects as they are stored. In particular, the programmer may choose each name to consist of a data-structure name and of an element name within the structure.

Implementation

Since the associative store removes the need for programmed allocation, it appears to be a perfect solution, except that its implementation is either not simple or not fast.

Wastes bit budget.   The fastest content-addressing implementations provide a 1-bit comparator for each of the m bits of the name field of each word. Relative to a direct-addressed memory, each word has m extra bits of memory. If a comparator takes twice the circuitry of a memory bit, additional cost per word is $m + 2 \times m = 3m$ bits. If, for example, the datum length is also m, such a memory takes four times as much circuitry as a directly-addressed memory of comparable speed and capacity. Put more vividly, one could have a direct-address memory of four times the capacity for the same cost. Which is more valuable?

Cheaper implementations are, of course, possible. The cheapest scans each word in turn. Now the extra cost is only the m extra storage bits in each word for the name, but the access is far slower. Intermediate implementations include a scheme with a 1-bit comparator per word, in which all words are simultaneously scanned serially for the search name.

Next-technology fallacy.   Through the years, proponents of content-addressed main memory have done cost estimates in current technology. Although appalled by the results, they have asserted that content-addressed memory will become attractive when the next technology appears and makes components cheap. This fallacy confuses the properties of the implementations with those of their realizations.

In *any* technology suitable for realizing the simultaneous comparison, and for any number of circuits one can assemble and afford, one can use the circuits either for content addressing or for about four times the capacity in directly-addressed memory. Regardless of technology, the architect must choose between function and capacity [Brooks, 1965].

Strangely enough, there was an *older* technology, the drum memory, where associative addressing could compete with direct addressing, but only because the drum's direct addressing wasted much access time. The only way to get something for nothing is to have previously gotten nothing for something.

Uses for Associative Addressing

In spite of its several proponents [Kiseda et al., 1961], associative addressing has not been widely adopted for main memory. Only an occasional design, such as the Goodyear Staran (1972), has in fact been implemented [Siewiorek et al., 1982, pp. 317–31]. The inherent cost of the interpretive name-location binding is acceptable only when early binding will not do what is wanted. For each postulated use, therefore, one must weigh whether the value of interpretive binding justifies its high implementation or performance cost.

Symbol table.   Some have justified content addressing in main memory because it eliminates the symbolic-name translation function of assemblers or compilers. But here interpretive binding is of little or no value—the work saved in program translation is trivial; the cost is high.

Table search.   Others have urged using associative memory as a mechanism for table-searching operations. But when one weighs the speedup in such operations versus their frequency of use, the high costs of associative addressing can rarely be justified.

Allocation.   When all is said and done, the principal justification for associative addressing must be that it provides a complete and elegant solution of the memory-allocation problem. But this benefit compares unfavorably with the alternative of four-fold capacity. Extra capacity has too many powerful uses—by allowing waste space for variable-sized segments, it can even be used to simplify allocation.

Special Addressing Functions

Content addressing comes into its own when the set of names to be bound is large but access to some small, ever-changing subset is much more frequent than average. The frequently used names can then be bound interpretively to a set of locations the size of a small working set, yet addressed with names

from the full set. This situation arises in segment-page tables and in cache systems.

3.2.3

Modal Mapping

In practice, address-mapping systems fall between the extremes of software rebinding and fully associative addressing. Achieving the flexibility needed without the costs of fully associative addressing has stimulated the invention of more sophisticated systems that exploit the different frequencies of the different sorts of rebindings needed. Tree 3-8 illustrates the main design choices for address mapping.

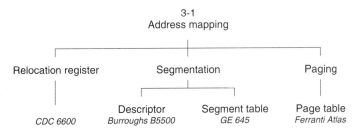

TREE 3-8   Design choices for address mapping.

Desiderata for address mapping.   Mapping machine-language object names (addresses) to locations should

1. Accommodate a variable set of named objects, with creation and destruction occurring during execution
2. Accommodate named objects of variable size
3. Preserve efficiency of memory allocation: All active objects (or active object elements) fit if the total memory needed is less than or equal to the total memory available
4. Allocate each object contiguous space (access to elements within objects is linear)
5. Ensure that each user can access only his own objects, regardless of the names he may accidentally or intentionally use, but allow explicit sharing of segments between users
6. Bind names to addresses such that accesses are fast and access mechanisms simple

The static programmed mapping of objects fails desiderata 1 and 2, and associative addressing fails to satisfy desideratum 6.

Relocation register.   A simple tool for address mapping is the *relocation register*, used by Kinslow [1964] as a special option on the IBM 7090 (1959), and later used on the 6600 and other machines. The relocation register stores a constant address value, which is added to the effective address as it is transmitted to memory (Figure 3-9). The application program itself has

no access to the register. The operating system can change the contents of the relocation register and does so prior to turning execution over to the application program. Program 3-10 gives the operation of the relocation register in the 6600.

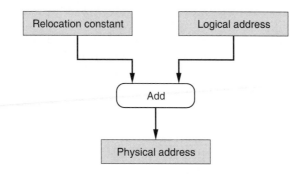

FIGURE 3-9   Address mapping with a relocation constant.

Limit register.   A `limit` indicates the extent of the allocated area and prevents the access by one program to the area of another program. In essence, the limit bounds the available name-space. The 6600 has a limit register, whose action is described in Section 14.2.3.

The use of a limit prevents a program from sharing procedures or data with other programs. The technique assumes that the program and all its data are confined to one contiguous memory area. When memory is filled sequentially, the external fragmentation problem is solved. When the time slices of the various programs are not equal, however, space is likely to be wasted. Relocation registers operate modally; that is, nothing in the individual address specifies that it is to be relocated or by how much. All are relocated alike.

Register pairs.   The DEC PDP10 (1968) and the Univac 1108 (1966) each provide two sets of relocation and limit registers—one applying to data addresses, the other applying to instruction addresses. Operation is still modal. A pure procedure and its data array can be handled gracefully, and, more important, different users can each use the same pure procedure with their several individual activation records and data. This advantage makes a qualitative difference in programming capability; going on from two sets to more sets makes no further qualitative change unless full generality is provided, as in segmentation.

```
location←map6600 address
ᴀ CDC 6600 address mapping
location←origin+adrcap|address
```

PROGRAM 3-10   Relocation register in the CDC 6600.

3.2.4

Segmentation

Name-Space Models

The name-space models embodied in high-level programming languages illustrate propriety and impropriety in name-space structures.

Elements within named objects are normally arranged in a certain sequence. Elements of different objects, however, have no such relationship to one another. The programmer's name-space is not one linearly organized entity, but a set of unrelated entities.

In APL, for example, the name-space is proper—it consists of a set of unrelated named objects, each of which may have an internal structure. No user action can determine or learn how these objects are placed in memory. No object is "adjacent" to another distinct object in the name-space.

In FORTRAN, on the other hand, the name-space is improperly structured. It comes close to consisting of disjoint objects, except that the provision of named COMMON areas reveals the memory mapping and shows adjacencies among objects. Furthermore, calculating the address of an array element beyond the boundary declared for that array can also reveal adjacencies: In many FORTRAN systems, the object accessed is different from that nominally addressed.

Segmentation provides a hardware mapping that implements an ideal and proper name-space model. The computer's address space is divided into disjoint chunks of contiguous addresses, called *segments*. The name of each program or data structure is compilatively bound to a distinct segment. Each segment is ideally the size of the program or data structure it contains, and it ideally changes size dynamically as that structure changes. Because a segment occupies a contiguous portion of memory, the elements within a structure can be addressed linearly within the segment, yet the several segments can be allocated and relocated independently.

This binding in principle costs drastically less than the associative store, since the independent objects in a program are far fewer than the individual elements. It is much more flexible, and indeed more proper, than a relocation register that moves a whole name-space bodily.

Dynamic Segment Allocation with a Segment Table

The indirect binding of the segment names with a segment table allows late binding of the object name to a segment name and thus aids the allocation of segments in memory.

Segment name.   The segment name is usually encoded and allocated to a few high-order bits of the machine-language address. These bits are then used as an index to a segment table. The table entries contain the memory address of the segment, as illustrated in Figure 3-11. Each segment is allocated independently, as a unit.

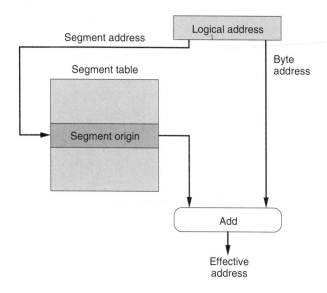

FIGURE 3-11   Segmentation using a segment table.

Table in registers.   When a segment table is implemented as a bank of registers, late binding can be quite fast. If the table entry (register content) is prefixed to the non-segment address part instead of being added to it, the time cost may be negligible. But the cost of many registers may be too high to allow each user to have large numbers of segments, as would be desirable.

Data descriptors.   Instead of accepting the limitations on segment number imposed by a small number of registers, one may put a segment table in memory. Each data reference now requires two memory accesses—one to find the governing mapping entry, and a second to fetch the data. For this high cost, one gets an essentially unlimited number of segments, so each may correspond to an individual program variable. This memory model approaches the ideal logical behavior.

The Burroughs B5500 (1964) incorporates this basic scheme by the use of *descriptors* (Program 3-12). The descriptor identifies the memory location of a segment by an origin and a length (`count`). Furthermore, the descriptor contains a code that identifies it as such and protects the descriptor against unintentional modification—that is, it is a distinct datatype, and typechecking is done. The descriptor is used to identify an item within the segment; an operand from the stack is interpreted as an element address relative to the segment origin.

Lookaside table.   It would be ideal to have both the large segment tables that tables in memory allow and the very rapid address-location mapping that tables in registers achieve. The most popular solution is to place the segment tables in memory, but to provide a small set of registers mirroring the most active entries, the *lookaside table*. If an entry is found in the lookaside table, access to the memory table is unnecessary.

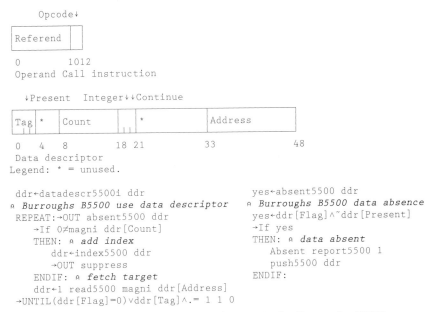

```
ddr←datadescr5500i ddr              yes←absent5500 ddr
ᴀ Burroughs B5500 use data descriptor  ᴀ Burroughs B5500 data absence
REPEAT:→OUT absent5500 ddr          yes←ddr[Flag]∧˜ddr[Present]
   →If 0≠magni ddr[Count]            →If yes
   THEN: ᴀ add index                 THEN: ᴀ data absent
       ddr←index5500 ddr                 Absent report5500 1
       →OUT suppress                     push5500 ddr
   ENDIF: ᴀ fetch target             ENDIF:
       ddr←1 read5500 magni ddr[Address]
→UNTIL(ddr[Flag]=0)∨ddr[Tag]∧.= 1 1 0
```

PROGRAM 3-12   Operand specification in the Burroughs B5500.

Sharing of information.   Segmentation allows several programs to share procedure and data segments. These programs need only use the same data descriptor or an identical entry in the segment tables to have access to the same object. The name of this object, even down to the argument used to address the segment table, need not be the same for the different programs (Figure 3-13). Such a common access, of course, does not guarantee a proper use of the access. In particular, the problem of interlocking—controlling shared access during modification of a datum—needs special attention.

Virtual Memory

With dynamic memory allocation there is no longer necessarily a one-to-one correspondence between physical memory and address space. In fact, there is no limit to the size of the address space other than the number of address bits available: Each of many time-sharing users may use not just all his portion of physical memory, nor even just all of installed memory, but rather all of addressable name-space, whether or not corresponding physical memory is installed. This addressable name-space is called the *virtual memory*.

Virtual memory frees the application programmer from a number of concerns that are not proper to his primary task. He no longer needs to introduce and manage overlays: All necessary routines are allocated separate space in virtual memory, and the management of the physical store is left to dynamic memory allocation. Also, some of his files may be placed entirely in virtual memory, eliminating the need to order the reading and writing of parts of these files as needed. Infrequently used procedures, such as error routines, may similarly be placed in virtual memory. If they are not needed, no time and real memory space are expended; if they are needed, no special

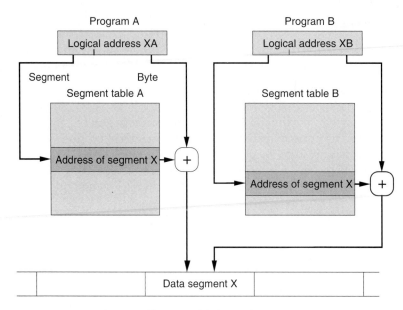

FIGURE 3-13   Sharing of information via segments.

action need be taken to fetch them. With all of address space at his disposal,
the user can also accommodate variable data structures. He need only place
the various objects sufficiently far apart in his address space.

The advantages of virtual memory cause the address space to be used
sparsely, but over its full range. They encourage a large address space, as
indeed is made available on modern machines (Table 3-14).

	Relocation register	Relocation table		
		Memory size in segments	Segment size in pages	Page size in bytes
Ferranti Mark 1		16	1	192
Ferranti Atlas		4096	1	4096
CDC 6600	×			
RCA Spectra 70		4096	1	4096
DEC PDP8		32	2	128
IBM System/370		256	16 32	4096 2048
IBM System/370		16	256 512	4096 2048
Cray 1	×			
DEC VAX11		2*21	1	512

TABLE 3-14   Dynamic relocation in various machines.

Virtual machine.   The concept of virtual memory can be extended to that of a
virtual machine. In a *virtual machine* each program not only has all of memory
to itself, but also has separate images of all working and control spaces.

Fragmentation

When segment sizes change dynamically, either allocations must change, or memory space must be wasted.

Internal fragmentation.   The simplest memory-allocation strategy for segments that change size is to allocate to each segment as much space as that segment uses when maximally extended. When the segment is not maximally extended, there is unused space within the segment's allocation. The available free memory is said to be *fragmented*: Instead of being in a single continuous block from which new allocations can be made, it is in fragments scattered uselessly about. Since these fragments are within segments, this condition is called *internal* fragmentation (Figure 3-15).

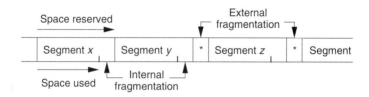

FIGURE 3-15   Internal and external fragmentation.

External fragmentation.   During program execution, segments that are created and then destroyed free space for the next segment to be allocated. However, the space rarely matches what is needed: Each new allocation is less than or equal to the free block of space. When it is less than the free block, the block gets divided into a new segment allocation and a small unallocated fragment. As the process continues, all the available free memory space tends to be divided into scattered fragments, so new allocations of contiguous blocks become impossible even with plenty of free memory. This phenomenon is called *external* fragmentation (Figure 3-15).

Garbage collection.   If programs and their data segments can be relocated during execution, an operating system can from time to time do *garbage collection*—the reassembly of unallocated fragments into a single large block of memory.

3.2.5
Paged Mapping

Working down from the memory models appropriate for programming languages, the designers of segmentation emphasized the disjunction of program variables; hence, they made segments of specifiable size, to match the sizes of program variables.

Meanwhile, hardware designers, motivated by high frequency of moving data between memory and backing store, also arrived at execute-time address binding via mapping tables. These designers emphasized speed and simplicity, so they divided the memory into *fixed-size* units of allocation, called *pages*.

Segmented and paged mapping each divide a machine's name-space into disjoint segments that are allocated independently and are accessed via execute-time table references.

Paging

Kilburn provided a primitive form of paging in the Ferranti Mark 1 (1951; Section 10.4). This machine's memory consists of 12 pages of 64 words each. For each page, the address of that page on the magnetic-drum store can be noted. This facility was not used by programmers, however. In contrast, the paging of Ferranti Atlas (1962) was deliberately designed and programmed to gain speed [Kilburn et al., 1961].

Page table.   The address space of the program is divided into pages of equal size. These pages are related through a table—the *page table*—with blocks of memory locations—called *frames*—that have the size of a page (Figure 3-16).

A program is distributed over the frames of memory as specified by the program's page table. Adjacent pages are not necessarily placed in adjacent frames.

In the Atlas, the table is placed in a separate set of 32 registers. This set indicates which page is located in which of the 32 frames. Each frame contains 512 words of memory.

The Atlas uses the table to store the frame content rather than the page reference. The table length shrinks, since there is a maximum of 256 pages in a program and only 32 frames in memory. Since the table has to be searched for the page identification, it is addressed associatively. This procedure differs from that of Figure 3-16, although not in principle.

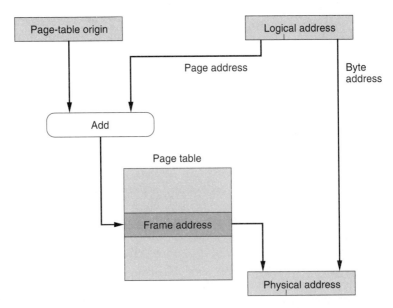

FIGURE 3-16   Address mapping with a relocation table.

```
                                      address70
┌──────────┬──────────┬──────────┐    ⍝ RCA Spectra 70 address allocation
│ Page     │ Byte     │          │    pagesize←2*12
│          │          │          │    ⍝ table allocation
└──────────┴──────────┴──────────┘    Frame←0+⍳12
0          12         24
Address format
```

```
location←map70 address;page;frame
⍝ RCA Spectra 70 address mapping
page←⌊address÷pagesize
frame←magni table[page;Frame]
location←(pagesize|address)+frame×pagesize
```

PROGRAM 3-17   Address mapping in the RCA Spectra 70.

When the table is placed in memory, it normally contains the page address as argument; its size is less critical, and direct addressing is less expensive. An example is the RCA Spectra 70 (1965). Program 3-17 gives the corresponding algorithm; it matches Figure 3-16 directly. The length of the table is specified, so that the memory area used is no longer than necessary.

Page size.   Paging resolves only the external fragmentation of memory. Since the program length is not likely to equal an integral number of pages, making the page size small reduces internal fragmentation.

A small page size, on the other hand, increases the page-table size, which either makes the register implementation more expensive, as in the Atlas, or uses more memory space, as in the Spectra 70. Furthermore, a large page is usually transmitted to a disk more efficiently than is an equivalent amount in smaller pages. Page sizes tend to average 2 K to 4 K bytes (Table 3-14).

Dynamic Allocation

In static allocation, when a program is made active, its page table is formed and placed in memory. The frames of memory are loaded from auxiliary storage with the corresponding procedures and data. When the operating system starts a program execution, it makes its page table active by pointing to its origin, as in the Spectra, or by loading the registers, as in the Atlas.

In *dynamic allocation* blocks of memory are allocated only when the program references the corresponding pages. In the extreme case, no memory is allocated at all as a program starts; then, the block containing the initial program section is allocated; then, the block containing the first data that are referenced is referenced, and so on.

Page fault.   A reference to a page that has no corresponding frame allocated is called a *page fault*. When a page fault occurs, execution is stopped, the desired page is fetched by the supervisor and is allocated to a frame, the page table is updated, and execution is resumed. Since transmission of the page takes time, another ready program is commonly run in the meantime.

A page fault is not a mistake, as is addressing the wrong location; it should be transparent to the problem program. When a page fault occurs, an instruction making multiple memory fetches must be interrupted such that it can be readily and automatically resumed.

The easiest way of interrupting an instruction is to nullify it completely, so that it is executed afresh when the program is resumed. Anticipating this

need may require a "dry run" by the implementation to see whether a page fault will occur. For the Translate operation (shown in Program 5-15 for the 360), the 370 must test both ends of the operands and the table for page faults. If one occurs, the program is suspended, and the needed pages are fetched before the Translate is actually executed.

When it is impractical to nullify an instruction after it has started, the instruction must be made resumable. This method, illustrated in the Zoo for the VAX/11 (Section 15.3), is also used in the Move Long instruction of the 370.

Working set.   Dynamic allocation would be highly unattractive if only a few items were needed from each page. Data processing, however, is economical exactly because information normally comes as a structure. Items needed in any part of a computation tend to cluster in the address space. This is called the principle of *locality*.

From the principle of locality, Denning [1968] derived the concept of the *working set*.   A working set is the set of pages referenced by a program during a given time period.   If this period is comparable to that needed to fetch a page, we have a measure of the number of frames a program requires.   Denning [1970] and others have observed that the principle of locality causes the working-set size of most programs to be nearly constant during the program's execution.

If there are not enough frames available for a program's working set, the program should not be placed in memory. Otherwise, excessive page faults will occur, and the bit traffic will increase. In the extreme case, the system is so occupied with swapping pages that hardly any program execution takes place, a phenomenon known as *page thrashing*.

When a new program is loaded, its working set should be determined by observing its behavior in time. Once the working set is known, the system can reserve enough frames when the program is allotted a time slice. Then, most-recently-used pages are usually loaded as a group (*prepaging*). As execution progresses, pages are loaded only as needed (*demand paging*).   When the working-set size is indeed constant, the new pages can replace pages that are no longer used.

Reference recording.   For each frame, special bits can record whether (and perhaps how often) the frame has been referenced or changed. The bits can be set by the operating system, and used by it as data for the page-replacement algorithm. In the 360 these bits are part of a separate control store (Program 3-18). A page that is referenced but not changed need not be written back to auxiliary store when it is replaced.

When a new page must be brought in, some old page must be selected to be replaced. Most operating systems use a Least-Recently-Used replacement algorithm and use the change bits, which are periodically reset, to select a not-used-recently page. The replacement algorithm must discriminate between newly fetched pages—sometimes called *virgin pages*—that have not yet had a chance to be used, and pages with actual low frequency of use.

Automatic paging.   Unlike segmentation, paging is not properly an architectural function. It is in essence an implementation of a large fast memory

PROGRAM 3-18   Reference and change bits in the IBM System/360 Model 67.

by means of a small fast memory and a large slow backing store. Ideally, it should be invisible in the architecture, both to the application program and to the supervisor program. Indeed, for the Atlas, all the necessary algorithms were built into read-only control store. This approach sacrifices flexibility; in particular, one loses the power for the supervisor to prepage a working set when a program is loaded. (Programs could, of course, be contrived so as to force access to each page in the working set as part of initialization.) Most machines do not do fully automatic paging, but rather leave some of the work and some of the decisions up to the supervisor program. So the page tables and controls show through into the supervision architecture. Paging is invisible to the application programmer in all machines.

Cache Memory

Paging uses a small fast memory, a large but slower backing store, and transfer algorithms to implement a storage system whose capacity is that of the larger component and whose speed approximates that of the faster component. The success of the tactic depends on program locality. The locality property is sufficiently pronounced that the same scheme can be used advantageously with two levels of electronic memory whose speeds may differ by as little as one order of magnitude [Wilkes, 1965]. Such two-level implementations are almost universal from microcomputers up. The small fast memory in two-level electronic memories is called a *cache*.

Most machines use a cache implemented completely in the hardware and not visible in the architecture at all. But cache management can be improved if it can be directly controlled by a programmer or a smart compiler that has global knowledge of data-usage patterns. Some designers have therefore exposed the cache in the architecture, allowing blocks of cache to be reserved or invalidated by the program as it deems best. The IBM 801 RISC computer (1978) has such controls available to the operating system.

The difference between paging and caching is one of degree only: Both are characterized by the formula for average access time

$$time \leftarrow ((1 - q) \times fasttime) + (q \times slowtime)$$

or by

$$time \leftarrow fasttime + q \times (slowtime - fasttime)$$

where q represents the fraction of all memory references that go to the slow memory. This formula is approximated by

$$time \leftarrow fasttime + q \times slowtime$$

when the speeds are quite different.

For caching, the ratio *slowtime* ÷ *fasttime* is on the order of 10; for paging, the ratio is on the order of 10,000. The strategy for paging is therefore quite different from that for caching: Execution is switched from one program to another when a page fault occurs, whereas execution is suspended rather than switched in case the cache does not contain the desired data.

Hennessy and Patterson [1990] give the authoritative treatment of caching and cache design, and caching's relationship to virtual memory.

3.2.6

Segmentation with Paging

Segmentation lifts the memory-allocation problem from the application programmer. He need not design and manage overlays, and he can use variable data structures. The allocation problem, however, is not eliminated; it is simply moved to the operating system.

In particular, with segments of various size, the replacement problem is difficult—the supervisor must find variable-sized, contiguous blocks in main memory when a new segment is allocated, and it must do garbage collection of fragments that can get very small. A combination of segmentation and paging therefore suggests itself, a solution first proposed by Dennis [1965], and Arden et al. [1966], and shortly afterward incorporated in the GE 645 (1965) and the 360 Model 67. Figure 3-19 gives a diagram for segmentation with paging.

Segments are made up of an integral number of independently allocated pages, so there is no external fragmentation. Backing-store transfers are multiples of whole pages, and can be made efficient. Execution can operate in part of a segment without the entire segment's being fetched.

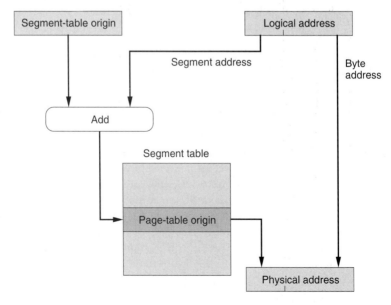

FIGURE 3-19   Segmentation with paging.

Figure 3-19 shows the translation of a logical address—the address supplied by the program—into a physical-memory address. The logical address consists of three parts: the segment, the page, and the byte address. In principle, segments and pages could be any length; in practice, everyone specifies lengths that are powers of the addressing radix, so the logical address can be divided into disjoint bit fields.

The Segment part of the address selects an entry within a user segment table. (The location of the segment table is specified by an origin address in a control register, set by the operating system when the program is loaded.) The entry in the segment table contains the address of the origin of a page table: One out of several page tables is selected.

The Page part of the logical address is used next, to select an entry within the page table. This entry contains the high-order bits of the actual memory address, the Frame address.

The low-order part of the memory address, the address within a page, is obtained directly from the corresponding part of the logical address. It is called the Byte address.

Each user has his own segment table. Different segment tables may have entries that point to the same page table; when users share a program or data, only one page table needs to be used and updated.

The length field in the segment table indicates the length of the associated page table. Although the segment table now takes more space, the total table space can be markedly reduced since the page tables no longer span most of the address space, but span only the total of the currently used segment sizes. Furthermore, segments that are not actively used are marked as such and need not have a page table in memory.

In the GE 645 each segment is a distinct name-space. Address calculation cannot affect the segment part of the logical address. In the Model 67 the segment can be changed by address calculation; the segments are successive partitions in one giant name-space.

The GE solution is the proper one. The Model 67 solution preserves compatibility with the other 360 models.

Implementation

Every reference to memory requires two sequential table references. Since the tables themselves are placed in memory, a three-to-one speed reduction can be expected, as compared to direct addressing. This radical increase in bit traffic is unacceptable. Suitable implementation methods, however, make it possible to keep this speed reduction to the order of 10 percent. For the Model 67, the implementation makes use of the set of lookaside registers shown schematically in Figure 3-20.

These Model 67 registers contain the most-recently-used logical addresses and their translation. Before starting the two-stage table lookup, the implementation looks in these registers to see if the current address is known—hence the name *lookaside* table. The collection of these is also known as *directory lookaside table* (DLAT).

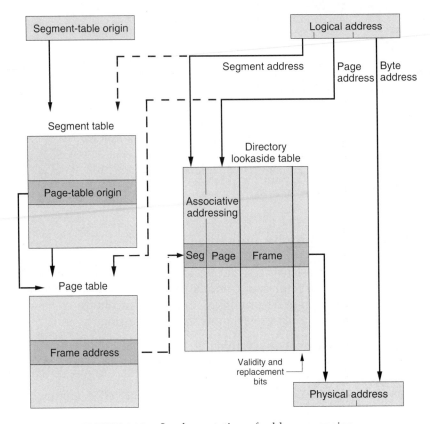

FIGURE 3-20   Implementation of address mapping.

Associative lookup.   The segment-page part of the logical address is compared simultaneously with the left part of all lookaside registers. If an equality results, the frame address in the matching register is used. The registers thus form an associative memory.

If the segment-page combination is not found in the associative memory, the formal route via the tables is followed, as shown by the dashed lines. The frame address obtained is used for the actual memory address. It also goes into a register with the corresponding segment-page. A subsequent associative lookup with the same segment-page now succeeds.

The lookaside registers are part of the implementation and are properly invisible to the architecture. If this is the case, different implementations may use different mechanisms. In the 360 and 370 the various models do use different numbers of registers, different modes of addressing these registers, and different replacement algorithms for the registers [Blaauw, 1976]. Replacement algorithms develop and use auxiliary information, such as the Validity and Replacement bits in Figure 3-20 and Program 3-18.

Dynamic address translation is an example of an architectural feature that is feasible only because the implementation does not follow the straightforward algorithm implied by architectural description.

3.2.7
Bibliography

Arden et al. [1966], Baylis et al. [1968], Belady [1966], Blaauw [1976], Brooker [1959], Burnett and Coffman [1970], Brooks [1965], Conti et al. [1968], Corbato et al. [1962], Denning [1968, 1970], Dennis [1965], Djordjevic et al. [1980a, 1980b], Fatheringham [1961], Gibson [1966], Hammerstrom and Davidson [1977], Howarth et al. [1961], M. Johnson [1982], Joseph [1970], Kilburn et al. [1961a, 1961b], Kinslow [1964], Kiseda et al. [1961], Mattson et al. [1970], McGee [1965], Parmelee et al. [1972], Seeber [1960], Siewiorek et al. [1982], A.J. Smith [1982], Thurber and Wald [1975], Wilkes [1965].

3.3
Address Modification by Indexing

Regular arrays, such as matrices and vectors, are by far the most common and important data structures in computing. Addressing array elements is therefore a key programming primitive. Computer architectures have, from the beginning, made special provision for such addressing.

Addressing array elements.   Naming an element of an array requires the array name, and an index for each dimension of the array. These make up a noun phrase—a composite address for the element.

If memory allocation allows each array to be located contiguously and homogeneously in directly addressed memory, element locations map directly from their indices, and elements can be fetched in any order. It is therefore worthwhile to use contiguous allocation and to preserve the composite name in instructions.

Access to an element of an array in memory requires computing a single address from the array-name-plus-indices of the composite address. This computation is called *address calculation*. When address calculation takes place interpretively and ephemerally as part of instruction execution, it is called *address modification*. The result is the *effective address*.

Design choices.   Tree 3-21 gives the design choices for address modification, showing the address components that are basic to the addressing of a data structure in memory.

Address Components

A general calculation of element addresses within an array contiguously stored in memory uses a *base address*, an *element address*, and a *displacement* (Figure 3-22).

Base address.   The *base address* specifies the location of the array in memory. Usually it is the address of the first or last element. The loader's memory-allocation algorithm determines this address component during the load procedure.

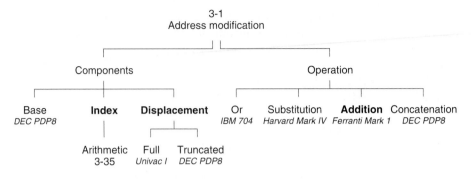

TREE 3-21   Design choices for address modification.

As the elements of the array are accessed, the value of the base address remains unchanged. A new base address is generated, however, each time memory is reallocated.

Element address.   The location of an element within a data structure is determined by the *element address*. This address component is relative to the base address and is consequently independent of the location of the structure in memory. The element address is changed during execution of the program by the algorithm that accesses the several data elements one by one.

Displacement.   The third address component, the *displacement*, determines the location of an item relative to the current element address.

There may be several data items or variables in each element of an array. For example, an array might represent a three-dimensional geometry, and its elements might each describe a vibrating point in space. For each point, a number of values can be given, such as velocity and acceleration in three dimensions. The displacement specifies the location of each such variable

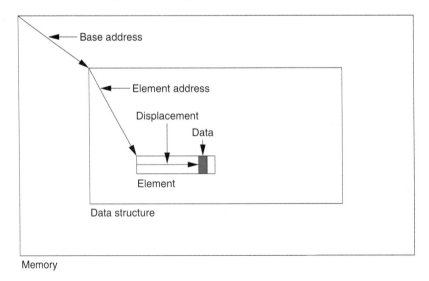

FIGURE 3-22   Address components.

relative to the element address. A commercial example is a customer file. The record relating to each customer forms one element, and the displacement can be used to locate fields such as name, address, account balance, and allowable credit.

The displacement need not point at items within the active element, but may instead point at the element's neighbors. Examples are the numerical methods for solving differential equations. Figure 3-23 shows the address calculation for a two-dimensional Poisson stencil that addresses right, left, upper, and lower neighbors of a three-field element.

As Figure 3-23 suggests, the displacement may have more than one component. In the case shown, it embodies both the relation of a point's address to the addresses of its neighbors and the selection among fields within the information describing a single point. Since both of these relations are bound early, at compile time, and are not changed during execution, the two displacement components can be combined into a single resultant displacement without loss of flexibility. This combining is done universally.

Multiple subscripts.   Should the element address be a single value, as assumed up to now, or a set of values that are combined at the moment of address modification? The mathematical formulations used in computing regularly use multiple subscripts. Nevertheless, it is more efficient to combine them first into a single value in an outer loop rather than add their values each time a modified instruction is executed.

For this reason, computers normally allow only one index value as an address component. In the IBM Stretch (1961) the use of multiple subscripts is facilitated by the operation Load Value With Sum (Program 3-24). This operation adds any selected number of index values and places the sum

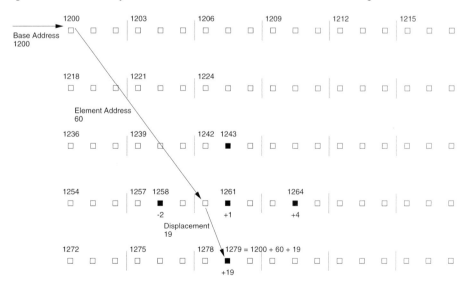

Ninety storage locations used for three-valued, two-dimensional array of 6 X 5 elements.
(Displacement shown for second value of an element and of its four neighbors.)

FIGURE 3-23   Use of displacement for Poisson stencil.

in another selected index. This instruction was a mistake for two reasons. First, the operation is improper. The index summation is chiefly useful in the innermost of nested loops, but it is very wasteful there; it should be compiled out. Second, the instruction is totally inconsistent in format and method of register specification with all other instructions.

```
┌─────────────────────┬────┬────────┐
│ Adrhalf             │ R1 │ Opcode │
└─────────────────────┴────┴────────┘
0                     19   23       32
Legend: R = register.

LVS;mask;sum;index
ᴀ IBM Stretch Load Value With Sum
  mask←Index+word×inst[ι16]/ι16
  sum←+/signmagni memory[mask∘.+Value]
  index←regout R1
  index[Value]←adrsize signmagnr sum
  R1 regin index
  signal7030X index
```

PROGRAM 3-24   Load Index Value With Sum in the IBM Stretch.

A machine that uses multiple subscripts as part of the address phrase is the Atlas (Program 3-25). This provision, however, seems to have been motivated as much by the availability of format space as by any perceived need for the function.

```
┌─────────┬──────┬──────┬──────────────────────┐
│ Opcode  │ X1   │ X2   │ Address              │
└─────────┴──────┴──────┴──────────────────────┘
0         10     17     24                      48
Legend: X = index.

address←adrmu3;index1;index2;displacement
ᴀ Ferranti Atlas addressing
  index1←magni reg[fld X1;]
  index2←magni reg[fld X2;]
  displacement←fld Address
  address←adrcap|index1+index2+displacement


instructionmu3
ᴀ Ferranti Atlas instruction allocation
ᴀ operation specification
  Opcode←0+ι10
ᴀ operand specification
  X1←10+ι7
  X2←17+ι7
  Address←24+ι24
```

PROGRAM 3-25   Double indexing in the Ferranti Atlas.

Effective Address Calculation

The first and fundamental contribution to calculating elements' *effective addresses* was the stored program, proposed by Eckert and Mauchly and documented by von Neumann in 1946 [Burks et al., 1946]. Placing the

Pseudocode

```
FOR  I=2 TO 4
  FOR  J=2 TO 5
    V[I;J] ← (1/4) * (V[I-1;J] + V[I;J-1]  + V[I;J+1] + V[I+1;J])
    END
  END
```

IBM 650 Program

Location	Operation	Data address	Instruction address	

⌐ *Initialization of outer (I) loop*

0300	RAL	0100	0301	Load address constant
0301	STDA	0500	0302	Store address in modified instruction
0302	RAL	0119	0303	Store row end in dummy test instruction
0303	STDA	0101	0400	

⌐ *Inner loop (I) address set-up and modification*

▶ 0400	RAL	0500	0401	Load upper neighbor's instruction
0401	AL	0103	0402	
0402	STDA	0500	0403	Load left neighbor's instruction
0403	AL	0115	0404	
0404	STDA	0501	0405	Load element's instruction
0405	AL	0103	0406	
0406	STDA	0505	0407	Load right neighbor's instruction
0407	AL	0103	0408	
0408	STDA	0502	0409	Load lower neighbor's instruction
0409	AL	0115		
0410	STDA	0503		

End of row test

| 0411 | SL | 0101 | 0410 | Test with dummy instruction |
| 0412 | BEQ | 0600 | 0500 | If beyond last value, skip to I scanning loop. |

⌐ *Calculation of Poisson stencil—bracketed addresses are modified*

0500	RAU	[1204]	0501	Load above neighbor, second value
0501	AU	[1219]	0502	Add left neighbor, second value
0502	AU	[1225]	0503	Add right neighbor, second value
0503	AU	[1240]	0504	Add below neighbor, second value
0504	DIV	0104	0505	Divide by 4
0505	STL	[1222]	0400	Store quotient in element, second value, and go around loop

⌐ *Outer(I)loop address modification*

▶ 0600	RAL	0500		Load upper neighbor address
0601	AL	0106		Add 3
0602	STDA	0500		Store in location 0500
0603	RAL	0101	0604	
0604	AL	0118	0605	Increment the row-end test
0605	STDA	0101	0606	to test the next row

⌐ *Outerloop end test*

| 0606 | SL | 0102 | 0607 | |
| 0607 | BMI | 0400 | 0608 | If not complete, scan next row |

⌐ *Constants*

0100	RAU	1201	0501	Initial value of instruction, less three
0101	RAU	[1252]	0501	Dummy instruction for row-end test
0102	RAU	1288	0501	Dummy instruction for matrix-end test
0103	+00	0003	0000	Address increment=3
0104	+00	0000	0004	Data constant=4
0115	+00	0015	0000	Address increment=15
0118	+00	0018	0000	Address increment=18
0119	RAU	1252	0501	Initial value of row-end dummy

PROGRAM 3-26 Poisson stencil by direct address modification—IBM 650.

instructions in addressable memory made the instruction in general, and the address field in particular, subject to modification as if they were data, thus allowing any element-addressing algorithm.

Programmed address modification.   Program 3-26 illustrates programmed address computation. The address field of the instruction must be incremented as the program proceeds from one element of the array of Figure 3-23 to the next. Since the Poisson stencil requires five accesses, the modification must be repeated as many times. (The program calculates only the 12 interior values of the mesh, leaving the boundary values unchanged. The second of the three values for each element is the datum for this calculation.) The real contribution of the stored program, however, was to make compilers possible.

Interpretive address modification.   Programmed address calculation was quite cumbersome in practice, since in a one-address machine each address calculation required three instructions. Moreover, changing instructions in memory makes a program hard to understand and maintain. In 1949 Kilburn proposed performing address modification dynamically as part of instruction execution [Kilburn, 1949b]. The address part of the instruction was added to the content of a register (Figure 3-27). The content of such a register was later termed an *index*, from standard mathematical usage.

Substitution.   An easier (and faster) form of address modification to implement is substitution. The Harvard Mark IV (1952) uses an I-J register for this purpose. Effective address calculation substitutes two address digits from an I register for two special (invalid) digits in the tens and hundreds part of the decimal address, and/or a single digit from the J register for the units digit. I and J can be used independently of each other.

Such partial substitution allows matrix addressing, but has the obvious impropriety that the matrix dimensions must match the addressing radix. It is never used now.

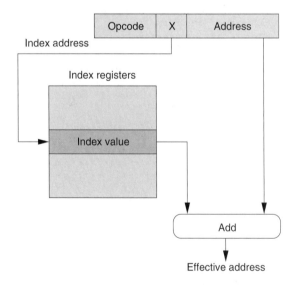

FIGURE 3-27   Address modification.

```
 ┌─────┬───┬────┬─────────┐   ┌──────────────────────────┐
 │ Op  │ * │ X0 │ Address │   │ Address                  │
 └─────┴───┴────┴─────────┘   └──────────────────────────┘
 0    5 7 10           20     0                          20
 Instruction                 Index
 Legend: Op = opcode; X = index; * = unused.


 inst←index1 inst;index;displacement
 ⍝ Ferranti Mark 1 instruction indexing
 →If¯(fld Opcode)∈ 1 3 5 7
 THEN: ⍝ index instruction
     index←reg[fld X0]
     displacement←magni inst
     inst←half magnr index+displacement
 ENDIF:
```

PROGRAM 3-28   Additive indexing in the Ferranti Mark 1.

Addition.   Adding the index to the address field is more proper and powerful than substitution. The Manchester machine has this facility (Program 3-28). An index is added to the entire instruction; it can also modify the operation code. This feature—considered interesting at the time—we would now reject as a violation of orthogonality.

The improvement of interpretive over programmed address modification can be appreciated by comparing Program 3-26 with an equivalent program

```
        Label     Operation          Symbolic  Literal   Comment
                                      operand   operand
                                      address   address

        InitRow Reset Add Index B         18    0018      Immediate
                                                          address-start
                                                          with first
                                                          non-boundary row.

   ┌──▶ InitCol Reset Add Index A        3.B    4003      Immediate effective
   │                                                      address-start
   │                                                      with first
   │                                                      non-boundary row.
   │
   │ ⍝  Inner Loop
 ┌─┼─▶ Left    Reset Add Lower    1201-3.A     3198      Index encoded
 │ │   Above   Add Lower          1201-18.A    3183      in address
 │ │   Right   Add Lower          1201+3.A     3204
 │ │   Below   Add Lower          1201+18.A    3219
 │ │           Divide                  four
 │ │   Result  Store Lower         1201.A      3201
 │ │
 │ │ ⍝  Address Modification
 │ │   IncreCol Add to Index A          3       0003      Immediate address
 │ │            Reset Add Index C       A       8005      Load A into C for
 │ │                                                      nondestructive
 │ │                                                      testing
 │ │            Subtract from Index C  15.B     4015      Immediate effective
 │ │                                                      address
 │ └──── NonZero Index C              Left                Branch if same row
 │     IncreRow
 │
 │              Add to Index B          18      0018
 │              Reset Add Index C        B      8006
 │              Subtract from Index C    72     0072
 └──────── NonZero Index C           InitCol

     ⍝  Constants
     four                              +00   0000 0004
```

PROGRAM 3-29   Poisson stencil by additive indexing in the IBM 650.

that uses an index. Program 3-29 shows that the index is incremented just once in the inner loop, which reduces the number of housekeeping instructions radically. The instructions remain unchanged, a first step toward making procedures reentrant.

Number of index registers. Program 3-30 derives its simplicity in part from the fact that only one data structure is involved; only one index is changed in the inner loop. When, in contrast, two matrices are multiplied to yield a third, the index register must be loaded with the proper index prior to each access. So multiple index registers have a definite advantage. Even though the cost of such registers was high for early computers, the Mark 1 supplied eight, and multiple index registers were normally made available. The number of index registers used in a single array operation depends on the number of distinct element addresses. Dyadic operations, which operate element by element, need only one. Matrix multiplication,

$$CD \leftarrow A + . \times B$$

requires three or more, depending on the ordering of the arrays. The incremental value of registers beyond one drops markedly because the outer members of a nest of loops are executed less often. A total of eight registers seems reasonable.

```
address←modify;index;value
A basic additive address modification
index←interpret reg[fld R;]
value←fld Address
address←index+value
```

PROGRAM 3-30   Basic additive indexing.

The IBM 704 (1955) has three index registers, each specified by a separate bit (Program 3-31). Its descendant, the IBM 7094 (1963), uses the three instruction bits more powerfully (and more properly) to address seven index registers. Table 3-32 shows the index-register space of various machines.

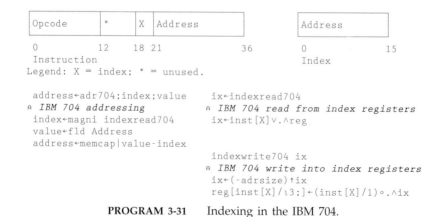

Opcode	*	X	Address		Address

```
0           12    18 21              36    0              15
Instruction                               Index
Legend: X = index; * = unused.
```

```
address←adr704;index;value     ix←indexread704
A IBM 704 addressing           A IBM 704 read from index registers
index←magni indexread704       ix←inst[X]∨.∧reg
value←fld Address
address←memcap|value-index
                               indexwrite704 ix
                               A IBM 704 write into index registers
                               ix←(-adrsize)↑ix
                               reg[inst[X]/ι3;]←(inst[X]/ι1)∘.∧ix
```

PROGRAM 3-31   Indexing in the IBM 704.

	Index Number	Index Size	Address size	Address modification
Ferranti Mark 1	8	20	10	$i \leftarrow i + x$
IBM NORC	3	4d	4d	$e \leftarrow a$ $e \leftarrow t + x$
IBM 704	3	15	15	$e \leftarrow a - \vee / x$
STC ZEBRA	15w	33	13	$i \leftarrow i + x$
IBM 1620	14m	5d	5d	$e \leftarrow a + x$
Bendix G20	63m	15	15	$e \leftarrow a + x + b$
IBM Stretch	16	24,s c	24	$e \leftarrow a + x$
Ferranti Atlas	127	24	24	$e \leftarrow a + x + x$
English Electric KDF9	15	15	15	$e \leftarrow a + x + b$
IBM 7094	7	15	15	$e \leftarrow a - x$
CDC 6600	8	18	18	$e \leftarrow a + x$ $e \leftarrow x + x$
CDC 6600 PPU	64m	12	12	$e \leftarrow a + x$
Burroughs B5500	m	15	15	$e \leftarrow b + t + x$
IBM System/360	15w	32	24	$e \leftarrow t + x + x$
Electrologica X8	7	18	18	$e \leftarrow a + x$
DEC PDP10	15	18	18	$e \leftarrow a + x$
DEC PDP11	8w*	16	16	$e \leftarrow a + x$
Intel 8080A	1w	16	16	$e \leftarrow x$
Cray 1	8 64	24	24	$e \leftarrow t + x$
Motorola M6800	1	16	16	$e \leftarrow t + x$
MOS 6502	2	8	16	$e \leftarrow a + x$ $e \leftarrow t + x$
DEC VAX11	16w*	32	32	$e \leftarrow a + x$ $e \leftarrow t + x$
Motorola MC68000	8	32	32	$e \leftarrow x$ $e \leftarrow t + x + x$
IBM 6150	16	32	32	$e \leftarrow t + x$ $e \leftarrow x + x$

Legend: a = full address; b = base; c = part of compound structure;
d = decimal; e = effective address; i = instruction;
m = index embedded in memory; p = prefix;
s = sign of index; t = truncated address;
w = index in general working store; x = index;
* = instruction address useable as index.

TABLE 3-32   Addressing modification in various machines.

Location of Address Components

Since the memory's address space is organized linearly, the address components must be added to obtain the effective address. During address modification, the address components should be readily available for this purpose—either in the instruction or in working registers.

Table 3-33 summarizes the nature of the address components; it helps us find the best location for each.

Element address.   Since the element address changes during program execution, it certainly should be placed in an index register.

Displacement.   The displacement does not change at all. It is logically associated with the operation code and therefore is properly placed in the address field of the instruction.

Base address.   The best location of the base address is less clear. For the early machines, additive indexing by more than one quantity was too ambitious in equipment (a three-input adder) or time (the extension of the addressing cycle). So the base address was combined either with the displacement or with the element address. Both combinations have disadvantages.

	Why	When	Who	Where
Base address	memory allocation	load time	operating system	register
Element address	data structure	execution time	compiler	register
Displacement	operation	translation time	user	instruction

TABLE 3-33   Nature of address components.

Base address combined with displacement.   Combining base address and displacement complicates loading, but is otherwise acceptable in a simple operating environment, since both are bound early. Within a multiprogramming environment, a procedure such as a matrix inversion should be usable on short notice and in intermixed fashion, with several data structures having different element spacings. Changing the base addresses in all instructions is clearly undesirable. Copying the entire structure as a value parameter also is undesirable. The only alternative then, is to duplicate the procedures, one per user space.

Combined base and element address.   Combining base address and element address causes no serious problems with multiprogramming, since each program needs its own copy of the changing element addresses anyway. As each program is activated, the proper base and element addresses can be placed in the index registers. This combination, however, violates orthogonality in that the address calculation is affected by the location of the array. If an element address is compared with a constant, as for the end of a row of a matrix, this constant must take into account the base address. Furthermore, when base addresses are changed dynamically, it is desirable to separate base and element addresses.

Separate base address.   The 360 design was motivated by the large address capacity desired. Since the displacement was truncated to preserve bit efficiency, a base address or an index had to be used to access all of memory. The preceding considerations led us to use a separate base address in the 360. During address modification not two, but three quantities are added, as shown in Figure 3-23 and Program 3-34. So the 360's address calculation resembles the double indexing of the Atlas, even though the motivations for these two designs are quite different. The 360 design is inconsistent, however, in not allowing a base and index in the SS and SI formats (Program 2-36).

Base-address space.   The 360 uses the same address space for the base and the element addresses; it even shares this space with operands and results. But Table 3-33 shows that these address components are determined at different moments by different procedures based upon different considerations. Not only is there no need to share a common set of registers, but sharing is not even advisable, since it gives the user access to the base address. Giving base

```
┌─────────┬───┬───┬───┬───────────────────────┐   ┌─────┬───────────────────────────────┐
│ Opcode  │R1 │X1 │B1 │D1                     │   │  *  │ Address                       │
└─────────┴───┴───┴───┴───────────────────────┘   └─────┴───────────────────────────────┘
0        8  12  16  20                    32      0     8                              32
RX instruction                                    Base or index
Legend: B = base; D = displacement; R = register; X = index; * = unused.
```

```
address←adr360bxd;base;index;displacement
⋔ IBM 360 base-index-displacement address
base←magni(0≠fld B1)∧reg[fld B1;Address]
index←magni(0≠fld X1)∧reg[fld X1;Address]
displacement←fld D1
address←base+index+displacement


address←adr360bd1;base;displacement
⋔ IBM 360 base-displacement address 1
base←magni(0≠fld B1)∧reg[fld B1;Address]
displacement←fld D1
address←base+displacement
```

PROGRAM 3-34   Address modes in the IBM System/360.

registers a separate space that is accessible only via the system software is more proper and is therefore preferable.

Combined base, index, and displacement.   At the other extreme of design choices, all three address components can be combined as an effective address in an address register.   Address modification is then no longer required. Addressing is indirect via the address register; the instructions need specify only one register address per operand, so the address phrase is fast in execution (low bit traffic) and efficient in specification (small bit budget). The disadvantage is that the addresses must be calculated by extra instructions prior to the use of the effective address.

These advantages and disadvantages explain the use of address registers at both ends of the computer-performance scale.   At the high end, the 6600 exemplifies this method. The time for the preliminary address computation is eliminated by using separate equipment in an overlapped implementation.

In early microprocessors the simplicity of delegating the effective address computation to the program is bought at expense in time, as the Intel 8080A (1974) shows (Section 16.1).   Later microprocessors have followed the same evolutionary trend in indexing, as have mainframes and minis.

3.3.1
Bibliography

Burks et al. [1946], Kilburn [1949b].

3.4
Index Arithmetic

The part of the architecture that changes the contents of the index registers is *index arithmetic*. The element address ideally resides in an index register, and

index arithmetic concerns algorithms for access within data structures.

Access within data structures. An access algorithm is determined by two factors: the order in which the user wants to process the data elements, and the mapping of the data structure onto the memory space. As an example, consider a matrix data structure whose elements are placed row by row in successive memory locations, as illustrated in Figure 3-23, and a user who wishes to access the elements in this matrix columnwise.

The access and the allocation order are, in principle, independent. A given data structure is mapped only once, but it may be accessed in many different orders. Furthermore, the mapping and access order actually employed may differ from the user's conception of those used. We consider four levels of awareness, using the mapping of Figure 3-23 as a concrete example:

- If the user is fully aware of the mapping and of the access order, he can access the column elements by using an initial element address of 0 and incrementing it by 18 each time a new element is desired. After the increment is applied four times, the process is repeated with each of the initial values 3, 6, 9, 12, and 15.
- If he is using a higher-level language, the user need not know the precise allocation of the data structures, even though he still specifies the access order. He may declare a matrix and access an element with a double index [I;J]. In the given example, he might use two nested FOR loops, using an increment of 1 in each case. The compiler might then translate the element address with an expression such as

$$element\ address\ \leftarrow\ (18\ \times\ I)\ +\ (3\ \times\ J)$$

- In yet higher-level languages, the user may need to specify neither the allocation nor the access order. An example is the APL matrix multiplication

$$A\ \leftarrow\ B\ +\ .\ \times\ C$$

in which the interpreter decides both allocation and order. It may even deviate from the customary order, provided the result is correct.
- Finally, the machine language may itself include higher-order data structures such as arrays. For array operations, neither the programmer nor the interpreter needs to bother about order.

Program primitives. The preceding examples show that index arithmetic is used in many contexts. Data structures also vary widely. It is difficult to predict, and dangerous to prescribe, the precise uses of index arithmetic. Generality is therefore a major requirement of the architecture.

Given generality, one wants frequently used operations to be straightforward. The linear address space of memory and the importance of sequential structures make a convenient linear scan desirable. The most common sequential structures are the *queue*, which has first-in-first-out (FIFO) addressing, and the *stack*, which has last-in-first-out (LIFO) addressing. The program primitives derived from accessing these structures are storing and fetching, combined with incrementing and decrementing the element address of the accessed location.

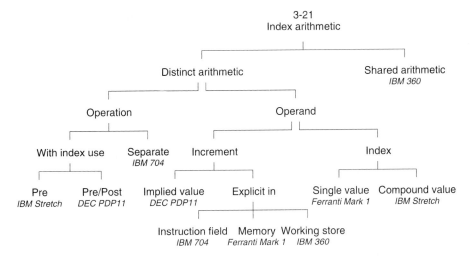

TREE 3-35 Design choices for index arithmetic.

Matrix addition, multiplication, transposition, and inversion are important program primitives in scientific computing. Most indexing systems were designed with matrix multiplication as the driving problem.

Design choices. The design choices for index arithmetic (Tree 3-35) reflect the desire for generality and for the straightforward implementation of the commonest program primitives.

3.4.1

General Index Operations

General index arithmetic operations are strongly determined by the nature of the index name-space.

Separate index space and operations. Index registers were originally considered a separate name-space from other working registers, such as accumulators. Index arithmetic had its own, quite limited, operation set, apart from regular arithmetic. The 704 even had a separate instruction format for index arithmetic (Program 3-52).

With a separate index space, the index length need be only as long as the address length. The index registers of the 704 were only 15 bits long—considerably shorter than the 704's 36-bit integer format.

Alternatively, the index word can be structured for extra function. The Stretch gave the index format the size of its 64-bit word. Signed bit addresses used 25 bits in that machine; the remaining space was used for quantities associated with the index, as shown in Program 3-51 and explained in Section 3.5.

Shared index space and operations. Since addresses are integers, and since the addressing operations are in integer arithmetic, a distinction between fixed-point arithmetic and index arithmetic is unnatural. The 360, therefore,

specifies a set of *general purpose registers*, which can be used for intermediate results in calculations as well as for addressing calculations, as indices. The 360 therefore needs no index-modification operations.

Index modification requires 12 and 26 percent of the operation set in the 704 and in the Stretch, respectively. Yet, the 360 can use many index operators—such as multiply, divide, and shift—that are not available in the 704 or in the Stretch.

Operation Set

Address and index arithmetic justifies integer arithmetic as a machinehood need; it is treated as a case of integer arithmetic in Section 5.3.

Architects have often limited separate index-arithmetic operations to load, store, add, subtract, and compare; they have justified multiply, divide, and logic only for other integer computations. Access within linearly mapped data structures, however, also justifies multiplication—preferably cumulative—and, to a lesser degree, shifting and masking.

The 6600 limits its index arithmetic in the classical way. It provides, however, a strong link between the 60-bit floating-point space and the 18-bit index and address spaces.

3.4.2
Queue Addressing

A one-dimensional array that is stored contiguously and in order may be sequentially accessed by generation of addresses in numerical order, spaced apart by element size. When this order is used in the same direction for reading and writing, the FIFO algorithm results, and the data structure is called a *queue*; reading and writing in opposite directions yields the LIFO algorithm, which applies to a *stack*.

FIFO algorithm.   Program 3-36 gives the functions for FIFO reading and writing. Writing in essence extends the queue on one end, and reading contracts it by deleting the information that is read from the other end. Exceptions, such as wanting to read from an empty queue, are ignored here.

```
data←readfifo size       writefifo data
 ⍝ read from fifo store   ⍝ write in fifo store
data←size↑store           store←store,data
store←size↓store
```

PROGRAM 3-36   FIFO addressing.

Application.   Each element of the queue is accessed only once for writing and only once for reading with pure FIFO addressing. Such actually is the case for true input and output operations—those to peripheral units that are not used as auxiliary store. These units—such as printers, communication units, and terminals—are sequential and *self-indexed*; that is, they present their locations in a fixed order.

An important application of the FIFO algorithm using implicit incrementing is the execution sequence of the instruction addresses.

3.4.3

Stack Addressing

The term *stack* suggests a pile of papers that becomes higher as it grows. It
indicates that there is no need to make all items shift location as more are
added. The stack is also called a *push-down* store. This term derives, by
analogy, from the spring-loaded mechanism for cafeteria trays and plates that
ensures easy access to the item on top. The item at the bottom is pushed down
deeper as the pile grows higher. In practical implementations, such shifting
is hardly ever done. The LIFO algorithm concerns access, not placement; no
data movement is required.

LIFO algorithm. Program 3-37 gives the reading and writing functions for a
stack. Reading is the same as for FIFO; it is called *pop* for a stack. Writing,
however, differs from FIFO; it adds a new element at the same end where the
structure is read. This operation is called *push*.

```
data←readlifo size    writelifo data
 ∩ read from stack    ∩ write in stack
data←size↑store       store←data,store
store←size↓store
```

PROGRAM 3-37   LIFO addressing.

Application.   The stack is frequently used in compilers and in operating
systems—for example, parsing expressions, searching tree structures, and
making nested references to subroutines. An architecture should certainly
provide for addressing this structure. The question is how extensive this
provision should be. Tree 3-38 gives the pertinent design choices.

Since LIFO addressing is useful for some objects among the total program
information, but not for all of them, no one has proposed addressing all of
memory in this fashion. Several designs, however, treat the working store
as a stack in view of its convenience in processing expressions [Allmark and

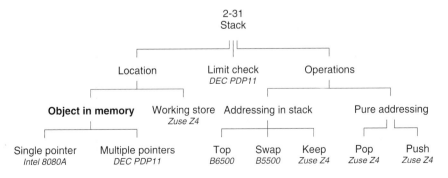

TREE 3-38   Design choices for stacks.

Lucking, 1962; Lonergan and King, 1961; Organick, 1973]. The pioneering Zuse Z4 (1945) addressed its two-register working store that way. Other examples are the English Electric KDF9 (1963) and the B5500. More common are facilities that allow the addressing of one or more stacks in memory, such as those in the DEC PDP11 (1970), the 8080A, and the Motorola MC68000 (1980).

We treat, in turn, these two approaches: LIFO addressing of the working store, and LIFO addressing of parts of the main store. We discuss the use of stacks in subroutine linkage in Section 6.4.

Stack as Working Store

In an expression such as
$$((a + b) \times (c + g\,d)) \div (e + f)$$
one cannot immediately see the proper execution order. Therefore, this expression is commonly transformed to the so-called *reversed Polish* notation of Lukasiewicz [1951]:
$$ab + cd + \times ef + \div$$
This expression is processed from left to right. Variables that are encountered are placed on the stack. When an arithmetic operator is encountered, it is applied to the two operands on top of the stack, and the result replaces them. The order of the Lukasiewicz notation is such that the proper operands are always on top of the stack, a property called *profitable surfacing*. The stack is therefore a natural candidate for addressing the working registers that contain the operands and results. Program 3-39 illustrates this use of a stack, as compared to the use of a directly addressed working store.

Repeated operands. Ockham's razor prescribes that each kind of function should be provided with as few distinct mechanisms as possible. So one should seek a single universally applicable method of addressing working storage. In considering LIFO for this use, one must determine that it handles all cases, else the advantages gained by its use may well be offset by the necessity of providing another, different method for handling other cases. In

```
lifoclassic      directclassic
push a           r1←a
push b           r1←r1 add b
add              r2←c
push c           r2←r2 add d
push d           r1←r1 multiply r2
add              r2←e
multiply         r2←r2 add f
push e           r1←r1 divide r2
push f           y←r1
add
divide
y←pop
```

A y←((a+b)×(c+d))÷(e+f)

PROGRAM 3-39   Procedure without repeated operands.

practice, the stack handles many frequent cases beautifully; it does not handle all cases well.

Consider the case of repeated operands, such as constants or intermediate results, illustrated by the square-root computation in Newton's iteration (Program 3-40). This method is represented by the expression

$$y \leftarrow 0.5 \times (y + n \div y)$$

In this expression, y is the current approximation, and n is the operand. Before being replaced by the result, y is used twice in each iteration. The number n and the constant 0.5 remain unchanged—they are required in each iteration. Adequate performance requires that all three operands be placed in the working store, and that no extra operations be necessary for addressing. A directly addressed working store satisfies these requirements.

Pure LIFO addressing cannot use an operand from the working store repeatedly, since each operation destroys its operands. The architecture assumes that all original operands are fetched from memory and that only intermediate results are left in the working store. In the stack example of Program 3-40 A, the constants 0.5 and n are fetched from memory each time they are used. Also, the variable y must be stored at the end of the iteration and then be fetched twice during the next iteration. The bit traffic consists of five references to memory for each iteration, whereas none is required, as shown by the loop of the direct-address procedure (B in Program 3-40).

Stack manipulations. Expanding the stack architecture can reduce memory references in such cases. An example is the operation Duplicate, which acts on the top operand of the stack. Another example is the general modification andkeep, used in stackroot (C in Program 3-40), which preserves one or both operands of an operation. This modification applies to all operations and therefore more or less doubles the operation repertoire.

At times it is necessary to reach deeper into the stack, as for the constant 0.5 in stackroot. This leads one to provide the operations Top, which places a copy of any operand out of the stack on top, as in stackroot, and Swap, which interchanges an operand out of the stack with the one on top. These two operations require addressing the working store. The

```
A                      B                       C

liforoot               directroot              stackroot
REPEAT:push n          r1←0.5                  push 0.5
   push y              r2←n                    push n
   divide              r3←y                    push y
   push y              REPEAT:r4←r2            REPEAT:divideandkeep
   add                    r4←r4 divide r3         add
   push 0.5               r3←r3 add r4            top ¯2
   multiply              r3←r3 multiply r1       multiply
   y←pop              →UNTIL test              →UNTIL test
→UNTIL test             y←r3                    y←pop
                                                clear
                                                clear
```

a y←0.5×(y+n÷y)

PROGRAM 3-40   Procedure with repeated operands.

original advantage of the stack—the elimination of the explicit working-store address—is therefore diminished. Also, the compiler must simulate the LIFO algorithm to determine where to find the operands.

Upon completion of the square-root procedure, the stack should be empty again; the repeatedly used operands n and 0.5 should be eliminated. Usually an operation such as Clear, which removes the top operand, is used for this purpose (as occurs twice in `stackroot`). Again, the compiler must keep track of the contents of the stack, to determine how many Clears to issue. So passes the hoped-for simplicity.

Stack size.   The compiler must take into account the number of working registers. A full stack is an exception condition that must be anticipated and resolved. The usual solution is to provide a large stack, partly in fast, and partly in slow realization, and an interruption upon overflow of the total allocated area.

Bit traffic.   In comparison to direct addressing, the LIFO algorithm does not decrease the number of memory references—the bit traffic. Rather, the examples of Programs 3-39 and 3-40 show that, in the case of repeated operands, the bit traffic can increase noticeably for the LIFO algorithm in its pure form.

Bit efficiency.   Profitable surfacing eliminates the need of register addresses, so the instructions have an increased bit efficiency. Also, the compiler need not address and allocate the register space. But some studies indicate that, because of repeated operands, the net instruction density with LIFO addressing is less, not greater, than with direct addressing [Myers, 1977a].

We conclude that the advantages of the stack organization for working store are overbalanced by the disadvantages. In the design of the 360, we decided that simple direct addressing of the working registers was preferable. This decision allowed the same set of registers to be used for operands and as index registers. The use of a stack as a working store is illustrated in the Z4 (Section 10.3).

Stacks in Memory

Quite apart from choosing how to address the working store, the designer must consider the access to stacks that appear as objects in memory. Since memory is accessible anyway by direct addressing, the designer can incorporate any of a range of functions, from completely automatic stack manipulation to no specialized function at all. In the most elaborate function, the top of the stack and its maximum extent are specified by pointers; the stack is reduced for all pop operations and extended by all push operations; alarms are given when an attempt is made to pop from an empty stack or to push onto a full one. Table 3-41 lists the stack-manipulation provisions of several machines.

	Separate instructions	With index use Pre	Post
Ferranti Mark 1	+ -		
IBM NORC	+		
IBM Stretch	+ - -1		+
Ferranti Atlas	+ -		+ -
CDC 6600	+ -	+ -	
DEC PDP8		+1	
DEC PDP11		-1	+1
Intel 8080A	+ +1 -1		
Cray 1	+ - ×		
Motorola M6800	+1 -1		
MOS 6502	+1 -1		
DEC VAX11		-1	+1
Motorola MC68000	+ -	-1	+1

Legend: + = add; - = subtract; × = multiply.

TABLE 3-41   Index arithmetic in various machines.

3.4.4

Incrementing

Successive elements of a queue in memory can be accessed for reading and for writing by incrementing the memory address; accessing the elements of a stack requires decrementing as well. Since the elements may vary in size, we first treat the general increment operation, which is equivalent to addition of an arbitrary value. Then we consider queue and stack addressing where the increment operation is combined with index use.

The value to be added to the element address, the *increment*, can be specified either explicitly or implicitly. Explicit specification usually uses a separate instruction that specifies the incrementing operation and its operand. The increment location can be memory or a register.

Increment in memory.   When indices are placed in general purpose registers, the normal Add can be used, which allows the memory address of the increment to be indexed.

Increment in register.   The 360 instruction Load Address is an example of a special increment instruction (Program 3-42; also Program 3-34). This instruction forms an effective address as usual—by adding the base address and element address (index) to the displacement. This effective address is not

Opcode	R1	X1	B1	D1

```
0       8  12  16  20              32
Legend: B = base; D = displacement;
        R = register; X = index.
```

```
LA:address
⋒ IBM 360 Load Address
address←adrcap|adr360bxd
reg[fld R1;]←word magnr address
```

PROGRAM 3-42   Incrementing with Load Address in the IBM System/360.

```
address←size incrll r;count              address←size decrll r;count
⍝ DEC PDP11 postincrement                ⍝ DEC PDP11 predecrement
address←size,memadr,magni regout r       count←(magni regout r)-size≠byte
count←address[Value]+size≠byte           Warning report(r=Sp)∧count=limitll
r regin word magnr count                 Spec report(r=Sp)∧count=limitll-16
                                         address←size,memadr,adrcap|count
                                         r regin word magnr address[Value]
```

PROGRAM 3-43   Postincrement and predecrement in the DEC PDP11.

used for a fetch; rather, it is placed in a specified register. The instruction Load Address can be used to add an increment, stored in one register, to the content of another register that is specified both as index register and as result register. So the index register gets incremented.

Since Load Address does not involve any main storage access, it is fast in execution. Because of its broad application, Load Address has become one of the two most used operations in the 360/370 family. (Branch On Condition is the other.)

Immediate increment.   The increment value can also be specified in the displacement field of the Load Address instruction. We return to this type of operand addressing—immediate addressing—in Section 3.5. It is appropriate for specifying constants in a program, but not when increments can vary.

Increment with Index Use

Linear mapping of the queue and stack onto memory allows the program primitives of Programs 3-36 and 3-37 to be implemented by an indexed read or write operation, which is combined with an index increment or decrement. The index is often called the *stack pointer*.

Position of stack and pointer.   How does the stack grow? From low to high memory addresses, or vice versa? Either direction is feasible. For a stack that grows from high to low, the Top operations can use a positive displacement relative to the pointer value. The stack is then conveniently placed at the high end of the available segment.

Does the pointer, when at rest, point to the top element of the stack (the position of the next Read) or to one position beyond the stack (the position of the next Write)? Again, either position is possible, but for variable-length data the choice follows from the stack position.

When the stack grows from high to low memory addresses, and the pointer points to the top element, a Pop becomes a Read followed by an increment corresponding to the size of the data just read, a so-called *postincrement*; Push is a Write preceded by a decrement, the *predecrement*. The And Save operations read with a displacement of zero or one times the element size and do not increment the pointer. This general and common solution is found in the 8080A, the PDP11 (Program 3-43) and DEC VAX11 (1978), and the MC68000.

When the stack grows upward, the pointer should point to the first position beyond the stack. Pop is now a Read with a predecrement; Push is a Write with a postincrement; the And Save operations require a displacement

of −1 or −2. These alternatives show that the architectural provision for sequential addressing is postincrement and predecrement. It is not preincrement and postdecrement, because data are addressed by their low-order memory position.

Explicit increment.   The Stretch contains one of the first examples of increment with index use. It combines an immediate increment with the use of the index in address modification, an index mode called *progressive indexing*. Program 3-44 shows this operation. (The flag and refill functions are explained in Section 3.5.) The increment value occupies the address field of the instruction. The displacement that normally occupies that location is implied to be zero.

Progressive indexing provides postdecrement instead of predecrement, because we used the queue—not the stack—as a program primitive (1957). The explicit increment allows an increment different from the data length, but it violates orthogonality by using the instruction address field differently from all other index operations. Using the explicit increment probably was a mistake.

Implied increment.   The 8080, PDP11, VAX11, and the MC68000 all have one or more system stacks, with an implied fixed data length, that are used in subroutine calling and interruption.

The PDP11 is illustrated in Program 3-45. The stack pointer (Sp) resides in one of the general registers and is processed by incr11 and decr11, shown in Program 3-43. A lower memory boundary of 256 is set for the stack.

The DEC and Motorola machines have postincrement and predecrement with variable sizes as an addressing mode, shown for the PDP11 in Program 3-43. Each register can serve as a stack pointer, and stored stacks can be maintained in memory.

Address		Op	X1	M0	L0		Bs	Offset	Opcode	X2

```
0                          24  28  32 35    41 44      51       60  64
Legend: Bs = byte size; L = length; M = address mode; Op = opcode;
        X = index.
```

```
address←adr7030m
ค IBM Stretch bit-address modes
→CASE fld M0                        C4: ค immediate address
C0: ค indexed address                   address←(ρAddress) magnr adr7030
    address←Address modify7030 X1       Invop report tomem
    →ENDCASE                            →ENDCASE
C1: ค increment                     C5: ค decrement
    address←X1 incr7030 fld Address      address←X1 incr7030-fld Address
    →ENDCASE                            →ENDCASE
C2: ค increment, count              C6: ค decrement, count
    address←X1 incr7030c fld Address     address←X1 incr7030c-fld Address
    →ENDCASE                            →ENDCASE
C3: ค increment, count, refill      C7: ค decrement, count, refill
    address←X1 incr7030cr fld Address    address←X1 incr7030cr-fld Address
    →ENDCASE                         ENDCASE:
```

PROGRAM 3-44   Progressive indexing in the IBM Stretch.

```
    push11 data                         data←pop11
  ⍝ DEC PDP11 write onto stack        ⍝ DEC PDP11 read from stack
    (word decr11 Sp) write11 data     data←read11 word incr11 Sp
```

PROGRAM 3-45   LIFO organization in the DEC PDP11.

3.4.5
Bibliography

Allmark and Lucking [1962], Blake [1977], Hauck and Dent [1968], Lonergan and King [1961], Lukasiewicz [1951], Mulder and Flynn [1992], Myers [1977a], Organick [1973], Pooch and Nieder [1973], Thomas and Necula [1977].

3.5
Address Levels

So far we have considered addresses as machine-language names for data. Such addresses are called *direct*. But an address need not necessarily name a data element; it may also refer to another address, a process called *indirect addressing*. The fruitfulness of indirection derives from its allowing the definition of complex data structures regardless of the linear memory structure.

In its simplest form, indirect addressing gives a chain of addresses. But, by associating a data item with each address, one can get a list of those items. Treating data that way (also called *list processing*) can solve the memory-allocation problem.

Conversely, an address need not name a data item; it itself can be used as the data item. This process is called *immediate addressing*. We recognize three levels of addressing: indirect, direct, and immediate.

3.5.1
List Processing

In a *list*, each data element is stored with at least one *chain address* or *pointer* that refers to its successor or predecessor. Program 3-46 gives the basic algorithm for scanning a simple forward chain and for constructing one.

If all the data structures used in a program are scalars or one-dimensional arrays (including higher-order arrays scanned in only one order), the use of chained addressing provides an effective solution to the memory-allocation problem. Varying numbers of varying-sized vectors can readily be allocated

```
    data←readchain
  ⍝ read chained
    data←memory[address;Data]
    address←magni memory[address;Address]


    writechain data
  ⍝ write chained
    memory[address;Data]←data
    address←magni memory[address;Address]
```

PROGRAM 3-46   Chained addressing.

without storage waste, and can be scanned rapidly and cheaply. All unused memory locations are kept chained together, so allocation is easy. This mode of working is called *list processing*, and there are higher-level programming languages such as LISP and FORTH that exploit its flexibilities.

Chained addressing sacrifices contiguity of allocation of array elements. The other cost is the storage space taken by the pointers. An obvious generalization is to allocate small blocks (of perhaps variable numbers) of elements contiguously, chaining them together. This saves pointer space but complicates the scanning algorithm.

A list provides a means of mapping a data structure onto linear memory. The primitive data structures are still the matrix, the vector, the queue, the stack, the file, the tree, and so on. The list is not another one of these data structures, but a means of implementing them.

Operations upon Lists

Besides scanning, the four basic operations applicable to a data structure implemented as a list are appending, truncating, inserting, and deleting [Blaauw, 1959]. The basic list primitive is the pointer, used as a means of indirection in a forward or a backward chain.

Forward chain. Forward-chained lists are an especially convenient representation that allows sequential data structures, such as files and queues, to be scanned with reading and writing in the same order. A pointer provides all the special function needed for chain management.

Backward chain. Backward chains also constitute a convenient implementation. As with the forward scan, a pointer suffices for chain management.

Two-way chain. One wants to be able to scan a list in both directions, as for the stack. The obvious solution is to provide each data item with two pointers, one to its successor, the other to its predecessor. An ingenious idea, whose inventor is unknown to us, implements the two by storing the EXCLUSIVE-OR of the forward and backward pointers, the *compressed* pointer, in the pointer space. During scan from either direction, one combines with an EXCLUSIVE-OR the address one came from with the pointer value to find where to go next. Reversal of direction in the middle of a scan is rapid, which is useful for a stack.

The program is radically simpler if one can do the EXCLUSIVE-OR logic in an index register—that is, if the index registers are part of the working store for integer arithmetic and logic.

Graphs. Chained addressing can be used for general graphs, by associating pointers to all connecting nodes with the element for each node [Iverson, 1962].

An interesting, common, and important special case of the general graph is the *binary tree*, where each element has exactly two successors and one predecessor. This binary tree is useful not only in its own right, but also as a representation of two-dimensional arrays—matrices. In this use, one pointer addresses an element's row successor; the other, its column successor. Matrices can then be scanned rapidly in either order.

Indirection

Important as the pointer may be, it is by no means the only application of indirection in addressing. When parameters are passed to a subroutine, the addresses of these parameters may be placed at an agreed-upon location. The subroutine can then obtain the parameters via one level of indirection. Or, when the actions of a program are traced, the operands of the subject program may be obtained indirectly by referring to the addresses of the subject instructions, but without executing these instructions. We observe that, in these cases, the target of indirection is not necessarily an integer address, but may be an address phrase.

3.5.2

Indirect Addressing

What machine-language facility should be provided to implement the pointer as a program primitive? All that is really needed is to make the content of an addressed location available as an address, a facility called *indirect addressing*.

Since the content of an index register can be used as an address, indirect addressing can be accomplished explicitly by the loading of an index register from memory. It can also be accomplished ephemerally as part of an addressing action, as shown in Tree 3-47.

Indirection as an Instruction

Tree 3-47 shows that indirect addressing poses an unusually large number of design choices. We first consider the specification of indirection by means of instructions.

Load index with integer.   In the 360 the loading of index registers can be done with full indexing power, and many registers are provided. A normal Load Register can therefore be used as a separate instruction to effect indirect addressing. An integer can be loaded from memory, from working store, or from an effective address (with Load Address, Program 3-42).

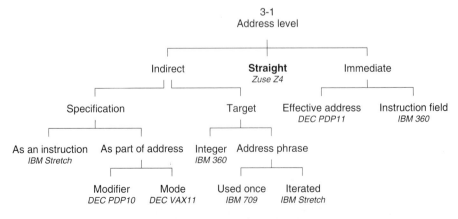

TREE 3-47   Design choices for address level.

The choice between indirect addressing as an independent instruction action and as part of address specification depends primarily on bit efficiency. A Load instruction requires 32 bits. The first option requires 1 bit per address field, or on the average 1 bit per instruction. The second requires a Load instruction whenever indirection is wanted. For the 360, where a Load cost 32 bits, more than one thirty-second, or 3 percent, of addresses would have to be indirect to justify the bit. The figures available to us suggested that the frequency was less than that. (Had the bit been justified, we would still have had the problem of fitting it into the address phrase.)

Indirection as Part of Addressing

Address modifier.   In the IBM 709 (1959), where indirect addressing first appeared, there are only three index registers, but there is plenty of space in the address-phrase format. So the architects chose to provide an indirection modifier as part of the address phrase. The 709 (Program 3-48) actually uses two bits as the indirection modifier, a squandering of the bit budget not found in modern machines.

Addressing mode.   For machines that have several addressing modes, such as postincrement and predecrement, the indirection mode can be obtained with less cost to the bit budget. The PDP11 (Program 3-49) uses 3 bits per address to specify one of eight addressing modes. Four of these modes are indirect, so 1 bit of the address phrase is spent for indirection after all. In the VAX11, however, only five out of 16 modes have indirection (Section 15.3); in the MC68000 only one out of eight primary modes specifies indirection (Section 16.4).

Multilevel indirection.   When the target address phrase can itself specify address indirection, multilevel indirection is possible. Through a programming error, a never-ending sequence may now result. Such a sequence is unlike an unending loop of instructions, which may be broken by an interruption after any instruction. Rather, the whole sequence belongs to one instruction, and special provisions must be introduced to stop the process.

Various machine designs have made various choices. In the 709 (Program 3-48) the operand specified by the effective address was parsed as an instruction format, but no further indirection was allowed.

Load index with effective address.   The instruction Load Value Effective (LVE) of the Stretch (Program 3-50) placed the effective address of an instruction that was addressed in memory in an index register. That addressed

```
 ┌──────────┬───┬───┬─────────┐
 │ Opcode   │ I │ * │ X │Address│
 └──────────┴───┴───┴─────────┘
 0          12  18  21        36
 Legend: I = indirect; X = index; * = unused.

  address←adr709
A IBM 709 addressing
  →If 3=fld Indirect
  THEN:inst[X,Address]←(read704 adr704)[X,Address]
  ENDIF:address←adr704
```

PROGRAM 3-48   Indirect addressing in the IBM 709.

Op	S	D	Address	Address

```
0    4   10  16              32               48
Legend: Op = opcode; D = destination; S = source.

address←size adr11 field;r;step;rf
⍺ DEC PDP11 addressing
r←fld field[R]
step←(size,word)[r∈Sp,Pc]
→CASE fld field[M]
  C0: ⍺ register                    C4: ⍺ predecrement
      address←size,regadr,r             address←size,1↓step decr11 r
      →ENDCASE                          →ENDCASE
  C1: ⍺ register indirect           C5: ⍺ predecrement indirect
      rf←magni read11 word,regadr,r     rf←magni read11 word decr11 r
      address←size,memadr,rf            address←size,memadr,rf
      →ENDCASE                          →ENDCASE
  C2: ⍺ postincrement               C6: ⍺ index+displacement
      address←size,1↓step incr11 r      address←size displ11 r
      →ENDCASE                          →ENDCASE
  C3: ⍺ postincrement indirect      C7: ⍺ index+displacement indirect
      rf←magni read11 word incr11 r     rf←magni read11 word displ11 r
      address←size,memadr,rf            address←size,memadr,rf
      →ENDCASE                        ENDCASE:
```

PROGRAM 3-49   Addressing modes in the DEC PDP11.

instruction could itself be a Load Value Effective, allowing indirection to any level. A special timeout was required to break endless pointer loops occurring within the execution of one instruction.

Adrhalf	R1	Op	X1

```
0                   19  23  28  32
Legend: Op = opcode; R = register; X = index.

LVE;inst0;index
⍺ IBM Stretch Load Value Effective
index←regout R1 WHERE inst0←inst
⍺ start time-out
REPEAT:inst←half read7030 adr7030
  ⍺ →OUT time-out exceeded
→UNTIL 'LVE '∨.≠oplist[decode inst;]
index[Value]←adrsize signmagnr adr7030
R1 regin index WHERE inst←inst0
signal7030X index
```

PROGRAM 3-50   Load Index Value Effective in the IBM Stretch.

Implied Target Location

In the simple forward chain, the target location of indirect addressing is usually implied. Because of the inherently sequential nature of list processing, it is not surprising that the application of chained addressing in computer architectures concerns primarily the structures we encountered in discussing the FIFO algorithm.

Instruction addressing.   The IBM 650 (1954) uses a simple form of chain addressing for the instruction address (Program 1-30). Chain addressing has also been used for channel commands, as illustrated by the control word of the

Stretch (Program 8-37). Both applications, however, are customarily served by implied FIFO addressing; the storage space for the address is saved.

Data structure addressing.   The Stretch control word is in format and usage close to its index word shown in Program 3-51. The chain address, which resides in the successor field, points to the index word to be used next in the addressing of the data structure.

The Stretch index word is inefficient in bit usage for the chaining of individual data elements; 64 bits per element are far too many. The index word, however, efficiently chains sequential data structures, such as files.

```
                       Sign↓↓Flag

│ Address            │ │ * │ Count     │ Next           │

0                      25 28            46               64
Legend:  * = unused.

index7030
a IBM Stretch index allocation
 Value←24,0+ι24
 Flag←25
a unused←26+ι2
 Count←28+ι18
 Next←46+ι18
```

PROGRAM 3-51   Index word of the IBM Stretch.

Provisions for Trees

The designers of the 704 made, perhaps inadvertently, superb special provisions for scanning binary trees implemented with lists. A special format used for setting and modifying index registers contains an operation code, an index specification, and two full 15-bit address fields. Special operations fetch each of these address fields into an index register (Program 3-52).

```
│ Op │ Decrement        │ X │ Address        │

0   3                  18 21                36
Legend:  Op = opcode;  X = index.

LXA;od                            LXD;od
a IBM 704 Load Index From Address  a IBM 704 Load Index From Decrement
 od←read704 fld Address            od←read704 fld Address
 indexwrite704 od[Address]         indexwrite704 od[Decrement]
```

PROGRAM 3-52   Add and decrement operations in the IBM 704.

McCarthy, in developing the LISP list-processing language, noticed the convenience of these 704 operations for handling binary trees. He incorporated into LISP the operators CAR (originally for Content of Address Register) and CDR (originally for Content of Decrement Register) for following the left and right links of the branching chain. These operators are very efficiently implemented with LXA and LXD of the 704 [McCarthy, 1960]. LISP proved enormously successful in implementing with lists many applications involving

memories full of variable-sized, rapidly changing trees and vectors on the 704 and its successors, the 709, 7090, and PDP10 family.

3.5.3

Immediate Addressing

The use of instruction bits as an operand is called *immediate addressing*. This procedure obviates a memory reference and yields the operand immediately. The operand location may be a special instruction field, as the 8-bit immediate field in the 360 (Program 3-53) or the address field, as in the VAX11, or it may be the effective address, as in the 360 Load Address (Program 3-42).

```
Opcode  Imm      B1  D1

0        8      16  20          32
Legend: B = base; D = displacement; Imm = immediate.

NI;od;rl                      MVI
 ∩ IBM 360 And Immediate       ∩ IBM 360 Move Immediate
 od←byte read360 adr360bd1     adr360bd1 write360 inst[Imm]
 →OUT suppress360
 rl←od∧inst[Imm]
 adr360bd1 write360 rl
 signal360Z rl
```

PROGRAM 3-53   Immediate addressing in the IBM System/360.

General address option.   Immediate addressing can be provided as a general option at the expense of some operation-code space. Such an option, however, must be limited to the data movement, arithmetic, and logical operations; branch operations must point somewhere. Even within the datatypes where the option applies, there are operations—such as Store—that do not allow immediate addressing. So, unlike an indirection modifier, an immediate modifier cannot be applied to all addresses. Its provision as an orthogonal modifier is therefore unnecessary—there will be meaningless combinations. The MC68000, which has immediate addressing as one of its address modes, uses the impossible mode combinations for other functions.

In the Stretch, immediate addressing is specified as an option for fixed-point arithmetic, logic, and index arithmetic (Program 3-54); the floating-point format does not match the address format.

```
Adrhalf            R1  Opcode

0                 19  23        32
Legend: R = register.

LVI;index
 ∩ IBM Stretch Load Value Immediate
 index←regout R1
 index[Value]←adrsize↑0,inst[Adrhalf]
 R1 regin index
 signal7030X index
```

PROGRAM 3-54   Immediate addressing in the IBM Stretch.

Extended field.   The PDP11 gives an elegant and quite general means of immediate addressing. The instruction format of Program 2-37 apparently does not allow this address mode. The instruction address, however, can be used as an index. It normally points at the first word following the instruction, which therefore can be fetched as data. The postincrement mode is then used to step the instruction address beyond the data.

Both operands can be immediate in the PDP11—a property that has little use. The PDP11 has the advantage that its word size of 16 bits matches the data size, the address size, and the basic instruction size.

Instruction field.   An alternative to a general immediate addressing option is to introduce a few instructions that provide the immediate address function for a limited number of cases. The 360 provides, besides Load Address, a limited set of explicit immediate operations, such as Move Immediate and And Immediate (Program 3-53).

Branch address.   The branch address does not follow the pattern of immediate, direct, and indirect addressing. It is normal to consider an effective memory address in a branch instruction as a branch address. This view equates an operand in, say, arithmetic with an instruction in branching. One can alternatively consider the branch address as the new content of the instruction address register. This view considers ordinary branching instructions to have immediate, not direct, addresses. We prefer this view, since it cleanly comprehends both architectures with implied instruction addresses and those, such as the PDP11, where the instruction address register is visible in the working store.

Decomposition.   Decomposition can be used to reduce the proliferation of combinations and options that can be specified in instructions. Addressing illustrates this principle. The MC68000 allows about 12 useful modes. When addressing actions, such as indirect addressing, are done by separate instructions, these modes are all available. The bit budget may balance about the same for these alternative means of specification, but both compilation and the controls of the implementation are simplified. In a RISC computer, such as the IBM 6150 (1986), only three basic addressing modes are provided (Program 3-55).

```
Opcode  Rb  Rc  Ihalf                    Op  Imm  Rb  Rc

0      8   12   16                 32     0   4    8   12   16
Legend:  Imm = immediate;  Op = opcode;  R = register.

  address←adr6150;index;displacement       address←adr6150x;base;index
ⵀ IBM 6150 signed address               ⵀ IBM 6150 base-index address
  index←magni regc                         base←magni reg[fld Rb;]
  displacement←radixcompi inst[Ihalf]      index←magni regc
  address←index+displacement               address←base+index


  address←adr6150b;index;displacement      data←regc
ⵀ IBM 6150 short byte address           ⵀ IBM 6150 register access
  index←magni regc                         data←(0≠fld Rc)∧reg[fld Rc;]
  displacement←fld Imm
  address←index+displacement
```

PROGRAM 3-55   Addressing modes in the IBM 6150.

	Immediate	Indirect		
		Referrer	Referee	Termination
IBM 704	field	address	address	one level
STC ZEBRA	field			
Bull Gamma 60	address	address		
IBM 1620	field	address	address	modifier
Bendix G20	address	field/addr.	field	one level
IBM Stretch	address	address	address	op code
Ferranti Atlas	address	~	~	~
English Electric KDF9	field	~	~	~
IBM 7094	field	address		
CDC 6600 PPU	field	field	address	one level
Burroughs B5500	field	descriptor	word	one level
IBM System/360	field			
DEC PDP8		address	address	one level
DEC PDP10		address	address	modifier
DEC PDP11	field	address	word	one level
Intel 8080A	field			
Cray 1	field			
Motorola M6800	field			
MOS 6502	field	address	address	one level
DEC VAX11	field	address	word	one level
Motorola MC68000	field			
IBM 6150	field			

Legend: address = effective address; field = instruction field;
word = memory word.

TABLE 3-56   Address levels in various machines.

Some of the variants of address levels in various machines are shown in Table 3-56.

3.5.4
Bibliography

Berkling [1971], Blaauw [1959], Iverson [1962], McCarthy [1960].

3.6
Rules of Good Practice

1. Segments of contiguous linearly addressed memory should be made available for accessing elements within data structures.
2. Direct addressing is superior to associative addressing for memory and for working store.
3. Direct addressing is superior to stack addressing for memory and for working store.
4. Indexing functions should include provisions for postincrement and predecrement of multiple stack pointers referring to memory.
5. Full arithmetic power should be available in index arithmetic.
6. Parsimony should be applied to addressing modes.
7. Decomposition of an addressing function by suitable index arithmetic instructions is preferable to the use of addressing modes.

3.7

Exercises

3-1 The problem of fragmentation is aggravated by a large page size, whereas using a small page size makes the page table become too large. Sketch a design for an address-translation system with two distinct page sizes, and discuss its advantages and disadvantages.

3-2 Explain the difference between:

a. An *effective address*, as the term is used in this chapter, and an assembly-language *label*

b. An *effective address* and assembly-language *label*, and an actual *memory address*

3-3 Suppose that you have to write the standard matrix routines for addition, multiplication, and transfer of sparse two-dimensional matrices. (A sparse matrix is one in which many of the elements are zero; they arise in many applications.) Describe how you would take advantage of each of the following addressing schemes in designing the data structures to be used in your package:

a. Direct

b. Sequential (say FIFO on tape)

c. Associative

d. Indirect

3-4 If register 5 holds a small positive integer i, the 360 instruction LA 5,1(5) replaces i by $i + 1$. Due to the conventions of 360 addressing, the high-order eight bits will be set to 0.

a. Explain what happens if i is not a small positive integer.

b. Discuss the design decisions leading to the anomaly of part a in terms of orthogonality, propriety, and transparency.

3-5 Economy of bits dictated that indirection be omitted as a standard 360 option. Since RX instructions mostly operate on halfwords or greater, the low-order bit of the instruction is always zero (except for Insert Character and Store Character, which could be treated as special cases). Discuss the suggestion that this bit be used as an indirect bit.

3-6 What is the relationship between implied address-modification schemes and the ease of generating efficient code for a given machine? Discuss the information a compiler must have to generate efficient code for the following:

a. The Stretch

b. A standard minicomputer such as the DEC PDP8

3-7 S. Cray uses no cache in the Cray 1 (1976).

a. What architectural features of the Cray 1 serve the same function as a cache?

b. What implementation or realization features of the Cray 1 reduce the need for a cache?

c. Explain how Cray's assumptions about the use of the machine justify such a design choice.

3-8 A characteristic of microprocessors is the abundance of addressing modes.

a. Explain how this characteristic is consistent with the application characteristics of microprocessors.

b. Offer an hypothesis as to why large-scale computers have not used so many addressing modes.

c. Justify your hypothesis from part b with at least two distinct arguments.

E

P   5   6   4

P 1 3 2

P 1 2 3

C

P 2   7

A

P 3   6 $6\frac{1}{2}$

P 1   10   6 11

D

B

P 6   7

P 4   6

Data

The computer architect selects not only what may be said in the computer's machine language (the instructions) but also what may be spoken about (the data). The data, like the instructions, are normally represented in bits. Bits are the principal raw material, and representation is a chief concern.

Datatypes. We consider a datatype to be provided in a machine architecture if and only if there are one or more operations that depend upon that datatype's allocation and encoding.

Bell and Newell [1971] have excellent discussions of datatypes. We summarize their key points here:

1. A datatype consists of a referent set (the set of concepts represented) and a representation (a set of bit patterns and the encoding and allocation that define the correspondence).

2. A processor's datatypes divide into two classes: those used to produce bit patterns with new meaning (*data* in the narrow sense), and the instructions and other status words used to control the computing system itself. These latter were treated in Chapter 2 and are not further discussed here.

3. Each datatype has a set of operations proper to it, and it is the existence of this set that establishes the distinctness of the datatype. Examples are *character strings*, which may be reallocated (moved), reencoded, and compared, but preserve their inherent meaning; *logical data*, which are subject to Boolean operations; and *numbers*, upon which arithmetic may be performed.

4. A datatype is made up of several subparts, which may themselves be datatypes. Conversely, structures of datatypes are possible, such as vectors and matrices. (Figure 4-1 shows the hierarchy of datatypes, as indicated by arrows.) So an array may have floating-point numbers as elements. Each floating-point number contains the exponent and the coefficient, which are each fixed-point numbers. A fixed-point number consists of a sign and digits; these in turn are represented as bit vectors.

5. Because of the hierarchical nesting, any item of data will be used at different times as if it were different datatypes—for example, it may

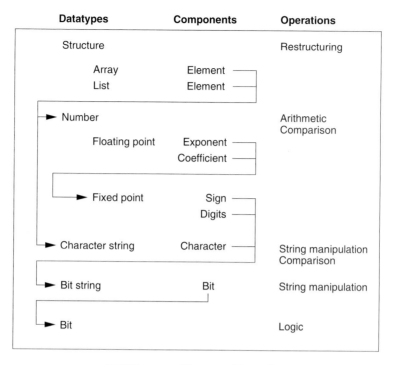

| Datatypes | Components | Operations |

Structure — Restructuring

Array — Element

List — Element

Number — Arithmetic / Comparison

Floating point — Exponent / Coefficient

Fixed point — Sign / Digits

Character string — Character — String manipulation / Comparison

Bit string — Bit — String manipulation

Bit — Logic

FIGURE 4-1   Datatype hierarchy.

be treated as an input datum, then moved as a character string, then added as a number, then interpreted as an instruction.

6. One can often embed one kind of representation in another so as to coalesce datatypes. Addresses are usually encoded as integers. Often they are allocated exactly the same as the integer datatype, so the two datatypes can be coalesced.

7. Bigger computers usually have more datatypes, because faster and more expensive hardware justifies more elaborate operation sets, and because the marginal cost of additional operations drops as the system grows.

8. Computers with longer word lengths usually have more datatypes. It is easier in implementation, and usually more fruitful conceptually, to get new ones by subdivision rather than by aggregation.

9. Datatypes tend to be added to a computer in a fixed order, since certain tasks must be performed by any computer.

These points, cogently stated by Bell and Newell, are well-established by experience. We believe that a somewhat more complex model is better than the single fixed order of datatypes described in point 9. This model can be derived from the historic development.

Historic development.   The representations of character strings and numbers spring from independent historical traditions.

Mechanical manipulation (other than communication) of character strings was first done on a large scale in tabulating machines that used decimal arithmetic and variable-length alphanumeric words. The Univac I provided

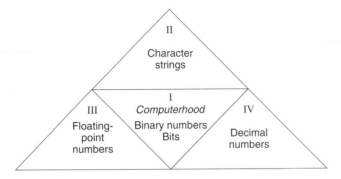

FIGURE 4-2   Datatype optionality.

alphanumeric characters in a fixed 12-character-per-word format (1951). The IBM 702 (1954) pioneered variable-length character strings.

For numbers, the abacus and the pioneering work of Schickard, Pascal, and Leibniz led to electromechanical desk calculators. These calculators in turn inspired the fixed-length scientific computers. The users of these computers accepted binary representation in exchange for higher performance. With some initial hesitation, they also accepted floating point as the most efficient way to solve the scaling problem.

Zuse's and Aiken's machines and the Princeton IAS (1952) provide no logical operations. The Cambridge EDSAC (1949) and the IBM 701 (1953) each provide a distinct logical datatype, with Shift and AND. The IBM 704 (1955) is more powerful with AND, OR, NOT, shift, and test facilities for logical vectors. The Univac 1103A (1956) has AND, EXCLUSIVE-OR, Extract, and shift.

The development of higher-level languages since 1954 has made it possible and desirable to combine the two parallel developments of so-called commercial and scientific computers. These languages have their own requirements for character strings (such as names of variables) and for numbers (such as array indices). In the early 1960s, attempts were made—most notably in the IBM Stretch (1961), the Burroughs B5500 (1964), and the IBM System/360 (1965)—to come to a design that would satisfy both the commercial and scientific requirements.

Computerhood.   As Bell and Newell suggest, certain operations and datatypes are necessary for a machine to do its own housekeeping. One might say that these are the consequences of *computerhood* itself. They include integers for counting and addressing, and bits for logical decisions.

Clearly, the fixed-point number can be made to serve each of these functions. Just as clearly, greater specialization can save memory space. These housekeeping datatypes are shown as the mandatory base, region I in Figure 4-2.

Optionality.   Increased CPU sophistication has expressed itself in new datatypes for two basic reasons. First, as machines found progressively wider application, users progressively recognized the need for new types. Second, as user experience accumulated, additional operations were justified by frequency of use. As Bell and Newell point out, there are only so many

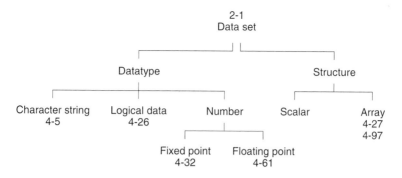

TREE 4-3   Design choices for data.

fruitful operations one can perform on any particular datatype, so increases in operation repertoire have usually been effected by providing more datatypes.

Inasmuch as these additional datatypes are not part of computerhood, however, they are optional and the performance/cost ratio of additional ones falls off rapidly. Text processing of all kinds is served by region II, character strings. The engineering and scientific applications are served with region III, floating-point numbers. For these applications, this type certainly is mandatory. The commercial application has classically been served with region IV, the decimal numbers. Now it is recognized that binary integers do just as well for these applications.

Obviously, many combinations of the regions are possible. The 360 and the B5500 include them all. The CDC 6600 (1964) has only I and III, as has the DEC PDP10 (1968). The minicomputers, except for the DEC PDP11/45 (1973), which also has III, usually have only region I. The Intel 8080A microcomputer (1974) also has only I, but includes a minimal provision for IV, as is the case for the Motorola MC68000 (1980). Many microcomputer systems use a separate chip to provide II. Tree 4-3 summarizes the datatypes treated in this chapter.

Paradigm.   Program 4-4 gives the basic activity of this chapter. A datum `data` is represented by the function `represent` and is recovered from its representation `rep` by `interpret`. Because the datum as such has no representation, it is called an *abstract datatype* [Naur, 1963]. APL is a nice means of conveying this notion, since it is reasonably successful at hiding the representation it uses for `data`.

A datum must be a member of a representable domain. For each member of this domain, a corresponding code value must be specified. This code is represented in bits (or decimal digits, if they are the minimal element), using the encoding function `magnr` (for *magnitude representation*). The interpretation steps are the exact reverse, using `magni` (for *magnitude interpretation*) (Program 1-31).

```
rep←size represent data                data←interpret rep
ᴀ basic representation                  ᴀ basic interpretation
rep←size magnr codesetιdomainιdata      data←domain[codeset[magni rep]]
```

PROGRAM 4-4   Basic representation and interpretation of data.

The pattern of the paradigm is found in all representation and interpretation functions. In general,

- Representation and interpretation functions may be many to one, but not one to many. Not all representations match the representation of their interpretation; an example is the 360 decimal sign in Program 4-54.
- The domain of the data to be represented may include concepts such as invalid, unspecified, undetermined, too large, or too small. Examples are found in the 6600 floating-point numbers (Table 4-82).
- Once a set of valid representations is established, the set of interpretations follows from the interpretation algorithm. One can also proceed in the reverse direction by first defining the set of valid concepts, and then using the representation algorithm to obtain the set of valid representations. The definition of the concept set, however, is usually more difficult than is the definition of the representation set, as is especially apparent for floating-point numbers.

4.1

Character Strings

Most modern machines (but not all) do a substantial amount of processing of alphanumeric character strings. This is necessary for the input and output of data from and to people. A substantial additional workload of character strings appears when a machine is used to process its own programs, expressed in symbolic assembler or higher-level languages.

The character-string datatype is not mandatory when a machine's program translation is done on another machine. A general purpose machine often performs program translation for embedded microcomputers.

Definition.   A computer has the character string as a datatype when it can manipulate a string of alphanumeric characters in a single operation. Some character-handling operations change the code or allocation of the data, but others change only the location of the character string. A computer that has the first type of operations, such as Translate or Edit For Print, clearly has the character string as datatype. Do computers that have only moving operations,

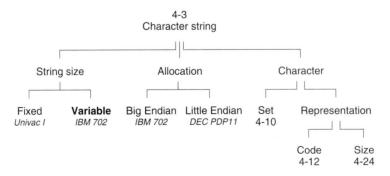

TREE 4-5   Design choices for character strings.

such as Load and Store, have a character-string datatype? We consider the character-string datatype to be absent when these operations are mere subsets of the logical and arithmetic operations and apply to only those strings whose lengths match the word sizes for logic or arithmetic. So we say that the Univac I, the 650, and most microcomputers do not have this datatype.

Structure.   A character string is simply structured—all the elements are of one type. Nevertheless, the datatype is not the character, but the string of characters, since both semantic interpretation and manipulative operations depend on the relationships among the characters in the string. Of course, a single character, and indeed an empty string, are proper special cases of the character string.

Representing alphanumeric data by character strings requires allocating fields for the string itself, allocating the characters within the string, and encoding them. The result is the design choices of Trees 4-5, 4-10, 4-12, and 4-24:

- Number of characters in the string, the *string size*
- Choice of the *character size*
- Choice of the *character set*
- *Encoding* of the characters in bits
- *Allocation* of the encoded characters, normally side by side

These choices are strongly related. The choice of character set strongly affects selection between the character sizes of 6 and 8 bits. Table 4-6 gives the parameter table for character-string formats.

	Field size in characters	Character set Code	Character set Size	Character size
Univac I	12	own	48	6
IBM 701	36	BCD	48	6
IBM 650	5	own	48	2d
IBM 704	6	BCD sc	48	6
IBM 705	1-ω	BCD cm	48	6
Bull Gamma 60	4×0-255	own	60	6
IBM 1401	1-ω	BCD cm	64	6
IBM 1620	2-ω÷2	BCD sc	49	2d
IBM Stretch	1-10	own	120	6-8
Ferranti Atlas	8	own	64	6
English Electric KDF9	8	own	94	6
Burroughs B5500	0-63	own	64	6
IBM System/360	1-256	EBCDIC	256	8
DEC PDP10	5	ASCII	128	7
Burroughs B6500	8 6	EBCDIC	64 256	6 8
DEC PDP11	2	ASCII	128	8
CDC Star100	0-ω	both	128 256	8
DEC VAX11	0-ω	ASCII	128	8

Legend: d = decimal digit; cm = commercial; sc = scientific;
        - = through; ω = memory size.

TABLE 4-6   Character strings in various machines.

4.1.1

String Size

The natural length of character strings is highly variable. Moreover, some strings may be treated individually in one case and as part of a larger string in another case. A record in a personnel file may contain fields for name and for address, and these in turn may contain other fields, such as the postal code. At times, one will manipulate only the postal code; at other times, the whole address; at still others, the whole record.

Length Distribution

Whereas the distribution of the used ranges and precisions of numbers is reasonably well-known, and desirable lengths cluster around a few values, fewer data are available on length distributions for character strings. The distributions themselves are smoother, with broad peaks.

Payroll example.   Table 4-7 shows the distribution of string lengths for a 5000-name payroll listing [Brooks, 1956]. The first name and surname are listed in full, one middle initial is given with no period, and the separating blanks are included in the count: for example, HELGA F THORVALDSDO(TTIR). This table is artificially cut off at 19—the names were forced to fit 19 characters throughout the payroll file. The proportion exceeding 19, and hence requiring abbreviation, is less than 1 percent. First names average about six letters. The distribution of Table 4-7 has the usual flat top.

The length variability inherent in the data means that no fixed-length character string can be used efficiently for names. For street addresses, error messages, running text, and so on, the situation is even worse. If one were designing a machine in the *four* format system, for example, and wanted a fixed string length, one might pick 16 characters, but one would surely need

Length	Percentage
8	.08
9	.37
10	1.81
11	4.04
12	7.83
13	12.94
14	16.98
15	18.54
16	15.40
17	11.28
18	7.16
≥ 19	3.57
Total	100.00

Average length is 14.6.

Given name, blank, initial, blank, surname.

TABLE 4-7   Distribution of lengths of names.

concatenation and multiword operations. If one has to have these operations anyway, perhaps eight characters (64 bits) would not be so bad a length—but then most fields would require multiple words, and padding with special blanks.

Fixed-Length Format

The first computer to provide a character-handling capability was the Univac I. It has fixed words of 12 characters each. The IBM 650 (1954; a Univac-philosophy machine) and its successors have fixed words of five characters, which is much too small.

Variable-Length Format

The second important business data-processing computer after the Univac I was the 702, which introduced variable-length character strings. This machine's family, the IBM 705 (1956) and its successors, was highly successful for commercial applications, and variable-length character strings became standard. The IBM 1401 (1960) and similar machines, such as the Honeywell 200 (1964), made this technique standard for small business computers as well. It is the preferable technique.

Char	Char	Char	Char	Char		Char

```
0     1     2     3     4                m
Legend:  Char = character;  m = no maximum.              ⍵ 4 16 ρbcd705
                                                     a  -&
 data705                                             1/JA
 ⍝ IBM 705 data representation                       2SKB
 ⍝ character encoding                                3TLC
 charcode←bcd705                                     4UMD
 ⍝ sign encoding                                     5VNE
 plus←3                                              6WOF
 minus←2                                             7XPG
 ⍝ byte allocation                                   8YQH   Legend:
 Zone←0+ι2                                            9ZRI   a = register mark
 Num←2+ι4                                             0rmp   g = group mark
 ⍝ data delimiter                                    #,$.   m = minus zero
 ⍝  - in register                                    @%*◊   p = plus zero
 regmark←'a'                                          ○○○○   r = record mark
 ⍝  - in memory                                      ○○○○   t = tape mark
 recordmark←'r'                                       t○○g   ○ = unassigned.
 ⍝ collating sequence
 collate←'  .◊g&$*-/,%#@pABCDEFGHImJKLMNOPQRrSTUVWXYZ0123456789'
```

PROGRAM 4-8   Variable-length character string in the IBM 705.

Programs 4-8 and 4-9 show the variable-length character-string format of the 705 and 360, respectively. Only the encoding set is given, since the general algorithms `alphai` and `alphar` of Program 1-38 apply.

Char	Char	Char	Char		Char

0   1   2   3   m

Legend: Char = character; m = maximum 256; ∘ = unassigned.

```
    data360                                   Q16 16 ρebcdic
  ∩ IBM 360 data representation      ∘∘∘∘ ∧-∘∘∘∘∘∘∘∘∘()
  ∩ character encoding               ∘∘∘∘∘∘/∘aj∘∘AJ∘1
    charcode←ebcdic                  ∘∘∘∘∘∘∘bks∘BKS2
  ∩ floating-point base              ∘∘∘∘∘∘∘∘clt∘CLT3
    base←16                          ∘∘∘∘∘∘∘∘dmu∘DMU4
  ∩ word allocation                  ∘∘∘∘∘∘∘∘env∘ENV5
    Address←8+ι24                    ∘∘∘∘∘∘∘∘fow∘FOW6
    Highbyte←ι8                      ∘∘∘∘∘∘∘∘gpx∘GPX7
    Lowbyte←24+ι8                    ∘∘∘∘∘∘∘∘hqy∘HQY8
  ∩ byte allocation                  ∘∘∘∘∘∘∘∘irz∘IRZ9
    Zone←ι4                          ∘∘∘∘¢!∘:∘∘∘∘∘∘∘∘
    Num←4+ι4                         ∘∘∘∘.$,#∘∘∘∘∘∘∘∘
                                     ∘∘∘∘<*%@∘∘∘∘∘∘∘∘
                                     ∘∘∘∘()'`∘∘∘∘∘∘∘∘
                                     ∘∘∘∘+;>=∘∘∘∘∘∘∘∘
                                     ∘∘∘∘|~?"∘∘∘∘∘∘∘∘
```

PROGRAM 4-9   Variable-length character string in the IBM System/360.

4.1.2

Character Choice

The most difficult choice in designing a computer character-string datatype is the selection of what characters to include in the character set.

Character classes.   Characters are either graphics or controls. *Graphics* are characters printed or displayed to the user; *controls* are characters sent in the data stream to control the process of communication and display, such as line feed, carriage return, and retransmit. Trees 4-10 and 4-11 show how the characters regularly used in computers can be organized into classes.

There are many coherent specialized classes of symbols, such as the mathematical, chemical, and biological. The number of distinct characters in each special class is usually limited, such as 26 for the English alphabet, 35 for the Cyrillic, 24 for the Greek, 23 for the Hebrew, and 28 for the Arabic.

The character sets in common use have been reflected in I/O devices such as terminals and printers. The sets and set-sizes of such devices have in turn constrained the evolution of character sets, and even of computer languages.

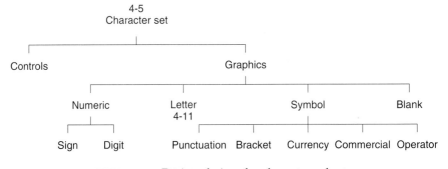

TREE 4-10   Design choices for character subsets.

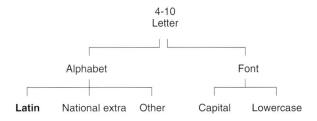

TREE 4-11   Design choices for letter subsets.

FORTRAN, for example, was constrained in case and symbol richness by the 48-character size of the BCD set. APL insisted on a rich character set in spite of the equipment limitations, but even here subscripts and superscripts were eliminated from the original language in going to the interactive version, which had to be handled on terminals.

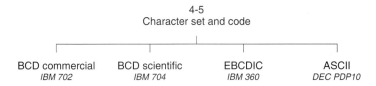

TREE 4-12   Design choices for character set and code.

BCD character set.   Early IBM computers used an existing punched-card printer mechanism, the IBM 407 tabulator. The print wheels of this printer rigidly limited the number of characters to 48 including blank.

Table 4-13 shows the *binary-coded-decimal* (BCD) character set of the 701 and 702 series. The name BCD reflects the encoding of the decimal part of the card code with a 4-bit binary code to form a 6-bit character code.

The character set contains only capital letters. The lowercase letters, as used by the Telex, would, in fact, have been more legible. Punched-card custom, however, made this option appear unacceptable for commercial applications.

Class	Graphics	t	c
Blank		1	1
Letters			
Capital	ABCDEFGHIJKLMNOPQRSTUVWXYZ	26	27
Digits	0123456789	10	37
Symbols			
Punctuation	. ◇ -	3	40
Commercial	& ☐ * / % # @	7	47
Currency	$	1	48

Legend: c = cumulative total; t = total per class.

TABLE 4-13   BCD 48-character set.

FORTRAN	Commercial	Card code	6-bit code	Bit pattern
=	#	8-3	0-11	001011
'	@	8-4	0-12	001100
(	%	0-8-4	1-12	011100
+	&	12	3-0	110000
)	◇	12-8-4	3-12	111100

TABLE 4-14   FORTRAN substitutions in BCD code.

Dual characters.   Backus and colleagues [1957], in developing FORTRAN, needed some symbols not available in BCD. They resolved to require only five such graphics: = ' (+). Because the 704 printer was limited to 48 characters plus blank, these new characters had to displace five other graphics. So a separate character set was adopted, substituting = ' (+) for # @ % & ◇ (Table 4-14).

Unfortunately, these substitute symbols were assigned the *same* codes as those they replaced, rather than five of the 16 unused 6-bit codes. The goal was for the keyboard, punch, and printing mechanisms to work without alteration. These encodings are called *duals*, because they are dually interpreted. One of these bit patterns stands sometimes for one character, sometimes for the other.

ASCII character set.   The American Standards Association, the European Computer Manufacturers Association, and the International Organization for Standardization (ISO) developed a code for information interchange that contains 95 graphics (including the blank) and 33 controls—128 characters, which can be directly encoded with 7 bits. Although the code should be formally known as the American version of the ISO code, it is commonly known as ASCII (American Standard Code for Information Interchange). Table

Class	Graphics	t	c
Blank		1	1
Letters			
Capital	ABCDEFGHIJKLMNOPQRSTUVWXYZ	26	27
Lower case	abcdefghijklmnopqrstuvwxyz	26	53
Digits	0123456789	10	63
Symbols			
Punctuation	. , : ; ! ? - ' " ·	10	73
Accents	`	1	74
Brackets	( ) [ ] { ~	6	80
Commercial	& * \ / % # @	7	87
Currency	$	1	88
Operators			
Logical	~ ∧ }	3	91
Relational	< = >	3	94
Arithmetic	+	1	95
Controls		33	128

Legend: c = cumulative total; t = total per class.

TABLE 4-15   ASCII character set.

4-15 shows the characters of this code [American National Standards Institute, 1968]. It is the code in widest use today.

EBCDIC character set. Because IBM was the first manufacturer to adopt the 8-bit byte, it had to develop an enlarged character code before the ASCII standard was developed. Customer horror at mass conversion of existing files argued strongly for an evolutionary step from BCD, which in turn descended from the Hollerith code for punched cards. The result was the Extended Binary Coded Decimal Interchange Code (EBCDIC).

The major decision in the design of the EBCDIC was to extend BCD, rather than to design an entirely new code. Data showed users to be holding at the very least 5 billion card images in BCD form, so in designing the 360 we decided that the new code should be easily translatable into BCD and Hollerith, and vice versa.

It is difficult to depict the real architectural process in a book such as this; the evolution of any major part of an architecture's design would take too much space. The EBCDIC design process is clear, typically complex, and describable in relatively short space. So we shall detail it here as our only real example of how the architectural process progresses—a mixture of evolution and design, of building from first principles and accepting very transitory technological constraints. For those wanting to compare this process with other similar ones, MacKenzie and others have documented the ASCII deliberations [MacKenzie, 1980], and Buchholz [1962, Chapter 6] has documented the design of the set for the Stretch.

The EBCDIC design consists essentially of four decisions: the desiderata and constraints, the size of the character set, the selection of the characters, and the assignments of encodings.

Desiderata and constraints. The principal desiderata and constraints established for the EBCDIC design follow:

1. The code was to be an extension of BCD, compatible except as in desideratum 2.
2. There were to be no duals—that is, the BCD duals had to be "unwound," and separate codes assigned for these graphics. The character set had to include at least 53 characters.
3. The character set was to be suitable for interchange. It had to fit all then-existing media and devices, including tape, disks, cards, printers, typewriters, and keypunches. These realization constraints were:
   - The typewriter allowed 88 characters plus blank (b).
   - The IBM bar printer allowed $52 + b$ or $64 + b$.
   - The IBM chain printer allowed $(240 \div n) + b$. The chain was 240 characters long. One could have an integral number n of repeats, or indeed a fractional number at some higher cost.
   - The keypunch's interpreting printer had a decoding mechanism that could be moved nine steps in one direction and seven in the other. It could interpret $(9 \times 7 = 63) + b$
   - Although blank did not need to occupy a spot on printer chains and bars since it could be printed by suppressing hammer firing, it occupied a code point.

4. The primary character set was to be representable in 6 bits, but 8-bit versions had to include the lowercase alphabet, distinguished by only one bit from the uppercase alphabet.
5. The character set was to be universal across Latin-alphabet natural languages. The alphabets had to include 29 letters, to accommodate the German, French, and the Scandinavian languages. (A whole separate language-by-language story shows why 29 is a suitable number for many European languages.)
6. The character set was to include the punctuation marks needed by natural language. These were operationally defined by the character set of a "correspondence" typewriter. This requirement meant adding to the unwound BCD the characters : ; ? " ! and, ideally, ¢.
7. The designers of the programming language PL/I wanted the FOR-TRAN operators and delimiters, plus the logical operators & | ˜ , the relational operators < > , and the brackets [ ].

Size of the printer subset of EBCDIC.   Considering these constraints and desiderata, the size z of the EBCDIC printer's uppercase subset becomes a mathematical exercise:

1. The upper limit for z, including blank, is 2^6, or 64.
2. The characters of z plus the 29 lowercase alphabetics had to be representable on the $88 + b$ characters of the typewriter. Hence, $z \le 89 - 29$, which reduces the maximum to 60.
3. The lower limit of z derives from the 48 of BCD plus 5 to unwind the duals; it is 53.
4. A 240-character chain printer could not accommodate five iterations of 53 characters each, but if restricted to four iterations, each could have 60 characters. With blank, it could give 61 characters, which is greater than the maximum of 60 for the typewriter's one-case subset. Therefore, $z = 60$ (including blank) was the best size.

Selection of graphics.   Consider the 70 candidates for the 60-character subset shown in Table 4-16. Clearly, something had to give.

Source	Graphics	t	c
Blank		1	1
Capital letters	ABCDEFGHIJKLMNOPQRSTUVWXYZ	26	27
Digits	0123456789	10	37
Symbols			
BCD - no dispute	. , - * /	5	42
BCD - commercial duals	# @ % & ◇	5	47
BCD - Fortran duals	= ' (+)	5	52
BCD - USA only	$	1	53
Correspondence	: ; ! ? - " ¢	7	60
PL/I	∧ ∨ ˜ < > [ ]	7	67
National use	three graphics	3	70

Legend: c = cumulative total; t = total per class.

TABLE 4-16   Candidates for inclusion in EBCDIC.

The steps taken to select a set of 60 graphics were as follows:

1. □ was discarded completely because it was used rarely, according to a customer survey.
2. & was made to serve both as the PL/I symbol for AND, and as a commercial character.
3. $ was dedicated as one of the three uppercase national-alphabet characters, to be replaced by other currency symbols (for example, the British pound symbol) as required. The Latin-alphabet languages needing larger alphabets fortunately do not use unique currency symbols. Notice that the national-alphabet symbols are duals (even multiples) by definition.
4. @ and #, whose usage is mainly in the United States, were dedicated as uppercase national-alphabet characters, along with $.
5. " ¢ ! were made lowercase national-alphabet characters, thereby getting them onto the typewriter but not onto the 60-character printer. These three plus the 59 uppercase characters were put on the 63 + b keypunch. This left one remaining code that could be printed on the keypunch; it was represented on the card by 0-2-8. This code was *specifically forbidden* to have a graphic, because that would violate typewriter and printer representability.
6. PL/I was forced to give up two graphics. The language designers chose to give up [ ]. This was a bad mistake—as delimiters, brackets are much

Class	Graphics	Subset p	k	t
Blank		1	1	1
Letters				
Capital	ABCDEFGHIJKLMNOPQRSTUVWXYZ	26	26	26
Lower case	abcdefghijklmnopqrstuvwxyz			26
Digits	0123456789	10	10	10
Symbols				
Punctuation	. , : ; ? - ' '	8	8	8
Brackets	( )	2	2	2
Commercial	& * / %	4	4	4
National use letters				
Capital	# @ $ (USA)	3	3	3
Lower case	! " ¢ (USA)		3	3
Operators				
Logical	~ |	2	2	2
Relational	< = >	3	3	3
Arithmetic	+	1	1	1
Subset total		60	63	89
Controls				64
Spares				103
Total				256

Legend: k = keyboard; p = printer; t = typewriter.

TABLE 4-17   EBCDIC character set.

more powerful than are operators in making a language easy to write, read, and parse. It would have been better to give up $< >$. (Even after the character set was frozen, the language designers could have used $< >$ as brackets rather than as operators. They chose not to; a bad decision, we believe.) The sets that resulted are shown in Table 4-17. Given the 60-character subset and the 63-character subset, the 89-character full set just adds the 26 lowercase letters.

4.1.3

Character Encoding

The character encoding is influenced by history as much as is the character choice.

Hollerith card code. For electrical reasons, in 1890 Hollerith used a 1-out-of-10 code employing 10 separate rows for the decimal digits. Two rows were used for control. This code was later extended to alphabetics by adding two hole positions to each column. Card rows 12, 11, and 0 were used as overpunches, each identifying a third of the alphabet, and rows 1 through 9 were used to distinguish letters.

In the 1920s a variety of punctuation and special symbols became necessary. The first three were satisfied by the 12-blank (&), 11-blank (-), and the now-usable 0-1 (/) combinations. Later needs were met by triple punching, rather dictated by the implementations of the IBM 402 and 407 tabulators. The triple punching uses a zone row plus 8-3 (for 11) and 8-4 (for 12). So the Hollerith code ended up with 48 characters including the blank, as shown in Figure 4-18.

BCD code. The designers of the 702 wanted a 6-bit version of the Hollerith code, one for which translations to 12-bit Hollerith would be very simple. They divided the 6-bit code into a 2-bit encoding of the zone rows (12, 11, 0

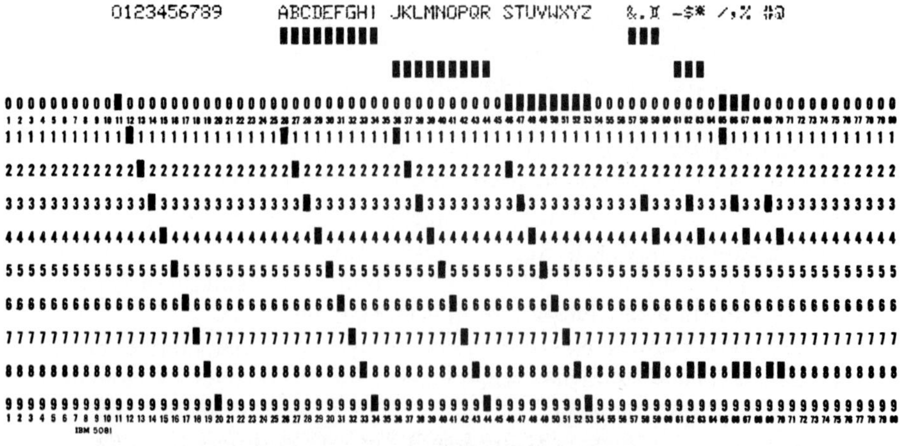

FIGURE 4-18 48-Character Hollerith card code.

```
tape←tbcd card;zone;num                    cardtape
ⱥ from hollerith to bcd                    ⱥ card column allocation
zone←+/card[Cardzone]× 3 2 1               Cardzone←0+ι3
num←+/card[Cardnum]×1+ι9                   Cardnum←3+ι9
→If(zone=1)∧num=0                          ⱥ tape byte allocation
THEN:zone←0                                bytesize←6
    num←10                                 Tapezone←0+ι2
ENDIF:tape←bytesizeρ0                      Tapenum←2+ι4
tape[Tapezone]←2 magnr zone
tape[Tapenum]←4 magnr num
```

PROGRAM 4-19   Code translation from Hollerith to BCD.

and blank) and a 4-bit encoding of the numeric rows (0, ..., 9, 8-3, 8-4). The numeric values, thought of as 0, ..., 9, 11, 12, were directly encoded in radix 2.

Program 4-19 gives the APL algorithms, and Table 4-20 shows the BCD code and the corresponding card code. Note the anomalous coding of zero.

Numeric	Zone bits 0 1			Numeric		Zone rows		
bits 2345	00	01	10	11	rows	b	0	11	12
0000		∘	-	+	b		0	-	+
0001	1	/	J	A	1	1	/	J	A
0010	2	S	K	B	2	2	S	K	B
0011	3	T	L	C	3	3	T	L	C
0100	4	U	M	D	4	4	U	M	D
0101	5	V	N	E	5	5	V	N	E
0110	6	W	O	F	6	6	W	O	F
0111	7	X	P	G	7	7	X	P	G
1000	8	Y	Q	H	8	8	Y	Q	H
1001	9	Z	R	I	9	9	Z	R	I
1010	0	∘	∘	∘	8-2	∘	∘	∘	∘
1011	=	,	$	.	8-3	=	,	$	.
1100	'	(	*	)	8-4	'	(	*	)

BCD 6-bit code   Hollerith card code
Legend: ∘ = unassigned; b = blank card row.

TABLE 4-20   Codes for 48-character set (FORTRAN set).

EBCDIC code.   Two additional requirements on the encoding itself were that:

- The collating sequence had to be acceptable when ordinary binary comparison is done; in particular, numerals had to fall after letters and other characters before letters, as in BCD.
- The characters had to be allocable to *sticks* (columns in the code table), so that expansion from 6- to 7- or 8-bit codes would be straightforward and without pitfalls. In particular, the 7- and 8-bit codes had to have whole sticks allocable to communication control characters.

The result is shown in Table 4-21 and in the card code of Table 4-22.

The first two bits divide the code table into four sticks. If these bits are elided and the second and fourth sticks overlaid, the result is a 6-bit code as compatible with BCD as the unwinding of duals will allow.

In the 8-bit version, the extra bits allow the special characters to be pulled out, so that *all* special characters collate below the alphabetics. No longer does / fall between R and S in the collating sequence, as it did in BCD!

Furthermore, the lowercase alphabet (third stick) differs from the uppercase alphabet in only one bit, as desired. The same unfortunately does not

Numeric bits 4567	Zone bits 0123															
	00 00	00 01	00 10	00 11	01 00	01 01	01 10	01 11	10 00	10 01	10 10	10 11	11 00	11 01	11 10	11 11
0000	∘	∘	∘	∘		&	-	∘	∘	∘	∘	∘	∘	∘	∘	0
0001	∘	∘	∘	∘	∘	∘	/	∘	a	j	∘	∘	A	J	∘	1
0010	∘	∘	∘	∘	∘	∘	∘	∘	b	k	s	∘	B	K	S	2
0011	∘	∘	∘	∘	∘	∘	∘	∘	c	l	t	∘	C	L	T	3
0100	∘	∘	∘	∘	∘	∘	∘	∘	d	m	u	∘	D	M	U	4
0101	∘	∘	∘	∘	∘	∘	∘	∘	e	n	v	∘	E	N	V	5
0110	∘	∘	∘	∘	∘	∘	∘	∘	f	o	w	∘	F	O	W	6
0111	∘	∘	∘	∘	∘	∘	∘	∘	g	p	x	∘	G	P	X	7
1000	∘	∘	∘	∘	∘	∘	∘	∘	h	q	y	∘	H	Q	Y	8
1001	∘	∘	∘	∘	∘	∘	∘	∘	i	r	z	∘	I	R	Z	9
1010	∘	∘	∘	∘	¢	!	∘	:	∘	∘	∘	∘	∘	∘	∘	∘
1011	∘	∘	∘	∘	.	$	,	#	∘	∘	∘	∘	∘	∘	∘	∘
1100	∘	∘	∘	∘	<	*	%	@	∘	∘	∘	∘	∘	∘	∘	∘
1101	∘	∘	∘	∘	(	)	˙	'	∘	∘	∘	∘	∘	∘	∘	∘
1110	∘	∘	∘	∘	+	;	>	=	∘	∘	∘	∘	∘	∘	∘	∘
1111	∘	∘	∘	∘	|	˜	?	"	∘	∘	∘	∘	∘	∘	∘	∘

Legend: ∘ = unassigned or control.

TABLE 4-21   EBCDIC code.

hold true for the three national-alphabet characters, which are encoded in the stick with the special characters.

The first stick is used exclusively for communication control characters, which enables them to be recognized simply.

Numeric rows	Zone rows			
	b	0	11	12
b	0	-	&	
1	1	/	J	A
2	2	S	K	B
3	3	T	L	C
4	4	U	M	D
5	5	V	N	E
6	6	W	O	F
7	7	X	P	G
8	8	Y	Q	H
9	9	Z	R	I
8-2	:	∘	!	¢
8-3	#	,	$	.
8-4	@	%	*	<
8-5	'	˙	)	(
8-6	=	>	;	+
8-7	"	?	˜	|

Legend: ∘ = unassigned;
b = blank row.

TABLE 4-22   EBCDIC card code.

ASCII code.   The designers of ASCII made the opposite decision—to scrap BCD and start over from first principles. (For reasons of commercial rivalry, they were determined *not* to be compatible with BCD.) Among things scrapped was the division of the 6-bit code into two zone bits and four numeric bits. Since card users, and BCD users, often use the zone and numeric fields of a

Numeric bits 3456	000	001	010	011	100	101	110	111
			Zone bits 0 1 2					
0000	∘	∘		0	@	P	'	p
0001	∘	∘	!	1	A	Q	a	q
0010	∘	∘	"	2	B	R	b	r
0011	∘	∘	⧣	3	C	S	c	s
0100	∘	∘	$	4	D	T	d	t
0101	∘	∘	%	5	E	U	e	u
0110	∘	∘	&	6	F	V	f	v
0111	∘	∘	'	7	G	W	g	w
1000	∘	∘	(	8	H	X	h	x
1001	∘	∘	)	9	I	Y	i	y
1010	∘	∘	*	:	J	Z	j	z
1011	∘	∘	+	;	K	[	k	{
1100	∘	∘	,	<	L	\	l	}
1101	∘	∘	-	=	M	]	m	˜
1110	∘	∘	.	>	N	∧	n	˜
1111	∘	∘	/	?	O	˙	o	∘

Legend: ∘ = unassigned or control.

TABLE 4-23   ASCII code.

single column to represent independent data, *there is not* and *never can be* a hardware device or program capable of translating BCD or EBCDIC to ASCII without column-by-column specification of how the code is to be interpreted. That is, a context-free translation is impossible. For example, N is encoded as 10 0101 in BCD. But, when a 10 0101 is encountered, is it to be translated into ASCII as N (100 1110) or as ASCII 5 (011 0101) combined with a separate overpunch?

The ASCII decision to scrap BCD compatibility is apparent from the code chart of Figure 4-23. The alphabets occupy two columns each, and all 16 code points of the column are used. Also, the collating sequence of the alphabetics versus the digits is reversed with respect to BCD, a second notable break with the past. Neither order is inherently better.

4.1.4

Character Size

At first glance, the character size is simply the ceiling of the logarithm of the size n of the character set, or $\lceil 2 \circledast n$ in APL notation. One wants sizes commensurate with other formats, however, so no one has built a machine with, for example, 7-bit characters.

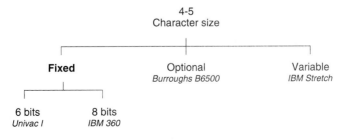

TREE 4-24   Design choices for character size.

Variable Character Size

Although methods for encoding characters with a length that depends on their characters' frequency of use are well-known [Huffman, 1952], and although such encodings may give noticeable improvement of bit efficiency, they are not used in the machine representation. It is too awkward to change memory allocation when one changes a variable's value from one 8-character string to another. In computers, character size is varied only for *all* the characters in a string, together.

Multiple character sets.   When variable character size is provided in a computer, the purpose is to accommodate a variety of character sets and encodings, each with its own character size—for example, decimal digits and alphanumeric characters. Such flexibility is particularly desirable in a period of transition from one character size to another, as from the 6-bit BCD to 7-bit ASCII or 8-bit EBCDIC.

The variable character size—called *variable byte size*—of the Stretch is an early manifestation of such a transition to a larger character size. The optional choice of 6 or 8 bits of the Burroughs B6500 (1968), however, is more easily justified than the full range from 1 to 8 bits in the Stretch or the Burroughs B1700 (1972).

Fixed Character Size

Six-bit characters.   Early computers with printer-limited character sets—such as the BCD set—needed no more than a 6-bit character size. Even the 650, whose code could accommodate a set of 100, could print only the 48 BCD characters.

As the desire for the lowercase alphabet grew, either a dramatic shift in character size was required or escape characters had to be employed.

Escape characters.   *Escape characters* are of two basic kinds: a *stable shift*, in which a mode or state variable is changed and stays changed until another case-shift character is encountered, and a *bouncing shift*, in which only the immediately succeeding character is interpreted from the alternate case. Many older teletypewriters used the stable shift (Table 4-25).

A basic disadvantage of the stable shift is that the mode must be known for the characters to be interpreted: The interpretation is not context-free. Furthermore, for both shifts the field length is context-dependent, which makes memory allocation and field addressing difficult [Brooks and Sweeney, 1957].

Seven-bit characters.   For both lower- and uppercase alphabets, 7 bits is the ideal; the ASCII code adopted this size. However, no machine has used a 7-bit character size exclusively.

Eight-bit characters.   Because we believed that text processing would be an application of steadily growing importance, we chose for the 360 what would give easy accommodation of the lowercase alphabet: the *four* format system and 8-bit characters [Amdahl et al., 1964]. Nearly all subsequent designs incorporate the same decision.

Code	Letters	Digits/symbols
11000	a	-
10011	b	?
01110	c	:
10010	d	who are you
10000	e	3
10110	f	national use
01011	g	national use
00101	h	national use
01100	i	8
11010	j	bell
11110	k	(
01001	l	)
00111	m	.
00110	n	,
00011	o	9
01101	p	0
11101	q	1
01010	r	4
10100	s	'
00001	t	5
11100	u	7
01111	v	=
11001	w	2
10111	x	/
10101	y	6
10001	z	+
00010	new line	new line
01000	line feed	line feed
11111		to letters
11011	to digits	
00100	blank	blank
00000	national use	national use

TABLE 4-25   Five-bit Teletype code.

Larger character size.   What will be the demand for yet larger character size? Is character-set size like memory size, growing continually with time as computers are used? Probably not. The absence of the lowercase alphabet seems to have been the only substantial artificial limitation on character sets designed into early computers, and providing it will probably suffice for general purpose computers forever. The stability of the 88-character set for typewriters is a comforting precedent here.

Scientific computing, and hence programming languages, would benefit from provision of full superscript and subscript fonts, but the chief limiting factor is printer design. The case-shift technique can handle the internal representation awkwardly but quite usably.

Yet, certain special applications require more. They usually require much, much more. Printing and publishing, for example, require large fonts, typically 200 characters each, and many sizes and shapes of such fonts. Font change is an ideal application for escape characters, and an 8-bit character suffices for representing the several members within each font.

Japanese and other languages with very large alphabets constitute a special case. Fortunately, 16 bits seem to suffice for Kanji, so computer architects can accommodate such languages by making sure pairs of 8-bit characters can be

handled gracefully, and that comparisons of character strings work properly when characters are paired (a concern that urges Big-Endian allocation).

Our own view is that 8 bits is large enough for the high-frequency byte sets, not only for now, but also for the foreseeable future, and that larger character sizes are wasteful. Provision must be made for two-byte encoding of oriental ideographs.

4.1.5
Character-String Allocation

In a byte-addressed computer, it is natural to allocate a character string to memory from left to right—the leftmost byte in the string gets the lowest address. In word-addressed computers, character allocation becomes a design decision between the Big Endian convention and the Little Endian convention. The two conventions are treated fully in Section 2.3.

4.1.6
Bibliography

Amdahl et al. [1964], Backus et al. [1957], Brooks [1956], Brooks and Sweeney [1957], Buchholz [1962], Huffman [1952], MacKenzie [1980], Zemanek [1965].

4.2
Logical Data

Logical data are most often used in decision making about character strings or numbers. They are rarely entered as such into a system, nor finally put out by the system, but are used chiefly for program housekeeping.

A logical or *Boolean* datum has two possible states, designated as *true* and *false*. It can be represented by a single bit, and it is the simplest datatype.

The proper operations for logical data include the Boolean functions of one and of two variables. Also, logical data result from the relational operations—the comparisons—even though their operands are character strings or numbers.

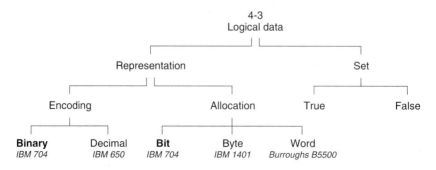

TREE 4-26   Design choices for logical data.

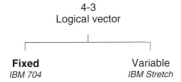

TREE 4-27   Design choices for logical data structures.

Structure.   Because the datatype is so simple, and because machines are principally designed to work with the larger representations required for characters and numbers, logical data are usually aggregated into vectors. Such higher-order structures are treated generally in Section 4.5. The logical vector, however, is so common that it is treated here with the logical element.

Trees 4-26 and 4-27 give the design choices for logical data; Table 4-28 gives the solutions found in various machines.

	Encoding True	False	Allocation	Vector size
Cambridge EDSAC	1	0	bit	17 35
Ferranti Mark 1	1	0	bit	40
IBM 701	1	0	bit	36
IBM 650	9	8	digit	d
IBM 704	1	0	bit	36
Univac 1103A	1	0	bit	36
Librascope LGP30	1	0	bit	31
Bull Gamma 60	1	0	bit	24
IBM Stretch	1	0	bit	1-64
CDC 6600	1	0	bit	60
CDC 6600 PPU	1	0	bit	6 12 18
Burroughs B5500	1	0	word bit	1 47
IBM System/360	1	0	bit	32 8-2048
DEC PDP8	1	0	bit	12
DEC PDP11	1	0	bit	8 16
Burroughs B1700	1	0	bit	1-24
Intel 8080A	1	0	bit	8
Cray 1	1	0	bit	64×64 64
Motorola M6800	1	0	bit	8
MOS 6502	1	0	bit	8
DEC VAX11	1	0	bit	8 16 32
Motorola MC68000	1	0	bit	8 16 32
IBM 6150	1	0	bit	16 32

Legend: d = decision only; - = through.

TABLE 4-28   Logical data in various machines.

4.2.1

Single Element

The need for a single logical variable is most obvious in decision making. Control structures, such as If-Then-Else, test an expression that reduces to a single Boolean variable.

Encoding

It seems obvious to represent *true* by 1 and *false* by 0, following the conventions of Boolean algebra. To do so remains, however, a design decision. Many names in this section and in Section 5.2, such as *all-ones count* instead of *all-trues count*, reflect this tacit decision. It is also assumed in the basic algorithm of Program 4-29.

```
vector←logici rep        rep←logicr vector
  ⌐ logical interpretation  ⌐ logical representation
vector←rep               rep←vector
```

PROGRAM 4-29   Basic logical interpretation and representation.

A machine that has not the bit, but a character or decimal digit as elementary unit of representation, needs a more deliberate design decision. In the 650, for example, a decimal digit value of 8 represents *true*, 9 represents *false*, and any other digit value is invalid in decision making.

Allocation

The allocation of a simple logical datum is trivial only when address resolution is to the bit; then, it need occupy only one bit. For coarser address resolution—the more common case—the designer is embarrassed by his riches. He must either select one bit out of a byte or word and waste the other bits, or extend his datatype to a vector. The latter option is usually taken.

The B5500 uses 1 of the 48 data bits in a word for decision making. In logical operations, however, 47 bits are used as a logical vector. The 360 tests the leftmost bit of an 8-bit byte in its Test And Set operation (Section 7.5), but it then sets all bits of this byte to one. The Stretch uses its bit addressing in decision making; otherwise, logic applies to vectors.

In the 1401, each character has an extra bit, the *word mark*, which serves dually as a logical variable and as the delimiter for a character string or number. The zone bits of the characters also serve as logical variables. There are no logical operations, so there is no logical datatype.

Flags.   The 1401 is an illustration of the combination of characters and numbers with logical information. The programmer may use this logical information to indicate the use of the data. Information bits of this type are generally called *flags*. Flags should be distinguished from *tags*, discussed in Section 2.3, which define the data to the computer and alter the interpretation accordingly.

In many applications there are two layers of data—one describing structure and one describing values. Figure 4-30 shows as an example a cross-section of a cylindrical nuclear power reactor. Some data describe the cross-section's shape; others, the value of physical entities.

In calculating neutron diffusion, heat flow, and so on, one must consider the geometry and, depending upon the region, choose data values (for example, for conductivity, neutron cross-section) corresponding to the appropriate material. Since this geometry is complex, it is not easily embodied in tests on bounds of index registers.

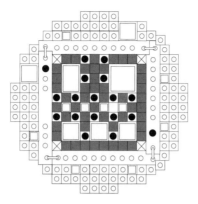

FIGURE 4-30   Cross-section of a cylindrical nuclear reactor.

Similarly, in business applications one has character strings, numbers, and several 1-bit indicators that some exceptional characteristic is present. Some computer designs, therefore, have included data flags, usually with special means for the flags to be used in controlling logic.

The Stretch may have been the first machine to embody a data flag [Buchholz, 1962]. Each fixed- and floating-point number contains up to 3 independent flag bits. Whenever a word in which a flag is set is fetched, a corresponding interrupt indicator, unique for each flag, is turned on.

Flags violate orthogonality by linking data handling or arithmetic with logic. As a result, bit efficiency suffers, since all data have flags, whether or not those flags are needed. Furthermore, it is not clear how the flags of a result should be set. Should one AND or OR the flags of the operands? How are flags to be set or reset? A separate bit map manipulated by logical operations is a cleaner solution by far.

4.2.2

Logical Vectors

In most applications, the logical data are represented by a vector, not by a string—the elements are independent of one another and could be reordered without a change of significance, if addresses referring to them were correspondingly changed.

Vector Size

One cannot look to application studies for design guidance on vector size. They yield little or no machine-independent data on bit-vector lengths. Design of bit-vector facilities must therefore be done by extrapolation from other architectural decisions.

Length.   Logical data are sometimes used as a bit map to represent a characteristic of the elements of a data array—for example, zero versus non-zero. Then, the size of the logical data is derived from the size of the array. Bit vectors of hundreds of elements would be desirable.

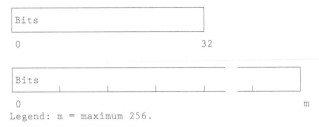

Legend: m = maximum 256.

PROGRAM 4-31   Logical vectors in the IBM System/360.

The secondary nature of logical data allows the architect to use formats that match the formats for character strings and numbers. In the 360 the formats for logical data are derived from the full-word integer format and from the variable-length character-string format. The first format gives a 32-element logical vector; the second gives an $n \times 8$ logical matrix, with $n \leq 256$ (Program 4-31).

4.2.3
Bibliography

Buchholz [1962], Sangren [1960].

4.3
Fixed-Point Numbers

Mathematics develops in succession the cardinal numbers, the integers, the rational numbers, the real numbers, and the complex numbers; each of these classes includes the preceding ones. Even the lowest class—that of the cardinal numbers—is too ambitious for a computer: The set has an unlimited range, which a machine just cannot represent. What *can* be represented is a subset of the rational numbers.

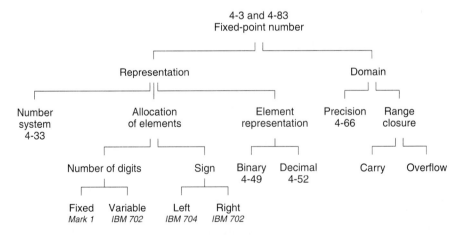

TREE 4-32   Design choices for fixed-point number.

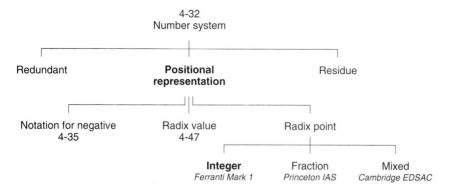

TREE 4-33   Design choices for number systems.

Programming languages usually recognize this limitation by offering "integers" and "real numbers." Both terms are misnomers; they stand for numbers that have fixed-point and floating-point representations. So we use the terms *fixed-point numbers* and *floating-point numbers*.

The selection of a number representation depends upon the range of the numbers and the amount of calculation to which they are subject. Range influences the choice between fixed point and floating point; amount of calculation influences the choice of radix between binary and decimal.

The representation of fixed-point numbers (Tree 4-32) involves several levels of encoding and allocation. The first encoding decision is that of the number system (Tree 4-33). The normal solution is to use positional representation, which expresses a positive number in terms of digits using an implied radix. A further encoding decision concerns the representation of negative numbers. With these encoding decisions goes an allocation decision. What is the order of the digits, and where is the sign placed?

A second level of representation decisions concerns the encoding of digits and the sign in terms of bits and the allocation of these bits in the available space. Tree 4-32 shows these design choices, as they are considered in this section.

4.3.1

Number Systems

Positional representation.   Computers represent positive integers in fixed point in the same way that those integers are represented in writing—that is, by the use of positional representation:

$$n = \sum a[i] \times r^i$$

where r is the radix, each $a[i]$ is a digit drawn from the set 0, 1 ... $r - 1$, and i is the positional index.

In APL, the Base Value (Decode) operator $\perp$ expresses this polynomial interpretation as used in `magni`, Program 1-31, the basic algorithm for positional interpretation of positive integers.

Conversely, the APL Representation (Encode) operator $\top$ expresses the derivation, by successive division, of the vector of digits from a given value and a vector of radices. This is the basic algorithm for positional representation. When the radix is constant, the number of digits is given by `size`, as shown in `magnr` (Program 1-31).

Why has positional representation survived as the dominant internal-representation technique in computers? Not merely because of inertia! As we shall see, designers have neither hesitated to use the unfamiliar for radices, negative numbers, and floating point, nor failed to propose unfamiliar number systems in the literature; they would have abandoned positional representation had it been advantageous to do so. But all the peculiar choices that have been used are within the framework of positional representation.

The ancient inventor of zero (and hence of positional representation) wrought well; positional representation has weighty advantages of efficiency over its rivals: With only a few symbols, any number can be represented or closely approximated; addition can be digit by digit and requires only a limited table; the same is true for subtraction and multiplication; comparison can be even faster than addition.

Redundant representations.   Positional representation is non-redundant—every representable value has a unique representation, and vice versa. *Redundant number systems* are rarely used as architectural representations because bit efficiency is an important desideratum for a computer number representation. (This requirement is strongest for memory and auxiliary store.) In implementations, however, numbers are often kept in redundant form. A sum may be preserved internally as a partial sum and a generated carry during a multiplication.

Residue number systems.   Integers can also be efficiently expressed as a vector of residues of a set of relatively prime moduli [Garner, 1959]. Arithmetic operations, including multiplication and division, can be done much faster on such representations than on positional ones, because the residues can be computed independently of each other. Such systems, however, have a crucial disadvantage that has inhibited their use in computers—there is no simple way to tell a positive number from a negative one, or to determine which of two numbers is larger. Svoboda used residue representation in the implementation of his EPOS computers [Oblonsky, 1980]. Program 4-34 gives representation and interpretation for positive integers.

```
number←resi rep;base;modulus;x          rep←n resr number
A positive residue interpretation        A residue representation
base←Φprimeρrep                          rep←(Φprime n)|number
number←0
modulus←1
x←0
REPEAT:number←number+modulus×(base[x]|number+modulus×ιbase[x])ιrep[x]
    modulus←modulus×base[x]
    x←x+1
→UNTIL x=ρrep
```

PROGRAM 4-34   Residue-number-system interpretation and representation

4.3.2

Notation for Negative Numbers

Whereas all computer designs use straightforward positional representation for positive integers, there are four commonly used computer notations for negative numbers, as shown in Tree 4-35:

- Signed magnitude
- Radix complement: 2's complement in binary, 10's complement in decimal
- Digit complement: 1's complement in binary, 9's complement in decimal
- Bias

Table 4-36 illustrates the representation and interpretation for each of these methods in a 3-bit binary machine.

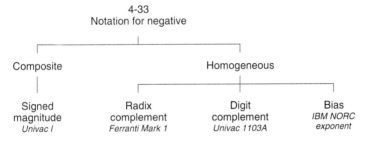

TREE 4-35   Design choices for the notation of negative numbers.

Criteria.   In each notation the sign is explicitly recognizable and can be represented with equal efficiency.

The four methods differ in their satisfaction of other important criteria:

- Uniqueness of *zero*
- *Symmetry* of representation range
- *Homogeneity* of the representation
- Ease of *conversion* to and from the conventional representation
- Ease of *implementation* of arithmetic operations
- Ease of *extended-precision operations*

Representation	Signed magnitude	Radix complement	Digit complement	Bias
000	0	0	0	‾4
001	1	1	1	‾3
010	2	2	2	‾2
011	3	3	3	‾1
100	‾0	‾4	‾3	0
101	‾1	‾3	‾2	1
110	‾2	‾2	‾1	2
111	‾3	‾1	‾0	3

TABLE 4-36   Notations for positive and negative numbers.

Characteristics	Signed magnitude	Radix complement	Digit complement	Bias
Zero	- -	++	- -	++
Symmetry	++	-	++	-
Homogeneity	- -	++	++	+
Conversion	++	-	-	- -
Implementation				
Add/subtract	- -	++	-	+
Multiply	+	+	-	-
Divide	+	-	-	-
Ext. precision	-	++	-	+

Legend: ++ = ideal; + = good; - = fair; -- = poor.

TABLE 4-37   Summary of notation characteristics.

Table 4-37 summarizes the properties of each notation with respect to these criteria.

Signed Magnitude

Signed magnitude is the obvious notation, since it matches the conventional written representation.

Program 4-38 gives the general algorithms for the interpretation and representation of numbers in this notation. Since not all numbers can be represented with a given number of digits—as specified by `size`—a positive excess is indicated by `xmax` and a negative excess by `xmin`. The functions of Program 4-38 apply to numeric scalars and vectors.

Zero. The first problem is zero, since signed-magnitude notation has $+0$ and -0. We consider a single zero definitely preferable, because of propriety. If the notation allows two zeros, as is the case here, then the arithmetic should accept both, but produce only the one with the positive sign. A comparison should recognize $+0$ as equal to -0; a zero test should ignore the sign. If the same format can be used as for logical data, then a logical operation such as a

```
↓Sign
┌─┬─────────────────────────────────┐
│ │Digits                           │
│ │                                 │
└─┴─────────────────────────────────┘

number←signmagni rep;modulus;value
⍝ signed-magnitude interpretation
modulus←radix*(0⌷¯1↑⍴rep)-1
value←radix⊥⍉rep
number← 1 ¯1[(⌊value÷modulus)∊minus]×modulus|value


rep←size signmagnr number;modulus;sign
⍝ signed-magnitude representation
modulus←radix*size-1
sign←((1↑plus),minus)[number<0]
rep←sign,⍉((size-1)⍴radix)⊤|number
⍝ domain signals
xmax←number≥modulus
xmin←number≤-modulus
```

PROGRAM 4-38   Signed-magnitude interpretation and representation.

FIGURE 4-39   Accumulator and MQ register in the IBM 704.

logical shift can produce a negative zero. A test other than the arithmetic sign test should be available to determine the value of the bit used for the sign.

How easy is it for the implementor always to produce a positive sign for a zero result? Harder than one would expect, although a modern machine can and should do it right. In the 704, $0 + (-0)$ gave $+0$; $(-0) + 0$ gave -0 (Section 11.4). In the 650, the designers fixed addition so that it would produce only $+0$, except when adding -0 to -0 (Program 1-41). Multiplication and division could even more easily produce -0 (Section 12.1). The same is true for the 360 decimal arithmetic. Load Complement in the 360 floating point changes the sign even if the number is zero.

Homogeneity.   A second problem is that the datatype is compound, consisting of distinct subparts that are treated differently by operations.

This inhomogeneity enters the architecture when a pair of integers makes one double-length number. The 650 solution is an accumulator with twice the normal number of digits and a single sign. The 704 uses a pair of registers, Acc and MQ, each with its own sign (Figure 4-39). The user must remember when the MQ sign participates and when it does not. Keeping the cases straight is complex because Acc and MQ are also used for logical data, which treat sign and digit positions alike.

The 650 can keep things simple for most cases, since it has only one sign. Division in the 650, however, places a quotient and remainder in the accumulator, each with its own sign. So there proves to be a second sign after all, with a set of rules to tell when it is active (Section 12.1).

So sign and digits each require an encoding decision, and their allocation is non-trivial.

Conversion.   Signed-magnitude notation has the clear advantage that it requires no extra actions in the conversion from and to conventional representation.

Implementation.   If two numbers with unlike signs are to be added, the addend is complemented before addition (Table 4-40). If a carry propagates through the high-order bit of the accumulator, the result has the opposite sign from that of the addend, and it must be *recomplemented*, requiring a second addition cycle. This cycle, however, can sometimes be combined with a subsequent operation.

Multiplication and division are simple. The absolute values are processed and an independent EXCLUSIVE-OR operation is performed on the signs. But, of course, the operands or results should be tested for zero, so as to produce the proper result signs.

Cumulative multiplication—adding a product to a previous result—is complicated, since the sign may change as the partial product is developed,

```
   Manual       Signed magnitude      Radix complement      Digit complement
───────────────────────────────────────────────────────────────────────────────

   125               +0125                 0125                  0125
    37               +0037                 0037                  0037
   ──── +            ──── +                ──── +                ──── +
   162               +0162                 0162                  0162


   125               +0125                 0125                  0125
    37     +0037 → +9962       0037 → 9962          0037 → 9962
   ──── -                 1                   1                  ──── +
    88               ──── +                ──── +                10087
                     +0088                 0088                  └──→1
                                                                 ──── +
                                                                 0088


  ¯125               -0125                 9875                  9874
    37     +0037 → -9962                   0037                  0037
   ──── +                1                 ──── +                ──── +
  ¯ 88               ──── +                9912                  9911
                     -0088


    37               +0037                 0037                  0037
  ¯125     -0125 → +9874                   9875                  9874
   ──── +                1                 ──── +                ──── +
  ¯ 88               ──── +                9912                  9911
                     -0087 ← +9912
                         1
                     ──── +
                     -0088


  ¯125               -0125                 9875                  9874
  ¯ 37               -0037                 9963                  9962
   ──── +            ──── +                ──── +                ──── +
  ¯162               -0162                 9838                  19836
                                                                 └──→1
                                                                 ──── +
                                                                 9837
```

TABLE 4-40   Examples of complementation in various notations.

which would require a recomplementation. According to the manual, the 650 provides cumulative multiplication; actually, it adds the absolute value of the partial sum to the absolute value of the product, with only the sign of the product determining the sign of the result (Section 12.1).

Application. Decimal radix representations usually have signed-magnitude notation to match conventional representation; many large computers provide such decimal datatypes. Microprocessors, however, often include provisions for unsigned decimal, which is equivalent to radix complement. The ease of multiple precision in complement notation—essential for microprocessors—is the compelling argument.

Radix Complement

Negative integers of n digits are represented in this notation by the complement of their magnitude upon $radix^n$. Program 4-41 gives the general interpretation and representation algorithms.

```
Digits
```

```
number←radixcompi rep;modulus;value
ᴀ radix-complement interpretation
modulus←radix*0⊥¯1↑ρrep
value←radix⊥⌽rep
number←value-(value≥modulus÷2)×modulus
```

```
rep←size radixcompr number;modulus
ᴀ radix-complement representation
modulus←radix*size
rep←⌽(sizeρradix)⊤number
ᴀ domain signals
xmax←number≥modulus÷2
xmin←number<-modulus÷2
```

PROGRAM 4-41   Radix-complement interpretation and representation.

Sign.   The sign of a number can be determined from the high-order digit. In binary, 0 indicates positive and 1 negative. In decimal, 0 through 4 can be positive and 5 through 9 negative if one opts for a nearly symmetrical number range (Program 4-41).

Zero.   There is only one zero, and it is represented by an all-zeros vector. The simple sign test interprets zero as positive. The single zero is one of the strong advantages of this notation.

Asymmetry of range.   Signed-magnitude notation can represent the absolute value of each representable negative number. In radix complement, however, there is one number, $-radix^{n-1}$, for which this is not the case. (See ¯4 in Table 4-36.) Any notation with a single zero will necessarily have an asymmetric range.

The asymmetric range manifests itself in a number of exceptions: Complementing a number may result in an overflow, or, if the radix point is considered to be just to the right of the sign digit in binary, multiplication of −1 by −1 results in an overflow.

Although the asymmetric range is at times unpleasant, it is not basically wrong. There are many actions whose results exceed the representable range, and this class is just slightly extended.

Homogeneity.   The datatype is simple, not compound. The high-order digit does, in fact, denote the sign, but it is part of the number and participates fully in arithmetic. In multiple precision, the low-order part can be treated as all-digits, without sign.

Conversion.   Numbers are printed in signed-magnitude notation; they are usually entered into a computer system with that notation. Since the external formats usually differ from internal formats, some conversion is required. When the internal representation uses radix-complement notation, an extra conversion step is always required. This step is not complex, however. It involves a sign test and, in case of minus sign, a complementation, or the equivalent, a subtraction from zero (Program 4-42).

```
sm←rcsm rc
ᴀ architecture: sm←(ρrc)signmagnr radixcompi rc
ᴀ implementation
→IF 1↑rc
THEN: ᴀ negative sign
    sm←1,(ρ1↓rc) magnr 1+magni˜rc
    →ENDIF
ELSE: ᴀ positive sign
    sm←rc
ENDIF:
```

PROGRAM 4-42   Conversion from radix complement to signed magnitude.

Implementation.   Radix complement is the most easily implemented notation. All numbers are simply added as if they were positive integers; the signs take care of themselves. No sign test need be performed to control the precomplementation necessary for subtraction; the subtrahend is always complemented. Recomplementation is never needed.   Indeed, the only complication is the detection of overflow.

Multiplication is also simple, using the algorithm of Booth [1951]. Even in cumulative multiplication, a difference in sign produces no problems.

Division is slightly more complex, owing to the asymmetric notation range; also, the conventional rules for the remainder sign are not convenient for radix complement.

Application.   When the binary radix is chosen, a radix conversion is necessary for a change to input or output format, and the extra complementation required by radix complement is only a minor added action. The good architectural and implementation characteristics then recommend the 2's-complement notation. It is consequently the most popular negative notation.

Digit Complement

Digit-complement notation is similar to radix complement, in that negative numbers are represented by their complement. The modulus, however, is not $radix^n$, but $radix^n - 1$. The formal name for this notation is *radix-minus-one complement*, or *diminished-radix complement*. We prefer *digit complement* as shorter and more descriptive.

Digit complement has the same representation range as signed magnitude. A negative number is represented by separately complementing each digit of the corresponding positive number on $radix - 1$; hence the name *digit complement*. Program 4-43 shows the general interpretation and representation algorithms; the 6600 (Section 14.2) is an example.

Sign and symmetry.   The high-order digit can be used to determine the sign of the number, as for radix complement.

The range of representable numbers is symmetric from $-(radix^{n-1} - 1)$ through $radix^{n-1} - 1$.

Zero.   There are two zeros, with all the problems discussed under signed magnitude. In fact, the notation of -0 is about as different from that for $+0$ as it could be, affecting all digits. In signed magnitude, only the sign is different.

```
┌─────────────────────────────────────────┐
│ Digits                                   │
│                                          │
└─────────────────────────────────────────┘
```

```
number←digitcompi rep;modulus;value
 ⍝ digit-complement interpretation
 modulus←(radix*0⊥¯1↑⍴rep)-1
 value←radix⊥⍉rep
 number←value-(value≥modulus÷2)×modulus


 rep←size digitcompr number;modulus
 ⍝ digit-complement representation
 modulus←(radix*size)-1
 rep←⍉(size⍴radix)⊤modulus|number
 ⍝ domain signals
 xmax←number≥modulus÷2
 xmin←number<-modulus÷2
```

PROGRAM 4-43   Digit-complement interpretation and representation.

Algebraic addition by complementation of the addend unfortunately produces the less desirable −0 for any zero sum, represented in binary by an all-ones vector. For this reason, the 1103 family and the 6600, which use this notation, perform subtraction rather than addition in their implementations, complementing the subtrahend when addition is to be performed. This causes subtraction of identical operands to yield +0. All operations correctly yield +0, except when −0 is added to −0, or +0 is subtracted from −0 (Table 4-44). **Implementation.**   During algebraic addition and subtraction, no sign test need be made to control precomplementation, which depends only on the operation.   Recomplementation is never required, but a low-order 1 must be added if and only if there is a carry from the high-order end.   On a parallel adder, this addition is accomplished by an *end-around carry* signal. This signal, however, makes the adder into a sequential circuit, which may have undesirable implementation consequences. With a serial adder, a second pass

Manual		Addition		Subtraction
13		01101		01101
13	01101 →	10010		01101
— -		——— +		——— -
0		11111		00000
13		01101		01101
¯13		10010	10010 →	01101
— +		——— +		——— -
0		11111		00000
0		00000		00000
0	00000 →	11111		00000
— -		——— +		——— -
0		11111		00000
¯0		11111		11111
¯0		11111	11111 →	00000
— +		——— +		——— -
0		11111		11111

TABLE 4-44   Sign of zero in digit complement.

Effective operands		Result	Assumed probability	Signed-magnitude recomplementation	Digit-complement end-around carry
+	+	+	0.25		
+	+	overflow	0.0	yes	
+	-	+	0.125		yes
+	-	-	0.125	yes	
-	+	+	0.125	yes	yes
-	+	-	0.125		
-	-	-	0.25		yes
-	-	overflow	0.0	yes	yes
		total	1.00	0.25	0.50

TABLE 4-45   Extra adder actions required by the sign notation.

over the sum must be made, just as with recomplementation. Alternatively the carry can be remembered and added during a subsequent operation.

Table 4-45 compares the extra actions of signed-magnitude and digit-complement notations. It shows that, for equal probability of the various signs and magnitudes and zero probability for overflow, the end-around carry occurs 50 percent of the time, and recomplementation occurs 25 percent of the time. But positive numbers and positive results occur more often than chance predicts. Sweeney [1965] shows that recomplementation happens in about 10 percent of additions.

Multiplication can use Booth's algorithm and hence is rather simple in digit complement. Cumulative multiplication has trouble with the end-around carry. Division has about the complexity of radix complement. Overflow detection is just as complex as with radix complement. Richards [1955], Phister [1958], and Hwang [1979] treat these matters in detail.

Application. Easy mental conversion is really the chief advantage of digit-complement notation. On all other counts, it has the worst features of both the signed-magnitude and the radix-complement notations.

Bias

In bias notation, a range of numbers spread about zero is shifted to a non-negative range by addition of a bias equal to the magnitude of the negative range. Table 4-36 demonstrates this shift. The table also shows that the bias notation is the only notation for which the positive range does not match the normal binary interpretation. Program 4-46 gives the relevant algorithms.

Sign, zero, homogeneity, and conversion.   The bias notation has only one zero, but it is not represented by an all-zeros vector. The datatype is homogeneous, not compound. The high-order digit denotes the sign, but it has an encoding opposite to the usual convention.

Conversion of numbers requires an addition and a conditional complementation.

Implementation. From Table 4-36 and Programs 4-41 and 4-46, one can see that the bias notation can be obtained from the radix-complement notation by

```
Digits
```

```
number←biasi rep;bias;value      rep←size biasr number;bias
⍝ bias interpretation            ⍝ bias representation
bias←⌊0.5×radix*0⊥¯1↑ρrep        bias←⌊0.5×radix*size
value←radix⊥⍉rep                 rep←⍉(sizeρradix)⊤number+bias
number←value-bias                ⍝ domain signal
                                 xmax←number≥bias
                                 xmin←number<-bias
```

PROGRAM 4-46   Bias interpretation and representation.

adding half the radix to the leftmost digit. In binary, the leftmost bit is just inverted. So bias notation has approximately the same characteristics as radix complement and is as easy to build.

Application.   When the bits of the bias notation are interpreted as an unsigned integer, the comparison sequence of the represented numbers is not changed. This property is not true for the other notations (Table 4-36). When bias notation is used for the exponent of floating-point representations, these representations can be compared by using the fixed-point comparison operations.

Bias is not used for fixed-point numbers. Consequently, when an arithmetic subroutine needs to perform exponent arithmetic, the programmer does not have the arithmetic to match the notation and must make suitable corrections.

Addition and subtraction require a correction that depends only on the operation, not on the data. For addition, the bias must be subtracted once as a correction; for subtraction, the bias must be added once.

For multiplication and division, however, corrections are rather complicated. It is better to pre- and postconvert the bias notation to and from radix-complement notation.

Inverted-Sign Notation

The desire to use fixed-point operations to compare floating-point numbers yields yet another notation in machines using digit-complement notation: digit complement with inverted sign. This notation cannot be obtained by shifting of the digit-complement number range; there is no bias. Another difference from bias notation is the two representations for zero. The 1103A and 6600 families use this notation.

4.3.3

Radix

Besides notation for negative numbers, positional representation involves the choice of a radix and of a radix point (Tree 4-32).

Radix Choice

The binary radix is perhaps the most conspicuous impropriety of computers. The whole modern world calculates in decimal, and with good reason: 1914 is much more easily remembered than 11101111010. So, why not conform? This issue was hotly debated during the early days of the computer, with the Harvard Mark I (1944), the Pennsylvania ENIAC (1946), the Univac I (1951) on the side of decimal and the IAS (1952), the Pennsylvania EDVAC (1952), and the Cambridge EDSAC (1949) on the side of binary. The binary side won, relegating decimal to auxiliary uses. Tree 4-47 shows the radices that have been tried.

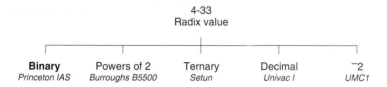

4-33
Radix value

| **Binary** | Powers of 2 | Ternary | Decimal | ⁻2 |
| *Princeton IAS* | *Burroughs B5500* | *Setun* | *Univac I* | *UMC1* |

TREE 4-47   Design choices for the radix value.

Theoretical argument.   There is a theoretical and a physical argument for binary. The theoretical argument says that the information content of an n-state device is $\log_2 n$ bits. If an n-state device has a relative cost of n, its relative efficiency is $(\log_2 n)/n$. The optimum of this expression has n equal to e (e=2.71828). The optimum integer value of n is 3, followed closely by 2.

This argument may be reasonable for a true n-state device such as the decimal element of the Mark I, which was a rotating switch of 10 positions. Most n-state devices, however, are built from two-state devices. In this case the cost of an n-state device is related to $\lceil \log_2 n$ [Buchholz, 1959]. The efficiency is thus $(\log_2 n) \div \lceil \log_2 n$. All powers of 2 have 100 percent efficiency, ternary has 80 percent efficiency, and decimal has 83 percent efficiency.

Physical argument.   Almost all physical phenomena that are used in the realization are harnessed most efficiently in binary devices. This technological factor is a strong force in favor of binary representation. There is a fundamental reason why the two-state bit is more economically and reliably realized than any higher-radix representor.

Any bounded continuous physical variable has two limits, which can be used to realize the two values of a bit. A transistor may pass a saturation current on one end of its operating range, and essentially no current at the other. Similarly, the armature of a relay may be pushed by a spring to one extreme of its motion, whereas the energized coil will pull it to the other extreme. For many such physical phenomena, the limits of the operation range are clearly defined and easily attained as operating points. It is easy to position some detectable threshold in the transition region between the extremes.

By defining two more thresholds (and thus two more regions of operation), one can represent a total of four values. Since these new regions have no natural operating points, but only arbitrary ones, their boundaries are more

difficult to distinguish and maintain stable over the life of the device. It is invariably less expensive and more reliable to use two binary devices than to represent four values by one device. A similar argument applies to three-state devices.

Higher powers of 2.   A radix that is a higher power of 2 has the advantage that numbers can be represented just as efficiently as in binary and yet are less voluminous and more memorable in visual appearance. Octal is optimal since its numerals are familiar. This may explain why an information-unit size of *three* is found in a few early machines. The Electrologica X8 (1965) has word length 27.

Binary, however, has won over decimal precisely because most users are no longer confronted with the internal representation of numbers. Therefore, the internal representation's ease of interpretation should no longer affect the data formats.

Ternary.   The Soviet SETUN (1959) was built with radix 3, apparently because of technological constraints. Three states of two magnetic cores represent each ternary digit; the fourth state, with both cores "on," is defined as invalid and is used for checking. So the number of cores that can switch at once is lower than with binary representation. The SETUN uses radix 9 analogously to octal for communication to the user [Ware, 1960].

Negative radix.   The use of a negative radix, in particular -2, has received substantial attention in the literature. Yuen has pointed out that this radix can compete only in special cases with binary. The representation range is highly asymmetric; sign recognition is much more complicated; implementation is more complex and harder to make fast; conversion to conventional representation is more complex; and the representation is less familiar [Yuen, 1975]. Nevertheless, the early Polish BINEG (1959) and its successors UMC1 (1961) and UMC10 (1963) use this radix [Pawlak and Wakulicz, 1957; Pawlak, 1959; Marczynski, 1980].

Position of the Radix Point

In computer fixed-point representations, the radix point is not explicitly represented. Its location is by definition *fixed*—that is, permanently and conventionally stationed at a particular place in the word. This position is then the implied representation of the point.

Scaling.   In most computers, mixed numbers, which have integral parts and fractional parts, are fundamentally treated as though they were integers. The radix point is not included in the representation—only the program knows where it is, and the location may not be explicitly stated there. It is up to the user to shift operands to align radix points for addition. More seriously, it is up to him to ensure, by shifting operands and their radix points, that products and quotients stay within allowable sizes. This process is called *scaling*.

Alternative positions.   There are two favorite locations for the radix point:

- Just to the right of the digits, the *integer notation*
- Just to the left of the digits, the *fractional notation*

In principle, the point could be between any two digits, the *mixed notation*, or even several digits to the right or left of the represented digits.

Surprisingly enough, where the implied radix point is located does matter, for this location determines how the results of multiplications and divisions will be aligned with respect to their operands in some sign notations.

The location of the radix point affects only double-length data, such as products or dividends. In integer notation the right half is aligned like a single-length operand; in fractional notation the left half is so aligned. All other choices of radix point line up on less simple boundaries, which explains why they are rarely used; an example is the Ferranti Mark 1 (1951).

Effect of sign notation. The implied position of the radix point matters only for complement notations (Table 4-48). In any notation, the multiplication of two n-bit (with sign) words yields $2n - 2$ bits of product, and a sign. In signed magnitude, the sign of the low-order word of a product or dividend is separate from the digits and is replicated in both the high-order words. So both words are aligned to match the operands. The double-length accumulator of early machines, such as the 704, illustrates this positioning (Figure 4-39).

In the complement notations the sign is treated as a digit, and a product or dividend digit fills what would properly be the sign bit of the low-order word. Only $(2n - 2 + 1)$ bits are produced by a multiplication, to fill a $2n$-bit space. The designer must decide whether to right-align the product (integer notation) or to left-align it (fractional notation).

For fixed-point arithmetic, we prefer the integer notation over the fractional notation, because integers occur more frequently than fractions. Entire classes of data are inherently integers: addresses, counts, and quantities of people, cars, and cents. Far fewer data are inherently pure fractions. Data that are part integer and part fraction, such as dollars and cents, can be converted as easily to the one as to the other. Most machines use integer notation.

Manual		Signed magnitude	Radix complement	Adjusted radix complement
Integer	Fraction			
8	0.5	+1000	01000	01000
8	0.5	+1000	01000	01000
—— ×	—— ×	—— —— ×	—— —— ×	—— —— ×
64	0.25	+0100 0000	00010 00000	00100 00000
8	0.5	+1000	01000	01000
¯4	¯0.25	-0100	11100	11100
—— ×	—— ×	—— —— ×	—— —— ×	—— —— ×
¯32	¯0.125	-0010 0000	11111 00000	11110 00000
2	0.125	0010	00010	00010
¯4	¯0.25	-0100	11100	11100
—— ×	—— —— ×	—— —— ×	—— —— ×	—— —— ×
¯8	¯0.03125	-0000 1000	11111 11000	11111 01000
Integer weight:		×16 ×1	×32 ×1u	×16 ×1
Fraction weight:		÷16 ÷256	÷8 ÷256u	÷16 ÷256

Legend: u = unsigned representation; operands in 5-bit registers;
        results in pairs of 5-bit registers;
        interpretation is either as an integer or as a fraction.

TABLE 4-48   Alignment of radix point.

Adjusted complement notation. An alternative solution for the complement notations is to keep the low-order sign position of a double-length quantity as a sign. For radix complement, this sign is always positive. For a single-length result, however, the low-order sign should be used as Table 4-48 illustrates. The ICL 1900 uses this notation.

Table 4-50 shows, for a number of machines, whether the product or quotient specification requires that fixed-point numbers be interpreted as fractional or integer notation.

4.3.4

Digit and Sign Allocation

The number system and notation encode a number in terms of digits and a sign. These lower-level concepts must then be allocated.

Digit allocation.   There is less agreement about the allocation of the digits of the number representation than one might think. In spoken German the order is hundreds, units, tens. A date of 1/2/3 may mean January 2, 1903, or 1 February 1903, or 1901, February 3.

In almost all computers, the digits are allocated from high order to low, relative to the addressing of memory (Section 2.2). This order matches conventional written representation.

The Manchester MU1 uses the reverse order to match the serial processing sequence—a reversal that permeates all representations, such as operations codes and instructions. But all that was needed was to reverse the human interfaces, such as switches and lights. Most early machines faced with the same serial implementation chose that route; we follow it in presenting the MU1 (Section 10.4).

Sign allocation.   The sign appears explicitly only in signed-magnitude notation. There is no "best" place for it, but since it has highest significance, it is preferably placed left of the high-order digit, as is done in speaking and writing.

Since the architectural preference is weak, the implementation desires usually dominate. If the arithmetic is parallel, it does not matter which bit is used for the sign. If the arithmetic is serial, as in the 650, the sign should be low order, since addition goes from low to high, and the sign must be known first.

The allocation of the sign usually shows in the architecture only. The 650 is exceptional, however, in that the sign of its number representation is not used in other datatypes, such as the character string or the instruction. In fact, the order is *not* part of the architecture.

Second-level representation.   The digits and the sign are the second-level components of a number. They must in turn be represented, which again involves encoding and allocation. The problems encountered in this second-level representation depend heavily upon the radix.

4.3.5

Binary Fixed Point

The binary integer is the basic datatype of a computer. Its design choices are shown in Tree 4-49.

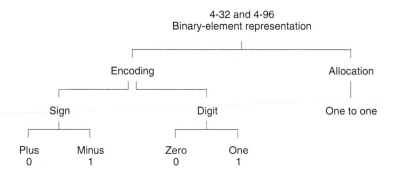

TREE 4-49   Design choices for binary fixed-point representation.

Number of Bits

For binary radix, each digit requires 1 bit, and the number of digits simply determines the length of the number in bits.

Address length.   For integers, length depends on range, and the most important range is the size of the name-space of the computing system itself. Therefore, choosing the lengths of addresses is a fundamental decision that affects datatype design.

As discussed in Section 2.3, one must distinguish physical-memory capacity from name-space size. The needs for each over any architecture's lifetime are difficult to predict. Nevertheless, 32 bits will, for many machines, suffice for directly addressed physical memory; 16 bits has proven to be too small for addressing a working set; 24 is marginal.

Data length.   The various data that binary integers may represent are commercial data, computational data, and theoretical data.

Commercial data.   The length of commercial data is discussed later for decimal integers. In absence of a decimal option, the binary integers must serve the purpose. Based on the desire to have some seven to 10 decimal digits, a binary length of 23 to 33 bits seems appropriate.

Computational data.   The values of physical entities that enter a computer are usually known to five or fewer decimal digits. Similarly, the results of a computation that are used to control physical equipment rarely need more than five decimal digits. When the intervening computation is simple and can easily be scaled, this size can be maintained throughout. This situation is typical for a control computer and explains in part the word size of 16 bits for mini- and microcomputers used in such applications. Examples in point are the formats of the DEC PDP11 (1970) and of the 8080A (Table 4-50), as well as the halfword format of the 360.

	Notation	Point	Allocation
Cambridge EDSAC	2-c	fraction	17 35
Ferranti Mark 1	2-c	mixed	20 40
Princeton IAS	2-c	fraction	40
IBM 701	s-m	both	s,17 35
IBM 704	s-m	both	s,35
Univac 1103A	1-c	integer	36
STC ZEBRA	2-c	~	33
Bendix G20	s-m	integer	ff,s,f,27
Bull Gamma 60	magnitude	integer	15 24
IBM Stretch	s-m	both	1-64,(s)
English Electric KDF9	2-c	integer	24 48 95
CDC 6600	1-c	~	18 60
CDC 6600 PPU	1-c	~	6 12 18
IBM System/360	2-c	integer	16 32
Electrologica X8	1-c	integer	27
DEC PDP8	2-c	integer	12
Honeywell H8200	s-m	integer	s,44
DEC PDP11	2-c	integer	16
Burroughs B1700	2-c	~	1-24
CDC Star100	2-c	integer	0-(2*16)-1
Intel 8080A	2-c	~	8 16
Cray 1	2-c	integer	24 64
Motorola M6800	2-c	~	8
MOS 6502	2-c	~	8
DEC VAX11	2-c	integer	8 16 32
Motorola MC68000	2-c	integer	8 16 32
IBM 6150	2-c	integer	32

legend: f = flag; s = sign; both = integer and fraction;
() =optional; - = through; ~ = no multiply or divide;
s-m = signed magnitude; 1-c = 1's complement;
2-c = 2's complement; numbers give number of digits.

TABLE 4-50   Binary fixed-point representation in various machines.

Computation requiring more digits than the input data possess usually involves scaling and is normally done in floating-point arithmetic; it is discussed later under that topic.

Theoretical data.   Theoretical values may pertain to a model of physical reality, as for theoretical physics or astronomy. In that case, a satisfactory precision is usually several times that of measurement values—10 to 15 decimal digits. If the theoretical values do not pertain to physical reality, as for number theory, any precision may be required. In this case, multiple precision is more valuable than a long word size.

The desirable lengths for mixed numbers are longer than those of integers. The fractional part is a net increase in the total precision with which numbers must be represented; the range of numbers needed is unchanged. Word lengths of 32, 36, 40, and 48 have found wide use for fixed-point mixed numbers.

In summary, 12 bits is clearly a minimum for integer data, even though microprocessors originally had to live with 8. The integers 0 through 4095 form about as small a set as one can use in any application. A more livable size is 16 bits for small machines. For general purpose machines, 24 bits appear minimal, with 32 to 36 bits apt to suffice for over 99 percent of uses. Von Neumann argues for 40 bits, but his argument includes mixed numbers

[Burks et al., 1946]. Table 4-50 shows the sign notation and the length used in a number of machines that have binary fixed-point formats.

Variable length.   Table 4-50 shows that the Stretch is exceptional in providing a variable-length binary integer arithmetic. Just as there is little real need for addressing resolution to the bit, the same arguments apply to a variable data length with bit resolution. Refinement is even less desirable when variability must be paid for with many instruction bits.   In the Stretch, the variable-length mechanism is shared with decimal arithmetic and logic, so the marginal implementation cost of variable binary fields is low.   The cost in bit budget and bit traffic, however, is high, which is why, in hindsight, we would not make that mistake again.

Encoding and Allocation

Digits.   The encoding representation of binary digits is trivial.

Sign.   The encoding of the sign must be decided for signed magnitude. The common choice is 0 for plus and 1 for minus.   The allocation of this sign bit appears trivial, but the Stretch gives an example where up to 8 bits are available as a sign byte.   The sign bit must be allocated within this byte (Section 13.3).

4.3.6

Decimal Fixed Point

Numerical input from people and output to people must be in radix 10. For applications in which true input and output are a major part of the total work, such as many file-maintenance tasks, it may be more economical to provide decimal datatypes and keep all files in decimal, than to convert inbound numbers to binary, perform arithmetic, and convert back. For this reason, decimal datatypes and arithmetic are usually provided, at least as an option, on computers intended for commercial applications.

Today's designer faces two major decisions concerning a decimal datatype. First, should one provide decimal arithmetic at all, or only binary arithmetic? Second, if decimal arithmetic is provided, should it operate on the character strings in which decimal numbers enter and leave the system, or should there be a different and more efficient packed decimal format for the sake of storage and memory efficiency?

The ability to store and move decimal digits in character form does not constitute a decimal datatype—there must be operations proper to decimal. So the 8080A, with its Decimal Adjust, just barely has a decimal data type. The unpacked decimal representation in the 360 is just a decimal representation, not a distinct datatype.

Decimal versus Binary

Binary numbers take less space than decimal ones do, by the ratio $(\log_2 10)/4 = 0.83$. The decimal efficiency is yet lower if the number sign is encoded as a decimal digit. On the other hand, a substantial fraction of

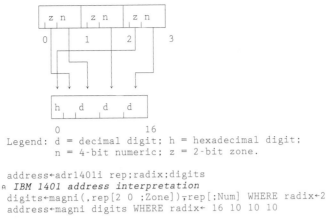

Legend: d = decimal digit; h = hexadecimal digit;
        n = 4-bit numeric; z = 2-bit zone.

```
address←adr1401i rep;radix;digits
⍝ IBM 1401 address interpretation
digits←magni(,rep[2 0 ;Zone]),⍤rep[;Num] WHERE radix←2
address←magni digits WHERE radix← 16 10 10 10
```

PROGRAM 4-51   Address interpretation in the IBM 1401.

commercial files consists of character strings such as names and addresses, rather than numbers; the added file-capacity cost of decimal over binary is lower than one would at first expect.

Historically, there have been intense emotional arguments for decimal arithmetic. An invalid argument often heard is that the proper handling of dollars and cents requires decimal arithmetic, since the rounding and conversion of fractions to and from binary would produce errors in the low-order place. Indeed it would, but the proper solution is to carry amounts in integers (cents) and insert the decimal point when printing.

Decimal addressing.   In the 1950s, commercial machines commonly used only decimal arithmetic, including decimal addressing. By 1960 the growing acceptance of assemblers and higher-level programming languages had diluted the force of the ease-of-use arguments for decimal addressing, the bit wastage had become larger as address spaces had grown, and the costly inefficiency had led architects to use the available bits, resulting in some very clumsy *mixed-radix addressing*. (The 1401 shows this clumsiness, as illustrated in Program 4-51.) These addressing systems no longer had the ease of use that was claimed for decimal arithmetic, and they required special arithmetic.

One of the 360's most salutary influences on computer technology was the displacement of decimal and mixed-radix addressing in commercial computers with binary addressing. More than any other technical decision, this one brought the commercial and scientific architectural traditions into a common stream. As a consequence, the choice facing today's designer is not whether to use binary or decimal, but whether to have a decimal type besides the standard binary one.

We now believe that the decimal datatype can be dispensed with completely; that the very most one should consider, even for machines intended primarily for commercial applications, is a minimal decimal datatype whose only operation is a decimal-addition correction. We therefore abbreviate the exhaustive delineation of the design space for decimal datatypes.

Design choices.   The design of decimal representation is relatively complex, second only to that for floating-point representation. Encoding and allocation must be designed for digits and sign. Tree 4-52 summarizes the design choices.

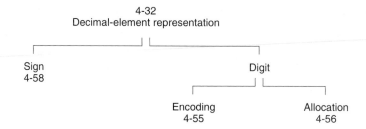

TREE 4-52   Design choices for decimal fixed-point representation.

Number of Digits

Like fixed-point binary numbers, decimal numbers have a well-defined usage distribution. They are mostly integers or dollar-and-cent amounts, representable as integral cents. Both range and precision are clustered narrowly.

Figure 4-53 shows distributions of lengths of some 400 decimal number fields from four payroll applications [Brooks, 1956]. Each field occurring in any file is counted once; fields are not weighted by frequency of use. The table and the Total figure show the aggregate of the four distributions.

In the distributions, many of the short fields are codes, as for marital status. These codes depend on particular programming choices. Many other short fields, however, are real data: age, number of dependents, tax rate, and so on.

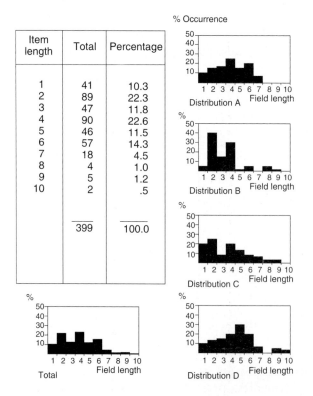

Item length	Total	Percentage
1	41	10.3
2	89	22.3
3	47	11.8
4	90	22.6
5	46	11.5
6	57	14.3
7	18	4.5
8	4	1.0
9	5	1.2
10	2	.5
	399	100.0

FIGURE 4-53   Lengths of decimal fields in some payroll programs.

```
                                              decimal360 size
┌───┬───┬───┬───┬───┬───┬───┬ ─ ─ ┬───┬───┐   ⍝ IBM 360 decimal number
│ d   d │ d   d │ d   d │ d │     │ d │ s │   ⍝ sign encoding
└───┴───┴───┴───┴───┴───┴───┴ ─ ─ ┴───┴───┘   plus← 10 12 14 15
  0       1       2       3           m       minus← 11 13
Legend: d = digit; m = maximum 16; s = sign. ⍝ allocation
                                              Sign←size-1
                                              Digits←⍳size-1


number←decimal360i rep;radix;decimals;plus;minus;Sign;Digits
⍝ IBM 360 decimal interpretation
decimals←magni digit wide rep WHERE radix←2
decimal360ρdecimals
number←signmagni decimals[Sign,Digits] WHERE radix←10
Invop report~decopt∧∧/inst[⍳4]
Data report∨/(decimals[Sign]<10),decimals[Digits]≥10


rep←size decimal360r number;radix;decimals;plus;minus;Sign;Digits
⍝ IBM 360 decimal representation
decimal360 size÷4
decimals←((size÷4) signmagnr number)[⍙Sign,Digits] WHERE radix←10
rep←byte wide digit magnr decimals WHERE radix←2
Decoflo report xmax∨xmin
```

PROGRAM 4-54   Decimal fixed-point number in the IBM System/360.

As the cumulative distribution shows, 97 percent of all such numbers have seven or fewer digits, and over 99 percent have nine or fewer digits.

Variable length.   The variable-length decimal representation was pioneered by the 702. Its number's variable length is consistent with its variable-length character strings'.

Since decimal field lengths are narrowly distributed, in contrast to character strings, there is no strong argument for making length variable. During the design of the 360, this point was the subject of extensive debate. In the *four* format system, a 64-bit double word would give 15 digits and a sign, and a 32-bit word would give seven digits and a sign; it seemed necessary to allow both lengths because of the substantial number of fields longer than seven digits. Faced with this alternative, we selected a variable–field-length format, since this would use the same concepts and machinery as does the variable-length character string. Furthermore, the COBOL standard required 16 digits and a sign—slightly too much for a full word. The selection of a maximum length of 31 digits plus sign, or 16 bytes, was governed by the *four* format system. The resulting format is shown in Program 4-54. The variations in length that occur in other computers are shown in Table 4-59. The IBM 1620 (1960) and 1401 are unusual in allowing any length that fits memory.

Encoding of Digits

The encoding of decimal digits has usually been 8421 from the IBM 604 calculator (1952) and the 702 computer (1954) on. The Harvard Marks II–IV use codes especially designed to facilitate arithmetic. Univac I uses the excess-three code, first used by Stibitz in the Bell Laboratory calculators. That code has a self-complementing property that was handy for Univac's serial-by-bit implementation. The 650 implementation uses in storage a 2-out-of-5 code that

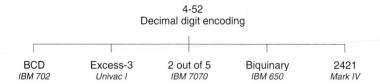

TREE 4-55 Design choices for decimal digit encoding.

allows only 10 valid combinations and uses the redundancy for checking. In a machine using ASCII or EBCDIC for alphanumeric characters, however, the 8421 code for digits is essentially dictated by their embedment in the character set. The design choices are listed in Tree 4-55.

Allocation of Digits

Even though decimal digits enter and leave a computer as parts of character strings, a digit carries less information than a character does. Memory, disk, and tape space are saved when decimal fields are stored efficiently. This fact forces difficult design choices. A decimal digit demands 4 bits; an alphanumeric character demands at least 6, but more commonly 8. How shall digit- and character-representation decisions be combined? Tree 4-56 and Figure 4-57 show four solutions:

- 4/8 (meaning 4 bits for a digit and 8 for a character and called *packed decimal*), used, for example, in the 360
- 6/6, used in the Univac I, IBM 705, IBM 1401
- 4/6, used in the Honeywell 800 (1961)
- 8/8 (*unpacked*), used in the 360, but not as an arithmetic datatype

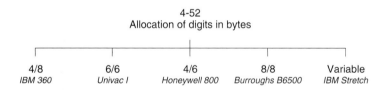

TREE 4-56 Design choices for decimal digit allocation.

Bit efficiency. Since the 6-bit character no longer satisfies modern text-processing requirements, the 6/6 and 4/6 solutions are no longer viable contenders. The packed 4/8 has bit efficiency equal to or better than that of the unpacked 8/8 solution, but it requires Pack and Unpack instructions and extra conversion actions.

How much more efficient is the packed solution? Consider 100 file characters; suppose 30 are alphabetic and 70 numeric. A numeric field

d d	d	d d d	d
0 8	0 6	0 6 12	0 8
4/8	6/6	4/6	8/8

Legend: d = digit; d/c = digit size/character size.

FIGURE 4-57 Decimal-digit allocation.

averages 5 digits, so there are 14 signs. These signs can be placed in a zone over a digit in the 8/8 solution. So 44 characters $(30+14)$ are alphanumeric or signed digits; 56 (4×14) are pure digits, which require 28 packed 4/8 bytes. The result is 100 bytes for 8/8 and 72 bytes $(44+28)$ for 4/8. This 28 percent difference must compensate for the extra time and equipment of packing and unpacking.

In all the foregoing discussion, the concern with efficiency of representation is not limited to memory usage, nor is it even principally preoccupied with that. The efficiency on tapes and disks is far more important, for it determines both capacities and effective data rates. The ultimate efficiency is binary representation; this is the strongest argument against decimal datatypes.

Conversion.   In the 8/8 solution the digit size is equal to the character size. If the encoding is also the same, there is no distinction between a digit and a numeric character.

Does this mean that the internal decimal-number format matches the I/O format? After all, the radix, the number system, and the character size and code are all the same. Not usually; the I/O format still requires editing, such as for output, insertion of punctuation, change of sign notation, and suppression of zero.

Sign Allocation

Decimal datatypes use signed magnitude, so one can choose whether to represent the sign with a bit, or whether to devote a whole digit for consistency. All the machines using 6-bit characters for decimal numbers—such as the Univac I, the 705, the 1401, and the Honeywell 200 (1964)—use one of the zone bits for the sign. The machines representing decimal digits with 4 bits, including the 650 and the 360, have dedicated a whole digit. Tree 4-58 shows the design choices for both the allocation and the encoding of signs. Table 4-59 gives examples.

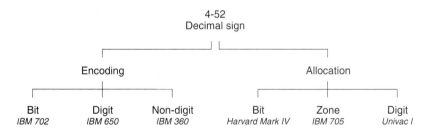

TREE 4-58   Design choices for decimal sign representation.

Sign Encoding

When only a single bit is available for the sign, the encoding decision is trivial: Plus is commonly 0, and minus is 1. When four bits are available, there is still a set of design choices. The Stretch uses all that is needed—one bit—and uses the remaining three bits as flags. An alternative is to encode the sign with four bits, as in the 360. The values 11 and 13 are recognized

	Number representation	Sign Code +	Code -	Size	Digit Code	Allocation system
Harvard Mark I	s-m	s,24	0	9	digit	1 of 10	1 in 1
Univac I	s-m	s,11	0	15	digit	excess-3	4 in 6
Harvard Mark IV	s-m	s,16	0	1	bit	2421	4 in 4
IBM 650	s-m	s,10	8	9	digit	~	1 in 1
IBM 705	s-m	1-256,s	11	10	zone	BCD*	4 in 6
IBM 1401	s-m	1-ω,s	00+	10	zone	BCD*	4 in 7
IBM 1620	s-m	2-ω,s	0	1	zone bit	BCD	4 in 5
IBM 7070	s-m	s,10	9	6	digit	2 of 5	1 in 1
IBM Stretch	s-m	1-16,(s),f	0	1	bit	BCD	4 in 4-8
Burroughs B5500	s-m	0-63,s	00+	10	zone	BCD	4 in 6
IBM System/360	s-m	1-31,s	10+	11+	digit	BCD	2×4 in 8
Honeywell H8200	s-m	s,11	1+	0	digit	BCD	3×4 in 2×6
Burroughs B6500	s-m	s,6 8 11	0	15	digit	BCD	4 in 8 6 4
Intel 8080A	t-c	2	~	~		BCD	2×4 in 8
Motorola M6800	t-c	2	~	~		BCD	2×4 in 8
MOS 6502	t-c	2	~	~		BCD	2×4 in 8
DEC VAX11	s-m	1-31,s	12+	13+	digit	BCD	2×4 in 8
Motorola MC68000	t-c	2	~	~		BCD	2×4 in 8

Legend: f = flag; s = sign; () = optional; - = through;
+ = more sign values; * = zero encoded as 1010;
ω = memory size; ~ = not applicable;
s-m = signed magnitude; t-c = 10's complement.

TABLE 4-59   Decimal fixed-point numbers in various machines.

as minus; the remaining non-decimal values are recognized as plus. These choices match the requirements of EBCDIC numerics with overpunched sign codes.

The all-decimal 650 uses a 9 for minus and an 8 for plus—an encoding that is neatly invisible in the architecture.

A Minimal Decimal Datatype

In binary computers with 8-bit bytes, decimal digits can be packed two to a byte, with signed-magnitude or 10's-complement notation. Addition, subtraction, and comparison can be programmed very simply if a Decimal Carry Status bit and a Decimal Adjust operation are provided. Section 16.2.5 illustrates the minimal decimal datatype for the 8080A.

4.3.7
Bibliography

Booth [1951], Brooks [1956], Burks et al. [1946], Buchholz [1959], Ercegovac [1973], Garner [1959], Hwang [1979], McKeeman [1967], Marczynski [1980], Oblonsky [1980], Pawlak [1959], Pawlak and Wakulicz [1957], Phister [1958], Richards [1955], Svoboda [1957], Sweeney [1965], Ware [1960], Yuen [1975].

4.4
Floating-Point Numbers

As Knuth [1981, vol. 2, p. 180] has pointed out, floating-point notation is as old as the Babylonians. Zuse, in his Z3 calculator (1941) and Z4 computer (1950), Stibitz, in his Bell Laboratory calculator Model V (1947), and Aiken, in his Mark II computer (1947), recognized the need for number ranges in excess of those expressible in fixed point, and they all used floating-point numbers and operations, the *floating point* datatype.

When computers became commercially available, however, the range problem was left at first for the programmer to solve by scaling, as in the 701. This method proved very tedious. (Any reader who has never programmed a mixed-precision fixed-point calculation should try to do one. See, for example, McCracken [1957, Chapter 4, Exercises 14 through 17]. McCracken's lucid chapter is also well worth reading.)

Users at Bell Laboratories, Los Alamos Scientific Laboratories, and elsewhere developed floating-point subroutines and then interpretive floating-point systems. As a result of this user experience and demand, the architects of the 704 (1955), a revision of the 701, included built-in floating point as a non-optional datatype. This contributed materially to the success of the machine and made FORTRAN conceivable. Since then, machines intended for scientific computing have included floating point, at least as an option.

Few early minicomputers include floating point, since they were used only rarely for substantial scientific computation. The PDP11s are a notable exception. Early microcomputers did not have floating point; their evolutionary recapitulation brought this capability, first as separate coprocessor chips, then as on-chip function.

Purpose.   Floating-point representation allows a large range for the representable numbers, with equal precision for each number. Floating-point equipment, of course, is slower and more expensive than comparable fixed-point equipment. Use of this representation, however, is much more efficient than the use of programmed scaling.

Floating point is one of the first successful steps toward a higher-level language, because it conceals the scaling occasioned by fixed-point representations: The user thinks in terms of numbers, not of their representations. Floating point is also a good example of an arithmetic technique stimulated by computer development. Although it was used earlier as "scientific notation" in physics and astronomy, the computer has markedly increased its application.

Nature of Floating Point

Floating point assumes a *base*, which is taken to a power specified by an *exponent* and subsequently multiplied by a *coefficient* (e.g., $.678 \times 10^2$). The sign of the number is embodied in the coefficient, as shown in fli (Program 4-60).

High-level representation.   Floating point places another encoding and allocation level above the two levels of fixed point. In flr (Program 4-60)

a number is first expressed in terms of a base, exponent, and coefficient, using the generic function `normalform`; the exponent and coefficient are then represented in fixed point with the methods of the previous section. Since the coefficient is usually not an integer, the parameter `point` is used to establish a radix point and the generic function `entire` is used to obtain a value that is representable in fixed point.

Exponent	Coefficient

```
number←fli rep;exponent;coefficient
⍝ general floating-point interpretation
exponent←interpret rep[Exp]
coefficient←interpret rep[Coef]
number←coefficient×base*exponent-point
```

```
rep←size flr number;exponent;coefficient
⍝ general floating-point representation
expzero normalform number
rep←sizeρ0
rep[Coef]←(ρCoef) represent entire coefficient
rep[Exp]←(ρExp) represent exponent
```

PROGRAM 4-60   Interpretation and representation of floating point.

Quasi-logarithmic representation.   A floating-point representation is quasi-logarithmic. An ordinary logarithm to base *base* of a number *number* consists of an integral part *exponent* and a fractional part *mantissa*:

$$number \ = \ base^{exponent+mantissa}$$

or

$$number \ = \ base^{exponent} \times base^{mantissa}$$

In contrast, in `fli` the floating-point exponent is indeed the integral part of the logarithm, but the base to the fractional power of the mantissa is exchanged for a coefficient:

$$number = coefficient \times base^{exponent}$$

This procedure vastly simplifies addition, which cannot be done with purely logarithmic representations.

Terminology.   The quasi-logarithmic form has led to the use of the term *mantissa* for the coefficient, which is mathematically incorrect. The term *fraction* is also undesirable, since the coefficient need not be a fraction at all. The term *coefficient* most accurately describes the function of this component.

The exponent is sometimes called the *characteristic*. But the exponent really *is* an exponent. The frequent use of bias sign notation for the exponent is at times given as a reason for a different name. But sign notation is not an issue at this level.

Design choices.   The quasi-logarithmic representation is not closed, is non-unique, and is compound. These attributes underlie the main design choices of this datatype, as shown in Tree 4-61. The key attributes of the high-level

encoding are the implied base, the range of the exponent, and the precision and radix point of the coefficient.

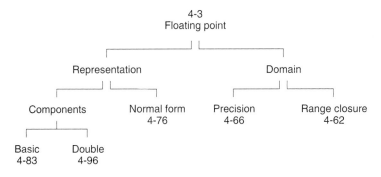

TREE 4-61   Design choices for floating-point numbers.

4.4.1

Closure

Since exponent and coefficient are both fixed-point numbers, the floating-point numbers are a subset of the rational numbers. The rational numbers exhibit *closure* with respect to the operations add, subtract, multiply, and divide. This closure means that any pair of rational operands yields a rational result for these operations. For the floating-point subset of the rational numbers, this property does not hold. Worse, the operations quite often produce results outside the subset. Tree 4-62 shows the designer's choices for whether and how to achieve closure.

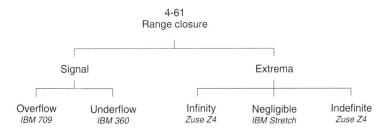

TREE 4-62   Design choices for floating-point range closure.

Representation example.   Table 4-63 lists as an example all 128 numbers represented by a floating-point format with three exponent bits and four coefficient bits, using radix-complement sign notation. In Figure 4-64 we show all positive numbers of Table 4-63 on the line of positive real numbers; the low-order end of the line is expanded to present the necessary details. As a comparison, Figure 4-64 also shows the numbers represented by the same seven format bits when interpreted as 2's-complement fixed point with an overlapping range.

Coefficient			0 000	1 001	2 010	3 011	$^-4$ 100	$^-3$ 101	$^-2$ 110	$^-1$ 111
0	0000		0zg	0 z	0 z	0 z	0	0　z	0　z	0　z
1	0001		1 g	2	4	8	0.0625 g	0.125 g	0.25 g	0.5 g
2	0010		2 g	4	8	16	0.125	0.25	0.5	1
3	0011		3 g	6	12	24	0.1875 g	0.375 g	0.75 g	1.5 g
4	0100	n	4 g	8 g	16 g	32 g	0.25	0.5	1	2
5	0101	n	5 g	10 g	20 g	40 g	0.3125 g	0.625 g	1.25 g	2.5 g
6	0110	n	6 g	12 g	24 g	48 g	0.375	0.75	1.5	3
7	0111	n	7 g	14 g	28 g	56 g	0.4375 g	0.875 g	1.75 g	3.5 g
$^-8$	1000	n	$^-8$ g	$^-16$ g	$^-32$ g	$^-64$ g	$^-0.5$	$^-1$	$^-2$	$^-4$
$^-7$	1001	n	$^-7$ g	$^-14$ g	$^-28$ g	$^-56$ g	$^-0.4375$ g	$^-0.875$ g	$^-1.75$ g	$^-3.5$ g
$^-6$	1010	n	$^-6$ g	$^-12$ g	$^-24$ g	$^-48$ g	$^-0.375$	$^-0.75$	$^-1.5$	$^-3$
$^-5$	1011	n	$^-5$ g	$^-10$ g	$^-20$ g	$^-40$ g	$^-0.3125$ g	$^-0.625$ g	$^-1.25$ g	$^-2.5$ g
$^-4$	1100		$^-4$ g	$^-8$	$^-16$	$^-32$	$^-0.25$	$^-0.5$	$^-1$	$^-2$
$^-3$	1101		$^-3$ g	$^-6$	$^-12$	$^-24$	$^-0.1875$ g	$^-0.375$ g	$^-0.75$ g	$^-1.5$ g
$^-2$	1110		$^-2$ g	$^-4$	$^-8$	$^-16$	$^-0.125$	$^-0.25$	$^-0.5$	$^-1$
$^-1$	1111		$^-1$ g	$^-2$	$^-4$	$^-8$	$^-0.0625$ g	$^-0.125$ g	$^-0.25$ g	$^-0.5$ g

Legend: g = grau; n = normalized; z = order of magnitude zero;
3-bit exponent and 4-bit coefficient; 2-complement notation.

TABLE 4-63   Value set of a small floating-point format.

Figure 4-64 suggests that the representable fixed-point numbers form a picket fence along the real-number line—finite in number, equally spaced. The floating-point representation has the same number of pickets, but they are not equally spaced.

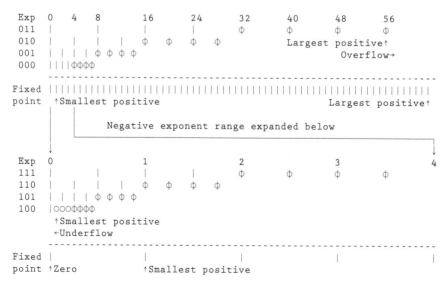

FIGURE 4-64   Representable numbers in fixed and floating point.

Augend	64	56	48	40	32	28	24	20	16	14	12	10	8	7	6	5	4	3.5	3	2.5
64	+	+	+	+	+	+	+	+	+	+	+	+	+	+	+	+	+	+	+	+
56	+	+	+	+	+	+	+	+	+	+	+	+	64	o	o	o	o	o	o	o
48	+	+	+	+	+	+	+	+	64	o	o	o	56	o	o	o	o	o	o	o
40	+	+	+	+	+	+	64	o	56	o	o	o	48	o	o	o	o	o	o	o
32	+	+	+	+	64	o	56	o	48	o	o	o	40	o	o	o	o	o	o	o
28	+	+	+	+	o	56	o	48	o	o	40	o	o	o	o	o	32	o	o	o
24	+	+	+	64	56	o	48	o	40	o	o	o	32	o	o	o	28	o	o	o
20	+	+	+	o	o	48	o	40	o	o	32	o	28	o	o	o	24	o	o	o
16	+	+	64	56	48	o	40	o	32	o	28	o	24	o	o	o	20	o	o	o
14	+	+	o	o	o	o	o	o	o	28	o	24	o	o	20	o	o	o	o	o
12	+	+	o	o	o	40	o	32	28	o	24	o	20	o	o	o	16	o	o	o
10	+	+	o	o	o	o	o	o	o	24	o	20	o	o	16	o	14	o	o	o
8	+	64	56	48	40	o	32	28	24	o	20	o	16	o	14	o	12	o	o	o
7	+	o	o	o	o	o	o	o	o	o	o	o	o	14	o	12	o	o	10	o
6	+	o	o	o	o	o	o	o	o	20	o	16	14	o	12	o	10	o	o	o
5	+	o	o	o	o	o	o	o	o	o	o	o	o	12	o	10	o	o	8	o
4	+	o	o	o	o	32	28	24	20	o	16	14	12	o	10	o	8	o	7	o
3.5	+	o	o	o	o	o	o	o	o	o	o	o	o	o	o	o	o	7	o	6
3	+	o	o	o	o	o	o	o	o	o	o	o	o	10	o	8	7	o	6	o
2.5	+	o	o	o	o	o	o	o	o	o	o	o	o	o	o	o	o	6	o	5

Legend: + = lack of range; o = lack of precision.

TABLE 4-65   Lack of closure in floating point.

Table 4-65 shows for the upper part of the domain of the numbers of Table 4-63 the pairs that give a sum inside the domain. The sparseness of Figure 4-64 graphically illustrates the two causes for the lack of closure. First, the representable numbers may not be precise enough; the unrepresentable numbers fall between the "pickets" of Figure 4-64. This lack of closure is caused by insufficient coefficient precision. Second, the results of the operations may be beyond the representable range; they fall beyond the fence of Figure 4-64. This lack of closure is a consequence of insufficient exponent range. Both causes for lack of closure are a consequence of the top-level encoding of a number by a pair of fixed-point numbers; they are independent of lower-level representation steps.

Precision Treatment

Precision treatment amounts to selecting a representable neighbor of an unrepresentable number. For example, how shall $-1 \div 2$ be represented in an integer datatype? The 704 and Bendix G20 (1961) get 0; the IBM NORC (1954) and the Ferranti Atlas (1962) get -1, depending upon their precision treatments and sign notations. Tree 4-66 gives the design choices for precision treatment that apply to fixed point as well as floating point.

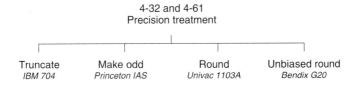

TREE 4-66   Design choices for precision treatment.

Truncation.   The simplest method of making a result fit the representation is to omit the excess low-order digits and leave the others unchanged. This method is called *truncation* or *chopping* (Program 4-67).

```
result←truncate number
ᴀ signed-magnitude or digit-complement truncation
result←(×number)×⌊|number

result←chop number
ᴀ radix-complement truncation
result←⌊number
```

PROGRAM 4-67   Precision treatment by truncation.

The effect of truncation depends upon the sign representation of the number; truncate, which applies to signed-magnitude and digit-complement notation, gives a bias toward zero. The radix-complement function chop has a bias toward negative infinity. Table 4-68 illustrates these cases, as well as the effect of the other precision treatments.

```
                        ¯2        ¯1         0         1         2

Truncate
   Signed magnitude  → →¯2 → → →¯1 → → → 0 ← ← ← 1 ← ← ← 2 ← ←
   Radix complement  ← ←¯2 ← ← ←¯1 ← ← ← 0 ← ← ← 1 ← ← ← 2 ← ←
   Digit complement  → →¯2 → → →¯1 → → → 0 ← ← ← 1 ← ← ← 2 ← ←
Make odd
   Signed magnitude  ← ← ← → → →¯1 ← ← ← → → → 1 ← ← ← → → →
   Radix complement  ← ← → → → →¯1 ← ← ← → → → 1 ← ← ← → → →
   Digit complement  → →¯2 → → → → → →¯0 → → → 1 ← ← ← → → →
Make odd and even
   Digit complement  ← ← ← → → →¯1 ← ← ← → → → 1 ← ← ← → → →
Round
   All notations     ← →¯2 ← ← →¯1 ← ← → 0 ← → → 1 ← → → 2 ← →
True round
   All notations     → →¯2 ← ← →¯1 ← → → 0 ← ← → 1 ← → → 2 ← ←
```

TABLE 4-68   Bias of precision treatment.

Making odd.   For binary radix, *making odd* forces the low-order digit to 1 by adding either one or zero (Program 4-69). Von Neumann introduced the concept for quotients in the IAS (Section 11.1). For higher radix, the action is more involved, but in principle is the same.

```
result←makeodd number
ᴀ signed-magnitude truncation to odd number
result←(×number)×(2|⌊|number)+⌊|number
```

PROGRAM 4-69   Precision treatment by making odd.

The effects of making odd are also sign-representation-dependent. For signed magnitude and radix complement, there is no bias. For digit complement, the negative numbers have a bias toward zero—that is, toward larger numbers. But when the negative numbers are made even in digit complement, the bias is removed. The magnitude of the deviation from the mean is twice as large for making odd as for rounding. Making odd is slightly more difficult to implement than truncation. Both methods ignore the digits that are discarded.

The NORC uses making odd in its decimal floating point. The coefficient uses signed magnitude, so no bias is introduced. Two exceptional provisions are revealing. If the retained coefficient digits are zero prior to the treatment or if all discarded digits are zero, the one is not added. So it is still possible to represent even integers, including zero.

Rounding.   *Rounding* selects the representable neighbor nearest to the given number; it is independent of the representation and is definitely the preferable treatment (Program 4-70).   Rounding has a considerably more involved implementation than truncation and making odd; it requires an addition, which may cause an overflow and may cost extra time. Nevertheless, von Neumann used it in multiplication, and the Univac 1103A had it as an option.

```
result←round number
a algebraic round
result←(×number)×⌊0.5+|number
```

PROGRAM 4-70   Precision treatment by rounding.

Unbiased rounding.   The rounding of Program 4-70 has a bias, a non-zero average error. Consider, in decimal, the rounding to an integer of uniformly distributed two-digit decimal fractions. The fraction 0.01 rounds down; it is matched in error by 0.99, which rounds up. Similar compensation occurs for all pairs *except* 0.00 and 0.50. *Unbiased rounding*, also called *symmetric rounding* (Program 4-71) rounds a fraction of 0.50 to the nearest even integer.

```
result←trueround number;bias
a unbiased algebraic round
bias←0.5≠2||number
result←(×number)×⌊(0.5×bias)+|number
```

PROGRAM 4-71   Precision treatment by unbiased rounding.

This type of precision treatment differs from ordinary rounding only when the given number is exactly between its two representable neighbors. For an even radix, the fractional part of the given number is then exactly one-half. The extra decision required by unbiased rounding and its marginal difference with ordinary rounding made it unattractive for early machine implementations. For modern machines it is quite feasible, but the tradition has persisted. The G20 incorporated this rounding.

```
result←round754 number
a IEEE 754 round modes
→CASE roundmode
   a unbiased round
C0:result←trueround number
   →ENDCASE
   a truncate to zero
C1:result←truncate number
   →ENDCASE
   a round upwards
C2:result←⌈number
   →ENDCASE
   a round downwards
C3:result←⌊number
ENDCASE:
```

PROGRAM 4-72   Optional precision treatment in the IEEE Standard.

Optional precision treatment.   Most modern machines still use truncation as the normal means of precision treatment in view of the expense of rounding and the not-too-unfavorable results of truncation. Some provide a rounding mode, as do the 1103A and the PDP11. The IEEE Standard gives four options: unbiased round, truncation, upward round, and downward round (Program 4-72). The last two options are used in interval arithmetic (Section 5.4). Table 4-73 shows a summary of the methods used and the operations to which they apply.

| | Fixed point | | Floating point | | |
	Truncate	Round	Truncate	Make odd	Round
Zuse Z4	~	~	+ × ÷ r		
Cambridge EDSAC	×	→			
Univac I	×	× ÷	~	~	~
IBM 701	× ÷	m	~	~	~
IBM 650	÷	→	+ × ÷		
IBM NORC	~	~		+ × ÷	
IBM 704	× ÷	m	+ × ÷		
IBM 705		→			
Univac 1103A	÷		+ × ÷		+ × ÷
Bull Gamma 60	÷		× ÷		
Bendix G20	~	~	÷		+ × u
IBM Stretch	m	m	+ × ÷		m
Ferranti Atlas	× ÷			+ × ÷	
English Electric KDF9		× ÷ m			+ × ÷ m
CDC 6600	~	~	+ × ÷		+ × ÷ m
Burroughs B5500	~	~			+ × ÷ i
IBM System/360	÷		+ × ÷		
Electrologica X8					+ × ÷
DEC PDP8	÷		~	~	~
DEC PDP11			+ × ÷		+ × ÷
Cray 1			+ × ÷		×
DEC VAX11	÷		i		+ × ÷
IEEE Standard 754	~	~			+ × ÷ u*

Legend: i = make integer; m = move; r = square root;
   u = unbiased round; + = add and subtract; → = shift right.
   ~ = not applicable; * = also directed rounding.

TABLE 4-73   Precision treatment in various machines.

Overflow and Underflow

The two classes of numbers that fall outside the representable range are *overflow* (when the exponent is larger than the representable positive exponent range) and *underflow* (when the exponent is smaller than the representable negative exponent range).

This lack of closure can be treated in two ways. First, the occurrence is signaled such that the program can take suitable action. Second, a special member of the representable domain, called an *extremum*, is chosen, such that the program can proceed undisturbed.

Out-of-Range Signal

An overflow or underflow may occur if either of two cases occurs:

- The program is invalid—that is, produces a wrong result.
- The program algorithm is valid, but the floating-point range is too narrow.

An interruption should be caused if either of these cases occurs. If no interrupt is given, and hence no fixup can occur, an indicator should be set to signal erroneous results. For enough information to be preserved that the program can extend the representation range, the exponent should be represented by its modular value, such that the correct exponent value can be reconstructed from the modular value and the overflow indication.

In the 360 the result of overflow was originally specified as unpredictable. The floating-point range was thought to be sufficient; it never is. As the machine entered production, this error had to be corrected; a modular exponent representation was used.

Extrema

Negligible. Figure 4-64 shows that the pickets tend to crowd together near zero. For a number between zero and the first non-zero picket, underflow occurs—which suggests that, when underflow occurs, the value of the number may have become negligibly small. In that event, there is no point in extending the floating-point range, and an interrupt is only a nuisance. Rather, the number can be recognized as the extremum *negligible* and be represented as such. Moreover, since negligible and zero have the same result when used as operands in arithmetic operations, they can use the same representation.

In the 360 an interrupt mask bit determines the representation for underflow in a modal way. When an underflow interrupt is given, the exponent is represented with its exact value except for the overflow bit. When the interrupt is masked off, the result is forced to zero (Program 4-91).

This mode solution aims to pass the problem to the user, but in practice the compilers may not offer user facilities to handle it. Moreover, the mode may cause complications in pipelined implementations. Therefore, it is more attractive either to substitute zero or to use an unmaskable interruption. The IEEE Standard (Program 4-78) makes the first choice.

Infinity. Just as zero is treated as the artificial neighbor of a number that underflows, so *infinity* can be defined as an artificial neighbor for a number that overflows. In contrast with zero, infinity does not have a neighbor number whose representation it can share with impunity. So a unique representation must be defined for positive and negative infinity.

Indefinite. Zuse used a consistent scheme for zero and infinity as representable members of the floating-point domain. He recognized that these two extrema do not close the domain; for example, infinity minus infinity, or zero times infinity, produce results that are still not representable. He solved the closure problem by introducing a third extremum, an *indefinite* operand, called *NaN*, not-a-number, in the IEEE Standard. Table 4-74 shows the rules that allow a consistent system to be defined.

Remarkably, Zuse's floating-point work was not known during the Stretch design. The Stretch uses infinity where indefinite should be employed. The 6600 is the first modern machine to have a complete set of extrema.

Add/subtract	Multiply	Divide	Compare
x ← n + n	x ← n × n	x ← n ÷ n	n >/=/< n
n ← n + ε	ε ← n × ε	ω ← n ÷ ε	n > ε
n ← ε + n	ε ← ε × n	ε ← ε ÷ n	ε < n
ω ← n + ω	ω ← n × ω	ε ← n ÷ ω	n < ω
ω ← ω + n	ω ← ω × n	ω ← ω ÷ n	ω > n
ω ← ω + ε	i ← ω × ε	ω ← ω ÷ ε	ω > ε
ω ← ε + ω	i ← ε × ω	ε ← ε ÷ ω	ε < ω
ω/i← ω + ω	ω ← ω × ω	i ← ω ÷ ω	ω u ω
ε ← ε + ε	ε ← ε × ε	i ← ε ÷ ε	ε = ε
i ← x + i	i ← x × i	i ← x ÷ i	x u i
i ← i + x	i ← i × x	i ← i × x	i u x
i ← i + i	i ← i × i	i ← i ÷ i	i u i

Legend: i = indefinite; n = representable number;
   u = unrelated; x = ω, ε, or n;
   ε = negligible or zero;
   ω = positive or negative infinity; / = or.

TABLE 4-74   Operations upon extrema.

Unordered.   The IEEE Standard also specifies the results of comparing extrema (rightmost column of Table 4-74). When at least one of the comparison operands is indefinite, the result is called *unordered*.

Encoding.   Zuse's Z4 uses a separate bit to identify the extrema (Program 4-75). The 6600 and IEEE Standard use a more economical representation by

```
┌Extremum
│ ↓Coefficient sign and leading digit

 │ │ Exp │ Coefficient                        │
 │ │     │                                    │

0 3     10                  32
Legend: Exp = exponent.
```

```
f14
ค Zuse Z4 floating-point number
ค base
base←2
ค sign encoding                 r←range4i rep
plus←1                          ค Zuse Z4 range interpretation
minus←0                         →IF rep[Extremum]
ค exponent allocation           THEN: ค extremum
Exp←3+ι7                              r←magni rep[Exp]
ค coefficient allocation              →ENDIF
Coef← 1 1 2 ,10+ι22             ELSE: ค normal range
ค extreme exponent                    r←(negnorm,posnorm)[rep[Coef[0]]]
extexp←radix*0⊥ρ1↓Exp           ENDIF:
ค extremum allocation
Extremum←0
ค radix point                   number←f14i rep;exponent;coefficient
point←0⊥ρ2↓Coef                 ค Zuse Z4 floating-point interpretation
ค range identifiers             exponent←radixcompi rep[Exp]
ค - normal range                coefficient←signmagni insertbit rep[Coef]
posnorm←0                       number←coefficient×base*exponent-point
negnorm←1
ค - extrema
zero←2
inf←3
posinf←4
neginf←5
indef←6
```

PROGRAM 4-75   Floating-point format and interpretation in the Zuse Z4.

indicating the extrema with distinct exponent values. Stretch uses a separate extremum bit and records the largest absolute exponent value encountered in the exponent field.

For the Z4 and the 6600, which have no interrupt, the extrema are highly desirable. For a machine with interrupts, the extrema are more of an option; however, programming practice has shown that this option is desirable.

4.4.2

Normal Form

The quasi-logarithmic form of floating point departs at critical points from the true logarithmic form. Most important, floating point can represent negative numbers and zero, which logarithms cannot. On the other hand, the exponent and mantissa part of a logarithm are each uniquely defined, which is not true of the exponent and coefficient of floating point.

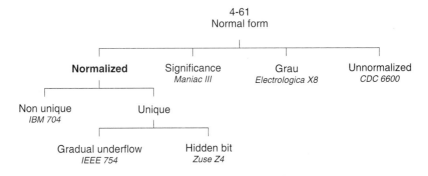

4-61
Normal form

TREE 4-76   Design choices for floating-point normal form.

Non-unique representation.   For a given number, we can select any exponent, provided the coefficient has enough precision. In practice, the precision of the coefficient is limited, which restricts the choice of exponent. Nevertheless, many representations may be equivalent and are therefore redundant. In Figure 4-64 half the pickets for binary base lie on top of the others; many lie on top of zero.

This lack of uniqueness leads to a second major design choice in floating point: the definition of a *normal form* (Tree 4-76). A normal form is equivalent to a selection rule for the exponent. Once it is known, the coefficient is unique. flr follows this approach (Program 4-60). The preferred representations are:

- Minimum exponent, or *normalized* form
- Minimum exponent magnitude, or *Grau* form
- Unique exponent, or *significance* form
- Arbitrary exponent, or *unnormalized* form

The term *minimum* refers to allowable exponent values; no representation discards significant high-order coefficient digits; one is choosing between the pickets of Figure 4-64 that are on top of one another. The various preferred representations, however, reflect different approaches to the low-order coefficient digits.

Normalized Form

In a *normalized number* the largest representable value of the coefficient (hence the minimum exponent) is selected (Program 4-77). Numbers of comparable magnitude have similar exponents. In the example of Table 4-63, the normalized form for the number 2 has exponent ‾1 and coefficient 4, or 111 0100; it is adjacent to 2.5, whose only possible representation, 111 0101, has the same exponent. The number with minimum exponent and zero coefficient conventionally represents zero.

```
    expzero normalize numexp;expnorm
  ⍝ normalized or specified exponent form
  →IF 0=1↑numexp
  THEN: ⍝ exponent for zero
      exponent←expzero
      →ENDIF
  ELSE: ⍝ minimal or specified exponent
      expnorm←⌊(1+base⊛|1↑numexp)+point-(⍴1↓Coef)×base⊛radix
      exponent←⌈/expnorm,1↓numexp
  ENDIF:coefficient←0⊥(1↑numexp)÷base*exponent-point
```

PROGRAM 4-77   Normalized form.

The normalized form is very common. It is particularly convenient when the exponent and coefficient are to be treated separately, as in mathematical subroutines.

Hidden bit.   The coefficients of all normalized numbers except zero have significant high-order digits. So, in base 2, the high-order coefficient bit is redundant. Zuse used only normalized numbers and eliminated the high-order bit of the coefficient from the floating-point format. One can imagine this bit being inserted as the number is interpreted and being removed as the number is represented—hence the name *hidden bit*. It is used in the PDP11 and the DEC VAX11 (1978). Some special exponent has to be reserved to represent zero.

Gradual underflow.   The exclusive use of the normalized form creates a gap around zero. In Table 4-63 it eliminates the representable numbers -0.25, -0.1875, -0.125, -0.0625, 0.0625, 0.125, 0.1875, and zero itself. This gap can be filled by allowing the numbers with smallest exponent value to have high-order non-significant digits (zeros, for positive numbers). The new pickets are spaced equal to the closest spacing; they are unique and include zero. This *gradual underflow* can be provided even if the hidden-bit notation is not used. Any normalized representation with unique zero is bi-unique: Not only does each bit string have only one interpretation, but each interpretation yields only one bit-string.

IEEE Standard.   The IEEE 754 Standard for floating-point arithmetic [IEEE, 1985; Stevenson, 1981] incorporates infinite and indefinite extrema, hidden bit, and gradual underflow (Program 4-78). Within the Standard 32- and 64-bit formats the exponent occupies 8 and 11 bits with a bias of 127 and 1023 respectively. This bias is one less than usual to balance the representation range. The largest exponent represents the infinities and indefinite. Table 4-79 shows the represented values for a short format of three exponent bits and four coefficient bits.

↓Sign

Exp	Coefficient

01   12   64

↓Sign

Exp	Coefficient

01   9   32

Legend: Exp = exponent.

```
f1754 size                              r←range754i rep;sign;exponent
⍝ IEEE 754 floating-point number        ⍝ IEEE 754 range interpretation
⍝ base                                   f1754ρrep
base←2                                   sign←rep[1↑Coef]
⍝ sign encoding                          exponent←1+biasi rep[Exp]
plus←0                                   →CASE((-extexp),extexp+1)ιexponent
minus←1                                  C0:→IFv/rep[2↓Coef]
⍝ exponent allocation                       THEN: ⍝ gradual underflow
Exp←1+ι 8 11[size=double]                       r←(posnorm,negnorm)[sign]
⍝ coefficient allocation                     →ENDIF
Coef← 0 0 ,(1+ρExp)+ιsize-(1+ρExp)        ELSE: ⍝ zero
⍝ radix point                                r←(poszero,negzero)[sign]
point←0⊥ρ2↓Coef                          ENDIF:→ENDCASE
⍝ extreme exponent                       C1:→IF1v/rep[2↓Coef]
extexp←(radix*0⊥ρ1↓Exp)-1                 THEN1: ⍝ indefinite
⍝ range identifiers                          r←indef
⍝ - normal range                             →ENDIF1
posnorm←0                                ELSE1: ⍝ infinite
negnorm←1                                    r←(posinf,neginf)[sign]
⍝ - extrema                              ENDIF1:→ENDCASE
poszero←2                                C2: ⍝ normalized range
negzero←3                                    r←(posnorm,negnorm)[sign]
posinf←4                                 ENDCASE:
neginf←5
indef←6


number←f1754i rep;exponent;coefficient         rep←insertbit rep
⍝ IEEE 754 floating-point interpretation        ⍝ expose hidden bit
f1754ρrep                                        rep[1]←1
exponent←1+biasi rep[Exp]
→IF exponent≠-extexp
THEN: ⍝ normalized range
   coefficient←signmagni insertbit rep[Coef]
   number←coefficient×base*exponent-point
   →ENDIF
ELSE: ⍝ zero and gradual underflow
   coefficient←signmagni rep[1↓Coef]
   number←coefficient×base*exponent+1-point
ENDIF:
```

PROGRAM 4-78   Floating-point format and representation in the IEEE Standard.

Significance Form

The substitution of representable neighbors for unrepresentable numbers introduces error. The architect who chooses the normalized form is, of course, aware of this fact, but he leaves the error analysis to the numerical analyst.

The designers of the Chicago Maniac III (1961) tried to encode the precision of a number in the representation [Ashenhurst and Metropolis, 1959]. They

Coefficient with hidden bit	Exponent −3 000	−2 001	−1 010	0 011	1 100	2 101	3 110	4 111
8 0(1)000	0	0.25	0.5	1	2	4	8	ω
9 0(1)001	0.03125	0.28125	0.5625	1.125	2.25	4.5	9	i
10 0(1)010	0.0625	0.3125	0.625	1.25	2.5	5	10	i
11 0(1)011	0.09375	0.34375	0.6875	1.375	2.75	5.5	11	i
12 0(1)100	0.125	0.375	0.75	1.5	3	6	12	i
13 0(1)101	0.15625	0.40625	0.8125	1.625	3.25	6.5	13	i
14 0(1)110	0.1875	0.4375	0.875	1.75	3.5	7	14	i
15 0(1)111	0.21875	0.46875	0.9375	1.875	3.75	7.5	15	i
‾8 1(1)000	‾0	‾0.25	‾0.5	‾1	‾2	‾4	‾8	-ω
‾9 1(1)001	‾0.03125	‾0.28125	‾0.5625	‾1.125	‾2.25	‾4.5	‾9	i
‾10 1(1)010	‾0.0625	‾0.3125	‾0.625	‾1.25	‾2.5	‾5	‾10	i
‾11 1(1)011	‾0.09375	‾0.34375	‾0.6875	‾1.375	‾2.75	‾5.5	‾11	i
‾12 1(1)100	‾0.125	‾0.375	‾0.75	‾1.5	‾3	‾6	‾12	i
‾13 1(1)101	‾0.15625	‾0.40625	‾0.8125	‾1.625	‾3.25	‾6.5	‾13	i
‾14 1(1)110	‾0.1875	‾0.4375	‾0.875	‾1.75	‾3.5	‾7	‾14	i
‾15 1(1)111	‾0.21875	‾0.46875	‾0.9375	‾1.875	‾3.75	‾7.5	‾15	i

Legend: exponent in 3-bit biased notation with bias 3;
        coefficient in 4-bit signed-magnitude notation,
        with hiddden bit and gradual underflow;
        extrema for infinity (ω) and indefinite (i).

TABLE 4-79   Value set of a reduced IEEE Standard format.

adjust exponents so that only significant coefficient digits are represented. Therefore, the three representations of the number 2 in Table 4-63 refer to three quite distinct numbers: All three have the value 2, but their average errors are 1, 1/2, and 1/4 respectively; there is no exact 2. Each representation has a unique meaning.

In Section 5.4 we shall see to what extent such significance information can be preserved consistently in so-called *significance arithmetic*.

Order-of-magnitude zero.   In the significance form a number with zero coefficient is considered a number with minimal significance. Since the unrepresented bits to the right of a fraction are in general not zero, the number is a band of uncertainty, evenly distributed about zero, whose extent is given by the exponent; one cannot even be sure of its sign. Such a number is called an *order-of-magnitude zero* (OMZ).

Because the OMZ has magnitude but minimal precision, it behaves peculiarly in arithmetic. For the representation of Table 4-63, $0.0625 + 0$ gives 0.0625, but $0.0625 + 0 \times 2^3$ gives 0×2^3.

In the Stretch, OMZs are allowed. Moreover, there is a range of values for negligible and its inverse, infinity. Creation of an OMZ sets a Lost Significance indicator, which can interrupt. In the 360 the creation of an OMZ also sets a Lost Significance indicator, which can interrupt, but true zero is not separately marked, nor is its arithmetic different.

One uses OMZs at his peril. The IEEE Standard recognizes only true zero and does not signal lost significance.

Grau Form

The *Grau* form selects where possible a zero exponent by taking the exponent's minimal absolute value (Program 4-80). This choice allows the integer coefficient value to be the same as the fixed-point representation of the given number [Grau, 1962]. For instance, the result of 2×1.5 has zero exponent and as coefficient the value 3; this is not true for the normalized or significance forms.

```
grau number
A grau normal form
 →IF 0=number
 THEN: A exponent for zero
     exponent←zero
     →ENDIF
 ELSE: A minimal exponent
     exponent←0⌊⌊(1+base⊛|number)+point-(ρ1↓Coef)×base⊛radix
 ENDIF:coefficient←number÷base*exponent-point
A exponent with minimal magnitude
 →WHILE(exponent<0)∧0=base|coefficient
     exponent←exponent+1
     coefficient←coefficient÷base
     →△
 ENDWHILE:
```

PROGRAM 4-80   Grau form.

The Grau form assumes an integer coefficient and an unbiased exponent placed leftmost in the format. In Table 4-63 the Grau representation is equal to the fixed-point representation for the integer range 0 through 7; the negative range -8 through -1 can also match fixed point when the exponent is represented as the EXCLUSIVE-OR of the coefficient sign and the exponent digits. For the entire coefficient range, -8 through 7, the floating-point representation is equal to the fixed-point representation. For a more realistic coefficient size, the range that matches fixed point may satisfy the requirements for housekeeping—such as address computation. So the fixed-point representation may be omitted entirely, as is the case for the Electrologica X8 (1965)—the design that pioneered the Grau form (Program 4-85). In machines that have both datatypes, the Grau form can be used to simplify conversion to and from fixed point.

The hidden bit cannot be used to make the Grau representation bi-unique, because more than half the representands are used. So even for binary radix there is not a redundant bit that can be "hidden." Gradual underflow, however, can be specified for the Grau form.

Unnormalized Form

The normalized form and the Grau form specify a preferred representation. Why not allow all equivalent representations without specifying a preferred one? As long as the preferred form can readily be obtained by Normalize operations, the results of arithmetic operations may be specified so as to simplify or speedup arithmetic implementation.

In the *unnormalized* form the exponent depends upon the operation. From an operation and its operands, a preferred exponent is derived that must be

↓Sign

	Exponent	Coefficient	

01   12   60

```
f16600
∩ CDC 6600 floating-point number
∩ base
 base←2
∩ exponent allocation                r←range6600i rep;sign;exponent;negzerox
 Exp←1+ι11                            ∩ CDC 6600 range interpretation
∩ coefficient allocation             sign←rep[1↑Coef]
 Coef←0,12+ι48                        exponent←digitcompi signinv rep[Exp]≠sign
∩ radix point                        negzerox←(exponent=0)∧rep[1↑Exp]=sign
 point←0                             →CASE(negzerox,(exponent=extexp),∧/rep=sign)ι1
∩ extreme exponent                   C0:  ∩ indefinite
 extexp←(radix*0⌊ρ1↓Exp)-1               r←indef
∩ range identifiers                      →ENDCASE
∩ - normal range                     C1:  ∩ infinity
 posnorm←0                               r←(posinf,neginf)[sign]
 negnorm←1                               →ENDCASE
 poszero←2                           C2:  ∩ zero
 negzero←3                               r←(poszero,negzero)[sign]
∩ - extrema                              →ENDCASE
 posinf←4                            C3:  ∩ normal range
 neginf←5                                r←(posnorm,negnorm)[sign]
 indef←6                             ENDCASE:


 numexp←f16600i rep;exponent;coefficient;number
∩ CDC 6600 floating-point interpretation
 exponent←digitcompi signinv rep[Exp]≠rep[1↑Coef]
 coefficient←digitcompi rep[Coef]
 number←coefficient×base*exponent
 numexp←number,exponent
```

PROGRAM 4-81   Floating point in the CDC 6600.

used if possible; otherwise, a smaller exponent is used. normalize (Program 4-77) allows unnormalized operation. The operand numexp is a two-element vector. The first element of numexp is the number to be represented; the second element is the preferred exponent for this representation. Observe that the normal form is used when the preferred exponent is omitted.

The 6600 follows the unnormalized form (Program 4-81). Its operations do not always preserve maximum precision (Section 5.4). Some other computers, such as the IBM 704, provide unnormalized Add operations. These are useful for converting from floating to fixed point.

Non-unique representation.   It is important that a floating-point system interpret all bit strings correctly—even unnormalized numbers encountered during normalized operation. Non-unique representations should always be interpreted correctly, as in fli (Program 4-60). These numbers, and other non-unique representations, should be so interpreted even if the result of an operation is specified to be in the preferred form. However, the designer of the implementation may decide to interpret the non-preferred representations more slowly.

Table 4-82 shows the domain closure and normal form of various machines.

	Range closure	Normal form	Order of magnitude
Zuse Z4	0 ω i	h	
IBM 650		n/u	OMZ
IBM 704		n/u	OMZ
Univac 1103A		n	
Bull Gamma 60		n	
Bendix G20		n/u	
IBM Stretch	∈ ω	n/u	OMZ
Chicago Maniac III		s	OMZ
Ferranti Atlas		n/u	OMZ
English Electric KDF9		n	OMZ
CDC 6600	0 ω i	u	OMZ
Burroughs B5500		n/u	
IBM System/360		n/u	OMZ
Electrologica X8		grau	
DEC PDP11		h	
CDC Star100	∈ ω i	n/u	OMZ
Cray 1		u	
DEC VAX11		h	
IEEE Standard 754	0 ω i	h	

Legend: h = normalized with hidden bit; i = indefinite;
n = normalized; s = significance; u = unnormalize
OMZ = order of magnitude zero; ∈ = negligible;
ω = inifinity; 0 = zero or ∈.

TABLE 4-82   Floating-point domain in various machines.

4.4.3
Compound Structure

We now turn to the third consequence of the top-level encoding of floating-point numbers: compound structure. This attribute derives from encoding a number with exponent, coefficient, and implied base, as shown in Tree 4-83. The two explicit components must be allocated within the floating-point format. This allocation decision should be consistent with the encoding and allocation of the constituent parts, as well as with the remainder of the data formats.

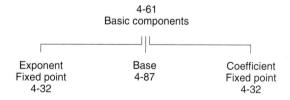

TREE 4-83   Design choices for basic floating-point components.

For optimal consistency,

- The entire compound floating-point number must be of a size commensurate with other formats.
- The exponent and the coefficient should each be severally manipulable in a simple way without special operations. Such manipulation is required, for example, when a power or a logarithm of a floating-point argument is taken.

- Since the integers are a subset of the rational numbers, fixed point should be a subset of floating point. All fixed-point operations can be applied to a subset of the floating-point domain, or a subset of the fixed-point operations can be applied to the entire domain.

Several corollaries follow:

1. The sign notation of the exponent should be the same as for fixed-point numbers.
2. The sign and the digits of the exponent should be adjacent and allocated as in fixed point.
3. The sign notation of the coefficient should be the same as for fixed-point numbers.
4. The sign and the digits of the coefficient should be adjacent and allocated as in fixed point.
5. The representations of fixed-point numbers and floating-point numbers should be identical in their common domain.
6. The floating-point representation should allow fixed-point comparison.
7. The representation of zero and sign should be the same as for fixed-point numbers.

As always, the field sizes for the exponent and the coefficient should be appropriate for the format system in use, *four, six,* or other.

It is impossible to satisfy all these desiderata simultaneously; different designers have sacrificed different ones, as illustrated in Table 4-84. The numbers at the head of each column correspond to the listed desiderata.

	Exponent		Coefficient		Format as fixed		
	(1)	(2)	(3)	(4)	(5)	(6)	(7)
Zuse Z4	~	×	~		~	~	~
IBM 650		×	×	×		n	n
IBM NORC	~	×	~	×	~	~	~
IBM 704		×	×			n	n
Univac 1103A		×	×			×	×
Bull Gamma 60		×				n	n
IBM 1620	×	×	×	×			
Bendix G20	×	×	×				×
IBM Stretch	×	×	×	×			
Chicago Maniac III		×	×	×			
Ferranti Atlas		×	×	×			n
English Electric KDF9		×	×				×
CDC 6600		×	×			n	n
Burroughs B5500	~	×	~		~	~	~
IBM System/360		×					n
Electrologica X8	×	×	×	×	×		
DEC PDP11		×					
CDC Star100	×	×	×	×			
Cray 1		×					×
DEC VAX11		×					
IEEE Standard 754	~	×	~		~	~	~

Legend: (1,3) sign notation as in fixed point; (2,4) contiguous allocation; (5) in common domain; (6) for comparison; (7) for zero and sign test; n = satisfied when normalized; × = satisfied; ~ = not applicable, since no fixed point.

TABLE 4-84   Floating-point criteria in various machines.

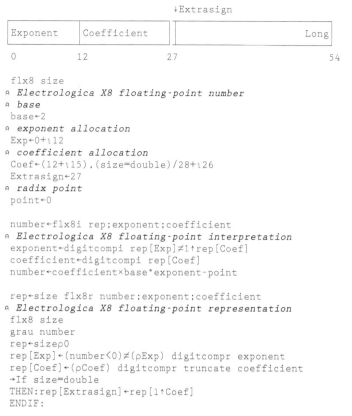

```
flx8 size
⍝ Electrologica X8 floating-point number
⍝ base
base←2
⍝ exponent allocation
Exp←0+⍳12
⍝ coefficient allocation
Coef←(12+⍳15),(size=double)/28+⍳26
Extrasign←27
⍝ radix point
point←0

number←flx8i rep;exponent;coefficient
⍝ Electrologica X8 floating-point interpretation
exponent←digitcompi rep[Exp]≠1↑rep[Coef]
coefficient←digitcompi rep[Coef]
number←coefficient×base*exponent-point

rep←size flx8r number;exponent;coefficient
⍝ Electrologica X8 floating-point representation
flx8 size
grau number
rep←sizeρ0
rep[Exp]←(number<0)≠(ρExp) digitcompr exponent
rep[Coef]←(ρCoef) digitcompr truncate coefficient
→If size=double
THEN:rep[Extrasign]←rep[1↑Coef]
ENDIF:
```

PROGRAM 4-85   Floating-point representation in the Electrologica X8.

Desiderata 1 through 4 concern the parts of the floating-point format. They can all be satisfied—as they are, for example, in the Stretch and the Electrologica X8.

Desiderata 5, 6, and 7 relate the floating-point format as a whole to fixed point; these tend to conflict with the first four.

Common domain as in fixed point.   The common-domain desideratum 5 aids in converting to and from fixed point, and ultimately I/O, formats.

Desideratum 5 is very demanding; we consider it for integer fixed-point data. (For fractional fixed point, similar requirements apply.) First, the representation of a zero exponent must be a zero string. Then, the coefficient must be an integer placed rightmost in the format, using the fixed-point sign notation (desideratum 3).

With signed magnitude, the coefficient sign position must match the fixed-point sign position. This match can be achieved without violating desideratum 4 when the sign is placed to the right of the digits, as in the Stretch.

When the sign notation is radix or digit complement, the exponent must be complemented for negative coefficient values. Because the exponent is zero in the common domain, the coefficient sign and digits can be adjacent (4).

The Electrologica X8 (Program 4-85) is the only example that meets desiderata 1 through 4 as well as the common-domain requirement of desideratum 5. The Stretch and 1620, which satisfy desiderata 1 through 4, fail

```
numexp←flbsi rep;exponent;coefficient;number
∩ bias signed-magnitude fractional interpretation
exponent←biasi rep[Exp]
coefficient←signmagni rep[Coef]
number←coefficient×base*exponent-point
numexp←number,exponent

rep←size flbsr numexp;exponent;coefficient
∩ bias signed-magnitude fractional representation
(1↑1↓numexp,-extexp) normalize numexp
rep←sizeρ0
rep[Coef]←(ρCoef) signmagnr truncate coefficient
rep[Exp]←(ρExp) biasr exponent
```

PROGRAM 4-86   Floating-point using signed magnitude and bias.

desideratum 5 because their coefficient is a fraction, whereas their fixed-point number is an integer.

Comparison with fixed point.   When floating-point numbers compare as if they were fixed point (desideratum 6), the operation set is reduced, and the comparison is fast. Both advantages are minor.

Desideratum 6 can be satisfied only when the floating-point representation is unique. Otherwise, differing bit patterns must compare equal, which is not the case in fixed point. When the representation is non-unique, one can still apply desideratum 6 to the normal form, but a distinct floating-point Compare operation should be provided.

The floating-point compare sequence can use fixed-point arithmetic when the following are true:

- The numbers are normalized.
- The exponent is to the left of the coefficient.
- The exponent is in bias or inverted-sign notation.
- The representation of the coefficient is the same as for fixed point.
- The sign position of the coefficient and fixed point are the same.

As a consequence, desideratum 1 is always violated if desideratum 6 is satisfied. Many early machines, such as the IBM 704 and Univac 1103A, allowed fixed-point comparison for floating-point numbers. Program 4-86 gives a representation that matches signed-magnitude fixed point.

Sign and zero as in fixed point.   Desideratum 7 allows the use of fixed-point sign and zero test. The exponent value for true zero must have a zero string as representation, and the coefficient sign position must match the integer sign position. These properties hold for representations that can be compared with fixed point, so desideratum 7 is always satisfied when desideratum 6 is satisfied.

4.4.4

Base

There are three radices involved in the floating-point representation: those of the exponent and coefficient representation and the implied base of which the exponent specifies the power.

The base must be a power (often 1) of the coefficient's radix. Otherwise, a shift of the coefficient digits—a basic action—would require a complex change

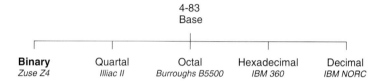

TREE 4-87   Design choices for floating-point base.

both in the exponent and in the coefficient. Tree 4-87 shows bases that have been used.

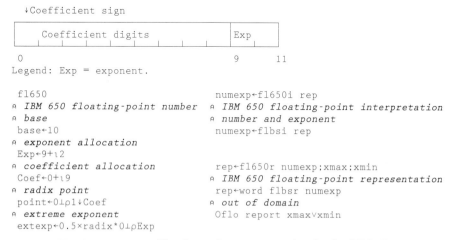

PROGRAM 4-88   Floating-point representation in the IBM 650.

Decimal base.   In computers whose integer format is exclusively decimal, such as the 650, decimal floating point is obviously preferred. Program 4-88 shows the floating-point representation of the 650. The 650 shares the use of f l b s i and f l b s r with the 704 (Program 4-89) and the 360; the only difference is in the choice of base and allocation.

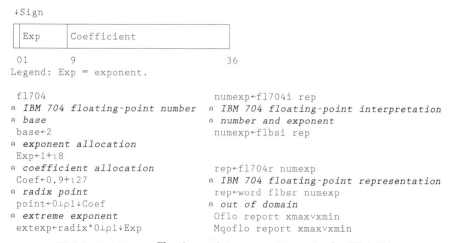

PROGRAM 4-89   Floating-point representation in the IBM 704.

Base→	Alignment-shift frequency					Normalization-shift frequency				
	2	4	8	16	32	2	4	8	16	32
Zero result→						1.42	1.42	1.42	1.42	1.42
Overflow→						19.65	10.67	6.52	5.50	5.69
Shift										
0	32.61	38.24	45.77	47.32	52.52	59.38	72.11	79.40	82.35	83.86
1	12.11	18.54	19.77	26.02	26.37	6.78	7.96	8.75	7.29	5.99
2	8.61	12.83	11.92	10.47	5.92	3.47	3.35	1.61	1.38	0.87
3	6.72	9.87	6.26	2.24	1.82	2.35	1.49	0.38	1.01	0.88
4	7.17	3.01	1.73	1.31	2.08	1.91	0.34	0.43	0.30	0.41
5	3.88	2.05	1.10	1.70	1.87	1.06	0.14	0.71	0.32	0.88
6	4.39	1.01	0.89	1.24		0.56	0.92	0.25	0.43	
7	4.82	0.72	1.52			0.48	0.18	0.22		
8	1.29	0.63	1.00			0.16	0.13	0.28		
9	1.28	0.94				0.14	0.15			
10	1.31	0.72				0.08	0.18			
11	0.48	0.97				0.09	0.17			
12	0.58	0.74				0.32	0.27			
13	0.38	0.27				0.55	0.52			
14	0.38					0.16				
15	0.32					0.02				
16	0.33					0.04				
17	0.32					0.09				
18	0.40					0.08				
19	0.48					0.07				
20	0.36					0.12				
21	0.53					0.07				
22	0.48					0.07				
23	0.33					0.09				
24	0.36					0.11				
25	0.36					0.16				
26	0.19					0.52				
	9.50	9.43	10.04	9.70	9.42	←Excessive shift				

TABLE 4-90   Implementation shifts for various floating-point radices.

Binary base. With binary coefficients, the binary base is used most frequently, starting with Zuse's Z3 and Z4.

Large base. Sweeney's study [1965], done in 1958 and later, clearly shows the implementation advantages of a large base. His data show that the frequencies of alignment and normalization shifts are sharply lower for higher bases—for example, for bases 8 and 16 (Table 4-90). The convergence of improvement is rapid: There is little gain in using a base of 16 over one of 8. One would select between these bases to match the format system.

The G20 pioneered the use of a higher power of 2 as base by selecting base 8. In designing the 360 we used a *four* system, so base 16, with 4-bit shifting units, was more suitable (Program 4-91). The University of Illinois has experimented with base 4 in the Illiac II (1961) and bases 256 and 16 in the Illiac III (1963) [Garner, 1976].

There is, of course, a price to the larger base. Normalization in base 2^p allows up to $p - 1$ high-order zeros. In effect, worst-case precision is reduced by $p - 1$ bits, and average precision is reduced by somewhat less. On the other hand, the exponent now requires $\log_2(\log_2 p)$ fewer bits for its expression. Equivalently, for a given-length floating-point word, the bits one loses in the fraction are somewhat—but not entirely—compensated in the exponent. For base 16, for example, one saves 2 bits in the exponent and loses 3 in worst-case precision; for base 256, 3 bits are saved and 7 are lost.

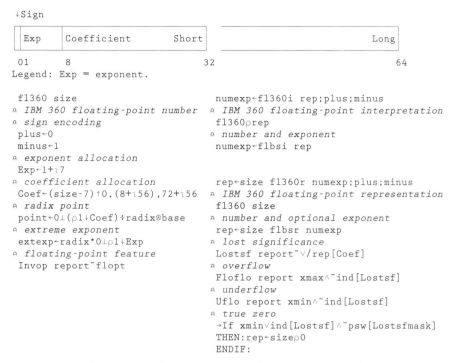

```
↓Sign

┌─┬───────┬─────────────────────────┬──────┬─┬────────────────────────────────────────────┬──────┐
│ │ Exp   │ Coefficient       Short │      │ │                                       Long │      │
└─┴───────┴─────────────────────────┴──────┴─┴────────────────────────────────────────────┴──────┘
 01      8                          32                                                       64
Legend: Exp = exponent.


 fl360 size                           numexp←fl360i rep;plus;minus
A IBM 360 floating-point number     A IBM 360 floating-point interpretation
A sign encoding                       fl360ρrep
 plus←0                             A number and exponent
 minus←1                              numexp←flbsi rep
A exponent allocation
 Exp←1+ι7
A coefficient allocation              rep←size fl360r numexp;plus;minus
 Coef←(size-7)↑0,(8+ι56),72+ι56     A IBM 360 floating-point representation
A radix point                         fl360 size
 point←0⊥(ρ1↓Coef)÷radix⊛base       A number and optional exponent
A extreme exponent                    rep←size flbsr numexp
 extexp←radix*0⊥ρ1↓Exp              A lost significance
A floating-point feature              Lostsf report˜∨/rep[Coef]
 Invop report˜flopt                 A overflow
                                      Floflo report xmax∧˜ind[Lostsf]
                                    A underflow
                                      Uflo report xmin∧˜ind[Lostsf]
                                    A true zero
                                      →If xmin∨ind[Lostsf]∧˜psw[Lostsfmask]
                                      THEN:rep←sizeρ0
                                      ENDIF:
```

PROGRAM 4-91   Floating-point representation in the IBM System/360.

In the 360, the loss in precision is quite acceptable for the long format. The short format, even if it had a true 24-bit fraction, would be unsuitable for error-propagating calculations, and losing 3 more still leaves 21, adequate for many calculations not given to error propagation.

Position of the Radix Point

In principle, any radix point can be used for the coefficient. The desire to match the fixed-point representation, however, favors either a pure integer or a pure fraction.

Multiple formats.   When floating-point formats of several lengths are available, a number should preferably have the same exponent in each. For normalized numbers, conversion from one format to the other is then by truncation or by addition of low-order bits. For an integer coefficient, this procedure poses a problem. The B5500, whose single-precision coefficient is an integer, keeps the exponent constant for single and double precision by using a fixed radix point and treating the low-order extension as a fraction (Program 4-92). The CDC STAR100 (1973), however, keeps the radix rightmost in all formats.

Magnitude range.   Table 4-93 shows that the fractional coefficient has a rather balanced magnitude range; when the exponent has the same range in the positive and negative directions, nearly every normalized number has a representable reciprocal. For an integer coefficient, this reciprocal property is not true. These range considerations are of major importance to the designer

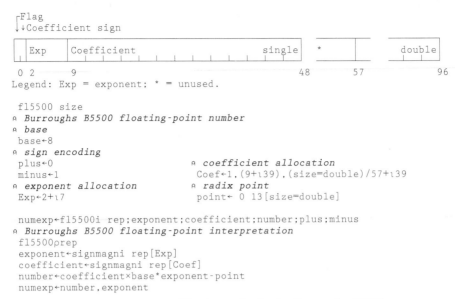

```
⌐Flag
↓↓Coefficient sign

│  ┌───┬──────────────────────────────────┬────────┐ ┌─┬────────┬─────────┐
│  │Exp│ Coefficient                      │  single│ │*│        │  double │
│  └───┴──────────────────────────────────┴────────┘ └─┴────────┴─────────┘
  0 2      9                                       48   57                96
Legend: Exp = exponent;  * = unused.

  fl5500 size
 ⋂ Burroughs B5500 floating-point number
 ⋂ base
  base←8
 ⋂ sign encoding
  plus←0                        ⋂ coefficient allocation
  minus←1                        Coef←1,(9+ι39),(size=double)/57+ι39
 ⋂ exponent allocation          ⋂ radix point
  Exp←2+ι7                        point← 0 13[size=double]

  numexp←fl5500i rep;exponent;coefficient;number;plus;minus
 ⋂ Burroughs B5500 floating-point interpretation
  fl5500ρrep
  exponent←signmagni rep[Exp]
  coefficient←signmagni rep[Coef]
  number←coefficient×base*exponent-point
  numexp←number,exponent
```

PROGRAM 4-92   Floating-point in the Burroughs B5500.

of arithmetic subroutines [Kuki and Ascoly, 1971] and influenced the choice of the bias.

Implementation.   Exponent determination in floating-point addition is independent of the radix point. For multiplication and division, the implementation is slightly easier for a fractional coefficient than for an integral one.

4.4.5

Range and Precision

What range is sufficient for floating point? What precision is adequate? The first question concerns the exponent length; the second, the coefficient length.

Exponent length.   Experience with the 704 family and the 1103A family confirmed the range of 2^{-128} to 2^{127} (10^{-38} to 10^{38}) as usually adequate. The designers of the Stretch, building on 704 experience, allowed more range, but chiefly because doing so was easy rather than because of user pressure. When

	Maximum			Minimum		
	Exponent	Coefficient	Value	Exponent	Coefficient	Value
IBM 704						
Fraction	2*127	2*0	2*127	2*⁻128	2*⁻1	2*⁻129
Integer*	2*127	2*27	2*154	2*⁻128	2*26	2*⁻102
B5500						
Fraction*	8*63	8*0	8*63	8*⁻63	8*⁻1	8*⁻64
Integer	8*63	8*16	8*79	8*⁻63	8*15	8*⁻48

Legend: * hypothetical radix point, other is actual.

TABLE 4-93   Representation range for fraction or integer coefficient.

	Range —		Precision
	Low	High	
Zuse Z4	-20	20	7
IBM 650	-50	50	8
IBM NORC	-50	50	13
IBM 704	-38	38	7
Univac 1103A	-38	38	7
Bull Gamma 60	-40	39	10
IBM 1620	-50	50	1-99
Bendix G20	-38	38	6 12
IBM Stretch	-154	154	14
Ferranti Atlas	-38	38	12
English Electric KDF9	-38	38	4 11
CDC 6600	-294	322	14
Burroughs B5500	-45	68	11 22
IBM System/360	-77	77	6 15
Electrologica X8	-616	616	3 11
DEC PDP11	-38	38	6 16
CDC Star100	-32 -9849	44 9877	7 14
Cray 1	-2466	2466	14
DEC VAX11	-38	38	7 16
IEEE Standard 754	-38 -307	38 307	7 15

Legend: range in integral powers of 10;
precision in equivalent decimal digits.

TABLE 4-94 Range and relative error in floating point.

the designers of the IBM 7094 (1963) went to a 72-bit double-precision word, they elected not to use any of the bits for increased range. This decision seems to have caused little user difficulty. On the other hand, designers of the Univac 1108 did allow for increased range in their 72-bit format. No strong case can be made for a range much larger than 2^{128}.

The early manuals for the Cray 1 (1976) specify a large and unbalanced exponent range: -16384 to $+8191$. The large range reflects Cray's philosophy that interruptions for overflow or underflow are expensive in pipelined implementations; the large range minimizes these. The unbalanced range is a matter of coding convenience. If the leftmost two digits of the exponent are 00 or 01, the exponent is negative. If they are 10, it is positive; 11 is reserved for tagging overflowed numbers, to be tested later by branching. The final design of the Cray 1, however, has a balanced exponent range (Section 14.4).

Coefficient length.   One can group large scientific computations into two classes according to whether rounding error is propagated throughout a long computation. Monte Carlo computations, data reduction, parameter studies involving millions of independent evaluations of a few formulas, finding roots of equations by iterative methods, integrations, and so on, make modest precision demands, for there is no cumulative precision loss. Matrix inversions, solutions of linear systems, solutions of partial differential equations, and solutions of systems of ordinary differential equations all require carrying many digits.

For the first class of computations, the 27-digit precision of the 1103A and the 704 is more than adequate. For the second, it is marginal at best and is often grossly insufficient. When the Stretch was designed (before the 7090 [1959]), it was intended chiefly for large computations, often partial differential

	Base	Radix	Exponent		Point	Coefficient	
			Code	Size		Code	Size
Zuse Z4	2	2	r-c	e,7	23	s-m	s,↓23
IBM 650	10	10	bias	2d	8	s-m	s,8d
IBM NORC	10	10	bias	2d	13	s-m	s,13d
IBM 704	2	2	bias	8	27	s-m	s,27
Univac 1103A	2	2	bias*	8	27	d-c	28
Bull Gamma 60	10	10	bias	3,1d	10	s-m	s,10d
IBM 1620	10	10	s-m	2d,s	2-100	s-m	2-100d,s
Bendix G20	8	2	s-m	s,6	7 14	s-m	s,7 14o
IBM Stretch	2	2	s-m	10,s,e	48	s-m	48,s,f
Chicago Maniac III	2	2	bias*	8	39	r-c	40
Ferranti Atlas	8	2	r-c*	8	13	r-c	s,13o
IBM 7094	2	2	bias	8	27 54	s-m	s,27 54
CDC 6600	2	2	˜d-c*	11	0	d-c	49
Burroughs B5500	8	2	s-m	s,6	0 13	s-m	s,13 26o
IBM System/360	16	2	bias	7	6 14	s-m	s,6 14h
Electrologica X8	2	2	d-c*	12	0	d-c	15 41
Burroughs B6500	8	2	s-m	s,6 15	0 13	s-m	s,13 26o
DEC PDP11	2	2	bias	8	23 55	s-m	s,↓23 55
IBM System/370	16	2	bias	7	6 14	s-m	s,6 14 28h
CDC Star100	2	2	r-c*	8 16	0	r-c	24 48
Cray 1	2	2	bias	15	48	s-m	s,48
DEC VAX11	2	2	bias	8	23 55	s-m	s,↓23 55
IEEE Standard 754	2	2	bias	8 11	22 51	s-m	s,↓22 51

Legend: d = decimal; e = extrema bit; f = flag bit; h = hexadecimal;
     o = octal; s = sign; d-c = digit complement;
     r-c = radix complement; s-m = signed magnitude; - = through;
     ↓ = hidden bit; * = negative coefficient inverts exponent;
     ˜ = sign inversion.

TABLE 4-95   Floating-point representation in various machines.

equations. High precision was mandatory, so the word size was made large, with 48 coefficient bits. The 6600 was intended for the same applications, and its designers also chose a 48-bit floating-point coefficient. The 7094 and Univac 1110 designers provided built-in double-precision hardware to handle this class of problems.

When the 360 was designed in 1962, a survey was made to attempt to discover the use of double-precision subroutines on the 7090s. Almost every user used them at one time or another; some quoted usage as high as 3 percent. We then surveyed users of the CDC 1604 (1960), which has a 48-bit word with a 36-digit coefficient. We found only one 1604 installation that had double-precision subroutines in its library, and that one reported little use. From this finding we concluded that a 48-bit floating-point word would be ideal. This conclusion agrees with von Neumann's original recommendation for a 40-bit fixed-point word.

For the 360, we decided to provide two precisions of floating-point—a short precision (21 effective binary digits) suitable only for computations not propagating rounding error, and a long precision (53 effective digits) intended for all matrix and differential-equation work. The flexibility of several different floating-point precisions turns out to be somewhat hard to use via higher languages, such as FORTRAN and PL/I.

Table 4-94 shows various machines' range and error in floating point; Table 4-95 shows floating-point representation choices.

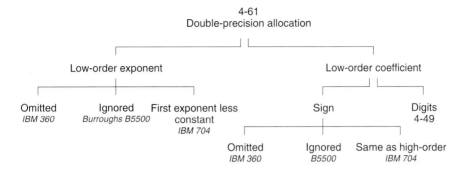

TREE 4-96   Design choices for double-precision floating point.

Double-precision formats.   One can provide a general double-precision datatype, usable for operands in registers or memory. Matrix inner products and some arithmetic-function subroutines require double-precision intermediate results to preserve normal precision even when the operands and final results are single precision [Wilkinson, 1963]. Some machines, therefore, limit the double-precision datatype to register operands only. Tree 4-96 gives the design choices for double-precision floating-point representation.

User pressure caused the provision of extended-precision floating-point in the 7094 (144-bit formats). Similarly, the B6500 and IBM System/370 (1971) introduced double-precision formats [Case and Padegs, 1978]. The Burroughs machines and the STAR100 extend the exponent as well. There is no evidence that use of these formats is high; they may not be worthwhile.

Temporary formats.   The IEEE Standard defines, for its short 32-bit format and for its long 64-bit format, temporary formats of at least 44 and 79 bits, respectively. These temporary formats are intended for intermediate results, so that arithmetic subroutines may produce results with the same accuracy as those of the normal arithmetic operations.

4.4.6
Bibliography

Ashenhurst and Metropolis [1959], Brent [1973], Case and Padegs [1978], Cody [1973], Cody and Kuki [1973], Garner [1976], D. Goldberg [1990], I.B. Goldberg [1967], Grau [1962], IEEE [1985], Knuth [1981], Kuki and Ascoly [1971], McCracken [1957], Morris [1971], Stevenson [1981], Sweeney [1965], Wilkinson [1963], Zuse [1936].

4.5
Arrays

4.5.1
The Array as Program Primitive

Data structures can be roughly divided into arrays and graphs. The first class has a homogeneous multidimensional structure; examples are vectors,

including stacks, and matrices. The second class has the structure of a network; an example is the tree.

Requirements

The array as a mathematical concept was well-established before computers were invented. Let us consider the mathematical object and its associated operations as the primitive used in programs.

Mathematical concept.   An array's elements are placed in groups of equal size. The number of elements in a group is called that group's *dimension*. Groups may again be placed in groups; the size of such a group is then a *higher dimension*. The number of times this process is repeated—the number of dimensions of the array—is the *rank* of the array.

The *matrix* is an array with rank 2; the *vector* has rank 1; a *scalar*, a single ungrouped element, has rank 0.

Homogeneity.   Arrays may be *homogeneous*, with all elements of the same datatype, or *inhomogeneous*. Array constructors (such as Insert and Delete) and selectors (such as Index) operate on arrays of both kinds. Inhomogeneous vectors are often called *records*; arrays of them are *files* or *structures*.

The conceptual economy of arrays, however, comes mostly from operating alike on all elements, which can be done only for homogeneous arrays. This section will treat only homogeneous arrays.

Element type.   In the simplest case, the element is some primitive datatype—a bit, a character, or a number.

Obstacles to Using Arrays as Entities

Even though the array is as common a program primitive as the individual variable, we find that most programs go through arrays element by element and ignore the inherent power of treating the structure as an entity. What obstacles cause the advantages present in principle to be ignored in practice?

Homogeneity of application.   Most mathematical array operators require homogeneous arrays.   Therefore, a first issue is whether real problems arising in nature are sufficiently homogeneous and exception-free to be so represented. For example, most of the early atmospheric models used for weather prediction were quite homogeneous.   Modern models, however, include complex boundary-layer behavior reflecting the geographic roughness of mountains and the thermal roughness of ocean currents. Similarly, the partial differential equations for neutron diffusion in a nuclear reactor (Figure 4-30) must cope with numerous internal materials boundaries. How many worthwhile problems have the homogeneity to allow a completely uniform treatment?

It may be countered that some of these boundaries can in turn be represented by arrays. Nevertheless, any non-uniformity of the problem or of its expression limits the gains to be derived from the use of arrays. Too often the real applications encountered have been less uniform than the simplified application used for driving the machine design, so performance has fallen short of expectations.

Sparsity.   Many arrays have few non-zero elements. Such arrays are called *sparse*. The elements near the diagonal of a matrix are often the only elements that are non-zero. Arrays representing boundaries in two-dimensional spaces also are usually sparse. Sparse arrays are commonly compressed to save storage space and processing time. Treating all elements—zero or non-zero— alike foregoes a good part of these savings.

Variability.   Array dimensions are likely to vary from one execution of the program to the next; they may even vary during execution. The static change causes an allocation problem that is independent of the use of arrays as a machine-language datatype. The dynamic change poses an allocation problem at run time. One solution may be to exclude operations that change the dimensions, but then the user is denied the full power inherent in the mathematical concept.

Language deficiency.   A machine-language facility must always be matched in some way by the higher-level programming languages. But most of these languages have only reluctantly adopted the numeric array, and then not always in standard form.

In FORTRAN I (1957) a DO facility made looping through vectors and larger arrays natural, even though these could not be specified as single entities. FORTRAN '77 provided array datatypes. ALGOL (1960) included arrays of like elements as distinct datatypes, but limited operations to the selection of single elements from these arrays.

Meanwhile, business data processing revealed the need for vectors and matrices whose elements were not alike—often were not even the same datatypes. Such vectors require much more elaborate declaration and element specification [Brooks, 1956]. Such records and files were provided in COBOL (1959). Again, little more than selection from these arrays was made available. PL/I (1964) provided a richer set of operations for these entities, there called *structures*.

In 1962 Iverson showed with APL the power that can be achieved with array operations that change structure (compression, expansion, etc.) and value (scalar arithmetic, reduction, generalized inner and outer product, etc.). This power was amply demonstrated in the interactive implementation of APL\360 and its many successors.

APL is widely used, but its use is only a fraction of that of common languages such as FORTRAN and COBOL. Therefore, the array facilities that are offered by various machines have required extensions to most of the programming languages.

Order of execution and intermediate results.   Another lack of efficiency arises from potential intermediate results and order of execution.

Assume the expression $(a + b) \times (c + d)$ is to be evaluated, with a, b, c, and d each a large numeric vector. If these vectors are treated as entities, many compilers would add a to b and c to d, then take the scalar product of the two sum vectors. If, however, the array is not available as a datatype and FOR statements are used instead, most programmers would use one all-encompassing FOR statement and evaluate for each index value the total expression within the loop. In such an evaluation, each operand and result element requires only one memory access; intermediate results are

easily accommodated in a small working store. The straightforward array computation, in contrast, would either require a vastly larger working store, or it would involve many more memory references. Modern optimizing compilers are indeed capable of transforming the array expression into the efficient implementation [Abrams, 1970; Cocke and Schwartz, 1970].

4.5.2
Machine-Language Elements

The machine-language equivalent of a numeric array must store the element representation in memory and must store the dimension information. Tree 4-97 gives the design choices.

Vectorial Mappings

Memory name-spaces have the structure of a matrix with the size of a byte or a word as the row dimension. Therefore, a numeric structure is best mapped in memory as a vector. With auxiliary dimensional information, such a vector can be treated as a more complex structure. For an array, this information can easily be outside the data proper. The shape operator of APL, the dyadic ρ, illustrates this point. For lists (Section 3.5), the information about the structure is usually intermixed with the data, which explains the difficulty of processing different elements concurrently.

Procrustean dimensions. Reflecting the array data structure into the memory name-space structure is improper and inefficient (Section 2.2). When the name-space is highly structured, the application structures must be commensurate in every dimension to give a good fit. The experience with two-dimensional indexing in the Harvard Mark IV (1952) confirms this property. It is therefore simpler and more general to stay with the vectorial name-space, as is usually done.

The most notable exception to the vectorial name-space is the Illiac IV [Barnes, et al., 1968], which provides 64 parallel-processing units arranged in an 8 by 8 array. The designers of the Illiac IV (1971) foresaw that processors would become relatively inexpensive. They wanted to harness this inexpensive processing power in a 16 by 16 array. Only one-quarter of this array was built; it was attached to a B6500. Considerable programming effort proved to be necessary to use the array to its intended advantage [Kuck,

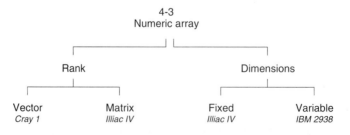

TREE 4-97   Design choices for arrays.

1968]. One reason was the need to fit the array onto the machine-imposed dimensions, a procrustean impropriety.

Generalized vector.   Some machines have a general numeric vector as datatype, and with good reason. Many numeric data structures are vectors. Also, many high-order structures can be processed as though they were vectors. Furthermore, since the single dimension of the vector matches the storage structure, it is much easier to achieve generality and avoid artificial limits. Examples are the IBM 2938 vector processor (1969), the CDC STAR100 (1973), the Cray family (1975), the Data General Eclipse (1978), and the 370 vector facility.

Dimensions

The dimension of a vector is a single integer. For arrays of higher rank, an integer is needed for each dimension. These integers are conveniently combined as a *dimension vector*. The key provision, then, is a single dimension value. This value can be used for the large class of vectors; it can also be used to delimit the dimension vector of higher-order regular arrays. The Cray 1 places the vector length in a register, whose use is implied in the vector operations.

Descriptor.   The indirect dimension specification via a data descriptor is particularly attractive, since the extra memory references to obtain the descriptor are incurred only once for an entire array, rather than once per element, as for scalars (Section 3.1).

4.5.3
Bibliography

Abrams [1970], Barnes et al. [1968], Brooks [1956], Cocke and Schwartz [1970], Kuck [1968].

4.6
Rules of Good Practice

The rules of good practice dealing with representation as such have been listed in Section 2.7. They concern (1) orthogonality, (2) level, (3) efficiency, (4) spare space, (5) policing, (6) commensurateness, (7) contiguity, (8) separation of data and control, and (9) alignment.

Rules peculiar to the representation of data in particular are given here:

10. At least one datatype should allow arbitrary bit configurations—the user may want to use the bit structure in a different way from any imagined by the architect (a refinement of rule 8).

11. Operations whose architecture assumes certain valid data encodings, such as decimal arithmetic, should catch the occurrence of invalid codes, but the mere movement of invalid data should not be inhibited (a refinement of rule 5).

12. Multiple equivalent representations should be avoided; in any case, they should be interpreted the same throughout.
13. An 8-bit byte is preferred for character representation.
14. Radix-complement is preferred for fixed-point number sign notation.
15. The IEEE Standard is preferred for floating-point number representation, in spite of its implementation costs.

4.7
Exercises

4-1 Show the program for the following operations in digit complement with radix B:

a. Addition

b. Multiplication

c. Division

4-2 Some numbers have no complement in the radix-complement notation. Enumerate the places in which this fact affects data formats and representation algorithms.

4-3 Can one make a floating-point representation that is unique and satisfies requirements 5, 6, and 7 of Table 4-84? Explain your answer.

4-4 Make a floating-point representation with signed-magnitude coefficient and Grau normal form.

4-5 Make a floating-point representation with multiple lengths and Grau normal form.

4-6 Prove that an end-around carry logically cannot go around more than once.

4-7 Determine the corrections needed in multiplication and division when using additive bias notation without first eliminating the bias.

4-8 Design a balanced ternary integer notation, with digits -1, 0, and 1. Give the representation and interpretation algorithms, and show how, for this notation,

a. Rounding can be accomplished by truncation.

b. The sign is determined by the leftmost digit.

c. Negation is performed.

4-9 Derive the formulas for the interval results that correspond to interval operands in

a. Addition

b. Multiplication

c. Division

4-10 Give an APL program for translation from BCD to EBCDIC.

4-11 Place the inverted sign notation in Tree 4-35 and Tables 4-36 and 4-37.

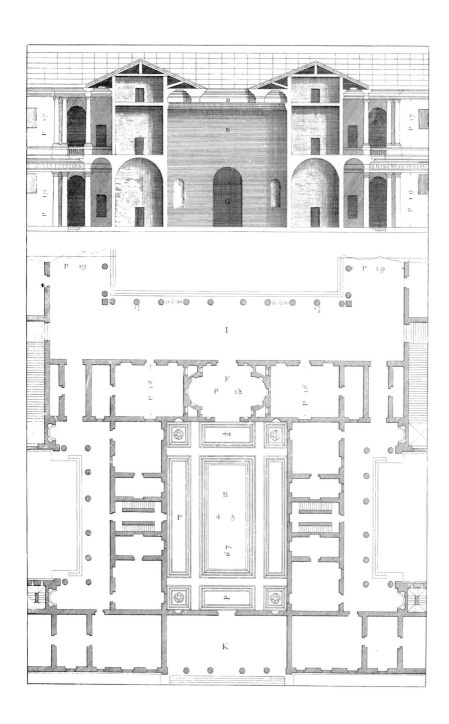

5

Operations

Overview of the Chapter

In this chapter we discuss the primary operations of a computer, those operations designed for manipulating data. We treat "machinehood" operations—address computation, instruction sequencing, I/O—in Chapters 3, 6, and 8.

Description in terms of abstract operations.   Chapter 4 shows that one can establish a correspondence between sets of data—character strings, logical elements, numbers—and their representations in a data format. Computer operations can therefore be described as *abstract operations*, defined in terms of their effects on representands, such as character strings or numbers, rather than in terms of their effects on representations, such as bit patterns. This abstract description is closer to the way people think about operations, without sacrificing accuracy. It also recognizes the orthogonality of representation and operation.

Operation steps.   Since a computer operation in fact works on representations, its description in terms of the underlying abstract operation must consist of several steps: the interpretations of the representands of the operands from the representations, the abstract operation itself, and the re-representation of the abstract result (Figure 5-1).

Each operand is first selected by addressing. The various bit patterns within the data format are next parsed by the allocation rules. These bit patterns are then decoded to determine the values of the data represented. An operation is then performed upon the operands to yield one or more results. The results are then represented: encoded, allocated, and placed at their addressed destination locations.

This dissection is useful for thinking for several reasons:

- The operand-interpretation process depends only on the datatype, not on the operation. So a designer can provide one interpretation specification per datatype and get consistency from operation to operation.
- Result representation likewise depends only on the datatype, not the operation.

- Most operation exceptions arise not in the abstract operation itself, but in the process of representing the abstract result within the domain of the datatype specification. Hence, having one representation procedure per datatype makes exception handling consistent.

Operation classes. Figure 5-1 furnishes not only a useful way of thinking about computer operations, but also a useful complexity ordering of operations. Each class includes the actions of all lower classes. We organize the chapter accordingly.

Section 5.1 treats data-handling operations. All computer operations include data handling. By *data-handling operations* we mean those that do nothing else—no arithmetic or logic. Data-handling operations can be ordered according to changes in allocation or coding. In *data movement* neither allocation nor coding changes—an unchanged bit pattern is copied from one place to another. The Move involves only the addressing of operand and result. Moves are equivalent to address changes and can be traded for address manipulations.

A second subclass—*format transformations*—changes allocation but not encoding. The decoding and encoding steps are not involved; both moves and format transformations are hence *code-independent*.

The last subclass of data handling is *code transformation*, which changes coding and in general requires reallocation. Here the decode and encode steps are not mutually inverse.

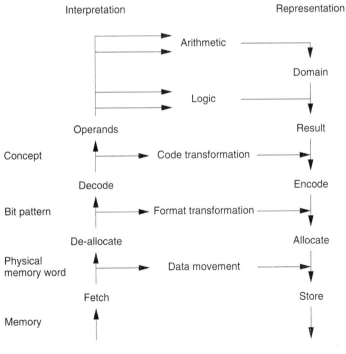

FIGURE 5-1   Operation steps.

In contrast with data handling, both logic and arithmetic transform operand values. They therefore involve all the coding and allocation steps of interpretation and representation.

Section 5.2 treats the logical operations. Computer binary logic is identical to mathematical binary logic. The operations have *closure*. The range of the binary logic operators is the same as the domain of the operands. Results are always straightforwardly representable.

Computer arithmetic does not have closure, because of finite domains and ranges. The result of an addition or division may be outside the representable domain because the result is too large, is too small, or requires too great a precision. We therefore separate machine-arithmetic operations into the *operation proper*, which produces the result—such as a sum or a quotient—in the rational number range, according to the normal rules of arithmetic; and the *representation function*, which maps this result, if necessary, onto the domain of the operand datatype, signaling any failure. Figure 5-1 shows this relation among operand, interpretation, operation, result, and representation for machine arithmetic [Geerdink, 1975].

Whereas the domain function is usually trivial for fixed-point arithmetic, it is rarely so for floating-point arithmetic. This difference turns out to be pervasive, so we treat the two types of arithmetic separately: fixed point in Section 5.3, and floating point in Section 5.4.

The relational operations, such as Equal, Greater, and Smaller, are peculiar in using operands from one datatype and yielding a result in another, the logical datatype; they are treated in Section 5.5.

The operations that are proper to numeric arrays as such—not just the elements of these arrays—are discussed in Section 5.6; they match the data of Section 4.5.

Operation description in APL.   Program 5-2 gives the basic steps of instruction execution. The operand representations `od` of size `size` and at an address specified by `adr` are obtained by `read`. A result value `result` is obtained by some operation upon the interpretations of the operands `operand`. (Any interpretation function of Chapter 4 can be substituted for the general expressions `interpret`, and any arithmetic or logic operator can replace `operation`.) The result `rl` is the representation of the value `result`. (The representation functions of Chapter 4 can replace `represent`.) Finally, `rl` is stored by `write` at a location specified by some addressing algorithm indicated by `adr3`.

Whereas the interpretation functions are virtually standard, the allocations vary widely.

```
operation;od1;od2;operand1;operand2;result;rl
ⱥ basic operation
od1←size1 read adr1
od2←size2 read adr2
operand1←interpret od1
operand2←interpret od2
result←operand1 operation operand2
rl←size3 represent result
adr3 write rl
signal rl
```

PROGRAM 5-2   Basic execution steps.

The domain function is incorporated in Program 5-2 in the representation function `represent` and in the signaling function `signal`. The domain function is assumed to be operation-independent and concerns only the result value `result` and its representation `rl`.

It turns out that the representation functions follow a standard pattern in all machines; the key differences in design are found in the signaling functions. These differences are aggravated by the different design decisions made outside the area of the operations, as in decision making and interrupt handling. We shall consider in this chapter only the basic messages that must be signaled. We treat the encoding of these messages and the actions they cause in Sections 6.2 and 7.2.

Design choices.   The classification implied by Figure 5-1 is expressed explicitly in Tree 5-3.

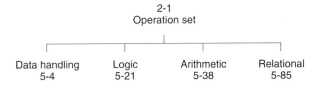

TREE 5-3   Design choices for operations.

5.1

Data Handling

Tree 5-4 shows the design choices for data handling, by which we mean all the operations that deal with data representations without interpreting data semantics—that is, the bottom three steps in Figure 5-1. A surprising variety of data-handling operations have been built into computers.

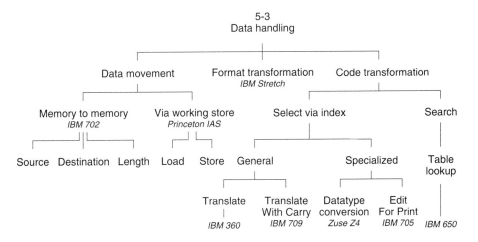

TREE 5-4   Design choices for data handling.

5.1.1

Data Movement, or Assignment

The simplest computer operation realizes the programming-language primitive of *assignment*, giving to a destination variable the value of a source variable. Although the operation is in fact copying, rather than moving, data, it is commonly called *data movement*.

Though simple, assignment is a high-frequency operation. Consider the preparation of a print record for a utility bill. One copies the name and address from a master file. One copies the date from an operating-system variable. Finally, one places into the print record the current billing data from the updated master file. Similarly, code generation during compilation is essentially the assembly, by copying, of bits and pieces from all over a skeleton library.

Tree 5-4 shows the design choices. Assignment inherently requires two operand specifications: source and destination. For the general case—the setting of one memory variable to the value of another—neither address can be abbreviated.

One-address computers, such as the Princeton IAS (1952), use a working-store register as intermediary for memory-to-memory move (as they also do with dyadic operations). They use two instructions, Load *source* and Store *destination*, to carry the two address phrases. Computers with two full addresses, such as the Univac Scientific 1103A (1956), effect the same data movement with one instruction, thereby saving one operation code (and only that—both one- and two-address machines need two address phrases).

For fixed-length data, the length is implied in the operation code, and few design issues arise. Because of the high frequency of data movement in both applications and housekeeping, many computers provide data movement for variable-length data, whether character strings, decimal strings, or vectors of numbers. (Most machines provide such variable-length Move operations for I/O.) Variable-length data movement raises several design issues.

Character-String Move

The character-string Move copies data without changing their value, encoding, or allocation (Program 5-5). Propriety dictates that the operation should be independent of the order of execution of any piecewise moves chosen by the implementation. This mandate is awkward to implement when the source and destination fields overlap, so overlap, though useful, is often forbidden, or propriety is violated.

Field specification.   The IBM 705 (1956), a one-address machine, adopts an unorthodox solution to the two-operand problem.   It does a variable-

```
move;data
ρ basic move
data←size read adr1
adr2 write data
```

PROGRAM 5-5   Basic Move.

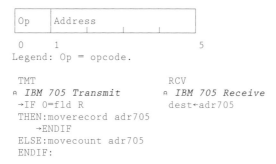

```
Op    Address
      |         |         |
0     1                           5
Legend: Op = opcode.

TMT                     RCV
 ⋀ IBM 705 Transmit      ⋀ IBM 705 Receive
  →IF 0=fld R             dest←adr705
  THEN:moverecord adr705
     →ENDIF
  ELSE:movecount adr705
  ENDIF:
```

PROGRAM 5-6   Move in the IBM 705.

length memory-to-memory Move, but introduces an architecturally visible destination register for this purpose (Program 5-6).

Field length.   Move is monadic and inherently involves one length. Any of the methods for length specification mentioned in Section 2.3 may be used, as Programs 5-6 through 5-8 illustrate. When the source and destination fields can be specified with different lengths, however, the operations can be used for movement or for format transformation. Additional design problems come with the additional function: whether to signal any length mismatch; whether to align to the left or the right end; and whether to fill with blank, zero, or a special fill character.

Source-destination overlap.   Most Move operations are implemented by transfering the data one word or byte at a time from the source to the destination. Such an implementation may change the data to be moved if the specified source and destination fields overlap. In a transfer from left to right one byte at a time, with the destination one byte to the right of the source, the leftmost source byte is propagated through the entire destination.

The abstract operation, however, calls for the data to remain intact even with a source-destination overlap (Program 5-5). A feasible implementation for this prescribed behavior is the use of a (maximum-string-length) buffer, or a right-to-left element transfer when overlap would cause trouble. Such an implementation was considered too expensive in early machines; most Move operations were defined in a less general way by just stating how the implementation worked and letting the programmer cope with the overlap (Program 5-7). If the overlapped Move architecture is defined as what the implementation does, building a compatible implementation with a different physical word size will be difficult.

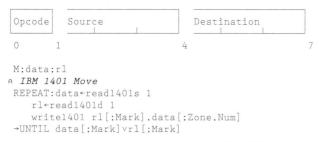

```
Opcode| Source            | Destination
      |        |          |        |          |
0     1                   4                    7

M:data:rl
 ⋀ IBM 1401 Move
 REPEAT:data←read1401s 1
     rl←read1401d 1
     write1401 rl[;Mark],data[;Zone,Num]
→UNTIL data[;Mark]∨rl[;Mark]
```

PROGRAM 5-7   Move in the IBM 1401.

Opcode	L0		B1	D1		B2	D2	

```
0        8       16  20              32  36              48
Legend: B = base; D = displacement; L = length.
```

```
MVC;source;dest;length;data
ⵁ IBM 360 Move
source←adr360bd2
dest←adr360bd1
length←1+fld L0
REPEAT: ⵁ move byte
    data←byte read360 source
    →OUT suppress360
    dest write360 data
    source←source+1
    dest←dest+1
    length←length-1
→UNTIL length=0
```

PROGRAM 5-8   Move Characters in the IBM System/360.

In any case, compatible implementations with different physical-memory word sizes will have conflicting preferences as to the amount of data to be transferred as a unit. In the IBM System/360 (1965), for example, the 1-byte–wide implementation of the Model 30 does the prescribed Move gracefully; it is inherently awkward for the 8-byte–wide implementation of the Model 75.

Program 5-8 shows the Move Characters operation of the 360. The operation specifies two left boundaries and one length. The length specification is limited to 256; this limitation is reasonable, but unfortunately does not match the length specification of the I/O moves (in range or encoding). The IBM System/370 (1971) remedies these shortcomings by the new operation Move Characters Long; it even handles overlap properly. Program 5-9 gives a similar operation for the DEC VAX11/780 (1978).

Table 5-10 shows the means for data movement (including format-field selection) in various machines.

Opcode	Source	Length	Dest	

```
0        8       16      24      32
Legend: Dest = destination.
```

```
MOVC3;source;dest;od;odend;rlend
ⵁ DEC VAX780 Move Characters
source←adr780str
dest←source[Size,Space],(adr780 byte)[Value]
regend780?6ρadrcap
od←read780 source WHERE ind[Fpd]←1
dest write780 od
odend←source[Value]+source[Size] WHERE ind[Fpd]←0
rlend←dest[Value]+dest[Size]
regend780 0,odend,0,rlend,0,0
status[Carry,Neg,Oflo]←0
status[Zero]←1
```

PROGRAM 5-9   Move Characters in the DEC VAX11/780.

	Memory-to-memory move	Field selection	Translation	Search
IBM 650				c word
IBM 705	$6 \times \omega \rightarrow$			
Bull Gamma 60	$24 \times 0 - 255$	24	$c \rightarrow c$ $d \leftrightarrow c$	
IBM 1401	$\leftarrow 7 \times \omega$			
IBM 1620	$\leftarrow 5 \times \omega \rightarrow$		$d \leftrightarrow c$	
IBM 7070	$100 \times \omega \rightarrow$		$d \leftrightarrow c$	c word
IBM Stretch	$\leftarrow 64 \times 2 * 12 \rightarrow$	64		
Burroughs B5500	$6 \times 63 \rightarrow$	48		word
IBM System/360	$8 \times 256 \rightarrow$		$c \rightarrow c$ $d \leftrightarrow c$	c
DEC PDP10	$36 \times \omega \rightarrow$			
DEC PDP11	2			
DEC VAX11	$8 \times \omega$	32	$c \rightarrow c$ $d \leftrightarrow c$	c

Legend: c = character; d = digit; ω = up to memory limit;
        ← = right to left; → = left to right;
        numbers give maximum field size.

TABLE 5-10   Move and field selection in various machines.

5.1.2

Format Transformation

Reallocation operators transform one machine field into another without changing the encoding. As an example, it should be easy to select the 4-bit B1 field of the instruction shown in Program 5-8, and to expand it to an 8-bit byte or 32-bit word, or reversely to insert the B1 field into the instruction from a byte or a word. If a single information-unit system has been used throughout the architecture, this generality can be achieved without loss of efficiency.

The process of reallocation is equivalent to the copying of a field from one set of bit locations to another. The two sets of locations may have different lengths; thus, the operation may involve truncation or extension. The main facilities provided for this purpose are field selection and shifting.

Field Selection

The most straightforward means of field selection is bit addressing, as illustrated in Program 5-11 by the Burroughs B1700 (1972). The B1700, like the IBM Stretch (1961), allows any string of bits in storage to be placed in any location of the accumulator. The beauty of the generality is offset by the inefficiency of specification, not to mention the cost of implementation.

For machines with byte or word addressing, reallocation of bits is less easily specified; it usually involves an auxiliary address component that extends the address resolution.

The logical operations can also be used for field selection. The AND provides a mask that selects fields; the OR allows the merging of fields; the Shifts can be used to position and extend fields.

Although shifting can be thought of as format transformation or reallocation, we treat all shifting under Logical Operations, Section 5.2.

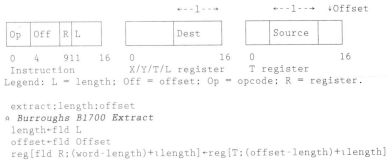

```
extract;length;offset
A Burroughs B1700 Extract
length←fld L
offset←fld Offset
reg[fld R;(word-length)+ιlength]←reg[T;(offset-length)+ιlength]
```

PROGRAM 5-11   Extract in the Burroughs B1700.

5.1.3
Code Transformation

Tree 5-4 shows the design choices.   One data representation in a machine
language can be transformed to another representation if the concept sets that
the two represent intersect. The closer the relation of the datatypes, the larger
the common intersection and the more profitable the code-transformation
operations in the machine language. These transformations are called *conversion* operations. Radix conversion, decimal packing, float, and fix operations
convert between various numeric representations.

Conversion operations.   The general abstract architecture of conversion
operations is given by Program 5-12. This program refers to the basic interpret and represent functions of Program 4-4, which can be replaced in each
specific instance by the corresponding functions of the given representations.

  For conversion to or from representations that are part of programming
languages, it is often difficult to provide an exactly corresponding machine-
language operation, and hazardous to approximate.   Nevertheless, the conversion to the print format—a frequently occurring programming-language
datatype—is found in several machines, as discussed at the end of this
subsection.

  In machine practice, of course, one short-circuits interpretation into concepts, and maps directly from one representation to the other. Where there
is a one-to-one correspondence between representations, a perfectly general
encoding transformation can be effected by either of two table techniques. One
can make a vector table of all the possible result encodings, ordered so the
argument encoding serves as the index. Then, result←table[argument]
will effect the transformation for any argument. Or, and this is especially
useful if the argument set is not densely encoded, one can make a two-column
matrix table such that the first column has all the argument values and the

```
convert;od;operand;rl
A basic conversion
od←size1 read adr1
operand←interpret od
rl←size2 represent operand
adr2 write rl
signal rl
```

PROGRAM 5-12   Basic conversion.

second all the corresponding results. Then, one searches for the argument and retrieves the result: `result←table[table[;0]ιargument;1]`

Conversion primitives.   The program primitives that can serve as general tools for code conversion can also be derived from the `interpret` and `represent` functions of Program 4-4.

Code dependence.   The operations of a machine language can always be made code-independent by making the necessary tables available to them. For arithmetic such a procedure is highly inefficient. For data handling, however, the character codes are dictated by various kinds of input and output equipment, such as keyboards and displays, and so are diverse and arbitrary. Hence, for these operations, code independence is highly desirable. An example is the transformation to print format.

Search

Table Lookup.   The IBM 650 (1954) facilitates code searching by the operation Table Lookup. A character can be used to yield a word, from which in turn a character can be extracted, as shown in Program 5-13.

The argument word of the Table Lookup is in a register—the Distributor `dist`—and is compared with the words in successive memory locations. Since the memory of the 650 is implemented as a drum, the successive comparisons are fast relative to all other sequences of operations. Words 0 through 47 of each successive drum band are compared in one drum rotation. Words 48 and 49 are skipped (to allow band-switching time), and the search continues on the next band. When the memory operand compares high or equal, the operation terminates and leaves the memory address accessible in the Lower Accumulator. So a left-aligned short argument filled out with zeros will find a table with a matching left-aligned argument followed by a function value.

The IBM 7070 (1960) and 7074 (1962)—descendants of the 650—also incorporate table-lookup operations. Because these machines have random-access memories rather than drums, the speed advantage of the Table Lookup is much smaller than for the 650.

*	Opcode	Address			Next			

```
0   1        3              7              11
Legend: * = unused.
```

```
TLU;origin;argument;value;index   value←table650 address;location
ᴀ IBM 650 Table Lookup            ᴀ IBM 650 table values
origin←adr650                     ᴀ valid locations in addressed track
argument←|signmagni dist          location←(50×⌊address÷50)+ι48
REPEAT: ᴀ search track            ᴀ values in track locations
    value←table650 origin            value←signmagni memory[memcap|location;]
    index←(argument≤|value)ι1        Invadr report location≥adrcap
    →If index=48
    THEN: ᴀ not found in track
        origin←origin+50
ENDIF:→UNTIL(index≠48)∨ind[Invadr]
→OUT ind[Invadr]
acc[(Sign,Lower)[Address]]←adrsize magnr origin+index
```

PROGRAM 5-13   Table Lookup in the IBM 650.

Opcode	L0		B1	D1		B2	D2	

```
0        8       16  20              32  36          48
Legend:  B = base;  D = displacement;  L = length.
```

```
TRT;origin;source;length;argument;r1
⋀ IBM 360 Translate And Test
origin←adr360bd2
source←adr360bd1
length←1+fld L0
REPEAT:  ⋀ translate byte
   argument←magni byte read360 source
   r1←byte read360 origin+argument
   →OUT suppress360
 ⋀ test for non-zero translation
   →IF∨/r1
   THEN:  ⋀ record source and translation
      reg[1;Address]←adrsize magnr source
      reg[2;Lowbyte]←r1
      →ENDIF                     length signal360TRT r1;none;more;last;cc
   ELSE:  ⋀ continue              ⋀ IBM 360 translate and test condition
      source←source+1            none←0=∨/r1
   ENDIF:  ⋀ count               more←length≠0
   length←length-1               last←length=0
→UNTIL(∨/r1)∨length=0            cc←1↑(none,more,last)/ 0 1 2
length signal360TRT r1           psw[Cc]←2 magnr cc
```

PROGRAM 5-14   Translate And Test in the IBM System/360.

Several later machines incorporate table-lookup operations—for example, the Univac 1110 (1970), the Manchester University MU5 (1974), and the latter's descendants, the ICL 2900s.

The 360 operation Translate And Test provides a multiple search using successive characters of a string as arguments into a table of function bytes (Program 5-14). The search succeeds when the function byte is non-zero. The address of the argument character and the function byte are the results. The multiple search enables any member of a class, such as delimiters or punctuation symbols, to be located in a single operation, with one table per class searched for.

Translation

The simplest use of a vector translation table is for character-by-character conversion. The table must be placed in an addressable section of memory, as opposed to working store. The conversion of a single character by an indexed fetch requires no special operation. It is convenient, however, to be able to convert a whole character string with a single instruction.

One of the first computers to translate a string of characters as a single operation was the IBM Harvest (1961). The translation operations of the 360 owe a debt to the Harvest's design. Program 5-15 shows the Translate operation of the 360. One address points to the character string to be translated, and the other address points to the translation table. Each character of the string is interpreted as a number and is used as an index into the translation table. The character found in the table is substituted for the original character. Since every character consists of 8 bits, the table has a maximum size of 256 8-bit characters.

Opcode	L0		B1	D1		B2	D2	

```
0        8       16  20              32  36              48
Legend: B = base; D = displacement; L = length.
```

```
TR;origin;dest;length;argument;rl
A IBM 360 Translate
origin←adr360bd2
dest←adr360bd1
length←1+fld L0
REPEAT: A translate byte
    argument←magni byte read360 dest
    rl←byte read360 origin+argument
    →OUT suppress360
    dest write360 rl
    dest←dest+1
    length←length-1
→UNTIL length=0
```

PROGRAM 5-15   Translate in the IBM System/360.

Reverse application.   The use of the search and translate primitives can also be reversed, as is obvious from the APL functions. Thus, by an algorithm due to Blaauw, Translate can be used for rearranging the order of the characters, with insertions and deletions [IBM, 1964]. In this algorithm, the normal roles of the operands are switched: The data to be arranged collectively form the table, and a format vector serves as the source byte string. For example, a result presented in decimal digits and placed adjacent to a radix point and separator symbol (.,39427053), when addressed with the index 2 3 4 1 5 6 7 0 8 9 (as by a Translate) yields the print format 394,270.53.

Translate With Carry.   As an extension of the translation concept, the table that is used for the translation of each character can be made dependent on the result of the preceding character translations. In this case, each character yields a result character and a carry index. The carry is combined with the table address to select the table to be used for the next character. This change

Opcode	Count	*		Address	

```
0            10      18 21              36
Legend: * = unused.
```

```
CVR;count;entry;argument;table
A IBM 709 Convert By Replacement From Accumulator
count←fld Count
entry←inst
→WHILE count≠0
    argument←magni(-byte)↑acc
    table←magni entry[Address]
    entry←read704 table+argument
    acc←(byteρ0),(-byte)↓acc
    acc[P+ιbyte]←acc[P+ιbyte]∨byte↑entry
    count←count-1
    →Δ
ENDWHILE:→If inst[20]
THEN:reg[0:]←(-adrsize)↑entry[Address]
ENDIF:
```

PROGRAM 5-16   Convert By Replacement in the IBM 709.

of table is equivalent to a finite-state-machine state change, and it is very powerful. It can be used, for example, to effect case shift in running teletype text.

The IBM 709 (1959) has a Convert operation in which the six 6-bit characters of a word are translated one by one by table reference. Each table entry contains a new table address; this action is equivalent to Translate With Carry (Program 5-16).

The carry tends to require several—often sparsely populated—tables. A typical application is the suppression of zeros in numbers that are to be printed.

Transformation to Print Format

Numbers are not usually printed as strings of digits, but are spaced and punctuated. This format is awkward for arithmetic, so a transformation from the internal to the print format is required. Preparing numbers for printing is one of the many functions called "editing." Figure 5-17 gives an example of the print editing of a pair of numbers.

```
            pattern
amount    DDD,DDS.DD  F reduction S.DD

            amount
01203456

            reduction
003

            pattern EDit amount,reduction
amount    12,034.56    reduction 0.03
```

FIGURE 5-17   Editing a number for print output.

The specific requirements for conventional printed representation are unusually complex. They are illustrated in Program 5-18.

```
    edit;od1;od2;number;mask;d;digits;numeric;l;amount;result;rl
 ⍝ basic print edit
 ⍝ fetch and interpret operands
 od1←size1 read adr1
 od2←size2 read adr2
 number←interpret od1
 mask←alphai od2
 ⍝ number to characters
 d←mask=digitinsert
 digits←'0123456789'[((+/d)ρ10)⊤|number]
 ⍝ spacing with comma and period
 numeric←(((~d)/mask),digits)[⍋⍋d]
 ⍝ zero suppress by fill character and floating dollar
 l←(numeric∊'123456789')ι1
 amount←((l-1)ρfill),'$',l↓numeric
 ⍝ credit indication
 result←amount,(number<0)/creditsymbol
 ⍝ represent and store result
 rl←size3 represent result
 adr3 write rl
```

PROGRAM 5-18   Typical edit function.

```
ED;pattern;digits;figures;fill;significant;j;k
ⴰ IBM 360 Edit
 Invop report˜decopt
ⴰ identify edit controls
 charcode[32 33 34]←'↑↓⊥'
ⴰ fetch and interpret pattern and digits
 pattern←alphai byte wide(size360 L0) read360 adr360bd1
 digits←magni digit wide(size360 L0) read360 adr360bd2
 figures←'0123456789+-+-++'[digits]
 →OUT suppress360
ⴰ initiate counts and significance
 j←k←significant←0
ⴰ select fill character
 fill←1↑pattern                      char←digitselect
ⴰ initiate condition code            ⴰ IBM 360 digit selection for edit
 psw[Cc]← 0 0                        char←figures[k]
 REPEAT: ⴰ process pattern           Data report char∈'+-'
     →CASE '↑↓⊥'ιpattern[j]          k←k+1
     C0: ⴰ digit selection           ⴰ zero test
         pattern[j]←digitselect      significant←significant∨char≠'0'
         →ENDCASE                    psw[Cc[0]]←psw[Cc[0]]∨char≠'0'
     C1: ⴰ significance start        char←(fill,char)[significant]
         pattern[j]←digitselect      →If(1=2|k)∧figures[k]∈'+-'
         significant←1               THEN: ⴰ sign test
         →ENDCASE                        psw[Cc]←(figures[k]='-')Φpsw[Cc]
     C2: ⴰ field separation              k←k+1
         pattern[j]←fill             ENDIF:
         significant←0
         psw[Cc]← 0 0
         →ENDCASE
     C3: ⴰ other characters
         pattern[j]←(fill,pattern[j])[significant]
     ENDCASE:j←j+1
 →UNTIL j=ρpattern
ⴰ record edited pattern
 adr360bd1 write360 byte alphar pattern
```

PROGRAM 5-19   Edit in the IBM System/360.

Zero suppression. Zeros to the left of the most significant digit are replaced by blanks or, when a monetary value is involved as in checks, by asterisks or dashes. Zero suppression stops at the radix point or one digit to its left, but in some applications a zero amount is entirely replaced by blanks.

In any polynomial representation, the scan direction for zero suppression is inherently opposite to that for addition. For the conventional implementation, a left-to-right scan is required with a 1-bit memory to remember the passing of a significant digit or the radix point. A one-character lookahead or one-character backtracking is required when the suppression stops one digit to the left of the radix point. Blanking of all-zero amounts requires a two-character lookahead or backtracking.

Floating currency symbol.   With money amounts, the rightmost zero suppressed is often replaced by a currency symbol as a precaution against fraud.

Grouping.   Digits are usually grouped into threes by a blank or grouping symbol, which is suppressed as if 0.

Radix point.   The radix point is indicated by a period in Anglo-Saxon countries and by a comma in continental Europe. The grouping symbol is conversely a comma and a high period.

Sign representation.   A positive sign is not usually printed. A negative sign is placed to the left of the most significant digit or to the right of the number. In billing applications, it may be replaced by a credit symbol or message.

Print-format conversion in various machines.   The number to be printed can be assumed to be decimal. (Radix conversion is properly a separate operation.) One of the first print-conversion operations is Store For Print of the IBM 702 (1954). The Edit operation of the 360 is almost code-independent (Program 5-19). It also expands the packed format into an unpacked format. Other machines show a trend toward generality through code independence (Table 5-20). Nevertheless, most FORTRAN and COBOL compilers do not generate the machine-language edit operations, because of slight semantic differences. Such specialized operations are low frequency at best, and should be left out.

	Left zeros	True zero	Money symbol	Space symbol	Radix point	Sign place	Sign symbol
IBM 705	∘			,	.	←	-
Bull Gamma 60	∘		marked	. ∘	any	← →	- +
IBM 1401	∘	∘	$	, .	, .	← →	- cr
IBM System/360	any		marked	any	any	marked	
Burroughs B6500	any	any	any	any	any	← →	any
DEC VAX11	any	any				← →	any

Legend: any = any symbol; ← = sign left; → = sign right; ∘ = blank;
    marked = place of symbol is recorded.

TABLE 5-20   Conversion to print format in various machines.

5.1.4
Bibliography

Geerdink [1975], IBM [1964].

5.2
Logic

Almost all applications use logical variables and operations in decision making. Logical operations can be implemented inexpensively, often as a byproduct of arithmetic circuits, and rapidly, due to the lack of carry propagation. Specifications costs (operation codes) often exceed implementation costs. Therefore, for these operations the key architectural problem is not what *can* be provided, but what *should* be provided.

We treat here only logical operators proper—those whose operands and principal results are logical data. We treat comparisons, whose results are also logical data, but whose operands are character strings or numbers, in Section 5.5.

Since most machines address groups of bits as the finest resolution, most logical operations apply to vectors of bits.

Design choices.   The dyadic operations upon a single pair of bits are called *connectives*. They typically work pairwise between corresponding bits of two (equal-length) logical vectors.

Using APL terminology (Section 9.3), we identify as a second class of vector operations the *composite* functions that are constituted from an operator and a dyadic scalar function; Reduction is the most common operator. In reduction, the dyadic logical function is repeatedly applied to each element and the previous partial result in one vector:

$$\oplus/v = v_1 \oplus (v_2 \oplus (v_{n-1} \oplus v_n)\ldots)$$

The third class is the Restructuring functions, in that the elements of logical vectors are rearranged. Shift is the most common. Tree 5-21 shows these design choices.

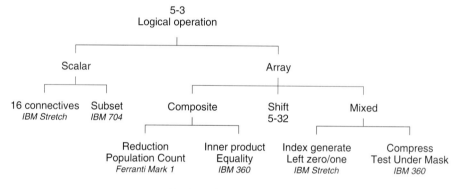

TREE 5-21   Design choices for logic operations.

5.2.1

Connectives

Complete set.   All 16 connectives of two binary variables can be specified by 4 bits (Table 5-22). With the proper 4-bit code, they can be built very simply. Program 5-23 illustrates the code used in the Stretch, for which Program 5-24 gives a feasible implementation.

Sufficient subsets of connectives.   Not all the 16 connectives shown in Table 5-22 need to be supplied. The most frequent functions AND, OR, and NOT constitute a *sufficient subset*, with which all 16 connectives can be effected; indeed, just AND and NOT constitute a sufficient subset. The NAND and the NOR are each a sufficient subset.

Partial set.   Are the 16 operation codes needed for the complete set profitably invested? Table 5-22 shows that the 16 connectives include the operations Set To 0 (NEVER) and Set To 1 (ALWAYS), which are niladic—they require no operand. Further, four operations are monadic, requiring only one operand, so providing all 16 connectives in a two-operand instruction wastes address bits. It also wastes opcode space, since several connectives can be obtained from others by interchanging operands. These facts explain why most machines limit their logical-operation repertoire to a partial set.

| Operands x→0011 | Name | Formula | Can be |
| 0 1 2   y→0101 | | | satisfied by: |
↓ ↓ ↓ ↓↓↓↓			
0 0000	never	0	immediate move
1 0001	and	x∧y	
2 0010	larger	x∧˜y	
3 0011	identity	x	move
4 0100	smaller	(˜x)∧y	commutation of (2)
5 0101	identity	y	move
6 0110	exclusive-or	x≠y	
7 0111	or	x∨y	
8 1000	nor	˜x∨y	
9 1001	equality	x=y	
10 1010	not	˜y	(6) with constant
11 1011	implication	x∨˜y	
12 1100	not	˜x	equivalent of (10)
13 1101	implication	(˜x)∨y	commutation of (11)
14 1110	nand	˜x∧y	
15 1111	always	1	immediate move

TABLE 5-22   Logical connectives of two variables.

Address	Op	X1	M0	L0	Bs	Offset	Con	Op	X2
0	24	28	32	35	41	44	51	55	60 64

Legend: Bs = byte size; Con = connective; L = length;
        M = address mode; Op = opcode; X = index.

```
C;od1;od2;size;od1size;r1size;operand1;operand2;result
ค IBM Stretch Connect
od1←(fld0 Byte) wide(fld0 L0) read7030 adr7030m
od2←8 wide memory[Acc+ιdouble-fld Offset]
size←(ρod2)L(1↑ρod1),8
od1size←((fld0 Byte)|fld0 L0)+8×L(fld0 L0)÷fld0 Byte
r1size←(double-fld Offset)Lod1size
operand1←(-r1size)↑,(-size)↑od1
operand2←(-r1size)↑,(-size)↑od2
result←operand1 connect7030 operand2
memory[(Acc+double-(r1size+fld Offset))+ιr1size]←result
ค counts and signals
memory[Leftzeros]←(ρLeftzeros) magnr resultι1
memory[Allones]←(ρAllones) magnr+/result
Partialfld report7030 r1size≠od1size
Tomem set7030 0
signal7030NZP magni result
```

PROGRAM 5-23   Logical connectives in the IBM Stretch.

```
r1←od1 connect7030 od2;c00;c01;c10;c11
ค IBM Stretch logical connective
c00←inst[Con[0]]∧(˜od1)∧˜od2
c01←inst[Con[1]]∧(˜od1)∧od2
c10←inst[Con[2]]∧od1∧˜od2
c11←inst[Con[3]]∧od1∧od2
r1←c00∨c01∨c10∨c11
```

PROGRAM 5-24   Feasible implementation of all logical connectives.

	Size	0	1	2 4	6	7	8	9	10 12	11 13	14	15
Cambridge EDSAC	35		∧									
Ferranti Mark 1	40		∧	≠								
IBM 701	36		∧									
IBM 704	36		∧			∨				~		
Univac 1103A	36		∧	≠								
STC ZEBRA	33	0	∧									
Bull Gamma 60	24	0	∧			∨				~		1
IBM Stretch	64	0	∧	<	≠	∨	⊽	=	~	≥	⊼	1
CDC 6600	60		∧	<	≠	∨		=	~	≥		
CDC 6600 PPU	18	0	∧	<	≠				~			1
Burroughs B5500	47	0	∧			∨		=	~			
IBM System/360	32	0	∧		≠	∨			~			1
DEC PDP8	12		∧			∨			~			
DEC PDP10	36	0	∧	<	≠	∨	⊽	=	~	≥	⊼	1
DEC PDP11	16	0		<	≠	∨			~			1
Intel 8080A	8	0	∧		≠	∨			~			1
Cray 1	64		∧	<	≠	∨		=				
Motorola M6800	8	0	∧		≠	∨			~			1
MOS 6502	8	0	∧		≠	∨						1
DEC VAX11	64	0	∧	<	≠	∨			~			1
Motorola MC68000	32	0	∧		≠	∨			~			1
IBM 6150	32	0	∧		≠	∨			~			1

Legend: maximum size shown; ⊽ = nor; ⊼ = nand.

TABLE 5-25   Logical operations in various machines.

The designers of programming languages have similarly limited themselves to partial sets, but not always to the same one. The partial subset of the machine language should therefore always include a sufficient subset. Because of their frequent use in formal and informal logic, the AND, OR, and NOT are definitely preferred. Table 5-25 shows the logical operations of various machines.

Masking.   The AND operation can be considered as the masking of one operand—the datum proper—with another operand, the *mask*. Where the mask bits are 1, the data bits are preserved; where the mask bits are 0, the data bits are set to 0. Hence, masking is a kind of selection.

One can select a single bit in a byte by using one of eight masks, each containing a single one (1000 0000, 0100 0000, 0010 0000 ... 0000 0001). In the 360 the immediate-addressed logical operations are often so used.

5.2.2

Composite Functions

The composite logical functions (Table 5-26) consist of an APL *operator* that applies a dyadic scalar function among the elements of a vector.

Reduction

The reduction operator / is most common. For example, ∧/a,b,c means a∧b∧c. The OR reduction gives the result "there is one"; the AND reduction gives "all are one"; the AND reduction of the inverse gives "all are zero"; the

Reduction	Inner product
∧/od ᴀ *all ones*	od1∧.=od2 ᴀ *equality*
∨/od ᴀ *any one*	
+/od ᴀ *population count*	

TABLE 5-26   Composite logical vector functions.

add reduction gives the "all ones" or *population count*; the add reduction of the inverse gives the "all zeros" count. These operations are often performed as an automatic auxiliary operation upon the result of a primary logical operation, yielding a secondary result. In the 360, the first two operations are recorded in the condition code (Program 5-28). The Stretch records the population count of all logical results in an auxiliary All Ones register (Program 5-23). In contrast, the CDC 6600 (1964) has a separate Population Count operation, which seems better (Section 2.2).

Inner Product

The generalized inner-product operator (APL .) applies two dyadic functions to two logical vectors. Vector equality is its main application; u∧.=v means ∧/u=v, where u and v are logical vectors. Vector equality is, however, often treated as a subset of comparison, where the rows of an array are interpreted as characters, or integers.

5.2.3
Mixed Functions

The third class of array functions operates upon one array, perhaps with another, to produce a restructured array, whose dimension may be different from that of either operand (Table 5-27).

Monadic	Dyadic
	ι index of
, ravel	, catenate
ρ shape	ρ reshape
	↑ take
	↓ drop
⍉ transpose	
⌽ reverse	⌽ rotate

TABLE 5-27   Mixed logical vector functions.

Compression

One logical vector can serve to select bits from another. Often, the selected bits are then further operated upon. The 360 operation Test Under Mask compresses a byte and applies the OR, AND, and AND NOT reduction to the result

to give a selective "there is one," "all ones," and "all zeros" test to any subset of a byte (Program 5-28). The compressed result is not available.

```
Opcode  Imm    B1  D1

0        8      16  20          32
Legend: B = base; D = displacement; Imm = immediate.

TM;od;mask                         signal360TM r1;allone;someone
⍝ IBM 360 Test Under Mask         ⍝ IBM 360 test under mask condition
od←byte read360 adr360bd1          allone←(0≠⍴,r1)∧∧/r1
→OUT suppress360                   someone←∨/r1
mask←inst[Imm]                     psw[Cc]←allone,someone
signal360TM mask/od
```

PROGRAM 5-28   Test Under Mask in the IBM System/360.

Index Of

When applied to logical data, the search or "index of" function, the APL ⍳, gives the "left-zero" count in searching for one, and the "left-one" count in searching for zero. The first is illustrated by the Stretch (Program 5-23).

Table 5-29 shows the non-scalar vector operations of various machines.

	Composite	Mixed
Ferranti Mark 1	+/	⍳1
IBM 701	∧/~	
IBM 650		⍳1
IBM 704	∧/~	
Univac 1103A		⍳1
Bull Gamma 60	∧/ ~∧/ ∨/ ~∨/	
IBM Stretch	∧/~ +/	⍳1
CDC 6600	+/	
IBM System/360	∧/~ ∨/	
DEC PDP11	∧/~	
Intel 8080A	∧/~	
Cray 1	∧/~ +/	⍳1
Motorola M6800	∧/~	
MOS 6502	∧/~	
DEC VAX11	∧/~	⍳1 ⍳0
Motorola MC68000	∧/~	
IBM 6150		⍳1

Legend: +/ = population count; ∧/~ = all zero;
        ∨/ = any one ; ⍳0 = leftmost 0;
        ⍳1 = leftmost 1.

TABLE 5-29   Logical vector operations in various machines.

Shift

The shift is used in data handling for field selection; in logic, for bit inspection; and in arithmetic, for programmed scaling, multiply, divide, and floating point. We choose to treat it here.

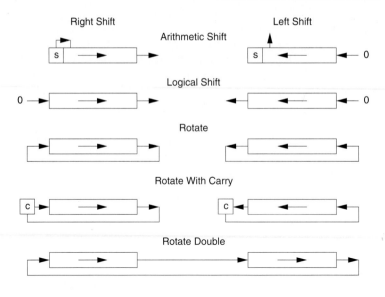

Legend: c = carry; s = sign.

FIGURE 5-30   Shift operations.

	Size	Logical				Arithmetic		Sd
		Shift		Rotate		Shift		
		Single	Double	Single	Double	Single	Double	
Cambridge EDSAC	35						←11→	o
Ferranti Mark 1	40						←80→	a
Princeton IAS	40					←1→		o
Univac I	s,11d	←9→				←9→		o
IBM 701	s,37					←37→	←37→	o
IBM 650	s,10d					←9,10→		o
IBM 704	s,37		←73	←36		←37→	←72→	o
Univac 1103A	36			36	72			o
STC ZEBRA	33		←1→					o
Bull Gamma 60	24	24→		24→				o
Ferranti Atlas	24	←24→		←24→		←24→	←40→	o
English Electric KDF9	48	←48→	←96→	←48→		←48→	←95→	a
CDC 6600	60			←60		60→		oa
CDC 6600 PPU	18	18→		←18				o
IBM System/360	32	←32→	←63→			←31→	←63→	o
DEC PDP8	12		←24→	←2c→			23→	oa
DEC PDP10	36	←36→	←72→	←36→	←72→	←35→	←70→	a
DEC PDP11	8 16	←1→		←1c		←15→	←31→	oa
IBM System/370	31d					←31→		a
Intel 8080A	8			←1c→				o
Cray 1	64	←64→	←128→					o
Motorola M6800	8	←1→		←1c→		←1→		o
MOS 6502	8	←1→		←1c→		←1		o
DEC VAX11	32			←32→		←31→	←63→	a
Motorola MC68000	32	←32→		←32→		←32→		o
IBM 6150	32	←32→				31→		o

Legend: a = direction determined by shift amount; c = through carry;
         d = decimal; o = direction determined by opcode; s = sign
         Sd = shift direction; ← = left shift; → = right shift;
         figures refer to maximum effective shift.

TABLE 5-31   Shift in various machines.

Definition. In a shift operation the minimal elements—usually the bits—are all moved some number of positions to the right or to the left. Many useful kinds of Shift can be defined (Figure 5-30) and have been used (Table 5-31).

In *logical shift* all operand bits are treated the same; in *arithmetic shift* the operand is considered a signed integer that is multiplied by a power of the radix. A logical shift can be *linear*—bits shifted out are lost, and bits shifted in are zero; or it can be *circular*, called Rotate—bits shifted out at one end are entered at the other end of the operand. The extent of the operand can be one word, or a word and a bit, called the *carry bit*, or two adjacent words.

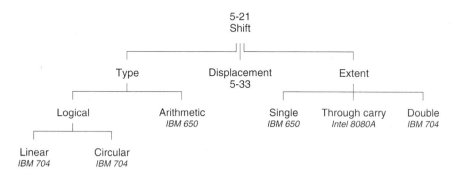

TREE 5-32   Design choices for shift.

The shift operation is basically dyadic, with a shift and a signed shift amount, although often the direction of shift is shown in the opcode instead of in the shift-amount sign. Use of the sign is better, for it simplifies indexing of shift amounts. Besides the various kinds of shifting actions, one has various options for specifying shifting (Trees 5-32 and 5-33). Provision for all kinds of shifts costs many operation codes. The DEC PDP10 (1968), which has a large opcode field, is the only machine in Table 5-31 to give such full generality.

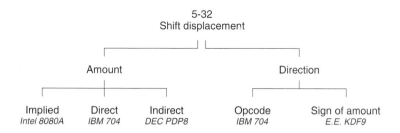

TREE 5-33   Design choices for shift displacement.

Logical shifts.   Program 5-34 shows the logical shift in the PDP10.

The circular logical shift corresponds to the APL function ⌽. Program 5-36 illustrates the use of the circular shift for field selection.

Arithmetic shifts.   The arithmetic shift is defined as multiplication of the integer operand by a power of the radix. This power is the shift amount, as shown in Program 5-35. An arithmetic right shift is equivalent to division with truncated quotient. Such a truncated quotient does not give the conventional

```
        Indirect↓

    ┌─────────┬───┬───┬─────────────────────────┐
    │Opcode   │R  │ X │ Address                 │
    └─────────┴───┴───┴─────────────────────────┘
    0         9   14  18                      36
    Legend: R = register; X = index.

    LSH;shift
    ⋒ DEC PDP10 Logical Shift
    shift←(×adr10)×64||adr10
    reg[fld R;]←wordρshiftΦreg[fld R;],shift↑0


    LSHC;shift;pair
    ⋒ DEC PDP10 Logical Shift Combined
    shift←(×adr10)×64||adr10
    pair←16| 0 1 +fld R
    reg[pair;]←(2,word)ρshiftΦ(,reg[pair;]),shift↑0


    ROT;shift                        ROTC;shift;pair
    ⋒ DEC PDP10 Rotate               ⋒ DEC PDP10 Rotate Combined
    shift←(×adr10)×64||adr10         shift←(×adr10)×64||adr10
    reg[fld R;]←shiftΦreg[fld R;]    pair←16| 0 1 +fld R
                                     reg[pair;]←(2,word)ρshiftΦ,reg[pair;]
```

PROGRAM 5-34   Logical Shift and Rotate in the DEC PDP10.

result for radix complement notation; for example, -3 divided by 2 should be -1; but a right-shifted -3 in radix complement notation becomes -2.

For signed-magnitude representation, the sign bit of the shiftand should not participate. For complement representation, the sign must be extended in a right shift. Since the arithmetic shift is an arithmetic operation, it should use the arithmetic-domain function, discussed in Section 5.3, to test result validity. In particular, overflows should be signaled. For radix-complement notation, the arithmetic left shift is the same as the logical left shift, except for the overflow test.

A circular shift has no arithmetic interpretation. The 6600, however, uses a circular shift to achieve its 1's-complement arithmetic left shift, which would work properly if only the 6600 signaled overflow.

For the binary radix, a left shift of 1 bit is equivalent to the addition of the number to itself. This fact is often used in implementations. Some simple architectures—such as the DEC PDP8 (1965) and microprocessors—that provide only a shift amount of one do not provide an arithmetic left shift. The right shift is usually omitted as well, although accomplishing it by programming takes far more effort.

For decimal radix, the arithmetic shift should be a whole digit at a time, for scaling decimal results. Because of sign representation, and so forth, the use of a binary shift usually does not meet the architecture of Program 5-35.

```
            arithshift;od;operand;result;r1
        ⋒ basic arithmetic shift
            od←size1 read adr1
            operand←interpret od
            result←entire operand×radix*shiftamount
            r1←size2 represent result
            adr2 write r1
            signal r1
```

PROGRAM 5-35   Basic arithmetic shift.

When we designed the 360, we thought the byte-resolution addressing and a one-digit shift would meet the need. They did not. The lack of a proper decimal shift in the 360 was corrected in the 370.

Shift amount.   The shift amount can result either directly from the problem statement or from the computation. Usually, the shift amount is specified immediately, in instruction fields that are otherwise used for address specification. This peculiarity is less undesirable than one might think, since a shift is often used to effect finer-resolution addressing. Moreover, indexing can be used to get an indirect specification. Addressing mechanisms, however, do not normally produce negative values. Yet it is desirable to specify the shift direction by means of the sign of the shift amount, and to be able to compute the sign indirectly. A high-order shift amount could be treated as a sign bit. More properly, however, the shift amount would be treated as a normal operand, assuming that immediate operand specification is available.

Scope of shift.   A double-length shift can be used in format transformations to split a format into fields, as illustrated in Program 5-36. In arithmetic a double-length shift is necessary to handle an arbitrary radix-point product or dividend.

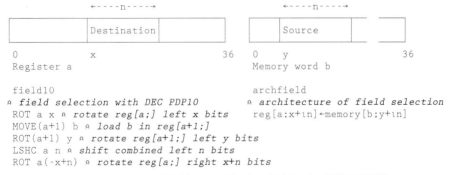

PROGRAM 5-36   Field assembly by shift in the DEC PDP10.

The double-length shift can be composed from single-length shifts by storing the bits that are shifted out in a carry bit. This Shift With Carry is particularly attractive when the shift amount is limited to 1. The Intel 8080A (1974) illustrates this method. Program 5-37 shows two of its four shift operations.

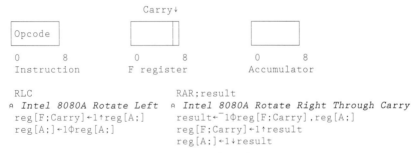

PROGRAM 5-37   Shift in the Intel 8080A.

5.3
Fixed-Point Arithmetic

Computer arithmetic operations are best understood as consisting of two steps. First, the operation as defined in mathematics is applied to the interpretations of the operand representations. Next, the mathematical result is changed by a domain function, if necessary, such that it can be represented in the datatype's domain. The arithmetic proper is representation-independent and needs little discussion; its design choices are shown in Trees 5-38 and 5-39. The re-representation of the result is representation-dependent and non-trivial.

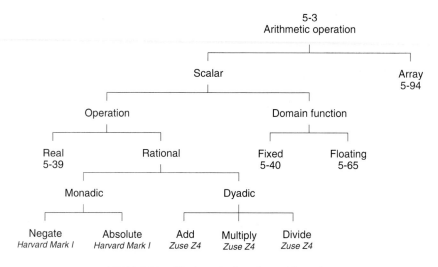

TREE 5-38   Design choices for arithmetic.

For fixed-point representation, the domain function usually does not change the mathematical result. When it does, however, it has a major effect on the result, such as changing large numbers to small ones. Discarding all overflows causes fixed-point addition to act like modular addition.

For floating-point representation, in contrast, the domain function often changes the result, but the effect on the result value is relatively small, being of the order of the representable precision. The consequence is, however, that floating-point arithmetic no longer follows major arithmetic laws.

Fixed-point and floating-point arithmetic are sufficiently different that they warrant separate treatments. The other representation choices, such as radix and length (Sections 4.3 and 4.4) hardly affect the operation proper and require

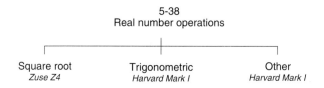

TREE 5-39   Design choices for real number operations.

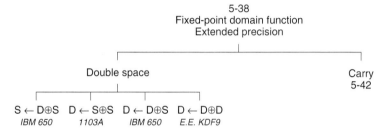

TREE 5-40   Design choices for fixed-point extended precision.

only incidental comment here. The design choices peculiar to fixed-point arithmetic (Tree 5-40) supplement those of Tree 5-38.

Modular arithmetic.   The most salient property of fixed-point arithmetic, as opposed to normal arithmetic, is the limited range of its numbers, the *representation range*.   The limited representation range makes fixed-point arithmetic similar to modular arithmetic. In many uses, such as most address arithmetic, the representation range is never exceeded and therefore presents no problem. The abundance of such applications is enough to justify this type of arithmetic. For all other applications, provisions are necessary either to signal an error or to extend the given range.

Although it would be preferable for fixed-point arithmetic to match regular arithmetic, the correspondence to modular arithmetic can be considered second-best. How close is this correspondence really?

Notation dependence.   In the usual architecture for signed magnitude, only the magnitude of the number obeys modular arithmetic, whereas the sign is treated independently. So the number as a whole does not follow modular arithmetic. In the complement notations, on the other hand, entire numbers follow modular arithmetic precisely. For digit complement, the modulus is one less than for radix complement.

Datatype mixing.   We normally consider any operation as proper to one datatype; when datatypes must be mixed, explicit type conversion is done. Numeric datatypes of various lengths are an exception. Program 5-2 shows that the domain function applies to the result field only and does not depend on operand datatypes. So there is no further mathematical complexity, or difficulty beyond specification costs, in allowing arithmetic operations upon mixed (numeric) datatypes. One may, for example, add a byte or a halfword to a full-word fixed-point number. We shall treat such mixed operations no further.

Secondary results.   For fixed-point arithmetic the key secondary result is the overflow information, lost by the application of the domain function. This information is readily available as a secondary result and is expensive to obtain otherwise. It is precisely what one needs for programming extended-precision operations. Less important, but easy to provide, are the secondary results indicating that the primary result is greater than, equal to, or less than zero.

5.3.1

Extended-Precision Arithmetic

Driving problem.   No matter what the limited number range of a computer may be, one will occasionally need to operate with larger numbers. The larger the word length, the rarer the problem—8-bit microprocessors do large amounts of extended-precision operation; 64-bit computers do much less.

The driving problem for designing the detailed properties of fixed-point arithmetic is extended-precision arithmetic, not because it is used so frequently, but because it overcomes the basic restriction introduced by fixed-point arithmetic itself.

Arithmetic on polynomial representations.   As children we all learned how to do arithmetic on multidigit numbers: One memorizes digit-pair addition and multiplication tables (which depend on the radix) and uses these tables in multidigit algorithms for combining the partial sums, differences, products, and quotients. These algorithms determine radix points as well.

These algorithms do not depend on the radix; they work as well for binary, octal, and hexadecimal as for decimal. They are in fact the algorithms for combining polynomials of the form

$$\sum_{i=0}^{n} c_i r^i$$

where all the polynomials have the same radix.

The standard digital arithmetic algorithms include rules for using operand signs and determining result signs. These rules *do* depend on the sign notation—in school children learn them for the signed-magnitude notation.

Metanumbers and metadigits.   Arithmetic on (arbitrarily) extended-precision fixed-point, fixed-length numbers is exactly this same polynomial arithmetic. For clarity, let us call each fixed-length element a *metadigit*, and each extended-precision number a *metanumber*. Metadigits are usually one full word long, whatever the computer's fixed-point word length. Each metadigit therefore has n or $n - 1$ bits, depending on the sign notation, and the radix of the metanumber is 2^n, 2^{n-1}, or $2^{n-1} - 1$ for radix complement, signed magnitude, and digit complement respectively. In addition/subtraction a carry/borrow of 1 bit must be propagated. In multiplication, the high-order half of one double-length metadigit product is added into the low-order half of the next metadigit product. Even metanumber division can be done by the usual long-division algorithm (as well as by neater ones).

Metanumber sign notation.   It is reasonable, although not necessary, to choose the same sign notation for the metanumber as for the single fixed-point numbers, the metadigits. So a single number is a subset of a metanumber, and the conventions for the single number can be extended to metanumbers.

The sign notation chosen for the metanumber yields the same advantages and disadvantages as for single numbers (Section 4.3). Furthermore, each

single number should act as a proper metadigit, hence have modular arithmetic. In particular, radix complement requires only one pass through the meta number, as opposed to the recomplementing or end-around carry passes of the other two notations.

Metadigit operation.   The traditional algorithms and their refinements all assume that the digit-by-digit operation is strictly modular with easy determination of carry, borrow, and high-order elementary product digit. This is true only for radix complement. Signed magnitude is not modular for subtraction; digit complement gives no simple carry indication when the modulus is reached or exceeded. These shortcomings are usually remedied by extending the number of digits of the metadigit by at least one. A common solution in early machines is to make a double-length accumulator, as found in the 650 and the 1103A.

5.3.2

Basic Operations

Addition and Subtraction

Subtraction is no more difficult than is addition of positive and negative operands; it will be subsumed under addition unless otherwise stated.

Effective addition and subtraction.   When we need to refer to the summing or differencing of magnitudes, we shall call these operations *effective addition* and *effective subtraction*, respectively.

Basic addition.   The basic fixed-point addition is given in Program 1-42. The terminology matches that of Program 5-2. Any of the interpretation and representation functions for numbers given in Section 4.3 may be substituted for `interpret` and `represent`. Secondary results generated by `signal` are those for overflow, extended precision, and sign recognition.

```
extadd;ad;au;metaΔad;metaΔau;addend;augend;sum;metaΔsm;sm
ᴀ basic extended addition
ᴀ fetch operands
 ad←size1 read adr1
 au←size2 read adr2
ᴀ interpret operands as meta digits
 metaΔau←interpret size3 wide au
 metaΔad←interpret size4 wide ad
ᴀ interpret metadigits as numbers
 augend←interpret metaΔau
 addend←interpret metaΔad
ᴀ addition
 sum←augend+addend
ᴀ represent result as meta digits
 metaΔsm←size5 represent sum
ᴀ represent meta digits
 sm←size6 represent metaΔsm
ᴀ store result
 adr3 write sm
```

PROGRAM 5-41   Basic extended-precision addition.

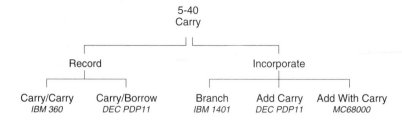

TREE 5-42   Design choices for carry in fixed-point extended precision.

Overflow.   When operands and results have equal lengths, an overflow can always be represented by 1 bit. In the case of variable-length numbers, several bits may be lost, yet a single overflow bit is enough of a warning signal. The programmer has the tools to preserve any desired result precision. It would be redundant to provide other means of preserving the lost information.

Extended-precision addition.   If all the metadigits of each metanumber have the same sign, the usual arithmetic rules apply unchanged. The digit-pair sums are formed by full-word addition instead of by lookup in a memorized addition table.

Program 5-41 shows that the extended-precision number, the metanumber, is, in turn, made up of fixed-point numbers. These fixed-point numbers are the metadigits of the extended-precision number system, the *metanumber system*.

The metadigit-by-metadigit addition or subtraction uses modular arithmetic and must provide a carry or borrow (Tree 5-42). The carries between metadigits differ for the three main sign notations, because negative numbers are represented and processed differently. The suitability of signed-magnitude, radix-complement, and digit-complement notation for extended addition is discussed next and is summarized in Table 5-43.

Signed-magnitude addition.   The metadigits are represented by the magnitude part of the notation. The sign of the low-order metadigits is redundant—a minor loss of efficiency. The metadigits have modular effective addition.

Effective subtraction requires a complementing prepass.

An early example of binary fixed-length signed-magnitude arithmetic is the IBM 704 (1955). The single accumulator of the 704 has two additional bits, the P and Q bits, which are extensions of the magnitude and effectively record overflow bits. (One bit would do nicely.) The carry of the metadigit addition is recorded in P and can be shifted to the low-order position for the next metadigit. A complement operation aids extended subtraction.

	Signed magnitude	Radix complement	Digit complement
Meta radix	radix*(n-1)	radix*n	(radix*n)-1
Sign treatment	separate	as a digit	as a digit
Complement	explicit	inherent	inherent
Carry	out of magnitude	out of sign	needs extra digit
Extra actions	recomplement	none	end-around carry

Legend: n = number of digits, including sign.

TABLE 5-43   Characteristics of extended-precision addition.

```
┌Sign
↓QP
  ┌─┬──────────────────────────────────────────┐
  │ │ │Digits                                   │
  │ │ │                                         │
  └─┴──────────────────────────────────────────┘
  0   3                                38
  Accumulator

  ADD:s;p;addend;augend;sum          CLA
  ⋒ IBM 704 Add                      ⋒ IBM 704 Load
   s←acc[Sign]                        acc[Sign,Accdigits]←read704 adr704
   p←acc[P]                           acc[Q,P]←0
   addend←signmagni read704 adr704
   augend←signmagni acc
   sum←augend+addend
   acc←accsize signmagnr sum
   →If sum=0
   THEN:acc[Sign]←s
   ENDIF:Oflo report p≠acc[P]
```

PROGRAM 5-44   Addition in the IBM 704.

The 650 uses decimal fixed-length signed-magnitude arithmetic. In contrast to the 704, the entire double-length accumulator participates in the addition. The carry appears in the low-order position of the left half of the accumulator (the Upper accumulator) and can be shifted to the right half (the Lower accumulator). Program 1-41 shows the arithmetic organ of the 650 and gives a typical add operation.

Radix-complement addition.   The modulus of radix-complement representation is $radix^n$, where n is the number of digits including the sign (Program 4-41).

The homogeneity of radix-complement notation greatly simplifies the extended-addition algorithm. There are no special actions for the sign bits: Addition and subtraction match modular arithmetic. No separate complement cycles are required; the carry or borrow out of the metadigit operation is easily propagated. This explains why radix complement is used exclusively by mini- and microcomputers (which must frequently perform extended-precision operations).

Add With Carry.   Adding the carry of two metadigits to the next pair of metadigits requires adding three quantities. When these are added in two operations, the first operation may produce the metadigit carry, which the second operation will reset and lose if it is held in a carry indicator. In double-length–accumulator machines, carries from the lower half are automatically accumulated in the upper half. In the IBM 701 (1953) family, where addition is only into the upper half, extra bits accumulate the carry. A more proper and more efficient solution is to preserve the carry in a separate location, and to add all three quantities in one operation, as does the Add With Carry of the 8080A (Program 5-45).

In radix complement, Add With Carry extends the partial sum of a meta-addition with another metadigit. So the sign secondary result of Add With Carry should apply to the new metaresult. Unfortunately, the 8080A sign secondary result reflects only the last metadigit and not the resulting metanumber, and gives a zero result even if only the high-order metadigit

```
┌─────┬───┐
│ Op  │ S │
│     │   │
└─────┴───┘
 0    5  8
Legend: Op = opcode; S = source.
```

```
ADC;ad;addend;augend;sum                    signal8080NZP r1
 ⋒ Intel 8080A Add With Carry                ⋒ Intel 8080A conditions
ad←read8080 word adr8080 Source             reg[F;Neg]←1↑r1
addend←radixcompi ad                        reg[F;Zero]←0=∨/r1
augend←radixcompi reg[A;]                    reg[F;Parity]←~2|+/r1
sum←augend+addend+reg[F;Carry]
reg[A;]←word radixcompr sum
signal8080C augend,addend,reg[F;Carry]
signal8080NZP reg[A;]
```

PROGRAM 5-45   Add With Carry in the Intel 8080A.

is 0. In the Motorola MC68000 (1980, Program 5-46) the zero condition is correctly applied to the full metaresult (at minimal implementation cost).

The investment for the "with carry" operations is two operation codes—a good investment in a processor with 8-bit word length. The implementation cost is negligible, since the low-order adder stage must have provisions for the input carry anyway.

Add Carry.   The DEC PDP11 (1970) needs the same function as the 8080A. Since the opcode space of the PDP11 is very tight for its two-operand operations, the designers chose to introduce the single-operand operations Add Carry (Program 5-47) and Subtract Borrow.

Add Carry works smoothly for double precision, but is awkward for other extended precision, for the reasons given. Therefore, the PDP11 also provides Branch On Carry and Set Carry operations.

For the 360, with its 32-bit words, the frequency of extended precision is even lower than for the PDP11. Still, two operation codes in each of two classes are devoted to this purpose. The operations could have been just Add With Carry, as in the 8080A, except for an architectural decision in the seemingly remote area of decision functions. For most operations, the 360 stores one of four secondary-result messages, encoded in a 2-bit condition code. Since the implied zero comparison requires three messages, there is no room for a

```
ADDX;dest;source;addend;augend;sum;sm
 ⋒ Motorola 68000 Add With Carry
source←size680 adr680(4×fld Rm),fld R2
addend←radixcompi read680 source
dest←size680 adr680(4×fld Rm),fld R1
augend←radixcompi read680 dest
sum←augend+addend+status[Extend]
sm←size680 radixcompr sum
dest write680 sm
→IF sum=0
THEN: ⋒ zero result
    status[Neg,Oflo]←0
      →ENDIF
ELSE: ⋒ non-zero result
    signal680NZO sm
ENDIF:signal680X
(ρsm) signal680C addend,augend,status[Extend]
```

PROGRAM 5-46   Add With Carry in the Motorola MC68000.

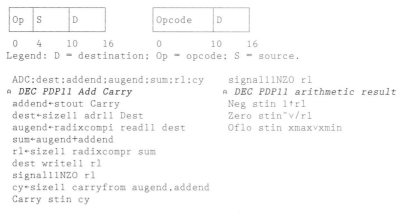

```
 Op  S    D              Opcode    D

0    4    10   16       0         10   16
Legend: D = destination; Op = opcode; S = source.

ADC;dest;addend;augend;sum;rl;cy     signal11NZO rl
ᴀ DEC PDP11 Add Carry                ᴀ DEC PDP11 arithmetic result
addend←stout Carry                   Neg stin 1↑rl
dest←size11 adr11 Dest               Zero stin~∨/rl
augend←radixcompi read11 dest        Oflo stin xmax∨xmin
sum←augend+addend
rl←size11 radixcompr sum
dest write11 rl
signal11NZO rl
cy←size11 carryfrom augend,addend
Carry stin cy
```

PROGRAM 5-47   Add Carry in the DEC PDP11.

message that can occur for any of these results. Therefore, the fourth message is devoted to overflow, regardless of sign. A separate set of operations, Add Logical and Subtract Logical, is used to record (in the condition code) the presence or absence of a carry.

Program 5-48 shows the actions of Add and Add Logical. They differ only in the setting of the condition code. It would have been better to record the carry separately in the PSW, and to use the operations Add With Carry and Subtract With Borrow, as does the MC68000.

```
 Opcode  R1  X1  B1  D1

0        8   12  16  20            32
Legend: B = base; D = displacement; R = register; X = index.

A;addend;augend;sum;xmax;xmin
ᴀ IBM 360 Add
addend←radixcompi word read360a adr360bxd
augend←radixcompi reg[fld R1;]
→OUT suppress360
sum←augend+addend                    signal360NZPO result;cc
reg[fld R1;]←word radixcompr sum     ᴀ IBM 360 arithmetic result
signal360NZPO sum                    cc← 2 1[result<0]
Oflo report xmax∨xmin                cc←(cc,0)[result=0]
                                     cc←(cc,3)[xmax∨xmin]
                                     psw[Cc]←2 magnr cc
AL;addend;augend;sum;xmax;xmin
ᴀ IBM 360 Add Logical
addend←magni word read360a adr360bxd
augend←magni reg[fld R1;]            signal360ZC rl;carry;nonzero
→OUT suppress360                     ᴀ IBM 360 logical result
sum←augend+addend                    carry←xmax
reg[fld R1;]←word radixcompr sum     nonzero←∨/rl
signal360ZC reg[fld R1;]             psw[Cc]←carry,nonzero
```

PROGRAM 5-48   Add and Add Logical in the IBM System/360.

Carry versus borrow in extended subtraction.   In radix complement, the extended-precision subtract is normally performed by adding the 2's complement of the subtrahend. This 2's complement is obtained from the 1's complement by adding 1 (a carry-in). The carry-out of a metadigit then

```
↓Sign
```

Upper	Lower

```
0                              36                            72
Accumulator
```

```
RA;ad;addend;augend;sum
Ɑ Univac 1103A Add
acc←extend word read1103 adr1103u
augend←magni acc
ad←extend word read1103 adr1103v
addend←magni ad
sum←augend+addend
acc←double zerocompr sum
adr1103u write1103 acc
```

PROGRAM 5-49   Addition in the Univac 1103A.

serves as the carry-in of the next-higher metadigit. The absence of a carry-in is equivalent to a borrow. Designers differ, however, in the treatment of the carry. In the 360, the carry is recorded as status, and a zero carry signifies a borrow. In the DEC tradition, however, the carry is inverted in subtraction, such that it is 1 for a borrow and 0 for no borrow. Table 5-50 indicates the choices made in various machines.

	What saved	Where saved	How used
Harvard Mark I	carry	memory word	Add Carry
IBM 701	overflow	P-bit	Shift
IBM 650	overflow	accumulator	Shift
IBM 704	overflow	P-bit	Shift
STC ZEBRA	carry	indicator	Add With Carry
IBM Stretch	carry	indicator	Branch
CDC 6600 PPU	overflow	accumulator	Shift
IBM System/360	carry	condition	Branch
DEC PDP8	carry	indicator	Add Carry
DEC PDP11	carry/borrow	condition	Add Carry
Intel 8080A	carry/borrow	condition	Add With Carry
Motorola M6800	carry/borrow	condition	Add With Carry
MOS 6502	carry	condition	Add With Carry
DEC VAX11	carry/borrow	condition	Add With Carry
Motorola MC68000	carry/borrow	condition	Add With Carry
IBM 6150	carry	condition	Add With Carry

TABLE 5-50   Extended addition and subtraction in various machines.

Digit-complement addition.   The modulus of digit-complement representation is $radix^n - 1$, with n the number of digits, including the sign. Upon addition, a carry is produced whenever the modulus is exceeded, but not when the modulus is reached, even though that value is interpreted as (negative) zero. Therefore, the result of the metadigit addition can best be recorded in an accumulator that is extended with at least 1 bit. A proper carry is preserved, and no end-around carry occurs in the metadigit; its modulus is again $radix^n$.

Program 5-49 describes the double-length accumulator and the corresponding addition of the 1103A.

Multiplication

Basic multiplication is given in Program 5-51. For fixed point, the limited representation range poses a design problem as to the product length.

```
multiply;mr;md;multiplier;multiplicand;product;pd
A basic multiplication
mr←size1 read adr1
md←size2 read adr2
multiplier←interpret mr
multiplicand←interpret md
product←multiplicand×multiplier
pd←size3 represent product
adr3 write pd
signal pd
```

PROGRAM 5-51   Basic fixed-point multiplication.

Product length.   The number of product digits is just less than or equal to the total number of digits of the multiplier and multiplicand. For variable-length numbers, this size poses no immediate problem; for fixed-length numbers, however, the product can occupy twice the operand size.

In contrast to fixed-length addition, where a single-length result and an overflow indication present the complete result, a single-length product represents only half the digits of the result; the exact result can no longer be reconstructed. Many fixed-length machines make the full product available in some way.

Von Neumann's design [Burks et al., 1946] developed the product in a two-word working store and allowed the programmer to store either half, or to shift the product before storing. The implementation of a full product requires no more equipment or operation time than would supplying just half the product digits. The double-length accumulators of the 650 and the 1103A, and the 704 accumulator-MQ (Figure 4-39) follow the von Neumann design. An alternative to a double-length working register is a pair of working registers, as found in the 360 (Program 5-52).

Another solution, which matches the program primitives and the basic paradigm, is to use a pair of multiply operations, one producing the low-order product digits and the other the high-order digits. This approach was first used in the Librascope LGP30 (1957; Program 5-53). The 6600 uses a

Opcode	R1	R2

```
0        8   12   16
Legend: R = register.
```

```
MR;multiplier;multiplicand;product;pd
A IBM 360 Multiply Register
multiplier←radixcompi reg[fld R2;]
multiplicand←radixcompi reg[odd R1;]
→OUT suppress360
product←multiplicand×multiplier
pd←double radixcompr product
reg[(even R1)+ι2;]←word wide pd
```

PROGRAM 5-52   Fixed-point multiply in the IBM System/360.

```
                        *↓
  ┌──────────────┬─────┬─┬──────────┬──┐
  │ *            │ Op  │*│ Address  │  │
  └──────────────┴─────┴─┴──────────┴──┘
  0              12   1618           31
```
Legend: Op = opcode; * = unused.

```
M;multilier;multiplicand;product          N;multilier;multiplicand;product
α LGP30 Multiply High                     α LGP30 Multiply Low
multiplier←radixcompi read30 adr30        multiplier←radixcompi read30 adr30
multiplicand←radixcompi acc               multiplicand←radixcompi acc
product←multiplicant×multiplier           product←multiplicant×multiplier
acc←word↑(2×word) radixcompr product      acc←word radixcompr product
```

PROGRAM 5-53   Fixed-point multiply in the LGP30.

similar approach to provide double-precision floating-point multiply; it has no fixed-point multiply.

Extended multiplication.   As with extended addition, extended fixed-length fixed-point multiplication follows the rules of digit-by-digit operation for positional representation. Again, the metadigits used correspond to a single fixed-length integer, and modular arithmetic is used. The double-length metadigit products form pairs of metadigits. All these metadigits are added using extended addition.

Cumulative multiplication.   A product that is added to an augend is called a *cumulative multiplication*. A cumulative multiplication is often as fast and as easy to implement as a normal multiplication and is found in many early machines, such as the Ferranti Mark 1 (1951), the Cambridge EDSAC (1949), and the IBM 650 (1954).

Multiply Step.   Multiplication and division are normally implemented using several cycles, whereas addition and subtraction need only one. A total machine implementation is much simpler if all its operations use only one cycle, so Seymour Cray, in Countess—an early machine in the 1103 family— provided only single-cycle operations and a Repeat operation.

One of the single-cycle operations, Multiply Step, examines the rightmost bit in a multiplier register, adds the multiplicand into an accumulator if the multiplier bit is 1, and then shifts both accumulator and multiplier 1 bit to the right. When it is iterated under program control, it effects multiplication.

```
  ┌──────────────┬─────┬─────┐
  │ Opcode       │ Rb  │ Rc  │
  └──────────────┴─────┴─────┘
  0              8    12    16
```
Legend: R = register.

```
M;multiplicand;multiplier;augend;product
α IBM 6150 Multiply Step
multiplicand←radixcompi reg[fld Rc;]
multiplier←+/(status[Mq; 30 31]/ ¯2 1),¯status[Cond;Carry]
augend←radixcompi reg[fld Rb;]
product← 0 4 ⊤augend+multiplier×multiplicand
status[Cond;Carry]←¯status[Mq;30]
reg[fld Rb;]←word radixcompr product[0]
status[Mq;]←(2 radixcompr product[1]),¯2↓status[Mq;]
```

PROGRAM 5-54   Multiply Step in the IBM 6150.

The technique has also been used in Van der Poel's ZEBRA (1959) and in several minicomputers and microprocessors (Program 5-54). It gives simple programming and respectable multiply performance without special cycling controls. As used with Repeat, the Multiply Step instruction does not have to be refetched as it is iterated, which helps performance radically.

Division

The basic fixed-point division is given in Program 5-55. The limited representation range again causes several length problems.

```
divide;dr;dd;divisor;dividend;quotient;remainder;qt;rm
ⁿ basic division
dr←size1 read adr1
dd←size2 read adr2
divisor←interpret dr
dividend←interpret dd
Dividecheck report divisor=0
→OUT suppress
quotient←dividend÷divisor
quotient←(×quotient)×⌊|quotient
remainder←dividend-quotient×divisor
qt←size3 represent quotient
rm←size4 represent remainder
adr3 write qt
adr4 write rm
signal qt
```

PROGRAM 5-55   Basic fixed-point division.

A quotient is infinitely long if it is a fraction that is not a multiple of a (negative) power of the radix. So 1 divided by 5 requires only one digit to the right of the radix point in a decimal machine, but is a repeating fraction in a binary machine. An exact result can be obtained for all divisions by producing a remainder as well as a quotient. The two results can be accommodated by treating one as a secondary result, or—better—by providing two separate quotient and remainder operations.

Remainder length.   The remainder must be smaller than the divisor; it can thus be provided in the divisor's length.

Dividend length.   When division is viewed as the inverse of multiplication, a double-length dividend is desirable, since otherwise a dividend smaller in absolute value than the divisor would yield a zero quotient and a remainder equal to the dividend. Hence, either explicitly or implicitly, a double-length dividend is common.

Quotient length.   There is no quotient defined for a zero divisor. In other cases, the integer quotient digits can always be represented if the quotient length is equal to the dividend length (Table 5-56). The smallest divisor—1 in fixed-point arithmetic—yields the maximum quotient; so the maximum quotient is equal to the dividend. The Stretch accordingly makes the quotient length equal to the dividend length; the quotient replaces the dividend, and a special remainder location stores the remainder as a secondary result.

| | Quotient length | | | |
| | Single | | Double | |
	Decimal	Binary	Decimal	Binary
Dividend	55	00110111	100	01100100
Divisor	7	0111	3	0011
Quotient	7	0111	33	00100001
Remainder	6	0110	1	0001

TABLE 5-56   Quotient length in division.

Most computers produce a single-length quotient from a double-length dividend. This solution is the more proper one, giving both quotient and remainder the normal datatype size. The double-length product is used much more frequently as a double-length operand in subsequent operations than is a double-length quotient. Restricting the quotient to single-length requires a rule constraining the upper half of the dividend to be smaller in magnitude than the divisor. This rule injects a major impropriety and a major practical awkwardness into the programming of fixed-point arithmetic.

| Division | Classical | | Chinal | |
examples	qt	rm	qt	rm
22÷ 7	3	1	3	1
22÷ ⁻7	⁻3	1	⁻4	⁻6
⁻22÷ 7	⁻3	⁻1	⁻4	6
⁻22÷ ⁻7	3	⁻1	3	⁻1

Legend: qt = quotient; rm = remainder

TABLE 5-57   Sign of remainder in division.

Remainder sign.   The sign of the remainder is traditionally defined to be the same as the sign of the dividend, unless the remainder is zero. Chinal [1972], however, has proposed to give the remainder the sign of the divisor

Steps		Classical		Chinal	
dd1←⌊dd÷mod		⌊125÷16		⌊125÷16	
First dividend	dd1	7	00000111	7	00000111
Divisor	dr	⁻3	1101	⁻3	1101
First quotient	qt1	⁻2	1110	⁻3	1101
First remainder	rm1	1	0001	⁻2	1110
dd2←(rm1×mod)+mod	dd	(1×16)+16	125	(⁻2×16)+16	125
Second dividend	dd2	29	00011101	⁻19	11101101
Divisor	dr	⁻3	1101	⁻3	1101
Second quotient	qt2	⁻9	(1)0111	6	0110
Final remainder	rm	2	0010	⁻1	1111
qt←(qt1×mod)+qt2		(⁻2×16)+⁻9		(⁻3×16)+6	
First quotient	qt1	⁻2	11100000	⁻48	11010000
Second quotient	qt2	⁻9	11110111	6	00000110
Final quotient	qt	⁻41	11010111	⁻42	11010110

Example: dd÷dr for 125÷⁻3 or 01111101÷1101 with mod 16.

TABLE 5-58   Examples of continued division.

```
┌────────┬────┬────┐
│ Opcode │ Rb │ Rc │
└────────┴────┴────┘
0        8   12   16
Legend: R = register.
```

```
D:divisor;drsign;dividend;ddsign;remainder;rmsign;quotient
A IBM 6150 Divide Step
divisor←radixcompi reg[fld Rc;]
drsign←divisor≥0
dividend←radixcompi reg[fld Rb;],status[Mq;0]
ddsign←dividend≥0
remainder←dividend+ 1 ‾1[ddsign=drsign]×divisor
rmsign←remainder≥0
reg[fld Rb;]←word radixcompr remainder
quotient←rmsign=drsign
status[Mq;]←1↓status[Mq;],quotient
status[Cond;Oflo]←ddsign=rmsign
status[Cond;Carry]←drsign=rmsign
```

PROGRAM 5-59   Divide Step in the IBM 6150.

(Table 5-57). The purpose of this uncommon rule is to produce a positive quotient extension, which is desirable when the division is continued with the remainder, as in Table 5-58. This rule, however, derives from the use of 2's-complement sign notation for the extended quotient. A remainder of desired sign can also be obtained by a suitable correction.

Extended division.   Just as division is more difficult to implement than multiplication, so extended division is more difficult to implement than is extended multiplication. The implementation algorithms are again a source of inspiration—both the deterministic ones, computing one metadigit of the quotient at a time, and the iterative ones, based on Newton's method. In either case, extended division is reduced to extended multiplication, and the normal Divide operation serves to provide an estimate of the metadigits of the quotient.

	Size		——————— Operation ———————				
	Single	Double	S←SOS	S←DOS	D←SOS	D←DOS	D←DOD
Cambridge EDSAC	17 35	70				+ ×	
Ferranti Mark 1	40	80	+		×	+	
Univac I	s,11d	s,22d	+ × ÷		×		
Princeton IAS	40	80	+ ÷		×		
IBM 701	s,2,36	s,2,72	+	÷	×		
IBM 650	s,10d	s,20d		÷	×	+	
IBM 704	s,2,36	s,2,72	+	÷	×		
Univac 1103A	36	72	+ ×	÷	×	+	
IBM Stretch	1-64	128				+ × ÷	
IBM Stretch	1-16d	32d				+ × ÷	
English Electric KDF9	48	96	+ × ÷	÷	×		+
IBM System/360	32 16	64	+	÷	×		
DEC PDP8	12	24	+	÷	×		
DEC PDP11	16	32	+ ×	÷	×		
DEC VAX11	8	16 32	+ × ÷		×		+ × ÷
Motorola MC68000	8 16	32	+	÷	×	+	+

Legend: d = decimal; D = Double; S = Single; O = operation;
         + = add and subtract; result of division applies to quotient.

TABLE 5-60   Extended-precision fixed point in various machines.

Divide step.   An attractive simplification is to eliminate the multiple-cycle Divide in favor of a one-cycle Divide Step, which is iterated under program control to effect division.   A typical Divide Step shifts the dividend and quotient each 1 bit to the left, attempts to subtract the divisor from the dividend, and generates a quotient bit of 1 if the subtraction does not change the dividend sign. If the subtraction is about to change the sign, the operation is suppressed, and a Divide Step generates a quotient bit of 0. In either case, the quotient bit is inserted into the rightmost position of the quotient register (Program 5-59). As with Multiply Step, Divide Step works smoothly with a Repeat operation.

Representation range, and hence the relative need for extended precision, is a key factor in design decisions for basic arithmetic operations. Table 5-60 shows the choices made with regard to precision in various machines.

5.3.3
Extension of the Operation Set

Frequency studies show that arithmetic operations beyond those already discussed are used infrequently. Nevertheless, several other arithmetic operations have been provided in some machines. Two sources of such operations are

- The variety of numeric datatypes, which requires conversion from one type to another
- Mathematics primitives that go beyond the basic operations

Table 5-61 shows fixed-point arithmetic operations in various machines.

Conversion

Datatype conversions are all governed by the interpretation and representation functions. They conform to Program 5-12 and include

- A change between fixed point and floating point (see Section 5.4 on floating point)
- A change in radix—for example, the 360 Convert To Binary (Table 5-61); the 8080A Decimal Adjust (Program 5-62) changes not the radix of an operand, but the radix of the result of an addition
- A change in allocation—for example, the decimal Unpack (Program 5-63) and Pack operations of the 360, which change packed decimal arithmetic data to unpacked decimal representation data, and vice versa

These operations can count on a reasonable (but not high) usage, since they are necessary for converting from external datatypes to the datatypes for which arithmetic is defined.

Supplementary Arithmetic Operations

Sign manipulation.   Negate and Make Absolute are frequently provided monadic operators (Table 5-61). Stretch includes these operators as modifiers of the basic arithmetic operations. Separate operations, as in the 360, are more proper and more efficient.

	Operation Binary	Operation Decimal	Secondary result
Harvard Mark I		+ × ÷ * ⊗ s	
Cambridge EDSAC	+ ×		
Ferranti Mark 1	+ +×		
Univac I		+ × ÷	
Princeton IAS	~ | + × ÷		
IBM 701	+ × ÷ r		
IBM 650		~ | + +× ÷	
IBM 704	~ | + × ÷ r		
IBM 705		~ + × ÷ r	
Univac 1103A	~ | + × +× ÷		
STC ZEBRA	+ M D		
Bull Gamma 60	~ + × ÷		
IBM 1401		~ +	
IBM Stretch	~ | + × +× ÷ d	~ | + × +× ÷ b	=0 <0 >0
English Electric KDF9	~ | + × ÷ d	b	
CDC 6600	+		
CDC 6600 PPU	+		
Burroughs B5500	d	+ b	
IBM System/360	~ | + × ÷ d	+ × ÷ b	=0 ≤0 c o
DEC PDP8	+ × ÷		c
DEC PDP11	~ + × ÷		=0 <0 c o
Intel 8080A	+	a	=0 <0 c x p
Cray 1	+		
Motorola M6800	~ +	a	=0 <0 c o x
MOS 6502	+	+	=0 <0 c o
DEC VAX11	~ + × +× ÷ d f	+ × ÷ b	=0 <0 c o
Motorola MC68000	~ + × ÷	~ +	=0 <0 c o e
IBM 6150	+ M D		=0 <0 >0 c o

Legend: a = decimal adjust; b = convert to binary; c = carry;
d = convert to decimal; e = extend bit;
f = convert to floating point; o = overflow;
p = parity; r = round; s = sine; x = auxiliary carry;
D = divide step; M = multiply step; ~ = negate;
| = make absolute; + = add and subtract;
+× = cumulative multiply.

TABLE 5-61   Fixed-point arithmetic operations in various machines.

Offset.   The Stretch also has an offset, which multiplies one operand by a power of the radix to aid alignment in addition. Offset is a bad idea. The 7 instruction bits required for specification are expensive; a fast implementation is also expensive; a slow one, useless. The function is better provided as a separate operation, the arithmetic shift. So our dictum that compound operations are not good architecture (Section 1.4) is exemplified.

Round.   Precision may be adjusted by necessity or by choice. Sometimes, products or quotients must be shortened by the datatype domain function.

```
DAA;carry10;addend;augend;sum
ᴀ Intel 8080A Decimal Adjust
carry10←9<magni digit wide reg[A;]
addend←16⊥6×reg[F;Carry,Carry4]∨carry10
augend←radixcompi reg[A;]
sum←augend+addend
reg[A;]←word radixcompr sum
reg[F;Carry,Carry4]←carry10∨reg[F;Carry],0
signal8080NZP reg[A;]
```

PROGRAM 5-62   Decimal Adjust in the Intel 8080A.

Opcode	L1	L2	B1	D1		B2	D2	

```
0        8   12  16  20            32  36            48
```
Legend: B = base; D = displacement; L = length.

```
UNPK;source;dest;12;11;hex
ᴀ IBM 360 Unpack
source←adr360bd2
dest←adr360bd1
12←fld L2
11←fld L1
ᴀ invert sign byte
hex←digit wide byte read360 source+12
(dest+11) write360.Φ[0] hex
→WHILE(11>0)∧12>0
   12←12-1
   11←11-1
  ᴀ expand low order hex to byte
  hex←digit wide byte read360 source+12
  (dest+11) write360(4ρ1).hex[1;]
  →If 11>0
  THEN: ᴀ expand high order hex to byte
     11←11-1
     (dest+11) write360(4ρ1).hex[0;]
  ENDIF:→Δ
ENDWHILE: ᴀ fill with zero
dest write360(11,byte)ρ(4ρ1),4ρ0
```

PROGRAM 5-63   Unpack in the IBM System/360.

Precision treatment becomes a matter of choice when excess result digits remain available, at least temporarily. Thus, in the Stretch, the accumulator has space for double-length results. The programmer can store rounded results by the operation Store Rounded, or truncated results by means of Store. Because of the temporary result space, rounding can be advantageously postponed until after a sequence of operations.

Precision analysis is part of the more general problem of error analysis, and automatic procedures are not nearly capable of solving this problem. Hence preserving excess digits (when possible) and providing a Round operation allows the programmer to decide how the precision should be treated.

Square root.   The Harvard Mark I (1944) and the ENIAC (1946) had the square-root operation for fixed point. The Zuse Z3 (1941) and Z4 (1945) and many modern machines have Square Root for floating point; it is part of the

Address		Op	X1	M0	L0		Bs	Offset	Opcode		X2

```
0                      24  28  32 35      41 44        51          60  64
```
Legend: Bs = byte size; L = length; M = address mode; Op = opcode;
         X = index.

```
A;od;operand;addend;augend;sum
ᴀ IBM Stretch Add
od←(fld0 L0) read7030 adr7030m
operand←factor7030×mem7030i od
augend←acc7030i
acc7030r operand                  sum←augend+neg7030×addend
addend←acc7030i                   acc7030r sum
operand report7030PF addend       Lostcarry report7030 sum≠acc7030i
```

PROGRAM 5-64   Variable-length addition in the IBM Stretch.

IEEE Standard. It occurs with low frequency, but a direct implementation is usually much faster than a programmed subroutine.

Conditional operations.   Sometimes, the action of arithmetic operations is made conditional, as a way of both making a test and effecting it in one operation. This combination is proper when the combined operation has a conceptual unity and when it requires no more parameters or operands than can normally be specified in one instruction. Such an operation avoids branching, thus speeding operation in pipelined machines.

Conditional move. One way of effecting the several outcomes of a test is to provide data moves whose source or destination depends on the test result. The Max, Min, and Sort functions in high-level language are all of this kind.

A machine-language analog proposed by Sites [1978] is a conditional swap of two registers if the Less Than condition code is on. The sequence

Conditional Swap A,B

would then leave the greater in register A and the lesser in B. Alternatively, the Max and Min operations may be provided as such, as in the Z4.

Conditional arithmetic.   A similar idea is to provide arithmetic operations whose behavior is conditional either on the result of some previous test, or on the result of some test performed during execution. The sign-manipulation operation Make Absolute can be considered a conditional operation whose behavior depends on an intermediate sign test.

Other conditional-arithmetic operations with similar usefulness have occasionally been used. Brooks proposed Augment, incorporated in the Stretch as Add To Magnitude, which, when it effectively differences two numbers, produces an ordinary difference if positive, and a zero otherwise [Brooks, 1956]. This operator provides efficient evaluation of piecewise-linear functions without branching. The Z4 has a monadic version of this operation; it gives the maximum of zero and the operand.

5.3.4
Bibliography

Atkins and Garner [1973], Brooks [1956], Burks et al. [1946], Chinal [1972], Garner [1965], Kulish [1977], Meggitt [1962], Sites [1978].

5.4
Floating-Point Arithmetic

The mathematical operations Add, Subtract, Multiply, and Divide are, in principle, the same for floating-point as for fixed-point arithmetic. The floating-point operations, however, necessarily *approximate* the mathematical operations. We consider this basic difference in general, and then discuss the individual operations, including format conversion and double precision. Tree 5-65 gives the operation design choices that are specific to floating point.

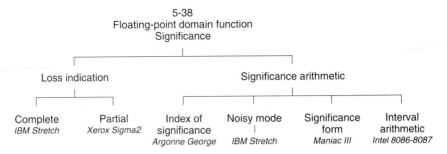

TREE 5-65   Design choices for floating-point arithmetic.

Laws of Floating-Point Arithmetic

Fixed-point arithmetic follows all the basic arithmetic laws, such as the associative and commutative laws, as long as the result of the operation remains in the representable domain. When a fixed-length result exceeds the representation range, all information can be preserved if the domain function is defined properly and the necessary information—such as an overflow indication, a high- and low-order product, and a remainder—is preserved. With this information and some extra work, the basic arithmetic laws can be preserved even when the result is outside the normal domain.

Approximate arithmetic.   In floating-point arithmetic, however, the domain function usually produces an approximation of the result. Preserving exact results would entail corrective action, which would in effect reintroduce programmed scaling and thus defeat the whole purpose of floating-point arithmetic. As a consequence, designers do not provide corrective action, and the lost precision becomes irretrievable. Table 5-66 lists the basic algebraic laws and shows their validity for floating point, assuming that the results are within the exponent range. The key law violated is the associative law. As a consequence, the distributive law fails, as do cancellation and solvability (Table 5-67).

```
Law and example              Applies to    Valid    Approximate  Not always

Associative
     a+(b+c)↔(a+b)+c            + ×                      ×            +
Commutative
     a+b↔b+a; a×b↔b×a           + ×         + ×
Distributive
   a×(b+c)↔(a×b)+(a×c)         (+ ×)                    (+ ×)
Identity
          a+0↔a; a×1↔a          + ×         + ×
Inverse
        --a↔a; ÷÷a↔a            - ÷          -                       ÷
Cancellation
        (a+b)=(a+c)↔b=c         + ×                      ×            +
Solvability
 (a+b)-b↔a; (a×b)÷b↔a         (+ -) (× ÷)                (× ÷)       (+ -)
```

Legend: ↔ = implies; (○ ○) = operation pair;
        laws apply only within domain.

TABLE 5-66   Floating-point algebraic laws.

Law and example	Gives	Result	Discrepancy
Associative			
$(4+0.75)+\overline{}3.5$	$4+\overline{}3.5$	0.5	
$4+(0.75+\overline{}3.5)$	$4+\overline{}3$	1	$0.5{\neq}1$
Distributive			
$3\times(2.5+\overline{}0.5)$	3×2	6	
$(3\times2.5)+(3\times\overline{}0.5)$	$7+\overline{}1.5$	5	$6{\neq}5$
Inverse			
$1\div(1\div1.75)$	$1\div0.5$	2	$1{\neq}2$
Cancelation			
$4+0.5$ versus $4+0.125$	4 versus 4	equal	$0.5{\neq}0.125$
Solvability			
$(2+0.75)-0.75$	$2.5-0.75$	1.75	$2{\neq}1.75$

Legend: representation of Table 4-63;
        precision treated by truncation.

TABLE 5-67   Examples of imprecise arithmetic.

Relative error.   The failure of the algebraic laws lies in the elementary floating-point operations. The floating-point result has a relative error, whose magnitude can be made smaller than or equal to $0.5 \times base^{1-p}$, where p is the number of coefficient digits, assuming normalized operands. This relative error assumes rounding; it is twice as large in case of truncation.

Approximate algebraic laws.   The relative error can be made acceptably small by providing enough coefficient digits. The algebraic laws of Table 5-66 that failed might nevertheless hold within a tolerance that has the magnitude of a small multiple of the relative error. Such laws can then be called *approximate algebraic laws*.

Table 5-66 shows that there is an approximate distributive law. The associative law and the corresponding cancellation and solvability laws, however, are approximate for multiplication and division, but not for addition. In fact, the associative law holds for effective addition, but not for effective subtraction (for which the cancellation and solvability laws therefore do not hold).

There is no bound to the error that is caused by the failure of the associative law for effective subtraction. Therefore, this deviation from normal arithmetic laws is much more serious than is the relative error of the individual operations. It is inherent in the use of any floating-point representation, quite apart from the choice of notation, radix, base, and number of allocated digits. It can be avoided only by careful numerical analysis of the calculation at hand.

In the first example of Table 5-67, if the numerical analyst knows the relative magnitude of the operands, he can select the proper order of operating on them; namely, to sum in order of increasing magnitude.

5.4.1

Significance

The failure of the associative law expresses itself in a loss of valid, or *significant*, coefficient digits. For a given algorithm this loss cannot be avoided, but it can be noted either by signaling its occurrence or by keeping track of its effect throughout the computation. The first method is called *lost-significance indication*; the second, *significance arithmetic*.

Lost-Significance Indication

Loss of significance arises only through an effective subtraction of two nearly equal numbers. The resulting intermediate coefficient has some left bits equal to 0s. After a left shift, 0s appear in the right part of the coefficient. These 0 bits, however, do not represent zero values; rather, they are placeholders or ignorance indicators. As computation proceeds using this result, these digits may take on all kinds of values even though they still have no meaning.

Several methods have been proposed to signal the loss of significance as part of an arithmetic operation.

Complete significance loss.   The most dramatic loss of significance is the generation of a zero coefficient. The result then constitutes the order-of-magnitude zero (OMZ). Depending on the definition of the domain of the representable floating-point numbers, the OMZ will be recognized as such or treated as a true zero. In any case, the generation of an OMZ may indicate a major flaw in the computational algorithm. Hence, many computers provide a signal, such as an interrupt or an indicator setting, when the OMZ is generated (Section 4.4). The Stretch was one of the first computers to provide an interrupt for this occurrence. The Z4 was the first computer to detect this case.

Partial significance loss.   One might want to signal a less extreme loss of significance. The Xerox Sigma7, for example, gives a lost-significance interruption on any postshift of more than two hexadecimal digits.

Significance Arithmetic

More refined than just signaling the occurrence of a major loss in significance is an accounting of the significance of all results that are produced. Even a piecemeal loss of significance, which in the end is just as bad as the more dramatic all-at-once loss, will be noticed.

The methods proposed for this purpose are the index of significance, unnormalized arithmetic, noisy mode, and interval arithmetic.

Index of significance. The computer George (1958), built at Argonne National Laboratory [Weik, 1961; Kassel, 1959], contains in its floating-point format six bits that indicate the number of significant coefficient digits. In an addition, the postnormalization right shift increases the index; a left shift reduces the index. Multiplication and division take the larger of the operand indices for the result [Gray and Harrison, 1959; Goldstein, 1963].

This scheme has substantial cost, not just in equipment, but also in precision itself. How much of one's wealth will one pay to an accountant to know how much one has? In George, would it have been better to use the six bits for added precision? We think so.

Unnormalized arithmetic.   Instead of carrying a low-order index of significance, suppose one chooses never to normalize. Then, the high-order zeros neatly and automatically serve as place markers, using exactly the space in the format that becomes available when significance is lost.

The significance indicator notes the occurrence of invalid digits. Unnormalized arithmetic, however, prevents the occurrence of invalid digits

by omitting the normalization. This method was used by Ashenhurst and Metropolis [1959] in the MANIAC III (1961) of the University of Chicago.

For an addition, the method is clear: Only the right shift for a carry overflow is performed. For multiplication, the method is less obvious. If normalization is eliminated here, the high-order part of the result will contain the left zeros of both operands. The product is much more reliable than those zeros indicate. To avoid this difficulty, the MANIAC III prenormalizes the large operand.

A second source of normalization in multiplication is the product value. With fully significant operands, a left zero may still arise ($3 \times 4 = 12$, but $3 \times 3 = 09$). In some such cases, the MANIAC III performs a left shift. Similar rules apply to division.

Whereas the significance indicator is too expensive, unnormalized arithmetic is too pessimistic. Normalized arithmetic gives more precise results than does unnormalized arithmetic, even though one does not know how precise the normalized results are. Sterbenz has pointed out that the trouble with significance arithmetic is its discrete nature [Sterbenz, 1974]. Significance is accounted for in whole bits; but significance is in fact lost in fractions of bits. Modern machines therefore have not adopted unnormalized arithmetic as a means of significance accounting.

Noisy mode. The term *noisy mode* is derived from the artificial introduction of noise into a computation. In shifting left, ones can be introduced from the right with as much justification as zeros. Therefore, in the noisy mode, ones are injected instead of zeros. (The normal mode is actually just as noisy as the noisy mode.) A computation can now be performed in both modes, and the results compared. The Stretch has this facility [Campbell, 1962].

	Noisy mode set to 0			Noisy mode set to 1	
6	000 0110 →	000 0110	6	000 0110 →	000 0110
⁻4	000 1100 →	000 1100	⁻4	000 1100 →	000 1100
— +	——— +	——— +	— +	——— +	——— +
2	111 0100 ←	000 0010	2.5	111 0101 ←	000 0010
	true value 2 = 6+⁻4			noisy range 2 - 2.5	
20	010 0101 →	010 0101	20	010 0101 →	010 0101
16	010 0100 →	010 0100	16	010 0100 →	010 0100
— -	——— -	——— -	— -	——— -	——— -
4	000 0100 ←	010 0001	7	000 0111 ←	010 0001
10	001 0101 →	001 01010 g	10	001 0101 →	001 01010 g
4	000 0100 →	001 00100	7	000 0111 →	001 00111
— -	———	——— -	— -	———	——— -
6	000 0110 ←	001 00110	3.5	111 0111 ←	001 00011
1.5	110 0110		1.5	110 0110	
— ×	——— ×	——— ×	— ×	——— ×	——— ×
8	001 0100		5	000 0101	
	true value 9 = 1.5×(10-(20-16))			noisy range 5 - 8	

Legend: representation of Table 4-63; precision treated by truncation; g = guard digit.

TABLE 5-68   Examples of noisy mode.

A first objection to performing a computation in both modes is that the computation takes twice as long. But the length may be reduced by using the noisy mode for only critical parts of the problem. A more fundamental objection is that the two modes present the extremes of each individual number, but not necessarily the extremes of a computation. Table 5-68 shows an example in which the true value is outside the range predicted by the two modes.

Interval arithmetic.   Table 5-68 indicates why noisy mode at times gives a misleading answer: Inserting ones instead of zeros does not always affect the final answer in the same direction; noise cancels noise. What would seem ideal is to carry a range, or *interval*, for each operand. Operations then calculate the interval for the result. This method is called *interval arithmetic*. Table 5-69 illustrates the rules of interval arithmetic for some arithmetic operations.

Interval arithmetic has been studied extensively [Moore, 1966]. It is expensive in time or equipment (each operation is done twice), and in space (each operand has two values defining the interval). By proper encoding, these expenses can be reduced but not eliminated. If one is willing to pay this price, then double-precision arithmetic might be a better investment even though it does not directly say how accurate the result is.

Interval arithmetic can also be programmed, provided that the proper rounding is available. To facilitate this programming, the IEEE Standard includes rounding operations that either uniformly take the next-higher representable point or uniformly take the next-lower one.

Concept	Rule	Example
Operand	od←od[0],od[1]	od1←8 7; od2←4 3
Addition	sum←od1+od2	sum←12 10
Subtraction	difference←od1-Φod2	difference←5 3
Multiplication	product←od1×od2	product←32 21
Division	qt←od1÷Φod2	qt←2.67 1.75
	quotient←(⌈qt[0]),⌊qt[1]	quotient←3 1

TABLE 5-69   Interval arithmetic for positive operands.

5.4.2

Basic Operations

Floating-point operations are as easy to specify architecturally as are fixed-point operations. The floating-point interpretation and representation functions need only be substituted for the corresponding fixed-point functions; addition (Program 5-71) serves as an example.

The implementation of floating point is much more complex than that of fixed point. For early computers, it was a major *tour de force* to implement floating point efficiently. It is not surprising that corners were cut that reflected back into the architecture—especially since one could argue that the floating-point results were known to be imprecise anyway. Once this tradition was established, it was—as always—hard to correct.

| | ——————— Operation ——————— | | Secondary |
	Binary	Decimal	result
Zuse Z4	~ | + ⌈ ⌊ × ÷ R r		=0 o
IBM NORC		~ | + × ÷ r	
IBM 704	+ × ÷		
Univac 1103A	+ × +× ÷		
Bull Gamma 60		~ | + × ÷	<0 =0 >0
Bendix G20	+ × ÷ f		
IBM Stretch	+ × +× ÷ r		<0 =0 >0
Chicago Maniac III	+ × ÷		
English Electric KDF9	~ | + × ÷		
CDC 6600	+ × ÷		
Burroughs B5500	+ × ÷ f		
IBM System/360	~ | + × ÷		=0 ≥0 o
Electrologica X8	+ × ÷		=0 ≥0 o
DEC PDP11	~ | + × ÷ f		<0 =0
Cray 1	+ × D R		
DEC VAX11	~ + × +× ÷ f		<0 =0
IEEE Standard 754	+ × ÷ r rm		

Legend: D = divide step; f = convert to fixed; o = overflow;
r =square root; R = reciprocal; rm = remainder; ~ = negate;
\| = make absolute; + = add and subtract; ⌈ = maximum;
⌊ = minimum; +× = cumulative multiply.

TABLE 5-70   Floating-point arithmetic in various machines.

In specifying a floating-point operation, let us assume that the operands are exact, and that we desire to represent the exact arithmetic result using the proper domain function in the desired normal form. A central problem for the architect is to give a feasible implementation of this architecture, to prove that such an ideal specification can be implemented efficiently.

Extrema.   The arithmetic operations should apply to the entire floating-point domain, including the extrema. Table 4-74 gives the results for extrema in the basic arithmetic operations, as defined for the 6600 and the IEEE Standard. These definitions match the mathematical concepts of operating with zero and infinity.

OMZ.   When an OMZ is defined to belong to the floating-point domain, it should give the proper result when used as an operand in an arithmetic operation. The OMZ, however, does not match a simple mathematical concept, so the results of operating with OMZs are representation-dependent.

Operation set.   Since the central problem is the feasible implementation of the basic operations, we discuss only these operations and the conversion to and from fixed point. The supplementary operations described for fixed point also apply to floating point. Tree 5-38 gives the design choices, and Table 5-70 shows the selections made in various machines.

Addition

Addition is frequent and should be fast. Unfortunately, it is one of the most complex operations to implement. As a consequence, the architecture that is implemented often departs from the ideal paradigm specified in Program 5-71. The complex part of this algorithm is the result representation `flr`, which includes the domain function and sets exception indicators.

```
fladd;ad;au;addend;augend;sum;sm
A basic floating-point addition
  ad←size1 read adr1
  au←size2 read adr2
  addend←fli ad
  augend←fli au
  sum←augend+addend
  sm←size3 flr sum
  adr3 write sm
  signal sm
```

PROGRAM 5-71   Basic floating-point addition.

Implementation steps. The basic addition architecture obtains its simplicity by interpreting the operands and subsequently representing the sum. This description accurately reflects the concepts, but it does not suggest a feasible implementation, since the builder cannot work with numbers, but must use adders and shifters to manipulate the representations of numbers.

The exponents of the two operands may differ, so the coefficients require an alignment, or *preshift*. The coefficient sum may have several leading zeros or may overflow, requiring a *postnormalization*. Handling these cases leads to the following implementation steps:

- Exponent comparison
- Preshift of the coefficient with smaller exponent, or setting one of the coefficients to zero in case of an excessive exponent difference
- Coefficient addition
- Rounding of the sum at the proper place
- Postnormalization of the sum, which may involve a postshift of one digit to the right or several digits to the left, with a corresponding exponent correction

Program 5-72 shows these steps in a feasible implementation algorithm.

```
impfladd;expdif;addend;augend;sum;guard;rndbit;stckbit;coef;shift;exp
A floating-point effective addition
A exponent comparison
expdif←(interpret au[Exp])-interpret ad[Exp]
sm←au
→If expdif<0
THEN: A swap operands
    sm←ad
    ad←au
    expdif←-expdif
ENDIF:→If1 expdif<ρCcoefficient
THEN1: A guard, round, and sticky bit
    guard←1↑ad[(-expdif)↑Coef]
    rndbit←1↓2↑ad[(-expdif)↑Coef]
    stckbit←v/2↓ad[(-expdif)↑Coef]
  A coefficient addition
    augend←interpret sm[Coef],0
    addend←interpret ad[(-expdif)↓Coef],guard
    sum←augend+addend+(0.5×rndbit)+0.25×stckbit
    coef←(2+ρCoef) represent trueround sum
  A post normalization
    shift←(1↓coef)ι1
    exp←(interpret sm[Exp])+1-shift
    sm[Exp]←(ρExp) represent exp
    sm[Coef]←(ρCoef)↑shift↓coef
ENDIF1:
```

PROGRAM 5-72   Feasible implementation of floating-point addition.

	Without prenormalization				With prenormalization		
			g				g
2	001 0001	→	001 00010	2	001 0001	→	111 01000
0.5	101 0100	→	001 00000	0.5	101 0100	→	111 00010
——— +	——————— +		———————— +	——— +	——————— +		———————— +
2	111 0100	←	001 00010	2.5	111 0101	←	111 01010

Legend: representation of Table 4-63; g =guard digit;
precision treated by truncation.

TABLE 5-73   Example of insufficient preshift in addition.

The implementation questions that affect the architecture are the amount of preshift that is considered excessive, and the width of the adder beyond the coefficient length.

Excessive preshift and prenormalization.   It is attractive to eliminate the shift and the addition entirely when the exponent difference is equal to or exceeds the digit length of the coefficient. Such a procedure, however, matches the basic architecture only when the unshifted operand is normalized. Table 5-73 illustrates a case of an erroneous result and illustrates how prenormalization avoids it.

The example of Table 5-73 is extreme. One of the operands is unnormalized, and the digits of the other are added to bits that are usually not significant. According to Sweeney's figures (Table 4-90), the excessive preshift occurs 10 percent of the time for a coefficient of 27 bits. If combined with only 2 percent unnormalized operands, the undesirable preshift would occur less than 0.2 percent of the time. The 360 design reflects this reasoning and does not prenormalize (Program 5-74).

Our present preference, however, is based not on the frequency of occurrence, but on the need to avoid exceptions where possible. We think that, for current implementations, it is both feasible and desirable to either prenormalize or fully extend the intermediate operands.

The 360 does not round its results, but rather uses truncation. In the case of excessive preshift, however, it applies the equivalent of rounding. Otherwise, an effective subtraction of two numbers with widely different exponents would reduce the magnitude of the coefficient of the largest by one

Opcode	R1	X1	B1	D1

```
0        8  12  16  20            32
Legend: B = base; D = displacement; R = register; X = index.

AD;au;ad;scale;addend;augend;sum;xmax;xmin
ᴀ IBM 360 Floating-point Add Long
  ad←fl360i double read360a adr360bxd
  au←fl360i flreg[rfl R1;]
  →OUT suppress360
  scale←base*(au[1]⌈ad[1])-point
  addend←scale×truncate ad[0]÷scale
  augend←scale×truncate au[0]÷scale
  sum←augend+addend
  flreg[rfl R1;]←double fl360r sum
  signal360NZPO sum
```

PROGRAM 5-74   Floating-Point Add in the IBM System/360.

	Without guard digit			With guard digit	
No guard digit needed					
					g
5	000 0101 →	000 0101	5	000 0101 →	000 01010
‾4	000 1100 →	000 1100	‾4	000 1100 →	000 11000
− +	──── +	──── +	− +	──── +	──── +
1	110 0100 ←	000 0001	1	110 0100 ←	000 00010
One guard digit needed					
					g
4	000 0100 →	000 0100	4	000 0100 →	000 01000
3.5	111 0111 →	000 0011	3.5	111 0111 →	000 00111
1	110 0100 ←	000 0001	0.5	101 0100 ←	000 00001

Legend: g = guard digit; representation of Table 4-63; precision treated by truncation.

FIGURE 5-75   Additions with and without guard digit.

in the low-order place. So truncation cannot really be maintained consistently in floating point.

Guard digit.   By how many digit positions beyond the coefficient length should the adder be extended to the right?

With a preshift of zero, all bits of both coefficients are added. When the coefficient of the smaller operand is shifted right, there is a larger number of sum digits. Since the final result-coefficient is limited to the representation size, the extra low-order digits are meaningful only if they are preserved in a subsequent normalization left shift.

It turns out that, for normalized operands, only one extra low-order digit—the *guard digit*—can conceivably be reintroduced in this manner. A large cancellation of higher-order digits, resulting in a large postshift, can occur only for an effective subtraction with a preshift of 0 or 1. In these cases, however, the intermediate sum is extended by at most one digit to the right. When the preshift exceeds 1, only one leading zero can be produced. So the left shift is at most 1, and again only one guard digit is required. Figure 5-75 shows examples of additions with and without guard digits.

In an extreme case the absence of the guard digit can cause an error equal to the base (Figure 5-75). This error is equivalent to a worst-case relative error of 900 percent in a decimal machine, or 100 percent in a binary machine; it is, of course, intolerable. The mere possibility of this anomaly requires extra code in arithmetic subroutines; the code must preserve the precision carefully.

The original design of the 360 had a guard digit in the short precision of six hexadecimal coefficient digits, but had none in the long precision of 14 such digits. The reasoning was that the long precision was good enough anyway. It was not. This inconsistency had to be remedied after the first machines were installed.

Rounded addition.   For rounding, only one more adder bit is needed. For unbiased rounding, the bits that are shifted out are inspected for the all-zeros condition. This condition is recorded in a *sticky bit*. The algorithm, shown in Program 5-72, shows that correctly rounded addition is quite feasible.

Multiplication

Floating-point multiplication can adhere to the ideal architectural specification with far less difficulty than can addition. Program 5-51 gives the basic architecture, and Program 5-76 gives as an example the 360 Multiply Long.

```
┌─────────┬────┬────┬────┬──────────────────┐
│ Opcode  │ R1 │ X1 │ B1 │ D1               │
└─────────┴────┴────┴────┴──────────────────┘
0         8    12   16   20                 32
Legend: B = base; D = displacement; R = register; X = index.

MD;multiplier;multiplicand;product
∩ IBM 360 Floating-point Multiply Long
multiplier←1↑fl360i double read360a adr360bxd
multiplicand←1↑fl360i flreg[rfl R1;]
→OUT suppress360
product←multiplicand×multiplier
flreg[rfl R1;]←double fl360r product
```

PROGRAM 5-76   Floating-Point Multiply in the IBM System/360.

Implementation steps. The feasible implementation of floating-point multiplication requires a coefficient multiplication and exponent addition (Program 5-77). These two actions can be performed independently. The product of two normalized operands requires a postshift left of one digit for about half the cases; otherwise it needs no shift at all. When the operands are not both normalized, a normalized result may be obtained by either of the following:

- Prenormalization of the coefficients and possibly one digit postnormalization
- Postnormalization applying to a larger number of digits

The two methods of normalization are architecturally equivalent if a double-length intermediate product is generated and rounding occurs after normalization. These implementation steps are relatively easy and should give no cause to deviate from the ideal architecture. Nevertheless, the 6600 multiplication only approximates the ideal; it prerounds the operands, but it does not postnormalize at all.

```
impflmpy;expmr;expmd;exp;coefmr;coefmd;coef
∩ floating-point multiplication
∩ prenormalization
mr←normalize mr
md←normalize md
∩ exponent addition              ∩ coefficient multiplication
expmr←interpret mr[Exp]           coefmr←interpret mr[Coef]
expmd←interpret md[Exp]           coefmd←interpret md[Coef]
exp←expmr+expmd                   coef←coefmr×coefmd
∩ exponent overflow              ∩ product normalization and truncation
Floflo report exp>maxexp          pd←(ρmr)ρ0
∩ exponent underflow              pd[Exp]←(ρExp) represent exp
Uflo report exp<minexp            pd[Coef]←(ρCoef) represent coef
```

PROGRAM 5-77   Feasible implementation for floating-point multiplication.

Division

In floating-point division, a single-length divisor and dividend usually produce a single-length quotient and no remainder, since most designers assume the operands to be inexact. The architecture for the 360 (Program 5-78) would match the ideal if only the representation function would specify rounding and zero would always have positive sign.

Opcode	R1	R2

```
0        8   12   16
Legend: R = register.
```

```
DDR;dr;dd;divisor;dividend;quotient;xmax;xmin
ቦ IBM 360 Floating-point Divide Register Long
divisor←1↑fl360i dr WHERE dr←flreg[rfl R2;]
dividend←1↑fl360i dd WHERE dd←flreg[rfl R1;]
Fldiv report divisor=0
→OUT suppress360
quotient←dividend÷divisor
flreg[rfl R1;]←double fl360r quotient
→If quotient=0
THEN:flreg[rfl R1;0]←dd[0]≠dr[0]
ENDIF:
```

PROGRAM 5-78   Long Floating-Point Divide in the IBM System/360.

Implementation steps.   The feasible implementation algorithm of floating-point division requires exponent subtraction and coefficient division, as shown in Program 5-79. These two actions are independent. With normalized operands, the quotient should be shifted right one digit in half the cases, and the exponent correspondingly increased.

Unnormalized operands are usually prenormalized in division, since the fast divide algorithms require normalized operands to avoid extensive alignment shifts.

```
impfldiv;expdd;expdr;exp;coefdd;coefdr;coef;normshift
ቦ floating-point division
ቦ prenormalization
dd←normalize dd
dr←normalize dr
ቦ exponent subtraction
expdd←interpret dd[Exp]          ቦ coefficient division
expdr←interpret dr[Exp]           coefdd←interpret dd[Coef]
exp←expdd-expdr                    coefdr←interpret dr[Coef]
ቦ exponent overflow               coef←coefdd÷coefdr
Floflo report exp>maxexp         ቦ quotient normalization and truncation
ቦ exponent underflow              qt[Coef]←(ρCoef) represent normalize coef
Uflo report exp<minexp           qt[Exp]←(ρExp) represent exp-normshift
```

PROGRAM 5-79   Feasible implementation for floating-point division.

Remainder.   The IEEE Standard prescribes a Remainder operation (Program 5-80). This operation requires an extrema test that incorporates the IEEE definition of normal and extreme actions. This test is described with the matrix `rngrem`. For a normal operation, the remainder is obtained as the difference of the dividend and the product of quotient and divisor. For an extreme result, the type of result is supplied by `rngrem` and encoded by `range754r`.

```
REM;r;divisor;dividend;quotient;remainder
ⁿ IEEE 754 Remainder
r←rngrem[range754i read adr2;range754i read adr1]
→IF r<0
THEN: ⁿ normal remainder
   divisor←fl754i read adr1
   dividend←fl754i read adr2
   quotient←trueround dividend÷divisor            show754 rngrem
   remainder←dividend-quotient×divisor    n  n  i  i -ω +ω  i
   adr3 size write fl754r remainder       n  n  i  i -ω +ω  i
   →ENDIF                                  n  n  i  i -ω +ω  i
ELSE: ⁿ extreme remainder                  n  n  i  i -ω +ω  i
   adr3 write size range754r r             i  i  i  i  i  i  i
   Dividecheck report r∊poszero,negzero    i  i  i  i  i  i  i
ENDIF:                                     i  i  i  i  i  i  i
```

Legend: i = indefinite; n = normal action; ω = infinite;
       operands: positive, negative, 0, -0, +ω, -ω, i.

PROGRAM 5-80   Remainder operation in the IEEE 754 Standard.

Conversion of Representation

Since the floating-point format does not match the normal I/O formats, a simple means of representation conversion may be provided. Such a conversion requires a change between

- Floating-point and fixed-point representations
- Fixed-point and character string representations

The radix conversion and the editing of input and output formats of the second step have been discussed. The transformation between fixed and floating format is usually performed as a separate step, since fixed-point representation is, as a rule, available as a separate datatype. The architecture of the conversions between floating-point and fixed-point representations is given in Program 5-81.

```
float;od;number;rl                    fix;od;number;rl
ⁿ basic fixed to floating conversion  ⁿ basic floating to fixed conversion
od←size1 read adr1                    od←size1 read adr1
number←interpret od                  number←fli od
rl←size2 flr number                  rl←size2 represent number
adr2 write rl                        adr2 write rl
signal rl                            signal rl
```

PROGRAM 5-81   Conversions between floating and fixed formats.

Float. Converting a fixed-point to a floating-point representation is called *floating* the number. Floating a number is easy when the fixed-point and floating-point representations coincide for the common part of their number ranges (Section 4.4).

When fixed-point and floating-point numbers have no common representation range, the format transformation must supply the proper exponent representation, and must change the coefficient representation as needed. Program 5-82 shows the 360 program for the transformation from the 2's-complement 32-bit fixed-point format of the 360 to its 64-bit floating-point format with coefficient represented in signed-magnitude and exponent in biased representation.

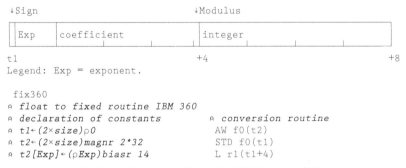

```
↓Sign                                    ↓Integer sign

  │ Exp │ coefficient        │           │ integer digits       │        │
  │     │                    │           │                      │        │
t1                                      +4                              +8
Legend: Exp = exponent.

   float360
 ∩ fixed to float routine IBM 360
 ∩ declaration of constants          ∩ conversion routine
 ∩ t1←(2×size)ρ0                        ST r1(t1+4)
 ∩ t1[Exp]←(ρExp)biasr 14               XI 128 t1(t1+4)
 ∩ t2←(2×size)magnr 2*31                LD t1 f0
 ∩ t2[Exp]←(ρExp)biasr 14               SD t2 f0
```

PROGRAM 5-82   Float in the IBM System/360.

These actions can be provided in a single instruction, as in the VAX 11. The gain in efficiency is small, however, since the frequency of the operation is low.

Fix.   In floating a number, precision is lost only if there are not sufficient coefficient digits. In fixing a number, the range is likely to be exceeded, since the very purpose of floating-point representation is to allow numbers beyond the range of the fixed-point representation. A range comparison must therefore precede the fixing operation, and proper action should be taken in case the number is outside the representable range.

A simple procedure for fixing a number is unnormalized addition to an auxiliary floating-point number with coefficient 0 and exponent corresponding to the fixed-point scaling that is desired. When the floating-point format is compatible with the fixed-point format, the only further step is a reallocation of the coefficient. In any case, the exponent of the result must be eliminated, and complementing may be required. Program 5-83 shows this program for the 360.

```
↓Sign                                    ↓Modulus

  │ Exp │ coefficient        │           │ integer              │        │
  │     │                    │           │                      │        │
t1                                      +4                              +8
Legend: Exp = exponent.

   fix360
 ∩ float to fixed routine IBM 360
 ∩ declaration of constants          ∩ conversion routine
 ∩ t1←(2×size)ρ0                        AW f0(t2)
 ∩ t2←(2×size)magnr 2*32                STD f0(t1)
 ∩ t2[Exp]←(ρExp)biasr 14               L r1(t1+4)
```

PROGRAM 5-83   Fix in the IBM System/360.

Extended Precision

Long precision.   The result of an arithmetic subroutine, such as a sine or exponential, should have the same accuracy as a sum or product. Since such a subroutine contains many steps, it is necessary to perform these steps with a higher precision than that required for the final result. The IEEE Standard therefore calls for a longer precision mode that applies to working store only.

Double-precision provisions. Since the driving problem for double precision floating is maintaining precision in intermediate results, a double-length format can be used in the working store. Table 5-84 shows the provisions for double precision in various machines.

	Coefficient		Operation				
	Single	Double	S←SOS	S←DOS	D←SOS	D←DOS	D←DOD
IBM 650	8d	18d	÷		+ ×		
IBM NORC	13d	26d	+ ÷		×		
IBM 704	27	54	÷		+ ×		
Bull Gamma 60	10d		+ × ÷		+ ×		
IBM Stretch	48	96	+ × ÷	÷	×	+ ×	
Chicago Maniac III	39	78			+ × ÷		
Ferranti Atlas	13	26	+ × ÷	÷	+ ×	+	
English Electric KDF9	40	79	+ × ÷	÷	×		+
IBM 7094	27	54	÷		+ ×		+ × ÷
Burroughs B5500	13o	26o	+ × ÷				+ × ÷
IBM System/360	6h	14h	+ ÷		×		+ × ÷
DEC PDP11	24	56	+ × ÷				+ × ÷
DEC VAX11	24	56	+ × ÷	m	m		+ × ÷

Legend: d = decimal; D = double; h = hexadecimal; m = move; o = octal;
r = square root; S = single; + = add and subtract;
o = operation; size indicated by number of coefficient digits;
result of division applies to quotient.

TABLE 5-84   Double-precision floating-point in various machines.

Arbitrary extended precision. Why does one want arbitrarily long extended precision in fixed point, and not in floating point? Extended precision serves those computations, such as in number theory or theoretical physics, that require extreme precision and hence many digits.

In fixed-point extended precision, the metadigits of the metanumber maintain constant scaling with respect to each other. The automatic scaling of floating point, however, turns out to be a disadvantage in this application. Metadigits that are represented by floating-point numbers should have an unvarying exponent, and the operations upon these metadigits should preserve this alignment. Neither normalized nor unnormalized arithmetic satisfies this requirement; a carry out of an addition is, in both cases, absorbed by the automatic scaling of the postnormalization, rather than being signaled for propagation to the next metadigit.

In fact, one wants all the attributes of fixed-point arithmetic and none of those of floating-point. Even the exponent digits can better be traded for coefficient digits. So the natural and best solution is to use fixed-point arithmetic for true extended precision.

5.4.3

Bibliography

Ashenhurst and Metropolis [1959], Aspinall and Patt [1985], Campbell [1962], Gentleman and Marovich [1974], Goldberg [1990, 1991], Goldstein [1963], Gray and Harrison [1959], Gross [1985], Hansen [1965], Kassel [1959], Kent [1977], Kuck et al. [1977], Kulish [1977], Malcolm [1972], Metropolis and Ashenhurst [1958, 1963], Moore [1966], Omondi [1994], Sterbenz [1974], Wadey [1960], Weik [1961], Yohe [1973].

5.5

Relational Operations

Relational operations test a specified relation among operands and produce a result that is true or false. They require specification of the relation and of the datatypes. The result is logical—commonly 1 bit. Since a full word is quite a lot to allocate for just 1 bit, the allocation of the relational result has attracted various solutions, as indicated in the design choices of Tree 5-85.

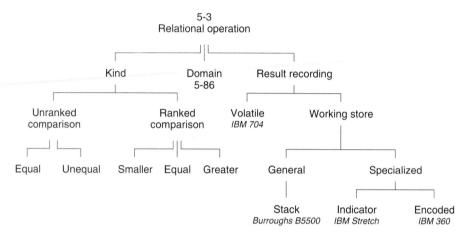

TREE 5-85   Design choices for relational operations.

5.5.1

Kinds of Relations

Mapping.   A relation is established by examining some datum and assigning it to one of a set of mutually exclusive and collectively exhaustive categories. A relation can formally be considered to be a mapping from an input *domain*, consisting of all possible values of the datum, to an output space or *range*, consisting of one point for each category.

In digital computers, both domain and range are discrete and finite. The mapping is always many to one, for that is the purpose of defining the relation. Since the spaces are discrete and finite, they can be considered one-dimensional without loss of generality. As a result, it can be shown that the mapping of any point—and hence of any relation—can be accomplished by a series of comparison operations, each of which divides the domain into two finite segments and establishes which segment contains the given point. A single comparison operation, such as testing the sign of a datum for negative, can be shown to be sufficient for programming all relations.

Interestingly enough, a zero/non-zero or an equal/unequal comparison is not sufficient by itself. Either one can be made sufficient by supplementing it with an operation to take the absolute value of an algebraic quantity, since $(0=X-|X|)$ can be used as a sign test [W.Y Stevens, 1958].

Program primitive.   The program primitive for the relational operations is the comparison. It is found in all machines, either explicitly as a Compare

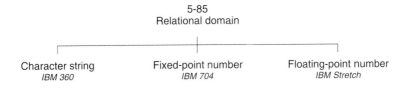

5-85
Relational domain

| Character string | Fixed-point number | Floating-point number |
| IBM 360 | IBM 704 | IBM Stretch |

TREE 5-86 Design choices for relational operation domain.

operation, or implicitly as a secondary operation that provides a sign test of
the primary result of a subtract. The price for using subtract is the destruction
of an operand. So the explicit Compare is preferable.

Which relations are encountered in programs, and which of these are
best implemented with the comparison? We treat, in order of increasing
complexity, unranked and ranked comparisons, with standards and among
data.

Unranked Comparison with N Standards

A datum is fairly often compared with a set of n values called *standards*.
The desired result is sometimes the 1-bit value of set membership—the datum
is equal to one member of the set or it is not equal to any. This test is useful
in an IF THEN ELSE control structure.

In other cases, the target is $n+1$ output points—the datum is equal to one
of the standards, which is identified, or it is equal to none. This corresponds
to the CASE control structure.

Program 5-87 gives the APL equivalents of these two unranked comparisons. It shows that the comparison with n standards can be implemented
with a search operation, as discussed in Section 5.1. In the absence of such an
operation, a comparison can be iteratively applied.

If n is equal to 1, the unranked comparison becomes a Compare For
Equality.

```
member                  search
true←datum∈standard     which←standardιdatum
```

PROGRAM 5-87   Unranked comparison with standards.

Ranked Comparison with N Standards

For the ranked comparison of a datum against n ordered standards the
output space has in general $(2 \times n) + 1$ points; the datum can be equal to one
of the n standards, or it can fall in one of the $n + 1$ regions they divide. This
operation is called *ranking* the datum. Program 5-88 describes this comparison
precisely.

Again this type of comparison can be implemented with a search operation, or a Compare can be applied iteratively.

```
ranking
which←(datum∈standard)+2×+/datum>standard
```

PROGRAM 5-88   Ranked comparison with standards.

```
K;cd;operand;comparand              KR
A IBM Stretch Compare               A IBM Stretch Compare Range
cd←(fld0 L0) read7030 adr7030m      cd←(fld0 L0) read7030 adr7030m
comparand←neg7030 mem7030i cd       comparand←neg7030 mem7030i cd
operand←scale7030 acc7030i          operand←scale7030 acc7030i
operand signal7030C comparand       operand signal7030R comparand


operand signal7030C comparand;ind   operand signal7030R comparand;ind
A IBM Stretch compare result        A IBM Stretch range result
ind←memory[Ind]                     ind←memory[Ind]
ind[Low]←operand<comparand          ind[Equal]←operand<comparand
ind[Equal]←operand=comparand        ind[High]←operand≥comparand
ind[High]←operand>comparand         ind[Tomem]←0
ind[Tomem]←0                        memory[Ind]←ind
memory[Ind]←ind
```

PROGRAM 5-89   Compare Range in the IBM Stretch.

The ranked comparison with just one standard is the Compare for greater, equal, or smaller.

Compare Range. The special case of ranked comparison with two standards corresponds to the common mathematical test $A \leq X \leq B$. Usually, only three of the five possible output cases are distinguished; the equals-to cases are each rolled together with one of the regions. This comparison is useful for testing not only data, but also the validity of subscripts, given a valid range. Most compilers and some machines incorporate comparisons of this type.

The Stretch provides this comparison by means of a Compare Range operation (Program 5-89). The sequence—Load X, Compare Range A, Compare Range B—sets the indicators: Low if $X \leq A$; Equal if $A < X < B$; High if $B \leq X$.

Comparison Among Data

The most complex type of comparison is the (unranked or ranked) comparison among data. Consider the task of evaluating a five-card poker hand. The goal is to detect one pair, two pairs, three of a kind, four of a kind, flush, straight, and straight flush, by testing the rank coordinate in most cases, only the suit coordinate in case of a flush, and both coordinates for a straight flush (Program 5-90).

For $n = 2$, comparison among data turns out to be the same as comparison with one standard. Either datum can be considered the standard, and the other

```
poker;rank;suit;count
A 5 2 ∧.=ρhand
rank←'234567890jqka'
suit←'shdc'
count←+/rank∘.=hand[;Rank]
highcard←2+⌈/rankιhand[;Rank]
onepair←1=+/count=2
twopairs←2=+/count=2
threeofkind←1=+/count=3
straight←4=+/(1↓count=1)∧⁻1↓count=1
flush←1=+/suitεhand[;Suit]
fullhouse←onepair∧threeofkind
fourofkind←1=+/count=4
straightflush←straight∧flush
```

PROGRAM 5-90   Evaluation of a poker hand.

is greater than, equal to, or less than it. For $n > 2$, comparison among data is clearly a different kind of operation. Instead of comparing one item with n standards, which produces n results, each item must be compared with each of the others.

The number of points in the output space of a comparison among data is complex to calculate, and it grows rapidly (Table 5-91).

Number of data	Comparison output points Unranked	Ranked
2	2	3
3	5	13
4	15	75

TABLE 5-91   Number of comparisons among data.

Because the results of such tests are hard to describe concisely and because the number of output points is large, general comparisons among data have not been implemented as machine operations.

Ordering of operands.   One important special case of comparison among data involves combining the test with data transpositions to order the set, partially or completely. The APL maximum and minimum reductions, for example, give partial ordering, yielding a single result. The APL grade-up and grade-down operators order their operand vectors completely, as do the COBOL and PL/I Sort operators.

The Harvest provides maximum reduction, minimum reduction, grade up, and another special case, Merge, as machine operations.

Requisite for machine operation.   This collection of compare operations confirms that, as a rule, the desirability of a proposed machine operation depends on

- The operation's frequency of use
- The time and space saved as compared to programmed implementation
- The number of parameters required

The case of comparison among data illustrates the last point especially well. The general case requires specification of many parameters, and, in this case, destinations for many outputs. This requirement is awkward and costly, so architects have not implemented it. The special cases that have been implemented, such as Sort in the Harvest, are attractive precisely because they are simply specified; there are few parameters.

5.5.2

Domain

The operands to be compared can be character strings, logical vectors, or fixed-point or floating-point numbers. A ranked comparison of character strings requires an ordering or *collating sequence* of the characters. To the degree that such a collating sequence is not universally established, it must be specified explicitly as part of the definition of comparison.

Extended operands.   Just as extended-precision arithmetic requires some architectural provisions, so comparison of extended fields or extended-precision numbers has its own architectural requirements.

The Stretch incorporates a Compare Conditional operation that changes the indicators only if the Equal indicator is set (Program 5-92). First, the most significant operand sections are compared with the normal Compare. Next, the subsequent lower-order sections are compared with Compare Conditional.

```
KE
⌐ IBM Stretch Compare If Equal
→If memory[Ind[Equal]]
THEN: ⌐ regular compare
     K
ENDIF:
```

PROGRAM 5-92   Compare Conditional in the IBM Stretch.

Extrema comparison.   A comparison should, of course, give the proper result for the entire operand domain; thus, floating-point extrema should be properly handled. The IEEE Standard 754 provides a special result, called *unordered*, in case one or both operands are Indefinite.

5.5.3

Result Recording

Since the result of most relational operations is a single bit, there are many ways to record it. Here we briefly summarize the options with regard to multiple operations and result location (see Section 6.2 for other alternatives).
Multiple operations.   Needing to record only 1 bit per relation makes it attractive to perform several tests, such that all six relations ($<$, $\leq$, $=$, $\geq$, $>$, and $\neq$) can be obtained with one Compare. Furthermore, a comparison can be combined with an arithmetic operation, provided its operands are implied.

	Alphanumeric		Fixed point		Floating point	
Univac I	u	volatile	r	volatile		
IBM 704			r	volatile		
IBM 705	r	indicator				
Univac 1103A			r	volatile	r	volatile
Bull Gamma 60	r	indicator	r	indicator	r	indicator
IBM 1401	u	indicator				
IBM Stretch			r	indicator	r	indicator
CDC 6600			r	volatile	r	volatile
Burroughs B5500	r	indicator	r	indicator	r	stack
IBM System/360	u	condition	r	condition	r	condition
DEC PDP10			r	volatile	r	volatile
DEC PDP11			r	condition	r	condition
Intel 8080A			r	condition		
Motorola M6800			r	condition		
MOS 6502			r	condition		
DEC VAX11	r	condition	r	condition	r	condition
Motorola MC68000			r	condition		
IBM 6150			r	condition		

Legend: r = ranked; u = unranked.

TABLE 5-93   Comparison in various machines.

When the first operand is taken to be the result of the arithmetic operation and the comparand is taken as zero, the familiar sign test is obtained.

Result location.   Architects have used almost all options for the result locations.   First, the location is volatile when the compare operation is combined with a conditional branch as one instruction. Next, the result bit, or bits, may be recorded in working store as a regular result. Or they may have a special location, either private to comparisons or shared with other inputs of the decision operations. Table 5-93 gives various machines' design decisions for comparison.

5.5.4
Bibliography

W.Y. Stevens [1958].

5.6
Numeric-Array Operations

We have met array operations upon character strings in Section 5.1, and upon logical vectors in Section 5.2. In this section, we examine operations upon numeric arrays. Since array operations are often independent of the datatype of the array element, some of the operations of this section are familiar by now. In contrast to the byte and the bit of the character and Boolean arrays, however, the numeric array normally requires a word for proper representation of each element. Therefore, the specific problems of array operations are particularly apparent for the numeric array.

We start with motivation: Why have array operations? Next, we look at the array as a macroconcept: What are its inherent consequences? Finally, we treat the array operations themselves.

5.6.1
Motivation

There are two major motivations for array processing. The architecture benefits from conciseness of expression, and hence from reduced instruction flow. The implementation gains speed in execution.

Conciseness of Expression

Data structures provide conceptual and programming economy of names and operations.

Systematic naming.   Arrays allow a systematic naming system for substructures and individual elements. Thus, they can be specified iteratively or recursively even for element-by-element operations. The array name enables—but does not require—array operations, which explains why many programming languages have the array as datatype, but limit themselves to the selection operations.

Concise operations.   Many useful operations can be specified for whole structures or substructures and imply operation upon every element. In a typical program, this procedure can eliminate a whole chunk of instructions. The operations as such are not eliminated, but are instead performed with one instruction fetch for the whole array, rather than one per element.

In many APL programs, use of arrays can eliminate a whole lower level of iteration structures, typically reducing the number of statements by a factor of 7. As a result, the program is easier to understand (for those who know the symbolism) and to verify for correctness.

Speed

The speed advantage of array operations stems from the conciseness of specification and the ease of parallel implementation.

Inherent speed.   Conciseness of expression results in fewer instructions, and therefore in a reduced instruction flow. The fraction of memory bandwidth so used approaches $1/64$ for the Illiac IV (1971); theoretically, it approaches 0 as vector lengths approach infinity for the CDC STAR100 (1973) and the IBM Harvest (1961).

Fast machines, however, are fundamentally memory-bandwidth limited. Furthermore, about one-half of the bit traffic is used for instructions, indexes, and indirect addresses. Therefore, if—by architectural magic—*all* instruction flow were eliminated, the performance ratio would at most be doubled.

Parallelism.   An entire arithmetic and logical unit can now be built as a single relatively inexpensive electronic component. Therefore, computer structures that can operate upon many data in parallel appear attractive. This kind of reasoning is behind the Holland and Solomon proposals of 1959 and 1963 [Gregory and Reynolds, 1963], and the Illiac IV of 1971 [Barnes et al., 1968]. In these designs, one instruction stream directs an array of processors all operating in lock step—a parallel organization that is known as *synchronous concurrency* or single instruction, multiple data (SIMD).

Array operations allow, but do not require, a one-element–to–one-processor mapping. Rigidity results from such a one-to-one reflection of the implementation into the architecture (Section 4.5). Therefore, many later designs—such as the IBM 2938 [Ruggiero and Corriell, 1969], the CDC STAR100 (1973), and the Cray 1 (1976)—do not exhibit the number of processors of the implementation and allow greater variability of the array dimensions.

5.6.2

Macroconcept

The major architectural design problems identified in the design choices of Tree 5-94 all stem from the fact that an array is a macroconcept. Because many elements are operated upon in one operation, the major design decisions made for single elements must be visited again.

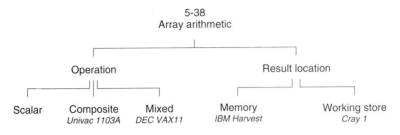

TREE 5-94   Design choices for array operations.

Result location

The first design decision to consider is the location of the result of the array operation. The key issue here is bit traffic.

Memory.   Memory-to-memory array operations are easily implemented, as experience with the Harvest has shown. They may be relatively slow, because they have noticeably more bit traffic than an all-encompassing loop that stores intermediate results in working registers. Consider $A \leftarrow D + B \times C$. If it is evaluated by array operations, it generates $(B \times C)$ as an intermediate result that takes a lot of memory space and generates a lot of bit traffic for its storage and subsequent retrieval. Looping through the elements $A_i \leftarrow D_i + B_i \times C_i$ need take neither main-memory space nor memory cycles for intermediate results.

Working store.   The Cray 1 provides a working store for numeric arrays. Whereas, for elementary operands, one has to decide on the number of intermediate results to be stored during the evaluation of an expression, one now must also decide on the size of these operands.

The Cray 1 sets a word limit of 64 elements to the size of the vectors that can be handled in one operation. This number, although undoubtedly arbitrary, is far better than the 8×8 of the Illiac IV. Sizes that are smaller as well as larger than the limit of 64 can be handled quite well, because only one dimension is at stake. Furthermore, because 64 is rather large, it is conveniently used as the dimension of a grid, as used in differential equations, or an integral fraction of such a grid. Although 64 is an arbitrary choice for such a dimension, the programmer often has a free choice for grid dimensions; so why not match this number? Therefore, more often than one might expect, the traveler happens to fit Procrustes's bed without any surgical effort on the part of his host.

Secondary Operations

We advised against secondary operations in Section 2.4, and look at the trouble they get us into now.

Inherent impropriety.   If one decides on a small condition code reflecting sign, zero, and overflow for elementary operands, how many bits should one provide for vector operands, and where should they be stored? The inherent impropriety of secondary operations comes home to roost.

The best solution still seems to have no secondary operations. But, if consistency with past practice forces one to keep going down that road, one

should at least arrange the secondary results as logical vectors, which can be scanned and operated upon as units.

Execution Time

Vector operations should allow several implementations. Although their performance advantage is at its best for parallel implementations, they should also allow more sequential implementations. In each case, but particularly in the slower implementations, the time for executing one vector operation may be noticeably longer than for operations on scalar operands.

Interrupt latency.   A long execution time gives a potentially long *interrupt latency* This problem arises for the Move Long of the 370, which is in fact a vector operation, on vectors of up to 16 K characters. The problem is even more severe for numeric vectors that are being added or multiplied. The solution is the same as for the 370 character strings. Either the latency is accepted (external interrupts may be handled by another processor), or the operation is made interruptible by exposing the necessary counts.

5.6.3

Operations

Iverson [1962] classifies the array operations as scalar, composite, and mixed operations.

Scalar Operations

Scalar operations between arrays apply a dyadic scalar function to corresponding elements of the two operand arrays. The operands should have the same dimension vector, which is also the dimension of the result. The actual dimension, however, is not important. A matrix addition yields the same result elements as a vector addition on the same sets of elements. This property follows from the commutativity of the scalar operators and the shape operator. Therefore, many array operations can be performed as vector operations.

Processors that have scalar array operations, such as the STAR100 and the Data General Eclipse, usually have the same functions as are available for single elements: add, subtract, multiply, and divide. The Cray 1, whose vector addition is shown in Program 5-95, is remarkable in having an inversion iteration step, rather than divide, for scalars and for arrays (Section 14.4).

Composite Operations

The composite operations are constituted from a scalar function and an operator. A well-known composite operation is the plus reduction, $+/$, summation across the elements of a vector. Another familiar example is the inner product of addition over multiplication, $A \leftarrow B + . \times C$, which is traditionally known as vector or matrix "multiplication."

```
ADVF;ad;au;sum;exp                          data←veck
⍝ Cray 1 Floating-point Add Vector          ⍝ Cray 1 vector k-operand
→OUT(fld Ri)∈(fld Rj).fld Rk                data←vec[fld Rk;⍳vl;]
ad←vflΔC1i veck
au←vflΔC1i vecj
sum←au[;,0]+ad[;,0]                          data←vecj
exp←au[;,1]⌈ad[;,1]                          ⍝ Cray 1 vector j-operand
veci vflΔC1r sum,exp                         data←vec[fld Rj;⍳vl;]


vector←vflΔC1i rep                           veci data
⍝ Cray 1 floating-point vector interpretation  ⍝ Cray 1 vector i-result
vector← 0 2 ρ0                               vec[fld Ri;⍳vl;]←data
→WHILE 0≠1↑ρrep
   vector←vector⍪flΔC1i rep[0;]
   rep← 1 0 ↓rep
   →Δ
ENDWHILE:
```

PROGRAM 5-95   Vector addition in the Cray 1.

Mixed Operations

Mixed operations are array operations that do not fit in the scalar or composite class, and hence are more irregular. Examples of mixed arithmetic array operations are the polynomial evaluation, as provided in the 1103A and the DEC VAX, and interpolation, as provided on the Harvard Mark I (1944).

5.6.4
Bibliography

Barnes et al. [1968], Gregory and Reynolds [1963], Iverson [1962], Ruggiero and Corriell [1969].

5.7
Rules of Good Practice

1. The architecture of an operation should adhere to the abstract operation definition. The domain function should be dependent only on the result value, not on the operation.
2. Each operation should yield a result that can, in turn, be used as an operand: It should be within the domain of the operation datatype.
3. Avoid the use of secondary operations.
4. Add With Carry is the preferred solution to extended fixed-point addition.
5. If Add With Carry yields a secondary result, it should reflect the partial metanumber rather than the metadigit.

5.8
Exercises

5-1 Which problems does a machine with 32-bit storage encounter with the architectural definition of Move characters, as defined in Program 5-8?

5-2 Give an APL description of the 705 operation Store For Print, based on the facts of Table 5-20 and Program 5-18.

5-3 Section 2.4 discusses minimal instruction sets. What functions must be included in Van der Poel's one instruction?

5-4 Determine a bound on the relative error generated by the addition of normalized floating-point numbers in base B without a guard digit, and with sufficient guard digits (relative error is equal to absolute error ÷ correct answer).

5-5 Do the field assembly by shifting using the operations of

a. The 360

b. The 8080A or Motorola M6800

5-6 Show how, with the shift operations of the 8080A or M6800, the decimal arithmetic shift can be performed.

5-7 Show how a 24-bit field in memory can be shifted 3 bits left using the 8080A or M6800 shift operations.

5-8 Give a translation of BCD to EBCDIC (Tables 4-20, 4-21)

a. Using the 360 Translate

b. Without instructions of this type

5-9 Write a 360 program to use the reverse application of indexing by using an index vector pattern as an argument to a 360 Translate to obtain digits from a number used as a table, so as to insert space and radix point as part of the conversion of numbers to the print format.

5-10 From the 360 Unpack operation, Program 5-63

a. Give an APL description of the inverse operation Pack.

b. Show, via a terminal implementation of APL (if available) that the two operations are mutually inverse.

5-11 Program the following double-precision operations for the IBM 650 in its machine language, using the standard grade-school polynomial algorithms and the 650 word as the metadigit. Provide the usual 650 domain function indications.

a. Addition

b. Multiplication

c. Division (develop a two-word quotient and a two-word remainder)

5-12 Write programs to calculate $C = A + . \times B$. A is a matrix with dimension vector 2 5, and B is a matrix with dimension vector 5 3. Assume that all matrices are stored in row order, and that all intermediate values stay nicely bounded, so that no scaling is necessary.

a. In APL without using $+.\times$

b. In some assembly language for a machine with indexing

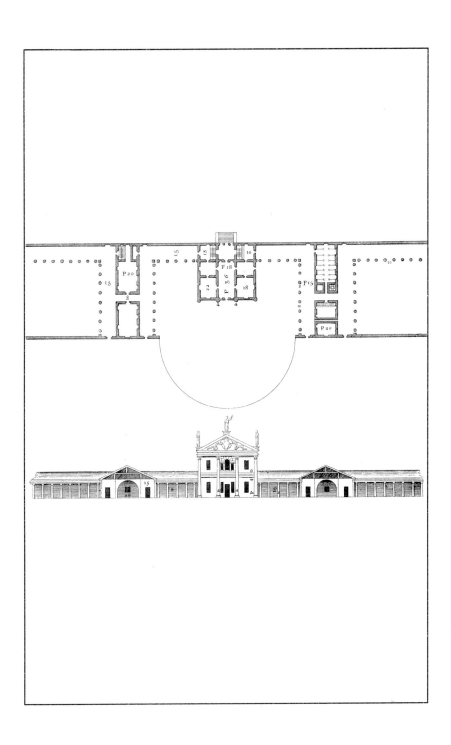

Instruction Sequencing

Overview of the Chapter

The preceding chapters showed that the syntax of machine language is rigid, and its vocabulary limited. Nevertheless, all computable procedures can be expressed in such languages by placing the instructions in the proper sequence and using the computer's ability to decide, to iterate, and to delegate. This ability to *control* is embodied in instructions that alter the instruction sequence, depending on the state of the machine or its environment. The conditions that may be tested, the nature of the tests, and the branching in sequence that ensues are all major design issues. Designers have expressed themselves with many original, ingenious, and even bizarre ideas for instruction sequencing.

High-level primitives. Whereas other computer instructions either express a complete thought-unit or are components of a solid sequence that does so, the expression of a control concept typically requires several instructions that are often separated from one another in the program. An iteration, for example, may require instructions just before the block to be iterated, and more at the end. A decision typically requires the expression of a test and the disjoint expression of two or more alternate action sequences. The primitive thought-units governing the sequence of operations are in fact higher-level than the branching operations with which they are usually expressed.

This fact has long been understood, at least implicitly. Burks, Goldstine, and von Neumann recognized it, and their seminal proposal for a stored-program computer included two languages—the machine language and a separate flow-charting language whose principal purpose was to display the flow of control [Burks et al., 1946].

Control structures. What then are the proper primitives for expressing sequencing? These primitives are perhaps best determined by studying those higher-level programming languages that have evolved without the constraints governing machine languages. A study of algorithms expressed in higher-level languages shows the utility, sufficiency, and naturalness of a certain set of general *control structures* that determine the flow of control in programs. It is our thesis that the sequencing operations in machine

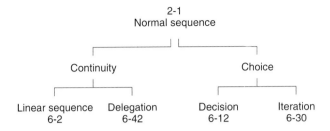

TREE 6-1   Design choices for instruction sequence.

languages are best understood and most effectively designed in terms of these higher-level control structures.   Therefore, we start in each of the following sections with these program primitives, and derive from them the corresponding machine language alternatives. Tree 6-1 shows the four main issues.

Meta-operation.   The simplest control structure is that of the plain linear sequence, or block. Its discussion in Section 6.1 includes the relative merits of *meta-operations*—operations that effect the execution of one or more other operations. These meta-operations attempt to capture the control structures as one unified operation. We encounter them in each section. The methodology called *structured programming* uses only those control structures that have a single begin and a single end, as found in the linear sequence [Dahl et al., 1972]. This limitation greatly improves the comprehensibility of a program. For, although the control structures are simple as such, they can result in great complexity when used intermixed. The structured-programming approach guarantees that the intermixing always has an orderly, or *nested*, organization.

Language level.   Section 6.2 discusses the control structures for decision, including IF THEN ELSE and CASE.

We address the question, Why are the program primitives themselves not made part of the machine language? We think the answer lies in the disparate nature of the control structure, in the difference between compilation and interpretation, and in the diversity of the programming languages.

Alternative solutions.   Section 6.3 treats iteration, with WHILE, REPEAT UNTIL, and FOR as control structures. Machine-language facilities for the FOR structure are an extension of index arithmetic.

Section 6.4 concerns delegation, with the function and the procedure call and, at the machine-language level, the Branch and Return operations as control structures. Delegation also involves state preservation.

6.1

Linear Sequence

Machine and high-level programming languages are both designed to express the step-by-step algorithms for the solution of problems. Both have the same

needs for expressing the sequence of steps to be performed. Sequencing operators in high-level languages are relatively unconstrained by hardware, so they more clearly express the essence of the sequencing to be performed.

Control Structure

The simplest structure is the linear sequence—or vector arrangement—of instructions. When instructions are arranged in a vector, each can be identified by the vector index of its position in memory—its address. To avoid confusion with address fields within an instruction, the address where the instruction resides is called its *location*.

Design choices.   As simple as the linear sequence is, it nevertheless calls forth some design choices, illustrated in Tree 6-2. What is the relation between successive steps of the algorithm? Where is the next instruction found? And when does the sequence end?

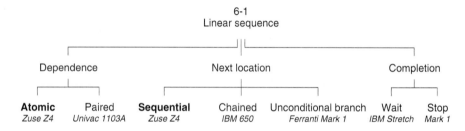

TREE 6-2   Design choices for linear sequence.

6.1.1
Functional Independence

Since a computer does one thing at a time, and one after another, the instructions to be executed always constitute independent syntactical units. This rule is of advantage to the machine implementer and to the user, since no implied syntactic information need be carried from one instruction to the next. (Machine state is, of course, carried forward.)

Nevertheless, a few machines have incorporated instructions that are functionally dependent semantically. An example is the Store Instruction Counter If of the IBM Stretch (1961), which stores the instruction address if the next instruction is a successful branch (Program 6-45).

Meta-operation.   Functional dependence characterizes a larger class of operations, the *meta-operations*, in which one operation governs the execution of one or more other operations.

Meta-operations are attractive when they match program primitives, such as control structures. Still, their application is severely limited by a number of fundamental requirements:

- The meta-operation action should be orthogonal to other design decisions. The operations that are involved should not be altered or

restricted, nor should other machine functions, such as interruptions, be affected. Nesting should be allowed.

- The meta-operation should be proper. It should match the program primitive exactly; a deviation, even at a minor point, may be fatal.
- The meta-operation should be general. If it matches the primitive of only a few languages, the users of other languages pay for a function they cannot use.

The examples of meta-operations in this chapter show the severity of these requirements.

6.1.2

Instruction Location

A linear sequence requires that a successor can be determined for each instruction. Program 6-3 gives the basic operation.

```
inst←ifetch
ᴀ basic instruction fetch
inst←(ilength×word) read iadr
iadr←iadr+ilength
```

PROGRAM 6-3   Basic instruction fetch.

Linear addressing.   Normally, the vector of instructions is placed linearly in memory, using an implied instruction address. This arrangement is illustrated for fixed instruction length by the IBM 704 (1955; Program 6-4), and for variable instruction length by the IBM System/360 (1965; Program 6-5).

```
inst←ifetch704
ᴀ IBM 704 instruction fetch
inst←read704 iadr
iadr←memcap|iadr+1
```

PROGRAM 6-4   Instruction fetch in the IBM 704.

Chained addressing.   Chained instruction addressing is illustrated by the IBM 650 (1954), Programs 1-30 and 1-43. The use of a chain address in each instruction is in general quite inefficient, and is justified only in special circumstances.

```
inst←ifetch360;iadr;length
ᴀ IBM 360 instruction fetch
ind[Program]←0
iadr←magni psw[Iadr]
length← 1 2 2 3[magni 2↑half read360a iadr]
inst←,(length×half) read360 iadr
→OUT suppress360
iadr←iadr+2×length
psw[Iadr]←adrsize magnr iadr
psw[Ilc]←2 magnr length
```

PROGRAM 6-5   Instruction fetch in the IBM System/360.

Unconditional branch. Use of an explicit instruction address becomes necessary when a linear sequence must be mapped on several disjoint storage sequences. The *unconditional branch* is used for that purpose.

The unconditional branch corresponds to the high-level primitive GO TO. It is also properly a component of the control sequences for decision and iteration.

6.1.3

Completion

A program usually has a well-defined end. When this end is reached in simple computers, such as programmable hand calculators, one wants to stop the sequencing mechanism and wait for human attention.

Early computers, such as the Ferranti Mark 1 (1951) and the Univac I (1951), had Stop operations. Computer operation, however, need stop only when the system is shut down. When a program is finished, it signals completion, which should result in the initiation or resumption of a supervisory program, which stays alert for the arrival of new tasks. Hence, one wants not a true Stop operation, but a Wait.

	Next location	Dependence	Completion
Harvard Mark I	i		Stop
Zuse Z4	i		Stop
Cambridge EDSAC	i		Stop
Ferranti Mark 1	i b		Stop
Univac I	i b		Stop
Princeton IAS	i b		Stop
IBM 701	i b		Stop
IBM 650	c		Stop
IBM 704	i b		Stop
IBM 705	i b		Stop
Univac 1103A	i b	Repeat	Stop
STC ZEBRA	c i b r s		
Bull Gamma 60	i		Stop
IBM 1401	i b		Stop
Bendix G20	i	Repeat	
IBM Stretch	i b r	Store If Branch	Wait
CDC 6600	i b		Stop
CDC 6600 PPU	i b r		Stop
Burroughs B5500	i b r		Stop
IBM System/360	i b		Wait
Electrologica X8	i		
DEC PDP8	i b s		Stop
DEC PDP11	i b r		Stop Wait
Intel 8080A	i b		Stop
Cray 1	i b		
Motorola M6800	i b r		Wait
MOS 6502	i b r		
DEC VAX11	i b r		Stop
Motorola MC68000	i b r		Wait
IBM 6150	i b r		Wait

Legend: b = absolute branch; c = chained; i = implied sequential; r = relative branch; s = skip; b r s are unconditional.

TABLE 6-6 Linear sequence in various machines.

Table 6-6 shows the solutions for linear sequencing that are adopted in various machines.

6.2
Decision

The provision of decision operations gives generality to procedures. Ideally, the same sequence of instructions would be used for many sets of data. In practice, the treatment of the various sets of data has much in common, but also has some distinctive parts. By incorporating treatment of all the cases in one procedure and using decisions to select the proper distinctive subprocedures for each case, similar procedures can be subsumed into a general one.

Control Structures

IF. The most elementary decision is represented by the ALGOL constructions

IF condition THEN then-block

and

IF condition THEN then-block ELSE else-block

Figure 6-7 shows a diagram for these structures.

Böhm and Jacopini [1966] have shown that, given IF THEN ELSE and the iterative structure WHILE, all other control structures can be synthesized without any other primitives; not even GO TO is needed.

CASE. In practice, IF THEN ELSE and WHILE are often too cumbersome, although not too limited, to serve as the only means of expression. Thus the CASE control structure seems to be a highly desirable addition to the basic two.

One can have conditions whose testing yields more than two useful results. A comparison of two numbers yields three results: low, equal, and high. Testing membership of a number in a range yields five results: low, equal to bottom bound, within, equal to top bound, and high. Testing whether an object is a member of a set yields $(1 + \rho\ set)$ results; for example, a character is A, B, C, ... Z, or is not a member of the set of Roman capitals.

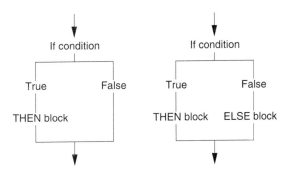

FIGURE 6-7 IF structures.

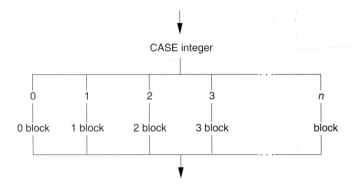

FIGURE 6-8   Diagram of CASE structure.

A multiple decision can, of course, be handled by a tree of two-way decisions. Equally clearly, this method is often awkward. So programming languages often have a set-member identification test, called CASE. This structure is shown in Figure 6-8. The syntax for the CASE statement in Pascal and an example of its use are shown in Program 6-9. Note that, in early Pascal, CASE does not handle non-membership.

```
Syntax:
        CASE <expression> of
            <case label list>: statement;
                    . . .
                    . . .
                    . . .
            <case label list>: statement
        END

Example:
        VAR I: integer;
        CASE I OF
            0 : x:= 0;
            1 : x:= x;
            2,3: x:= x*x
        END
```

PROGRAM 6-9   The CASE statement in Pascal.

OUT.   Another desirable addition to the basic control structures is a set of GO TOs with a common address, here called OUT (Figure 6-10).

A use for OUT is to branch without return to an exception-handling routine that handles errors or other unlikely events from any of many validity tests in a program. In contrast to GO TO, OUT should terminate the pending control structures.

Branches

The diagrams of Figures 6-7 and 6-8 correspond to a flow chart, or mental image. In contrast, Figure 6-11 shows diagrams of the control structures in the linear ordering demanded by the vectorial nature of memory. It also shows that the implementation of each structure requires two or more branches.

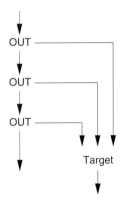

FIGURE 6-10   Action of the OUT statement.

Why not have instructions that more closely match the control structures instead of composing them of branches? This approach is possible but costly, and it requires limiting generality. Let us see why.

Disparity of actions.   The THEN block and the ELSE block each have begin and end delimiters. Since one of the two blocks must be skipped, an action is potentially required at the beginning of each. This situation rules out one single instruction. For the CASE statement, this fact is all the truer.

Diversity of higher languages.   There are two IF structures, and most—but not all—languages have them. Far fewer languages have CASE structures;

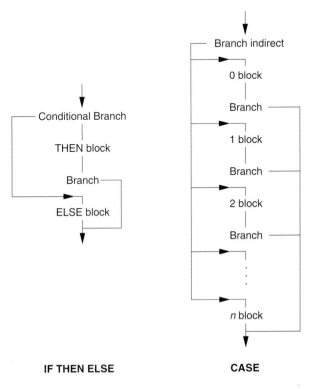

IF THEN ELSE   **CASE**

FIGURE 6-11   Decisions implemented with branches.

and the languages that have them usually differ and are not necessarily ideal. This diversity of languages is even more pronounced for the more complex structures such as FOR, WHILE, and REPEAT UNTIL.

Design Choices

Decisions involve three rather separate sets of design choices. The first is the specification of the condition of the IF structure. Tree 6-12 shows that the main issues here are the explicitness, the encoding, and the spaces of the condition.

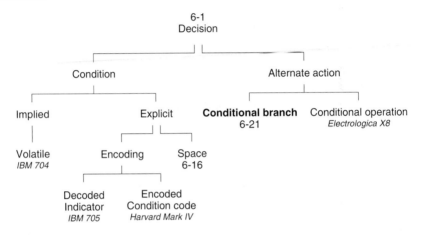

TREE 6-12   Design choices for decision.

The second issue is the specification of the alternative actions, as contained in the blocks of both the IF and CASE structures.

A third issue arises from the decomposition of a single decision-control structure into a set of branches. What is the branching factor and branch target, and how do we reconstruct the whole from the parts? These issues are shown in Tree 6-21.

6.2.1

Condition

The condition of an IF structure is a logical value, which may be true or false. This value may be the result of any valid expression using the operations of Chapter 5, provided that the final operation is either logical or relational.

One might think that there is not much to be said about the condition. After all, it is just 1 bit. But the condition is just one of those points where designers have exerted great ingenuity. Therefore, it is worthwhile to trace carefully the basic specification choices of Tree 2-7.

Implied Condition

Since the domain of the condition is simply true or false, the first issue of interest is whether the condition is implied or is specified explicitly.

Volatile condition. In early designs the condition was often specified as the outcome of a relational operation; the 704 Compare Accumulator To Storage is an example (Program 6-23). In such a case the condition is obtained and applied in one instruction; it is not available for further inspection—it is volatile.

The volatile condition violates orthogonality by coupling an expression with a branch to be taken. Since there are many different expressions and many different ways of branching, the number of combinations proliferates rapidly.

Explicit Condition

Separating the specification of a condition from the specification of branch target improves both the understanding and the quality of the design. Such separation is achieved by making the condition explicit, and hence durable and visible. Any desired expression can produce this condition; any desired branching can be specified for this condition (Figure 6-13).

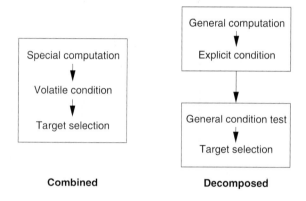

FIGURE 6-13   Separation of condition and target specification.

Encoding the Condition

Indicator.   When the condition is either true or false, 1 bit suffices. One indicates true; zero, false. Such a 1-bit encoded condition is called an *indicator*.

Condition code. Multivalued conditions can be considered as sets of binary conditions that are mutually exclusive. Thus, an arithmetic result may be any one of positive, zero, negative, or not representable; in a dyadic comparison, the first operand may be larger than, equal to, or smaller than the second operand; a message sent to a peripheral processor may be accepted or rejected because the processor is busy, not operational, or not able to perform the request.

Two bits can convey one of the four conditions in each of the examples given. Such a joint encoding of conditions is called a *condition code.*

In the 360 several mutually exclusive sets of four or fewer conditions are each encoded in a 2-bit condition code (Table 6-14).

| | Code value | | | Signal |
	00	01	10	11	function
Logic	=0	≠0			signal360Z
Test Under Mask	∧.=0	∧/∈0 1		∧.=1	signal360TM
Addition	=0	<0	>0	oflo	signal360NZPO
Logical addition	=0	≠0	=0	≠0	signal360ZC
	˜carry	˜carry	carry	carry	signal360ZC
Comparison	=	<	>		signal360C
Start I/O	ready	pending	busy	absent	signal360IO
Instruction bit	8	9	10	11	

TABLE 6-14   Condition code in the IBM System/360.

Unfortunately, we overdid the encoding—four codes are not always sufficient. In addition and subtraction, it is desirable to record the carry-out independently of the sign status; six cases result. The carry can then be used in extended precision.

Condition operator. Regardless of whether or not the four conditions are encoded, one wants to test functions of them in making a decision. Thus, one may wish to branch for a representable arithmetic result, which implies a positive, negative, or zero result.

The condition operator for the 360 is shown in the Branch On Condition operation of Program 6-15, and is indicated at the bottom of Table 6-14. The 4-bit mask is ANDed with the four (decoded) conditions, and the OR of the result determines branching. 0000 and 1111 turn the Conditional Branch into a No Operation and Unconditional Branch, respectively.

```
     Mask↓
┌─────────┬────┬────┬────────────────┐
│ Opcode  │ X1 │ B1 │ D1             │
└─────────┴────┴────┴────────────────┘
0        8   12   16   20            32
Legend: B = base; D = displacement; X = index.

     BC
   ⋀ IBM 360 Branch On Condition
     →If fld Mask[magni psw[Cc]]
     THEN:psw[Iadr]←adrsize magnr adr360bxd
     ENDIF:
```

PROGRAM 6-15   Branch On Condition in the IBM System/360.

An extension of the 360 condition code to 3 bits, as suggested previously, would require an 8-bit condition operator. The 8 bits would not fit in the instruction format—another instance of the bit budget's causing a conflict between design goals.

Allocating the Condition

Allocation requires a space and an index to address the condition within that space. All conceivable spaces have been used for allocating the condition; we treat them here in order.

General working store. For machines that place results in a working store, it seems proper to use the working store as a place for the condition. After

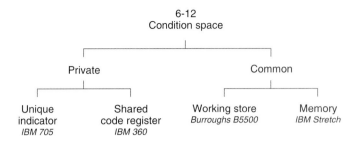

6-12
Condition space

Private

Unique
indicator
IBM 705

Shared
code register
IBM 360

Common

Working store
Burroughs B5500

Memory
IBM Stretch

TREE 6-16   Design choices for condition space.

all, that is where the condition would appear following the evaluation of the conditional expression of the IF statement.

The Burroughs B5500 (1964) uses this approach. Its working store is organized as a stack: The condition resides at the top, in the rightmost bit.

Many early machines, such as the Mark 1, use the accumulator sign as a condition. This method, however, is neither orthogonal, nor general, nor proper. First, the condition is obtained "free" only if the sign test is indeed required. Second, the use of a condition operator to test multiple conditions is not possible. Third, many tests such as I/O status require considerable ingenuity to have the result end up in the accumulator sign.

The successors of the very early machines abandon the accumulator sign as universal condition and provide a set of branches with implied condition, resulting in a proliferation of operations. Table 6-17 shows the list of branches for the IBM 705 III (1957) as an illustration.

Private working store.   Many conditions are the result of secondary operations. For an arithmetic operation, the sign, a zero, and the overflow condition of the result can be efficiently determined while the operation is performed; in addressing a peripheral unit, its status is of necessity known to the central unit.

These side effects, though improper, are part of most operations because of their apparent gain in efficiency. The instruction usually has no bits left to specify a different general register for these secondary results, as well as the primary results, such as a sum or product.

Therefore, the conditions that arise as secondary results of an operation are normally retained in an implied location of their own. This location could be an implied general register, but it is usually a private working store.

TRH Compare High	TRA Any I/O Or Check Signal
TRE Compare Equal	TSA Synchronizer Any
TZB Zero Bit (1,2,4,8,A,B, or C)	TRC Read/write Check
NTR Normalize One Digit	TRR Tape Read
TRZ Zero	TMC Machine Check
TRP Positive	TTC Transmission Check
TOC Overflow Check	TEC Echo Check
TSC Sign Check	TIC Instruction Check
TAA/TAF Switch (A,B,C,D,E, or F)	TRS Last Selected Signal

TABLE 6-17   Specialized branches in the IBM 705 III.

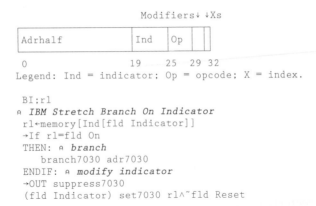

PROGRAM 6-18   Branch On Indicator in the IBM Stretch.

Indicator register. In an *indicator register* each condition has a private location. The Stretch uses a 64-bit indicator register, with a 6-bit field to address it (Program 6-18).

Since not all indicators can be on at once, their representation is redundant, which adds to the status of the processor and makes the storing and restoring of the status more expensive.

Testing indicators can be quite simple: The indicator is selected by an address, and the test succeeds if the indicator is 0 or 1, as specified by a condition operator (Program 6-18). After the test, the indicator may be left unchanged or set to 0.

The use of indicators is particularly attractive when the number of conditions is small. This case is typical in mini- and microcomputers. Programs 6-19 and 6-22 show the Intel 8080A (1974) and the DEC PDP11 (1970) as examples.

The PDP11 follows the basic indicator scheme by providing individual tests.   But it violates the spirit of the indicator scheme by occasionally combining two indicators in one test. It is hard to preserve generality with the indicator approach.

The number of functions of n independent conditions goes as $2 * 2 * n$; 2 bits yield 16 functions; 3 bits, 256 functions; and 4 bits, 65,536 functions, as we saw with the condition code.

The 8080A follows the Stretch, except that it does not turn off the indicator (Program 6-19).

Condition register. When all mutually exclusive, simultaneously available conditions are encoded in a condition code, a private time-shared working store, the *condition register*, can be dedicated for the code. No address is needed to specify the condition.

The time sharing of the condition register means that successive conditions may wipe out their predecessors. Two consequences follow: First, between

```
JP;branch                          true←condition8080;cond
A Intel 8080A Branch On Condition  A Intel 8080A condition test
  branch←magni ifetch8080 adrsize    cond←(Zero,Carry,Neg,Parity)[fld Rp]
  →If condition8080                  true←reg[F;cond]=fld On
THEN:iadr←branch
ENDIF:
```

PROGRAM 6-19   Conditional Branch in the Intel 8080A.

the setting of the condition and its use some simple housekeeping should be possible without destroying the condition. A Load, for instance, should not change the condition code. Second, it should be convenient to store and refetch the condition from memory.

Saving the condition.   The condition, whether expressed as indicators or as a condition code, is a part of machine state and must be saved whenever a status switch is performed. Moreover, it may have to be saved on subroutine entry if a branch after the subroutine depends on the condition value before the subroutine. Therefore, it is common to provide automatic saving as part of an interruption, and sometimes it is provided for all calling sequences. In the 360, the condition code is made part of the Program Status Word, so it is saved upon all status switches. Moreover, the Branch And Link operation, provided for the purpose of subroutine linkage, also saves the condition code (Program 6-48).

Memory.   The most general location for the condition is memory; the condition has a regular memory address. The Stretch provides an example of treating any bit in memory as a condition in the operation Branch On Bit (Program 6-20).

Branch On Bit has an interesting implementation history. Since its frequency of use was expected to be low, the implementers were encouraged to reduce its cost. So the operation was implemented with variable-length store operations. The successor to the addressed word was always fetched and restored, whether or not it was needed, making operation speed slower than floating-point divide. Thus, the frequency of use was indeed low.

For housekeeping purposes—particularly for the control and synchronization of I/O—most computers have a variety of status bits whose values must be tested. Some machines address these bits by embedding them as implied locations in the memory address space.

The PDP11 uses this method. Therefore, ordinary arithmetic, logic, and compare instructions suffice to perform all device error and status checking. With memory address 65388 assigned to the status register for the Model PC11 paper-tape punch, a simple arithmetic sign test checks for error conditions:

        TST 65388 ; check sign of punch status location
        BMI error ; if minus, branch to punch error handler

                                          Modifiers↓ ↓Xs2

Address		X1	Op	Adrhalf2		Opcode	

0   24 28 32   51   60 64
Legend: Op = opcode; X = index.

```
BB;od;r1
ρ IBM Stretch Branch On Bit
od←1 read7030 adr7030
→If od=fld On2
THEN: ρ branch
    branch7030 adr7030s2
ENDIF: ρ modify bit
r1←(fld Invert)≠od∧˜fld Reset2
adr7030 write7030 r1
```

PROGRAM 6-20   Branch On Bit in the IBM Stretch.

6.2.2

Alternative Action

Having specified the condition, one must indicate which action corresponds to each of its values. This indication is normally accomplished by giving the start address of the desired sequence as the target of a conditional branch instruction. As an alternative, each individual instruction may indicate whether or not it participates in the desired sequence, thus making the operations conditional.

Conditional Branch

Conditional branch involves the design choices of the branching factor, the addressing of the branch target, and the branch trace (Tree 6-21).

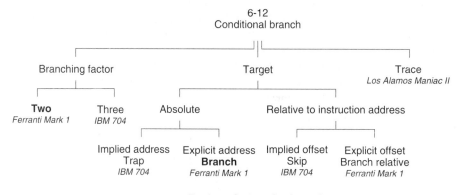

TREE 6-21   Design choices for branching.

Branching factor. The branches that implement an IF structure must have a branching factor of 2. The CASE structure requires a branching factor of n. A branching factor of 3 was provided in some early machines (Table 6-26) such as the 704 (Program 6-23).

Branch target. Of the two branch targets for the IF structure, one can be conveniently implied as the continuation of the linear sequence; the other must be specified differently. There are two independent design choices: whether the branch addresses will be *absolute* or *relative* to the instruction address at the branch point; and whether the branch addresses will be *implied* or *explicit*.

Branch absolute. The conditional branch with specified absolute branch address is the most frequent branch structure. Branch Conditional of the 360 is a typical example of a conditional branch (Program 6-15). The branch address is specified as an operand; the non-branch address is implied.

Branch relative. Specified relative branch addresses are common. The PDP11 is a good example (Program 6-22). The exclusive use of relative branches allows a section of program to be relocated without modification.

```
BLT;iadr;offset
ค DEC PDP11 Branch On Less
→If≠/stout Neg,Oflo
THEN:iadr←magni reg[Pc;]
     offset←2×radixcompi inst[Offset]
     reg[Pc;]←word magnr iadr+offset
ENDIF:
```

PROGRAM 6-22   Jump in the DEC PDP11.

Whereas one may want to use only relative branches for decisions in a code segment, the repertoire should include absolute branches as well; they are useful for the OUT, CALL, and RETURN control structures.

Skip.   The implied relative target, or *skip*, is usually used to make formats work when they have no room for target addresses. Depending on the condition, one or more instructions are skipped; these skipped instructions are almost invariably unconditional branches.

An interesting example is the 704 Skip On Comparison (Compare Accumulator To Storage, CAS) (Program 6-23). The sole operand field specifies a memory location to be tested. The three-way result is effected by skips: If the accumulator is greater than memory, two instructions are skipped; if the two are equal, one instruction is skipped; if the accumulator is less than memory, no instruction is skipped.

Opcode	*	X	Address

```
0            12   18 21              36
Legend: X = index; * = unused.
```

```
CAS;comparand;operand
ค IBM 704 Skip On Comparison
comparand←signmagni read704 adr704
operand←signmagni acc
iadr←iadr+(operand>comparand)+operand≥comparand
```

PROGRAM 6-23   Skip On Comparison in the IBM 704.

Interesting as CAS may be, it does not naturally match the IF THEN ELSE program primitives. Moreover, the skipping technique offers no space advantage—the implied addresses must be specified in the unconditional branches after all. If the skipped instructions are of variable length, there is no time advantage either—the branches must be fetched for their length to be determined.

Trap.   A branch with implied absolute target address is called a *trap*. Examples of instructions that trap for an explicitly stated condition are rare. They save the space of an address, but the program must cope with a fixed target location. The trap is attractive only for exception handling, as in the OUT structure. A nice example is the Motorola MC68000 traps (1980; Program 6-24).

```
TRAPL                      TRAPV
ค Motorola 68000 Trap Low  ค Motorola 68000 Trap On Overflow
Trap[fld R2] report 1      Oflotrap report status[Oflo]
```

PROGRAM 6-24   Trap in the Motorola MC68000.

Opcode	Select	Origin	Limit	Case 0		Case 1	Case limit
0	8	16	24	32		48	48+16×limit

```
CASEB;select;start;end;case;iadr
ⓐ DEC VAX780 Case Byte
select←magni read780 adr780 byte
start←magni read780 adr780 byte
end←magni read780 adr780 byte
case←select-start
iadr←magni reg[Pc;]
→IF case≤end
THEN:reg[Pc;]←long magnr iadr+2×case
    →ENDIF
ELSE:reg[Pc;]←long magnr iadr+2×end+1
ENDIF:
```

PROGRAM 6-25   Case in the DEC VAX11/780.

Indirect branch.   The CASE is efficiently programmed on machines whose branch addresses can be indexed to target a table of unconditional branches. So the frequency of the CASE structure argues for modifiable branch addresses. This function is readily available by giving the branch address the same format as the operand address, as is done in most computers.

The n-way branching of the CASE control structure requires so many operands that, in most computers, it has not been implemented as a separate operation. Nevertheless, the CASE is found in the DEC VAX11 (1978; Program 6-25). The variable instruction length of the VAX allows an efficient specification of the n targets.

Branch Trace.   The collection of taken branch addresses is equivalent to a forward chain through a set of routines. It thus allows a forward trace of a program. Since there is no backward chain, a trace in the opposite direction, which is so desirable in debugging, is more difficult. A proposed solution has been to store the instruction address of each executed branch instruction in a Path Address location, or to store a series of these in stacked fashion.

The Los Alamos Maniac II (1958) provides a branch trace function, called a Pathfinder. Most architects have judged this function too limited for its expense, especially since structured programs make the need less vital, and software diagnostics provide more powerful debugging aids.

Conditional Operation

Instead of using the condition of an IF structure to control the sequence of instructions, as in the case of branching, one can use the condition to change the operations in the sequence that follows the test.

Suppression.   A general technique for effecting alternate actions is the use of instruction suppression, depending on the value of some condition bit presumably set by the condition of an IF structure.

In the IBM 604 (1952) plugboard-controlled electronic computer, each instruction has a suppression bit, which can be controlled by a condition bit or its inverse, or left unset. If the suppression bit is 1, the instruction is not executed. An IF THEN ELSE structure is accomplished by setting all

	Condition space	Branch factor	Branch target	Trace	Conditional operation
Zuse Z4	w	2	s		
Cambridge EDSAC	w	2	b		
Ferranti Mark 1	v i w	2	b s		
Univac I	v	2	b		
Princeton IAS	w	2	b		
IBM 701	i w	2	b		
IBM 650	i w	2	b		
IBM NORC	v i	2 3	b		
IBM 704	v i w	2 3	t b s	trap	
IBM 705	i w	2	b		
Univac 1103A	v w	2	b		
STC ZEBRA	w	2	s		yes
Bull Gamma 60	i	2	b r		
IBM 1401	i m	2	b		
IBM Stretch	i m	2	b		
CDC 6600	v	2	b		
CDC 6600 PPU	i w	2	b r		
Burroughs B5500	w	2	b r		
IBM System/360	c	2	b		
Electrologica X8	i	2	b		yes
DEC PDP8	w	2	s		
DEC PDP11	c	2	r		
Intel 8080A	i	2	b		
Cray 1	w	2	b		
Motorola M6800	i	2	r		
MOS 6502	i	2	r		
DEC VAX11	c m	2	r		
Motorola MC68000	i c	2	t r		
IBM 6150	v i	2	t b r		

Legend: b = absolute branch; c = condition code; i = indicator;
m = memory; r = relative branch; s = skip; t = trap;
v = volatile; w = working store; b r s t are conditional.

TABLE 6-26   Decision in various machines.

the instructions in the then-block from the condition bit, and the instructions in the else-block from its inverse.

The Electrologica X8 (1965) employs a similar technique. Its instruction format (Program 6-27) contains two precondition bits, which specify suppression of the instruction based on two condition bits. The instruction also contains two postcondition bits, which specify the setting of the condition code. One bit of the condition code is general and can be specified by the precondition to suppress the instruction if the bit is 0 or 1. The other condition bit indicates an overflow and can be specified to suppress only if set to 1. The precondition bit can also specify the absence of suppression.

Suppression is a meta-operation, and the Electrologica X8 illustrates the problems discussed in Section 6.1. The operation matches the IF THEN ELSE structure for one condition and the IF THEN structure for the overflow condition. Generality is violated, however, by not providing the precondition specification in all instruction formats. Also, nesting of decisions is not allowed.

The Electrologica X8 method uses its bit budget efficiently when the THEN- and ELSE-blocks are short, but it increases the bit traffic since in-

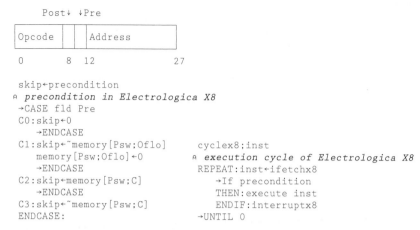

```
         Post↓  ↓Pre

     ┌─────────┬─┬─────────────┐
     │ Opcode  │ │ Address     │
     └─────────┴─┴─────────────┘

     0       8  12             27

  skip←precondition
 ᴀ precondition in Electrologica X8
  →CASE fld Pre
  C0:skip←0
     →ENDCASE
  C1:skip←¯memory[Psw;Oflo]          cyclex8:inst
     memory[Psw;Oflo]←0            ᴀ execution cycle of Electrologica X8
     →ENDCASE                        REPEAT:inst←ifetchx8
  C2:skip←memory[Psw;C]                →If precondition
     →ENDCASE                         THEN:execute inst
  C3:skip←¯memory[Psw;C]              ENDIF:interruptx8
  ENDCASE:                          →UNTIL 0
```

PROGRAM 6-27   Suppression in the Electrologica X8.

structions that are suppressed must still be fetched. A very similar technique has been proposed by Nievergelt and Irland [Nievergelt and Irland, 1970].

6.2.3
Bibliography

Böhm and Jacopini [1966], Burks et al. [1946], Dahl et al. [1972],   Nievergelt and Irland [1970], Tanenbaum [1978], Wolczko and Williams [1994].

6.3
Iteration

Since every step must be specified, a computer saves effort only if a set of instructions, once specified, can be executed many times with different data. This repetition is used not only for whole programs, but also for program segments. A basic structure is therefore the *iteration*.

Control Structures

Iterations are of three basic kinds, most clearly delineated by the WHILE, the REPEAT UNTIL, and the FOR constructions of ALGOL, Pascal, and PL/I (Figure 6-28). Each iteration structure involves at least a *scope* (*What* is to be iterated?) and a *termination* condition (*When* should iteration be stopped?). Since an iteration is a control structure, one must be able to nest iterations of any kind in any fashion.

WHILE.   In a WHILE structure, the number of iterations is contingent upon some computational result that is modified within the iteration. The sequential searching of a table is a good example.

WHILE requires specification of

1. The *start* of the scope

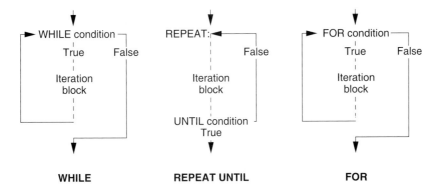

FIGURE 6-28   Iteration Structures.

2. The *end* of the scope (or the location of the first instruction after the structure)
3. The *termination* condition

In ALGOL and PL/I, a WHILE statement gives items 1 and 3; an END statement gives item 2.

Very few machines have made explicit provisions for WHILE iteration, for the same reasons as for the IF and CASE structures. In most machines, the WHILE is programmed by a test of the WHILE condition, using a conditional branch at the start of the scope and a completely separate unconditional branch at the end of the scope (Figure 6-29).

REPEAT UNTIL. Figure 6-28 shows that REPEAT UNTIL is almost equivalent to the WHILE structure. The terminating condition, however, must be known prior to the iteration for WHILE; it may be produced in the iteration for REPEAT UNTIL. As a consequence, REPEAT UNTIL cannot do an iteration zero times.

Several languages incorporate REPEAT UNTIL structures, including Pascal, BLISS, and PL/I.

The REPEAT UNTIL requires the same specifications as the WHILE, but now the REPEAT gives the start of the scope, and the UNTIL gives the end of the scope and the termination condition. Therefore, the structure is

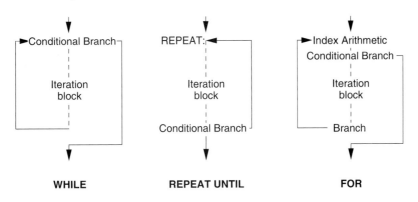

FIGURE 6-29   WHILE, REPEAT UNTIL, and FOR in machine language.

conveniently programmed by a conditional branch at the end of the scope with the start as target.

FOR. In FOR, the number of iterations is a part of the iteration structure itself, and the iteration operation could be equally well expressed as DO N TIMES, so far as control of instruction sequencing alone is concerned. The FOR structure, however, also allows specification of address modification; its more general form is:

FOR I = initial value TO last value BY increment UNLESS condition

Such an iteration corresponds closely to the way one thinks for some operations. For other operations, as APL experience has shown, the thought unit is really a multielement data structure, such as a vector or an array, and iteration is merely a cumbersome element-by-element mechanism for specifying operations upon the data structure as a whole. Moreover, the iteration mechanism implies an ordering of execution not inherent in the array concept.

If one specifies a dummy variable, initializes it outside the structure, counts it, and tests it, one can always subsume the FOR structure into the WHILE structure. Similarly, by the use of the UNLESS option, one can always subsume the WHILE and the REPEAT UNTIL into the FOR. In the absence of UNLESS, the cost is higher; a branch out of the FOR is the ugliest kind of GO TO. It violates the integrity of the FOR structure since it may leave variables and storage allocations unterminated. As long as the language has insufficient array operations, one wants not only the WHILE and REPEAT UNTIL, but the FOR as well.

FOR requires specification of

- The *start* of the scope
- The *end* of the scope
- The *name* of the control variable
- Its *initial* value
- Its *last* value
- Its *increment*
- An optional *early termination* condition

An END statement gives the end of the scope. The FOR statement gives all other parameters.

Diversity of higher languages. The large number of parameters to be specified for the FOR structure presents a challenge to the computer architect to satisfy the high-level construct with something more than just a branch. However, this large number of parameters has also resulted in a diversity of decisions in the higher languages.

Design Choices

Since the WHILE and REPEAT UNTIL structures can be implemented with the conditional and unconditional branch, they introduce no basic new design choices. The FOR, however, introduces the design choices for initiation, incrementing, and termination. Therefore, the FOR structure constitutes the driving problem for the design of iteration functions in machine language.

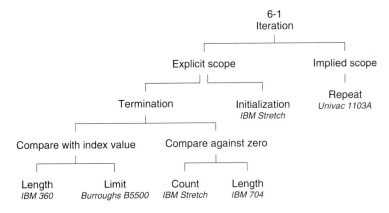

TREE 6-30 Design choices for iteration.

The design choices for initiation and termination are shown in Tree 6-30. The general means for incrementing have been discussed in Section 3.4; we discuss incrementing here only where it is combined with provisions for termination.

Most computers make some provision for the FOR structure; a few have embodied the structure directly, but always in restricted form. We first consider the general case, and then discuss some more restrictive versions that have been designed.

Since the designs that incorporate initialization also include incrementation, and those that include incrementation also include termination, we start with the latter, and subsequently consider how incrementation and initialization can be added. Table 6-31 gives the iteration functions of various machines.

	Operation	Condition	Action	Implied scope
		Explicit scope		
IBM 704	-	>≤	b	
Univac 1103A	-1	≥0	b	repeat
STC ZEBRA	+2	=0	i	repeat
Bull Gamma 60	-1	=0	b	
IBM Stretch	-1	=0 ≠0	b i	
English Electric KDF9		=0		repeat
Burroughs B5500	‾1	=0	b	
IBM System/360	-1 +	≠0 ≥ <	b	
DEC PDP8	+1	=0	s	
DEC PDP10	+1 -1	< ≤ = ≥ > ≠	b s	
DEC PDP11	-1	≠0	-r	
DEC VAX11	+1 -1 +	< ≤ > ≥	r	
Motorola MC68000	-1	≠0	r	

Legend: + = add; - = subtract; +1 = increment; -1 = decrement;
b = branch; i = initialize; r = relative branch;
-r = relative branch, backwards only; s = skip.

TABLE 6-31 Iteration in various machines.

6.3.1

Termination

Termination in general involves a termination condition and a branch target.

Termination Condition

Any termination condition may occur in a WHILE or REPEAT UNTIL and in the UNLESS of the FOR. This condition is conveniently implemented with a conditional branch. The TO statement is more specific and may be combined with the incrementation of the BY, as we shall see.

Branch Target

The implied/explicit, absolute/relative address alternatives considered for the decision structures are, in principle, also usable for the iteration structures. But the implied-absolute combination—trap—makes little sense and does not occur.

The implied-relative combination—skip—serves in iteration structures, as in IF THEN ELSE, only to provide space for a branch address that cannot be accommodated in the format, as in the DEC PDP8 (1965) Increment And Skip If Zero (Program 6-32).

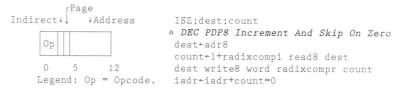

```
             ┌Page
   Indirect↓│  ↓Address        ISZ:dest:count
                               ⋒ DEC PDP8 Increment And Skip On Zero
   ┌──┬─┬─┬──────┐             dest←adr8
   │Op│ │ │      │             count←1+radixcompi read8 dest
   └──┴─┴─┴──────┘             dest write8 word radixcompr count
    0   5    12                iadr←iadr+count=0
   Legend: Op = Opcode.
```

PROGRAM 6-32   Increment And Skip On Zero in the DEC PDP8.

Iterative structures most commonly use the specified absolute or relative branch addresses. The relative address must, however, be backward for the REPEAT UNTIL, as illustrated in Figure 6-29.

In the WHILE and FOR, branching should be forward. Several designs have nevertheless combined incrementing intended for a FOR structure and its test with a branch-back. The 704 Branch On Increment (Transfer And Increment Index, TIX), Program 6-33, branches as long as the termination condition is not reached, and therefore needs to be placed at the end of the iteration scope.

6.3.2

Incrementation

In the FOR structure an increment is added to an index value, and a termination test is performed. First, both the increment and the iteration scope are explicit, and hence general. Second, the increment is implied. Third, both the scope and the increment are implied.

Increment and Branch

The 704 TIX (Program 6-33) decrements an index value by a specified decrement value and branches to the specified start of the iteration scope; no decrement and no branch occur when the index value is less than or equal to the decrement value. By using the decrement field as comparand as well as increment, one two-address instruction can specify all the parameters that are necessary for the FOR structure.

```
Op Decrement       X  Address

0   3               18 21              36
Legend: Op = opcode; X = index.

 TIX;index;decrement;ix
 ⍝ IBM 704 Branch On Increment
 index←magni indexread704
 decrement←fld Decrement
 →If index>decrement
 THEN: ⍝ decrement and branch
    ix←adrsize magnr index-decrement
    indexwrite704 ix
    iadr←target704 fld Address
 ENDIF:
```

PROGRAM 6-33   Branch On Increment in the IBM 704.

Subtractive indexing.   The bit efficiency of TIX depends on the implied comparand, which in turn depends on incrementing the index value toward zero. One could use negative index values and increment them, one could use subtractive indexing (as the 704 does), or one could use positive index values with decrementing and additive indexing. In the last case, arrays are scanned backward, which is improper and causes programmer errors.

In the 704, the address part of the instruction, containing base address and displacement, refers to the end of the data structure—the limit. The index contains an element address that is subtracted from the limit. At the start of the iteration, the index contains the length of the data structure,

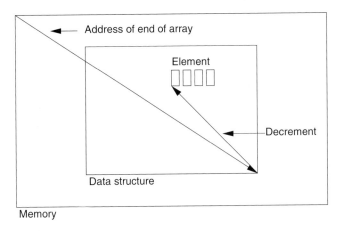

FIGURE 6-34   Subtractive indexing in the IBM 704.

Opcode	R1	R2	B1	D1	

```
0        8   12   16   20              32
Legend: B = base; D = displacement; R = register; X = index.
```

```
BXH;increment;value;sum;odd2;comparand
A IBM 360 Branch On Index High
increment←radixcompi reg[fld R2;]
value←radixcompi reg[fld R1;]
sum←value+increment
odd2←1+2×⌊0.5×fld R2
comparand←radixcompi reg[odd2;]
→If sum>comparand
THEN:psw[Iadr]←adrsize magnr adr360bd1
ENDIF:reg[fld R1;]←word radixcompr sum
```

PROGRAM 6-35   Branch On Index High in the IBM System/360.

and the effective address points to the first element of the structure. As the computation proceeds, the index is decremented after each iteration, and the effective address moves forward in normal fashion through the data structure (Figure 6-34).

Subtractive indexing has not been used again. The fact that everything occurs just backward from the expectation of the normal user is a perpetual source of errors; subtraction is simply not proper to address formation.

Additive indexing.   The regular additive indexing of address modification can be preserved by using one more operand in the termination instruction. The 360 Branch On Index High (BXH) and Branch On Index Low Or Equal (BXLE) match the incrementation requirements of the BY and the termination requirements of the TO by specifying two operands in registers for these purposes, as shown in Program 6-35 for BXH. The instructions are furthermore designed to be placed at the start of the scope, thus allowing zero iterations.

Although the BXH and BXLE provide a general FOR, they are relatively rarely used, for several interesting reasons. One reason is slow implementation. More important, the operations use three registers, a number most compiler designers consider excessive. When the compiler does not have three free registers for a BXLE, a slowdown occurs.

Implied Increment

DO *N* TIMES.   A FOR iteration with implied increment of 1 is equivalent to DO *N* TIMES and requires specification of

1. The *start* of the scope
2. The *end* of the scope
3. The *name* of the control variable
4. The *number* of iterations

In ALGOL and PL/I, a FOR statement provides specifications 1, 3, and 4; 2 is specified by an END statement.

If the control variable is not used for indexing operands, specification 3 is eliminated. Furthermore, the variable can be counted down, which allows an implied end value of zero. Here too, as in FOR, combining the iteration

```
┌─────────┬────┬────┬────┬─────────────┐
│ Opcode  │ R1 │ X1 │ B1 │ D1          │
└─────────┴────┴────┴────┴─────────────┘
0         8    12   16   20            32
Legend: B = base; D = displacement; R = register; X = index.

BCT;count
⋒ IBM 360 Branch On Count
count←(magni reg[fld R1;])-1
→If count≠0
THEN:psw[Iadr]←adrsize magnr adr360bxd
ENDIF:reg[fld R1;]←word magnr count
```

PROGRAM 6-36   Branch On Count in the IBM System/360.

test with the necessary branch at the end of the scope is most economical, but does not accommodate a count of zero.

Branch and count.   A branch combined with a simple count is often provided for loop closing. The increment is the implied value -1. Therefore the count is not useful for indexing data. Program 6-36 shows the 360's Branch On Count (BCT).

Implied Scope

The limitations occasioned by implication are even more severe when the scope is implied, for example, to be of a fixed length such as one or two instructions.

Repeat.   The Univac 1103A (1956) has the FOR iteration built-in as the meta-operation Repeat (Program 6-37).

The number of iterations, n, is specified in the first address field. The scope is restricted to one full instruction, so the end is implied. This restriction is not so painful as one might imagine, since this scope is a full two-address instruction and powerful operators are included. Table search, vector inner product, and polynomial evaluation can each be done by a Repeat followed by a suitable single instruction.

Modification, by increments of 0 or 1, of the first and second address in the instruction to be repeated, is controlled respectively by the `incru` and `incrv` bits. The repeated instruction simply remains in the Instruction Register, so a Repeat loop requires no instruction flow—a big gain.

Side effect.   In the 1103A, resuming sequencing after Repeat is peculiarly painful. One would expect it to be easy; since the scope is restricted to one instruction, the Instruction Address could simply be incremented. But the implementers chose to save (costly vacuum-tube) hardware by using the instruction counter to count down the repeat control variable. This implementation forced the architecture to specify resumption of sequencing from the implied location `F1(6)`. So the last address in the format for Repeat is used to allow one to give a value to be stored at location 6 before execution begins. When Repeat ends, the instruction address is set to 6. But this operation has the undesirable side effect of changing the contents of location 6. In this machine, an awkward architectural impropriety follows directly from corner cutting in the implementation—that is, failure to provide the proper counting register.

```
         ↓Control
┌──────┬──┬─────────────┬─────────────────┬──────┐
│Op    │  │Count        │Addressv         │      │
└──────┴──┴─────────────┴─────────────────┴──────┘
0      6  9             21                36
Legend: Op = opcode.
```

```
  RP;cont;incru;incrv;count
A Univac 1103A Repeat
  cont←fld Control[0]
  incru←fld Control[1]
  incrv←fld Control[2]
  count←fld Count
  memory[F1;Addressv]←inst[Addressv]
A fetch instruction to be repeated
  inst←ifetch1103
A Repeat as subject instruction
  →ERROR(fld Opcode)=61
A mark instruction address for branch
  iadr←¯1
  →WHILE(cont∨count≠0)∧iadr=¯1
      execute inst
      inst[Addressu]←adrsize magnr(fld Addressu) incr1103 incru
      inst[Addressv]←adrsize magnr(fld Addressv) incr1103 incrv
      count←count-1
      →Δ
  ENDWHILE:→If(fld Opcode)∈ 34 35
  THEN: A record control and count for TJ and EJ branches
      mq[]←0
      mq[Addressv]←cont,incru,incrv,(ρCount) magnr count
  ENDIF:iadr←F1⌈iadr
```

PROGRAM 6-37   Repeat in the Univac 1103A.

Meta-operation.   Because Repeat is a meta-operation, it imposes inter-instruction syntax constraints—the 1103A's Repeat better not be followed by another Repeat. Such constraints are awkward for both the implementer and the compiler writer.

Low-level Repeat.   A lower-cost sibling of the 1103A, called Countess, used Repeat with the low-level operations Multiply Step and Divide Step to allow efficient programming of multiplication and division, which were not built-in. The implementation of these operations required no internal repetition, so the machine was substantially simpler to build. From a different point of view, one could say that the user had to have the multiplication and division functions, which require internal repetition. By the use of Repeat, the designers gave the programmer access to this mechanism.

Two-instruction scope.   The Repeat, to be useful, must apply to a complete action.   Therefore, in single-address machines, the one-instruction scope restriction of the 1103A's Repeat would destroy most of Repeat's value. The single-address Bendix G20 (1961) incorporated a Repeat with a scope of two instructions.

Because of the meta-operation nature of Repeat, the extended scope raises complications, too.   The more comprehensive the scope, the more private resources the meta-operation must have.   Moreover, the meta-operation and its scope together form a unit that is difficult to interrupt.   If interruption is allowed, the private registers must be made visible so that they can be

saved and restored. Yet, there must be rules that prevent their being used for anything except the meta-operation.

Zero-instruction scope.   Van der Poel's STC ZEBRA (1959) provides low-level operations with the repeat function as a part of the instruction to be repeated; thus, at least the scope problems are solved.

Meta-operation.   The fundamental difficulty of the Repeat is that the meta-operations violate the definition of an instruction as the minimal syntactically independent program element; all the complexities follow necessarily from that violation. Moreover, other iterators, such as the Count And Branch, offer all the termination functions of the Repeat and more general incrementation, without violating syntactical independence. For these reasons, the Repeat is not widely used in later machines.

6.3.3

Initialization

Initialization occurs only once per control structure, whereas incrementation and termination testing occur once per iteration. Therefore, implied initialization is meaningful only when the FOR structure itself is iterated. Although this is still a frequent occurrence, initialization's gain in program-bit efficiency is low indeed.

Implied initialization.   The Stretch contains an example of implied initialization (Program 6-38). A single instruction increments an index, reduces a count, and tests this count for zero. In case of zero count, the index and the count are replaced by new initial values. These new values are chain addressed by the *refill* address. In turn, this refill address is replaced by a new refill address.

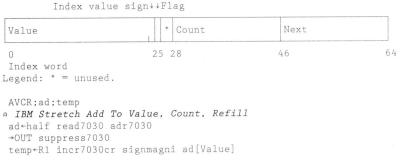

```
AVCR;ad;temp
Ɐ IBM Stretch Add To Value, Count, Refill
  ad←half read7030 adr7030
  →OUT suppress7030
  temp←R1 incr7030cr signmagni ad[Value]
```

PROGRAM 6-38   Index arithmetic in the IBM Stretch.

The chain addressing of the Stretch indexing used an extra address in each index word. Sequential addressing with an occasional branch address, however, is normally more efficient. The Refill scheme was not emulated in later designs.

Compiler effects.   Hand-coded examples can produce strong frequency arguments for specialized instructions, such as TIX, BXH, BXLE, BCT, and even for the Stretch Increment, Count, And Refill operations [Blaauw, 1959].

The actual iteration mechanism used in programs is largely determined by compilers.

The 704 TIX was introduced for the purpose of aiding loop closing. Because it had to be placed at the end of an iteration instead of the start, it did not cover the cases needed by FORTRAN. For many years it was not used in FORTRAN-generated programs.

Because many fast compilers cannot afford the special-case analysis that is required for the use of specialized operations, inclusion of specialized operations in an operation set is justified only if

1. An efficient universal mechanism is also provided
2. Their specialization gives a significant reduction in space and time
3. Their frequency of use is substantial
4. The compiler writers agree

Condition 1 is satisfied for the 360 by Branch On Condition; condition 2, by the elimination of one instruction in space and execution per iteration. Condition 3, however, is barely met by Branch On Count (with 2.5 percent usage), and hardly by BXLE and BXH—with a combined 0.25 percent usage, as compared with a 25 percent usage of Branch On Condition.

6.3.4
Bibliography

Blaauw [1959].

6.4
Delegation

Delegation of control allows a recurring function to be detailed only once and to be called from many places (Figure 6-39). This subroutine technique abbreviates the program representation, thus saving space; it also introduces modularity, separates programming responsibilities, and simplifies making changes in the function.

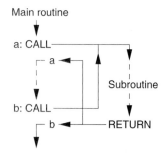

FIGURE 6-39   Subroutine structure.

Control Structures

Function reference.   A major use of the subroutine is to implement the mathematical concept of a *function reference*, found in languages such as FORTRAN, ALGOL, PL/I, and APL. Function reference is an implied subroutine call that, because it returns only a single variable, can be simplified by parameter implication.

Procedure call. Higher-level languages further distinguish between function reference and a more elaborate *procedure call* by the scope of the variables and the number of possible variables returned or affected.

Subroutine call.   Although the difference between function reference and procedure call—with respect to the variables involved—is of major importance to the programmer and the compiler, the instruction sequence can be treated, in both cases, as the call of a closed subroutine, or *subroutine call* for short. The primitive language elements associated with this control structure are CALL, SAVE, and a single inverse for both of these, RESTORE-RETURN, commonly abbreviated RETURN.

Linkage conventions.   Early computers made only primitive provisions for subroutine calling, usually providing only a mechanism for saving a return address. Programmers used other operations of machines to handle the remaining tasks. Because of the high frequency of subroutines and the desirability of easy substitution of one for another, calling sequences quickly became standardized and idiomatic. They are commonly known as the *linkage conventions* for operating systems.

The software linkage conventions make subroutine calling in an operating system appear very complex. Yet, performing subroutine calling swiftly can have a marked effect on performance. Modern computers embody major parts of the CALL, SAVE, and RETURN primitives in hardware.

Requirements

The fundamental issues of the subroutine call are:
- How is the call effected?
- How is the return effected?
- How are parameters passed—both ways?
- How is the machine state preserved?

These issues must each be viewed in relation to the requirements of nesting, reusability, re-entrancy, and recursion.

Nesting.   Orthogonality demands that a computer be capable of multiple levels of subroutines. That is, a subroutine must be allowed to call other subroutines. Generality demands that there not be an arbitrary limit to the allowable depth of nesting.

Reusability.   Subroutines, like all programs, can be classified according to their reusability properties. Since a subroutine's very purpose is to allow a single program to be used from many places, a *non-reusable* subroutine is useless.

```
Tick: PROC(N);
       DECLARE (I,N) FIXED B
       DO FOR I=1 TO N;
       action
       END;
       RETURN;
```

PROGRAM 6-40   A serially-reusable subroutine.

A *serially reusable* subroutine may have only one execution underway at any time, but once that one has completed, another may begin. Program 6-40 is serially reusable; the local variable I that controls the iteration is restored to its initial value only upon the subroutine's completion.

Re-entrancy.   The same copy of a *re-entrant* subroutine may be used concurrently by two or more invocations. Such a subroutine may not modify itself in any way, and it must be provided a separate data space (called an *activation record*) for each invocation. Such a program is also called *pure procedure*, since it does not include any activation-dependent part.

A common method of handling re-entrant subroutines is for each caller to provide the subroutine with activation record space, which the subroutine uses for temporary memory.

Recursion.   A *recursive* subroutine is one that calls itself in the course of its own execution. Such a subroutine cannot expect the caller to furnish its activation data spaces, since there are no distinct callers. The common solution is to have the subroutine request the operating system to allocate such spaces. Since the calls to a recursive subroutine are well-nested, the activation records can be stacked, allowing simple management. Such simple management is not possible for the general re-entrant subroutine, for time may be allocated to the different callers in unpredictable ways.

In short, the re-entrant and recursive subroutines are more constrained than the serially reusable subroutine, but not in the same way. Neither is a special case of the other.

Coroutines.   When two procedures are symmetrically related such that each calls the other and, upon return, proceeds from where it left off, they are called *coroutines*. The coroutine may be considered as a generalization of the subroutine in which the master–slave relationship is replaced by a coordinate one [Knuth, 1968]. Alternatively, the coroutine may be considered a specialization of the subroutine where entry is not at the beginning, but at the point where the routine stopped [Wirth, 1976].

Not-well-nested calls.   Complications in the design of Call, Save, and Return conventions arise from the desire to have subroutine structures that are not well-nested, as illustrated in Figure 6-41. The 360 Supervisor operations Link and Transfer Control [Witt, 1966] are illustrated in this figure. Rather complex linkage conventions have been devised to meet all these needs.

Interrupt handling.   A program interruption can usefully be viewed as a kind of subroutine call. All the parameter-passing and state-saving requirements of the subroutine apply with full force. Program structure and code generation are more uniform if the subroutine linkage and the interruption linkage are

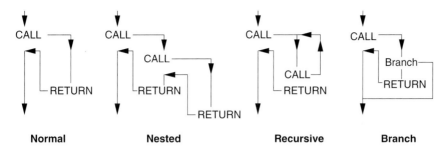

FIGURE 6-41   Subroutine linkages.

the same. Interrupt handling imposes one new constraint on the linkage: The interrupted program, the caller, cannot be assigned any responsibility for parameter-passing and state-saving.

Design Choices

Tree 6-42 shows the architectural approaches to meeting the subroutine call requirements. The provisions for Call, Return, Parameter passing, and State-saving are discussed later. (State-saving is considered further in Section 7.5, as part of interrupt handling.) A comprehensive, but limited, meta-operation, the Execute, that matches the entire control structure, is described at the end of the current section.

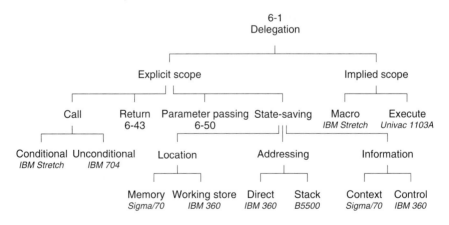

TREE 6-42   Design choices for delegation.

6.4.1

Call and Return

Call.   The call as such is basically an unconditional branch. Since the subroutine is roughly equivalent to an operation, there is no more point to making the call conditional than to making Add or Subtract conditional.

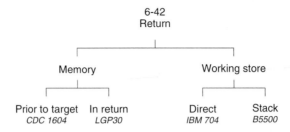

TREE 6-43   Design choices for delegation return.

Nevertheless, Table 6-44 shows that several machines, including the Stretch (Program 6-45), provide a conditional call.

Return.   Upon completion or failure, a subroutine must return sequencing control to the calling program. Since a subroutine may be called from many locations, it cannot know the return address, or *link* (which must be passed, implicitly or explicitly, by the caller). If the return address is the next address in sequence after the call, it is easiest to calculate and plant the return address as part of the same operation that calls the subroutine, for the address is most easily calculated then.

Direct insertion.   Even the minimal Librascope LGP30 (1957), which has only 16 operations, has a Return Address operation that increments the Instruction Address and stores it in the address field of a specified instruction. This

	Call	Return address	Passing or saving What	Where	Implied routine
Zuse Z4	c u	implied			
Ferranti Mark 1	b	memory			
Univac I	b	memory			
IBM 704	u a	direct			
Univac 1103A	u a	memory			
STC ZEBRA	b	direct			x
Bull Gamma 60	b	memory			x
IBM Stretch	c u a	direct			x m
CDC 6600	u a	target-1			
CDC 6600 PPU	u a	target-1			
Burroughs B5500	u a	stack	context	stack	
IBM System/360	u a	direct	control	direct	x
DEC PDP8	u a	target-1			
DEC PDP11	u a	direct	linkage	stack	
Intel 8080A	c u a	stack			
Cray 1	u a	direct			
Motorola M6800	c u a	stack			
MOS 6502	u a	stack			
DEC VAX11	u a	stack	context	stack	
Motorola MC68000	u a r	stack			
IBM 6150	u a	direct			

Legend: a = absolute; b = branch used as call; c = conditional call;
        m = macro facility; r = relative; u = unconditional call;
        x = execute; direct = directly addressed working store.

TABLE 6-44   Delegation in various machines.

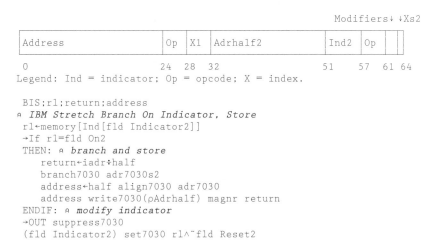

```
                                              Modifiers↓ ↓Xs2

Address                 Op  X1  Adrhalf2          Ind2  Op

0                       24  28  32               51   57  61 64
Legend: Ind = indicator; Op = opcode; X = index.

 BIS;rl;return;address
 ⍝ IBM Stretch Branch On Indicator, Store
 rl←memory[Ind[fld Indicator2]]
 →If rl=fld On2
 THEN: ⍝ branch and store
    return←iadr÷half
    branch7030 adr7030s2
    address←half align7030 adr7030
    address write7030(⍴Adrhalf) magnr return
 ENDIF: ⍝ modify indicator
 →OUT suppress7030
 (fld Indicator2) set7030 rl∧˜fld Reset2
```

PROGRAM 6-45   Branch On Indicator and Store in the IBM Stretch.

operation still requires the caller to know the location of the return instruction within the subroutine.

In the Stretch, instruction-address storing is specified in a halfword prefix, called Store Instruction Counter If (Program 6-45). The prefix can be attached to any halfword branch operation, giving also a conditional subroutine call. This provision appears more general than and just as easy as a single branch and link—but it is *not*. The linking prefix constitutes a meta-operation that violates orthogonality in various ways.

Direct insertion of the return address in the return branch makes the subroutine non-relocatable and non-reenterable.

Reference via memory.   Later machines such as the CDC 1604 (1960) also provide an indirect branch. The return address is then planted in the first word of the subroutine, whose location is standard, and the Call branched to the second word. The Return branches indirectly to the first word and thence home. The caller need do nothing beyond the second word of the callee.

This kind of facility is common in modern minicomputers. Table 6-44 gives examples. Such a linkage does not yield re-enterable subroutines.

Reference via working store.   In the 704, the return address and the parameters are passed through use of an index register. The branching operation (TSX, originally called Transfer And Set Index) specifies a branch address and one of the three index registers (Program 6-46). Before branching,

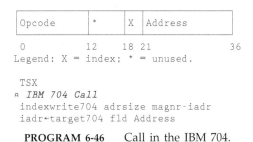

```
Opcode          *   X  Address

0               12  18 21              36
Legend: X = index; * = unused.

 TSX
 ⍝ IBM 704 Call
  indexwrite704 adrsize magnr-iadr
  iadr←target704 fld Address
```

PROGRAM 6-46   Call in the IBM 704.

```
Calling routine                 Subroutine

TSX 4,jack──────────────→jack: CLA 4,1*
address of parameter 1          ADD 4,2*
address of parameter 2          ST  4,3*
address of result               TRA 4,4
resume computation←─────────────┘
```

PROGRAM 6-47   Calling sequence in the IBM 704.

the updated Instruction Address is stored in the specified index register. (Actually, the 2's complement is stored, because of the subtractive indexing of the 704.) Then the branch is effected. In the subroutine, the index can be used, with or without indirect addressing, for fetching parameters from the calling sequence, and for the return branch.

Program 6-47 illustrates the 704 subroutine call. By a universal software convention, index register 4 (of the set 1 2 4) is reserved for subroutine calls. Nestable subroutines are responsible for saving and reloading it. Few subroutine calling sequences have been devised that are as fast, cheap, and powerful.

The 360 Call (BAL), shown in Program 6-48, closely resembles the 704 TSX; the call specifies a general purpose register for storing the return address.

BAL embodies a poor architectural decision; it stores not only the return link, but also machine status bits. So far, so good; the essential part of machine status must be preserved by caller or subroutine. But since the address field is only 24 bits, the status is stored in the upper eight bits of the specified register rather than in a separate register. This approach was designed to conserve registers and to give a "free" Store Status operation. This shortcut, however, has complicated the inevitable growth of the 360 architecture to 31-bit addresses. BAL is the only CPU operation whose action depends on the maximum length of addresses being 24 bits (although I/O control words and status words also do so).

Reference via working stack.   When subroutines are nested, all the registers or other special mechanisms used to set up the outer call and its return must be freed for use by the inner call and its return. After the inner subroutine returns, the registers must be restored for use by the outer subroutine. For pure nesting, a LIFO memory of return addresses is desirable. In the B5500 a stack is elegantly used for this purpose.

Opcode	R1	X1	B1	D1

```
0       8   12  16  20          32
Legend: B = base; D = displacement; R = register; X = index.

BAL;branchadr
⋀ IBM 360 Call
  branchadr←adr360bxd
⋀ preserve status
  reg[fld R1;]←psw[Ilc,Cc,Programmask,Iadr]
⋀ branch
  psw[Iadr]←adrsize magnr branchadr
```

PROGRAM 6-48   Call in the IBM System/360.

Reference via memory stack.   The use of a memory stack for return addresses is illustrated by the 8080A (Program 6-49).

```
┌─────────┬─────────────────────┐     ┌─────────┐
│ Opcode  │ Address             │     │ Opcode  │
└─────────┴─────────────────────┘     └─────────┘
0         8                  24        0         8
Call                                   Return

CALL;branchadr                         RET
 ⍝ Intel 8080A Call                     ⍝ Intel 8080A Return
   branchadr←magni ifetch8080 adrsize   iadr←magni pop8080
   push8080 adrsize magnr iadr
   iadr←branchadr
```

     PROGRAM 6-49   Call and Return in the Intel 8080A.

6.4.2

Parameter Passing

A subroutine usually operates upon data furnished by the calling program, and usually furnishes it one or more results. These data and results are called *parameters*. The proper method for passing these parameters is an issue that programming language designers have widely debated. Shall copies of the actual values of parameters be passed, or shall the names (that is, the addresses) of parameters be passed? The choice affects speed; it also affects the results if the subroutine alters a parameter. For example, in the APL header

$$a \leftarrow b \ function \ c$$

b and c are passed by value; function cannot alter them. a also is passed by value only, and only outward to a's correspondent in the calling statement. Indeed, function cannot read a's previous value. Besides the *formal* variables b and c, function may also use *global* variables, whose scope is shared with the calling routine, say d and e. APL is unusually constrained in parameter passing; most other languages give more flexibility. (Most other languages also require explicit declaration of shared global variables, which is proper.)

    The APL example raises another issue—shall a fixed number of parameters be passed and returned? In most languages, the number of parameters is not fixed, although return of a single value is usually conveniently specified by substituting it for the function reference, as with the SIN function in the FORTRAN statement

$$Y = RADIUS * SIN(X)$$

    For clarity of program structure and simplicity of debugging and maintenance, explicit parameter-passing is better than using global variables, the "Direct" option in Tree 6-50.

    To accommodate the requirements of the various higher-level languages, parameter passing should allow the following four programming primitives:

- The parameter values are passed.
- The addresses of the parameters are passed.
- The address of a *parameter list* is passed.
- The values or names of the parameters are placed in the calling program itself, relative to the return address, which then is the only thing passed.

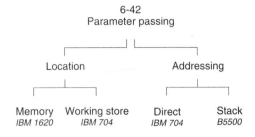

6-42
Parameter passing

TREE 6-50   Design choices for parameter passing.

As with the return address, the parameter passing should take into account relocation, reentrance, and recursion of the subroutine.

Passing via working store.   When the number of parameters to be passed is small and fixed, it is fast—but not general—to pass them in the working store.

Passing via stack.   A stack is ideal for managing the parameter passing in nested subroutines. The operands needed by the subroutine are conveniently left on the top of the stack, and the results are left there. Because a subroutine needs no temporary memory of its own beyond the stack, it may be used recursively—that is, in its execution it may transfer control to itself. This property greatly increases the generality and power of subroutine usage.

Multiple stacks.   In practice, two stacks are ideal—one for return addresses and one for parameter-passing. The Burroughs B6700 (1971), which allows for several stacks in a *cactus stack* arrangement, is probably the most sophisticated machine in its stack structure [Organick, 1973]. Perhaps the designers of the B6700 went too far in adding complex stack function, thus violating parsimony.

The use of stacks is convenient for well-nested subroutines, but it demands that they be well-nested. When tasks are switched in response to external interruptions, for example, they must not share a common subroutine control stack, for LIFO behavior cannot be guaranteed. So, many microprocessors that use a single stack for subroutine and interruption control demand unusual programmer precautions.

Few machines have made explicit provision for coroutine linkages; but these can be handled neatly in machines that provide stack mechanisms for

```
     JSR:dest
   ⋀ DEC PDP11 Call
   ⋀ fetch instruction address
     dest←word adr11 Dest
   ⋀ test address
     Invop report dest[Space]=regadr
     Spec report 1=2|dest[Value]
     →OUT suppress11
   ⋀ push linkage pointer onto stack
     push11 regout fld Source[R]
   ⋀ store instruction address
     (fld Source[R]) regin reg[Pc:]
   ⋀ new instruction address
     reg[Pc:]←word magnr dest[Value]
```

PROGRAM 6-51   Call in the DEC PDP11.

Routine #1 is operating, it then executes:

    MOV #PC,-(R6)
    JSR PC,@(R6)+

with the following results:

1) PC2 is popped from the stack
   and the SP autoincremented

2) SP is autodecremented and the
   old PC (i.e. PC1) is pushed

3) control is transferred to the
   location PC2 (i.e. routine #2)

Routine #2 is operating, it then executes:

    JSR PC ,@(R6)+

with the result the PC2 is exchanged
for PC1 on the stack and control is
transferred back to routine #1.

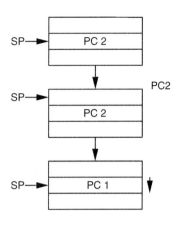

FIGURE 6-52   Coroutine linkage in the DEC PDP11 [Digital, 1971b, p. 146].

subroutine call. The PDP11 subroutine call can be used in this way, by using the stack and the Call operation of Program 6-51.

Figure 6-52 shows an example of coroutine linkage in the PDP11. The linkage handles control flow; parameters are passed by the stack, and state-saving is the responsibility of each coroutine.

6.4.3

State Preservation

One purpose of a subroutine is to hide from the user the details of a calculation and to present merely the results, just as a built-in machine operation does. So it is desirable for a subroutine to be free of *side effects*—changes to any part of the machine state other than the result parameters.

But the subroutine itself needs to use the working store, the Instruction Address, and other machine components in carrying out its task. So the caller or callee must save at least those parts of machine state that (a) the subroutine corrupts, and (b) the caller values.

Who shall do the saving? How much state shall be saved? Where?

Who saves?   In the simplest discipline, the caller saves all the machine state, before calling, in a memory area belonging to it. For several reasons, this solution is too simple for maximum effectiveness.

Subroutines and calling programs are regularly written by different persons. Therefore, the caller and callee should like to know as little as possible about each other. If the caller saves, it must assume that all state will be corrupted. If the subroutine saves, it must assume all state to be valuable. More state must be saved than the logically necessary minimum.

It is much easier to determine accurately the portion of machine state corrupted by a subroutine than to determine the part valuable to a caller. Moreover, the latter portion is apt to change—with disastrous consequences— when the calling program is modified. Good programming discipline therefore strongly argues for making saving and restoring a subroutine responsibility. Economy urges the same strategy, for there are usually many more calls than subroutines. The desire to treat interruption-entered subroutines like call-entered ones also favors this solution, for, in the interrupt case, only the called routine can do the required saving and restoring.

How much is saved?   For machines with only a few words of state, it is simplest to save all the state other than the memory. The LGP30, for example, has two words; the 704, about six. But for a machine with multiple accumulators, many index registers, and so forth, saving all is very wasteful. Few subroutines will need to use, and will corrupt, all those facilities. It may be better for the subroutine to save and restore only those parts of the caller's state that it needs to use, except when the machine incorporates a high-speed facility that saves all the state faster than it can save part.

Where is state saved?   If the subroutine saves state in its own space, it is no longer pure procedure and cannot be used reentrantly and recursively. Therefore the caller furnishes a *save area*—or *activation record*—of proper size, such as a stack, to a subroutine whenever it calls it, passing its address as a parameter. The subroutine saves and restores as need be, using this area.

Life is still more complex when security and privacy considerations require that neither caller nor callee trust the other or access the other one's data [Saltzer and Schroeder, 1975].

6.4.4

Meta-operation

The difficulty of defining a meta-operation for delegation is due to parameter passing. We consider two cases, each restricted in some way: the macroinstruction, which has only one result and only one or two operands, and the Execute, which has a scope of just one instruction.

Macroinstruction

The *macroinstruction* is a subroutine call that resembles a normal instruction. It indicates the location of the subroutine that is to perform its function, and passes to this subroutine the operands that are obtained as part of a normal operand fetch.

The Stretch instruction Load Transit And Set (Program 6-53) places the operand in a special Transit register, places a 7-bit pseudo-operation code in a working register, sets an indicator, and subsequently causes an interrupt. Interrupt handling should call the desired subroutine.

The subroutine call was indistinguishable from a regular instruction. In fact, decimal multiply and divide used the same mechanism (but not the same operation code) for a programmed implementation.

Another example of a macroinstruction is the extra code of the Ferranti Atlas (1962).

Address		Op	X1	M0	L0		Bs	Offset	Opcode		X2

```
0                              24  28  32 35    41 44       51        60  64
Legend: Bs = byte size; L = length; M = address mode; Op = opcode;
        X = index.
```

```
LTRS;operand
⋀ IBM Stretch Load Transit And Set
 operand←mem7030i(fld0 L0) read7030 adr7030m
 Transit write7030 trans7030r neg7030×operand
 memory[Leftzeros]←7 magnr 96
 memory[Allones]←inst[Offset]
 (Binarytransit.Decimaltransit)[fld Decimal] set7030 1
```

PROGRAM 6-53   Load Transit And Set in the IBM Stretch.

Execute

The Execute operation was first designed for the Stretch and copied in the IBM 709 (which was delivered before the Stretch, in 1959). It is now widely used. Consider the Execute of the 360 (Program 6-54). All primitives of the subroutine call are represented in the Execute, albeit in restricted form.

Call and Return.   The effective address is treated as the called address. The return address is implied to be that following the Execute. Since the subroutine is only one instruction long, the instruction-address register is not needed to sequence the subroutine, so it automatically holds the return address.

Parameter passing.   The calling program is allowed to pass 1 byte of explicit parameter—the low-order byte of the specified General Purpose Register. This is ORed with the second byte of the executed instruction, thus allowing modification of the part of an instruction not affected by indexing. Other parameters, especially addresses, are passed implicitly in the working store and in other parts of the machine state.

Opcode	R1	X1	B1	D1

```
0        8   12  16  20             32
Legend: B = base; D = displacement; R = register; X = index.
```

```
 EX;instinfo;modifier
⋀ IBM 360 Execute
⋀ preserve instruction information
 instinfo←psw[Ilc,Iadr]
 modifier←(0≠fld R1)∧reg[fld R1;Lowbyte]
⋀ fetch subject instruction
 psw[Iadr]←adrsize magnr adr360bxd
 inst←ifetch360
⋀ modify instruction
 inst[Imm]←inst[Imm]∨modifier
⋀ restore instruction information
 psw[Ilc,Iadr]←instinfo
⋀ test if subject instruction is Execute
 Execute report 68=fld Opcode
 →OUT suppress360
⋀ execute subject instruction
 execute inst
```

PROGRAM 6-54   Execute in the IBM System/360.

State-saving and restoration.   Program 6-54 shows that the instruction-length code is saved and restored. The instruction address is also preserved, but it is replaced by a successful branch in the subject instruction.

Recursion.   Execute is a meta-operation under whose control any other operation can be executed; it may therefore require some private hardware. If it does, Execute may not take another Execute instruction as its operand. In the 360, for example, such an attempt triggers an interruption.

Even if private hardware is not needed, problems arise because of the violation of the independent-instruction concept. For example, an Execute referring to itself causes an unending loop. The Stretch's solution is to place a time limit on the Execute execution. Another problem is the definition of the interrupt address when the target of an Execute generates an interruption.

Instruction modification.   An Execute operation can be used in a section of pure procedure to address a modifiable instruction within an activation record. This technique allows, but controls, the use of instruction modification in protected or even read-only memory; microcomputers and airborne computers often have most of their memory in this form to save cost and weight.

Interpretation.   A useful special case of the one-instruction subroutine technique occurs in interpretive routines where a machine is interpreting statements in its own language intermixed with pseudo-instructions. Some computers that have no built-in floating-point operations, for example, are used via an interpreter in which floating-point instructions are treated like subroutine calls. In such a case, the interpreter can use Execute to interpret machine-language instructions directly, without transplanting them into itself.

General interpretation does not work in the 360 because Execute uses a base register for addressing, rather than a private resource as a meta-operation should. Therefore, a target instruction cannot use the same base register—a violation of generality.

Program monitoring.   In program monitoring, including tracing, the object instruction of an Execute operation should be prevented from changing the instruction address that controls the monitoring routine.

In the Stretch, for example, there are two execute operations, designed so that one can be used for one-instruction subroutines and the other for program monitoring. They are called Execute and Execute Indirect And Count. Each causes a single instruction to be fetched from an addressed location and to be executed, except that execution may not change the Instruction Address. If the object instruction specifies a branch operation (which would cause such a change), branching is suppressed and the execute exception indicator is actuated, which may interrupt the (monitoring) program. Moreover, the object instruction is not allowed to change the state (enabled or disabled) of the interrupt system.

Execute Indirect And Count (Program 6-55) specifies an object-instruction address, which points to the object instruction. After the object instruction is performed, the object-instruction address is incremented according to the length of the object instruction. This last feature is particularly convenient in a computer that has instructions of different lengths; it uses equipment that the computer must have anyway.

```
EXIC;iloc;iadr
ᴀ IBM Stretch Execute Indirect And Count
iloc←word align7030 adr7030
iadr←half×magni(ρAdrhalf) read7030 iloc
ᴀ start time-out if exec=0
exec←1
Invadr report7030 iloc<16×word
→OUT suppress7030
execute ifetch7030
iloc write7030(ρAdrhalf) magnr iadr÷half
```

PROGRAM 6-55   Execute Indirect And Count in the IBM Stretch.

The main interpretive loop for performing a control trace in the Stretch reduces to Execute Indirect And Count, specifying the object-instruction address, followed by an absolute branch to the execute instruction. When a branch occurs in the object program, this loop is interrupted, and a suitable routine records the tracing data and changes the object-instruction address.

An obvious extension of the execute operations would be to have the Execute Indirect And Count operation change the object-instruction address automatically when the object instruction is a branch. One would still want an alarm to the supervisory program, however, so the Stretch does not have this function.

6.4.5
Bibliography

Buckle [1978], Digital Equipment Corporation [1971b], Katevenis [1983], Knuth [1968], Naur [1963], Organick [1973], Saltzer and Schroeder [1975], Wirth [1976], Witt [1966], Wolczko and Williams [1994].

6.5
Rules of Good Practice

1. Instructions should be syntactic entities, independent of their predecessor(s) or successor(s).
2. The establishment of a condition for branching should not be combined with the use of this condition in deciding on the branch target.
3. Forward and backward branching should be equally convenient.
4. An operation that can be used to implement the FOR structure should allow zero iterations.
5. All functions designed to implement control structures should allow nesting and recursion.
6. A Wait operation, rather than a machine stop, should be provided for the completion of a process.
7. Meta-operations that implement control structures should match the primitive exactly, should be generally usable, and should not restrict or alter the subject machine functions; nesting should be allowed.

6.6

Exercises

6-1 A conditional branch is specified by a condition test and a set of alternative actions. These two specifications may be contained together in one instruction, or may be separated into two instructions.

a. If certain instructions are prohibited from changing the condition codes, what additional advantage is there to separation? To what instructions would you apply this prohibition to maximize the advantage?

b. What additional problem of separation must the architect address if the machine is designed for multiprogramming? How is this problem solved in the 360?

6-2 In a branch instruction it is necessary to specify the branch address. Many machines use the same addressing mechanism to specify branch addresses and to specify operands for arithmetic instructions. Name three such machines.

6-3 The PDP11 provides some branch instructions that use the standard memory-addressing mechanism, and others that use a special addressing mechanism. Since the standard addressing mechanism is general enough to specify all possible branch addresses, why is a second, special mechanism provided? Give at least two reasons why the standard addressing mechanism is provided in addition to the special mechanism.

6-4 Consider an experimental computer whose entire instruction sequencing apparatus consists of a 1-bit condition register, CC, and three operations:

Unconditional Branch (address), (offset)

Conditional Branch (address), (offset)

Return

The Conditional Branch succeeds if CC=1; otherwise, it falls through. Upon any successful branch, the return address is the address of the branch plus the signed offset, which can have a value from -1, 0, 1, or 2.

Show how one can implement the following control structures:

a. IF THEN

b. IF THEN ELSE

c. WHILE

d. REPEAT UNTIL

e. DO FOREVER

f. CASE

6-5 Design a REPEAT instruction (operations and formats) for the 360 with a control scope of

a. One instruction

b. Two instructions

6-6 Design a parameter-passing mechanism using a stack for the 360.

6-7 Would you prefer conditional Wait over unconditional Wait? Why?

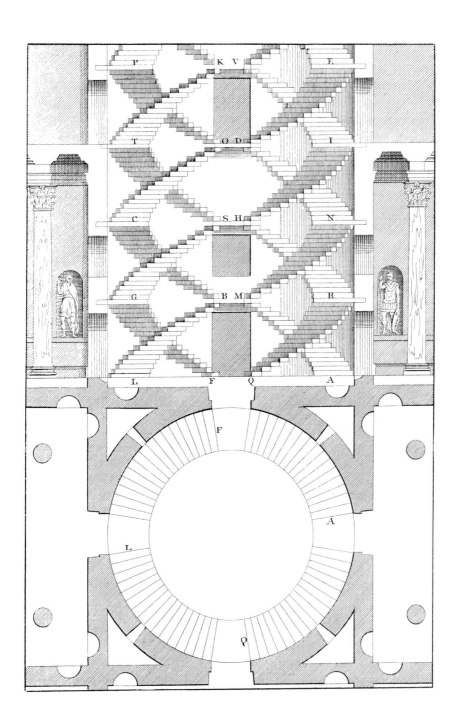

Supervision

Supervision is necessary for *efficiency* and *reliability*. Efficiency demands that the resources of the system—such as memory space, processor time, and peripheral devices—be used by a program no more and no longer than necessary. Reliability requires that the result of a program be correct in the presence of malfunction. The malfunction may be caused by the hardware, some other program, malicious or inadvertent human interference, or the program itself.

Since programs fail, something must control their behavior for the sake of other programs and for their own sake. This control function can be provided in part by the machine architecture and in part by a control program, the *supervisor* or *operating system*. The supervisor does this task and manages the system resources for efficiency.

It would be ideal if the supervisor were itself faultless; it customarily is not.

The design of a robust supervisor requires considerable skill. The machine architecture functions that allow a supervisor to exercise and retain control, although limited in number, must likewise be carefully designed.

The essential architectural requirement for the supervisor is the ability to seize control from a user program. Three corollaries follow: (1) the system must allow concurrency, if only in an elementary way; (2) the actions of the user program should be so limited that it cannot in any way seize control from the supervisor or spoil its integrity; (3) the state of the user program should be so preserved that the user program can be resumed unchanged. Tree 7-1 shows the design choices.

There are at least two programs within a typical computer system—the supervisor and a user program. Since there is commonly more than one user program in a machine simultaneously, the architecture of supervision should provide for a multiplicity of programs.

The two main types of multiplicity are multiprogramming and multiprocessing. In *multiprogramming*, one processor executes in succession parts of several programs. In *multiprocessing*, more than one processor executes several programs concurrently.

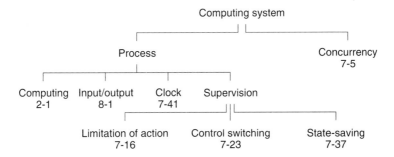

TREE 7-1   Design choices for a computing system.

Since the literature presents many kinds of concurrency, we start Section 7.1 with a classification. Next we review the many—often mixed—motives for concurrency. We conclude that, apart from extreme speed, the most common arguments again are efficiency and reliability, but that these do not necessarily lead to concurrency in each case. This analysis helps us to decide on suitable configurations for concurrency.

Since concurrency involves interaction through shared resources, architectural functions for signaling and interlocking are needed for proper synchronization, as discussed in Section 7.2.

Section 7.3 shows that the basic architectural requirement for preserving the integrity of a system is a limitation of the user functions. This limitation can be achieved by restricting the user operations, by restricting the access of the user to storage, or by doing both. These protection functions drastically improve the efficiency and reliability of a system.

Section 7.4 examines the functions of the machine architecture that enable the switching of control between the supervisor and the user program. The most demanding is the interruption system. This system turns out to be a rudimentary concurrent processor. The design of this processor requires an analysis of the functions that are necessary to manage the system resources and to respond to external and internal stimuli.

Section 7.5 considers the extent of program state and the means of preserving it during control switching.

Section 7.6 discusses supervisory tools such as clocks, the operator console, and initial program loading.

7.1

Concurrency

7.1.1

Perspective

The terms *concurrency, multiplicity,* and *parallelism* abound in computer literature, with a variety of definitions. One of our purposes in this chapter is to distinguish among them and give examples of each.

Concurrency in a system means that actions take place simultaneously; it is more easily achieved and more effectively practiced in the implementation than in the architecture. A good part of hardware implementation is inherently concurrent. Furthermore, refined implementation techniques of parallelism, overlap, pipelining, and lookaside are well-established.

Any laboratory can build an array of microprocessors. But it is much harder to give such an array a proper architecture, so that a programmer can readily invoke the functions proper to his problem. Indeed, good architectural concurrency is achieved much less dramatically and far less often than implementation concurrency.

A computer *system* is a communicating collection of equipment including at least one processor.

Communication is a prerequisite for a system. Two computers, half a world apart, communicating via a satellite, form a system. Our definition pragmatically excludes communication that requires human assistance. Two computers in the same room that communicate via an operator-carried diskette do not constitute a system.

A *processor* is an instruction sequencer and interpreter. It can be recognized by the presence of an Instruction Address. The sequence of instructions that the processor executes is an *instruction stream* [Flynn, 1966]. So not only a CDC 6600 PPU (1964), but even a VAX DMA (channel) is a processor.

Systems that include several processors are called *multiprocessors*. Since I/O channels are in fact processors, the class of multiprocessors turns out to be larger than one would expect.

Multiprocessors proceed *synchronously* when they maintain a fixed, step-by-step relationship. The Harvard Mark II (1947), for example, is such a system; it has two processors driven by a single clock. Each of several synchronous processes can safely depend on the progress of the others.

Otherwise, multiprocessors are called *asynchronous*. One such process typically knows the time any other starts, but not when the other completes or reaches any intermediate milestones.

Architectural concurrency.   A system has *architectural concurrency* when the events within that system that can be observed externally appear to proceed simultaneously and under separate controls.

Architectural concurrency is visible to the user and should match the logical independencies of parts of his computing task. The most familiar example is the concurrency of a CPU and an I/O processor.

Implementation concurrency.   A system has *implementation concurrency* when the events within that system actually proceed simultaneously. In contrast to architectural concurrency, implementation concurrency is invisible to the user.

Implementation concurrency arises from independencies in the definition of the computer architecture. A 32-bit fixed-point load instruction, for example, inherently allows the implementation complete freedom to fetch 1, 2, 4, ..., 128, or some other number of bits at a time; it also allows the implementation to process this instruction concurrently with preceding and following instructions in a pipelined fashion.

Relation of architecture and implementation.   There need not be a one-to-one correspondence between architectural function and implementation facilities.

A multiprocessor architecture may quite feasibly be implemented by a single processor. The 10 peripheral processing units of the CDC 6600 (1964), for example, are really virtual machines whose arithmetic functions are implemented by a common processor. In the sharing of equipment by the central processor and I/O processors, as in the IBM System/360 Model 30 multiplexor subchannels, the channels are architecturally a set of processors within a multiprocessor.

Conversely, a single processor architecture may be implemented by several concurrent processors. An example is the 6600, which incorporates one logical unit, one integer-add unit, one floating-add unit, two multiply units, one divide unit, two increment units, one shift unit, and one branch unit. All these units can operate concurrently, even though the machine language invokes them sequentially.

Simultaneity.   To say that events are *simultaneous* is to use a term whose precise definition gives trouble to physicists and philosophers. People say of a multiprogrammed computer system that programs of many users are proceeding "simultaneously" at the terminals, although the CPU is executing only one at a time. What is simultaneous on the macroscopic system scale is sequential and time sliced on the microscopic machine language scale. A sequentially programmed implementation is used for the concurrent system architecture.

People also say that, during a single program's time slice, the CPU and the I/O channels proceed "simultaneously," whereas, from the point of view of the memory bus of the machine implementation, the requests may be handled in a strictly sequential fashion.

Similarly, in a parallel implementation there is one wire per bit to be processed, and all are processed "simultaneously." A closer look reveals that a parallel addition may be implemented with some form of serial carry propagation.

The whole matter of simultaneity is rather like grayness in an engraving. When one looks closely, he sees a fine structure of black and white lines. Because computer systems have a vertical stratification where each architecture is implemented with the architecture of a lower level, concurrency is recursive—the black and white lines themselves often have a yet finer structure.

	Purpose	Appearance
Architecture	orthogonality propriety	multiple processes
Implementation	super speed efficiency availability	one process

TABLE 7-2   Architectural and implementation of concurrency.

7.1.2

Motivation

Why do things concurrently? Well, why do things sequentially? Concurrent solution, not sequential solution, is proper to many applications. Much of the sequential ordering in our use of computers is the result of implementation decisions, rather than of sequential constraints inherent in the applications.

Inherent Concurrency

A chef cooks many dishes concurrently in order to serve them at the same time, all hot. Many computing applications have a similar structure—the task itself involves subtasks that must proceed concurrently.

Consider the control of an industrial process, an airplane, a battle, or an orbiting astronomical observatory. In each of these cases, the subtasks are synchronized to the external timing of chemical or mechanical processes. In an airplane, for example, the altitude, velocity, and engine power must each be separately sensed and controlled, all at once. A computer system serving many on-line terminals has this very characteristic.

Human beings, however, have a single stream of consciousness: They think about things sequentially (even though they have concurrent alarm processors that can interrupt). Therefore, a system that interacts with a real-time environment is normally structured into a limited number of sequential processes. Each interacts with part of the environment.

Simulated concurrency. The classical computer configuration has concurrent I/O processes interacting with the environment, and one central processor that handles all other data processing. The central processor's single instruction stream is improper, since it does not match the several concurrent tasks to be processed. This mismatch is undetectable on the outside of the system because the outside communicates with the concurrent I/O processors.

Internally this mismatch is acceptable—any application that can be accomplished by multiple concurrent processors can, in principle, be met by a single processor, if it is sufficiently fast. Processors are digital and operate with discrete actions. They necessarily sample and change the processes they control at discrete intervals. Because of this discretization, the time-sliced attention of a single system has the same effect as multiple processors, so long as the system maintains the necessary sampling rates for all the sensors and controllers.

In short, inherent concurrency in an application always allows, but never demands, full concurrency in the system designed to perform that application.

Range of solutions. A demand that inherently calls for many things to be done "at the same time" can be handled in many ways. At one extreme, each person or process is furnished with a private computer, such as a personal computer. Then each independent task is pursued concurrently, though slowly. At the other extreme, a single, completely sequential fast computer undertakes all jobs, serving a queue of users who wait for attention if necessary, but whose work is finished quickly once it has begun. For every

proposed set of processes, one can propose a range of configurations bounded by these two extremes.

Because concurrent subprocesses are easily simulated on a single central processor, the decision to provide multiple central processors in the architecture is dominated by the implementation questions: What is fast? What is efficient? What is reliable?

Multiprocessing for Speed at Any Price

For some applications, absolute performance is all-important. If one wants to intercept a missile, for example, speed is everything; cost is secondary. If the required speed is above that achievable by a sequential organization in available technology, the only alternative is concurrent organization.

Cost of communication.   The joint performance of concurrent processors is always lower than the sum of the performances of these processors when operating independently. The communication that makes these processors operate as a multiprocessing system decreases the total system performance because of physically longer path lengths, synchronization delays, and contention for shared resources.

Concurrency brings an additional user overhead as well. To achieve the speed potential of concurrency the computing task must be carefully divided into parts that can be performed concurrently.

Single processor competitive.   A multiprocessor motivated by speed must still compete with a single system using a pipelined implementation, perhaps with multiple arithmetic-and-logical units.   In such a system, the implementation dynamically selects strings of instructions that can be performed simultaneously. Concurrency is sought within one program segment, rather than among several program segments as in the multiprocessor. Because of the greater integration of design and the absence of programmed interlocks, a pipelined processor is often more efficient than a multiprocessor of equal weight.

Multiprocessing for Efficiency

Proper use of concurrency can give a system a better cost/performance ratio. How does such an improvement come about? Several methods have been proposed [Blaauw, 1964].

The idle resource.   The saying goes, "You can't get something for nothing." A more precise statement is, "You can get something for nothing only if you have previously gotten nothing for something"—that is, if you have bought capacity that is idle.

Adding concurrency to compensate for speed mismatches or idleness due to specialization is a design exercise that can be repeated on many levels. It is a major reason why economies of scale can be achieved in computing systems.

When a CPU cannot fully use its memory bandwidth, one might, for example, augment the system.   The provision of this extra logic yields performance corresponding to that added component and may yield more,

since memory cycles otherwise idle can now contribute; the system efficiency is improved.

Likewise, a fast CPU may often wait for a slow disk. This speed mismatch can be partially offset by adding other disks. The throughput improvement can be more than proportional to the added cost, since otherwise-idle CPU power is harnessed.

Volume manufacturing. The combined volume of the component processors may make them cheaper than component count would suggest. So several small units with better total performance than one large unit may be heavier but cheaper.

The Carnegie–Mellon C.mmp, for example, is designed to give an attractive cost/performance ratio on this logic. It consists of 16 DEC PDP11s (1970). Although it is hard to identify comparable costs (the engineering costs of the C.mmp are not accounted for), the C.mmp supposedly outperforms a more expensive uniprocessing DEC PDP10 (1968) [Fuller, 1976]. Since many of the PDP11s are idle at any given time, such a claim would seem inconceivable except for the volume-manufacturing advantage of the entire PDP11 assembly. With modern microprocessors as elements, the potential effect is even greater.

Geographic distribution. When data are collected and distributed over geographically separate locations, local processors may so reduce the volume of data transmission that they more than pay for their extra cost. With processing costs decreasing more rapidly than transmission costs, this advantage is becoming more pronounced.

Since most data are used where they are generated, local processors can a priori be expected to be efficient. But when the application inherently demands a common database, as does airline-reservation processing, decentralization may or may not pay, depending on the transmission costs that can be saved.

Incidental motives. Geographic distribution often springs from non-technical considerations, such as autonomous control at the local installation. Or an enterprise may elect to augment an owned machine into a multiprocessing system rather than selling it and buying a bigger uniprocessor.

Component pooling. In principle, the cost/performance ratio may be improved by pooling memory, storage, and peripheral equipment among several CPUs whose tasks may be mostly independent. Pooling is even more attractive when not only storage, but also stored information, can be shared—for example, systems programs on a shared disk.

Multiprocessing installations based solely on equipment pooling are rare, since the cost of equipment interconnection usually matches the savings in equipment. The introduction of switching into what otherwise would be a simple connection always involves some cost and performance penalty. The gating, selection, priority determination, and powering not only involve additional equipment, but also cause additional access time. Furthermore, the concurrent use of one resource by several processors results in delays, called *interference*, when one processor cannot access the resource because another processor is using it.

Memory bottleneck. Main memory is the most critical resource to be shared. The speed with which the total bit traffic of an application can be handled is determined, to a major degree, by the time required for memory access. Adding more processors does not help once memory access is saturated.

It would be nice if memory access were so fast that it could naturally satisfy several processors. The realization technology of memory, however, is silicon, like that of processors. For such a technology, the implementation can nicely match the access offered by a memory system with the memory access required by one or two processors and their I/O processors. But sharing that access with more processors only lowers the processors' effective performance. A faster technology does no good: The processor–memory balance is determined by the implementation, not by the realization. This phenomenon is sometimes incorrectly called the *von Neumann bottleneck*.

Functional specialization.   The several processors in a multiprocessing configuration may each be specialized for a distinct part of the common task, thereby effecting economies. The I/O channel is a prime example. When something must wait substantial intervals for some external activity, such as I/O, it is usually cheaper to build a small, slow processor to do the I/O (and the waiting), while most of the system continues its activity as another processor.

Specialization has also been explored for the main processors, leading to division of labor among them. The so-called *front-end/back-end* configurations or *attached server processors* (ASPs) allocate pure computing to the back-end processor and editing and communications functions to the front-end unit.

A single CPU must be able to perform a variety of tasks, but may not be equally adept at each. In particular, speedup by parallel implementation is less fruitful in character-oriented operations than in word-oriented floating-point operations. In compiling or editing, the processing speed of a highly parallel CPU may be only a little greater than that of a narrower CPU. A functional division of work among the CPUs may therefore result in an improved cost/performance ratio, even after the overhead involved.

Multiprocessing for Availability

From the very beginning, computer system designers have taken one of two approaches. Some, led originally by von Neumann (Institute for Advanced Study), have assumed that a collection of hardware will work as specified. Malfunctions are unfortunate exceptions that programmers must detect, avoid, or correct. Others, led originally by Aiken (Harvard) and Stibitz (Bell Labs), have assumed that any collection of hardware will fail, and that designs must provide for the detection and correction of the effects of malfunctions.

Computer families such as those of the IBM 704 (1955), the Univac 1103A (1956), and the 6600, reflect the "will work" assumption. Computer families such as the Univac I (1951), the IBM 650 (1954), the IBM 705 (1956), the IBM System/360 (1965), reflect the "will fail" assumption (Table 7-3).

Early military systems, such as the SAGE air-defense system (ca. 1958) led the way in the provision of redundancy to provide fail-safe systems.

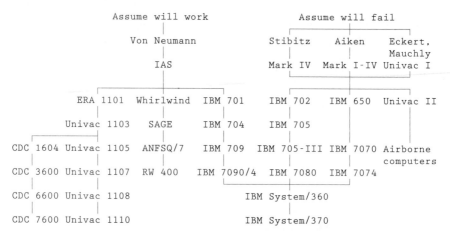

TABLE 7-3   Reliability in several computer families.

Milestones include the IBM Stretch (1961), which introduced built-in error correction in memory, as well as error correction in disks and tapes; and airborne computers, which introduced triple-modular redundancy as an error-correction technique around 1962.

Ramo and Wooldridge introduced the dynamically reconfigurable computer in their RW-400 [Porter, 1960]. These ideas and those from SAGE and the Burroughs D825 (1960) led Mitre Corporation to fail-soft and fail-safe concepts, incorporated into the 360-based special systems for the FAA.

Reconfiguration time.   The system components that communicate in the performance of a given task are said to form a *configuration*. *Reconfiguration* is the reconnection of system components so as to cut failing components out of the system and perhaps to replace them with spares.

The time required to reconfigure when a malfunction occurs is a critical systems parameter. *Reconfiguration time* includes the time required for fault detection, fault location, partitioning of the system into working configuration and non-working parts, and program restart.

Reconfiguration time is critical only with respect to the time allowed for completing a task. When the application allows enough time, reconfiguration may be entirely manual, and multiprocessing is unnecessary. In a payroll application, for example, reconfiguration is often achieved by carrying the whole job from one system to another. When time constraints allow, such use of multiple independent systems is superior to multiprocessing, because multiple independent systems have greater overall reliability.

Independent systems are more reliable for the same reason that they are lower in cost and higher in speed: they have less circuitry.

More and more applications, however, require reconfiguration times of a few minutes, seconds, or fractions of seconds. For these, a multiprocessor must be able to reconfigure itself without manual intervention.

Fail safe.   A *fail-safe* system can perform its prescribed task even when any major system component fails. Each system component must have a potential replacement that is redundant. Also, each component must be isolated so that its failure does not affect other components.

The simplest fail-safe system is the dual symmetric or *standby* system, such as the Harvard Mark II (1947) and SAGE. Here the entire system required for the full workload is duplicated, so the total system has 50 percent total redundancy. The two subsystems communicate at several points, and reconfiguration time can be on the order of a few instruction execution times. Processing proceeds in duplicate and in parallel, with internal checks for each subsystem. The reconfiguration task can be minimal; hardware can implement it.

Fail soft.   In a *fail-soft* system, the workload is partitioned into *essential* and *deferrable* tasks. When a malfunction occurs, the system performs only its essential tasks .

Fail-soft design provides two advantages. First, only the processing power for the essential workload needs duplication. Second, in the absence of malfunction, the duplicated processing power can perform the deferrable workload. This workload can include diagnostic programs to detect, at an early and convenient time, actual or potential equipment malfunction. As a result, efficiency and availability improve.

A typical fail-soft configuration consists of two equal or unequal CPUs with a complement of storage and I/O equipment. The smaller CPU must be able to perform the essential tasks, whereas the processing power of both CPUs must be able to perform the overall workload, including any work previously deferred.

Multiplicity.   Instead of using two computers each of power p to do a p-sized workload fail-safely, one can use more smaller computers and reduce redundancy below 50 percent. Three computers, each of power $p/2$, would yield 33 percent redundancy. At first glance, it appears that, the more computers in a system, the lower the cost. This oversimplified conclusion ignores the multiprocessing and multiprocessing overheads. So the number of CPUs within a multiprocessing system designed for availability may be expected to be small. As a typical example, assume a normal workload requiring two computers and an essential workload requiring one. Then a three-computer system could provide fail-safe operation for the entire workload, and, upon the occurrence of double malfunction, fail-soft operation for the essential workload.

Modularity.   A system is said to be *modular* with respect to some components if such components can be included or excluded individually, with the system always able to use those that are included. Most systems are therefore modular with respect to disk drives and printers.

Although system components may be *logically* independent, they may still be *physically* dependent, because they share common implementation or realization—for example, a common frame and common power supplies; physical as well as logical independence is required for improved system availability.

Increased modularity is not the only, or necessarily the best, way to increase availability. The savings in equipment of an integrated design can increase the reliability and, in turn, the availability of the overall system. This increase in system availability through component reduction may outstrip

the increase in availability that physically independent modules would have provided.

We have ourselves seen one dramatic instance in which a buyer's specifications overprescribed *how* availability was to be achieved, rather than *what level* of availability was desired. The modularity required by his specification in fact yielded a system with lower availability, due to the numerous interconnection components, than a more integrated system of equal power would have provided. Of course, cost, power, cooling, and maintenance were also larger for the modular system. (In the event, doctrine triumphed over sense; the customer got the modular system on which he insisted.)

7.1.3

Configuration

The desire to put order into the bewildering profusion of concurrent systems—actual or just on paper—has led to several proposals for classification [Flynn, 1966; Händler, 1975; Enslow, 1974; Delesalle, 1981].

Flynn Notation

Flynn uses four letters in his notation. The second letter is always I for instruction stream, and the fourth is always D for data stream; the first and third letter are each either S for single or M for multiple (Table 7-4).

Instruction stream	Data stream	
	Single	Multiple
Single	SISD	SIMD
Multiple	MISD	MIMD

TABLE 7-4   Flynn notation.

SISD. A processor with a single instruction stream and a single data stream (e.g., the 704) is called *SISD* and represents the conventional processor. Machines that have major implementation concurrency, such as the Stretch (1961) and the Cray 1 (1976), are called *confluent* SISD machines.

SIMD. A processor with a single instruction stream and multiple data streams (e.g., the Illiac IV of 1972) is called *SIMD*. This class refers to a uniprocessor that can handle larger datatypes, usually arrays, treating each element the same. From our perspective, SIMD merely deals with larger data structures, which are not the subject of this chapter.

MISD. The class *MISD* represents multiple instruction streams applied to a single data stream. Flynn uses the plugboard tabulating machine as an example. He states that this category has received little attention. The reason, we believe, is that this organization in its strict sense is not practical.

MIMD. The last class, *MIMD*, refers to a system with multiple instruction streams, each with its own data stream. From our perspective the MIMD is the multiprocessor and applies to all machines of this section.

Design Choices

Tree 7-5 shows our classification of concurrency.

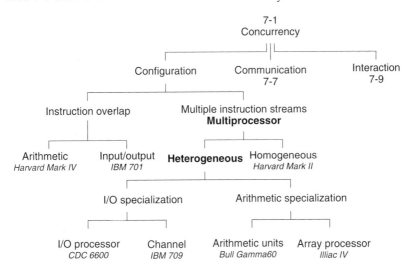

TREE 7-5   Design choices for concurrency.

Instruction overlap.   The first architectural alternative is between concurrent execution of single instructions and multiple instruction streams. The first case is called *instruction overlap*; it involves only one instruction stream.

Pipelining.   Many computers, beginning with the IBM Stretch, have had multiple successive instructions in different stages of execution at once. This technique is called *pipelining*.   When it is well-done, it is entirely in the implementation and is not visible in the architecture.

Arithmetic overlap.   Many machines have achieved speedup by incorporating, in the implementation, multiple operation units, specialized for the several arithmetic operations, and operating concurrently.   The Harvard Mark IV (1952) is a rare example where this multiplicity is exhibited as synchronous concurrency in the architecture.

The Mark IV incorporates two accumulators, a multiplier, and a divider. Multiply takes seven instruction times; divide, 21; so the user can have multiplication, division, and addition proceeding concurrently (Figure 7-6).

Architecturally visible arithmetic overlap is not attractive. It is a concession to the implementation and imposes an improper burden on the user; for a compiler it is an unbidden complication. When the concurrency in the implementation is hidden from the architecture, one can achieve an equivalent gain in efficiency and preserve freedom in the implementation. The 6600 is a good example; its implementation is highly concurrent, yet its architecture is compatible with the CDC 6400 (1966), which has no arithmetic concurrency.

The synchronous approach may incorporate some tolerance. If the Store is given too early, the machine waits for the division to complete.   So the user can ignore the precise timing and treat the synchronous concurrency as though it were asynchronous.

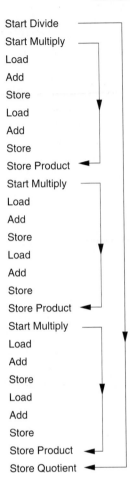

FIGURE 7-6   Example of Harvard Mark IV overlap.

Input/output overlap.   Many early machines overlapped a single I/O operation with CPU operation. This asynchronous concurrency is still normal procedure for microprocessors. The evolution of I/O systems is traced in Chapter 8.

Multiprocessor.   The alternative to concurrent single operations is concurrent instruction streams in the multiprocessor. This class is a much more proper architectural concept; it constitutes the major branch in our design tree.

The first distinction is between homogeneous and heterogeneous multiprocessors.

Homogeneous multiprocessor.   In a *homogeneous multiprocessor* configuration, all processors are architecturally alike. Each processor has all necessary functions; yet, each one's role in the system may differ.

The interaction of multiple processors implies the ability to initiate, synchronize, or terminate one process by another. This ability in turn implies some sort of supervisory program. In earlier systems, even when the processors were alike in nature, they were different in role: one executed the

supervisory program governing the others. The Burroughs D825 (1960) seems to have been the first multiprocessor system to adopt the philosophy that supervision is allotted to a program, not to a machine, and that the supervisory task, like all others, runs on whatever processor next comes to service the single queue of pending tasks [J.P. Anderson et al., 1962].

Heterogeneous multiprocessor.   A multiprocessor whose processors are differently specialized in function is called a *heterogeneous multiprocessor*. The chief subclass consists of systems that are specialized for the I/O function.

Input/output specialization.   An I/O processor may be specialized so that it can do only I/O, as is a 360–370 channel or a DEC Direct Memory Access (DMA) unit. Otherwise, the I/O processor may have general purpose function, as does a 6600 PPU.

Inclusive processing specialization.   The typical representative of inclusive processing specialization is a classical processor with an attachment capable of processing higher datatypes directly. A 360 Model 65 with a 2938 Array Processor attachment has inclusive processor specialization. (The Model 65 could have done the array processing with subroutines; it commonly does so.) It also has exclusive I/O specialization—the Model 60 main processor cannot possibly do normal I/O without the channels, nor can the channels do arithmetic.

The Illiac IV also falls into this class. It has one specialized matrix processor (instead of 64), one general purpose processor (a Burroughs 6700), and a complement of I/O channels.

Exclusive processing specialization.   The Bull Gamma 60 (1959) is the main, and probably the only, commercially offered representative of exclusive processing specialization. The Gamma 60 encountered all the problems of controlling concurrent processes that use multiple processors, and solved them elegantly.

The Gamma 60 has an arithmetic processor, a logic processor, a comparison processor, and several I/O processors, all capable of functioning concurrently, each with its own instruction stream. They are exclusive processors: The arithmetic processor can neither perform logic nor compare [Dreyfus, 1959b].

The Gamma 60 proves very hard to program. The instruction sequences that each processor can handle are just not natural in a computation. Arithmetic is usually intermixed with logic; they are not a separate activity. As a consequence the programs constantly switch from processor to processor, which reduces the system performance to that of a single processor without concurrency.

The Gamma 60 teaches two lessons. First, a processor operating concurrently should be capable of handling a sequence of instructions that is a unit from the user's point of view, not just from the implementation's point of view. An I/O operation, a matrix inversion, and a syntax analysis are such units. Each can be considered a process and can therefore be dedicated to a separate processor.

Second, the architect should not outguess the implementer. The thought behind the Gamma 60 was that, while an arithmetic operation was in progress, the logic unit and the compare unit should be exploited. Those resources,

however, are not idle at all, since most processors use the arithmetic circuits to do logic and comparison. If those resources are idle, as is the case in the Gamma 60 design, the cost of using them as concurrent processors is disproportionate to the benefit gained.

Fine granularity. Exclusive processing specialization, in particular when each processor is capable of only one, of a few operations (as in early dataflow proposals [Dennis and Misunas, 1974]), is called a multiprocessor with *fine granularity*, as opposed to *coarse granularity* of full processing ability. The main problem that fine granularity must overcome is the increased bit-traffic that its specialization involves.

Basic configurations. Tree 7-5 shows that there are only two basic configurations for architectural concurrency: instruction overlap and multiprocessing. This parsimony has two causes:

- Multiprocessing includes some extreme cases. Most notably, the instruction set of a processor can be so specialized that it performs only one operation. In that case, no instruction stream is needed; only the data must be offered.
- The interconnection of processors to form a concurrent system still forms a separate class of design choices (Section 7.1.4).

7.1.4

Communication

We now consider the communication of the system components in a multiprocessor. Tree 7-7 shows the main design choices. The design of a computer network and its taxonomy, however, are beyond the scope of this book. A detailed treatment of that subject may be found in the work of Anderson and Jensen [G.A. Anderson and Jensen, 1975].

Basic communication alternatives. The processors within a multiprocessor system may communicate in two basic ways: either directly by transmitting information via a connecting link, or indirectly by placing this information in a shared storage medium. Several elements may occur in the path from a processor to the interconnection or to the shared medium.

Figure 7-8 gives a simplified diagram of the arrangement of a processor, a memory, an I/O processor, a control unit, and an I/O device. The diagram indicates several possible connections between processors.

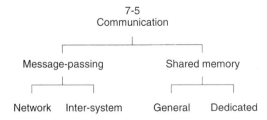

TREE 7-7   Design choices for multiprocessor communication.

Transmission

Networks and carrier lines.   Most systems allow for transmission of information over the communication lines of a local or public network (see A in Figure 7-8). The simplest way to connect two processors is to use the extant apparatus, software, and protocols. The rate of communication is determined primarily by line capacity. Although this method is simple, the line capacity limitations are severe. So this technique is used chiefly for processors that are geographically separated.

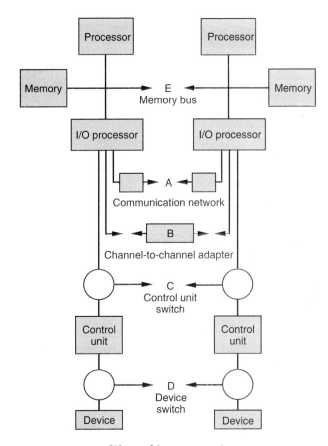

FIGURE 7-8   Ways of interconnecting computers.

Direct channel-to-channel transmission.   More direct, more rapid, and more difficult is transmission directly from the I/O processor of one machine to that of another. Usually some adapter is required to make an I/O processor appear to be a device to the other I/O processor (see B in Figure 7-8).

The main application of this type of interconnection is in a multiprocessing system emphasizing medium reconfiguration time or equipment specialization.

Shared Storage

When two or more processors have access to a common storage medium, one processor can read information placed in that medium by another processor. In contrast to transmission, sending and receiving need not be synchronized, and there need not be a one-to-one relation between recording and retrieving. Which storage medium to share is determined by access time, transmission rate, capacity, and cost per bit.

Shared peripheral devices.   Shared devices are useful for restart information, which allows recovery upon reconfiguration.

Disks may be pooled for residence of programming systems. Disks are also useful as a means of communication between specialized CPUs to achieve improved turn-around time. Thus, a control unit may be switched from the I/O processor of one system to that of another (see C in Figure 7-8).

D in Figure 7-8 shows the sharing of devices, such as tape drives, by their being attached to two control units, rather than by sharing the control units between I/O processors. This choice makes the control unit part of the architecture. Solution C is preferable because the control unit can be invisible to the user.

Shared memory.   The sharing of memory is shown by E in Figure 7-8. Such configurations are called *closely coupled*; all previous interconnections are called *loosely coupled*.

Configurations can share all their memory, or they can combine shared memory with private memory. Where one program is executed in turn by different processors, it is desirable that the locations of instructions and associated data have the same address for every processor.

The most critical application of shared memory is in a multiprocessing system requiring very short reconfiguration time. Shared memory is also used in multiprocessor systems designed just for speed, where one problem is partitioned and parts executed on several processors concurrently. Typically, two to 16 CPUs are connected to the memory system.

7.1.5
Bibliography

G.A. Anderson and Jensen [1975], J.P. Anderson et al. [1962], Arvind and Iannucci [1983], Astrahan et al. [1956], Baer [1976], Blaauw [1964], Delesalle [1981], Dennis and Misunas [1974], Dreyfus [1959b], Enslow [1974], Flynn [1966, 1972a, 1972b, 1974, 1995], Fuller [1976], Gill [1958], Händler [1975], Hord [1982], Keedy [1979], Nicolau and Fisher [1984], Porter [1960], Smith [1978], Tjaden and Flynn [1970].

7.2
Interaction

The interaction of multiple processes requires that they be able to signal each other in order to synchronize their activities when necessary. It also requires that the processes be interlocked so that they do not read and modify variables in an interlaced fashion (Tree 7-9).

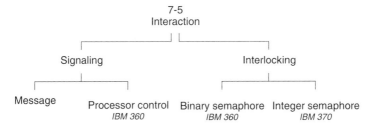

TREE 7-9   Design choices for interaction.

7.2.1

Signaling

The synchronization of processes can occur on the message or on the processor level. On the *message level*, processors exchange messages that may cause one process to wait for other processes. On the *processor level*, a processor is assigned to a process by another processor and terminates either of its own accord or by initiative of another processor. Processor signaling includes the signaling between a process and the processor that executes it, for identification and relocation purposes.

Message Signaling

Before one processor sends information to another, it must alert the receiving processor. Once alerted, the recipient can allocate the proper memory area and signal the sender that it is ready to transfer the incoming data under control of a Read command. The transmitting processor then transfers data under control of a Write command.

Attention signal.   The signal of one processor to another is called an *attention signal*; it can be the same as that sent by a device that requires attention. When transmission is complete, both receiving and transmitting processors can be interrupted.

Message alert.   For communication through a common storage facility, the receiving processor must be alerted that another processor has stored a message for it. This alerting can be programmed, of course, by polling a signal bit.

Processor Signaling

Traditionally, individual physical processors show in the architecture; the allocation of processors to them is done by the supervisor. One might propose making the physical processors invisible to the machine architecture, by presenting the supervisor with a large number of virtual processors and mapping the virtual processors onto the physical ones. But this approach is unattractive because the scheduling of processes and their memory allocation is complex, and the allocation algorithms are subject to change. Moreover, the occurrence

	Means of signaling	Types of signals	Memory interlock
Bull Gamma 60	direct	chain	integer
IBM Stretch	interrupt	general	
CDC 6600 PPU	direct	exchange jump	
Burroughs B5500	interrupt	general	
IBM System/360	instruction	byte	binary
IBM System/370			integer

TABLE 7-10   Interaction in various machines.

of the scheduling action is infrequent, so a hardware implementation can produce no major performance gains.

Dispatching.   Dispatching should be distinguished from initialization. *Initialization* is the preparation of data, procedures, and control information so that a process can start execution. *Dispatching* is the assignment of a processor to an initialized process. A supervisor can initialize as many processes as are ready, but it can dispatch only as many processes as there are processors.

One processor can dispatch a task on another when the proper signals are defined. The Start Input/Output operation in the 360 is an example. The main processor sends a signal that causes the I/O channel to start its execution.

In a loosely coupled multiprocessing system, one must both reinitialize the memory of a processor, after it has been down for repair, and dispatch the processor. For this reason, one processor should have means for initiating the initial program loading of another processor. In a multiprocessor with shared memory, only the processor need be dispatched—for example, by loading its Program Status Word (PSW).

Termination.   One process must be able to terminate another process, if only because malfunction may have confused it. For main processors an interruption can serve as a termination signal.

Malfunction alerting.   The properly operating part of the system must be alerted when an undesired event occurs in another part of the system. The undesired event may be caused by a program or by the hardware. Program mistakes, as such, do not require multiprocessing, but only a supervisory program.

Although an interruption and a programmed restart may make it possible for the processor to recover from an intermittent malfunction, another must take over when the malfunction is solid. The 360 provides a hardware-generated malfunction signal that can be used to interrupt another processor.

Identification

A process does not necessarily, or easily, know the processor to which it is assigned. Yet this knowledge is desirable, if only in case of machine malfunction.

Processor identification.   The IBM System/370 (1971) assigns each main processor a unique permanent number at the time of manufacture. The

number is passed on to other processors as part of a malfunction alert or other processor-to-processor signaling. If a program wants to know the number of its current host, it issues the privileged operation Store CPU Address.

Preferred storage.   Processor-specific spaces—such as interrupt vector locations—that are embedded in memory address space, will fall on top of the spaces of other processors in a multiprocessor unless special provisions are made. The 360 solves this by giving each processor in a system a distinct prefix that is attached to all addresses smaller than 4096, covering the area where spaces are embedded (Program 7-11).

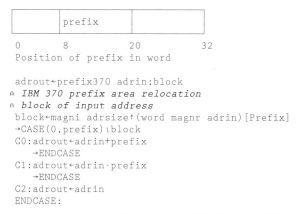

```
adrout←prefix370 adrin;block
 ∩ IBM 370 prefix area relocation
 ∩ block of input address
   block←magni adrsize↑(word magnr adrin)[Prefix]
   →CASE(0.prefix)ιblock
   C0:adrout←adrin+prefix
      →ENDCASE
   C1:adrout←adrin-prefix
      →ENDCASE
   C2:adrout←adrin
   ENDCASE:
```

PROGRAM 7-11   Prefix in the IBM System/370.

7.2.2

Interlocking

When any storage medium is shared among two or more processes with write authority, interlocks must be provided to prevent logic errors. Suppose, for example, that each of two processes is incrementing a shared event counter. One reads the counter, increments it, and writes it. Meanwhile, the other reads the original value, increments it, and then writes it. One of the two updates is lost.

Critical Section

The interlocking problem, when it occurs in memories, is called the *critical-section* problem; when in disk stores, the *record-out* problem. The term *critical section* derives from the necessity of executing several instructions as a block, without interruption in one processor nor meddling in the relevant memory by another.

Atomic actions.   In a multiprogrammed uniprocessor each instruction execution is usually an indivisible action, called *atomic*. Following each instruction, but only then, an interrupt may occur, and the processor may switch to another process. Macroscopically the various processes appear concurrent, but microscopically the instructions are executed sequentially.

In a tightly coupled multiprocessor, an instruction is no longer an indivisible action. Access to memory is usually granted for the duration of one memory cycle, not for that of an entire instruction. Also, an instruction that places a byte from a register into memory may in some implementations read one or more words, replace the byte in that set of words, and store these words as an entity. So even the neighborhood of a result may be altered.

Programmed Interlock

In a multiprogrammed uniprocessor, or its equivalent, the critical-section problem can be solved by disabling the interruption system upon entering the section and re-enabling it upon exiting the section. The sections should be kept small enough so that the interrupt latency is acceptable. The usual approach is to make the entrances and exits of interacting procedures each a critical section. The remainder of these procedures can then be normal, since the critical section sees to it that only one process can enter at a time.

For a multiprocessor the disabling strategy fails. Since each processor may be executing a disabled process, several processes may succeed in entering a critical section simultaneously.

Dekker first gave a programmed solution for two-processor conditions. [Dijkstra, 1968, p. 58]. The solution was later generalized to n processors by Dijkstra [1965] and later improved. The trouble with these solutions, however, is their complexity and the presence of active wait loops. Programmed solutions without active wait loops have since been found [Yang and Anderson, 1995].

Architectural Provisions

Because the architectural functions are too elementary, programmed interlock primitives become too complex. Therefore, the next step is to find a compound architectural function that is acceptable.

Binary semaphore. To this end, Dijkstra [1968] proposed the *semaphore* as a new datatype. The two operations defined for this datatype are called P (or *wait*) and V (or *signal*, or *post*).

The semaphore has two states, which we shall call 0 and 1. Initially it must be 1. Wait is placed at the start of a critical section; it inspects the semaphore. If the semaphore is 1, the process proceeds; otherwise, it waits till it becomes 1. When the process proceeds, the semaphore is set to 0. Post is placed at the end of a critical section; it sets the semaphore to 1.

Program 7-12 shows the action of the Wait and Post operations. Each is postulated to be atomic, as noted by the comments "serialize memory" and "end serialization." The memory is said to be *serialized* because the interleaving of accesses is forbidden.

Test And Set. The semaphore can easily be represented by a bit in memory. The Post operation can be performed by a Store, which need not be indivisible. The only new architectural function that is needed is an atomic Wait. This operation must contain a read, a write, and a decision. The decision, however, can be deferred, so long as the read and write are one atomic action.

```
wait:free                          post
 ⍝ test semaphore                   ⍝ set semaphore
 REPEAT: ⍝serialize memory          ⍝ serialize memory
    free←semaphore                  semaphore←1
    semaphore←0                     ⍝ end serialization
  ⍝ end serialization
→UNTIL free
```

PROGRAM 7-12   Operations upon a semaphore.

The Test And Set operation of the 360, proposed in 1963 by Dirac, gives this function. Test And Set reads a byte from memory, records the state of the leftmost bit of this byte (the semaphore bit) in the condition code, and sets the byte to all ones as one atomic action (Program 7-13) [Dirac, 1963].

```
┌─────────┬───┬────┬────────────────┐
│ Opcode  │ * │ B1 │ D1             │
└─────────┴───┴────┴────────────────┘
0         8     16   20             32
Legend: B = base; D = displacement; * = unused.

 TS
 ⍝ IBM 360 Test And Set
 ⍝ serialize memory
 ⍝ test leftmost bit in byte
  psw[Cc]←2 magnr 1↑byte read360 adr360bd1
 ⍝ set byte to all ones
  adr360bd1 write360 byteρ1
 ⍝ end serialization
```

PROGRAM 7-13   Test And Set in the IBM System/360.

Test And Set should be followed by a branch (Program 7-14). So a sufficient and general means for interlocking is provided. Some issues involved in such interlocking are discussed under "Synchronization" in [Hennessy and Patterson, 1990].

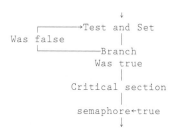

PROGRAM 7-14   Critical section programmed with Test And Set.

Implementation consequences.   The atomicity requirement of Test And Set has noticeable implementation consequences. The latency of memory, normally related to one access, is now related to two, unless the Test And Set logic is made part of memory.

General semaphore.   The binary semaphore can be generalized by extending its domain to positive integers. Post now increases the semaphore value by 1; Wait inspects the semaphore for 0 and decreases it by 1 if the semaphore is not 0. The process waits if the semaphore is 0 at the moment of inspection.

The general semaphore can conveniently be used to allow a given number of processes, instead of just one, to enter a region [Keedy et al., 1979].

Compare And Swap.   The binary behavior of Test And Set has been generalized in the 370 to Compare And Swap (Program 7-15).

opcode	R1	R2	B1	D1

```
0        8   12  16  20               32
Legend: R = register; B = base; D = displacement.

 CS;operand;comparand
 ∩ IBM 370 Compare and Swap
 ∩ serialize memory
 ∩ compare operands
 operand←radixcompi reg[fld R1;]
 comparand←radixcompi,word read360 adr360bd
 psw[Cc]←2 magnr operand≠comparand
 ∩ swap operands
 →IF operand≠comparand
 THEN:reg[fld R1;]←word radixcompr comparand
     →ENDIF
 ELSE:adr360bd write360 reg[fld R2;]
 ENDIF:
 ∩ end serialization
```

PROGRAM 7-15   Compare And Swap in the IBM System/370.

Compare And Swap compares a memory operand, the semaphore, with a comparand. If they are equal, the memory operand is replaced by a successor value; otherwise, the memory operand is copied into a register. The result of the comparison is noted in the condition register. The entire operation is indivisible.

7.2.3

Bibliography

Bershad et al. [1992], Dijkstra [1965, 1968], Dirac [1963], Hennessy and Patterson [1990], Keedy et al. [1979], Lamport [1987], Yang and Anderson [1995].

7.3

Integrity

What hardware facilities does a supervisor require if it is to keep control of an unspecified, uncooperative set of user programs?

Basic premise.   If a supervisor is indeed going to exercise control, it must be able to limit the actions of the user programs. A user program, on the other hand, should not be able to limit the supervisor in any way, let alone remove the limitations the supervisor imposes.

Since any corruption of the supervisory program limits its proper operation, the storage area where it resides must be protected against writing. It should also be protected against reading: The user should not be able to know

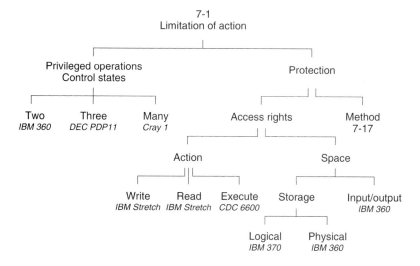

TREE 7-16   Design choices for integrity provision.

the password of a system programmer who is allowed to make changes in the program. Furthermore, the user should not be able to know what actions the supervisor takes to limit or free him. Since each action involves an operation and operands, there are two ways to achieve these restrictions:

- *Privileged operations*: The operations that exercise control are reserved for the supervisor.
- *Capabilities*: The operands that are capable of control are accessible only to the supervisor.

We treat the privileged operations first; we treat the method of capabilities as part of storage protection. Trees 7-16 and 7-17 show the pertinent design choices; the selections made in various machine designs are shown in Table 7-21.

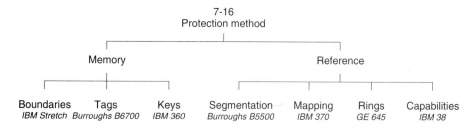

TREE 7-17   Design choices for protection method.

7.3.1

Privileged Operations

Since privileged operations can be invoked only by the supervisory program, memory protection and I/O mechanisms can both be managed in the same way by such operations. In practice, the number of privileged operations

a	SPM	Set Program Mask	c	RDD	Read Direct
c	LPSW	Load PSW	c	WRD	Write Direct
a	SSK	Set Storage Key	c	SIO	Start Input/Output
c	SSM	Set System Mask	c	HIO	Stop Input/Output
a	ISK	Insert Storage Key	c	TIO	Test Input/Output
		Diagnose	c	TCH	Test Channel

TABLE 7-18   Privileged operations in the IBM System/360.

needed is rather small, as shown for example in Table 7-18, but their frequency is moderately high.

Control modes.   The computer must know whether or not a privileged operation is allowed. This awareness implies at least two modes of operation, here called *privileged mode* and *user mode*. Various other names are in use, such as *supervisor, control, master,* or *kernel* on the one hand, and *problem, normal,* or *slave* on the other.

In the 360 the modes are distinguished by bit 15 of the PSW, a part of the control store illustrated in Program 7-38.

Hierarchy of Control

Who controls the controller? For computers this problem is simplified by assuming the critical parts of the supervisor to be perfect—an assumption one does not make for people. But, since a program is made by people, it must be thoroughly tested before one can really trust it. Hence it may be expedient to run a supervisor as a user program during its development, or to use several supervisors simultaneously in one multiprogramming system under control of a supervisor of supervisors, or *hypervisor*. Thus, a hierarchy of control must be established.

Multiple modes.   Two control modes are necessary for a system using privileged operations. A hierarchy of control, however, does not demand a hierarchy of modes; two are sufficient. The solution is to pass on all actions that are privileged at some level to the top level, which can then decide whether or not to perform them as requested. Thus, the 370 virtual machine system VM/370 uses just two modes to accomplish three levels of control: a hypervisor, a virtual supervisor, and a virtual problem level. The hypervisor catches and simulates privileged instructions attempted under the virtual supervisor. It also catches privileged instructions attempted under the virtual problem level and reflects them to the virtual operating system at the virtual supervisor level.

The PDP11 has three modes: the Kernel, Supervisor, and User mode, recorded in Processor Status Word bits 0 and 1 (Program 7-27). A privileged operation, however, is valid only in the Kernel mode. It is ignored in the Supervisor and User mode. The last two modes select the working registers to be used, to speed up context switching.

In the PDP11 the I/O operations use regular load and store operations with special addresses. They are controlled as part of memory protection and need no privileged operations. This example illustrates the interchangeability of privileged operations with memory protection.

7.3.2

Memory Protection

Purpose

The purpose of protection may be security, privacy, diagnostics, or—more likely—a combination thereof.

Security.   Preventing system collapse due to unintentional or malicious acts of users is called system *security*. Security preserves the integrity of both the supervisor and the user programs.

Privacy.   By guaranteeing *privacy*, protection keeps unauthorized users from accessing data and programs.

Diagnostics.   Protection also gives an early warning of errors in programs or addressing hardware. Since an addressing violation is caught as it occurs, the cause of the error is much easier to find.

Access Rights

Access rights specify the type of access that is allowed and the resources that are protected.

Write protection.   Preventing unauthorized writes is essential for the security of the supervisor and of other users; it also ensures repeatability of the active program—a major diagnostic aid.

Read protection.   Unauthorized reading does not immediately destroy information, but it violates privacy.

Execute protection.   Preventing unauthorized execution is essential for security.   Diagnostics are aided by preventing "excursions"—the execution of arbitrary bit patterns after an erroneous branch address.

Memory.   Memory must be protected, since it contains vital portions of the supervisor. Memory may be protected at the logical level or at the physical level. Either one is satisfactory, but the logical level is more proper.

Peripheral.   If the supervisor manages the peripheral devices securely and provides the I/O services, then the devices and the areas of memory that the peripheral devices use in transmission need no further protection. In some applications, however, it is convenient to let the user pass to the supervisor the memory areas read or written. Some of these areas are even determined as the process proceeds. So it is more proper to have memory protection for I/O as well.

Method

As stated, memory may be protected by checking the logical address or the physical address (Tree 7-16). Since location protection was used earlier than address protection, we treat them in this order [Saltzer and Schroeder, 1975].

Clear. Whatever method is used, some basic precautions are in order. For example, storage should be cleared before it is made available to a new user.

Boundaries. One of the earliest methods of memory protection is to limit access to a contiguous memory area. The Stretch pioneered this method (Program 7-19).

```
      Inv protect7030 address;wordadr;upper;lower
   ⍝ IBM Stretch storage protection
   wordadr←⌊address÷word
   ⍝ invalid address
   Invadr report7030 address≥memcap
   →OUT suppress7030
   →If(enable∨exec)∧(wordadr≥32)∨wordadr∊ 1 2 3
   THEN: ⍝ not permanently allowed
     ⍝ permanently protected
     Inv report7030 wordadr∊ 1 2 3
     ⍝ protected by bounds
     upper←wordadr<magni memory[Upperbound]
     lower←wordadr≥magni memory[Lowerbound]
     Inv report7030 memory[Boundbit]=upper∧lower
   ENDIF:
```

PROGRAM 7-19   Protection boundaries in the IBM Stretch.

The memory area is defined by two address values, which are part of the control store of the Stretch. Normally the area delimited by the upper and lower bounds is valid, but the Stretch can also specify the reverse: The bounded area is invalid, and the remainder of memory is valid—a facility intended for the supervisor. The basic problem with the contiguous area, however, is that programs are usually not contiguous, since they use common subroutine libraries.

Tags. In the Burroughs B6700 (1971) each memory word contains a bit that prevents writing into that word when it is on. This method allows discontiguous areas, but at a high expense to the bit budget. To distinguish read, write, and execute protection would be even more expensive. Therefore, the B6700 supplements the method with protection of reading and execution via segmentation.

Keys. The methods discussed so far are geared to two programs: a supervisor and one user. The normal time-sharing case, however, has several programs entered in memory. Thus, the supervisor must change the contents of the boundary registers as part of resource management, or worse, it must change tags in memory words at that time.

The 360 gives each program in memory a 4-bit *key*. Program locations may be discontiguous, but at a resolution of 2048-byte blocks, rather than at the word resolution of previous methods. Each block has a 4-bit *lock* that the key of the accessing processes must match. The all-zeros key is a pass key; an all-zeros lock is open to all (Program 7-20).

Once memory is provided with locks, keys can be given to peripheral processes as easily as to the current process. The 360 includes keys in its channel status words (Program 8-38) as well as in its PSW (Program 7-38).

The size of the key allows 15 programs to be in memory simultaneously. We thought this number was reasonably generous, but it turned out to be too

```
 adrcheck360 location;key;lock
A IBM 360 address check
A memory capacity
 Invadr report location≥memcap
A protection
→If protopt
THEN:key←magni psw[Key]
    lock←magni keys[⌊location÷block;]
    Protect report(key≠0)∧(0≠lock)∧key≠lock
ENDIF:
```

PROGRAM 7-20   Protection in the IBM System/360.

skimpy. The CDC STAR100 (1973) uses a 12-bit protection key and issues four keys to each task.

Address mapping.   Address mapping introduced the distinction between the logical and the physical address. Protection is best applied at the logical level. Address mapping is in itself, however, also a method of protection. The 6600, which has contiguous mapping via a reference address, uses it to restrict access to a contiguous area; the area starts at the reference address and is limited by a specified length.

Segmentation and paging allow discontiguous mapping, and therefore discontiguous protection (Section 3.2). Mapping can easily differentiate the various access rights by specifying them in the segment tables.

Rings.   The MULTICS system introduced a hierarchical protection method called *rings of protection* [Organick, 1972, Chapter 5]. A ring is a key that matches not on equal, but rather on equal or larger. Rings are numbered from 0 to n from inside out ($n = 7$ in the Honeywell 6180; $n = 63$ in the early papers). A process that is executing in ring i has access rights only to segments in rings with a number equal to or larger than i. Conversely, a segment belongs to ring i if it is accessible only to processes in rings with number equal to or smaller than i.

Figure 7-22 illustrates the ring-protection concept as applied to a simple system of segments A, B, C, and D, and rings 0, 1, 2, and 3. Segment D is accessible to processes executing in segments A, B, and D, but not to segment

	Access rights	Protection method	Delimiter resolution	Space	P
IBM Stretch	r w	boundaries	64-bit word	memory	
English Electric KDF9		boundaries	32 words	memory, I/O	
CDC 6600	e r w	mapping	60-bit word	memory	
Burroughs B5500		segment	48-bit word	memory, I/O	p
IBM System/360		4-bit key	2*11 bytes	memory, I/O	p
GE 645		64 rings	1024 words		
DEC PDP11		stack limit	256 bytes	memory	p
IBM System/370		mapping	2*11 bytes	memory	p
Cray 1		mapping	16 words	memory	
DEC VAX11	r w	mapping	512 bytes	memory	p
IBM System/38		capability		memory	

Legend: e = execute; p = P = privileged operation; r = read; w = write.

TABLE 7-21   Integrity in various machines.

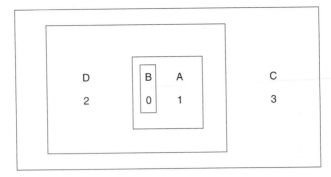

FIGURE 7-22   Rings as a series of concentric lines of defense.

C. Segment B is protected from the other segments, and segment C is accessible to the other three segments.

In the simple ring structure, a user process executing in an outer ring cannot transfer control to an inner, supervisory ring. Humble access, however, is allowed into designated *gate* locations in the inner segment.

The simple ring structure was further generalized to allow a segment to reside in a band of rings, rather than just in a single ring. Also, a band was subdivided into bands of write access, read access, execute access, inward ring-crossing access, and no access allowed at all. These bands add greatly to the usefulness of the ring structure, but are not crucial to its supervisory power.

The principal advantage of the ring structure is that it allows the building of a hierarchy of software layers to be built between the machine and the user, with careful policing of the interactions between the layers.

Capabilities.   In the methods of memory protection encountered so far, the access rights concern reading, writing, and execution. These rights can be refined by recognizing control information—including the information that specifies the address protection—as a separate information class. Such a protection system requires changing the protection control by writing into the locations that specify the protection—locations that only the supervisor can change.

More generally, all resources can be managed by establishing access rights, called *capabilities*, and in turn treating the capabilities as a resource [Dennis and Van Horn, 1966; Wilkes, 1972].

The systematic use of capabilities obviates the use of privileged operations and their associated modes. Capabilities are used in the IBM System/38 (1980).

7.3.3

Bibliography

Beerstis [1980], Dennis and Van Horn [1966], Fabry [1974], Graham and Denning [1972], Houdek et al. [1981], Lampson [1969], Levy [1984], Needham and Wilner [1972], Needham and Walker [1977], Organick [1972], Saltzer and Schroeder [1975], Schroeder and Saltzer [1972], Wilkes [1972; 1982].

7.4

Control Switching

A basic assumption for the modern computer is that a supervisory program, rather than a human operator, is in charge of the minute-by-minute operation. The human operator, if present, serves as hands and feet for the supervisor: He inserts diskettes, mounts tapes, removes printer output, and performs other tasks under its instructions. He also serves as agent of last resort when a supervisor bug or a hardware malfunction debilitates the supervisor.

A supervisory program requires three types of control switches:

- *Dispatch*: The supervisor gives control to the user.
- *Humble access*: The user yields control.
- *Interruption*: The supervisor takes control.

7.4.1

Interruption

Interruption, taking control, embodies the essence of supervision. The supervisor can seize control only if there is a process concurrent with the user program that monitors it.

An *interruption* is a control switch away from the program under execution to another program—almost invariably the supervisor. (Trees 7-23 and 7-28 give the design choices.) Customarily, a set of conditions is provided, any of which, when satisfied, may cause a control switch.

Each of these conditions must be specified as part of the architecture. The designer of the supervisor is not as free to invent conditions for switching from the user program to the supervisor, as he is for the opposite case. He is peculiarly constrained by the machine architecture.

Once a control switch takes place, the supervisor resumes execution at a location related to the interrupt condition but specified by the supervisor. The supervisor recognizes the interruption, but proceeds on its own terms.

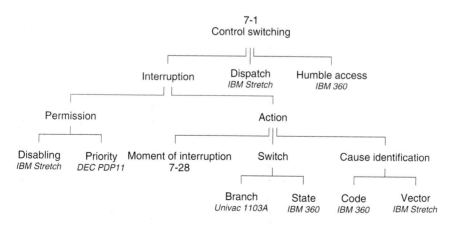

TREE 7-23   Design choices for control switching.

Historical Development

The 1103A had the first true interruption facility—one with the ability to resume the interrupted program. The purpose was for the 1103A to operate in batch mode until an aircraft wind tunnel was ready to release its pulse of air. Then the machine was to be instantaneously and momentarily dedicated to the capture and reduction of data from the wind tunnel [Mersel, 1956].

Instruction address switch.   The 1103A architecture provides two fixed addresses. Upon receipt of the external signal, the instruction address was dumped into one of these and reloaded from the other. The interrupting program is responsible for saving all other components of machine state and for restoring them before resuming execution of the interrupted program.

Input/output conditions.   The Lincoln Lab TX2 (1959) generalizes the single interruption condition of the 1103A to a set of conditions that can be turned on by the normal I/O devices, not just by a special one.

General purpose interruption.   The Stretch incorporates three notions, each of which stimulated development of an interruption system. First, it has up to 32 I/O channels, each executing its own instruction sequence concurrently and asynchronously, but capable of only normal transmission. Since each channel is in fact an independent processor, a generalized mechanism was needed for reporting I/O completions and exceptional events to the central processing unit. Second, the designers adopted a philosophy of full checking of errors and full policing of invalidities, so they needed an economical way of reporting these. Third, the machine is designed to be multiprogrammed, so means for the supervisor to take control from user programs have to be provided.

A general purpose interruption system—including 64 indicators, masking, and disabling—addresses these separate and disparate needs [Brooks, 1958]. Although Stretch's standard supervisor did not fully exploit these facilities, they were used and proved in an extensive multiprogramming experiment carried out by Codd and his colleagues [Codd et al., 1959; Buchholz, 1962, Chapter 13].

Protected control state.   The interruption system of the 360 derives from that of the Stretch, but incorporates a significant advance: Whereas the Stretch assumes that user programs have been prevented by the compiler from disabling protection, the 360 uses its interruption system as a defense against sloppy or malicious users. A privileged state is reserved for the supervisor, and the crucial control operations are limited to this state. The user can invoke supervisory functions only by requesting them from the supervisor.

Control state-saving.   The Stretch leaves all state-saving to the supervisory program. The 360, instead, automatically saves one word of control information, the PSW, and replaces this control information with the status of the supervisor. The operation Load PSW allows the supervisor to reverse the PSW exchange when ready to resume the interrupted program.

Working store saving.   The RCA Spectra 70 (1965) expands the 360 state-saving by storing several registers as part of the interrupt action.

Stacked context.   The PDP11 further improved the automatic saving of control information by using a stack. This stack makes it easier to allow interruptions of an interrupting program.

Interrupt Conditions

The program primitives for the interrupt conditions derive from the system-management functions of the supervisor.

Resource allocation.   The main management function of the supervisor is the allocation of resources. The principal resource is the CPU time, which is usually managed by allotting time slices to each of the user programs.

Service requests.   The supervisor must also respond to external signals, such as those from the operator console or from other processors. And it must handle the internal service requests from the user program, such as requests for exception handling and warnings of machine malfunction. Most of the program primitives mentioned are satisfied by a status switch initiated by an interruption.

Asynchronous conditions.   Interruptions whose timing is independent of the execution of the interrupted program are called *asynchronous*. Events outside a program's executions, such as the completion of a peripheral operation, always cause asynchronous operations; sometimes, pipelined implementations cause them even for execution-occasioned events whose causing instruction can no longer be identified.

In a uniprogrammed system, the user program can control its I/O safely and efficiently. In a multiprogramming system, only the supervisor can know the total set of requests pending for a peripheral device. So efficient use of a device requires that all scheduling be done by the supervisor and that all completions and other events be reported to the supervisor.

A completion ordinarily occurs during execution of a user program different from the one to which the I/O activity pertains; the supervisor must get control so it can process the scheduling. These considerations also apply to the more general multiprocessing system.

Management through polling.   The supervisor can manage peripheral and external processes by inquiring periodically about their progress, a method called *polling*.

As soon as computers had concurrent I/O action, as in the Univac I, they provided for explicit inquiry as the means for a CPU to test I/O completion and errors. When a program reached the point where it needed the data previously ordered to be read, for example, it tested to see whether reading was complete, and, if not, went into a wait loop repeating the test.

Management through interruption.   Multiprogramming urged changes in the polling mode of operation for two reasons. First, when the CPU has to wait, one wants to switch it to some other task, and that task cannot incorporate the I/O polling operation for an independent program. Second, many computers, such as those doing file maintenance, are essentially I/O limited. So, when a peripheral operation finishes, efficient operation dictates that the next one be

started at once, not after some CPU task finds it convenient to poll the I/O system. The Stretch and the 360, both designed for multiprogramming operation, adopted a philosophy of immediate interprocess reporting of completions and of untoward events by means of interruptions.

Interruption versus polling.   The opposite philosophy is vividly summarized in words attributed to Seymour Cray, designer of the 6600: "Don't tell me about [such events] when I'm doing something else; all I can do is save them for handling later. Instead you save them. When I'm ready to handle them, I'll ask."

The implication is that it is more efficient to complete bursts of CPU work without interpolated task switches than it is to strain to the utmost to give immediate response to peripheral events. This approach clearly applies to jobs that are computer-limited; it may well apply in most cases. Whether or not it does apply, however, is a question of fact, to be established by measurement for the given application.

What is unquestionably true is that the supervisor and perhaps the machines are *simpler* when synchronization is done by polling than when it is done by interruption. On the other hand it is also true that some peripheral processes demand a fast response, which can be achieved most effectively by interruption.

Even though the choice between interruption and polling may be application-dependent, we believe that the computer architecture should allow, but not dictate, the use of interruption.

External signals.   If a supervisor, not a human operator, is to control ordinary operations, there must be a means whereby the operator can break in, even on the supervisor.

Similarly, in a multiprocessing system, one CPU should be able to signal another and seize control. Such a provision allows an outside machine to diagnose and correct failing hardware or supervisory software.

Synchronous conditions.   An interrupt caused by some act of the instruction being executed is called a *synchronous interruption*: The occasion of interruption is synchonized with the execution of the interrupted program. Such an interrupt is also called a *trap*.

Exception monitoring.   The user program may request the system to watch for exceptional conditions—for example, data-caused invalidities such as overflow, underflow, and division by zero. Upon the occurrence of such an exception the user-provided error routine can be executed. The supervisor does not necessarily need to be involved in this case. Most program exceptions, however, must invoke the supervisor. Even those for which the user might provide a fixup must invoke the supervisor when no fixup is provided, so a default procedure can be followed. So it is customary to route all program exceptions to the supervisor, leaving it to accommodate user-provided fixups.

One-instruction fixup.   The Stretch intended to improve exception monitoring by allowing a one-instruction interrupt routine. As shown in Program 7-25, the interruption system effectively inserted one full-length instruction, which

could be a subroutine call, into the sequence of the interrupted program, allowing a *one-instruction fixup* to be performed without the overhead of control switching and state-saving.

A one-instruction subroutine is of little value in a single-address computer: Most conceptual units of action require more than one instruction (see Section 6.4).   In the Stretch, however, one frequent need could be so met: the adjustment after floating underflow, where a common repair is to substitute zero for the underflowed number. In practice, floating-point underflow was so common that even this fixup turned out to be too slow; a zero substitution was then built into the hardware. Thereafter, the one-instruction fixup had little usefulness.

System security functions.   The three areas where errors can be observed are

- Machine-language syntax mistakes, such as invalid operation codes
- Machine-language domain mistakes, such as invalid addresses or memory protection violations
- Hardware malfunctions that are detected as such; for instance, parity failures

A hardware malfunction may, of course, manifest itself as a program malfunction. The reverse, however, should never be the case for a good machine implementation. Invalidities and malfunctions should be reported immediately to the supervisor, preferably through the interruption mechanism.

Invalidity policing.   Many early machines and many modern mini- and microcomputers have been designed without invalidity policing. Since programming errors are much more common than hardware malfunctions, our position is that a machine should

- Perform no operation when presented with an instruction that violates the machine's language syntax
- Indicate that an incorrect specification has occurred

One might consider a form of policing that merely renders the invalid instruction inoperative and sets a bit to be tested at a checkpoint. The argument for immediate testing (and reporting) is that, once the invalidity has been attempted and suppressed, later instructions do not accomplish dependably useful work. In fact, they propagate the error far and wide, making both diagnosis and recovery much more difficult. Moreover, policing is important to keep the design open-ended. Otherwise, the spaces saved for the future are not really saved.

Table 7-29 indicates with the letter p which computers have some kind of validity checking for program syntax.

Hardware malfunctions. The health of the machine's realization is of utmost interest to the supervisor. A main power failure or other processing unit malfunction requires preemptive response.

Can a supervisor achieve much that is useful when it must use a malfunctioning machine? In some cases, no. But the supervisor can help the system to recover even in case of a power failure. The power supply usually has enough

```
     indicator360
   ∩ IBM 360 indicators
   ∩ machine check              ∩ - invalid divisor
    Machine←0                    Divide←9
   ∩ program check              ∩ - decimal overflow
    Program←1+ι15                Decoflo←10
   ∩ - invalid operation       ∩ - zero decimal divisor
    Invop←1                      Decdiv←11
   ∩ - privileged operation    ∩ - floating-point overflow
    Priv←2                       Floflo←12
   ∩ - execute error           ∩ - floating-point underflow
    Execute←3                    Uflo←13
   ∩ - protection violation    ∩ - lost significance
    Protect←4                    Lostsf←14
   ∩ - invalid address         ∩ - zero floating divisor
    Invadr←5                     Fldiv←15
   ∩ - specification error     ∩ supervisor call
    Spec←6                       Svc←16
   ∩ - invalid data            ∩ external signal
    Data←7                       External←17
   ∩ - binary overflow         ∩ input/output
    Oflo←8                       Io←18+ι7
```

PROGRAM 7-24   Indicators of the IBM System/360.

reserve to last a fraction of a second. In that period, the system workload can be brought to an end in such a fashion that later resumption will be more elegant.

Malfunction reporting represents an interaction between the realization of a computer and its architecture. The realization itself appears to the architecture as an "external device" that occasionally requires attention.

Indicators.   The interrupt conditions, called *indicators*, are usually ordered as a control store. Program 7-24 shows the indicators for the 360.

Summary indicators.   The one-instruction fixup of the Stretch requires a distinct indicator for each condition with a distinct fixup. As a result, there are 34 synchronous indicators. Since the processor must inspect the indicator bits and the supervisor must manipulate them, there has been an effort to reduce their number. The 360 has only 16 synchronous indicators because similar conditions are grouped into a *summary indicator*. The PDP11 reduces the number to eight.

In the 360, Machine Check summarizes the report of a large number of error-checking circuits. Once a Machine Check has been reported, a diagnostic program is used to identify the particular trouble. The use of summary indicators is a reasonable solution for rare events.

Permission for Interruption

When two or more interrupt conditions arise simultaneously, which shall be handled first? In the simplest case the architecture gives a fixed order that embodies the supervisor's preference. At design time, however, this preference may not be known, and it may not always be the same. To be general, the machine architecture must give the supervisor means to establish a hierarchy; the condition the supervisor considers most important at a given moment is handled first.

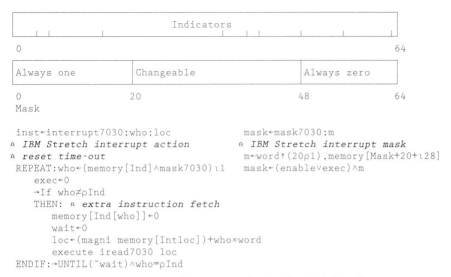

```
inst←interrupt7030:who:loc              mask←mask7030:m
ᴀ IBM Stretch interrupt action          ᴀ IBM Stretch interrupt mask
ᴀ reset time-out                        m←word↑(20ρ1),memory[Mask+20+ι28]
 REPEAT:who←(memory[Ind]∧mask7030)ι1     mask←(enable∨exec)∧m
    exec←0
    →If who≠ρInd
    THEN: ᴀ extra instruction fetch
       memory[Ind[who]]←0
       wait←0
       loc←(magni memory[Intloc])+who×word
       execute iread7030 loc
 ENDIF:→UNTIL(~wait)∧who=ρInd
```

PROGRAM 7-25   Interrupt action in the IBM Stretch.

Disabling.   Many interrupt handlers contain a short critical section for preserving the old and establishing the new machine state. The latter must not be interrupted at all, lest the state be irretrievably lost. Commonly, the whole interruption mechanism is *disabled* during such critical sections. Interruptions may occur again when the interruption system is *enabled*.

Disregarding.   The supervisor architect may consider some conditions included by the machine architect not to be worth interrupting for. Therefore, the interruption system should provide a means to *disregard* those conditions.

The basic mechanisms that are used to give permission for interruption are the mask and the priority code.

Disabling by masking.   A summary mask bit can solve the critical-section problem. When the mask bit is 1, the system is enabled; any interruption is allowed. When the mask bit is 0, the system is disabled; all interruptions are inhibited. (The interruption system can be disabled at the start of a critical section, and re-enabled at the end.) Because this mask bit applies to all interruption causes, it is called a *summary* mask bit.

In the Stretch a summary mask bit is implied: Disabling and enabling are combined with unconditional branch operations, which furnish the interruption-routine address and store the resumption address.

Disregarding by masking.   Because a summary mask bit cannot disregard a particular condition, the Stretch provides an explicit mask as well. This mask corresponds bit for bit with the 64 indicators that record the interrupt conditions. An interrupt condition is considered only when its corresponding mask bit is 1, as illustrated in line three of Program 7-25. This program shows that, if more than one condition is satisfied and masked on, the leftmost one is taken. So the fixed order of the indicators determines their hierarchy, within the set masked on.

Masking does not necessarily make sense for all conditions; moreover, it is costly in machine state. The full masking of the Stretch was later cost-reduced

Cause	Priority	Mask bit in PSW	Location of PSW Old	New	Class
Machine malfunction	1	13	48	112	3
Program error	2	36+ι4	40	104	2
Humble access (SVC)	2		32	96	1
Timer	3	7	24	88	0
Peripheral signal	4	0+ι7	56	120	4
External signal	3	7	24	88	0

TABLE 7-26   Interrupt classes of the IBM System/360.

so that 20 indicators were permanently masked on, 28 were program maskable, and 16 were permanently masked off—they could only be tested by branch operations (Program 7-25). Given today's hardware costs, the design would surely have had full masking.

Classes of interruptions.   In the 360 the interrupt conditions are combined into five classes, each with its own location for the old and new PSW (Table 7-26), and each class separately maskable by 1 or more mask bits. Subsequent interrupts within a class should be disabled by setting the mask bits of that class to zero until the critical section for that class is completed.

Priority by masking.   If each interruption class is maskable, the interrupt handler can precisely and completely control the order of handling of all interrupt classes. When a condition causes an interrupt, a new mask is supplied that disables the class of that condition and all classes of lesser importance as defined by the programmer. Then the system is re-enabled. When multiple masked-on interrupts occur at once, they are taken in the order established by the architecture. But each time the system is re-enabled, there will be an immediate interrupt until the (program-defined) highest class is serviced; only then are all other conditions masked off. After that, the server restores the mask that it found. Full, as opposed to summary, masking allows maximum flexibility.

Priority level.   A priority code in hardware simplifies the programming to establish a hierarchy of interrupt conditions. Here each condition, or group of conditions, has a *priority level*, as expressed in a code. The processor also

```
          Priority↓  ↓Trace
        ┌─────┬─┬───┬───┐
        │Mode │*│   │Cdn│
        └─────┴─┴───┴───┘
        0    5  8  12  16
        Legend: Cdn = condition;  * = unused.

        status11
        ⋀ DEC PDP11 status
        ⋀ control modes            ⋀ trace mode
          Currentmode←0+ι2           Trace←11
          Previousmode←2+ι2        ⋀ conditions    ⋀ mode encoding
        ⋀ register set              Neg←12           Kernel←0
          Regset←4                  Zero←13          Supervisor←1
        ⋀ interrupt priority        Oflo←14          User←2
          Priority←8+ι3             Carry←15
```

PROGRAM 7-27   Processor status word of the DEC PDP11.

has a level, the *current level*. Interrupt conditions with a higher priority than the current level are honored and cause a status switch.

The priority level is illustrated by the PDP11. The current priority level is contained in the PSW and can have values 0 through 7. Value 0 is equivalent to disregarding (Program 7-27).

Moment of Interruption

Once an interrupt condition arises and is verified for enabling and priority, exactly when is the interruption taken?

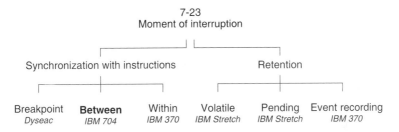

TREE 7-28   Design choices for moment of interruption.

Breakpoint.   The National Bureau of Standards' DYSEAC (1954) and the Lincoln Laboratories' TX2 use a *breakpoint* bit in each instruction to specify whether a status switch is allowed at the end of that instruction.   The breakpoint, when properly used, avoids switching the content of working store: A switch is allowed only when that content is no longer significant.

The breakpoint reduces the bit efficiency of the instructions. More important, the breakpoint assumes a cooperative user—an unacceptable assumption in most modern environments.

Interruption between instructions.   According to our definition in Section 6.1, an instruction is the minimal unit of computer action. So, in most computers, it is the maximal unit that is executed as a block without interruption; interruption occurs only in between complete instructions.

Life is not so simple, however, when interruption is used as the means of synchronizing concurrent processes, such as I/O transfers and CPU programs. Some such processes have a *maximum wait time* (MWT) and must receive CPU attention within the MWT after the interrupt condition arises. Some check sorters, for example, transmit the sorting key from the check to the computer while keeping the paper in flight toward the sorting gates. The computer must respond with a gate selection before the document reaches the gates.

Any process for which a MWT is specified is called a *real-time process*. In any computer designed for real-time processes, the shortest MWT bounds the length of time during which the computer is uninterruptible, and it can become an important bound on the maximum execution time of any instruction. In the 360, for example, the character-string instructions are limited to strings of length 256, so that their execution time is on the same order of magnitude as Divide, and their provision does not significantly raise the shortest MWT.

Interruption within instructions.   Users of the 360 found the limitation of character-string instructions to 256 bytes to be a severe constraint, substantially complicating compilers.   So the 370 designers provided Move Long and Compare Logical Long operations, treating field lengths of up to 16 million (2^{24}) bytes. Such instructions had to be made interruptible by asynchronous conditions.

There are several options for interrupting instructions in midflight. For many operations, the first store (to memory or register) is the last action of the operation. If this change in the visible state of the machine has occurred, the instruction is finished. If it has not, the instruction can be *nullified*, leaving no evidence that it was ever started. Other operations, such as the 370 long moves and comparisons, lend themselves to somewhat better treatment. They can be stopped and restarted easily, because they involve very little internal state. The long instructions have addresses and counts specified in the general registers. When such instructions are interrupted, the relevant general registers are updated, but the Instruction Address is not. Upon return to the interrupted program, the interrupted instruction is resumed. The process is straightforward only because resumption and initial start have been designed to be identical [Case and Padegs, 1978].

The DEC VAX11 (1978) illustrates an intermediate solution. To preserve generality of addressing, the original addresses and counts need not be placed in registers. When an instruction is interrupted, however, the current values are placed in preassigned registers. The machine status contains an *in process* signal; this signal indicates that the instruction must be resumed using the values in the registers.

	Condition		Means of permission	Moment of interrupt	Cause identified	R
	sync	async				
IBM 650	m		mask	between		
Univac 1103A		e	none	between		
Lincoln Lab TX2				breakpoint		
Bull Gamma 60	m p i	e		between		
Bendix G20	p h t i		mask	between		d
IBM Stretch	m p i		mask	between	vector	d
Ferranti Atlas	m p	e		between	vector	d
English Electric KDF9	p h	e	none	between	code	s
Burroughs B5500	m p h t i	e	priority	between	vector	s
IBM System/360	m p h t i	e	mask	between	code PSW	d
DEC PDP8	i	e	mask	between		
DEC PDP11	m p h i		priority	between	vector	s
IBM System/370	m p h t i	e	mask	within	code PSW	d
Intel 8080A		e	mask	between	vector	
Cray 1	m p h i		mask	between	bit PSW	d
Motorola M6800	h	e	mask	between	vector	
MOS 6502	h	e	mask	between	vector, bit	s
DEC VAX11	m p h t i	e	priority	within	vector	s
Motorola MC68000	m p h i	e	priority	between	code PSW	s
IBM 6150	m p h t i	e	mask	between	code PSW	

Legend: d = direct return address; e = external; h = humble access;
i = input/output; m = machine error; p = program;
R = return address; s = stacked return address; t = timer.

TABLE 7-29   Interruption in various machines.

Instruction ending.   What happens to an instruction when it causes a synchronous interruption? There are four main possibilities:

- The instruction is *completed*: All instruction actions are performed. An overflow in an addition, for example, may be signaled, but all other instruction actions are performed as usual.
- The instruction is *suppressed*: The instruction is treated as a No Operation; hence, it is not executed at all. An example is a protected-data-address violation.
- The instruction is *nullified*: The instruction is not executed, nor is the instruction address advanced. This action is desirable when the interrupt handler can remove the cause of the interruption; the instruction can then be retried. An example is a page fault (Section 3.2).
- The instruction is *terminated*: None, part, or all of the instruction is executed. This specification gives full freedom to the implementer but minimal certainty to the user. It is a major impropriety.

Retention of Conditions

What shall be done about an interrupt condition that is not serviced? Lack of service because of disregarding means "I'm not interested; forget it"; in the case of disabling, it means "I'm busy with more important matters; wait."

Synchronous conditions.   Distinguishing between synchronous and asynchronous conditions helps here, too. Synchronous interruptions that indicate an invalidity should be handled at once if the programmer wants to handle them at all.

For example, a floating-point underflow can be serviced by replacing the result with a zero. If this action is not taken, the result is likely to be in error. Therefore, the synchronous interruption when serviced is a request for immediate action. When it is not serviced, it becomes an error signal—a quite different matter.

The synchronous condition that is not serviced can be turned off at once; more usefully, it can be left on as a record that one or more conditions of that type occurred while the mask was off. In that case, the program should test, record, and reset the conditions before enabling them. The indicators in the Stretch can be used for this purpose.

Volatile conditions.   In the 360 and most subsequent designs, the synchronous interrupt conditions are no longer part of the program status; they are *volatile*. A volatile condition must have the highest priority: The condition is lost when another interrupt intervenes. This priority, however, applies to *reporting*. The urgency of *handling* the interruption is low: Once the interruption is made, the interruption routine can readily be interrupted for other causes.

The masking technique is well-suited for volatile conditions. Although, in the 360, synchronous conditions have priority over asynchronous conditions (Table 7-26), the new PSW of the program interruptions can leave the asynchronous interruptions enabled. Consequently, the program-generated interruptions, although recorded first, are treated last (Table 7-30). In the 360

Event	State	Priority	Mask bits
Divide instruction	execution		5 7 enabled
Timer interruption	pending	3	7 used
Channel 5 interruption	pending	4	5 used
Integer divide interruption	taken	2	not maskable
Old in 40 new from 104	PSW switch		5 enabled
Channel 5 interruption	taken	4	5 enabled
Old in 56 new from 110	PSW switch		none enabled
Process channel interruption	execution		none enabled
Load PSW from 56	return		5 enabled
Process divide error	execution		5 enabled
Load PSW from 40	return		5 7 enabled
Timer interruption	taken	3	5 7 enabled
Old in 24 new from 88	PSW switch		none enabled
Process timer	execution		none enabled

TABLE 7-30   Order of interrupt handling in the IBM System/360.

the synchronous conditions that are masked off are ignored and vanish. Their occurrence can be recorded only by taking the interruption.

Program event recording.   The 370 can record the occurrence of synchronous and several other conditions through program-event recording.

Pending conditions.   Asynchronous conditions usually report completions or troubles in concurrent processes. The supervisor must handle each event sooner or later. When several conditions share one indicator, provision must be made to retain these conditions. If six tape drives report read completions, for example, each potentially requires attention.

Asynchronous conditions can usually be kept *pending* by retaining them in the device that causes the interruption, since a device usually produces at most one condition of a given type. A condition must be retained until it can be asynchronously serviced; it can be kept as long as needed.

Cause Identification

When an interruption occurs, what caused it, and when does one want to know this cause?

Manner of identification.   The two basic means of identifying the cause of an interruption are

1. A routine that is initiated
2. A code that is passed as a parameter

Method 1 uses an implied branch or a PSW switch that is specific to each cause. This method is called *vectored interrupt*, since there is a vector whose elements specify the next instruction for each interrupt condition.

Method 2 assumes that a common routine is initiated, but that a code unique to each cause is available.

Moment of identification.   The choice between the two methods is influenced by the moment at which the cause of interruption needs to be known.

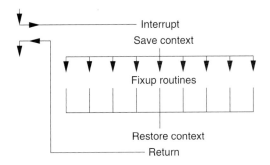

FIGURE 7-31   Structure of an interrupt handler.

If status must be switched by programming, the interrupt routines have an initial common part concerned with state-saving (Figure 7-31). The interruption cause should then be preserved by a code that can be used in a CASE statement after the state has been saved. If, on the other hand, sufficient status is saved automatically, the specific routine is preferable: The CASE statement can be executed as part of the interruption.

The Stretch was the first computer to provide vectored interrupt; it uses a branch table for control switching. An interruption address specifies the start address of this 64-word table. A leftmost-one identifier gives the index of the leftmost masked-on indicator whose value is one. This index is added to the interruption address to give the address of the instruction to be executed next. Normally this instruction is a subroutine call. Program 7-25 illustrates this process.

The Stretch leaves all state-saving, including even the saving of the instruction address, to the interrupting routine. We expected programmed saving of as little state as necessary to be faster than the automatic saving

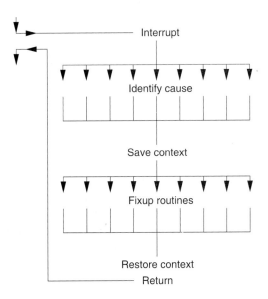

FIGURE 7-32   Structure of the interrupt handler for the IBM Stretch.

of the entire machine state. Probably it was not. Likewise, the manner and timing of cause identification was not convenient (Figure 7-32).

The 360 identifies each of its five classes of interrupt conditions (Table 7-26) by a distinct PSW switch (Program 7-33). A code in the old PSW further identifies the cause within the class. This solution is justified when the amount of status saving differs for the various classes, or when a common routine can treat all cases within a class. For some classes, such as syntax errors and I/O interruptions, these assumptions are valid. For other classes, such as the external interruptions, a greater differentiation in routines would be better, in particular if the context is saved automatically.

```
interrupt360;who;class
 ∩ IBM 360 interrupt action
 REPEAT: ∩ test interrupt sources
    →WHILEv/ind∧mask360
        who←(ind∧mask360)ι1
        ind[who]←0
        class←class360[who]
      ∩ record interrupt cause
        psw[Intcode]←code360 class
      ∩ store program status
        Oldpsw[class] write360a psw
      ∩ new program status
        psw←double read360a Newpsw[class]
        →Δ
 ENDWHILE:→UNTIL 0=psw[Wait]
```

PROGRAM 7-33   Interrupt action in the IBM System/360.

Implementation

The part of the interruption system that monitors the interrupt conditions can be viewed as a set of primitive processors that are active concurrently with the normal instruction processor.

Simplicity of interrupt. Concurrent processors need not take any time away from the normal instruction execution. Even the decision whether or not to interrupt can usually be combined with other internal control actions and need not lengthen the normal instruction cycle. Therefore, the interrupt as such is simple and easy to implement.

Complexity of interrupt.   A computer implementation often becomes complex when several actions interact, even if each of them is simple. The implementation of the Stretch experienced this with regard to interrupt and pipelined execution, called *lookahead* in that machine [Buchholz, 1962].

Most very fast computer implementations use pipelining to give several levels of overlap of instruction fetch and execution. In the 360 Model 91, for example, as many as 5 instructions are in process at a time, with some undergoing instruction fetch, others engaged in effective address calculation, others awaiting data fetch, and so on [S.F. Anderson, 1967].

Pipelining works well only when the sequence of instructions is predictable; data-controlled branching (as opposed to index-controlled looping) and interruption cause severe performance loss. More seriously, the possibility

of interruption and the complexity of associating a synchronous interruption with the instruction that occasions it add greatly to the design problems of a pipelined machine. Either one makes the hardware quite complex, or one compromises the architecture. So the manual may state that the synchronous interrupt relates to "one of the preceding n instructions." This concept is called *imprecise interrupt*. The 360 Model 91 is an example [S.F. Anderson, 1967].

Since such vagueness carries its own costs, we believe the designers must face the hardware complexities. R.P. Case observes that, in spite of the hardware complexities, the 370 supercomputer designers returned to precise interrupts after the Model 91 [Gifford et al., 1987].

7.4.2

Dispatching

Program states. The users of a time-sharing system are at any moment either *active* (if they have requested system use) or *inactive* (if they have not done so). When the aggregate memory requirement of the active users exceeds the available capacity, they have to await their turn.

A program that is actually placed in memory is called *entered*; the others are called *not entered* (Figure 7-34). This is a useful distinction because fetching a program with its data from backing store may take as long as executing it.

In a uniprocessor, only one of the programs that are entered is executed at a given moment; its state is called *executing*. The other programs may be waiting for input/output (the *not ready* state) or they may have all necessary

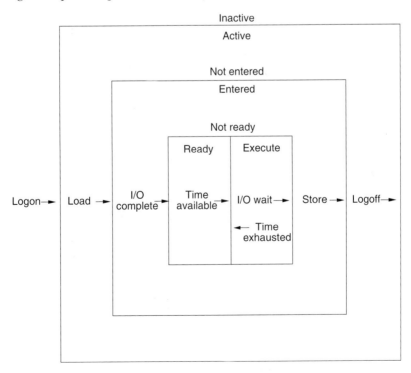

FIGURE 7-34   Program states.

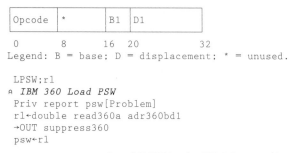

```
LPSW;r1
a IBM 360 Load PSW
  Priv report psw[Problem]
  r1←double read360a adr360bd1
  →OUT suppress360
  psw←r1
```

PROGRAM 7-35   Load PSW in the IBM System/360.

information and just be waiting for a processor (the *ready* state). The supervisor *dispatches* a program on a processor when it changes that program's state to executing.

A switch from the supervisor to a user program is always initiated by the supervisor. The point where the user program is to start or resume execution should be implied or explicitly stated as part of the switch operation.

In the 360 the instruction address is part of the PSW (Program 7-38). The supervisor uses the privileged operation Load PSW to switch to the user mode (Program 7-35).

In the PDP11 the control store is embedded in memory; the privileged status of the PDP11 can therefore be changed by storing a word at the memory address of the PSW. Since the user mode has its own instruction address, the address of the next instruction is known at the moment of switching.

In both examples the dispatch operation is clearly designed to match the information structures of the interruption.

7.4.3

Humble Access

The case in which the user program yields control is far less demanding than the case in which the supervisor takes control. Some instruction can be specified that causes the control to change. But the supervisor—not the program—must specify the point at which the supervisor starts execution; the user program can access the privileged program only on the latter's own terms.

The requirements for humble access prove to be similar to those for interruption, although some are less critical. The return address need not necessarily be preserved automatically; it can be passed as a parameter. Also, it is not essential to identify the detailed cause of humble access at once; it too can be passed as a parameter. Finally, there is no need for masking or disabling the humble access.

Use of interruption system.   Since interruption requires control switching, it is not surprising that the interruption system is used almost universally for humble access and intentional control switching, even though the uses of interruption and humble access are quite different.

Intentional interruption.   The Stretch uses the interruption system in a rather crude way for humble access. The compiler produces an invalid instruction

which the supervisor recognizes as such; no hardware expense whatever is invested.

Supervisor Call instruction. In the design of the 360 we considered a deliberate error an improper means for humble access, since it implies a semantics for reserved operation codes. So we provided the Supervisor Call instruction of Program 7-36. Since the operation causes a PSW switch, it is equivalent to an interruption.

```
                               SVC
 ┌──────────┬───────────┐      ᴀ IBM 360 Supervisor Call
 │ Opcode   │ Imm       │        psw[Intcode]←half magnr fld Imm
 └──────────┴───────────┘        ind[Svc]←1
 0          8          16
 Legend: Imm = immediate.
```

PROGRAM 7-36   Supervisor Call in the IBM System/360.

Dedicating a specific operation such as SVC (Supervisor Call) to humble access is explicit and orthogonal. Furthermore, it has the advantage that the operation can be augmented with power to pass parameters to the supervisor it invokes. The 360's SVC, for example, passes a code indicating which of 256 different supervisory functions one wants.

So the main purpose of humble access is quite distinct from that of the interruption system, yet both use one mechanism. The designer should be aware of this coincidence, lest he copy this combined solution because of mere inertia when changed circumstances dictate separate designs for the two purposes.

7.4.4
Bibliography

S.F. Anderson [1967], Brooks [1958], Buchholz [1962], Case and Padegs [1978], Codd et al. [1959], Gehringer and Colwell [1986], Gifford et al. [1987], Hunt [1980], Katevenis [1983], Lampson [1982], Mersel [1956].

7.5
State-Saving

The cause of an asynchronous interruption is independent of the program that is in execution. For that program the moment of switching is arbitrary, and the switching action must be transparent: Eventually the interrupted program must be resumed as though no interruption had occurred.

This need for transparency at an arbitrary moment requires preserving the entire state of the user program. Since often the caller of a subroutine wants to do just that, the method of state-saving for interruption is usually, and properly, tied to the design of the subroutine-calling sequence. Tree 7-37 gives the pertinent design choices, and Table 7-39 the methods adopted in various machines.

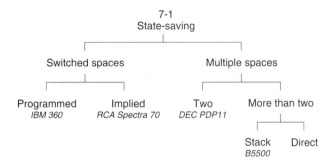

TREE 7-37 Design choices for state-saving.

Program State

The state of a program is defined by the content of its storage spaces—that is, the used parts of memory, working, and control store.

A user program that is in execution may in principle occupy any part of memory except those locations that the architecture has assigned for control functions, such as a vector of interrupt addresses. The working store is, as a rule, entirely available to the user program. The control store, on the other hand, often contains functions not available to the user program. The state of a program is determined not only by the parts of control store that it can change, such as an instruction address or a condition code, but also by the parts that it cannot change, such as protection registers.

In the 360 we made a deliberate effort to reduce the control information by crowding it into the 64-bit PSW (Program 7-38). The design of other machine functions, such as the arithmetic carry, suffered from this space limitation (Section 5.3). As early as 1965, the 360 Model 67, which needed more control

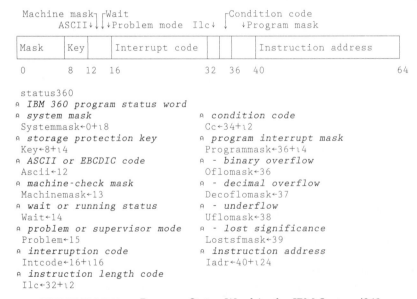

PROGRAM 7-38 Program Status Word in the IBM System/360.

	Working store	Control store
Honeywell 800	x spaces	
IBM Stretch	programmed	programmed
Ferranti Atlas	programmed	3 spaces
CDC 6600	exchange	exchange
Burroughs B5500	stacked	stacked
IBM System/360	programmed	5 spaces
RCA Spectra 70	2 spaces	
DEC PDP11	2 spaces	3 spaces
Cray 1	exchange	exchange
Motorola M6800	stacked	stacked
MOS 6502	programmed	stacked
Motorola MC68000	2 pointers	stacked
IBM 6150	x spaces	spaces

Legend: x = programmable number of spaces.

TABLE 7-39   Context preservation in various machines.

space for address mapping, used an extra control space of 16 registers, of 32 bits each. The PDP11 has a 16-bit PSW, but it also uses parts of memory and the working store for control purposes.

Preservation action.   When the state of a machine is changed from executing one program to executing another, all the storage spaces that are time-shared, called the *program context*, must be preserved as part of the old state.

Memory preservation.   Memory should have sufficient space for the active parts of the user program as well as the critical routines of the supervisor. Therefore, the part of the user program state that is in memory can be preserved at the moment of mode switching merely by leaving it alone.

This passive way of preserving memory state is possible because memory is not time-shared at the moment of switching. From a larger time perspective, of course, memory *is* time-shared. The exact purpose of the control switch may indeed be the management of time-shared memory spaces.

Virtual machine.   The possibility of preserving program state extends the concept of virtual memory (each user has his own memory) to that of the *virtual machine* (each user has his own machine). A hypervisor can now supervise other supervisors, each operating in its own virtual machine.

7.5.1

Context Switching

The program context is placed in a reusable resource, such as working registers, whose current content of the resource must be preserved upon a control switch. For working and control registers, the preservation space is either memory or a second set of registers. Either the content of the registers is switched, or the name of the registers is switched.

Programmed Context Switching

The minimal context switch affects only the instruction address. A new instruction address must be specified somehow, and the current instruction address must be kept available.

The Stretch is an example of minimal context preservation. At the moment of interruption one extra instruction, at an implied location, is performed. The instruction address, which points to the location where the interrupted program is to be resumed, is kept unchanged. Program 7-25 illustrates this action.

When the extra instruction is a subroutine call that stores the instruction address and branches, the return address is preserved and an interrupt handling routine initiated. As a first action, the interrupt handler normally preserves part or all of the remaining context, which comprises about 32 words of 64 bits. This preservation must be performed without changing the context, which is possible in the Stretch with a multiword Move, because the registers are embedded in the memory name-space. Prior to the resumption of the interrupted program, the context must be restored (Figures 7-31 and 7-32).

The Intel 8080A (1974) has about the same provision as the Stretch. Upon an interruption a Restart (subroutine call) is performed, which stores the return address and branches to the interrupt handler. The context of the 8080A is about eight registers of 8 bits. The operation set has no convenient Move as does the Stretch.

Automatic Context Switching

How much of the working and control-store spaces should be switched automatically?

Control-store switching. The 360 automatically stores the control store by switching PSWs (Program 7-33). The extended control of the Model 67 and the 370, however, is not switched.

The 360 does not switch the working store automatically. This choice was made partly for hardware simplicity, partly on the theory that saving the entire context automatically would take more time than saving only the necessary parts under program control. Alas, supervisors, such as MVS/360 and EOS/360, cannot conveniently discriminate so finely. They save the entire context anyway.

Working-store switching. Given today's ratios of logic costs to other system costs, the entire context of the 360 should be saved automatically. In fact, the designers of the Spectra 70 departed from the 360 architecture at exactly this point: Its first six general purpose registers are stored at a fixed set of locations. This arrangement is an improvement on the 360 design, although the partial store detracts from the generality of the registers.

Multiple context switches. When one interruption interrupts the handling of another interruption, each should have its own area for the part of the context that is saved automatically. The 360, which saves only the PSW, has a different

save area for the old PSW of each of its five classes of interrupt conditions, and it has five locations for the five possible new PSWs.

Nested context switches.   When interruptions of the same class are allowed to interrupt each other (i.e., when their context switches are nested), the saved context must in turn be saved. This task can be done by automatically stacking the saved areas. The PDP11 stacks the saved PSW and instruction address, as shown in Program 7-40, thus allowing nested interruptions.

The Cray 1 machine state includes the address of the Exchange Package, the place where the state to be swapped is stored. This feature allows programmed stacking, or even more flexible techniques.

Restoration.   Automatic state-saving upon interruption must be complemented by automatic or facile state restoration when the interrupted program is resumed.

```
interrupt11;who;old;new          progint11;who;nr
ᵃ DEC PDP11 interrupt action     ᵃ DEC PDP11 programmed interrupt
progint11                        who←7-(7↑read11 byte,memadr,Piw)⍳1
REPEAT: ᵃ search indicators      →If who>magni stout Priority
    who←ind⍳1                    THEN: ᵃ record request number twice
    →If who≠ρind                     nr←byte magnr who×34
    THEN: ᵃ process indicator        (byte,memadr,Piw+1) write11 nr
        ind[who]←0                   Pir report 1
        old←stout⍳word           ENDIF:
        push11 old
        push11 reg[Pc;]
        reg[Pc;]←read11 word,memadr,Intvec[who]
        Spec report 1=2|magni reg[Pc;]
        new←read11 word,memadr,2+Intvec[who]
        new[Previousmode]←old[Currentmode]
        (⍳word) stin new
        wait←0
ENDIF:→UNTIL˜wait
Bpt report stout Trace
```

PROGRAM 7-40   Interrupt action in the DEC PDP11.

7.5.2

Multiple Contexts

The alternative to context switching is to have multiple contexts, preferably one context per interruption class. This alternative avoids context saving only if nested interruptions *within* a class do not occur [Eickemeyer and Patel, 1987].

The PDP11 has two sets of working store. One set belongs to the User mode, whereas the other is shared by the Supervisor and Kernel mode. Since the Supervisor and Kernel modes are intended to handle most supervisory actions of the PDP11, context switching occurs mainly in going to and from the User mode. These switches are simplified by the double register set. The switches between Kernel and Supervisor mode are programmed as part of the supervisor. Therefore, the contents of the registers are usually predictable and need not be saved automatically.

7.5.3
Bibliography

Eickemeyer and Patel [1987], England [1975].

7.6
Tools of Control

7.6.1
Clock

The supervisor must be able to seize control from a user program when it pleases, at the very least to avoid the possibility of an endless loop.

Not only is some form of interruption required to handle the endless-loop problem, but so is some form of *terminator*, a mechanism *outside* the program sequence that can determine when to interrupt it. Furthermore, since the supervisor acts in real time, it must often know the *time of day* in communicating with the user, if only to mark messages and output with a time stamp.

The time stamp serves also as a *unique identifier*. A program that is run twice may yield different results because of changes in the data or program text; a time stamp helps distinguish the outputs. So the time stamp is one of three uses of the clock.

We first consider the program primitives and design choices for a clock (Trees 7-41 and 7-44).

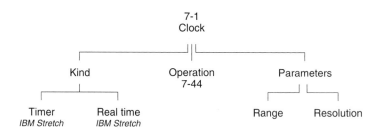

TREE 7-41   Design choices for clocks.

Timer

The simplest form of terminator is a clock that interrupts after a fixed time period, ensuring the supervisor an opportunity to alter time and resource allocation after each period. Other schemes include a counter that interrupts after a specified number of instructions and a separate processor that interrupts after completing a loop of its instructions. The clock, the counter, and the auxiliary processor are essentially isomorphic in function; the counter actually

	Operation Set	Read	Run	Bits	Range	Resolution in ..m...u...n..
IBM Stretch	s	s u	a	19	8 min	1m
Burroughs B5500		s u		6	1 sec	16m67
IBM System/360	s	s u	a	32	15 hours	13u
DEC PDP11	s		a	1	16 msec	16m67
IBM System/370				51	143 years	1u
CDC Star100	s u	s u	s u	24	16 sec	1u
Cray 1	u	u	u	64	7200 years	12n5
DEC VAX11	s	s	a	32	1 hour	1u

Legend: a = always; d = decimal; s = supervisor; u = user;
resolution shown in milli(m)-micro(u)-nano(n)-seconds,
where 3n5 means 3.5 nanoseconds.

TABLE 7-42   Timer in various machines.

tallies a warped sort of time; the processor's program loop implicitly specifies a fixed interval.

Following the Stretch, most machines have provided some form of program-readable, program-settable clock. Such a facility serves several purposes. For the terminator function, one clearly wants an alarm clock, such as a variable that is ticked up and compared to a program-settable comparand. This system is provided in the 370 [Case and Padegs, 1978]. A simpler device is a clock whose initial value is program-settable and that ticks down to 0. The 360 Elapsed Time Clock is typical. Ideally, one wants a separate terminator for each concurrent process in a multiprogrammed system, keeping *process time*, as does the stopwatch in a basketball game or each of the clocks on a chess timer. Clearly, software realization is an option, given a single hardware alarm clock. Equally clearly, such a basic, universal, and well-specified function is a natural candidate for hardware implementation.

If, as is true in many machines, interruption may occur only after one instruction is completed and before the next, endless-loop conditions arising within an instruction cannot be broken by interruptions. Indirect addressing, for example, may potentially loop. Execute instructions may form a ring. Each instruction must be examined to ensure that stopping is certain, or special provisions must be made. In the Stretch, indirect addressing and Execute operations are monitored by an auxiliary clock with a 1 ms fixed interval (Section 6.4).

Table 7-42 describes the parameters for timers in various machines.

Real-Time Clock

A quite separate need is for a program to know what the time is by the standard of the external world. Resource allocation and charging require such knowledge, as does much extra-system communication.

Standard time is measured in awkward units, due in part to Babylonian precedent and in part to the fundamental incommensurability of the earth's daily rotation and yearly revolution. Computer clocks usually solve the hour-minute-second problem by counting seconds and 2^{-n} fractions thereof. Software does base conversion, handling the calendar problem as well.

| | Operation | | | Bits | Range | Resolution in |
	Set	Read	Run			..m...u...n..
IBM Stretch		s u	a	36	2 years	1m
CDC 6600 PPU		u	a	12	4 msec	1u
DEC PDP10	s	s	s u	18	143 years	10u
IBM System/370				51	143 years	1u
CDC Star100		s u	a	47	9 years	1u
Cray 1	s	s u	a	64	7200 years	12n5
DEC VAX11	s	s	a	32	497 days	10m

Legend: a = always; d = decimal; s = supervisor; u = user;
resolution shown in milli(m)-micro(u)-nano(n)-seconds,
where 3n5 means 3.5 nanoseconds.

TABLE 7-43   Real-time clock in various machines.

The real-time clock must be settable, for it may be stopped for machine repair and, in any case, must be initialized. It should be sufficiently accurate to need only very rare adjustments.

Synchronization.   Clocks and timers in the processors of a multiprocessing system should be synchronized. One solution is to provide only one set of time functions for the entire system. As an alternative, the implementation should ensure proper synchronization of the systems—something difficult to achieve when system components are far apart. Although, in principle, it can never be done exactly, in practice it can be done as precisely as necessary.

Table 7-43 shows the parameters of real-time clocks of various machines.

Unique-Identifier Generator

One use of a real-time clock is as a generator of unique values. If a clock has enough range that it will not repeat, its values can be so used.

The number of unique identifiers needed by a system will usually be far fewer than the clock pulses in a system lifetime, even though the maximum rate of demand may be equal to or exceed the clock-pulse rate. So a clock is not an efficient generator of unique identifiers, and identifier bits can be saved by providing a separate mechanism for identifier generation. This mechanism should increment by one each time it is read.

A similar non-timing use of a clock is to use the low-order bits of the clock as a pseudo-random number. This artifice is improper also, since the programmer must ensure that he does not call for these values on a cyclic basis, else the randomness is ruined.

Parameters

Trees 7-41 and 7-44 show that terminators, as well as real-time clocks, require decisions about range, resolution, and operations for setting, reading, and running.

Range.   How many bits should be used to express time? The range of a clock determines the time before turnover. This range must be at least so large that the supervisor will surely look at the clock several times during the range interval and so can maintain a longer-range software clock. If the entire desired range is maintained in hardware, the supervisor is simplified.

Resolution.   The resolution or precision of a clock is the minimum interval measured.

Over the years, the resolution required by the most demanding computer applications has become steadily finer. On the 360, the basic decision was to position the bits in the word so that the format would allow a resolution of $1 \div 300 \times 2^{-8}$ seconds, or 13.02 microseconds. Timers with this resolution are available on some models. The standard timer is counted down by five in bits 0 to 23 each 1/60 second, or by six each 1/50 second, depending on the main power frequency, thus counting integral numbers of 1/300 second.

On the 370, both the range and the resolution of the 360's clock are extended. The range has a period of about 143 years; the resolution is about a microsecond, with format space to extend it compatibly to 0.25 nanoseconds.

On the Cray 1, the timer has a resolution of one machine-clock pulse. This interval is the shortest meaningful one possible and guarantees unique names. Such design is highly realization-specific, however.

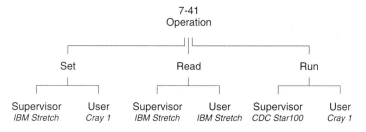

TREE 7-44   Design choices for clock operation.

Operations.   Clocks must be settable and readable. If the clocks are assigned fixed memory locations, no special operations are necessary, but the locations must be protected.

Tables 7-42 and 7-43 show that some clocks are set only by the supervisor. The STAR100 has a separate timer for the supervisor and for the user. When the clock is implemented with a backup battery, it needs to be set less often.

7.6.2

Interpretive Console

The break between the mostly uniprogrammed second-generation computers and the mostly multiprogrammed third-generation and later computers is nowhere so visible as in their consoles.

In a uniprogrammed machine, one console serves many essentially distinct purposes:

- Interaction of user and program at execution time
- Operator control for supervisory functions
- Tape- and disk-mounting messages
- Hardware maintenance

Terminal.   In a multiprogrammed machine the interaction of a user with his program at execution time   requires that a console be linked with the user's program. If multiple users are to interact with their several programs at once, there must be multiple user consoles. User consoles are called *terminals*, because once their function has been separated from other console functions, they can be located at the end of communication links.

The provision of many terminals dictates that their keys and switches not control the CPU hardware directly, and that their lights and displays not show hardware status directly. Instead, each must be treated as an I/O device. The keys represent so many bits of input; the display represents so many bits of output. No fixed meaning is attached to either; the program interprets and defines the console. The Stretch was the first machine to incorporate this concept, so far as we know [Brooks, 1962].

Operator console.   For machines with an operator, including one mounting tapes or disks, the operator's console likewise needs to communicate with a program, the supervisor, not with the hardware, so an interpretive console is proper for this function. Because of its intense use and the likelihood of system delay during its use, one can justify a considerably more elaborate facility for this purpose than for an ordinary user terminal. Cathode-ray tubes for very high display rates are common. The 6600 was one of the first to use two—one normally dedicated to tape- and disk-mounting messages. Such separation of function allows the mounting message console to be physically located among the tape drives or in the tape vault, separate from the main control station.

Maintenance console.   With the user and operator functions handled separately, the hardware maintenance console no longer need intrude on the computer architecture. It can be completely part of the implementation.

Hardware maintenance requires local control, but a remote terminal may also be provided for maintenance; then the hardware can be diagnosed from a central location where expertise and experience are concentrated. This concentration has become more necessary as machines have become more reliable; no one machine experiences enough failures to give its maintainers extensive diagnostic experience.

7.6.3
Initial Program Load

Initial program loading (IPL) initiates a processor when the contents of memory or of the control store are not suitable for processing. Such a situation occurs after the initial power on (hence the name). It may also occur after a machine or supervisor failure. The first instance may be automated—as is the case with most modern machines. The latter instance cannot be automated within a single processor, but automation can be obtained in a multiprocessing environment (Section 7.2).

Initial program load usually consists of the following sequence:

- Resetting several storage devices

- Reading from a predefined input device into a predefined area of memory
- Loading of part of the control store from a predefined set of memory addresses
- Starting instruction execution

7.6.4

Bibliography

Brooks [1962], Case and Padegs [1978].

7.7

Rules of Good Practice

1. The source of a synchronous interruption should be uniquely identifiable; there should be no imprecise interruption.
2. Address protection should apply to units in the name-space, not in the physical memory space.
3. The entire control state should be preservable to allow virtual machines.
4. Input, output, and external service requests should be made available by indicators that can be disregarded, to allow both polling and interrupt handling.

7.8

Exercises

7-1 Explain any reasons for using multiprocessing in the following circumstances:

a. The Internal Revenue Service wants a new computer for processing tax returns. It must process 140 million tax returns per year (not all on April 15).

b. NASA wants a new computer to regulate the manned spacestation. The computer must automatically monitor and control all functions, such as oxygen supply, rocket guidance, and health status.

7-2 For a two-processor system with all storage shared, explain how processor-based virtual storage and paging could introduce problems, and indicate a possible solution.

7-3 Suppose that, in the system of Exercise 7-2, an exposed cache is used in each processor. Explain possible problems, and give a proposed solution for each.

7-4 If a processing unit and part of memory are packaged as a single unit with one power supply, would a power failure in this single unit affect operations for each of the multiprocessing configurations in the text? Are any of the configurations fail-soft?

7-5 Would the Stretch design have been better if all indicators had had a changeable mask? Consider cost and actual programming ease and speed.

7-6 What function would be lost if a user could not protect his own information against his own errors?

7-7 Suggest a way to obtain the interrupt breakpoint at lower bit cost than 1 bit per instruction. How does your solution differ from programmed polling?

7-8 The Intel 8259 chip, which provides interrupt handling for the 8080, generates an address that is specific for each interrupt case. Would you prefer an interrupt code over the branch address? Why do you think the architects selected the address method?

7-9 Which indicators are permanently masked on in the Stretch and in the 360 (see the Zoo)? Note differences, and state which solution you prefer and why.

7-10 Devise a scheme by which a user can execute a program without the ability to read or copy it.

7-11 In many applications it is desirable for multiple users to share data in a common memory. Show how segmentation with paging allows this sharing. Extend the scheme to allow shared reading access but write access for only one user.

Input/Output

Overview of the Chapter

An input/output (I/O) operation is a Move operation to or from the space of an I/O device, so the design tree for I/O operation (Tree 8-1) is in first instance very simple. With the Move as such already treated (Section 5.1), the only new aspects are the I/O spaces and their specification. Nevertheless, no part of a computer manual is so difficult to read and understand as the section treating I/O operation. Why is that so? Why are the spaces and formats of I/O more complex than those governing the CPU operation?

Confounding of implementation and architecture. A first reason is that, in I/O operations, the implementation tends to intrude into the architecture. The fine implementation detail makes the architecture complex indeed to understand. Sometimes the implementation detail is visible necessarily. Too often it is visible unnecessarily and improperly: The architecture itself receives elaboration that is not proper to the architecture, or that includes irrelevant implementation material. I/O design demands a strict adherence to the separation of architecture and implementation.

In this chapter, as elsewhere, we omit concepts that are implementation only. The organization of a time-shared bus or an asynchronous buffer may be of vital interest to an implementer, but it need not affect the architecture.

Properties of input/output operations. Much of the strangeness of I/O operations derives from the wide differences between I/O devices and CPUs. Most of these differences arise from the mechanical motion common to most I/O devices. Many properties of I/O devices, including their slow operation, specialization, and inherent unreliability, follow from the devices' mechanical motion. Section 8.1 treats these properties.

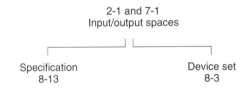

TREE 8-1 Design choices for input/output spaces.

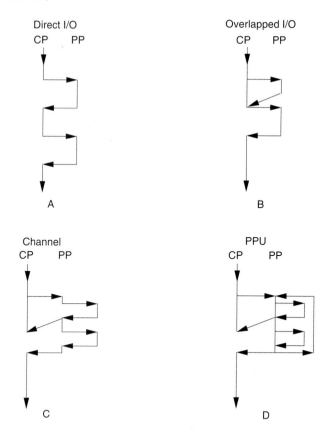

Legend: CP = computing process; PP = peripheral process; I/O = device process. The arrows indicate the relation between these processes.

FIGURE 8-2   Concurrency of peripheral processes.

Asynchronous processes.   A CPU executes a single process, sequenced by its own instruction stream and clocked autonomously. Actual writing on a disk or to a communication line is a separate process, asynchronous to that of the CPU and clocked by the I/O device. I/O systems communicate between the CPU process and the necessarily autonomous devices. As computers have evolved, this communication has evolved through a complete cycle.

The simplest machines finesse communication of these asynchronous processes by having the CPU wait as necessary to synchronize with the device. Such CPU inefficiency has led to separate simple, perhaps specialized, processors for I/O. They do the waiting, and their task then becomes synchronization among processors.

Figure 8-2 gives a diagram of the four types of I/O operation:

1. *Direct input/output*—the computing process waits.
2. As the computing process becomes more powerful, waiting becomes more costly, making *overlapped operation* desirable.
3. A separate processor, the *channel*, is attached to do some of the I/O processing; it is cheap enough that it can afford to wait.

4. The I/O processor becomes a complete processor, the *peripheral proces-sor*, for which in turn overlapped operation often becomes desirable.

In *direct input/output*, the CPU process reads by taking a single byte or word from the I/O process and writes by making a single byte or word available to the I/O process. It may stop and wait if an input chunk is not ready, or if an output chunk has not been written by the I/O process (Section 8.2). The I/O process is very simple; it only transmits a chunk of data at a time to the CPU process from the medium, or vice versa.

In *overlapped operation*, the I/O process has become more capable. When-ever it is started, it transfers one block of data between the device and a buffer known to the CPU, while the CPU keeps on executing instructions. Section 8.3 treats this case. Section 8.5 treats the specialized I/O processor, the *channel*, which can now execute its own sequence of operations.

The *peripheral processor* handles I/O transfers by direct I/O or overlapped operation exactly as in parts A and B of Figure 8-2 (Section 8.4). The historical development reflected in Figure 8-2 comes full circle, ending where it began, but with a dedicated I/O processor carrying it out. There obviously can be recursion on this cycle.

Note that, in part D of Figure 8-2, the peripheral process is shown to start the main process, although the converse is also possible.

Device diversity.   The final cause of the complexity of I/O operation is the diversity of the I/O devices that are attached to computers. There are dozens of different devices, and each has special logical properties that must be exploited if a program is to take full advantage of the device.

We do not treat devices as such; nevertheless, it is desirable to develop some uniform way of relating all these devices to any one of many different computers. This I/O interface relation is treated in Section 8.6.

8.1

Input/Output Devices

A general purpose central processor is made into an application-specific data-processing system by equipping it with a program and a set of suitably specialized I/O devices. The variety of applications is very great; the variety of I/O devices is correspondingly great, as shown in Tree 8-3. By 1975, for example, some 80 distinct I/O devices were available from IBM alone for attachment to IBM System/370 (1971) computers. Many of these devices had properties inherently and fundamentally different from other devices, due to their intended uses. Even more had incidental differences arising from market pressures or different designers' views of excellence.

8.1.1

Purposes of Devices

Custom has lumped together all the devices involving mechanical motion, treating transmission to and from these devices as a special operation, called

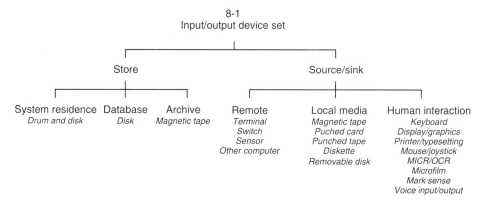

8-1
Input/output device set

Store

Source/sink

System residence	Database	Archive	Remote	Local media	Human interaction
Drum and disk	*Disk*	*Magnetic tape*	*Terminal*	*Magnetic tape*	*Keyboard*
			Switch	*Puched card*	*Display/graphics*
			Sensor	*Punched tape*	*Printer/typesetting*
			Other computer	*Diskette*	*Mouse/joystick*
				Removable disk	*MICR/OCR*
					Microfilm
					Mark sense
					Voice input/output

TREE 8-3   Design choices for input/output devices.

input/output. The access time and other general properties deriving from motion are so different from those of purely electronic apparatus as to make this distinction useful. One might say the difference between access times (a factor of 10^4) has completely dominated distinctions based on purpose and function.

Classification of input/output devices.   Yet distinctions based on function are more fundamental than those based on speed, for the functional distinctions are technology-independent. The most important functional distinction divides the computing system not into the two parts of Figure 8-4, but rather into the three of Figure 8-5, thus subdividing I/O operation into a store, and a source and sink.

The *store* is the part of the system where data is stored for later retrieval by the system itself. *Source/sink* or *true input/output* is the part of the system where data enter from or depart to the outside world.

Store

The store includes the memory and any auxiliary devices whose purpose is to hold data for later use in the same system. Such devices can fruitfully be considered as memory-extension devices, even though they may have separate name-spaces. Because of the relatively high cost of all-electronic memories, almost all systems include auxiliarly mechanical-storage devices as well.

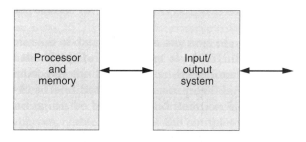

FIGURE 8-4   Two-part conception of a computer system.

Auxiliary storage devices serve three distinct purposes: system residence, database, and archival store. Each purpose has different requirements, so devices with properties appropriate to each have been developed. These specializations, however, are only approximate. There has been a historic shift in usage: The drum was used first as main memory, then as database, then as system residence, and now hardly at all.

System residence.   After main memory, the most important storage is the system residence. Its purpose is to serve as an extension of the main memory, containing working sets of active programs, especially the queues, tables, and code segments of the operating system itself. It may also store high-usage data directories and parts of the program library.

On paging and virtual-memory systems, this extension is called the *backing store*; on other systems, it is usually called the *system residence device*. Its requirements are quick access and high data rates. It needs capacities in the tens of millions of bytes.

Today the system residence is most often implemented by a moving-head disk or an electronic store configured to simulate a disk. In first- and second-generation systems, it was most often implemented by magnetic tape, although drums were sometimes used.

Database.   Many systems require access to large amounts of data, stored in a *database*. Because many systems operate on-demand services, usually initiated from remote terminals, these systems require continual and unpredictable access to large databases. Such databases are usually implemented on disks today, although many other kinds of devices have been used.

On-line database devices are characterized by (1) access on the order of tens to hundreds of milliseconds, (2) modest data rates, but (3) very large capacities and low cost per bit. Capacities range from 10^5 to 10^{12} bytes.

A less demanding database requirement is also common—files of data that are batch-processed (so they can be passed sequentially). This class of use includes working space for large sorts. This function is often implemented by magnetic tapes, although disks are also commonly used.

Archive.   Almost all data-processing systems require the production, storage, and occasional retrieval of *archives*—data saved to meet yet unspecified needs. This function demands high capacity, minimal cost per bit, a data rate governed chiefly by the rate of generation (rather than the rate of reference), and very relaxed access time. Today it is most often implemented by magnetic tape, removable disks, diskettes, and tape cartridges.

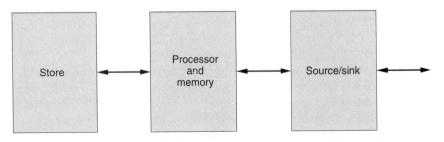

FIGURE 8-5   Three-part conception of a computer system.

Source and Sink

A processing system can be considered as part of a larger overall system, with which it communicates via *source-sink devices,* but over which it has no direct control. The source/sink devices can be classified by their relation to this larger system (Tree 8-3).

Effect of Properties on the Input/Output Architecture

The purposes of storage devices are quite distinct from those of source/sink devices. The two classes should be considered separately even if designer finally chooses a common control technique for both. Storage and source/sink were separated, for example, in the Ferranti Atlas (1962), where Kilburn and his colleagues treated the drum and memory together, and all other I/O separately. The result was far cleaner and faster drum use as part of the one-level store.

Furthermore, the access, data rate, and reliability requirements of storage devices are typically far greater than those of source/sink devices, so different technologies and control techniques are appropriate.

Finally, most source/sink devices will continue for many years to involve mechanical motion or speed-limited remote transmission. Storage devices, on the other hand, are now often realized in all-electronic technology, drastically reducing the 10^4 gap between memory and device access times. Then, an attachment method quite distinct from that used for source/sink devices, and much more intimate than today's methods, is called for.

8.1.2

Motion

Most I/O devices use motion, which is the greatest difference between them and the modern CPU, where only electrons and fans move.

Why do I/O devices use motion?

Motion of the medium.   Storage devices exist to provide cheaper storage of information than is possible in a main memory. The saving is accomplished by sharing the reading and writing circuits over a large number of bits, which are selected by moving the recording medium. A key technical problem then becomes how to select. So time is often used as a dimension of selection by moving a medium, such as a magnetic disk, past a read/write mechanism. This sequential operation can lower the cost per bit, at the expense of slow access.

Motion of the mechanism.   Time can also be traded for equipment in source/sink devices. In printing, for example, a column of jets of ink can print a character in a succession of strokes; a moving type element, such as a daisywheel, can print a succession of characters; a print chain can pass by a line. In all these cases, the mechanism moves over the medium.

Motion of the information.   Wave motion can also store information, as in the classical acoustic and electric delay lines, and in the newer optical delay lines.

In delay lines, neither medium nor mechanism moves, but the information does, and slower access is traded for cheaper storage.

Consequences of Motion

Magnetic tape was the first I/O system used on commercial computers. Indeed, the Univac I (1951) had no other I/O device (except for a console typewriter). Punched cards were read and punched on off-line card-to-tape and tape-to-card machines; printing was done on off-line tape printers. There-fore, through the years, the reading and writing of tape has been the driving problem for the design of I/O operation. The reader will be able to explain many developments and characteristics of I/O systems when he sees them as responses to this particular driving problem.

The logical consequences of the sequential operation commonly found in I/O devices are asynchronism, slow and varying access, concurrency, slow data-rates, and time urgency.

Asynchronism.   Due to mechanical tolerances, the motors that provide motion can rarely be conveniently operated in synchrony with one other. So the I/O process is a transmission of data between two inherently asynchronous processes—that of the device and that of the CPU.

Slow access.   When many bits share the access mechanism, a given bit cannot usually be read immediately when it is requested. (This property is called *latency*). The tape must move; the disk head must move; the disk, drum, or chain must rotate.

Since mechanical motion is much slower than electronic propagation, the access to information on mechanical I/O devices may typically be more than 10 ms, or more than 10^4 to 10^5 times as long as required for CPU main memories.

Concurrency.   Four orders of magnitude is an immense ratio. Imagine a CPU doing an operation each second; a disk half-rotation 10^4 slower takes three hours! It is as if a person doing additions, and capable of doing one per second, sent a friend off 100 kilometers by car to fetch each next addend.

While a disk turns half around or a tape accelerates to reading speed, a workstation CPU can execute perhaps 100,000 instructions. This opportunity is almost irresistible; most designs allow the I/O process to be concurrent with the CPU process, so that this computing capacity can be used.

Indeed, because access times are so slow, one wants to have several accesses under way at once. The ordinary I/O system therefore operates a multiplicity of I/O processes, all concurrent with one other and with the CPU.

Widely varying access times.   Access varies greatly because of medium motion. Finding an arbitrary bit may take quite a long while. Finding the next bit on the track is very quick—a fraction of a microsecond.

Therefore, if there is the slightest chance (better than about 1 in 10^4) of needing the next datum after finding the one sought, one is well-advised to read it also into memory. This logic leads inescapably to the reading and writing of data in blocks whose size is limited chiefly by the cost and

availability of memory space. If it takes a long time to go to the well, one should bring back as much water as the bucket will hold.

Slow data rate.   Not only is access slow, but also the transmission of data from a device, once a block is found, is often (but by no means always) slow compared to a memory-to-memory transmission. So programs using a lot of data, such as file-maintenance programs, are usually limited by I/O data rate. Therefore, the CPU is capable of operating and doing the computing for several I/O processes concurrently.

Amdahl's rule.   The combination of slow access and slow data rate has led programmers to structure programs into well-defined internal and I/O tasks. Amdahl has discovered that the resulting ratio of I/O operation to computing has held approximately constant over a wide range of jobs and over at least the years 1956 to 1968. He finds that I/O traffic is 1 bit per instruction executed by the CPU; this traffic includes all accesses to disks and drums [personal communication; also Amdahl, 1970].

Time urgency.   I/O devices often have time urgencies, of two types: those in which timely response is essential to *correct* operation (such as a check sorter), and those in which timely response is necessary for *efficient* operation (such as a tape drive). All high-inertia devices capable of intermittent operation fall at least into the latter category. After reading a record, the mechanism will disengage and decelerate unless another read instruction is received within some specified time. The rated reading speed can be attained only if the mechanism is not allowed to disengage. A *cache* can be used effectively with such an I/O device.

8.1.3
Input/Output Spaces

I/O devices that serve as stores usually have their own name-spaces.

Addressing.   By its nature, an I/O device space favors either sequential or direct addressing.

Self-indexing.   A sequential-access device presents successive information units automatically, without the explicit modification of addresses necessary in a memory-to-memory block transmission. Such devices are said to be *self-indexing*, which is equivalent to first-in first-out (FIFO) addressing. After a read or a write, the medium is automatically positioned for the next operation. The advantage of this property is simplicity; the chief disadvantage is the difficulty of backing up.

Reversibility.   A tape, however, can also be read backward, which in principle gives LIFO addressing. Since the data unit is normally a character, the process would deliver a reversed sequence of characters. Therefore, some I/O processors, such as the IBM System/360 (1965) channels, place this sequence into memory with a reversed address sequence, which stores the record in memory with normal character sequence.

Private name-spaces.   When the I/O name-space is directly addressed (for example, in disks), that address space is normally private to the device. Source/sink devices may also have private spaces—for example, a communication system with line and terminal addresses, and a graphic screen with x and y pixel coordinates.

Implied block length.   Devices themselves often impose a physical-block structure on the contained data, independently of its logical structure. For a disk, each track is a physical block, and the cylinder defined by a single positioning of the access arm constitutes a higher-level block. On tape, the necessity of leaving a gap for deceleration and acceleration between separate tape motions defines blocks as the units written and read without stopping the tape. A printed line has an obvious physical-block structure.

Specialization

Storage media often require functions other than data selecting, reading, or writing—functions proper to the medium or the device, and usually concerned with the handling of the medium itself.

Auxiliary functions.   Printers, for example, normally have controllable paper movement, allowing skipping to the bottom of a page for a total, or skipping to the top of the next page. They may allow various type fonts, and may allow selection among fixed formats such as letterheads. Some allow programmed control of a knife that cuts separate sheets from a continuous paper roll.

Reciprocating transmission.   Some devices cannot be operated satisfactorily by block transmissions of data; they require the high-speed alternation of reading and writing. A check sorter, for example, sends a line of data to the computer, which must quickly return the resultant pocket-selection information. A scanner of instrumentation sensors may require a steady stream of sensor addresses from the computer, to allow some to be sampled more frequently. After receiving a particular address, the scanner returns the specified datum.

8.1.4
Malfunctions

A major cause of failure in I/O is the physical motion of a medium relative to an access mechanism. Friction, aerodynamic flutter, and medium wear all take their toll.

Moreover, the relative motion of the medium means that information flows to and from that medium over an inherently changeable path, such as a magnetic field through an air gap. The medium itself has inherent inhomogeneities; interchangeability of media among read/write stations implies yet greater variability.

Because of these reasons,

- I/O processes have radically *higher malfunction rates* than do CPU processes. Intermittent malfunctions must be considered normal, and malfunction recovery must be automatic or under programmed control.
- Devices have not only a high rate of intermittent failures, but also a high rate of *complete failures.* A system should be designed to operate while some devices are undergoing repair.
- The *mechanisms of malfunction* are *different* from one device to another. Extensive and specific error-recovery procedures must be devised to match the high-frequency malfunctions of each type. In MVS/360, these procedures account for a significant fraction of the I/O control program. Moreover, the I/O-control hardware design must allow the program to sense information about device state, and control instructions (as opposed to data) must be transmitted to the device.

Since each device has its own modes of malfunction, the designer must develop strategies for recovery that usually require action sequences more complex than the logical power of the device proper has historically been able to accomplish. Some of these sequences have always been reasonable for the I/O controller, which must have considerable logical power for its other functions; other sequences have historically required full programming power—a PPU or a CPU. Now that microprocessors have very low cost, systems are being designed such that each device has its own local processor that handles error recovery.

The procedures for magnetic-tape error recovery have had time to evolve considerable sophistication. To give a feel for this part of the I/O control task, we describe one particular set of such procedures in painful detail. The procedures described are those of the IBM Model 3480 tape drive, which records data at 38,000 bits/inch/track, uses 18 tracks, and moves tape 2 meters/second for a maximum data rate of 3 MB/second. Some 20 different kinds of malfunction indications can arise during operation of the tape. We describe the recovery procedure used for only one, a Data Check.

Malfunction mechanisms. High-density tape recording depends on very close contact between the head and the tape. If a stray particle of dust (such as a wear product from the tape itself) is borne along on the flying tape, it causes a momentary separation between the tape and the head. Since the tape is flexible, aerodynamic flutter may prolong this separation. So intermittent read errors are common, and they tend to occur in clusters spaced along a track or group of adjacent tracks.

A second error, called *skew*, occurs because 18 bits are written simultaneously on as many heads. When the tape is read on a different mechanism, a very small difference in head alignment will destroy this simultaneity. On 38,000 bit/inch tape, for example, an alignment difference of 1/38,000 inch—less than 0.00003 inches—between the reading heads and the writing heads will misplace a bit into the next byte.

Coding strategies. Redundant coding is used on the tape to allow error detection and error correction. Each 18-bit group along the tape has an error-correction code.

```
    message                    out←dr cycliccheck in
1 1 1 0 1 1 0 0 1          ⍝ cyclic check of a message
                              out←in,((ρdr)ρ2)⊤(2⊥dr)|-2⊥in,dr
    divisor
1 1 0 1

    divisor cycliccheck message
1 1 1 0 1 1 0 0 1 1 0 1 1
```

PROGRAM 8-6   Cyclic group error-correcting check.

Next, data are recorded with a cyclic group-error–correction code, arranged to allow correction of a group of bits. This especially helps when multiple consecutive errors occur in one track. The calculation is made on all the bits in an n-byte block, treated as a single vector. Program 8-6 shows such a code on a small scale.

Finally, a longitudinal parity is applied to each track of a block, as shown in Program 8-7.

```
    out←longparity in                     longparity ⍉(4ρ2)⊤⍳5
⍝ odd-parity byte per message     0 0 0 0
    out←in,[0]~≠/in                       0 0 0 1
                                          0 0 1 0
                                          0 0 1 1
                                          0 1 0 0
                                          1 0 1 1
```

PROGRAM 8-7   Longitudinal parity check.

Data Check Recovery Procedures

Retry procedures.   Experimental data show that backspacing and re-reading the failing block often correct intermittent errors that cannot be corrected by decoding alone. Surprisingly, the probability of a successful read from a retry remains significant even after scores of unsuccessful retries on the same block. The Data Check recovery strategy thus specifies that many retries be attempted.

Tape (and head) cleaning.   Since dust particles are often responsible for trouble, the tape head incorporates a knife that scrapes the tape. If four normal retries fail, the tape may be "shoeshined" past this knife. Then, further retries are attempted. This whole sequence of four retries followed by a tape-cleaning action may be iterated several times.

Reverse reading.   Reading in the reverse direction is sometimes successful when retry fails. The procedure mandates multiple tries at reading in the reverse direction if the first retries fail.

Erase gap.   The tape head incorporates both writing and reading magnetic-field gaps, arranged so the presence and correct parity of a byte can be sensed immediately after the byte is written. If a block is defectively written, writing is retried. Failure of retry suggests a worn spot in the tape surface, so the prescribed procedure calls for writing an interblock gap, then attempting to write the block on a different part of the tape. Erase Gap is a control instruction interpreted by the device.

Data compression.   Once an I/O system has logical power enough to handle error recovery, it can do other complex parts of the task as well. The 3480 control unit does automatic data compression, extension buffering, and data blocking, for example.

8.1.5
Bibliography

Amdahl [1970], Renwick and Cole [1971].

8.2
Direct Input/Output

Concept

The simplest I/O control system specifies a memory-to-I/O Move in the same manner as a memory-to-memory Move. A distinct operation code must be used to mark one of the addresses as outside the memory name-space, unless the device space is embedded in the memory name-space.

Implementing this simple specification is itself simple. The I/O process waits for execution in the device to complete, then proceeds on to the next instruction.

Significance.   The earliest computers used this kind of direct input/output. The great waste of CPU cycles in I/O waiting was a major shortcoming. But a concurrent processor—such as a PPU—or a channel, uses direct input/output very effectively, for the cycles wasted waiting are cheap. Virtual PPU processors are nearly "free." So direct I/O is still the basic technique, although at first glance it might appear to be painfully awkward and thoroughly obsolete. Not only I/O processors, but also minicomputers and microcomputers still use it.

8.2.1
Input/Output Operations

Direct I/O operations must specify a direction of information flow, in or out, and select between two sources/destinations, the I/O medium and the device itself. The resulting four operations are often called

- Read (in from medium)
- Write (out to medium)
- Sense (in from device)
- Control (out to device)

Read and Write

The I/O move can be specified in many ways, as discussed in Section 5.1 for moves generally. In particular, one may have a block move, or one may

```
↓Modifier                          *↓
┌──┬─────┬──┬───────────┬──┐
│* │     │Op│* │Address  │  │
└──┴─────┴──┴───────────┴──┘
0         12  1618        31
Legend: Op = opcode; * = unused.

I;byte
ᴀ Librascope LGP30 Read From Paper Tape
byte← 6 4[fld Mod]
acc←byte↓acc,byte↑tape[0;]
tape← 1 0 ↓tape


P;byte
ᴀ Librascope LGP30 Print On Flexowriter
byte← 6 4[fld Mod]
flexo←6↑(byte↑acc), 1 0
```

PROGRAM 8-8   Input/output instructions of the LGP30.

have an elementary one-character move. Since the basic assumption of direct I/O is simplicity, a frequent decision is to provide a one-character move and expect the block move to be programmed by iteration.

One-character Move.   The LGP30 (1957), a minimal computer, is an example of extreme I/O simplicity (Program 8-8).   There is only one I/O device, a Flexowriter typewriter/paper-tape reader.   The operation Input shifts one character from the paper tape into the accumulator. The operation Print prints the symbol given as an immediate datum in the address field.

Since one character is treated at a time, the rules are few.   There is no overlap; the process is slow. If one wants to optimize device actions, such as the engaging and disengaging of the tape movement to get maximum speed, the programmer must do the timing.   Many computers, from the Ferranti Mark 1 (1951) and STC ZEBRA (1959) down to the Intel 8080A (1974) and the Motorola M6800 (1975) and their successors, have this type of I/O facility.

Block Move.   The IBM 702 (1954) and IBM 705 (l956) provide a direct-I/O system that was much easier to use than the one-character Move.   The

```
┌──┬─────────────────────┐
│Op│Address              │
└──┴─────────────────────┘
0  1                    5
Legend: Op = opcode.

RD;dest                          SEL
ᴀ IBM 705 Read                   ᴀ IBM 705 Select Device
dest←adr705                       select←adr705
dest write705 iodata,recordmark   iostate[select]←busy
iostate[]←ready


WR;source;length
ᴀ IBM 705 Write
source←adr705
length←(source↓magni memory)ɩmagni recordmark
iodata←length read705 source
iostate[]←ready
```

PROGRAM 8-9   Input/output instructions of the IBM 705.

machines operate on variable-length fields throughout, so a variable-length
I/O Move is a simple and natural operation, using the automatic successor-
address-generating mechanism available for internal operations. Furthermore,
since the variable-length Move can be of up to 256 bytes, block sizes on tape
can vary to suit the needs of the application. The Read and Write instructions
are given in Program 8-9.

Auxiliary direct input/output.   Although the main I/O control system in the
360 embodies quite a different philosophy, the 360 contains a primitive but
complete direct-I/O control system, intended as an auxiliary. The operations
are Read Direct and Write Direct (Program 8-10); they allow an 8-bit data
byte and an 8-bit control byte to be transmitted between a single port and a
memory location specified by the address. The control byte can be used to
specify an address in an I/O device name-space.

Why was this auxiliary direct-I/O system provided? The chief purpose
was communication among multiple CPUs, where promptness, directness,
and synchrony with program execution are vital. A secondary motivation
was provision for unspecified future I/O devices that might be inherently
unfittable to the main I/O control system.

In the 370, the anticipated future I/O devices led to extensions of the
channel function, making direct I/O unnecessary in the view of the designers.
They dropped it from the 370 architecture.

```
┌─────────┬──────────┬─────┬─────────────────────┐
│ Opcode  │ Imm      │ B1  │ D1                   │
└─────────┴──────────┴─────┴─────────────────────┘
0         8          16   20                    32
Legend:  B = base;  D = displacement;  Imm = immediate.
```

```
RDD                              WRD
ค IBM 360 Read Direct           ค IBM 360 Write Direct
  Invop report~diropt             Invop report~diropt
  Priv report psw[Problem]        Priv report psw[Problem]
  →OUT suppress360                →OUT suppress360
  signalout←inst[Imm]             signalout←inst[Imm]
  adr360bd write360 directin      directout←byte read360 adr360bd
```

PROGRAM 8-10   Direct input/output in the IBM System/360.

Sense and Control

In practice, controlling a device for a proper transmission may require actions considerably more diverse than just Read or Write. Table 8-11 shows that,
in the IBM 701 (1953), control instructions to the device are specified by distinct
operations, such as Read Select (which not only specifies a device, but engages
clutches to start motion), Write End Of File, and Rewind Tape. Sensing and
controlling of device state is somewhat more general, being specified by a
single operation (Sense), whose address specifies the device and/or condition
sensed; the operation also provides a general control operation for the printer,
card punch, console lights, and switches. Thus the CPU architecture reflects
the properties of the I/O devices.

```
a CPY Copy And Skip      a WEF Write End Of File
a RDS Read Select        a SNS Sense
a RDB Read Backwards     a REW Rewind Tape
a WRS Write Select       a LDA Locate Drum Address
```

TABLE 8-11   Input/output instructions of the IBM 701.

The diverse properties of the I/O devices must inevitably be incorporated into the application design and the application program itself. This diversity should not be gratuitously evident in the system. So the CPU, the memory, and the operating-system supervisor should not be affected by the diversity of I/O device properties or the peculiar properties of any device. One wants to quarantine this complexity to its own quarters.

Control information.   This quarantining is substantially aided by recognizing that the I/O flow involves transmission to and from not only the I/O medium (screens, paper, magnetic tape, or cards), but also the device itself (display, printer, tape drive, or card reader). Each of the auxiliary medium-handling functions, such as line skipping, can be considered as actions taken by the device upon receipt of appropriate instructions from the CPU.

If the instructions to the device are packaged in some suitably uniform way, they can be transmitted exactly as though they were data. The device particularities re-emerge only as these instructions are interpreted by the device (Figure 8-12).

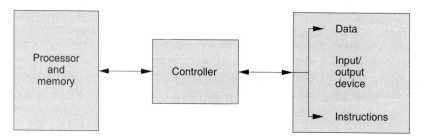

FIGURE 8-12   Packaging of sense and control information as data.

Furthermore, if control instructions are so packaged, any number of intermediate transmissions can be performed on the I/O data-and-control information stream without damaging it. A stream of print data and interspersed paper movement instructions can be spooled onto disk for later execution.

Sense information.   Not only is there an outflow of control data to the device, but there is also an inflow of data from the device about its own state, the *sense information.* A tape read operation may terminate successfully, for example, or it may terminate because a fuse blew. The program needs to know which.

Sense information, like control information, can be packaged uniformly and interspersed with data read from the medium. In this case, the I/O control system need not be aware of the interpretation of the device state data.

This generalized approach is important because Sense and Control are often more frequently used than Read and Write; they were first used in the IBM Stretch (1961) computer [Buchholz, 1962] (Section 13.3).

8.2.2
Specification of Outboard Resources

A direct input/output operation must specify not only the participating region in memory, but also the device itself and perhaps the participating region in the device's name-space. In many systems, the I/O operation must also specify the path to the device through an I/O attachment network. Tree 8-13 shows the alternatives for these specifications.

Path Addressing

In a memory-to-memory move, the routing of the transmission does not concern the programmer and is therefore concealed from him. Things are not so clean for I/O configurations. For reliability and economy, there are often several possible paths between a CPU and an I/O device, and path specification is often left to the (operating system) programmer. Most large computer systems allow a complex I/O configuration.

Control units and devices. Most I/O contraptions consist of two parts: the mechanism that moves and the electronics that control the motion, amplify and discriminate signals read, and provide the writing currents.

Attachment tree. When magnetic-tape recording was new, the electronics were costly. Any given tape mechanism was inherently idle for a significant fraction of time, while reels were mounted. Furthermore, interspersed access

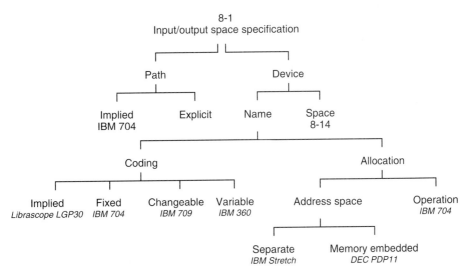

TREE 8-13   Design choices for input/output space specification.

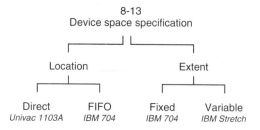

TREE 8-14   Design choices for device space specification.

to multiple files required each active stream to be mounted, even though not all data streams were needed or could be used at once.

It seemed logical that the costly electronics be time-shared among several mechanisms—only one in a set would be in motion at a time. So it became standard practice to separate the mechanisms and the electronics, the latter being grouped into what is called a *control unit*, which is shared among several mechanisms. (In fact, some part of the electronics has always been kept with the mechanism; that combination is called the *I/O device*) Similar logic led to sharing transmission units. Thus was born the attachment tree (Figure 8-15). The original justification for an I/O attachment tree was the high relative cost of the potentially sharable electronics. Since these electronic costs have dropped precipitously, this justification no longer applies. Practice over three decades has, of course, adapted to the tree, creating secondary reasons for keeping the structure; so it survives.

Attachment network.   When an I/O operation is initiated, the desired path may be busy for several independent reasons. The transmission unit may be busy, the control unit may be busy, or the device itself may be busy. So that idle path components can be used to bypass busy ones, various deviations from the simple tree structure occur, such as devices that are switchable between control units, and control units that are switchable between transmission units. So the attachment tree becomes an attachment network (Figure 8-16).

Queuing for the use of resources must be done at each of the three levels! Completion reporting and reallocation must be done for each. So the complexity of the I/O control program is compounded. Moreover, the attachment-tree structure assumes that any data transmission activity will occupy only one device and one control unit per transmission unit. In fact, although only one transmission is indeed in progress at a time, multiple actions other than transmissions may be under way at one time; they too must be controlled via the transmission unit and control unit.

For example, since Seeks and Rewinds do not involve continuous data transmission, they do not require the transmission unit and can be carried out by the control unit (or device, in case of Rewind). Nevertheless, the I/O process must be notified, or be able to learn, about normal completions, malfunctions, and operator-originated Attention Requests. This requirement is awkward when the control unit is busy reading or writing on some other device.

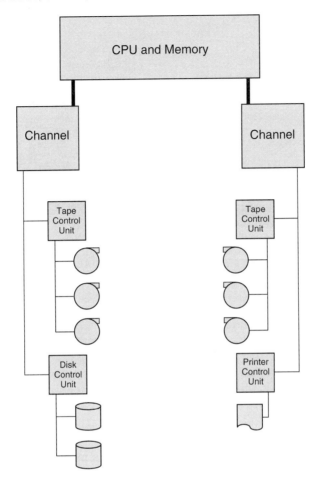

FIGURE 8-15   Attachment tree of the IBM System/360.

Complex path addressing.   The addressing of an I/O network structure can be solved by giving a separate name to each unique pathway from the memory to a given device. The operating system then requests a particular name. This scheme is used in the OS/360 and its descendants to handle the non-treelike complexities of the configuration.

Address allocation.   If the path needs specification, the most common solution is to combine it with device specification. In the 360 a 2-byte address field, the *device address*, is used to designate channel, control unit, and device (Figure 8-17). The first byte cleanly specifies the channel, 0 to 6, each of which may have up to 256 devices.

The second byte specifies the control unit and the device proper as follows:

- For each device that has a private control unit, the control unit and the device together have one unique 1-byte address, 0 to 255, as shown in the left part of Figure 8-17.
- For devices that share a control unit, a variable number of low-order bits specifies the device; the high-order bits specify the control unit, as in the right part of Figure 8-17.

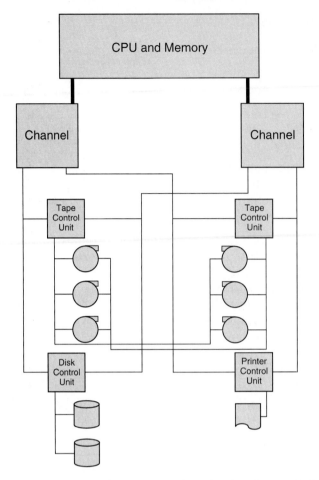

FIGURE 8-16   Attachment network in the IBM System/360.

Clean design.   All of the nasty complexities just described arise from allowing the topology of the attachment network, an implementation issue, to protrude into the architecture. A much cleaner and more general solution is for the machine architecture to conceal all multiplexing of equipment in the implementation and to handle all contention there. Today a designer would provide one (perhaps virtual) I/O processor per device, with no perceivable boundary between the two, and no visible control unit at all. It is not evident that such a stratagem adds anything significant to hardware cost; it surely effects substantial savings on control-program complexity and cost.

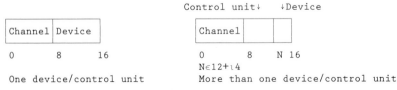

FIGURE 8-17   Input/output path address in the IBM System/360.

Device Addressing

In the simplest form, each device has a unique device address.

Implied address. The Librascope LGP30 (1957), which has only one device (paper tape) for reading and for writing, uses the operation code to imply this device. Similarly the ZEBRA uses a register address.

Fixed addresses.   Other early computers, such as the 701, have a limited number of devices, so each device has the same address in all installations.

Installation-dependent addresses.   As the number of potential devices increased beyond that used in any particular configuration, it became undesirable to use more and more address space; the device addresses were then determined for each installation.

Changeable addresses. Early tape systems incorporated a dial on each drive by which the operator could alter the drive's address at will. The purpose was to allow one drive to be reading or writing a file while later volumes of the same file were mounted on another. When reading was complete, the operator renamed the newly readied drive with the address of the old one and continued the program. This method simplified programming, but led to operator errors and made it very difficult to link malfunctions with particular physical drives.

By the time the 360 was designed, I/O control programs were in universal use; they allowed logical naming and renaming of devices, so the manual renaming feature was not a part of the 360 and subsequent IBM tape drives.

Separate name-space.   The earliest computers and many others indicate, through the operation code of the I/O instruction, that the specified address lies in a separate device name-space, instead of in main memory. The Read Select instruction of the IBM 709 (1959) illustrates this way of addressing (Program 8-18).

```
┌──────────────┬─────┬───┬─────────┐
│Opcode        │  *  │ X │Address  │
│              │     │   │       │ │
└──────────────┴─────┴───┴─────────┘
0              12    18 21              36
Legend: X = index;  * = unused.

RDS:address:channel
ᐱ IBM 709 Read Select
address←adr704
channel←⌊address÷512
direction[channel]←in
iostate[channel]←busy
```

PROGRAM 8-18   Read Select in the IBM 709.

Joint name-space. In most minicomputers and microcomputers, the device addresses lie within the memory name-space. A reference to such an address activates the device instead of fetching or storing in the corresponding memory location. Essentially, the designer has chosen to sacrifice one memory word per device to avoid having a separate name-space for the set of devices. A prominent example is the DEC PDP11 (1970), as illustrated in Program 8-19.

```
namellio
ⓐ DEC PDP11 device addresses
   Ttyinw←memcap-142          Disk256w←memcap-210
   Ttyoutw←memcap-138         Disk64w←memcap-242
   Ptpinw←memcap-150          Dectapew←memcap-288
   Ptpoutw←memcap-146         Diskcrdw←memcap-256
   Clockw←memcap-154          Tapew←memcap-176
   Realtimew←memcap-160
   Printerw←memcap-178
```

PROGRAM 8-19   Device addressing in the DEC PDP11.

Indirect addressing.   Because device addressing varies from installation to installation, as well as during the life of any one installation, it is desirable both in separate and joint name-spaces to be able to specify the device indirectly. The indexing facilities for a memory address usually suffice for this purpose.

Private Spaces

If a device has its own directly addressed internal name-space, a *private* or *internal* address is required to specify locations such as tracks and blocks. The one-level store of the Atlas makes the private space of a drum available as a direct-storage address by embedding it in the memory name-space. This approach is particularly attractive for storage devices (Section 3.2).

In contrast to storage devices, most source/sink devices have self-indexing storage media. Nevertheless, even these devices may contain internal spaces that should be program-accessible. Examples are registers that contain parameter settings, such as transmission rate or stacker selection. This type of internal addressing is often treated as control information. In mini- and microprocessors, however, these control registers are often embedded in the memory name-space. An 8080A that is used to control a terminal or printer will directly address each of the registers of that device.

8.2.3
Bibliography

Buchholz [1962], L.D. Stevens [1952].

8.3
Single-Instruction Overlap

The grave shortcomings of direct I/O are:

- The processor must wait for slow I/O action.
- It is difficult to program CPU timing to match device timing.

So single-instruction overlap is a natural advance from direct I/O for processors that handle the I/O process as part of computation.

8.3.1

Transmission

Overlapped I/O is used in one of the earliest commercially available computers, the 701. Table 8-11 gives a list of the I/O instructions of the 701; a few
representative operations are explicated in Program 8-20.

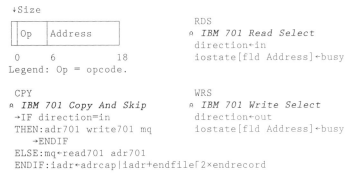

```
↓Size
                                      RDS
 ┌──┬──────────┐                      ⋒ IBM 701 Read Select
 │Op│ Address  │                        direction←in
 └──┴──────────┘                        iostate[fld Address]←busy
 0    6        18
 Legend: Op = opcode.


 CPY                                  WRS
 ⋒ IBM 701 Copy And Skip              ⋒ IBM 701 Write Select
 →IF direction=in                       direction←out
 THEN:adr701 write701 mq                iostate[fld Address]←busy
    →ENDIF
 ELSE:mq←read701 adr701
 ENDIF:iadr←adrcap|iadr+endfile⌈2×endrecord
```

PROGRAM 8-20   Input/output instructions of the IBM 701.

The 701's I/O configuration is more complex than that of the LGP30, so
an I/O device address must be specified as well as a memory address. But,
because of the self-indexing property of the devices, only the memory address
needs to change during a block transmission.

Since the 701 is a single-address machine, it needs two instructions for the
two addresses. So a Read Select that specifies the device address is followed
by a Copy And Skip that gives the memory address. This sequence allows
one 36-bit word to be read from a device into memory.

The multiplier-quotient register (MQ) serves as the buffer necessitated
by synchronization. The MQ also does automatic word assembly when a
magnetic tape is read, shifting 6 bits at a time to assemble six 6-bit bytes into
a word. Card readers, printers, punches, and drums all transfer 36-bit words
in parallel. Program 8-21 shows this operation.

Use of overlap. The 701 illustrates that the time available to the main process
during the instruction overlap can be put to good use by selecting the next
word of the memory block that is to be read or written. Block moves are
accomplished by a programmed iteration, which Program 8-22 shows for the
701. The program must avoid using the MQ; it is busy performing the I/O.

In practice, one wants to do more than just transmit a block. The
block move as programmed in Program 8-22 contains only one block-length

```
    transfer701 device
  ⋒ IBM 701 simplified input/output transmission
   REPEAT:→WAIT iostate[device]=busy
      →IF direction=in
      THEN:mq←iodata
         →ENDIF
      ELSE:iodata←mq
      ENDIF:iostate[device]←ready
   →UNTIL endfile∨endblock
```

PROGRAM 8-21   Operation of input/output in the IBM 701.

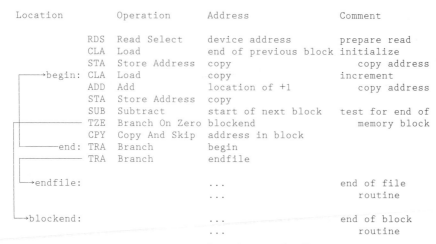

Location	Operation		Address	Comment
	RDS	Read Select	device address	prepare read
	CLA	Load	end of previous block	initialize
	STA	Store Address	copy	copy address
begin:	CLA	Load	copy	increment
	ADD	Add	location of +1	copy address
	STA	Store Address	copy	
	SUB	Subtract	start of next block	test for end of
	TZE	Branch On Zero	blockend	memory block
	CPY	Copy And Skip	address in block	
end:	TRA	Branch	begin	
	TRA	Branch	endfile	
endfile:			. . .	end of file
			. . .	routine
blockend:			. . .	end of block
			. . .	routine

PROGRAM 8-22   Copy loop in the IBM 701.

specification (that of the memory block), implied by the difference between END and START. For block moves, however, the block on the device may be longer or shorter, and it must be specified.

In the 701, occurrence of the end of a block on the device sets a testable trigger. Likewise, occurrence of the end of the I/O medium itself (for example, a reel of tape or a deck of cards), called End of File in IBM terminology, sets a testable trigger.

These tests are incorporated in the Copy operation. Copy And Skip not only copies, it also skips the next two instructions when the end of an I/O block is encountered; it skips only one instruction when an end of file is encountered (Programs 8-20 and 8-22).

Word and block overlap.   The 701 illustrates overlapped single-word transmission, as does the DEC PDP8 (1965; see Chapter 15). Overlapped block transmission is illustrated by the Univac I and the IBM 650 (1954; see Section 12.1).

8.3.2

Buffering

In direct I/O the details of the data transmission belong to the I/O program and are not part of the architecture. In overlapped transmission, however, the processor proceeds while transmission is in progress, and the architecture must state whether, where, and when these data can be accessed. So instruction overlap inherently involves the concepts of testing, buffering, and synchronization.

Buffer.   A space that participates in transmission to and from a device is called a *buffer*. Fundamentally, a buffer is a storage that can be read and written under control of either of two asynchronous processes. It is therefore capable of passing data between them.

If data are read or written sequentially, the buffer can be used to reduce the effective access time of the I/O device. In the case of writing, the buffer

```
   readbuffer                        writebuffer
 ∩ empty buffer                    ∩ fill buffer
   REPEAT:→WAIT buffer=full          REPEAT:→WAIT buffer=empty
     buffer←empty                      buffer←full
   →UNTIL 0                          →UNTIL 0
```

PROGRAM 8-23   Basic buffer.

is filled by the Write operation at electronic speeds; then, data are transferred from the buffer to the I/O device as its own motion allows, while program execution proceeds. In the case of reading, the first record from the device is loaded into the buffer either automatically, before the first Read operation is executed by the computer, or by a dummy Read. Each subsequent Read transfers a data block from the buffer at electronic speeds and reloads it at device speeds (Program 8-23). The 650 is an example of automatic preload and postempty; the Univac I requires the programmer to "prime the pump" of the buffers (Section 10.5).

Buffer allocation.   The buffer can share part of the main computer space, or it can have a dedicated space. Block sizes on the I/O medium are limited by the size of buffer provided. As an example, the Cray 1's (1976) disk controller has two buffers, each with 512 words of 64 bits each.

Shared buffer space.   An example of a buffer that shares processor space is the MQ register in the 701. It is an extreme example, since the sharing of the MQ register conflicts with operations such as multiply and divide. Therefore, the overlap of instruction execution is only partially possible.

Dedicated name-space.   The Univac I uses magnetic tapes and a dedicated buffer accommodating 60 words of 12 bytes each.

Dedicated memory space.   Whereas the Univac I makes its buffer a separate space, the PDP11 dedicates part of memory as a buffer. The high-order addresses are reserved for I/O devices. There are no I/O operations. For instance, a Move to location 65394 (which is `memcap-142`; see Program 8-19) places a byte in the teletype print buffer and prints the character.

Similarly, the 650's optional tape system includes a 60-word buffer, which is embedded in the name-space (9000–9059) and can also be used as fast memory.

Multiple buffers.   Program 8-23 illustrates that a buffer should not be accessed by the main process while the I/O operation is loading or emptying it. The delay associated with this inaccessibility can be reduced by providing two or more buffers for each device. One buffer can be filled while the other is emptied. Now not only can the CPU act instantaneously and proceed, but the slower of the processes, the I/O transfer, can proceed at its maximum possible rate, for there is an empty buffer available for it.

```
   readalt                           writealt
 ∩ empty alternate buffers         ∩ fill alternate buffers
   REPEAT:→WAIT buffer1=full          REPEAT:→WAIT buffer1=empty
     buffer1←empty                      buffer1←full
     →WAIT buffer2=full                 →WAIT buffer2=empty
     buffer2←empty                      buffer2←full
   →UNTIL 0                          →UNTIL 0
```

PROGRAM 8-24   Alternating buffers.

Multiple buffering requires cycling to switch the roles of the buffers when filling and emptying are complete. The basic operation of a two-buffer system, showing the interlocking, is shown in Program 8-24.

More than two buffers per device may be used; an advantage is derived only if the frequency of Write (or Read) operations in the CPU program is highly variable. Multiple buffers then smooth the variability.

Private buffers.   Heretofore, we have assumed that each I/O device has its own buffer or set of buffers. Such a system of *private buffers* is always simplest. In fact, sometimes a device's requirements are so particular that a private buffer is the only economical choice. A chain printer, for example, scans its buffer many times during the printing of a single line to determine hammer firing. The buffer is necessarily integrated very closely with the device. Similarly, a parallel card reader requires a "corner-turning" buffer, read in row-by-row and out column-by-column. Such specialized buffers should be part of the I/O device and need not be visible as separate entities in the architecture.

Common buffers.   The essential general requirement is that an I/O system have one buffer, or set of buffers, for each I/O transfer that is to proceed concurrently. A magnetic-tape configuration may have six drives, but if only two of them read or write at any one time, only two buffers sets are necessary. Such common buffers are usually part of the I/O system, not part of the device. They should share some generally accessible space. In such a system, of course, interlocking is more complex.

8.3.3

Synchronization

As soon as one moves away from direct I/O, it becomes necessary to synchronize the processor with the device. If, during writing, a buffer has been loaded and transfer to tape has begun, the program must not dump another load into the buffer until the first has been cleared. Similarly, the main process must not read data from a buffer until it has arrived there from the device.

How is this synchronization accomplished? The answer is simple to state, but painful in practice—the programmer does it.

Consider as an extreme example the card reader on the 701. Cards are read row-by-row, 9-edge first. The brushes for 72 columns can be mapped by plugboard into two 36-bit words. Only 72 of the 80 card columns can be read. By user convention, columns 1 through 72 were taken, a convention that survives today in the specifications for FORTRAN and the MVS/360 Job Control Language.

Some 270 ms after Read Select is given, the clutch on the reader has engaged, and the card has moved so that the 9-row is under the brushes. Since the card moves steadily, the holes of the 9-row stay under the brushes for only 0.57 ms. During this interval, the program must issue two Copy instructions. The first copies the left word; the second copies the right word.

Fifteen ms elapse before the holes of the 8-row are under the brushes. During this interval, the program may go about other business. Then it

must issue two more Copy instructions while the 8-row is passing by. The 701 manual gives the duration of each operation, and the programmer sums the durations of his interspersed instructions to check against the timing constraints.

Wait condition. The 701 has one major concession to human fallibility and laziness. If a Copy instruction is given too early, it does not produce wrong results; it merely causes the CPU to stop and wait until the I/O device arrives at the point of synchronism. This technique is always available to the designer when one of two asynchronous processes is stoppable and is faster than the other.

The card punch, printer, magnetic tapes, and magnetic drum of the 701 are controlled and timed in essentially the same fashion. Indeed, the drum data rate is constrained by the timing of the tightest possible copy loop.

This direct, although primitive, means of synchronization gives the programmer the possibility of achieving concurrency between computing and some of the I/O operation.

In practice this procedure is very tedious, so the 701 programmers use it only to overlap I/O operation with the computing directly associated with it, such as binary–decimal radix conversion.

Polling. The PDP8 family has overlapped I/O facilities very similar to those of the 701. Section 15.1 in the Zoo shows the machine's organization. The operation I/O Transfer (IOT) specifies a transfer of one 12-bit word between the CPU accumulator and the specified device (Program 8-25). Input is distinguished from output by assigning two device addresses to devices that may do both.

Each PDP8 device has a one-word buffer and a control flag that is set to 1 when the buffer is filled on input or emptied on output. IOT goes one step further than Copy And Skip in the 701 because it allows the device flag to be polled. The instruction includes a 3-bit field `Iop` that governs the transfer. Bit `Iop2` clears the device flag. Bit `Iop4` tests the flag; `Iop1` skips the next instruction if the flag is 1. `Iop4` causes the transfer between accumulator and device.

During input, the program sits in a loop waiting for the flag to come on, indicating a full buffer word. Then the flag `IOT BR` causes the loop branch to be skipped and the device buffer to be read into the accumulator. DCA then stores the accumulator content in memory (Program 8-26). A similar sequence occurs for output.

The flag may also be used to generate an interrupt when it is set, so that the program may do independent processing while waiting for the device.

```
          Iop↓
                          IOT
 ┌──┬───┬────┐            ⋀ DEC PDP8 Input/Output Transfer
 │Op│Dev│ Op │            interface[Dataout]←acc
 └──┴───┴─┬┬─┘            interface[Deviceadr]←inst[Device]
 0   3    9 12            interface[Iomod]←inst[Iop4,Iop2,Iop1]
                          iadr←iadr+interface[Ioskip]
 Legend: Dev = IO device;  acc←(acc⋀~interface[Clear])∨interface[Datain]
         Iop = IO modifiers;
         Op = Opcode.
```

PROGRAM 8-25   Input/Output Transfer in the DEC PDP8.

```
IOT     Skip next instruction if flag set
JMP     Branch to previous instruction
DCA     Store and clear accumulator
```

PROGRAM 8-26   Input loop in the DEC PDP8.

This interruption facility lets the PDP8 have a fixed-buffer I/O system even though the buffer is minimal (one word).

Testing.   Testing a single flag to determine whether an I/O operation is in progress or completed is not enough. If an operation was completed successfully, the next can begin, and the held-up computer process can be restarted; but if the operation stopped because of failure, a retry must be attempted instead. So three conditions of a transmission must be distinguished:

- In progress
- Complete and satisfactory
- Complete and failed

With programmed testing of indicators as the means of synchronizing, at least two indicators must be tested before a second operation is executed.

Buffer delay.   A buffer acts as a delay mechanism. Two kinds of actions are required to pass information through it—filling and emptying. These actions may be overlapped such that, for a series of n transmissions, $n + 1$ actions are necessary. Before a series of Read operations, a dummy or automatic read must fill the buffer initially. Similarly, if each Write does an implied test of the previous one, after a series of Writes, a dummy Write or a test must verify that the last Write was satisfactory.

8.4

Peripheral Processor

The most proper and the most satisfactory form of I/O operation dedicates a separate processor to each I/O process concurrently sharing main memory. Such a processor is called a *peripheral processor*, or *peripheral processing unit* (PPU), as distinct from the central processing unit (CPU).

Concept

Because the PPU is separate from the CPU, the complexities of I/O control can be separated from the application programs. Since the PPU shares a memory with the CPU, the main process can treat its I/O operation as a Move. Since the PPU does nothing but carry on one I/O process at a time, and since I/O data rates are typically much slower than processor ones, a set of PPUs can share cyclically one implementation. That is, each PPU may be a virtual processor.

Table 8-27 shows the types of concurrency of the I/O operation. The CDC 6600 (1964) is the only commercially available processor with a PPU; both the 6600 and its PPU are listed. For systems using a channel (Section 8.5), a single entry suffices, since the channel has no private memory as far as the

	Type of concurrency	Processor space	Device named by
Zuse Z4	d word	stack	operation
Cambridge EDSAC	d byte	memory	operation
Ferranti Mark 1	d byte	memory	operation
Univac I	d block	buffer	operation
IBM 701	d word	mq register	operation
IBM 650	d block	fixed area	operation
IBM 704	o word	mq register	operation
IBM 705	d block	memory	address
Univac 1103A	o word	memory	address
STC ZEBRA	d byte	accumulator	operation
Lincoln Lab TX2	PPU	memory	PPU
Bull Gamma 60	channel	memory	operation
IBM 1401	d byte	accumulator	operation
IBM Stretch	channel	memory	address
CDC 6600	PPU	memory	PPU
CDC 6600 PPU	d block	memory	field
Burroughs B5500	channel	memory	memory
IBM System/360	channel	memory	address
DEC PDP8	d word	accumulator	field
DEC PDP11	o word	memory	location
Intel 8080A	d byte	accumulator	implied
Cray 1	channel	memory	operation
DEC VAX11	channel	memory	address
Motorola MC68000	d byte	memory	memory
IBM 6150	channel	memory	address

Legend: d = direct I/O; field = instruction field;
        o = overlapped I/O; fixed area = fixed memory area.

TABLE 8-27   Peripheral operation in various machines.

architecture is concerned. Table 8-27 also gives various examples of systems in which the main processor performs the I/O process either by direct I/O or by overlapped operation.

The PPU is a general purpose processor with I/O instructions. General purpose processing is discussed in the preceding chapters, and the I/O instructions are treated in Sections 8.2 and 8.3. Therefore, little needs to be said about the architecture of the peripheral processor—we mention just its bias to the I/O task, the sharing of memory, and the supervision of a system consisting of a CPU and its PPUs.

8.4.1

Bias of the PPU to the Input/Output Task

Identical architecture.   The first system using a peripheral processor is the Lincoln Laboratory TX2 [Forgie, 1957]. It is an extreme example and needs little explanation: The peripheral processors are each identical with the main processor. Each I/O device has associated with it a virtual PPU identical to the CPU but with its own instruction address. The PPU and the CPU share memory and all working registers. In fact, the PPUs even share the implementation of the CPU.

When a device needs service, any lower-priority CPU or PPU sequence is interrupted as soon as allowable, and the device then runs until the sequence ends. Because the single working store is shared by all processors, interruption

without state-saving is possible only from time to time. A breakpoint bit in each instruction indicates when higher-priority sequences are allowed to interrupt (Section 7.4).

The programmer determines allocation of memory and working-register space; the assumption is that the processes will cooperate. The architectural concurrency is not exploited by the implementation. The design is inexpensive but slow, as might be expected for a pioneering effort.

Biased architecture.   Since the PPU has a special task to perform, its architecture, although general purpose in nature, may be biased toward that particular task. The 6600 PPU (Section 14.3), is an example. Its architecture has minimal arithmetic, and is biased toward control.

In the 6600, each system incorporates 10 PPUs with approximately the same architecture as that of the CDC 160A (1960). These PPUs are implemented as 10 sets of registers time-sharing a single arithmetic unit [Thornton, 1970]. The architectural concurrency is reflected in implementation concurrency where it matters: in concurrent CPU and I/O operation. The virtual concurrency of the PPUs saves equipment and, because of the slow device operation, yields sufficient speed. The PPU concept is continued in the CDC 7600 (1969), where one CPU may have from 8 up to 42 PPUs.

8.4.2

Main Memory Sharing

Since an I/O operation is a Move of data between the main processor's memory and an I/O device, the I/O process shares the main memory with the main process and perhaps with other peripheral processes. The most general design is to allow the peripheral process access to the entire main memory.

Addressing

The allocation of memory space for I/O operation is a major concern for an operating system. Sections 3.2 and 3.3 explained two main methods for relocating data: The logical address may be mapped upon a physical location via a page table, or the effective address may be dynamically modified via an index register.

Address mapping.   The PPU and the CPU should ideally address data in the same name-space. If the CPU has virtual memory, with logical-to-physical address mapping, the PPU should ideally have it also.

But, whereas the CPU can suspend its problem-process execution when a page fault occurs, and wait while its supervisory process fetches the new page, a PPU usually cannot. Its process must be clocked by the external device—a spinning disk, or a communication wire that cannot heed "Wait a moment." Indeed, in the middle of a block transmission, even the extra time implied by just doing address mapping may be too long. So it is common, although awkward and improper, for PPUs not to have address mapping even when the associated CPUs do.

The Model 67, which introduced address mapping for the 360, is an example: The addresses of I/O data do not go through address mapping. The

time intervals between bytes coming from fast I/O devices are too short for dynamic address mapping. Since CPU programs work with virtual addresses, and the I/O process with real ones, many complications result. Most of these complications affect the operating system; an occasional one constrains the application programmer. These complications are not necessary; the byte-interval time constraint can be solved by buffering in the peripheral processors.

Transmission Between Memory and the Device

The action of the I/O process proper consists, in its simplest form, of a Read (a transmission of data from an I/O device to a main memory) or a Write (a transmission from memory to device). For the PPU this transmission has two parts: the transmission between CPU and PPU, and the transmission between PPU and device.

Each CDC 6600 PPU (1964) has a private memory of 4096 12-bit words. Each also has access to the 6600 CPU memory. (The CPU word size is 60 bits.) The PPU accesses CPU memory either by single words or by block transfers to its own memory (Program 8-28). Similarly, each PPU can address the system's 12 I/O ports and control a one-word transfer or a block transfer between the PPU and the port (Program 8-29). In between the transmissions, the PPU performs the necessary format transformations.

Dual length.   A memory-to-memory move in a CPU needs specification of only one length, since source and destination are under control of the same program. In I/O transmission, however, the program has no control over block length on the I/O medium. This structure may differ from device to device. Therefore, the memory buffer area must have some size specified to ensure that locations are not overwritten unintentionally.

```
 Op    X              Op    X    D

 0     6    12        0     6    12           24
Legend: D = displacement; Op = opcode; X = index.


 CRD
 ∩ CDC 6600 PPU Read Word From CPU Memory
 (fld X) writeΔppu cpuword readΔcpu magni acc


 CWD
 ∩ CDC 6600 PPU Write Word Into CPU Memory
 (magni acc) writeΔcpu cpuword readΔppu fld X


 CRM
 ∩ CDC 6600 PPU Read Block From CPU Memory
 0 writeΔppu word magnr iadr
 (fld D) writeΔppu(cpuword×adrΔppux) readΔcpu magni acc


 CWM
 ∩ CDC 6600 PPU Write Block Into CPU Memory
 0 writeΔppu word magnr iadr
 (magni acc) writeΔcpu(cpuword×adrΔppux) readΔppu fld D
```

PROGRAM 8-28   Transmission between the CDC 6600 CPU and PPU.

Op	X		Op	X	D

```
0      6      12    0      6      12     18
Legend: D = displacement; Op = opcode; X = index.
```

```
IAM;address;count                          IAN
ᴀ CDC 6600 PPU Read Block                   ᴀ CDC 6600 PPU Read Word
memory[0;]←word magnr iadr                  acc[Lower]←readΔio fld X
address←fld D
REPEAT:→IF iostate[fld X;Active]
   THEN: ᴀ read word and count
       address writeΔppu readΔio fld X
       address←address+1
       count←(digitcompi acc)-1
       acc←accsize digitcompr count
       →ENDIF
   ELSE: ᴀ mark final word with zero
       address writeΔppu wordρ0
ENDIF:→UNTIL(count=0)∨˜iostate[fld X;Active]
iadr←magni memory[0;]
```

```
OAM;address;count                          OAN
ᴀ CDC 6600 PPU Write Block                  ᴀ CDC 6600 PPU Write Word
memory[0;]←word magnr iadr                  (fld X) writeΔio acc[Lower]
address←fld D
REPEAT:→If iostate[fld X;Active]
   THEN: ᴀ write word and count
       (fld X) writeΔio word readΔppu address
       address←address+1
       count←(digitcompi acc)-1
       acc←accsize digitcompr count
ENDIF:→UNTIL(count=0)∨˜iostate[fld X;Active]
iadr←magni memory[0;]
```

PROGRAM 8-29   Direct input/output in the CDC 6600 PPU.

It follows that there are inherently two lengths. Since the block length on the device may be too short, just right, or too long for the memory buffer length, the I/O control program must provide gracefully for all these contingencies.

Word assembly and disassembly.   Many I/O devices are, like magnetic tape, arranged for only byte-to-byte transmission. If memory is wider than a byte, the I/O control system must assemble words from bytes or disassemble words into bytes. This process may or may not be visible to the user. In a 6600 PPU, for instance, the program assembles 12-bit bytes into 60-bit words for transmission to the central processor memory. In contrast the 709 channels assemble 6-bit bytes to 36-bit words without explicit program control; a channel—unlike a PPU—has no general program control.

8.4.3
Supervision

The PPU serves one process at a time; there is no switching among processes. Supervisory requirements all concern the protection of processes in the CPU.

Memory protection.   For reasons given in Section 7.3, the transmission of I/O data to and from memory should be subject to memory protection. Preferably

the protection method used in the main processor should also be employed for I/O data; this requirement may be a serious constraint on the method to be selected.

The 709 had no protection at all for CPU or channel. The Stretch had some: It used boundary registers for the CPU. A full complement of boundary registers for all channels was considered too expensive, so I/O operation was not protected. This was clearly a half-way solution.

The 360's lock and key method was selected precisely because it could also be used for I/O operations. When, in the 370, relocation became generally available, it also gave a means of main-memory protection. Since 370 channel addresses are not mapped, however, this method cannot be generally used for I/O protection.

Contention. Since PPU instruction execution is subject to the timing constraints of the I/O device, and since the PPUs and CPUs share the same memories, memory implementations universally give PPUs priority over CPUs when both request access simultaneously.

Matters are not so simple, however, for resolving access contention among several I/O processes. A customary solution—and one adopted in the 360 channels—is to establish a fixed priority ordering. It is then possible to do a worst-case analysis and determine for each process the maximum data rate that can be handled without the possibility of overrun. Each user then configures his system with the fastest devices on the fastest channels, and so on.

Synchronization

The designer of a system with PPUs must choose whether the CPU or a PPU runs the supervisor, because both have full processing power. He subsequently can decide to use polling or interrupting as a means of synchronization (Section 7.4).

In the 6600 the CPU can be started by a PPU, and one PPU is customarily dedicated to running the operating system for the entire system. The 6600 makes no provision for the CPU to interrupt the PPUs or to read the PPU status. On the other hand, a PPU can issue an Exchange Jump (Program 8-30), which interrupts the CPU and causes a status switch (Program 8-31). Moreover, a PPU can poll the instruction address of the CPU, so it can monitor the progress of the CPU process.

Initiation and termination. The initiation of one process by another requires an operation that specifies the process to be initiated and passes the necessary parameters; termination requires issuing an interrupting or halting signal. In the 6600 the PPU has the initiative, so all the PPUs are started by the initial dead-start sequence and run until power-off.

```
                   EXN
 ┌─────┬─────┐
 │ Op  │  X  │     ⋀ CDC 6600 PPU Force Exchange Jump In CPU
 └─────┴─────┘       controlΔcpu magni acc
 0     6     12
 Legend: Op = opcode; X = index.
```

PROGRAM 8-30   Exchange Jump in the CDC 6600 PPU.

```
exchange address;oldpack;newpack
ⴴ CDC 6600 exchange of context
oldpack←(16,word)ρ0
oldpack[ι3;6+ιadrsize]←adrsize magnr iadr,origin,limit
oldpack[3;9+ι3]←mask
oldpack[4 5 ;ιecssize]←ecssize magnr ecsorigin,ecslimit
oldpack[ι8;24+ιadrsize]←x
oldpack[ι8;42+ιadrsize]←adr
oldpack[8+ι8;]←reg
newpack←memory[address+ι16;]
iadr←magni newpack[0;6+ιadrsize]
origin←magni newpack[1;6+ιadrsize]
limit←magni newpack[2;6+ιadrsize]          interrupt6600
mask←newpack[3;9+ι3]                      ⴴ CDC 6600 interrupt action
ecsorigin←magni newpack[4;ιecssize]      ⴴ serialize indicator
ecslimit←magni newpack[5;ιecssize]       →If ind∧0=1|iadr
x←newpack[ι8;24+ιadrsize]                THEN:ind←0
adr←newpack[ι8;42+ιadrsize]                ⴴ end serialization
reg←newpack[8+ι8;]                          exchange exadr
memory[address+ι16;]←oldpack             ENDIF: ⴴ end serialization
```

PROGRAM 8-31   Status exchange in the CDC 6600 CPU.

In Tree 7-7, we saw that concurrent processes communicate either by transmission of a signal, or by the sharing of dedicated memory areas, or the sharing of general memory areas. The greater the degree of dedication, the easier it is for receiving processes to monitor the presence of inbound messages. So signaling is invariably used in CPU–PPU communications to obtain a fast response in communication, initiation, and termination, whereas storage is used for data passing.

8.4.4
Bibliography

Forgie [1957], Thornton [1970].

8.5
Channel

Concept

A *channel* is a peripheral processor so specialized for the transmission of I/O data that it cannot perform the normal main-processor operations, even at reduced power or efficiency. Since transmission is most of I/O activity, a channel does most of the I/O work, in terms of time fraction.

A channel cannot, however, handle most of the I/O work in terms of fraction of functions. Channels cannot, in most machines, count and sequence retries and tape-cleaning operations when a tape-read operation fails. Nor can the channel handle the complexities of the end of an I/O file when error situations are encountered. Whereas the burden of transmission remains with the I/O process, the burden of controlling the complete I/O operation is now upon a CPU process.

The channel must internally execute precisely the same set of transmission functions performed by a PPU. It is directed to do so by a sequence of comprehensive instructions, called a *channel program*. In contrast to the PPU, however, the channel has no explicit memory space of its own; the channel program therefore resides in main memory.

8.5.1

Channel Architecture

Since the channel is a special purpose processor, we must investigate which of the computer attributes discussed in Chapters 2 through 7 apply to the channel. The analysis demonstrates the lack of generality of the channel as compared to the PPU.

Representation

Data. Since a channel does nothing to data except move them, it has only one datatype, which normally is simply structured. The only choice that remains is the resolution; it was 36 bits in the 709, grew to 64 bits in the Stretch, and shrank to 8 bits in the 360. Figure 8-32 shows the data format of the 360 channel. All data, including control information, are constrained to the 8-bit byte format.

```
Bytes

0                                                              m
Legend: m = maximum 64k.
```

FIGURE 8-32   Data format for the IBM System/360 channel.

Instructions.   An I/O transfer typically occurs between the device and a contiguous block in memory. Of the various means to specify the memory area's extent, length is the most common.

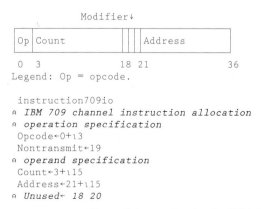

```
                    Modifier↓
  ┌──┬───────────┬───┬─────────┐
  │Op│Count      │││  │Address  │
  └──┴───────────┴───┴─────────┘
  0  3           18 21          36
Legend: Op = opcode.

  instruction709io
  ∩ IBM 709 channel instruction allocation
  ∩ operation specification
  Opcode←0+ι3
  Nontransmit←19
  ∩ operand specification
  Count←3+ι15
  Address←21+ι15
  ∩ Unused← 18 20
```

PROGRAM 8-33   Channel instruction in the IBM 709.

Program 8-33 shows the instruction of the 709 channel. It was called a Channel Control Word (CCW), a term the 360 borrowed. The term *Control Word* unfortunately obscures the fact that it refers to an instruction; that confusion undoubtedly hurt the design of the 360, by hindering us in thinking of the channel as a processor.

The 709 channel-instruction format (Program 8-33) shows that the memory area is specified by an origin address and length, here called *Count*. Besides the address and length fields, only an operation-code field is necessary. The same components are found in the 360 channel instruction (Program 8-34), except that the operation code is supplemented by a set of modifier bits.

Opcode	Address		Mod	*	Count	
0	8		32	40	48	64

Legend: Mod = modifier; * = unused.

```
ccw360
∩ IBM 360 channel control word
   Opcode←0+ι8                        ∩ skip block
   Address←8+ι24                         Skip←35
∩ chain data                         ∩ programmed interrupt
   Cd←32                                 Pci←36
∩ chain command                      ∩ permanent zero
   Cc←33                                 Zero←37+ι3
∩ suppress length indication         ∩ unused←40+ι8
   Sli←34                               Count←48+ι16
```

PROGRAM 8-34   Instruction (CCW) format of the IBM System/360 channel.

Addressing

A channel should be able to address an object anywhere in memory, preferably without restrictions as to resolution and extent. The 360 channel has the full memory name-space of any 360 processor: 2^{24} bytes, addressed by 24 bits.

Data fields may begin and end anywhere. On any particular system, the attached memory complement may be less than 2^{24} bytes. In this case, as with addresses in the CPU, the memory name-space is appropriately truncated, and addresses beyond the limit are rejected as invalid.

The length of the field may be up to 2^{16} bytes. The choice of this maximum length was not dictated by the CCW bits available for specifying it, nor by any inherent limitation imposed by I/O devices, but just by the desire to reduce implementation cost.

CCWs themselves are constrained to begin on double-word boundaries; that is, their address must be a multiple of eight.

The remarks concerning address mapping made for the PPU apply equally to the channel.

Operations

The channel has operations for moving data, for controlling the I/O device, and for sequencing the channel's own instruction execution.

IOCD	Count Control And Disconnect
IOCP	Count Control And Proceed
IORP	Record Control And Proceed
TCH	Branch In Channel
IOCT	Count Control And Branch
IORT	Record Control And Branch
IOSP	Signal Control And Proceed
IOST	Signal Control And Branch

TABLE 8-35   Instructions of the IBM 709 channel.

Move. Since the physical-block size of the I/O medium does not necessarily correspond to the size of the data areas used in the main process, data movement may involve

1. Movement between a large memory area and many physical blocks on the medium (for example, disk tracks or tape records). Such an action requires at least one operand per block specifying the proper subset of the memory field. The last block must be identified as such if one wants to specify all these moves as a single I/O transmission.
2. Movement between many memory fields and one physical block, operations sometimes called *Gather Write* and *Scatter Read*. Each memory field requires one operand to specify it. These operations are useful in sorting on disks and tapes and in file maintenance applications.
3. Movement of portions of a physical block into memory, skipping over other portions. The reason is to save memory space. Each contiguous portion to be transmitted requires a specification; a separate specification identifies each portion to be passed over without transfer to memory. From the memory's point of view, this procedure is the same as item 1.

In each of these movements, several memory fields must be specified, each with a start address and a length. Since such operand specifications are long and operation specifications are short, it is customary to dedicate a whole I/O instruction to each block, with the result that a whole set of instructions is required to specify a single operation. This grouping of instructions for one transmission is called *data chaining*.

Besides the need for a sequence of operations to handle multiple data movements, there is a need for a series of different operations, all auxiliary to one desired data movement. A disk Write, for example, is often followed by a Read to confirm that the record was correctly written. Since a disk Seek often precedes a Read or Write, a single Write may require the sequence Seek, Write, Seek, Read. Similarly, a Rewind often follows a tape Read or Write. This grouping of instructions for a single I/O action is sometimes called *command chaining*.

The transmission of data to or from any area of memory via a channel was introduced on the 709 [Christiansen, et al., 1957]. The 709 channel provides only transmission; but the transmission operations allow considerable flexibility. Gather–Read and Scatter–Write are possible, incommensurate records and memory areas can be handled, and iteration is possible via a branch in the channel program. Table 8-35 gives the complete instruction repertoire of the 709 channel. The I/O systems of the Stretch and the 360 follow the 709 concept.

Channel operations.   Since the coupling of the CPU process with the I/O device is accomplished via the channel, the channel should transmit control and sense information as well as data. The channel program needs the full set of operations for general I/O: Read, Write, Sense, and Control.

The 360 channel incorporates all four. Because control is generalized to transmit data bytes to the device itself, which does the interpretation as to control action, the channel is independent of the particular control needs of each device. This generalization also keeps the channel operation set short, as illustrated in Table 8-36.

```
Read                Sense
Read Backwards      Control
Write               Transfer In Channel
```

TABLE 8-36   Instructions of the IBM System/360 channel.

Read transfers bytes from the device to the memory block specified in the CCW, placing successive bytes in ascending memory locations.

Read Backward transfers bytes from the device's medium to memory, placing successive bytes in *descending* memory locations. It is valid only for tape; the tape actually moves backward under the reading head. At first glance, one would consider replacing the operation by a normal Read preceded by a separate Control specifying the backward direction (a more orthogonal solution). But this would not work; the operation must reverse the direction of both the channel and the I/O device atomically.

Write transfers bytes from memory to the device's medium. There is no corresponding backward operation, because tape drives do not write backward.

Sense causes data about the state of the device to be transferred to the memory block specified by the CCW.

Control transfers bytes to the device's control registers. Most control actions are immediately specified by the particular operation code of the Control command. If more information is needed, it is fetched from the memory block specified by the CCW.

Transfer In Channel is Branch in the CCW sequence.

The transmission operations are modified by mode bits that allow transmission of multiple physical blocks and multiple memory data areas in a single I/O program. The Chain Data bit (Cd) specifies whether the current operation is to be continued with the memory area specified in the next CCW. The Chain Command bit (Cc) specifies whether, upon completion of the current operation, the next CCW in memory is to be fetched and executed, that is, whether both the memory field and the command of the next CCW are interpreted. The Chain Command bit is ignored when the Chain Data bit is set.

The Chain Data bit provides scatter/gather transmission. The Chain Command bit allows several transmissions, that is several blocks on the I/O medium, to follow each other without CPU action. This bit can also be considered as an end-of-instruction-stream marker, as we shall see.

Block sizes on the medium may be variable, as in magnetic tape; they may be fixed, as on cards; or they may be variable with fixed maxima, as on disks.

In the 360 channel, the end of a block is specified by completion of a CCW whose Chain Data bit is 0. If the physical block on the device is longer than that in memory, writing is completed with nulls whose encoding is part of the device specification; reading is completed without transfer of data to memory.

A length error is noted if the physical block on the medium is longer or shorter than the memory area specified by the CCW. The Suppress Length Indicator (Sli), when set to 1, indicates that the CPU program does not wish to be informed when such a length error occurs.

The Skip Block bit (Skip), when set to 1, tells the channel not to transfer to memory the information obtained from the device on Read, Read Backward, or Sense. This mode is useful if memory buffer area is scarce, physical records are long, and only a fixed part of each record is needed.

Instruction Sequencing

Linear sequence. In the 709 and the 360 the channel instructions are executed in the order of their memory locations. They include an unconditional branch, Transfer In Channel, as an aid in allocating the channel programs to memory. One use of this branch is by the operating system to knit a single user's channel program into the longer one prepared by the operating system, and actually issued. So the operating system can protect itself while giving the user the flexibility the channel program affords.

The Stretch sequenced channel instructions by an explicit successor address, called Next (Program 8-37). This design is less efficient than ordered execution, but noteworthy in that the channel instruction format is the same as that of index words, allowing interchangeable use in file-maintenance applications.

Stop. Since the channel function is rather limited, most channel programs consist of few instructions. So most designs do not devote a separate instruction to stopping the channel process, but rather allow this specification in each instruction. Table 8-35 illustrates this case for the 709, where the term *Proceed* explicitly specifies continuation; the Chain Command bit of the 360 channel instruction, Program 8-34, has a similar function.

Decisions. Since channels lack comparison operations, the normal control structures are not possible. This lack of decision making is the greatest weakness of the channel; the main processor must still do the I/O control.

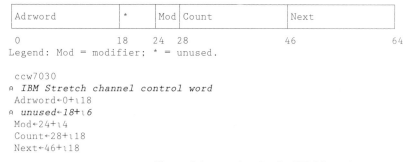

Adrword		*	Mod	Count		Next	

```
0                       18    24  28               46              64
Legend: Mod = modifier;  * = unused.

  ccw7030
⍺ IBM Stretch channel control word
  Adrword←0+ι18
⍺ unused←18+ι6
  Mod←24+ι4
  Count←28+ι18
  Next←46+ι18
```

PROGRAM 8-37   Channel instruction in the IBM Stretch.

As a consequence, the channel must pass to the CPU the information that would most affect decisions, the sense information.

The 360 channel does have a conditional branching facility, but it is highly specialized and limited. Depending on the outcome of various operations, devices may send a Status Modifier signal when they complete operation. If command chaining is specified, the next CCW in sequence is skipped when the Status Modifier signal is received upon completion of a CCW. By specifying the skipped CCW as an unconditional branch, a program can select between alternate CCW sequences depending on the bit sent by the device.

This selection is most frequently used with disk operations consisting of searches dependent on a program-specified key, followed by a read or write to the record containing the key. The search CCW specifies command chaining and is immediately followed by an unconditional branch back to itself, forming a tight loop. When the key is found (an event detected at the device), the device returns the Status Modifier signal, the channel skips the unconditional branch, and executes the Read or Write CCW.

Supervision

Since the channel has minimal processing power, it cannot monitor CPU process completion. On the other hand, the CPU usually needs to know about the channel process's completion. This asymmetry arises because I/O operation is slow, there often is a queue of pending I/O tasks, and these tasks limit the throughput rate. It is desirable to initiate another channel process as soon as one completes.

Completion. Channels normally report completion by setting a (maskable) interrupt signal of the CPU. The supervisor is then free to use a polling or interrupting strategy for responding to channel completion. The 709 allows polling through a Branch On Channel In Operation (e.g., TAO) instruction.

The 360 architecture allows a polling philosophy by means of the CPU operations Test I/O and Test Channel. But OS/360 and DOS/360, and their descendants, all use an interruption philosophy.

```
       ↓Zero

    ┌─────┬───────────────────────┬──────────────┬─────────────────┐
    │ Key │ Address               │ Status       │ Count           │
    └─────┴───────────────────────┴──────────────┴─────────────────┘
    0    4  8                      32             48                64
    Channel status word


       ↓Zero

    ┌─────┬───────────────────────┐        csw360
    │ Key │ Address               │        ∩ IBM 360 channel status word
    └─────┴───────────────────────┘        Key←0+ι4
    0    4  8                      32       Zero←4+ι4
    Channel address word                    Address←8+ι24
                                            Status←32+ι16
    caw360                                  Count←48+ι16
    ∩ IBM 360 channel address word          ∩ status field allocation
    Key←0+ι4                                   status360io
    Zero←4+ι4
    Address←8+ι24
```

PROGRAM 8-38 Channel address and status words in the IBM System/360.

Status reporting.   Mere news of completion is rarely enough—the CPU needs various information parameters distinguishing among a variety of untoward events and normal, correct completion. The 360 channel reports such status through a Channel Status Word (CSW), as illustrated in Program 8-38. More elaborate status information can be obtained via Sense operations.

Intermediate synchronization.   Occasionally it is necessary for a channel and a CPU to operate in close synchrony.   Consider a system receiving and processing a continuous stream of data telemetered from a spacecraft. The I/O process does not complete, and the CPU process cannot wait for that completion before beginning to use the data, as it would in a normal application. Some form of cyclic buffering must therefore be used, and two processes must be synchronized whenever a buffer is filled (Program 8-39).

```
readstream                      writestream
ᴀ process continuous input   ᴀ deliver continuous input
 REPEAT:→WAIT buffer1=full       REPEAT:overrun←buffer1≠empty
    buffer1←empty                  buffer1←full
    process                        overrun←overrun∨buffer2≠empty
    →WAIT buffer2=full             buffer2←full
    buffer2←empty                →UNTIL overrun
    process                      errormessage
 →UNTIL 0
```

PROGRAM 8-39   Buffer action for a continuous data stream.

The main process can test the progress of the channel if the CPU can get access to the Next Instruction Address of the channel. On the 360, Test Channel (Program 8-40) allows such access. (For finer-grained synchronization, one could even give access to the CCW in progress; this is not done in the 360.)

Alternatively, the channel can signal completion to the CPU. This function could be performed by a separate channel operation, executed after each buffer filling. Since data continue to arrive, however, the channel now must fetch and execute two instructions (CCWs) in the interval between data bytes—a demand that could be met by sufficient data buffering in the channel.

To obviate such buffering, each 360 channel instruction (Program 8-34) incorporates a modifier bit specifying whether the CPU is to be signaled upon completion of the associated data transmission operation. This bit is called the Program-Controlled Interruption (Pci) bit.

```
┌─────────┬───┬────┬──────────────┐
│ Opcode  │ * │ B1 │ D1           │
└─────────┴───┴────┴──────────────┘
0         8   16   20             32
Legend: B = base; D = displacement; * = unused.
```

```
TCH;address;channel;state        signal360TCH state;cc
ᴀ IBM 360 Test Channel          ᴀ IBM 360 test channel condition
 Priv report psw[Problem]         cc←(state=ready,pending,burst,absent)⍳1
 →OUT suppress360                 psw[Cc]←2 magnr cc
 address←adr360bd
 channel←⌊address÷256
 signal360TCH stateio[channel]
```

PROGRAM 8-40   Test Channel in the IBM System/360.

8.5.2

Main Processor Actions

The CPU performs both essential and residual I/O operations. The essential operations concern initiation and termination of the channel program, as for the PPU. Residual operations are those operations that the channel could have performed, but that are still assigned to the CPU because it is more powerful.

Initiation.   There is a crucial difference with respect to initiative between the general purpose PPU and the special purpose channel. Since the channel has no logical power, it cannot take the initiative in controlling the system operation, as the PPU can. In short, a channel cannot contain a supervisor; a PPU can. Therefore, initiation of the channel is always from the CPU. The operation Start I/O of the 360 (Program 8-41) is an example.

```
  Opcode   *       B1  D1

  0        8      16  20              32
  Legend: B = base; D = displacement; * = unused.

  SIO;address;channel;state        signal360IO state;cc
∩ IBM 360 Start Input/Output   ∩ IBM 360 input/output condition
  Priv report psw[Problem]         cc←(state=ready,pending,busy,absent)ıl
  →OUT suppress360                  psw[Cc]←2 magnr cc
  address←adr360bd1
  channel←⌊address÷256
  device←256|address
  state←stateio[channel]
  →If state=ready
  THEN:stateio[channel]←busy
  ENDIF:signal360IO state
```

PROGRAM 8-41   Start input/output in the IBM System/360.

The initiation of a channel program requires specifying the channel, specifying the device, the location of the first channel instruction to be executed, and possibly the status of the channel. The effective address of Start I/O is partitioned into channel specification and path specification. In contrast, the initial instruction address, which is 24 bits long, is communicated by using shared storage. A Channel Address Word (CAW) is placed at a dedicated location; the CAW contains the address of the initial CCW and the applicable protection key. For the 360, the channel status is limited to the protection key; other channels might require a priority indication.

Termination.   Normally the channel process will stop of its own accord. Rarely, but occasionally, the CPU will need to stop the channel—for example, if its instruction stream gets into an endless loop. Table 8-42 shows the four I/O instructions of the CPU for the 360. The 370 added four new I/O operations. A new Start I/O Fast Release allows the CPU to proceed without waiting

```
  d SIO   Start Input/Output   d TIO   Test Input/Output
  d HIO   Stop Input/Output    d TCH   Test Channel
```

TABLE 8-42   Channel instructions of the IBM System/360 and System/370.

for the channel to determine if the device is available. Halt Device allows one device to be stopped without affecting other subchannels. Clear I/O stops a subchannel immediately, without waiting for an I/O completion. Store Channel I/O identifies the channel by model, version, and serial number to aid diagnosis and recovery.

Residual functions.   In contrast to the 360, the CPU instructions devoted to I/O in the 709 (Table 8-43) deal with the detailed actions of the I/O operation. The 709 channel handles only transmission independently. All control functions are left to the main processor.

```
RDS  Read Select             T*O  Branch On Operational
WRS  Write Select            T*N  Branch On Not-operational
BST  Backspace Tape          T*R  Branch On Redundancy Check
BSF  Backspace File          T*F  Branch On End Of File
WEF  Write End Of File       SC*  Store Channel Status
REW  Rewind Tape             LC*  Load Channel Status
LDA  Locate Drum Address     PSE  Plus Sense
CPY  Copy                    MSE  Minus Sense
CAD  Copy And Add Logical        Legend: * = channel A...F.
```

TABLE 8-43   Input/output instructions of the IBM 709.

8.5.3

One Architecture, Multiple Implementations

The channel is a specialized processor; it is supposed to do just one thing—transmission—and do that well. Given the wide range of device data rates, designers often make different implementations—some fast, some inexpensive.

Implementation for maximum speed.   A channel that must accommodate fast disk and tape transmission rates typically has a dedicated implementation optimized for speed. It must have sufficient buffering for channel-instruction fetch in midstream; bytes that are inadvertently missed in transmission should be signaled as *channel-overrun* conditions. In short, the exclusive specialization for fast transmission leads to the conceptual structure of a grown-up buffer, rather than a processor.

Implementation for minimum cost.   Most of the channels of an average computer system have a relatively low data rate. So, just as for the PPU, virtual channels with a shared implementation seem called for. The Stretch I/O system, for example, provides 32 architectural channels implemented by a single mechanism, the Exchange [Buchholz, 1962, Chapter 16].

The existence of several types of channels in the 360 and 370 is fundamentally motivated by this desire to share implementations among virtual channels, called *subchannels* in 360 terminology. Unfortunately, we let second-order architectural differences creep in between multiplex and simplex channels.

How the 360 Channel Should Have Been Designed

It is clear now that the basic architectural-channel concept for the 360 should have been a set of logical or virtual PPUs, each identified with one

device and capable of controlling one I/O action at a time, and that all channels should have been architecturally identical and independent of one other. The concept of the 360 subchannel anticipates the one-channel-per-device ideal; the 370 XA architecture channel approaches it, finally. The 370 still does not have PPUs.

8.5.4
Bibliography

Akela and Siewiorek [1991], D.T. Brown et al. [1972], Buchholz [1962], Case and Padegs [1978], Chen and Patterson [1994], Christiansen et al. [1957], Dugan [1983], Frankovich and Peterson [1957], Padegs [1964].

8.6
Device Interfaces

The preceding sections implicitly included I/O devices as parts of the entire computer system. The machine language provides for communication among CPUs, PPUs or channels, and all kinds of devices. The physical connection of devices does not, of course, show in the architecture; it is an implementation and realization concern.

The architecture, implementation, and realization of I/O devices are constantly evolving. New kinds of devices, such as laser printers, facsimile machines, and CD-ROMs have become available. Processors are evolving independently. Moreover, the user often must obtain his processors and I/O devices from a variety of manufacturers.

This state of affairs suggest that one define a computer system as limited to CPUs and PPUs (or channels), separate from I/O devices and their particularized control units. In this case the architecture must specify the machine-language definition of the interfaces to which I/O devices attach, whether they are different for different kinds of devices, or whether they are standardized for all devices or for groups of device types.

Interface architecture can be defined at a moderately high level, just as is arithmetic architecture. Indeed, this is desirable if one wants a single interface to couple to a wide variety of devices. Alternatively, the designer may save control hardware by harnessing the program power of the processor to generate the sequence of orders and tests, or even the sequence of pulses, involved in establishing and maintaining communication between an I/O process in the system and the asynchronous, independently-clocked process in the device. In this case the machine language for I/O control becomes very low-level, very hardware-specific. This alternative is commonly used in microprocessors and small minicomputers.

Readers of a miniprocessor or microprocessor specification, such as the PDP8, are confronted with remarkably contrasting descriptions. The instructions are described with high-level concepts, such as addition and logic. But when the description turns to the connection of external devices, it deals with individual signals and their sequences. It is not often easy to ascertain what

is the purpose of these sequences and whether they are complete, logically correct, and free from deadlock or monopolization.

8.6.1

Concepts

Mastering this considerable complexity is aided by recognizing the vertical recursion of architecture in the communication between the central system and the peripheral device, or more generally between autonomous system components.

Protocol.   Processes communicate on a high level by exchanging messages. This exchange must follow a defined pattern, called a *protocol*, to ensure that messages are not lost, that messages are properly ordered and recognized, and that the exchange can be initiated and terminated in an orderly fashion.

Services.   To communicate in accordance with the protocol, each process uses underlying programs that reside in its processor and provide the necessary communication functions. These functions are called the *services* provided by the underlying layer. In other words, the architecture of each layer is implemented by the services of the underlying layer. This procedure is repeated recursively. Figure 8-44 shows the OSI-ISO terminology for communication between system components in a computer network.

Interface.   The downward recursion in architecture for communicating processors stops at a lowest level where the logical interface signals are those that have a direct physical realization. These logical signals are called *interface* signals. Program 8-45 gives the interface signals of the PDP8.

These signals are the minimum provision for attaching a processor or device to an interface. For each signal, there are also realization specifications that govern the connection.   At the realization level, for example, pulse voltages and durations, line impedances, and even the sizes, shapes, number, and locations of pins on the plug must match [Vissers, 1977]. But this provision is by no means sufficient: The use of these signals in interchanging messages via this interconnection must follow the protocol.

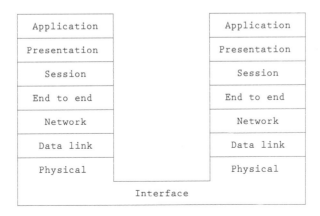

FIGURE 8-44   Communication layers.

```
interface8
ᴀ DEC PDP8 interface allocaticn
 Break←0
 Cycle←1                          Outputdata←32+ι12
 Dataadr←2+ι12                    Datain←44+ι12
 Incr←14                          Ioskip←56
 Direction←15                     Clear←57
 Inputdata←16+ι12                 Int←58
 Noincr←28                        Iomod←59+ι3
 Breakrequest←29                  Dataout←62+ι12
 Control←30+ι2                    Deviceadr←74+ι6
```

PROGRAM 8-45   Input/output interface of the DEC PDP8.

8.6.2

Standard Interfaces

Historical Development

In early computers, each I/O device was attached to the computer in any way that seemed simple to engineer. In the 701 a 6-bit bus ran between the low-order six bits of the Multiplier-Quotient register to the (single) tape-control unit. Similarly, a 36-bit bus ran between the entire MQ register and a switch selecting among the drum, the card reader, the punch, and the printer. The Univac I had only magnetic tapes and a console typewriter attached; their attachment was also ad hoc.

Proliferation.   The number and variety of I/O devices attachable to any given computer model increased sharply by the early sixties, as production runs went into the hundreds and customer diversity increased.

Furthermore, any new I/O device, such as the disk, needed to be attached to many quite different computers, each with a different I/O attachment philosophy. IBM alone had some six product families in 1963; its 1301 disk was attached to five of these families. Each family required a different 1301 control unit. Univac's situation was similar.

Stretch's standard interface.   Since these problems were already evident when the Stretch was designed (1955 to 1959), Buchholz incorporated configuration flexibility and attachment economies into its generalized I/O system by providing one standard interface between the channels and the I/O control units [Buchholz, 1962, Chapter 12]. Essentially, every device was to be made to look like a magnetic-tape unit, with suitable generalization in control and sensing. This approach would solve both problems: All devices would look alike to the channel, and all channels and machines would look alike to the devices. In practice, of course, this sweeping generalization is only almost true; various qualifications have to be appended.

IBM System/360 standard interface.   Whereas the Stretch was a limited-production supercomputer, adoption of a standard I/O interface on the 360 affected the entire product line, and the industry. The standard interface on the 360, and followed by many other systems, follows the Stretch in being 1 byte wide.

Advantages of standardization.   The use of a standard I/O interconnection essentially decouples the design and introduction of I/O devices from the design and introduction of CPU-memory subsystems.   The most obvious advantages are

- Different users can have radically different I/O configurations without special engineering.
- A user can change I/O configurations without changes to his CPU-memory subsystem; this procedure allows easy configuration growth, shrinkage, or updating.
- A user can change CPU-memory subsystems without altering I/O configurations; weekend conversions become possible.
- Since only one kind of control unit need be designed, manufactured, stocked, maintained, and programmed for each I/O device, costs drop substantially.
- I/O channels can be designed in a few types differing only in data rate, with substantially lower costs.
- New technologies can be introduced by any manufacturer on either side of the interconnection without affecting designs on the other. Each side can then achieve its natural lifetime without becoming obsolete through changes on the other.
- Much I/O software can be used for all devices.

Hardware costs of standardization.   Standardization of many designs necessarily means designing each differently from the way it would be designed alone. The differences always tend toward increasing the amount of hardware in order to reduce the total system costs (including engineering and software), and even, in the best case, to reduce hardware costs themselves because of quantity production.   The constraints of standardization are chiefly at the implementation level, with some implications for architecture and realization.

8.6.3

Interface Width

The most obvious and pervasive difference among I/O devices is in the number of bits handled in parallel. Disks and communication lines are 1 bit wide; tapes are 1 byte wide; drums, fixed-head disks, and so on, can be any convenient width; card readers, punches, and printers are many bits wide or have separate buffers. So widths of 1, 9, 32–128 bits are typical, for example, on 360 devices.

The most painful case: wide devices on wide machines.   Consider a wide I/O device such as a redundant array of inexpensive disks (RAID) or the multitrack drum of the 701. The most straightforward attachment engineers the width of the device to match that of the CPU memory word (Figure 8-46).

Such an interface is specific to the memory implementation of the CPU; so it limits the set of CPUs to which the device simply attaches. More seriously, it locks the disk array evolution, in width and datarate, to that of the host CPU.

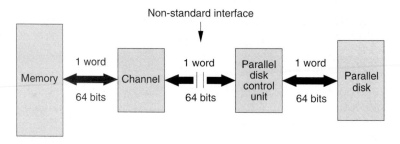

FIGURE 8-46   Non-standard interface between memory and RAID disk.

If one instead chooses a standard I/O interface 1 byte wide, as might be natural for a tape drive, both the disk control unit and the PPU or channel have to do extra work, as Figure 8-47 shows. Moreover, the datarate of the transfer may be limited by the disassembly of words into bytes and the reassembly into words.

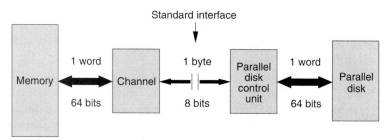

FIGURE 8-47   Width adaption between memory and parallel disk (or RAID).

Much less painful: 1-bit–wide devices.   By far the largest amount of I/O traffic is to and from disks, and a disk head is inherently 1 bit wide. For this case the byte-wide standard interface action becomes that of Figure 8-48. Each of the channel and the control unit do one stage of disassembly and reassembly, whereas a single mechanism could do the whole job. The penalties are modest.

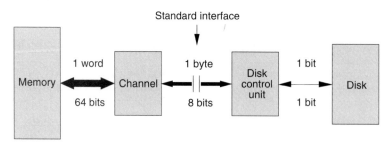

FIGURE 8-48   System/360 Standard I/O Interface controlling a disk.

An Example—The IBM System/360 Interface

Architecture.   The *architecture* of the 360 interface is partially represented by the following rules:

1. Data transmission is in 8-bit bytes; that is,

$$0 = 8 \mid \text{blocklength-in-bits}$$

and, equally important, there is no other modular constraint on blocklength.

2. The operations Read (including Read Backward, Skip, etc.) and Write control data transmission in blocks to and from the I/O medium.

3. All device-dependent control-and-sense information is transmitted in blocks between the control unit and the memory as if it were data, by the operations Control and Sense.

4. The device-independent commands are:

> Write
> Read
> Read Backward
> Control
> Sense
> Transfer In Channel (Branch)

These device-independent commands are not transmitted as though they were data. Instead, they are presented to the control unit across the interface by means of distinguished control signals.

5. Besides the large set of device-dependent conditions that can be read by a Sense command, there is a smaller set of device-independent inbound signals. Such signals are not transmitted as data blocks, but are rather transmitted on distinguished lines and stored into a Control Status Word in memory upon execution of Start I/O, Test I/O, Halt I/O, or upon completion of a channel process. These 16 conditions report various completions, invalidities, and malfunctions of the device, the control unit, or the channel:

Attention	Program-controlled interruption
Status unavailable	Incorrect length
Control unit end	Program check
Busy	Protection check
Channel end	Channel data check
Device end	Channel control check
Unit check	Interface control check
Unit exception	Chaining check

6. There are certain syntax constraints, too lengthy to specify here, on the sequence of commands and signals. See the *IBM System/360 Principles of Operation* [IBM, 1964].

7. There are defined semantics, also too lengthy to specify here, for each command and signal. See the manual.

The syntax of the architecture of the interface is almost independent of that of the channel. One could change Channel Control Word formats radically without affecting the interface; indeed, one could abandon channels and substitute direct I/O control or I/O peripheral processors without affecting interface architecture.

The converse is less true; interface architecture is a starting point for I/O control architecture.

Implementation.   The implementation of the 360 interface involves many decisions: the number of datapaths, the number and encoding of the control and signal lines, the nature of the send-acknowledge-respond-acknowledge communication protocol, the means of device selection, and so on. These matters are fully discussed in [Blaauw, 1976, Chapter 9].

1-Bit Wide Standard Interfaces

The byte-wide standard interface reflects the assumption that the tape drive is the archetypal I/O device. This assumption made sense in 1964; the 360 was one of the first systems whose principal operating systems mandated the inclusion of a disk in the I/O configuration. Today the disk is the archetypal device. Communication lines, now pervasive, are also 1 bit wide. Consequently new standard interfaces have adopted 1 bit as the standard width, avoiding the penalties of Figure 8-48. Figure 8-49 shows the arrangement.

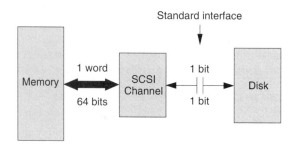

FIGURE 8-49   One-bit wide SCSI Standard I/O Interface

The SCSI interface.   Personal computers and workstations have adopted a 1-bit–wide *Standard Computer Serial Interface* (SCSI, pronounced "scuzzy"). Many such systems have different interfaces to their attached hard disks and displays, but use SCSI for miscellaneous devices.

Serial optical interfaces.   Fiber optics offers such fast transmission speeds that even 1-bit–wide connections do not limit the fastest I/O devices. Many systems, including the IBM 370 family, are using serial optical channels and connections to save I/O connection costs and permit longer connections.

8.6.4
Bibliography

Blaauw [1976], Buchholz [1962], IBM [1964], Knoblock et al. [1975], Matula [1967], Vissers [1977].

8.7

Exercises

8-1 In the 360 channel programs, a single block transfer, as specified by a single CCW, can be terminated by reaching the end of the physical block on the device or by completion of the block transfer specified by the Count field. For the eight combinations of settings of the CD, CC, and SLI bits, consider reasonable actions for the system to take in the cases of

a. Normal termination (count exhaustion and physical-block end coincide)

b. Termination by the end of the physical block with count not exhausted

c. Termination by count exhaustion with more data in physical block

If possible, check your determinations against the table in the chaining section of the *IBM System/360 Principles of Operation* [IBM, 1964].

8-2 Optional Data Break hardware may be purchased for the PDP8 to allow block transfers between memory and a high-speed device, transfers at data rates higher than direct programming can achieve. The hardware contains a word counter and a memory pointer register, both of which the program loads initially. An IOT instruction then initiates the transfer. The program then loops, waiting for the device flag to be set, indicating the end of the transfer. This type of transfer does not disturb the accumulator contents, so the CPU may do some unrelated processing in the wait loop.

Show how these Data Break facilities can be used with the interruption facility described in Section 7.3 to serve as an elementary memory-buffered I/O channel.

8-3 In what ways is the TX2 I/O system like the PPU system of the 6600? In what ways is it different [Forgie, 1957]?

8-4 How does the implementation on a single machine simplify process synchronization among the virtual processors of the TX2 [Forgie, 1957]?

8-5 Determine and sketch the particular I/O attachment network for some computer at your installation.

Part II
A Computer Zoo

ADVERTISEMENT.

THE works of the famous ANDREA PALLADIO, published by himself at *Venice* in the year 1570. have been universally esteemed the best standard of architecture hitherto extant. The original work written in Italian being very scarce, several have attempted to translate the same into English, and to copy his excellent and most accurate wooden prints on copper plates.

IN particular, two persons have published what they honour with the title of PALLADIO's works: The first, and in all respects the best of the two, was done in the year 1721. by Mr. LEONI; who has thought fit not only to vary from the scale of the originals, but also in many places to alter even the graceful proportions prescribed by this great master, by diminishing some of his measures, enlarging others, and putting in fanciful decorations of his own : and indeed his drawings are likewise very incorrect ; which makes this performance, according to his own account in the preface, seem rather to be itself an original, than an improvement on PALLADIO.

THE other work (published in the year 1735.) is done with so little understanding, and so much negligence, that it cannot but give great offence to the judicious, and be of very bad consequence in misleading the unskilful, into whose hands it may happen to fall.

TO do justice therefore to PALLADIO, and to perpetuate his most valueable remains amongst us, are the principal inducements to my undertaking so great and laborious a work ; in executing of which, I have strictly kept to his proportions and measures, by exactly tracing all the plates from his originals, and engraved them with my own hands : So that the reader may depend upon having an exact copy of what our author published, without diminution or increase ; nor have I taken upon me to alter, much less to correct, any thing that came from the hands of that excellent artist.

FROM the same motive I have chosen to give a strict and literal translation, that the sense of our author might be delivered from his own words.

Scotland-Yard,
June, 1737.

Guide to the Zoo

In the first eight chapters, we have examined, one by one, the design decisions facing a computer architect. Here we present a collection of sketches of machine architectures, chosen to be representative and interesting.

Such a collection is vital to our study for several reasons:

1. We have drawn especially upon these machines for illustrative examples in Part I. Here one can see the examples in detail and in context.

2. Each machine is an integrated collection of decisions, and the integration itself demands study. The reader can see here how the alternative chosen for one design decision constrains and fits the choices for another—for example, how instruction formats and data formats interact.

3. One can compare specimens, noting similarities and differences arising from different market objectives, different technology ratios governing implementation, different historical forces at work, and purely personal differences in the styles of the designers.

4. We exhibit individual computers in the context of their families, as they evolved over four decades. So the sketches provide material for studying the process of architectural evolution: the squeezing of ever more function and ever larger address spaces into ever more cramped formats.

Isaac Ware, Palladio's translator whose "Advertisement" appears opposite, felt keenly the importance of reproducing superb architectural specimens, and of doing so faithfully. So do we. Unlike Ware, we can praise the collectors who have preceded us.

Like most zoos, this Computer Zoo is organized into "houses" of related families and specimens. The houses group schools of design, some named after influential designers.

Criteria of selection. The hardest part of developing such a collection of machines is pruning the list of candidates. Any computer fancier will find that some of his favorites have been omitted; so have some of ours.

We have limited the members of the Zoo to real machines, actually built and used. These designs alone have had to accommodate tradeoffs and issues forced by consistency, functional needs, and implementation costs.

We present the architectures that have had greatest influence on later designs or have introduced radically new ideas that proved important. We

have made no attempt to select especially current architectures; the specimens are chosen for the ideas they illustrate.

Machine descriptions.   We have abbreviated the descriptions to sketches consisting mostly of programs, tables, and diagrams. Our driving goal was to provide the specific detail that exhibits all levels of design decisions, rather than to give a superficial overall summary. A detailed description has the advantage that it is subject to criticism and correction. We hope that corrections will come forth where we are in error.

From the descriptions, a computer-wise reader can write plausible programs in the machine language. Writing such programs is the only way we know to grasp how an architecture works.

For fuller descriptions, we give references to the literature. The original manuals are essential—but not always adequate—in supplying further information; the early papers are especially valuable for explaining the design objectives and the reasoning behind specific decisions. Many of the early papers have been reprinted in the great books by Bell and Newell [1971], Siewiorek, Bell, and Newell [1982], and Randell [1973, 1975].

9.1
Generations and Families

9.1.1
Computer Generations

Computers realized in a particular technology are called a *generation*. Table 9-1 shows the divisions that are commonly accepted. We use generation 0 to recognize that there were fully programmable electromechanical computers before there were any electronic computers. The boundary between generations 3 and 4 is fuzzy; most authors consider it to be as we have shown.

	Architecture	Implementation	Realization	(Start)
0	(Classical computer)	Parallel	Electromechanical	(1944)
1	Classical computer	Series, Parallel	Vacuum tubes	(1948)
2	Interruption, Supervision	Pipeline, Microcode	Transistors, Core storage	(1955)
3	Memory mapping, Peripheral processors	Microcode	Integrated circuits	(1965)
4	Vector arithmetic, Networks	Cache	Very Large Scale Integration	(1975)

TABLE 9-1   Computer generations.

This customary division into generations has nothing to do with computer architecture; it is a division based on realization technology alone. Not only is there a dramatic difference in capability and appearance from one realization generation to the next, but also, once a new realization emerges, it replaces the preceding generation. Vacuum tubes were completely displaced by discrete transistors and core storage, only to be displaced in turn by integrated logic and memory circuits.

The picture is quite different for architecture. Once a classical architecture was established in the first generation, it endured. New functions—such as those for supervision, memory management, and communication with peripheral devices—have appeared, but they have been orthogonal to the functions of the classical architecture, and have been added to it. Even details of the architecture often survive several generations of implementation and realization. One reason is that useful programs have very long lifetimes. As a program is used, it is extended and modified. It is not uncommon to find much-modified survivors more than 20 years old. Because reprogramming old applications is distasteful and expensive, there is a ready market for new computers that are at least upward compatible from old ones—computers that extend an old architecture.

Therefore, an architecture appears to be timeless, in contrast to its transient realizations. The fundamental implementation techniques are also timeless. The basic algorithms were all developed in the first generation, with macrotechniques—such as pipelining, microcoding, and lookaside—exploited on top of these algorithms. Since an implementation must match a stable architecture to a changing realization, different demands are made upon implementation's wide arsenal of techniques in each generation.

9.1.2

Architectural Eras

The stability of computer architecture is not caused merely by the inertia of programming investment. One can identify several eras in computer architecture, each marked by an entirely new field of application or way of using the computer. The more important architectural eras are illustrated by Table 9-2, which gives typical examples. Thus the minicomputer era, which placed the computer as an instrument in the laboratory, started afresh with new architectures and new programs, not tied to previous practice. Yet the minicomputer architecture was, at the start, not very different from the classical architecture and indeed converged to it in time.

The convergence has become striking in recent years. Hennessy and Patterson [1990] can completely cover the architecture and implementation of today's four major microprocessor families with a single description and an appendix of differences. These microprocessor families drive personal computers, workstations, superminicomputers, and high-performance graphics computers. Only supercomputers and minisupercomputers now have distinctive architectures, and convergence between microprocessor and supercomputer architecture proceeds apace. Intel's i860 RISC microprocessor includes vector and graphics datatypes and operations.

Era	Type	Example	Start
0	Pioneer computer	Mark I, Zuse Z4, ENIAC	1940
1	Classical computer	MU1, Univac, IBM 704	1950
2	Supervised computer	IBM Stretch	1955
3	Supercomputer	IBM Stretch, CDC 6600	1960
4	Time-shared computer	GE 645	1965
5	Minicomputer	DEC PDP8, PDP11	1970
6	Microprocessor	Intel 8080A	1975
7	Workstation	Motorola MC68000	1980

TABLE 9-2   Architectural eras.

The tendency for architectural concepts to converge has been explained concept by concept in Part I. In the Zoo we illustrate this convergence in the various houses (Figure 9-3). Because of this convergence, we can use a standard pattern to organize the sketches, and a common description structure to display our specimens.

9.1.3
Architectural Families

Each house of the Zoo contains several related species. A set of computer architectures embodying the same detailed design decisions is called a *computer family*. We try to depict each specimen within the context of its family; usually, one member suffices to illustrate the family.

Family members may be siblings—of the same era but specialized for different uses—or they may be ancestors and descendants. A descendant architecture is often an extension of the ancestor architecture; it is often created by the same design team. But sometimes another computer manufacturer propagates that family descent. Often one manufacturer decides explicitly to adopt a popular architecture and thus to inherit ready-built system and application software. The crossing of manufacturer boundaries happens in other ways, too: by corporate merger or split-off, movement of a key designer, or the considerable influence on any designer of the first machine he learned.

Just as all family members may not come from one manufacturer, so all the machines from one maker need not have any family resemblance at all. Corporations are not monoliths, and independent or competing design groups within one manufacturer often produce architectures that are radically different. Many published classifications of computer families treat *family* and *manufacturer* as identical, an error that confuses and conceals the conceptual evolutions that have occurred.

We discuss the family structures of a few prominent families and the product lines of a few prominent manufacturers to illustrate these points.

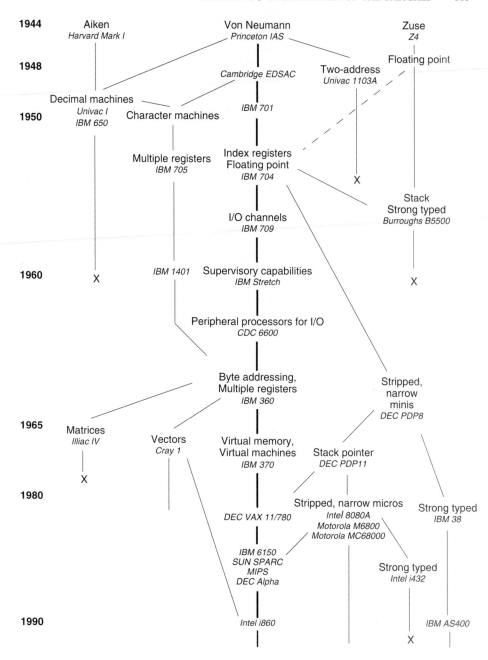

FIGURE 9-3   Divergence and convergence in computer architecture.

9.2

Organization of the Sketches

The sketches are organized like Part I, with a numbered section in each corresponding to the numbered chapters of the first part. Especially important

implementation considerations, and those that seriously affected the architecture, are mentioned in a separate section.

We use a canonical outline for the sketches to aid comparison among machines. We have held closely to its top level, usually have followed the second level, and have departed from the lower levels as the machine seemed to dictate. We show it here with section numbers, of which only the top levels are shown in the sketches themselves:

Machine designation
1. Highlights
    1.1 History
        Architects; dates; family tree
    1.2 Noteworthy
        New and useful ideas introduced in the machine; ideas that the machine exemplifies well
    1.3 Peculiarities
        Ideas that did not survive
    1.4 Descendants
        How ideas continued in further generations
2. Machine Language
    2.1 Language Level
        Design philosophy
    2.2 Unit System
    2.3 Spaces
        Memory name-space;   working store; control store; embedding; programming model
    2.4 Operand Specification
        Number of addresses; address phrase
    2.5 Operation Specification
        Mnemonics; types of control
    2.6 Instruction Structure
        Machine-language syntax; instruction format; status format
3. Addressing
        Direct addressing
    3.1 Address Mapping
    3.2 Address Modification by Indexing
        Address calculation
    3.3 Index Arithmetic
        Index operations; stack and list addressing
    3.4 Address Level
        Indirect addressing; immediate addressing
4. Data
    4.1 Character Strings
        Character set and size; character string formats
    4.2 Logical
        Logical formats
    4.3 Fixed-Point Numbers
        Radix; notation; allocation
    4.4 Floating-Point Numbers
        Format; representation; closure and normal form
5. Operations
    5.1 Data Handling
        Data movement; format and code transformation
    5.2 Logic
        Connectives; vector operations; shifts

The formal descriptions in APL are interleaved with the text of the appropriate sections.

9.3

The Formal Descriptions—Executable Simulators

The machine descriptions in the Zoo constitute, for each machine, an *executable architectural simulator*, covering almost all of the sequencing, but usually only a subset of the operations. The most vivid understanding of a design comes from running sample programs on this simulator in a suitable environment.

But even if such a safari experience is not immediately feasible, we have tried to make the visit to the Zoo rewarding by exhibiting the specimens in a way that helps individual and comparative study.

A computer's architecture consists of a static *structure* (the spaces, registers, memory) and dynamic *actions* (the processes of sequencing, instruction fetching, effective address evaluation, arithmetic). As Part I illustrates, architectures have similar structures and actions. The details differ widely from machine to machine.

We describe architectures using the overall method of description introduced in Section 1.3, with APL functions. More specifically, we have adopted a single style of formal description, a common static hierarchy of descriptive functions for describing structure, a common dynamic hierarchy for describing action, a set of general utility functions used throughout, and a common nomenclature.

The detailed functions must be machine-specific. To show the commonalities, we describe each machine with a set of machine-specific functions that mostly correspond to a canonical set. Section 9.3.1 describes this common basis, or canonical set. The particular machine-specific functions are given with the pertinent machine descriptions.

All of these functions use the same general utility functions, which are described in Section 9.3.2.

Programming models. In these diagrams we supplement the formal APL descriptions with geometric representations of the static structures. We represent only the data and address flow, not including the control and status bits. Usually we do not represent the I/O system at all. These diagrams provide a mental picture of most of the objects that the programming language talks about. Many details cannot be shown; the APL descriptions are normative.

To aid comparison, register widths are drawn to scale. Except where otherwise noted, we have used a scale of 24 bits/inch; machines too wide to fit our page constraint at that scale are represented at 36 or 48 bits/inch, as necessary. In each diagram heavier lines indicate the wider dataflows in that diagram; we do not attempt exact or consistent correspondence between line weight and dataflow width.

9.3.1

Machine-Specific Functions

Identifying suffix.   Each machine's machine-specific functions are given the canonical names, distinguished by an identifying suffix. For example, the functions of the DEC PDP11 (1970) description in the Bell house have suffix 11. When the suffix is not specified, we represent it with a hyphen, for example, `initiate-`.

Static Hierarchy of Declaration Functions

Static structures need to be declared as part of a program's environment. APL does not provide declaration as such; the convention is to accomplish it by functions that create and initialize variables. We use a static hierarchy

Initiation tree	Spaces, parameters, and allocations
initiate-	
format-	radix digit byte half word double quad long
	adrsize adrcap
configure-	memcap
space-	memory reg iadr ind cond status
name-	
address-	memadr regadr Size Space Value
control-	
instruction-	Op* Address R* X* B* L*
indicator-	Neg Pos Zero Oflo Carry
status-	
data-	charcode plus minus Upper Lower Zone Num Sign
decimal-	plus minus Sign Digits
fl-	base plus minus point extexp Exp Coef

Legend: - = machine suffix; * = postfix;
      initial capital signifies allocation index.

TABLE 9-4   Static hierarchy of declaration functions in a machine description.

of functions that declares and initializes the units, spaces, and names of a machine description. The hierarchy is static in the sense that these objects exist all the time in the machine; they need to be declared and initialized only once prior to executing a program. These objects and structures do not change. The content of the spaces, however, does change as the computer executes a program.

The description-program structure is a hierarchy because each function is called by just one higher function. The top of the hierarchy starts with the function `initiate-` (`initiate11` for the PDP11). Executing `initiate-` declares the entire name and space structure of a computer.

Table 9-4 shows the static hierarchy we use in all machine descriptions. First, the units and dimensions are established by `format-`, with parameters radix, digit, and so on. Then `configure-` gives the dimensions that vary among the installed machines, such as memory capacity; `space-` creates the machine spaces; `name-` specifies the allocation of entities (such as stack pointers) and subspaces (such as fields) within these spaces; `control-` and its subfunctions give the parameters and allocations necessary for status and instructions; and `data-` and its subfunctions give this information for data interpretation and representation.

Some function and variable names have a postfix to distinguish multiple occurrences. For example, an instruction format may contain three register fields with names R1, R2, and R3.

Variables named with an initial capital specify the allocation of the element named. Their chief function in the descriptions is mnemonic; Exp, for example, tells where the exponent is found in the data word. For the IBM 704 (1955), Exp is set to $1 + \iota 8$ when the machine is declared, specifying that the exponent field occupies 8 bits, starting at bit 1. Such variables' values differ from one machine to another, but rarely change within one machine's description.

When a certain concept does not apply to a given machine, it is omitted. We compress layers of the hierarchy when a layer has only one subconcept.

For example, if the only function of `control-` is `instruction-`, `control-` is replaced by `instruction-`.

`initiate-` always starts the static hierarchy declarations, but once its existence is known it is an obvious function; therefore we often do not show it in the machine descriptions.

Dynamic Function Hierarchy

Computers cycle between fetching and executing instructions. After each instruction is complete, interruptions and stopping conditions are tested; then the cycle iterates.

This cyclic action and all the subaction are described by a dynamic function hierarchy. Program 9-5 shows its general pattern. `cycle-` is the top node of the hierarchy. This hierarchy is dynamic: The functions called depend upon the machine state—notably, the instruction stream and the data content. Furthermore, `cycle-` repeats for the duration of a computing process.

```
cycle-
REPEAT:execute ifetch-
     interrupt-
 →UNTIL stop-
Legend: - = machine suffix.
```

PROGRAM 9-5   Basic execution cycle.

Basic cycle.   `cycle-` in general comprises the function `ifetch-`, which delivers the instruction `inst` to the function `execute` (generally followed by the function `interrupt-`), and some means of stopping, such as the variable `stop` in the PDP11, or the function `stop8080` in the Intel 8080A (1974).

Instruction execution.   Instruction execution, initiated by `execute`, involves an instruction `inst`, whose operation is specified by capitalized mnemonics, such as `INR` for the increment instruction of the 8080A. For most machines, only a sample of instructions is given. Within these instructions, usually-uniform addressing functions, (`adr-`) and storage access functions (`read-` and `write-`) are used, as well as the general interpretation and representation functions. The family of `signal-*` functions sets conditions as indicated by mnemonic suffixes, represented here by *; for example, `signal8080NZP` sets the Negative, Zero, and Parity conditions. `suppress-` aborts a function in case of an error condition.

Instruction Syntax

There are three major areas of interest in computer operation: the machine cycle (including the fetching of instructions), the decoding of instruction bits to determine operation and operands, and the actions of the various operations and addressing modes. Each of these concepts is orthogonal to the others. Yet in many machine descriptions, such as the early APL description of the IBM System/360 (1965; see Programs 1-21 and 1-22), the details of instruction decoding and instruction execution are presented as an integral part of the machine cycle. We keep these concepts separate; we use a single general

function `decode` to describe the parsing and decoding of all instruction formats for all binary machines.

This general function uses two machine-specific tables to control instruction parsing—a table of instruction formats, declared by the machine-specific function `syntax-`; and a table of the alphabetic mnemonics for the operation codes proper, declared as the character matrix `oplist`. The oplist table enables us to call the various specific operation functions by mnemonic name. It does not correspond to any physical structure in the computer; it is a description artifact.

Instruction-format syntax.   The function `syntax-` gives the syntactic patterns of the machine language. `syntax-` is part of the static hierarchy; its purpose is not execution, but merely specification. From `syntax-` a Boolean array `form` and a vector `orop` are derived. `form` and `orop` are used in our simulations to obtain the mnemonic name of an instruction from the character matrix `oplist`.

Syntactic patterns and operation groups.   `syntax-` describes the various instruction formats. Each row contains one distinct format, consisting of various fixed format-designation bits, some operation-code bits, and other fields. Corresponding to each row in `syntax-` is a contiguous group of rows in the `oplist` matrix, showing the several operations specified by the operation-code bits of that pattern. The letters shown in front of `syntax` rows designate format types. The formats in each type differ only in the values of fixed bits. The same letters in `oplist` show which format type goes with each operation group. An auxiliary vector `orop` gives the origin and extent within `oplist` of each opcode group.

As an example, Program 9-6 shows that the 8080A has the distinct syntactic pattern types marked a through h. Several types have more than one pattern. The type marked g, which consists of the field `Opr` and six fixed bit-values, occurs twice. The two occurrences of type g are the tenth and eleventh entries of the list of syntactic patterns. They differ only in the fixed bit-values. The field `Opr` has 2 bits, thus allowing four operations, for each occurrence. The

```
orop      syntax8080
 0     a 0 1 ,Dest,Source
 1     b 0 1 1 1 0 1 1 0
 2     c 0 0 ,Dest,Ops
10     d 1 0 ,Opd,Source
18     e 1 1 ,Rp,On,Ops
26     f 0 0 ,Opd, 0 1 0
34     f 0 0 ,Opd, 1 1 1
42     f 1 1 ,Opd, 0 1 1
50     f 1 1 ,Opd, 1 1 0
58     g 1 1 ,Opr, 1 0 0 1
62     g 1 1 ,Opr, 1 1 0 1
66     h 0 0 ,Rp, 0 0 0 1
67     h 0 0 ,Rp, 0 0 1 1
68     h 0 0 ,Rp, 1 0 0 1
69     h 0 0 ,Rp, 1 0 1 1
70     h 1 1 ,Rp, 0 0 0 1
71     h 1 1 ,Rp, 0 1 0 1
72
```

PROGRAM 9-6   Example of `orop` and `syntax` from the Intel 8080A.

```
a→MOV        ORA        STA        DI
b→HLT        CMP        LDA        EI
c→NOP        e→RT       f→RLC      f→ADI      h→LXI
  →h           →gh        RRC        ACI      h→INX
  →f         JP           RAL        SUI      h→DAD
  →h           →f         RAR        SBI      h→DCX
  INR        CL           DAA        ANI      h→POP
  DCR          →gh        CMA        XRI      h→PUSH
  MVI          →f         STC        ORI
  →f         RST          CMC        CPI
d→ADD        f→STAB     f→JMP      g→RET
  ADC        LDAB
  SUB        STAD         OT         PCHL
  SBB        LDAD         IN         SPHL
  ANA        SHLD         XTHL     g→CALL
  XRA        LHLD         XCHG
```

PROGRAM 9-7   Example of oplist from the Intel 8080A.

opcodes belonging to these patterns start at entries 58 and 62 in oplist (specified by orop[9] and orop[10]).

In Program 9-6 the values of orop are shown vertically to the left of the syntactic patterns; we omit these values in the regular machine descriptions.

Program 9-6 also illustrates that a syntactic pattern may be a special case of another pattern. Pattern type b is a special case of pattern type a, and the two patterns of type g are special cases of type e. In these cases the more general pattern is always placed first. In searching for a match, the function decode proceeds from bottom to top; it tries the special-case (later) patterns before the general patterns.

Operation list.   oplist is a character matrix with one mnemonic per row. Program 9-7 shows oplist in five columns to give a more compact figure on the page. The start of each opcode group is marked to the left of the column by an arrow and the identifying letter of its corresponding syntactic pattern. The first operations of the groups belonging to pattern type g are shown to be RET and CALL. Only four of the eight available code slots for type g are used.

When an entry in oplist is used, not for an operation, but rather to accommodate one or more special-case patterns, the type letters of the special-case pattern (preceded by an arrow) are placed in the table. For example, in Program 9-7 the second and sixth entries of type e are each used for patterns g and h. Program 9-7 does not show that pattern b is a subsidiary of pattern a because the move instruction MOV occupies the oplist entry (only specific source and destination-field values of MOV are designated for pattern b).

The lowercase letters and the arrows of Program 9-7 are not part of oplist. They are placed in the table to clarify how the decoding structure of the syntax affects the interpretation of oplist. In particular, they show which code slots are free for assigning new operations.

In some machines, such as the 704, oplist is sparse and large. In such cases, we show oplist compressed, with the blank entries omitted.

Decode.   To simplify its action, the general function decode uses the Boolean array form to find the mnemonic function name that belongs to an instruction inst (Program 9-8). The three-dimensional logical array form is a digest of the instruction syntax, with one plane for each pattern and a 2-bit row for each

```
r←decode inst;f;type
⍝ opcode decoding
f←form[;⍳⍴inst;]
type←+/∨\⌽1↓((∨/f)∧.≥inst)∧((</f)∧.≤inst)
r←orop[type]+magni(∧/f[type;;])/inst
```

PROGRAM 9-8   Operation-code decoding.

bit in a pattern. The four combinations of the two bits indicate respectively that the instruction bit must be either 1 or 0, or that it belongs to either the opcode field or to another field.

The general function `decode` exhibits the full power of APL, but to the APL novice it will undoubtedly appear incomprehensible. Since it is a service function, we just describe its overall function—those familiar with APL can discern the details. `decode` first matches the dimension of `form` to the length of `inst`; then it finds the type of instruction by assuring that those bits that must be 1 or 0 within a pattern indeed match, and by selecting the first pattern that matches searching, bottom to top; finally, it determines the specific instance of that type—hence, the operation of the instruction. More precisely, the index of the mnemonic of the name in `oplist` is found. `form` and `orop` are machine-specific; they are not shown in the machine descriptions, since their information is inherent in the instruction syntax of the given machine; they are derived from that information automatically.

As an example, consider an 8080A instruction `DCR` that refers to destination register 3. Program 9-7 shows that syntactic pattern `c` is used, and that the instruction is the fifth in that group (starting with zero). The instruction has pattern 00011101. As `decode` inspects this bit pattern, it finds no match for the left two bits and the rightmost three or four bits (searching from bottom to top) until the pattern `c`, which requires only a match on the left two bits. This pattern is selected, and the rightmost three bits signify the fifth entry in the group.

Mnemonics.   Mnemonics used as operation names consist of capital letters. We use the mnemonics of the assembly language of the computer when possible. Where the assembly mnemonics use symbols other than capital letters (as occurs in some early machines), or where no mnemonics are established, we use our own mnemonics.

Summary description.   The first line of each instruction function is a comment that summarizes that function's content. We use standard terms to obtain a common description for all machines. For example, in the instruction ANS of the IBM 701 (1953), we use And To Memory rather than Extract, the term used in the original manual (Program 11-56).

Instruction lists.   For each machine, we give the complete listing of the mnemonics, the letter identifying the syntactic pattern type, and the summary descriptions. (For the 360 and the DEC VAX11/780, these lists are compressed.) As we discuss a group of instructions, such as fixed-point arithmetic, we shall repeat the listing of that group unless all members of the group are fully described.

Universal assembly language.   We use a simple universal assembly language for all machines we describe. Each instruction is represented by its

mnemonic, followed by the decimal representation of all variable instruction fields (e.g., address and index fields) in their left-to-right order. For the 8080A, the three instructions that move the content of register 1 to register 2, decrement register 5, and subtract the content of register 3 from the accumulator, give the following assembly string: MOV 2 1 DCR 5 SUB 3.

Machine-specific assembler.   From `syntax` one can generate a machine-specific assembler that adheres to the universal assembly-language syntax. This assembler changes a character string into the bit patterns of the machine-language instructions. The assembler is useful as a means of demonstrating and testing the machine descriptions.

9.3.2

General Description Functions

By a *general* description function, we mean one, such as `decode`, that is the same in each machine description. These functions are written to be independent of machine radix, sign notation, instruction syntax, and so forth, so they may take these machine attributes as parameters.

Interpretation and representation functions.   Sometimes one thinks of a group of bits as individual bits, making up a bit vector. At other times, one thinks of the group as an encoding for some concept. This distinction, which can be left implicit in informal discourse, must be made explicit, in the formal descriptions, by interpetation and representation functions. In describing addition, for example, it is much clearer and more intuitive to use the concepts of numbers, integers, and integer addition from arithmetic, than merely to describe mechanical operations on the bits of the representations of the operands. Section 1.3 introduced the interpretation functions as they apply to the IBM 650 (1954). We restate them here for reference.

To describe an arithmetic operation in terms of numbers, one needs an interpretation function to decode the operand bit vectors as numbers, and a representation function to re-encode the numerical result as a bit vector. We encounter interpretation and representation functions for magnitudes, characters, integers, and floating-point numbers.

```
    value←magni rep                 number←magn0i rep;modulus;value
  ⍝ magnitude interpretation      ⍝ high zero magnitude interpretation
    value←radix⊥⍉rep                modulus←radix*0⌽¯1↑⍴rep
                                    value←radix⊥⍉rep
                                    number←value+modulus×value=0

    rep←size magnr value
  ⍝ magnitude representation
    rep←⍉(size⍴radix)⊤value
```

PROGRAM 9-9   Unsigned integer interpretation and representation.

Magnitudes

`magni` and `magnr` are the universal interpretation and representation functions that convert a representation vector of digits (`rep`) into an unsigned

scalar (`value`), and vice versa; they use the APL functions decode (⊥) and encode (⊤) respectively. The radix (`radix`) may have any value; usually it is binary. `magni` and `magnr` apply also to a vector of numbers; the representation of the vector is a matrix in which each row represents an element of the vector. Encode, and hence `magnr`, always yields an array of exactly the specified size; overflows are lost unless explicitly tested for; high-order zeros fill in.

Computer designers often need 1-origin indexing; for example, one may want a field of 8-bit length to represent lengths of 1 to 256, rather than 0 to 255. The commonest solution is to interpret the all-zeros representation as the representation modulus (256, in the example). `magn0i` does just that.

Instruction-field value.   `fld` gives the integer value of a field in an instruction. The desired field is specified by the integer vector `field`, which serves as a vector index to select the digits of the instruction `inst`. The function `magni` interprets the selected digits as an integer. Normally the digits are bits; in decimal machines such as the 650 they are decimal digits.

`fld0` varies from `fld` in interpreting the all-zero fields as the interpretation modulus, as explained for `magn0i`. So a 4-bit all-zeros field is interpreted as 16, rather than as zero.

```
value←fld field                  value←fld0 field
ค instruction field decoding   ค instruction field with high zero
value←magni inst[field]          value←magn0i inst[field]
```

PROGRAM 9-10   Instruction-field value.

Instruction execution.   `execute` executes the instruction represented by the bit pattern `inst`. It uses `decode` to find the mnemonic name of the operation specified by `inst` as a character vector from the matrix `oplist`. The instruction that belongs to `inst` is performed by executing (⍎) this character string as a function name.

```
execute inst
ค instruction execution
⍎oplist[decode inst;]
```

PROGRAM 9-11   Instruction execution.

Exception reporting.   Computers typically note exceptional conditions by setting a bit in an indicator vector `ind`. The general function `report` serves this purpose. The presence or absence of the condition that must be recorded is passed by the formal parameter `condition`. The index of the bit to be set is given by the integer scalar `which`. The recording is cumulative, using a logical OR; when `condition` is a vector, the OR encompasses all vector elements. So the indicator `which` will be 1 when one or more exception conditions occur, or when it was 1 prior to the operation.

```
which report condition
ค set identified indicator if any condition true
ind[which]←∨/ind[which],condition
```

PROGRAM 9-12   Indicator setting.

Invalid operation.   Program 9-13 shows the use of `report` in the function that signals an invalid operation code. In a machine that has this kind of policing, such as the 650, the function `i` is placed in each unused row of `oplist`. When an invalid operation code is specified in an instruction, the function `i` is selected and executed. Its action consists in making the invalid-operation indicator (`Invop`) 1.

```
            i
          ⍝ invalid operation
            Invop report 1
```

PROGRAM 9-13   Invalid-operation reporting.

Width adjustment.   `wide` shapes an array `in` into a matrix `out`, with row dimension specified by `size`. When the input and output are incommensurate, high-order zeros are used as fill elements. If a 32-bit operand is to be placed in an 8-bit–wide memory, 8 `wide` gives the operand the shape of four 8-bit words.

```
          out←size wide in;dimension
        ⍝ width adjustment
          dimension←(⌈(ρ,in)÷size),size
        ⍝ extend with zero as needed
          out←dimensionρ(-×/dimension)↑,in
```

PROGRAM 9-14   Width adjustment.

Characters

Character strings are a common machine datatype. In APL, we treat them as character vectors. The representation of a character vector, `rep`, has a bit or digit vector for each character, so it is a matrix.

The general interpretation and representation functions for characters convert between the representation matrix and the character-string vector, using a character-code table vector, `charcode`, in which each character of the character set is placed at the location whose index matches the character's binary code.

```
  string←alphai rep                 rep←size alphar string
⍝ character string interpretation  ⍝ character string representation
  string←charcode[magni rep]         rep←size magnr charcodeιstring
```

PROGRAM 9-15   Character-string interpretation and representation.

Integers

The functions that are commonly used to interpret digit vectors and signs as signed fixed-point integers, and the function inverses, are shown in Program 9-16. They apply to scalar numbers and to vectors of numbers with corresponding matrix representations. In each case the radix (`radix`) is kept general. The representation functions set the global variables `xmax` and `xmin` when the numbers are too large or too small to be fully represented in the specified size. These variables are often used in setting overflow and underflow indications.

```
number←signmagni rep;modulus;value
A signed-magnitude interpretation
modulus←radix*(0⊥¯1↑ρrep)-1
value←radix⊥⌽rep
number← 1 ¯1[((⌊value÷modulus)∈minus]×modulus|value


rep←size signmagnr number;modulus;sign
A signed-magnitude representation
modulus←radix*size-1
sign←((1↑plus),minus)[number<0]
rep←sign,⌽((size-1)ρradix)⊤|number
A domain signals
xmax←number≥modulus
xmin←number≤-modulus


number←radixcompi rep;modulus;value
A radix-complement interpretation
modulus←radix*0⊥¯1↑ρrep
value←radix⊥⌽rep
number←value-(value≥modulus÷2)×modulus


rep←size radixcompr number;modulus
A radix-complement representation
modulus←radix*size
rep←⌽(sizeρradix)⊤number
A domain signals
xmax←number≥modulus÷2
xmin←number<-modulus÷2


number←digitcompi rep;modulus;value
A digit-complement interpretation
modulus←(radix*0⊥¯1↑ρrep)-1
value←radix⊥⌽rep
number←value-(value≥modulus÷2)×modulus


rep←size digitcompr number;modulus
A digit-complement representation
modulus←(radix*size)-1
rep←⌽(sizeρradix)⊤modulus|number
A domain signals
xmax←number≥modulus÷2
xmin←number<-modulus÷2
```

PROGRAM 9-16   Signed-integer interpretation and representation functions.

Carry.   Several machines make arithmetic carry visible in the architecture.
Since we usually describe an arithmetic operation in terms of the represented
values, the carry, which is representation-dependent, has to be specifically
identified in our descriptions. For radix complement, the function `carryfrom`
gives the carries that result from the addition of several operands. The digit
positions at which the carry is obtained are identified by a vector of exponents
of the moduli. For example, the carry out of the eighth and the fourth digit
positions (counted from the right), when adding 6 and 13 in 2's complement,
is given by `8 4 carryfrom 6 13` and results in `0 1`.


```
carry←expmod carryfrom operands
A carry in addition
carry←(radix*expmod)≤+/(radix*expmod)∘.|operands
```

PROGRAM 9-17   Carry from bit positions.

Floating-Point Numbers

Bias notation.   The bias notation (Program 9-18 and Section 4.3) is widely used for floating-point exponents. Bias notation is a variant of radix-complement notation: When the sign bit of a radix-complement representation is inverted, a bias notation is obtained.

```
  number←biasi rep;bias;value    rep←size biasr number;bias
A bias interpretation           A bias representation
  bias←⌊0.5×radix*0⌈¯1↑⍴rep        bias←⌊0.5×radix*size
  value←radix⊥⍉rep                 rep←⍉(size⍴radix)⊤number+bias
  number←value-bias               A domain signal
                                  xmax←number≥bias
                                  xmin←number<-bias
```

PROGRAM 9-18   Bias interpretation and representation.

Sign inversion and negative zero in digit complement.   Since `signinv` inverts the sign bit of a representation, `signinv size radixcompr number` is equivalent to `size biasr number`. Applying `signinv` to a digit-complement representation, however, does not yield the same result as `size biasr number`.

`zerocompr` gives a negative zero result as required by one-complement addition that is implemented with a subtractor (Section 14.1.5).

```
  rl←signinv od        rep←size zerocompr number
A sign inversion     A negative zero complement representation
  rl←((⍴od)↑1)≠od      rep←size magnr number+number≥(radix*size)-1
```

PROGRAM 9-19   Sign inversion.

Hidden bit.   For the hidden bit floating-point notation, as in the Zuse Z4 (1945) or the DEC PDP11 (1970), the number of coefficient bits is one larger than the number of bits actually recorded. To manage this difference, the index of the hidden bit in the representation index of the coefficient, `Coef`, is made the same as the index for the sign bit. `insertbit` sets the hidden bit to 1. `hidebit` makes it equal to the sign and thus "hides" it effectively.

```
      rep←hidebit rep      rep←insertbit rep
    A hide hidden bit    A expose hidden bit
      rep[1]←rep[0]         rep[1]←1
```

PROGRAM 9-20   Hidden bit.

Rounding and truncation.   Program 9-21 gives the three most frequently used means of representing an unrepresentable fraction by a representable integer, as discussed in Section 4.4. Truncation in signed-magnitude or digit-complement notation is toward zero, conforming to normal usage. `truncate` takes the integer part of the absolute value of a number. The sign is restored by multiplying the result by the *signum* of the number; `×number` is 1 for a positive number, 0 for zero, and −1 for a negative number.

Radix-complement truncation is toward negative infinity. The APL function `⌊` describes this action.

```
      result←truncate number
    ⍝ signed-magnitude or digit-complement truncation
      result←(×number)×⌊|number
```

```
                              result←trueround number;bias
      result←round number      ⍝ unbiased algebraic round
    ⍝ algebraic round          bias←0.5≠2||number
      result←(×number)×⌊0.5+|number   result←(×number)×⌊(0.5×bias)+|number
```

PROGRAM 9-21   Various fraction-to-integer conversion options.

Normalization. `normalize` splits a number `numexp` into the exponent part (`exponent`) and the coefficient part (`coefficient`) of floating-point representation and normalizes it to the desired extent. This action is influenced by the desired exponent value for zero and for unnormalized numbers. `expzero` yields the exponent of zero. The preferred exponent of an unnormalized number is passed, together with the number, in the formal parameter `numexp`. When unnormalized operation is desired, `numexp` should be a two-element vector consisting of the number to be represented and that number's preferred exponent.

```
      expzero normalize numexp;expnorm
    ⍝ normalized or specified exponent form
      →IF 0=1↑numexp
      THEN: ⍝ exponent for zero
          exponent←expzero
          →ENDIF
      ELSE: ⍝ minimal or specified exponent
          expnorm←⌊(1+base⍟|1↑numexp)+point-(⍴1↓Coef)×base⍟radix
          exponent←⌈/expnorm,1↓numexp
      ENDIF:coefficient←0⊥(1↑numexp)÷base*exponent-point
```

PROGRAM 9-22   General normalization.

When normalized operation is desired, `numexp` should be a scalar or one-element vector that contains only the number to be represented. The exponent that is specified for unnormalized operation is used only when the high-order coefficient bits can be represented. Otherwise the (larger) exponent that gives a normalized coefficient is used.

The parameter `point` gives the number of coefficient digits to the right of the radix point. For an integer coefficient, as in the CDC 6600 (1964), `point` is zero; for a pure fraction, as in the 704, `point` is equal to the coefficient length minus 1 (for the sign bit).

Biased-signed-magnitude representation.   Program 9-23 gives a floating-point interpretation and representation used in several machines; it does not apply to all machines, and it is not necessarily preferred (Section 4.4). The general functions `flbsi` and `flbsr` show that, in this representation, the exponent is an integer, represented with biased notation; the coefficient is represented with signed-magnitude notation; truncation is used for precision treatment; the exponent of zero has the minimal representable value `-extexp`; and unnormalized representation is allowed. The general functions `flbsi` and `flbsr` are independent of the allocation of the exponent (`Exp`) and coefficient (`Coef`) digits, and of the choice of radix (`radix`), base (`base`), and radix point (`point`).

```
numexp←flbsi rep;exponent;coefficient;number
ᴀ bias signed-magnitude fractional interpretation
exponent←biasi rep[Exp]
coefficient←signmagni rep[Coef]
number←coefficient×base*exponent-point
numexp←number,exponent


rep←size flbsr numexp;exponent;coefficient
ᴀ bias signed-magnitude fractional representation
(1↑1↓numexp,-extexp) normalize numexp
rep←sizeρ0
rep[Coef]←(ρCoef) signmagnr truncate coefficient
rep[Exp]←(ρExp) biasr exponent
```

PROGRAM 9-23   Floating-point bias-signed-magnitude representation.

Conventions for Control Structures

The high level of abstraction of APL eliminates, to a large extent, the need for the classical control structures, especially iteration. Nevertheless, there are occasions, such as in `normalize` (Program 9-22), when there is a real need for such a control structure. The use of APL's GOTO-type branches at such times would be confusing. We define some control structures here and use them throughout.

The If-then-else, If-then, Repeat-until, While, Out, Error, and Where structures are implemented in normal APL with labels, such as THEN, ELSE, and ENDIF, and functions, such as IF, If, CASE, WHILE, OUT, and WHERE. The names of the labels and functions are largely self-explanatory. Multiple occurrences of control structures in a function are rare; they are handled by attaching a numeric suffix to the identifiers.

Decision.   We distinguish two If structures, for implementation convenience. The fully capitalized IF specifies an If-then-else structure; the initially capitalized If specifies an If-then structure.

```
label←IF condition              label←If condition
label←(ELSE,THEN)[condition]    label←(ENDIF,THEN)[condition]


label←CASE number
label←≛'C',⍕number
```

PROGRAM 9-24   Decision structures.

Scope.   The scope of structures is marked by prescribed labels and functions. In decision and WHILE, the functions come first, and the label ENDIF, END-WHILE is attached to the first statement after the structure. In REPEAT, the order is reversed.

Repeat.   The start of the repeat loop is the label REPEAT; the loop is closed by the function UNTIL.

```
label←UNTIL condition
label←(~condition)/REPEAT
```

PROGRAM 9-25   Repeat structure.

While.   The end of a while loop is marked by the label ENDWHILE. The loop is closed by △, a function that causes a branch to WHILE; this function just precedes ENDWHILE. All decision and iteration functions return a label. WHILE uses a stack △△ to preserve a return address in case the condition is 1. The return address is obtained from the line count □lc.

```
label←WHILE condition           label←△
label←(~condition)/ENDWHILE      label←1↑△△
△△←(condition/□lc[1]),△△         △△←1↓△△
```

PROGRAM 9-26   While structure.

Escape.   The general escape function is OUT; it terminates function execution—usually, the execution of an instruction—when its condition is satisfied. The function ERROR, also shown in Program 9-27, is functionally equivalent to OUT; the purpose of ERROR is to indicate that a condition has arisen that is recognized as erroneous, but whose precise consequences are not known or are not considered worth describing.

```
label←OUT condition    label←ERROR condition
label←condition/0      label←condition/0
```

PROGRAM 9-27   Escape functions.

Qualification.   WHERE is used as a general qualifying function (Program 9-28). The expression to the right of WHERE is executed prior to and independently of the expression to the left. We use WHERE to place a minor expression, such as a radix change, in the same line of a major expression, such as a representation action.   Although there is a direct APL equivalent to WHERE in some APL dialects, we use WHERE because of clarity.

```
out←left WHERE right
out←left
```

PROGRAM 9-28   Qualifying function.

Synchronization.   We use the generic monadic function WAIT occasionally as a synchronization primitive to indicate that execution is suspended until the operand becomes 1. WAIT assumes that a concurrent process can change the operand; the function may be implemented in various ways to allow such a change to occur.

Although the implementations of the control structures are shown here as a matter of interest, the programs in which they appear are best understood by referring to the common meaning of these structures.

Glossary

A glossary of terms used in the descriptions is given in Tables 9-29, 9-30, and 9-31. Terms, such as product or augend, that directly match the concepts to which they refer, are not placed in the glossary; they are usually scalar values. Abbreviated names, such as pd or au, refer to representations in bits

Term	Use	Type
acc	accumulator	vector
ad	representation of addend	vector
address-	specifies address components	function
Address	allocation of address field in instruction	vector
adr-	generates address	function
adrcap	address capacity	integer
adrsize	size of address in representation units	integer
alpha-*	interprets or represents character data	function
au	representation of augend	vector
B*	allocation of base field in instruction	vector
bias*	interprets or represents biased notation data	function
byte	size of a character in representation units	integer
Carry	allocation of carry indicator	integer
carryfrom	determines carry out of given bit positions	function
char	representation of character	vector
charcode	character set in code order	vector
Coef	allocation of coefficient in format	vector
cond	condition	boolean
configure-	specifies configuration	function
control-	allocates control space	function
cycle-	execution cycle	function
D*	allocation of displacement in instruction	vector
data-	codes and allocates data	function
dd	representation of dividend	vector
decimal-	codes and allocates decimal numbers	function
decimal-*	interprets or represents decimal data	function
decode	decodes opcode	function
decr-	decrements	function
dest	destination address	integer
Dest	allocation of destination field in instruction	vector
df	representation of difference	vector
digit	size of a decimal digit in bits	integer
Digits	allocation of digits in number	vector
digitcomp*	interprets or represents digit-complement data	function
digitzero	represents in digit complement with negative zero	function
double	double the number size	integer
dr	representation of divisor	vector
execute	executes instruction	function
Exp	allocation of exponent in format	vector
extexp	extreme exponent value	integer

Legend: - = machine suffix; * = postfix.

TABLE 9-29   Glossary of variables and functions: a through e.

for binary radix and in digits for decimal radix. An initial capital signifies an allocation index. Names with a machine-identifier suffix (-) apply to machine-specific functions. Names without a suffix are constants or variables. Postfixes distinguish multiple occurrences of allocation vectors, or variables such as od1 and od2. The interpretation functions have the postfix i, whereas the representation functions have the postfix r.

Term	Use	Type
fl-	codes and allocates floating-point number	function
fl-*	interpretes or represents floating-point data	function
fld*	evaluates an instruction field	function
format-	specifies radix and units	function
half	half the word size	integer
iadr	address of next instruction	scalar
ifetch	reads instruction from memory	function
ilength	evaluates instruction length	function
incr-	increments	function
ind	indicators	vector
indicator-	allocates indicator	function
initiate-	initiates spaces and values	function
inst	instruction	vector
instruction-	allocates instruction fields	function
interrupt-	interrupts instruction stream	function
ix	representation of index	vector
L*	allocation of length field in instruction	vector
length	operand size in bytes	integer
long	multiple of the word size	integer
Lower	allocation of low-order part of a space	vector
M*	allocation of address mode field in instruction	vector
magn*	interprets or represents magnitude	function
md	representation of multiplicand	vector
memadr	address applies to memory	integer
memcap	memory capacity in words	integer
memory	main memory	matrix
minus	code for minus sign	integer
mn	representation of minuend	vector
mq	multiplier-quotient register	vector
mr	representation of multiplier	vector
name-	specifies names in spaces	function
Neg	allocation of negative indicator	integer
Num	allocation of numeric part of a character	vector
od*	representation of operand	vector
Oflo	allocation of overflow indicator	integer
Op*	allocation of operation code in instruction	vector
oplist	mnemonic operation codes	matrix
pd	representation of product	vector
plus	code for plus sign	integer
point	radix point of coefficient	integer
pop-	reads from stack	function
Pos	allocation of positive indicator	integer
push-	writes onto stack	function

Legend: - = machine suffix; * = postfix.

TABLE 9-30   Glossary of variables and functions: f through p.

Term	Use	Type
qt	representation of quotient	vector
quad	four times the word size	integer
R*	allocation of register field in instruction	vector
radix	principal radix	integer
radixcomp*	interprets or represents radix-complement data	function
read-	reads from memory	function
reg	working store	matrix
regadr	address applies to register	integer
report	sets indicator bit on condition	function
rl	representation of result	vector
rm	representation of remainder	vector
sb	representation of subtrahend	vector
Sign	allocation of sign in number	integer
signal-*	sets result indicators	function
signmagn*	interprets or represents sign-magnitude data	function
size	operand size in representation units	integer
Size	allocation of operand size in compound address	integer
size-	determines data size	function
sm	representation of sum	vector
Source	allocation of source operand field in instruction	vector
Space	allocation of space identifier in compound address	integer
space-	specifies spaces	function
status	status bits	vector
status-	allocates status bits	function
stop	stop condition	boolean
stop-	tests conditions to control stopping	function
suppress-	tests conditions to suppress further execution	function
Upper	allocation of high-order part of a space	vector
Value	allocation of address value in compound address	integer
wide	shapes to satisfy the given width	function
word	size of a number in bits	integer
write-	writes into memory	function
X*	allocation of index field in instruction	vector
xmax	value too large for representation	boolean
xmin	value too small for representation	boolean
Zero	allocation of zero indicator	integer
zerocompr	represents in digit-complement with negative zero	function
Zone	allocation of the zone part of a character	vector

Legend: - = machine suffix; * = postfix.

TABLE 9-31   Glossary of variables and functions: q through z.

9.4

General Exercises

The following exercises are usable with almost every machine. They probe addressing, indexing, arithmetic, character handling, and sequencing. We have found that working the same exercise for several machines is helpful in understanding differences.

9-1 Matrices A and B have dimensions 1 5 and 5 3 respectively.
Write a program to calculate C = A +.× B (matrix inner product). Assume all matrices are stored in row order and that all intermediate quantities stay nicely bounded, so that no scaling need be done. When convenient, calculate the vector inner products in double or mixed precision.

9-2 In a stream of 1000 characters of running text, characters are to be replaced according to the following table:

.	'
3	9
A	Z
J	6
any invalid character	blank

All other valid characters are to remain unaltered. There are 48 characters in the set. Assume any 48-character set appropriate for the machine in question, or use that of Table 4-13.

Write a program, assuming that input and output are in memory.

9-3 Design, for the given machine, the architecture for the following additional instructions:
a. Square Root
b. Sine
c. Left Zero Count

Work within the applicable design decisions of the given machine. Select or design an appropriate instruction format, and use an available operation code. Pay attention to representation range, condition setting, and exception indication. Briefly state the design alternatives you considered, and argue for your choice. Do not give implementation algorithms.

9-4 Design, for the given machine, a suitable set of subroutines to provide the following additional instructions:
a. Square Root
b. Sine
c. Left Zero Count

Devise for each instruction an appropriate instruction format and a unique invalid operation code. Your subroutines are called by the interrupt handler, and the entire instruction is passed to each of them. Work within the applicable design decisions of the given machine.

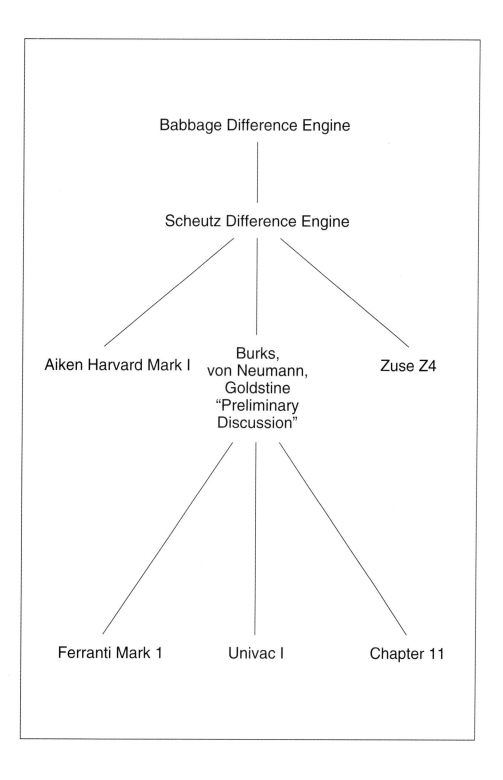

Pioneer House

The Classical Computer

As computer designs move from one generation to the next, the architecture of these generations evolves cumulatively; the advances of previous generations are retained, and new concepts are added. Indeed, the first-generation architecture is quite complete; it reappears in the mini era, and again in the micro era. We call it the *classical* computer architecture. Table 10-1 shows its emergence in the first generation and the contributions of that generation's pioneers; it is the subject of this chapter and the next.

Costliness. In his thorough study of Babbage's Analytical Engine, Bromley remarks that "this computer is *too much* like a modern computer" (his italics, [Bromley, 1982]). This observation is true of most pioneering computer designs. Indeed, it is remarkable how quickly the Difference Engine (1859), Aiken's Mark I (1944), Zuse's Z4 (1945), Kilburn's Mark 1 (1951), and Eckert and Mauchly's Univac I (1951) converge toward the classical computer, which is epitomized by the machines of the next chapter.

Why did the classical computer emerge so rapidly and persist so tenaciously? We believe the answer is found in the costliness constraint illustrated throughout Part I. Costliness and its various ramifications explain why the classical direct addressing was not abandoned for associative addressing, and

Concept	Innovator	Date
Arithmetic	Schickard	1624
Sequence control	Jacquard et al.	1804
Decision	Babbage	1867
Binary radix	Atanasoff et al.	1940
Floating point	Zuse	1941
Working store	Zuse	1941
Stored program	Eckert, Mauchly	1944
Multiple processors	Aiken	1947
Logic	Kilburn	1949
Indexing	Kilburn	1949
Byte addressing	Buchholz	1954
Directly-addressed registers	Buchholz	1956

TABLE 10-1   Classical computer architecture.

why the classical machine-language level was not abandoned by bridging the semantic gap either upward toward a high-level language or downward by adopting microcoding as the machine language. It also explains why elaborate and unbalanced instruction sets quickly converge to the almost standard instruction set of the classical computer.

Bibliography

Bromley [1982], R.E. Smith [1989].

10.1

Difference Engines of Babbage and Scheutz

10.1.1

Highlights

History

The Difference Engine is a nineteenth-century precursor of the computer. It differs from the earlier hand calculators in performing a sequence of operations. It is not yet a computer, since it has no decision power.

Architects. Charles Babbage was the main architect of the Difference Engine; the idea of a difference machine was presented earlier by Johann H. Müller.

Dates. Müller's idea for a machine that could calculate and print numerical tables dates back to 1784 through 1786. Charles Babbage designed such a machine in the years 1821 to 1833. Babbage completed only a model of the calculating part of the machine. In 1843 the father and son Georg and Edvard Scheutz completed their first Difference Engine in Stockholm, Sweden. The architecture of the machine was based upon Babbage's ideas. The implementation was their own; the machine was built by Edvard Scheutz at his home from 1837 to 1843 [Lindgren, 1987].

Family tree. Johan W. Bergström in Stockholm manufactured a copy of the Scheutz machine and completed it in 1852; Bryan Donkin & Co. in London manufactured a third machine and completed it in 1859. We describe the third machine.

Noteworthy

The Difference Engine is a special purpose calculator with just one operation. The original contents of the n registers are set by hand. Then, the repetition of this single operation tabulates any $(n - 1)$-degree polynomial. Since polynomials can approximate many functions successfully, the Difference Engine's range of application is surprisingly wide.

Fixed subroutine. The single operation of the Difference Engine consists of a sequence of additions, an incrementation, an edit, and an output operation. Therefore, the machine can be viewed as a calculator with a permanently fixed subroutine of classical operations.

Vector addition. During the basic cycle all the differences of each order are added to the corresponding differences of the next-lower order, with the first difference being added to the function value. This operation is equivalent to a vector addition. Babbage and Scheutz departed from the ideal, however, by adding the even-order differences to the odd-order differences in one parallel action and the odd to the even in a subsequent parallel action. This departure

from the ideal is visible in the architecture; it requires a different setting for the starting values.

Typesetting output.   From Müller on, a major objective of the Difference Engine was the elimination of the manual typesetting of tables. Babbage did not succeed in building an output unit, but the Scheutzes, who had experience with printing equipment, built a typesetting output. The machine directly produced the matrices used for casting lead type.

Print edit.   The Scheutz prototype impressed leading zeros into the output matrix. The user subsequently removed these zeros by hand to achieve the conventional presentation format. In the second and third machine, leading zeros were automatically replaced by blanks.

Peculiarities

Positive integers.   Babbage used one decimal-digit position for the sign: An even digit represented plus; an odd digit, minus. The Scheutz Engine had only positive numbers. The user could obtain a sequence of negative function values by re-entering the complement of the difference values as the function value went through zero.

Ascending edit.   The print-edit mechanism of the second Scheutz Engine assumed ascending function values. When the number of zeros to be suppressed increased, the zeros were not properly suppressed. This shortcoming was remedied in the third engine.

10.1.2
Machine Language

Language Level

The language is entirely at the hardware level.

Design philosophy.   The engine has no decision power and no status, no instructions; hence, no language as such.

```
initiateΔD
ᴀ initiation of the Difference Engine
formatΔD
spaceΔD
nameΔD
```

PROGRAM 10-2   Initiation of the Difference Engine.

Unit System

Scheutz's Difference Engine has a precision of 15 decimal digits, of which the high-order eight are printed. The argument has five digits.

```
formatΔD
ᴀ Difference Engine information units
ᴀ representation radix
  radix←10
ᴀ information units
  word←15
  argsize←5
  printsize←8
ᴀ register capacity
  regcap←5
```

PROGRAM 10-3   Basic parameters of the Difference Engine.

Spaces

The only spaces are the difference and function registers and the argument counter. The highest difference is not changed during operation; a constant fourth difference means any quartic function can be generated. All registers can be set manually.

Configuration.   The Scheutz Engine has four differences and one function value. Babbage admired the Scheutz machine and helped to make it known. He pointed out that tables requiring five to eight differences can be made in two passes. In the first pass the fourth difference is tabulated; in the second pass this difference is entered by hand on each cycle.

Babbage's original plans called for six differences of 18 digits; his incomplete model has three differences of five digits.

```
spaceΔD                        nameΔD
ᴀ Difference Engine spaces     ᴀ Difference Engine space names
ᴀ registers                    ᴀ function value
  reg←?(regcap,word)ρradix       Fn←0
  arg←?argsizeρradix           ᴀ differences in registers
                                 Δ1←1
                                 Δ2←2
                                 Δ3←3
                                 Δ4←4
```

PROGRAM 10-4   Spaces of the Difference Engine.

Programming model.   The odd-numbered registers are updated in the first half of a cycle; the even-numbered registers and the function value are updated in the second half of a cycle.

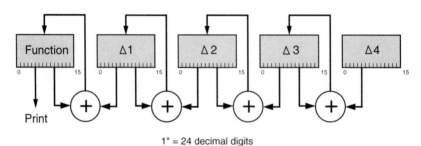

1" = 24 decimal digits

FIGURE 10-5   Programming model for Babbage's Difference Engine.

10.1.3

Data

Fixed-Point Numbers

Notation.   Signed-magnitude notation is used.

FIGURE 10-6   Fixed-point numbers in the Difference Engine.

Radix choice.   Decimal is natural for the user. Digits are directly implemented by the gears of the registers.

10.1.4

Operations

Add.   Two vector additions, each applying to vectors of two numbers, are performed. If the number of differences had been larger, the vectors would have increased in size accordingly, without loss of time.

```
OP;addend;augend;sum;char              char←editΔD rep;l
 ⍝ Difference Engine Operation          ⍝ Difference Engine Edit for Print
 ⍝ add even to odd differences          l←(rep≠0)⍳1
 addend←magni reg[Δ4,Δ2;]               char←(1↑' ').'0123456789'[1↓rep]
 augend←magni reg[Δ3,Δ1;]
 sum←augend+addend
 reg[Δ3,Δ1;]←word magnr sum
 ⍝ add odd to even differences
 addend←magni reg[Δ3,Δ1;]
 augend←magni reg[Δ2,Fn;]
 sum←augend+addend
 reg[Δ2,Fn;]←word magnr sum
 ⍝ increment argument
 arg←argsize magnr l+magni arg
 ⍝ edit for print
 char←(editΔD arg).editΔD reg[Fn;⍳printsize]
 ⍝ impress argument and function
 impress char
```

PROGRAM 10-7   Operation of the Difference Engine.

Increment.   A fixed value of 1 increments the argument. This operation was known from serial-numbering devices for bank notes.

Print edit.   Experience proved the need for deleting leading zeros. We show the architecture of this mechanism in its form for the third engine; it is applied twice: once for the function value and once for the argument.

10.1.5

Instruction Sequencing

The user operates the machine by turning the crank manually. Each operation requires 38 revolutions. At the completion of one operation, the next starts automatically, as the user keeps turning.

The same fixed sequence is iterated; there are no conditional operations.

10.1.6

Input/Output

Devices

Typesetting.   One output line is impressed upon the lead-casting print-matrix for each operation. Then, the matrix advances to allow impressing the next line.

Bell.   Babbage's model included a bell that sounded as the sign changed. This idea was probably borrowed from Müller's design; the Scheutz machine does not use a bell.

10.1.7

Implementation Notes

Engineering level.   What Babbage, with a grant of £17,000, and aided by the eminent mechanic Joseph Clement, could not do in 12 years, Edvard Scheutz accomplished alone at home, while a student at a technical institute, in 6 years at his father's expense. Perhaps the best explanation of this paradox is that Babbage's machine was heavily overdesigned, whereas Scheutz's machine was underengineered.

The Scheutz Engine was a table model weighing 400 kilograms and operated by hand. Babbage's design was on a larger physical scale and would have filled a room; it would have weighed more than 2000 kilograms and might have required a steam engine to run.

Reliability.   The Babbage design included several features intended for reliable operation. The first Scheutz machine was basically a feasibility model and was not very reliable. The second and third machines, however, were built by professionals following the original plan and were used as production machines. Although much more reliable than the prototype, they still did not have the robustness that continued use would require.

Speed.   Lindgren, to whom we owe most of the material presented in this section, estimates that the Scheutz machine could give about 63 lines of results in 1 hour.

In the Scheutz machine, one-half of the operation time is used for carry propagation. Babbage recognized that carry propagation time was critical, and incorporated a parallel method.

10.1.8
Bibliography

Lindgren, M., 1987: *Glory and Failure: The Difference Engines of Johann Müller, Charles Babbage and Georg and Edvard Scheutz*. Linköping, Sweden: Linköping Studies in Arts and Science. Also Cambridge, MA: MIT Press, 1990 (our defining reference).

C. Babbage [1837], G.H.P. Babbage [1910], Bromley [1982].

10.1.9
Exercises

10-1 Give the formal description of the Difference Engine planned by Babbage.

10.2
Harvard Mark I

10.2.1
Highlights

History

Architects.   Howard H. Aiken was the initiator and main architect of the Harvard Mark I. Clair D. Lake was the chief designer of the IBM implementation team, which also included Benjamin G.M. Durfee and Francis E. Hamilton. The Mark I was realized in standard IBM electromechanical rotating-counter technology.

Dates.   Aiken [1937] proposed to build the Sequence Controlled Automatic Calculator, later called the Mark I. The machine was put into operation in May 1944; it was dedicated on August 7, 1944.

Noteworthy

Rich operation repertoire.   The Mark I has Logarithm, Exponential, Sine, and Interpolation operations. Sign control allows combinations of negation and absolute value. Provisions are made for extended precision, rounding, zero suppression, shifting, and copying of a sign. Input is from a card reader and three paper tapes, and output is to a card punch and two printers.

Table-oriented.   Whereas the Difference Engine was designed as a special purpose machine for making tables, the Mark I is a general purpose computer. Nevertheless, the Mark I was used extensively in making tables. The architecture reflects this table orientation in the Interpolate operation. Such a function is no longer important in computers—their ubiquity has drastically reduced the need for tables and their interpolation.

Non-dense memory name-space.   There are 72 general memory locations and several special locations whose numeric addresses are spread throughout address space.

Minimal decision.   The original Mark I had minimal decision ability, but in 1946 conditional subroutines were installed [R.N. Bloch, 1947].

Concurrency.   The Mark I instruction has three fields, each of which can specify an action that may or may not relate to the actions specified in the other fields. Moreover, single-instruction overlap is used for operations with a long execution time. Finally, dyadic operations, such as Multiply, are broken down in parts, such as Load Multiplicand, Load Multiplier, and Store Product, which are specified in different instructions. The other fields of these instructions may specify unrelated actions, such as Reset Register, Read Tape, or Print.

One- and two-address instructions. Even though the unit of specification of the Mark I deals with only one operand or result, many instructions show the classical one-address and two-address patterns. We describe the instruction syntax from that point of view.

Scaling via plugboard.   Tabulating machines used plugboards extensively to define datapaths and to specify sequence. The Mark I deviated from standard practice in not using plugging for sequence control and instruction specification. This major advance toward the classical computer made the Mark I much easier to program than the ENIAC, which followed standard plugboard programming.

The Mark I maintained tabulating practice in using plugging to control number alignment. Since plugging is laborious and error-prone, the exigencies of regular operation of the Mark I more or less forced the use of a standard plugging convention (with 16 digits to the right of the decimal point).

Peculiarities

High precision.   The 23 digits and sign of the Mark I are equivalent to 77 binary digits. This high precision eased the scaling problem in the Mark I; it also slowed down complex machine operations such as Sine so much that programmed lower-precision calculation was often faster. The more complex functions were little used, so later they were removed.

Demanding synchronization.   When concurrent operations need operands, or deliver results, these operations must be immediately attended to in the Mark I; otherwise, an error results. Since many operations vary in length, the programmer must provide for the worst case. The multiplier must be presented at the third cycle following the multiplicand; the product then becomes available from 3 to 15 cycles later. Unless the programmer knows the nature of the multiplier, he must begin to wait for the product at cycle 3, thus losing potential performance.

No Load.   The elementary transfer of information is the Add. A Load is decomposed into two actions: a Clear followed by an Add. Since many special locations have individual Clears, there are many operations.

Memory-mapped function.   Most memory locations of the Mark I are implemented as adders. This mapping of the Add function upon memory would not show in the architecture if all memory locations had the same function.   Aiken took the functional mapping one step further, however, by associating some functions—such as extended precision, rounding, zero suppression, and various (plugged) shifts—with selected memory locations. This kind of memory-mapped function is readily apparent in the architecture.

Implementation detail. Throughout the architecture, little details reflect the implementation. Each of the two types of input switches, for example, has its own negation modifier. For interpolation, a sequence relay must be picked up and an intermediate result register cleared, neither of which actions has much meaning to the programmer.

Descendants

After completing the Mark I (1944), Aiken completed the relay Mark II (1947), the vacuum tube Mark III (1950), and the vacuum tube and diode Mark IV (1952). This impressive record of constructing four machines, each with a different technology, in a short time period was the result of a deliberate design philosophy: use of a proven technology with liberal tolerances, and careful attention to maintainability through use of replaceable components, permanent oscilloscopes, and permanently mounted neon indicator lights.

None of the Mark I through IV machines had stored programs; their architectures differed noticeably. They do not constitute a computer family.

10.2.2

Machine Language

Language Level

The language level is low. The Mark I is essentially a horizontally microprogrammed machine whose individual bus transfers and function-unit timings are the concern of the programmer. As is usual with such a low-level language, concurrent operations can be programmed whenever instruction fields are free and no bus conflicts will occur.

On the other hand, the language has some high-level primitives— interpolation and transcendental functions can each be invoked with one action. Once started, some functional units—such as multiply—operate independently for many machine cycles, yielding their results at specified later times.

Design philosophy.   The Mark I makes the transition from tabulator to computer. This transition was accomplished through sequence control, as reflected in the original name, "Automatic Sequence-Controlled Calculator."

```
      initiateΔMKI
  ℝ initiation of the Harvard Mark I
      formatΔMKI
      configureΔMKI
      spaceΔMKI
      nameΔMKI
      instructionΔMKI
```

PROGRAM 10-8   Initiation of the Harvard Mark I.

Unit System

The size of the binary instruction word is equal to the number of decimals in the data word, so the same type of tape reader can read instructions and data. One row of bits contains an instruction; a decimal value takes four rows.

Configuration.   The address capacity is 256 words. The actual memory is 72 words, 56 of which are used only as general locations, 8 only as special purpose locations, and 8 as both. The instruction tape can have any capacity; we set it arbitrarily at 100 to make our description executable.

```
formatΔMKI                        configureΔMKI
ᴀ Harvard Mark I information units ᴀ configuration for the Harvard Mark I
ᴀ representation radix            ᴀ memory capacity
radix←2                           memcap←72
ᴀ information units               tapecap←100
half←12
word←24
adrsize←8
ᴀ address capacity
adrcap←2*adrsize
```

PROGRAM 10-9   Basic parameters of the Harvard Mark I.

Spaces

Memory name-space.   The 256 addressable locations in the name-space are only sparsely implemented; the space is dense for locations 1 through 72.

```
spaceΔMKI
ᴀ Harvard Mark I spaces           ᴀ control store
ᴀ memory                          ᴀ - instruction address
 memory←?(adrcap,word)ρ10          iadr←?tapecap
ᴀ instruction store              ᴀ - function switches
 tape←?(tapecap,word)ρradix        fnsw←?6ρradix
ᴀ working store                  ᴀ - stopped state
ᴀ - carry bits                     stop←?radix
 carry←?3ρradix                   ᴀ - latent action list
                                   latentlist← 0 4 ρ' '
```

PROGRAM 10-10   Spaces of the Harvard Mark I.

Working store.   The carry-out from locations 64, 68, and 72 is stored for extended precision and testing.

Control store.   The instruction store is a 24-hole paper tape. The manual function switches control major functions, such as sine or logarithm.

Embedding.   Sixty manually set 24-digit registers are embedded in the name-space. These switches are intended for constants. Another switch is

```
nameΔMKI
ᴀ Harvard Mark I space names
ᴀ memory embedding
ᴀ general locations              ᴀ sine
 Loc←1+ιmemcap                    Sine1s←200
ᴀ switches                       Sine2s←136
 Sw←73+ι60                       Sine3s←201
ᴀ independent variable switch    ᴀ normalize
 Ivs←141                          Norm←135
ᴀ low-order product or quotient  ᴀ printer
 Lpqs←160                         Print1s←162
ᴀ tolerance                      Print2s←163
 Tols←72                         ᴀ punch
ᴀ logarithm                       Punchs←164
 Logs←133
 Logd←123

ᴀ source and destination addresses
 Adrsource←Loc,Sw,Ivs,Lpqs,Tols,Logs,Sine1s,Sine2s,Sine3s,Norm
 Adrsource←Adrsource,Print1s,Print2s,Punchs
 Adrdest←Loc,Logd,Norm
```

PROGRAM 10-11   Embedding in the Harvard Mark I.

intended for independent variables. The scattered allocation of the addresses of the special locations seems designed to minimize the number of instruction bits that are 1.

Functions often have multiple inputs or outputs, which have different plugging (radix point). Sine has one direct output and two plugged outputs.

Operand Specification

Number of addresses. A two-address format specifies addition and subtraction; many other operations use a one-address format.

Operation Specification

Mnemonics. The mnemonics shown (Table 10-14 and Program 10-12) are our own; Aiken used numeric codes.

```
a→ADD                                                            DP3
b→AC1   c→TLD   c→DR    c→      d→RD1   e→EXS           f→        DP4
  AC2     EXD     MD              RD2     f→PN                   g→CIR
                  LOG             RD3     PNC           RTS      g→CEX
                  EXP                                   INS      g→CSN
  AC3             INT    LWD    LWS
  AC4             SIN    UPD    UPS       ST1           CLG
        P1D                               ST2
        P2D                               ST3           RC1
    c→      c→IN1   d→      d→                           RC2
  SI2       IN2     INH    T2N    RS1     TLC
        PR1         IN3     CP1    T1N    RS2    PIT
        PR2                 CP2           RS3
        PNS         RP1     CPN
                    RP2            T2F                   DP1
                                   T1F                   DP2
```

PROGRAM 10-12   Operation-code list of the Harvard Mark I.

Instruction Structure

Machine-language syntax. The first syntactic pattern a is a two-address format; the patterns marked b, c, and d are one-address; the patterns marked e and f are for operations without address in the Source field; and the three patterns g are for operations specified in the Mod field.

```
  syntaxΔMKI
a Source.Dest.Seq.Mod
b Source.  1 1 0 0  .Opcode.Seq.Mod    f Source.Dest.Seq.  0 1  .Opm
c Source.  0 1 0 0 1  .Opa.Seq.Mod     f Source.Dest.Seq.  1 0  .Opm
c Source.  0 1 0 1 0  .Opa.Seq.Mod     g Source.Dest.Seq.  0 0 0 1 0 0
c Source.  0 1 1 0 0  .Opa.Seq.Mod     g Source.Dest.Seq.  0 0 0 1 0 1
c Source.  0 1 1 1 1  .Opa.Seq.Mod     g Source.Dest.Seq.  0 0 0 1 1 1
c Source.  1 0 0 1 0  .Opa.Seq.Mod
d 1 0 0 0 1  .Ops.Dest.Seq.Mod
d 1 0 0 1 0  .Ops.Dest.Seq.Mod
d 1 1 0 0 0  .Ops.Dest.Seq.Mod
e 1 0 0 0 0 1 1 0  .Dest.Seq.Mod
```

PROGRAM 10-13   Instruction syntax of the Harvard Mark I.

⍝ *fixed-point arithmetic*
```
d UPS Read Upper 71
d LWS Read Lower 71
a ADD Add Or Clear
c UPD Add Or Clear Upper 71
c LWD Add Or Clear Lower 71
b AC1 Add 64 W Carry To 65
b AC2 Add 65 W Carry From 64
b AC3 Add 68 W Carry To 69
b AC4 Add 69 W Carry From 68
c TLD Add Or Clear Tolerance
c MD  Multiplicand
c DR  Divisor
f DP1 Divide Precision 1
f DP2 Divide Precision 2
f DP3 Divide Precision 3
f DP4 Divide Precision 4
c LOG Logarithm
f CLG Clear Logarithm Argument
c EXP Exponential
e EXS Exponent
c EXD Add To Exponent
g CEX Clear Exponent
c SIN Sine Argument
b SI2 Plugged Sine Argument
g CSN Clear Sine Argument
c INT Interpolate
d INH Interpolation Interval
f INS Interpolate Sequence
g CIR Clear Intermediate Register
```
⍝ *sequencing*
```
f TLC Tolerance Stop
```

⍝ *input/output*
```
f RC1 Read Card Feed 1
f RC2 Read Card Feed 2
d RD1 Read Tape 1
d RD2 Read Tape 2
d RD3 Read Tape 3
f ST1 Step Tape 1
f ST2 Step Tape 2
f ST3 Step Tape 3
f RS1 Step Tape 1 Backwards
f RS2 Step Tape 2 Backwards
f RS3 Step Tape 3 Backwards
c IN1 Select Tape 1
c IN2 Select Tape 2
c IN3 Select Tape 3
f PIT Position Tape
f RTS Reset Tape Selection
c PNS Punch Value Or Stop
f PN  Punch
f PNC Punch And Complete
d CPN Clear Punch
c PR1 Print On Printer 1
c PR2 Print On Printer 2
c P1D Add To Printer 1
c P2D Add To Printer 2
c RP1 Round Printer 1
c RP2 Round Printer 2
d CP1 Clear Printer 1
d CP2 Clear Printer 2
d T1N Printer 1 On
d T2N Printer 2 On
d T1F Printer 1 Off
d T2F Printer 2 Off
```

Legend: W = With.

TABLE 10-14   Instruction list of the Harvard Mark I.

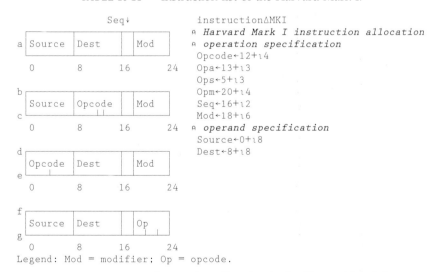

PROGRAM 10-15   Instruction allocation in the Harvard Mark I.

10.2.3

Addressing

Direct addressing.   A valid address causes the corresponding memory content to be placed on the bus; otherwise, nothing is placed on the bus. If two words appear on the bus at the same cycle, they are ORed together. The result is usually erroneous.

```
sourceΔMKI;source              od←signΔMKI od;neg
ᴀ Harvard Mark I data source   ᴀ Harvard Mark I negation
source←fld Source              →CASE 1 2 3 6 14 ιfld Mod
clear←source=fld Dest          C0:neg←minus≠od[Sign]
→CASE(clear,source∈Adrsource)ιl     →ENDCASE
C0: ᴀ clear memory location    C1:neg←minus=od[Sign]
    bus←wordρ0                      →ENDCASE
    →ENDCASE                   C2:neg←(fld Source)∈Ivs,Sw
C1: ᴀ memory data on bus            →ENDCASE
    bus←signΔMKI memory[source;]  C3:neg←(fld Source)∈Loc,Sw
    →ENDCASE                        →ENDCASE
C2: ᴀ control action           C4:neg←minus=memory[70;Sign]
    bus←wordρ0                      →ENDCASE
    execute word↑inst[Source]  C5:neg←0
ENDCASE:                       ENDCASE:→If neg
                               THEN: ᴀ complement operand
                                   od←9-od
                               ENDIF:
```

PROGRAM 10-16   Memory read in the Harvard Mark I.

Sign control.   Reading may be combined with negation and absolute value, as specified by the modifier field. The sign control is complicated because memory and the Ivs switch require different timing, specified by different modifiers. Modifier code 14 gives conditional negation of the number on the bus, depending upon the sign of the number in location 70.

```
destΔMKI;dest
ᴀ Harvard Mark I destination action   C1: ᴀ augment memory location
dest←fld Dest                             augmentΔMKI dest
→CASE(clear,dest∈Adrdest)ιl               →ENDCASE
C0: ᴀ clear memory location           C2: ᴀ control action
    memory[dest;]←0                        execute word↑(8ρ0),inst[Dest]
    →ENDCASE                          ENDCASE:
```

PROGRAM 10-17   Memory write in the Harvard Mark I.

Address Modification

The only address modification is the nullification of invalid addresses, a form of damage limitation without true policing.

Address Level

All addressing is direct, and there is no provision for address calculation. Arrays are not intended to reside in memory, but to enter element by element from a card reader or paper tape.

10.2.4
Data

The only datatype is the fixed-point number.

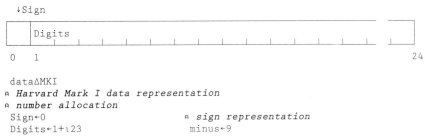

```
dataΔMKI
ⱥ Harvard Mark I data representation
ⱥ number allocation
 Sign←0                        ⱥ sign representation
 Digits←1+ι23                   minus←9
```

PROGRAM 10-18   Data specification in the Harvard Mark I.

Fixed-Point Numbers

Notation and allocation.   The memory implementation, derived from accounting machines, assumes digit-complement decimal notation. Digit complement is more convenient than radix complement for setting switches by hand.

10.2.5
Operations

Fixed-Point Arithmetic

In a memorandum, Aiken envisaged many functions, such as anti-trigonometric functions, as primitive operations. He proposed evaluating many standard functions, such as the hyperbolic ones, by programmed routines [Aiken, 1937]. As built, the Mark I operation set has fewer primitives than

```
d UPS Read Upper 71            c LOG Logarithm
d LWS Read Lower 71            f CLG Clear Logarithm Argument
a ADD Add Or Clear             c EXP Exponential
c UPD Add Or Clear Upper 71    e EXS Exponent
c LWD Add Or Clear Lower 71    c EXD Add To Exponent
b AC1 Add 64 W Carry To 65     g CEX Clear Exponent
b AC2 Add 65 W Carry From 64   c SIN Sine Argument
b AC3 Add 68 W Carry To 69     b SI2 Plugged Sine Argument
b AC4 Add 69 W Carry From 68   g CSN Clear Sine Argument
c TLD Add Or Clear Tolerance   c INT Interpolate
c MD  Multiplicand             d INH Interpolation Interval
c DR  Divisor                  f INS Interpolate Sequence
f DP1 Divide Precision 1       g CIR Clear Intermediate Register
f DP2 Divide Precision 2
f DP3 Divide Precision 3
f DP4 Divide Precision 4
Legend: W = With.
```

TABLE 10-19   Fixed-point instructions of the Harvard Mark I.

the memorandum proposes. It thus constitutes a first step toward obtaining complex functions from routines, as is done in the classical computer.

Location 71 can be accessed in the normal fashion, or its 12-digit upper and lower parts can be accessed separately with the operations UPS and LWS for reading and UPD and LWD for adding and clearing. This facility aids in using the 24-digit word as two 12-digit words. Similarly, the tolerance location—location 72—can be added to or cleared with TLD.

The instruction Logarithm gives the base-10 logarithm, and Exponential gives the power of 10. Interpolation requires a specific ordering and spacing of the instructions INT, INH, INS, and CIR.

Load and Store.   Neither Load nor Store is available, but a prior Clear can produce their effect. The Clear is obtained by specifying the register address in both the Source and the Dest fields without further sign control.

Add.   Since the addend can be changed by Absolute Value and/or by Negation as part of the operand fetch, there is no need for Subtract.

```
augmentΔMKI dest;radix
ᴀ Harvard Mark I augment memory
radix←10
addend←digitcompi bus
augend←digitcompi memory[dest;]
sum←augend+addend
memory[dest;]←word digitcompr sum
```

PROGRAM 10-20   Add to memory in the Harvard Mark I.

Multiply.   We detail Multiply as an example of the more complex operations such as Divide, Logarithm, Exponential, Sine, and Interpolate.

Latent operations.   The more complex operations of the Mark I have instruction overlap. We describe these concurrent processes with a description artifice, a FIFO list of future actions latentlist. The function postop places actions on this list and extends the list as needed. latentsource and latentdest execute actions from this list. The list is shortened each cycle. Multiplication can start when the operation MD presents the multiplicand. This operation posts the demand for the multiplier, the latent operation MR, allowing two intervening cycles for building a multiplication table. The programmer does not give an explicit MR instruction; two cycles later, the MR latent operation is executed, and whatever is on the bus is taken into the multiplier. MR in turn posts the latent operation PD, which presents the product in due course. The latent action list corresponds to dispersed control circuitry.

Timing.   Each operation has its specific timing rules. In Multiply, the number of cycles that intervene between MR and PD depends upon the number of odd and even multiplier digits that are non-zero, as is shown in mpytime.

Plugging.   Digits from the double-length product are placed upon the single-length bus via plugging. The general function plug represents this plugging as an indexed selection of the output digits from the input digits. The specific plugging used is represented by pdwire and is constant for an entire program. The programmer must specify the pluggings separately.

```
MD;radix
ⱥ Harvard Mark I Multiplicand
radix←10
multiplicand←digitcompi bus
2 postop ' MR'


MR;radix;multiplier
ⱥ Harvard Mark I Multiplier
radix←10
multiplier←digitcompi bus
product←multiplicand×multiplier
mpytime postop 'PD  '


PD;radix;pd
ⱥ Harvard Mark I Product
radix←10
pd←(2×word) digitcompr product
bus←bus⌈pdwire plug pd
memory[Lpqs;]←word↓pd
```

```
place postop code;c
ⱥ Harvard Mark I post latent operation
→If place≥1↑platentlist
THEN: ⱥ extend latent list
        latentlist←((place+1),4)↑latentlist
ENDIF:c←(code≠' ')/ιρcode
latentlist[place;c]←code[c]


time←mpytime
ⱥ Harvard Mark I multiply time
time←3+⌈/+⌿(half,2)ρbus≠0


out←wire plug in
ⱥ Harvard Mark I plugging
out←in[wire]
```

PROGRAM 10-21   Multiply in the Harvard Mark I.

The low-order product digits, unaffected by plugging, can be obtained by addressing location 160, called `Lpqs`.

10.2.6

Instruction Sequencing

The instruction overlap of the Mark I, as illustrated above for multiplication, implies that concurrent processes place source data on the bus or read destination data from the bus during the basic execution cycle. Each basic cycle starts by placing the source data, if any, on the bus; then `latentsource` inspects `latentlist` for a latent operation that places data on the bus; next the destination actions are executed; then `latentdest` may cause a latent operation to use the data on the bus; finally, an operation specified in the modifier field is executed. The bus is local to a single execution cycle and is not otherwise available to the programmer.

```
cycleΔMKI;inst;clear;bus
ⱥ basic cycle of the Harvard Mark I
REPEAT:inst←ifetchΔMKI
    sourceΔMKI
    latentsourceΔMKI
    destΔMKI
    latentdestΔMKI
    execute(-word)↑inst[Mod]
→UNTIL stopΔMKI
```

```
latentsourceΔMKI
ⱥ Harvard Mark I latent source
⍙, 1 2 ↑latentlist


latentdestΔMKI
ⱥ Harvard Mark I latent destination
⍙, 1 ¯2 ↑latentlist
```

PROGRAM 10-22   Basic cycle of the Harvard Mark I.

Latent-operation specification.   `latentlist` can specify the name of a source and the name of a destination operation. The first two characters represent the source operation, such as `PD` in multiply. `latentsource` executes them. The last two characters are the destination operation, such as `MR` in multiply.

Linear Sequence

Next instruction.   Instruction fetch simply means stepping the instruction tape. In our description this action amounts to incrementing the location where the tape is read, as specified by `iadr`. The tape is usually glued into an endless loop, so instruction addressing is modular.

```
inst←ifetchΔMKI
 ⍝ Harvard Mark I instruction fetch
inst←tape[iadr;]
iadr←tapecap|iadr+1
```

PROGRAM 10-23   Instruction fetch in the Harvard Mark I.

Completion.   A full Stop is specified by a 3 in the 2-bit `Seq` field of each instruction; a 1 in the `Seq` field specifies a `go` signal. The absence of `go` is equivalent to Wait. The Wait is terminated by the first concurrent operation that is encountered, such as PD. In our description the latent operation list is searched for the first posted operation during Wait.

```
halt←stopΔMKI;run                   TLC
 ⍝ Harvard Mark I stop and wait     ⍝ Harvard Mark I Tolerance Stop
 REPEAT: ⍝ shorten latent list       stop←stop∨~carry[2]
    latentlist← 1 0 ↓latentlist
    run←(1=fld Seq)∨∨/' '≠, 1 4 ↑latentlist
    halt←(stop∨3=fld Seq)∨(~run)∧0=1↑ρlatentlist
 →UNTIL halt∨run
```

PROGRAM 10-24   Stop and Wait in the Harvard Mark I.

Decision

Conditional stop.   The tolerance location can be used to check a value against a tolerance. First, one subtracts the value from the tolerance location; then, Tolerance Check (TLC) causes the machine to stop if an immediately preceding subtraction in the tolerance location gives a negative result.

Iteration

Iteration is achieved by looping the instruction tape.

10.2.7

Supervision

Concurrency

Almost all operations except Add and Clear take more than one cycle and can overlap other operations with synchronous concurrency. Multiply and Divide cannot overlap each other, but use the bus only for initiation and completion, so they can overlap Add, Print, and so on. But other operations—Exponential, Logarithm, Sine, and Interpolation—can only overlap operations that do not use the bus. As a result, concurrency is rather limited.

10.2.8
Input/Output

Devices

Three punched-paper-tape readers, two card readers, one card punch, and two typewriters, used as printers, provide the I/O.

Source and sink.   Paper tapes are used as input for the interpolation instruction or as value tapes.

Direct Input/Output

Each device has its own instructions, except that the paper-tape unit used for interpolation is first selected and then implied in positioning and interpolation.

```
f RC1 Read Card Feed 1           c PNS Punch Value Or Stop
f RC2 Read Card Feed 2           f PN  Punch
d RD1 Read Tape 1                f PNC Punch And Complete
d RD2 Read Tape 2                d CPN Clear Punch
d RD3 Read Tape 3                c PR1 Print On Printer 1
f ST1 Step Tape 1                c PR2 Print On Printer 2
f ST2 Step Tape 2                c P1D Add To Printer 1
f ST3 Step Tape 3                c P2D Add To Printer 2
f RS1 Step Tape 1 Backwards      c RP1 Round Printer 1
f RS2 Step Tape 2 Backwards      c RP2 Round Printer 2
f RS3 Step Tape 3 Backwards      d CP1 Clear Printer 1
c IN1 Select Tape 1              d CP2 Clear Printer 2
c IN2 Select Tape 2              d T1N Printer 1 On
c IN3 Select Tape 3              d T2N Printer 2 On
f PIT Position Tape              d T1F Printer 1 Off
f RTS Reset Tape Selection       d T2F Printer 2 Off
```

TABLE 10-25   Input/output instructions of the Harvard Mark I.

Read and Write.   Punching can either be overlapped with computation (PN) or non-overlapped (PNC). Rounding and zero suppression are directly associated with the printing process. Tapes are synchronous with calculation.

Sense and Control.   All devices have manual power control; the typewriters can also be switched off and on under program control.

10.2.9
Implementation Notes

The Mark I was realized with IBM tabulator components. Plain digits were implemented as rotary switches, with 10 detented positions. Operation was parallel by word, with the digits time-encoded as a one-out-of-10 pulse.

Speed.   The basic machine cycle is 0.3 seconds. Multiply requires $8+n$ cycles; Divide, $6 + 2 \times n$; Logarithm, $1148 \times n$; Exponential, $172 + 2 \times n$; and Sine, 199 cycles (1 minute). The variable n has a different value for each function; it varies between 1 and 24.

Reliability. "Before using the Exponential unit, one should test it for known values." This admonition from the manual applies to all the more complicated functions of the Mark I. The main cause of failure in this electromechanical machine was dust on the rotating contacts. On the other hand, once in operation, the machine ran day and night.

A log was kept of machine throughput. When, during a certain period, the machine showed poor performance at night, Aiken paid a surprise visit and found the operator and his friends dancing in the computer room; the machine had been stopped because its noise interfered with the music.

10.2.10
Bibliography

Staff of the Computation Laboratory, 1946: "The Manual of Operation of the Automatic Sequence Controlled Calculator." *Annals of the Computation Laboratory of Harvard University*, **1**. Cambridge, MA.: Harvard University Press (our defining reference). Rpt. with additional foreword and introduction as volume 8 of the Charles Babbage Institute Reprint Series. Cambridge, MA: MIT Press, 1985.

Aiken [1937], Aiken and Hopper [1946], Blaauw [1952], Bloch [1947], Staff of the Computation Laboratory, [1946].

10.2.11
Exercises

10-2 How conveniently can Interpolate use the tables that are produced by the Mark I?

10-3 Division produces a quotient and no remainder; its machine-language specification is consistent with that for multiply. Give the formal description of the division instructions.

10.3
Zuse Z4

10.3.1
Highlights

History

Architect.   Konrad Zuse was the chief architect. He was also responsible for the implementation, and for the realization of the relay processor and its mechanical memory.

Dates.   Although the first model of the Zuse Z4 was completed in 1945, the machine had to be rebuilt because of direct and indirect damage from World War II. The rebuilt Z4 was installed in 1950 at the Eidgenössische Technische Hochschule (ETH) in Zürich, where it remained operational until 1955. Later, it was sold to Dr. H. Schardin's Research Laboratory of St. Louis, near Basel [Zuse, 1962]. In 1959 the Z4 was bought back by the Zuse company and in 1960 it was made available to the Deutches Museum in Munich, Germany.

Family tree.   The Z1 (1936) was an experimental mechanical calculator with a mechanical memory. The Z2 (1939), a test model, combined the mechanical memory with an arithmetic unit of relays. The Z3 (1941), also an experimental prototype, used a relay memory and arithmetic unit, a photographic-film sequence tape, and floating-point arithmetic (only 14-bit coefficient). It was the first program-controlled processor. The Z4 is a direct descendant of the Z3; it differs by a larger set of instructions and by a word size of 32 bits, as opposed to the 22 bits of the Z3. Of crucial difference are the conditional operations later incorporated in the Z4 at the suggestion of A. Speiser [Schwartz, 1981].

Noteworthy

Floating point.   Binary normalized floating point is the Z4's only number representation; the floating-point representation's design was far ahead of its time.

Complete set of extrema.   Infinity, negative infinity, zero or negligible, and indefinite are part of the representation and are consistently used in its arithmetic. This design predates the incomplete extrema of the IBM Stretch (1961) by more than 15 years, and the complete set of extrema of the CDC 6600 (1964) by about 20 years; it is now part of the IEEE Standard 754 [IEEE, 1985].

Hidden bit.   Normalized representation with binary radix makes the leftmost coefficient bit redundant. Zuse eliminated this bit, as did Bell in the DEC PDP11 (1970). This hidden bit is also part of the IEEE Standard.

Rich arithmetic.   The operation set includes Negate, Make Absolute, Add, Subtract, Maximum, Minimum, Multiply, Divide, Reciprocal, Square, Square

Root, Times Two, Times Three, Times Ten, Times Pi, and Divide By Two, Three, Five, Seven, and Pi. This set exceeds the demands of a classical machine, but is quite suitable for a machine with limited subroutine facilities.

Conversion to and from decimal.   Numbers are converted from decimal to binary floating point on input from buttons, and back to decimal on output to lights.

Stack.   The working store is a stack with a maximum depth of 2. This function fits well in a design with a relatively fast memory; it predates the English Electric KDF9 (1963) and Burroughs B5000 (1963) stacks by more than 15 years.

No Operation.   The No Operation (like the other features described) reflects the extensive experience that the designer had with the use of his preceding machines.

No stored program.   The program was punched into a plastic tape—used movie film—quite separate from the mechanical memory used for the data.

Subroutine.   A second punched plastic tape could be used either for data, or as a secondary program tape; a limited subroutine facility.

Reliability.   Although the Z4 at times failed for prolonged periods [Stiefel, 1951], it was still one of the most reliable computers of its generation. At the ETH the machine normally ran unattended throughout the night. Zuse's engineering skill shows in details such as current-free switching of relays and his inexpensive, yet reliable, mechanical memory.

Peculiarities

What was done in the Z4 was done well. Taking into account the limitations we have mentioned, there are few peculiarities.

Minimal decision.   Originally, the Z4 had no decision-making power: It was in principle a calculator, like the Z3. Prior to the Z4's installation at the ETH, however, three conditional operations were added to the design.

Limited stack functions.   The stack, although short, works perfectly general for dyadic operations. For monadic operations, however, only one value may be placed in the stack.

Sign code.   The Z4 is a rare example of encoding plus as 1 and minus as 0.

Three infinities.   Unsigned infinity, produced by division by zero, is distinguished from positive and negative infinity, produced by positive and negative overflow.

Implementation effects.   The mechanical memory did not allow a Load to be followed immediately by a Store. Furthermore, a stored number could only be loaded again after at least three intervening instructions. The instruction Space is intended to be used for proper timing.

Descendants

The Z4 was the last of the line.

10.3.2

Machine Language

Language Level

Design philosophy.   The Z4 and its ancestors were intended and used for extensive engineering calculations; the design emphasized arithmetic.

```
initiate4
A initiation of the Zuse Z4
format4
configure4
space4
name4
instruction4
f14
```

PROGRAM 10-26   Initiation of the Zuse Z4.

Unit System

The Z4 has the (by now) familiar 8-bit byte and 32-bit word. The byte applies not to a character, however, but to the instruction tape that has two displaced 4-bit rows for each instruction. The installed machine has just 64 words in its memory; this size is comparable to that of the Harvard Mark I's memory (1944).

```
format4                        configure4
A Zuse Z4 information units   A configuration for the Zuse Z4
A representation radix        A memory capacity
radix←2                        memcap←adrcap
A information units           A tape capacity
byte←8                         tapecap←100
word←32                        tapecap1←100
adrsize←6
A address capacity
adrcap←radix*adrsize
A stack capacity
stackcap←2
```

PROGRAM 10-27   Basic parameters of the Zuse Z4.

Configuration.   Instruction memory was, of course, unlimited. We use the value 100 merely as an instance for the main and secondary tape.

Spaces

Memory name-space.   The memory name-space is homogeneously and fully used.

Working store.   The stack used as working store is implicitly addressed in true LIFO fashion. There is no direct addressing or programmed access to the stack pointer.

Control store. Binary status bits control the action of the stack on storing, the conditional skip, the use of the subprogram tape instead of the main program tape, and the action of the Signum instruction.

Switches and display. The manual entry buttons and the display lights allow entry and display of floating-point data. The thirteen entry buttons allow serial entry of a sign, a decimal point (comma), one to six decimal digits, and an exponent code. The decimal point may precede any one of the decimal digits—absence of decimal point signifies an integer. The exponent code is preceded by a slash; codes 1 through 6 indicate the decimal exponents 6, 12, 18, −6, −12, and −18; code 0 specifies an extremum. The display lights have columns for a sign, six decimal digits, decimal points, and an encoded power of 10.

```
space4                                  name4
A Zuse Z4 spaces                        A Zuse Z4 space names
A memory                                A - extrema lights
  memory←?(memcap,word)ρradix           Zero←0
A working store                         Infinite←1
  reg←?(stackcap,word)ρradix            Posinfinite←2
A instruction store                     Neginfinite←3
  tape←?(tapecap,byte)ρradix            Uflo←4
A instruction or data store             Indefinite←5
  tape1←?(tapecap1,byte)ρradix
A control store
A - instruction addresses
  iadr←?tapecap
  iadr1←?tapecap1
A - stack pointer
  sp←?stackcap+1
A - stopped state                       A input/output spaces
  stop←?radix                           A - entry buttons: 0123456789-,/
A -keep state                             entry←?13ρradix
  keep←?radix                           A - display: sign, 6 digits, exponent code
A - skip state                            display←?2,(6ρ10),7
  skip←?radix                           A - extrema lights
A - subprogram state                      light←?6ρradix
  sub←?radix                            A - protocol panels and pointer
A - signum switch                         protocol←? 10 5 ρradix
  sgnsw←?radix                            prp←? 11 5
```

PROGRAM 10-28 Spaces of the Zuse Z4.

Extrema lights. Extreme results are indicated by lights for the six extreme results: zero, unsigned infinity, positive infinity, negative infinity, underflow, and indefinite. Underflow is represented by a zero; overflow, by positive or negative infinity.

Protocol. The progress of a program and the corresponding actions required from the operator can be monitored by a display of eleven rows of five panels. Each one of these panels, except those in the first row, can be illuminated by instructions. At most one panel is lit at a time.

Programming model. The dataflow is simple; the instruction flow, simpler. We do not show the stack pointer which is not explicitly visible to the programmer. The light vertical separators within the registers show the format divisions of the only datatype, the floating-point number. Multiplication,

division, square root, and so forth are accomplished by control actions using the registers, adder, and dataflow visible in the static structure.

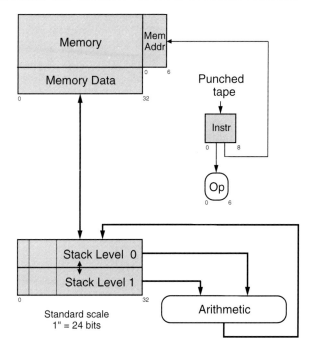

FIGURE 10-29   Programming model for the Zuse Z4.

Operand Specification

Number of addresses.   The Z4 uses true zero addressing: The one-address format is used only for Load and Store. The Z4 was clearly the first machine with a zero-address format; the Z4 and the Princeton IAS (1952) were the first to have the one-address format.

Operation Specification

The Z4 has 60 operations, a marked increase over the 18 operations of the Z3.

a→NOP	MPY	MP3	SQR	RD	PRO	RD0	IND	
	DIV	DV3	REC	WR	PR2	RD1	NFR	
ST	MAX	DV5	ABS	WRK	PR4		CL	
LD	MIN	DV7	SGN	PRT	PR6		STC	
b→LD1	HLV		MXP	PDN	CR		SKC	c→STE
SUB	DBL	MPP	IN1	PLT	TAB	ZER	CLC	RET
SBR	NEG	DVP	KP	PUP	PCH	POS		STN
ADD	TEN	SQ	SP	PR	PCP	INF		

PROGRAM 10-30   Operation-code list of the Zuse Z4.

Types of control.   Control is governed by instructions and the few modes they set. There are no indicators.

```
    ⌐ floating-point arithmetic      ⌐ sequencing
a LD  Load                        a NOP No Operation
b LD1 Load Immediate 1            b STC Stop On Condition
a ST  Store                       b SP  Space
b KP  Keep                        b SKC Skip On Condition
b NEG Negate                      b CL  Call
b ABS Make Absolute               b CLC Call On Condition
b ADD Add                         c RET Return
b SUB Subtract                      ⌐ supervision
b SBR Reverse Subtract            c STE Start Execution
b MAX Maximum                     c STN Start Number
b MXP Maximum Positive              ⌐ input/output
b MIN Minimum                     b RD  Read Switches
b MPY Multiply                    b WR  Display
b DBL Multiply By Two             b WRK Display And Keep
b MP3 Multiply By Three           b PR  Print
b TEN Multiply By Ten             b PR0 Print 0
b MPP Multiply By Pi              b PR2 Print 2
b DIV Divide                      b PR4 Print 4
b HLV Divide By Two               b PR6 Print 6
b DV3 Divide By Three             b CR  Carriage Return
b DV5 Divide By Five              b TAB Tabulate
b DV7 Divide By Seven             b RD0 Read Tape 0
b DVP Divide By Pi                b RD1 Read Tape 1
b REC Reciprocal                  b PCH Punch
b SQ  Square                      b PCP Punch Program
b SQR Square Root                 b PRT Protocol Right
b SGN Signum                      b PDN Protocol Down
b IN1 If Indefinite Then One      b PLT Protocol Left
b ZER Zero Test                   b PUP Protocol Up
b POS Positive Test
b INF Infinite Test
b IND Indefinite Test
b NFR Non-Fraction Test
```

TABLE 10-31   Instruction list of the Zuse Z4.

Instruction Structure

Machine language syntax.   The three instruction types are reflected in the instruction syntax and in the instruction-field allocation.

```
      syntax4
a Opcode,Address
b 0 1 ,Opb
c 0 0 1 0 0 0 ,Opc
```

PROGRAM 10-32   Instruction syntax of the Zuse Z4.

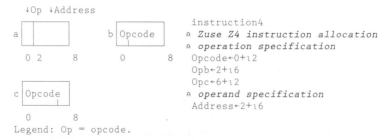

```
↓Op ↓Address
                          b Opcode    instruction4
a ┌────┬──────┐                         ⌐ Zuse Z4 instruction allocation
  │    │      │          │              ⌐ operation specification
  └────┴──────┘          0        8   Opcode←0+ι2
  0 2        8                         Opb←2+ι6
                                       Opc←6+ι2
c ┌──────────┐                          ⌐ operand specification
  │ Opcode   │                         Address←2+ι6
  └──────────┘
  0          8
Legend: Op = opcode.
```

PROGRAM 10-33   Instruction allocation in the Zuse Z4.

Instruction format.   The instruction format is the earliest example of the extended operation code.

10.3.3

Addressing

Direct addressing.   Reading and writing are simple because of the uniform data size.

```
data←read4 address        address write4 data
A Zuse Z4 read from memory A Zuse Z4 write into memory
data←memory[address;]      memory[address;]←data
```

PROGRAM 10-34   Memory read and write in the Zuse Z4.

Address Modification

Addressing is straightforward. There is no address modification; address calculation is not possible.

```
address←adr4
A Zuse Z4 addressing
address←fld Address
```

PROGRAM 10-35   Addressing in the Zuse Z4.

Stack addressing.   The stack operates with a predecrement pop and a postincrement push. Instructions check the stack capacity to prevent pushing into a full stack or popping from an empty stack. The Z4 deviates from normal stack operation by insisting upon a single entry in the stack for a Store or a monadic operation.

```
data←pop4                 push4 data
A Zuse Z4 read from stack  A Zuse Z4 write onto stack
sp←sp-1                   reg[sp;]←data
data←reg[sp;]             sp←sp+1
```

PROGRAM 10-36   Stack read and write in the Zuse Z4.

10.3.4

Data

The Zuse Z4 has no characters, logic, or fixed-point numbers.

Floating-Point Numbers

Closure and normal form.   A complete set of extrema closes the floating-point range.   Positive and negative overflow give positive and negative infinity, respectively.   These two extrema are distinguished from unsigned infinity, the result of division by zero.   Indefinite and negligible (equated with zero)

anticipate the 6600 and IEEE Standard 754. Truncation is used for precision treatment: "a real tragedy, but we saw no way to change it" [Speiser, 1989].

Floating-point formats. The Z4 floating-point datatype follows the Z3 design, except for the critical improvement of increasing the coefficient field from 13 to 23 bits.

A separate bit is allocated to signal the extrema. This arrangement is similar to the Stretch design, but is less efficient than the design of the 6600, which encodes the extrema in the exponent field. The choice of 7 exponent bits gives a range of about 10^{20} to 10^{-20}. The coefficient magnitude of 24 bits (including the hidden bit) gives accuracy of about seven decimal digits.

The coefficient allocation separates the sign and leftmost represented bit from the other 22 coefficient bits.

```
┌Extremum
│ ↓Coefficient sign and leading digit
↓ ↓
  ┌┬─────┬───────────────────┐
  │││ Exp │ Coefficient       │
  └┴─────┴───────────────────┘
0   3     10                  32
Legend: Exp = exponent.
```

```
f14                              r←range4i rep
⍝ Zuse Z4 floating-point number  ⍝ Zuse Z4 range interpretation
⍝ base                           →IF rep[Extremum]
base←2                           THEN: ⍝ extremum
⍝ sign encoding                        r←magni rep[Exp]
plus←1                                 →ENDIF
minus←0                          ELSE: ⍝ normal range
⍝ exponent allocation                  r←(negnorm,posnorm)[rep[Coef[0]]]
Exp←3+⍳7                         ENDIF:
⍝ coefficient allocation
Coef← 1 1 2 ,10+⍳22
⍝ extreme exponent               rep←range4r r
extexp←radix*0⌊⍴1↓Exp            ⍝ Zuse Z4 range representation
⍝ extremum allocation            rep←word⍴0
Extremum←0                       rep[Extremum]←1
⍝ radix point                    rep[Exp]←(⍴Exp) magnr r
point←0⌊⍴2↓Coef
⍝ range identifiers
⍝ - normal range
posnorm←0
negnorm←1                        ⍝ action code
⍝ - extrema                      ⍝ - operand 1 as result
zero←2                           o1←¯1
inf←3                            ⍝ - operand 2 as result
posinf←4                         o2←¯2
neginf←5                         ⍝ - normal action
indef←6                          n←¯3
```

PROGRAM 10-37   Floating-point format and range representation in the Zuse Z4.

Floating-point range.   range4i determines the range of a floating-point representation: positive or negative normal range, or one of the five extrema. range4r represents an extreme result; it is not used for normal results. The exponent codes for the extrema are our assumption.

Floating-point representation.   In the normal range, the Z4 has binary radix complement for the exponent and binary signed magnitude for the coefficient. The functions hiddenbit and insertbit hide and expose the hidden bit, as shown in Section 9.3. When the exponent is too large or too small for

```
number←fl4i rep;exponent;coefficient
⍝ Zuse Z4 floating-point interpretation
exponent←radixcompi rep[Exp]
coefficient←signmagni insertbit rep[Coef]
number←coefficient×base*exponent-point

rep←fl4r number;exponent;coefficient;xmax;xmin
⍝ Zuse Z4 floating-point representation
→IF number=0
THEN: ⍝ zero extremum
   rep←range4r zero
   →ENDIF
ELSE:⍝ normalize number
   →CASE(exponent<(-extexp),extexp)⍳1
   C0: ⍝ underflow
      rep←range4r zero
      light[Uflo]←1
      →ENDCASE
   C1: ⍝ normal range
      rep←wordρ0
      rep[Coef]←hidebit(ρCoef) signmagnr truncate coefficient
      rep[Exp]←(ρExp) radixcompr exponent
      →ENDCASE
   C2: ⍝ overflow
      rep←range4r(posinf,neginf)[coefficient<0]
   ENDCASE:
ENDIF:
```

PROGRAM 10-38   Floating-point interpretation and representation in the Zuse Z4.

the normal range, the signed infinity or zero extremum is represented. The underflow light distinguishes this zero result from a true zero.

10.3.5

Operations

Floating-Point Arithmetic

The arithmetic operations clearly exceed the classical repertoire. Selected immediate operands are supplied for Load, Multiply, and Divide. The seven range tests place their result in the stack; there are no indicators.

a	LD	Load	b	DIV Divide
b	LD1	Load Immediate 1	b	HLV Divide By Two
a	ST	Store	b	DV3 Divide By Three
b	KP	Keep	b	DV5 Divide By Five
b	NEG	Negate	b	DV7 Divide By Seven
b	ABS	Make Absolute	b	DVP Divide By Pi
b	ADD	Add	b	REC Reciprocal
b	SUB	Subtract	b	SQ Square
b	SBR	Reverse Subtract	b	SQR Square Root
b	MAX	Maximum	b	SGN Signum
b	MXP	Maximum Positive	b	IN1 If Indefinite Then One
b	MIN	Minimum	b	ZER Zero Test
b	MPY	Multiply	b	POS Positive Test
b	DBL	Multiply By Two	b	INF Infinite Test
b	MP3	Multiply By Three	b	IND Indefinite Test
b	TEN	Multiply By Ten	b	NFR Non-Fraction Test
b	MPP	Multiply By Pi		

TABLE 10-39   Floating-point instructions of the Zuse Z4.

Load and Store.   The Load and Store show the typical stack access. No load is allowed when the stack is full; a Store may have only one entry in the stack.

```
LD                          ST;od                  KP
⍝ Zuse Z4 Load              ⍝ Zuse Z4 Store        ⍝ Zuse Z4 Keep
→OUT sp=2                   →OUT sp≠1              →OUT sp≠1
push4 read4 adr4            od←pop4                keep←1
                           adr4 write4 od
                           →If keep
LD1                         THEN:push4 od
⍝ Zuse Z4 Load Immediate 1  ENDIF:keep←0
→OUT sp=2
push4 fl4r 1
```

PROGRAM 10-40   Load and Store in the Zuse Z4.

Keep.   In the `keep` mode the stack content is preserved during a Store or Punch. This mode is entered by the Keep instruction and reset upon use—a limited application of the keep concept.

Add and Maximum.   Add and Maximum show the handling of operands that may be extrema. `range4i` classifies each operand according to the seven

```
ADD;ad;au;r;addend;augend;sum        MAX;od1;od2;r;operand1;operand2;maximum
⍝ Zuse Z4 Add                        ⍝ Zuse Z4 Maximum
→OUT sp≠2                            →OUT sp≠2
ad←pop4                              od1←pop4
au←pop4                              od2←pop4
r←rngadd[range4i au;range4i ad]      r←rngmax[range4i od1;range4i od2]
→CASE(o1,o2,n)ιr                     →CASE(o1,o2,n)ιr
C0: ⍝ augend                         C0: ⍝ operand 1
    push4 au                            push4 od1
    →ENDCASE                            →ENDCASE
C1: ⍝ addend                         C1: ⍝ operand 2
    push4 ad                            push4 od2
    →ENDCASE                            →ENDCASE
C2: ⍝ normal sum                     C2: ⍝ normal maximum
    addend←fl4i ad                      operand1←fl4i od1
    augend←fl4i au                      operand2←fl4i od2
    sum←augend+addend                   maximum←operand1⌈operand2
    push4 fl4r sum                      push4 fl4r maximum
    light[Zero]←sum=0                   →ENDCASE
    →ENDCASE                         C3: ⍝ extreme maximum
C3: ⍝ extreme sum                       push4 range4r r
    push4 range4r r                  ENDCASE:
ENDCASE:
```

```
     show4 rngadd                           show4 rngmax
n   n o1   ω +ω -ω  i          n  o1 o1   i +ω o1   i
n   n o1   ω +ω -ω  i          o2  n  0   i +ω o1   i
o2 o2  0   ω +ω -ω  i          o2  0  0   i +ω -ω   i
ω   ω  ω   ω  i  i  i          i   i  i   ω  i  i   i
+ω +ω +ω   i +ω  i  i          +ω +ω +ω   i +ω +ω   i
-ω -ω -ω   i  i -ω  i          o2 o2 -ω   i +ω -ω   i
i   i  i   i  i  i  i          i   i  i   i  i  i   i
```

```
Legend: i = indefinite; n = normal action; ω = infinity;
        o1 = operand 1; o2 = operand 2;
        operands: positive, negative, 0, ω, +ω, -ω, i.
```

PROGRAM 10-41   Add and Maximum in the Zuse Z4.

ranges given in fl4i. The range matrices rngadd and rngmax give the code for the required action or extreme result. An action is either a normal operation, or the use of an operand as the result.

Multiply and Divide.   We illustrate the multiplication. Again, the ranges of the operands are used to decide upon a normal operation or an extreme result. Divide is similar except for its normal operation and its rangematrix rngdiv (Program 10-42).

```
MPY;mr;md;r;multiplier;multiplicand;product              show4 rngmpy
A Zuse Z4 Multiply                               n   n   0   ω  +ω  -ω   i
→OUT sp≠2                                        n   n   0   ω  -ω  +ω   i
mr←pop4                                          0   0   0   i   i   i   i
md←pop4                                          ω   ω   i   ω   i   i   i
r←rngmpy[range4i md;range4i mr]                 +ω  -ω   i   i  +ω  -ω   i
→IF r=n                                         -ω  +ω   i   i  -ω  +ω   i
THEN: A normal product                           i   i   i   i   i   i   i
   multiplier←fl4i mr
   multiplicand←fl4i md                                  show4 rngdiv
   product←multiplicand×multiplier              n   n   ω   0   0   0   i
   push4 fl4r product                           n   n   ω   0   0   0   i
   →ENDIF                                        0   0   i   0   0   0   i
ELSE: A extreme product                         ω   ω   i   i   i   i   i
   push4 range4r r                             +ω  -ω   ω   i   i   i   i
ENDIF:                                          -ω  +ω   ω   i   i   i   i
                                                 i   i   i   i   i   i   i
```

Legend: i = indefinite; n = normal action; ω = infinity;
         operands: positive, negative, 0, ω, +ω, -ω, i.

PROGRAM 10-42   Multiply in the Zuse Z4.

Other arithmetic operations.   The remaining arithmetic operations are all monadic. For these monadic operations the result classification can be specified by a range vector. We illustrate the Square and Square Root. Square Root gives an indefinite result for a negative operand, including negative infinity.

```
SQ;od;r;operand;result       SQR;od;r;operand;result
A Zuse Z4 Square              A Zuse Z4 Square Root
→OUT sp≠1                     →OUT sp≠1
od←pop4                       od←pop4
r←rngsq[range4i od]           r←rngsqr[range4i od]
→IF r=n                       →IF r=n
THEN: A normal square        THEN: A normal root
   operand←fl4i od              operand←fl4i od
   result←operand*2            result←⌊operand*0.5
   push4 fl4r result           push4 fl4r result
   →ENDIF                       →ENDIF
ELSE: A extreme square       ELSE: A extreme root
   push4 range4r r              push4 range4r r
ENDIF:                       ENDIF:
```

```
      show4 rngsq                   show4 rngsqr
 n   n   0   ω  +ω  +ω   i     n   i   0   ω  +ω   i   i
```

Legend: i = indefinite; n = normal action; ω = infinity;
         operands: positive, negative, 0, ω, +ω, -ω, i.

PROGRAM 10-43   Square and Square Root in the Zuse Z4.

Reverse Subtract interchanges minuend and subtrahend; there is no Reverse Divide. Maximum Positive gives the maximum of zero and the operand.

Range tests.   Signum matches its mathematical concept, as also found in APL: positive numbers are replaced by 1, negative numbers by -1, and zero by 0. As an alternative, the signum switch `sgnsu` can cause zero to be replaced by indefinite. The instruction If Indefinite Then One does just that—all other operands are left unchanged.

```
SGN;r                              IN1;od
A Zuse Z4 Signum                   A Zuse Z4 If Indefinite Then One
 →OUT sp≠1                          →OUT sp≠1
 r←rngsgn[sgnsw;range4i pop4]       od←pop4
 →CASE(posnorm,negnorm)ιr           →If indef=range4i od
 C0:push4 fl4r 1                    THEN: A replace operand by 1
    →ENDCASE                             od←fl4r 1
 C1:push4 fl4r ¯1                   ENDIF:push4 od
    →ENDCASE
 C2:push4 range4r r
 ENDCASE:                           NFR;od;r
                                    A Zuse Z4 Non-Fraction Test
                                     →OUT sp≠1
       show4 rngsgn                  od←pop4
 +   -   +   ω   +   -   i           r←rngnfr[range4i od]
 +   -   i   ω   +   -   i           →CASE(posnorm,inf)ιr
                                     C0: A normal range
                                         push4 fl4r ¯1 1[(|fl4i od)≥1]
    POS;r                               →ENDCASE
  A Zuse Z4 Positive Test            C1: A infinite
   →OUT sp≠1                             push4 fl4r 1
   r←range4i pop4                       →ENDCASE
   →IF r∈posnorm,zero,posinf         C2: A other ranges
  THEN: A positive                       push4 fl4r ¯1
     push4 fl4r 1                    ENDCASE:
     →ENDIF
  ELSE: A not positive
     push4 fl4r ¯1                         show4 rngnfr
  ENDIF:                              +   +   0   ω   ω   ω   i
```

```
Legend: i = indefinite; ω = infinity;
        + = positive result; - = negative result;
        operands: positive, negative, 0, ω, +ω, -ω, i.
```

PROGRAM 10-44   Range tests in the Zuse Z4.

The other five range tests each place 1 or -1 in the stack depending upon the test. These values, the Z4 equivalent of a logical result, can be used by the conditional operations.

10.3.6

Instruction Sequencing

Sequence control.   The Z4 initially had just No Operation and Stop for sequence control. As later modified, the Z4 has a Conditional Skip as well: A successful Conditional Skip causes the processor to skip all subsequent instructions until a Start Execution (operation code 68) is encountered.

```
cycle4                                  inst←ifetch4
A basic cycle of the Zuse Z4            A Zuse Z4 instruction fetch
REPEAT:→IF skip=0                       →IF sub=0
   THEN: A normal execution             THEN: A main program
      execute ifetch4                      inst←tape[iadr;]
      →ENDIF                               iadr←tapecap|iadr+1
   ELSE: A skip until Start Execution      →ENDIF
      skip←68≠decode ifetch4            ELSE: A subprogram
ENDIF:→UNTIL stop                          inst←tape1[iadr1;]
                                           iadr1←tapecap1|iadr1+1
                                        ENDIF:
```

PROGRAM 10-45   Basic cycle and instruction fetch of the Zuse Z4.

Linear Sequence

Next instruction.   The instruction tape is stepped to fetch the next instruction either from the main program tape or from the subprogram tape, as indicated by the sub mode.

The Space instruction is a No Operation that retards the machine cycle, such that repeated and successive memory access is possible. If the stack is not empty, the instruction is ignored.

```
NOP                                 SP
A Zuse Z4 No Operation              A Zuse Z4 Space
                                    →OUT sp≠0
                                    A retard machine cycle

SKC
A Zuse Z4 Skip On Condition
   →OUT sp≠1                        STC
   skip←1=f14i pop4                 A Zuse Z4 Stop On Condition
   →If skip                         →OUT sp≠1
   THEN: A reset protocol           stop←1=f14i pop4
      prp← 0 0
      protocol[;]←0
   ENDIF:
```

PROGRAM 10-46   No Operation and conditional operation in the Zuse Z4.

Decision

Conditional operation.   There are three conditional operations. Each inspects the stack for the value 1 and no other content. If so, the skip, stop, or sub mode is turned on. In each case the stack becomes empty; the skip action also resets the protocol.

Iteration

No iteration facilities are available, except that the instruction tape can be spliced into a loop.

Delegation

Subprogram.   A single subroutine can be installed on the secondary tape unit (four more tape units were envisaged but never installed). The Call can be conditional and unconditional. No parameters can be passed on the stack.

Return is unconditional from subprogram to main program, or from main program to a stop.

```
CL                                 RET
ค Zuse Z4 Call                     ค Zuse Z4 Return
 →OUT sp≠0                          →IF sub
 sub←1                              THEN: ค return to main program
                                          sub←0
                                          →ENDIF
CLC                                ELSE: ค stop main program
ค Zuse Z4 Call On Condition              sp←0
 →OUT sp≠1                                stop←1
 sub←1=f14i pop4                   ENDIF:
```

PROGRAM 10-47   Delegation in the Zuse Z4.

10.3.7

Input/Output

Devices

Store.   Punched tape is used for intermediate data storage—a modification made at the request of the ETH [Speiser, 1980].

Source and sink.   Manual buttons are available as input; display lights and a typewriter are available for output.

```
b RD   Read Switches        b RD0 Read Tape 0
b WR   Display              b RD1 Read Tape 1
b WRK  Display And Keep     b PCH Punch
b PR   Print                b PCP Punch Program
b PR0  Print 0              b PRT Protocol Right
b PR2  Print 2              b PDN Protocol Down
b PR4  Print 4              b PLT Protocol Left
b PR6  Print 6              b PUP Protocol Up
b CR   Carriage Return
b TAB  Tabulate
```

TABLE 10-48   Input/output instructions of the Zuse Z4.

Print instructions must follow immediately after a Display instruction. Printing is either with encoded exponent or with zero, two, four, or six digits after the decimal point. The decimal points are vertically aligned.

Direct Input/Output

Read and Write.   The reading from the buttons and the writing onto the display includes decimal to binary and binary to decimal conversions, respectively. We illustrate a typical action on the protocol.

10.3.8

Implementation Notes

The Z4 used 2200 relays. The mechanical memory was a Zuse invention.

```
PRT
ᴀ Zuse Z4 Protocol Right
prp[1]←5|prp[1]+1
→If prp[0]>0
THEN: ᴀ light panel
    protocol[:]←0
    protocol[prp[0]-1;prp[1]]←1
ENDIF:
```

PROGRAM 10-49   Protocol action in the Zuse Z4.

Speed.   Addition takes 0.5 to 1.25 seconds; multiplication, 3.5 seconds; division and square root, 6.75 seconds. Memory access is usually overlapped with arithmetic; otherwise it takes 0.5 seconds. The average speed is 1000 arithmetic operations per hour [Speiser, 1980].

The square-root implementation algorithm used a non-restoring method invented by Zuse.

10.3.9
Bibliography

Eidgenösse Technische Hochschule–Zürich, Institute for Applied Mathematics, 1952: *User Manual Z4* (German). Zürich: Eidgenösse Technische Hochschule.

Speiser, A.P., 1989: Letter to the authors.

Stiefel, E., 1951: Letter to Zuse. Document 017/002 Computer archive GMD, Schloss Birlinghoven, Sankt Augustin, Germany.

Ceruzzi [1981], IEEE [1987], Schwartz [1981], Speiser [1980], Zuse [1936, 1962, 1980, 1991].

10.3.10
Exercises

10-4 Assuming consistency with the instructions in this section, give the formal descriptions of the Z4 instructions

a. NEG, ABS, SUB, SBR, MXP, MIN

b. DBL, MP3, TEN, MPP

c. DIV, HLV, DV3, DV5, DV7, DVP, REC

d. ZER, INF, and IND

10.4

Ferranti Mark 1 (Manchester MU1)

10.4.1

Highlights

History

Architect.   Thomas Kilburn was the architect [Kilburn, 1949a, 1949b].

Dates.   The Ferranti Mark 1 is the result of several redesigns of the machine that Kilburn originally developed from 1946 through 1949 at Manchester University, building upon the Princeton IAS (1952) machine concepts. The machine was produced by the Ferranti corporation. The first Ferranti machine was installed in 1951; the last one was delivered in 1957 [Lavington, 1978].

Family tree.   The Manchester machine was at a later time renamed the MU1. It was the first of the series MU1 through MU5 that Kilburn designed. This series contained many novel architectural concepts. The members of the series differ to such an extent, however, that they do not constitute a family. We present the Ferranti machine (referred to as Mark 1 [Ferranti, 1954]), but note significant differences with the earlier Manchester machine (referred to as MU1).

Noteworthy

The Mark 1 constitutes a major step toward the establishment of the classical computer. Although it starts with the IAS concepts, its indexing, logic, and drum backing-store make it a pioneering effort on its own. The changes from the MU1 move the architecture toward the classical computer; they clearly show experience with actual use.

Indexing.   Kilburn invented address modification by indexing. His Mark 1 incorporates indexing in its almost ultimate form. Whereas the Harvard Mark III (1950) has partial substitution of the address by the index, the Mark 1 has additive indexing. Kilburn immediately saw the need for more than one index register, so the Mark 1 has eight; he also provided Index Add and Subtract, whereas the later IBM 704 (1955) has only Index Load and Store.

Multiple instruction formats.   The Mark 1 has single- and double-length instructions where other machines of its time adhered to one single length.

Logical connectives.   Perhaps owing to M.H.A. Newman's prior cryptological experience during World War II, the Mark 1 is the first computer with the classical logical operations. The Mark 1 has the essential set of connective operations And and Exclusive Or (which can be used as a Not). The MU1 also had Or.

Logical vector operations.   The Sideways Add—also known as Plus Re-duction, Population Count, or All-Ones Count—and the Normalize, which includes a Left-Zero Count, are available as logical vector operations.

Jump.   Besides the usual absolute Branch, a Relative Branch, or Jump, is available in the MU1.

Subroutine return.   The Mark 1 provided a convenient subroutine return.

Backing store.   Besides the main memory of 1024 halfwords of 20 bits, the Mark 1 has a drum backing-store extendable to 16 K words of 40 bits. One or two pages of 64 halfwords can be exchanged between main store and backing-store in a single operation; the store is two-level. Since the source of the page is program-accessible, a programmed one-level store is in principle feasible, but it was not implemented for this machine. (One-level store appeared in Kilburn's Ferranti Atlas [1962], implemented in hardware.)

Clock.   The MU1 was the first machine to have a program-readable clock; the clock was not part of the Mark 1.

Peculiarities

Instruction indexing. In one respect the indexing of the Mark 1 has not been copied in later designs: The indexing affects the entire instruction, not just the address field.

Mixed notation.   The position of the radix point is neither integer, nor fractional, but two digits from the left of the representation.

No plain Multiply.   Multiplication is either cumulative or subtractive—that is, the product is either added to an augend or subtracted from a minuend.

No Divide.   The absence of division foreshadows that of many later machines.

Indirect Branch.   In the MU1 all Branches and Jumps obtain the new instruction address from the addressed memory location, *not* as an immediate value from the instruction. This awkward procedure is changed in the Mark 1 to the classical solution.

Extended instruction format.   The second word of a double-length instruction does not follow the first word, but is obtained from a location that is addressed by the first word. The next instruction address, however, is that following the first word.

Asymmetry.   The MU1 instruction set is remarkably asymmetrical. It contains Index Subtract, but not Index Add; Left Shift, but not Right Shift; Or To Memory, but not And To Memory. In the case of Index Subtract, the choice is defensible; in other cases, the reason is less obvious. In the Mark 1, most (but not all) asymmetries are filled in.

Backwards bits.   The numeric digits as well as the instruction bits are displayed from left to right in ascending order of powers of 2. This reversed direction permeates the machine's manual and was a handicap for the pro-grammers. Since only the display is involved in this reversal, the reversal is not inherent in the design. Our description uses the conventional digit order.

10.4.2

Machine Language

Language Level

Design philosophy.   The Mark 1 solves the difference in length between data and instructions elegantly. Instruction addressing is always to the halfword (in contrast with the IAS), whereas data fetches and stores are always full words (in contrast with the Cambridge EDSAC [1949] and the IBM 701 [1953]).

```
initiate1
ᴀ initiation of the Ferranti Mark 1
format1
configure1
space1
instruction1
data1
```

PROGRAM 10-50   Initiation of the Ferranti Mark 1.

Programming model.   The Mark 1 is plainly modeled on the IAS machine (Section 11.1, Figure 11-4).   The most notable difference is of course the index registers. We introduce here the descriptive convention of abbreviating connections between registers and the Memory Data Register, which is in most machines connected to most registers.

Unit System

The MU1 had a word size of 32 bits; it was increased to 40 bits in the Mark 1 production models to obtain greater precision [Lavington, 1978].

```
format1
ᴀ Ferranti Mark 1 information units
ᴀ representation radix
radix←2                              configure1
ᴀ information unit                   ᴀ configuration for the Ferranti Mark 1
adrsize←10                           ᴀ memory capacity in half words
half←20                              memcap←768
word←40                              ᴀ drum capacity in pages
double←80                            drumcap←512
page←64                              ᴀ tape capacity in 5-bit bytes
                                     tapecap←100
```

PROGRAM 10-51   Basic parameters of the Ferranti Mark 1.

Configuration.   Installed memory capacity is 768 halfwords—three quarters of the addressing capacity. Installed drum capacity is 512 pages, or 32 K halfwords—one half of the capacity. The tape capacity is arbitrary.

Spaces

Memory name-space.   The Mark 1 has halfword addressing for its halfword instructions and indices; numbers are always full words. The result is one of the cleanest designs for these information sizes.

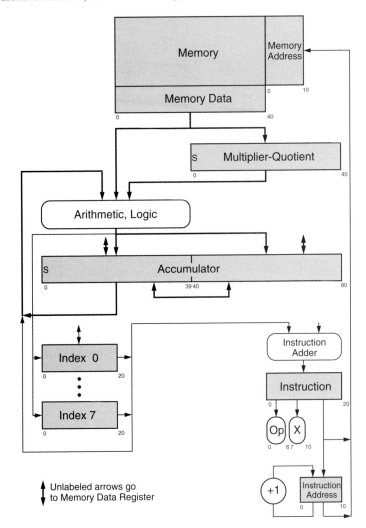

FIGURE 10-52   Programming model for the Ferranti Mark 1.

```
space1
⍝ Ferranti Mark 1 spaces
⍝ memory                             ⍝ - indicator
 memory←?(memcap,half)ρradix          ind←?radix
⍝ working store                      ⍝ - stop condition
⍝ - accumulator                       stop←?radix
 acc←?doubleρradix                   ⍝ manual control
⍝ - multiplicand                     ⍝ - data switches
 mq←?wordρradix                       switch←?halfρradix
⍝ - indices                          ⍝ - stop switch
 reg←?8ρradix*half                    stopsw←?radix
⍝ control store                      ⍝ input/output
⍝ - instruction address              drum←?(drumcap,page,half)ρradix
 iadr←?memcap                         tape←?(tapecap,5)ρradix
```

PROGRAM 10-53   Spaces of the Ferranti Mark 1.

Working store. In contrast to the IAS, the accumulator has double word size. There are eight index registers—the full complement for a classical machine. In comparison, the 701 family, which started with no indexing, for many years had only three registers. The IBM 7094 (1963) finally went to eight registers.

Auxiliary store. A drum auxiliary store has potentially 64 times the capacity of memory. In the MU1 a sixty-fifth halfword is associated with each page of 64 halfwords and preserves the track number from which the page has been read; in the Mark 1 the track number is noted in the accumulator.

Operand Specification

Number of addresses. The one-address format is used throughout.

Address phrase.   With the invention of indexing the concept of an *address phrase* emerges. The classical phrase, consisting of an index field and an address field, appears for the first time in the MU1.

Operation Specification

Mnemonics. The Mark 1 uses the teletype character codes as operation codes. The character is a letter or a special symbol, such as a colon or pound symbol. The mnemonics in the operation list follow this convention, but replace the non-alphabetic symbols each by multiple characters.

```
a→STP              J        S      b→WS
   SBB      C      K        T        WT
   NOP      D      L        U        WU
   ADB      E      M        V        WV
   STA      F      N       →b        WW
   STB      G      P        X        WX
   PCH      H      Q        Y        WY
   A        I      R        Z        WZ
```

PROGRAM 10-54   Operation-code list of the Ferranti Mark 1.

The unused operation code gives undefined actions; it is not policed.

Indicator.   There is only one indicator, set by the result of index arithmetic (Table 10-56).

Instruction Structure

Machine-language syntax. Two syntactic patterns are used.

```
    syntax1
a Opcode.Unused.X0.Address
b 1 1 1 0 0 .Unused.X0.Address.Page.Unp. 1 1 .Opw.Unt.Track
```

PROGRAM 10-55   Instruction syntax of the Ferranti Mark 1.

Instruction format. The double-length instruction format is used for transfer between the electronic memory and the magnetic drum store. The second instruction word, called a magnetic instruction, does not follow the first word; it resides in the memory location addressed by the (indexed) first word.

```
          ∩ address arithmetic              ∩ sequencing
    a A    Load Index                  a NOP No Operation
    a STB  Store Index                 a H   No Operation
    a ADB  Add To Index                a STP Stop
    a SBB  Subtract From Index         a Z   Stop On Switch
          ∩ logic and shift            a E   Branch
    a Q    And                         a C   Branch On Plus
    a L    Exclusive Or                a D   Branch On Minus
    a S    Population Count            a I   Branch On Index Plus
    a U    Arithmetic Shift            a STA Store Return Address
    a V    Normalize                        ∩ input/output
          ∩ fixed-point arithmetic     b WS  Check Drum Against Page
    a P    Load Upper                  b WT  Check Drum Against D Page
    a Y    Load MQ                     b WU  Drum To Page
    a M    Store Upper                 b WV  Drum To D Page
    a R    Store Upper And Clear       b WW  Page To Drum
    a J    Add To Upper                b WX  D Page To Drum
    a N    Add To Lower                b WY  Drum To Page And Note
    a K    Subtract From Upper         b WZ  Drum To D Page And Note
    a X    Multiply Cumulative         a G   Store Switches
    a T    Multiply Subtractive        a F   Read Tape
                                       a PCH Punch Tape
    Legend: D = Double.
```

TABLE 10-56   Instruction list of the Ferranti Mark 1.

```
a │Op  │ * │X0│Address      │     b │Op  │ * │X0│Address │Page│Op │ Track      │

   0    5 7 10           20          0    5 7 10          20   25  30          40
Legend: Op = opcode; X = index; * = unused.
```

```
instruction1
∩ Ferranti Mark 1 instruction allocation
∩ operation specification           ∩ operand specification
Opcode←0+ι5                            X0←7+ι3
Opw←27+ι3                              Address←10+ι10
Unused←5+ι2                            Page←20+ι4
Unp←24                                ∩ Drum page
                                      Track←30+ι10
```

PROGRAM 10-57   Instruction allocation in the Ferranti Mark 1.

10.4.3

Addressing

Little-Endian direct addressing.   The high-order half (left half) of a number is placed in the higher-addressed adjacent memory location, so a memory dump cannot be read as one long vector of words.   This Little-Endian approach foreshadows the DEC PDP11's (1970) "backwards byte."

```
          data←size read1 address
          ∩ Ferranti Mark 1 read from memory
          data←,memory[address+Φιsize÷half;]


          address write1 data;size
          ∩ Ferranti Mark 1 write into store
          size←ρdata
          memory[address+Φιsize÷half;]←half wide data
```

PROGRAM 10-58   Memory read and write in the Ferranti Mark 1.

Address Modification

There is no index mode; all instructions are modified to their full length by a halfword index. As an exception, the index arithmetic operations are always without address modification.

```
inst←index1 inst;index;displacement      address←adr1
ᴀ Ferranti Mark 1 instruction indexing   ᴀ Ferranti Mark 1 addressing
→If˜(fld Opcode)∈ 1 3 5 7                 address←fld Address
THEN: ᴀ index instruction
   index←reg[fld X0]
   displacement←magni inst
   inst←half magnr index+displacement
ENDIF:
```

PROGRAM 10-59   Instruction modification in the Ferranti Mark 1.

Index Arithmetic

A useful minimum of index arithmetic operations—Load, Store, Add, and Subtract—is provided without instruction modification.

```
a A   Load Index    a ADB Add To Index
a STB Store Index   a SBB Subtract From Index
```

TABLE 10-60   Index arithmetic instructions of the Ferranti Mark 1.

Index operations. All index arithmetic operations, except Store Index, set an indicator, which shows the sign of the result. They are the only operations that set an indicator.

```
SBB;subtrahend;minuend;difference        A;index
ᴀ Ferranti Mark 1 Subtract From Index    ᴀ Ferranti Mark 1 Load Index
subtrahend←radixcompi half read1 adr1    index←radixcompi half read1 adr1
minuend←reg[fld X0]                       reg[fld X0]←index
difference←minuend-subtrahend            signal1P index
reg[fld X0]←difference
signal1P difference
                                         signal1P result
                                         ᴀ Ferranti Mark 1 index result
STB                                      ind←result≥0
ᴀ Ferranti Mark 1 Store Index
adr1 write1 half radixcompr reg[fld X0]
```

PROGRAM 10-61   Index arithmetic in the Ferranti Mark 1.

10.4.4

Data

The double-length accumulator is divided into Upper and Lower halves.

Logical

Logical formats. The logical datatype uses a full word as a bit vector.

Upper	Lower	

```
0                                          40                      80
Accumulator

data1
A Ferranti Mark 1 data representation
A number allocation
 Sign←0
A accumulator allocation
 Upper←ιword
 Lower←word+ιword
```

PROGRAM 10-62   Data specification in the Ferranti Mark 1.

Fixed-Point Numbers

Notation and allocation.   Binary radix complement is used. The binary point is assumed to be between the second and third digit in the Multiply and Normalize operations. The upper accumulator is the most frequently used part of the accumulator.

10.4.5

Operations

Logic

Connectives.   The And and Exclusive Or are a meager, but sufficient set to perform all logical connectives. The MU1 had the Or as well and experimented with to-memory operations.

```
a Q    And                 a U    Arithmetic Shift
a L    Exclusive Or        a V    Normalize
a S    Population Count
```

TABLE 10-63   Logical and shift instructions of the Ferranti Mark 1.

```
Q;od
A Ferranti Mark 1 And
od←word read1 adr1
acc[Upper]←acc[Upper]∧od
```

PROGRAM 10-64   And in the Ferranti Mark 1.

Vector operations.   The number theorists at Manchester suggested the Population Count. It and the Left-Zero Count of the MU1 together provide a powerful set of operations for bit strings [Buchholz, 1962; Appendix]. In the Mark 1 the Left-Zero Count is combined with a (left or right) Shift to give Normalize as an aid to programmed floating point.

```
S;count
A Ferranti Mark 1 Population Count
count←+/word read1 adr1
acc[Upper]←word magnr count
```

PROGRAM 10-65   Population Count in the Ferranti Mark 1.

Shift.   The shift repertoire of the MU1 was minimal; only a one-bit left shift. The use of the fast Multiply into the double-length accumulator was considered sufficient. The Mark 1 has the classical full arithmetic right and left shift. The shift direction is determined by the sign of the shift amount—an important innovation.

```
V;shift
ⴰ Ferranti Mark 1 Normalize
shift←¯2+accι˜acc[0]
acc←double radixcomprↆ(radixcompi acc)×radix*shift
adrl writel half radixcompr shift


U;shift
ⴰ Ferranti Mark 1 Arithmetic Shift
shift←radixcompi inst[Address]
acc←double radixcomprↆ(radixcompi acc)×radix*shift
```

PROGRAM 10-66   Arithmetic Shift and Normalize in the Ferranti Mark 1.

Fixed-Point Arithmetic

There is no sign control and no Divide in the Mark 1.

a	P	Load Upper	a	J	Add To Upper
a	Y	Load MQ	a	N	Add To Lower
a	M	Store Upper	a	K	Subtract From Upper
a	R	Store Upper And Clear	a	X	Multiply Cumulative
			a	T	Multiply Subtractive

TABLE 10-67   Fixed-point instructions of the Ferranti Mark 1.

Load and Store.   Load and Store apply to the upper half of the accumulator. The Load Upper resets the lower half of the accumulator.

```
P
ⴰ Ferranti Mark 1 Load Upper
acc←double↑word readl adrl
```
```
M
ⴰ Ferranti Mark 1 Store Upper
adrl writel acc[Upper]
```

```
Y
ⴰ Ferranti Mark 1 Load MQ
mq←word readl adrl
```
```
R
ⴰ Ferranti Mark 1 Store Upper And Clear
adrl writel acc[Upper]
acc[]←0
```

PROGRAM 10-68   Load and Store in the Ferranti Mark 1.

Add and Subtract.   Subtract matches Add with respect to the upper accumulator, but not for the lower accumulator. Add To Lower can be used to load the lower when it follows Load Upper.

```
J;addend;augend;sum
ⴰ Ferranti Mark 1 Add To Upper
addend←radixcompi word readl adrl
augend←radixcompi acc[Upper]
sum←augend+addend
acc[Upper]←word radixcompr sum
```
```
N;addend;augend;sum
ⴰ Ferranti Mark 1 Add To Lower
addend←radixcompi word readl adrl
augend←radixcompi acc
sum←augend+addend
acc←double radixcompr sum
```

PROGRAM 10-69   Add in the Ferranti Mark 1.

Multiply.   Multiply Cumulative matches Multiply Subtractive. The mixed notation requires the 2-bit shift of the product.

```
T:multiplier;multiplicand:minuend:result
⍝ Ferranti Mark 1 Multiply Subtractive
multiplier←radixcompi word readl adr1
multiplicand←radixcompi mq
minuend←radixcompi acc
result←minuend-4×multiplicand×multiplier
acc←double radixcompr result
```

PROGRAM 10-70   Multiply in the Ferranti Mark 1.

Random.   At the suggestion of A. M. Turing, who worked at Manchester University from 1948 until his death in 1954 [Lavington, 1978], the MU1 had a Random function. It produced a random number from an oscillator, not a pseudo-random one from an algorithm. This idea proved to be a poor one for computer simulations because of debugging difficulty and was not put in the Mark 1.

The truly random function is preferable for generating cryptographic codes or running lotteries. For computer simulations, however, the pseudo-random function is much to be preferred. The ability to repeat a program exactly makes debugging much easier.

10.4.6

Instruction Sequencing

In the basic cycle, indexing is part of instruction fetch and thus precedes execution; the entire instruction, not just the address, is modified.

```
cycle1
⍝ basic cycle of the Ferranti Mark 1
REPEAT:execute ifetch1
→UNTIL stop
```

PROGRAM 10-71   Basic cycle of the Ferranti Mark 1.

The sequencing instructions of the Mark 1 are a major step toward the classical repertoire. The ability to store the instruction address (not yet in the MU1) makes the use of subroutines convenient.

```
a NOP No Operation      a E    Branch
a H   No Operation      a C    Branch On Plus
a STP Stop              a D    Branch On Minus
a Z   Stop On Switch    a I    Branch On Index Plus
                        a STA  Store Return Address
```

TABLE 10-72   Sequencing instructions of the Ferranti Mark 1.

Linear Sequence

Next instruction.   Instruction fetch includes instruction indexing with `index1` (Program 10-59). The double-length instruction has operation code 28. The second halfword is obtained from the memory location that is addressed in the first halfword. The double-length instruction is an innovation; the particular solution has not been followed in later machines.

```
inst←ifetch1
A Ferranti Mark 1 instruction fetch
inst←index1 half read1 iadr
→If 28=fld Opcode
THEN: A fetch second half
    inst←inst,half read1 adr1
ENDIF:iadr←iadr+1
```

PROGRAM 10-73   Instruction fetch in the Ferranti Mark 1.

Completion.   The absolute stop has operation code all-zero to reveal erroneous branches more readily. The conditional stop controlled by a switch is used for on-line program debugging.

```
E                             STP
A Ferranti Mark 1 Branch   A Ferranti Mark 1 Stop
  iadr←adr1                   stop←1
```

PROGRAM 10-74   Unconditional Branch and Stop in the Ferranti Mark 1.

Decision

Conditional branching.   The conditional branches are symmetric for the accumulator, but not for the index. All branches are direct and can be indexed.

```
STA
A Ferranti Mark 1 Store Instruction Address
adr1 write1 half magnr iadr
                              D
                              A Ferranti Mark 1 Branch On Minus
Z                             →If acc[Sign]
A Ferranti Mark 1 Stop On Switch   THEN:iadr←adr1
stop←stopsw                   ENDIF:
```

PROGRAM 10-75   Return and Conditional Branch in the Ferranti Mark 1.

Delegation

Subroutine return.   The next instruction address can be stored by STA. When this address is subsequently loaded in an index, a clean subroutine return can be made.

10.4.7

Input/Output

Devices

Store.   Using the drum as backing-store required that memory be divided into pages of 64 halfwords each. In the MU1 eight pages were available. As a programming convention, two pages were swapped with the drum, one-and-one-half pages were permanently resident, and one-and-one-half pages were working space. Three pages were at the discretion of the user [Campbell-Kelly, 1980b]. The Mark 1 has 12 pages.

Source and sink.   A paper-tape reader and punch, a teletypewriter, a set of input switches, and an audible hoot are available. The hoot was separately controlled on the MU1, but is combined with the stop instructions of the Mark 1.

```
b WS   Check Drum Against Page      a G    Store Switches
b WT   Check Drum Against D Page    a F    Read Tape
b WU   Drum To Page                 a PCH  Punch Tape
b WV   Drum To D Page
b WW   Page To Drum
b WX   D Page To Drum
b WY   Drum To Page And Note
b WZ   Drum To D Page And Note
Legend: D = Double.
```

TABLE 10-76   Input/output instructions of the Ferranti Mark 1.

Direct Input/Output

The paper tape and the switches are controlled by direct I/O. The drum is controlled by the double-length I/O instructions.

```
F                              G
∩ Ferranti Mark 1 Read Tape    ∩ Ferranti Mark 1 Store Switches
adr1 write1(-word)↑tape[0;]    adr1 write1 switch
tape← 1 0 ↓tape

PCH
∩ Ferranti Mark 1 Punch Tape
tape←tape⊤5↑half read1 adr1
```

PROGRAM 10-77   Tape and switch instructions in the Ferranti Mark 1.

Input/output operations.   Transfer from drum to memory and reverse can be a page or a double page at a time. When a double page has an even page

```
WS;data;check
∩ Ferranti Mark 1 Check Drum Against Page
data←memory[(page×fld Page)+ιpage;]
check←∧/,drum[fld Track;;]=data
iadr←iadr+2×check

WU;data
∩ Ferranti Mark 1 Drum To Page
data←drum[fld Track;;]
memory[(page×fld Page)+ιpage;]←data

WX;data
∩ Ferranti Mark 1 Double Page To Drum
data←memory[(page×fld Page)+ιpage;]
drum[fld Track;;]←data
inst[Page]←inst[Page]≠ 0 0 0 1
data←memory[(page×fld Page)+ιpage;]
drum[(fld Track)+1;;]←data

WY
∩ Ferranti Mark 1 Drum To Page And Note
WU
acc[half+ιhalf]←half magnr fld Track
```

PROGRAM 10-78   Drum transfer instructions in the Ferranti Mark 1.

address, an even–odd pair of successive pages is interchanged; when the page address is odd, the odd page and its predecessor are transmitted. A bit-by-bit compare instruction can check a preceding transfer—a much-needed facility. The page number on the drum (called a half-track) can be placed in the upper accumulator.

10.4.8
Implementation Notes

Speed. Multiplication time is 2.16 ms.

10.4.9
Bibliography

Ferranti, 1954. *The Manchester Universal Electronic Computer, Instructions in the Radix 32 Code.* Computer Dept., Ferranti Ltd, Morton. Courtesy, National Archive for the History of Computing, Manchester University (our defining reference).

Bowker, G. and R. Giordano, eds., 1993: "Special issue on Computing in Manchester." *IEEE Ann Hist Comput*, **15**, 3: 6–62.

Kilburn, T., 1949a: "The Manchester University Digital Computing Machine." *Report of a Conf. on High Speed Automatic Calculating Machines*, 119–22.

Kilburn, T., 1949b: "The University of Manchester High-Speed Digital Computing Machine." *Nature*, **164**: 684.

Lavington, S.H., 1978: "The Manchester Mark 1 and Atlas: A Historical Perspective." *Comm. ACM*, **21**, 1: 4–12.

Ralston, A., 1980. "Random Number Generation on the Ferranti Mark 1." *Ann Hist Comput*, **2**, 3: 270–71.

Buchholz [1962], Buckle [1978], Campbell-Kelly [1980b, 1995], Croarken [1993], Edwards et al. [1980], Kilburn [1956], Lavington [1975, 1977, 1980, 1993], Morris and Ibbett [1979], Pickstone and Bowker [1993], Williams and Kilburn [1948; 1952], Woods and Wheen [1983].

10.4.10
Exercises

10-5 What problems would you encounter if you tried to make the Mark 1 instruction set symmetric?

10-6 Assuming consistency of design, give the formal descriptions for the Mark 1

    a. Address arithmetic and logic instructions ADB, L
    b. Fixed-point arithmetic instructions K, X
    c. Sequencing instructions C, I
    d. Input/output instructions WT, WV, WW, WZ

10-7 How does the Normalize instruction distinguish an all-zero vector from an all-one vector?

10.5
Univac I

10.5.1
Highlights

History

Architects.   The Univac I was designed at Eckert-Mauchly by a team under John W. Mauchly and J. Presper Eckert, Jr. Apparently, Mauchly was the chief architect; Eckert, the chief engineer.

Dates.   The first Univac system was delivered to the National Bureau of the Census in Washington, D.C. and passed its acceptance test in March 1951 [Eckert et al., 1952].

Family tree.   Eckert and Mauchly had been major contributors to the ENIAC, built at the University of Pennsylvania's Moore School, but since ENIAC was not a stored-program machine, the Univac's architecture represents quite a fresh start. Eckert and Mauchly developed the Binac—a smaller, more specialized machine—during the same period. The Electrodata 205 (later, Burroughs 205, 210) and the IBM 650 (1954) were modeled largely on the Univac I [Stern, 1981].

Noteworthy

Characters.   The Univac is a true character machine, with no discernible substructure below the character.

Elaborate working store.   The working store has seven different locations, whose capacity ranges from one to 60 words.

Return instruction.   A Return operation used in a calling sequence inserts a subroutine's return address into a branch.

Trap.   Upon overflow, a trap to location 0 may be taken, thus allowing a standard fixup routine [Mersel, 1956].

Peculiarities

Tape input/output only.   Except for the operator keyboard and console typewriter, all I/O is handled through magnetic tapes; printer output is first placed on tape and then printed off-line from this tape.

Paired instructions.   Two instructions are placed in one word. These instructions are always executed as a pair, even when the first instruction is a Branch. Moreover, the branch target address is always taken from the second instruction. Branching can be only to the first instruction of a pair.

Minimal logic.   There are no logical connectives, but there are four shifts and a masked read operation, which yields AND if the memory values are logical.

10.5.2

Machine Language

Language Level

Design philosophy.   The Univac addresses commercial data processing, the traditional realm of punched-card accounting machines.

Unit System

The character is the basic unit; one decimal digit is represented by one character. The address size is three digits; the address capacity, 1000.

```
formatΔU                        configureΔU
⍝ Univac I information units    ⍝ configuration for the Univac I
⍝ principal radix               ⍝ memory capacity
radix←10                        memcap←adrcap
⍝ information units             ⍝ number of tape units
word←12                         tapecap←10
half←6                          ⍝ tape size
adrsize←3                       tapesize←1000
⍝ address capacity
adrcap←radix*adrsize
```

PROGRAM 10-79   Basic parameters of the Univac I.

Configuration.   The memory capacity is equal to the address capacity; 10 tape units is the maximum configuration. The tape size of 1000 is an arbitrary choice.

Spaces

Memory name-space.   The 1000 memory locations are used homogeneously and completely; there is no embedding. The name-space is cyclic.

```
spaceΔU                         array←any dim
⍝ Univac I spaces               ⍝ Univac I random array
⍝ memory                        array←charΔU[?dimρρcharΔU]
memory←any memcap,word
⍝ working store
⍝ - distributor                 ⍝ input/output
dist←any word                   ⍝ - input block
⍝ - accumulator                 in←any 60,word
acc←any word                    ⍝ - tape units
⍝ - multiplier/divisor          tape←any tapecap,tapesize,word
mq←any word                     ⍝ - tape unit switch
⍝ - extractor                   tapesw←?tapecap
f←any word                      ⍝ - tapelock
⍝ - transfer pair               lock←?tapecapρ2
v←any 2,word                    ⍝ - breakpoint switch
⍝ - transfer blockette          bps←?2
y←any 10,word                   ⍝ - branch breakpoint buttons
⍝ control store                 bpb←?11ρ2
⍝ - instruction address         ⍝ - output breakpoint switch
iadr←?adrcap                    bpo←?3
⍝ - indicators                  ⍝ - comparison light
ind←?2ρ2                        light←?2
```

PROGRAM 10-80   Spaces of the Univac I.

Working store.   The working store is one of the most elaborate for an early machine. The accumulator and MQ register are also found in the IAS design. Distinctive for the Univac are the distributor (a programmable memory-data register); an extraction register f; a register pair u, v; a register set y for a 10-word blockette; and an input buffer in for a 60-word block. Since the memory is implemented as a set of 10-word delay lines, the transfer buffers radically speed up pair and blockette moves, avoiding latency both for data fetches and instruction fetches. The distributor is a free gift from the implementation, but, since it lacks generality, later designs (except for the 650) discard it.

The function any (Program 10-80) makes a pseudo-random character array, similar to the random digit array produced by the random function ?.

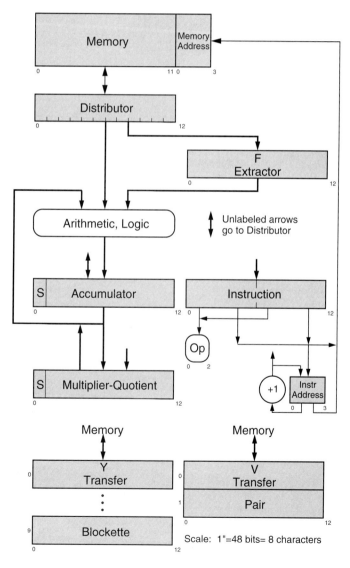

FIGURE 10-81   Programming model for the Univac I.

Control store. There are three sets of manual switches for program control and on-line debugging—there are 13 switches in all.

Programming model. The Distributor doubles as a result location in multiplication and division. Storing of register contents is quite restricted, but the Instruction Address can be stored.

Operand Specification

Number of addresses. The Univac has one-address operand specification without any special means for address modification. The address phrase is just the address field.

Operation Specification

Mnemonics. For each operation code, the character itself is used as the mnemonic. Where these characters are alphabetic, we use them in oplist. For other characters—such as semicolon, period, minus, and the digits—we use conventional mnemonics.

```
   a→                                        b→KEY
                   BPS                       b→STI
          ASR      SR                        b→STI
          ASL      SL                        b→TYP
          IR       A        J
          IRB      B        K        S
          RD       C        L        T
          RDB      D        M        U
          WR       E        N        V
          RW       F                 W
          WRL      G        P        X
          RWL      H        Q        Y
          STP               R        Z
```

PROGRAM 10-82   Operation-code list of the Univac I.

```
      ∩ logic and shift          a M    Multiply
  a E    Extract                 a P    Multiply D
  a SL   Shift Left              a N    Multiply Negative
  a SR   Shift Right             a D    Divide
  a ASL  Arithmetic Shift Left      ∩ sequencing
  a ASR  Arithmetic Shift Right  a STP  Stop
      ∩ fixed-point arithmetic   a BPS  Breakpoint Stop
  a B    Load                    a U    Branch
  a F    Load Extractor          a Q    Branch On Equal
  a L    Load MQ                 a T    Branch On Greater
  a V    Load D                  a R    Return
  a Y    Load Blockette             ∩ input/output
  a K    Load MQ And Clear       b KEY  Keyboard Input
  a H    Store                   a IR   Initial Read Tape
  a G    Store Extractor         a RD   Read Tape
  a J    Store Distributor       a IRB  Initial Read Tape Backward
  a W    Store D                 a RDB  Read Tape Backward
  a Z    Store Blockette         b STI  Store Input
  a C    Store And Clear         a WR   Write Tape
  a A    Add                     a WRL  Write Tape Low Density
  a X    Add Distributor         b TYP  Print
  a S    Subtract                a RW   Rewind Tape
                                 a RWL  Rewind Tape And Lock

Legend: D = Double.
```

TABLE 10-83   Instruction list of the Univac I.

Types of control.   The place of the two 6-character instructions in each 12-character word is identified by `Left` and `Right`.

```
control∆U
⋀ Univac I control allocation
⋀ instruction place
Left←ιhalf
Right←half+ιhalf
⋀ field allocation
instruction∆U
indicator∆U
```

PROGRAM 10-84   Control specification of the Univac I.

Instruction Structure

Machine-language syntax.   The syntactic patterns of the Univac are character patterns, not bit patterns.   There is one major pattern, with an operation code, a modifier, an unused character, and an address field.   Four separate patterns—each with modifier character 0—are recognized.

```
syntax∆U
a Opcode.Mod.Unused.Address
b '10'.Unused.Address
b '30'.Unused.Address
b '40'.Unused.Address
b '50'.Unused.Address
```

PROGRAM 10-85   Instruction syntax of the Univac I.

Instruction format.   The two halfword instructions that reside in one 12-character word are executed as a pair, as is particularly evident from the Branch instructions.   The operation code is alphanumeric; addresses are decimal digits only; the modifier is either a digit or the minus sign.

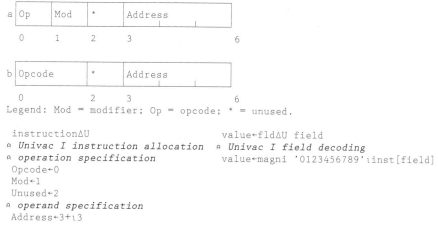

```
a | Op   | Mod  | * | Address          |
   0      1      2   3                  6

b | Opcode      | * | Address          |
   0             2   3                  6
Legend: Mod = modifier; Op = opcode; * = unused.
```

```
instruction∆U                       value←fld∆U field
⋀ Univac I instruction allocation   ⋀ Univac I field decoding
⋀ operation specification             value←magni '0123456789'ιinst[field]
Opcode←0
Mod←1
Unused←2
⋀ operand specification
Address←3+ι3
```

PROGRAM 10-86   Instruction allocation in the Univac I.

In our descriptions, the function `fld∆U` is equivalent to the general function `fld`, but applies to characters rather than digits.   The value of an

instruction field is interpreted in fldΔU by first translating the numeric characters of the field into digits and then interpreting this decimal-representation vector.

The modifier field is used to indicate a shift amount, a breakpoint selection in branches, and a tape number in I/O.

Status format.   There is a Stop indicator and a Trap indicator.

```
        indicatorΔU
      ⋒ Univac I indicators
        Stop←0
        Trap←1
```

PROGRAM 10-87   Indicators in the Univac I.

10.5.3

Addressing

Direct addressing.   The addressable unit is the 12-character word, with each byte represented in the implementation by 6 bits. Addressing is direct to any of the 1000 words.

```
    data←readΔU address              address writeΔU data
  ⋒ Univac I read from memory      ⋒ Univac I write into memory
    data←memory[address;]            memory[address;]←data
```

PROGRAM 10-88   Memory read and write in the Univac I.

Address Modification

There are no address-modification provisions.

Address calculation.   Instructions are fetched to the accumulator and modified by explicit programming, just as if they are data. Since only three-digit addresses are used, address arithmetic is cyclic modulo 1000.

Groups of two, 10, and 60 words can be moved as entities. The pairs may start at any address, but keep the same high-order address digits; for example, 123 is followed by 124, but 439 is followed by 430. For a group of 10 or 60, the low-order digit is simply ignored; for example, address 257 moves, in order, 250 through 259. This peculiarity is due to the implementation, which consisted of 10-word-long acoustic delay lines.

```
    address←adrΔU2                      address←adrΔU
  ⋒ Univac I pair addressing         ⋒ Univac I addressing
    address←(10×⌊adrΔU÷10)+10|adrΔU+ι2    address←fldΔU Address


    address←adrΔU10                     address←adrΔU60
  ⋒ Univac I blockette addressing    ⋒ Univac I block addressing
    address←(10×⌊adrΔU÷10)+ι10          address←(10×⌊adrΔU÷10)+ι60
```

PROGRAM 10-89   Addressing in the Univac I.

10.5.4

Data

The 10 decimal digits are recognized as a special subset of the characters; some operations are invalid or undefined on other characters. The minus symbol represents the negative sign, and 0 represents the plus sign.

```
dataΔU
ᴀ Univac I data representation
ᴀ character encoding              ᴀ sign encoding
charcode←charΔU                   plus←'0'
ᴀ word allocation                minus←'-'
Sign←0                            ᴀ modulus
Digits←1+ι11                      modulus←radix*0⊥ρDigits
```

PROGRAM 10-90   Data specification in the Univac I.

Character Strings

Character set and size.   The 64 character codes are almost fully used. The characters shown are defined for the unityper (Univac typewriter output) and differ slightly for the off-line devices.

```
┌─────────────────────────────────────────────────────────────────────────┐
│ Char   Char   Char   Char   Char   Char   Char   Char   Char   Char   Char   Char │
│     |      |      |      |      |      |      |      |      |      |      |        │
└─────────────────────────────────────────────────────────────────────────┘
 0                                                                        12
Legend: Char = character.

irtz   Legend:
Δ,"b   i = space
-.|:   Δ = space
0;)+   r = carriage return
1AJ/   t = tab
2BKS   z = stop
3CLT   b = breakpoint (typewriter stop).
4DMU
5ENV
6FOW
7GPX
8HQY
9IRZ
'#$%
&c*=
(@?
```

PROGRAM 10-91   Character set and format in the Univac I.

Character-string formats.   A word can contain 12 characters, but there are no specific data-handling operations, except for Compare, which correctly orders alphanumeric words.

Fixed-Point Numbers

Notation and allocation.   Negative numbers are represented with signed-magnitude notation. Decimal digits are encoded in 6 bits with the excess-three

code; the left two code bits are 0 on writing and are often ignored on reading. This encoding is invisible to the programmer.

Our interpretation and representation functions convert the 12 characters of a word to a number, and vice versa. When the representation part of an operation overflows, a trap to memory location 000 is taken. If the modifier character of the current instruction is minus, the computer stops prior to the trap.

Sign	Digits										

0   1   12

```
number←integerΔUi rep
ⲁ Univac I integer interpretation
number← 1 ‾1[rep[Sign]=minus]×magni '0123456789'⍳rep[Digits]
```

```
rep←integerΔUr number;digits
ⲁ Univac I integer representation
digits←(ρDigits) magnr|number
rep←(plus,minus)[number<0],'0123456789'[digits]
Trap report modulus≤|number
Stop report(minus≠inst[Mod])∧ind[Trap]
```

PROGRAM 10-92   Fixed-point number in the Univac I.

10.5.5

Operations

Logic

Masked selection.   The Extract instruction uses the content of the extractor location f to specify selected characters from a word in memory to replace corresponding accumulator characters; the others are left unchanged, a first step toward format transformation.

```
E;select                        bit←n parity char;radix;nr
ⲁ Univac I Extract              ⲁ character code parity
select←(6 parity f)/⍳word       nr←charcode⍳char WHERE radix←2
acc[select]←(readΔU adrΔU)[select]    bit←2|+/n magnr nr
```

PROGRAM 10-93   Extract in the Univac I.

Arithmetic shift.   The arithmetic shift leaves the sign unchanged. The modifier indicates the shift amount, which must be 1 through 9 for the right shift; otherwise, the accumulator is cleared and the machine stops. The left shift may be zero, which constitutes a Noop; in particular, the all-zeros halfword is convenient as a Noop, and the operation-code character of ASL is "0."

Logical shift.   All characters, including the sign, are shifted. Again, the modifier must be 1 through 9.

```
ASL;shift;rl                           ASR;shift;rl
ᴀ Univac I Arithmetic Shift Left       ᴀ Univac I Arithmetic Shift Right
shift←fldΔU Mod                         shift←fldΔU Mod
→IF shift≤9                            →IF(shift>0)∧shift≤9
THEN: ᴀ shift 0 through 9              THEN: ᴀ shift 1 through 9
   rl←shift↓acc[Digits],shiftρ'0'         rl←(shiftρ'0'),(-shift)↓acc[Digits]
   acc[Digits]←rl                         acc[Digits]←rl
   →ENDIF                                 →ENDIF
ELSE: ᴀ clear and stop                 ELSE: ᴀ clear and stop
   acc[]←'0'                              acc[]←'0'
   Stop report 1                         Stop report 1
ENDIF:                                 ENDIF:
```

PROGRAM 10-94   Arithmetic Shift in the Univac I.

```
SL;shift                               SR;shift
ᴀ Univac I Shift Left                  ᴀ Univac I Shift Right
shift←fldΔU Mod                         shift←fldΔU Mod
→IF(shift>0)∧shift≤9                   →IF(shift>0)∧shift≤9
THEN: ᴀ shift 1 through 9              THEN: ᴀ shift 1 through 9
   acc←shift↓acc,shiftρ'0'               acc←(shiftρ'0'),(-shift)↓acc
   →ENDIF                                 →ENDIF
ELSE: ᴀ clear and stop                 ELSE: ᴀ clear and stop
   acc[]←'0'                              acc[]←'0'
   Stop report 1                         Stop report 1
ENDIF:                                 ENDIF:
```

PROGRAM 10-95   Logical Shift in the Univac I.

Fixed-Point Arithmetic

Since data movement occurs via working-store locations, there are many Load and Store instructions. There is no sign control on loading; no Negate or Make Absolute.

```
a B   Load                  a Z   Store Blockette
a F   Load Extractor        a C   Store And Clear
a L   Load MQ               a A   Add
a V   Load D                a X   Add Distributor
a Y   Load Blockette        a S   Subtract
a K   Load MQ And Clear     a M   Multiply
a H   Store                 a P   Multiply D
a G   Store Extractor       a N   Multiply Negative
a J   Store Distributor     a D   Divide
a W   Store D
Legend: D = Double.
```

TABLE 10-96   Fixed-point instructions of the Univac I.

Load and Store.   The distributor is automatically loaded as part of loading the accumulator and MQ register; it does not participate in the double and blockette loads. There is no Store MQ.

C and K place the accumulator content in memory or in the MQ, then clear the accumulator. V, Y, and the other loads and stores from the two-word and 10-word registers use their peculiar cyclic-address functions. Loading the input block occurs from tape only; there is no operation.

Add and Subtract.   Add and Subtract follow the classical pattern. No conditions are set, but positive or negative overflow causes a trap, as shown

```
B                                  Y
ค Univac I Load                    ค Univac I Load Blockette
  dist←readΔU adrΔU                  y←readΔU adrΔU10
  acc←dist


                                   K
F                                  ค Univac I Load MQ And Clear
ค Univac I Load Extractor            mq←acc
  f←readΔU adrΔU                      acc[]←'0'



L                                  C
ค Univac I Load MQ                 ค Univac I Store And Clear
  dist←readΔU adrΔU                  adrΔU writeΔU acc
  mq←dist                            acc[]←'0'



V                                  J
ค Univac I Load Double             ค Univac I Store Distributor
  v←readΔU adrΔU2                    adrΔU writeΔU dist
```

PROGRAM 10-97   Load and Store in the Univac I.

in the representation function. Add Distributor is like Add but does not read from memory; the distributor contents are added to the accumulator. Since the memory is serial, Add Distributor is five times as fast as Add, on the average.

Subtract changes the sign of the addend by inverting the low-order character bit of the sign; this operation is equivalent to taking the neighbor of an odd–even pair of the character set. This peculiar behavior is encapsulated in the function neg ΔU. For ordinary sign characters, things work as one would expect. There is no invalidity policing on sign characters.

```
A;addend;augend;sum          S;addend;augend;sum
ค Univac I Add                ค Univac I Subtract
  dist←readΔU adrΔU             dist←negΔU readΔU adrΔU
  addend←integerΔUi dist       addend←integerΔUi dist
  augend←integerΔUi acc        augend←integerΔUi acc
  sum←augend+addend            sum←augend+addend
  acc←integerΔUr sum           acc←integerΔUr sum


  rl←negΔU od
ค Univac I negate
  rl←charΔU[(,Φ 32 2 ρcharΔU)ιod[Sign]],od[Digits]
```

PROGRAM 10-98   Add and Subtract in the Univac I.

Multiply and Divide.   Multiplication shows that numbers are treated as fractions. The double-length product is placed in the accumulator and distributor. The extractor is used during multiplication and is unpredictable after the operation; after the single-length Multiply, the distributor is unpredictable also.

Divide produces both a rounded and unrounded quotient, but no remainder.

Compare.   Comparison is between the accumulator and the MQ register. The operation is combined with branching and is shown as part of those instructions.

```
M;multiplier;multiplicand;product
A Univac I Multiply
multiplier←integerΔUi mq
dist←readΔU adrΔU
multiplicand←integerΔUi dist
product←multiplicand×multiplier
acc←integerΔUr round product÷modulus
f←any word
dist←any word


P;multiplier;multiplicand;product
A Univac I Multiply Double
multiplier←integerΔUi mq
multiplicand←integerΔUi readΔU adrΔU
product←multiplicand×multiplier
acc←integerΔUr truncate product÷modulus
dist←integerΔUr(×product)×modulus||product
f←any word


D;divisor;dividend;quotient
A Univac I Divide
divisor←integerΔUi mq
dividend←integerΔUi readΔU adrΔU
quotient←dividend÷divisor+divisor=0
acc←integerΔUr round quotient×modulus
dist←integerΔUr truncate quotient×modulus
```

PROGRAM 10-99   Multiply and Divide in the Univac I.

10.5.6

Instruction Sequencing

The basic cycle treats instructions as a pair. An arithmetic overflow causes a
trap to location 0. The Stop indicator causes the processor to stop.

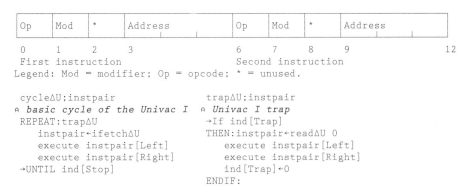

```
| Op | Mod | * | Address | Op | Mod | * | Address |

0    1     2   3          6    7     8   9           12
First instruction              Second instruction
Legend: Mod = modifier; Op = opcode; * = unused.

cycleΔU;instpair              trapΔU;instpair
A basic cycle of the Univac I A Univac I trap
REPEAT:trapΔU                 →If ind[Trap]
   instpair←ifetchΔU          THEN:instpair←readΔU 0
   execute instpair[Left]        execute instpair[Left]
   execute instpair[Right]       execute instpair[Right]
→UNTIL ind[Stop]                 ind[Trap]←0
                              ENDIF:
```

PROGRAM 10-100   Basic cycle of the Univac I.

Sequencing instructions.   We show all sequencing instructions in detail.

Linear Sequence

Next instruction.   Normal sequential execution is under control of the
instruction address. Instructions are fetched two at a time; the left is executed
first. Since halfwords are not addressable, branching can be only to a left

instruction. The zone bits of an instruction are only retained for the opcode character.

```
inst←ifetchΔU                    inst←dropzoneΔU inst;drop
ᴀ Univac I instruction fetch     ᴀ Univac I drop instruction zone bits
inst←dropzoneΔU readΔU iadr       drop←(1+ι5),7+ι5
iadr←adrcap|iadr+1                inst[drop]←charΔU[16|charΔUιinst[drop]]
```

PROGRAM 10-101   Instruction fetch in the Univac I.

The instruction pair is completely executed before a new pair is fetched. A branch specified in a left instruction is effected after the right instruction is executed, and the address in the right instruction not only specifies the operand of that instruction, but also becomes the branch target. Any test specified in a left instruction is done before the right instruction is executed.

```
U                    address←targetΔU;inst
ᴀ Univac I Branch    ᴀ Univac I branch target
iadr←targetΔU        inst←instpair[Right]
                     address←fldΔU Address
```

PROGRAM 10-102   Unconditional Branch in the Univac I.

Completion.   The Stop indicator is set by the Unconditional Stop instruction, upon overflow; by the Breakpoint Stop, when the corresponding switches are set; and by Conditional Branch, when the specified breakpoint buttons are set (a tracing facility).

```
STP                    BPS
ᴀ Univac I Stop        ᴀ Univac I Breakpoint Stop
Stop report 1          Stop report bps
```

PROGRAM 10-103   Stop in the Univac I.

Decision

Conditional branching.   The type of conditional branch is specified in the operation code. The condition is volatile; it is produced by a comparison and is used immediately in the branch decision. The conditions are not symmetric.

```
Q                                  T
ᴀ Univac I Branch On Equal         ᴀ Univac I Branch On Greater
Stop report bpb[10,fldΔU Mod]      Stop report bpb[10,fldΔU Mod]
→If∧/acc=mq                        →If(integerΔUi acc)>integerΔUi mq
THEN:iadr←targetΔU                 THEN:iadr←targetΔU
    light←1                        ENDIF:
ENDIF:
```

PROGRAM 10-104   Conditional Branch in the Univac I.

Delegation

Return.   Return inserts the updated instruction address into a Noop and Unconditional Branch instruction pair, which it then stores in memory. Return is used as a left instruction preceding a Branch to form a subroutine link.

```
R
ᴀ Univac I Return
adrΔU writeΔU '000000U00','0123456789'[adrsize magnr iadr]
```

PROGRAM 10-105   Return in the Univac I.

10.5.7
Supervision

Control Switching

The trapping of the arithmetic operations for overflow constitutes a primitive interruption system.

10.5.8
Input/Output

Devices

Source and sink.   Except for the console switches and a console typewriter, there are only tape drives—up to 10 of them. All other I/O is off-line.

b KEY Keyboard Input	a WR Write Tape	
a IR Initial Read Tape	a WRL Write Tape Low Density	
a RD Read Tape	b TYP Print	
a IRB Initial Read Tape Backward	a RW Rewind Tape	
a RDB Read Tape Backward	a RWL Rewind Tape And Lock	
b STI Store Input		

TABLE 10-106   Input/output instructions of the Univac I.

Overlapped Input/Output

One input and one output can proceed concurrently with each other and with CPU operation. After the 60-word input buffer is initially primed by reading one block from a tape drive, each successive input operation transfers one 60-word block to main memory. The CPU proceeds, while the buffer refills by reading the next block from tape.

An output operation transfers from memory to buffer, after which the CPU proceeds. The buffer then empties by writing a tape block. The output buffer is invisible to the user.

Read and Write.   Tape reading is into the buffer in with Initial Read Tape followed by one or more plain Reads.

TYP Types a word from memory, then stops if the breakpoint switch is on. KEY stops the computer, which resumes after a word is entered from the keyboard.

Sense and Control.   Control functions are not separate from reading and writing, except for tape rewinding. There are two types of Write, differing in density, and three types of Read, differing in direction and buffering. Read Backward saves rewinding during tape sorting.

```
IR;n                                WR;n
ᴀ Univac I Initial Read Tape        ᴀ Univac I Write Tape
n←unitΔU                            n←unitΔU
→OUT n≥tapecap                      →OUT n≥tapecap
in←tape[n;ι60;]                     →If lock[n]=0
tape[n;;]←60Θtape[n;;]              THEN:tape[n;ι60;]←readΔU adrΔU60
                                        tape[n;;]←60Θtape[n;;]
                                    ENDIF:
RD;n
ᴀ Univac I Read Tape
n←unitΔU                            n←unitΔU
→OUT n≥tapecap                      ᴀ Univac tape unit selection
adrΔU60 writeΔU in                  →IF inst[Mod]='Δ'
in←tape[n;ι60;]                     THEN: ᴀ selection by switch
tape[n;;]←60Θtape[n;;]                 n←tapesw
                                        →ENDIF
                                    ELSE: ᴀ programmed selection
STI                                    n←'-123456789'ιinst[Mod]
ᴀ Univac I Store Input              ENDIF:Stop report n≥tapecap
adrΔU60 writeΔU in
in[;]←'0'
```

PROGRAM 10-107   Input/output Read and Write in the Univac I.

10.5.9
Implementation Notes

Operation is serial by character and bit using mercury delay lines 10 words long, which explains the 10-word transfer buffer Y. Instructions cannot be refetched in fewer than 10 word times, so a 10-word memory-to-memory transfer programmed as a loop takes about 180 word times. The buffer does this transfer in about 20 word times. The accumulator-MQ is in a two-word–long delay line, so the register V gives zero-latency access to the A, L pair.

Speed. Add is 0.5 ms; Multiply, 2 ms; and Divide, 4 ms.

10.5.10
Bibliography

Esch, R. and P. Calingaert, 1957: *Univac I, Central Computer Programming*. Cambridge, MA: Harvard University Computation Laboratory (our defining reference).

Eckert et al. [1952], Mersel [1956], Stern [1981].

10.5.11
Exercises

10-8 Assuming consistency of design, give the formal descriptions for the Univac instructions H, G, W, Z, X, and N.

11

Von Neumann House

Von Neumann's Contribution

The issues of priority, contribution, and influence in the formation of the conceptual structure of the automatic computer have been debated and litigated at length. It is clear that Babbage was first, by a century. Not much else is indisputable.

Regardless of who had what idea when, the 1946 paper by Burks, Goldstine, and von Neumann, "Preliminary Discussion of the Logical Design of an Electronic Computing Instrument," certainly crystallized much of the extant thinking and galvanized many research groups into attempts to build electronic computers. In the event, it was the single most influential document; it constituted the beginning of computer science. Wilkes says of his midnight reading of a draft, "I recognized this at once as the real thing, and from that time on never had any doubt about the way computer development would go" [Wilkes, 1985].

It seems clear that the principal author of the document was John von Neumann, even though the ideas came from several people, including especially Eckert and Mauchly. Hence, the term *von Neumann computer* has come into widespread use. It is often used pejoratively, but this use scarcely does justice to the document's substantial contribution.

A von Neumann computer is commonly defined loosely as a computer that sequentially (architecturally, at least) executes a single stream of instructions. A *non–von Neumann computer*, then, is one that has concurrent processes. By convention, I/O concurrency does not count, so the IBM System/360 (1965), with concurrent channel programs, is a von Neumann computer. The CDC 6600 (1964), with 10 peripheral processors and one CPU, is a debatable case under this loose definition.

Using a sharper definition, we include, in the von Neumann *house*, computers having the salient features proposed in the "Preliminary Discussion" paper:

- Single stream of instructions sequenced by an instruction counter
- Instructions stored with data in an addressable memory
- Instructions encoded as numbers, so modifiable by arithmetic operations

- Radix two
- Word length long enough for scientific computing
- Single-address, single-operation instructions
- Single accumulator with a multiplier-quotient register

These features serve as the foundation for the classical computer, but they are by no means the complete set. Rather, the history of the von Neumann house shows that it was necessary to add features, such as indexing, logic, registers, and floating point, to obtain an efficient computer.

Bibliography

Atanasoff [1940], Burks et al. [1946], von Neumann [1943, 1963], Wilkes [1985].

11.1
Princeton IAS

11.1.1
Highlights

History

We start with the complete Princeton IAS design as published in [Burks et al., 1946], even though the IAS was not built exactly as described.

Dates.   Part I, the most often quoted paper, is dated June 28, 1946. Of Part II, Volume 1 is dated April 1, 1947; Volume 2, April 15, 1948; and Volume 3, August 16, 1948. Volume 4 of Part II was announced in Volume 3, but apparently it was never published. Part II deals primarily with programming, but contains some changes to the original proposal. We describe the original design, but note the later changes.

Six years after the publication of the first IAS paper, Bigelow completed the IAS computer at the Institute of Advanced Study, and the Moore School of Electrical Engineering at the University of Pennsylvania completed the EDVAC, based on the IAS concepts.

Family tree.   The IAS design inspired the designs of many other computers. We describe in this Zoo the Cambridge EDSAC (1949) and the IBM 701 (1953). Some others were the Los Alamos Maniac (1952), the University of Illinois Illiac (1952), the Ordvac (1952), the MIT Whirlwind (1953), the Rand Corporation Johnniac (1954), the Stockholm Besk (1954), and the Amsterdam Mathematical Centre Arra (1954). The Manchester Ferranti Mark 1 (1951) and Univac I (1951), although influenced by the IAS, are nevertheless pioneering efforts of their own; we place them in the Pioneer House (Chapter 10).

Unfortunately, all IAS-type machines were different, so programs were not interchangeable.

Noteworthy

Stored program.   By uniting the instruction and the data store into one memory, the IAS solved the most bothersome programming problem of early computers: addressing elements within an array. But this solution was almost immediately made obsolete by Kilburn's invention of address modification through indexing. The basic ability to treat instructions as data, however, remained; it cleared the way for programming languages.

Consistency.   The IAS design excels through consistency. To be sure, some of this consistency is the result of omitting necessary functions, such as logic and I/O, as well as of ignoring bit efficiency. Nevertheless, the design is strikingly clean and thorough. Furthermore, this consistency is not accidental: Von Neumann explicitly emphasized it.

In a sense, the IAS design also exemplifies the difficulties encountered in achieving consistency: the allocation of incommensurate objects and pressures from the implementation. (See the following comments on *rounding*.)

Incommensurate units. The key architectural problem of the von Neumann design is the incommensurateness of its data and instructions—exactly the two items one would like to treat alike in the stored-program design. The IAS design solves this problem by using 40 bits for all data and 20 bits for all instructions, with addressing resolution always 40 bits. The cost of this solution is a Left and Right version of Branch and of Store Address. Most other members of the house choose to gain bit efficiency by having halfword data—at the expense of complication.

Load.   A small example of clean design is the Load instruction. We might overlook it as obvious, but no design tradition had been established at this point; the EDSAC is an example of a less clean alternative: It has no Load, but combines clearing with storing.

Peculiarities

No logic.   Having no logic also means having no logical shift. Logic emerges only slowly in the von Neumann house (another contrast with Kilburn's Manchester design). The arithmetic shifts are accurately called Multiply By Two and Divide By Two, deemphasizing their shifting property.

No integers.   All numbers are treated as fractions; even such obvious integers as addresses are left-aligned in the instruction.

No multiple lengths.   Product and dividend are single-length data—a defensible decision.

Rounding.   As an outstanding numerical analyst, von Neumann was fully aware of the rounding problem, and he treated it thoroughly. The product is a rounded high-order fraction with the remainder of the product placed in the MQ.

For the quotient, however, von Neumann used "making odd" to simplify the implementation. He said that "this occasionally produces results with unfamiliar and even annoying aspects (e.g., when quotients like $0 \div y$ or $y \div y$ are formed), but it is nevertheless unobjectionable and self-consistent on the basis of our general principles" [Burks et al., 1946].

Address capacity.   The address capacity is large for its time; it could even have been four times larger by using two spare instruction bits. Interestingly enough, other members of the house have smaller word and address sizes. At that time, reliable memory implementation was the first concern; the need for a large memory was less urgent.

No input/output.   The omission of a design for the I/O mechanism is conscious; the need for I/O is mentioned in the IAS paper, but the paper leaves that problem to be solved later.

11.1.2

Machine Language

Language Level

Design philosophy.   The IAS design is aimed at scientific and engineering computation.   Floating point was considered, but von Neumann and his collaborators deemed programmed scaling to be more amenable to error analysis, and therefore better for the programmer.

```
            initiateΔIAS
          ⍝ initiation of the Princeton IAS
            formatΔIAS
            configureΔIAS
            spaceΔIAS
            instructionΔIAS
            dataΔIAS
```

PROGRAM 11-1   Initiation of the Princeton IAS.

The only control information is the instruction; the IAS has no indicators.

```
 formatΔIAS                          configureΔIAS
⍝ Princeton IAS information units   ⍝ configuration for the Princeton IAS
⍝ representation radix              ⍝ memory capacity
 radix←2                             memcap←adrcap
⍝ information units
 half←20
 word←40
 adrsize←12
⍝ address capacity
 adrcap←radix*adrsize
```

PROGRAM 11-2   Basic parameters of the Princeton IAS.

Spaces

Memory name-space.   Memory is homogeneous throughout its 4096 words; there is no embedding. We assume a configuration with the full addressing capacity populated.

```
            spaceΔIAS
          ⍝ Princeton IAS spaces
          ⍝ memory
            memory←?(memcap,word)ρradix
          ⍝ working store              ⍝ control store
          ⍝ - accumulator              ⍝ - instruction address
            acc←?wordρradix              iadr←0.5×?2×adrcap
          ⍝ - multiplier/quotient      ⍝ - stopped state
            mq←?wordρradix               stop←?radix
```

PROGRAM 11-3   Spaces of the Princeton IAS.

Working store.   Working store has two identical registers called A and R, or AR; for uniformity we use `acc` and `mq`.

Control store.   The instruction address is treated as an integer, with or without a fraction of one-half. The only other control state is the stopped state.

Programming model.   The IAS model epitomizes the von Neumann design. Notice the inability to save the Instruction Address.

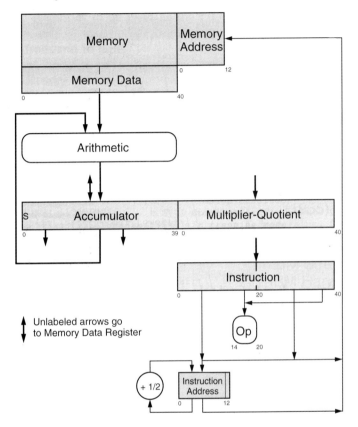

FIGURE 11-4   Programming model for the Princeton IAS.

Operand Specification

Number of addresses.   Instructions are uniformly one-address, with a single simple address field as the address phrase.

Operation Specification

The 22 operations are more or less classical, with the exception of the rounding in Multiply. Only 22 of the 64 codes are used. The coding, represented by position in Program 11-5, follows the numbering in the IAS paper. The mnemonics are our own.

```
a→        SA     BCR
   L      LMQ    ST
   LN     AMQ    SAL
   LA     MPY    SAR
   LNA    DIV    ASL
   A      BL     ASR
   S      BR     STP
   AA     BCL
```

PROGRAM 11-5   Operation-code list of the Princeton IAS.

```
  ∩ address arithmetic       a A    Add
a SAL Store Address Left      a AA   Add Absolute
a SAR Store Address Right     a S    Subtract
  ∩ logic and shift           a SA   Subtract Absolute
a ASL Shift Arithmetic Left   a MPY  Multiply
a ASR Shift Arithmetic Right  a DIV  Divide
  ∩ fixed-point arithmetic      ∩ sequencing
a L   Load                    a STP  Stop
a LMQ Load MQ                 a BL   Branch Left
a AMQ Load from MQ            a BR   Branch Right
a ST  Store                   a BCL  Branch Conditional Left
a LN  Negate                  a BCR  Branch Conditional Right
a LA  Make Absolute
a LNA Negate Absolute
```

TABLE 11-6   Instruction list of the Princeton IAS.

Instruction Structure

Instruction format.   There is only one format, so only one syntactic pattern.

```
        syntaxΔIAS
     a Address.Unused.Opcode
```

PROGRAM 11-7   Instruction syntax of the Princeton IAS.

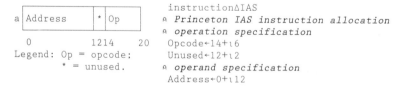

```
a Address    * Op
  0        1214   20
  Legend: Op = opcode;
         * = unused.
```

```
instructionΔIAS
∩ Princeton IAS instruction allocation
∩ operation specification
  Opcode←14+ι6
  Unused←12+ι2
∩ operand specification
  Address←0+ι12
```

PROGRAM 11-8   Instruction allocation in the Princeton IAS.

11.1.3
Addressing

Direct addressing.   Memory access follows the simplest paradigm.

```
data←readΔIAS address              address writeΔIAS data
 ⍝ Princeton IAS read from memory   ⍝ Princeton IAS write into memory
data←memory[address;]              memory[address;]←data
```

PROGRAM 11-9   Memory read and write in the Princeton IAS.

Address Modification

There is no explicit address modification.

```
address←adrΔIAS
 ⍝ Princeton IAS addressing
address←fld Address
```

PROGRAM 11-10   Addressing in the Princeton IAS.

Address calculation.   Two Store Address instructions (into the left and right halfwords) greatly ease address calculation, but still cannot compete with indexing. The address field is leftmost in the accumulator.

```
SAL;od                                  SAR;od
 ⍝ Princeton IAS Store Address Left      ⍝ Princeton IAS Store Address Right
od←readΔIAS adrΔIAS                      od←readΔIAS adrΔIAS
od[Address]←acc[Address]                od[half+Address]←acc[Address]
adrΔIAS writeΔIAS od                    adrΔIAS writeΔIAS od
```

PROGRAM 11-11   Store Address in the Princeton IAS.

11.1.4
Data

The only datatype is the fixed-point number.

Fixed-Point Numbers

Notation and allocation.   Binary, with radix complement, is the ideal choice. Many contemporary designers made different choices; almost all today's designs agree with the IAS.

```
┌──────────────────────────────────────────┐
│ Digits                                    │
│                                           │
└──────────────────────────────────────────┘
  0                                      40

dataΔIAS
 ⍝ Princeton IAS data representation
 ⍝ modulus
modulus←radix*word-1
```

PROGRAM 11-12   Fixed-point number in the Princeton IAS.

Numbers were considered fractions, something that shows only in Multiply, Divide, and—strangely—Store Address. The change of Part II, Volume 2, places the address field rightmost in the instruction and the source field of Store Address rightmost in the accumulator—a deliberate step toward integers.

11.1.5

Operations
Logic

Shift. There are no logical connectives. The two shifts were initially classified as Multiply By Two and Divide By Two (Program 11-13). But Part II, Volume 1, changes the left shift to an end-around shift, so that the high-order non-sign digit from the accumulator enters the low-order position of the MQ, the accumulator sign remains unchanged, the MQ shifts logically one place to the left, and zero shifts into the accumulator.

```
ASL;operand
 ⍝ Princeton IAS Shift Arithmetic Left
 operand←radixcompi acc
 acc←word radixcompr operand×2


ASR;operand
 ⍝ Princeton IAS Shift Arithmetic Right
 operand←radixcompi acc
 acc←word radixcompr⌊operand÷2
```

PROGRAM 11-13   Arithmetic Shift in the Princeton IAS.

Fixed-Point Arithmetic

Load and Store.   Load and Add include sign control, with Negate and Absolute Value as orthogonal options. The design is inconsistent in omitting Store MQ.

```
L                               LN;operand
 ⍝ Princeton IAS Load            ⍝ Princeton IAS Negate
 acc←readΔIAS fld Address         operand←radixcompi readΔIAS adrΔIAS
                                  acc←word radixcompr-operand


LMQ
 ⍝ Princeton IAS Load MQ         LA;operand
 mq←readΔIAS adrΔIAS              ⍝ Princeton IAS Make Absolute
                                  operand←radixcompi readΔIAS adrΔIAS
                                  acc←word radixcompr|operand

AMQ
 ⍝ Princeton IAS Load from MQ
 acc←mq                          LNA;operand
                                  ⍝ Princeton IAS Negate Absolute
                                  operand←radixcompi readΔIAS adrΔIAS
ST                               acc←word radixcompr-|operand
 ⍝ Princeton IAS Store
 adrΔIAS writeΔIAS acc
```

PROGRAM 11-14   Load and Store in the Princeton IAS.

Add and Subtract.   The description paper makes no mention of overflow in Add (or in Subtract, Make Absolute, or Negate). Scaling is a programming responsibility, and lost high-order digits are to be detected by programmed checking.

Extended-precision addition is to be programmed by splitting the number into a signed high-order part and one or more unsigned (positive) 39-bit low-order parts. During addition, these parts are checked for positive sign. Von Neumann was apparently well-aware of the decisive advantage of radix-complement notation for extended-precision arithmetic.

```
A;addend;augend;sum
ᴀ Princeton IAS Add
addend←radixcompi readΔIAS adrΔIAS
augend←radixcompi acc
sum←augend+addend
acc←word radixcompr sum


AA;addend;augend;sum
ᴀ Princeton IAS Add Absolute
addend←radixcompi readΔIAS adrΔIAS
augend←radixcompi acc
sum←augend+|addend
acc←word radixcompr sum


S;subtrahend;minuend;difference
ᴀ Princeton IAS Subtract
subtrahend←radixcompi readΔIAS adrΔIAS
minuend←radixcompi acc
difference←minuend-subtrahend
acc←word radixcompr difference


SA;subtrahend;minuend;difference
ᴀ Princeton IAS Subtract Absolute
subtrahend←radixcompi readΔIAS adrΔIAS
minuend←radixcompi acc
difference←minuend-|subtrahend
acc←word radixcompr difference
```

PROGRAM 11-15   Add and Subtract in the Princeton IAS.

Multiply.   Multiply gives a rounded high-order product in the accumulator and the signed remainder of the product in the MQ (as clarified in Part I). Von Neumann decided against cumulative multiplication because its traditional implementation treats numbers as integers, not as fractions. (But compare the IAS with the EDSAC and the MU1.)

```
MPY;multiplier;multiplicand;product
ᴀ Princeton IAS Multiply
multiplier←radixcompi readΔIAS adrΔIAS
multiplicand←radixcompi mq
product←multiplicand×multiplier
acc←word radixcompr round product÷modulus
mq←word radixcompr product-modulus×radixcompi acc
```

PROGRAM 11-16   Multiply in the Princeton IAS.

Divide.   The IAS paper gives the non-restoring division algorithm as the implementation of Divide. Only the iterative step and a final quotient correction are used. Without further provisions, the quotient is always odd, which is indeed the intention, since "making odd" is proposed as the precision treatment. So a zero dividend divided by a positive divisor gives as quotient 1 and as remainder the negative of the divisor! The IBM NORC (1954) also uses "making odd," but omits that action when the fractional part of the number to be rounded is zero.

```
DIV;divisor;dividend;quotient;remainder
ᴀ Princeton IAS Divide
divisor←radixcompi readΔIAS adrΔIAS
dividend←radixcompi acc
→IF divisor≠0
THEN:quotient←⌊dividend÷divisor
    mq←word radixcompr quotient+⁻2|quotient
    remainder←dividend-divisor×radixcompi mq
    acc←word radixcompr remainder
    →ENDIF
ELSE:mq←(1↑acc),(⁻1↓⁻1↓acc),1
    acc←word↑⁻1↑acc
ENDIF:
```

PROGRAM 11-17   Divide in the Princeton IAS.

Division by zero is allowed, but gives a meaningless result. It gives no warning.

11.1.6

Instruction Sequencing

The basic cycle continues fetching instructions until a Stop instruction occurs.

```
cycleΔIAS
ᴀ basic cycle of the Princeton IAS
REPEAT:execute ifetchΔIAS
→UNTIL stop
```

PROGRAM 11-18   Basic cycle of the Princeton IAS.

Linear Sequence

Next instruction.   Instruction fetch obtains an instruction pair and uses either the left or right half thereof, depending upon the fractional part of the instruction address. The memory name-space is cyclic.

```
inst←ifetchΔIAS;instpair
ᴀ Princeton IAS instruction fetch
instpair←half wide readΔIASⱢiadr
inst←instpair[0.5=1|iadr;]
iadr←adrcap|iadr+0.5
```

PROGRAM 11-19   Instruction fetch in the Princeton IAS.

Unconditional Branch.   The operation code effectively extends the branch address to the halfword resolution.

```
BL                                  BR
ⴰ Princeton IAS Branch Left    ⴰ Princeton IAS Branch Right
iadr←adrΔIAS                        iadr←adrΔIAS+0.5
```

PROGRAM 11-20   Unconditional Branch in the Princeton IAS.

Completion.   The only stop is the plain programmed Stop.

```
STP
ⴰ Princeton IAS Stop
stop←1
```

PROGRAM 11-21   Stop in the Princeton IAS.

Decision

Conditional branching.   The only branch condition is the accumulator sign. Testing for positive or zero and not for negative violates generality.

```
BCL                                 BCR
ⴰ Princeton IAS Branch Left on Plus  ⴰ Princeton IAS Branch Right on Plus
→If 0≤radixcompi acc                 →If 0≤radixcompi acc
THEN:iadr←adrΔIAS                    THEN:iadr←adrΔIAS+0.5
ENDIF:                              ENDIF:
```

PROGRAM 11-22   Conditional Branch in the Princeton IAS.

11.1.7
Input/Output

No provision for transferring data in or out is prescribed; that is left to be designed by the implementer.

Devices

Backing store.   The paper [Burks, 1946] mentions several magnetic-wire storage units.

Source and sink.   The paper also mentions the desirability of viewing tubes for graphical display of results and a typewriter for feeding data directly into the computer. It envisages off-line transfer from the magnetic-wire units to a Teletype printer.

11.1.8
Implementation Notes

The IAS paper proposes the Selectron—a specialized cathode-ray device—as the storage medium.

11.1.9
Bibliography

Burks, A.W., H.H. Goldstine, and J. von Neumann, 1946: "Preliminary Discussion of the Logical Design of an Electronic Computing Instrument." Report to U.S. Army Ordnance Department. Also in A.H. Taub, ed., *Collected Works of John von Neumann*. New York: Macmillan, 1963; **5**: 34–79. Reprinted in Bell and Newell [1971], 92–119 (our defining reference).

Everett [1952], Metropolis and Worlton [1980], Metropolis et al. [1980], von Neumann [1963, 1993].

11.1.10
Exercises

11-1 Describe how you would generalize the two IAS shift operations. Give a formal description.

11-2 Design an alternative to the IAS Divide. Give the formal description. Briefly defend your design choices, taking into account von Neumann's arguments.

11-3 Extend the IAS operations in a consistent manner to include Square Root; give the formal description and state the reasons for your design choices.

11.2
Cambridge EDSAC

11.2.1
Highlights

The Electronic Delay-Storage Automatic Calculator (EDSAC) built at Cambridge, England, is a typical member of the von Neumann House. It is representative of the kinds of departures that were made from the Princeton IAS (1952) design. It may have been the first von Neumann computer to have run.

History

The EDSAC was influential in focusing attention on the problem of programming a computer. The book that describes the basics of programming the EDSAC [Wilkes, 1951] was reprinted as late as 1959. The concept of the subroutine is introduced there.

Architect.   Maurice V. Wilkes designed the EDSAC for the Cavendish Laboratories at Cambridge.

Dates.   The EDSAC began to work in May and was demonstrated at a conference in June 1949 [Wilkes, 1985]. The machine was used until July 1956; it was modified in the course of that period.

Family tree.   The EDSAC did not give rise to a machine family; the EDSAC 2 is a quite different machine.

Noteworthy

Halfword addressing.   The EDSAC differs from the IAS in using halfword data and addressing to the halfword, as well as to the word. The accumulator is two words long.

Rounding.   As a consequence of multiple data sizes, the decision to round depends on the programmer. Rounding is a separate operation.

Minimal logic.   An And and two Shift instructions are provided.

Output check.   Store For Print helps in checking for correct output.

Peculiarities

Small memory capacity.   Only one-eighth the capacity proposed for the IAS is available: 1024 halfwords. One spare instruction bit could have been used for expansion. Wilkes perceived that a reliable memory technology was the chief challenge in implementing the IAS concept, so he made memory small.

No Load.   In contrast to the IAS, the EDSAC has a Store And Clear operation, but no Load.

No plain Multiply.   Multiplication is either cumulative or subtractive—conforming to the Ferranti Mark 1 (1951), rather than the IAS.

No Divide.   Division must be programmed.

No plain Branch.   For an unconditional Branch, one must use Branch On Accumulator Sign; the sign of the accumulator content must be known.

Shift-amount specification.   An n-bit shift is specified by an address value of 2^{n-2}—a cause of much confusion for programmers [Campbell-Kelly, 1980a].

Incommensurate sizes.   Of a potential 18-bit halfword and 36-bit word, only 17 and 35 bits, respectively, are usable, a concession to the implementation. Two halfwords do not make a full word. If the left and right halfwords from a memory location are combined in the accumulator, a *sandwich* bit in the middle of the full word is left out.

```
          initiateΔE
        ⌐ initiation of the Cambridge EDSAC
          formatΔE
          configureΔE
          spaceΔE
          instructionΔE
```

PROGRAM 11-23   Initiation of the Cambridge EDSAC.

11.2.2

Machine Language

Language Level

Design philosophy.   The language level is similar to that of the IAS, and it is likewise quite close to the implementation.

Unit System

The information units are multiples or fractions of the 36-bit word, but are affected by the lost bit. The accumulator is therefore 70 bits, not 72 bits.

```
 formatΔE                                configureΔE
⌐ Cambridge EDSAC information units     ⌐ configuration for the Cambridge EDS
⌐ representation radix                  ⌐ memory capacity
 radix←2                                  memcap←adrcap
⌐ information units
 half←18
 word←36
 short←17
 long←35
 accsize←70
 adrsize←10
⌐ address capacity
 adrcap←radix*adrsize
```

PROGRAM 11-24   Basic parameters of the Cambridge EDSAC.

Spaces

Memory name-space. Instead of the 12-bit IAS address field, the EDSAC has only 10 address bits. Since addressing is to the halfword, a more than eight-fold reduction of the IAS memory capacity (in bits) results.

```
space∆E
A Cambridge EDSAC spaces
A memory
memory←?(memcap,half)ρradix
A working store            A control store
A - accumulator            A - instruction address
acc←?accsizeρradix         iadr←?adrcap
A - multiplier             A - stopped state
mq←?longρradix             stop←?radix
```

PROGRAM 11-25   Spaces of the Cambridge EDSAC.

Working store. The accumulator has 70 bits to accommodate a full cumulative product—another departure from the IAS design. The MQ register is used only for multipliers; there is no Divide.

Programming model. The separate multiplier register makes cumulative multiplication possible, noticeably accelerating vector inner-product computa-

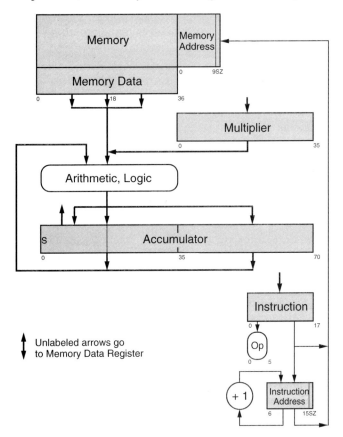

FIGURE 11-26   Programming model for the Cambridge EDSAC.

tion. Notice the size bit on the Instruction Address and the Memory Address Register.

Operand Specification

Address phrase. The address phrase always consists of the address field and the size modifier.

Mnemonics. All instructions are represented by a single letter, as shown in Program 11-27 and Table 11-28. Although the letters have little mnemonic value, they are an early example of a serviceable identification.

```
          a→      I
                  O       F       L
                                  X
          E                       G
          R       S               A
          T       Z       H
          Y               N       C
          U                       V
```

PROGRAM 11-27   Operation-code list of the Cambridge EDSAC.

```
      ∩ logic and shift          a V Multiply Cumulative
  a C And                        a N Multiply Subtractive
  a L Shift Left                 a X Round Short
  a R Shift Right                a Y Round Long
      ∩ fixed-point arithmetic       ∩ sequencing
  a H Load MQ                    a Z Stop
  a U Store                      a E Branch On Positive
  a F Store From Printer         a G Branch On Negative
  a T Store And Clear                ∩ input/output
  a A Add                        a I Read
  a S Subtract                   a O Print
```

TABLE 11-28   Instruction list of the Cambridge EDSAC.

Operation Specification

Instruction format. The spare bit of the instruction was used at a later time to specify address modification.

```
    *↓        Size↓       instruction∆E
                              ∩ Cambridge EDSAC instruction allocation
  ┌─┬────┬─┬─────────┬─┐       ∩ operation specification
  a│Op  │ │Address  │ │          Opcode←0+ι5
  └─┴────┴─┴─────────┴─┘          Unused←5
   0    6           17        ∩ operand specification
  Legend: Op = opcode;            Address←6+ι10
          * = unused.             Size←16
```

PROGRAM 11-29   Instruction allocation in the Cambridge EDSAC.

Instruction Structure

Machine-language syntax. There is just one syntactic pattern, but, as usual, the fields are not all used in all instructions.

```
                    syntaxΔE
            a Opcode,Unused,Address,Size
```

PROGRAM 11-30   Instruction syntax of the Cambridge EDSAC.

11.2.3

Addressing

Direct addressing.   Full-word addressing requires an even address.

```
       data←size readΔE address
     A Cambridge EDSAC read from memory
     →IF size=short
     THEN:data←1↓memory[address;]
          →ENDIF
     ELSE:data←1↓,memory[(2×⌊0.5×address)+Φι2;]
     ENDIF:


       address writeΔE data;size
     A Cambridge EDSAC write into memory
     →IF short=ρ,data
     THEN:memory[address;]←0,data
          →ENDIF
     ELSE:memory[(2×⌊0.5×address)+Φι2;]←half wide 0,data
     ENDIF:
```

PROGRAM 11-31   Memory read and write in the Cambridge EDSAC.

Address Modification

A single index register (called B-register) following the Manchester design was incorporated around 1954; we present the original machine.

```
     address←adrΔE                  size←sizeΔE
   A Cambridge EDSAC addressing   A Cambridge EDSAC data size
     address←fld Address            size←(short,long)[fld Size]
```

PROGRAM 11-32   Addressing in the Cambridge EDSAC.

A size modifier chooses between the two data sizes. The dual data sizes, also found in the 701, add a substantial complication to the ancestral IAS design.

11.2.4

Data

Logical

The EDSAC can use short and long words as logical data.

Fixed-Point Numbers

Notation and allocation.   The EDSAC follows the IAS in using 2's-complement notation. Numbers are interpreted as fractions.

0   17   35

FIGURE 11-33   Fixed-point number in the Cambridge EDSAC.

11.2.5

Operations

Logic

Connectives.   The only connective operation is the And, which is more than the IAS provides.

```
       C
     ∩ Cambridge EDSAC And
     acc←accsize↑mq∧long↑sizeΔE readΔE adrΔE
```

PROGRAM 11-34   And in the Cambridge EDSAC.

Shift.   Two instructions perform arithmetic left and right shift. The shift amount is specified by a bit in the address field—*not* by the value of the address field.

```
       L;shift;operand
     ∩ Cambridge EDSAC Shift Left
     shift←2+9⌊inst[ΦAddress]ι1
     operand←radixcompi acc
     acc←accsize radixcompr operand×2*shift


       R;shift;operand
     ∩ Cambridge EDSAC Shift Right
     shift←2+9⌊inst[ΦAddress]ι1
     operand←radixcompi acc
     acc←accsize radixcompr⌊operand×2*-shift
```

PROGRAM 11-35   Arithmetic Shift in the Cambridge EDSAC.

Fixed-Point Arithmetic

Load and Store.   There is no accumulator Load; the accumulator can be cleared upon storing.

```
     H
   ∩ Cambridge EDSAC Load MQ
   mq←long↑sizeΔE readΔE adrΔE


     U                           T
   ∩ Cambridge EDSAC Store     ∩ Cambridge EDSAC Store And Clear
   adrΔE writeΔE sizeΔE↑acc     adrΔE writeΔE sizeΔE↑acc
                                acc[]←0
```

PROGRAM 11-36   Load and Store in the Cambridge EDSAC.

Add and Subtract.   Short operands are extended to the right because of the fractional interpretation. Overflow detection must be programmed.

```
      A;addend;augend;sum
    A Cambridge EDSAC Add
      addend←radixcompi accsize↑size∆E read∆E adr∆E
      augend←radixcompi acc
      sum←augend+addend
      acc←accsize radixcompr sum


      S;subtrahend;minuend;difference
    A Cambridge EDSAC Subtract
      subtrahend←radixcompi accsize↑size∆E read∆E adr∆E
      minuend←radixcompi acc
      difference←minuend-subtrahend
      acc←accsize radixcompr difference
```

PROGRAM 11-37   Add and Subtract in the Cambridge EDSAC.

Multiply.   Multiplication is either cumulative or subtractive. The accumulator can accommodate a full product, but overflow can still occur because of the cumulative nature of the operation.

```
      V;multiplier;multiplicand;augend;product
    A Cambridge EDSAC Multiply Cumulative
      multiplier←radixcompi mq
      multiplicand←radixcompi long↑size∆E read∆E adr∆E
      augend←radixcompi acc
      product←augend+multiplicand×multiplier
      acc←accsize radixcompr product


      N;multiplier;multiplicand;minuend;product
    A Cambridge EDSAC Multiply Subtractive
      multiplier←radixcompi mq
      multiplicand←radixcompi long↑size∆E read∆E adr∆E
      minuend←radixcompi acc
      product←minuend-multiplicand×multiplier
      acc←accsize radixcompr product
```

PROGRAM 11-38   Multiply in the Cambridge EDSAC.

Round.   Wilkes mentions two Round instructions [Wilkes and Renwick, 1949a], but only the Round Long appears in later publications; the Round Short is replaced by a No Operation. A single bit is added 1 bit to the right of the word length. This type of rounding is correct only for positive numbers.

```
      Add one X↓            Add one Y↓
    ┌──────────────┬─────────────────┬──────────────────────────────┐
    │        short │           long  │                      accsize │
    └──────────────┴─────────────────┴──────────────────────────────┘
    0              17                35                             70
    Accumulator
```

```
    X;round                        Y;round
  A Cambridge EDSAC Round Short  A Cambridge EDSAC Round Long
    round←2*accsize-half           round←2*accsize-word
    acc←accsize magnr round+magni acc   acc←accsize magnr round+magni acc
```

PROGRAM 11-39   Round in the Cambridge EDSAC.

11.2.6

Instruction Sequencing

Linear Sequence

Next instruction. The basic cycle and instruction fetch have the elementary classical function. There is no unconditional branch.

```
cycleΔE
⍝ basic cycle of the Cambridge EDSAC
REPEAT:execute ifetchΔE
→UNTIL stop
```

PROGRAM 11-40   Basic cycle of the Cambridge EDSAC.

```
inst←ifetchΔE
⍝ Cambridge EDSAC instruction fetch
inst←short readΔE iadr
iadr←adrcap|iadr+1
```

PROGRAM 11-41   Instruction fetch in the Cambridge EDSAC.

Completion. When the computer stops, a bell sounds.

```
Z
⍝ Cambridge EDSAC Stop
stop←1
⍝ sound bell
```

PROGRAM 11-42   Stop in the Cambridge EDSAC.

Decision

Conditional branching. Two branches are provided; in each, zero is included with the positive numbers.

```
E
⍝ Cambridge EDSAC Branch On Positive
→If 0≤radixcompi acc
THEN:iadr←adrΔE
ENDIF:
```

```
G
⍝ Cambridge EDSAC Branch On Negative
→If 0>radixcompi acc
THEN:iadr←adrΔE
ENDIF:
```

PROGRAM 11-43   Conditional Branch in the Cambridge EDSAC.

11.2.7

Input/Output

Devices

Source and sink.   Five-bit paper tape is used as input. The output is a teleprinter using a 5-bit code.

Direct Input/Output

Read and Write.   Read fetches one 5-bit byte and stores it into the low-order bits of the addressed memory location. Writing is from the high-order bits of the memory location. Store From Printer reads back into memory the byte actually printed, sensed from the position of the teleprinter head. It can be used to check what is printed.

```
     I                                O
     ⋀ Cambridge EDSAC Read           ⋀ Cambridge EDSAC Print
       adrΔE writeΔE(-sizeΔE)↑tape[0;]   printer←5↑sizeΔE readΔE adrΔE
       tape← 1 0 ↓tape


     F
     ⋀ Cambridge EDSAC Store From Printer
       adrΔE writeΔE sizeΔE↑printer
```

PROGRAM 11-44   Input/output Read and Write in the Cambridge EDSAC.

11.2.8

Implementation Notes

Wilkes followed Aiken in using a conservative realization. Since he wanted to get a running machine for programming experience, he used the existing acoustic delay-line technology from World War II radars as the basis for the memories his team designed and built. Liberal engineering tolerances were applied.

11.2.9

Bibliography

Campbell-Kelly, M., 1992a. "The Airy Tape: An Early Chapter in the History of Debugging." *IEEE Ann Hist Comput*, **14**, 4: 16–25.

Wilkes, M.V., and W. Renwick, 1949a: "The EDSAC." *Report of a Conference on High Speed Automatic Calculating-Machines* (Cambridge, UK: 22–25 June 1949), 9–12. Reprinted in Randell [1973], 389–93 (our defining reference).

Wilkes, M.V., D.J. Wheeler, and S. Gill, 1951; 1959: *The Preparation of Programs for an Electronic Digital Computer*. Reading, MA: Addison-Wesley.

Wilkes, M.V., 1952: "The EDSAC Computer." *Review of Electronic Digital Computers, Proc., AIEE-IRE 1951 Joint Computer Conf.*, 79–83.

Bowden [1953], Campbell-Kelly [1980a, 1992b], Needham [1992], Wheeler [1992], Wilkes and Renwick [1949b], Wilkes [1949, 1985, 1992].

11.2.10

Exercises

11-4 Improve the architecture of the EDSAC shifts. Give the formal description and briefly argue for your design choices.

11-5 Consistently extend the EDSAC operation set with Divide. Give the formal description and arguments for your design choices.

11.3
IBM 701

11.3.1
Highlights

History

Architects.   Nathaniel Rochester was the chief architect.

Dates.   The 701 was designed from 1951 to 1953. Eighteen 701s were delivered in the period from 1953 through 1955.

Family tree.   The 701 is the only machine in the von Neumann-house that established a family on its own, as shown in the frontispiece to Chapter 12. The family also includes the DEC PDP10 and PDP20, and the GE 645 (1965).

Noteworthy

The 701 is a good example of a von Neumann computer. It is binary, has a 36-bit word, and has as working store an accumulator and a multiplier-quotient register. Buchholz gives the rationale for choosing memory size, word length, no checking, the signed-magnitude representation, division (vs. none), I/O, and variable-length tape records [Buchholz, 1953].

Input/output devices.   The 701 differs most markedly from other Princeton IAS machines by its rich complement of directly attached high-speed I/O devices, using IBM's highly developed electromechanical punched-card machine technology. The complement includes a card reader, a card punch, a printer, magnetic drums, and magnetic tapes. The direct I/O uses the shifting circuits of the MQ to disassemble words into bytes, and vice versa, as magnetic tape requires.

Peculiarities

Signed magnitude. The 701 differs from other IAS machines in using signed-magnitude number representation—a step backward.

Cramped addressing.   The 701 has addressing resolution to the 18-bit halfword. The addressing scheme became quite complex as the memory capacity grew from 4096 to 8192 halfwords, which exceeds the addressing capacity of a 12-bit address field. Memory-bank selection is controlled by the low-order address bit, by a modal control bit, and by the instruction address.

Cramped opcode. A thirty-third operation code is shoehorned into 5 bits by use of the same code for Extract, which references only full words, and for Store Address, which references only halfwords.

Overflow bits.   The size of the accumulator is inconsistent with the word size because a Q and a P bit are included for overflow detection. These Q and P bits are highly improper; they require explicit specification almost every

instruction's description. They are also unnecessary, since the 701 also has an overflow indicator—a much better solution.

Overlapped input/output. The program control of I/O allows computation to be interspersed in the middle of card reading, card punching, or line printing, but the programmer is responsible for counting the milliseconds until the next I/O action is due.

11.3.2

Machine Language

Language Level

The language level is quite low, as in the IAS. The 701 designers saw engineering computation as a production process similar to data processing with punched-card equipment, so they paid special attention to on-line high-speed source/sink equipment.

Unit System

Bytes are 6 bits; other unit sizes are 18 bits and 36 bits. Later family members include 72-bit and 144-bit units. The byte size affects only magnetic-tape reading and writing.

```
initiate701                        format701
A initiation of the IBM 701        A IBM 701 information units
  format701                        A representation radix
  configure701                       radix←2
  space701                         A information units
  control701                         byte←6
  data701                            half←18
  initiate701io                      word←36
                                     adrsize←12
                                     accsize←38
  configure701                       adrcap←radix*adrsize
A configuration for the IBM 701
A memory capacity
  memcap←2×adrcap
```

PROGRAM 11-45   Basic parameters of the IBM 701.

Configuration.   We describe the 8 K halfword configuration.

Spaces

Working store.   All accumulator arithmetic results go into the accumulator sign and 35 low-order digits, with only carries into Q and P. The whole accumulator, except the sign, participates in shifts.

The sign of the 36-bit multiplier-quotient register MQ does not participate in shifts. MQ is also used as the I/O data register.

```
     space701
   ⍺ IBM 701 spaces
   ⍺ memory                          ⍺ control store
     memory←?(memcap,half)ρradix    ⍺ - double memory
   ⍺ working store                     es2←?2
   ⍺ - accumulator                  ⍺ - instruction address
     acc←?accsizeρradix               iadr←?memcap
   ⍺ - multiplier/quotient          ⍺ - indicators and lights
     mq←?wordρradix                   ind←?4ρradix
   ⍺ - manual entry                 ⍺ - stop condition
     switch←?6ρradix                  stop←?radix
```

PROGRAM 11-46   Spaces of the IBM 701.

Control store.   The instruction address is capable of addressing all of memory. For data addressing, the choice between electrostatic (cathode-ray tube) storages 1 and 2 is made by the mode bit es2.

Programming model.   Figure 11-47 shows the programming model. Except for the P, Q bits and the sign complications, it is essentially that of the IAS.

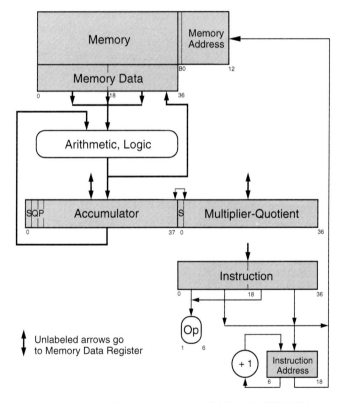

FIGURE 11-47   Programming model for the IBM 701.

Operand Specification

Address phrase.   The address phrase consists of one-address instructions, with the address applying to half- or full-word resolution, depending upon the size specification.

Operation Specification

The 701 does not use typical mnemonics for its operation codes; the names are rather lengthy, such as "MPY ROUND." We use the IBM 704 (1955) mnemonics, since almost all 701 instructions occur also in the 704. This convention aids comparison between the two machines.

a→HTR	NOP	MPY	RDS	b→ANS
TRA	ADD	MPR	RDB	
TOV	CLA	DVH	WRS	
TPL	ADM	RND	WEF	
TZE	STO	LLS	REW	
SUB	STA	LRS	LDA	
CLS	STQ	ALS	SNS	
SBM	LDQ	ARS	CPY	

PROGRAM 11-48   Operation-code list of the IBM 701.

```
    ⌐ address arithmetic           ⌐ sequencing
 a STA Store Address            a NOP No Operation
    ⌐ logic and shift           a HTR Stop And Branch
 b ANS And To Memory            a TRA Branch
 a ALS Shift Arithmetic Left    a TPL Branch On Plus
 a LLS Shift Arithmetic Long Left   a TZE Branch On Zero
 a ARS Shift Arithmetic Right   a TOV Branch On Overflow
 a LRS Shift Arithmetic Long Right   ⌐ input/output
    ⌐ fixed-point arithmetic    a CPY Copy And Skip
 a CLA Load                     a RDS Read Select
 a LDQ Load MQ                  a RDB Read Backwards
 a CLS Load Negative            a WRS Write Select
 a STO Store                    a WEF Write End Of File
 a STQ Store MQ                 a SNS Sense
 a ADD Add                      a REW Rewind Tape
 a ADM Add Absolute             a LDA Locate Drum Address
 a SUB Subtract
 a SBM Subtract Absolute
 a MPY Multiply
 a MPR Multiply R
 a DVH Divide Or Halt
 a RND Round From MQ
 Legend: R = Rounded.
```

TABLE 11-49   Instruction list of the IBM 701.

Instruction Structure

Machine-language syntax.   To solve the lack of opcode space, the 701 uses a separate syntactic pattern for size bit 1 and opcode 13, which applies to the And instruction. For size bit 0, opcode 13 identifies Store Address. The meaning of the size bit is not altered; the And has word resolution, and Store Address has halfword resolution.

```
        syntax701
      a Size,Opcode,Address
      b 1 0 1 1 0 1 ,Address
```

PROGRAM 11-50   Instruction syntax of the IBM 701.

Instruction format. The instruction formats satisfy the two syntactic patterns. The syntactic patterns show how 33 opcodes are squeezed into a 5-bit opcode field.

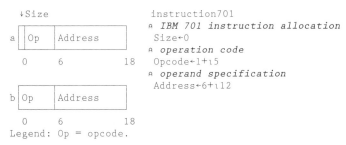

```
↓Size                              instruction701
                                   ⍝ IBM 701 instruction allocation
 a │Op │Address │                  Size←0
                                   ⍝ operation code
   0    6            18            Opcode←1+ι5
                                   ⍝ operand specification
                                   Address←6+ι12
 b │Op │Address │

   0    6        18
Legend: Op = opcode.
```

PROGRAM 11-51   Instruction allocation in the IBM 701.

Status format. The 701 was one of the first computers to use status, in the form of four indicators and one mode bit. There are indicators for accumulator overflow, improper copy, improper divide, and invalid tape read, as shown in the description of the 704.

11.3.3

Addressing

Direct addressing. The memory read and write functions apply to halfwords and full words.

```
data←size read701 address;location    address write701 data;location
⍝ IBM 701 read from memory            ⍝ IBM 701 write into memory
location←address+ιsize÷half           location←address+ι(ρ,data)÷half
data←,memory[location;]               memory[location;]←half wide data


size←size701
⍝ IBM 701 size
size←(half,word)[fld Size]
```

PROGRAM 11-52   Memory read and write in the IBM 701.

Address resolution. The address has halfword resolution—the 12-bit address field addresses 4096 halfwords. Since memory capacity is 8192 halfwords, the mode bit es2 is used to distinguish each of the lower and upper banks of 4096 halfwords, when halfwords are addressed. When full words are addressed, the even–odd pair of halfwords containing the addressed halfword is fetched, but the low-order bit determines which bank is used. So 1962 and 1963 address distinct full words in different memory banks. Likewise, 1962 and 1963 address distinct halfwords in the same memory bank.

The addressing scheme is further complicated by the use of a different set of rules for instruction addresses.

```
address←adr701
ⱥ IBM 701 addressing
→IF plus=fld Size
THEN: ⱥ half word addressing
    address←(adrcap×es2)+fld Address
    →ENDIF
ELSE: ⱥ full word addressing
    address←2×fld ¯1ΦAddress
ENDIF:
```

PROGRAM 11-53   Addressing in the IBM 701.

Address calculation.   The programmer modifies instructions by loading them into the accumulator, incrementing them, testing them, and returning them to memory by Store Address. The address arithmetic is modulo 4096 and must take into account the rules for half- and full-word addressing. Since Store Address does not affect the Size field, this consideration is usually trivial.

```
STA;od
ⱥ IBM 701 Store Address
od←half read701 adr701
od[Address]←acc[2+Address]
adr701 write701 od
```

PROGRAM 11-54   Store Address in the IBM 701.

11.3.4

Data

The peculiar accumulator size requires separate field allocation.

```
 ⌈Sign                                    ↓Sign
 ↓QP

 ┌┬┬──────────────────────────┐     ┌─┬──────────────┬──────┐
 │││ Digits                    │     │ │ Digits       │      │
 └┴┴──────────────────────────┘     └─┴──────────────┴──────┘
 0  3                       38        0                    36
 accumulator                          MQ

 data701
 ⱥ IBM 701 data representation
 ⱥ fixed-point number
 ⱥ - sign encoding
  plus←0
  minus←1                     ⱥ accumulator allocation
 ⱥ - word allocation           Q←1
  Sign←0                       P←2
  Digits←1+ι35                 Accdigits←3+ι35
```

PROGRAM 11-55   Data specification in the IBM 701.

Character Strings

Six 6-bit bytes occupy a 36-bit word in I/O.

Character set and size.   There is no CPU dependence upon the character encoding, which is BCD; there are no specific data-handling operations.

Logical

Logical formats. A logical vector is a 36-bit word—never a halfword—in the one and only logical operation, And To Memory. *True* is "1"; *false* is "0."

Fixed-Point Numbers

Notation and allocation. The 701 uses binary, signed-magnitude representation. Numbers are interpreted as fractions, as in the IAS.

11.3.5

Operations

Logic

Connectives. The only logical operation is And To Memory. The instruction is called Extract, but should not be confused with the quite different Extract used in the Univac.

```
ANS;od1;od2
ҩ IBM 701 And To Memory
od1←word read701 adr701
od2←acc[Sign,Accdigits]
adr701 write701 od1∧od2
```

PROGRAM 11-56   And To Memory in the IBM 701.

Shift. All shifts are arithmetic. They apply either to the accumulator or to the accumulator and MQ. The P and Q bits participate; the sign does not,

```
ALS;shift
ҩ IBM 701 Shift Arithmetic Left
shift←256|adr701
Oflo report shift↑acc[Accdigits]
acc[Q,P,Accdigits]←(accsize-1)↑shift↓acc[Q,P,Accdigits]

LLS;shift
ҩ IBM 701 Shift Arithmetic Long Left
shift←256|adr701
Oflo report shift↑acc[Accdigits],mq[Digits]
acc[Q,P,Accdigits]←(accsize-1)↑shift↓acc[Q,P,Accdigits],mq[Digits]
mq[Digits]←(word-1)↑shift↓mq[Digits]
acc[Sign]←mq[Sign]

ARS;shift
ҩ IBM 701 Shift Arithmetic Right
shift←256|adr701
acc[Q,P,Accdigits]←(-(accsize-1))↑(-shift)↓acc[Q,P,Accdigits]

LRS;shift
ҩ IBM 701 Shift Arithmetic Long Right
shift←256|adr701
mq[Digits]←(-word-1)↑(-shift)↓acc[Q,P,Accdigits],mq[Digits]
acc[Q,P,Accdigits]←(-(accsize-1))↑(-shift)↓acc[Q,P,Accdigits]
mq[Sign]←acc[Sign]
```

PROGRAM 11-57   Arithmetic Shift in the IBM 701.

except that, in the long-Left Shift, the accumulator sign is made equal to the MQ sign, and that, in the long-Right Shift, the reverse occurs.

Fixed-Point Arithmetic

The 701 generally follows the IAS instruction set, but there is a Store MQ. Load Absolute, on the other hand, is omitted even though Add Absolute is available.

a	CLA	Load	a	SUB Subtract
a	LDQ	Load MQ	a	SBM Subtract Absolute
a	CLS	Load Negative	a	MPY Multiply
a	STO	Store	a	MPR Multiply R
a	STQ	Store MQ	a	DVH Divide Or Halt
a	ADD	Add	a	RND Round From MQ
a	ADM	Add Absolute		

Legend: R = Rounded.

TABLE 11-58   Fixed-point instructions of the IBM 701.

Load and Store.   These instructions illustrate memory access for halfwords and full words. Because of the fractional interpretation, halfwords are extended to the right to make a full word. Because of the peculiar accumulator length, the P and Q bits require extra specification.

```
CLA
ℵ IBM 701 Load
acc[Sign,Accdigits]←word↑size701 read701 adr701
acc[Q,P]←0


CLS
ℵ IBM 701 Load Negative
acc[Sign,Accdigits]←word↑size701 read701 adr701
acc[Sign]←¯acc[Sign]
acc[Q,P]←0


STO
ℵ IBM 701 Store
adr701 write701 half wide size701↑acc[Sign,Accdigits]
```

PROGRAM 11-59   Load and Store in the IBM 701.

Add and Subtract.   The signed zero—a consequence of signed-magnitude notation—is quite noticeable in these instructions. We illustrate the Add; Add Absolute and Subtract follow Add.

```
ADD;s;p;addend;augend;sum
ℵ IBM 701 Add
s←acc[Sign]
p←acc[P]
addend←signmagni word↑size701 read701 adr701
augend←signmagni acc
sum←augend+addend
acc←accsize signmagnr sum
→If sum=0
THEN:acc[Sign]←s
ENDIF:Oflo report p≠acc[P]
```

PROGRAM 11-60   Add in the IBM 701.

Multiply and Divide.   Multiplication always sets the P and Q bits to 0. The rule for setting the accumulator and MQ signs includes the special treatment of the sign of zero. For Divide, see the 704 description (Section 11.4), which follows the 701 except for the halfword operands.

```
MPY;mr;multiplier;multiplicand;product;pd
A IBM 701 Multiply
mr←word↑size701 read701 adr701
multiplier←magni mr[Digits]
multiplicand←magni mq[Digits]
product←multiplicand×multiplier
pd←(accsize+word-1) magnr product        MPR
acc←accsize↑pd                           A IBM 701 Multiply Rounded
mq[Digits]←accsize↓pd                    MPY
acc[Sign]←mq[Sign]←mq[Sign]≠mr[Sign]     RND
```

PROGRAM 11-61   Multiply in the IBM 701.

Rounding.   Rounding treats the MQ as an extension of the accumulator. The number in both registers together is rounded to the accumulator length. Actually, only the high-order MQ bit participates.

```
RND;p;number;result
A IBM 701 Round From MQ
p←acc[P]
number←0.5×signmagni acc,1↑mq[Digits]
result←round number
acc←accsize signmagnr result
Oflo report p≠acc[P]
```

PROGRAM 11-62   Round in the IBM 701.

11.3.6
Instruction Sequencing

The basic cycle is elementary, but the instruction fetch is complicated by the two-bank memory system. The instruction address increments cyclically within each bank; halfword 4095 has 0 as its successor; 8191 is followed by 4096. We show all sequencing instructions.

```
cycle701                         inst←ifetch701
A basic cycle of the IBM 701     A IBM 701 instruction fetch
REPEAT:execute ifetch701         inst←half read701 iadr
→UNTIL stop                      iadr←(adrcap|iadr+1)+adrcap×iadr≥adrcap
```

PROGRAM 11-63   Basic cycle and instruction fetch of the IBM 701.

Linear Sequence

Next instruction.   Branching is also complicated by the memory-addressing scheme. The Size field indicates the memory bank in the unconditional branch.

Completion.   Stop And Branch stops the machine, but sets the instruction address.

```
TRA                                      HTR
A IBM 701 Branch                         A IBM 701 Stop And Branch
  iadr←(fld Address)+adrcap×fld Size       iadr←(fld Address)+adrcap×fld Size
                                           stop←1


NOP
A IBM 701 No Operation
```

PROGRAM 11-64   Stop And Branch in the IBM 701.

Decision

Conditional branching.   The operation code specifies the condition of the conditional-branch operations. The branch target is limited to the bank where the current instruction resides, as indicated by the function `target701`. There are no provisions for iteration or delegation.

```
TZE                              TOV
A IBM 701 Branch On Zero         A IBM 701 Branch On Overflow
  →If 0=signmagni acc              →If ind[Oflo]
  THEN:iadr←target701             THEN:iadr←target701
  ENDIF:                                 ind[Oflo]←0
                                  ENDIF:


TPL
A IBM 701 Branch On Plus         address←target701
  →If plus=acc[Sign]             A IBM 701 branch target
  THEN:iadr←target701              address←(fld Address)+adrcap×iadr≥adrcap
  ENDIF:
```

PROGRAM 11-65   Conditional Branch in the IBM 701.

11.3.7
Supervision

There is no supervisory capability. The only mode is the one that governs the scope of halfword data addresses. This mode is explicitly set by the I/O instruction Sense, as though the mode were an I/O device.

11.3.8
Input/Output

Devices

Store.   There are four magnetic drums, each capable of storing 2048 full words.

```
initiate701io                    device701
A IBM 701 input/output initiation A IBM 701 device address
  format701io                      Drum←128+ι4
  space701io                       Tape←256+ι4        Reader←2048
  device701                        Printer←512+ι10    Switch←69+ι6
                                   Punch←1024+ι2      Light←64+ι5
```

PROGRAM 11-66   Input/output–device addresses of the IBM 701.

Source and sink.   Card reader, card punch, printer, magnetic tape, and graphical display with both viewing tube and camera are all provided. Six console sense switches and four programmable console lights are also provided; they are read and set directly with the Sense instruction.

Direct Input/Output and Overlapped Input/Output

The 701 has direct program control of I/O via Read Select and Write Select instructions to set up the paths and start the mechanisms moving; and via Copy instructions to specify each data word's location in memory. The I/O devices each feed through the multiplier-quotient register. This action was discussed in Chapter 8.

```
a CPY Copy And Skip    a WEF Write End Of File
a RDS Read Select      a SNS Sense
a RDB Read Backwards   a REW Rewind Tape
a WRS Write Select     a LDA Locate Drum Address
```

TABLE 11-67   Input/output instructions of the IBM 701.

Read and Write.   Copy And Skip copies to or from memory via MQ; the instruction skips to the third successor after copying if it encounters an end of record, and to the second successor if there is an end of file.

```
RDS                              format701io
a IBM 701 Read Select            a IBM 701 input/output parameters
direction←in                     a maximum number of devices
iostate[fld Address]←busy        devcap←14
                                 a direction
                                 in←0
WRS                              out←1
a IBM 701 Write Select           a status
direction←out                    ready←0
iostate[fld Address]←busy        busy←1


CPY                              space701io
a IBM 701 Copy And Skip          a IBM 701 input/output spaces
→IF direction=in                 direction←?ρ2
THEN:adr701 write701 mq          iostate←?devcapρ2
   →ENDIF
ELSE:mq←read701 adr701
ENDIF:iadr←adrcap|iadr+endfile⌈2×endrecord
```

PROGRAM 11-68   Input/output Read and Write in the IBM 701.

Sense and Control.   Sense And Skip tests the sense switches on the console. Locate Drum Address specifies the drum start address for a copy sequence.

11.3.9

Implementation Notes

The implementation is parallel. The main memory is Williams-tube technology, with one CRT for each of the 36 bits, and 4096 spots on a CRT. Refresh cycles come automatically.

Speed.   Add takes 60 μs; Store, also 60 μs; Multiply and Divide each take 456 μs; a branch takes 48 μs. Memory cycle time is 12 μs, and the clock cycle is 1 μs.

Reliability.   The mean error-free time of memory is on the order of tens of minutes, so programmed checking and backing up of memory to drum are standard practice on the 701. The CPU is totally unchecked; I/O has single-bit parity checking.

11.3.10
Bibliography

IBM Corporation, 1953: *Principles of Operation Type 701 and Associated Equipment*. IBM Form 24-6042-2. New York: IBM Corp. (our defining reference).

Hurd, C.C., ed., 1983: "Special Issue: IBM 701." *Ann Hist Comput*, 5, 2: 110–219.

Buchholz [1953], Frizzell [1953], Ross [1953], L.D. Stevens [1952].

11.3.11
Exercises

11-6 Assuming consistency with the instructions presented in this section, give the formal descriptions of LDQ, STQ, ADM, SUB, and SBM.

11-7 Assuming that the 704 arithmetic has been changed consistently from that of the 701, give the formal description of DVH. Note that there is no DVP in the 701.

11-8 Extend the instruction set of the 701 with Square Root. Give a formal description, and briefly argue for your design choices. What are the greatest difficulties that you encounter?

11.4
IBM 704

11.4.1
Highlights

History

Architects.   Gene Amdahl was the IBM 704's chief architect.

Dates.   The IBM 704 was announced in 1954 and delivered in late 1955. In the period from 1955 to 1960, 123 machines were delivered [Bashe, 1986].

Noteworthy

The 704 follows the 701 in using binary 36-bit words, signed-magnitude number representation, accumulator and MQ working store, P and Q overflow bits, and copy-logic I/O. But the 704 also introduces into the Princeton IAS (1952) design several basic functions of the classical architecture.

Floating point.   Floating point is standard, non-optional. The 704 firmly established floating point as the way to do scientific and engineering calculations.

Indexing.   Three index registers are provided as standard, non-optional. Floating point and indexing made FORTRAN feasible; it was developed for this machine.

Enlarged address space.   The cramped 12-bit address space of the 701 is expanded to 15 bits. Moreover, address resolution goes from halfwords to full words. These two changes yield a 16-fold expansion of normal addressing.

Full-word instructions.   The enlarged address field requires abandoning halfword instructions, resulting in 36-bit instructions. This switch from the famine of the cramped halfword to the feast of the full word has at least two consequences:

- Liberal instruction set: Nine bits are available for the opcode in most instructions. So the 33 operations of the 701 are more than doubled to 86 in the 704, with plenty of room for expansion in later family members.
- Compound instructions: The newly gained space also allows a two-address instruction format for a few operations. Among others, these operations include a one-instruction loop-closer that decrements and tests the index, and a one-instruction subroutine linkage.

Immediate addressing.   The decrement field of the instruction is used as an immediate value in index arithmetic.

Logic.   The 701's single logical instruction was augmented with the classical set of And, Or, and Not, all operating upon the accumulator.

Trapping.   A trapping mode causes a trap after each normal successful branch, making program tracing faster.

Peculiarities

The 704 design reflects experimentation with new machine functions such as indexing.

Subtractive indexing.   Index values are subtracted from an indexed address to provide the effective address. This subtraction allows arrays to be scanned forward by decrementing the index toward an implied limit of zero.

ORed index values.   Three index bits, one per index, occur in every instruction. They can be set in any combination; the values of the indices are ORed together and the result subtracted from the specified address.

One's complement.   Besides the normal signed-magnitude notation for fixed-point arithmetic, there is also what is in effect a 1's-complement Add called Add and Carry Logical Word. This operation uses the P bit of the accumulator with end-around carry out of P, but does not affect the accumulator sign. It is provided for check-summing blocks of I/O data.

Liberal operation-code space.   The cramped opcode space of the 701 is replaced with a space that can hold more than 1064 codes. Fewer than one-tenth of these codes are used in the 704, and about one-fifth are used in the last descendant.

Cyclic memory.   Effective address computation works modulo the particular installed capacity of 4 K, 8 K, or 32 K, thus rendering programs incompatible among machines with different installed capacities.

11.4.2

Machine Language

Unit System

The 704 follows the 701 with a 36-bit word and a 6-bit byte, but deletes the halfword.

```
initiate704                            format704
a initiation of the IBM 704            a IBM 704 information units
configure704                           a representation radix
format704                              radix←2
space704                               a information units
control704                             byte←6
data704                                word←36
                                       adrsize←radix⊛memcap
                                       accsize←38
configure704
a configuration for the IBM 704
a memory capacity
memcap←2*15
```

PROGRAM 11-69   Basic parameters of the IBM 704.

Configuration.   The address size is shown in Program 11-69 to depend upon the installed memory configuration. We show the programs in general form, but give the maximum capacity as the normal configuration.

Spaces

Memory name-space. The omission of the 701 halfword gives a substantially cleaner memory name-space.

Working store.   Unfortunately, the accumulator P and Q bits continue in the 704. MQ continues to be used as the I/O data register, both in parallel transfers to drum, cards, or printer, and as the byte assembler/disassembler for transfers from and to tape.

The size of the three index registers depends upon the installed memory capacity.

```
space704
ค IBM 704 spaces              ค control store
ค memory                      ค - instruction address
  memory←?(memcap,word)ρradix   iadr←?memcap
ค working store               ค - indicators and lights
ค - accumulator                 ind←?4ρradix
  acc←?accsizeρradix          ค - manual entry
ค - multiplier/quotient         switch←?6ρradix
  mq←?wordρradix              ค - stop condition
ค - indices                     stop←?radix
  reg←?(3,adrsize)ρradix      ค - trapping mode
                                trap←?radix
```

PROGRAM 11-70   Spaces of the IBM 704.

Control store. The instruction address is also limited to the installed memory capacity. A trapping-mode bit is placed in the control store.

Programming model. The programming model for the 701 is extended with three index registers.

Operation Specification

Three different operation-code lengths are used, to wedge a large instruction set into some tight formats.

Operand Specification

Address phrase. The 704 address phrase has an address and an index field. The phrase is not used uniformly; operations whose mnemonic contains an X have no indexing and use only the address field in the address phrase.

Instruction Structure

Machine-language syntax. The 704 uses an entirely new instruction syntax—one that clearly deviates from the IAS pattern. The a format is used for index incrementing, the b pattern for single-address instructions, and the c pattern for instructions with extended operation code.

Instruction format. The decrement field contains an immediate value that is used in index arithmetic. For these instructions, the index field is not part of the address phrase, but rather specifies the index register that is both operand and result. This a format is essentially a three-address format. Format b is one-address; format c is zero-address.

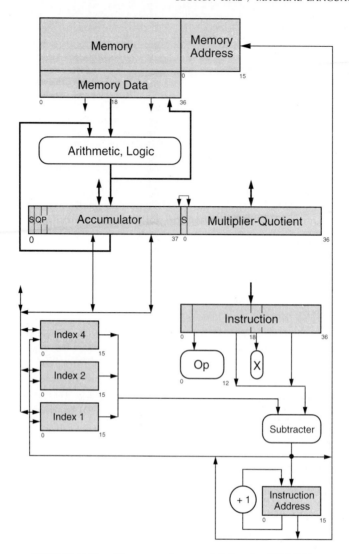

FIGURE 11-71   Programming model for the IBM 704.

a→→b	TQP	LDA	LLS	SBM	COM
TXI	MPY	CLA	BST	CAL	ETM
TIX	DVH	CLS	LRS	ORA	RND
TXH	DVP	LXA	ALS	LXD	DCT
→b	FDH	LDQ	WEF	STQ	c→PBT
TNX	FDP	STO	ARS	ORS	SSM
TXL	FMP	SLW	REW	SLQ	LTM
b→HTR	FAD	STA	WRS	SXD	RTT
TRA	FSB	STD	b→TNZ	PDX	
TTR	ANS	STP	TMI	MSE	
TLQ	CAS	CPY	TNO	LGL	
TSX	ACL	PAX	MPR	RQL	
TZE	ADD	PXD	UFM	c→CLM	
TPL	ADM	PSE	UFA	LBT	
TOV	SUB	NOP	UFS	CHS	
TQO	HPR	RDS	ANA	SSP	

PROGRAM 11-72   Operation-code list of the IBM 704.

a	*address arithmetic*		a	*floating-point arithmetic*
b	LXD Load Index From Decrement		b	FAD F Add
b	LXA Load Index From Address		b	UFA Unnormalized Add
b	PXD Index To Decrement		b	FSB F Subtract
b	PDX Decrement To Index		b	UFS Unnormalized Subtract
b	PAX Address To Index		b	FMP F Multiply
b	SXD Store Index In Decrement		b	UFM Unnormalized Multiply
b	STA Store Address		b	FDH F Divide Or Halt
a	*logic and shift*		b	FDP F Divide Or Proceed
c	COM Not		a	*sequencing*
b	ANA And		b	NOP No Operation
b	ANS And To Memory		b	HPR Stop
b	ORA Or		b	HTR Stop And Branch
b	ORS Or To Memory		b	TRA Branch
b	LGL Shift Logical Left		b	TTR Branch After Trap
b	ALS Shift Arithmetic Left		b	TPL Branch On Plus
b	LLS Shift Arithmetic Long Left		b	TMI Branch On Minus
b	ARS Shift Arithmetic Right		b	TNO Branch On No-Overflow
b	LRS Shift Arithmetic Long Right		b	TZE Branch On Zero
b	RQL Rotate MQ Left		a	TXL Branch On Index Low Or Equal
a	*fixed-point arithmetic*		b	TNZ Branch On Non-zero
c	CLM Clear Magnitude		a	TXH Branch On Index High
b	CLA Load		b	TOV Branch On Overflow
b	LDQ Load MQ		b	TQP Branch On MQ Plus
b	CLS Load Negative		b	TLQ Branch On MQ Low
b	CAL Load Logical		b	TQO Branch On MQ Overflow
b	STO Store		a	TNX Branch On No-Increment
b	STD Store Decrement		b	CAS Skip On Comparison
b	STP Store Prefix		c	DCT Skip On Division
b	STQ Store MQ		c	PBT Skip On P Bit
b	SLQ Store Upper MQ		c	LBT Skip On Low Order Bit
b	SLW Store Logical		c	RTT Skip On Tape Redundancy
c	CHS Negate		a	TIX Branch On Increment
c	SSP Make Absolute		a	TXI Branch And Increment
c	SSM Negate Absolute		b	TSX Call
b	ADD Add		a	*supervision*
b	ADM Add Absolute		c	ETM Enter Trapping Mode
b	ACL Add And Carry Logical		c	LTM Leave Trapping Mode
b	SUB Subtract		a	*input/output*
b	SBM Subtract Absolute		b	CPY Copy And Skip
b	MPY Multiply		b	RDS Read Select
b	MPR Multiply R		b	WEF Write End Of File
b	DVH Divide Or Halt		b	WRS Write Select
b	DVP Divide Or Proceed		b	PSE Plus Sense
c	RND Round From MQ		b	MSE Minus Sense
			b	BST Backspace Tape
			b	REW Rewind Tape
			b	LDA Locate Drum Address

Legend: F = Floating-point; R = Rounded.

TABLE 11-73   Instruction list of the IBM 704.

```
    syntax704
a Opcode,Decrement,X,Address
b 0 0 0 ,Opn,Unused,X,Address
b 1 0 0 ,Opn,Unused,X,Address
c 0 0 0 1 1 1 1 1 0 0 0 0 ,Une,Ope
c 1 0 0 1 1 1 1 1 0 0 0 0 ,Une,Ope
```

PROGRAM 11-74   Instruction syntax of the IBM 704.

Status format.   The 704 indicators are the same as the 701 indicators, except that the Copy indicator is replaced by Floating-Point Overflow.

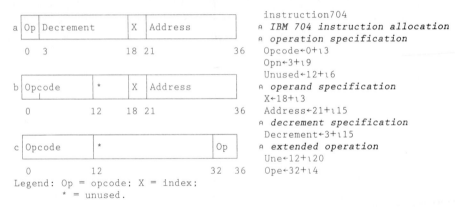

Legend: Op = opcode; X = index;
        * = unused.

PROGRAM 11-75   Instruction allocation in the IBM 704.

```
indicator704
ᴀ IBM 704 indicators
ᴀ accumulator overflow    ᴀ improper divisor
  Oflo←0                    Divide←2
ᴀ mq overflow             ᴀ invalid tape read
  Mqoflo←1                  Tapecheck←3
```

PROGRAM 11-76   Indicators in the IBM 704.

11.4.3

Addressing

Direct addressing.   There is no abbreviation; all addresses are given in full. The name-space is cyclic: 4 K, 8 K, or 32 K in circumference. All address and index arithmetic is modulo installed capacity.

```
data←read704 address           address write704 data
ᴀ IBM 704 read from memory     ᴀ IBM 704 write into memory
  data←memory[memcap|address;]   memory[memcap|address;]←data
```

PROGRAM 11-77   Memory read and write in the IBM 704.

Address Modification

The 3-bit index specification field X uses a separate bit for each index, so it is possible to specify more than one index. In that case the Or of the specified indices is taken as shown in indexread704. Conversely, one index-arithmetic result can be placed in more than one index register. (See indexwrite704 in Program 11-78.)

```
address←adr704;index;value    ix←indexread704
ᴀ IBM 704 addressing          ᴀ IBM 704 read from index registers
  index←magni indexread704      ix←inst[X]∨.∧reg
  value←fld Address
  address←memcap|value-index
                              indexwrite704 ix
                              ᴀ IBM 704 write into index registers
                                ix←(-adrsize)↑ix
                                reg[inst[X]/ι3;]←(inst[X]/ι1)∘.∧ix
```

PROGRAM 11-78   Addressing in the IBM 704.

In addressing, the index value obtained from the index registers is sub-tracted from the value specified in the address field of the instruction.

Index Arithmetic

One or more indices can be loaded from the decrement or address part of a memory word (LXD LXA) or accumulator (PDX PAX). The Or of the specified indices can be stored in the decrement part of a memory word (SXD) or the accumulator (PXD). Addition and subtraction of decrements to the address field in the index word is combined with branching. Due to the P and Q bits, the allocation of the decrement field in the accumulator has to be relative to the P bit in the accumulator (Program 11-80).

```
b LXD Load Index From Decrement  b PAX Address To Index
b LXA Load Index From Address    b SXD Store Index In Decrement
b PXD Index To Decrement         b STA Store Address
b PDX Decrement To Index
```

TABLE 11-79   Index arithmetic instructions of the IBM 704.

```
PXD:ix                           PDX
a IBM 704 Index To Decrement     a IBM 704 Decrement To Index
ix←(-ρDecrement)↑indexread704      indexwrite704 acc[P+Decrement]
acc[P+Decrement]←ix WHERE acc[]←0
```

PROGRAM 11-80   Index arithmetic in the IBM 704.

Index operations.   The index-modification operations are not indexable. Since the index registers are 12, 13, or 15 bits in size, not all 15 decrement bits are necessarily used. The remaining index operations are combined with branching; we discuss them with the branching operations.

List addressing.   The load operations LXD and LXA proved to be very useful for list processing, with the Decrement and Address fields giving their names to the LISP operators CDR and CAR (Program 11-81).

```
LXA;od                             LXD;od
a IBM 704 Load Index From Address  a IBM 704 Load Index From Decrement
od←read704 fld Address             od←read704 fld Address
indexwrite704 od[Address]          indexwrite704 od[Decrement]


SXD;od
a IBM 704 Store Index In Decrement
od←read704 fld Address
od[Decrement]←(-ρDecrement)↑indexread704
(fld Address) write704 od
```

PROGRAM 11-81   List-processing instructions in the IBM 704.

Address Level

Immediate addressing.   The decrement is used as an immediate quantity in index arithmetic.

11.4.4

Data

The data specification of the 704 follows that of the 701, except that the new floating-point type needs specification.

Character Strings

Character set and size.   The 704 has six 6-bit bytes per 36-bit word, as does the 701. Encoding, and the absence of special character operations, also follow the 701.

Logical

Logical formats.   Each word holds a 36-bit logical vector.

Fixed-Point Numbers

Notation and allocation.   The 704 follows the binary, signed-magnitude notation and allocation of the 701 (Program 11-55).

Floating-Point Numbers

It is a pity that von Neumann decided against floating point in the IAS design. Otherwise, he certainly would have set an example of greater cleanliness than that found in most contemporary designs (other than the unknown work of Zuse). Most likely he would have addressed rounding and consistency of representation, both of which are lacking in the 704.

Closure and normal form.   Both normalized and unnormalized operands are recognized and produced. Exponent overflow and underflow set an indicator.

Floating-point representation.   The 704 uses binary, signed-magnitude fractional representation for the coefficient, and bias representation for the

```
↓Sign
  ┌─┬──────┬──────────────────────┐
  │ │Exp   │Coefficient           │
  └─┴──────┴──────────────────────┘
 01      9                      36
Legend: Exp = exponent.
```

```
  f1704                            numexp←f1704i rep
  ⍀ IBM 704 floating-point number  ⍀ IBM 704 floating-point interpretation
  ⍀ base                           ⍀ number and exponent
    base←2                           numexp←flbsi rep
  ⍀ exponent allocation
    Exp←1+⍳8
  ⍀ coefficient allocation
    Coef←0.9+⍳27                   rep←f1704r numexp
  ⍀ radix point                    ⍀ IBM 704 floating-point representation
    point←0⍳ρ1↓Coef                  rep←word flbsr numexp
  ⍀ extreme exponent              ⍀ out of domain
    extexp←radix*0⍳ρ1↓Exp           Oflo report xmax∨xmin
                                    Mqoflo report xmax∨xmin
```

PROGRAM 11-82   Floating-point interpretation and representation in the IBM 704.

exponent. These choices grew into an informal standard for the IBM house; they are found, for example, in the IBM 650 (1954) and the 360. The bias in the 701 family is +128. The functions `flbsi` and `flbsr` show this design (Section 9.3).

When unnormalized results are specified in an operation, the result of the exponent value must be specified to the representation function (`flbsr`). Since one usually wants the representation function governed by the exponents of the unnormalized operands, the interpretation function (`flbsi`) must return it. The two-element vector `numexp` gives, in its first element, the value of the number and, in its second element, the associated exponent.

11.4.5

Operations

Logic

Connectives. AND and OR functions are provided in both to-accumulator and to-memory operations—a consistent expansion of the single And To Memory of the 701. The Not operation is inconsistent in being accumulator-to-accumulator. The accumulator for the logical datatype is the vector [P, Digits]. The sign bit never participates. The Not is also inconsistent in inverting the Q bit, which does not participate in And and Or.

```
  COM
  ⋀ IBM 704 Not
  acc[Q,P,Accdigits]←˜acc[Q,P,Accdigits]

  ANA:od1:od2                 ORA:od1:od2
  ⋀ IBM 704 And               ⋀ IBM 704 Or
  od1←read704 adr704          od1←read704 adr704
  od2←acc[P,Accdigits]        od2←acc[P,Accdigits]
  acc[P,Accdigits]←od1∧od2    acc[P,Accdigits]←od1∨od2
  acc[Sign,Q]←0               acc[Sign,Q]←0

  ANS:od1:od2                 ORS:od1:od2
  ⋀ IBM 704 And To Memory     ⋀ IBM 704 Or To Memory
  od1←read704 adr704          od1←read704 adr704
  od2←acc[P,Accdigits]        od2←acc[P,Accdigits]
  adr704 write704 od1∧od2     adr704 write704 od1∨od2
```

PROGRAM 11-83   And, Or, and Not in the IBM 704.

Arithmetic shift. Following the 701 design, the 704 has four arithmetic shifts.

```
  b LGL Shift Logical Left          b ARS Shift Arithmetic Right
  b ALS Shift Arithmetic Left       b LRS Shift Arithmetic Long Right
  b LLS Shift Arithmetic Long Left  b RQL Rotate MQ Left
```

TABLE 11-84   Shift instructions in the IBM 704.

Logical shift. New are a rotation of the entire MQ and a Long Logical Left Shift, which is logical only in the sense that the MQ sign participates; the accumulator sign still remains unchanged.

```
┌Sign
│QP                                        ↓Sign
│
│ │  ┌─────────────────────────────┐      │ ┌──────────────────────┐  ┌────┐
│ │  │ Digits                      │      │ │ Digits               │  │    │
│ │  └─────────────────────────────┘      │ └──────────────────────┘  └────┘
0   3                              38     0                          36
Accumulator                              MQ register
```

```
LGL;shift
ค IBM 704 Shift Logical Left
shift←256|adr704
Oflo report shift↑acc[Accdigits].mq
acc[Q,P,Accdigits]←(accsize-1)↑shift↓acc[Q,P,Accdigits].mq
mq←word↑shift↓mq


RQL
ค IBM 704 Rotate MQ Left
mq←(256|adr704)Φmq
```

PROGRAM 11-85   Logical Shift in the IBM 704.

Fixed-Point Arithmetic

The fixed-point arithmetic instruction set expands the 701 set. Operations are provided for loading, storing, and check-summing words treated as bit vectors, called "logical" words. All three operations use the P bit as the high-order bit of the accumulator, rather than the sign bit. Add Logical uses an end-around carry from P, so that check-summing of blocks of data will give the same probability of detection for multiple high-order-bit errors as multiple low-order-bit errors. Add Logical turns out to be the mathematical equivalent of providing loading, storing, and algebraic addition (but not subtraction) of 1's-complement numbers.

c	CLM Clear Magnitude	c	CHS Negate
b	CLA Load	c	SSP Make Absolute
b	LDQ Load MQ	c	SSM Negate Absolute
b	CLS Load Negative	b	ADD Add
b	CAL Load Logical	b	ADM Add Absolute
b	STO Store	b	ACL Add And Carry Logical
b	STD Store Decrement	b	SUB Subtract
b	STP Store Prefix	b	SBM Subtract Absolute
b	STQ Store MQ	b	MPY Multiply
b	SLQ Store Upper MQ	b	MPR Multiply R
b	SLW Store Logical	b	DVH Divide Or Halt
		b	DVP Divide Or Proceed
		c	RND Round From MQ

Legend: R = Rounded.

TABLE 11-86   Fixed-point instructions of the IBM 704.

Load and Store.   With a new instruction format for the 704 come load and store operations for the various instruction fields, such as the Decrement and the Prefix (P and the two highest-order regular digits). The ability (inherent in 701 addressing) to store the left part of the MQ is preserved in the 704 with the operation Store Upper MQ.

The 704 instructions differ from those of the 701 in lacking size selection and having indexing.

Add and Subtract.   New are the sign handling and 1's-complement addition. The Carry Logical refers to the end-around-carry of 1's-complement addition.

```
CLA                                      STO
∩ IBM 704 Load                           ∩ IBM 704 Store
acc[Sign,Accdigits]←read704 adr704        adr704 write704 acc[Sign,Accdigits]
acc[Q,P]←0


                                         STD;od
CAL                                      ∩ IBM 704 Store Decrement
∩ IBM 704 Load Logical                    od←read704 adr704
acc[P,Accdigits]←read704 adr704           od[Decrement]←acc[P+Decrement]
acc[Sign,Q]←0                             adr704 write704 od
```

PROGRAM 11-87   Load and Store in the IBM 704.

```
SUB;s;p;subtrahend;minuend;difference    ADM;s;p;addend;augend;sum
∩ IBM 704 Subtract                        ∩ IBM 704 Add Absolute
s←acc[Sign]                               s←acc[Sign]
p←acc[P]                                  p←acc[P]
subtrahend←signmagni read704 adr704       addend←signmagni read704 adr704
minuend←signmagni acc                     augend←signmagni acc
difference←minuend-subtrahend             sum←augend+|addend
acc←accsize signmagnr difference          acc←accsize signmagnr sum
→If difference=0                          →If sum=0
THEN:acc[Sign]←s                          THEN:acc[Sign]←s
ENDIF:Oflo report p≠acc[P]                ENDIF:Oflo report p≠acc[P]


ACL;addend;augend;sum;carry              CHS
∩ IBM 704 Add And Carry Logical           ∩ IBM 704 Negate
addend←magni read704 adr704               acc[Sign]←~acc[Sign]
augend←magni acc[Q,P,Accdigits]
sum←augend+addend
carry←word carryfrom augend,addend
acc[Q,P,Accdigits]←(word+1) magnr sum+carry
```

PROGRAM 11-88   Add and Subtract in the IBM 704.

Divide.   Multiply and Divide are similar to the 701 operations, except that Divide Or Proceed is not available in the 701. In this operation, division is suppressed when the `Divide` indicator is set, which occurs when the divisor is smaller (in absolute value) than the high-order part of the dividend (including when the divisor is zero).

```
DVP;dr;divisor;dividend;quotient;remainder
∩ IBM 704 Divide Or Proceed
divisor←magni dr[Digits] WHERE dr←read704 adr704
dividend←magni acc[Q,P,Accdigits],mq[Digits]
Divide report divisor≤dividend÷2*word-1
→OUT ind[Divide]
quotient←⌊dividend÷divisor
remainder←divisor|dividend                      DVH
acc[Accdigits]←(ρAccdigits) magnr remainder     ∩ IBM 704 Divide Or Halt
mq[Digits]←(ρDigits) magnr quotient             DVP
mq[Sign]←acc[Sign]≠dr[Sign]                        stop←ind[Divide]
```

PROGRAM 11-89   Divide in the IBM 704.

Compare.   Comparison is combined with branching, as shown later.

Floating-Point Arithmetic

All floating-point operations, except division, are available with normalized and unnormalized result.

```
b FAD F Add                    b FMP F Multiply
b UFA Unnormalized Add         b UFM Unnormalized Multiply
b FSB F Subtract               b FDH F Divide Or Halt
b UFS Unnormalized Subtract    b FDP F Divide Or Proceed
Legend: F = Floating-point.
```

TABLE 11-90   Floating-point instructions of the IBM 704.

Floating-point Add and Subtract.   The description of the floating-point operations is close to the implementation level; Add is described in 11 elaborate steps. The design reflects von Neumann's cautious approach toward floating point. Program control of the process is made as complete as possible by the unnormalized operations and by preserving low-order coefficient bits in the MQ. We show both normalized and unnormalized addition to illustrate their differences.

Again, we have to mind our Ps and Qs. If they are not both zero, the operation will be in error, which we approximate by showing the instruction as suppressed. Note that, because of the P and Q bits, the fields in the accumulator have an allocation index that is 2 larger than in a regular word.

Apart from these improprieties, the key issues are truncation and order-of-magnitude zero. The number with largest exponent is not truncated at all, since it fits the accumulator; the other operand is truncated if, after shifting,

```
FAD;sr;ad;au;s;scale;addend;augend;sum;rl
A IBM 704 Floating-point Add
→OUTv/acc[Q,P]
ad←fl704i sr WHERE sr←read704 adr704
au←fl704i acc[Sign,Accdigits]
s←acc[Sign],sr[Sign]
scale←base*(au[1]⌈ad[1])-2×point
addend←scale×truncate ad[0]÷scale
augend←scale×truncate au[0]÷scale
sum←augend+addend
acc[Sign,Accdigits]←fl704r sum
rl←fl704i acc[Sign,Accdigits]
mq←fl704r(sum-rl[0]),rl[1]-point
→If(0=sum)v(rl[1]+point)≤au[1]⌈ad[1]
THEN:acc[]←0
    acc[Sign]←s[au[1]>ad[1]]
    mq←fl704r sum,(au[1]⌈ad[1])-point
    mq[Exp]←0
ENDIF:

UFA;sr;ad;au;s;scale;addend;augend;sm;rl
A IBM 704 Unnormalized Add
→OUTv/acc[Q,P]
ad←fl704i sr WHERE sr←read704 adr704
au←fl704i acc[Sign,Accdigits]
s←acc[Sign],sr[Sign]
scale←base*(au[1]⌈ad[1])-2×point
addend←scale×truncate ad[0]÷scale
augend←scale×truncate au[0]÷scale
sm←(augend+addend),au[1]⌈ad[1]
acc[Sign,Accdigits]←fl704r sm
rl←fl704i acc[Sign,Accdigits]
mq←fl704r(sm[0]-rl[0]),rl[1]-point
→If 0=v/acc[P+1↓Coef]
THEN:acc[Sign]←s[au[1]>ad[1]]
ENDIF:
```

PROGRAM 11-91   Floating-point Add in the IBM 704.

it does not fit the accumulator and MQ. The sign of zero also complicates the operation; the original signs of the accumulator and of the memory operand are recorded in s, and one of them is selected in case of a zero result. The sign of a zero is the sign of the operand with the smaller (!) exponent, or, if equal, the original sign of the accumulator.

The interpretation function f1704i returns the value of an operand and its exponent as a tuple. In normalized addition the representation function f1704r is supplied with the value of the sum and no preferred exponent; it gives the normalized result. In unnormalized addition the largest exponent is supplied with the value of the sum as a preferred exponent; the unnormalized result uses that exponent if possible.

The exponent of the result in MQ is made point less than the exponent in the accumulator. In case the high-order bits of the sum are all zeros prior to normalization, a true zero is assumed in normalized operation, and an order-of-magnitude zero is assumed in unnormalized operation. The true zero has minimal exponent and zero coefficient in the accumulator, and minimal exponent, but not necessarily zero coefficient, in the MQ. The order-of-magnitude zero exponent is equal to the largest operand exponent. Observe that the representation function assigns the preferred exponent (if any) to a zero value.

Floating-point Multiply and Divide.   We show both normalized and unnormalized Multiply, to illustrate the design approach. The normalized multiplication actually normalizes only one bit position at most, which guarantees a normalized result only when both operands are normalized prior to the operation. The difference in normalization action is expressed by the preferred exponent that is supplied to the representation function f1704r. For FMP, this exponent is one less than for UFM, which causes the representation function to attempt a 1-bit normalization.

```
FMP;sr;mr;mc;s;pd;rl                 UFM;sr;mr;mc;s;pd;rl
ⴰ IBM 704 Floating-Point Multiply    ⴰ IBM 704 Unnormalized Multiply
→OUTv/acc[Q,P]                       →OUTv/acc[Q,P]
sr←read704 adr704                    sr←read704 adr704
mr←f1704i sr                         mr←f1704i sr
mc←f1704i mq                         mc←f1704i mq
s←(plus,minus)[mq[Sign]≠sr[Sign]]    s←(plus,minus)[mq[Sign]≠sr[Sign]]
pd←(mc[0]×mr[0]),mc[1]+mr[1]-1       pd←(mc[0]×mr[0]),mc[1]+mr[1]
acc[Sign,Accdigits]←f1704r pd        acc[Sign,Accdigits]←f1704r pd
rl←f1704i acc[Sign,Accdigits]        rl←f1704i acc[Sign,Accdigits]
mq←f1704r(pd[0]-rl[0]),rl[1]-point   mq←f1704r(pd[0]-rl[0]),rl[1]-point
→If 0=v/acc[P+1↓Coef]                mq[Sign]←acc[Sign]←s
THEN:acc[Q,P,P+Exp]←0
   mq[Exp]←0
ENDIF:mq[Sign]←acc[Sign]←s
```

PROGRAM 11-92   Floating-point Multiply in the IBM 704.

The high-order part of the product appears in the accumulator with the low-order part (unnormalized) in the MQ. The P and Q bits remain unchanged, except when a true zero is recognized in the accumulator. The sign of zero gives the usual troubles. Zero treatment is otherwise the same as in addition.

Floating-point Divide has two variants: Floating Divide Or Halt stops the machine when a zero divisor is encountered; Floating Divide Or Proceed

suppresses the division and proceeds. Both give zero-divide behavior when unnormalized operands would generate a quotient overflow.

Floating-point Compare.   The floating-point format was carefully chosen to allow fixed-point comparison to work properly. The fixed-point compare and branch operations all apply.

11.4.6

Instruction Sequencing

Normal sequencing proceeds under control of the instruction address. Since all instructions are one word long, the control is simple.

```
  cycle704                       inst←ifetch704
a basic cycle of the IBM 704   a IBM 704 instruction fetch
  REPEAT:execute ifetch704       inst←read704 iadr
  →UNTIL stop                    iadr←memcap|iadr+1
```

PROGRAM 11-93   Basic cycle and instruction fetch of the IBM 704.

A rich set of sequencing operations is provided.

```
b NOP No Operation                   b TQP Branch On MQ Plus
b HPR Stop                           b TLQ Branch On MQ Low
b HTR Stop And Branch                b TQO Branch On MQ Overflow
b TRA Branch                         a TNX Branch On No-Increment
b TTR Branch After Trap              b CAS Skip On Comparison
b TPL Branch On Plus                 c DCT Skip On Division
b TMI Branch On Minus                c PBT Skip On P Bit
b TNO Branch On No-Overflow          c LBT Skip On Low Order Bit
b TZE Branch On Zero                 c RTT Skip On Tape Redundancy
a TXL Branch On Index Low Or Equal   a TIX Branch On Increment
b TNZ Branch On Non-zero             a TXI Branch And Increment
a TXH Branch On Index High           b TSX Call
b TOV Branch On Overflow             c ETM Enter Trapping Mode
                                     c LTM Leave Trapping Mode
```

TABLE 11-94   Sequencing and supervisory instructions of the IBM 704.

Linear Sequence

Next instruction.   The trapping mode, when enabled, causes a trap for each successful branch. The function `target704` illustrates this action. A return from the trap-handling routine requires a branch without trapping: Branch After Trap is provided for just this purpose.

Completion.   The No Operation and the Stop And Branch are the same as in the 701; the plain Stop is new.

```
  TRA                          address←target704 address
a IBM 704 Branch             a IBM 704 branch or trap
  iadr←target704 adr704        →If trap
                              THEN: a save old address and trap to 1
                                 memory[0:Address]←(ρAddress) magnr iadr-1
  TTR                            address←1
a IBM 704 Branch After Trap  ENDIF:
  iadr←adr704
```

PROGRAM 11-95   Unconditional Branch in the IBM 704.

Decision

Conditional branching.   Most decision operations are conditional-branch instructions (called "Transfers") whose address specifies the branch target location and whose condition is specified by the operation code—for example, Branch On Minus.

```
TNO                                      TMI
 ⌐ IBM 704 Branch On No-Overflow         ⌐ IBM 704 Branch On Minus
 →If~ind[Oflo]                           →If minus=acc[Sign]
 THEN:iadr←target704 adr704              THEN:iadr←target704 adr704
 ENDIF:ind[Oflo]←0                       ENDIF:


TXH;index;decrement                      TLQ;operand;comparand
 ⌐ IBM 704 Branch On Index High          ⌐ IBM 704 Branch On MQ Low
 index←magni indexread704                operand←signmagni mq
 decrement←fld Decrement                 comparand←signmagni acc
 →If index>decrement                     →If operand<comparand
 THEN:iadr←target704 fld Address         THEN:iadr←target704 adr704
 ENDIF:                                  ENDIF:


CAS;comparand;operand                    PBT
 ⌐ IBM 704 Skip On Comparison            ⌐ IBM 704 Skip On P Bit
 comparand←signmagni read704 adr704      iadr←iadr+acc[P]
 operand←signmagni acc
 iadr←iadr+(operand>comparand)+operand≥comparand
```

PROGRAM 11-96   Conditional Branch in the IBM 704.

A second large class comprises tests that, when successful, cause the next instruction to be skipped. CAS, for example, skips one instruction when the operands (fixed-point or floating-point) are equal, and skips two instructions when the accumulator operand is greater than the memory operand. The address field may be used for a comparand address, as in CAS, or for operation-code expansion, as in PBT.

The branches that test the overflow indicators reset these indicators, as in TNO.

Stevens analyzes the decision operations of the 704 fully and insightfully [W.Y. Stevens, 1958].

Iteration

Incrementation and termination.   One-instruction loop-closing is provided by TIX and TNX, whose format contains the index decrement, which is also used as the comparand. TXI—Branch And Increment—simply applies the decrement to the index and then branches unconditionally.

```
TIX;index;decrement;ix                   TNX;index;decrement;ix
 ⌐ IBM 704 Branch On Increment           ⌐ IBM 704 Branch On No-Increment
 index←magni indexread704                index←magni indexread704
 decrement←fld Decrement                 decrement←fld Decrement
 →If index>decrement                     →IF index>decrement
 THEN: ⌐ decrement and branch            THEN: ⌐ decrement
    ix←adrsize magnr index-decrement        ix←adrsize magnr index-decrement
    indexwrite704 ix                        indexwrite704 ix
    iadr←target704 fld Address              →ENDIF
 ENDIF:                                  ELSE: ⌐ branch
                                            iadr←target704 fld Address
                                         ENDIF:
```

PROGRAM 11-97   Increment and branch in the IBM 704.

Delegation

Call and return.   The Call instruction TSX puts the *complement* of its own instruction address into the specified index register.   Because indexing is subtractive, use of this register in the subroutine causes the calling instruction's address to be added to the specified address. Parameters or their addresses are put in the calling sequence after TSX. They are then easily accessed by indexing their displacements with the calling address. Return is just as easily effected.

```
TSX
ⲁ IBM 704 Call
  indexwrite704 adrsize magnr-iadr
  iadr←target704 fld Address
```

PROGRAM 11-98   Call in the IBM 704.

11.4.7

Supervision

The trapping mode is a primitive supervisory mode that monitors all successful branches.

Integrity

Invalidities of all sorts cause a machine halt. Divide Or Proceed allows the programmer to avoid halt on invalid division; the action is suppressed and an indicator set. There is no memory or other protection.

11.4.8

Input/Output

Devices

Store.   The set of four drums of the 701 is expanded to eight, each still with 2048 words. Ten magnetic tapes can also be used for storage.

PROGRAM 11-99   Input/output devices of the IBM 704.

Source and sink.   Card punch and reader, a printer, and a cathode-ray tube serve as source and sink.

Direct Input/Output

Switches and lights are controlled by direct I/O, using Sense instructions. Copy operations act as direct I/O, effecting parallel transfers to/from the MQ from/to the card reader, punch, and printer. The main CPU process stops automatically until the completion of a parallel transfer between the MQ and an I/O device.

Overlapped Input/Output

In serial output transfers, such as transfers to tape, the main process proceeds as soon as the MQ is loaded from memory. It is up to the programmer to avoid using the MQ for the requisite interval while the serial transfer is taking place. A Write Select with a special address of 217 serves as a control operation to delay CPU operation until the MQ is free.

The I/O instructions are as in the 701, except that the Sense instruction is split in two; the names Plus Sense and Minus Sense refer to the code, not to the semantics.

```
b CPY Copy And Skip       b MSE Minus Sense
b RDS Read Select         b BST Backspace Tape
b WEF Write End Of File   b REW Rewind Tape
b WRS Write Select        b LDA Locate Drum Address
b PSE Plus Sense
```

TABLE 11-100   Input/output instructions of the IBM 704.

Read and Write.   Copy And Skip performs the basic I/O data transfer and also two implied tests, skipping two instructions on end of record (e.g., on tape) and one instruction on end of file, as shown for the 701.

Sense and Control.   The action of the Sense instructions depends upon the (indexed) address. For example, upon Plus Sense, address 96 turns off all four lights; 97 through 100 turn on individual lights; 113 through 118 cause a skip if the corresponding switch is on; 225 and 226 each give a signal at the cardpunch's plugboard; 240 causes a skip depending upon a condition on the printer plugboard—for example, out of paper; 361 through 372 each give an impulse at the printer's plugboard. Upon Minus Sense, the addresses 97 through 100 sense one of the lights and indicators; if it is on, a skip occurs and the light is turned off.

```
PSE:class
ϱ IBM 704 Plus Sense
 class←(adr704< 96 97 101 113 119 225 227 240 241 251)ι1
 →CASE 6 0 1 6 2 6 3 6 4 5 6[class]
 C0:lights←0
    →ENDCASE
 C1:lights[adr704-97]←1
    →ENDCASE
 C2:iadr←iadr+switch[adr704-113]
    →ENDCASE
 C3:punchin[adr704-225]←1
    →ENDCASE
 C4:iadr←iadr+printout              MSE
    →ENDCASE                        ϱ IBM 704 Minus Sense
 C5:printin[adr704-241]              →Ifν/lights∧adr704=97+ι4
    →ENDCASE                        THEN:lights[adr704-97]←0
 C6:                                     iadr←iadr+1
 ENDCASE:                           ENDIF:
```

PROGRAM 11-101   Input/output Sense and Control in the IBM 704.

11.4.9

Implementation Notes

The 704 was made of the same 1-MHz vacuum-tube circuitry as the 701, but it had a magnetic core memory, which was reliable, instead of the Williams Tube memory of the 701. It proved to be a reliable workhorse.

11.4.10

Bibliography

IBM, 1955: *IBM Electronic Data-Processing Machines Type 704 Manual of Operation.* Form 24-6661-0. New York: IBM Corp. (our defining reference).

Burks [1946], Bashe [1986], Greenstadt [1957], Grumette [1958], W.Y. Stevens [1958].

11.4.11

Exercises

11-9 Assuming consistency with the instructions in this section, give the formal descriptions of:

    a. The index instructions PAX, SXD and the shifts ALS, LRS

    b. The load and store instructions CLM, LDQ, STP, STQ, SLQ, SLW

    c. The floating-point arithmetic instructions FSB, UFS, FDH, FDP

    d. The sequencing instructions TNZ, TXL, TQP, TQD, LBT, TXI, ETM, and LTM.

11-10 "If the divide-check indicator and light are on, the indicator and light are turned off, and the calculator takes the next instruction in sequence. If the indicator and light are off, the calculator skips the next instruction and proceeds from there" [IBM, 1955]. Give the formal description of DCT from the machine descriptions in this section and from this manual text.

11-11 How would you improve the floating-point operation of the 704? Give the formal description for addition and multiplication following your design. Preserve consistency with the unaltered parts of the 704 design.

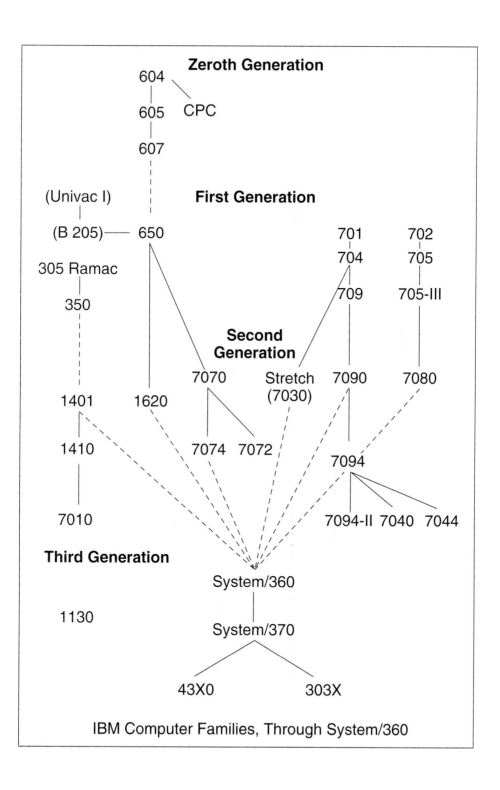

IBM Computer Families, Through System/360

12

IBM House

IBM Computer Families

Architectural diversity.   Untangling IBM computer architectures requires recognizing several independent archetypes, produced by independent teams essentially uninfluenced by one another. These independent origins are spread out over many years, reflecting a philosophy of decentralized management. What is remarkable is not that the computer products are so diverse, but that they share so much conceptual structure—another demonstration of convergence toward the classical computer.

The history of IBM machine families divides into two periods: before and after the IBM System/360 in 1964. This division came about through IBM's decision to replace six then-current product families by a single new one. The new family was quite successful commercially, and therefore it also achieved the desired conceptual unification—those six family trees essentially end in 1964. Had the 360 not been an overwhelming market success, the earlier families would have continued. The frontispiece shows the families of this period.

Since 1964, two diversifying forces have continued to operate on IBM machines. First, the 360 product family as it has evolved has split, with major architectural extensions (called *XA*, Extended Architecture, and *ESA*, Enterprise Systems Architecture) being devised for and incorporated in high-performance models (made by the Data Systems Division), but not in middle-sized and smaller models, made by other divisions.

Second, the creation of whole new architectures has continued.   Each was originally intended for markets with price objectives putatively too low to be met satisfactorily with 360/370 implementations.   Each of the new architectures has in turn sired a product line of successors, some merely more powerful implementations of the original architectures, some incorporating architectural extensions.   Figure 12-1 shows the families of the post-1964 period.

The commercial success of the IBM Personal Computer not only created a whole new market, but also started a major product line that promises to equal that of the 360 in lifetime and number of models, although not in performance scope. It also started a third period of IBM architectural history.

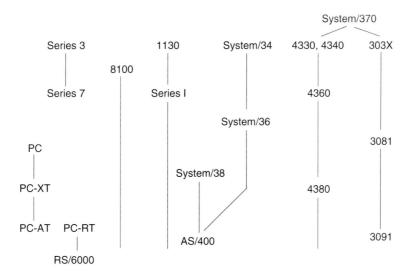

FIGURE 12-1   IBM computer families from the IBM System/360 to 1990.

What is architecturally remarkable about this product family is that the 8086 (1976) family architecture it incorporates is not IBM's, but Intel's (Section 16.1).

IBM Prehistorical Computers

IBM introduced its first versions of stored-program electronic computers in 1953, relatively late. The company had, however, built both programmable computers and electronic computers before that. The evolution of electromechanical punched-card tabulators and calculators had proceeded through the 1930s and early 1940s in Endicott, New York, culminating in a plugboard-programmed electromechanical calculator, the 602A. Endicott engineers had also implemented and realized the Harvard Mark I (1944) according to Howard Aiken's architecture.

Electronics engineers at Endicott devised a plugboard-programmed punched-card electronic calculator, the 604, which integrated well into punched-card procedures and was a commercial success. It had 10 words of data memory, capacity for programs of up to 60 two-address instructions, and data-dependent branching. Straightforward successors of more power were the 605 and 607.

A non-straightforward successor was the Card-Programmed Calculator. This machine incorporated a 605 plugged to execute a set of standard subroutines, an electromechanical memory of 16 words, and a 407 tabulator that read punched-card programs of any length. Each card carried one three-address instruction, which typically invoked a floating-point subroutine on the 605.

Meanwhile, IBM electronics engineers built an electronic scientific computer, paper-tape programmed, called the Selective Sequence Electronic Calculator. Wallace Eckert was the chief architect.

Pre-1964 Architectures

Three groups, two in Poughkeepsie and one in Endicott, all developed stored-program electronic computers as IBM's initial commercial offerings.

IBM 701 (1953).   The genius of the 701 was its rich set of directly attached I/O devices: a fast printer, a fast card reader, magnetic tapes, and a magnetic drum.   These devices allowed much faster job turnaround than did other contemporary scientific machines, which did not have direct card readers and printers and so required awkward card–tape and tape–printer conversion steps. As a consequence, the 701 and its successors were better received than their competitors, even though the latter were perhaps 50 percent faster in raw computing performance, for equivalent prices.

IBM 702 (1954).   A second Poughkeepsie group designed the 702 for large tape-to-tape file-maintenance ("commercial") applications, such as those being done on the Univac I (1951).

The independence of the 701 and 702 groups shows not only in the radically different computer architectures, but even in the tape standards: The 701 uses odd parity; the 702, even.

IBM 650 (1954).   The Endicott group built a card-in, card-out machine that integrated powerfully into standard punched-card procedures. The 650 was therefore a roaring success; some 1800 were sold, an order of magnitude more copies than those of any other contemporary machine.   The 650's magnetic drum and conservative circuitry proved remarkably reliable among first-generation machines, so there was little pressure to go to another realization for many years.

The 701 and 702, on the other hand, used Williams-tube memories that were expensive and not reliable. The appearance of magnetic-core memories enabled an early change of technology.   With it came modest architectural change as the 702 sired the IBM 705 (1956), and major architectural redesign as the 701 sired the 704 (1955).

The next substantial change was in I/O control, the provision of semi-autonomous I/O channels performing elaborate sequences and reading and writing concurrently with CPU processing. This concept led to the IBM 709 and the 705 III (1957).

Transistor circuits led to the reimplementation of the 705 III as the IBM 7080 (1961), and the re-realization of the 709 as the 7090 (1959). The 650 sired two transistorized descendants—the 7070 (1960) in Poughkeepsie and, later, the 1620 (1960), a small scientific computer, in Endicott.

IBM 1401 (1960).   Meanwhile, two significant developments were afoot. One was the invention of the magnetic disk. This device was introduced in the 305 computer, which did little else but maintain large files on disk. The other was the development of the high-speed chain printer, which required a substantial magnetic-core memory to control printing. Around this memory the designers wrapped a radically different and rather minimal architecture for commercial data processing—the 1401.

The 1401, like the 650, slipped naturally into punched-card installations. The whole 1401 system was a more economical and faster printer than three

407 card printers. Its printer nose inveigled the computer camel into the office; once the computer was there, people discovered its capabilities. Some 12,000 machines were installed, creating the second major market expansion for computers.

Each of these second-generation machines—the 1401, 7070, and 7090—sired others, with no substantial architectural innovations.

IBM Stretch.   In 1955, while the 704 was still dominant in scientific computing and transistor technology was developing rapidly, Dunwell and Palmer led IBM in a bold decision to make a scientific supercomputer—the IBM Stretch, which reigned as the fastest supercomputer from 1961 until the CDC 6600 in 1964.

The Stretch explored a host of innovations in architecture and implementation; we treat it in the Explorer House, Section 13.3.

Post-1964 Architectures

IBM System/360 descendants.   The 360 architecture has shown remarkable endurance. Four major steps mark its post-1964 evolution. In 1970 the IBM System/370 extended the architecture modestly in several directions, removing limitations. In 1972 a major modification—virtual-memory and virtual-machine capability—was made without a name change. Then, in 1982, came a major extension—one originally planned in 1964: The 370 XA (for Extended Architecture) extended the address size from 24 bits to 31 bits. In 1988 came the 370 ESA. This modification provided for every general purpose register a corresponding 32-bit Access Register that points to one of many disjoint address spaces. Each reference using the general purpose register as a base address is automatically modified to point into the associated address space.

Many manufacturers have made many implementations of each of these architectures. The 370 architecture has been implemented in an option card to be added to an IBM PC. At the other end of the spectrum are the Fujitsu scientific supercomputers.

Non-360 families.   As each implementation technology has appeared, it has seemed to some IBM engineers that cost/performance ratios could be improved, especially at the low end of the several markets, if only the constraints of the 360/370 compatibility were removed. This idea, and the relative independence of IBM's product divisions, has led to several new, conceptually unrelated product families:

- Series/1, a classical binary minicomputer
- System/32 family, character-oriented for small businesses
- System/38, an object-oriented architecture
- Series 7, a data acquisition minicomputer
- 8001 (UCC) family, a microcomputer architecture oriented toward communications
- The Displaywriter, oriented toward word processing
- The Personal Computer family, using the Intel 8086 family CPUs discussed in Section 16.1

- The AS/400 family, a descendant of the Systems 32 and 38

Of these families, only the System/38 is of much architectural interest, although the System/34–AS/400 family and the Personal Computer family have been major commercial successes. PCs and their clones number in the tens of millions. That fact changes the computer world and strongly shapes the IBM world.

Operating systems. IBM's post-1964 computers are best classified in terms of the several major operating systems (with their concomitant language, utility, and applications programs) that IBM evolved. Those for 360s and 370s are shown in Figure 12-2. They provide the inertia that keeps architectures alive; they furnish both the constraints and the incentives shaping architectural evolution. The dashed lines show systems that sprang from OS/360, sometimes as derivatives, sometimes as reactions against it.

Bibliography

Bashe et al. [1986], Bender et al. [1960], Phelps [1980], Pugh [1995], Svigals [1959].

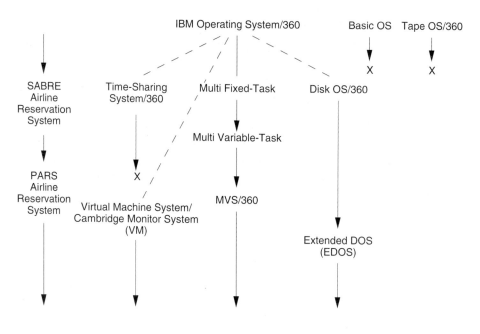

Legend: X = discontinued.

FIGURE 12-2   Major IBM Operating Systems.

12.1
IBM 650

12.1.1
Highlights

History

Architect.   The chief architect was Ernest Hughes; the chief implementer was Frank Hamilton.

Dates.   The IBM 650 was announced on July 2, 1953; first delivery was in December 1954; the last unit was sold in 1962 [Bashe et al., 1986].

Family tree.   This chapter's frontispiece shows the family tree.

Noteworthy

The 650 was the first machine with over 1000 copies (about 1800 in fact [Bashe et al., 1986]), about an order of magnitude more than predecessors and contemporaries. It introduced computing into hundreds of businesses and colleges.

The 650 is, like its ancestor the Univac I, a decimal version of the proposed computer described by Burks, Goldstine, and von Neumann [1946] and built as the Princeton IAS computer (1952). It has a fixed word length, a working store, and simple single-address instructions of uniform length.

Decimal.   The architecture is purely decimal; no representation finer than the decimal digit is discernible. Likewise, one cannot tell the allocation and encoding of the sign—it is a pure datum. The machine is exceptionally clean in these respects.

Unlike the Univac I, the 650 divides the word into decimal digits rather than alphanumeric characters. All arithmetic and addressing are decimal. Characters are represented by digit pairs. In branching there is even a primitive logical datatype mapped upon the decimal digit.

The word length of 10 digits enhances the decimal feel of the machine, so obviously designed for hand coding before even assembly programs were in use.

Embedding.   The working-store registers that are normally implied in the instruction can also be addressed with storage addresses—a novel feature.

Signed-magnitude notation.   The 650 deviates from the IAS design, as did the Univac, in the use of signed-magnitude notation.

Working store.   The 650 deviates even further from the IAS design by using a double-length accumulator and a distributor, but no MQ. The relationship between the halves of the 650's accumulator is, however, very like that of the 704's accumulator and MQ (Figure 11-71, Programs 11-85 and 12-18).

Fixed-point arithmetic.   Although only fixed-point arithmetic is provided in the original machine, there is a Shift And Count operation for normalization in floating-point subroutines.

Table lookup.   The 650 is a drum machine. This technology gave it a major advantage in reliability over electrostatic-storage machines, such as the 701; the disadvantage was dramatically lower speed. A search operation, however, can be performed at drum-scanning speed, without waiting for drum rotations for instructions. It is used successfully in the Table Lookup instruction. As core storage eventually replaced the drum, the speed advantage of the Table Lookup disappeared; its frequency of use no longer justifies the function today.

Policing.   The 650, like the Univac, polices invalid operation codes, invalid addresses, and invalid data.

Concurrent input/output.   I/O uses fixed-size, concurrently operated buffers to allow transmission to and from unsynchronized mechanical devices. I/O was originally by punched cards and printer only. During its life the machine was enhanced by tapes, disks, and communications.

Options.   The 650 architecture was incrementally, but substantially, extended over its long life. Added one by one were character I/O, index registers, masking, floating point, and a 60-word supplementary fast memory motivated by reading and writing tapes and disks. We describe the original basic machine, with some reference to later extensions.

Peculiarities

Chained instructions.   Since an instruction cannot squeeze into a halfword, but a full word is rather long for one instruction, the designers used the spare instruction space to provide for chaining the instruction vector. Each instruction contains an implied branch; there is no need for a separate unconditional branch.

No logic.   Following the IAS and Univac, the 650 has no logical connectives.

Cumulative multiply.   The cumulative multiply reflects some shortcuts in the implementation. A partial product can overflow into the multiplier digits, resulting in a useless and erroneous product.

Descendants

The 7070 (1960) succeeded the 650 and preserved the thoroughly decimal fixed-word-length structure. It added record-control words (descriptors) to control internal and I/O moves. Its flexible field-definition facility is a very livable technique in a fixed-word-length architecture. The 7070 spaces include three accumulators and 99 registers for indexing. The 7070 continues to use table lookup, but the realization-derived advantage is gone, since the machine uses core storage instead of the 650 drum.

12.1.2

Machine Language

Language Level

Design philosophy.   The 650 is a direct descendant of the Univac I, with fixed-length decimal data words and instructions, aimed at the commercial market.

Unit System

Taking 4 bits for a decimal digit, the word size of the 650 roughly matches that of the IAS.

```
initiate650                      format650
ᴀ initiation of the IBM 650      ᴀ IBM 650 information units
format650                        ᴀ representation radix
configure650                     radix←10
space650                         ᴀ information units
name650                          word←11
control650                       accsize←21
data650                          adrsize←4
                                 byte←2
                                 ᴀ address capacity
configure650                     adrcap←2000
ᴀ configuration for the IBM 650
ᴀ memory capacity
memcap←adrcap
```

PROGRAM 12-3   Basic parameters of the IBM 650.

Spaces

Memory name-space.   Only 2000 addresses out of a name-space of 10,000 are used for memory addressing. Of the remainder, 6000 were later used for indexing, and some of the remaining 2000 for fast memory.

Working store.   The IAS accumulator and MQ are combined into one double-length Accumulator. The Distributor (visible storage register) is a typical Univac trait. The content of the 1-bit remainder-sign register is specified only following the execution of a Divide.

```
space650
ᴀ IBM 650 spaces                 ᴀ control store
ᴀ memory                         ᴀ - instruction address
memory←?(memcap,word)ρradix      iadr←?memcap
ᴀ working store                  ᴀ - indicators
ᴀ - accumulator                  ind←?4ρ2
acc←?accsizeρradix               ᴀ - manual entry
ᴀ - distributor                  switch←?wordρradix
dist←?wordρradix                 ᴀ - stop enable switches
ᴀ - remainder sign               mask←?3ρ2
rmsign←?radix                    ᴀ input/output
                                 cardin←(10,word)ρradix
                                 cardout←(10,word)ρradix
```

PROGRAM 12-4   Spaces of the IBM 650.

```
name650
ᴀ IBM 650 space names
ᴀ memory embedding
ᴀ - lower accumulator   ᴀ - switches
Accl←8002                Switch←8000
ᴀ - upper accumulator   ᴀ - input/output transfer
Accu←8003                Input←1+ι10
ᴀ - distributor          Output←27+ι10
Dist←8001
```

PROGRAM 12-5   Embedding in the IBM 650.

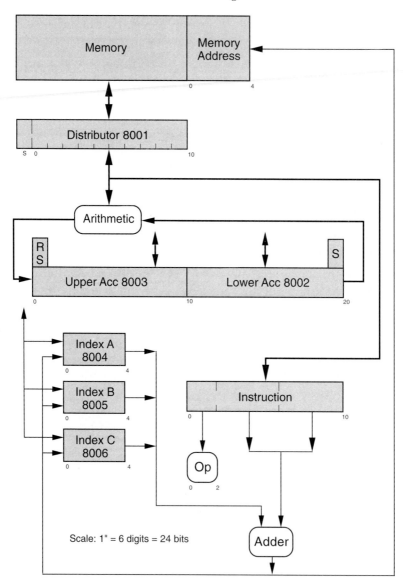

FIGURE 12-6   Programming model for the IBM 650.

Optional. Later additions are three index registers and a 60-word immediate-access memory, which also serves as the buffer for reading and writing tape.

Control store. The control store contains five indicators and three stop-control switches: one for stop codes, one for overflows, and one for all other invalidities and machine malfunctions. When a switch is not set to stop, in the first two cases the machine proceeds. In the case of invalidities and machine malfunctions, it traps to the console decimal switches, which usually contain an instruction.

Embedding. The Distributor, the upper and lower part of the Accumulator, and a 10-digit (plus sign) set of decimal switches on the console are embedded in memory name-space.

Within each 50-word band, locations 1 through 10 may be used for input and locations 27 through 36 may be used for output, as shown in name650 (Program 12-5).

Programming model. We show the addresses of the embedded registers. We also show the optional index registers, which are not included in the formal descriptions, but are described in the text. The absence of an Instruction Address is striking (Figure 12-6).

Operand Specification

Number of addresses. The 650 is a one-address machine with an explicit next-instruction address.

Address phrase. The address phrase is just a four-digit field; it occurs twice in the instruction. Index specification is encoded in the high-order digit.

Operation Specification

Out of a space of 100 operation codes, 44 codes were used initially.

Mnemonics. Systematic and serviceable mnemonics are used (Program 12-7).

```
a→NOOP    STL      i        RAU      i
  STOP    STU      i        RSU      i
  i       STDA     i        i        i
  i       STIA     i        i        i
  i       STD      BRNZU    DIVRU    TLU
  i       i        BRNZ     RAL      i
  i       i        BRMIN    RSL      i
  i       i        BROV     RAABL    i
  i       i        i        RSABL    i
  i       i        i        LD       i
  AU      SRT      i        RD       BRD10
  SU      SRD      i        PCH      BRD1
  i       i        i        i        BRD2
  i       i        i        i        BRD3
  DIV     i        i        i        BRD4
  AL      SLT      i        i        BRD5
  SL      SCT      i        i        BRD6
  AABL    i        i        i        BRD7
  SABL    i        i        i        BRD8
  MULT    i        i        i        BRD9
```

PROGRAM 12-7   Operation-code list in the IBM 650.

```
     ⌐ data handling                   a MULT  Multiply
a TLU    Table Lookup                  a DIV   Divide
     ⌐ logic and shift                 a DIVRU Divide Without Remainder
a SLT    Shift Arithmetic Left             ⌐ sequencing
a SCT    Shift Arithmetic Left And Count a NOOP  No Operation
a SRT    Shift Arithmetic Right         a STOP  Stop
a SRD    Shift Arithmetic Right R       a BRD1  Branch On Digit 1
     ⌐ fixed-point arithmetic          a BRD2  Branch On Digit 2
a RAU    Load Upper                     a BRD3  Branch On Digit 3
a RAL    Load Lower                     a BRD4  Branch On Digit 4
a LD     Load Distributor               a BRD5  Branch On Digit 5
a RAABL  Load Lower Absolute            a BRD6  Branch On Digit 6
a RSU    Load Upper Negative            a BRD7  Branch On Digit 7
a RSL    Load Lower Negative            a BRD8  Branch On Digit 8
a RSABL  Load Lower Negative Absolute   a BRD9  Branch On Digit 9
a STU    Store Upper                    a BRD10 Branch On Digit 10
a STL    Store Lower                    a BRMIN Branch On Minus
a STD    Store Distributor              a BRNZ  Branch On Non-zero
a STDA   Store Data Address             a BRNZU Branch On Non-zero Upper
a STIA   Store Instruction Address      a BROV  Branch On Overflow
a AU     Add Upper                          ⌐ input/output
a AL     Add Lower                      a RD    Read Card
a AABL   Add Lower Absolute             a PCH   Punch Card
a SU     Subtract Upper
a SL     Subtract Lower
a SABL   Subtract Lower Absolute
Legend: R = Rounded.
```

TABLE 12-8   Instruction list of the IBM 650.

Instruction Structure

Machine-language syntax.   All instructions conform to the same syntactic pattern.

```
        syntax650
    a Unused,Opcode,Address,Next
```

PROGRAM 12-9   Instruction syntax of the IBM 650

Instruction format.   The instruction uses only the digit positions of a word, not the sign.

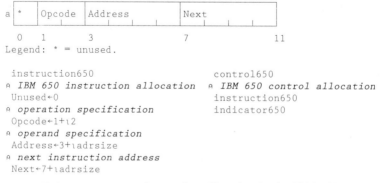

```
a | *  │Opcode │Address      │ Next
  |    │       │             │

  0   1        3             7              11
Legend: * = unused.
```

```
  instruction650                control650
  ⌐ IBM 650 instruction allocation  ⌐ IBM 650 control allocation
  Unused←0                      instruction650
  ⌐ operation specification     indicator650
  Opcode←1+ι2
  ⌐ operand specification
  Address←3+ιadrsize
  ⌐ next instruction address
  Next←7+ιadrsize
```

PROGRAM 12-10   Instruction allocation in the IBM 650.

Status format.   Invalid operation codes and invalid addresses are policed. There is also a machine-malfunction indicator.

```
     indicator650
   A IBM 650 indicator allocation
   A programmed stop                A invalid operation code
    Progr←0                          Invop←2
   A overflow                       A invalid address
    Oflo←1                           Invadr←2
   A machine malfunction            A absolute stop
    Mach←2                           Stop←3
```

PROGRAM 12-11   Indicators in the IBM 650.

12.1.3

Addressing

Direct addressing. The embedding of the working store into memory space complicates the reading from memory. Embedding does not apply to writing into memory.

```
   data←read650 address                 address write650 data
 A IBM 650 read from store            A IBM 650 write into memory
  →CASE(Switch,Dist,Accl,Accu)⌷address   Invadr report address≥adrcap
  C0:data←switch                       →OUT ind[Invadr]
     →ENDCASE                          memory[memcap|address;]←data
  C1:data←dist
     →ENDCASE
  C2:data←acc[Sign,Lower]
     →ENDCASE
  C3:data←acc[Sign,Upper]
     →ENDCASE
  C4:data←memory[memcap|address;]
     Invadr report address≥adrcap
  ENDCASE:
```

PROGRAM 12-12   Memory read and write in the IBM 650.

Address Modification

In the basic machine, which our APL programs describe, addressing is direct only, without indexing. The indexing option encodes the index address in a complex way. Main-memory addresses, 0000 thorough 1999, are augmented by 0, 2000, 4000, or 6000 to specify no indexing, or additive indexing by each of the three registers respectively. The embedded working-store addresses, 8000 through 9999, are augmented by 0, 200, 400, or 600 to specify the same indexing.

```
        address←adr650
      A IBM 650 addressing
        address←fld Address
```

PROGRAM 12-13   Addressing in the IBM 650.

Address calculation. The Store Data Address and Store Instruction Address replace the content of the data or instruction-address field of the distributor with the content of the corresponding field in the lower accumulator, leaving

the rest of the distributor unchanged. The new value of the distributor is
stored, and it remains available for immediate use.

```
STDA
⍝ IBM 650 Store Data Address
dist[Address]←acc[(Sign,Lower)[Address]]
adr650 write650 dist
```

```
STIA
⍝ IBM 650 Store Instruction Address
dist[Next]←acc[(Sign,Lower)[Next]]
adr650 write650 dist
```

PROGRAM 12-14   Store Address in the IBM 650.

Index Arithmetic

The indexing option (not included in the APL description) includes
immediate-address load, add, subtract, and branching operations for each of
the index registers A, B, C (RAA, RSA, AXA, SXA, NZA, BMA for index A).

Address Level

All addressing is direct; there is no indirect addressing, and only the
index arithmetic operations have immediate addressing. They have no direct
addressing.

12.1.4
Data

The position of the sign has no visible relation to the digit positions. In our
APL description we allocate the sign immediately to the left of the high-order
digit.

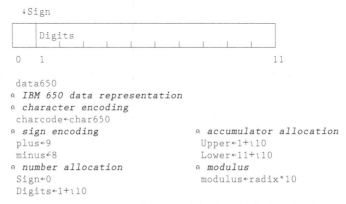

```
data650
⍝ IBM 650 data representation
⍝ character encoding
charcode←char650
⍝ sign encoding                ⍝ accumulator allocation
plus←9                         Upper←1+⍳10
minus←8                        Lower←11+⍳10
⍝ number allocation            ⍝ modulus
Sign←0                         modulus←radix*10
Digits←1+⍳10
```

PROGRAM 12-15   Data specification in the IBM 650.

Character Strings

Character set and size. Translation between the internal decimal encoding and the card or printer encoding is by optional hardware. There are no operations on this datatype as such, but the encoding is such that a decimal comparison orders the characters in the proper BCD collating sequence.

In Program 12-16, the blank shows as a blank in the top-left corner of the character display; unused codes are marked by a small circle.

Character-string formats. Each character occupies two digits, giving five characters to the word.

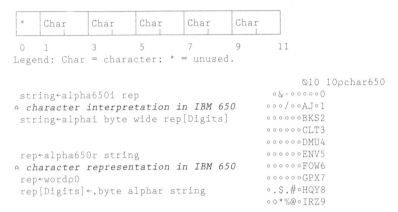

PROGRAM 12-16   Character string in the IBM 650.

Fixed-Point Numbers

Notation and allocation. Signed magnitude is used for signed integers. Zero sums and differences are forced to plus zero; zero products, quotients, and shift results are not. The double-length accumulator helps in programming extended-precision arithmetic.

Radix choice. Unlike most other "decimal" machines, the decimal radix is used exclusively throughout. So the minimal unit of the machine is the decimal digit.

Logical Variables

Ten-digit logical vectors can be tested, but not otherwise operated upon. False is encoded as 9; true, as 8.

Floating-Point Numbers

The floating-point option follows the 704 in using signed magnitude for the coefficient and bias notation for the exponent (Section 4.4). The exponent is in the low-order two digits of the word, so that it is encountered first in the serial implementation.

12.1.5

Operations

Data Handling

Table search. The Table Lookup operation performs a streaming comparison of the distributor's contents against the contents of memory, stopping when the memory value is equal to or exceeds the value of the distributor in absolute value. The origin of the search is determined by the data address of the instruction. The search proceeds with a band of 50 addresses at a time. The data address identifies such a band, not an address within the band. The auxiliary function `table650` presents the content of such a band. For each band of 50 addresses, the last two, addresses 48 and 49, are not searched. The main function TLU searches the band for the first value equal to or larger than the argument. If none is found, the index value is 48, and the search is repeated.

```
TLU;origin;argument;value;index   value←table650 address;location
∩ IBM 650 Table Lookup            ∩ IBM 650 table values
origin←adr650                     ∩ valid locations in addressed track
argument←|signmagni dist          location←(50×⌊address÷50)+ι48
REPEAT: ∩ search track            ∩ values in track locations
   value←table650 origin            value←signmagni memory[memcap|location;]
   index←(argument≤|value)ι1      Invadr report location≥adrcap
   →If index=48
   THEN: ∩ not found in track
      origin←origin+50
ENDIF:→UNTIL(index≠48)∨ind[Invadr]
→OUT ind[Invadr]
acc[(Sign,Lower)[Address]]←adrsize magnr origin+index
```

PROGRAM 12-17   Table Lookup in the IBM 650.

Logic

The 650 has no logical connectives. A left-zero count is combined with the Shift Arithmetic Left And Count.

Shift. All shifts specify the amount of shift, 0 through 9, by the units digit of the address. For Shift Arithmetic Right and Shift Arithmetic Left, a digit of 0 means no shift; for Shift Arithmetic Right Rounded and Shift Arithmetic Left And Count, it means a shift of 10. Even though only the low-order address digit is used, the high-order address digit is still tested for a valid address.
   Shift Arithmetic Right Rounded shifts the entire accumulator right by the specified amount, then rounds the result according to the value of the highest-order digit that is shifted out of the lower accumulator.
   Shift Arithmetic Left And Count shifts the entire accumulator left until a non-zero digit is in the high-order position, but does not shift by more than the specified amount. The amount shifted, plus the 10's complement of the amount specified, is then placed in the two low-order accumulator positions (the exponent field in the floating-point option). For a shift of zero places or of

one place, however, the amount recorded has both digits zero, or the leftmost digit zero—a clear accommodation of the implementation.

The Arithmetic Shift is shown in Program 12-18.

```
↓Sign
┌──────────────────────────────┬──────────────────────────────────────┐
│  Upper                       │  Lower                                │
└──────────────────────────────┴──────────────────────────────────────┘
0   1                          11                                     21
Accumulator
```

```
SLT;operand;shift
∩ IBM 650 Shift Arithmetic Left
operand←magni acc[Upper,Lower]
shift←fld ‾1↑Address
acc[Upper,Lower]←(accsize-1) magnr operand×radix*shift
Invadr report adr650≥adrcap


SCT;operand;maxshift;shift
∩ IBM 650 Shift Arithmetic Left And Count
operand←magni acc[Upper,Lower]
maxshift←fld0 ‾1↑Address
shift←maxshiftL(0≠acc[Upper,Lower])ι1
acc[Upper,Lower]←(accsize-1) magnr operand×radix*shift
→CASE 0 1 ιshift
C0:acc[‾2↑Lower]←0
   →ENDCASE
C1:acc[‾2↑Lower]←0,10|(-maxshift)+shift
   →ENDCASE
C2:acc[‾2↑Lower]←2 magnr(10-maxshift)+shift
ENDCASE:Oflo report 0=acc[1↑Upper]
Invadr report adr650≥adrcap


SRT;operand;shift
∩ IBM 650 Shift Arithmetic Right
operand←magni acc[Upper,Lower]
shift←fld ‾1↑Address
acc[Upper,Lower]←(accsize-1) magnrLoperand÷radix*shift
Invadr report adr650≥adrcap


SRD;operand;shift
∩ IBM 650 Shift Arithmetic Right Rounded
operand←magni acc[Upper,Lower]
shift←fld0 ‾1↑Address
acc[Upper,Lower]←(accsize-1) magnrL0.5+operand÷radix*shift
Invadr report adr650≥adrcap
```

PROGRAM 12-18   Arithmetic Shift in the IBM 650.

Fixed-Point Arithmetic

All arithmetic operations use the entire 20-digit accumulator as an entity; an Add Lower can spill a carry or borrow into the Upper (half); an Add Upper that causes a sign change will complement the Lower (half). There is only one accumulator sign (except after a Divide). Table 12-19 shows the fixed-point instructions of the 650.

```
a RAU    Load Upper                         a AU    Add Upper
a RAL    Load Lower                         a AL    Add Lower
a LD     Load Distributor                   a AABL  Add Lower Absolute
a RAABL  Load Lower Absolute                a SU    Subtract Upper
a RSU    Load Upper Negative                a SL    Subtract Lower
a RSL    Load Lower Negative                a SABL  Subtract Lower Absolute
a RSABL  Load Lower Negative Absolute  a MULT  Multiply
a STU    Store Upper                        a DIV   Divide
a STL    Store Lower                        a DIVRU Divide Without Remainder
a STD    Store Distributor
a STDA   Store Data Address
a STIA   Store Instruction Address
```

TABLE 12-19   Fixed-point instructions of the IBM 650.

Load and Store. Loading (called Reset Add or Reset Subtract) includes sign control. The Absolute option applies only to loading the lower accumulator.

Store Upper normally stores the upper accumulator with the accumulator sign. When the remainder sign is valid, however, that sign is used instead of the accumulator sign. Division sets the remainder sign to a valid + or − (encoded as 9 or 8). A Load or multiplication makes the remainder sign invalid (encoded as a 0).

```
RAU;addend                                 STU
⋂ IBM 650 Load Upper                       ⋂ IBM 650 Store Upper
dist←read650 adr650                        →IF rmsign∈plus,minus
addend←signmagni dist                      THEN:dist←rmsign,acc[Upper]
acc←accsize signmagnr addend×modulus          →ENDIF
rmsign←0                                   ELSE:dist←acc[Sign,Upper]
                                           ENDIF:adr650 write650 dist


RSABL;subtrahend
⋂ IBM 650 Load Lower Negative Absolute     STL
dist←read650 adr650                        ⋂ IBM 650 Store Lower
subtrahend←signmagni dist                  dist←acc[Sign,Lower]
acc←accsize signmagnr-|subtrahend          adr650 write650 dist
rmsign←0
```

PROGRAM 12-20   Load and Store in the IBM 650.

Add and Subtract. The instructions that refer to the upper part of the accumulator have no absolute-value sign control of the addend.

An overflow is signaled by use of the values `xmax` and `xmin`, generated by the representation function `signmagnr`.

Multiply and Divide. Multiplication is cumulative in that the content of the lower accumulator is added to the magnitude of the product. The content of the upper accumulator is used as multiplier. As the multiplication proceeds, the multiplier digits are used left to right, and the product is developed in the accumulator. If the original content of the lower accumulator is not zero and is sufficiently large, the partial product may carry into low-order multiplier digits that are still to be processed. This behavior causes a highly unorthodox product specification.

The product digits are determined from the accumulator and distributor digits interpreted as positive magnitudes. The product sign is determined from multiplier and multiplicand signs, without forcing a positive zero.

```
AABL;addend;augend;sum;xmax;xmin
⍝ IBM 650 Add Lower Absolute
dist←read650 adr650
addend←signmagni dist
augend←signmagni acc
sum←augend+|addend
acc←accsize signmagnr sum
Oflo report xmax


SU;subtrahend;minuend;difference;negzero;xmax;xmin
⍝ IBM 650 Subtract Upper
dist←read650 adr650
subtrahend←signmagni dist
minuend←signmagni acc
difference←minuend-subtrahend×modulus
negzero←(acc[Sign]=minus)∧(dist[Sign]=plus)∧difference=0
acc←accsize signmagnr difference
→If negzero
THEN:acc[Sign]←minus
ENDIF:Oflo report xmax∨xmin
```

    PROGRAM 12-21   Add and Subtract in the IBM 650.

In division the divisor resides in the distributor; the dividend in the accumulator is replaced by the remainder and quotient. The quotient sign, like the product sign, is simply formed from the operand signs; a zero is not forced positive. The two entities placed in the accumulator each have a sign, which is inconsistent with its normal interpretation and results in the extra rules for the remainder sign.

```
MULT;multiplier;multiplicand;augend;sum;product
⍝ IBM 650 Multiply
multiplier←magni acc[Upper]
dist←read650 adr650
multiplicand←magni dist[Digits]
augend←magni acc[Lower],(⍴Lower)⍴0
sum←augend+multiplicand×multiplier
⍝ overflow of product into multiplier
product←sum+multiplicand×⌊sum÷modulus*2
acc[Upper,Lower]←(accsize-1) magnr product
acc[Sign]←(plus,minus)[acc[Sign]≠dist[Sign]]
Oflo report product≠magni acc[Upper,Lower]
rmsign←0


DIV;divisor;dividend;quotient;remainder
⍝ IBM 650 Divide
dist←read650 adr650
divisor←magni dist[Digits]
dividend←magni acc[Upper,Lower]
(Oflo,Stop) report divisor≤dividend÷modulus
→OUT ind[Oflo]
quotient←⌊dividend÷divisor
remainder←dividend-quotient×divisor
acc[Lower]←(⍴Lower) magnr quotient
acc[Upper]←(⍴Upper) magnr remainder
rmsign←acc[Sign]
acc[Sign]←(plus,minus)[acc[Sign]≠dist[Sign]]
```

    PROGRAM 12-22   Multiply and Divide in the IBM 650.

Floating-Point Arithmetic

The optional floating-point operations are what one would expect. Only the upper accumulator participates in addition and division. Results are normalized and rounded.

12.1.6

Instruction Sequencing

The `Next` instruction-address field of each instruction specifies the successor instruction. Since the working store is addressable, instructions may be executed from the Distributor, the Accumulator, the Console Switches, and so on.

```
cycle650                          inst←ifetch650
a basic cycle of the IBM 650      a IBM 650 instruction fetch
 REPEAT:execute ifetch650         ind[Progr,Mach,Stop]←0
       interrupt650               inst←read650 iadr
 →UNTIL stop650                   iadr←fld Next


 yes←stop650
 a IBM 650 stop condition
 yes←v/ind[Stop].mask∧ind[Progr,Oflo,Mach]
```

PROGRAM 12-23   Basic cycle and instruction fetch of the IBM 650.

Linear Sequence

Next instruction.   An unconditional branch is not needed; the `Next` instruction address field serves as such.

Completion.   The Stop instruction sets the stop indicator, causing a machine stop if the corresponding mask switch is on.

a	NOOP	No Operation	a	BRD7	Branch On Digit 7
a	STOP	Stop	a	BRD8	Branch On Digit 8
a	BRD1	Branch On Digit 1	a	BRD9	Branch On Digit 9
a	BRD2	Branch On Digit 2	a	BRD10	Branch On Digit 10
a	BRD3	Branch On Digit 3	a	BRMIN	Branch On Minus
a	BRD4	Branch On Digit 4	a	BRNZ	Branch On Non-zero
a	BRD5	Branch On Digit 5	a	BRNZU	Branch On Non-zero Upper
a	BRD6	Branch On Digit 6	a	BROV	Branch On Overflow

TABLE 12-24   Sequencing instructions of the IBM 650.

Decision

Conditional branching.   Branching operations, when successful, cause the next-instruction address to be taken from the data-address field, rather than from the `Next` field.

Branch On Digit (1 to 10) tests the distributor digit specified (in 1-origin, right to left). If it is 8 (minus), the branch succeeds; if 9 (plus), the branch

fails. All other digit values are invalid here; the machine stops if the `Stop` indicator is enabled by its mask switch.

```
STOP                              NOOP
 ᴀ IBM 650 Stop                    ᴀ IBM 650 No Operation
 ind[Progr]←1

                                  BRD1
 BRMIN                             ᴀ IBM 650 Branch On Digit 1
 ᴀ IBM 650 Branch On Minus         brd650 1
 →If acc[Sign]=minus
 THEN:iadr←adr650
 ENDIF:                            brd650 n
    .                             ᴀ IBM 650 branch on digit n
                                  →CASE(plus,minus)ιdist[11-n]
 BROV                             C0: ᴀ no branch
 ᴀ IBM 650 Branch On Overflow        →ENDCASE
 →If ind[Oflo]                    C1: ᴀ branch
 THEN:iadr←adr650                     iadr←adr650
    ind[Oflo]←0                       →ENDCASE
 ENDIF:                           C2: ᴀ error stop
                                     ind[Stop]←1
                                  ENDCASE:
```

PROGRAM 12-25   Conditional branching in the IBM 650.

12.1.7
Supervision

Interruption.   There is a rudimentary interrupt system for machine errors. When the stop condition of the Machine Error indicator in not enabled by its mask switch, it causes a trap. The next instruction is now taken from the console switches, word 8000, instead of from the specified location. There is no status preservation whatever; there is no way to know where the offending trap occurred. Moreover, the Distributor and Accumulator are reset; the main purpose is to get a fresh restart after an intermittent error.

Integrity

Policing.   Invalid instruction codes, addresses, character codes, and branch test values cause a machine stop under control of the error mask switch.

```
interrupt650                    regreset650
 ᴀ IBM 650 interrupt action      ᴀ IBM 650 register reset
 →If ind[Mach]∧~mask[Mach]        acc[]←0
 THEN:regreset650                 dist[]←0
    iadr←8000                     rmsign←0
 ENDIF:
```

PROGRAM 12-26   Interruption action in the IBM 650.

12.1.8

Input/Output

Devices

Store.   Tape and disk storage were provided later as an option.

Source and sink.   A card reader serves as source; the sink is a card punch. Both are housed in one unit (type 533). Printing was originally off-line from punched cards, using regular tabulating machines. One such machine, the IBM 407, was soon directly attached. To the program it looks like a card punch, except for using different buffer locations.

Overlapped Input/Output

The several I/O processes proceed concurrently with one other and with the CPU, exactly as in the Univac I. The card machinery is slow enough that buffering can be on the drum—the drum rotates at least once during each card hole time. The optional tape and disk demand asynchronous buffering to match their clocks; the optional core memory (addresses 9000–9059) meets that need. Tape block size, like that in the Univac I, is limited to the 60-word size of the buffer. It may be used as a smaller buffer, by programming.

Read and Write.   Reading and punching cards consists, in the program, of moving a 10-word vector to (and from) addressed memory areas, from (and to) I/O buffers. The reading and punching actions themselves are indicated by read650io and write650io, but we do not show them.

```
        RD
      ⌐ IBM 650 Read Card
        memory[Input+50×⌊adr650÷50;]←cardin
        cardin←read650io


        PCH
      ⌐ IBM 650 Punch Card
        cardout←memory[Output+50×⌊adr650÷50;]
        write650io cardout
```

PROGRAM 12-27   Input/output Read and Write in the IBM 650.

12.1.9

Implementation Notes

The 650 follows the Aiken approach of a conservative implementation and realization. A digit-serial implementation is used. The registers are built from condenser circuits that need periodic refreshing. This realization was chosen to avoid the Eckert–Mauchly patents on drum revolvers [Bashe, 1986].

Speed.   The magnetic-drum main memory had a remarkably fast revolution time of 4.8 ms; average access time was 2.4 ms. The time needed to transmit a word was 96 μs; the clock cycle was 8 μs.

Production. Early IBM computers were tested, tuned, and corrected for about 1 month after final assembly at the plant. The test team went as "customer engineers" with the computer to the customer site. As the large series of increasingly reliable 650s was produced, it became possible for the first time to eliminate this costly test period at the plant. Processors worked correctly as soon as assembly was completed.

12.1.10
Bibliography

IBM, 1955: *Manual of Operation, Type 650 Magnetic Drum Data-Processing Machine*. IBM Form 22-6060-1. New York: IBM Corp. (our defining reference).

Brooks and Iverson [1963] describes the 650 with most of its options, including programming examples.

Hurd, C.C., ed., 1986: "Special Issue: IBM 650." *Ann Hist Comput*, **8**, 1: 3–88.

Bashe et al. [1986], Burks [1946], Carr III [1959c], Gordon [1956], Hughes [1954], Royse [1957].

12.1.11
Exercises

12-1 For the 650, compare the use of serial datapaths with the use of parallel ones: How does implementation choice affect performance?

12-2 Assuming realistic cost ratios on registers, gates, and memory, how does the choice between serial and parallel datapaths influence the cost?

12-3 Assuming consistency with the 650 descriptions of this section, give the descriptions of RAL, LD, RSU, RSL, RAABL, SABL, STD, AU, SL, DIVRU, BRNZ, and BRNZU.

12.2
IBM 705

12.2.1
Highlights

History

Architect.   Werner Buchholz was the chief architect.

Dates.   In 1953 the IBM 702 was announced for delivery in 1955. About 15 702s were delivered. In 1954 the IBM 705 was announced, to be delivered in 1956.

Family tree.   Major family members are the IBM 702, 705, 705 III, and 7080. This chapter's frontispiece shows the family tree. The 705 is more precisely identified as the 705 I; a minor extension is the 705 II; the 705 III (1957) is a major extension. The 7080 is a transistorized version of the 705 III using IBM Stretch (1961) technology.

Noteworthy

This interesting and original family introduced (1) sets of registers as working store, (2) variable-length data words, (3) variable-length registers, and (4) efficient and flexible data formats on tape. We describe the 705 because its 16 registers are a major innovation and a significant step toward the classical-computer architecture.

Characters.   The 705 is a character machine. In the 6-bit BCD representation of digits and characters, the zone and numeric parts (derived from the corresponding card rows) are more readily distinguished than in the Univac I.

Sign in zone.   The signed-magnitude representation of the numbers has the sign over the low-order digit—a favorite punched-card representation.

Variable-length data.   Data fields have variable length. The variable length of a register determines the length of its contents. In memory the length is specified by the sign of a number or by the record mark for a character string.

Byte resolution.   Variable-length data implies address resolution to the byte—a new departure.

Registers.   The one main accumulator and 15 auxiliary accumulators constitute a working store of 16 registers. Four zone bits of the address part of an instruction specify the register.

Fixed-length, aligned instructions.   Instructions are 5 bytes long and are aligned on 5-byte boundaries. In effect, the word length is 5 bytes.

Block move.   An aligned block move, both internal and I/O, takes advantage of the 5-byte–wide memory.

Condition code.   The 15 auxiliary registers share a zero indicator, which becomes the (unintentional) prototype of a condition code.

Peculiarities

Variable register size.   The variable register size (inspired by tabulating machines) is achieved by providing two 256-character circular stores.   For register 0 (the main accumulator), both boundaries can be moved within the first store; the remaining 15 registers (auxiliary accumulators) share the second ring and are marked off with fixed low-order starting points (on the right) and movable high-order delimiters (on the left).

Growing registers.   The registers accommodate the result of an arithmetic operation; a carry beyond the register end causes the delimiter to be moved. At first glance, provision of variable-length registers seems to disprove the modular nature of fixed-point arithmetic. In fact, the growth of a register may conflict with an adjacent register, and thus the contents of the register must have a definite size allocated when they are stored in memory.

Shared sign.   The 15 auxiliary registers share not only a zero indicator (quite defensible), but also one sign (hardly defensible).

Mixed-radix addressing.   Memories of up to 10,000 bytes are addressed by four decimal-address digits. As more memory capacity became necessary, the 705 used up to four binary zone bits, which eventually gave 160 K addressing in the 7080. A corollary of this addressing scheme was that unsigned mixed-radix address arithmetic had to be provided.

Field addressing.   The address points to the rightmost byte of a data field. When multiples of five characters are moved in one operation, the leftmost group is specified by the address of its rightmost character. When multiple single characters are moved, the leftmost character is addressed.   Clearly, consistency is sacrificed for ease of implementation.

Programmable address register.   To specify the two addresses of a memory-to-memory move, a separate instruction loads the destination address into an address register. The content of this register can be used in several subsequent move instructions. This chaining technique is not encouraged in the 705; the 1401 (1960) exploits it fully.

Delimiting.   Several different characters serve as delimiters: in the registers, the register mark; in memory, the record mark and the group mark; on tape, the tape mark. Delimiting is also by a sign zone and by register length—even if that register does not otherwise participate in the operation. The delimiter characters prevent the processing of binary data in the 705.

Edit.   The Store For Print operation is one of the first attempts to aid the complex format transformation required for conventional printing.

Zero divided by zero.   As in other early designs, some situations are considered too rare and too bothersome to be handled properly. In the 705,

division of zero by zero does not turn on the overflow indicator (as it normally does for a divisor that is too small); the user is advised to check the dividend for zero.

Normalize step.   Leftmost-zero digits can be removed one at a time, effectively shrinking the register that holds the number.

Program-generated error.   The Store Numeric instruction has the dubious honor of being perhaps the first instruction to enable the programmer to create a parity error.

Descendants

The 705 III introduces much-needed address arithmetic, but not yet indexing, which appears in the 7080. The 705 III also introduces memory-buffered channels, an idea that Buchholz proposed for the 702 but that was not accepted at that time [Bashe, 1986]. The channels are asynchronous concurrent specialized processors (DMAs, in DEC parlance). Other new functions of the 705 III are setting and testing individual bits, a subroutine call, memory blanking, and extensions of several 705 instructions.

12.2.2

Machine Language

Language Level

Design philosophy.   The 702 family aimed at commercial data processing and tried to give the equivalent of established punched-card techniques.

Unit System

The basic parameters reflect the 6-bit character, which holds a 4-bit decimal digit in its numeric part. Unlike the Univac and the 650, the parts of a character are often interpreted individually, so the individual element is binary, even though the arithmetic is decimal.

```
initiate705                        format705
a initiation of the IBM 705        a IBM 705 information units
configure705                       a principal radix
format705                          radix←2
space705                           a information units
data705                            a - in bits
control705                         digit←4
                                   byte←6
                                   a - in bytes
configure705                       word←5
a configuration for the IBM 705    regsize←16
a memory capacity                  accsize←256
memcap←20000                       a address capacity
                                   adrcap←80000
```

PROGRAM 12-28   Basic parameters of the IBM 705.

Configuration. The initial memory capacity offered was 20 Kbytes, twice the 702 capacity; the capacity of the 705 III was eventually 80 Kbytes.

Spaces

Memory name-space. Memory is addressable to the byte.

```
space705
A IBM 705 spaces                        A control store
A memory                                A - instruction address
 memory←?(memcap,byte)ρradix             iadr←?adrcap
A working store                         A - indicators
A - registers                            ind←?9ρradix
 reg←?(2,accsize,byte)ρradix            A - component selection
A - sign and zero                        select←?10000
 sign←?2ρradix                          A - manual alteration
 zero←?2ρradix                           alter←?6ρradix
A - accumulator starting point         A - mask switches
 accstart←?accsize                       mask←?6ρradix
A - destination address                A - stopped state
 dest←?adrcap                            stop←?radix
                                        A input/output control
                                         iostate←?30ρradix
```

PROGRAM 12-29   Spaces of the IBM 705.

Working store. The 16 registers of the 705 are built from two circular 256-byte stores (Figure 12-30). The first store contains register 0; the second contains registers 1 through 15. Register 0 has a variable low-order starting point; the other 15 registers have fixed starting points 16 characters apart. The high-order (left) end of each register is delimited by a register mark. By placing the register mark sufficiently far to the left, one may make the registers 1 through 15 overlap. Thus, when register 5 is 50 characters long, it overlaps registers 6, 7, and 8. Register 6 is 34 characters long and overlaps 7 and 8; 7 overlaps 8 and has a length of 18 characters; register 8 is two characters long.

Shared indicators. There are two sign and two zero indicators; the first of each is for register 0; the second of each is shared by registers 1 through 15.

Address register. The programmable address register `dest` is used in move operations.

Control store. The 705 still reflects hands-on debugging practice with testable alteration switches, and indicators controlled by mask switches that either cause a stop or allow testing by branches.

The `select` register specifies a device, indicator, or switch to be tested or reset.

Operand Specification

Number of addresses. The 705 is a two-address computer. Each instruction contains one memory address and one register address. Occasionally, the register address bits are used as an operation modifier.

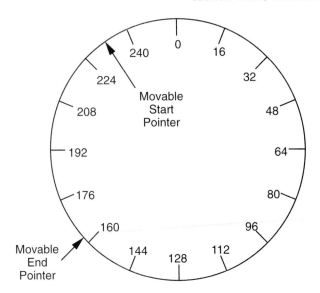

Register 0, Accumulator, 256 bytes

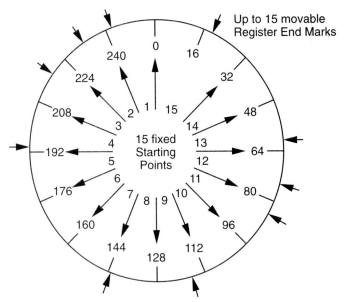

Registers 1–15, 256 bytes collectively

FIGURE 12-30   Working store in the IBM 705.

Operation Specification

Mnemonics. The 705 uses the character representation of the opcode bits as an instruction name. Originally, these characters were the 26 letters and the digits 1 through 9; in the extensions of the 705 III other characters were used, such as the slash. Besides these single symbols, however, the manuals also give two- or three-character mnemonics; we use these mnemonics.

```
a→i          i          i          i
 TR          i          HLT        NOP
 SEL         RWW        TRH        SET
 CTR         SGN        TRE        SHR
 CMP         RCV        TRP        LNG
 SPR         MPY        TRZ        RND
 ADM         DIV        TRS        ST
 UNL         NTR        SUB        ADD
 LOD         RD         RSU        RAD
 TMT         WRE        WR         TRA
 i           i          i          i
 i           i          i          i
 i           i          i          i
 i           i          i          i
 i           i          i          i
 i           i          i          i
```

PROGRAM 12-31   Operation-code list of the IBM 705.

```
    ⋒ data handling              ⋒ sequencing
a TMT Transmit                a NOP No Operation
a RCV Receive                 a HLT Stop
a SPR Store For Print         a TR  Branch
    ⋒ fixed-point arithmetic  a NTR Branch On Normalize
a LOD Load                    a TRS Branch On Signal
a SGN Load Sign               a TRA Branch On Any
a SHR Shorten Accumulator     a TRE Branch On Equal
a LNG Lengthen Accumulator    a TRZ Branch On Zero
a SET Set Register Mark       a TRH Branch On High
a UNL Store                   a TRP Branch On Positive
a ST  Store Numeric               ⋒ input/output
a ADD Add                     a RD  Read
a RAD Reset And Add           a RWW Read While Writing
a ADM Add To Memory           a WR  Write
a SUB Subtract                a WRE Write Erase
a RSU Reset And Subtract      a SEL Select Device
a MPY Multiply                a CTR Control
a DIV Divide
a RND Round
a CMP Compare
```

TABLE 12-32   Instruction list of the IBM 705.

Instruction Structure

Machine-language syntax.   A single syntactical pattern is used.

```
        syntax705
     a Opcode,R,Address
```

PROGRAM 12-33   Instruction syntax of the IBM 705.

Instruction format.   The instruction format in Program 12-34 graphically illustrates the scramble for bits as the family evolved. First, just four numeric fields (bytes 1 2 3 4) were used to give addressing up to 10,000; then, the zone bits of byte 1 were put to work; next, one of the two zone bits of byte 4 was used in the 705 III; finally, the second zone bit of byte 4, the last available bit, was used in the 7080. (Note the reversal of the zone bits.) The zone bits of bytes 2 and 3 were used from the beginning to specify the 16 registers.

Status format.   All indicators can be tested by conditional branches. The two comparison indicators remain unaltered until the next comparison. The six

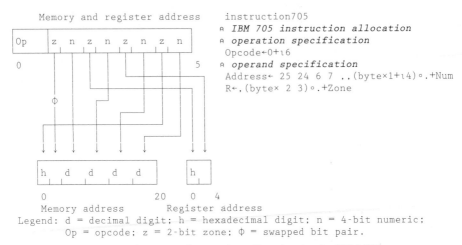

```
       Memory and register address        instruction705
                                          ⍝ IBM 705 instruction allocation
 ┌──┬──────────────────────────────┐      ⍝ operation specification
 │Op│ z  n  z  n  z  n  z  n        │       Opcode←0+⍳6
 └──┴──────────────────────────────┘      ⍝ operand specification
 0                                 5       Address← 25 24 6 7 ,,(byte×1+⍳4)∘.+Num
                                          R←,(byte× 2 3)∘.+Zone
         Φ


         ↓  ↓  ↓  ↓  ↓  ↓        ↓  ↓
       ┌──────────────────────┐ ┌──────┐
       │ h   d   d   d   d    │ │ h    │
       └──────────────────────┘ └──────┘
       0                 20      0    4
       Memory address       Register address
 Legend: d = decimal digit; h = hexadecimal digit; n = 4-bit numeric;
         Op = opcode; z = 2-bit zone; Φ = swapped bit pair.
```

PROGRAM 12-34   Instruction allocation in the IBM 705.

exception indicators cause a stop when the corresponding mask switch is set.
The Any indicator summarizes the error indicators.

```
       indicator705
       ⍝ IBM 705 indicators
       ⍝ comparison
        High←0
        Eq←1
       ⍝ overflow              ⍝ error
        Oflo←2                  Machine←5
       ⍝ invalid operation     Inout←6
        Invop←3                 Record←7
       ⍝ invalid sign          ⍝ summary
        Sign←4                  Any←8
```

PROGRAM 12-35   Indicators of the IBM 705.

12.2.3

Addressing

Direct addressing of memory.   The address points to the rightmost byte of
the field in memory. In reading from memory, the length of the data must be
specified by the receiving register's length.

```
data←size read705 address            address write705 data;size
⍝ IBM 705 read from memory           ⍝ IBM 705 write into memory
data←memory[memcap|Φaddress-⍳size;]  size←1↑ρdata
                                     memory[memcap|Φaddress-⍳size;]←data
```

PROGRAM 12-36   Memory read and write in the IBM 705.

Direct addressing of registers.   In reading from registers, the entire register
participates. In writing from register to memory, the register field length
determines the memory field length.

```
data←read705reg r;loc            r write705reg data;size;loc;rl
⍝ IBM 705 read from register     ⍝ IBM 705 write into register
loc←Φ(regstart705 r)-⍳regsize705 r   size←1+1↑⍴data
data←reg[r≠0;accsize|loc;]        loc←Φ(regstart705 r)-⍳size
                                  rl←(byte alphar regmark)⍔data
                                  reg[r≠0;accsize|loc;]←rl
```

PROGRAM 12-37   Register read and write in the IBM 705.

Address interpretation.

Address interpretation.   For an address to be obtained, the unscrambled instruction bits are interpreted binarily in groups of four, yielding five digits (Program 12-34). Then, these digits are interpreted as a number in a mixed hexadecimal–decimal radix system.

```
address←adr705;radix;digits      start←regstart705 r
⍝ IBM 705 addressing             ⍝ IBM 705 register starting position
radix←2                          →IF r=0
digits←fld digit wide Address    THEN: ⍝ accumulator
radix← 16 10 10 10 10               start←accstart
address←magni digits               →ENDIF
                                 ELSE: ⍝ registers 1-15
                                   start←accsize|-regsize×r-1
                                 ENDIF:
```

PROGRAM 12-38   Addressing in the IBM 705.

Operand delimiting.   The starting position of register 0 is determined by the value accstart; for the other registers, it is fixed at the appropriate multiple of the register size 16 (Figure 12-30 and Program 12-38).

The size of numeric operands in memory is delimited at the left by the encounter of a non-numeric character (such as a signed digit of an adjacent field).

The register size is determined by the first register mark to the left of the starting position of the register.

```
size←size705
⍝ IBM 705 memory operand size
size←1+((alphai memory[Φ⍳adr705;])∈'0123456789')⍳0
```

```
size←regsize705 r
⍝ IBM 705 register operand size
size←(Φ(1+regstart705 r)Φalphai reg[0≠r;;])⍳regmark
```

PROGRAM 12-39   Operand and register size in the IBM 705.

12.2.4

Data

The 705 has character strings and decimal fixed-point numbers; there is no logical datatype.

Character Strings

Character set and size. The 705 character set deviates from the usual BCD by the position of blank and the use of many (non-printable) delimiters. Because the tapes used even parity and the tape-reading circuitry required some bit to be 1 in each byte, the all-zeros combination was not allowed in the character set read or written in I/O; it was conveniently available as a register mark.

Char	Char	Char	Char	Char		Char

```
0     1     2     3     4                 m
Legend: Char = character; m = no maximum.
```

```
                                                   ◊ 4 16 ρbcd705
                                              a -&
data705                                       1/JA
ᴀ IBM 705 data representation                 2SKB
ᴀ character encoding                          3TLC
  charcode←bcd705                             4UMD
ᴀ sign encoding                               5VNE
  plus←3                                      6WOF
  minus←2                                     7XPG
ᴀ byte allocation                            8YQH  Legend:
  Zone←0+ι2                                   9ZRI  a = register mark
  Num←2+ι4                                    0rmp  g = group mark
ᴀ data delimiter                             #,$.  m = minus zero
ᴀ - in register                              @%*◊  p = plus zero
  regmark←'a'                                 ○○○○  r = record mark
ᴀ - in memory                                ○○○○  t = tape mark
  recordmark←'r'                             t○○g  ○ = unassigned.
ᴀ collating sequence
  collate←' .◊g&$*-/,%#@pABCDEFGHImJKLMNOPQRrSTUVWXYZ0123456789'
```

PROGRAM 12-40   Data specification in the IBM 705.

Character-string formats. Character strings are up to 128 bytes long in single byte increments and of unlimited length in groups of five.

Fixed-Point Numbers

Notation and allocation. The representation is decimal signed magnitude. In memory, the sign is over the low-order digit. In the registers, the sign is separate from the numerics. The representation and interpretation functions assume the memory format; the register format is given by read705num and write705num.

```
data←read705num r;zone              r write705num data;zone
ᴀ IBM 705 read number from register  ᴀ IBM 705 write number into register
data←read705reg r                    r write705reg(-ρdata)↑data[;Num]
zone←(plus,minus)[sign[0≠r]]         zone←magni data[(1↑ρdata)-1;Zone]
data[(1↑ρdata)-1;Zone]←2 magnr zone  sign[0≠r]←zone∊minus
                                     zero[0≠r]←∧/10=magni data[;Num]
```

PROGRAM 12-41   Numeric read and write in the IBM 705.

The representation of the decimal zero deviates from binary-coded decimal; it is binary ten, not binary 0, because of the tape-recording constraint.

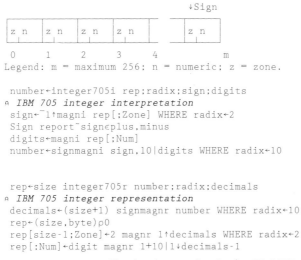

```
                                    ↓Sign
   ┌─────┬─────┬─────┬─────┬─────┐ ┌─────┐
   │ z n │ z n │ z n │ z n │     │ │ z n │
   └─────┴─────┴─────┴─────┴─────┘ └─────┘
   0     1     2     3     4       m
   Legend: m = maximum 256; n = numeric; z = zone.

   number←integer705i rep;radix;sign;digits
   ᴀ IBM 705 integer interpretation
   sign←¯1↑magni rep[;Zone] WHERE radix←2
   Sign report˜sign∈plus,minus
   digits←magni rep[;Num]
   number←signmagni sign,10⊥digits WHERE radix←10


   rep←size integer705r number;radix;decimals
   ᴀ IBM 705 integer representation
   decimals←(size+1) signmagnr number WHERE radix←10
   rep←(size,byte)ρ0
   rep[size-1;Zone]←2 magnr 1↑decimals WHERE radix←2
   rep[;Num]←digit magnr 1+10|1↓decimals-1
```

PROGRAM 12-42   Fixed-point number in the IBM 705.

12.2.5

Operations

Data Handling

Data movement.   The word and the byte Move are distinguished by the register address. `moverecord`, specified by register address 0, moves records of 5-byte words that must be aligned on word boundaries and are terminated by a record mark.   The byte Move moves a field of bytes whose length is determined by the length of the register that is specified in the instruction. The register does not otherwise participate in the instruction; both moves are memory to memory.   In each case, the destination area is specified by the address register `dest`. This register is normally set by a preceding RCV instruction; chaining is used at the programmer's risk.

```
RCV                                 TMT
ᴀ IBM 705 Receive                   ᴀ IBM 705 Transmit
dest←adr705                         →IF 0=fld R
                                    THEN:moverecord adr705
                                       →ENDIF
                                    ELSE:movecount adr705
                                    ENDIF:


moverecord source;data              movecount source;count;data
ᴀ IBM 705 move words until mark     ᴀ IBM 705 move characters by count
Invop report 4≠5|source,dest        count←regsize705 fld R
→ERROR ind[Invop]                   REPEAT:data←1 read705 source
REPEAT:data←word read705 source       source←source+1
   source←source+word                 dest write705 data
   dest write705 data                 dest←dest+1
   dest←dest+word                     count←count-1
→UNTIL recordmark=alphai data[4;]   →UNTIL count=0
```

PROGRAM 12-43   Move in the IBM 705.

Format and code transformation.   Store For Print uses a memory field as its pattern and replaces this pattern with the content of a register. As a first action, the code is transformed to turn an all-zeros byte into the decimal zero character (001010). Next, the sign (blank or minus) is placed rightmost in the field; digits are placed one by one right to left, skipping periods and commas; leading zeros are replaced left to right by blanks up to the decimal point.

```
SPR;data;string;source;d;b;rl
A IBM 705 Store For Print
data←alphai read705reg fld R
A numeric zero becomes ten
data←('rmp',data)[(' -&',data)ιdata]
A sign rightmost
string←' -'[sign[0≠fld R]]
source←adr705-1
REPEAT:d←alphai 1 read705 source
    →IF d∈'..'
    THEN: A skip delimiter
        string←d,string
        →ENDIF
    ELSE: A insert character
        string←(⁻1↑data),string
        data←⁻1↓data
    ENDIF:source←source-1
→UNTIL 0=ρdata
A blank left zeros
b←(string∈'0rmp,')ι0
rl←(bρ' '),b↓string
adr705 write705 byte alphar rl
```

PROGRAM 12-44   Store (Edit) For Print in the IBM 705.

Fixed-Point Arithmetic

The fixed-point instruction set is remarkably complete. The Shorten and Lengthen instructions are equivalent to arithmetic shifts.

a LOD Load	a ADD Add	
a SGN Load Sign	a RAD Reset And Add	
a SHR Shorten Accumulator	a ADM Add To Memory	
a LNG Lengthen Accumulator	a SUB Subtract	
a SET Set Register Mark	a RSU Reset And Subtract	
a UNL Store	a MPY Multiply	
a ST Store Numeric	a DIV Divide	
	a RND Round	
	a CMP Compare	

TABLE 12-45   Fixed-point instructions of the IBM 705.

Load and Store.   Lengthen extends the accumulator by moving the starting point to the right. The data are extended with zeros, and a register mark is always placed to the right of the starting point. Shorten operates in the opposite direction, but does not set a register mark.

The register mark (left end) of a register can be set to a position specified by the memory address field. The instruction Round places the starting point (right end) of register 0 to the left, but first adds 5 in the leftmost place that is discarded. Load Sign removes a sign zone from memory and places it in a register.

```
LOD;od;size                          ST;od;Next
⍝ IBM 705 Load                       ⍝ IBM 705 Store Numeric
size←regsize705 fld R                od←read705num fld R
od←size read705 adr705               adr705 write705 od
(fld R) write705reg od               Next←memcap|adr705-1↑od
                                     →If 0=magni memory[Next;Zone]
                                     THEN:memory[Next;Zone]←2 magnr plus
                                     ENDIF:
```

PROGRAM 12-46   Load and Store in the IBM 705.

```
LNG;fill
⍝ IBM 705 Lengthen Accumulator
accstart←accsize|accstart+adr705
fill←byte alphar regmark,adr705ρ'0'
reg[0;accsize|accstart+1-⍳1↑ρfill;]←fill
reg[0;accsize|accstart+1;]←byte alphar regmark
```

```
SHR;number                           SET;data;result
⍝ IBM 705 Shorten Accumulator        ⍝ IBM 705 Set Register Mark
accstart←accsize|accstart-adr705     data←alphai read705reg fld R
number←integer705i read705num 0      result←(-adr705)↑(adr705ρ'0'),data
sign[0]←number<0                     (fld R) write705reg byte alphar result
zero[0]←number=0
```

PROGRAM 12-47   Register-size adjustment in the IBM 705.

Add and Subtract. The arithmetic operations use special sign control when reading and writing in the registers. The length of the destination register is the largest of the memory length, the result length, and the original register length. Thus, results can overflow beyond the preset register length (even into adjacent registers), which is signaled to an overflow indicator.

```
ADD;addend;augend;sum;rlsize
⍝ IBM 705 Add
addend←integer705i size705 read705 adr705
augend←integer705i read705num fld R
sum←augend+addend
rlsize←⌈/size705,(regsize705 fld R),⌊1+10⊛|sum+sum=0
Oflo report rlsize>regsize705 fld R
(fld R) write705num rlsize integer705r sum
```

```
RAD;addend;rlsize
⍝ IBM 705 Reset And Add
addend←integer705i size705 read705 adr705
rlsize←size705⌈regsize705 fld R
Oflo report rlsize>regsize705 fld R
(fld R) write705num rlsize integer705r addend
```

PROGRAM 12-48   Fixed-point addition in the IBM 705.

Multiply and Divide. Multiply and Divide use only register 0. They adjust the accumulator to fit the result up to a length of 128 digits. The other half of the accumulator stores the multiplier and the remainder, respectively. These two values can be recovered by giving Shorten with a length of 128.

Compare. Comparison uses the collating sequence collate, as shown in Program 12-42, which follows the punched-card convention. It is a superset of the BCD character set and collating sequence (Figure 12-40). A positive or

zero result gives a high or equal comparison. In comparing a numeric register value against a numeric memory value, the memory sign (in the zone bits) participates, but the register sign (in the sign register) does not participate, which gives awkward compare results.

```
CMP;operand;comparand;result
A IBM 705 Compare
comparand←alphai(regsize705 fld R) read705 adr705
operand←alphai read705reg fld R
result←(pcollate)⊥(collateιoperand)-collateιcomparand
ind[High,Eq]←(result>0),result=0
```

PROGRAM 12-49   Fixed-point comparison in the IBM 705.

12.2.6

Instruction Sequencing

With a fixed instruction length, the basic instruction cycle is simple, except that the instruction address must have its low-order digit equal to 4 or 9; that is, instructions must be aligned on word boundaries.

```
cycle705                           inst←ifetch705
A basic cycle of the IBM 705      A IBM 705 instruction fetch
REPEAT:execute ifetch705          Invop report 4≠5|iadr
→UNTIL stop705                    →ERROR ind[Invop]
                                   inst←,word read705 iadr
                                   iadr←adrcap|iadr+word
true←stop705
A IBM 705 stop condition
true←∨/stop,mask∧ind[Invop,Machine,Inout,Record,Oflo,Sign]
```

PROGRAM 12-50   Basic cycle and instruction fetch of the IBM 705.

```
a NOP No Operation          a TRA Branch On Any
a HLT Stop                  a TRE Branch On Equal
a TR  Branch                a TRZ Branch On Zero
a NTR Branch On Normalize   a TRH Branch On High
a TRS Branch On Signal      a TRP Branch On Positive
```

TABLE 12-51   Sequencing instructions of the IBM 705.

Decision

Conditional branching.   The conditional branches are not orthogonal. Their number increases drastically in the 705 III.

```
TR                    HLT
A IBM 705 Branch      A IBM 705 Stop
iadr←adr705           stop←1
```

PROGRAM 12-52   Unconditional Branch and Stop in the IBM 705.

Branch On Normalize tests the left digit of a number in a register for zero; if the digit is zero, it deletes it by moving the left end of the register, and branches.

Branch On Any resets the Any indicator, but not the indicator that caused it to be set. A sequence of subsidiary branches can localize the particular active indicator.

```
TRE                                    TRP
ⁿ IBM 705 Branch On Equal              ⁿ IBM 705 Branch On Positive
→If ind[Eq]                            →If⁻sign[0≠fld R]
THEN:iadr←adr705                       THEN:iadr←adr705
ENDIF:                                 ENDIF:


NTR;data                               TRA
ⁿ IBM 705 Branch On Normalize          ⁿ IBM 705 Branch On Any
data←read705reg fld R                  →If ind[Any]
→If(10=magni data[0;Num])∧1<1↑ρdata    THEN:iadr←adr705
THEN:iadr←adr705                            ind[Any]←0
   (fld R) write705reg 1 0 ↓data       ENDIF:
ENDIF:
```

PROGRAM 12-53   Conditional Branch in the IBM 705.

12.2.7

Input/Output

Devices

Store. The 705 can use one or more magnetic drums, each with a capacity of 60,000 characters. Up to 10 magnetic-tape units can be attached.

Source and sink. A card reader serves as source; sinks are a printer, a card punch, and a console typewriter.

Direct Input/Output

Writing onto the typewriter is non-concurrent; the CPU waits.

Overlapped Input/Output

All other I/O operations are concurrent with processing.

```
a RD   Read                 a WRE Write Erase
a RWW  Read While Writing   a SEL Select Device
a WR   Write                a CTR Control
```

TABLE 12-54   Input/output instructions of the IBM 705.

Read and Write.   There are remarkably few I/O instructions, since all control actions are specified with a single Control instruction; sensing is done with branches preceded by Select. This parsimonious design philosophy is continued in the Stretch and in the 360.

Write Erase blanks the memory area from which data are written as part of the write operation—a remarkable instruction, in view of the unreliability of writing on magnetic tape.

Sense and control.   Each I/O device, as well as the maskable indicators and the alteration switches, has a distinct identifier; Select Device selects one of these by setting the selection register.   Once selected, a device may be interrogated with Branch On Signal.

12.2.8
Bibliography

Bashe [1986], IBM, 1959: *IBM 705 Data Processing System.* IBM Form A22-6506-0. New York: IBM Corp. (our defining reference)

12.2.9
Exercises

12-4 How would you restore orthogonality of branching in the IBM 705?

12-5 Assuming consistency of design, give the formal description of the instructions UNL, SUB, RSU, RND, TR, TRZ, and TRH.

12-6 Why is it necessary for the Lengthen instruction to place a register mark to the right of the accumulator? Why is it unnecessary for the Shorten instruction to do so?

12.3
IBM 1401

12.3.1
Highlights

History

Architects.   Architectural responsibility changed considerably during development. Francis O. Underwood had a major role in the architectural design; he was responsible for the use of a word mark as data delimiter [Bashe, 1986].

Dates.   The IBM 1401 was a highly successful computer; more than 12,000 systems were sold [Bashe, 1986]. The machine was announced in October 1959, with delivery in 1960.

Family tree.   The 1401 was intended for printing and accounting functions and as such replaced the IBM 407 card accounting machine.

Noteworthy

The early 1401 is a simple machine, operating memory-to-memory with variable-length data and instructions and with a limited operation repertoire for 6-bit characters and decimal numbers. Typically, the first version of the 1401, which we present here, has no Multiply or Divide, but it does have Zero Suppress and Edit.

Memory-to-memory operation.   The 1401 is one of the first machines to operate memory-to-memory without intermediate registers that are visible in the architecture.

Variable length.   Both data and instructions are variable in length. It is one of the first computers with variable-length instructions. (Another, more primitive example is the Ferranti Mark 1.)

No policing.   The architecture is not policed. Since the architecture invites exploration of undefined functions, an apocryphal architecture came into use, which was carefully copied in the 360 emulator.

Direct input/output.   Since the machine was conceived as a print-buffer controller, the I/O devices were attached directly (with a "native" interface). The printer was the new chain printer, much more powerful than predecessors, and it was in itself a key to the 1401's success.

Sense switches.   An operator panel designed for on-line debugging and machine-language programming reflects the assumptions of no assembler and no debugging software.

Peculiarities

Byte addressing.   As in the 705, addressing is to the byte. Addressing is at the right end for data, but at the left end for instructions, according to which byte is needed first by the implementation.

Word marks.   A seventh bit in each byte is used to mark the unaddressed end of entities. This explicit delimiter avoids the delimiting characters of the 705.

Chained operation.   Two registers address the source and the destination field of an operation. At the end of the operation, they generally point to the fields placed left-adjacent to these. A subsequent instruction can use these addresses implicitly by omitting its own address fields of the instruction, thus achieving great abbreviation.

Mixed-radix addressing.   The 1401 relived the 705 evolution, progressively robbing zone bits to extend the limited three-digit decimal address.

Descendants

IBM 1410.   The 1410, a 1401 successor, has a 5-byte–wide parallel-memory implementation; as a consequence, its architecture moves toward the classical, away from the (byte-serial–derived) innovations of the 1401: five-digit addresses, fixed-length instructions, plain decimal addressing and arithmetic, 15 signed index values. Store Address, Multiply, and Divide are no longer options. A 650-style Table Lookup is provided, even though the motivating drum memory is gone.

12.3.2
Machine Language

Language Level

Design philosophy.   The 1401 is an I/O engine—a computer primarily devoted to I/O controller functions—that started as a printer buffer. The growth of memory and I/O configurations meant that the machine was designed not all at once, but as a series of additions: tape, disk, inquiry station, teleprocessing, and indexing. All these additions give the machine an implementation-derived architecture, strongly affected by the byte-serial datapath.

Unit System

The 6-bit byte is extended with a word mark. The address capacity is achieved with three decimal digits and four zone bits, similar to, but not quite the same as, in the 705. The initial capacity in bytes is surprisingly small; it reflects the task of an I/O controller.

```
format1401
A IBM 1401 information units
A principal radix
radix←2
A information units
digit←4
byte←7
A address capacity
adrcap←16000
```

```
configure1401
A configuration for the IBM 1401
A memory capacity
memcap←1400
```

PROGRAM 12-55   Basic parameters of the initial IBM 1401.

```
space1401
A IBM 1401 spaces
A memory
memory←?(memcap,byte)ρradix
A working store
A - operand addresses
source←?adrcap
dest←?adrcap
A control store
A - instruction address
iadr←?adrcap
A - modifier
mod←?byteρradix
A - indicators
ind←?9ρradix
A - manual control
switch←?2ρradix
A - stopped state
stop←?radix
```

```
name1401
A IBM 1401 space names
A memory embedding
A - card input
Cardin←1+ι80
A - card output
Cardout←101+ι80
A - print output
Printout←201+ι100
A switch names
Io←0
Process←1
```

PROGRAM 12-56   Spaces and embedding of the IBM 1401.

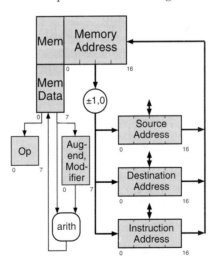

FIGURE 12-57   Programming model for the IBM 1401.

Spaces

Memory name-space.   The 1401 follows the 705 tradition of byte addressing.

Working store.   The 1401 design trades data registers, such as an accumulator, for address registers. Since the content of these registers always represents a number, the registers are described as numeric values; the implementation of each would be a 4-digit, 16-bit register (one hex digit and three decimal ones; see Program 12-64).

Control store.   The modifier of an instruction can be chained; hence, it is part of the control store.

Embedding.   About one-quarter of the initial memory capacity is used for I/O buffers.

Programming model.   Figure 12-57 shows the programming model. The address flow is wider than the dataflow, and addresses occupy most of the register space. The address incrementer provides for chaining of all fields, including the instruction.

Operand Specification

Number of addresses.   The 1401 is a two-memory–address computer. Because of chaining, however, most instructions can have two, one, or zero explicit addresses. For two addresses, both the source and the destination address registers are loaded and used. For one address, either both address registers get the same value, or the destination address is chained. For zero addresses, the current contents of both address registers are used.

Operation Specification

Mnemonics.   The character interpretation of the 6-bit operation code is used as a mnemonic. We present these mnemonics, except when they are digits or symbols. In the latter case we use two- or three-letter mnemonics.

```
a→
   IO1      CLR                    A
   IO2      S          K           B
   IO3                 L           C
   IO4                 M           D
   IO5      V          N           E
   IO6                             F
   IO7
            Y
            Z
                       RS          RA
   MA       SWM                    STP
                                   CWM
```

PROGRAM 12-58   Operation-code list of the IBM 1401.

```
       ⌐ address arithmetic        ⌐ sequencing
    a MA  Modify Address        a N    No Operation
       ⌐ data handling          a STP  Stop
    a M    Move                 a B    Branch Conditional
    a D    Move Numeric         a V    Branch On Word Mark
    a Y    Move Zone               ⌐ input/output
    a CLR Clear Memory          a IO1  Read
    a CWM Clear Word Mark       a IO2  Print
    a SWM Set Word Mark         a IO3  Print And Read
    a Z    Suppress Zero        a IO4  Punch
    a E    Edit                 a IO5  Read And Punch
       ⌐ fixed-point arithmetic a IO6  Print And Punch
    a L    Load                 a IO7  Print Read And Punch
    a A    Add                  a K    Select Stacker
    a RA  Reset Add             a F    Control Carriage
    a S    Subtract
    a RS  Reset Subtract
    a C    Compare
```

TABLE 12-59   Instruction list of the IBM 1401.

Instruction Structure

Machine-language syntax.   The minimal syntax used in decoding instructions is a 6-bit operation code (a word mark equal to one). Depending upon the size specified by the next word mark, the address and modifier registers may be loaded as part of the instruction fetch.

```
             syntax1401
           a 1.Opcode
```

PROGRAM 12-60   Instruction syntax of the IBM 1401.

Instruction format.   The instruction consists of a basic single operation field with optional address and modifier fields.

```
    a│Opcode│ Source              │ Destination        │ Mod │

    0     1                      4                     7     8
    Legend: Mod = modifier.
```

```
    instruction1401
  ⌐ IBM 1401 instruction allocation
  ⌐ operation specification
    Opcode←1+ι6
```

PROGRAM 12-61   Instruction allocation in the IBM 1401.

Status format.   There is an overflow indicator and a comparison indicator; also, the printer-carriage tape channels 9 and 12 and the last card of the

```
       indicator1401
     ⌐ IBM 1401 indicators
     ⌐ overflow              ⌐ input/output   ⌐ error
       Oflo←0                  Chan9←2          Read←5
     ⌐ compare not equal      Chan12←3         Punch←6
       Neq←1                   Lastcard←4       Print←7
                                                Machine←8
```

PROGRAM 12-62   Indicators in the IBM 1401.

card-reader punch can be sensed; finally, errors in the I/O devices and in the processor are indicated.

12.3.3
Addressing

Direct addressing.   In reading from memory, either the source or the destination address register is used. The address in the register is reduced by the size of the operand during reading. In either case a size is specified, but the size of the source is the lesser of the specified size and the operand size derived from the word mark. Writing uses the destination address.

```
 data←read1401s size                  size←size1401 address
 ⍝ IBM 1401 read source from memory    ⍝ IBM 1401 operand size
 size←size⌊size1401 source            size←1+memory[Φιaddress+1;Mark]ιl
 source←source-size
 data←memory[source+1+ιsize;]


 data←read1401d size                   write1401 data;size
 ⍝ IBM 1401 read destination from memory  ⍝ IBM 1401 write into memory
 dest←dest-size                        size←1↑ρdata
 data←memory[dest+1+ιsize;]            memory[dest+1+ιsize;]←data
```

PROGRAM 12-63   Memory read and write in the IBM 1401.

Address specification.   In address interpretation, the four digits are obtained from two zones and three numeric fields; next, these digits are interpreted in the mixed hexadecimal–decimal radix. The order of the zone bits differs from that for the 705.

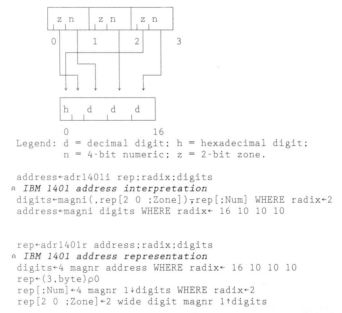

Legend: d = decimal digit; h = hexadecimal digit;
        n = 4-bit numeric; z = 2-bit zone.

```
 address←adr1401i rep;radix;digits
 ⍝ IBM 1401 address interpretation
 digits←magni(,rep[2 0 ;Zone])⍪rep[;Num] WHERE radix←2
 address←magni digits WHERE radix← 16 10 10 10


 rep←adr1401r address;radix;digits
 ⍝ IBM 1401 address representation
 digits←4 magnr address WHERE radix← 16 10 10 10
 rep←(3,byte)ρ0
 rep[;Num]←4 magnr 1↓digits WHERE radix←2
 rep[2 0 ;Zone]←2 wide digit magnr 1↑digits
```

PROGRAM 12-64   Address interpretation and representation in the IBM 1401.

Address Modification

Address chaining.   An instruction may omit either the destination address, or both addresses. When an address is omitted, the previous contents of its address register are used as the starting address for the datum. As characters are accessed one by one, the address register is counted down (for data), so it ends up pointing to the right end of the preceding memory field.

Address Arithmetic

Address addition.   The instruction MA became necessary to perform addition upon addresses in the mixed hexadecimal-decimal radix.

```
MA;size;addend;augend;sum
ᴀ IBM 1401 Modify Address
addend←adr1401i read1401s 3
augend←adr1401i read1401d 3
sum←augend+addend
write1401 adr1401r sum
```

PROGRAM 12-65   Address addition in the IBM 1401.

12.3.4

Data

The 1401 has as datatypes character strings and decimal numbers.

```
↓Mark                                              Q4 16pbcd1401
 _____     _____
| Char | Char | Char |  |    | Char |             ○-&
|_____|_____|_____|  |____|_____|             1/JA
  0      1      2              m                   2SKB
Legend: Char = character; m = no maximum.         3TLC
                                                  4UMD
data1401                                          5VNE
ᴀ IBM 1401 data representation                    6WOF
ᴀ character encoding                              7XPG
charcode←bcd1401                                  8YQH
ᴀ sign encoding                                   9ZRI
plus← 0 1 3                                        0+mp
minus←2                                           #.$.
ᴀ byte allocation                                 @%*◇   legend:
Mark←0                                            ○○○○    m = minus zero
Zone←1+ι2                                         ○○○○    p = plus zero
Num←3+ι4                                          ○○○○    ○ = unassigned
```

PROGRAM 12-66   Data specification in the IBM 1401.

Character Strings

Character set and size.   The 1401 character set deviates from BCD in representing distinct plus and minus zeros.

Character-string formats. The character string's variable length is determined by the word mark.

Fixed-Point Numbers

Notation and allocation.   Numbers have a variable length specified by a
word mark; they use signed-magnitude notation. The high-order zone bits
represent an overflow digit that participates in interpretation and representation and (in part) facilitates address arithmetic. In interpretation, the zone bits
of the high-order character are concatenated to the numeric bits.

The digit zero is represented by a binary ten (1010). The sign is in the
zone of the low-order digit. A word mark is placed in the high-order byte.

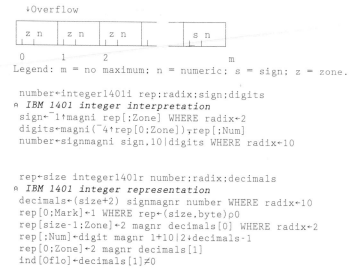

```
number←integer1401i rep;radix;sign;digits
⍝ IBM 1401 integer interpretation
sign← ̄1↑magni rep[;Zone] WHERE radix←2
digits←magni( ̄4↑rep[0;Zone]);rep[;Num]
number←signmagni sign,10|digits WHERE radix←10


rep←size integer1401r number;radix;decimals
⍝ IBM 1401 integer representation
decimals←(size+2) signmagnr number WHERE radix←10
rep[0;Mark]←1 WHERE rep←(size,byte)ρ0
rep[size-1;Zone]←2 magnr decimals[0] WHERE radix←2
rep[;Num]←digit magnr 1+10|2↓decimals-1
rep[0;Zone]←2 magnr decimals[1]
ind[Oflo]←decimals[1]≠0
```

PROGRAM 12-67   Fixed-point number in the IBM 1401.

12.3.5

Operations

Data Handling

Data handling is provided by move operations (including word-mark
manipulation) and print-edit operations.

a	M	Move	a	CWM	Clear Word Mark
a	D	Move Numeric	a	SWM	Set Word Mark
a	Y	Move Zone	a	Z	Suppress Zero
a	CLR	Clear Memory	a	E	Edit

TABLE 12-68   Data-handling instructions of the IBM 1401.

Data movement.   The plain Move, M, stops as soon as either a source or a
destination word mark is sensed; Move With Mark, L, ignores the destination
word mark. These operations inherently proceed one byte at a time, right to
left, which explains the results for overlapping fields. Chaining of source and

destination address is allowed; chaining just the destination address is also allowed in the plain Move—but not for other operations.

Clear sets a group of bytes to blank. Clearing starts at the location addressed by the source and proceeds downward, down to and including the first address that is a multiple of 100; it may be chained. The other move operations shown affect only a single byte; they may be chained too. Set Word Mark sets the word mark in the source and in the destination byte.

```
M:data;rl                                 L:data
a IBM 1401 Move                           a IBM 1401 Move with Mark
REPEAT:data←read1401s 1                   REPEAT:data←read1401s 1
   rl←read1401d 1                            dest←dest-1
   write1401 rl[;Mark],data[;Zone,Num]      write1401 data
→UNTIL data[;Mark]∨rl[;Mark]              →UNTIL data[;Mark]


D:data;rl                                 CWM
a IBM 1401 Move Numeric                    a IBM 1401 Clear Word Mark
data←read1401s 1                           memory[source,dest;Mark]←0
rl←read1401d 1                             source←source-1
write1401 rl[;Mark,Zone],data[;Num]        dest←dest-1


CLR;size                                  SWM
a IBM 1401 Clear Memory                    a IBM 1401 Set Word Mark
size←1+100|source                          memory[source,dest;Mark]←1
source←source-size                         source←source-1
memory[source+1+ιsize;]←0                  dest←dest-1
```

PROGRAM 12-69   Move in the IBM 1401.

Format and code transformation.   Suppress Zero prepares a number for printing by blanking leftmost zeros and removing the sign. Edit does a more complete job; it uses a pattern for the result, as in the 705 Store For Print. Edit provides punctuation and sign indication on the right. An expanded print-edit option has asterisk protection, floating dollar sign, sign indication on the left, and blank for an entirely zero field.

Logic

Connectives.   There are no logical connectives. Branches are called *logical operations* and are indeed the only way to do logic.

Fixed-Point Arithmetic

There are just five basic arithmetic operations; of these, Multiply and Divide are options.

a	L	Load	a	S	Subtract
a	A	Add	a	RS	Reset Subtract
a	RA	Reset Add	a	C	Compare

TABLE 12-70   Fixed-point instructions of the IBM 1401.

Add and Subtract.   The size of the destination field determines the maximum operand size; a word mark encountered earlier in the source field shortens that

operand. Chaining is allowed. It can effect vector addition. When only the source address is specified, both operands are obtained from the same field; in that case, Add doubles the operand and Subtract gives a zero result.

```
A;size;addend;augend;sum
ⓐ IBM 1401 Add
  size←size1401 dest
  addend←integer1401i read1401s size
  augend←integer1401i read1401d size
  sum←augend+addend
  write1401 size integer1401r sum
```

PROGRAM 12-71   Addition in the IBM 1401.

Compare.   The basic machine provides only comparison for equality; greater/less comparison is an option. The destination field determines the size of the fields to be compared; a shorter source field gives an inequality indication. Chaining is not possible, since the fields are scanned left to right until an inequality is sensed; after the comparison, the source and destination addresses are unpredictable.

```
C;size;od1;od2
ⓐ IBM 1401 Compare
  size←size1401 dest
  →IF size>size1401 source
  THEN:ind[Neq]←1
       →ENDIF
  ELSE:od1←alphai 0 1 ↓read1401s size
       od2←alphai 0 1 ↓read1401d size
       ind[Neq]←∨/od1≠od2
  ENDIF:source←?source
  dest←?dest
```

PROGRAM 12-72   Comparison in the IBM 1401.

12.3.6

Instruction Sequencing

Linear Sequence

Next instruction.   The instruction fetch obtains a 1-byte operation code followed by zero, one, or two addresses, in turn followed by zero or one modifier field (Program 12-61). These alternatives give six possible lengths. All other lengths are in error, but are not policed. When a single-address field is present, the destination field is left unchanged for the move operations L and M; for all other operations, the destination address is made equal to the source address.

Unconditional branch.   There are two branch operations; both have many options. The unconditional branch is a special case of the conditional branch.

```
┌────────┬──────────────────────┬──────────────────────┬────────┐
│Opcode  │ Source               │ Destination          │ Mod    │
└────────┴──────────────────────┴──────────────────────┴────────┘
0        1                      4                      7        8
Legend: Mod = modifier.
```

```
 inst←ifetch1401                        cycle1401:ilength
 ⍝ IBM 1401 instruction fetch           ⍝ basic cycle of the IBM 1401
 ⍝ operation code                       REPEAT:execute ifetch1401
 inst←memory[iadr;]                      →UNTIL stop
 ⍝ addresses and modifiers
 ilength←1+memory[iadr+1+ι8;Mark]ι1
 →CASE ilength                          N
 C1: ⍝ opcode only                      ⍝ IBM 1401 No Operation
     →ENDCASE
 C2: ⍝ modifier
     mod←memory[iadr+1;]                 STP
     →ENDCASE                           ⍝ IBM 1401 Stop
 C3:→ERROR 1                            stop←1
 C4: ⍝ source
     source←adr1401i memory[iadr+1+ι3;]
     →If⁓(alphai inst[Opcode])∈'LM'
     THEN:dest←source
     ENDIF:→ENDCASE
 C5: ⍝ source and modifier
     source←adr1401i memory[iadr+1+ι3;]
     mod←memory[iadr+4;]
     →ENDCASE
 C6:→ERROR 1
 C7: ⍝ source and destination
     source←adr1401i memory[iadr+1+ι3;]
     dest←adr1401i memory[iadr+4+ι3;]
     →ENDCASE
 C8: ⍝ source, destination, and modifier
     source←adr1401i memory[iadr+1+ι3;]
     dest←adr1401i memory[iadr+4+ι3;]
     mod←memory[iadr+7;]
     →ENDCASE
 C9:→ERROR 1
 ENDCASE:iadr←adrcap|iadr+ilength
```

PROGRAM 12-73   Basic cycle and instruction fetch of the IBM 1401.

Decision

Conditional branching.   The action of Branch Conditional B depends upon the instruction length. When B has just one address and no modifier, it is unconditional. With one address and a modifier, branching is conditional upon an indicator or one of the six console sense switches, as specified by the modifier. The nine indicators are selected by the modifier characters Z through %; a blank modifier gives an unconditional branch; for any other modifier, no branch occurs. (With a full set of optional features, the 1401 has 22 indicators.)

With two addresses and a modifier, the branch is conditional upon the character specified by the destination field. This test occurs also when neither an address nor a modifier are specified; the destination is chained, which makes it easy to search a character string by a sequence of branch instructions. The modifier is also preserved as last specified.

The Branch On Word Mark tests the presence of a word mark and the bit pattern of a zone, or both, as specified by the modifier.

```
B;true                            V;data;match;true
⍝ IBM 1401 Branch Conditional    ⍝ IBM 1401 Branch On Word Mark
→CASE 4 5 8 1 ⍳ilength            data←,read1401d 1
  C0: ⍝ unconditional branch      match←mod[Zone]∧.=data[Zone]
      true←1                      →CASE magni mod[¯2↑Num]
      →ENDCASE                    C0:→ERROR 1
  C1: ⍝ branch on condition       C1: ⍝ branch on word mark
      true←condition1401              true←data[Mark]
      →ENDCASE                        →ENDCASE
  C2: ⍝ branch on character       C2: ⍝ branch on zone
      true←∧/1↓mod←,read1401d 1        true←match
      →ENDCASE                        →ENDCASE
  C3: ⍝ branch on character       C3: ⍝ branch on word mark or zone
      true←∧/1↓mod←,read1401d 1        true←data[Mark]∨match
      →ENDCASE                    ENDCASE:→If true
  C4:→ERROR 1                     THEN:iadr←source
ENDCASE:→If true                  ENDIF:
THEN:iadr←source
ENDIF:


true←condition1401;mask;who
⍝ IBM 1401 branch condition
mask←(⍴ind)⍴1
mask[Read,Print,Punch,Machine]←~switch[Io,Io,Io,Process]
who←'Z/9@Apm+% '⍳alphai mod
true←((mask∧ind), 1 0)[who]
→If who=Machine
THEN:ind[Machine]←0
ENDIF:
```

PROGRAM 12-74   Branch Conditional in the IBM 1401.

12.3.7

Input/Output

Devices

Store.   Peripheral storage is on cards or on magnetic tape, or (at a later time) on disk.

Source and sink.   A card reader serves as source; sinks are a card punch (housed with the card reader as the IBM 1402) and the IBM 1403 chain printer.

Direct Input/Output

The I/O operation is basically non-overlapped, but—as indicated in the instruction list—reading, punching, and printing can be specified jointly. In such a case, reading and punching *are* overlapped; printing precedes the other operations, but starts them earlier than when specified separately. An optional print buffer allows high-speed transfer to the buffer followed by overlapped printing, reading, and punching. Tape operation is non-overlapped; it uses the Move and Load operations.

Read and Write.   The modifier specifies printing with or without word marks. The source address, when present, specifies an unconditional branch following the I/O operation.

```
a I01 Read            a I06 Print And Punch
a I02 Print           a I07 Print Read And Punch
a I03 Print And Read  a K   Select Stacker
a I04 Punch           a F   Control Carriage
a I05 Read And Punch
```

TABLE 12-75   Input/output instructions of the IBM 1401.

Sense and Control.   Select Stacker specifies via the modifier where a card that has just been read can be stacked. This selection can be based upon the content of that card, but must be completed within 10 ms after the Read to be effective. The same operation also works for the punch stacker; there is no timing constraint. Control Carriage specifies via its character modifier the line spacing of the paper, with reference to a forms-control paper tape on the printer.

12.3.8
Implementation Notes

The 1401 is serially organized, with 1-byte–wide datapath and hardwired controls. The two 16-bit address registers are more costly than the 7-bit data registers in such a dataflow.

Realization note.   The 1401 was one of the earlier machines to use solid-state technology (discrete transistors).

12.3.9
Bibliography

IBM, 1959: *General Information Manual, 1401 Data Processing System.* IBM Form D24-1401-0 9/59. New York: IBM Corp. (our defining reference).

Bashe [1986].

12.3.10
Exercises

12-7 Give the formal description of Y, assuming consistency with D.

12-8 Give the formal description of S, RA, and RS, knowing that they are consistent partners of A and that the reset makes one operand zero prior to the operation.

12-9 Compare the Add of the 1401 with that of the 705. Comment at least on the quality of design of the data sizes and overflow.

12-10 Why is a relative comparison so much more complex than compare for equality that it warrants a special option?

12-11 Why are sense switches no longer used?

12.4
IBM System/360

12.4.1
Highlights

History

Architects. G. M. Amdahl , F. P. Brooks, Jr., and G. A. Blaauw were the chief architects.

Dates. The 360 was announced in April 1964; first deliveries were made in 1965.

Family tree. See this chapter's frontispiece.

Noteworthy

The 360 merges some six commercially successful computer families into a common architecture.

Compatible family. The 360 architecture was designed deliberately to span a wide performance range with a compatible set of machine implementations, and to last through generations of future implementations [Brooks, 1965]. Whereas, in the past, families arose with more or less compatible members, the 360 developers aimed at strict compatibility from the outset. Moreover, the policing of unused spaces was intended to allow future upward- and downward-compatible extensions.

Eight-bit byte. The 8-bit byte of the 360 allows the use of a character set that includes lowercase alphabetic characters and a full set of punctuation; it is a major break with second-generation machines' architectures.

Address capacity. A second major break with the pioneer era is the address size of 32 bits. This size was intended from the outset to be available when needed, even though it was initially held at 24 bits, as presented here [Brooks, 1965]. The 32-bit address was somewhat compromised, yet it was sufficiently guarded to make the shift to it feasible in the 370-XA and ESA.

General purpose registers. In the 360 the address size matches the word size. So the indexing and fixed-point calculation coalesce, and data registers need no longer be distinguished from index registers. The main working registers are called *general purpose registers*.

Alignment. In the IBM Stretch (1961), lack of alignment caused a noticeable reduction in performance. The 360 requires that information units with a fixed length of a word, halfword, or double word must be aligned on multiples of their lengths.

Condition code.   The condition code gives an orthogonal separation of test causes and branch actions, with freedom of specification in each case.

Supervision.   The 360 pioneered a supervisory system that is logically shielded from inadvertent or intentional interference by user programs.

Test And Set.   The 360 was designed for multiprogramming, with multi-processing an important option. As part of this aim, Jules Dirac invented the Test And Set instruction to solve the critical-section problem; this instruction anticipated the concept of the software semaphore. It provides an atomic combination of actions with which software semaphores can be implemented.

Standard interface.   A standard architectural, electrical, and mechanical inter-connection of all computers to all devices gives great flexibility in configuring systems and in accommodating technological developments.

Peculiarities

Floating point.   The floating-point design of the 360 followed the successful IBM 704 design more closely than appears desirable in retrospect. Moreover, some deviations that were made are debatable. The use of a hexadecimal base was intended to speed up the implementation, yet the resulting loss in precision was underestimated. The absence of a guard digit in the 64-bit format had to be corrected soon after the first machines were delivered.

Inconsistencies.   In spite of deliberate efforts to keep the architecture clean, the 360 shows several inconsistencies. Some were fixed soon after delivery of the machines began. Some are of minor consequence; we note them as we encounter them in the description. One of the most obvious is the address phrase, which is either base-index–displacement or just base-displacement.

Base registers.   Whereas index and working registers are properly combined into general purpose registers, the base registers should have been separate from these, and accessible only to the control program.

Crowded PSW.   The 360 packs all control information of the current program into one 64-bit word, the Program Status Word (PSW). The information is made to fit at the expense of some poor design decisions, such as awkward extended-precision arithmetic and a 24-bit instruction address, which in turn is reflected in the Branch And Link instruction. The 370 allows much more status information.

Channels.   The I/O channels are too limited in function. They should have been generalized processors (perhaps virtual processors, just as the Control Data 6600 peripheral processors were).

Descendants

The 360 had many generations of descendants. Most of the original design remained unchanged, but function was added in an upward-compatible

manner. Thus, the 370 (1970) introduced address mapping, whereas the XA extended architecture (1984) provided the 32-bit address, plus a vector-arithmetic option (1987). The EA Enterprise Architecture (1988) added access registers for more address spaces.

12.4.2
Machine Language

Language Level

Design philosophy.   The 360 is a deliberate attempt to roll the function of the 704–7090 technical scientific family, that of the 705–7080 commercial data-processing family, that of the 650–7070 decimal family, and that of the 1401–1410 accounting family into one compatible family covering a wide range of performance.   The design at various points includes specific functions reminiscent of those machines.   Nevertheless, the design is basically a new departure, embodying many concepts introduced in the Stretch.

Unit System

The 8-bit byte results in a set of units that are all powers of 2—except initially the address size. `block` is the memory size that is protected as an entity.

```
format360                       configure360
∩ IBM 360 information units      ∩ configuration for the IBM 360
∩ principal radix               ∩ memory capacity
 radix←2                          memcap←radix*20
∩ information units             ∩ operation options
 digit←4                         ∩ - decimal
 byte←8                           decopt←1
 half←16                         ∩ - floating point
 adrsize←24                       flopt←1
 word←32                         ∩ - protection
 double←64                        protopt←1
 block←2048                      ∩ - direct control
∩ address capacity               dircopt←1
 adrcap←radix*adrsize           ∩ number of channels
                                  chancap←8
```

PROGRAM 12-76   Basic parameters of the IBM System/360.

Configuration.   One of the ways to serve as successor to a wide variety of machines is to provide options. In the 360, the most important options are floating point for the engineering-scientific applications and decimal for the commercial applications. In later generations, decimal was made standard, as was memory protection. Direct I/O control was dropped (a mistake).

The physical-memory size of 1 MB in Program 12-76 is just an arbitrary choice for descriptive purposes; 16 MB could be installed in larger models.

```
space360                              name360
⍺ IBM 360 spaces                      ⍺ IBM 360 space names
⍺ memory                              ⍺ memory
memory←?(memcap,byte)ρradix           ⍺ - old and new program status
⍺ working store                       Oldpsw←24+8×⍳5
⍺ - general registers                 Newpsw←88+8×⍳5
reg←?(16,word)ρradix                  ⍺ - channel instruction address
⍺ - floating-point registers          Caw←72
flreg←?(4,double)ρradix
⍺ control store
⍺ - indicators
ind←?25ρradix
⍺ - status word
psw←?doubleρradix
⍺ - stopped state
stop←?radix
→If protopt
THEN: ⍺ - protection key
   keys←?((⌈memcap÷block),4)ρradix
ENDIF:
```

PROGRAM 12-77   Spaces and embedding of the IBM System/360.

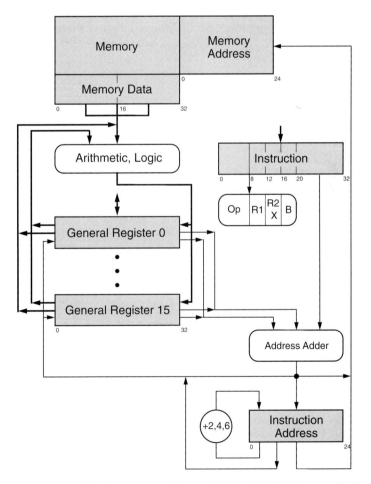

FIGURE 12-78   Basic programming model for the IBM System/360.

Spaces

Memory name-space.   Memory name-space is linear, not cyclic; addresses that exceed the installed capacity are invalid.

Working store.   Besides the sixteen 32-bit general purpose registers, there are four 64-bit floating-point registers. These spaces are kept separate to allow fast implementation and to give a larger total working store.

Control store.   There is a 64-bit PSW. Twenty-five indicators represent interruption causes, some of which are stored in the PSW at the moment of interruption. The stop condition is set only by manual control, such as the initial program load button; program control does not change it.

Embedding.   The 360 does not use fully embedded spaces (spaces accessible in two ways), but uses fixed memory addresses for control. The state information that is used and preserved during an interruption (the old and new PSWs) resides in memory, as does the initial instruction address for a new channel program.

Programming models.   Page size limitations make it easiest to diagram the machine with three models. Figure 12-78 shows the basic fixed-point arithmetic and instruction execution mechanism. Figure 12-79 shows the additional static structure used in floating-point operation. Figure 12-80 shows the model of the character processing and decimal arithmetic, which is quite similar to that of the 1401 (Figure 12-56). Only this part of the machine uses 6-byte instructions, and the simultaneous availability of two running addresses is crucial to the byte-by-byte operation.

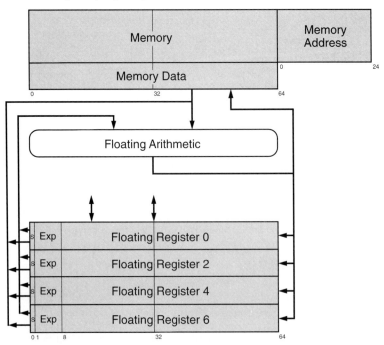

FIGURE 12-79   Floating-point model of the IBM System/360.

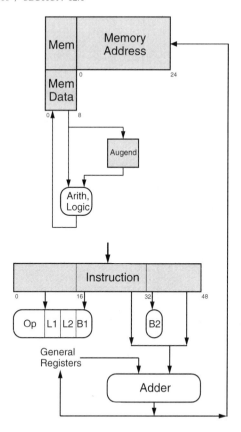

FIGURE 12-80   Character and decimal model of the IBM System/360.

Operand Specification

Number of addresses.   The 360 is a two-address machine—in a dyadic operation one operand is replaced by the result. The addresses are either register addresses or memory addresses; all four combinations occur.

Address phrase.   To allow 24- or 32-bit addresses without sacrificing bit efficiency, the direct address in the instruction is truncated to 12 bits, with the full address residing in a base register. To keep object allocation independent of addressing in the object, an index address is provided. This provision applies only to the memory-to-register format, however; in memory-to-memory formats the index and base must (improperly) use the same register.

Operation Specification

Mnemonics.   We use the official mnemonics in the operation list (Program 12-82). Unused operation codes are policed as invalidities (i).

Types of control.   The control information consists of instructions, indicators, and the PSW.

⌐ *data handling*
MVC   Move(Zones/Numeric)
MVO   Move With Offset
MVI   Move Immediate
PACK Pack
UNPK Unpack
TR   Translate(And Test)
ED   Edit(And Mask)
⌐ *logic and shift*
N   And(Register)
NC   And Characters
NI   And Immediate
O   Or(Register)
OC   Or Characters
OI   Or Immediate
X   Exclusive Or(Register)
XC   Exclusive Or Characters
XI   Exclusive Or Immediate
TM   Test Under Mask
SL   Shift Left(D)(Arithmetic)
SR   Shift Right(D)(Arithmetic)
⌐ *fixed-point arithmetic*
L   Load(Register)
LH   Load Half
IC   Insert Character
LTR   Load Register And Test
LA   Load Address
LM   Load Multiple
ST   Store
STH   Store Half
STC   Store Character
STM   Store Multiple
CV   Convert To Decimal/Binary
LPR   Make Absolute
LNR   Negate Absolute
LCR   Negate
ALR   Add(Logical)(Register)
AH   Add Half
S   Subtract(Logical)(Register)
SH   Subtract Half
M   Multiply(Register)
MH   Multiply Half
D   Divide(Register)
C   Compare(Logical)(Register)
CH   Compare Half
CLC   Compare Logical Character
CLI   Compare Logical Immediate

⌐ *decimal arithmetic*
ZAP   Decimal Load
AP   Decimal Add
SP   Decimal Subtract
MP   Decimal Multiply
DP   Decimal Divide
CP   Decimal Compare
⌐ *floating-point arithmetic*
L   F Load(Register)Short/Long
LT   F Load Register And Test Short/Long
ST   F Store Short/Long
LPR   F Make Absolute Short/Long
LNR   F Negate Absolute Short/Long
LCR   F Negate Short/Long
A   F/U Add(Register)Short/Long
S   F/U Subtract(Register)Short/Long
M   F Multiply(Register)Short/Long
D   F Divide(Register)Short/Long
HR   F Halve Register Short/Long
C   F Compare(Register)Short/Long
⌐ *sequencing*
BC   Branch On Condition/Count(Register)
BX   Branch On Index High/Low Or Equal
BAL   Call(Register)
EX   Execute
⌐ *supervision*
SVC   Supervisor Call
TS   Test And Set
SPM   Set Program Mask
LPSW Load PSW
SK   Set/Insert Storage Key
SSM   Set System Mask
⌐ *input/output*
RDD   Read Direct
WRD   Write Direct
SIO   Start Input/Output
HIO   Stop Input/Output
TIO   Test Input/Output
TCH   Test Channel

Legend: D = Double; F = Floating-Point; U = Unnormalized;
        () = option; / = alternative.

TABLE 12-81   Compressed instruction list of the IBM System/360.

Instruction Structure

Machine-language syntax. There are seven main syntactic patterns (Program 12-83).

Instruction format. Some fields have multiple names, such as R2, X1, and L1—a distinction that shows the function of the field (Program 12-84). In the manual, even more synonyms are used to identify a first and a second operand.

a→i	LPDR	b→STH	STD	c→SSM	e→i	g→STM
i	LNDR	LA	i	i	MVN	g→LM
i	LTDR	STC	i	LPSW	MVC	
i	LCDR	IC	i	i	MVZ	
SPM	HDR	EX	i	WRD	NC	
BALR	i	BAL	i	RDD	CLC	
BCTR	i	BCT	i	BXH	OC	
BCR	i	BC	i	BXLE	XC	
SSK	LDR	LH	LD	SRL	i	
ISK	CDR	CH	CD	SLL	i	
SVC	ADR	AH	AD	SRA	i	
i	SDR	SH	SD	SLA	i	
i	MDR	MH	MD	SRDL	TR	
i	DDR	i	DD	SLDL	TRT	
i	AWR	CVD	AW	SRDA	ED	
i	SWR	CVB	SW	SLDA	EDMK	
LPR	LPER	ST	STE	d→→g	f→i	
LNR	LNER	i	i	TM	MVO	
LTR	LTER	i	i	MVI	PACK	
LCR	LCER	i	i	TS	UNPK	
NR	HER	N	i	NI	i	
CLR	i	CL	i	CLI	i	
OR	i	O	i	OI	i	
XR	i	X	i	XI	i	
LR	LER	L	LE	→g	ZAP	
CR	CER	C	CE	i	CP	
AR	AER	A	AE	i	AP	
SR	SER	S	SE	i	SP	
MR	MER	M	ME	SIO	MP	
DR	DER	D	DE	TIO	DP	
ALR	AUR	AL	AU	HIO	i	
SLR	SUR	SL	SU	TCH	i	

PROGRAM 12-82   Operation-code list of the IBM System/360.

```
        syntax360
    a 0 0 ,Opcode,R1,R2
    b 0 1 ,Opcode,R1,X1,B1,D1
    c 1 0 0 0 ,Ops,R1,R2,B1,D1
    d 1 0 0 1 ,Ops,Imm,B1,D1
    e 1 1 0 1 ,Ops,L0,B1,D1,B2,D2
    f 1 1 1 1 ,Ops,L1,L2,B1,D1,B2,D2
    g 1 0 0 1 0 0 0 0 ,R1,R2,B1,D1
    g 1 0 0 1 1 0 0 0 ,R1,R2,B1,D1
```

PROGRAM 12-83   Instruction syntax of the IBM System/360.

Indicators. The first indicator summarizes machine malfunction; the next 15 identify program exceptions; indicator 16 is used for humble access; indicator 17 summarizes concurrent external events; the last seven indicators are for concurrent I/O events (Program 12-85).

Status format.   The PSW contains the mode bits, the interrupt mask bits, the interruption cause, and the instruction address. The crowded PSW allows only 24 bits for the instruction address (Program 12-86). The 370 required more status information, which forced a larger PSW and made a 32-bit instruction address possible.

12.4.3

Addressing

Direct addressing.   Memory read and write can be specified either with or

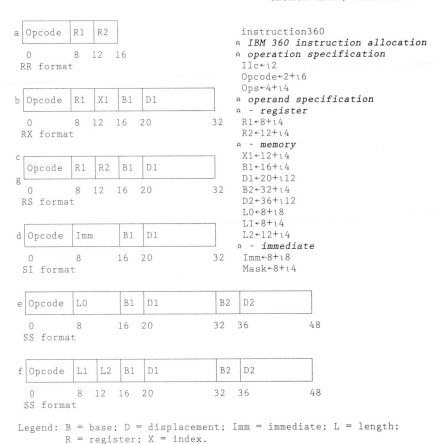

```
a  Opcode  R1  R2

   0        8   12  16
   RR format


b  Opcode  R1  X1  B1  D1

   0        8   12  16  20        32
   RX format


c
g  Opcode  R1  R2  B1  D1

   0        8   12  16  20        32
   RS format


d  Opcode  Imm     B1  D1

   0        8       16  20        32
   SI format


e  Opcode  L0      B1  D1        B2  D2

   0        8       16  20        32  36          48
   SS format


f  Opcode  L1  L2  B1  D1        B2  D2

   0        8   12  16  20        32  36          48
   SS format
```

```
instruction360
A IBM 360 instruction allocation
A operation specification
  Ilc←ι2
  Opcode←2+ι6
  Ops←4+ι4
A operand specification
A - register
  R1←8+ι4
  R2←12+ι4
A - memory
  X1←12+ι4
  B1←16+ι4
  D1←20+ι12
  B2←32+ι4
  D2←36+ι12
  L0←8+ι8
  L1←8+ι4
  L2←12+ι4
A - immediate
  Imm←8+ι8
  Mask←8+ι4
```

Legend: B = base; D = displacement; Imm = immediate; L = length;
        R = register; X = index.

PROGRAM 12-84   Instruction allocation in the IBM System/360.

```
indicator360
A IBM 360 indicators
A machine check
  Machine←0
A program check
  Program←1+ι15
A - invalid operation
  Invop←1
A - privileged operation
  Priv←2
A - execute error
  Execute←3
A - protection violation
  Protect←4
A - invalid address
  Invadr←5
A - specification error
  Spec←6
A - invalid data
  Data←7
A - binary overflow
  Oflo←8
A - invalid divisor
  Divide←9
A - decimal overflow
  Decoflo←10
A - zero decimal divisor
  Decdiv←11
A - floating-point overflow
  Floflo←12
A - floating-point underflow
  Uflo←13
A - lost significance
  Lostsf←14
A - zero floating divisor
  Fldiv←15
A supervisor call
  Svc←16
A external signal
  External←17
A input/output
  Io←18+ι7
```

PROGRAM 12-85   Indicators in the IBM System/360.

without alignment, so two sets of read and write functions are provided in

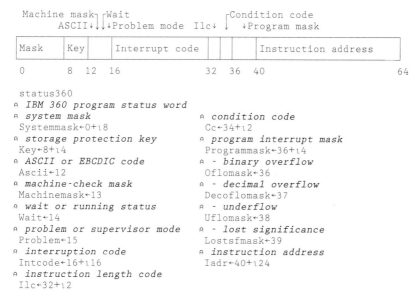

```
Machine mask┐┌Wait                        ┌Condition code
       ASCII↓│↓↓Problem mode  Ilc↓ │   ↓Program mask

┌────────┬─────┬───────────────────┬──┬──┬───────────────────────┐
│ Mask   │ Key │   Interrupt code  │  │  │  Instruction address  │
└────────┴─────┴───────────────────┴──┴──┴───────────────────────┘
0        8    12   16                32  36  40                      64
```

status360
A IBM 360 program status word
A system mask   A condition code
  Systemmask←0+ι8   Cc←34+ι2
A storage protection key   A program interrupt mask
  Key←8+ι4   Programmask←36+ι4
A ASCII or EBCDIC code   A - binary overflow
  Ascii←12   Oflomask←36
A machine-check mask   A - decimal overflow
  Machinemask←13   Decoflomask←37
A wait or running status   A - underflow
  Wait←14   Uflomask←38
A problem or supervisor mode   A - lost significance
  Problem←15   Lostsfmask←39
A interruption code   A instruction address
  Intcode←16+ι16   Iadr←40+ι24
A instruction length code
  Ilc←32+ι2

PROGRAM 12-86   Program Status Word in the IBM System/360.
```

our description. The first set of functions checks for alignment; then it calls the second set. The location is checked for validity and memory protection (Program 12-118).

```
data←size read360 address;location    address write360 data;location
A IBM 360 read from memory            A IBM 360 write in memory
  location←address+ιsize∔byte           location←address+ι(ρ,data)∔byte
  adrcheck360 location                  adrcheck360 location
  data←,memory[memcap|location;]        →OUT suppress360
                                        memory[location;]←byte wide data


data←size read360a address            address write360a data;size
A IBM 360 read aligned from memory    A IBM 360 write aligned in memory
  Spec report 0≠(size∔byte)|address     size←ρ.data
  data←size read360 address             Spec report 0≠(size∔byte)|address
                                        address write360 data

PROGRAM 12-87    Memory read and write in the IBM System/360.
```

Address Mapping

There is no address mapping, a design decision that had to be reversed almost as soon as systems were delivered. The Model 67 (1965) was introduced with address mapping—the whole family followed suit later.

Address Modification

Addresses are modified with a base, index, and displacement, or just with a base and displacement. Also shown are auxiliary functions for specifying a field length and for specifying the odd or even member of a register pair.
```

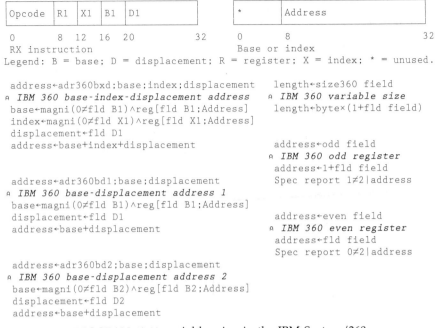

```
address←adr360bxd;base;index;displacement      length←size360 field
ᴀ IBM 360 base-index-displacement address      ᴀ IBM 360 variable size
base←magni(0≠fld B1)∧reg[fld B1;Address]          length←byte×(1+fld field)
index←magni(0≠fld X1)∧reg[fld X1;Address]
displacement←fld D1
address←base+index+displacement                address←odd field
                                               ᴀ IBM 360 odd register
                                                  address←1+fld field
address←adr360bd1;base;displacement               Spec report 1≠2|address
ᴀ IBM 360 base-displacement address 1
base←magni(0≠fld B1)∧reg[fld B1;Address]
displacement←fld D1                            address←even field
address←base+displacement                      ᴀ IBM 360 even register
                                                  address←fld field
                                                  Spec report 0≠2|address
address←adr360bd2;base;displacement
ᴀ IBM 360 base-displacement address 2
base←magni(0≠fld B2)∧reg[fld B2;Address]
displacement←fld D2
address←base+displacement
```

PROGRAM 12-88   Addressing in the IBM System/360.

Index Arithmetic

Index operations.   Using general registers for both data and addresses eliminates the need for separate index-arithmetic instructions.

Address Level

Indirect addressing.   Indirect addressing is achieved by loading a register with a separate instruction, and then indexing or basing with it.

Immediate addressing.   Immediate addressing is specified not in the address phrase but through distinct operations.

12.4.4
Data

Character Strings

Character set and size.   The 8-bit EBCDIC character set was designed specifically for the 360. The upper four bits of a byte are the zone part; the lower four bits are the numeric part. The code is discussed more fully in Section 4.1.

Character string formats.   A character string is up to 256 bytes long. In later generations, this length is extended to 16,384 bytes.

Char	Char	Char	Char		Char
0	1	2	3		m

Legend: Char = character; m = maximum 256; ○ = unassigned.

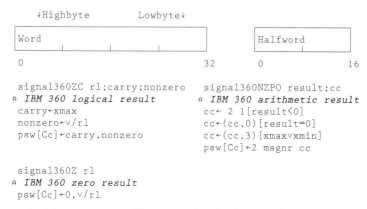

```
data360                                    Q16 16 ρebcdic
⍺ IBM 360 data representation     ○○○○  ∧-○○○○○○○0
⍺ character encoding              ○○○○○○/○aj○○AJ○1
charcode←ebcdic                   ○○○○○○○bks○BKS2
⍺ floating-point base             ○○○○○○○○clt○CLT3
base←16                           ○○○○○○○○○dmu○DMU4
⍺ word allocation                 ○○○○○○○○○env○ENV5
Address←8+ι24                     ○○○○○○○○○fow○FOW6
Highbyte←ι8                       ○○○○○○○○○gpx○GPX7
Lowbyte←24+ι8                     ○○○○○○○○○hqy○HQY8
⍺ byte allocation                 ○○○○○○○○○irz○IRZ9
Zone←ι4                           ○○○○¢!○:○○○○○○○
Num←4+ι4                          ○○○○.$,#○○○○○○○○
                                  ○○○○<*%@○○○○○○○○
                                  ○○○○()`'○○○○○○○○
                                  ○○○○+;>=○○○○○○○○
                                  ○○○○|~?"○○○○○○○○
```

PROGRAM 12-89   Character string in the IBM System/360.

Logical

Logical formats. The logical data match the character string and the numeric formats; they are either a string of up to 256 bytes or a word. Results are tested for zero or not zero using `signal360Z` (Program 12-90).

```
↓Highbyte          Lowbyte↓
```

Word				Halfword	
0			32	0	16

```
signal360ZC r1;carry;nonzero       signal360NZPO result;cc
⍺ IBM 360 logical result           ⍺ IBM 360 arithmetic result
carry←xmax                         cc← 2 1[result<0]
nonzero←∨/r1                       cc←(cc,0)[result=0]
psw[Cc]←carry,nonzero              cc←(cc,3)[xmax∨xmin]
                                   psw[Cc]←2 magnr cc

signal360Z r1
⍺ IBM 360 zero result
psw[Cc]←0,∨/r1
```

PROGRAM 12-90   Binary number in the IBM System/360.

Fixed-Point Numbers

Notation and allocation. The 360 provides binary radix-complement notation and decimal signed-magnitude notation. Results of addition and subtraction are normally tested for negative, zero, positive, or overflow. In the multiple-precision operations, a carry and a zero result are noted.

Decimal numbers. Decimal digits are represented with 4-bit binary encoding. Two digits are placed in one byte. Half of the rightmost byte represents the sign.

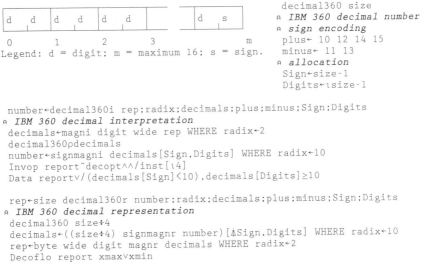

```
                                        decimal360 size
  ┌───┬───┬───┬───┬───┬───┬─   ─┬───┬───┐  ⋀ IBM 360 decimal number
  │ d   d │ d   d │ d   d │    │ d │ s │  ⋀ sign encoding
  └───┴───┴───┴───┴───┴───┴─   ─┴───┴───┘  plus← 10 12 14 15
  0       1       2       3          m    minus← 11 13
  Legend:  d = digit;  m = maximum 16;  s = sign.   ⋀ allocation
                                        Sign←size-1
                                        Digits←ιsize-1
```

```
number←decimal360i rep;radix;decimals;plus;minus;Sign;Digits
⋀ IBM 360 decimal interpretation
decimals←magni digit wide rep WHERE radix←2
decimal360ρdecimals
number←signmagni decimals[Sign,Digits] WHERE radix←10
Invop report˜decopt⋀⋀/inst[ι4]
Data reportv/(decimals[Sign]<10),decimals[Digits]≥10
```

```
rep←size decimal360r number;radix;decimals;plus;minus;Sign;Digits
⋀ IBM 360 decimal representation
decimal360 size÷4
decimals←((size÷4) signmagnr number)[⊿Sign,Digits] WHERE radix←10
rep←byte wide digit magnr decimals WHERE radix←2
Decoflo report xmaxvxmin
```

PROGRAM 12-91   Decimal number in the IBM System/360.

Signs and digits are distinguished and checked as such. The sign codes are chosen to facilitate conversion from 6-bit BCD to 8-bit EBCDIC.

Floating-Point Numbers

Closure and normal form.   The 360 uses normalized and unnormalized representations, much like the 704; the underlying biased-exponent signed-magnitude fractional-coefficient functions `flbsi` and `flbsr` are the same as those used in the 704 (Section 9.3). Lost significance, underflow, and overflow are signaled. A true zero is generated if the exponent underflows or if lost significance occurs and the corresponding mask bit is off.

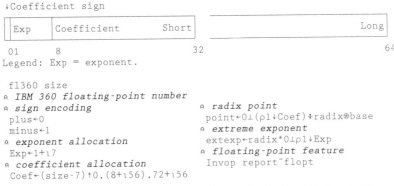

```
  ↓Coefficient sign
 ┌┬─────┬────────────────┬───────┐  ┌────────────────────────────────────┐
 ││ Exp │ Coefficient    Short  │  │                              Long  │
 └┴─────┴────────────────┴───────┘  └────────────────────────────────────┘
  01    8                   32                                         64
  Legend: Exp = exponent.
```

```
  fl360 size
  ⋀ IBM 360 floating-point number
  ⋀ sign encoding                    ⋀ radix point
    plus←0                             point←0⊥(ρ1↓Coef)÷radix⊛base
    minus←1                           ⋀ extreme exponent
  ⋀ exponent allocation               extexp←radix*0⊥ρ1↓Exp
    Exp←1+ι7                         ⋀ floating-point feature
  ⋀ coefficient allocation            Invop report˜flopt
    Coef←(size-7)↑0,(8+ι56),72+ι56
```

PROGRAM 12-92   Floating-point format in the IBM System/360.

Floating-point format.   A short 32-bit format and a long 64-bit format are available. The short one may have been a mistake.

Floating-point representation.   The 360 uses the hexadecimal base to reduce shifting.

```
numexp←f1360i rep;plus;minus
⍝ IBM 360 floating-point interpretation
f1360ρrep
⍝ number and exponent
numexp←flbsi rep

rep←size f1360r numexp;plus;minus
⍝ IBM 360 floating-point representation
f1360 size
⍝ number and optional exponent
rep←size flbsr numexp
⍝ lost significance
Lostsf report˜∨/rep[Coef]
⍝ overflow
Floflo report xmax∧˜ind[Lostsf]
⍝ underflow
Uflo report xmin∧˜ind[Lostsf]
⍝ true zero
→If xmin∨ind[Lostsf]∧˜psw[Lostsfmask]
THEN:rep←sizeρ0
ENDIF:
```

PROGRAM 12-93   Floating-point interpretation and representation in the IBM 360.

12.4.5

Operations

Contrary to our normal procedure, we do not repeat in this section all the instructions of the 360 that occur in Part I.

Data Handling

All data-handling operations except Move Immediate are memory to memory.

```
e MVC  Move                f PACK Pack
e MVZ  Move Zones          f UNPK Unpack
f MVO  Move With Offset    e TR   Translate
e MVN  Move Numeric        e TRT  Translate And Test
d MVI  Move Immediate      e ED   Edit
                           e EDMK Edit And Mark
```

TABLE 12-94   Data-handling instructions of the IBM System/360.

Data movement.   The moves are byte-by-byte operations. Move Zone and Move Numeric move only the corresponding part of each byte, leaving the other part of the destination byte unchanged. Move Immediate moves one instruction byte to memory.

Format and code transformation.   Translate And Test and Edit are shown in Section 5.1. The Edit instructions are the end of a tradition started with the 705; their complexity spoils their usefulness. The Translate instructions, in contrast, are simple and versatile. Unpack is the inverse of Pack. The zone of the unpacked digits is 0101 when the ASCII bit of the PSW is one, and 1111 otherwise.

```
MVC;source;dest;length;data        PACK;source;dest;12;11;hex
A IBM 360 Move                     A IBM 360 Pack
source←adr360bd2                   source←adr360bd2
dest←adr360bd1                     dest←adr360bd1
length←1+fld L0                    12←fld L2
REPEAT: A move byte                11←fld L1
   data←byte read360 source       A invert sign byte
   →OUT suppress360               hex←digit wide byte read360 source+12
   dest write360 data             (dest+11) write360,Φ[0] hex
   source←source+1                →WHILE(11>0)∧12>0
   dest←dest+1                        12←12-1
   length←length-1                    11←11-1
→UNTIL length=0                        A byte to low order hex
                                      hex←(4ρ0),4↓,byte read360 source+12
                                      →If 12>0
MVI                                   THEN: A byte to high order hex
A IBM 360 Move Immediate              12←12-1
adr360bd1 write360 inst[Imm]          hex[ι4]←4↓,byte read360 source+12
                                      ENDIF:(dest+11) write360 hex
                                      →Δ
                                   ENDWHILE: A fill with zero
                                   dest write360(11,byte)ρ0
```

PROGRAM 12-95   Move and Pack in the IBM System/360.

```
TR;origin;dest;length;argument;rl
A IBM 360 Translate
origin←adr360bd2
dest←adr360bd1
length←1+fld L0
REPEAT: A translate byte
   argument←magni byte read360 dest
   rl←byte read360 origin+argument
   →OUT suppress360
   dest write360 rl
   dest←dest+1
   length←length-1
→UNTIL length=0
```

PROGRAM 12-96   Translate in the IBM System/360.

Logic

Connectives.   And, Or, and Exclusive Or are provided; the Not can be obtained from an Exclusive Or with one of its operands all-ones.

b	N	And		b	X	Exclusive Or
e	NC	And Characters		e	XC	Exclusive Or Characters
d	NI	And Immediate		d	XI	Exclusive Or Immediate
a	NR	And Register		a	XR	Exclusive Or Register
b	O	Or		d	TM	Test Under Mask
e	OC	Or Characters				
d	OI	Or Immediate				
a	OR	Or Register				

TABLE 12-97   Logical connectives of the IBM System/360.

Vector operations.   Test Under Mask examines selected bits of a byte. The condition code is 0 when all tested bits are 0 (including when no bits are tested); the code is 1 when some, but not all tested bits, are 1; it is 3 when all tested bit are 1. The 360 does not follow the Stretch in providing a population count or a left-zero count.

```
OC;source;dest;length;crl;rl        NI;od;rl
A IBM 360 Or Characters             A IBM 360 And Immediate
source←adr360bd2                    od←byte read360 adr360bd1
dest←adr360bd1                      →OUT suppress360
length←1+fld L0                     rl←od∧inst[Imm]
crl←byteρ0                          adr360bd1 write360 rl
REPEAT: A or byte                   signal360Z rl
    od2←byte read360 source
    od1←byte read360 dest
    →OUT suppress360
    rl←od1∨od2                      XR;od1;od2;rl
    dest write360 rl                A IBM 360 Exclusive Or Register
    source←source+1                 od2←reg[fld R2;]
    dest←dest+1                     od1←reg[fld R1;]
    length←length-1                 rl←od1≠od2
    crl←crl∨rl                      reg[fld R1;]←rl
→UNTIL length=0                     signal360Z rl
signal360Z crl


TM;od;mask                         signal360TM rl;allone;someone
A IBM 360 Test Under Mask          A IBM 360 test under mask result
od←byte read360 adr360bd1          allone←(0≠ρ,rl)∧∧/rl
→OUT suppress360                   someone←∨/rl
mask←inst[Imm]                     psw[Cc]←allone,someone
signal360TM mask/od
```

PROGRAM 12-98   And and Or in the IBM System/360.

Shift.   The 360 has a complete set of word and double word, logical and arithmetic, left- and right-shifts.

```
c SLL   Shift Left       c SLA  Shift Left Arithmetic
c SLDL  Shift Left D      c SLDA Shift Left D Arithmetic
c SRL   Shift Right      c SRA  Shift Right Arithmetic
c SRDL  Shift Right D     c SRDA Shift Right D Arithmetic
Legend: D = Double.
```

TABLE 12-99   Shift instructions of the IBM System/360.

```
SLA;operand;shift;result;rl;xmax;xmin    SLDL;od;shift;rl
A IBM 360 Shift Left Arithmetic          A IBM 360 Shift Left Double
operand←radixcompi reg[fld R1;]          od←,reg[(even R1)+ι2;]
shift←64|adr360bd1                        →OUT suppress360
result←operand×radix*shift               shift←64|adr360bd1
rl←word radixcompr result                rl←double↑shift↓od
reg[fld R1;1↓ιword]←1↓rl                 reg[(even R1)+ι2;]←word wide rl
signal360NZPO radixcompi reg[fld R1;]
Oflo report xmax


SRA;operand;shift;result;xmax;xmin
A IBM 360 Shift Right Arithmetic
operand←radixcompi reg[fld R1;]
shift←64|adr360bd1
result←⌊operand÷radix*shift
reg[fld R1;]←word radixcompr result
signal360NZPO radixcompi reg[fld R1;]
```

PROGRAM 12-100   Logical and Arithmetic Shift in the IBM System/360.

An arithmetic shift is treated as a multiplication with a power of 2; the sign remains unchanged, and the arithmetic conditions are set. In the logical shifts all bits participate; no condition is set.

Fixed-Point Arithmetic

Fixed-point arithmetic is memory to register or register to register. The memory operand is a word or a halfword. The sign-control instructions are only register to register. The instructions A and AL are shown in Section 5.3.

b	L	Load	b	S	Subtract	
b	LH	Load Half	b	SH	Subtract Half	
b	IC	Insert Character	a	SR	Subtract Register	
a	LR	Load Register	b	SL	Subtract Logical	
a	LTR	Load Register And Test	a	SLR	Subtract Logical Register	
b	LA	Load Address	b	M	Multiply	
g	LM	Load Multiple	b	MH	Multiply Half	
b	ST	Store	a	MR	Multiply Register	
b	STH	Store Half	b	D	Divide	
b	STC	Store Character	a	DR	Divide Register	
g	STM	Store Multiple	b	C	Compare	
b	CVD	Convert To Decimal	b	CH	Compare Half	
b	CVB	Convert To Binary	a	CR	Compare Register	
a	LCR	Negate	b	CL	Compare Logical	
a	LPR	Make Absolute	e	CLC	Compare Logical Character	
a	LNR	Negate Absolute	d	CLI	Compare Logical Immediate	
b	A	Add	a	CLR	Compare Logical Register	
b	AH	Add Half				
a	AR	Add Register				
b	AL	Add Logical				
a	ALR	Add Logical Register				

TABLE 12-101   Fixed-point instructions of the IBM System/360.

Load and Store.   There are various loads and stores; a single character can be inserted, and a group of consecutive registers can be loaded and stored.

```
LA;address                            STH;od
ᴀ IBM 360 Load Address                ᴀ IBM 360 Store Half
address←adrcap|adr360bxd                od←reg[fld R1;half+ıhalf]
reg[fld R1;]←word magnr address        adr360bxd write360a od

IC;od                                 LM;test;size;od
ᴀ IBM 360 Insert Character            ᴀ IBM 360 Load Multiple
od←byte read360 adr360bxd             ᴀ alignment test
→OUT suppress360                        test←word read360a adr360bd1
reg[fld R1;Lowbyte]←od                 →OUT suppress360
                                       size←1+16|(fld R2)-fld R1
                                       od←(size×word) read360 adr360bd1
LCR;result;xmax;xmin                   reg[16|(fld R1)+ısize;]←word wide od
ᴀ IBM 360 Negate
result←-radixcompi reg[fld R2;]
reg[fld R1;]←word radixcompr result   CVD;result;r1;xmax;xmin
signal360NZPO result                  ᴀ IBM 360 Convert To Decimal
Oflo report xmax                        result←radixcompi reg[fld R1;]
                                        r1←double decimal360r result
                                        adr360bxd write360a r1
```

PROGRAM 12-102   Monadic binary arithmetic in the IBM System/360.

Radix conversion operations.   The conversion operations are not part of the decimal option; rather, they are intended to be used most when one machine does not have the hardware decimal datatype installed.

Add and Subtract.   Logical Add and Subtract differ from regular Add and Subtract only in the setting of the condition register. Since these logical operations are intended for multiple-precision arithmetic, no halfword operations are supplied.

```
AH;addend;augend;sum;xmax;xmin
ᴀ IBM 360 Add Half
addend←radixcompi half read360a adr360bxd
augend←radixcompi reg[fld R1;]
→OUT suppress360
sum←augend+addend
reg[fld R1;]←word radixcompr sum
signal360NZPO sum
Oflo report xmaxᵥxmin
```

```
                                      MR;multiplier;multiplicand;product;pd
SLR;addend;augend;sum;xmax;xmin       ᴀ IBM 360 Multiply Register
ᴀ IBM 360 Subtract Logical Register   multiplier←radixcompi reg[fld R2;]
addend←1+magni~reg[fld R2;]           multiplicand←radixcompi reg[odd R1;]
augend←magni reg[fld R1;]             →OUT suppress360
sum←augend+addend                     product←multiplicand×multiplier
reg[fld R1;]←word radixcompr sum      pd←double radixcompr product
signal360ZC reg[fld R1;]              reg[(even R1)+ι2;]←word wide pd
```

PROGRAM 12-103   Dyadic binary arithmetic in the IBM System/360.

Multiply and Divide.   Multiply Half has a single length result and ignores overflow. Divide yields a quotient and remainder. The 64-bit dividend resides in an odd/even register pair; the 32-bit divisor is either in a register or in memory; there is no halfword divisor. The 32-bit remainder and quotient replace the dividend in the even- and odd-numbered registers respectively, just as in the 704 and the 650. A divide exception occurs when the quotient cannot be represented properly, whether because of zero divisor or just overflow.

Compare.   The regular comparisons assume radix-complement notation. The logical comparisons assume magnitude notation and use the logical formats; they allow character comparisons based upon the collating sequence of the character code.

```
CLI;operand;comparand                operand signal360C comparand;cc
ᴀ IBM 360 Compare Logical Immediate  ᴀ IBM 360 comparison condition
operand←magni byte read360 adr360bd1 cc← 1 2[operand>comparand]
comparand←fld Imm                    cc←(cc,0)[operand=comparand]
→OUT suppress360                     psw[Cc]←2 magnr cc
operand signal360C comparand
```

PROGRAM 12-104   Binary comparison in the IBM System/360.

Decimal Arithmetic

Decimal arithmetic uses variable-length operands and is memory to memory. The mnemonic of decimal Load is derived from Zero and Add Positive.

f ZAP	Decimal Load	f MP	Decimal Multiply
f AP	Decimal Add	f DP	Decimal Divide
f SP	Decimal Subtract	f CP	Decimal Compare

TABLE 12-105   Decimal instructions in the IBM System/360.

Decimal Add and Subtract.   The sign of zero is always plus, except when an overflow creates an apparent zero; in that case the sign of the number to be represented is maintained.

```
ZAP;result;xmax;xmin
ᑎ IBM 360 Decimal Load
result←decimal360i(size360 L2) read360 adr360bd2
adr360bd1 write360(size360 L1) decimal360r result
signal360NZPO result
Decoflo report xmaxᵥxmin


AP;addend;augend;sum;xmax;xmin
ᑎ IBM 360 Decimal Add
addend←decimal360i(size360 L2) read360 adr360bd2
augend←decimal360i(size360 L1) read360 adr360bd1
→OUT suppress360
sum←augend+addend
adr360bd1 write360(size360 L1) decimal360r sum
signal360NZPO sum
Decoflo report xmaxᵥxmin


MP;mr;mc;multiplier;multiplicand;product;pd;xmax;xmin
ᑎ IBM 360 Decimal Multiply
multiplier←decimal360i mr←(size360 L2) read360 adr360bd2
multiplicand←decimal360i mc←(size360 L1) read360 adr360bd1
product←multiplicand×multiplier
pd←(size360 L1) decimal360r product
→If(product=0)∧≠/((magni ⁻4↑,mr),magni ⁻4↑,mc)∈ 11 13
THEN:pd←byte wide(⁻4↓,pd),digit magnr 11
ENDIF:adr360bd1 write360 pd
```

PROGRAM 12-106   Decimal arithmetic in the IBM System/360.

Decimal Multiply and Divide.   The sign of a zero product is determined by the sign of the multiplier and multiplicand. In Divide the dividend is replaced by quotient and remainder, with the remainder size equal to the divisor size. The quotient sign is determined from dividend and divisor. The division operates as though an integer result is wanted; when the divisor size exceeds 8 bytes, or is larger than or equal to the dividend size, then the division is suppressed with the operands unchanged.

Decimal Compare.   Decimal comparison is upon the interpretation of the operands: Plus and minus zero compare equal; a field with high-order zeros compares equal to the same field without some of those high-order zeros. (This behavior is different from that of the 705 family.)

Floating-Point Arithmetic

Floating-point arithmetic is memory to register or register to register; the operands are either short or long. In the mnemonics, E designates short and D long (double). If a long operand in memory or in a register is accessed as though it were short, the operation works correctly; the converse is not always true. The instruction MD is shown in Section 5.4.

b	LE	F	Load Short	b	SE	F	Subtract Short
b	LD	F	Load Long	b	SD	F	Subtract Long
a	LER	F	Load Register Short	a	SER	F	Subtract Register Short
a	LDR	F	Load Register Long	a	SDR	F	Subtract Register Long
a	LTER	F	Load Register And Test Short	b	SU	U	Subtract Short
a	LTDR	F	Load Register And Test Long	b	SW	U	Subtract Long
b	STE	F	Store Short	a	SUR	U	Subtract Register Short
b	STD	F	Store Long	a	SWR	U	Subtract Register Long
a	LCER	F	Negate Short	b	ME	F	Multiply Short
a	LCDR	F	Negate Long	b	MD	F	Multiply Long
a	LPER	F	Make Absolute Short	a	MER	F	Multiply Register Short
a	LPDR	F	Make Absolute Long	a	MDR	F	Multiply Register Long
a	LNER	F	Negate Absolute Short	b	DE	F	Divide Short
a	LNDR	F	Negate Absolute Long	b	DD	F	Divide Long
b	AE	F	Add Short	a	DER	F	Divide Register Short
b	AD	F	Add Long	a	DDR	F	Divide Register Long
a	AER	F	Add Register Short	a	HER	F	Halve Register Short
a	ADR	F	Add Register Long	a	HDR	F	Halve Register Long
b	AU	U	Add Short	b	CE	F	Compare Short
b	AW	U	Add Long	b	CD	F	Compare Long
a	AUR	U	Add Register Short	a	CER	F	Compare Register Short
a	AWR	U	Add Register Long	a	CDR	F	Compare Register Long

Legend: F = Floating-Point; U = Unnormalized.

TABLE 12-107   Floating-point instructions of the IBM System/360.

Floating-point Load and Store.   For short operands, the low-order 32 bits of the registers remain unchanged. Unnormalized operands are accepted in normalized operations, and vice versa. The function rfl checks that the floating-point register address has the value 0, 2, 4, or 6, and converts the address into an index to be used in the descriptions.

Floating-point Add and Subtract.   Add and Subtract resemble the 704 operations, except that there are no P and Q bits and that the result is not extended in a MQ register. In long precision, low-order digits are discarded

```
AD;au;ad;scale;addend;augend;sum;xmax;xmin
⋒ IBM 360 Floating-Point Add Long
ad←fl360i double read360a adr360bxd
au←fl360i flreg[rfl R1;]
→OUT suppress360
scale←base*(au[1]⌈ad[1])-(point+1)
addend←scale×truncate ad[0]÷scale              STD
augend←scale×truncate au[0]÷scale       ⋒ IBM 360 Floating-Point Store Long
sum←augend+addend                         Invop report˜flopt
flreg[rfl R1;]←double fl360r sum          →OUT suppress360
signal360NZPO sum                         adr360bxd write360a flreg[rfl R1;]
```

```
AUR;au;ad;scale;addend;augend;sm;xmax;xmin
⋒ IBM 360 Unnormalized Add Register Short
ad←fl360i flreg[rfl R2;ιword]
au←fl360i flreg[rfl R1;ιword]
→OUT suppress360
scale←base*(au[1]⌈ad[1])-(point+1)
addend←scale×truncate ad[0]÷scale
augend←scale×truncate au[0]÷scale         address←rfl Reg
sm←(augend+addend).au[1]⌈ad[1]          ⋒ IBM 360 floating-point register
flreg[rfl R1;ιword]←word fl360r sm        address←4|⌊0.5×fld Reg
signal360NZPO sm[0]                       Spec report˜(fld Reg)∊2×ι4
```

PROGRAM 12-108   Floating-point Add and Store in the IBM System/360.

beyond the result length; in short precision, one guard digit is preserved. This inconsistency was quickly corrected; a guard digit was added for long precision, too. The sign of zero is always positive.

Floating-point Multiply and Divide.   The results of Multiply and Divide are always normalized; their operation is straightforward, except that the sign of zero is computed from the operand signs, which may result in a negative zero.

```
ME;mr;md;multiplier;multiplicand;product;xmax;xmin
ᴀ IBM 360 Floating-Point Multiply Short
multiplier←1↑fl360i mr WHERE mr←word read360a adr360bxd
multiplicand←1↑fl360i md WHERE md←flreg[rfl R1;ɩword]
→OUT suppress360
product←multiplicand×multiplier
flreg[rfl R1;ɩword]←word fl360r product
→If product=0
THEN:flreg[rfl R1;0]←md[0]≠mr[0]
ENDIF:


DDR;dr;dd;divisor;dividend;quotient;xmax;xmin
ᴀ IBM 360 Floating-Point Divide Register Long
divisor←1↑fl360i dr WHERE dr←flreg[rfl R2;]
dividend←1↑fl360i dd WHERE dd←flreg[rfl R1;]
Fldiv report divisor=0
→OUT suppress360
quotient←dividend÷divisor
flreg[rfl R1;]←double fl360r quotient
→If quotient=0
THEN:flreg[rfl R1;0]←dd[0]≠dr[0]
ENDIF:
```

PROGRAM 12-109   Floating-point Multiply and Divide in the IBM System/360.

Floating-point Compare.   Comparison is upon the interpretation of the numbers: Zeros with different sign or exponent compare equal; normalized and unnormalized versions of the same number compare equal.

12.4.6

Instruction Sequencing

Possible interrupts are taken before each instruction. When an external stop occurs, the pending interrupts are registered, but are not executed.

```
cycle360                         inst←ifetch360;iadr;length
ᴀ basic cycle of the IBM 360     ᴀ IBM 360 instruction fetch
REPEAT:interrupt360              ind[Program]←0
   execute ifetch360             iadr←magni psw[Iadr]
→UNTIL stop                      length← 1 2 2 3[magni 2↑half read360a iadr]
interrupt360                     inst←,(length×half) read360 iadr
                                 →OUT suppress360
                                 iadr←iadr+2×length
                                 psw[Iadr]←adrsize magnr iadr
                                 psw[Ilc]←2 magnr length
```

PROGRAM 12-110   Basic cycle and instruction fetch of the IBM System/360.

Next instruction. The instruction length is specified in the first two instruction bits: The instruction stream must have halfword alignment. `fetch360` first fetches 2 bytes with alignment check and determines the instruction length. Then the instruction is fetched to its full extent and the instruction address is updated. The instruction length is recorded in the PSW for use by the supervisory program.

```
b BC   Branch On Condition          b BAL  Call
b BCT  Branch On Count              a BALR Call Register
a BCR  Branch On Condition Register b EX   Execute
a BCTR Branch On Count Register
c BXLE Branch On Index Low Or Equal
c BXH  Branch On Index High
```

TABLE 12-111   Sequencing instructions of the IBM System/360.

Linear Sequence

Unconditional branch. An unconditional branch can be specified as a case of the Branch On Condition.

Completion. There is no Stop instruction. A wait can be obtained by loading a PSW with the wait bit on.

Decision

Conditional branching. The branch condition may be any selection of the four values that the condition code in the PSW can assume. Each value of the condition code is specified by a bit of the mask field of the Branch On Condition instructions. A mask of four ones makes the branch unconditional; four zeros give a No Operation. Branching is effected by changing the `Iadr` field of the PSW.

```
BC
a IBM 360 Branch On Condition
→If fld Mask[magni psw[Cc]]
THEN:psw[Iadr]←adrsize magnr adr360bxd
ENDIF:
```

PROGRAM 12-112   Conditional Branch in the IBM System/360.

Iteration

Incrementation and termination. Iteration is by a simple count or by incrementing an index and testing it against a comparison value. The latter case, as in `BXH`, requires three registers and a memory address—more than a normal format contains. The register address of the comparand is obtained from the register address of the increment by forcing the comparand address to be odd. Increment and comparand may, but need not, coincide. The registers are used in address modification prior to any change caused by the iteration. The instruction `BCT` is shown in Section 6.3. A zero register address in the `R2` field signifies no branching in `BCTR` (and `BALR`).

```
    BCTR;count
A   IBM 360 Branch On Count Register
    count←(magni reg[fld R1;])-1
    →If(count≠0)∧(fld R2)≠0
    THEN:psw[Iadr]←reg[fld R2;Address]
    ENDIF:reg[fld R1;]←word magnr count


    BXH;increment;value;sum;odd2;comparand
A   IBM 360 Branch On Index High
    increment←radixcompi reg[fld R2;]
    value←radixcompi reg[fld R1;]
    sum←value+increment
    odd2←1+2×⌊0.5×fld R2
    comparand←radixcompi reg[odd2;]
    →If sum>comparand
    THEN:psw[Iadr]←adrsize magnr adr360bd1
    ENDIF:reg[fld R1;]←word radixcompr sum
```

PROGRAM 12-113   Iteration in the IBM System/360.

Delegation

Call.   The 360 Call (Branch And Link) stores the necessary status, instruction length, condition code, program mask, and instruction address in a register. Then, the new instruction address is placed in the PSW.

```
    BAL;branchadr
A   IBM 360 Call
    branchadr←adr360bxd
A   preserve status
    reg[fld R1;]←psw[Ilc,Cc,Programmask,Iadr]
A   branch
    psw[Iadr]←adrsize magnr branchadr
```

PROGRAM 12-114   Call in the IBM System/360.

Execute.   Execute preserves the instruction length and address and restores this information after the subject instruction is executed.

```
    EX;instinfo;modifier
A   IBM 360 Execute
A   preserve instruction information
    instinfo←psw[Ilc,Iadr]
    modifier←(0≠fld R1)∧reg[fld R1;Lowbyte]
A   fetch subject instruction
    psw[Iadr]←adrsize magnr adr360bxd
    inst←ifetch360
A   modify instruction
    inst[Imm]←inst[Imm]∨modifier
A   restore instruction information
    psw[Ilc,Iadr]←instinfo
A   test if subject instruction is Execute
    Execute report 68=fld Opcode
    →OUT suppress360
A   execute subject instruction
    execute inst
```

PROGRAM 12-115   Execute in the IBM System/360.

12.4.7

Supervision

Concurrency

Processor interconnection.   The communication between processors is the object of a special multisystem option [Blaauw, 1964].

Process Interaction

The most elementary communication between 360 processors is by reception of external signals as interruptions and by issuance of signals through direct output. A multisystem feature deals with the problems of malfunctioning processors, the sharing of the fixed memory locations that are used for interrupt control, and processor identification.

Critical section.   Test And Set is an atomic operation that serializes memory access, such that, at one instant, only one process or processor can observe and change a semaphore bit.

```
TS
⋀ IBM 360 Test And Set
⋀ serialize memory
⋀ test leftmost bit in byte
 psw[Cc]←2 magnr 1↑byte read360 adr360bd1
⋀ set byte to all ones
 adr360bd1 write360 byteρ1
⋀ end serialization
```

PROGRAM 12-116   Critical-section control in the IBM System/360.

Integrity

Privileged operations.   Logical integrity is ensured by the use of privileged operations that can be executed only when the system is in the supervisory mode. These privileged operations are Load PSW, Set/Insert Storage Key, Set System Mask, Diagnose, and all I/O operations. The instruction Diagnose has no mnemonic and no uniform syntax or semantics. Its function varies from implementation to implementation, since it is intended for maintenance.

```
a SVC   Supervisor Call    a SSK  Set Storage Key
d TS    Test And Set       c SSM  Set System Mask
a SPM   Set Program Mask   a ISK  Insert Storage Key
c LPSW  Load PSW                  Diagnose
```

TABLE 12-117   Supervisory instructions of the IBM System/360.

Protection.   We show memory protection and the checking for valid addressing in one function. The 360 uses a lock-and-key protection system that applies to memory blocks. A zero key acts as a pass key; a zero lock is open to all; otherwise, the lock and key must be equal.

```
adrcheck360 location;key;lock
ᴀ IBM 360 address check
ᴀ memory capacity
 Invadr report location≥memcap
ᴀ protection
 →If protopt
 THEN:key←magni psw[Key]
      lock←magni keys[⌊location÷block;]
      Protect report(key≠0)∧(0≠lock)∧key≠lock
 ENDIF:
```

PROGRAM 12-118   Protection in the IBM System/360.

The privileged instruction Set Storage Key gives a new key value to a storage block. The key is 4 bits long and is specified by the left four bits of a low-order byte in a register. Insert Storage Key performs the complementary operation by reading a key from the key storage into a register. The key in the PSW is changed with Load PSW.

```
SSK;address
ᴀ IBM 360 Set Storage Key
 address←magni reg[fld R2;Address]
 Invop report˜protopt
 Priv report psw[Problem]
 Invadr report address≥memcap
 Spec report 0≠16|address
 →OUT suppress360
 keys[⌊address÷block;]←reg[fld R1;4↑Lowbyte]
```

PROGRAM 12-119   Protection change in the IBM System/360.

Control Switching

Interruption.   The interrupt system repeatedly inspects the indicators after each instruction execution until the wait bit becomes 1. During inspection, the leftmost masked indicator that is 1 is processed by recording its cause in the PSW, then storing the PSW and fetching a new PSW from memory locations that correspond to the class of the interruption. This process continues as long as there are still masked indicators that are 1 (each time using the mask of the recently loaded PSW; Program 12-121).

Humble access.   Supervisor Call places the Immediate field of the instruction into the PSW as a programmed message to the operating system.

```
SVC                              LPSW;rl
ᴀ IBM 360 Supervisor Call       ᴀ IBM 360 Load PSW
 psw[Intcode]←half magnr fld Imm  Priv report psw[Problem]
 ind[Svc]←1                       rl←double read360a adr360bd1
                                  →OUT suppress360
                                  psw←rl
```

PROGRAM 12-120   Humble access and dispatching in the IBM System/360.

```
interrupt360;who;class                    true←suppress360
a IBM 360 interrupt action                a IBM 360 operation suppression
 REPEAT: a test interrupt sources          true←∨/(ind∧mask360)[Program]
    →WHILE∨/ind∧mask360
      who←(ind∧mask360)ι1
      ind[who]←0                           class←class360
      class←class360[who]                  a IBM 360 interrupt classes
    a record interrupt cause               class←(ρind)ρ0
      psw[Intcode]←code360 class           class[Machine]←3
    a store program status                 class[Program]←2
      Oldpsw[class] write360a psw          class[Svc]←1
    a new program status                   class[External]←0
      psw←double read360a Newpsw[class]    class[Io]←4
      →Δ
ENDWHILE:→UNTIL 0=psw[Wait]

mask←mask360
a IBM 360 interrupt mask
mask←(ρind)ρ1
mask[Machine]←psw[Machinemask]
mask[Oflo,Decoflo,Uflo,Lostsf]←psw[Programmask]
mask[Io,External]←psw[Systemmask]

code←code360 class
a IBM 360 interrupt code
 →CASE class
C0:code←(-half)↑Φ(ιbyte)∈extadr
    →ENDCASE
C1:code←psw[Intcode]
    →ENDCASE
C2:code←half magnr who
    →ENDCASE
C3:code←?halfρradix
    →ENDCASE
C4:code←,byte magnr channeladr,deviceadr
ENDCASE:
```

PROGRAM 12-121   Interruption action in the IBM System/360.

Dispatching.   Suspended and new programs are dispatched with the privileged instruction Load PSW.

State Preservation

Context switching.   Other than the PSW, all context must be switched by programming.

```
                SPM;od
                a IBM 360 Set Program Mask
                od←reg[fld R1;2↓Highbyte]
                psw[Cc,Programmask]←od
```

PROGRAM 12-122   Status change in the IBM System/360.

Tools of Control

Clock.   The 360 has both a Time-of-Day Clock and an Interval Timer, which counts down and interrupts at 0.

Initial program load.   A built-in loading sequence is actuated by console button or a signal from another processor.

Diagnose instruction.   The Diagnose instruction, defined differently for different implementations, does direct I/O to the machine's own implementation as if it were an external device. It can both set and read state.

12.4.8
Input/Output

Devices

Store.   Many kinds of disks, tapes, and other storage devices have served the 360 and its successors.

```
c RDD   Read Direct     d SIO   Start Input/Output
c WRD   Write Direct    d HIO   Stop Input/Output
                        d TIO   Test Input/Output
                        d TCH   Test Channel
```

TABLE 12-123   Input/output instructions of the IBM System/360.

Source and sink.   Similarly, many source and sink devices have been attached: communications devices, printers, card readers and punches, check sorters, terminals, graphics displays.

Direct Input/Output

As an option, external signals can be sent and received by the Write Direct and Read Direct. The immediate field of these instructions serves as a synchronizing prompt.

```
RDD                                WRD
ᴀ IBM 360 Read Direct              ᴀ IBM 360 Write Direct
Invop report~diropt                  Invop report~diropt
Priv report psw[Problem]             Priv report psw[Problem]
→OUT suppress360                     →OUT suppress360
signalout←inst[Imm]                  signalout←inst[Imm]
adr360bd write360 directin         directout←byte read360 adr360bd
```

TABLE 12-124   Direct input/output in the IBM System/360.

Channel

Input/output operation.   The privileged operation Start Input/Output initiates a channel operation. The device and channel are specified by parts of the effective address. The original state of the channel is recorded in the condition code, then is set to Busy. Testing the channel without starting it is possible with Test Channel. That instruction also notes the type of transmission of the channel.

```
SIO;address;channel;state            signal360IO state;cc
 ∩ IBM 360 Start Input/Output        ∩ IBM 360 input/output condition
 Priv report psw[Problem]             cc←(state=ready,pending,busy,absent)ιl
→OUT suppress360                      psw[Cc]←2 magnr cc
 address←adr360bd1
 channel←⌊address÷256
 device←256|address
 state←stateio[channel]
→If state=ready
THEN:stateio[channel]←busy
ENDIF:signal360IO state


 TCH;address;channel;state            signal360TCH state;cc
 ∩ IBM 360 Test Channel              ∩ IBM 360 test channel condition
 Priv report psw[Problem]             cc←(state=ready,pending,burst,absent)ιl
→OUT suppress360                      psw[Cc]←2 magnr cc
 address←adr360bd
 channel←⌊address÷256
 signal360TCH stateio[channel]
```

PROGRAM 12-125   Input/output instructions in the IBM System/360.

12.4.9
Implementation Notes

The 360 architecture was initially implemented in six models that spanned a wide performance range [W.Y. Stevens, 1964]. These simultaneous implementation efforts at different locations in the United States and in Europe tested the architecture for its implementability and helped ensure its integrity.

12.4.10
Bibliography

IBM Corporation, 1967: *IBM System/360 Principles of Operation.* Form A22-6821-6. New York (our defining reference).

IBM Corporation, undated: *System/370 Extended Architecture Principles of Operation.* Armonk, NY: IBM Corp.

IBM Corporation, 1965: *System/370 Principles of Operation.* Armonk, NY: IBM Corp.

IBM Corporation, 1988: *System/370 Enterprise Systems Architecture Principles of Operation.* Armonk, NY: IBM Corp.

Amdahl et al. [1964], Blaauw and Brooks [1964], Blaauw [1964], Blakernay et al. [1967], Brooks [1965], Brown et al. [1964], Campbell-Kelly [1995], Conti [1964], Conti et al. [1968], Davis and Goodman [1978], Dugan [1983], Evans [1986], Moore et al. [1987], Murphy and Wade [1970], Padegs [1968, 1981], Pugh et al. [1991], Pugh [1995], Scalzi et al. [1989], W.Y. Stevens [1964], Tucker [1986].

Brooks and Iverson [1969] gives a full architectural description with programming examples.

Padegs [1983] discusses the System/370 Extended Architecture. Padegs et al. [1988] discusses the vector architecture.

12.4.11

Exercises

12-12 Describe MVZ and MVN, basing your comments on the short description in this section, and assuming consistency with the rest of the architecture.

12-13 Give a description of the logical operations that are not shown in this section, assuming consistency with OC, NI, and XR.

12-14 Give the description of SLL, SRL, SRDL, SLDA, and SRDA, assuming consistency with SLDL, SLA, and SRA.

12-15 Give a description of the binary arithmetic operations L, LH, LR, ST, STC, STM, CVB, LNR, LTR, AR, ALR, S, SH, SR, LSL, M, MH, C, CH, CLC, CR, CL, and CLR, assuming consistency with the arithmetic instructions shown in this section and in Section 5.3.

12-16 Describe D and DR basing your comments on the text of this section and assuming consistency with the rest of the architecture.

12-17 Give the formal description of the decimal operations SP, DP, and CP, basing your comments on the text of this section, and assuming consistency with the rest of the architecture.

12-18 Give the formal description of the floating-point operations that are not shown in this section or in Chapter 5, assuming consistency with STD, AD, AUR, ME, MD, and DDR.

12-19 Give the formal description of BCR, BXLE, and BALR, basing your comments on instructions shown in this section and in Section 6.3.

12-20 Describe ISK as the inverse operation of SSK.

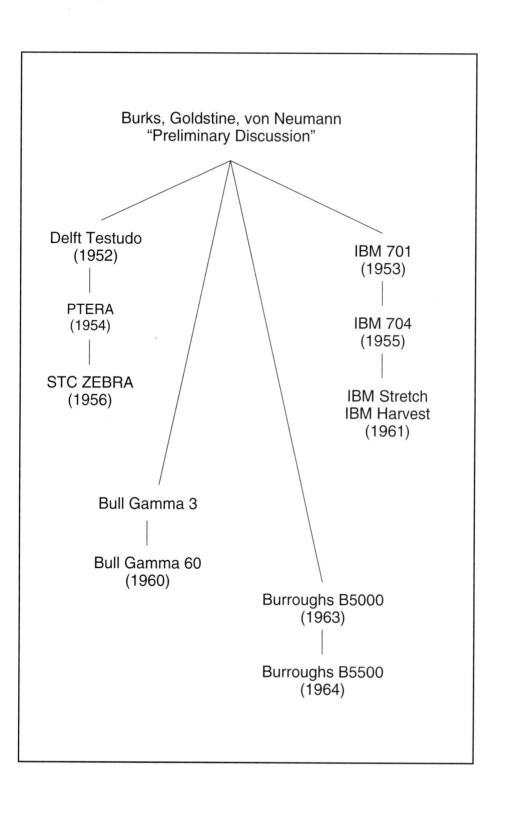

Burks, Goldstine, von Neumann
"Preliminary Discussion"

Delft Testudo
(1952)

PTERA
(1954)

STC ZEBRA
(1956)

IBM 701
(1953)

IBM 704
(1955)

IBM Stretch
IBM Harvest
(1961)

Bull Gamma 3

Bull Gamma 60
(1960)

Burroughs B5000
(1963)

Burroughs B5500
(1964)

13

Explorer House

Exploring the Classical Computer

The previous chapters have shown how the architecture of computers converges to the classical architecture: Complex and infrequent instructions, such as logarithm and sine, are eliminated; frequent and simple instructions, such as logical connectives and shifting, are incorporated; address resolution is to the word or byte; address modification is by indexing; multiple registers are available; floating point is used for scientific and engineering computation; and decision, iteration, and delegation are by suitable orthogonal branches. Thus, in the 1980s, computer architecture has stabilized and consolidated around a register-base RISC-type architecture, sometimes called the *Load-Store* architecture. Most new commercially produced computer architectures resemble one another, at least within the broad outline of the classical computer.

It is instructive, therefore, to look back to the architectural ferment of the 1950s and early 1960s, when many new concepts were introduced. Some concepts dominated and became part of the classical design. Some survived, but had little influence on other machines. Some died.

In this House we place a sample of specimens that explore the limits of the design space of the classical computer. Thus the STC ZEBRA (1959) challenged the classical instruction specification and instruction fetch; the Bull Gamma 60 (1960), the single instruction stream; the IBM Stretch (1961), the addressing resolution, the character size, and the index as a single entity; and the Burroughs B5500 (1964), the direct addressing of the working store. Each of these machines was sold commercially, but only the B5500 established a family. Nevertheless, the ZEBRA can be studied as an early example of a single-execution-cycle computer, a philosophy made popular in the RISC computers; the Gamma 60, as a useful exploration of the design of a concurrent machine; and the Stretch, as the first supercomputer. Hence, for their failures as well as for their successes, these machines are well worth their places in the Zoo.

13.1
STC ZEBRA

13.1.1
Highlights

History

Architect.   W. L. van der Poel was both the architect and the implementer of the STC ZEBRA.

Dates.   The architecture of the ZEBRA was first published in 1956.

Family tree.   Van der Poel built his first computer, Testudo (Latin for "turtle"), from 1947 to 1952 for the Technical University of Delft; it was the first computer in the Netherlands and remained in use until 1964. In 1953 Van der Poel completed PTERA for the Dutch Postal Telephone and Telegraph system; PTERA worked until 1958. In 1952 he experimented with a minimal design, later called ZERO. This model ran for a few weeks and served as a test model for the ZEBRA. His theoretical one-instruction machine was part of his Ph.D. thesis [1956, 1962], as is the architecture of the ZEBRA, presented here. The ZEBRA became commercially available through Standard Telephone and Cables (STC) in 1959. Sixty machines were sold. Strict upward program compatibility was maintained throughout the ZEBRA's evolution, including a later transistorized implementation.

Noteworthy

No operation code.   The ZEBRA has no operation code, but has many modifiers. (The one-instruction computer, in contrast, has neither operation code nor modifiers.) The ZEBRA illustrates three ways in which operation codes can be eliminated:

1. A modifier-specified subset of a fixed sequence of operations (here, Skip, Store, Load, Clear, Shift, Add, and Input/Output) is specified by each instruction. This technique is used in each of the three DEC PDP8 (1965) microinstructions.
2. The results of secondary operations are obtained from specific locations—here, the AND of two registers is available from register 24. This technique is used extensively in the Burroughs B1700 (1972).
3. The use of a memory or register location initiates an operation—here, Write, Punch, and Read. This technique is used in the DEC PDP11 (1970) for I/O data movement and operation. In the ZEBRA, I/O data movement is a separate action that precedes or follows the actual Punch or Read action. These operations could be described with a separate instruction and syntactic pattern. We follow Van der Poel, however, in describing the ZEBRA as a one-instruction machine.

Many modifiers.   Van der Poel mentions the influence of microcoding (as proposed by Wilkes) upon his use of many modifiers in an instruction and cites the ZEBRA, the Zuse Z22 (Fromme), and the Vienna Mailüfterl (Zemanek) as designs that influenced one another.

There are potentially 4096 combinations of the twelve 1-bit modifiers. More combinations are useful than one might expect, because subcycles of the classical machine operation, such as instruction fetch and instruction address increment, are separately controlled. Actually, the 12 modifiers do not really suffice, since Van der Poel found it necessary to reinterpret some combinations of modifier values. Nevertheless, a 12-bit operation code is far more than a classical operation set requires, and bit efficiency argues strongly for a shorter operation code. Therefore, a multitude of modifiers is found only occasionally, and then only partially, in later designs such as the PDP8.

Explicit instruction fetch.   Modifiers in each instruction specify the manner of fetching the next instruction. Instructions that fetch the next instruction from memory often alternate with instructions that specify data access to memory, but this need not be the case, nor need the instructions be fetched from memory; they may be obtained from a register.

Multiply Step and Divide Step.   The ZEBRA anticipates to some extent the RISC computer. Each instruction uses only one pass through the dataflow of the machine. Hence there is no Multiply or Divide; just one step out of these operations is performed.

Repeat.   The address field of an instruction may be used as a count to repeat an instruction pair a specified number of times.

Register capacity.   The ZEBRA has a liberal 5-bit register address. Many of the 32 register addresses are assigned to special purposes, however, and six registers were not implemented.

Instruction manipulation.   A ZEBRA instruction is a dynamically manipulable information unit. Whereas, in the Princeton IAS (1952), an instruction residing in memory might have its address field altered during a calculation (an intractable practice soon to be replaced by indexing), in the ZEBRA an instruction may also reside and be modified in one of several registers. So it is not possible to follow the flow of a program by just noting the instructions in memory. Rather, the content of several functionally different registers must be monitored if the flow and action of a program is to be known. This so-called *underwater* programming makes the program intractable indeed. The reader may see for himself by deducing the action of the multiplication program from the top part of Program 13-20 without consulting the bottom part of that program. (Special trace programs helped in debugging.)

Serial synchronous output.   Communication to the teletypewriter is via a single bit that is kept 0 or 1 for periods based on the drum revolution time to match the Teletype timing specifications.

Peculiarities

Implementation influence.   Many design decisions follow from the 1-bit serial datapath and the drum memory. In such an implementation, adders

are relatively inexpensive—five adders and a counter can be identified in the architecture, twice the normal requirement for arithmetic, indexing, and instruction-address update. Proper placement of instructions and data around the drum circumference and clever elimination of many instruction fetches from memory give an order-of-magnitude speed improvement—the ZEBRA outdoes the IBM 650 (1954) by repeating as well as modifying instructions stored in registers.

Thirty-three–bit word size.   The word size of 33 bits is derived from the number of normal multiply steps that can be done in one 32-word drum revolution (followed by a thirty-third sign step).

The position of working store.   The working-store register set is conceived as a fast secondary memory, not as a large number of accumulators. All actions are through an accumulator pair. Loading data from memory into a register requires two steps: from memory into the accumulator or MQ, then from there into the register.

Inhomogeneous working storage.   General purpose registers are mixed with special purpose registers, such as the accumulators and registers that provide a latent action (e.g., the logical AND).

Instruction modification.   The ZEBRA follows the Ferranti Mark 1 (1951) in modifying the entire instruction by indexing or incrementing. Unlike in the Mark 1, this action is not an accidental result of implementation convenience, but rather was deliberately planned to give the repeat function.

Lack of orthogonality.   The specification of Multiply Step and Divide Step actions each uses an unused modifier combination. Although these actions are conceptually similar, they differ noticeably in detail.

13.1.2
Machine Language
Language Level

Design philosophy.   ZEBRA stands for Very Simple Binary Calculating Engine (in Dutch). "Very Simple" refers to implementation simplicity, which at times interferes with architectural simplicity. Van der Poel does not mind using tricks in writing programs. (He wrote a paper on trickology.) The standard software package, LOT, was developed while the machine was designed, and influenced its architecture. So the architecture is an exercise of minimal function put to surprisingly effective use.

Unit System

The ZEBRA does not exhibit a typical unit size of 4, 6, or 8. Characters, which might have dictated such a unit, are not emphasized in the ZEBRA. A 5-bit Teletype code is used, and 13 characters are packed in two 33-bit words.

Configuration.   Although there can be as many as 22 registers, there are normally 16; addresses 0 through 3, and 22 through 31, are used in a special way.

```
initiateΔZ                         formatΔZ
ⁿ initiation of the STC ZEBRA      ⁿ STC ZEBRA information units
  formatΔZ                         ⁿ representation radix
  configureΔZ                        radix←2
  spaceΔZ                          ⁿ information unit
  nameΔZ                             word←33
  instructionΔZ                      adrsize←13
  dataΔZ
  iospaceΔZ

                                   configureΔZ
                                   ⁿ configuration for the STC ZEBRA
                                   ⁿ memory capacity
                                     memcap←radix*adrsize
                                   ⁿ register capacity
                                     regcap←16
                                   ⁿ tape capacity
                                     tapecap←100
```

PROGRAM 13-1   Basic parameters of the STC ZEBRA.

Spaces

Memory name-space. The maximum memory capacity is 8 K words; the first 32 locations cannot be used.

```
  spaceΔZ                          nameΔZ
ⁿ STC ZEBRA spaces                 ⁿ STC ZEBRA space names
ⁿ memory                          ⁿ register names
  memory←?(memcap,word)ρradix     ⁿ - accumulator
ⁿ working store                     Acc←2
  reg←?(regcap,word)ρradix        ⁿ - multiplier-quotient
  oflo←?radix                       Mq←3
  carry←?radix                    ⁿ - multiplicand
ⁿ control store                     Md←15
  inst←?wordρradix                ⁿ - return address
  altinst←?wordρradix               Return←4
ⁿ manual entry
  switch←?7ρradix
```

PROGRAM 13-2   Principal spaces of the STC ZEBRA.

Working store.   Besides the set of registers (which includes an accumulator and MQ), there is an overflow and a carry bit.

Control store.   There is no specific instruction address; the alternate instruction `altinst` may be used to obtain a linear instruction sequence, but may also contain data. Seven switches can be tested by the program.

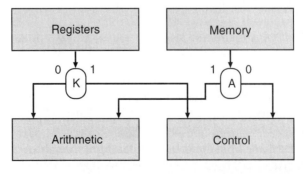

FIGURE 13-3   Programming model for the STC ZEBRA.

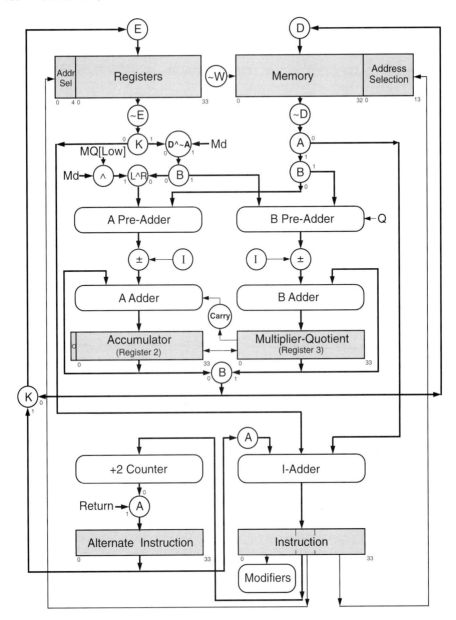

FIGURE 13-4   Detailed programming model for the STC ZEBRA.

Embedding.   An accumulator, an MQ register, a multiplicand register, a return address, and six I/O registers are embedded in the working store.

Programming model.   The simple programming model shown (Figure 13-3) follows that of Van der Poel. The connections are from storage to the arithmetic unit or to the instruction control unit. K determines the connection of the registers to these units; A, the memory connections.

The switches K and A give four main operation types:

- 0 0: Registers are used in arithmetic; an instruction is fetched from an addressed memory location.

- 0 1: Register and memory data are used in arithmetic; an alternate instruction is used for the next instruction.
- 1 0: Registers index the instruction fetched from memory; arithmetic is mainly limited to shifts and counts, but may add the multiplicand.
- 1 1: Registers index the alternate instruction; memory data are used in arithmetic.

The detailed programming model, Figure 13-4, shows how the ZEBRA machine language is in effect microcoded. The operation code, called `Modifiers`, is fully decoded. Each bit controls gates directly. There is no instruction counter; instruction sequencing is explicit, as in the IBM 650.

Operand Specification

Number of addresses.   There is a memory address and a register address, but the use of the accumulators suggests one-address operation.

Address phrase.   Besides the address fields for memory and registers, several modifiers specify storage use and access.

Operation Specification

Types of control.   The ZEBRA uses no indicators. Decisions are made directly upon the accumulator and MQ contents.

Instruction Structure

Machine-language syntax.   There is no opcode field; hence there is only one syntactic pattern. The right-to-left order of the modifiers indicates their precedence, if any.

Mnemonics.   The modifier mnemonics are those used by Van der Poel. For the test, register address, and memory address fields, we use our machine-independent naming convention.

```
        syntaxΔZ
     a A,K,Q,L,R,I,B,C,D,E,V,Test,W,Reg,Address
```

PROGRAM 13-5   Instruction syntax of the STC ZEBRA.

Instruction format.   Most modifiers have a single controlling function, so they are found in just one or a complementary pair of description functions. Q appears only in the incrementing action of the MQ adder, and E and W appear just in register and memory read and write. Two operations, however, are controlled by a combination of modifiers at the expense of simplicity: L with R is used in Multiply Step, and not-A with D is used in Divide Step.

13.1.3

Addressing

Direct addressing.   The ZEBRA requires addressing of memory, registers, and a pair of accumulators. These spaces are directly addressed from a corresponding instruction field.

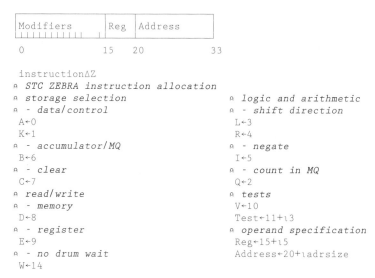

PROGRAM 13-6   Instruction allocation in the STC ZEBRA.

Memory access. The choice between reading and writing is made by modifier D. The presence or absence of reading or writing is controlled by W, the (do not) wait modifier; when W is 0, drum access takes place and the processor waits until the drum sector of the data is under the read/write head. When W is 1, the memory address may be used for other purposes, such as counting.

```
data←readΔZ address                 address writeΔZ data
ᴀ STC ZEBRA read from memory        ᴀ STC ZEBRA write into memory
→IF 0=fld D,W                       →If 2=fld D,W
THEN:data←memory[address;]          THEN:memory[address;]←data
    →ENDIF                          ENDIF:
ELSE:data←wordρ0
ENDIF:
```

PROGRAM 13-7   Memory read and write in the STC ZEBRA.

Register access.   Reading from and writing into registers is complicated by many special purpose register locations. For a register set of 16, only 14 registers are actually installed; 0 and 1 contain constants. Four of the installed registers have special purposes: 2, 3, 4, and 15 are the accumulator, MQ, return, and multiplicand, respectively. The high-order addresses are all special: 22 is a spare; 23 is the maximum-negative number; 24 gives the AND of the accumulator and MQ; address 25 is a synonym for the accumulator on reading and sends a signal to the Teletype; 26 through 30 each read a bit from paper tape or record a bit of the code to be punched; 31 causes a paper-tape read or write action.

When writing to memory is specified by D but the arithmetic section is not specified by A, then the multiplicand Md is selected without further control for arithmetic use by regselectΔZ. This action may be used in a Divide Step. Normal register access may simultaneously be used for control purposes.

Accumulator access.   We identify the two accumulators as Acc and Mq for their part in multiplication and division, in conformity with other machines. The choice between these two registers is made by modifier B.

```
data←readregΔZ;r                         writeregΔZ data;r
ᴀ STC ZEBRA read from register          ᴀ STC ZEBRA write into register
→IF 0=fld E                              →If fld E
THEN:r←fld Reg                           THEN:r←fld Reg
   →CASE(r<1,2,regcap,23,24,25,26,31)ι1      →CASE(r<4,regcap,26,31)ι1
   C0: ᴀ (0) zero                           C0: ᴀ (0...3) read only
      data←wordρ0                              →ENDCASE
      →ENDCASE                             C1: ᴀ (4...regcap-1) present
   C1: ᴀ (1) one                              reg[fld Reg;]←data
      data←(-word)↑1                          →ENDCASE
      →ENDCASE                             C2: ᴀ (regcap...25) absent
   C2: ᴀ (2...regcap-1) present               →ENDCASE
      data←reg[fld Reg;]                   C3: ᴀ (26...30) punch-code bit
      →ENDCASE                                punchcode[r-26]←data[Sign]
   C3: ᴀ (regcap...22) absent                 →ENDCASE
      data←wordρ0                          C4: ᴀ (31) (punch into tape)
      →ENDCASE                             ENDCASE:
   C4: ᴀ (23) maximal negative          ENDIF:
      data←word↑1
      →ENDCASE
   C5: ᴀ (24) And of acc and MQ
      data←reg[Acc;]∧reg[Mq;]
      →ENDCASE
   C6: ᴀ (25) accumulator
      data←reg[Acc;]
      →ENDCASE
   C7: ᴀ (26...30) tape-code bit        data←regselectΔZ
      data←wordρreadcode[r-26]           ᴀ STC ZEBRA select register source
      →ENDCASE                           →IF 1=fld A,D
   C8: ᴀ (31) (read from tape)          THEN: ᴀ divide step
      data←wordρ0                           data←reg[Md;]
   ENDCASE:→ENDIF                           →ENDIF
ELSE: ᴀ no read                         ELSE: ᴀ normal register
   data←wordρ0                             data←(0=fld K)∧readregΔZ
ENDIF:                                   ENDIF:
```

PROGRAM 13-8   Register read and write in the STC ZEBRA.

Address Modification

An index from working store may modify an instruction, so the ZEBRA registers contain indices as well as numbers, and as such they anticipate the general registers of the IBM System/360 (1965). As in the Mark 1, however, the entire instruction, not just the address field, is modified.

```
                    address←adrΔZ
                  ᴀ STC ZEBRA addressing
                    address←fld Address
```

PROGRAM 13-9   Addressing in the STC ZEBRA.

13.1.4

Data

The ZEBRA recognizes logical data and numbers; both have the 33-bit format. The accumulator is placed to the left of the MQ in shifting, and is extended by an overflow bit in shifting and arithmetic.

Fixed-Point Numbers

Notation and allocation.   Radix complement is used. The leftmost and the rightmost bit can be selected separately with `Sign` and `Low`.

```
↓Overflow
┌─┬──────────────────────────────────────┬─┬───────────────────────────┐
│ │Accumulator                           │ │Mq                         │
└─┴──────────────────────────────────────┴─┴───────────────────────────┘

┌────────────────────────────────────────┐   dataΔZ
│                                        │   ⌐ STC ZEBRA data representation
└────────────────────────────────────────┘   ⌐ fixed-point number allocation
 0                                     33   Sign←0
Memory and register word                    Low←32
```

PROGRAM 13-10   Data formats in the STC ZEBRA.

13.1.5

Operations

The execution of an instruction consists of a sequence of eight actions, most of which are individually controlled. The first of these, `SKIP`, conditionally changes the current instruction into a No Operation. We discuss the eight actions in our usual order; shifting is described under fixed-point arithmetic.

```
executeΔZ;acc;mq
⌐ execution of STC ZEBRA
⌐ skip                          ⌐ add to accumulator
 SKIP                            ADDA
⌐ store accumulator or MQ       ⌐ add to MQ
 ST                              ADDB
⌐ clear                         ⌐ input/output
 CLR                             IO
⌐ shift                         ⌐ load registers
 SRL                             LD
```

PROGRAM 13-11   Operation in the STC ZEBRA.

Logic

Connectives.   The only explicit connective is the AND of the accumulator and MQ that can be read from register 24. The other connectives require extra actions. Thus OR can be obtained by adding the operands and subtracting their AND.

Fixed-Point Arithmetic

Store.   Store places the accumulator or the MQ in memory when D is equal to 1 and W is 0 (Program 13-7), independently of A (in spite of the simplified programming model).

```
ST
∩ STC ZEBRA Store
→IF fld B
THEN: ∩ store MQ
        adrΔZ writeΔZ reg[Mq;]
        →ENDIF
ELSE: ∩ store accumulator
        adrΔZ writeΔZ reg[Acc;]
ENDIF:
```

PROGRAM 13-12   Store in the STC ZEBRA.

Load. Load Register places the original contents of the accumulator or MQ in the specified register when K is equal to 0; when K is 1, the alternate instruction is loaded into the specified register. Writing into a register occurs only when E is 1 and the register address is valid (Program 13-8). After the general registers are loaded, the accumulator and MQ content is changed as a result of a possible Clear, Shift, and Add action. All actions of Load Register occur at the end of the execution sequence.

```
LD
∩ STC ZEBRA Load Register
→CASE 0 1 ιfld K,B
CO: ∩ from accumulator              ∩ update accumulator
    writeregΔZ reg[Acc;]              reg[Acc;]←1↓acc
    →ENDCASE                         oflo←1↑acc
C1: ∩ from MQ                        ∩ update MQ
    writeregΔZ reg[Mq;]               reg[Mq;]←mq
    →ENDCASE
C2: ∩ from alternate instruction
    writeregΔZ altinst
ENDCASE:
```

PROGRAM 13-13   Load in the STC ZEBRA.

Clear.   Clear resets the accumulator or MQ when C is equal to 1. The accumulator and overflow bit are combined to form a 34-bit quantity.

```
CLR
∩ STC ZEBRA Clear
∩ take or clear accumulator
acc←(2≠fld C,B)∧oflo,reg[Acc;]
∩ take or clear MQ
mq←(3≠fld C,B)∧reg[Mq;]
```

PROGAM 13-14   Clear in the STC ZEBRA.

Shift.   L and R specify a 1-bit left or right shift of the accumulator concatenated with the MQ. When both shifts are specified, the right shift takes precedence. On right shift, the low-order bit of the accumulator enters MQ, and the overflow bit will enter the accumulator. This shift is the only way to retrieve the overflow bit. On left shift, the high-order bit of the MQ enters the accumulator. The bit shifted from accumulator to MQ, or reverse, is replaced by a zero when the Clear modifier C is one.

Add and Subtract.   The sign of the addend, and hence the choice between addition and subtraction, is specified by I. The accumulator and the MQ each

```
            SRL
         ⍝ STC ZEBRA Shift
          →CASE inst[R,L]⍳1
          C0: ⍝ right shift
              mq←((0=fld C)∧¯1↑acc),¯1↓mq
              acc←¯1↓0,acc
              →ENDCASE
          C1: ⍝ left shift
              acc←1↓acc,(0=fld C)∧mq[Sign]
              mq←1↓mq,0
              →ENDCASE
          C2: ⍝ no shift
          ENDCASE:
```

PROGRAM 13-15   Arithmetic Shift in the STC ZEBRA.

have an adder and a preadder. During every execution sequence, the preadders add the memory operand, the register operand (or the multiplicand), and a carry in. The adders then add these partial sums to the accumulator and MQ, respectively. Various parts of this action can be suppressed by modifiers. A carry out of the preadder is ignored.

Multiply step.   In the accumulator preadder, the register operand is replaced by the multiplicand Md when both left and right shift are specified and the low-order multiplier bit in the MQ is 1. For a typical Multiply Step, the normal register operand would be 0, such that the multiplicand is (or is not) added to the shifted partial product, depending upon the multiplier bit. This action allows the normal register selection to be used for other purposes, such as retrieving the next instruction.

Accumulator addition.   The preadder delivers a 33-bit addend to the accumulator adder. This addend is sign-extended by 1 bit and added to the accumulator and overflow bit. The 34-bit sum replaces the accumulator and overflow as part of the actions of LD.

```
  ADDA;addendmem;addendreg;ad;addend;augend;sum
⍝ STC ZEBRA Add To Accumulator
  addendmem←radixcompi(2=fld A,B)∧readΔZ adrΔZ
  →IF reg[Mq:Low]∧3=fld L,R
  THEN: ⍝ multiplicand as operand
      addendreg←radixcompi reg[Md;]
      →ENDIF
  ELSE: ⍝ normal register operand
      addendreg←radixcompi(0=fld B)∧regselectΔZ
  ENDIF:ad←word radixcompr negΔZ×addendreg+addendmem+carryΔZ
  addend←radixcompi ad
  augend←radixcompi acc
  sum←augend+addend
  acc←(word+1) radixcompr sum
```

```
  value←carryΔZ;shift;conflict                          sign←negΔZ
⍝  STC ZEBRA carry from mq to accumulator          ⍝ STC ZEBRA negate
  shift←1+2=fld L,R                                    sign← 1 ¯1[fld I]
  conflict←(shift=2)∧(2|addendreg)∧2|addendmem
  carry←carry≠fld I
  value←shift×carry∧(8=fld V,Test)∧~conflict
```

PROGRAM 13-16   Add To Accumulator in the STC ZEBRA.

Extended addition. The carry-out of MQ is added into the accumulator when V is 1 and Test is 0. This action allows double-precision addition. The carry is shifted left 1 bit when L is specified. In that case, the carry is ORed with the carry out of the low-order register and memory addition. A carry is lost when both carries are 1—the programmer should beware! Also, the carry is not shifted right when a right shift is specified.

Increment and Decrement. In the MQ preadder, the carry-in is controlled by modifier Q and gives an explicit means of incrementing or decrementing depending upon the modifier I.

MQ addition. The MQ is added to the 33-bit result of its preadder. A carry-out from the 33-bit sum is placed in carry and may be added to the accumulator in the next cycle, as we have stated.

```
ADDB;addendmem;addendreg;addend;augend;sum
⍝ STC ZEBRA Add To MQ
addendmem←radixcompi(3=fld A,B)∧readΔZ adrΔZ
addendreg←radixcompi(fld B)∧regselectΔZ
addend←negΔZ×addendreg+addendmem+fld Q
augend←radixcompi mq
sum←augend+addend
mq←word radixcompr sum
carry←word carryfrom augend,addend
```

PROGRAM 13-17   Add To MQ in the STC ZEBRA.

13.1.6

Instruction Sequencing

Linear Sequence

Next instruction. In a simple linear sequence, successive instructions are stored in alternate memory slots to allow time for a single-cycle execution between each instruction fetch. The locations between instructions, on any of the 256 tracks, can be used for data. When every position around the circumference of the drum is used, maximum speed is achieved. Instructions with A contain a data address; their successor is obtained from altinst. Instructions without A read a new instruction from memory, while the current instruction

```
cycleΔZ                              ifetchΔZ;index;instvalue
⍝ basic cycle of the STC ZEBRA      ⍝ STC ZEBRA instruction fetch
REPEAT:ifetchΔZ                      index←magni(fld K)∧readregΔZ
   executeΔZ                         →IF fld A
→UNTIL 0                             THEN: ⍝ alternate instruction
                                         instvalue←magni altinst
                                         altinst←reg[Return;]
SKIP                                     →ENDIF
⍝ STC ZEBRA Skip                     ELSE: ⍝ branch
→If¨conditionΔZ                          instvalue←magni readΔZ adrΔZ
THEN: ⍝ make No Operation                altinst←word magnr 2+magni inst
   inst←(ɩword)∊A,W                  ENDIF:inst←word magnr index+instvalue
ENDIF:
```

PROGRAM 13-18   Basic cycle and instruction fetch of the STC ZEBRA.

is incremented by 2 and is stored in altinst; meanwhile, arithmetic can be performed with an operand from a register. A simple linear sequence alternates instructions with and without modifier A.

With K present and E absent, the entire instruction (and hence its address field) can be indexed.

Unconditional branch.   The explicit instruction address (not A) of the ZEBRA effectively provides an Unconditional Branch. This instruction address resembles that of the 650 and can be used to optimize drum access at the expense of program tractability.

Decision

Conditional operation.   The Test condition makes every instruction conditional. When the condition is true, the instruction is executed. When the condition is false, the instruction is changed into a No Operation by making modifiers A and W equal to 1, and all others 0.

Conditional Branch.   The conditional-operation mechanism changes an Unconditional Branch into a Conditional Branch.

Condition.   Modifier V specifies two sets of eight conditions. When V is zero, the accumulator sign, the MQ sign, a 0 or not-0 accumulator value, or the low-order MQ bit serve as the test-criterion set. The unused conditions are always satisfied. When V is 1, a panel switch is selected to be tested. (The last switch acts inversely.) Test value 0 is always satisfied.

```
  true←conditionΔZ;test
 ⍝ STC ZEBRA test condition
 →IF fld V
 THEN: ⍝ test acc and mq
    test←1,reg[Acc;Sign],reg[Mq;Sign],(~v/reg[Acc;]),reg[Mq;Low], 1 1 1
    →ENDIF
 ELSE: ⍝ test manual switches
    test←1,switch= 1 1 1 1 1 1 0
 ENDIF:true←test[fld Test]
```

PROGRAM 13-19   Condition in the STC ZEBRA.

Completion.   A stop is achieved by a loop under control of switch 7. When this normally closed switch is opened, the loop is broken, and processing can proceed.

Iteration

Incrementation and termination.   Iteration can be achieved by incrementing the address field by 2 during each iteration, using the implied-instruction– fetch action for not-A. When the address overflows, it increments the register address. The new register address may be used to fetch an instruction that terminates the iteration.

Multiply example.   To show the functioning and programming of the ZEBRA, we show Van der Poel's general fractional multiply program. (There are

```
adr     memory          md in acc, mr in MQ
100     E 0 5 101       acc to 5, inst+2 to altinst, ifetch from 101
101     ACE 0 15 102    acc to 15, clear acc, 102 to acc, ifetch from altinst
102     ALRW 0 0 0      mpy step, ifetch from altinst
103     KLRCE 0 6 104   clear acc, mpy step, altinst to 6, ifetch from 104
104     KLRW 0 5 8162   mpy step, inst+2 to altinst, ifetch from 5
105     LRI 0 0 106     negative mpy step, inst+2 to altinst, ifetch from 106


from    inst            altinst             execution actions
100     E 0 5 101       unknown             (md to 5)
101     ACE 0 15 102    E 0 5 103           md to 15, clear acc, ALRW 0 0 0 to acc
alt     E 0 5 103       (from 4)            ALRW 0 0 0 to 5
103     KLRCE 0 6 104   E 0 5 105           clear acc, mpy step 1, E 0 5 105 to 6
104     KLRW 0 5 8162   KLRCE 0 6 106       mpy step 2
  5     ALRW 0 0 0      KLRW 0 5 8164       mpy step 3, count 2
alt     KLRW 0 5 8164   (from 4)            mpy step 4
  5     ALRW 0 0 0      KLRW 0 5 8166       mpy step 5, count 2
...     ...             ...                 ...
  5     ALRW 0 0 0      KLRW 0 5 8190       mpy step 29, count 2
alt     KLRW 0 5 8190   (from 4)            mpy step 30
  5     ALRW 0 0 0      KLRW 0 6 0          mpy step 31, count 2
alt     KLRW 0 6 0      (from 4)            mpy step 32
  6     E 0 5 105       KLRW 0 6 2          (acc to 5)
105     LRI 0 0 106     E 0 5 107           negative mpy step 33
```

PROGRAM 13-20   Multiply example in the STC ZEBRA.

several variants.) Our general assembler notation starts with the mnemonic instruction name and then gives the numeric value of all specifiable fields of the syntactic pattern. For the ZEBRA, we use as a mnemonic the name of all modifiers that are 1 (an X is used when all modifiers are 0). Van der Poel uses a similar notation, with a few shortcut conventions.

The top part of Program 13-20 illustrates the storage content prior to execution. The multiplicand resides in the accumulator, and the multiplier in MQ; memory locations 100 through 105 contain instructions. The general function of each instruction is noted and can be verified from the machine description. The instruction fetch concerns the successor instruction.

The bottom part of Program 13-20 shows the order in which the instructions are executed and their meaning in the multiplication process. The content of altinst is shown next to the current instruction to clarify the program—a practice followed by Van der Poel.

The first four instructions move the multiplicand from the accumulator into register 15, then move the instruction that is in location 102 via the accumulator into register 5 and the instruction that is in location 100 twice via altinst into register 6. In the process, this instruction fetches the instructions from locations 101 and 103. (It stores the accumulator content twice into register 5, the first action being meaningless.) At the end of the multiplication, the same instruction is executed from register 6 and causes the instruction fetch from location 105; the incidental storing of the accumulator is again meaningless and destroys the content of 5, which was a key instruction in the multiplication loop.

The multiplication loop uses an instruction from register 5 alternating with an instruction in altinst that performs the count. When the count overflows, the next instruction is taken from register 6 and the process is terminated. Von Neumann's multiplication algorithm is used, which uses a

final subtraction to correct for negative sign. The algorithm uses every slot on the drum circumference optimally. Side effects in the process are indicated in parentheses.

13.1.7
Input/Output

Devices

Source and sink.   The source is a 5-bit paper-tape reader; sinks are a 5-bit paper-tape punch and a 1-bit serial teletypewriter. At a later time, a telephone dial and the keyboard of the Teletype were added as a source, thus enabling conversational operation.

Direct Input/Output

Read and Write.   Paper-tape I/O takes place when register address 31 is specified. For reading, E is 0; for writing, E is 1.

```
IO                                        iospaceΔZ
⍝ STC ZEBRA Input and Output              ⍝ STC ZEBRA peripheral spaces
→CASE(25 57 31 63 =fld E,Reg)ι1           ⍝ paper tape input
  C0: ⍝ write to teletype                 readtape←?(tapecap,5)ρradix
      type←reg[Acc;Sign]                  readcode←?5ρradix
      →ENDCASE                            ⍝ paper tape output
  C1:→If fld A                            punchtape← 0 5 ρ0
      THEN: ⍝ write to teletype           punchcode←?5ρradix
           type←reg[Acc;Sign]             ⍝ teletype output
      ENDIF:→ENDCASE                      type←?radix
  C2: ⍝ read from tape
      readcode←readtape[0;]
      readtape← 1 0 ↓readtape
      →ENDCASE
  C3: ⍝ punch into tape
      punchtape←punchtape,punchcode
      punchcode←5ρ0
      →ENDCASE
  C4: ⍝ no input/output operation
ENDCASE:
```

PROGRAM 13-21   Input/output Read and Write in the STC ZEBRA.

Register 25 transmits a single bit to the Teletype when E is 0 or when E and A are 1. The standard output routine transmits with the exact interval of 20 ms per high/low sequence by using just two revolutions of the drum.

13.1.8
Implementation Notes

The ZEBRA has serial-by-bit implementation. Memory is a drum with 10 ms revolution time; 32 words are placed on a track. Several tracks are made read-only to protect the system software.

Timing.   Programmed multiplication takes slightly more than one drum revolution; division, slightly more then two revolutions; square root, 26 ms.

Drum-access efficiency.   A meter on the front panel indicates the drum access from the minimum of 3 percent (one hit per revolution) to 100 percent. The average hit ratio was 70 percent [Van der Poel, 1990].

13.1.9
Bibliography

Van der Poel, W.L., 1952: "A Simple Electronic Digital Computer." *Applied Scientific Research*, **B.2**: 367–400.

Van der Poel, W.L., 1956, 1962: *The Logical Principles of Some Simple Computers*. Ph.D. Thesis, University of Amsterdam. Excelsior, The Hague, The Netherlands.

Van der Poel, W.L., 1959: "ZEBRA, A Simple Binary Computer." *Proc. ICIP* (UNESCO, Paris), 361–5. Reprinted in Bell and Newell [1971], 200–4.

Van der Poel, W.L., 1962b: "Micro-Programming and Trickology." W. Hoffmann, ed., *Digitale Informationswandler*. Braunschweig: Vieweg, 269–311 (our defining reference).

Van der Poel, W.L., 1988: "Early Dutch Computer." *Ann Hist Comput*, **10**, 3: 221.

Van der Poel, W.L., 1990, 1992: Letters to the authors of this book.

13.1.10
Exercises

13-1 Make the NOT of a logical vector in the accumulator of the ZEBRA.

13-2 Make the EXCLUSIVE OR of two logical vectors that are in the accumulator and in the MQ of the ZEBRA.

13-3 Give a precise execution time for Program 13-20.

13-4 Annotate, in the manner of Program 13-20, Van der Poel's restoring division program; in memory locations 100 through 102 are the instructions KE 0 7 101, KQLDW 0 6 8130, and AQIVW 1 15 0; in register 6, the instruction AQIVW 1 15 0; in register 7, a return instruction; memory location 103 not used. The positive dividend is in the accumulator and MQ. The positive divisor is placed negatively in register 15.

13-5 Give, for a linear series of instructions, the two sets of alternating modifier values, and, for each of these, the modifiers and fields that can still be selected.

13.2
Bull Gamma 60

13.2.1
Highlights

History

Architect.   Philippe Dreyfus was the architect.

Dates.   The Bull Gamma 60 was published in 1957 and was presented in 1958 at the Eastern Joint Computer Conference. The first copies of the machine were delivered in 1960.

Family tree.   The Gamma 60 was preceded by the Gamma 2 calculator (1951), the highly successful Gamma 3 calculator (1952), and the stored-program computer Gamma ET (1956) [Leclerc, 1990]. The Gamma 60 did not establish a family. Only 19 machines were delivered, of which 13 remained for some time in actual use [Mounier-Kuhn, 1990]. The smaller and more classical Gamma 10 (1964) managed to restore some of Bull's share of the computer market.

Noteworthy

The Gamma 60 was an early attempt to unite commercial and scientific computer designs. Toward this end, the machine had character handling, binary arithmetic and logic, decimal floating point, and extensive I/O facilities. Most noteworthy, however, are the multiprocessing facilities of the system.

Exclusive multiprocessing.   The central computing facilities of the Gamma 60 are distributed over four processors whose abilities do not overlap; the central Supervisory Processor distributes the workload over these processors, as well as over several I/O processors. All these processors operate concurrently. When a program demands the facilities of a processor that is busy, the activities of that processor are scheduled by building a chain of tasks. The central supervisor computes addresses, takes decisions, and performs other supervisory tasks.

No embedding.   The Gamma 60 is, for its time, remarkably general and clean: It has no embedding of registers in memory, no special control functions implied by registers, except in the comparator.

Relative addressing.   Addressing relative to the instruction address is a basic addressing mode for data and branch addresses.

Long fields.   Comparison and translation apply to fields of up to 256 words. There are, however, no facilities for extended arithmetic.

Decimal floating point.   Floating point has a decimal base, exponent, and coefficient. Since the computer is otherwise binary, decimal digits are

represented with binary encoding. The location of the decimal point within the coefficient may be specified by the programmer. This ability covers only a small part of the floating-point domain; it is an attempt to match the needs of scientific and commercial computing.

Compare For Range.   Comparison is against a single value and against a range of values specified by an upper and lower limit, as in the IBM Stretch (1961).

Translation.   Character strings may be translated under control of a pattern string.

Elaborate indicators.   Each processor has up to 24 indicators. These indicators identify many logical and arithmetic conditions, such as bit-by-bit implication and exclusion, all-zeros and all-ones bit vectors, six comparison results, but no carry or overflow indication. The indicators are used by a conditional branch, which tests for a bit to be 1, but not for a bit to be 0, which explains in part why there are so many indicators.

Execute.   The Gamma 60 is (with the ZEBRA and the Stretch) one of the first computers to execute a word in a register as a single instruction.

Virtual elements.   Multiprocessing confronted the designers with the critical-section problem, which they solved elegantly by extending the concept of multiple processing elements with that of multiple virtual elements.

Peculiarities

Limited address capacity.   The basic address capacity of the Gamma 60 is 4096 24-bit words. This capacity could be expanded to a maximum of 32 K words. Since the system assumes that several programs are executed concurrently, this capacity is inadequate even for the Gamma 60's time.

Six-bit byte.   The 6-bit byte is assumed and leads to the 24-bit word. In the translator, some means are provided to handle 8-bit bytes.

Instruction modification in memory.   The design has several instructions that are intended to be modified in memory during execution. Thus branches may be changed to No Operation, and vice versa.

Little attention to policing.   The system has no protection and no formal interruption. It is not clear what happens when a fault or error is encountered.

13.2.2
Machine Language

Language Level

Design philosophy.   The Gamma 60 design was ahead of its time in trying to combine commercial and scientific computing (as in the IBM System/360,

1965), to see I/O processing as a concurrent independent activity (as in the CDC 6600 peripheral processors, 1965), to delegate certain processing tasks to coprocessors (as in the DEC PDP11 (1970) floating-point processor, 1973), and to recognize the importance of multiprocessing. The design identified specific needs of, for instance, an assembler, data converter, and commercial/scientific processor and intended the logical processor, translator, and arithmetic processor for each of these. But the design had too fine granularity; it did not give each processor sufficient processing power of its own, which caused extra interaction (spoiling bit efficiency and bit traffic). Also, the processing tasks suffered under the small memory capacity, and the cost of concurrency in equipment (many registers) and time (the common use of memory) were underestimated.

Unit System

The Gamma 60 uses the *six* unit system. The character size is six, and the word (the *catene*) has 24 bits. Floating point has double word size. The arithmetic accumulator has twice that size again.

```
initiate60                                  format60
A initiation of the Bull Gamma 60           A Bull Gamma 60 information units
format60                                    A representation radix
configure60                                 radix←2
space60                                     A information units
name60                                      digit←4
control60                                   byte←6
fl60                                        adrsize←15
                                            word←24
                                            double←48
configure60                                 accsize←96
A configuration for the Bull Gamma 60       A address capacity
A memory capacity                           adrcap←radix*adrsize
memcap←adrcap                               A register capacity
A number of elements                        regcap←4
ecap←11
```

PROGRAM 13-22   Basic parameters of the Bull Gamma 60.

Configuration. The maximum address capacity is 32 K 24-bit words, similar to that of the IBM 704 (1955) or the Univac 1103. This small capacity is a serious limitation for a machine with memory-coupled multiprocessing abilities. The number of concurrent processors is typically 12: five for central processing and seven for peripheral processing.

Spaces

Memory name-space. Memory is shared by all processors.

Working store. The central register rcb belongs to the central processor. The logical registers g and k are part of the logical processor. (In the Bull Gamma manual, logical register g is called l; we rechristen it to avoid the ambiguity between lowercase L and the numeral 1.) The accumulator acc is part of the arithmetic processor.

```
space60                              name60
∧ Bull Gamma 60 spaces               ∧ Bull Gamma 60 space names
∧ memory                             ∧ elements
memory←?(memcap,word)ρradix          Arith←0
∧ working store                      Logic←1
∧ - central register                 Transl←2
rcb←?wordρradix                      Comp←3
∧ - logical registers                Drum←4
g←?wordρradix                        Cardreader←5
k←?wordρradix                        Cardpunch←6
∧ - arithmetic accumulator           Printer←7
acc←?accsizeρradix                   Magntape←8
∧ - addresses                        Tapereader←9
reg←?(ecap,regcap)ρadrcap            Tapepunch←10
∧ control store                      ∧ chain address allocation
∧ - instruction address              Last←0
iadr←?ecapρadrcap                    Next←1
∧ - indicator
ind←?(ecap,word)ρradix
∧ - chain addresses
cadr←?(ecap,2)ρadrcap
∧ - current element
rne←?ecap
∧ - next instruction
nadr←?adrcap
```

PROGRAM 13-23   Spaces of the Bull Gamma 60.

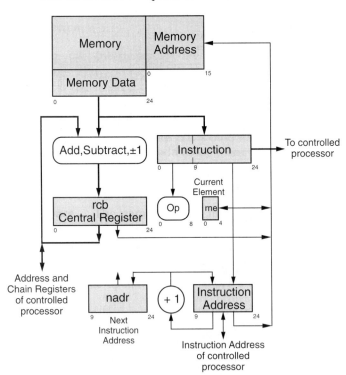

FIGURE 13-24   Central Processor of the Bull Gamma 60.

Control store.   Each processor has up to four address registers `reg`, an instruction address, 24 indicators, and two chain addresses `cadr`. The processor currently being served by the central processor is identified by `rne`. The address to be used next in the chain for a processor and the last address of the chain are located in the pair of chain addresses. The next instruction address `nadr` is used by the central processor in branching.

Processing elements.   Besides the central processor, the processors are: the floating-point arithmetic processor, the binary logical-and-arithmetic processor, the character- and bit-string translator, the character-string comparator, and seven I/O-device processors. In principle this number of processors could be extended.

Embedding.   There is no memory embedding. The address registers of each processor normally have no specialized tasks.

Programming model.   Each of the five processors has its own programming model. We show only that for the Central Processor, Figure 13-24, and that

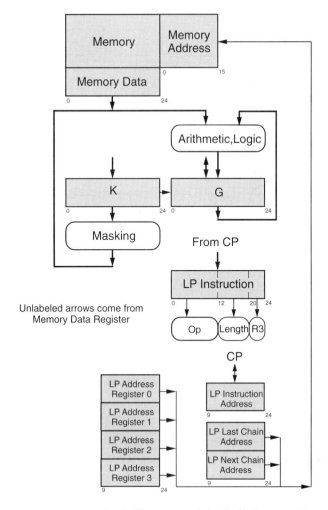

FIGURE 13-25   Logic Processor of the Bull Gamma 60.

for the Logic Processor, Figure 13-25, which does the fixed-point arithmetic as well as logic.

The central processor is essentially a supervisory machine, and its principal datatype is the address, for it does address arithmetic and branching for all the processors. Especially noteworthy are the *nadr*, the next instruction address, and the *rne*, which governs which processor is currently addressed.

The Logic Processor looks very familiar, except that the arrangement of K and G is unorthodox for an accumulator-MQ combination. The real power of the LP lies in the masking facilities that accomplish flexible subfield selection from K. Most of the processors have their own index and chain registers. Note the absence of a path from the Instruction Register to the Instruction Address. Branching for the LP is handled by the CP.

Operand Specification

Number of addresses.   The arithmetic processor has three-address operation; all other processors have two-address operation.

Address phrase.   The typical memory-address phrase has a 15-bit address field and two modifier bits; it occurs only once in the instruction format (Program 13-29). Several processors use up to three 4-bit fields that each specify a register address with 2 bits and its mode with the other 2 bits.

Operation Specification

Mnemonics.   The mnemonics are in principle those of the manufacturer; they are derived from French terms. We change mnemonics that are used twice (notably in the arithmetic processor ADD, SOU, MUL, and DIV). The number of characters in the mnemonic indicates the type of operation. One character is used for address arithmetic, two characters for instruction sequencing, four characters for supervision, and three characters for all other operations.

a→RI	FZ	b→BR	TRR	→g	i	i
GE	FU	c→CNRM	f→FAD	g→TCK	g→GMI	
RE	DI	CHLD	FSU	TCL	CAT	
TA	PC	CINT	FMP	TKL	CET	
RA	i	i	FDV	MCL	CAM	
TB	i	PROT	DIR	IKL	CEM	
RB	i	LIBE	TER	FZL	TCA	
GB	i	SIMU	MPD	FUL	BPT	
AB	i	STOP	DPD	ADD	TBP	
SB	i	d→G	ISI	SOU	TIP	
CB	i	R	PVA	MUL	TVM	
SQ	i	A	CVA	DIV	MVT	
SI	i	S	CAL	FCL	MVM	
FJ	i	e→CMP	ARR	INT	RCL	
FT	i	CDB	i	REU	FIN	
FI	i	EFL	→g	CBL	i	

PROGRAM 13-26   Operation-code list of the Bull Gamma 60.

The codes within each group of the opcode list are our assumption.

Instruction list.   We present the instructions of all processors in one conventional list. The instructions with one, two, or four mnemonic characters

belong to the central processor. The other processors all have three-character mnemonics for their instructions. The arithmetic processor performs all floating-point instructions; the logical processor, all logic, shift, and fixed-point arithmetic; the comparator, the four data-handling instructions with format e; and the translator, the 13 data-handling instructions with format g.

	⌐ *address arithmetic*				⌐ *fixed-point arithmetic*	
d	G	Load Address		g	TCL	Load
d	R	Store Address		g	TKL	Load From K
d	A	Add Address		g	TCK	Load K
d	S	Subtract Address		g	ADD	Add
a	TB	Load		g	SOU	Subtract
a	SQ	Load Indirect		g	MUL	Multiply
a	GB	Load Immediate		g	DIV	Divide
a	RB	Store		g	CBL	Compare
a	PC	Increment			⌐ *floating-point arithmetic*	
a	DI	Decrement		f	TER	F Move
a	AB	Add Immediate		f	ISI	F Negate
a	SB	Subtract Immediate		f	PVA	F Make Absolute
a	CB	Compare Immediate		f	FAD	F Add
a	FZ	Set All Zero		f	FSU	F Subtract
a	FU	Set All One		f	FMP	F Multiply
	⌐ *data handling*			f	FDV	F Divide
e	EFL	Blank		f	DIR	F Remainder
e	TRR	Move		f	ARR	F Round
e	CMP	Compare		f	CVA	F Compare
e	CDB	Compare For Range		f	CAL	F Compare Absolute
g	RCL	Translate		f	MPD	F Add Exponent
g	FIN	End Translate		f	DPD	F Subtract Exponent
g	GMI	Load Table			⌐ *sequencing*	
g	CAT	Translate From Card		b	BR	Branch
g	CET	Translate From IBM Card		a	FJ	Set Branch Off
g	BPT	Translate From Paper Tape		a	FT	Set Branch On
g	CAM	Translate Card To Packed		a	FI	Reverse Branch
g	CEM	Translate IBM Card To Packed		a	RI	Store Instruction Address
g	TCA	Translate To Card		a	SI	Execute
g	TBP	Translate To Paper Tape			⌐ *supervision*	
g	TIP	Translate To Print		c	STOP	Stop
g	MVM	Translate Packed To Packed		c	CNRM	Element Change
g	TVM	Translate To Packed		c	CHLD	Element Change And Hold
g	MVT	Translate From Packed		c	CINT	Element Interrupt
	⌐ *logic and shift*			c	PROT	Protect Access
g	FCL	Not		c	LIBE	Free Access
g	INT	And		c	SIMU	Fork
g	REU	Or		a	TA	Load Indicator
g	FZL	Fill Zero		a	RA	Store Indicator
g	FUL	Fill One		a	GE	Set Element Number
g	IKL	Shift From K		a	RE	Store Element Number
g	MCL	Rotate				

Legend: F = Floating-Point.

TABLE 13-27   Instruction list of the Bull Gamma 60.

Instruction Structure

Machine-language syntax. The central processor uses the first four syntactic patterns. The other processors use the last four patterns, all of which start with three 1s. Each of those processors has only one syntactic pattern to decode. Although the syntactic patterns of these processors are mutually distinct, they

need to be distinct only from the patterns of the central processor. Some details of the syntactic patterns are our conjecture.

```
syntax60
a 1 0 ,Opcode,Relative,Indirect,Address
b 0 0 ,Cdn,Relative,Indirect,Address
c 0 1 ,Opc,Count,Relative,Indirect,Address
d 1 1 0 ,Opa,Ra,Relative,Indirect,Address
e 1 1 1 1 ,Opd,R0,Relative,Indirect,Address
f 1 1 1 0 ,Ope,Point,R1,R2,R3
g 1 1 1 0 1 1 1 0 ,Opl,L0,R3
g 1 1 1 0 1 1 1 1 ,Opl,L0,R3
```

PROGRAM 13-28   Instruction syntax of the Bull Gamma 60.

Instruction format.   The instruction formats match the syntactic-pattern groups. With one format per processor (other than the central processor), it frequently happens that fields are not used.

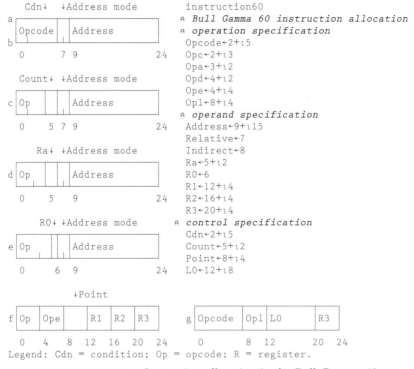

PROGRAM 13-29   Instruction allocation in the Bull Gamma 60.

Status format.   Each processor has 24 indicators, which are tested for branching by the central processor. The first machine-error indicator summarizes the other machine-error indicators. Indicator bits are used for different purposes in the various processors, as indicated in the comments of indicator60. Some indicators, such as the comparison indicators, are set by more than one processor.

```
indicator60
ᴀ Bull Gamma 60 Indicator
ᴀ machine error            ᴀ logical exclusion       ᴀ arithmetic
 Mach←0                      Kegn←12                   Pos←15
 Datapath← 3 4               Keg←13                    Neg←16
 Comparator← 5 6            ᴀ logical implication      Zero←17
 Counter← 7 8               Kign←14                   ᴀ comparison
ᴀ program error             Kig←15                     Ne←18
 Length←1                   Gikn←16                    Le←19
 Invop←2                    Gik←17                     Ge←20
ᴀ iteration                ᴀ all-one/zero comparand   Eq←21
 End←9                      One1←14                    Ls←22
 Cont←10                    Zero1←15                   Gr←23
ᴀ logical cover             One0←16
 Kcgn←10                    Zero0←17
 Kcg←11
```

PROGRAM 13-30   Indicators in the Bull Gamma 60.

13.2.3

Addressing

Direct addressing.   An address has three attributes: the data space, the data size, and the address value (see address60, Program 13-31). When the first two attributes are not specified, a single word in memory is the default. Reading is from memory or from a processor register. An operation normally places its result in a processor register. As an extra action, the result may be written into memory as well. The data size is one word or a multiple thereof.

```
data←read60 address;size;loc        address write60 data;size;loc
ᴀ Bull Gamma 60 read from memory    ᴀ Bull Gamma 60 write into memory
address←¯3↑address                  address←¯3↑address
size←word⌈address[Size]             size←word⌈address[Size]
→CASE address[Space]                →OUT address[Space]≠memadr
C0: ᴀ memory                        loc←address[Value]+ιsize÷word
   loc←address[Value]+ιsize÷word    memory[loc;]←word wide size↑data
   data←,memory[loc;]
   →ENDCASE
C1: ᴀ arithmetic accumulator        address60
   data←size↑acc                    ᴀ Bull Gamma 60 address allocation
   →ENDCASE                         ᴀ address attributes
C2: ᴀ logical register              Space←0
   data←g                           Size←1
ENDCASE:                            Value←2
                                    ᴀ space identifiers
                                    memadr←0
                                    accadr←1
                                    logadr←2
```

PROGRAM 13-31   Memory read and write in the Bull Gamma 60.

Address Modification

The main address mode, adr60, has a relative-address option and an indirect-address option, which may be specified independently of each other. Indirect addressing applies to one address level only.

Address calculation.   The address modes of the arithmetic and logical processors differ from the main addressing mode. The modes of adr60a

```
address←adr60
⍝ Bull Gamma 60 addressing
address←(fld Address)+iadr[rne]×fld Relative
→If fld Indirect
THEN:address←magni memory[address;Address]
ENDIF:
```

PROGRAM 13-32   Addressing in the Bull Gamma 60.

apply to arithmetic operands and results; adr60g applies to the logical result. The options specified in the field r are:

- Memory address as specified by an address register reg
- The same, but with the content of the address register being postincremented
- The accumulator or g register content
- Memory address for long precision data

```
address←adr60a r;value              address←adr60g;value
⍝ Bull Gamma 60 arithmetic address  ⍝ Bull Gamma 60 logical address
value←reg[Arith;fld 2↓r]            value←reg[Logic;fld 2↓R3]
→CASE fld 2↑r                       →CASE fld 2↑R3
C0: ⍝ register address              C0: ⍝ register address
   address←memadr,double,value         address←memadr,word,value
   →ENDCASE                            →ENDCASE
C1: ⍝ postincrement address         C1: ⍝ postincrement address
   address←memadr,double,value         address←memadr,word,value
   reg[Arith;fld 2↓r]←value+2          reg[Logic;fld 2↓R3;]←value
   →ENDCASE                            →ENDCASE
C2: ⍝ accumulator                   C2: ⍝ logic register
   address←accadr,accsize,0            address←logadr,word,0
   →ENDCASE                         ENDCASE:
C3: ⍝ long precision
   address←memadr,accsize,value
ENDCASE:
```

PROGRAM 13-33   Arithmetic and logical addressing in the Bull Gamma 60.

Index Arithmetic

Stack and list addressing.   The advancing of the arithmetic- and logical-processor addresses is suitable for list addressing; there is no decrement to facilitate stack addressing.

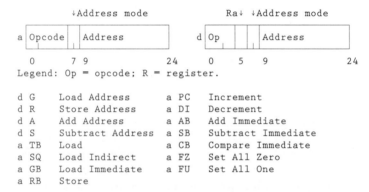

a	Opcode		Address		d	Op			Address	

↓Address mode   Ra↓ ↓Address mode

```
0       7 9          24  0   5 9             24
Legend: Op = opcode; R = register.
```

d	G	Load Address	a PC	Increment
d	R	Store Address	a DI	Decrement
d	A	Add Address	a AB	Add Immediate
d	S	Subtract Address	a SB	Subtract Immediate
a	TB	Load	a CB	Compare Immediate
a	SQ	Load Indirect	a FZ	Set All Zero
a	GB	Load Immediate	a FU	Set All One
a	RB	Store		

TABLE 13-34   Address operations of the Bull Gamma 60.

Address operations.   All address instructions are executed by the central processor. The first four instructions change the address in one of the address registers of the processor that is currently being controlled by the central processor. The other 11 instructions apply to register `rcb` of the central processor.

Address register operations.   The four operations Load, Store, Add, and Subtract apply to the address register `Ra` of the processor `rne` (*Registre Numero d'Elément*) that is currently under control of the central processor. The addresses are treated as 15-bit positive quantities. No indicators are set.

```
G;od                                  R;od
ค Bull Gamma 60 Load Address         ค Bull Gamma 60 Store Address
od←(read60 adr60)[Address]            od←word magnr reg[rne;fld Ra]
reg[rne;fld Ra]←magni od              adr60 write60 od


A;addend;augend;sum                   S;subtrahend;minuend;difference
ค Bull Gamma 60 Add Address          ค Bull Gamma 60 Subtract Address
addend←magni read60 adr60             subtrahend←magni read60 adr60
augend←reg[rne;fld Ra]                minuend←reg[rne;fld Ra]
sum←augend+addend                     difference←minuend-subtrahend
reg[rne;fld Ra]←adrcap|sum            reg[rne;fld Ra]←adrcap|difference
```

PROGRAM 13-35   Address register operations of the Bull Gamma 60.

Address preparation operations.   The 24-bit register `rcb` (*registre centrale binaire*) of the central processor serves as an address accumulator. This register can be loaded and stored directly from and to memory. The 15-bit address part of `rcb` can be loaded immediately by an effective address, and the total register content can be replaced by the storage word that is addressed by the address part of `rcb`. The register can also be reset to all-zeros and all-ones.

```
TB                                    RB
ค Bull Gamma 60 Load                 ค Bull Gamma 60 Store
rcb←read60 adr60                      adr60 write60 rcb


SQ                                    FZ
ค Bull Gamma 60 Load Indirect        ค Bull Gamma 60 Set All Zero
rcb←read60 magni rcb[Address]         adr60 write60 wordρ0


GB
ค Bull Gamma 60 Load Immediate
rcb[Address]←adrsize magnr adr60
```

PROGRAM 13-36   Load and Store Address in the Bull Gamma 60.

Increment and Decrement.   Incrementing applies to the address portion of a memory word. The original content of the word remains in `rcb`. The instruction seems intended for list processing. Decrementing is intended for iteration; it applies to a count in a full word. When the count is 0, it is set at a new initial value, not unlike the Refill of the Stretch. Otherwise, the count is reduced by 1. The outcome of the test is noted in two indicators.

```
PC;od;count                         DI;count
ⱥ Bull Gamma 60 Increment           ⱥ Bull Gamma 60 Decrement
od←rcb←read60 adr60                 rcb←read60 adr60
count←magni od[Address]             count←magni rcb
od[Address]←adrsize magnr count+1   ind[rne;9+ι15]←?15ρradix
adr60 write60 od                    →IF count=0
                                    THEN: ⱥ reset
                                      ind[rne;End,Cont]← 1 0
                                      adr60 write60 read60 adr60+1
                                      →ENDIF
                                    ELSE: ⱥ continue
                                      ind[rne;End,Cont]← 0 1
                                      adr60 write60 word magnr count-1
                                    ENDIF:
```

PROGRAM 13-37   Increment and Decrement Address in the Bull Gamma 60.

Address arithmetic and comparison.   Addition, subtraction, and comparison have rcb and one memory word as operands. The results are 15-bit addresses and leave the other bits of rcb unchanged. All six relations of operand and comparand are indicated by individual indicators.

```
AB;addend;augend;sum               operand signal60C comparand
ⱥ Bull Gamma 60 Add Immediate      ⱥ Bull Gamma 60 compare signal
addend←adr60                       ind[rne;Gr]←operand>comparand
augend←magni rcb[Address]          ind[rne;Ge]←operand≥comparand
sum←augend+addend                  ind[rne;Eq]←operand=comparand
rcb[Address]←adrsize magnr sum     ind[rne;Le]←operand≤comparand
                                   ind[rne;Ls]←operand<comparand
                                   ind[rne;Ne]←operand≠comparand
CB;operand;comparand
ⱥ Bull Gamma 60 Compare Immediate
operand←magni rcb[Address]
comparand←adr60
operand signal60C comparand
```

PROGRAM 13-38   Add and Compare Address Immediate in the Bull Gamma 60.

13.2.4

Data

Character Strings

Character set and size.   The 60-character set is that of Bull, but conversion from IBM cards is facilitated (Program 13-39). The character set is encoded in such a way that the numeric values of the codes match the collating sequence. The alphabetic character set is organized in two columns, anticipating the ASCII code. Scientific and commercial characters are part of the set.

Character string formats.   Four 6-bit characters are placed in a word. Strings of words are handled as character strings in the comparator and in the translator.

Logical

Logical formats.   The data of the logical processor have 24-bit word size and are interpreted as logical vectors in the registers g and k.

Fixed-Point Numbers

Notation and allocation.   The logical processor interprets 24-bit words as positive binary numbers. In the central processor, the 15-bit address format is used in the address registers `reg` or as a low-order field in the word format of the central register `rcb`.

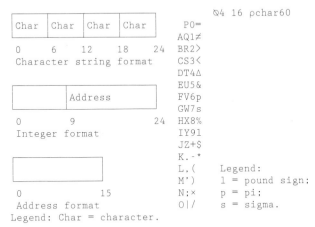

```
                                        ◊4 16 ρchar60
┌──────┬──────┬──────┬──────┐
│ Char │ Char │ Char │ Char │       PO=
└──────┴──────┴──────┴──────┘       AQ1≠
0      6     12     18     24       BR2>
Character string format             CS3<
                                    DT4Δ
┌─────────────┬─────────────┐       EU5&
│             │   Address   │       FV6p
└─────────────┴─────────────┘       GW7s
0             9            24       HX8%
Integer format                      IY91
                                    JZ+$
┌───────────────────────────┐       K.-*
│                           │       L,(        Legend:
│                           │       M')        1 = pound sign;
└───────────────────────────┘       N;×        p = pi;
0                          15       0|/        s = sigma.
Address format
Legend: Char = character.
```

PROGRAM 13-39   Fixed-point formats in the Bull Gamma 60.

Floating-Point Numbers

Floating-point format.   The arithmetic processor uses a double-word floating-point format with decimal base and representation. The exponent and coefficient allocation applies to decimal digits. The arithmetic accumulator contains two floating-point formats.

```
↓Coefficient sign
┌─┬───┬───────────────────────────────────────────┐
│ │Exp│ Coefficient                               │
└─┴───┴───────────────────────────────────────────┘
0    8                                           48
01 2  3   4   5   6   7   8   9  10  11  12  13 (decimal)
Legend: Exp = exponent.
```

```
f160
∩ Bull Gamma 60 floating-point number
∩ base
  base←10
∩ sign encoding
  plus←0
  minus←1
∩ decimal exponent allocation
  Exp←1+ι2
∩ decimal coefficient allocation
  Coef←0,3+ι10                      signal60NZP result
∩ radix point                       ∩ Bull Gamma 60 floating-point result
  point←10                          ind[Arith;Neg] ←result<0
∩ extreme exponent                  ind[Arith;Zero]←result=0
  extexp←40                         ind[Arith;Pos] ←result>0
```

PROGRAM 13-40   Floating-point format of the Bull Gamma 60.

Arithmetic results are noted in the indicators. Because the branch succeeds only for indicators that are set, it is not possible to branch for a non-0 result in one operation.

Floating-point representation.   Floating-point numbers are represented in 13 decimal digits, of which the first two are abbreviated: Decimal digit position 0 is the number sign, represented with 1 bit; decimal digit position 1 is the high-order exponent digit, represented with 3 bits. The decimal format is mapped as a 48-bit binary format by `flbin60r`; `flbin60i` maps from binary to decimal.

The exponent has a range from −40 through 39 and is represented with a bias of 40. The coefficient is represented as a signed-magnitude fraction.

```
number←fl60i rep;radix;dec;exponent;coefficient
ค Bull Gamma 60 floating-point interpretation
dec←flbin60i double↑rep
exponent←¯40+magni dec[Exp] WHERE radix←10
coefficient←signmagni dec[Coef]
number←coefficient×base*exponent-point


rep←fl60r numexp;radix;dec;low;exponent;coefficient;lower;xmax;xmin
ค Bull Gamma 60 floating-point representation
dec←low←13ρ0 WHERE radix←10
→CASE(numexp[1]= 11 12)ι1
C0: ค normalized
    (-extexp) normalize numexp[0]
    lower←coefficient-truncate coefficient
    →ENDCASE
C1: ค normalized and rounded
    (-extexp) normalize numexp[0]
    coefficient←round coefficient
    →If(|coefficient)=10*10
    THEN:exponent←exponent+1
        coefficient←coefficient÷10
    ENDIF:lower←0
    →ENDCASE
C2: ค programmed point
    exponent←point-numexp[1]
    coefficient←numexp[0]×base*numexp[1]
    lower←coefficient-truncate coefficient
ENDCASE:dec[Exp]←(ρExp) magnr exponent+40
dec[Coef]←(ρCoef) signmagnr truncate coefficient
→ERROR xmax∨xmin
low[Exp]←(ρExp) magnr(exponent+30)×lower≠0
low[Coef]←(ρCoef) signmagnr truncate lower×base*10
rep←(flbin60r dec),flbin60r low


dec←flbin60i bin;radix
ค Bull Gamma 60 floating-point from binary
dec←magni digit wide bin[0],0,1↓bin WHERE radix←2


bin←flbin60r dec;radix
ค Bull Gamma 60 floating-point to binary
bin←,digit magnr(dec[1]+8×dec[0]),2↓dec WHERE radix←2
```

PROGRAM 13-41   Floating-point representation in the Bull Gamma 60.

Closure and normal form.   A floating-point result can be represented in normalized form, in rounded normalized form, and with programmed exponent. The normalized representation is placed leftmost in the accumulator. The non-representable low-order coefficient digits are placed, as a proper floating-point number, rightmost in the accumulator, with the same sign and with an exponent that is 10 less than the exponent of the primary result. Arithmetic normally uses only single-precision operands. If the low-order part of the accumulator is to be used, the full accumulator must be stored; then each part can be used separately. In the rounded normalized representation, the low-order result is used to round the primary result and is then set to 0.

Programmed point.   The programmer can indicate in the arithmetic instructions the number of digits to the right of the radix point that should appear in the coefficient. This capability gives an unnormalized range, with exponent 0 through 10, which can be used for fixed-point calculations. High-order digits that cannot be represented with this program-specified point are lost, and set an error indication. Low-order digits are recorded in the low-order accumulator, as for normalized operation.

13.2.5

Operations

Data Handling

The comparator performs the Move, Compare, and Blank operations. The processor has three address registers, which are used in a more or less dedicated way. The comparator instructions have syntactic pattern e. The translator performs the translation operations using syntactic pattern g. We summarize only the operation of the translator.

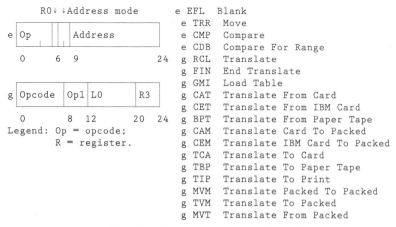

e	EFL	Blank
e	TRR	Move
e	CMP	Compare
e	CDB	Compare For Range
g	RCL	Translate
g	FIN	End Translate
g	GMI	Load Table
g	CAT	Translate From Card
g	CET	Translate From IBM Card
g	BPT	Translate From Paper Tape
g	CAM	Translate Card To Packed
g	CEM	Translate IBM Card To Packed
g	TCA	Translate To Card
g	TBP	Translate To Paper Tape
g	TIP	Translate To Print
g	MVM	Translate Packed To Packed
g	TVM	Translate To Packed
g	MVT	Translate From Packed

TABLE 13-42   Data-handling operations of the Bull Gamma 60.

Data movement.   Register 0 specifies the source operand. The destination is specified by register 1 or 2, depending upon the R0 field of the instruction. The

register content is updated as the operation proceeds. The effective address specifies the operand length. The eight low-order bits of the address are used, allowing lengths of 0 to 255. An excessive length is signaled.

```
TRR;size;source;dest              EFL;size;dest
A Bull Gamma 60 Move              A Bull Gamma 60 Blank
 →OUT rne≠Comp                     →OUT rne≠Comp
 size←word×256|adr60               size←word×256|adr60
 source←size,reg[Comp;0]           dest←size,reg[Comp;0]
 dest←size,reg[Comp;1+fld R0]      dest write60 0
 dest write60 read60 source        reg[Comp;0]←dest[1]+adr60
 reg[Comp;0]←source[1]+adr60       Length report60 adr60>255
 reg[Comp;1+fld R0]←dest[1]+adr60
 Length report60 adr60>255
```

PROGRAM 13-43   Variable-length move in the Bull Gamma 60.

Comparison.   Comparison is left to right, and stops when an inequality is recognized. The register contents are unpredictable at the end of the operation. Comparison is word-by-word unsigned binary and is valid for unsigned decimal data and for characters. All-zero and all-one operands are signaled.

```
CMP;size;od;cd;operand;comparand
A Bull Gamma 60 Compare
 →OUT rne≠Comp
 size←word×256|adr60
 →If size≠0
 THEN:od←read60 size,reg[Comp;0]
    cd←read60 size,reg[Comp;1+fld R0]
    operand←magni od
    comparand←magni cd
    operand signal60C comparand
    reg[Comp;0]←?adrcap
    reg[Comp;1+fld R0]←?adrcap         who signal60Z od
    0 signal60Z od                   A Bull Gamma 60 all zero/one result
    1 signal60Z cd                    ind[Comp;(Zero0,Zero1)[who]]←~∨/od
    Length report60 adr60>255         ind[Comp;(One0,One1)[who]]←∧/od
 ENDIF:
```

PROGRAM 13-44   Variable-length compare in the Bull Gamma 60.

Compare for range.   The three address registers specify the operand, the upper boundary, and the lower boundary. The indicators are set as applying to the range specified by these boundaries.

Format and code transformation.   The translator handles translation to and from the formats and codes of the I/O devices and a packed format in memory that represents quantities with fewer bits than the 48 bits required by floating point (such as small integers). The translation uses a table and a pattern that directs the character-by-character use of the table in translating a source word-string to a destination string. Loading the table, or specifying the type of translation, prepares the operation. The actual operation starts with Translate and ends when the data or pattern so indicate.

```
CDB;size;od;operand;upper;lower
ᴀ Bull Gamma 60 Compare For Range
→OUT rne≠Comp
size←word×256|adr60
→If size≠0
THEN:od←read60 size,reg[Comp;0]
    operand←magni od
    upper←magni read60 size,reg[Comp;1]
    lower←magni read60 size,reg[Comp;2]
    ind[Comp;Gr]←(operand>upper)∧operand>lower
    ind[Comp;Ge]←operand=upper
    ind[Comp;Eq]←(operand≤upper)∧operand≥lower
    ind[Comp;Ne]←(operand<upper)∧operand>lower
    ind[Comp;Le]←operand=lower
    ind[Comp;Ls]←(operand<upper)∧operand<lower
    1 signal60Z od
    reg[Comp;ι3]←?3ρadrcap
    Length report60 adr60>255
ENDIF:
```

PROGRAM 13-45   Variable-length compare for range in the Bull Gamma 60.

Logic

The logical processor performs logic and shifting. Each instruction has a length field $L0$ that specifies a selection, shift, or rotation of an operand in combination with a logical operation. Lengths and shifts are specified from the right end of the register. The operands are in the registers g and k, and the result is normally placed in g. Results may also be stored in memory, with or without advancing the content of the register specified by $R3$.

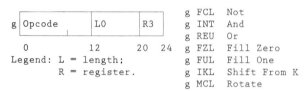

g	Opcode	L0	R3

0   12   20   24
Legend: L = length;
        R = register.

g FCL   Not
g INT   And
g REU   Or
g FZL   Fill Zero
g FUL   Fill One
g IKL   Shift From K
g MCL   Rotate

TABLE 13-46   Logical and shift operations of the Bull Gamma 60.

Connectives.   There is a classical subset of connectives. Logic is upon the rightmost $L0$ bits of the registers, leaving the other bits of the result register g unchanged.

```
FCL;length                    INT;length
ᴀ Bull Gamma 60 Not           ᴀ Bull Gamma 60 And
→OUT rne≠Logic                →OUT rne≠Logic
length←-fld L0                length←-fld L0
g←(length↓g),length↑~g        g←(length↓g),length↑g∧k
adr60g write60 g              adr60g write60 g
```

PROGRAM 13-47   Logical connectives in the Bull Gamma 60.

Vector operations.   Some vector reductions are available as a secondary result of fixed-point comparisons (Program 13-53).

Shift.   Fill Zero and Fill One shift the content of g to the right and fill the vacated bits with 0s or 1s, respectively. These instructions can be used in

programmed arithmetic right shift. Shift From K fills the vacated bits of g
from k. Left shift can be obtained with Fill Zero followed by a Rotate.

```
FUL;shift                        IKL;shift
ⴰ Bull Gamma 60 Fill One        ⴰ Bull Gamma 60 Shift From K
→OUT rne≠Logic                   →OUT rne≠Logic
shift←-fld L0                     shift←-fld L0
g←((|shift)ρ1),shift↓g           g←(shift↑k),shift↓g
adr60g write60 g                 k←shift⌽k
                                 adr60g write60 g


MCL;shift
ⴰ Bull Gamma 60 Rotate
→OUT rne≠Logic
shift←-fld L0
g←shift⌽g
adr60g write60 g
```

PROGRAM 13-48   Shift and Rotate in the Bull Gamma 60.

Fixed-Point Arithmetic

The arithmetic of the logical processor uses a specified number of rightmost bits from k and all the bits of g, both interpreted positively, and places
the result in g. g can be stored in memory at the end of each instruction,
except for TCL and TCK. Overflow or carry are not signaled.

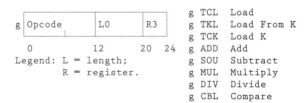

g	Opcode	L0	R3			g	TCL	Load
						g	TKL	Load From K
						g	TCK	Load K
	0	12	20	24		g	ADD	Add
Legend: L = length;						g	SOU	Subtract
R = register.						g	MUL	Multiply
						g	DIV	Divide
						g	CBL	Compare

TABLE 13-49   Fixed-point arithmetic operations of the Bull Gamma 60.

Load and Store.   Loading of g and k is from memory, with or without
postincrementing of the specified address register. The data are rotated right
by L0 bits as they are placed in the register. In moving from k to g, the
specified low-order bits of k are placed in g with high-order zero extension.

```
TCK;shift;data                   TKL;length
ⴰ Bull Gamma 60 Load K          ⴰ Bull Gamma 60 Load From K
→OUT(rne≠Logic)∨8≤fld R3         →OUT rne≠Logic
shift←-fld L0                    length←-fld L0
data←read60 adr60g               g←(-word)↑length↑k
k←shift⌽data                     adr60g write60 g
```

PROGRAM 13-50   Fixed-point Load in the Bull Gamma 60.

Add and Subtract.   The rightmost L0 bits of k are added to, or subtracted
from, the entire register g, and are placed in that register.

```
ADD;length;addend;augend;sum
⍝ Bull Gamma 60 Add
 →OUT rne≠Logic
 length←-fld L0
 addend←magni length↑k
 augend←magni g
 sum←augend+addend
 g←word magnr sum
 adr60g write60 g
```

PROGRAM 13-51 Fixed-point Add in the Bull Gamma 60.

Multiply and Divide. The multiplier in the L0 rightmost bits of k is multiplied with the contents of g; the product replaces g. The divisor is in the L0 rightmost bits of k. The dividend is in g and is replaced by the remainder and the quotient. Avoiding quotient overflow is the programmer's responsibility.

```
MUL;length;multiplier;multiplicand;product
⍝ Bull Gamma 60 Multiply
 →OUT rne≠Logic
 length←-fld L0
 k←(-word)↑length↑k
 multiplier←magni k
 multiplicand←magni g
 product←multiplicand×multiplier
 g←word magnr product
 adr60g write60 g

DIV;length;divisor;dividend;quotient;remainder;qt;rm
⍝ Bull Gamma 60 Divide
 →OUT rne≠Logic
 length←-fld L0
 k←(-word)↑length↑k
 divisor←magni k
 dividend←magni g
 quotient←⌊dividend÷divisor+divisor=0
 qt←(word+length) magnr quotient
 →ERROR xmax∨xmin∨divisor=0
 remainder←dividend-divisor×magni qt
 rm←(|length) magnr remainder
 g←rm,qt
 adr60g write60 g
```

Program 13-52 Fixed-point multiplication and division in the Bull Gamma 60.

Compare. Comparison is between the rightmost L0 bits of k and l, which are treated as positive quantities. The six possible relations are noted in the

```
CBL;length;operand;comparand
⍝ Bull Gamma 60 Compare
 →OUT rne≠Logic
 length←-fld L0
 operand←magni length↑g
 comparand←magni length↑k
 operand signal60C comparand
 (length↑k) signal60L length↑g
```

```
k signal60L g
⍝ Bull Gamma 60 logical result
⍝ cover
 ind[Logic;Kcg]←∧/k∨g
 ind[Logic;Kcgn]←~∧/k∨g
⍝ exclusion
 ind[Logic;Keg]←~∨/k∧g
 ind[Logic;Kegn]←∨/k∧g
⍝ implication
 ind[Logic;Kig]←∧/k≤g
 ind[Logic;Kign]←~∧/k≤g
 ind[Logic;Gik]←∧/g≤k
 ind[Logic;Gikn]←~∧/g≤k
```

PROGRAM 13-53 Fixed-point comparison in the Bull Gamma 60.

indicators. For both bit vectors also, the results of the logical-vector scan operations—cover, exclusion, and mutual implication and their inverses—are noted as secondary results.

Floating-Point Arithmetic

Floating-point operations are usually three address; each address is specified via an address register, possibly with postincrementing, and may apply either to memory or to the accumulator. The accumulator may not be used as the second operand. The operands are normally single precision. The result appears in the accumulator, and consists normally of two floating-point formats. The result may also be stored in memory. The result sign and zero condition are set in the indicators.

```
                    ↓Point

      f Opcode         R1  R2  R3

        0        8  12  16  20  24

      f TER   F Move           f DIR   F Remainder
      f ISI   F Negate         f ARR   F Round
      f PVA   F Make Absolute  f CVA   F Compare
      f FAD   F Add            f CAL   F Compare Absolute
      f FSU   F Subtract       f MPD   F Add Exponent
      f FMP   F Multiply       f DPD   F Subtract Exponent
      f FDV   F Divide
      Legend: F = Floating-Point; R = register.
```

TABLE 13-54   Floating-point instructions of the Bull Gamma 60.

Floating-point move and sign control.   Move interprets the operand and allows a change of representation. If the R1 field specifies the accumulator, the high-order and the low-order accumulator are retrieved, and both participate, allowing a round or left shift of the coefficient. Negate and Make Absolute move data, but do not allow a change of coefficient or a round; only the sign of the operand is changed.

```
TER;source;operand                 ISI
∩ Bull Gamma 60 Floating-Point Move ∩ Bull Gamma 60 Floating-Point Negate
→OUT rne≠Arith                     →OUT rne≠Arith
source←adr60a R1                   acc←accsize↑read60 adr60a R1
operand←f160i read60 source        acc[1↑Coef]←¯acc[1↑Coef]
→If accadr=source[Space]           (adr60a R3) write60 acc
THEN: ∩ low-order accumulator used signal60NZP f160i acc
   operand←operand+f160i double↓acc
ENDIF:acc←f160r operand,fld Point
(adr60a R3) write60 acc
signal60NZP operand
```

PROGRAM 13-55   Floating-point monadic operations in the Bull Gamma 60.

Floating-point Add and Subtract.   Addition and subtraction allow full address control of both operands and the result. The 10 decimal digits to the right of the coefficient may be preserved in the low-order accumulator.

```
FAD;source;addend;augend;sum
ᴀ Bull Gamma 60 Floating-Point Add
→OUT rne≠Arith
source←adr60a R2
→ERROR accadr=source[Space]
addend←fl60i read60 source
augend←fl60i read60 adr60a R1
sum←augend+addend
acc←fl60r sum,fld Point
(adr60a R3) write60 acc
signal60NZP sum
```

PROGRAM 13-56   Floating-point addition in the Bull Gamma 60.

Floating-point Multiply and Divide.   Multiplication is similar to addition and subtraction. The low-order product digits may be preserved in the low-order accumulator. The two division operations FDV and DIR both place the quotient (controlled by Point) in the low-order accumulator, and the remainder in the high-order accumulator. In DIR both the remainder and the quotient are stored at the end of the operation when double precision is specified. In FDV the quotient is moved from the lower to the upper accumulator and is then stored with single precision. Zero divisor and lost high-order–quotient digits are signaled.

```
DIR;source;divisor;dividend;qt;remainder
ᴀ Bull Gamma 60 Floating-Point Remainder
→OUT rne≠Arith
source←adr60a R2
→ERROR accadr=source[Space]
divisor←fl60i read60 source
dividend←fl60i read60 adr60a R1
quotient←dividend÷divisor+divisor=0
qt←double↑fl60r quotient,fld Point
remainder←dividend-divisor×fl60i qt
acc←(double↑fl60r remainder,11),qt
(adr60a R3) write60 acc
signal60NZP remainder
```

PROGRAM 13-57   Floating-point remainder in the Bull Gamma 60.

Other floating-point operations.   Round rounds the high-order accumulator based upon the contents of the low-order accumulator. This instruction is

```
MPD;radix;dec;addend;exponent;sum
ᴀ Bull Gamma 60 Floating-Point Add Exponent
→OUT rne≠Arith
radix←2
acc←accsize↑read60 adr60a R1
dec←flbin60i double↑acc
addend←fld Point
radix←10
exponent←magni dec[Exp]
sum←exponent+addend
dec[Exp]←(ρExp) magnr sum
→ERROR exponent≥80
acc←(flbin60r dec),double↓acc
radix←2
(adr60a R3) write60 acc
signal60NZP fl60i acc
```

```
ARR;radix;dec;low;coefficient;round
ᴀ Bull Gamma 60 Floating-Point Round
→OUT rne≠Arith
dec←flbin60i double↑acc
low←flbin60i double↓acc
radix←10
coefficient←magni dec[1↓Coef]
round←coefficient+low[Coef[1]]≥5
dec[1↓Coef]←10 magnr round
→ERROR coefficient=10*10
acc←accsize↑flbin60r dec
radix←2
(adr60a R3) write60 acc
signal60NZP fl60i acc
```

PROGRAM 13-58   Floating-point Round and Add Exponent in the Bull Gamma 60.

useful to round a result with programmed point. A coefficient overflow resulting from the round presumably gives an error indication.

Add and Subtract Exponent change the exponent without affecting the coefficient. The maximum adjustment is 15. There is no warning of an exponent overflow or underflow in these operations.

Floating-point Compare. Comparison is either with signed value or with absolute value of the comparand and operand. The indicators of the arithmetic processor are set according to the comparison result by signal60C (Program 13-58).

```
CVA;source;operand;comparand
A Bull Gamma 60 Floating-Point Compare
→OUT rne≠Arith
source←adr60a R2
→ERROR accadr=source[Space]
comparand←f160i read60 source
operand←f160i read60 adr60a R1
operand signal60C comparand
```

PROGRAM 13-59   Floating-point Compare in the Bull Gamma 60.

13.2.6

Instruction Sequencing

Next instruction. The central processor fetches the instructions of all processors from the common memory. When a given processor completes an instruction, the central processor fetches the next instruction and increments the instruction address of that processor. The next instruction is executed either by the central processor or by the given processor. The central processor performs address arithmetic and branches, and notes the end of an instruction sequence. A processor stops when its instruction address is made 0. When all instruction addresses are 0, the system stops. As long as not as not all processors are stopped, a processor that is ready for another instruction is selected by ese160.

```
cycle60                                 inst←ifetch60
A basic cycle of the Bull Gamma 60      A Bull Gamma 60 instruction fetch
REPEAT:execute ifetch60                 rne←ese160
→UNTIL stop60                           inst←read60 iadr[rne]
                                        iadr[rne]←iadr[rne]+1
                                        →ERROR iadr[rne]=adrcap
out←stop60
A Bull Gamma 60 stop condition
out←∧/iadr=0                            rne←ese160
                                        A Bull Gamma 60 element selection
                                        rne←0⊥1↑(?ecap)⌽(iadr≠0)/⍳ecap
which report60 condition
A Bull Gamma 60 set indicator on condition
ind[rne;which]←∨/ind[rne;which],condition
```

PROGRAM 13-60   Basic cycle and instruction fetch of the Bull Gamma 60.

Sequencing instructions. Sequencing instructions are executed by the central processor. There is only one branch instruction, but there are means to change its operation, to store the instruction address, and to execute a one-instruction subroutine.

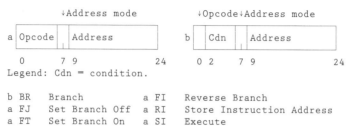

<table>
<tr><td colspan="3">↓Address mode</td><td colspan="3">↓Opcode↓Address mode</td></tr>
</table>

Legend: Cdn = condition.

b BR   Branch   a FI   Reverse Branch
a FJ   Set Branch Off   a RI   Store Instruction Address
a FT   Set Branch On   a SI   Execute

TABLE 13-61   Sequencing instructions of the Bull Gamma 60.

Linear Sequence

Unconditional Branch.   The Unconditional Branch and the No-Operation are special cases of the Conditional Branch.

Decision

Conditional branching.   The Branch is conditional upon one of the indicators of the current processor. The 5-bit condition field in the instruction specifies, in order, a 0 bit, the 24 indicator bits numbered right to left, six more 0 bits, and a 1 bit. Therefore, the all-zeros condition—as well as the all-zeros word—is a No-Operation, and the all-one condition is an Unconditional Branch. As a Branch is performed, its updated instruction address is preserved as $nadr$ in the central processor to be used by a subroutine call.

The three branch-manipulation instructions change a Branch instruction in memory into one of the following: a No-Operation, by making its condition field all-zeros; an Unconditional Branch, by making the condition field all-one; or a different Branch, by taking the inverse of all condition bits.

```
BR:od                                    FJ:od
ด Bull Gamma 60 Branch                   ด Bull Gamma 60 Set Branch Off
od←Φind[rne;]                            od←read60 adr60
→If(0,od, 0 0 0 0 0 1)[fld Cdn]          od[Cdn]←0
THEN: ด branch and trace                 adr60 write60 od
   nadr←iadr[rne]
   iadr[rne]←adr60
ENDIF:
```

PROGRAM 13-62   Conditional Branch in the Bull Gamma 60.

Iteration

Incrementation and termination.   Decrement (Program 13-37) may be used to close an iteration loop.

Delegation

Call and return.   A subroutine call is accomplished by Branch. The return address is the address following the Branch, as preserved in $nadr$ in the central processor. This return address must be saved during the first instruction of the subroutine. Store Instruction Address stores the address obtained from $nadr$

in the low-order 15 bits of a memory word and makes the nine high-order bits 0, which turns it into a No-Operation. A return Branch can refer to it with indirection.

```
RI
A Bull Gamma 60 Store Instruction Address
  adr60 write60 word magnr nadr
```

PROGRAM 13-63   Store Instruction Address in the Bull Gamma 60.

Execute. A word in memory is addressed from the address field of rcb and executed as an instruction. The next instruction is the instruction following the Execute, unless the subject instruction is a successful Branch, in which case the instruction sequence continues at the branch target address.

```
SI
A Bull Gamma 60 Execute
  execute read60 magni rcb[Address]
```

PROGRAM 13-64   Execute in the Bull Gamma 60.

13.2.7

Supervision

Concurrency

The Central, Translate, Logical, Arithmetic, and I/O processors operate concurrently and require means of scheduling and synchronization. The real concurrency of these processing elements is extended to a virtual concurrency (interleaving) of tasks by means of virtual elements that schedule and synchronize the various tasks that are in memory. As a general technique, the start addresses of instruction sequences that apply to a (virtual) element are chained to establish an order of execution. There is a set of instructions called *coupures* (*cutting points*)—all those shown in Table 13-65 with format c. These instructions manipulate these chains and cause the attention of an element to change from one sequence to another.

Supervisory instructions. The supervisory instructions handle the concurrency of actual or virtual processing elements (four-character mnemonics) and status changing (two-character mnemonics). All these instructions are executed by the central processor and as such are privileged.

Process Interaction

Completion. A sequence of instructions is terminated by a Stop instruction. The Stop instruction then determines the next task of this processor, as described by next60.

Task chain. Each processor has a pair of chain addresses in the address array cadr. This pair refers to the chain of addresses in memory that describes the

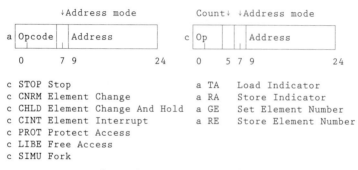

		↓Address mode			Count↓ ↓Address mode			
a	Opcode	Address		c	Op		Address	
	0	7 9	24		0 5 7 9			24

c STOP	Stop	a TA	Load Indicator
c CNRM	Element Change	a RA	Store Indicator
c CHLD	Element Change And Hold	a GE	Set Element Number
c CINT	Element Interrupt	a RE	Store Element Number
c PROT	Protect Access		
c LIBE	Free Access		
c SIMU	Fork		

TABLE 13-65   Supervisory instructions of the Bull Gamma 60.

list of tasks that is in memory for that processor. Each task starts with a
coupure, such as CNRM, that calls a real or virtual element. The instruction
word following the *coupure* is reserved for the chain pointer to the next task.
The next instructions in memory constitute the task to be performed. The
Next entry of cadr is the chain address for the sequence of instructions that
forms the next task for this processor. The Last entry is the chain address of
the last task for this processor. A Next entry that is 0 indicates that there is
no chain of tasks for this processing element. An instruction address that is 0
indicates an idle processor.

```
STOP                          address←next60 rne
ᴀ Bull Gamma 60 Stop          ᴀ Bull Gamma 60 next task of element
→OUT join60 iadr[rne]         address←cadr[rne;Next]
iadr[rne]←next60 rne          →CASE(0,cadr[rne;Last])ιaddress
                              C0: ᴀ empty chain
                                  →ENDCASE
                              C1: ᴀ terminate chain
                                  cadr[rne;]←0
                                  address←address+1
                                  →ENDCASE
                              C2: ᴀ reduce chain
                                  cadr[rne;Next]←adrcap|magni read60 address
                                  address←address+1
                              ENDCASE:
```

PROGRAM 13-66   Stop and get next task in the Bull Gamma 60.

Next task.   The function next60 obtains the next task for a processor.
next60 examines the Next entry of cadr for the current processing element
rne. If the Next address is 0 (case 0) then there is no further task, and the
instruction address of that processor is set to 0. When the address is non-0,
then there is a task to be done, and the instruction address is set to the first
instruction of that task, which is the instruction following the chain address.
The Next entry of cadr is also updated. Two cases are distinguished here. If
the Next entry is equal to the Last entry (case 1), there is no successor task,
and both entries are made 0. Otherwise (case 2), the successor task address is
fetched from memory and is placed in the Next entry, leaving the Last entry
unchanged.

Integrity

Critical section.   The critical-section problem is solved for the Gamma 60 by using a virtual element and chaining access to this virtual element in the same manner as for real elements. The virtual element and its chain addresses consist of two successive words in memory. The semaphore of the element is the leftmost bit of the first word; the two chain addresses are the rightmost 15 bits in each of the two words. PROT is used to obtain access to this element and to protect it from further use. LIBE frees the element after use.

```
PROT;nt;lt;last                                LIBE;nt;next;lt;last;nw
ῃ Bull Gamma 60 Protect Access                 ῃ Bull Gamma 60 Free Access
→OUT join60 iadr[rne]                          →OUT join60 iadr[rne]
nt←read60 adr60                                nt←read60 adr60
→CASE(nt[0],magni nt[Address])ι0               next←magni nt[Address]
C0: ῃ free access                              lt←read60 adr60+1
    adr60 write60 word↑1                       last←magni lt[Address]
    iadr[rne]←iadr[rne]+1                       →CASE(0,last)ιnext
    →ENDCASE                                   C0: ῃ empty chain
C1: ῃ start chain                                  adr60 write60 0
    nt[Address]←adrsize magnr iadr[rne]            →ENDCASE
    adr60 write60 nt                           C1: ῃ terminate chain
    (adr60+1) write60 nt                           adr60 write60 word↑1
    iadr[rne]←next60 rne                           (adr60+1) write60 0
    →ENDCASE                                       rne chain60 next
C2: ῃ extend chain                                 →ENDCASE
    last←adrcap|magni read60 adr60+1           C2: ῃ reduce chain
    lt←read60 last                                 nw←read60 next
    lt[Address]←adrsize magnr iadr[rne]            nt[Address]←nw[Address]
    last write60 lt                                adr60 write60 nt
    (adr60+1) write60 lt                           rne chain60 next
    iadr[rne]←next60 rne                       ENDCASE:
ENDCASE:                                       iadr[rne]←iadr[rne]+1
```

PROGRAM 13-67   Critical-section control in the Bull Gamma 60.

Access to virtual element.   Sequences that want access to a virtual element must give a Protect Access instruction and must reserve the next instruction word for the chain of access addresses. Protect Access inspects the first word of the virtual element pair, the next address word, called nt.   When the semaphore is 0, it is changed to 1 and is stored in memory. Memory access does not have to be atomic, since the supervisor is the only processor that executes these instructions, and it uses no concurrency. Also, the supervisor is supposed to be in control of memory allocation.   The second case the Gamma 60 distinguishes is a semaphore that is set without an address chain's being established. In this case, the address part of nt is 0. Protect Access now records the updated instruction address (the address of the empty word following Protect Access) in the address part of nt and also in its successor word in memory. This duplication signifies that the chain consists of only one entry. In the third case, a chain that is established is extended by placing the updated instruction address at the address specified by the successor word and by subsequently entering the updated instruction address in the successor word. In the last two cases, the task involved is stopped, and the processor proceeds to the next pending task, if any.

Freeing access to the virtual element.   When the use of a virtual element is completed, access to the virtual element is granted through the Free Access instruction. When the next address of the virtual element is zero, a simple request is processed, which leaves the chain empty. The semaphore is reset by recording all-zeros in the first virtual element word. When the next and the last address entries of the virtual element are equal, than the last request of a chain is processed. Both words of the virtual element are set to 0, which also resets the semaphore. Otherwise, the chain is not empty and is now reduced. The process indicated by the next address may proceed, and is allowed to do so by chaining its chain address to the chain for that processor (Program 13-68). The next process in the chain is noted in the virtual element by obtaining it from the chain location in memory.

Control Switching

Chaining real elements.   Chaining of a real element resembles that of a virtual element except that the Next and Last addresses in cadr are now used, and that there is no semaphore. The function next60 corresponds to Free Access, and chain60 corresponds to Protect Access. If the processor is stopped (its instruction address is 0), the processor is started at the new task by making its instruction address 1 larger than the chain address. If the processor is active and the Next address is 0, there is no chain, and the chain is stored by placing the new address in the Next and Last location. If there is a chain, then it is extended by storing the new chain address at the memory location indicated by Last and in the Last location of cadr.

```
rne chain60 address                    wait←join60 address;cnt
ⴰ Bull Gamma 60 chain task             ⴰ Bull Gamma 60 join tasks
→CASE(iadr[rne],cadr[rne;Next])ι0        cnt←magni memory[address;Count]
  C0: ⴰ free access                      memory[address;Count]←2 magnr 0⌈cnt-1
     iadr[rne]←address+1                 wait←cnt>0
     →ENDCASE                            →If wait
  C1: ⴰ start chain                      THEN:iadr[rne]←next60 rne
     cadr[rne;]←address                  ENDIF:
     →ENDCASE
  C2: ⴰ extend chain
     memory[cadr[rne;Last];Address]←adrsize magnr address
     cadr[rne;Last]←address
ENDCASE:
```

PROGRAM 13-68   Chaining and joining in the Bull Gamma 60.

Joining tasks.   In a simple sequence, a task may be started as soon as the preceding task is completed. In a more complex sequence, it may be necessary for several tasks to complete before a new task can be started. A count field in the word following a coupure makes it convenient to control the completion of several tasks. Counting applies to the access of both real and virtual elements. join60 simply reduces the content of the 2-bit count field and leaves the count 0 once it reaches 0. The chaining action of the coupure is ignored, and the process is simply terminated when the count is not 0. If three sequences must be joined, the count must be originally 2, and only the third execution of that coupure will be allowed to proceed. (Re)setting the count in the instruction is a programming responsibility.

Dispatching.   There are four coupures that initiate the action of an element. The Element Change coupure is used when one processor completes its task and the program wants to continue with another processor. The number of the new element is obtained from the effective address and is tested for an existing address, other than 0 (the supervisor). Then the join test is performed. If this test is satisfied, then the instruction sequence is chained to the desired processor chain. In any event, the task of the current processor is terminated, and a new task is requested.

```
CNRM                                    SIMU
∩ Bull Gamma 60 Element Change          ∩ Bull Gamma 60 Fork
→ERROR(adr60≥ecap)∨adr60=0                →OUT join60 iadr[rne]
→OUT join60 iadr[rne]                     rne chain60 iadr[rne]
adr60 chain60 iadr[rne]                   iadr[rne]←adr60
iadr[rne]←next60 rne
```

PROGRAM 13-69   Dispatching and switching in the Bull Gamma 60.

Interruption.   The coupure Element Change And Hold is the same as Element Change, except that the current task is continued. Element Interrupt is also a variant of Element Change; it interrupts the new element, but provides no means to resume the interrupted program. These two coupures are intended not for basic supervisory control, but rather for error recovery.

Fork.   The Fork instruction starts a new process in the current element at the next instruction address, and at the same time branches to a specified address, where it continues. If it is desired to have a multiple fork, the Fork can be repeated several times.

State Preservation

Context switching.   The indicators of the current processor can be stored and loaded. The element number can also be stored and loaded by the supervisor. The latter action changes the control of the processor, disregarding the chain of processor tasks.

```
TA                                      GE
∩ Bull Gamma 60 Load Indicator          ∩ Bull Gamma 60 Set Element Number
ind[rne;]←read60 adr60                    →ERROR adr60≥ecap
                                          rne←adr60


RA                                      RE
∩ Bull Gamma 60 Store Indicator         ∩ Bull Gamma 60 Store Element Number
adr60 write60 ind[rne;]                    adr60 write60 word magnr rne
```

PROGRAM 13-70   Status control in the Bull Gamma 60.

13.2.8

Input/Output

The I/O processors operate essentially as peripheral processors. A processor is started by calling it with a coupure. The list of I/O processors is given in name60 (Program 13-23).

Devices

Store.   The 25,600 words of the drum are addressable to the word.

Source and sink.   There are up to 18 units of 8-bit magnetic tape; 80-column card readers and card reader-punches; 5- and 8-channel paper-tape readers and punches; and printers with 120 print positions.

13.2.9
Implementation Notes

Residue error detection.   Three memory bits are added to each 24-bit word to record a modulo 7 sum for error detection.

Timing.   Memory has an 11 μs cycle. An operand fetch requires 33 μs. Instruction fetch, priority resolution, and transmission from the central processor to another processor takes 66 μs. When all processors operate, about all memory cycles are needed, ignoring conflicts.

The logical processor operates bit-serially. Addition takes 130 μs; multiplication, 500 μs.

Floating-point addition and subtraction take 100 μs; multiplication, 300 μs; division, 600 μs.

Technology.   The processors are built with discrete transistors; memory uses ferrite cores.

13.2.10
Bibliography

Compagnie des Machines Bull, undated: *Idée Directrice du Gamma 60.* Reference manual. Paris, France. (our defining reference).

Dreyfus, P. 1959a: "System Design of the Gamma 60." *Proc., AIEE–ACM–IRE 1958 Western Joint Computer Conf.,* **13**: 130–32.

Dreyfus, P. 1959b: "Programming Design Features of the GAMMA 60 Computer." *Proc., AIEE–ACM–IRE 1958 Eastern Joint Computer Conf.,* **14**: 174–81.

Leclerc [1990] and Mounier-Kuhn [1990].

13.2.11
Exercises

13-6 Give the description of the address arithmetic instructions SB and FU, assuming consistency with the address-arithmetic instructions shown in this section.

13-7 Give the description of the logical instructions REU and FZL, assuming consistency with the logical instructions shown in this section.

13-8 Give the description of the fixed-point arithmetic instructions TCL and SOU, assuming consistency with the fixed-point arithmetic instructions shown in this section.

13-9 Give the description of the floating-point arithmetic instructions PVA, FSU, FMP, FDV, CAL, and DPD, assuming consistency with the floating-point arithmetic instructions shown in this section.

13-10 Give the description of the sequencing instructions FT and FI, assuming consistency with the sequencing instructions shown in this section.

13-11 Give the instruction sequence for an arithmetic right shift and for a logical left shift in the logical processor.

13.3

IBM Stretch

13.3.1

Highlights

History

Architects.   Stephen Dunwell was the project manager. The principal architect was Werner Buchholz.

The IBM Stretch (IBM 7030) supercomputer was designed to meet the scientific-computation needs of the Los Alamos Scientific Laboratory and of other similar customers.   The Stretch had a goal of being "100 times the 704" in performance. The technologies available included memories six times faster than the IBM 704's (1955) and circuits about 10 times faster. The Stretch supercomputer was to achieve the remainder of the speedup by architectural and implementation innovation. The designers were not only not constrained by component count, but they were driven to find new ways to use components to achieve effective performance. The Stretch's performance finally turned out to be about 50 times the 704's.

The Stretch is an excellent example of both the implementation strategies and the architectural strategies used in all supercomputers to achieve performance gains beyond what realization-technology advances offer.   The implementation strategies are treated in the implementation notes at the end of this section.

Dates.   The first customer shipment was in 1961; nine systems were installed in all. The project began in 1955.

Family tree.   See the frontispiece to Chapter 12. The Stretch is immediately descended from the 704, and is an architectural sibling of the IBM 709.

Noteworthy

A major new operating concept for which the machine was explicitly planned was *multiprogramming*, the time-sharing of the central computer among several independent application programs.

Supervisory facilities.   The most important architectural innovations are the whole range of supervisory facilities provided to enable the system to be multiprogrammed and to be operated under control of a supervisory program, rather than of a human operator. The Stretch pioneered many facilities that have become commonplace today:

- Maskable and vectored interruption
- Memory protection
- Interval timer and real-time clock
- Wait instead of Halt

- Program-interpreted operator's console; the lights and switches are set and interpreted entirely by the supervisory program, rather than reflecting and governing the hardware directly

Speedup facilities.   The architectural strategies for higher performance focus on better use of the memory bandwidth:

- Multiple concurrent processors, to the extent that the applications can use the concurrency; in the Stretch, the separate I/O processors are an example
- More complex instruction formats, to maximize their bit efficiency (the effect is to reduce the number of fetches per instruction); the Stretch carries this concept very far
- More registers, thus eliminating average address length and reducing Loads and Stores; the Stretch introduces large address-register sets, but has only two data registers
- More symmetric and complete operation sets, reducing instructions that just permute operands or branch addresses; examples in the Stretch are Reciprocal Divide, symmetric sign control, Connect with 16 connectives, and fully symmetric Branch On Condition and Branch On Bit
- More powerful operations, limited ultimately by the number of operands required for superoperations (the effect is to reduce the number of instructions per program); examples in the Stretch are Add To Memory, Cumulative Multiply, Store Square Root, and Add To Magnitude
- Interruption mechanisms monitoring for exceptional conditions, to avoid explicit tests and pollings

Large memory.   The memory name-space is 256 K 64-bit words, or 2 million 8-bit bytes, much the largest of any machine of its time, and eight times that of its predecessor, the 704.

Separate I/O computer.   I/O transmissions are handled by some 17 concurrently operating channels, which are—architecturally and in implementation—processors separate from the CPU.

Specialized coprocessor.   The IBM Harvest (IBM 7950) coprocessor (1961) provides high-speed logical and table-lookup operations on very long character vectors. It is memory-coupled to the Stretch CPU and operates concurrently with it.

Systematic and rich operation set.   The Stretch has many new operations, and an unusually symmetric operation set defined by base operations plus orthogonal modifiers. Branching is symmetric, with testing separated from branch-address specification.

Powerful indexing.   The I/O control word has the identical format as the index word, enabling reading, processing, and writing to be controlled with the same control-word sequences. The index registers include not only value, but also count and next-index fields, enabling tight loop-closing. Autoincrementing and decrementing is provided, enabling an index to be changed after each use without any extra instructions.

Bit addressing. Every bit in memory is addressable, and a data field of any length up to 64 bits may be specified. Moreover, the fields may be subdivided in bytes of 1 to 8 bits. These fields participate in logic, and in binary or decimal, signed or unsigned, fixed-point arithmetic.

Immediate addressing. All applicable addressing operations can be performed with an immediate operand.

Execute operation Execute interprets a word in memory or in a register as an instruction. Execute Indirect And Count establishes a pseudo instruction counter that is updated and that reflects the result of branch operations as subject instructions. Execute operations may have Execute operations as subject instruction for multiple levels.

Indicator register. All status is grouped in one 64-bit indicator register. These indicators are uniformly accessible for testing, storing, and restoring.

Peculiarities

Architectural elaboration. Several concepts are carried to the limit, beyond what we would today recognize as good practice:
- Bit resolution in addressing
- Variable byte size
- Boundary-free alignment
- Large, complex set of instruction formats
- Full variable-field-length arithmetic for fixed-point integers
- Rich operation set; designed, as it is, for assembly-language programming, it provides many operations that a compiler would not use in code generation, such as Add To Memory, Add To Magnitude, and Store Zero

Embedding. Little programming advantage is gained by embedding almost the entire working and control store in memory, but substantial implementation cost is incurred in terms of complexity and time.

Data flags. Data words carry up to three flag bits, or tags, that can cause interruption when the words are fetched, and that can be set and tested by program. Considering its infrequent use, this mechanism is space-costly.

Secondary results for logical operations. Logical operations yield not only a bit vector, but also the All-Ones Count and the Left-Zeros Count characterizing that result.

Left-aligned address. The address occurs first in the format, since addresses vary in the number of low-order bits that are truncated.

Floating-point extrema. The floating-point extrema are less complete than are the earlier extrema of the Zuse Z4 (1945) and the later CDC 6600 (1964) extrema. They establish extreme ranges rather than extreme values.

Noisy mode. Floating-point operations have two symmetric modes, one of which brings zeros into low-order positions, the other of which brings

ones into those positions, upon left shifting and normalization. Neither mode is really "noisier" that the other; they just make opposite choices for non-significant bits, so that a calculation can be run twice and the degree of significance loss can be estimated, even though it cannot be assuredly bounded.

Limited supervisory mode.   Although extensive provisions are made for supervision, there is no supervisory mode as such, and there are no privileged operations. The compilers are expected to intercept operations that should be restricted to the supervisor. The Enabled/Disabled mode does control access to address protection and the interrupt mask.

Intractably complex.   The interaction of the peculiarities mentioned is in itself a source of complexity. Thus it is not immediately evident what is the result of loading a signed operand with byte size 5 and length 2. Similarly, the combination of embedding, multiple indicators, and multilevel executes causes situations that are hard to predict even when the well-documented manual is consulted.

13.3.2

IBM Harvest Coprocessor

One of the Stretch copies was equipped with a coprocessor for performing logical and table-lookup operations on very long character vectors [Buchholz, 1962, Chapter 17]. The IBM Harvest (IBM 7950) coprocessor (1961) is large, having approximately twice as many transistors as the Stretch itself.

Data streaming.   The Harvest, like today's vector machines, aims at utilizing the memory bandwidth by avoiding instruction flow. An operation, perhaps quite a complex one, is set up by an elaborate instruction, some 200 bits. Then two character vectors are streamed into the operation (and a result vector is streamed out) at memory-limited data rates, without any more instruction fetch. A single instruction execution might last 1/2 hour or longer. The programming model is shown in Figure 13-71 [Herwitz and Pomerene, 1960].

Indexing.   Three nested levels of indexing on each input stream, each index with value, count and next-index fields, can perform elaborate cyclic patterns of memory fetching in forming the character streams. Completion of the count of one index causes the index to reset to the next index word, and causes the index level above to increment and count. Two nested levels of indexing on the output stream give yet more pattern power.

Operation units.   An arithmetic and logical unit (ALU) does byte-by-byte logical operations, sums, differences, and comparisons, producing a stream of bytes or, for comparisons, a stream of result bits.
   A table-lookup unit (TLU) includes a Table Address Assembler, which assembles sequences of bytes into addresses, adds them at flexible offsets to a table base address, and streams these addresses off into memory. Either counting or incidence marking at the addressed locations is performed in the memories themselves, or else streams of byte fields return. The other part

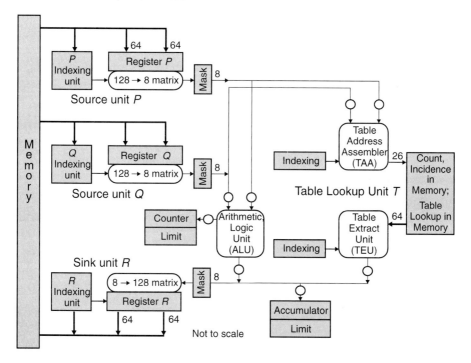

FIGURE 13-71   Programming model for the IBM Harvest Processing Unit.

of the TLU, a Table Extract Unit, selects the wanted fields from the memory words returned.

An auxiliary operations unit can count, for example, the number of byte comparisons that are equal, and can interrupt when the count reaches a threshold. A similar unit can sum the bytes coming in, as signed or unsigned numbers, and can interrupt when the sum reaches a threshold. The input streams or the outputs of the ALU or TLU can be directed to these counters and summers.

Special setups of this coprocessor are built into hardware to do merge sorting and collating.

Data monitoring and adjustments.   Sets of sixteen 1-byte–wide comparators sit astride the data-stream paths at various points. When any passing byte matches one of the 16 comparands, a distinctive output signal is generated. Each of these signals can be set up to cause an automatic stream adjustment: increment or reset index levels, suppress the data-stream byte, substitute another byte, increment the counter, or stop the Harvest and interrupt the Stretch to come do some programmed adjustment.

Applications.   Typical applications (besides cryptography) well-suited to the Harvest are: generation of all eight-note sequences from an encoding of a melody; generation and counting of English trigraphs from a prose text; translation of Roman numerals via table lookup with table switching [Buchholz, 1962, pp. 267–71]; and discrimination between English and Dutch texts by Bayesian analysis using letter frequency tables.

13.3.3

Machine Language

Language Level

Design philosophy. The Stretch's language is well above the implementation. It is designed for coding in assembler. Because of the slow main memory, efficient use of the memory bandwidth receives very great emphasis. There are many instruction formats, tightly packed.

Unit System

The Stretch uses the *four* system of units, with 4-bit register addresses, 8-bit bytes, 64-bit words, and a 128-bit accumulator with 8-bit sign register. The address size includes 24 bits and a sign bit.

```
initiate7030                          format7030
∩ initiation of the IBM Stretch       ∩ IBM Stretch information units
format7030                            ∩ principal radix
configure7030                         radix←2
space7030                             ∩ information units
name7030                              half←32
control7030                           word←64
data7030                              double←128
                                      adrsize←25
                                      ∩ address capacity
configure7030                         adrcap←radix*adrsize-1
∩ configuration for the IBM Stretch
∩ memory capacity
memcap←radix*20
```

PROGRAM 13-72   Basic parameters of the IBM Stretch.

Configuration. The address capacity is measured in bits; it is equivalent to 2 MB, assuming 8-bit bytes. We show a small `memcap` configuration.

Spaces

Memory name-space. The name-space is linear. It is a seamless vector of bits that can be addressed by word, halfword, or bit.

Working store. The working store and most of the control store are embedded in the main name-space, besides being separately addressable. As a consequence, the space specification is short and the name specification (Program 13-74) is long.

```
space7030
∩ IBM Stretch spaces        ∩ - stopped state
∩ memory                    stop←?radix
memory←?memcap∘radix        ∩ - wait state
∩ control store             wait←?radix
∩ - instruction address     ∩ - interrupt enable
iadr←half×?memcap÷half      enable←?radix
                            ∩ - execute state
                            exec←?radix
```

PROGRAM 13-73   Spaces of the IBM Stretch.

Control store.   Non-embedded control store is for the instruction address, stopping by manual control, waiting, enabling of the interruption mechanism during normal instruction sequencing, and enabling as part of an execute operation.

Embedding.   Almost the entire working and control stores are accessible as memory, but a variety of rules governs the use of these locations as operands or instructions. Arithmetic is done in a single double-length accumulator-MQ combination (Acc and Signreg), as in the 704, except that separate registers are available for the multiplier in cumulative multiplication (Factor), for the remainder in division (Remainder), and for an operand in macro-operations (Transit).

```
name7030
ᴀ IBM Stretch space names
ᴀ memory names
ᴀ - zero                              ᴀ - all ones count
  Zero←0+ιword                          Allones←(7×word)+44+ι7
ᴀ - timer                             ᴀ - double-word accumulator
  Timer←(1×word)+ι19                    Acc←8×word
  Clock←(1×word)+28+ι36               ᴀ - sign byte
ᴀ - interrupt address                   Signreg←10×word
  Intloc←(2×word)+ι18                 ᴀ - indicators
ᴀ - protection boundaries               Ind←(11×word)+ιword
  Upperbound←(3×word)+ι18            ᴀ - interrupt mask
  Lowerbound←(3×word)+half+ι18         Mask←12×word
  Boundbit←(3×word)+half+25          ᴀ - remainder
ᴀ - maintenance                         Remainder←13×word
  Maintenance←4×word                 ᴀ - factor
ᴀ - channel address                     Factor←14×word
  Chanadr←(5×word)+12+ι7            ᴀ - transit
ᴀ - other CPU                           Transit←15×word
  Othercpu←(6×word)+ι19             ᴀ - 16 index words
ᴀ - left zero count                     Index←16×word
  Leftzeros←(7×word)+17+ι7
```

PROGRAM 13-74   Embedding of the IBM Stretch.

Register file.   The Stretch is, along with the IBM 705 (1956), one of the first machines to provide a register file, here used as a set of 16 full-word index registers.

Programming model.   Stretch is best modeled as an instruction computer (Figure 13-75), and two execution units, one for floating point (Figure 13-76) and one for byte, bit, and decimal manipulation (Figure 13-77). Although there is extensive pipelining within and especially between the units, it does not show in the architecture.

The instruction processor essentially has a 24-bit datapath, for address arithmetic. It is distinctive because of the long, multi-component index registers.

The floating-point processor model is distinctive in having a single accumulator, quite long, with specialized Factor and Remainder registers besides. The Factor Register permits clean cumulative floating-point multiplication.

The Bit–Byte Processor is remarkable for the richness and power of its selection facilities, combined with the weakness of its serial ALU. The generalized bit-field manipulation task is difficult, and its inherent cost shows

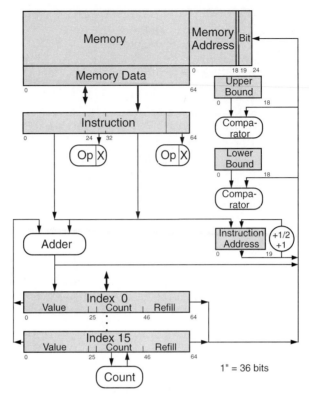

FIGURE 13-75   Instruction processor model for the IBM Stretch.

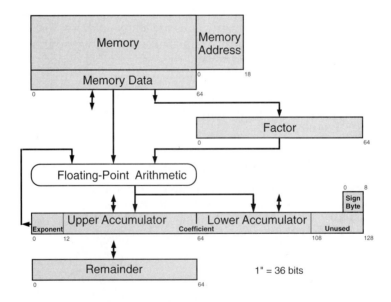

FIGURE 13-76   Floating-point processor model for the IBM Stretch.

in the amount of register and selection logic. Figure 13-77 follows Buchholz [1962, p. 23].

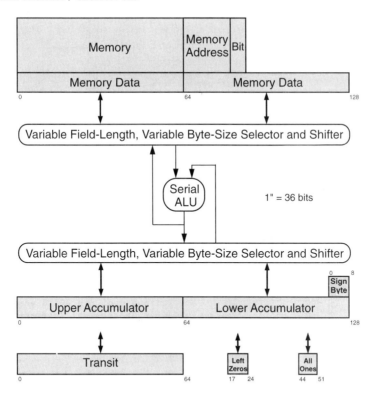

FIGURE 13-77   Bit–byte processor model for the IBM Stretch (After [Buchholz, 1962]).

Operand Specification

Number of addresses.   Most instructions are single-address. The exceptions are a very general two-address Move (Transmit), several two-address memory-to-index register operations, and several two-address Call (Branch And Store) instructions (Program 13-82).

Address phrase.   The address phrase consists of an 18-, 19-, or 24-bit direct or immediate address, generally indexed by one index register, specified by a 4-bit or 1-bit index address.

Operation Specification

Mnemonics.   We use the manufacturer's mnemonics where alphabetic characters are used. We do not follow the manufacturer in the use of arithmetic symbols, such as +, but rather replace these by letters. We also do not follow the use of one mnemonic for more than one instruction.

Instruction Structure

Machine-language syntax.   There are 16 syntactic patterns and 13 pattern groups. The patterns occupy either 64 or 32 bits. The patterns i, l, and m appear as the right part of patterns d, e, and f. The distinctness of the patterns is best seen from the Type field (bits 24 through 27), which is 1 0 0 0 in patterns

	ᴀ *address arithmetic*			a	KFE	Compare Field If Equal
j	LX	Load Index			ᴀ *floating-point arithmetic*	
j	LV	Load Value		h	FL	F Load
j	LC	Load Count		h	DL	Load D
j	LR	Load R		h	FLWF	F Load With Flag
j	LVE	Load Value Effective		h	DLWF	Load With Flag D
k	LVS	Load Value With Sum		h	FLFT	F Load Factor
k	LVI	Load Value I		h	FST	F Store
k	LVNI	Load Value Negative I		h	SLO	F Store Low Order
k	LCI	Load Count I		h	FSRD	F Store Rounded
k	LRI	Load R I		h	FSRT	F Store Root
j	SX	Store Index		h	FA	F Add
j	SV	Store Value		h	DA	Add D
j	SC	Store Count		h	FAMG	F Add To Magnitude
j	SR	Store R		h	DAMG	Add To Magnitude D
j	SVA	Store Value In Address		h	FADM	F Add To Memory
j	AV	Add To Value		h	FAMM	F Add Magnitude To Memory
j	AVC	Add To Value, Count		h	SHF	Shift Coefficient
j	AVCR	Add To Value, Count, R		h	AF	Add To Coefficient
k	AVI	Add I To Value		h	AE	Add To Exponent
k	ACI	Add I To Count		h	AEI	Add I To Exponent
k	AVCI	Add I To Value, Count		h	FM	F Multiply
k	AVRI	Add I To Value, Count, R		h	DM	Multiply D
k	SVI	Subtract I From Value		h	FMA	F Multiply Cumulative
k	SCI	Subtract I From Count		h	FD	F Divide
k	SVCI	Subtract I From Value, Count		h	DD	Divide D
k	SVRI	Subtract I From Value, Count, R		h	FRD	F Reciprocal Divide
j	KV	Compare Value		h	FK	F Compare
j	KC	Compare Count		h	FKR	F Compare Range
k	KVI	Compare Value I		h	FKM	F Compare Magnitude
k	KVNI	Compare Value Negative I		h	FKMR	F Compare Magnitude Range
k	KCI	Compare Count I			ᴀ *sequencing*	
i	R	R Index		i	NOP	No Operation
i	RCZ	R Index On Zero Count		d	NOPS	No Operation, Store
j	RNX	Rename Index		i	B	Branch
	ᴀ *data handling*			d	BS	Branch, Store
c	T	Move		i	BR	Jump
	ᴀ *logic and shift*			d	BRS	Jump, Store
b	C	Connect		g	BB	Branch On Bit
b	CM	Connect To Memory		m	BI	Branch On Indicator
b	CT	Connect For Test		f	BIS	Branch On Indicator, Store
	ᴀ *fixed-point arithmetic*			l	CB	Branch On Count
a	L	Load		e	CBS	Branch On Count, Store
a	LWF	Load With Flag		l	CBR	Branch On Count, R
a	LFT	Load Factor		e	CBRS	Branch On Count, R Store
a	LCV	Load Converted		i	EX	Execute
a	LTRS	Load Transit And Set		i	EXIC	Execute Indirect And Count
a	LTCV	Load Transit Converted			ᴀ *supervision*	
a	ST	Store		i	BE	Branch Enabled
i	Z	Store Zero		d	BES	Branch Enabled, Store
a	SRD	Store Rounded		i	BD	Branch Disabled
a	A	Add		d	BDS	Branch Disabled, Store
a	AMG	Add To Magnitude		i	BEW	Branch Enabled, Wait
a	ADM	Add To Memory		d	BEWS	Branch Enabled, Wait, Store
a	AMM	Add Magnitude To Memory			ᴀ *input/output*	
a	INCM	Increment Memory		d	RD	Read
a	M	Multiply		d	RDS	Read And Suppress
a	MA	Multiply Cumulative		d	W	Write
a	D	Divide		d	WS	Write And Suppress
a	CV	Convert		d	CTL	Control
a	DCV	Convert D		d	CTLS	Control And Suppress
a	K	Compare		d	CCW	Copy Control Word
a	KF	Compare Field		d	REL	Release
a	KR	Compare Range		d	RELS	Release And Suppress
a	KFR	Compare Field Range		d	LOC	Locate
a	KE	Compare If Equal		d	LOCS	Locate And Suppress

Legend: D = Double; F = Floating-Point; I = Immediate; R = Refill.

TABLE 13-78   Instruction list of the IBM Stretch.

a→A	AMG	b→C	i	i	FD	DD	EXIC	AVCR	AVRI
LCV	LTCV	CM	i	i	FAMG	DAMG	BEW	SX	SCI
L	LWF	CT	RELS	i	FLWF	DLWF	Z	SV	LVNI
→b	→b	i	i	→f	FAMM	i	i	SC	KCI
ADM	AMM	c→T	i	i	FSRD	FSRT	i	SR	LVS
LFT	INCM	d→RD	d→BES	e→CBS	FKM	SHF	NOP	KC	KVNI
ST	SRD	W	i	e→CBRS	FKMR	AEI	i	LVE	SVI
→b	→b	CTL	BDS	f→BIS	FMA	i	i	SVA	SVCI
K	KF	LOC	i	g→BB	FRD	i	i	RNX	SVRI
KE	KFE	RDS	BS	h→FA	DA	i→BE	j→LX	k→ACI	1→CB
KR	KFR	WS	i	FL	DL	R	LV	LVI	1→CBR
→b	→b	CTLS	BRS	FADM	FLFT	BD	LC	LCI	m→BI
M	MA	LOCS	i	FST	SLO	RCZ	LR	LRI	
CV	DCV	CCW	BEWS	FK	AF	B	KV	KVI	
D	LTRS	REL	i	FKR	AE	EX	AV	AVI	
→b	→b	i	NOPS	FM	DM	BR	AVC	AVCI	

PROGRAM 13-79   Operation-code list of the IBM Stretch.

a through g, x x 1 0 (x is *don't care*) in h, 0 0 0 0 in i and k, x x x 1 in j, and x 1 0 0 in l and m. The pairs i k and l m are distinguished by extensions to the left and right. The word formats a through g are distinguished by Type bits in the second halfword in a similar way as for the halfword formats.

```
  syntax7030
a Address, 1 0 0 0 ,X1,M0,L0,Byte,Offset,Nosign,Negate2,Decimal,Opvl,1,X2
b Address, 1 0 0 0 ,X1,M0,L0,Byte,Offset,Con,Opcn, 1 1 1 ,X2
c Address, 1 0 0 0 ,X1,Adrhalf2,R2,Backward,Immediate,Swap, 1 0 ,X2
d Address, 1 0 0 0 ,X1,Adrhalf2,Opcode2, 1 0 0 0 0 ,X2
d Address, 1 0 0 0 ,X1,Adrhalf2,Opcode2, 0 0 0 0 0 ,X2
e Address, 1 0 0 0 ,X1,Adrhalf2,R2,Advance2, 1 0 0 1 0 ,On2,Xs2
e Address, 1 0 0 0 ,X1,Adrhalf2,R2,Advance2, 1 0 0 1 1 ,On2,Xs2
f Address, 1 0 0 0 ,X1,Adrhalf2,Indicator2, 1 0 0 0 ,Reset,On2,Xs2
g Address, 1 0 0 0 ,X1,Adrhalf2, 1 1 1 0 0 0 0 0 0 ,Invert,Reset2,On2,Xs2
h Adrword,Norm,Absolute,Negate,Opfl, 1 0 ,X1
i Adrhalf,Opcode, 0 0 0 0 0 ,X1
j Adrhalf,R1,Opxd,1,X1
k Adrhalf,R1, 1 0 0 0 0 ,Opxi
l Adrhalf,R1,Advance, 1 0 0 1 0 ,On,Xs
l Adrhalf,R1,Advance, 1 0 0 1 1 ,On,Xs
m Adrhalf,Indicator, 1 0 0 0 ,Reset,On,Xs
```

PROGRAM 13-80   Instruction syntax of the IBM Stretch.

Types of control.   Control allocation is very elaborate. Besides the many instruction formats, there are various index fields and 64 indicators to be allocated.

```
          control7030
        ⋒ IBM Stretch control allocation
          instruction7030
          index7030
          indicator7030
```

PROGRAM 13-81   Control allocation in the IBM Stretch.

Instruction format.   The 13 syntactic-pattern groups are summarized as 10 instruction formats. The address field is leftmost in the instruction and appears as a 24-bit address, a 19-bit halfword address, and an 18-bit word

address. The 4-bit index-address field is rightmost in the halfwords of the format. In some formats this field is truncated to 1 bit to fit the format, which leaves the choice between no indexing and indexing with register 1. The immediate index-arithmetic format is the only format without an indexed address field. To improve clarity, the various modifier bits of the syntactic patterns are shown as opcode bits in the formats.

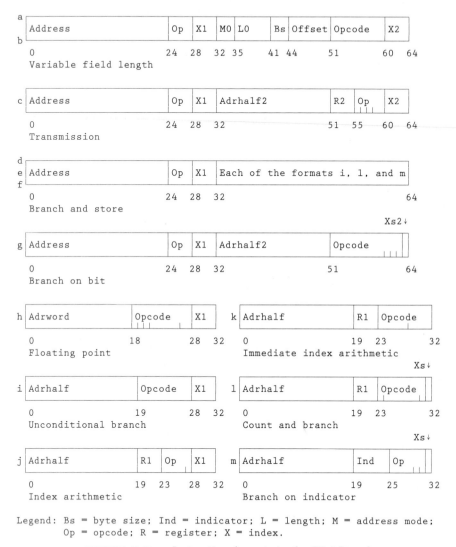

Legend: Bs = byte size; Ind = indicator; L = length; M = address mode;
        Op = opcode; R = register; X = index.

FIGURE 13-82   Instruction formats in the IBM Stretch.

Instruction allocation.   The allocation function shows the many fields and modifier bits of the instructions. The suffix 2 relates a field in the second halfword to a corresponding field in the first halfword. The address type field is used implicitly in the syntax; it is used explicitly in decoding the address lengths of the various instructions.

```
instruction7030
ᴀ IBM Stretch instruction allocation
ᴀ operation specification              ᴀ transmission
 Opcode←19+ι4                           Backward←55
 Opfl←21+ι5                             Immediate←56
 Opxd←23+ι4                             Swap←57
 Opxi←28+ι4                            ᴀ fixed-point arithmetic
 Opcode2←51+ι4                          Nosign←51
 Opvl←54+ι5                             Negate2←52
 Opcn←55+ι2                             Decimal←53
ᴀ operand specification               ᴀ connectives
ᴀ - address type                       Con←51+ι4
 Type←24+ι4                            ᴀ floating-point arithmetic
ᴀ - displacement                       Norm←18
 Address←0+ι24                          Absolute←19
 Adrword←0+ι18                          Negate←20
 Adrhalf←0+ι19                         ᴀ index arithmetic
 Adrhalf2←32+ι19                        Advance←23+ι2
ᴀ - index                              Advance2←55+ι2
 X1←28+ι4                              ᴀ branch
 X2←60+ι4                               Indicator←19+ι6
 Xs←31                                  Indicator2←51+ι6
 Xs2←63                                 Invert←60
ᴀ - register                           Reset←29
 R1←19+ι4                               Reset2←61
 R2←51+ι4                               On←30
ᴀ - variable length                    On2←62
 M0←32+ι3
 L0←35+ι6
 Byte←41+ι3
 Offset←44+ι7
```

PROGRAM 13-83   Instruction allocation in the IBM Stretch.

Status format.   The Stretch introduced the concept of summarizing status in a single bit vector, the 64-bit indicator register. Most bits signal errors or results (Program 13-127). Only bit 63, the floating-point noisy-mode bit, acts as a controlling switch. Bits 41 through 47, the Programmed indicators, are intended to be set by the general Load and Store instructions. Bit 14 of the indicator register is unused.

Indicator types.   Indicators are used in branching and interruption. The first 20 indicators always interrupt when the system is enabled; the next 28 may be masked; the last 16 never interrupt. Indicators that report events and stay on until turned off by programming or interruption are called *permanent*; indicators that are set on or off by successive events are called *temporary*.

13.3.4

Addressing

Direct addressing.   Addressing is direct to the word, halfword, or bit. Variable-length data are specified by a start bit-address and field length in bits. Variable-length fields may fall anywhere in the memory bit string: There are no alignment constraints for such fields. Bytes may overlap word boundaries.

Reading distinguishes immediate data obtained from the instruction from data obtained directly from memory. Immediate data are derived from the address field. Direct data are specified by a scalar address and are subject to

```
 ┌Machine checks        Transmission┐  ┌Programmed
 │   ↓Timer,external        Flags↓   │  │        Noisy mode↓
 ↓   │                               ↓  ↓        │
┌────┬──┬───────────────┬────┬──┬──────┬───────┐
│    │  │ I/O │ Exceptions        │    │  │Index │ Result│
│    │  │     │                   │    │  │      │       │
└────┴──┴─────┴───────────────────┴────┴──┴──────┴───────┘
0    4  6     15                  35   41 48    55       64
111111111111111111111mmmmmmmmmmmmmmmmmmmmmmmmmmmmmm0000000000000000
ppppppppppppppppppppppppppppppppppppppptttttppppppppppptttttttttttttttttttp
Legend: m = masked; p = permanent; t = temporary.
```

```
indicator7030
ค indicators IBM Stretch
ค equipment              ค result exception     ค index result
Machine←0                Lostcarry←22           Countzero←48
Instcheck←1              Partialfld←23          Valueneg←49
Instreject←2            Zerodivisor←24          Valuezero←50
Exchangecheck←3          ค floating point       Valuepos←51
ค attention              Imaginaryroot←25       Indexlow←52
Timer←4                  Lostsgnf←26            Indexequal←53
Externalcpu←5            Lowsgnf←27             Indexhigh←54
ค i/o reject             Expflagpos←28          ค to-memory operation
Exchangecheck←6          Floflo←29              Tomem←55
Unitnotready←7           Exphigh←30             ค arithmetic result
Channelbusy←8            Explow←31              Neg←56
ค i/o status             Fluflo←32              Zero←57
Exprogramcheck←9         Expflagneg←33          Pos←58
Unitcheck←10             Remainderuflo←34       Negsign←59
Endexception←11          ค flags                Low←60
Endoperation←12          Dataflags←35+13        Equal←61
Channelsignal←13         Indexflag←38           High←62
ค unused←14              ค transit mode         ค noisy mode
ค instruction            Binarytransit←39       Noisy←63
Invop←15                 Decimaltransit←40
Invadr←16                ค programmable
Unendingseq←17           Programmed←41+17
Execute←18
Datastore←19
Datafetch←20
Instfetch←21
```

PROGRAM 13-84   Indicators in the IBM Stretch.

protection (Program 13-125). Writing applies only to memory; it is suppressed when a location is protected or some other program error is detected.

```
data←size read7030 address;location    address write7030 data;location
ค IBM Stretch read from memory          ค IBM Stretch write in memory
→IF 1=ppaddress                         location←address+ιpdata
THEN: ค immediate data                  Datastore protect7030 location
   data←size↑address                    →OUT suppress7030
   →ENDIF                               memory[location]←data
ELSE: ค normal address
   location←address+ιsize
   Datafetch protect7030 location
   data←memory[memcap|location]
ENDIF:
```

PROGRAM 13-85   Memory read and write in the IBM Stretch.

Address Modification

Index word. The 64-bit index word contains a signed index value represented with signed-magnitude notation, the index proper; an unsigned 18-bit count to

be counted down during an iteration; a next-index address, which addresses another index word in memory to replace the current word when the count reaches 0; and an index flag that sets an indicator and therefore can be used in branching and interruption. The 16 index words are embedded in memory; they are accessed by `regin` and `regout`. The secondary result of an indexing action is noted in the five index indicators.

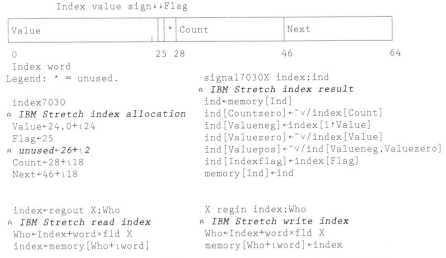

PROGRAM 13-86   Index format and access in the IBM Stretch.

Address calculation.   The primary indexing mode uses base-displacement address modification. This mode varies according to the size of the address

```
address←adr7030
⍝ IBM Stretch indexed address
→CASE((inst[ΦType]ι1)= 3 1 2)ι1
C0: ⍝ bit address
    address←Address modify7030 X1
    →ENDCASE
C1: ⍝ word address
    address←Adrword modify7030 X1
    →ENDCASE
C2: ⍝ short-index address
    address←Adrhalf modify7030 Xs
    →ENDCASE
C3: ⍝ half-word address
    address←Adrhalf modify7030 X1
ENDCASE:


address←adr7030h2
⍝ IBM Stretch half-word address-2
address←Adrhalf2 modify7030 X2


address←adr7030s2
⍝ IBM Stretch short-index address-2
address←Adrhalf2 modify7030 Xs2
```

```
address←adr7030m
⍝ IBM Stretch bit-address modes
→CASE fld M0
C0: ⍝ indexed address
    address←Address modify7030 X1
    →ENDCASE
C1: ⍝ increment
    address←X1 incr7030 fld Address
    →ENDCASE
C2: ⍝ increment, count
    address←X1 incr7030c fld Address
    →ENDCASE
C3: ⍝ increment, count, refill
    address←X1 incr7030cr fld Address
    →ENDCASE
C4: ⍝ immediate address
    address←(ρAddress) magnr adr7030
    Invop report tomem
    →ENDCASE
C5: ⍝ decrement
    address←X1 incr7030-fld Address
    →ENDCASE
C6: ⍝ decrement, count
    address←X1 incr7030c-fld Address
    →ENDCASE
C7: ⍝ decrement, count, refill
    address←X1 incr7030cr-fld Address
ENDCASE:
```

PROGRAM 13-87   Addressing in the IBM Stretch.

(the presence or absence of low-order address bits), the size of the index field (normally 4 bits, occasionally 1 bit), and the halfword of the instruction to which it applies. The index value is signed; the displacement is unsigned.

A secondary indexing mode applies only to bit addressing. This mode allows three increment and three decrement submodes (called *progressive* indexing), an immediate address, and base-displacement modification.

Address modification.   The 24-bit signed index value is algebraically added to the direct address to yield the effective address. A zero index address implies no indexing. The resulting address is always a bit address. Word and halfword addresses must be extended with low-order 0 bits; corresponding low-order bits of the index value do not participate in the addition, but the index sign does. The absolute value of the sum of index and displacement is used as an address.

Alignment.   Index, floating-point, and I/O control words are aligned on a word boundary; instructions are aligned on a halfword. Alignment is enforced by ignoring the low-order five or six address bits; there is no alarm if these bits are not 0.

```
address←A modify7030 X;size;ix;index;displacement
⍝ IBM Stretch address modification
size←radix*adrsize-0⊥1+⍴A
ix←(0≠fld X)∧(regout X)[Value]
index←size align7030 signmagni ix        out←size align7030 in
displacement←size×fld A                   ⍝ IBM Stretch alignment
address←|index+displacement               out←(×in)×size×⌊|in÷size
```

PROGRAM 13-88   Address modification and alignment in the IBM Stretch.

Stack and list addressing.   Progressive indexing gives automatic incrementing and decrementing of index values after each use, anticipating the postincrement of the DEC PDP11 (1970). So progressive indexing is suitable for lists. It is not suitable for stacks, since there is no predecrement. The increment and decrement may be with counting, and, if so, with or without a refill. This refill of an index word gives smooth list-pointer following.

```
address←X incr7030 addend;augend;index;sum
⍝ IBM Stretch increment
index←regout X
augend←signmagni index[Value]
sum←augend+addend
index[Value]←adrsize signmagnr sum
address←|augend
X regin index
signal7030X index


address←X incr7030c addend;augend;index;sum;count
⍝ IBM Stretch increment, count
index←regout X
augend←signmagni index[Value]              address←X incr7030cr addend;next
sum←augend+addend                          ⍝ IBM Stretch increment, count, refill
index[Value]←adrsize signmagnr sum         address←X incr7030c addend
address←|augend                            →If memory[Ind[Countzero]]
count←(magni index[Count])-1               THEN: ⍝ refill
index[Count]←(⍴Count) magnr count            next←word×magni(regout X)[Next]
X regin index                                X regin word read7030 next
signal7030X index                          ENDIF:
```

PROGRAM 13-89   Increment, decrement, count, and refill in the IBM Stretch.

The Next field, which specifies an index word used for a refill, is a word address. The progressive indexing modes set the index indicators; they are set prior to a possible refill.

Index Arithmetic

Index operations.   The rich set of index arithmetic instructions illustrates the consequences of the compound structure of the index word. Each component needs its Load and Store—and possibly an Add, Subtract, and Compare—but it must also be possible to invoke the count and refill actions. These requirements result in some 30 of the 34 instructions, which in turn are a sizeable part of the total 118 machine instructions.

```
j LX    Load Index                 k AVI  Add I To Value
j LV    Load Value                 k ACI  Add I To Count
j LC    Load Count                 k AVCI Add I To Value, Count
j LR    Load R                     k AVRI Add I To Value, Count, R
j LVE   Load Value Effective       k SVI  Subtract I From Value
k LVS   Load Value With Sum        k SCI  Subtract I From Count
k LVI   Load Value I               k SVCI Subtract I From Value, Count
k LVNI  Load Value Negative I      k SVRI Subtract I From Value, Count, R
k LCI   Load Count I               j KV   Compare Value
k LRI   Load R I                   j KC   Compare Count
j SX    Store Index                k KVI  Compare Value I
j SV    Store Value                k KVNI Compare Value Negative I
j SC    Store Count                k KCI  Compare Count I
j SR    Store R                    i R    R Index
j SVA   Store Value In Address     i RCZ  R Index On Zero Count
j AV    Add To Value               j RNX  Rename Index
j AVC   Add To Value, Count
j AVCR  Add To Value, Count, R
Legend: I = Immediate; R = Refill.
```

TABLE 13-90   Index arithmetic instructions of the IBM Stretch.

Index Load and Store.   Most index arithmetic instructions use a halfword address. In loading an index value, however, the halfword bit of the address is ignored, and word addressing is used. Since the index fields do not fit the halfword, they are extended on storing and truncated on fetching.

```
LX;index;address                   SVA;od;size;index
ᴀ IBM Stretch Load Index           ᴀ IBM Stretch Store Value In Address
address←word align7030 adr7030     od←half read7030 adr7030
index←word read7030 address        size← 18 19 18 24 18[od[ΦType]ι1]
R1 regin index                     index←regout R1
signal7030X index                  od[ιsize]←size↑index[1↓Value]
                                   adr7030 write7030 od
                                   signal7030X index

SC;index
ᴀ IBM Stretch Store Count
index←regout R1
adr7030 write7030(-half)↑index[Count]
signal7030X index
```

PROGRAM 13-91   Index Load and Store in the IBM Stretch.

Store in address field.   A computed value can be fitted easily in the address field of an instruction with variable field-length bit addressing. The length

of an address field depends upon the instruction format, however, so the assembler is aided by Store Value In Address, which gives the address field the length specified by the `Type` field.

Index addition.   The index value addition and its modification give the same functions as found in progressive indexing, except that the index value is not used as an address.

```
AVC;ad;temp
 ⍝ IBM Stretch Add To Value, Count
 ad←half read7030 adr7030
 →OUT suppress7030
 temp←R1 incr7030c signmagni ad[Value]
```

PROGRAM 13-92   Index addition in the IBM Stretch.

Indirect addressing.   Load Value Effective provides infinite-level indirect addressing, with a distinct index applied at each level. The instruction loads the effective address of a subject instruction in a specified index register. When the subject instruction is another LVE, the action repeats. Since an unending loop could easily be established, a time-out of 1 ms (about 100 levels) is used, as indicated by comments.

```
LVE;inst0;index
 ⍝ IBM Stretch Load Value Effective
 index←regout R1 WHERE inst0←inst
 ⍝ start time-out
 REPEAT:inst←half read7030 adr7030
   ⍝ →OUT time-out exceeded
 →UNTIL 'LVE '∨.≠oplist[decode inst;]
 index[Value]←adrsize signmagnr adr7030
 R1 regin index WHERE inst←inst0
 signal7030X index
```

PROGRAM 13-93   Loading of effective address in the IBM Stretch.

Cumulative indexing.   A ghastly example of inconsistent and over-rich architecture, Load Value With Sum, treats the address as a bit vector designating the 16 index registers, and sums those whose designator bits are 1. The selected value fields form a matrix. The signed-magnitude values of each row form a vector, and the sum reduction of that value is placed in the value field of the specified index.

```
LVS;mask;sum;index
 ⍝ IBM Stretch Load Value With Sum
 mask←Index+word×inst[⍳16]/⍳16
 sum←+/signmagni memory[mask∘.+Value]
 index←regout R1
 index[Value]←adrsize signmagnr sum
 R1 regin index
 signal7030X index
```

PROGRAM 13-94   Cumulative indexing in the IBM Stretch.

Index renaming.   Although 16 indices have proved to be generally adequate, even without the count and refill options, Rename Index is intended to extend this number with virtual indices. The specified index is stored at the location

specified by the `Next` field of index zero. Then, the addressed word replaces the specified index, and its address is in turn recorded in the `Next` field of index 0. Thus an index word in an arbitrary memory location can be mapped onto an index register.

```
RNX;next;index
∩ IBM Stretch Rename Index
next←word×magni memory[Index+Next]
next write7030 regout R1
memory[Index+Next]←(ρNext) magnr⌊adr7030÷word
index←word read7030 word×magni memory[Index+Next]
R1 regin index
signal7030X index
```

PROGRAM 13-95   Index renaming in the IBM Stretch.

Address Level

Immediate addressing.   The Stretch first formalized the concept of immediate addressing.   It is used extensively.   Immediate operands applying to the various index fields are obtained from the first 19 or 18 bits of the address field. The immediate operand is not indexed.

```
LVI;index
∩ IBM Stretch Load Value Immediate
index←regout R1
index[Value]←adrsize↑0.inst[Adrhalf]
R1 regin index
signal7030X index
```

PROGRAM 13-96   Immediate index load in the IBM Stretch.

Immediate index addition.   All options of counting and refilling are available with immediate addition and subtraction.

```
AVRI;temp
∩ IBM Stretch Add Immediate To Value, Count, Refill
temp←R1 incr7030cr half×fld Adrhalf
```

PROGRAM 13-97   Immediate index add in the IBM Stretch.

Immediate index comparison.   Index comparison sets a separate set of index indicators. The immediate field is extended with low-order bits in comparing the index value. The count comparison requires only an 18-bit immediate field.

```
KVI;operand;comparand                   operand signal7030XC comparand;ind
∩ IBM Stretch Compare Value Immediate   ∩ IBM Stretch compare index
comparand←half×fld Adrhalf              ind←memory[Ind]
operand←signmagni(regout R1)[Value]     ind[Indexlow]←operand<comparand
operand signal7030XC comparand          ind[Indexequal]←operand=comparand
                                        ind[Indexhigh]←operand>comparand
                                        ind[Indexflag]←(regout R1)[Flag]
KCI;operand;comparand                   memory[Ind]←ind
∩ IBM Stretch Compare Count Immediate
comparand←fld Adrword
operand←magni(regout R1)[Count]
operand signal7030XC comparand
```

PROGRAM 13-98   Immediate index compare in the IBM Stretch.

13.3.5
Data

Character Strings

Character set and size.   Stretch was the first 8-bit byte machine. It includes a new 120-character set, with upper- and lowercase alphabets that differ in the low-order code bits. The set was not used in any later machine. The subscript numerals and some of the special characters are not found in current 8-bit sets.

```
data7030                                       ◊16  16ρchar7030
⋒ IBM Stretch data representation    [&cks08∘∘∘∘∘∘∘∘∘
⋒ character encoding                 α⊃+CKSΔΔ∘∘∘∘∘∘∘∘
 charcode←char7030                   →]$dlt19∘∘∘∘∘∘∘∘
⋒ sign encoding                      ≠O=DLTΔΔ∘∘∘∘∘∘∘∘
 plus←0                              ∧←*emu2.∘∘∘∘∘∘∘∘
 minus←1                             ≡(EMUΔ:∘∘∘∘∘∘∘∘
                                     ↑ι/fnv3-∘∘∘∘∘∘∘∘
                                     ρ)FNVΔ?∘∘∘∘∘∘∘∘
 signal7030NZP result;ind            ∨%.gow4∘∘∘∘∘∘∘∘∘
⋒ IBM Stretch numeric result         ∈\;GOWΔ∘∘∘∘∘∘∘∘∘  Legend:
 ind←memory[Ind]                     ↓◊'hpx5∘∘∘∘∘∘∘∘∘  α = plus-minus;
 ind[Neg]←result<0                   ω|"HPXΔ∘∘∘∘∘∘∘∘∘  ∈ = exclusive-or;
 ind[Zero]←result=0                  >⌗aiqy6∘∘∘∘∘∘∘∘∘  ω = double bar;
 ind[Pos]←result>0                   ≥!AIQYΔ∘∘∘∘∘∘∘∘∘  ι = not;
 ind[Negsign]←result<0               <@bjrz7∘∘∘∘∘∘∘∘∘  ρ = root;
 memory[Ind]←ind                     ≤˜BJRZΔ∘∘∘∘∘∘∘∘∘  Δ = subscript digit.
```

PROGRAM 13-99   Data specification and character set in the IBM Stretch.

Character string formats.   Character strings may be 1 through 64 bits long, beginning at any bit. Byte size may be 1 through 8 bits. A 7-bit byte accommodates the new character set; a 6-bit byte, the standard BCD set. Note that alphabetical and numerical strings, and fields in file records, can use different byte sizes freely and easily. There are no character-handling operations other than those that are part of the logical and arithmetic operations.

Logical

Logical formats.   Any bit vector of 1 through 64 bits can be treated as a single operand. Logical data are treated as consisting of bytes. The accumulator has 8-bit bytes by definition. The size of the memory bytes is specified in the instruction.

Secondary results.   The arithmetic value of a logical or arithmetic result is noted in the indicators. Many other secondary results are noted as part of the operation or result representation.

Fixed-Point Numbers

Notation.   Fixed-point numbers use signed-magnitude notation. The radix is 2 or 10, depending upon the `Decimal` modifier. The sign and digits are in turn represented in bits. The notation may include flag bits. Negative zero is signaled by the negative sign indicator. Our manual does not detail the occurrence of negative zero; hence it is not described.

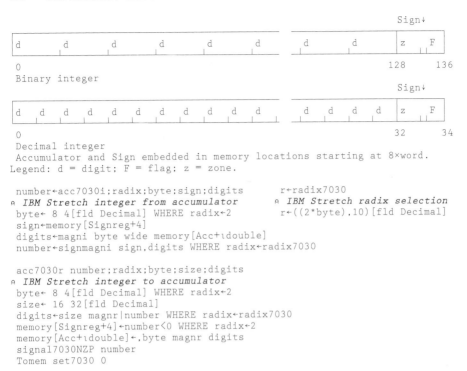

```
number←acc7030i;radix;byte;sign;digits       r←radix7030
ⓐ IBM Stretch integer from accumulator     ⓐ IBM Stretch radix selection
byte← 8 4[fld Decimal] WHERE radix←2         r←((2*byte),10)[fld Decimal]
sign←memory[Signreg+4]
digits←magni byte wide memory[Acc+ιdouble]
number←signmagni sign,digits WHERE radix←radix7030

acc7030r number;radix;byte;size;digits
ⓐ IBM Stretch integer to accumulator
byte← 8 4[fld Decimal] WHERE radix←2
size← 16 32[fld Decimal]
digits←size magnr|number WHERE radix←radix7030
memory[Signreg+4]←number<0 WHERE radix←2
memory[Acc+ιdouble]←,byte magnr digits
signal7030NZP number
Tomem set7030 0
```

PROGRAM 13-100   Accumulator operand representation in the IBM Stretch.

Accumulator operand allocation.   The fixed-point allocation is complex because of its many generalized modifiers and because the accumulator allocation differs from the memory allocation. The numeric field is divided into bytes. In binary arithmetic, all bits in a numeric byte are used to form a digit. In decimal arithmetic, only the four low-order bits are numeric. The high-order bits in the byte (if any) are zone bits. In the accumulator, the byte size is 8 for binary arithmetic, and 4 for decimal arithmetic. The sign is placed to the right of the digits in a sign byte. In decimal arithmetic, the accumulator uses two 4-bit bytes for the sign, which differs from the sign byte in memory.

Memory operand allocation.   In memory, the byte size is instruction-specified. Signed fields may carry a 1- to 3-bit flag field that can be set and tested. A sign byte of size 1 contains the sign; for sizes 2 through 4, there are one to three flags to the right of the sign; for sizes 5 through 8, there are up to four zone bits to the left of the sign. In signed operation the three flag indicators are set. If there are fewer than three flags, the remaining flag indicators are set to 0. Unsigned operands have no sign byte, and hence no flags and no binary zones.

Floating-Point Numbers

Closure and normal form.   Operands may be normalized or unnormalized. Results are or are not normalized depending upon the normalization modifier. A number is interpreted as being in the positive or negative extremum range when the high-order exponent bit, the extremum bit, is on. Arithmetic operations with normal operands may cause an exponent overflow or underflow

Sign↓

```
┌──────────────────────────────────────────┬─────┐
│ d d    d     d     d     d     d     d    │ z  F│
│ └─    └──   └──   └──   └──   └──   └──    │ └┴  │
```

0   44   50
Signed binary memory integer with size 50 and byte size 6

↓Zone

```
┌───────────────────────────────────────────┐
│ d   d    d    d    d    d    d    d    d    │
│ └┴  └┴   └┴   └┴   └┴   └┴   └┴   └┴   └┴   │
```

0   9
Unsigned decimal memory integer with size 43 and byte size 5
Legend: d = digit; F = flag; z = zone.

```
number←mem7030i rep;radix;byte;signbyte;sign;zone;digits
ᴀ IBM Stretch integer from memory
byte←fld0 Byte WHERE radix←2
→IF fld Nosign
THEN: ᴀ unsigned
   sign←plus
   →ENDIF
ELSE: ᴀ signed
   signbyte←(-byte)↑rep
   sign←signbyte[0⌈byte-4]
   Dataflags set7030 3↑(1⌈byte-3)↓signbyte
   rep←(-byte)↓rep
ENDIF:zone←0,(0⌈byte-4)×fld Decimal
digits←magni zone↓byte wide rep
number←signmagni sign,digits WHERE radix←radix7030

od←od mem7030r number;radix;byte;size;digits;Num;rep;signbyte
ᴀ IBM Stretch integer to memory
byte←fld0 Byte WHERE radix←2
size←⌈(ρod)÷byte
digits←size magnr|number WHERE radix←radix7030
rep←,byte magnr digits WHERE radix←2
Num←(Φ(ρod)ρbyte↑ 8 4[fld Decimal]ρ1)/ιρod
→If˜fld Nosign
THEN: ᴀ signed
   signbyte←(-byte)↑od
   signbyte[0⌈byte-4]←number<0
   rep←rep,signbyte
ENDIF:od[Num]←((-ρod)↑rep)[Num]    ideal report7030PF fitted
signal7030NZP number               ᴀ IBM Stretch partial field report
Tomem set7030 1                    Partialfld report7030(|ideal)≠|fitted
```

PROGRAM 13-101   Memory operand representation in the IBM Stretch.

from the normal range into the extremum range. This case is noted by the `Floflo` and `Fluflo` indicators. Operands in the positive extremum range act as pseudo-infinite values and give extreme results that relate to the exponent values of the operands; operands in the negative extremum range are considered negligible and may give normal or extreme results. Extreme results created by extreme operands set the `Expflagpos` or `Expflagneg` indicator. The extremum system is not complete, however. Indefinite results, such as for a positive pseudo-infinite number added to a negative pseudo-infinite number, are not recognized; the result is made pseudo-infinite instead. Within the normal range, two upper ranges of positive exponent values are noted that set the `Exphigh` and `Explow` indicators (Program 13-103). Underflow produces a true 0.

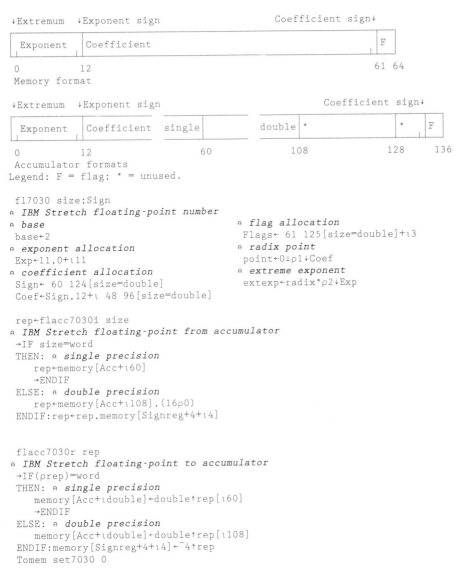

Legend: F = flag; * = unused.

```
f17030 size;Sign
A IBM Stretch floating-point number
A base                             A flag allocation
base←2                            Flags← 61 125[size=double]+ι3
A exponent allocation              A radix point
Exp←11,0+ι11                      point←0⌷ρ1↓Coef
A coefficient allocation           A extreme exponent
Sign← 60 124[size=double]         extexp←radix*ρ2↓Exp
Coef←Sign,12+ι 48 96[size=double]


rep←flacc7030i size
A IBM Stretch floating-point from accumulator
→IF size=word
THEN: A single precision
    rep←memory[Acc+ι60]
    →ENDIF
ELSE: A double precision
    rep←memory[Acc+ι108],(16ρ0)
ENDIF:rep←rep,memory[Signreg+4+ι4]


flacc7030r rep
A IBM Stretch floating-point to accumulator
→IF(ρrep)=word
THEN: A single precision
    memory[Acc+ιdouble]←double↑rep[ι60]
    →ENDIF
ELSE: A double precision
    memory[Acc+ιdouble]←double↑rep[ι108]
ENDIF:memory[Signreg+4+ι4]←¯4↑rep
Tomem set7030 0
```

PROGRAM 13-102   Floating-point number allocation in the IBM Stretch.

Floating-point format.   Floating point has a single 64-bit format in memory with 12-bit exponent, 49-bit coefficient, and three data flag bits. These flags may be used to mark singular numbers. The accumulator accommodates a single and a double format. The two accumulator formats differ only by the coefficient being either 48 or 96 bits. The accumulator format departs from the memory format by placing the sign and flag bits in the sign register. Mapping to and from the accumulator format occurs with flacc7030i and flacc7030r.

Floating-point representation.   Exponent and coefficient are binary signed magnitudes with the sign to the right of the digits, in accordance with the fixed-point formats. As a floating-point word is interpreted, the Dataflag indicators may be set (usually for the memory operand) or left unchanged

(usually for the accumulator operand).   Representation may be with or without noise (low-order 1 bits entered instead of 0 bits during left shift in normalization) as specified by the Noisy indicator.

```
 numexp←fl7030i rep;exponent;coefficient;number
ᴀ IBM Stretch floating-point interpretation
 fl7030ρrep
 exponent←signmagni rep[Exp]
 coefficient←signmagni rep[Coef]
 number←coefficient×base*exponent-point
 numexp←number,exponent


 numexp←fl7030if rep
ᴀ IBM Stretch floating-point interpretation with flag
 numexp←fl7030i rep
 Dataflags set7030 rep[Flags]


 rep←size fl7030r numexp;exponent;coefficient;noise
ᴀ IBM Stretch floating-point representation
 fl7030 size WHERE rep←sizeρ0
 (1↓numexp) normalize(-fld Norm)↓numexp
 noise←0⌊memory[Ind[Noisy]]×(×1↑numexp)×(base*(1↓numexp)-exponent)-1
 rep[Coef]←(ρCoef) signmagnr truncate coefficient+noise
 rep[Exp]←(ρExp) signmagnr exponent
 Floflo report7030(˜memory[Ind[Expflagpos]])∧exponent≥extexp
 Fluflo report7030(˜memory[Ind[Expflagneg]])∧exponent≤-extexp
 Exphigh report7030(exponent≥2*9)∧exponent<extexp
 Explow report7030(exponent≥2*6)∧exponent<2*9
 signal7030NZP 1↑numexp
```

PROGRAM 13-103   Floating-point representation in the IBM Stretch.

13.3.6

Operations

Data Handling

Fields of 1 through 64 bits may be moved arbitrarily via the accumulator.

Data movement.   The two-address multiple-word Move illustrates the use of modifiers in the Stretch. Only one instruction is involved, but the modifiers result in many operations. A block of 64-bit words is moved from a source memory location (including the working store) to a destination location.

The Backward modifier gives a choice between decrementing or incrementing the source and destination addresses. Decrementing can be useful when the source and destination fields overlap. The Immediate modifier specifies the choice between an immediate length from 1 through 16, as specified by the R2 field, and a direct length of 1 through 256 K, as specified by the Count field of index R2. The Swap modifier gives the option of moving blocks from source to destination versus swapping source and destination blocks.

```
T;step;length;dest;source;od
ᴀ IBM Stretch Move
ᴀ direction of move
step←word× 1 ⁻1[fld Backward]
→IF fld Immediate
THEN: ᴀ immediate length
    length←fld0 R2
    →ENDIF
ELSE: ᴀ direct length
    length←magn0(regout R2)[Count]
ENDIF:dest←word align7030 adr7030
source←word align7030 adr7030s2
REPEAT:→CASE fld Swap
    C0: ᴀ transmit
        dest write 7030 word read7030 source
        →ENDCASE
    C1: ᴀ swap
        od←word read7030 dest
        dest write7030 word read7030 source
        source write7030 od
    ENDCASE:length←length-1
    dest←dest+step
    source←source+step
→UNTIL length=0
```

PROGRAM 13-104   Move in the IBM Stretch.

Logic

The Connect instructions can specify each of the 16 logical connectives of two variables. The three instructions vary with respect to the place or absence of the primary result: in the accumulator, in memory, or no primary result. Secondary results are: several indicators, a left-zero count, and an all-ones count. No flags are signaled.

```
b C     Connect
b CM    Connect To Memory
b CT    Connect For Test
```

TABLE 13-105   Logical connectives of the IBM Stretch.

Connectives.   The Connect is plagued by the extraneous byte size. The memory-operand length is specified by L0 (where zero is interpreted as 64); the operand is formed in a matrix of bytes of size Byte (where zero is interpreted as 8). These bytes are extended byte-by-byte with 0s to 8 bits, the byte size of the accumulator. The high-order byte, however, is extended only when it is complete. The accumulator field starts at the right with the position given by the Offset field. The accumulator field ends at the left, with the high-order accumulator bit, unless the memory field indicates a shorter field. The result size is the smallest of the extended-memory operand and the accumulator field. The result replaces the accumulator field; accumulator bits outside the result field remain unchanged.

The 16 connectives are specified in a symmetrical way by the four Conn bits. Each of these bits, when 1, specifies one of the four possible combinations of corresponding bits of the two operands. Connective bit 0 specifies that both operand bits must be 0; bit 1, that they must be 0 and 1; bit 2, that they must be 1 and 0; and bit 3, that both must be 1. The OR of the specified combinations gives the resulting connective. Thus the AND is specified by connective bit 3

```
C;od1;od2;size;od1size;rlsize;operand1;operand2;result
ᴀ IBM Stretch Connect
 od1←(fld0 Byte) wide(fld0 L0) read7030 adr7030m
 od2←8 wide memory[Acc+ɩdouble-fld Offset]
 size←(ρod2)⌊(1↑ρod1),8
 od1size←((fld0 Byte)|fld0 L0)+8×⌊(fld0 L0)÷fld0 Byte
 rlsize←(double-fld Offset)⌊od1size
 operand1←(-rlsize)↑,(-size)↑od1
 operand2←(-rlsize)↑,(-size)↑od2
 result←operand1 connect7030 operand2
 memory[(Acc+double-(rlsize+fld Offset))+ɩrlsize]←result
ᴀ counts and signals
 memory[Leftzeros]←(ρLeftzeros) magnr result⍳1
 memory[Allones]←(ρAllones) magnr+/result
 Partialfld report7030 rlsize≠od1size
 Tomem set7030 0
 signal7030NZP magni result


 r1←od1 connect7030 od2;c00;c01;c10;c11
ᴀ IBM Stretch logical connective
 c00←inst[Con[0]]∧(˜od1)∧˜od2
 c01←inst[Con[1]]∧(˜od1)∧od2
 c10←inst[Con[2]]∧od1∧˜od2
 c11←inst[Con[3]]∧od1∧od2
 r1←c00∨c01∨c10∨c11
```

PROGRAM 13-106   Logical connectives of the IBM Stretch.

being 1 and the others being 0; the OR is specified by connective bits 1, 2, and 3 being 1, and bit 0 being 0.

Vector operations.   The left-zero count and the all-ones count are recorded in dedicated memory locations. The result is also treated as a number, and is tested as such for positive, negative, and 0. The partial field indicator is set when some memory operand bits do not participate in the operation.

Shift.   Shifting operations are neither provided nor necessary. A variable-field-length Load addressing the accumulator as the memory operand accomplishes the same result.

Fixed-Point Arithmetic

Fixed-point arithmetic includes the classical set of Load, Store, Add, Multiply, Divide, and Compare. Novel variants are Add To Magnitude, Compare Range, and Compare If Equal. Many modifiers apply to the operands. The

a	L	Load	a INCM	Increment Memory
a	LWF	Load With Flag	a M	Multiply
a	LFT	Load Factor	a MA	Multiply Cumulative
a	LCV	Load Converted	a D	Divide
a	LTRS	Load Transit And Set	a CV	Convert
a	LTCV	Load Transit Converted	a DCV	Convert D
a	ST	Store	a K	Compare
i	Z	Store Zero	a KF	Compare Field
a	SRD	Store Rounded	a KR	Compare Range
a	A	Add	a KFR	Compare Field Range
a	AMG	Add To Magnitude	a KE	Compare If Equal
a	ADM	Add To Memory	a KFE	Compare Field If Equal
a	AMM	Add Magnitude To Memory		

Legend: D = Double.

TABLE 13-107   Fixed-point instructions of the IBM Stretch.

```
value←factor7030;power                result←scale7030 operand
ᴀ IBM Stretch factor                  ᴀ IBM Stretch scale and truncate to zero
→IF fld Decimal                       result←(×operand)×⌊|operand÷factor7030
THEN: ᴀ decimal
   power←(fld Offset)÷4
   value←10*⌊power                    sign←neg7030
   Invop report7030 0≠1|power         ᴀ IBM Stretch negate
   →ENDIF                             sign← 1 ¯1[fld Negate2]
ELSE: ᴀ binary
   power←fld Offset
   value←2*power
ENDIF:
```

PROGRAM 13-108   Fixed-point sign and precision control in the IBM Stretch.

sign modifier Negate obviates the need for Subtract. Numbers may be signed or unsigned, binary or decimal, with a length of 1 to 64 bits, and a relative offset of 0 to 127 bits in the accumulator. All these cases are treated (slowly) by the variable-field-length arithmetic unit.

Fixed-point modifiers.   Any integer operation specifies a memory field of 1 to 64 bits and an accumulator offset of 0 to 127 bits. The Offset modifier applies a binary or decimal shift to the memory operand, thus multiplying this operand with a power of 2 or 10. So all variable-field-length instructions incorporate a shift. The decimal shift must be a multiple of 4 bits. When an operand from the accumulator is used to obtain a result in memory, the offset has the effect of scaling down the accumulator operand by a power of 2 or 10, as in scale7030. The Decimal modifier affects the interpretation and representation functions (Program 13-101). The Negate2 modifier is applied to the result of an interpretation function.

Load and Store.   Load resets the entire accumulator before loading an integer from the specified field. The address mode may cause the integer to be immediate or direct, and, if direct, with or without incrementing, counting, and refilling. The integer may or may not be signed, and the result may be negated and displaced in the accumulator. The flags of the accumulator are set to 0. In Load With Flag the flags of the memory operand, if any, are placed in

```
L;od;operand;result                   LWF;od;operand;result;flags
ᴀ IBM Stretch Load                    ᴀ IBM Stretch Load With Flag
od←(fld0 L0) read7030 adr7030m        od←(fld0 L0) read7030 adr7030m
operand←mem7030i od                   operand←mem7030i od
result←neg7030×operand×factor7030     result←neg7030×operand×factor7030
acc7030r result                       acc7030r result
memory[Signreg+5+ι3]←0                →IF fld Nosign
result report7030PF acc7030i          THEN: ᴀ unsigned
                                           flags←3ρ0
                                           →ENDIF
                                      ELSE: ᴀ signed
ST;sfld;od;operand;rl;result               flags←3↑(¯3⌊(fld0 Byte)-1)↑od
ᴀ IBM Stretch Store                   ENDIF:memory[Signreg+5+ι3]←flags
sfld←(4⌊8-fld0 Byte)+ιfld0 Byte       result report7030PF acc7030i
od←Φ(fld0 L0)ρΦmemory[Signreg+sfld]
operand←acc7030i
result←scale7030 neg7030×operand
rl←od mem7030r result
adr7030m write7030 rl
result report7030PF mem7030i rl
```

PROGRAM 13-109   Load and Store instructions in the IBM Stretch.

the accumulator flags. Store places the accumulator integer with its flag and zone bits in memory. The `Offset` field now scales the integer down.

Load Factor loads the Factor register that is used as a multiplicand in cumulative multiplication. The Factor register has the same word format as the Remainder and the Transit registers (Program 13-112).

Sixty-four–bit integer format. The Transit, Remainder, and Factor registers each have a unique 64-bit integer format. This format has 15 hexadecimal or decimal digits and a sign; each figure is represented as a 4-bit byte.

Add and Subtract. The function of Add and Add To Memory follows from the memory and accumulator formats and the modifier functions. The two instructions illustrate the setting of the `Negsign`, `Tomem`, and `Partialfld` indicators. In Add, the first two indicators are set when the result is placed in the accumulator by `acc7030r`; in Add To Memory, they are set by `mem7030r`. `Partialfld` indicates in both instructions that significant bits of the addend are not used because they are beyond the augend and result size. If the operation still does not fit because of a carry, or because a negative result is placed in an unsigned memory field, the `Lostcarry` indicator is set. The operation Add To Magnitude is illustrated in the subsection on floating-point arithmetic (Program 13-116).

```
ADM;od;operand;dest;au;augend;addend;sum;sm
⋒ IBM Stretch Add To Memory
operand←scale7030 acc7030i              A;od;operand;addend;augend;sum
dest←adr7030m                           ⋒ IBM Stretch Add
au←(fld0 L0) read7030 dest               od←(fld0 L0) read7030 adr7030m
augend←mem7030i au                       operand←factor7030×mem7030i od
od←au mem7030r|operand                   augend←acc7030i
addend←(×operand)×mem7030i od            acc7030r operand
operand report7030PF addend              addend←acc7030i
sum←augend+neg7030×addend                operand report7030PF addend
sm←au mem7030r sum                       sum←augend+neg7030×addend
dest write7030 sm                        acc7030r sum
Lostcarry report7030 sum≠mem7030i sm     Lostcarry report7030 sum≠acc7030i
```

PROGRAM 13-110   Fixed-point addition in the IBM Stretch.

Multiply and Divide. Multiplication treats the operands as in addition. The operands are restricted to 48 or fewer bits, however, otherwise a `Partialfld` indication is given. Cumulative Multiply adds the accumulator content to the product of the multiplier in memory and the multiplicand in the Factor register. Division does not force the usual fixed-point constraint.

Programmed decimal operations. Decimal Multiply, Cumulative Multiply, and Divide are not performed directly. Instead, the Transit register is loaded, the all-zeros count is set to 0, 64, and 32, respectively, and the `Decimal-transit` indicator is set. This action causes an interruption to the operating system, which calls a system subroutine that effects the operation.

Hardware macro-instruction. Load Transit And Set loads a memory operand into the embedded Transit register, sets the offset value of the instruction in the all-ones register, places the operation code 96 in the Left-Zero Register, and notes the radix choice by setting either the binary or decimal transit indicator.

```
       MA;multiplicand;multiplier;augend;product
     ⍝ IBM Stretch Multiply Cumulative
       multiplicand←neg7030×mem7030i(fld0 L0) read7030 adr7030m
       →IF fld Decimal
       THEN: ⍝ programmed decimal
           Transit write7030 trans7030r multiplicand
           memory[Leftzeros]←7 magnr 64
           memory[Allones]←inst[Offset]
           Decimaltransit set7030 1
           →ENDIF
       ELSE: ⍝ binary
           multiplier←trans7030i memory[Factor+ιword]
           Partialfld report7030(2*48)≤multiplicand,multiplier
           augend←acc7030i
           product←augend+multiplicand×multiplier×factor7030
           acc7030r product
       ENDIF:
```

PROGRAM 13-111   Fixed-point multiply in the IBM Stretch.

This (maskable) indicator normally causes an interruption that services the macro-operation. Decimal multiply and divide have similar actions, but place different operation codes in the Left-Zero Register.

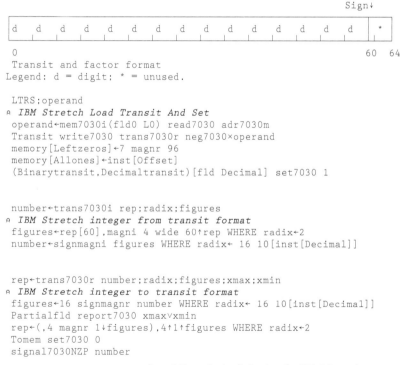

```
                                                          Sign↓
┌───┬───┬───┬───┬───┬───┬───┬───┬───┬───┬───┬───┬───┬───┬───┐
│ d │ d │ d │ d │ d │ d │ d │ d │ d │ d │ d │ d │ d │ d │ d │ * │
└───┴───┴───┴───┴───┴───┴───┴───┴───┴───┴───┴───┴───┴───┴───┘
0                                                     60   64
Transit and factor format
Legend: d = digit; * = unused.
```

```
       LTRS;operand
     ⍝ IBM Stretch Load Transit And Set
       operand←mem7030i(fld0 L0) read7030 adr7030m
       Transit write7030 trans7030r neg7030×operand
       memory[Leftzeros]←7 magnr 96
       memory[Allones]←inst[Offset]
       (Binarytransit,Decimaltransit)[fld Decimal] set7030 1
```

```
       number←trans7030i rep;radix;figures
     ⍝ IBM Stretch integer from transit format
       figures←rep[60],magni 4 wide 60↑rep WHERE radix←2
       number←signmagni figures WHERE radix← 16 10[inst[Decimal]]
```

```
       rep←trans7030r number;radix;figures;xmax;xmin
     ⍝ IBM Stretch integer to transit format
       figures←16 signmagnr number WHERE radix← 16 10[inst[Decimal]]
       Partialfld report7030 xmax∨xmin
       rep←(,4 magnr 1↓figures),4↑1↑figures WHERE radix←2
       Tomem set7030 0
       signal7030NZP number
```

PROGRAM 13-112   Load Transit And Set in the IBM Stretch.

Radix conversion.   Radix conversion acts as a Load with the radix choice inverted after the memory integer is obtained. A separate operation loads the Transit register instead of the accumulator. Radix conversion is needed by the subroutines that give programmed decimal multiplication and division.

```
LCV;operand;result;flags;zone
ᴀ IBM Stretch Load Converted
operand←mem7030i(fld0 L0) read7030 adr7030m
result←neg7030×operand×factor7030
memory[Signreg+5+ι3]←0
inst[Decimal]←~inst[Decimal]
acc7030r result
result report7030PF acc7030i
```

PROGRAM 13-113   Fixed-point radix conversion in the IBM Stretch.

Fixed-point comparison.   The accumulator is compared with a memory operand. In Compare, the entire accumulator to the left of the offset point participates. In Compare Field, the number of accumulator bytes is made equal to the number of memory bytes.

Extended comparison.   Compare If Equal can be used to implement a series of comparisons that proceed from high to low collating order.

Range comparison.   Compare followed by Compare Range gives a comparison of the accumulator against a range specified by a lower boundary addressed in Compare and an upper boundary in Compare Range. An equal indication is obtained when the accumulator is equal to or larger than the lower boundary, and is smaller than the upper boundary.

```
K;cd;operand;comparand
ᴀ IBM Stretch Compare
cd←(fld0 L0) read7030 adr7030m
comparand←neg7030×mem7030i cd
operand←scale7030 acc7030i
operand signal7030C comparand


KE
ᴀ IBM Stretch Compare If Equal
→If memory[Ind[Equal]]
THEN: ᴀ regular compare
   K
ENDIF:


KFR;cd;operand;comparand
ᴀ IBM Stretch Compare Field Range
cd←(fld0 L0) read7030 adr7030m
comparand←neg7030×mem7030i cd
operand←field7030 scale7030|acc7030i
operand signal7030R comparand
```

```
operand signal7030C comparand;ind
ᴀ IBM Stretch compare result
ind←memory[Ind]
ind[Low]←operand<comparand
ind[Equal]←operand=comparand
ind[High]←operand>comparand
ind[Tomem]←0
memory[Ind]←ind


operand signal7030R comparand;ind
ᴀ IBM Stretch range result
ind←memory[Ind]
ind[Equal]←operand<comparand
ind[High]←operand≥comparand
ind[Tomem]←0
memory[Ind]←ind


out←field7030 in;n;modulus
ᴀ IBM Stretch field comparison
n←⌈(fld0 L0)÷fld0 Byte
→IF fld Decimal
THEN: ᴀ decimal
      modulus←10*n
      →ENDIF
ELSE: ᴀ binary
      modulus←256*n
ENDIF:out←modulus|in
```

PROGRAM 13-114   Fixed-point comparison in the IBM Stretch.

Floating-Point Arithmetic

Floating point has the classical instruction set: Load, Store, Add, Multiply, Divide, Compare. It also has the extensions encountered in fixed point: Load With Flag, Add To Magnitude, Add To Memory, Cumulative Multiply, and Compare Range. Special to the floating-point set are Square-Root and Reciprocal Divide. Four operations apply to the coefficient or exponent subfields. All operations have a Negate, Absolute, and Normalized modifier. Applicable operations can be specified with double format in the accumulator.

```
h FL    F Load                     h SHF   Shift Coefficient
h DL      Load D                   h AF    Add To Coefficient
h FLWF  F Load With Flag           h AE    Add To Exponent
h DLWF    Load With Flag D         h AEI   Add I To Exponent
h FLFT  F Load Factor              h FM    F Multiply
h FST   F Store                    h DM    Multiply D
h SLO   F Store Low Order          h FMA   F Multiply Cumulative
h FSRD  F Store Rounded            h FD    F Divide
h FSRT  F Store Root               h DD    Divide D
h FA    F Add                      h FRD   F Reciprocal Divide
h DA      Add D                    h FK    F Compare
h FAMG  F Add To Magnitude         h FKR   F Compare Range
h DAMG    Add To Magnitude D       h FKM   F Compare Magnitude
h FADM  F Add To Memory            h FKMR  F Compare Magnitude Range
h FAMM  F Add Magnitude To Memory
Legend: D = Double; F = Floating-Point; I = Immediate.
```

TABLE 13-115   Floating-point instructions of the IBM Stretch.

Floating-point Add and Subtract.   Add shows the general pattern of a floating-point operation. Operations with extreme operands have the operand with largest exponent as a result. `extadd7030` gives the ascending order of the operand exponents and the upper and lower boundaries of the normal range in the sort index s. When both operands are below the lower boundary, the largest of the two is taken. Otherwise, the last element of the sort index determines which extreme operand is used as result or whether a normal operation is performed.

The normal operation preshifts and truncates the operands. The preshift is also used with an order-of-magnitude zero. An excessive preshift is noted. The addend has its sign changed, as specified by the modifiers. The result is or is not normalized, depending upon the corresponding modifier, and secondary results, such as flags, are signaled (Program 13-103).

Augment.   Add To Magnitude, also known as Augment, increases or decreases the magnitude of the augend without changing its sign. The magnitude is never decreased below 0. This function was proposed by Brooks and Murphy [Buchholz, 1962, p. 86]. The largest magnitude of a and b can be obtained by performing $a - b + b$ with two augment instructions.

Exponent and coefficient operations.   These operations act upon the floating-point number in the accumulator. Shift Coefficient moves the coefficient left or right according to the shift amount specified in the 12 high-order bits of the effective address; the rightmost bit is the shift sign. Add To Exponent adds the exponent of the memory operand to the exponent of the accumulator operand.

```
FA;au;ad;scale;addend;augend;sum
ⴰ IBM Stretch Floating-Point Add
ad←fl7030if word read7030 adr7030
au←fl7030i flacc7030i word
→CASE extadd7030 au[1],ad[1]
C0: ⴰ normal sum
   Lowsgnf report7030 48<|au[1]-ad[1]
   scale←base*(au[1]⌈ad[1])-point
   addend←scale×truncate ad[0]÷scale
   augend←scale×truncate au[0]÷scale
   sum←(augend+flsign7030 addend),au[1]⌈ad[1]
   Lostsgnf report7030(sum[0]=0)∧(ad[0]≠0)∨au[0]≠0
   →ENDCASE
C1: ⴰ augend as sum
   sum←au
   →ENDCASE
C2: ⴰ addend as sum
   sum←(flsign7030 ad[0]),ad[1]
ENDCASE:flacc7030r word fl7030r sum


DAMG;au;ad;scale;addend;augend;sum
ⴰ IBM Stretch Add To Magnitude Double
ad←fl7030if word read7030 adr7030
au←fl7030i flacc7030i double
→CASE extadd7030 au[1],ad[1]
C0: ⴰ normal sum
   Lowsgnf report7030 48<|au[1]-ad[1]
   scale←base*(au[1]⌈ad[1])-point
   addend←scale×truncate ad[0]÷scale
   augend←scale×truncate au[0]÷scale
   sum←((×augend)×0⌈(|augend)+flsign7030 addend),au[1]⌈ad[1]
   Lostsgnf report7030(sum[0]=0)∧(ad[0]≠0)∨au[0]≠0
   →ENDCASE
C1: ⴰ augend as sum
   sum←au
   →ENDCASE
C2: ⴰ addend as sum
   sum←(flsign7030 ad[0]),ad[1]
ENDCASE:flacc7030r double fl7030r sum
```

```
result←flsign7030 operand
ⴰ IBM Stretch sign change
→If fld Absolute
THEN: ⴰ make absolute
   operand←|operand
ENDIF: ⴰ negate
result← 1 ⁻1[fld Negate]×operand



case←extadd7030 odsexp;s
ⴰ IBM Stretch addition extrema
s←Δextexp,odsexp,-extexp
→IF∧/s[0 1]∈ 1 2
THEN: ⴰ both negligible
   case←s[1]
   Expflagneg report7030 1
   →ENDIF
ELSE: ⴰ normal or infinite
   case←s[3]
   Expflagpos report7030 s[3]∈ 1 2
ENDIF:
```

PROGRAM 13-116   Floating-point addition in the IBM Stretch.

```
SHF;shift;Coefmag
ⴰ IBM Stretch Shift Coefficient
shift←signmagni 1Φ12↑adrsize signmagnr adr7030
Coefmag←12+ι96
Lostcarry report7030 shift↑memory[Acc+Coefmag]
memory[Acc+Coefmag]←96↑shift↓memory[Acc+Coefmag]
Tomem set7030 0
```

```
AEI;Exp;addend;augend;sum
ⴰ IBM Stretch Add Immediate To Exponent
Exp←11,1+ι10
addend←signmagni(adrsize signmagnr adr7030w)[Exp]
augend←signmagni memory[Acc+Exp]
sum←augend+addend
memory[Acc+Exp]←(ρExp) signmagnr sum
memory[Extremum]←xmax∨xmin∨memory[Extremum]∨od[Extremum]
signal7030NZP fl7030i flacc7030i word
Tomem set7030 0
```

PROGRAM 13-117   Exponent and coefficient operations in the IBM Stretch.

Floating-point Compare.   The floating-point comparisons set the fixed-point indicators. Extreme operands are compared on the basis of their sign and exponent value. Compare Magnitude compares the magnitude of the accumulator operand with the memory operand (whose sign is under modifier control).

```
FK:operand:comparand
⍝ IBM Stretch Floating-Point Compare
od←fl7030if flacc7030i word
cd←fl7030i word read7030 adr7030
→If∧/extexp≤|od[1],cd[1]
THEN: ⍝ extreme comparison
    od[0]←(×od[0])×base*od[1]
    cd[0]←(×cd[0])×base*cd[1]
ENDIF:od[0] signal7030C flsign7030 cd[0]
```

PROGRAM 13-118   Floating-point comparison in the IBM Stretch.

13.3.7

Instruction Sequencing

The basic execution cycle of Stretch has the classical pattern, including an interrupt facility. The instruction fetch obtains either a word or a halfword; the word length occurs only when the `Type` field of the instruction has value 8. Instructions set the `Instfetch` indicator when protection is violated. Moreover, during normal instruction fetch, addresses below 32 are not valid.

Instruction modification.   For the full-word instructions with syntactic patterns a or b (as recognized by instruction bit 59 being 1), the length, byte size, and offset fields may be modified by the value field of index X2.

```
cycle7030
⍝ basic cycle of the IBM Stretch
REPEAT:interrupt7030
    execute ifetch7030
→UNTIL stop


inst←ifetch7030
⍝ IBM Stretch instruction fetch
inst←iread7030 iadr
Invadr report7030 iadr<32
iadr←iadr+0⍳ρinst



inst←iread7030 address:size
⍝ IBM Stretch read instruction from memory
size←(half,word)[8=magni memory[memcap|address+Type]]
Instfetch protect7030 address+⍳size
inst←imodify7030 memory[memcap|address+⍳size]
```

```
inst←imodify7030 inst:Fields:value
⍝ IBM Stretch instruction modification
→If(word↑inst)[59]
THEN: ⍝ modify fields
    Fields←L0,Byte,Offset
    value←L|adr7030h2÷half
    inst[Fields]←(ρFields) magnr value
ENDIF:
```

PROGRAM 13-119   Basic cycle and instruction fetch of the IBM Stretch.

Sequencing instructions.   Sequencing has provisions for decision, iteration, and delegation, including Execute.

```
i NOP   No Operation                    l CB    Branch On Count
d NOPS  No Operation, Store             e CBS   Branch On Count, Store
i B     Branch                          l CBR   Branch On Count, R
d BS    Branch, Store                   e CBRS  Branch On Count, R Store
i BR    Jump                            i EX    Execute
d BRS   Jump, Store                     i EXIC  Execute Indirect And Count
g BB    Branch On Bit
m BI    Branch On Indicator
f BIS   Branch On Indicator, Store
Legend: R = Refill.
```

TABLE 13-120   Sequencing instructions of the IBM Stretch.

Linear Sequence

Next instruction.   Instructions must be aligned on halfword boundaries. The instruction address register increments by one or two halfwords, as appropriate to the format.

Unconditional branch.   Unconditional branches have direct or relative addresses subject to address modification. The instruction address is changed only when the branch address is valid, is not protected, and is not produced as part of a direct or indirect Execute, as shown in `branch7030`.

```
B                                 branch7030 address
ค IBM Stretch Branch              ค IBM Stretch branch test
  branch7030 adr7030                Invadr report7030 address<32
                                    Instfetch protect7030 address
                                    Execute report7030 exec=1
                                  →OUT suppress7030
BR                                iadr←address
ค IBM Stretch Jump
  branch7030 iadr+adr7030
```

PROGRAM 13-121   Unconditional Branch in the IBM Stretch.

Completion.   Because the Stretch was designed for multiprogramming, it does not have a Stop instruction, as earlier machines do. Branch Enabled and Wait (Program 13-128) puts the processor into a quiescent state until an interruption occurs.

Decision

Conditional branching.   Decisions may be on any bit in memory or on any of the 64 indicators. A 64-bit Branch On Bit tests and optionally sets or inverts any memory bit. The `On2` modifier determines whether the test is for true or false. A 32-bit Branch On Indicator depends symmetrically on any of the

```
BB;od;r1                          BI;r1
ค IBM Stretch Branch On Bit       ค IBM Stretch Branch On Indicator
  od←1 read7030 adr7030             r1←memory[Ind[fld Indicator]]
→If od=fld On2                    →If r1=fld On
THEN: ค branch                    THEN: ค branch
   branch7030 adr7030s2              branch7030 adr7030
ENDIF: ค modify bit               ENDIF: ค modify indicator
r1←(fld Invert)≠od∧~fld Reset2    →OUT suppress7030
adr7030 write7030 r1              (fld Indicator) set7030 r1∧~fld Reset
```

PROGRAM 13-122   Conditional Branch in the IBM Stretch.

indicators being true or false, and can reset it. The bit or indicator is not changed when the branch address causes an exception.

Iteration

Incrementation and termination.   Branch On Count is a one-instruction loop-closer. The address is advanced with an increment of a halfword, an increment of a word, a decrement of a word, or is not advanced, as specified by the `Advance` modifier. The count reaching, or not reaching, 0 is used as a criterion that causes the branch. Branch On Count, Refill re-initializes the index when the count becomes 0.

```
CBS;addend;temp;return;address
⍝ IBM Stretch Branch On Count, Store
addend←(0,half,word,-word)[fld Advance2]
temp←R2 incr7030c addend
→If memory[Ind[Countzero]]=fld On2
THEN: ⍝ branch and store
    return←iadr÷half
    branch7030 adr7030s2
    address←half align7030 adr7030
    address write7030(ρAdrhalf) magnr return
ENDIF:
```

PROGRAM 13-123   Branch and count in the IBM Stretch.

Delegation

Call and Return.   A Store Instruction Counter If operation can be prefixed to any halfword branch, making the latter a Call. This compound instruction saves the updated instruction address when the Call succeeds. Branch On Bit cannot be so extended. We illustrate the storing of the return address in Branch On Count, Store. The return address is stored with halfword resolution, but replaces only the first 19 bits of the halfword (normally a Branch instruction).

State preservation.   The block Transmit (Program 13-67) and the embedded addresses allow state to be saved or restored with one instruction.

Execute.   Any unprotected word may be used as a subject instruction in Execute. In particular, locations below address 32, which normally may not contain instructions, are accessible. The control signal `exec` assures that— during an execute instruction—the interrupt system is active even if otherwise disabled (`mask7030`, Program 13-126). Since execute instructions may call execute instructions, a time-out is started to prevent never-ending recursions. Execute enables one-instruction subroutines, chosen by indexing—a partial mechanization of the Case structure.

Execute Indirect And Count implements automatic tracing. It establishes a pseudo instruction address in the first 19 bits of a word location in memory, such as an index word (but not in a location below address 16). A regular instruction fetch using the pseudo instruction address and an instruction execution now take place.

```
EX                                 EXIC;iloc;iadr
ⴲ IBM Stretch Execute              ⴲ IBM Stretch Execute Indirect And Count
ⴲ start time-out if exec=0          iloc←word align7030 adr7030
  exec←1                            iadr←half×magni(ρAdrhalf) read7030 iloc
  execute iread7030 adr7030        ⴲ start time-out if exec=0
                                     exec←1
                                     Invadr report7030 iloc<16×word
                                    →OUT suppress7030
                                     execute ifetch7030
                                     iloc write7030(ρAdrhalf) magnr iadr÷half
```

PROGRAM 13-124   Execute instructions in the IBM Stretch.

13.3.8

Supervision

Concurrency

Processor interconnection.   The Stretch's CPU instruction and execution units, the 16-channel I/O exchange, the high-speed disk synchronizer, and the Harvest coprocessor (1961) each access the memory system directly through the memory bus unit. All operate concurrently.

Process Interaction

Signaling.   The Stretch and the Harvest signal by mutual interruption. The I/O subsystems signal the Stretch by interruption.

Integrity

Privileged operations.   There are no privileged operations; the compiler substitutes supervisor calls for dangerous instructions.

Protection.   A fixed area and an area specified by two boundary addresses are protected. Data in word address 0 and in the addresses 4 through 31 are permanently available, whereas data with addresses 1, 2, or 3 are permanently protected in the enabled state. The supervisor sets the boundary addresses. An application program is normally confined to this contiguous block of addresses. The boundary registers are embedded in the word with address 3,

```
      Inv protect7030 address;wordadr;upper;lower
    ⴲ IBM Stretch storage protection
      wordadr←⌊address÷word
    ⴲ invalid address
      Invadr report7030 address≥memcap
     →OUT suppress7030
     →If(enable∨exec)∧(wordadr≥32)∨wordadr∊ 1 2 3
      THEN: ⴲ not permanently allowed
        ⴲ permanently protected
          Inv report7030 wordadr∊ 1 2 3
        ⴲ protected by bounds
          upper←wordadr<magni memory[Upperbound]
          lower←wordadr≥magni memory[Lowerbound]
          Inv report7030 memory[Boundbit]=upper∧lower
      ENDIF:
```

PROGRAM 13-125   Protection in the IBM Stretch.

and must be set by the supervisor while interruption is disabled (which also disables protection). The Bound bit, if 0, determines that access is allowed between the boundaries; if 1, access is allowed outside the boundaries. The Datastore, Datafetch, or Instfetch indicators are set when the bounds are violated. The Invadr indicator is set when the memory capacity is exceeded.

Control Switching

Interruption. The Stretch was the first machine to provide interruption that depended upon multiple maskable indicators. It is a vectored interruption—the indicator number is used to select an instruction from an interrupt table. The table base, Intloc, is programmable. That and the mask allow any interrupt priority scheme to be programmed. mask7030 controls the enabling and masking of the indicators with indicators 20 through 27 maskable by the corresponding bits of the mask register. Upon interruption, the instruction in the appropriate part of the interrupt table is executed. Unless it is a branch, it does not affect the instruction counter. So one-instruction fixup subroutines can be executed without context switching.

```
inst←interrupt7030;who;loc          mask←mask7030;m
 ⍝ IBM Stretch interrupt action      ⍝ IBM Stretch interrupt mask
 ⍝ reset time-out                    m←word↑(20ρ1),memory[Mask+20+⍳28]
 REPEAT:who←(memory[Ind]∧mask7030)⍳1  mask←(enable∨exec)∧m
     exec←0
     →If who≠ρInd
     THEN: ⍝ extra instruction fetch
         memory[Ind[who]]←0
         wait←0
         loc←(magni memory[Intloc])+who×word
         execute iread7030 loc
 ENDIF:→UNTIL(˜wait)∧who=ρInd
```

PROGRAM 13-126   Interruption action in the IBM Stretch.

Indicator control.   Error conditions can turn on permanent indicators by means of report7030. Temporary indicators can be set by set7030. suppress7030 is used to terminate instructions based upon indicator settings.

```
which report7030 condition
 ⍝ IBM Stretch conditional indicator setting
 memory[Ind[which]]←∨/memory[Ind[which]],condition
```

```
which set7030 value                 true←suppress7030
 ⍝ IBM Stretch indicator setting     ⍝ IBM Stretch operation suppression
 memory[Ind[which]]←value            true←∨/memory[Ind]∧mask7030
```

PROGRAM 13-127   Indicator setting and use in the IBM Stretch.

Supervisory instructions. Supervisory actions are the enabling and disabling of interruptions and entering of the wait state. All these actions are combined with an Unconditional Branch, which may include storing of the return address.

```
i BE    Branch Enabled              i BEW   Branch Enabled, Wait
d BES   Branch Enabled, Store       d BEWS  Branch Enabled, Wait, Store
i BD    Branch Disabled
d BDS   Branch Disabled, Store
```

TABLE 13-128   Supervisory instructions of the IBM Stretch.

Humble access.   Humble access is provided by the Load Transit And Set instructions (Program 13-112).

Dispatching.   Branch Enabled can be used to dispatch a user program, whereas Branch Disabled may be used to start a supervisory service routine; they set the enable bit to 1 and 0, respectively. Waiting is combined with enabling, such that the wait can be terminated by an interruption.

```
BEW                                  BD
  IBM Stretch Branch Enabled, Wait     IBM Stretch Branch Disabled
  branch7030 adr7030                   branch7030 adr7030
  →OUT suppress7030                    →OUT suppress7030
  enable←1                             enable←0
  wait←1
```

PROGRAM 13-129   Enable, disable, and wait in the IBM Stretch.

State Preservation

Context switching.   All interrupts act like subroutine calls. The block Move facilitates context switching.

Tools of Control

Interpretive console.   The operator's console is for the first time merely an I/O device, whose function is defined by the supervisory program.

Clocks.   There is a real-time clock and an interval timer, which interrupts.

13.3.9
Input/Output

Channel

The I/O exchange implements (with one commuted datapath and memory) 16 logical channels that handle all source–sink I/O. The high-speed disks have a separate, concurrent, high-data-rate channel.

Input/output operations.   Buchholz designed the perfectly general read, write, control I/O operation set. Only the sense of the IBM System/360 (1965) is missing, with a Copy, Release, and Locate provided instead. The operations with the Suppress option suppress interruption upon completion of the operation when no exceptional conditions occur, so polling can be used instead of interruption to test normal completion.

```
d RD    Read                    d CCW   Copy Control Word
d RDS   Read And Suppress       d REL   Release
d W     Write                   d RELS  Release And Suppress
d WS    Write And Suppress      d LOC   Locate
d CTL   Control                 d LOCS  Locate And Suppress
d CTLS  Control And Suppress
```

TABLE 13-130   Input/output instructions of the IBM Stretch.

Read and Write.   Read and Write start the channel moving data between memory and the I/O device's medium. The block of data to be moved is identified in memory by a channel control word. This control word has a format similar to that of the index word, except that the value field contains a word address—not a bit address—and that three modifier bits are used for chaining of memory fields, transfer of multiple device blocks, and skipping memory access on reading.

Sense and Control.   Control and the Sense type instructions start the channel-data transfer between memory and the I/O device's control unit.

```
| Adrword            | * | Mod | Count          | Next              |

0                   18  24   28               46                 64
Legend: Mod = modifier; * = unused.
```

```
ccw7030
⋀ IBM Stretch channel control word
  Adrword←0+ι18
⋀ unused←18+ι6
  Mod←24+ι4
  Count←28+ι18
  Next←46+ι18
```

PROGRAM 13-131   Channel control word in the IBM Stretch.

Interfaces

Stretch has the first device-independent standard I/O interface. All devices transmit 8-bit bytes, as if they were tape-driven.

13.3.10
Implementation Notes

The implementation strategies used in supercomputers to achieve performance beyond realization advances include the following:

Enhanced memory bandwidth.   Multiple concurrently operating memories can feed one bus. Stretch seems to have pioneered this concept, with two-way and four-way address interleaving among boxes. Ultimately, the memory bus system became the bottleneck.

Concurrent operation.   Several instructions or several programs may be executed at once. Concurrency among programs is architecturally visible. Concurrency in instruction execution may or may not be visible. Stretch

pioneered *pipelined execution*, with up to 11 sequential instructions under execution at once. It is architecturally invisible. An Instruction Box (I-Box) does all instruction fetching, effective address calculation, index arithmetic, and index-dependent conditional branching. It dispatches effective addresses to the memory and to the Data Box (D-Box). Hardware checks for memory access-order conflicts and forces instruction execution to produce results as if sequential. When the data come from memory, the D-Box associates them with their operations and executes them. Finally, a D-Box Store Buffer executes Stores [Buchholz, 1962, Chapter 15].

Checking.   The main memory provides single-error correction and double-error detection (SECDED) on 64-bit words. (The Stretch is the first machine to do so.) Datapaths are extensively checked, by parity or duplication.

Multiple units.   Separate concurrently operating units performed instruction arithmetic and fetch, and operation execution.

13.3.11
Bibliography

Buchholz, W., ed., 1962: *Planning a Computer System.* New York: McGraw-Hill.

IBM Corporation, 1961: *Reference Manual, 7030 Data Processing System.* Form A22-6530. White Plains, N.Y (our defining reference).

Bloch [1959], Blosk [1960], Campbell et al. [1962], Cocke and Kolsky [1959], Codd et al. [1959], Dunwell [1957], MacKenzie [1991], Snyder [1977].

13.3.12
Exercises

13-12 Give the description of the index arithmetic instructions LV, LC, LR, LVNI, LCI, LRI, SX, SV, SR, AV, AVI, ACI, AVCI, SVI, SCI, SVRI, KV, KC, KVNI, R, and RCZ, assuming consistency with the index arithmetic instructions shown in this section.

13-13 Give the description of the connective instructions CM and CT, assuming consistency with the connective instruction C shown in this section.

13-14 Give the description of the fixed-point instructions LFT, LTCV, AMG, AMM, M, KF, and KFE, assuming consistency with the fixed-point instructions shown in this section.

13-15 Give the description of the floating-point instructions FL, DL, FLWF, DLWF, FLFT, FST, DA, FAMG, FADM, FAMM, AF, AE, FM, DM, FKR, FKM, and FKMR, assuming consistency with the floating-point instructions shown in this section.

13-16 Give the description of the sequencing and supervisory instructions BS, BRS, CB, CBR, CBRS, BE, BES, BDS, and BEWS, assuming consistency with the sequencing and supervisory instructions shown in this section.

13.4
Burroughs B5500*

13.4.1
Highlights

History

Architects.   Robert Barton was the principal architect, at least of the ancestral machines.

Dates.   The Burroughs B5000 (1963) was produced in limited quantities, and was quickly succeeded by (and field modified to) the B5500, which we treat as the archetype. The concepts date essentially from 1963.

Noteworthy

The B5500 exemplifies the high-level language orientation, address segmentation, descriptors, control words, and stack that characterize the whole family.

High-level machine language.   The Burroughs B5500 family explores the feasibility of designing machines to be programmed in high-level language only. ALGOL 60 is the language selected, and facilities to interpret block-structured address scopes are provided. Even the operating system is written in ALGOL. Programs are designed not to be modified at run time. Very powerful subroutine and parameter-passing facilities are provided.

Nevertheless, there is a machine language under the ALGOL—there had to be, for run-time binding of such high-level constructs is just too inefficient. Moreover, customers immediately demanded COBOL and FORTRAN as well. An ALGOL-only machine would not have survived.

Address segmentation.   Just as the Ferranti Atlas (1962) introduced paging and the one-level store, so the B5500 introduced address segmentation with dynamic relocatability. The machine is designed to be run under an operating system and incorporates a supervisory mode, limited memory protection, and interruption with automatic state-saving.

Descriptors and control words.   The machine language uses descriptors to characterize data objects: instructions address the descriptor, which gives data location, index range, presence in memory, and so forth. Control words are used for state preservation in iteration, delegation, and interruption.

Stack.   The machine language is distinguished by the organization of working store into a stack, so that most operations require no address at all, yielding zero-address instructions.

---

*   Edward Brownlee and Jesse L. Thrall helped with the research for this sketch.

Forty-eight–bit word.   The machine is a good exemplar of the *six* units system, with 6-bit bytes and 48-bit words.

Multiprocessing.   Multiprocessing is provided for two processors in master–slave relationship.

Peculiarities

Target-language dependence.   ALGOL proved to be an unfortunate language choice, since it never became popular.   Some of the ALGOL-facilitating properties proved awkward for COBOL and FORTRAN.

Single stack.   The use of one stack for arithmetic and parameters and also for addresses is messy, as the manipulations of the various reference registers demonstrate. Not all parameters that should be accessible in the B5500 stack can be reached [Hauck and Dent, 1968]. Separate stacks for addresses and data would have been much cleaner, as in the English Electric KDF9 (1963).

Dual modes.   The B5500 architecture contains two disjoint modes—a word mode and a character mode. These modes are essentially different machines. The stack proves to be unsuitable for character data.

Twelve-bit instructions.   Instructions are made up of 12-bit *syllables*.   The syllable is too spacious for the zero-address instructions, and too cramped for the one-address instructions. A wide variety of address implication and abbreviation schemes is used to make the one-address instructions possible.

Limited address field.   The address field of an instruction is 10 bits, which is utterly inadequate. The design piles complexity upon complexity to compensate.

No modifiers.   Instructions have no modifiers. The instruction Move Pointers essentially uses two modifiers that are derived from the stack. Some groups of instructions actually have modifiers encoded in the operation code.

No integer.   All numeric data are in floating-point format; there is no integer datatype. The floating-point coefficient, however, is integral, not fractional, so the integer subset has a 0 exponent. Furthermore, arithmetic favors the 0 exponent.

Rounding.   The floating-point round is unbiased, with the sign of the number as the criterion for choosing between equidistant neighbors.

Complete sets of relations.   For each of the comparison types—character immediate, character string, and floating point—all six relations have separate instructions.   This proliferation is necessary because the operands are not symmetrically addressed and the branch conditions are asymmetric.

Poor bit-traffic.   Performance is inherently hurt by the high degree of run-time binding, particularly by the extra bit-traffic occasioned by indirect addressing via descriptors.

Hardware-oriented description.   The description of the architecture carries unnecessary implementation detail. Thus, mention of the registers that contain

the top two levels of the stack and their use for different purposes in the character mode forces the reader to verify whether a true stack is described and to what extent the word and character modes are independent. Similarly, other registers of the implementation are described.

Descendants

The B5500 was reimplemented as the B5700 in 1970. Earlier, in 1968, the B6500 had been delivered; it was a significant architectural rework, consolidating the two modes, extending the word size to 51 bits and the address field to 20 bits, using instructions with 8 to 96 bits, making double precision dependent upon the tag (and hence self-declaring), and redefining the various control words. The B6700 (1971) is a faster reimplementation, with little architectural change, of the B6500, and the B7700 (1973) is an upward-compatible successor of the B6700.

13.4.2

Machine Language

Language Level

Design philosophy.   The machine is designed as a word machine and a character machine with quite disjunct instruction and operand types, but with common control and addressing. Since these machines do not operate concurrently, we treat them as a single machine.

Unit System

In spite of the many novel features of the B5500, the byte size is still 6 bits, and the address size is still limited to 15 bits, as in the IBM 704 (1955). Addresses apply to 48-bit words. The character mode treats a word as eight 6-bit bytes.

```
initiate5500                               format5500
ᴀ initiation of the Burroughs B5500        ᴀ Burroughs B5500 information units
format5500                                 ᴀ principal radix
configure5500                              radix←2
space5500                                  ᴀ information unit
control5500                                byte←6
data5500                                   word←48
                                           double←96
                                           adrsize←15
                                           adrcap←radix*adrsize

configure5500
ᴀ configuration for the Burroughs B5500
ᴀ memory capacity
memcap←radix*adrsize
```

            PROGRAM 13-132   Basic parameters of the Burroughs B5500.

Configuration.   Maximum memory capacity is 32 K 48-bit words; this inadequate size is corrected in the B6500.

Spaces

Memory name-space.   Memory is homogeneous, without hierarchy.

Working store.   Working store is a stack of 48-bit words, placed as a variable-length, variable-location segment in memory. The implementation places the top two levels in hardware registers. Although this implementation does not seem to affect the architecture, the B5500 manual unfortunately describes the instructions in terms of these registers, thus introducing unnecessary detail. Our description notes for the working store only the stack pointer address sp. The top word of the stack usually contains an address or a descriptor; the next stack word down quite often contains a data word.

In the word mode, 48-bit words are placed from memory into the stack and moved from the stack to memory. Arithmetic and logic use the words on the stack. The field operations of the word-mode address fields in the top levels of the stack use the byte and bit address parts of source and dest. In the character mode, the stack is not used for data, but operands are specified in memory by the word, byte, and bit address parts of source and dest.

Control store.   Control store is elaborate. There are the usual instruction address (incremented a quarterword at a time) and indicators (a set of 62). The program reference address points to the program reference table, which contains operands and descriptors. The descriptors make this table similar to a segment table. The stack reference address points to the start or end of a parameter list in the stack. This start or end is a pointer to the next reference point down the stack, thus establishing a chain of references. The character mode uses a source and destination address, each comprising a word, byte, and bit component; the word mode knows only the byte and bit components.

```
space5500
 ⋒ Burroughs B5500 spaces
 ⋒ memory                              ⋒ - normal state
   memory←?(memcap,word)ρradix           normal←?radix
 ⋒ working store                       ⋒ - subprogram level
 ⋒ - stack pointer                       sublevel←?radix
   sp←?adrcap                           ⋒ - character mode
 ⋒ control store                         charmode←?radix
 ⋒ - instruction address               ⋒ - temporary program level
   iadr←0.25×?4×adrcap                    variant←?radix
 ⋒ - indicators                        ⋒ - action suppression
   ind←?62ρradix                         suppress←?radix
 ⋒ - program reference                 ⋒ - stopped state
   progref←64×?adrcap÷64                 stop←?radix
 ⋒ - stack reference                   ⋒ - mark signal
   stackref←?adrcap                      mark←?radix
 ⋒ - character addresses               ⋒ - processor number
   source←?adrcap,8,byte                 procnr←1+?radix
   dest←?adrcap,8,byte                 ⋒ - stop switch
                                         stopswitch←?radix
```

PROGRAM 13-133   Spaces of the Burroughs B5500.

There are six overall states:

- Supervisor versus normal state
- Program level versus sublevel state

- Word versus character mode
- Normal versus variant state
- Normal versus suppressed state
- Running versus stopped state

Moreover, in the word mode, the `mark` signal indicates that the top section of the stack contains parameters; in the character mode, the signal is a true/false condition. The system allows dual processors. A switch determines which processor is number 1; the other processor is then number 2. Only processor 1 can be in the supervisory state; both can be in normal state. For manual control, there is a stop switch.

Programming model.   The B5500 requires two models, one for the Word mode (Figure 13-134) and one for Character mode (Figure 13-135). The word-mode model is essentially a pure stack machine.

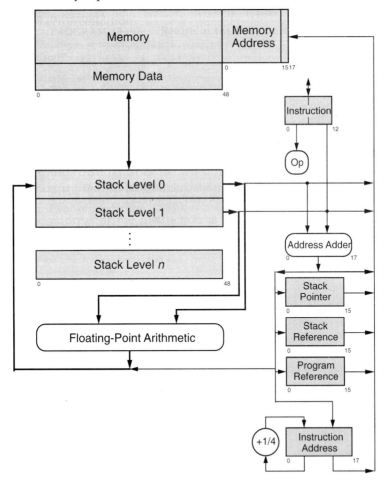

FIGURE 13-134   Word processor model for the Burroughs B5500.

Character mode has an action very similar to that of the IBM 1401 (1960), and the model shows the similarities. Almost all of the register positions are used for address registers. The datapath proper is only six bits wide.

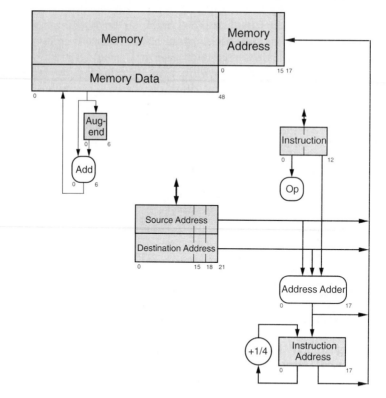

FIGURE 13-135   Character processor model for the Burroughs B5500.

Operand Specification

Number of addresses.   The design is pure zero-address; one-address instructions occur only for Load and Store type operations.

Address phrase.   The address phrase contains just one address field; structuring is delegated to descriptors.

Operation Specification

Mnemonics.   We use Burroughs' three-character mnemonics system, into which we fitted their three 4-character mnemonics O(P)DC, D(E)SC, and L(I)TC.

Code list.   Of the 653 available operation codes, 143 are used. The first 87 (formats a through e) sparsely occupy the 589 code slots of the word mode; the last 56 (format f) barely fit the 64 slots of the character mode.

Word mode instructions.   We show the instruction list of the word mode separate from that of the character mode in Tables 13-138 and 13-137. The word mode is the principal mode and centers around addressing, floating-point arithmetic, sequencing, supervision, and I/O.

a→ADD	MUL	FTC	IP1	RDV	CMN	SDA	STC	CNE
DLA	DLM	MOP	ISD	FBS	d→LTC	SSA	SEC	CEG
PRL	RTR	LOD	LEQ	CTF	d→ODC	SFD	CRF	CGR
LNG	LND	DUP	BBW	b→ISO	d→DSC	SRD	JNC	BIS
CID	STD	TOP	IP2	CBR	e→NOP	SES	JFC	BIR
GEQ	NEQ	IOR	ISN	DIA	e→XRT	TEQ	JNS	OCV
BBC	SSN	LBC	LSS	DIB	e→DEL	TNE	JFW	ICV
BRT	XIT	HP2	BFW	TRB	f→EXC	TEG	RCA	CEL
ITI	DIV	LFC	IIO	FCL	BSD	TGR	ENS	CLS
LOR	DLD	ZP1	EQL	FCE	BSS	SRS	BNS	FSU
CIN	COM	TUS	SSP	c→INX	RDA	SFS	RSA	FAD
GTR	LQV	IDV	IFT	COC	TRW	TEL	SCA	TRP
BFC	SND	SFI	CTC	MKS	SED	TLS	JRC	TRN
RTN	XCH	SFT	LBU	CDC	TDA	TAN	TSA	TRZ
SUB	CHS	FTF	LFU	SSF	ZP1	BIT	JRV	TRS
DLS	RTS	MDS	TIO	LLL	TBN	INC	CEQ	

PROGRAM 13-136   Compressed operation-code list of the Burroughs B5500.

A *address arithmetic*
f TSA Transfer Source
f TDA Transfer Destination
f SES Set Source
f SED Set Destination
f RSA Recall Source
f RDA Recall Destination
f SSA Store Source
f SDA Store Destination
f SFS Increment Source
f SFD Increment Destination
f SRS Decrement Source
f SRD Decrement Destination
f BSS Increment Source Bit
f BSD Increment Destination Bit
A *data handling*
f TRS Move Characters
f TRN Move Numeric
f TRZ Move Zone
f TRW Move Words
f TRP Move Program
f TBN Blank Non-Numeric
f TLS Character Less
f TEL Character Equal Or Less
f TEQ Character Equal
f TEG Character Greater Or Equal
f TGR Character Greater
f TNE Character Unequal
f CLS String Less
f CEL String Equal Or Less
f CEQ String Equal
f CEG String Equal Or Greater
Legend: B = Backward.

f CGR String Greater
f CNE String Unequal
f TAN Character Test
A *logic and shift*
f BIS Set Bit
f BIR Reset Bit
f BIT Test Bit
A *decimal arithmetic*
f FAD Decimal Add
f FSU Decimal Subtract
f ICV Decimal To Binary
f OCV Binary To Decimal
A *sequencing*
f ZP1 Stop On Switch
f JFW Jump
f JRV Jump B
f JFC Jump On Mark
f JRC Jump On Mark B
f BNS Begin Loop
f ENS End Loop
f JNS Leave Loop
f JNC Leave Loop On Mark
f SCA Store Instruction Address
f RCA Recall Instruction Address
f CRF Modify Next Instruction
f STC Store Tally
f SEC Set Tally
f INC Increment Tally
A *supervision*
f EXC Leave Character Mode

TABLE 13-137   Character mode instruction list of the Burroughs B5500.

Character-mode instructions.   The character mode is always at the subprogram level and has as a restricted purpose: the selection, movement, and testing of character strings, decimal fields, and bits. Sequencing emphasizes iteration. Supervision is minimal: return to word mode.

⌐	*address arithmetic*		a	SUB F	Subtract
d	ODC	Operand Call	a	DLS	Subtract D
d	DSC	Descriptor Call	a	MUL F	Multiply
c	COC	Construct Operand Call	a	DLM	Multiply D
c	CDC	Construct Descriptor Call	a	DIV F	Divide
a	PRL	Program Release	a	DLD	Divide D
e	XRT	Set Variant	a	IDV F	Divide To Integer
a	FTC	Stackref To Address	a	RDV F	Remainder
a	FTF	Stackref To Stackref	a	LSS F	Less
a	CTC	Address To Address	a	LEQ F	Less Or Equal
a	CTF	Address To Stackref	a	EQL F	Equal
c	SSF	Move Pointers	a	GEQ F	Greater Or Equal
c	INX	Add Addresses	a	GTR F	Greater
c	LLL	Lookup Link List	a	NEQ F	Not Equal
b	DIA	Immediate Source	⌐		*sequencing*
b	DIB	Immediate Destination	e	NOP	No Operation
⌐	*data handling*		a	ZP1	Stop On Switch
b	TRB	Move Field	a	BFW	Branch
b	ISO	Select Field	a	BBW	Branch B
b	FCL	Low Field	a	LFU	Branch Word
b	FCE	Equal Field	a	LBU	Branch Word B
⌐	*logic and shift*		a	BFC	Branch On Condition
a	LNG	Not	a	BBC	Branch On Condition B
a	LND	And	a	LFC	Branch Word On Condition
a	LOR	Or	a	LBC	Branch Word On Condition B
a	LQV	Equivalence	b	CBR	Branch On Non-zero
a	MDS	Set Flag	c	MKS	Mark Stack
a	MOP	Reset Flag	a	XIT	Exit
a	TOP	Test Flag	a	BRT	Return
a	FBS	Search Flag	a	RTN	Return Normal
⌐	*floating-point arithmetic*		a	RTS	Return Special
a	LOD	Load	⌐		*supervision*
d	LTC	Load Immediate	c	CMN	Enter Character Mode
a	STD	Store	a	ITI	Inspect Interrupt
a	SND	Store And Keep	a	SFI	Store For Interrupt
a	ISD	Store Integer	a	SFT	Store For Diagnose
a	ISN	Store And Keep Integer	a	IP1	Dispatch One
a	CID	Store Integer On Demand	a	IP2	Dispatch Two
a	CIN	Store And Keep Integer On Demand	a	COM	Humble Access
a	XCH	Swap	a	HP2	Stop Two
a	DUP	Duplicate	a	RTR	Read Time
e	DEL	Delete	a	IFT	Diagnose
a	CHS F	Negate	⌐		*input/output*
a	SSP F	Make Absolute	a	IIO	Start IO
a	SSN F	Negate Absolute	a	IOR	Release IO
a	ADD F	Add	a	TIO	Test IO
a	DLA	Add D	a	TUS	Test IO Status

Legend: B = Backward; D = Double; F = Floating-Point.

TABLE 13-138   Word mode instruction list of the Burroughs B5500.

Instruction Structure

Machine-language syntax.   The syntax has five pattern groups for the word mode and one pattern for the character mode. The 13-bit patterns are formed by 12 instruction bits with the character-mode bit to their right.

Types of control.   The B5500 has very diverse control. Besides the familiar instruction, indicator, and data allocations, there are two descriptors and seven control words. Descriptors specify operands and program segments; control words preserve status in iteration, marking parameters in the stack, subroutine

```
         syntax5500
       a Opcode,0,Ope, 0 1 0
       b L0,1,Ope, 0 1 0
       c Opcode, 1 0 0 0 0 1 0
       d Referend, 0 0 0
       d Referend, 1 0 0
       d Referend, 1 1 0
       e 0 0 0 0 0 0 1 0 1 1 0 1 0
       e 0 0 0 0 0 0 1 1 0 0 0 1 0
       e 0 0 0 0 0 0 1 1 0 1 0 1 0
       f L0,Opc,1
```

⌐ *Last pattern bit is the mode bit.*

PROGRAM 13-139   Instruction syntax of the Burroughs B5500.

return, interruption control, and program dispatch. Variations of descriptors are used for I/O control. When fields occur in more than one descriptor or control word, we declare them only once.

```
       control5500
     ⌐ Burroughs B5500 control allocation
       instruction5500                loop5500
       indicator5500                  mark5500
       data5500                       return5500
       datadescr5500                  int5500
       program5500                    ini5500
```

PROGRAM 13-140   Control allocation in the Burroughs B5500.

Instruction format.   The six syntactic pattern groups give three distinct instruction formats. The first format contains just opcode bits, as found in three pattern groups. The second format has a 6-bit length field, as found in two patterns. The third format has one 10-bit address field, the `Referend`; it occurs in the instructions that refer to data in memory.

```
a ┌─────────────┬──┐
c │ Opcode      │  │          instruction5500
e │          └┴─┘  │          ⌐ Burroughs B5500 instruction allocation
  0            12            ⌐ operation specification
                              Opcode←0+ι6
b ┌──────┬──────┬──┐          Ope←7+ι3
  │ L0   │ Op   │  │          Opc←6+ι6
f └──────┴┴┴────┘             ⌐ descriptor specification
  0      6      12            Referend←0+ι10
                              ⌐ - length
         Opcode↓              L0←0+ι6

d ┌───────────┬──┐
  │ Referend  │  │
  └───────────┴──┘
  0         1012
Legend: L = length; Op = opcode; Mode bit not shown.
```

PROGRAM 13-141   Instruction allocation in the Burroughs B5500.

Status format.   Each processor has 14 indicators (including a spare) for causes such as memory-parity error, invalid address, stack overflow, arithmetic overflow, underflow, and invalid division. The first three of these may occur

independently; the others are encoded with the same four bits, and only the first occurring condition is recorded. The indicator set for processor 1 starts at indicator 48; the set for processor 2 starts at indicator 32. Indicators 0 through 32 are used for I/O operation (not shown).

```
indicator5500                      which report5500 condition;procind
A Burroughs 5500 indicators        A Burroughs B5500 indicator setting
A memory error                     procind← 48 32[procnr=2]
  Memerror←0                       →If(which<3)∨~∨/ind[procind+3+ι11]
A invalid address                  THEN: A no conflict
  Invadr←1                            (procind+which) report condition∧normal
A stack overflow                      suppress←∨/suppress,condition
  Stoflo←2                         ENDIF:
A exclusive indicators
  Attention←4
  Ready←5
  Chain←6
  Absent←7
  Flagerror←8
  Index←9
  Uflo←10
  Floflo←11
  Oflo←12
  Divide←13
```

PROGRAM 13-142   Indicators in the Burroughs B5500.

Indicators are set only in the normal mode, not in supervisory mode. Setting an indicator also sets the status signal suppress, which may cause further execution of the current instruction to be suppressed.

```
data←length read5500 address;location
A Burroughs B5500 read from memory
location←address+ιlength
data←.memory[memcap|location;]
Invadr report5500 location≥memcap

address write5500 data;location
A Burroughs B5500 write into memory
location←address+ι(ρdata)÷word
memory[memcap|location;]←word wide data
Invadr report5500 location≥memcap

data←size read5500c adr;start;length;od
A Burroughs B5500 read bit string
start←byte⊥1↓adr
length←⌈(start+size)÷word
od←length read5500 1↑adr
data←size↑start↓od

adr write5500c data;start;length;od;rl
A Burroughs B5500 write bit string
start←byte⊥1↓adr
length←⌈(start+ρdata)÷word
od←length read5500 1↑adr
rl←(start↑od),data,(start+ρdata)↓od
adr[0] write5500 rl
```

PROGRAM 13-143   Memory read and write in the Burroughs B5500.

13.4.3

Addressing

Direct addressing.   `read5500` and `write5500` fetch and store one or more of the 48-bit words used in the word mode.

Character-mode reading and writing has bit resolution specified by a three-element address contained in `source` and `dest`. The first address element identifies a word in memory; the second element, one of the 8 bytes in a word; and the third element, one of the 6 bits in a byte. `read5500c` and `write5500c` fetch and store the necessary memory words and delete or attach bits to the left and right of the desired field.

Stack addressing.   The system stack is addressed with a postdecrement pop and a preincrement push. Its upward growth is limited by the start of the program reference table `progref`.

```
data←pop5500                        push5500 data
⋒ Burroughs 5500 read from stack    ⋒ Burroughs 5500 write onto stack
data←memory[sp;]                    sp←sp+1
sp←sp-1                             Stoflo report5500 sp≥progref
                                    →OUT suppress
                                    memory[sp;]←data
```

PROGRAM 13-144   System stack access in the Burroughs B5500.

Segmentation

Data descriptors are used for segmentation. When a descriptor is accessed whose `Present` bit is off, an interrupt signals that the described segment is not in memory. The operating system can then load the segment. This is straightforward when less than a full memory complement is installed, so all segment names are distinct.

Address Modification

Address calculation.   The action of calculating addresses is unbelievably complicated, but it preserves full dynamic program relocatability through indefinitely deep-nested subroutine calls, including recursive calls.

Address modification adds a 10-bit displacement to a 15-bit base address to obtain a full 15-bit address. The base may refer to the program reference table `progref` or, in case of a subroutine, to a local parameter list `stackref`, to a global parameter list, or to the integer part of the instruction address. The choice among these bases is determined in `adr5500` by `sublevel` and `mark` and by the high-order displacement bits.

The program level uses always the program reference table. On the subroutine level, the high-order displacement bits give a choice between addressing via the program reference table, via a parameter list, or via the instruction address. `parameter5500` shows that `mark` gives a choice between a local and a more global parameter list. Addressing relative to the instruction address is allowed only in operand or descriptor call operations, as conveyed by the register field `r`; otherwise, the program reference table is used.

```
address←r adr5500 field;base;displacement
ⁿ the Burroughs B5500 base addressing
→CASE(sublevel,field[ι3])ι0
   ⁿ program level                      address←r adr5500f ddr
C0: ⁿ segment table base                ⁿ Burroughs B5500 flagged address
   base←progref                         →IF ddr[Flag]
   displacement←magni field             THEN: ⁿ direct address
   →ENDCASE                                  address←magni ddr[Address]
   ⁿ subprogram level                        →ENDIF
C1: ⁿ segment table base                ELSE: ⁿ base address
   base←progref                              address←r adr5500 ⁻10↑ddr
   displacement←magni 1↓field           ENDIF:
   →ENDCASE
C2: ⁿ parameter base                     base←parameter5500;mscw
   base←parameter5500                    ⁿ Burroughs B5500 parameter base
   displacement←magni 2↓field            →IF mark
   →ENDCASE                              THEN: ⁿ global parameter
C3: ⁿ relative base                           mscw←1 read5500 progref+7
   base←(progref,ιadr)[r]                     base←magni mscw[Stackref]
   displacement←magni 3↓field                 →ENDIF
   →ENDCASE                              ELSE: ⁿ local parameter
C4: ⁿ subtract from parameter base            base←stackref
   base←parameter5500                    ENDIF:
   displacement←-magni 3↓field
ENDCASE:address←adrcap|base+displacement
```

PROGRAM 13-145   Addressing in the Burroughs B5500.

The Operand Call and Descriptor Call operations use the address modification of adr5500 with their 10-bit Referend field as argument. All other operations use a word at the top of the stack as argument. adr5500f shows that the flag bit of the word on the stack distinguishes an operand from a descriptor. When the flag is 1, the address part of the descriptor is used as address; otherwise, the 10 low-order bits of the operand are used as input to the address modification of adr5500.

Temporary level change.   A subprogram in the word mode can be set temporarily to the program level by the Set Variant instruction. The level is returned to the sublevel by variant5500, which is part of the Operand Call, Descriptor Call, Load, and Store operations. When Set Variant is given just prior to these instructions, they can use the segment table with a displacement of up to 1024, instead of 512. This mechanism is solely occasioned by the cramped 10-bit Referend field of the instructions.

```
XRT                           variant5500
ⁿ Burroughs B5500 Set Variant ⁿ Burroughs B5500 level variation
   sublevel←0                    sublevel←sublevel∨variant
   variant←1                     variant←0
```

PROGRAM 13-146   Level change in the Burroughs B5500.

Bit-address modification.   Whenever a character mode byte or word operation is executed, its bit address is aligned to the next byte or word, an action described by align5500. add5500c adds an increment to a bit-address value using the word-byte-bit radix of the bit-addressing notation.

```
adr←unit align5500 adr;radix:value    sm←au add5500c addend;radix
ᴀ Burroughs B5500 align to unit        ᴀ Burroughs B5500 add bit address
radix←adrcap,8,byte                    radix←adrcap,8,byte
value←magni adr                        sm←3 magnr(magni au)+addend
adr←3 magnr value+unit|-value
```

PROGRAM 13-147   Bit-address modification in the Burroughs B5500.

Address Level

Indirect addressing.   There is no address mode in the instruction that uses an operand as an address, but the flag bit of a descriptor causes such action.

Immediate addressing.   Load Immediate is the only instruction that uses instructions bits as an operand.

Index Arithmetic

Addressing operations.   The addressing instructions deal in the word mode (syntax groups a through e) with the use and construction of data descriptors, the manipulation of addresses and pointers, and indexing actions. Since the byte and bit parts of the source and destination registers are used in the specification of bit fields, these registers can also be set in the word mode. In the character mode (syntax group f) the full source and destination registers can be set, stored, and updated.

```
d ODC Operand Call              f TSA Transfer Source
d DSC Descriptor Call           f TDA Transfer Destination
c COC Construct Operand Call    f SES Set Source
c CDC Construct Descriptor Call f SED Set Destination
a PRL Program Release           f RSA Recall Source
e XRT Set Variant               f RDA Recall Destination
a FTC Stackref To Address       f SSA Store Source
a FTF Stackref To Stackref      f SDA Store Destination
a CTC Address To Address        f SFS Increment Source
a CTF Address To Stackref       f SFD Increment Destination
c SSF Move Pointers             f SRS Decrement Source
c INX Add Addresses             f SRD Decrement Destination
c LLL Lookup Link List          f BSS Increment Source Bit
b DIA Immediate Source          f BSD Increment Destination Bit
b DIB Immediate Destination
```

TABLE 13-148   Addressing instructions of the Burroughs B5500.

Data descriptor.   A data descriptor normally points to a scalar or a vector (Program 13-149). The Address field gives the address of the object; the Count field gives its size. A zero size indicates a scalar located at the specified address. A larger size signifies a vector that starts at the given address to which an index must be added in order to obtain the desired element. The Integer bit indicates that the associated data has been declared as an integer; it is used in Store Integer On Demand (Program 13-176). The Continue bit indicates chained vectors, as used in Program Release (Program 13-154).

↓Present Integer↓↓Continue

Tag	*	Count		*		Address	

```
0    4    8         18 21        33              48
```
Data descriptor
Legend: * = unused.

```
datadescr5500                           ddr←datadescr5500i ddr
ᵃ Burroughs B5500 data descriptor       ᵃ Burroughs B5500 use data descriptor
Tag← 0 1 3                              REPEAT:→OUT absent5500 ddr
Flag←0                                      →If 0≠magni ddr[Count]
Present←2                               THEN: ᵃ add index
Count←8+ι10                                  ddr←index5500 ddr
Integer←19                                   →OUT suppress
Continue←20                             ENDIF: ᵃ fetch target
Address←33+ιadrsize                          ddr←1 read5500 magni ddr[Address]
ᵃ Unused←(4+ι4),18,21+ι12               →UNTIL(ddr[Flag]=0)∨ddr[Tag]∧.= 1 1 0
```

```
ddr←datadescr5500r address
ᵃ Burroughs B5500 make data descriptor
ddr←wordρ0
ddr[Tag]← 1 0 0
ddr[Present]←1
ddr[Address]←adrsize magnr address
```

PROGRAM 13-149   Data descriptor in the Burroughs B5500.

Tag.   Three tag bits are used to distinguish the various information types. The leftmost bit (the Flag bit), when 0, identifies an operand; when 1, a descriptor or control word. The next bit, when 0, identifies a data descriptor; when 1, the third tag bit (the fourth bit of the word) gives a choice between a program descriptor (when 1) and a loop, return, interrupt, or initiate control word (when 0). The decoding of the tag in the B6500 distinguishes more cases, such as single and double operands.

Index action.   The index value is the next item below the descriptor in the stack. The index should be a floating-point value in the integer domain with a maximum of 1023, since its 10 low-order bits are used. This 10-bit integer is checked against the boundaries of the index range: 0 and the vector length specified by the Count field of the descriptor. A correct index is added to the

```
ddr←index5500 ddr;rl;index;address      yes←absent5500 ddr
ᵃ Burroughs B5500 indexing              ᵃ Burroughs B5500 data absence
rl←integer5500 pop5500                   yes←ddr[Flag]∧⁻ddr[Present]
index←magni ⁻10↑rl                       →If yes
Index report5500 index<0                THEN: ᵃ data absent
Index report5500 index≥magni ddr[Count]     Absent report5500 1
→If suppress                                push5500 ddr
THEN: ᵃ index out of range              ENDIF:
    push5500 rl
    →ENDIF
ELSE: ᵃ index within range
    address←(magni ddr[Address])+index
    ddr[Address]←adrsize magnr address
    ddr[Count]←0
ENDIF:
```

PROGRAM 13-150   Index action in the Burroughs B5500.

Address field of the descriptor, and the count is made 0, indicating a single element. Groups of vector descriptors can be themselves described by vector descriptors, so n-dimensional arrays can be handled by repeatedly accessing and indexing descriptors until a data element or a control word is found.

Segment absent. When a descriptor refers to data that are not yet in memory (the flag bit is 1, but the Present bit is 0), then an interrupt is signaled, the descriptor is pushed onto the stack, and no further action takes place, as described by absent5500. This action matches the general approach of pushing data or control words that are in error onto the stack for error analysis or, in the case of a segment fault, for fetching of the data. When the segment has been loaded, the supervisor must set the Present bit to 1.

Operand Call. The instruction Operand Call places an operand on top of the stack. First, adr5500 obtains an address from the 10-bit Referend field of the instruction. Next, odcall5500 interprets the word at this address. Four types of data, distinguished by the number of leftmost ones of the Tag field, cause appropriate action:

- An operand is pushed onto the stack.
- A data descriptor delivers an operand that is pushed onto the stack.
- A control word is pushed as an operand onto the stack.
- A program descriptor refers to a subroutine that should deliver a result that is pushed as an operand onto the stack. This subroutine is entered as described by entry5500 (Program 13-190).

```
ODC;address                              odcall5500 address:od
A Burroughs B5500 Operand Call           A Burroughs B5500 operand call
address←1 adr5500 inst[Referend]         od←1 read5500 address
odcall5500 address                       →CASE od[Tag]⍳0
variant5500                              C0:  A operand
                                              push5500 od
                                              →ENDCASE
COC;od;ddr                               C1:  A data descriptor
A Burroughs B5500 Make Operand Call           push5500 datadescr5500i od
od←pop5500                                    →ENDCASE
ddr←pop5500                              C2:  A control word
push5500 od                                   push5500 od
push5500 ddr WHERE ddr[Flag]←1                →ENDCASE
sp←sp-1                                  C3:  A program descriptor
odcall5500 sp+1                               0 entry5500 od
                                         ENDCASE:
```

PROGRAM 13-151   Operand call in the Burroughs B5500.

Make Operand Call. The instruction Make Operand Call changes a data word containing an address into a data descriptor by setting the data word's flag bit to 1. Then, it executes this word according to odcall5500. The address is assumed to be just below the corresponding data at the top of the stack. Thus a result at the top of the stack can be stored at an address that was placed on the stack prior to computation of the result.

Program descriptor. A program descriptor contains the start address of a subroutine. The routine is a program segment and is available if the segment

is in memory, as should be indicated by the `Present` bit. The mode of the routine is indicated by the `Charmode` bit. When `Argument` is 1, the parameters of the routine are on the top section of the stack; otherwise, the parameters are at the place indicated by `Stackref`.

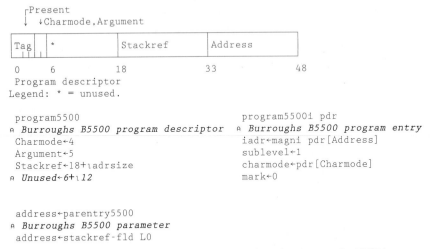

```
  ┌Present
  │  ↓Charmode,Argument
  ↓

│Tag│ * │      Stackref      │    Address       │

0     6            18             33                48
Program descriptor
Legend: * = unused.
```

```
program5500                            program5500i pdr
ꓮ Burroughs B5500 program descriptor   ꓮ Burroughs B5500 program entry
Charmode←4                             iadr←magni pdr[Address]
Argument←5                             sublevel←1
Stackref←18+ιadrsize                   charmode←pdr[Charmode]
ꓮ Unused←6+ι12                         mark←0


address←parentry5500
ꓮ Burroughs B5500 parameter
address←stackref-fld L0
```

PROGRAM 13-152   Program descriptor in the Burroughs B5500.

Parameter list entry.   The stack reference address points to the top of the parameter list; hence an entry in the parameter list can be found with `parentry5500` that subtracts the value of the field L0 from `stackref`.

Descriptor Call.   The instruction Descriptor Call places a data descriptor on top of the stack. As in Operand Call, a base-displacement addition is performed by `adr5500`. `ddcall5500` interprets the word found at this address and distinguishes four cases:

```
DSC;address                            ddcall5500 address;ddr
ꓮ Burroughs B5500 Descriptor Call      ꓮ Burroughs B5500 descriptor call
address←1 adr5500 inst[Referend]       ddr←1 read5500 address
ddcall5500 address                     →CASE ddr[Tag]ι0
variant5500                            C0: ꓮ operand
                                           push5500 datadescr5500r address
                                           →ENDCASE
CDC;od;ddr                             C1: ꓮ data descriptor
ꓮ Burroughs B5500 Make Descriptor Call     →OUT absent5500 ddr
od←pop5500                                 →If 0≠magni ddr[Count]
ddr←pop5500                                 THEN: ꓮ add index
push5500 od                                    ddr←index5500 ddr
push5500 ddr WHERE ddr[Flag]←1             ENDIF:push5500 ddr
sp←sp-1                                     →ENDCASE
ddcall5500 sp+1                         C2: ꓮ control word
                                           push5500 datadescr5500r address
                                           →ENDCASE
                                       C3: ꓮ program descriptor
                                           1 entry5500 ddr
                                       ENDCASE:
```

PROGRAM 13-153   Descriptor call in the Burroughs B5500.

- An operand causes a descriptor that points to the memory address of the operand to be constructed and pushed onto the stack.
- A data descriptor is indexed when it points to a vector, then is pushed onto the stack.
- A control word is treated as an operand; hence a descriptor pointing to its address is constructed and pushed onto the stack.
- A program descriptor is used for subroutine entry, as for operand call. The type of calling function (operand call or descriptor call) is noted in the entry and return actions of the subroutine, as indicated by the left argument (0 or 1) of entry5500.

Make Descriptor Call.   The instruction Make Descriptor Call is identical to Make Operand Call, except that ddcall5500 is used.

Program and data release.   A program or data segment that is no longer needed can be deleted by the supervisor. As a first step, the Present bit is set to 0; then the program space can be added to available space by suitable supervisory actions. Program Release provides this first step if the program is in the supervisory mode. In the normal mode, an interrupt is given, signaling a request either for chaining to another data or program segment if the Continue bit is on, or for completing if that bit is off.

```
PRL;od;address;ddr
A Burroughs B5500 Program Release
od←pop5500
→OUT absent5500 od
address←adr5500f od
ddr←1 read5500 address
→IF normal
THEN: A normal state
    Chain report5500 ddr[Continue]
    Ready report5500~ddr[Continue]
    (progref+9) write5500 word magnr address
    →ENDIF
ELSE: A control state
    ddr[Present]←0
    address write5500 ddr
ENDIF:
```

PROGRAM 13-154   Program release in the Burroughs B5500.

Address-field handling.   The word mode has instructions, such as Stackref To Address, that interchange the stackref or address field of a word in the second level of the stack with one of these fields in the top level of the stack. The top level is subsequently deleted. All four combinations occur.

Set or store pointers.   Move Pointers performs one of four push or set-pointer actions with the stack reference or stack pointer, depending upon the low-order two bits of the top of the stack. The top level (an extended instruction) is deleted, and the next level is used either to set or to receive one of these values.

```
SSF;od;rl
ⱥ Burroughs B5500 Move Pointers
od←pop5500
rl←pop5500
→CASE magni ‾2↑od
C0: ⱥ push stack reference
    rl[Stackref]←adrsize magnr stackref
    push5500 rl
    →ENDCASE
C1: ⱥ set stack reference
    stackref←magni rl[Stackref]
    sublevel←1
    →ENDCASE
C2: ⱥ push stack pointer
    rl[Address]←adrsize magnr sp        FTC;od;rl
    push5500 rl                         ⱥ Burroughs B5500 Stackref To Address
    →ENDCASE                            od←pop5500
C3: ⱥ set stack pointer                 rl←pop5500
    sp←magni rl[Address]                rl[Address]←od[Stackref]
ENDCASE:                                push5500 rl
```

PROGRAM 13-155   Pointer movement in the Burroughs B5500.

Address addition.   The address fields of the two top levels of the stack are added, and the sum is placed in the top level, with the second level deleted.

```
INX;au;ad;augend;addend;sum
ⱥ Burroughs B5500 Add Addresses
au←pop5500
ad←pop5500
augend←magni au[Address]
addend←magni ad[Address]
sum←augend+addend
au[Address]←adrsize magnr sum
push5500 au
```

PROGRAM 13-156   Address addition in the Burroughs B5500.

Stack and list addressing.   Lookup Linked List searches a list for an element greater than or equal to the operand on top of the stack. The words are linked by the Address field of each entry. The test is performed upon the 24 high-order coefficient bits of each entry. The test criterion is in the top of the stack; the address of the head of the list is in the next stack entry. The entry that meets the test is pushed upon the stack. The address of that entry is made into a descriptor, and again is pushed onto the stack.

```
LLL;od1;od2;field;test;address
ⱥ Burroughs B5500 Lookup Link List
od1←pop5500
od2←pop5500
field←9+ι24
test←magni od1[field]
REPEAT: ⱥ test for greater or equal
    address←magni od2[Address]
    od2←1 read5500 address
→UNTIL(magni od2[field])≥test
push5500 od2
push5500 datadescr5500r address
```

PROGRAM 13-157   Linked list search in the Burroughs B5500.

Immediate bit-addressing. In the word mode, the 6-bit L0 field can be used to set the byte and bit parts of the `source` and `dest` address registers. These are the only parts of these registers that are available in the word mode and are used for the addressing of bit fields in the stack.

String address manipulation. In the character mode the addresses in `source` and `dest` can be loaded, stored, and updated in several ways.

The Transfer instructions select three byte-aligned characters that are specified by the designated address register and use the three high-order bits of this string as a new byte-address, and the 15 low-order bits as a new word-address for the designated register.

The Set instructions give the word address a parameter value and sets the byte and bit part of the address to 0.

The Recall instructions obtain an address from the parameter list. If the word is a descriptor without data, an interrupt is signaled and no further action takes place. Otherwise, the address field of the word is used to set the word address. The byte address is set to 0 if the flag is 1; when the flag is 0, the three bits to the left of the address are used to set the byte address. The bit address is always set to 0.

The Store instructions complement the Recall instruction; they write the word address in the `Address` field and the byte address in the three bits to the left of this field.

```
TDA;od
⋀ Burroughs B5500 Transfer Destination
dest←byte align5500 dest
od←(3×byte) read5500c dest
dest[0]←magni 3↓od
dest[1]←magni 3↑od


RDA;ddr
⋀ Burroughs B5500 Recall Destination
ddr←1 read5500 parentry5500
→OUT absent5500 ddr
dest[0]←magni ddr[Address]
dest[1]←magni(~ddr[Flag])∧ddr[30+ι3]
dest[2]←0


BSS;size
⋀ Burroughs B5500 Increment Source Bit
size←fld L0
source←source add5500c size



SSA;od
⋀ Burroughs B5500 Store Source
source←byte align5500 source
od←1 read5500 parentry5500
od[Address]←adrsize magnr source[0]
od[30+ι3]←3 magnr source[1]
od[Flag]←0
parentry5500 write5500 od
```

```
DIA
⋀ Burroughs B5500 Immediate Source
→OUT 0=fld L0
source[1 2]←(fld 3↑L0),fld 3↓L0


SES;od
⋀ Burroughs B5500 Set Source
od←1 read5500 parentry5500
source[0]←magni od[Address]
source[1 2]←0


SRS;size
⋀ Burroughs B5500 Decrement Source
size←byte×fld L0
source←byte align5500 source
source←source add5500c-size
```

PROGRAM 13-158   Source and destination operations in the Burroughs B5500.

Character-address increment. The LO field of the instruction can be used to increment a bit address or to increment or decrement a byte-aligned byte address.

13.4.4

Data

All word-mode operands have a Flag bit that is normally 0.

Character Strings

Character set and size. The 6-bit character set has 64 characters using Burroughs' own encoding. Several arithmetic symbols, such as $\geq$, $\times$, and $\neq$, are added to the usual 48-character set.

Character-string formats. In word mode, eight characters are packed in one word. In character mode, strings starting and ending at individual characters can be addressed (and single bits can be addressed).

Logical

Logical formats. The low-order bit of the logical vector serves as a Boolean condition for test operations and branches. A 47-bit logical vector is used in the logical connectives. The vector includes the Boolean condition bit.

```
↓Flag                                    Boolean↓
  ┌┬──────────────────────────────────────────┐
  ││Logic                                      │
  └┴──────────────────────────────────────────┘
  0                                          48

  data5500
  ⍝ Burroughs B5500 data allocation
  ⍝ logic allocation
  Logic←1+⍳47
  Boolean←47
  ⍝ decimal numbers
  decimal5500
```

PROGRAM 13-159   Logical vector in the Burroughs B5500.

Fixed-Point Numbers

Notation and allocation. There is no binary fixed-point datatype. A subset of floating point appears as 40-bit signed-magnitude integers, embedded in a 48-bit word. The word mode also allows variable-length binary fields to be moved and compared.

Decimal numbers. Decimal representation uses the usual 6-bit BCD decimal code. The sign is encoded in zone bits of the low-order byte. Minus is encoded as 2 (zone 10); the other three zone-bit combinations are taken as plus.

Decimal representation. Decimal numbers have sign-magnitude notation, with the sign and digits binary encoded. The zones of all bytes other than

the low-order byte are ignored on interpretation and are set to zero during representation. The length of the representation has a maximum of 63 digits.

```
0     6    12    18    24                      m
Legend: m = maximum 63×6; n = numeric; s = sign; z = zone.
```

```
decimal5500
ค Burroughs B5500 decimal number
ค sign encoding
plus← 0 1 3
minus←2
ค byte allocation
Zone←ι2
Num←2+ι4
```

```
number←decimal5500i rep;od;radix;sign;digits
ค Burroughs B5500 decimal interpretation
od←byte wide rep
sign← ¯1↑magni od[;Zone] WHERE radix←2
digits←magni od[;Num]
number←signmagni sign,digits WHERE radix←10
```

```
rep←length decimal5500r number;radix;decimals;zones;numerics
ค Burroughs B5500 decimal representation
decimals←(length+1) signmagnr number WHERE radix←10
zones←(ρZone) magnr(-length)↑1↑decimals WHERE radix←2
numerics←(ρNum) magnr 1↓decimals
rep←,zones,numerics
```

PROGRAM 13-160   Decimal format and representation in the Burroughs B5500.

Floating-Point Numbers

Closure and normal form.   Overflow and underflow are signaled by the indicators Floflo and Uflo. Precision is treated with rounding. Normalized and unnormalized operands are allowed. Arithmetic on integers yields integer results where possible.

Floating-point format.   The floating-point base is octal. The single-precision format has a 7-bit exponent and a coefficient with sign and 13 octal digits. In

```
0 2     9                                    48         57            96
Legend: Exp = exponent; * = unused.
```

```
f15500 size
ค Burroughs B5500 floating-point number
ค base
base←8
ค sign encoding
plus←0                          ค coefficient allocation
minus←1                           Coef←1,(9+ι39),(size=double)/57+ι39
ค exponent allocation           ค radix point
Exp←2+ι7                           point← 0 13[size=double]
```

PROGRAM 13-161   Floating-point format in the Burroughs B5500.

double precision the coefficient has 26 octal digits; the sign and exponent field are unused in the second word (the B6500 uses these exponent bits to enlarge the exponent). The radix point has 13 octal digits to the left in both formats; this positioning makes the single-precision coefficient an integer.

Floating-point representation.   Signed-magnitude notation is used for the coefficient and for the exponent. An all-zeros exponent has value 0. This representation makes it easy to use a floating-point word as an integer in part of the floating-point range.

```
numexp←f15500i rep;exponent;coefficient;number;plus;minus
ค Burroughs B5500 floating-point interpretation
f15500ρprep
exponent←signmagni rep[Exp]
coefficient←signmagni rep[Coef]
number←coefficient×base*exponent-point
numexp←number,exponent


rep←size f15500r numexp;exponent;coefficient;plus;minus;xmax;xmin
ค Burroughs B5500 floating-point representation
f15500 size
0 normalize numexp
rep←sizeρ0
rep[Exp]←(ρExp) signmagnr exponent
rep[Coef]←(ρCoef) signmagnr round5500 coefficient
Floflo report5500 xmax
Uflo report5500 xmin
```

PROGRAM 13-162   Floating-point representation in the Burroughs B5500.

Make integer.   integer5500 attempts to give a floating-point word a 0 exponent—hence the appearance of an integer. If the absolute value of the represented number is too large to allow a 0 exponent, the integer overflow indicator Oflo is turned on.

```
rep←integer5500 rep                result←round5500 number;bias
ค Burroughs B5500 make integer    ค Burroughs B5500 round
numexp←f15500i rep                 bias←(0.5≠1|number)∨number>0
rep←(ρrep) f15500r numexp[0],0     result←(×number)×⌊(0.5×bias)+|number
Oflo report5500∨/rep[2+ι7]
```

PROGRAM 13-163   Convert to integer in the Burroughs B5500.

Rounding.   For positive numbers, an integer-and-a-half rounds upward; for negative numbers, an integer-and-a-half rounds toward 0.

13.4.5
Operations

Data Handling

The character mode contains the data-handling instructions, such as moves and compares. The word mode has four bit-string moves and compares.

f	TRS	Move Characters	f	CLS	String Less
f	TRN	Move Numeric	f	CEL	String Equal Or Less
f	TRZ	Move Zone	f	CEQ	String Equal
f	TRW	Move Words	f	CEG	String Equal Or Greater
f	TRP	Move Program	f	CGR	String Greater
f	TBN	Blank Non-Numeric	f	CNE	String Unequal
f	TLS	Character Less	f	TAN	Character Test
f	TEL	Character Equal Or Less	b	TRB	Move Field
f	TEQ	Character Equal	b	ISO	Select Field
f	TEG	Character Greater Or Equal	b	FCL	Low Field
f	TGR	Character Greater	b	FCE	Equal Field
f	TNE	Character Unequal			

TABLE 13-164   Data-handling instructions of the Burroughs B5500.

Data movement.   Move Characters applies to strings of 0 through 63 characters. The source and destination addresses are specified by source and dest. In a preliminary action these addresses are byte-aligned. The L0 field of the instruction gives the number of characters to be moved. A length of 0 gives byte alignment without further action. Otherwise, the character string is moved, and the source and dest are updated to point at the first character beyond the string that was moved.

```
TRS;size;od                              TRN;size;od;sign
ᴀ Burroughs B5500 Move Characters      ᴀ Burroughs B5500 Move Numeric
  size←byte×fld L0                        size←byte×fld L0
  source←byte align5500 source           source←byte align5500 source
  dest←byte align5500 dest                dest←byte align5500 dest
  →OUT size=0                             →OUT size=0
  od←size read5500c source               od←byte wide size read5500c source
  dest write5500c od                     sign←¯1↑magni od[;Zone]
  source←source add5500c size            od[;Zone]←0
  dest←dest add5500c size                dest write5500c,od
                                         source←source add5500c size
                                         dest←dest add5500c size
TRW;size;od                              mark←sign=minus
ᴀ Burroughs B5500 Move Words
  size←word×fld L0
  source←word align5500 source           TBN;size;od;test;blanks
  dest←word align5500 dest             ᴀ Burroughs B5500 Blank Non-Numeric
  →OUT size=0                             size←byte×fld L0
  od←size read5500c source               dest←word align5500 dest
  dest write5500c od                     →OUT size=0 WHERE mark←1
  source←source add5500c size            od←byte wide size read5500c dest
  dest←dest add5500c size                test←(0=magni od)∨0≠magni od[;Zone]
                                         blanks←byte×testı1
                                         dest write5500c blanksρ 1 1 0 0 0 0
TRP;size;source;od                       dest←dest add5500c blanks
ᴀ Burroughs B5500 Move Program           mark←size=blanks
  size←byte×fld L0
  dest←byte align5500 dest
  source←(Liadr),((8×1|iadr)+2|fld L0),0
  →OUT size=0
  od←size read5500c source
  dest write5500c od
  source←source add5500c size
  iadr←source[0]+source[1]÷8
  dest←dest add5500c size
```

PROGRAM 13-165   Move in the Burroughs B5500.

Move Words is like Move Characters, but applies in alignment and size to words, not to characters. Move Numeric moves only the numeric part of the characters and makes the zones zero; it notes the sign of the string in the `mark` bit. Move Zones similarly moves only the zones, but it leaves the numeric part of the receiving string unchanged and does not test the sign.

Blank Non-Numerics replaces successive characters by blank characters until a non-zero numeric character is encountered; then it stops. A completely blanked string is signaled by the `mark` indicator.

Move Program moves the L0 bytes that start at the next instruction address to the location specified by `dest`. Execution proceeds at the aligned location following the last transferred byte. In this operation the register `source` is not used or changed; a local value derived from `iadr` is used instead.

Format and code transformation. Single character comparison (such as TGR) is immediate against the L0 field of the instruction. Strings of characters are compared by CLS, and so forth, using the byte-aligned `source` and `dest` registers and a size specified by L0. Character Test is an immediate comparison against the L0 field for greater than or equal if the characters are not signed zeros (with a binary code value of 42 or 26), and for equal to if the characters are such signed zeros.

```
TGR;od                                    CLS;size;od1;od2
ᴀ Burroughs B5500 Character Greater       ᴀ Burroughs B5500 String Less
source←byte align5500 source              size←byte×fld L0
od←byte read5500c source                  source←byte align5500 source
mark←(magni od)>fld L0                     dest←byte align5500 dest
                                          →OUT size=0
                                          od1←size read5500c source
                                          od2←size read5500c dest
TAN;od;except                             mark←(magni od1)<magni od2
ᴀ Burroughs B5500 Character Test          source←source add5500c size
source←byte align5500 source              dest←dest add5500c size
od←byte read5500c source
→IF(magni od)∈ 42 26
THEN: ᴀ signed zero
   mark←(magni od)=fld L0
   →ENDIF
ELSE: ᴀ other character
   mark←(magni od)≥fld L0
ENDIF:
```

PROGRAM 13-166   Character compare and test in the Burroughs B5500.

In the word mode, bit fields within a word can be specified with the byte and address fields of registers `source` and `dest` and with a length given by L0. In Move Field such a bit-field is moved from the top of the stack to the corresponding field in the next stack entry. In Low Field and Equal Field two fields are compared binarily. Select Field takes a field from the top of the stack and places it right-aligned as a new entry in the stack. Selection is cyclic in this operation. The size specification is peculiar. The left three bits of L0 specify the number of bytes involved, and the right three bits of L0 specify the number of bits dropped from the end of the field.

```
TRB;sts;std;size;od;rl                FCL;sts;std;size;od1;od2;operand;comparand
ᴀ Burroughs B5500 Move Field          ᴀ Burroughs B5500 Low Field
sts←byte⊥source[1 2]                  sts←byte⊥source[1 2]
std←byte⊥dest[1 2]                    std←byte⊥dest[1 2]
size←(48-sts)⌊(48-std)⌊fld L0         size←(48-sts)⌊(48-std)⌊fld L0
od←pop5500                            od1←pop5500
rl←pop5500                            comparand←magni od1[sts+ιsize]
rl[std+ιsize]←od[sts+ιsize]           od2←pop5500
push5500 rl                           operand←magni od2[std+ιsize]
                                      push5500 od1
                                      push5500(-word)↑operand<comparand
ISO;size;sts;od;rl
ᴀ Burroughs B5500 Select Field
size←(byte×fld 3↑L0)-fld 3↓L0
sts←byte⊥source[1 2]
od←pop5500
rl←(-word)↑od[word|sts+ιsize]
source←source add5500c byte×fld 3↑L0
push5500 rl
```

PROGRAM 13-167   Field selection and comparison in the Burroughs B5500.

Logic

The word mode has four logical connectives and four flag operations. In the character mode, bit fields can be set, reset, and tested.

a	LNG	Not	a	MDS	Set Flag	f	BIS	Set Bit
a	LND	And	a	MOP	Reset Flag	f	BIR	Reset Bit
a	LOR	Or	a	TOP	Test Flag	f	BIT	Test Bit
a	LQV	Equivalence	a	FBS	Search Flag			

TABLE 13-168   Logical operations of the Burroughs B5500.

Connectives.   The connectives NOT, AND, OR, and EQUIVALENCE operate on the 47-bit logical vectors of words obtained from the stack. The flag bit of the first operand is propagated.

```
LNG;od                        LQV;od1;od2
ᴀ Burroughs B5500 Not         ᴀ Burroughs B5500 Equivalence
od←pop5500                    od1←pop5500
od[Logic]←~od[Logic]          od2←pop5500
push5500 od                   od1[Logic]←od1[Logic]=od2[Logic]
                              push5500 od1
```

PROGRAM 13-169   Logical connectives in the Burroughs B5500.

Flag operations.   The flag of the word at the top of the stack can be set to 0 or 1; it can also be made into a Boolean condition and pushed onto the stack. Search Flag searches a vector of words that are placed sequentially in memory for the first non-data item (with flag on). The address of this word is made into a descriptor and replaces the start address of the vector that was on top of the stack.

Bit logic.   In the character mode, variable-length bit fields can be set to 0 or 1. A single bit can be tested for 0 and 1.

```
MDS;od                              FBS;od;address;data
ค Burroughs B5500 Set Flag          ค Burroughs B5500 Search Flag
od←pop5500                          od←pop5500
od[Flag]←1                          address←magni od[Address]
push5500 od                         REPEAT: ค test for flag on
                                       data←1 read5500 address
                                       address←adrcap|address+data[Flag]=0
TOP;od                              →UNTIL data[Flag]=1
ค Burroughs B5500 Test Flag         push5500 datadescr5500r address
od←pop5500
push5500 od
push5500(-word)↑od[Flag]
```

PROGRAM 13-170   Flag operations of the Burroughs B5500.

```
BIR;od                              BIT;bit
ค Burroughs B5500 Reset Bit  ค Burroughs B5500 Test Bit
od←(fld L0)ρ0                       bit←1 read5500c source
dest write5500c od                  mark←bit=2|fld L0
dest←dest add5500c fld L0
```

PROGRAM 13-171   Bit operations of the Burroughs B5500.

Fixed-Point Arithmetic

Decimal arithmetic is limited to addition, subtraction, and conversion to and from binary floating point. These operations are performed in the character mode.

```
f FAD Decimal Add        f ICV Decimal To Binary
f FSU Decimal Subtract   f OCV Binary To Decimal
```

TABLE 13-172   Decimal operations of the Burroughs B5500.

Add and Subtract.   Decimal addition and subtraction is on byte-aligned character fields, starting at the source and dest addresses, and with a common length specified by L0. A zero result with both operands −0 has negative sign. The address registers are postincremented by the operand size. Negative or positive overflow set the mark signal.

```
FAD;size;ad;au;addend;augend;sum;sm
ค Burroughs B5500 Decimal Add
size←byte×fld L0
source←byte align5500 source
dest←byte align5500 dest
→OUT size=0                         →If(sum=0)∧minus=magni ad[size- 5 4]
ad←size read5500c source            THEN: ค sign of zero
au←size read5500c dest                 sm[size- 5 4]←au[size- 5 4]
addend←decimal5500i ad              ENDIF:dest write5500c sm
augend←decimal5500i au              source←source add5500c size
sum←augend+addend                   dest←dest add5500c size
sm←(fld L0) decimal5500r sum        mark←xmax∨xmin
```

PROGRAM 13-173   Decimal addition in the Burroughs B5500.

Radix conversion.   Conversion is floating point to and from decimal. The decimal field is addressed via a byte-aligned address register and has the length specified by L0, but with a maximum of 8 bytes. The binary floating-point word is addressed with a word-aligned address register. Only the

coefficient field of the word participates. In decimal-to-binary operation, no overflow can occur. In binary-to-decimal operation, an overflow is noted in the `mark` signal.

```
ICV;size;od;operand;rl                OCV;size;od;operand;rl
⋒ Burroughs B5500 Decimal To Binary  ⋒ Burroughs B5500 Binary To Decimal
size←byte×8Lfld L0                    size←byte×8Lfld L0
source←byte align5500 source         source←word align5500 source
dest←word align5500 dest              dest←byte align5500 dest
→OUT size=0                           →OUT mark WHERE mark←size=0
od←size read5500c source             od←word read5500c source
operand←decimal5500i od              operand←signmagni od[1,9+ι39]
rl←0,(word-1) signmagnr operand      rl←(8Lfld L0) decimal5500r operand
dest write5500c rl                   dest write5500c rl
source←source add5500c size          source←source add5500c word
dest←dest add5500c word              dest←dest add5500c size
                                     mark←xmax∨xmin
```

PROGRAM 13-174   Radix conversion in the Burroughs B5500.

Floating-Point Arithmetic

Floating-point operations include Load and Store, stack manipulation, sign control, arithmetic, and comparison. The arithmetic operations are in single and double precision.

```
a LOD Load                                  a ADD F Add
d LTC Load Immediate                        a DLA Add D
a STD Store                                 a SUB F Subtract
a SND Store And Keep                        a DLS Subtract D
a ISD Store Integer                         a MUL F Multiply
a ISN Store And Keep Integer                a DLM Multiply D
a CID Store Integer On Demand               a DIV F Divide
a CIN Store And Keep Integer On Demand      a DLD Divide D
a XCH Swap                                   a IDV F Divide To Integer
a DUP Duplicate                             a RDV F Remainder
e DEL Delete                                a LSS F Less
a CHS F Negate                              a LEQ F Less Or Equal
a SSP F Make Absolute                       a EQL F Equal
a SSN F Negate Absolute                     a GEQ F Greater Or Equal
                                            a GTR F Greater
                                            a NEQ F Not Equal
Legend: D = Double; F = Floating-Point.
```

TABLE 13-175   Floating-point instructions of the Burroughs B5500.

Load and Store.   Load and Store use the top of the stack as a direct address when that word is a descriptor (the flag is set), or as one of the various base addresses at the program or subprogram level. This address is used to read a word from memory and place it in the stack. `variant5500` sets the processor to the subprogram level if the `variant` status is 1, then resets this status.

Load Immediate pushes the 10-bit `Referend` field, extended to word size, as an operand upon the stack.

Store Integer places an integer copy of the data on the stack, then stores this integer, unless the integer overflows and becomes a floating-point value.

Store Integer On Demand acts the same if the `Integer` bit of the data descriptor on the top of the stack is 1; otherwise, a normal floating-point store is performed.

```
LOD;ddr
ค Burroughs B5500 Load
ddr←pop5500
→OUT absent5500 ddr
push5500 1 read5500 1 adr5500f ddr
variant5500




STD;ddr
ค Burroughs B5500 Store
ddr←pop5500
→OUT absent5500 ddr
(0 adr5500f ddr) write5500 pop5500
variant5500
```

```
LTC
ค Burroughs B5500 Load Immediate
push5500(-word)↑inst[Referend]



SND;ddr;data
ค Burroughs B5500 Store And Keep
ddr←pop5500
→OUT absent5500 ddr
data←pop5500
(0 adr5500f ddr) write5500 data
push5500 data
variant5500
```

```
CID;ddr
ค Burroughs B5500 Store Integer On Demand
ddr←pop5500
push5500 ddr
→IF ddr[Integer]
THEN: ค store integer
    ISD
   →ENDIF
ELSE: ค store
    STD
ENDIF:
```

```
ISD;ddr;r1
ค Burroughs B5500 Store Integer
ddr←pop5500
→OUT absent5500 ddr
r1←integer5500 pop5500
push5500 r1
push5500 ddr
→OUT suppress
STD
```

PROGRAM 13-176   Load and Store in the Burroughs B5500.

Stack service. Swap interchanges the two top levels of the stack. Duplicate places a copy of the top level on top of the stack. Delete eliminates the item at the top of the stack.

```
XCH;od1;od2                 DUP;od
ค Burroughs B5500 Swap     ค Burroughs B5500 Duplicate
od1←pop5500                 od←pop5500
od2←pop5500                 push5500 od
push5500 od1                push5500 od
push5500 od2
```

PROGRAM 13-177   Swap and Duplicate in the Burroughs B5500.

Floating-point sign change.   All three sign-change options operate purely on the coefficient sign. They apply to single and double precision. Since they ignore the coefficient value, a negative 0 may be created.

Floating-point Add and Subtract.   Addition and subtraction are each defined for single and double precision.   When the exponents of the two single-precision operands are equal, then this exponent value becomes the preferred exponent for an unnormalized result; otherwise, the result is normalized. Encompassing an integer datatype within the floating-point datatype by this kind of unnormalized mode is an attractive idea. The operands and the result each occupy two successive stack locations.

```
CHS;od
ค Burroughs B5500 Floating-Point Negate
od←pop5500
push5500 od WHERE od[1]←˜od[1]
```

```
ADD;ad;au;sm
ค Burroughs B5500 Floating-Point Add
ad←f15500i pop5500
au←f15500i pop5500
→IF au[1]=ad[1]
THEN: ค attempt integer add
     sm←(au[0]+ad[0]),ad[1]
     →ENDIF
ELSE: ค normalized add
     sm←au[0]+ad[0]
ENDIF:push5500 word f15500r sm
```

```
DLS;od1;sb;od2;mn;df;rl
ค Burroughs B5500 Subtract Double
od1←pop5500
sb←f15500i od1,pop5500
od2←pop5500
mn←f15500i od2,pop5500
→IF mn[1]=sb[1]
THEN: ค attempt integer subtract
     df←(mn[0]-sb[0]),mn[1]
     →ENDIF
ELSE: ค normalized subtract
     df←mn[0]-sb[0]
ENDIF:rl←double f15500r df
push5500 word↓rl
push5500 word↑rl
```

PROGRAM 13-178   Floating-point Add and Subtract in the Burroughs B5500.

Floating-point Multiply and Divide.

Multiply attempts, like Add, to obtain an integer result from integer operands. The condition applied in multiplication is that the exponents of both operands be 0. Division does not attempt to preserve integer values; it always normalizes. Divide Integer and Remainder, however, attempt to give an integer quotient or remainder, respectively.

```
MUL;mr;md;pd
ค Burroughs B5500 Floating-Point Multiply
mr←f15500i pop5500
md←f15500i pop5500
→IF(md[1]=0)∧mr[1]=0
THEN: ค attempt integer multiply
     pd←(md[0]×mr[0]),0
     →ENDIF
ELSE: ค normalized multiply
     pd←md[0]×mr[0]
ENDIF:push5500 word f15500r pd
```

```
DLD;od1;dr;od2;dd;quotient;qt
ค Burroughs B5500 Divide Double
od1←pop5500
dr←f15500i od1,pop5500
Divide report5500 dr[0]=0
→OUT suppress
od2←pop5500
dd←f15500i od2,pop5500
quotient←dd[0]÷dr[0]
qt←double f15500r quotient
push5500 word↓qt
push5500 word↑qt
```

```
RDV;dr;dd;quotient;remainder;rm
ค Burroughs B5500 Floating-Point Remainder
dr←f15500i pop5500
Divide report5500 dr[0]=0
→OUT suppress
dd←f15500i pop5500
quotient←truncate dd[0]÷dr[0]
remainder←dd[0]-quotient×dr[0]
rm←integer5500 word f15500r remainder
→If suppress
THEN:rm[]←0
ENDIF:push5500 rm
```

PROGRAM 13-179   Floating-point Multiply and Divide in the Burroughs B5500.

Floating-point Compare.

All six comparison relations that are available for a single character and for a character string are also provided for single-precision floating-point operands (including integers).

```
GTR;comparand;operand
A Burroughs B5500 Floating-Point Greater
comparand←1↑fl5500i pop5500
operand←1↑fl5500i pop5500
push5500(-word)↑operand>comparand
```

PROGRAM 13-180   Floating-point Compare in the Burroughs B5500.

13.4.6

Instruction Sequencing

The basic processing cycle is classical, with interrupt and a stop condition. The mode bit is attached to the instruction that is fetched to govern interpretation according to the syntactic patterns that apply to the word or the character mode.

```
cycle5500                                inst←ifetch5500;od
A basic cycle of the Burroughs B5500     A Burroughs B5500 instruction fetch
REPEAT:interrupt5500                     od←1 read5500⌊iadr
   execute ifetch5500,charmode           inst←(word÷4)↑(word×1|iadr)↓od
→UNTIL stop                              iadr←iadr+0.25
```

PROGRAM 13-181   Basic cycle and instruction fetch of the Burroughs B5500.

All instructions occupy a 12-bit syllable. Instruction fetch, in principle, fetches a full 48-bit word specified by the integer part of the instruction address, and selects the desired quarterword specified by the fractional part of the instruction address.

Sequencing instructions are needed in both modes. The various types of instructions, however, are divided unequally over the two modes. Word mode knows absolute and relative branches, subroutine entry, and return. Character mode has only relative branches; it has no subroutine entry, but does have iteration, and storing and recovery of the instruction address.

e	NOP	No Operation	f	BNS	Begin Loop
a	ZP1	Stop On Switch	f	ENS	End Loop
f	ZP1	Stop On Switch	f	JNS	Leave Loop
a	BFW	Branch	f	JNC	Leave Loop On Mark
a	BBW	Branch B	c	MKS	Mark Stack
a	LFU	Branch Word	a	XIT	Exit
a	LBU	Branch Word B	a	BRT	Return
f	JFW	Jump	a	RTN	Return Normal
f	JRV	Jump B	a	RTS	Return Special
a	BFC	Branch On Condition	f	SCA	Store Instruction Address
a	BBC	Branch On Condition B	f	RCA	Recall Instruction Address
a	LFC	Branch Word On Condition	f	CRF	Modify Next Instruction
a	LBC	Branch Word On Condition B	f	STC	Store Tally
b	CBR	Branch On Non-zero	f	SEC	Set Tally
f	JFC	Jump On Mark	f	INC	Increment Tally
f	JRC	Jump On Mark B			

Legend: B = Backward.

TABLE 13-182   Sequencing instructions of the Burroughs B5500.

Linear Sequence

Next instruction.   Normal sequencing occurs by incrementing the instruction address by 0.25.

Unconditional branch.   The set of branches includes forward and backward relative branches because the branch offset is limited and unsigned. Furthermore, branches may refer to quarterword syllable addresses or to fullword addresses. In the word mode, the top of the stack determines if the branch address is absolute or relative. When the flag is 0, Branch treats the 12 low-order bits of the entry as a syllable offset; Branch Word treats the low-order 10 bits as a word offset. When the flag is 1, the entry at the top of the stack is a data descriptor, and the full 15-bit address is used as an absolute branch address (via a program descriptor for relocatability). The corresponding backward branches differ only in the sign of the offset.

In the character mode, the branch is always relative and uses the L0 field as a syllable offset that is applied forward or backward.

```
BFW;od;offset                      LBU;od;offset
A Burroughs B5500 Branch           A Burroughs B5500 Branch Word Backward
od←pop5500                         od←pop5500
→IF˜od[Flag]                       →IF˜od[Flag]
THEN: A syllable jump              THEN: A word jump backwards
    offset←magni od[3↓Address]         offset←magni od[5↓Address]
    iadr←iadr+0.25×offset              iadr←iadr-offset
    →ENDIF                             →ENDIF
ELSE: A word branch                ELSE: A word branch
    →OUT absent5500 od                 →OUT absent5500 od
    iadr←magni od[Address]             iadr←magni od[Address]
ENDIF:                             ENDIF:
```

```
JFW
A Burroughs B5500 Jump
iadr←iadr+0.25×fld L0
```

PROGRAM 13-183   Unconditional Branch in the Burroughs B5500.

Completion.   The No Operation syllable has no action. The B5500 does not have a wait status. The Stop instruction, which occurs in both the word and character modes, stops the processor when the Stop Switch is activated.

```
NOP                                ZP1
A Burroughs B5500 No Operation     A Burroughs B5500 Stop On Switch
                                   stop←stopswitch
```

PROGRAM 13-184   No Operation and Stop in the Burroughs B5500.

Decision

Conditional branching.   Usually, testing and branch action are separated. In word mode, the branch address is assumed to be at the top of the stack, and the condition's value bit is the Boolean bit of the logical word just below the top. The condition fails if the Boolean is 1; in that case, both the branch

address and the test word are removed from the stack. When the condition succeeds, an unconditional branch occurs which may cause a syllable jump or a word branch; again, both the branch address and the condition are removed from the stack. If the unconditional branch fails because of data absence, the branch address and the condition remain on the stack. In character mode, the `mark` indicator stores the condition. A full set of relations is provided for the comparisons.

```
BBC;od1;od2
 ∩ Burroughs B5500 Branch On Condition Backward
 od1←pop5500
 od2←pop5500
 →If˜od2[Boolean]            CBR;od1;od2;start;size;zero
 THEN:push5500 od2           ∩ Burroughs B5500 Branch On Non-zero
     push5500 od1            od1←pop5500
     BBW                     od2←pop5500
     →OUT suppress           →If˜fld L0[5]
     od2←pop5500             THEN: ∩ preserve test word
 ENDIF:                          push5500 od2
                             ENDIF: ∩ test field
                             start←byte⊥source[1 2]
                             size←fld L0[ι4]
                             zero←˜∨/od2[word|start+ιsize]
                             →CASE(zero,fld L0[4])ι1
                             C0: ∩ no branch
                                 →ENDCASE
                             C1: ∩ branch forward
                                 push5500 od1
                                 BFW
                                 →ENDCASE
                             C2: ∩ branch backward
                                 push5500 od1
                                 BBW
                             ENDCASE:

 JRC
 ∩ Burroughs B5500 Jump On Mark Backward
 →If mark=0
 THEN:iadr←iadr-0.25×fld L0
 ENDIF:
```

PROGRAM 13-185   Conditional Branch in the Burroughs B5500.

Branch On Non-Zero. In this word-mode instruction, the top of the stack is used as branch address. The next stack level is tested for a zero field. The start of this field is determined by the byte- and bit-address part of `source`. The length of the field is determined by the first four bits of the L0 field. The stack level that contains the field is eliminated if the low-order bit of the L0 field is 1; otherwise, it is preserved. In case the field is 0, no branch occurs, and the branch address is eliminated. Otherwise, a forward or backward branch is performed, depending upon the next-to-last bit of the L0 field.

Iteration

In word mode there seems to be no fast loopcloser or other iterative construct. The character mode has a repeat, which is controlled by a loop

control word. The scope of the repeat is unlimited and marked by a Begin
Loop and an End Loop syllable. The number of times that the loop is repeated
is determined by the 6-bit `Repeat` field. The use of the stack for loop control
words makes it possible to nest multiple loops.

```
loop5500
ค Burroughs B5500 loop control        ค Burroughs B5500 make loop control
Syllable←10+ι2                        lcw←wordρ0
Repeat←12+ι6                          lcw[Tag]← 1 1 0
ค Unused←2,4+ι6                       lcw[Repeat]←6 magnr count
                                      lcw[Stackref]←adrsize magnr dest[0]
                                      lcw[Syllable]←2 magnr 4×1|iadr
                                      lcw[Address]←adrsize magnr|iadr
loop5500i lcw
ค Burroughs B5500 use loop control
iadr←0.25×magni lcw[Address,Syllable]
```

```
lcw←loop5500r count
```

PROGRAM 13-186   Loop control in the Burroughs B5500.

Incrementation and termination.   Begin Loop starts a loop by constructing
a loop control word that includes the count (from the `L0` field) and the start
address (the next instruction syllable address). The loop is a repeat structure,
so a start count of 0 and a start count of 1 have the same effect. The loop
count is limited to 63, but nesting can be used to increase this number. The
control word is pushed onto the stack. The scope of the loop is indicated by
the End Loop instruction. This latter instruction takes the loop control word
from the stack, reduces the count by 1, and tests the count for 0. If the count
is not 0, the instruction address is set to the start of the loop, and the control
word is pushed again onto the stack. Leave Loop jumps out of the loop and
eliminates the loop control word. The programmer must see to it that the
jump is beyond the corresponding End Loop, but not beyond a surrounding

```
BNS                                   JNS;lcw
ค Burroughs B5500 Begin Loop          ค Burroughs B5500 Leave Loop
  push5500 loop5500r 0⌈(fld L0)-1       iadr←iadr+0.25×fld L0
                                        lcw←pop5500


ENS;lcw;count
ค Burroughs B5500 End Loop            JNC
  lcw←pop5500                         ค Burroughs B5500 Leave Loop On Mark
  count←magni lcw[Repeat]              →If mark=0
  →If count≠0                          THEN: ค leave loop
  THEN: ค repeat loop                     JNS
     lcw[Repeat]←6 magnr count-1       ENDIF:
     loop5500i lcw
     push5500 lcw
  ENDIF:
```

PROGRAM 13-187   Increment and branch in the Burroughs B5500.

loop; otherwise, the words on the stack no longer match the various nested scopes.

Delegation

The subroutine enter-and-return actions are designed to handle any depth of delegation, including recursion. Working store can readily be stored and restored.

Parameter passing. The parameters used in a subroutine are intended to be brought to the stack from the program reference table specified by progref. A mark-stack control word, mscw, should separate the parameters from the underlying data on the stack. The mscw contains the current stack reference and program reference addresses, and the mark and sublevel bits. The stack is marked by the Mark Stack instruction (Program 13-190), which also places the address of the mark stack word in the stack reference address. Thus a chain of control words is established. The parameters of the subroutine are pushed above the mark-stack word.

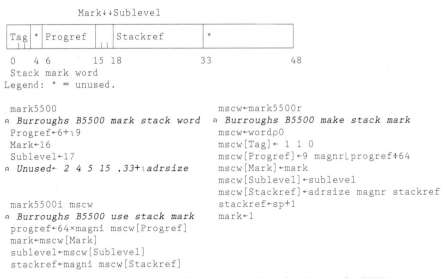

```
          Mark↓↓Sublevel
┌─────┬─┬────────┬─┬──────────┬─────────────┬────────┐
│Tag  │*│Progref │ │Stackref  │      *      │        │
└─┬─┬─┴─┴────────┴─┴──────────┴─────────────┴────────┘
0    4 6          15 18          33              48
Stack mark word
Legend:  * = unused.
```

```
 mark5500                                  mscw←mark5500r
ᴀ Burroughs B5500 mark stack word         ᴀ Burroughs B5500 make stack mark
 Progref←6+ɩ9                              mscw←wordρ0
 Mark←16                                   mscw[Tag]← 1 1 0
 Sublevel←17                               mscw[Progref]←9 magnrɩprogref≑64
ᴀ Unused← 2 4 5 15 ,33+ɩadrsize           mscw[Mark]←mark
                                           mscw[Sublevel]←sublevel
                                           mscw[Stackref]←adrsize magnr stackref
 mark5500i mscw                            stackref←sp+1
ᴀ Burroughs B5500 use stack mark          mark←1
 progref←64×magni mscw[Progref]
 mark←mscw[Mark]
 sublevel←mscw[Sublevel]
 stackref←magni mscw[Stackref]
```

PROGRAM 13-188   Mark-stack control in the Burroughs B5500.

Call.   After the stack is marked and the parameters are pushed on the stack, subroutine entry can be by Operand Call or Descriptor Call. These instructions should fetch the program descriptor of the subroutine and place a return control word, rcw, above the parameters in the stack. The rcw contains the return instruction address and the byte and bit part of the source and destination addresses. Again, the stack reference address—pointing to a preceding mark-stack word—is recorded, and the stack-pointer value is placed in stackref. Thus the chain of control words is extended.

↓Cltype   ↓Syllable

Tag	S	D		S	D	Stackref		Address	

```
0    4   7    12 15 18                  33              48
Return word
Legend: D = destination: S = source.
```

```
return5500                         rcw←return5500r call
ᴀ Burroughs B5500 return word      ᴀ Burroughs B5500 make return word
Cltype←2                           rcw←wordρ0
Sbit←4+ı3                          rcw[Tag]← 1 1 0
Dbit←7+ı3                          rcw[Cltype]←call
Syllable←10+ı2                     rcw[Sbit]←3 magnr source[1]
Sbyte←12+ı3                        rcw[Dbit]←3 magnr dest[1]
Dbyte←15+ı3                        rcw[Sbyte]←3 magnr source[2]
                                   rcw[Dbyte]←3 magnr dest[2]
                                   rcw[Stackref]←adrsize magnr stackref
return5500i rcw                    rcw[Syllable]←2 magnr 4×1∣iadr
ᴀ Burroughs B5500 use return word  rcw[Address]←adrsize magnr∟iadr
source[1]←magni rcw[Sbyte]         stackref←sp+1
source[2]←magni rcw[Sbit]          mark←0
dest[1]←magni rcw[Dbyte]
dest[2]←magni rcw[Dbit]
iadr←0.25×magni rcw[Address,Syllable]
stackref←magni rcw[Stackref]
sp←stackref
```

PROGRAM 13-189   Return word in the Burroughs B5500.

Enter action.   The details of subroutine entry are shown in entry5500. After checking of the presence of the routine in memory, the Argument and Chain bits of the descriptor are used to distinguish three major cases of entry. Argument indicates that the procedure requires parameters. If indeed the mark bit is set, then the arguments should be on the stack. The return word is pushed on top of the arguments, and the descriptor is used to set the instruction address and other status (Program 13-152). The subroutine may be either in the word or in the character mode. When mark is not set, the parameters are missing, no entry takes place, and the descriptor is just pushed onto the stack.

When no parameters are required and character mode is specified, the subroutine is not entered, and the descriptor is again pushed onto the stack. If word mode is specified, however, the subroutine is entered without parameters (called *accidental entry*). A mark-stack word and return word are pushed onto the stack, and the subroutine is entered at the address specified by the program descriptor. The stack reference address is set to the address specified in the descriptor, presumably pointing to parameters found elsewhere.

Return action.   restore5500 returns from a subroutine; it obtains the return control word and mark-stack word from the stack, uses them to restore the control registers, and sets the stack pointer to the stack reference. The stack pointer now addresses the mark-stack word below the parameter area. Thus the calling program can be restored to its status prior to entering the parameters on the stack. If both mark and sublevel are on, the list of

control words is searched for a word with 0 mark. That word is placed in program reference location 7.

```
call entry5500 pdr                          exit5500 address;od;rcw
A Burroughs B5500 subroutine entry          A Burroughs B5500 subroutine exit
→OUT absent5500 pdr                         od←pop5500
→CASE pdr[Argument.Charmode]ιl             →OUT absent5500 od
CO: A parameters required                   rcw←1 read5500 address
   →IF mark                                 Flagerror report5500~rcw[Flag]
   THEN: A parameters in stack             →If suppress
       push5500 return5500r call            THEN: A interrupt
       program5500i pdr                         push5500 rcw
       →ENDIF                                   push5500 od
   ELSE: A no parameters                    ENDIF:→OUT suppress
       push5500 pdr                         restore5500 rcw
   ENDIF:→ENDCASE                          →CASE rcw[Cltype]
C1: A special descriptor                    CO: A operand call
   push5500 pdr                                 odcall5500 od
   →ENDCASE                                     →ENDCASE
C2: A accidental entry                      C1: A descriptor call
   push5500 mark5500r                           push5500 od
   push5500 return5500r call                    ddcall5500 sp
   program5500i pdr                         ENDCASE:
   stackref←magni pdr[Stackref]
ENDCASE:

                                            restore5500 rcw;mscw
                                            A Burroughs B5500 restore registers
MKS;mscw                                    return5500i rcw
A Burroughs B5500 Mark Stack                mscw←pop5500
mscw←mark5500r                              mark5500i mscw
push5500 mscw                              →WHILE mscw[Mark]∧sublevel
→If sublevel∧mscw[Mark]=0                      mscw←1 read5500 magni mscw[Stackref]
THEN: A extra reference                        (progref+7) write5500 mscw
   (progref+7) write5500 mscw                  →Δ
ENDIF:                                      ENDWHILE:
```

PROGRAM 13-190   Subroutine entry and return in the Burroughs B5500.

Mark-stack instruction.   Mark Stack constructs a mark-stack word, pushes it onto the stack, and records its memory location in stackref. If the program is on a sublevel without parameters in the stack (mark is off) then the mark-stack word is also stored in program reference location 7. At the end of the operation, the mark bit is turned on (see mark5500r).

Return instructions.   All Return instructions are in the word mode. Exit returns from a subroutine by using restore5500 after checking the flag bit of the return word. When a subroutine is entered by an operand call or a descriptor call, the instructions Return Normal or Return Special can be used. They call upon exit5500, which checks flag and tag bits, then uses restore5500 for the actual return, and finally performs either an operand or descriptor call, depending upon the syllable type bit. Return Special obtains the mark-stack word from the stack (following the return word) and not from the stack reference register, as does Return Normal. Return (BRT) is used for the return from a subroutine that is entered by a Branch; the stack is not searched in this case. Return treats the word on top of the stack as a program

descriptor whose stack reference points to a mark-stack word. Both words are restored, depending upon the usual flag test.

```
RTN                                    RTS
ᴀ Burroughs B5500 Return Normal        ᴀ Burroughs B5500 Return Special
exit5500 stackref                      exit5500 sp


XIT;rcw;mscw                           BRT;pdr
ᴀ Burroughs B5500 Exit                 ᴀ Burroughs B5500 Return
rcw←1 read5500 stackref                pdr←pop5500
push5500 rcw                           Absent report5500~pdr[Present]
Flagerror report5500~rcw[Flag]         push5500 pdr
→OUT suppress                          →OUT suppress
restore5500 pop5500                    pdr←pop5500
                                       sp←magni pdr[Stackref]
                                       iadr←magni pdr[Address]
                                       mark5500i pop5500
```

PROGRAM 13-191   Return in the Burroughs B5500.

Store and recall instruction address.   Two character-mode instructions allow assembly-level programming of a subroutine in character mode. Store Instruction Address stores its own instruction address in a word in the parameter list. The fields where the word address and syllable address are stored conform to the format of a return control word. The flag bit is made 0, however, and thus distinguishes the word from a normal return control word. This distinction is used in Recall Instruction Address, which furthermore tests the Present bit of the control word to give a segmentation interruption if needed. The address of the instruction is updated after storing, and hence also after fetching.

```
SCA;od
ᴀ Burroughs B5500 Store Instruction Address
od←1 read5500 parentry5500
od[Address,Syllable]←(adrsize+2) magnr 4×iadr
od[Flag]←0
parentry5500 write5500 od


RCA;od
ᴀ Burroughs B5500 Recall Instruction Address
od←1 read5500 parentry5500
→CASE od[Flag,Present]ι0
C0: ᴀ syllable address
    iadr←0.25×1+magni od[Address,Syllable]
    →ENDCASE
C1: ᴀ address absent
    Absent report5500 1
    →ENDCASE
C2: ᴀ word address
    iadr←magni od[Address]
ENDCASE:
```

PROGRAM 13-192   Move instruction address in the Burroughs B5500.

Instruction modification.   Modify Next Instruction replaces the L0 field of the following character-mode instruction with six low-order bits obtained from the parameter list. Through this meta-instruction a calculated value can be substituted for the L0 field of any character-mode instruction. If the calculated value is 0 (which normally gives a meaningless character-mode instruction), a jump is performed instead. The offset of this jump is obtained from the newly fetched (but not yet executed) instruction.

```
CRF;od
 ⍝ Burroughs B5500 Modify Next Instruction
 od←1 read5500 parentry5500
 inst←ifetch5500
 →IF(magni ¯6↑od)≠0
 THEN: ⍝ modify and execute
     inst[L0]←¯6↑od
     execute inst
     →ENDIF
 ELSE: ⍝ jump
     iadr←iadr+0.25×fld L0
 ENDIF:
```

PROGRAM 13-193   Instruction modification in the Burroughs B5500.

Counter. In the character mode, the program reference address can be used as a tally (or counter), to be set, incremented, and stored. The program reference is not a complete address (it refers to blocks of 64 words); the tally uses only the low-order six bits of this 9-bit address.

```
SEC                              STC;r1
 ⍝ Burroughs B5500 Set Tally      ⍝ Burroughs B5500 Store Tally
 progref←64×fld L0                 r1←word magnr⌊progref÷64
                                   parentry5500 write5500 r1

INC
 ⍝ Burroughs B5500 Increment Tally
 progref←4096|progref+64×fld L0
```

PROGRAM 13-194   Tally operations in the Burroughs B5500.

13.4.7

Supervision

Concurrency

Full provision is made for dual processors, as well as for concurrent I/O operations. The processors have a master–slave relationship: the master can start and stop the slave.

Supervisory operations.   All supervisory instructions are in word mode, except, of course, the instruction that switches from character to word mode. The instructions deal with mode change, interrupt handling, dispatching, and stopping processors. The operation Diagnose is intended for maintenance purposes only.

```
f EXC Leave Character Mode    a IP1 Dispatch One
c CMN Enter Character Mode    a IP2 Dispatch Two
a ITI Inspect Interrupt       a COM Humble Access
a SFI Store For Interrupt     a HP2 Stop Two
a SFT Store For Diagnose      a RTR Read Time
                              a IFT Diagnose
```

TABLE 13-195   Supervisory instructions of the Burroughs B5500.

Mode change.   Enter Character Mode uses a control word to set the word and byte part of dest. The sublevel and charmode states are set, and the mark signal and progref address are made 0. The instruction address is not altered; the switch to character mode is made "in line." The instruction address is pushed as part of a return control word onto stack. The stack pointer is copied into the stack reference.

```
CMN;od
⋒ Burroughs B5500 Enter Character Mode
od←pop5500
→OUT absent5500 od                EXC;old;rcw
push5500 od                       ⋒ Burroughs B5500 Leave Character Mode
dest[0]←magni od[Address]         old←iadr
push5500 return5500r 0            rcw←1 read5500 stackref
→If od[Flag]=0                    Flagerror report5500˜rcw[Flag]
THEN: ⋒ byte address              push5500 rcw
   dest[1]←magni od[30+ι3]        →OUT suppress
ENDIF:progref←0                   return5500i pop5500
sublevel←1                        mark5500i pop5500
charmode←1                        charmode←0
mark←0                            →If 1=fld L0
                                  THEN: ⋒ leave in line
                                     iadr←old
                                  ENDIF:
```

PROGRAM 13-196   Mode change in the Burroughs B5500.

Leave Character Mode is the inverse of Mark stack, followed by Enter Character Mode. The stack reference address points to a return control word. After the flag bit is checked, the return word is used to set the byte and bit part of the source and destination addresses and the instruction address. Next, a mark-stack word is obtained from the stack and used to set the original stack reference address, the program reference address, as well as the mark and sublevel status bits. The charmode bit is set to 0. When the L0 field has the value 1, the processor does not proceed at the address specified by the Enter Character Mode instruction, but proceeds in line.

Process Interaction

Signaling.   Message passing is by shared memory with mutual interruption for signaling. The instruction Stop Processor 2 causes that processor to save its status and to halt such that it can be reinitiated without loss of information.

Integrity

Protection.   The supervisory state is protected by privileged instructions. Array bounds are checked automatically when a vector descriptor is used to form an effective address. This mechanism catches the most common

memory violation in compiler-generated code—one that can be caught only at execution time. I/O can only be initiated in supervisory state.

Privileged operations.   Interrupt interrogation, dispatching, and stopping are valid only in the supervisory state, as are Diagnose and various I/O operations. Privileged operations are ignored in the normal mode; they do not cause an interruption.

Control Switching

Interruption action.   Upon interruption, the machine goes into supervisory mode. A single operation causes branching to the appropriate interruption routine. Return to user mode is by a Dispatch operation.

Every instruction cycle tests if any indicator is set. If so, the indicator is processed if the system is in the normal mode. The B5500 uses the action of regular instructions for storing the machine status (SFI) and for finding an interrupt cause (ITI, Program 13-200). After storing the machine status, the program reference address is reset, and the modes are set to supervisor, program level, and word mode; the mark signal is reset. Processor 1 proceeds to handle an interruption; processor 2 is stopped.

```
interrupt5500                          reset5500
A Burroughs B5500 interrupt action   A Burroughs B5500 reset
suppress←0                             progref←0
→If normal∧∨/ind                       normal←0
THEN: A inspect indicator              sublevel←0
   SFI                                  charmode←0
   reset5500                            mark←0
   stop←procnr=2
   →OUT stop
   ITI
ENDIF:
```

PROGRAM 13-197   Interruption action in the Burroughs B5500.

State Preservation

Context switching.   At the moment of interruption, the interrupt status is placed in control words. In the character mode, a loop control word is pushed onto the stack to preserve the word part of the destination address. Next, in both modes, the interrupt control word and the return control word are placed in the stack. Finally, another control word, the initiate control word, is placed in the program reference table and points at the stack.

Interrupt control word.   The interrupt control word resembles the mark-stack word by preserving the program reference address, mark, and sublevel. The interrupt word, however, does not contain a stack reference address, but places the variant bit in one of the bits of that field.

Above the interrupt control word, a return word (Program 13-189) is placed. It contains the instruction and stack reference addresses, and the source and destination byte and bit addresses. The implementation uses bit 2 of this word as well as several bits that are marked "unused" in these control words.

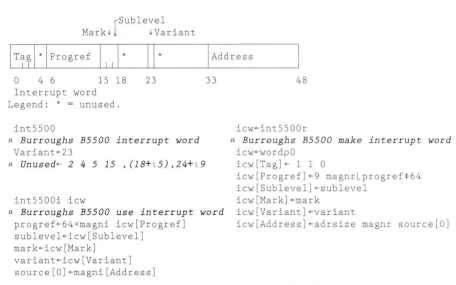

```
int5500                                    icw←int5500r
ꓮ Burroughs B5500 interrupt word           ꓮ Burroughs B5500 make interrupt word
  Variant←23                                  icw←wordρ0
ꓮ Unused← 2 4 5 15 ,(18+ι5),24+ι9            icw[Tag]← 1 1 0
                                             icw[Progref]←9 magnrⵏprogref÷64
                                             icw[Sublevel]←sublevel
int5500i icw                                 icw[Mark]←mark
ꓮ Burroughs B5500 use interrupt word         icw[Variant]←variant
  progref←64×magni icw[Progref]              icw[Address]←adrsize magnr source[0]
  sublevel←icw[Sublevel]
  mark←icw[Mark]
  variant←icw[Variant]
  source[0]←magni[Address]
```

PROGRAM 13-198   Interruption control in the Burroughs B5500.

Initiate control word. Since the interrupt handling routine uses its own stack, the stack pointer of the interrupted program is saved in the initiate control word. The character-mode bit is also saved in this word.

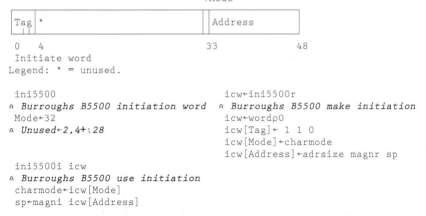

```
ini5500                                    icw←ini5500r
ꓮ Burroughs B5500 initiation word          ꓮ Burroughs B5500 make initiation
  Mode←32                                    icw←wordρ0
ꓮ Unused←2,4+ι28                             icw[Tag]← 1 1 0
                                             icw[Mode]←charmode
                                             icw[Address]←adrsize magnr sp
ini5500i icw
ꓮ Burroughs B5500 use initiation
  charmode←icw[Mode]
  sp←magni icw[Address]
```

PROGRAM 13-199   Dispatch control in the Burroughs B5500.

Interruption instructions. The non-privileged instruction Store For Interrupt, SFI, pushes the loop control word onto the stack in character mode, then, in both modes, it pushes the interrupt control word and the return control word onto the stack, and places the initiate control word in location 8 of the program reference table.

Store For Diagnose uses the functions of SFI, followed by a reset. Processor 1 then obtains a word from storage location 0 and uses its address field to set the instruction address. Processor 2 is stopped, since it is depends on Processor 1 to diagnose it.

Indicators do not cause an interruption in the supervisory state, but may be inspected with Inspect Interrupt. The functions of this instruction are also

used in the interruption action of the normal mode. The indicator that is on and has highest priority (according to a built-in hierarchy) is selected. If any such indicator is found, then the instruction address is made equal to its value, and the indicator is turned off (vectored interrupt). The stack pointer is set to the fixed value 64.

```
ITI;prior;who                        SFI
ρ Burroughs B5500 Inspect Interrupt  ρ Burroughs B5500 Store For Interrupt
→OUT normal                          →If charmode
ρ parity, address, I/O, printer      THEN:push5500 loop5500r 0
prior←(48+ι2),(18+ι3),(23+ι4),21+ι2  ENDIF:push5500 int5500r
ρ disk, processor1, processor2       push5500 return5500r 0
prior←prior,(27+ι5),(50+ι12),32+ι14  (progref+8) write5500 ini5500r
who←ind[prior]ι1
→If who≠ρprior
THEN: ρ service                      SFT;od
   iadr←prior[who]                   ρ Burroughs B5500 Store For Diagnose
   ind[prior[who]]←0                 SFI
   sp←64                             reset5500
ENDIF:                               stop←procnr=2
                                     →OUT stop
                                     od←1 read5500 0
                                     push5500 od
                                     iadr←magni od[Address]
```

PROGRAM 13-200   Interruption instructions in the Burroughs B5500.

Dispatching.   The supervisor on processor 1 can dispatch a program by pushing the initiate control word on its stack and then executing Dispatch One, which in turn uses the initiate, return, interrupt, and loop control words to (re)establish the environment of the program. Programs on processor 2 can only be dispatched by processor 1, since the supervisor is always on that processor. Processor 1 places the initiate control word in memory location 8, after which the stop signal of processor 2 must be reset.

Humble access.   An Attention indicator can be set in the normal state to force an interrupt. In the supervisory state, the instruction is ignored.

```
IP1                                  COM
ρ Burroughs B5500 Dispatch One       ρ Burroughs B5500 Humble Access
→OUT normal                          →OUT~normal
ini5500i pop5500                      (progref+9) write5500 push5500
return5500i pop5500                  Attention report5500 1
int5500i pop5500
→If charmode
THEN: ρ restore dest word address    IP2
   dest[0]←magni pop5500[Stackref]   ρ Burroughs B5500 Dispatch Two
ENDIF:                               →OUT normal
                                     8 write5500 pop5500
                                     ρ signal processor 2 to start
```

PROGRAM 13-201   Dispatch and humble access in the Burroughs B5500.

Tools of Control

Timer.   A 6-bit counter steps every sixtieth of a second and goes from 63 to 0 once every 1.07 seconds. At that moment an interrupt occurs, which the

supervisor can use to update a software clock. Read Timer places its result on top of the stack.

13.4.8
Input/Output

Devices

The devices are drum, disk, magnetic tape, punched cards, line printer, plotter, and console keyboard-printer.

Channel

The channels are fairly conventional. Any processor can use any channel. Any device can be reached via any channel through a fully general crosspoint switch.

Input/output instructions.   All I/O instructions, except for the test instructions, are privileged.

```
a IIO Start IO     a TIO Test IO
a IOR Release IO   a TUS Test IO Status
```

TABLE 13-202   Input/output instructions of the Burroughs B5500.

13.4.9
Implementation Notes

Only the top two levels of the stack are implemented by registers; other levels are contained in memory. This implementation adversely affects the machine's performance.

The memory is built of independent modules so that up to six simultaneous accesses (two CPUs, four channels) can be under way at once. Otherwise, memory is slow for its time, with a 6 μs or 4 μs cycle. Average add time is 3 μs; average multiply time, 30 μs.

13.4.10
Bibliography

Rosin, R.F., ed., 1987: "Special Issue: The Burroughs B5000." *Ann Hist Comput*, **9**, 1: 6–93.

Burroughs Corporation, 1964: *Burroughs B5500 Reference Manual*. Detroit, MI (our defining reference).

Barton [1961], Bock [1963], Carlson [1963], Doran [1975], Hauck and Dent [1968], Lonergan and King [1961], Maher [1961].

13.4.11

Exercises

13-17 a. Given Y and Z, vectors, F a function of X a vector, write a program to evaluate one iteration of the vector assignment

$$Z[I] \leftarrow Y[I] + F\ X([I])$$

Assume all descriptors, and so forth, are already in place.

b. How many syllables does your program require?

c. How many syllables would be redundant except for misplacement of operands in the stack?

An answer to a:

OPDC	I	Stack index for Z
DESC	Z	Index, stack address of Z
OPDC	I	Stack index of Y
OPDC	Y	Fetch Y[I]
MKS		Mark stack to receive argument X
OPDC	I	Stack index
OPDC	X	Fetch X[I]
OPDC	F	Call F (program descriptor) to evaluate F(X)

Note the similarity of calling and indexing sequences:

ADD	
XCH	Swap, putting address of Z(I) on top, store per address
STD	

13-18 How would you cause a loop to perform a string of instructions 100 times and how 101 times?

13-19 Give the description of the addressing instructions FTF, CTC, CTF, DIB, TSA, SED, RSA, SDA, SFS, SPD, SRD, and BSD, assuming consistency with the addressing instructions shown in this section.

13-20 Give the description of the data handling and decimal instructions TLS, TFL, TEQ, TGR, TNE, CEL, CEQ, CEG, CGR, CNE, TCE, and FSU, assuming consistency with the data handling and decimal instructions shown in this section.

13-21 Give the description of the instructions LND, LOR, NOP, and BIS, assuming consistency with the logical instructions shown in this section.

13-22 Give the description of the floating-point instructions ISN, CIM, DEL, SSP, SSN, DLA, SVB, DLM, DIV, LSS, LEQ, EQL, GEQ, and NEQ, assuming consistency with the floating-point instructions shown in this section.

13-23 Give the description of the sequencing instructions BBW, LFU, JRV, BFC, LFC, LBC, and JFC, assuming consistency with the sequencing instructions shown in this section.

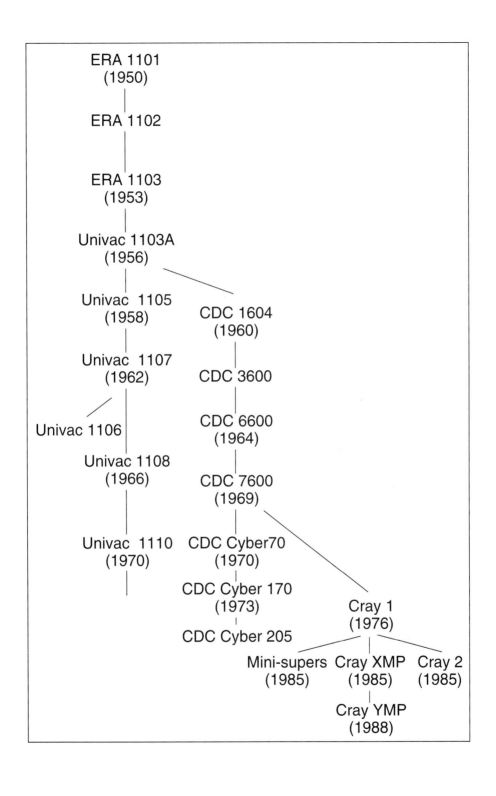

14

Cray House

Seymour Cray

Seymour Cray pioneered high-speed scientific computers from the first generation, and he was the outstanding designer until his death in 1996. Some of the machines mentioned in this House are Cray's own designs; others are designs of his school, usually done by teams in businesses he has left.

The computer family tree reflects Cray's own career. He started in 1951 with Engineering Research Associates (ERA), a start-up company in St. Paul, Minnesota. The ERA 1101 (binary for "13"), a 24-bit parallel, binary computer, was their first product (1952), built on contract for the Navy's cryptological service. In 1952, ERA was bought by Univac to become its scientific computer division. In 1953, the 1103, the first machine Cray influenced, was announced. Cray was later the principal designer of the Naval Tactical Data System Computer.

In 1958, Cray joined former colleagues William Norris and James Thornton at the new Control Data Corporation. Their first products were the CDC 1604 (1960), a high-speed scientific machine, and the CDC 160 (1960), a 12-bit, small, binary data processor. In 1960, work began on the CDC 6600, an innovative and powerful machine first shipped in 1964.

Cray seems to enjoy building computers, and not to enjoy the necessary duties of a corporation officer. Moreover, in 1972 CDC saw its future in mass-market machines; Cray saw his in supercomputers. So an amicable parting occurred.

Cray founded Cray Research, Incorporated. Their first machine, the Cray 1 (1976), was generally considered the world's fastest until 1985, when the Cray 2 was delivered. CDC has continued building supercomputers of the Cray school, including the Cyber 205. Meanwhile, Univac also has continued building scientific computers in the Univac scientific family.

Once again, Cray and corporate life diverged, and Cray left Cray Research to found his own laboratory, Cray Computers, Inc. (which closed in 1995). There the Cray 3 was developed. Cray Research, Inc.'s own engineering laboratories also continued developing machines of the Cray school, the Cray Y-MP and then the C-90. So there have been four organizations building Cray-school computers.

Cray's machines all reflect certain objectives and assumptions from which the characteristics of his style follow clearly. First, he aims at any time to make the fastest possible scientific computer that can be economically marketed to the supercomputer user community, which he knows intimately. He is monumentally unconcerned about other segments of the market, and the concept of a market-covering computer family would be only a distraction from making the top machine as fast as possible. Hence his successive machines have made only minimal concessions to compatibility with their predecessors, and none to compatibility with junior versions.

Second, he designs for a community that will be doing essentially all its programming in one high-level language—FORTRAN. (C later joined the fold.) The friendliness of the machine language to the user is of no concern at all—only suitability for compiler targeting. Thus he designs an implementation first, and the architecture is derived from the implementation in such a way as to use bit-budget and memory bandwidth with maximum efficiency. Formats, data representations, and operation semantics are all dictated by the naturalness, economy, and speed of their implementations. His designs in any generation define one pole of the hardware-derived versus programming-derived architectural spectrum.

Third, he is concerned with the design of the whole computer and its conceptual integrity. To achieve such integrity, he undertakes the design of machines only where he believes he can maintain intellectual grasp of the whole design, and he insists on working with very small development teams, in isolation from bureaucratic influences and from any market conception but his own.

Whereas we have argued strongly for the careful separation of architecture, implementation, and realization, a very important component of Cray's genius is his total overview of all three aspects and the facility with which he trades back and forth among them.

Fourth, in the area of realization, Cray has usually avoided forefront technology, but has driven the established technologies that he has chosen much harder than is customary. (His unsuccessful choice of gallium arsenide for the Cray 3 and Cray 4 was an exception.) Cray has said that refrigeration is the chief concern of the supercomputer designer, and he uses refrigeration to permit high-power, high-speed operation of components.

Supercomputers

The Application Domain

There has always been a class of scientific-computing applications whose importance cost-justifies long runs on the fastest available machines. Indeed, the standard big problems always seem to take one three-shift week of computer time, no matter what machine the technology offers.

The first-generation computers (see the frontispiece to this chapter) were briefly used to make mathematical tables, whose publication was an efficient means of sharing broadly the power of these unique resources. Of the first-generation commercial implementations of the Princeton IAS (1952)

machine—the ERA 1101 (1952) and the IBM 701 (1953)—many copies found their way into what is often called the *high-speed scientific* or *number-crunching* environment. These applications can be generally characterized as requiring inversion, eigenvalues, and eigenvectors of matrices; or as requiring solutions to partial differential equations or to systems of ordinary differential equations. In recent decades, finite-element analysis has become an important special case.

These mathematical techniques require floating-point arithmetic, array data structures, high numerical precision, and an unusually high proportion of multiplications. Although both computers and mathematical techniques have evolved immensely over 40 years, these characteristic properties, and the insatiable demand for number-crunching, have remained invariant.

Important applications include fluid dynamics (flow over vehicles, weather models, propagation of explosions); oscillation and deformation studies (electrical and mechanical); linear programming; seismic analysis; and diffusion (neutron, charge, heat, and mass).

What Is a Supercomputer?

At all times, computers specialized for the needs of the high-performance scientific applications have been developed. These machines are now known as *supercomputers*. The name implies an architecture specialized for the high-performance scientific applications. Thus an extra-big, extra-fast cryptanalytic engine or database transaction processor is not called a supercomputer. The term also implies an extra-fast implementation (and a high price) relative to those of its contemporary machines.

The Royal Succession

Although several early one-of-a-kind supercomputers were built (e.g., the IBM NORC, Univac LARC [Eckert, 1957]), the first commercial supercomputer built in quantity was the IBM 7030, or Stretch (Section 13.3). It reigned as the world's fastest until 1964, when CDC introduced Seymour Cray's CDC 6600. The 6600, a very successful machine, became the standard; it was succeeded in 1969 by its very similar descendant, the CDC 7600. After Cray left CDC, CDC continued to build supercomputers of this family, rechristened *Cyber*. The Cyber 205 is a good example.

Meanwhile, in 1976 Cray Research introduced the Cray 1. In 1985 it introduced the Cray 2 and the Cray X-MP, and in 1988 the Cray Y-MP. Competitors include the Fujitsu VP-400, the Hitachi S-810/20, and the NEC SX-2, although the Cray Y-MP is generally regarded as the fastest of this set.

Most early supercomputers achieved their high speed by means of (1) realizations with the fastest available components, and (2) implementations with pipelined execution of scalar instructions. By and large these means did not show in the architectures, although one occasionally saw a quirk such as restrictions on branches to and operations upon instructions nearby in the instruction stream, or traps imprecisely timed even when the causing condition could in principle be identified with a guilty instruction.

Some supercomputers provided multiple independent adders, multipliers, and dividers, with the program being responsible for the scheduling and allocation. Such provisions are often architecturally visible. (In the 6600, a hardware "scoreboard" does that scheduling invisibly.)

Whereas scalar execution streams can have pipeline implementations with little architectural visibility, such features as vector-arithmetic operations and parallel instruction streams are not easy to hide. Taking advantage of them usually requires restructuring existing programs.

Array data structures inherently occur in many supercomputer applications. Many algorithms are readily vectorizable, a reorganization that can often be done by a compiler. So vector arithmetic was the first peculiar architectural feature to be put into supercomputers. Even so, it often happens that as many as half of the executed program operations remain scalar. In such a case, even if the vector code were infinitely fast, the speedup would be only a factor of 2.

Some existing algorithms are readily parallelizable—that is, they lend themselves to reexpression so as to utilize multiple concurrent arithmetic units. As with vectorization, the fraction of many existing programs that can be simply parallelized remains modest, often allowing speedups by only small factors. Vectorization and parallelization are almost independent program transformations. Some applications allow one, some the other, some neither, and a few, both.

Machines such as the Cray Y-MP offer all of vectorization; parallel-program segment execution by multiple vector-arithmetic units; and concurrent independent adders, multipliers, and dividers inside each unit.

Miura [1986] characterizes vectorization as a "mature technology" that has realized a high fraction of its inherent potential. Although the clock cycle time of realizations has continued to drop—from 12.5 ns on the Cray 1 (1976) to 4.1 ns on the Cray 2 (1985) to 2.2 ns on the Cray T90 (1995)—some think that the component speed limit is near.

Moreover, the mass market for personal computers has made special componentry for supercomputers steadily less performance/cost effective. For these reasons, there is a concentration of intense efforts on parallelism (fine and coarse grained) as the direction of development for supercomputer architectures.

Minisupercomputers

The Cray 1 derives its high-speed scientific-computing performance from several independent factors:

- An architecture providing scores of registers in working store, thus abbreviating instructions and reducing instruction fetches
- A pipelined implementation for vector arithmetic with scores of real registers, thus reducing data access time
- Multiple arithmetic units in the implementation
- Pipelined instruction fetch and execution for scalar instructions
- Very fast main-memory realization
- Very fast logic realization

The advent in the 1980s of very-large-scale integration (VLSI), and of complementary metal-oxide semiconductors (CMOS) in particular, radically reduced per-circuit cost and allowed large numbers (30,000 to millions) of circuits to be realized on one chip. A consequence was the new economic attractiveness of building a rich architecture and an implementation similar to that of the Cray 1 with cheap realization technology. The resulting machines are called *minisupercomputers*. Some have the exact Cray-1 architecture and run its software; others have different architecture, but all emphasize vector operations and floating-point computation.

Minisupercomputers are quite different from *superminicomputers*. The latter are minicomputer descendants whose architectural and implementation word lengths evolved upward (to between 32 and 64 bits) until they are distinguishable from mainframes only by ancestry. The DEC VAX 11/780 is called a "superminicomputer"; the IBM System/370 Model 4381 is called a "mainframe." Both have essentially the same cost, performance, software support, and applications.

The VAX11/8600 is a superminicomputer; the Convex is a minisupercomputer. Costs are comparable; the Convex is biased toward vector floating-point operations, and hence performs them much faster than the VAX11/8600.

Bibliography

Elzen and MacKenzie [1994] gives an excellent and extended treatment of the development of supercomputers, and especially of the roles of Seymour Cray and Cray Research, Incorporated.

Elzen and MacKenzie [1991] emphasizes Cray's own role.

MacKenzie [1991] treats the stimulating roles of Los Alamos and Livermore in the development of supercomputers.

Ibbett and Topham [1989] in two volumes gives a crisp treatment of both uniprocessor and parallel supercomputer evolution and concepts.

Brooks, Sutherland, et al. [1995], Appendix A, recaps the evolution of parallel supercomputers.

S. Chen [1984], Eckert [1957], Fernbach [1986], Fuchs and Poulton [1985], Hwang et al. [1981], Hwang [1984], Karin and Smith [1987], Kung [1982], Lincoln [1977], Lukoff et al. [1959], Miura [1986].

14.1
Univac 1103A

14.1.1
Highlights

History

Architects. Arnold A. Cohen was the chief architect; Seymour Cray was one of the designers.

Dates. The 1103 was announced and delivered in 1953. The 1103A was first delivered in 1956.

Family tree. The Univac 1100 Scientific family is the longest-lived of computer families; it started with the Engineering Research Associates 1101 in 1952 and continues to the present day.

The 1101 is a 24-bit, single-address, drum-memory, parallel, binary computer of the Princeton IAS (1952) school. It departs from the IAS concepts in using 1's-complement notation. Double-precision arithmetic, very necessary for a 24-bit machine, is facilitated, as are logical operations on bit vectors. The 1101 was announced in 1950 and delivered in 1952. The 1102 had essentially the same architecture [Tomash and Cohen, 1979].

The 1103 broke with the ERA architecture, in going to a 36-bit word. The 1103, which had no floating-point hardware, was quickly superseded by the 1103A (1956)—the Univac Scientific Computer—which had floating point as an option.

The 1103A was a popular scientific computer. With an 8 μs memory cycle, it was inherently faster in its primitives than its competitor, the IBM 704 (1955), with a 12 μs memory cycle. As Bell and Newell [1971] say, "At the time both were used, it was not clear which computer was better."

With hindsight, we believe four factors account for the 704's eventual market dominance. In declining order of importance:

- A directly attached card reader and printer on the 704 gave quicker turnaround than the off-line printer of the 1103A.
- Floating point was standard on the 704, so the user community assumed it. That assumption enabled FORTRAN. Floating point was optional on the 1103A.
- The 704 had indexing; the 1103A had more limited address modification.
- The memory of the 704 was all fast, up to 32 K. The 1103A had up to 12 K of fast memory and 32 K of addressable main memory on drum. This memory-system disadvantage detracted from the 1103A's memory cycle-time advantage.

Noteworthy

The 1100 family is characterized by binary radix, 36-bit words, and 1's-complement notation. The 1103A explores many fresh ideas and makes many departures from the IAS model. These departures make it the most fascinating family member; we treat it in detail.

Two addresses.   The 1103A uses two full addresses, coming as it does at the end of a period when small memory capacities made that reasonable. Yet, it is not a clean example, since it also uses an accumulator and MQ register.

One's complement.   The 1103A is a good exemplar of 1's-complement sign notation, even in floating point. Note especially the left extensions of operands.

Floating point.   Arithmetic operations can (under mode control) produce rounded results. Special operations facilitate fixed–floating and floating–fixed conversion.

Repeat.   The meta-instruction Repeat executes its successor instruction a specified number of times. The working store combines imaginatively with the two-address instruction to give some very pretty single-instruction operations, especially powerful when iterated by Repeat. These include

- Cumulative Multiply, giving vector inner product
- Add Then Multiply, giving polynomial evaluation
- Equality and Threshold Branches, giving streaming table lookup

Vector operations.   An architectural strategy widely used in supercomputers to improve memory-bandwidth utilization is to harness uniformity in data structures, providing one instruction to specify operation on a whole array of operands.

The fact that one wants to do *exactly* the same thing to every corresponding pair of two arrays, or to every element of one array, radically reduces the Shannon-information cost per element operation.

In a single-address machine, the memory cycles approximately alternate between instruction fetches and data fetches. That is, the *instruction fraction* of memory bandwidth is normally about 0.5.

When one processes arrays with single instructions (or cache-trapped loops), the instruction fraction of the memory bandwidth tends toward 0. The 1103A provides excellent examples of this phenomenon, as in a vector inner-product calculation (cumulative multiplication) using Repeat, or in streaming table lookup (equality search) using Repeat.

Sequencing.   The sequencing instructions include a fast loop-closing operation, a subroutine call, and a parameter-passing supervisor call. The two-address format allows a two-way branch with two target addresses, which can be used to make a one-instruction iteration loop.

Interrupt.   The first-ever interruption system is provided as a special feature.

Policing.   Checks are made for invalid operations, invalid operands, and floating-point overflow. The interrupt is not yet used to signal these instances; the machine stops.

Peculiarities

Name-space.   The name-space is singularly awkward. The upper half addresses drum locations, with a manually changeable logical-to-physical mapping (variable-size interlace and spare tracks). The lower half is partly occupied with core-memory addresses in optional complements, partly with working-store addresses, and is in part invalid. Addressing is cyclic, not linear, with multiple cycles. Moreover, the cycles that occur in incrementing during the Repeat differ from those encountered in incrementing the instruction address.

Two-address plus accumulator.   The use of the accumulator and MQ in conjunction with the two-address memory-to-memory operation is not self-evident; since it is not consistently applied, it needs frequent explanation.

Embedded accumulator.   Only the lower half of the double-length accumulator is embedded in the memory name-space. In loading the accumulator with an operand from memory the operand normally is sign extended to double length. When the embedded accumulator is specified, however, the extension of the lower accumulator would cause loss of information; hence an exception is made (at times).

Negative zero.   The 1103 has two zeros, one negative, a property inherent in 1's-complement notation. The 1103A is an object lesson on the troubles two zeros create. In Chapter 4 we discussed the use of a subtractor, instead of an adder, in arithmetic to obtain a positive, instead of a negative, zero in most (but not all) cases. Since negative zeros can be created in many operations, such as Load Negative, the programmer must be constantly aware of their existence. In Branch On Equal, for instance, a negative zero is considered unequal to a positive zero. Worse, the equality test of the Branch On Equal instruction changes a negative zero to a positive zero after the test, such that a second invocation of Branch On Equal branches where the first did not branch.

Inconsistencies.   The architectural design is very close to what is easily feasible in the implementation. Many architectural inconsistencies follow: Logical operations each have a different appearance; shift amounts are specified in different ways; the destination location is usually specified by the v-address, but at times by the u-address; the accumulator and MQ may be (but not in all cases) used as embedded operands, and at times the results can be surprising.

Descendants

The 1105 (1959) is essentially an 1103A with I/O channels. The channels could not be programmed.

The pressure for indexing broke the two-address 36-bit architecture. The 1107 (1962) architecture was quite new—one memory address with one address for the 16-register working store, but still with only 16-bit memory addresses.

Later Univac Scientific machines are essentially smooth descendants from the 1107, until the architecture breaks again to accommodate yet larger addresses.

14.1.2

Machine Language

Language Level

Design philosophy.   The machine language follows directly from the implementation—it is very low level.

Unit System

Addressing is to the 36-bit word. Six-bit bytes are used on tape.

```
format1103                      configure1103
⍝ Univac 1103A information units  ⍝ configuration for the Univac 1103A
⍝ representation radix           ⍝ memory capacity
radix←2                          memcap←2*12
⍝ information units              ⍝ drum capacity
byte←6                           drumcap←2*14
adrsize←15
word←36
double←72
⍝ address capacity
adrcap←radix*adrsize
```

PROGRAM 14-1   Basic parameters of the Univac 1103A.

Configuration.   Installed capacity of memory may be 4 K, 8 K, or 12 K.

Spaces

Memory name-space.   Memory consists of a high-speed (core) memory and a drum store that is directly addressed to the word. The upper half of the name-space, starting at Drum, is used for drum memory.

```
space1103                        name1103
⍝ Univac 1103A spaces            ⍝ Univac 1103A space names
⍝ memory                         ⍝ fixed memory addresses
memory←?(memcap,word)ρradix      F1←0
⍝ drum store                     F2←1
drum←?(drumcap,word)ρradix       F3←2
⍝ working store                  F4←3
⍝ - accumulator                  ⍝ embedding
acc←?doubleρradix                Mq←25×2*9
⍝ - multiplier/quotient          Acc←26×2*9
mq←?wordρradix                   Drum←2*14
⍝ control store
⍝ - instruction addresss
iadr←?adrcap                     ⍝ in/out spaces
⍝ - round/truncate mode          ⍝ - serial
fltruncate←?radix                ioa←?8ρradix
⍝ - indicators                   ⍝ - parallel
ind←?5ρradix                     iob←?wordρradix
⍝ - stop switch                  ⍝ - typewriter
stopsw←?3ρradix                  twr←?byteρradix
⍝ - branch switch                ⍝ - punch
branchsw←?3ρradix                hpr←?byteρradix
                                 ⍝ - external signal
                                 signal←?radix
```

PROGRAM 14-2   Spaces of the Univac 1103A.

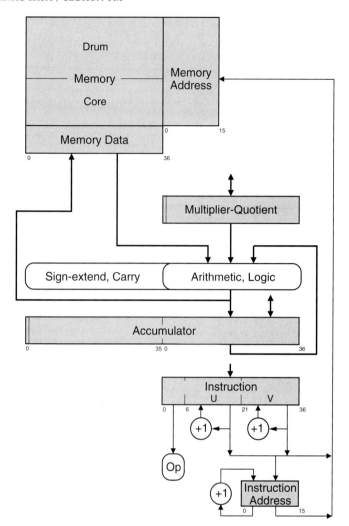

FIGURE 14-3 Programming model for the Univac 1103A.

a→i	i	i	i	b→FR
FP	RA	IJ	PR	b→LT
FI	→b	TJ	i	b→MJ
UP	RS	EJ	→b	b→MS
NP	i	QJ	FA	b→PU
→b	i	→b	FS	b→RP
i	i	SJ	FM	b→ER
i	CC	ZJ	FD	b→EW
i	i	i	i	
TP	SP	QT	MP	
TM	SA	QA	MA	
TN	SN	QS	DV	
IP	SS	LA	SF	
TU	AT	LQ	→b	
TV	ST	→b	→b	
EF	RJ	PS	→b	

PROGRAM 14-4 Operation-code list of the Univac 1103A.

Working store.   The 1103A has both a double-length accumulator and a multiplier-quotient register, thus permitting cumulative multiplication.

Control store.   Besides the instruction address, there are a floating-point truncation-mode bit, three stop switches, three branch switches, and a stop condition.

Embedding.   The first four memory addresses are reserved as fixed addresses for: F1, an instruction address following a Repeat and the return address of Supervisor Call; F2, the target of a Supervisor Call; F3, an instruction that is inserted when an interrupt occurs; and, F4, the location receiving MQ during a Cumulative Multiply operation.

The group of addresses starting at Mq all refer to the MQ register; the group of addresses starting at Acc all refer to the Accumulator.

Programming model.   The 1103A differs from the IAS model in having a double-length accumulator and a separate MQ register, enabling not only cumulative multiplication, but cumulative multiplication at double precision. This is especially important for calculating vector inner products, the crucial step in preserving accuracy in matrix multiplication and inversion.

Operand Specification

Number of addresses.   There are two address fields—the u-address and the v-address—that are used in conjunction with an accumulator and MQ register.

```
      ρ address arithmetic             ρ floating-point arithmetic
a TU Store U-address           a FA F Add
a TV Store V-address           a FS F Subtract
      ρ logic and shift        a FM F Multiply
a QT And                       a FI F Multiply Cumulative
a CC Exclusive Or              a FP F Multiply Polynomial
a QS Extract                   a FD F Divide
a SF Left-zero Shift           a NP F Pack
a LA Rotate                    a UP F Unpack
b LT Rotate Accumulator        b FR Set F Round
a LQ Rotate In MQ                   ρ sequencing
a SP Rotate Positive           a PS Stop
a SN Rotate Negative           b MS Stop On Switch
a SA Rotate Sum                b MJ Branch On Switch
a SS Rotate Difference         a EJ Branch On Equal
      ρ fixed-point arithmetic  a ZJ Branch On Zero
a TP Load                      a TJ Branch On Greater
a TN Negate                    a SJ Branch On Sign
a TM Make Absolute             a QJ Branch On MQ Sign
a RA Add                       a IJ Count And Branch
a AT Add To Accumulator        b RP Repeat
a QA Add Masked By MQ          a RJ Call
a RS Subtract                  a IP Supervisor Call
a ST Subtract From Accumulator      ρ input/output
a MP Multiply                  b ER Read
a MA Multiply Cumulative       b EW Write
a DV Divide                    b PU Punch
                               a PR Print
                               a EF Control

Legend: F = Floating-Point.
```

PROGRAM 14-5   Instruction list of the Univac 1103A.

Operation Specification

Mnemonics. The mnemonics that are used are derived from the instruction specification given in the 1103A manual (Program 14-4).

Instruction list. There are 50 instructions, divided more or less evenly among logic, fixed-point arithmetic, floating-point arithmetic, and sequencing. The floating-point operations are optional (Program 14-5).

Instruction Structure

Machine-language syntax. There are two main syntactic patterns. The most common pattern has two address fields; in the other, one address field is replaced by a control field and a count field.

```
     syntax1103
a Opcode.Addressu.Addressv
b 0 0 0 1 0 1 .Control.Count.Addressv
b 0 1 0 0 1 0 .Control.Count.Addressv
b 1 0 0 1 0 1 .Control.Count.Addressv
b 1 0 1 1 1 0 .Control.Count.Addressv
b 1 1 0 0 1 1 .Control.Count.Addressv
b 1 1 1 1 0 1 .Control.Count.Addressv
b 1 1 1 1 1 0 .Control.Count.Addressv
b 1 1 1 1 1 1 .Control.Count.Addressv
```

PROGRAM 14-6   Instruction syntax of the Univac 1103A.

Instruction format. Only a limited number of instruction fields is used; the control and count field are not always used when they appear in the format. Occasionally, the seven low-order bits of the v-address are used for a shift amount.

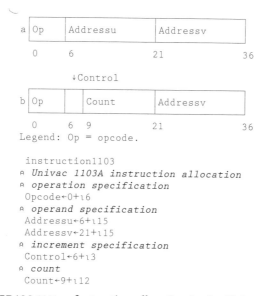

Legend: Op = opcode.

```
    instruction1103
a Univac 1103A instruction allocation
a operation specification
 Opcode←0+ι6
a operand specification
 Addressu←6+ι15
 Addressv←21+ι15
a increment specification
 Control←6+ι3
a count
 Count←9+ι12
```

PROGRAM 14-7   Instruction allocation in the Univac 1103A.

Status format. Five indicators are used for stop conditions.

```
 indicator1103
ᴀ Univac 1103A indicator allocation
ᴀ invalid operation code
 Invop←0
ᴀ invalid address
 Invadr←1
ᴀ overflow
 Oflo←2
ᴀ floating-point overflow
 Floflo←3
ᴀ programmed stop
 Stop←4
```

PROGRAM 14-8   Indicators of the Univac 1103A.

14.1.3

Addressing

All addresses have 15 bits, with no abbreviation and no indexing. The Repeat instruction may increment one or both addresses of the repeated successor instruction dynamically. Usually, the u-address specifies a source operand; the v-address specifies a source and/or a destination.

Direct addressing. Reading and writing can be from and to (core) memory, accumulator, MQ register, and drum. Reading can deliver one word or a double word. A double word is either the accumulator content or a sign-extended word from memory, MQ, or drum.

```
data←size read1103 address              address write1103 data
ᴀ Univac 1103A read from store          ᴀ Univac 1103A write into store
→CASE(address<memcap,Mq,Acc,Drum)ι1     →CASE(address<memcap,Mq,Acc,Drum)ι1
C0:data←extend memory[address;]         C0:memory[address;]←(-word)↑data
   →ENDCASE                                →ENDCASE
C1:Invadr report 1                      C1:Invadr report 1
   data←0                                  →ENDCASE
   →ENDCASE                             C2:mq←(-word)↑data
C2:data←extend mq                          →ENDCASE
   →ENDCASE                             C3:acc←data
C3:data←acc                                →ENDCASE
   →ENDCASE                             C4:drum[address-Drum;]←(-word)↑data
C4:data←extend drum[address-Drum;]      ENDCASE:
ENDCASE:data←(-size)↑data
```

```
r1←extend od
ᴀ Univac 1103A sign extension
r1←(wordρod[0]),od
```

PROGRAM 14-9   Memory read and write in the Univac 1103A.

The type of storage to which an address refers is determined by comparing the address to the range delimiters memcap, Mq, Acc, and Drum, and searching for the first 1. As an example, a memory address compares low to all delimiters, so it is recognized as case 0. A memory address exceeding the memory capacity, but smaller than the MQ reference, is recognized as case 1; it sets the invalid-address indicator, which causes a stop.

Address Modification

Except for the Repeat, which increments the address fields of its subject instruction, the u- and v-addresses are used unmodified.

```
address←adr1103u                    address←adr1103v
 ⋀ Univac 1103A u-address           ⋀ Univac 1103A v-address
address←fld Addressu                address←fld Addressv


yes←regadr address
 ⋀ Univac 1103A register address
yes←(address≥Mq)∧address<Drum
```

PROGRAM 14-10   Addressing in the Univac 1103A.

`regadr` tests whether the accumulator or MQ, as opposed to the memory or drum, is addressed. This function is used in instructions that prohibit the addressing of these registers.

Address calculation.   The u- and the v-address of an instruction word can be loaded by TU and TV from the corresponding field of another word—a minimal aid to address calculation.

```
TU;od1;od2                          TV;od1;od2
 ⋀ Univac 1103A Store U-address     ⋀ Univac 1103A Store V-address
Invadr report regadr adr1103v       Invadr report regadr adr1103v
→OUT stop1103                       →OUT stop1103
od1←word read1103 adr1103u          od1←word read1103 adr1103u
od2←word read1103 adr1103v          od2←word read1103 adr1103v
od2[Addressu]←od1[Addressu]         od2[Addressv]←od1[Addressv]
adr1103v write1103 od2              adr1103v write1103 od2
```

PROGRAM 14-11   Store Address in the Univac 1103A.

14.1.4

Data

Logical

Logical formats.   The format of the logical vector is the 36-bit word.

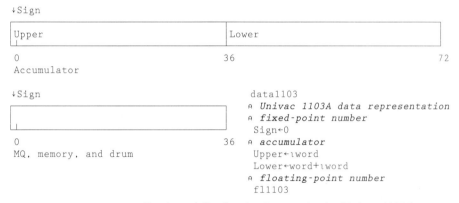

PROGRAM 14-12   Logic and fixed-point formats in the Univac 1103A.

Fixed-Point Numbers

Notation and allocation.   Binary digit-complement is used as a long-standing tradition, starting with the ERA design, and maintained throughout the CDC 6600 family.

Floating-Point Numbers

Closure and normal form.   Floating point is normalized; precision treatment is either by rounding or by truncation, depending upon the truncation-mode bit.

Floating-point format.   The floating-point allocation is identical to that of the 704.

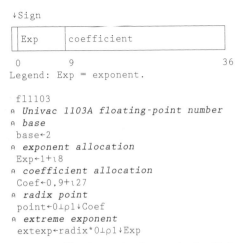

```
↓Sign
```

Exp	coefficient

```
0       9                              36
Legend: Exp = exponent.
```

```
 fl1103
∩ Univac 1103A floating-point number
∩ base
 base←2
∩ exponent allocation
 Exp←1+ι8
∩ coefficient allocation
 Coef←0,9+ι27
∩ radix point
 point←0⊥ρ1↓Coef
∩ extreme exponent
 extexp←radix*0⊥ρ1↓Exp
```

PROGRAM 14-13   Floating-point format in the Univac 1103A.

```
 number←fl1103i rep;exponent;coefficient
∩ Univac 1103A floating-point interpretation
 exponent←biasi rep[Exp]≠rep[1↑Coef]
 coefficient←digitcompi rep[Coef]
 number←coefficient×base*exponent-point

 rep←fl1103r number;exponent;coefficient;xmax;xmin
∩ Univac 1103A floating-point representation
 (-extexp) normalize number
 rep←wordρ0
 rep[Coef]←(ρCoef) digitcompr round1103 coefficient
 rep[Exp]←(number<0)≠(ρExp) biasr exponent
 Floflo report xmax∨xmin

 out←round1103 number
∩ Univac 1103A floating-point round
 →IF fltruncate
 THEN:out←truncate number
     →ENDIF
 ELSE:out←round number
 ENDIF:
```

PROGRAM 14-14   Floating-point representation in the Univac 1103A.

Floating-point representation.   The exponent is represented with bias notation; the coefficient, with digit complement. The use of complement notation for the coefficient has as a consequence that the exponent digits must be inverted, when the coefficient is negative, to obtain a fixed-point comparison sequence.

14.1.5

Operations

Data Handling

There are no data-handling operations as such, but logic provides mask-controlled extracting and inserting for subfields, characters, and individual bits. The Load operations (Program 14-20) serve as memory-to-memory moves.

Logic

Connectives.   The And is between a memory operand and the MQ with the result zero-extended in the accumulator. The result is also written in the memory location specified by the v-address. The Exclusive Or, however, is between two memory operands. The result replaces the u-operand and the lower accumulator, leaving the upper accumulator unchanged. Note that the lower accumulator receives the u-operand prior to the addressing of the v-operand (which may refer to the accumulator).

```
QT;od                                QS;od
⋒ Univac 1103A And                   ⋒ Univac 1103A Extract
od←word read1103 adr1103u              acc[Lower]←mq∧word read1103 adr1103u
acc←(-double)↑mq∧od                    mq←˜mq
adr1103v write1103 acc                 od←mq∧word read1103 adr1103v
                                       acc←(-double)↑od∨acc[Lower]
                                       mq←˜mq
CC;od                                  adr1103v write1103 acc
⋒ Univac 1103A Exclusive Or
acc[Lower]←word read1103 adr1103u
od←word read1103 adr1103v
acc[Lower]←od≠acc[Lower]
adr1103u write1103 acc
```

     PROGRAM 14-15   And, Exclusive Or, and Extract in the Univac 1103A.

Extract.   The four potential operands (two from memory, one from the accumulator, and one from the MQ) are effectively put to use in Extract. Here MQ serves as a mask, determining which bits are taken from the first and which from the second operand. The result is sign-extended and placed in the accumulator; it is also placed at the v-address location. The description is complicated by the need to show the action when the accumulator or the MQ is specified by the v-address.

Vector operations.   A left-zero count, combined with a corresponding left shift, gives a normalization operation in the accumulator. Since the accumulator has double word length, the word from memory is loaded (zero-extended)

in the accumulator, then it is rotated to the upper accumulator for the actual normalization. A count is recorded in the v-address location; it indicates the left shift that will restore the original accumulator content.

```
SF;shift;od
ⴰ Univac 1103A Left-zero Shift
Invadr report regadr adr1103v
→OUT stop1103
acc←double read1103 adr1103u
acc←wordΦacc
shift←⁻1+accι˜acc[0]
acc←shiftΦacc
od←word read1103 adr1103v
od[Addressv]←adrsize magnr 72|36-shift
adr1103v write1103 od
```

PROGRAM 14-16   Left-zero Shift in the Univac 1103A.

Shift.   All shifts are left circular. The shift amount is specified by the seven low-order digits of the count or v-address field. The combination of Load and Shift in one instruction gives powerful aligning of word subfields. The combination of shift with sign control, addition, and subtraction is more or less ad hoc; it uses a one-address format and takes the memory operand as an unsigned positive quantity.

```
a LA Rotate                a SP Rotate Positive
b LT Rotate Accumulator    a SN Rotate Negative
a LQ Rotate In MQ          a SA Rotate Sum
                           a SS Rotate Difference
```

TABLE 14-17   Shift instructions of the Univac 1103A.

Rotate.   Rotate Positive and Rotate Negative split the loaded word into k bits in the upper accumulator, and $36-k$ in the lower.

```
LT;shift;rl                            LA;shift
ⴰ Univac 1103A Rotate Accumulator      ⴰ Univac 1103A Rotate
shift←128|fld Count                    acc←double read1103 adr1103u
acc←shiftΦacc                          shift←128|adr1103v
→IF 2|fld Control                      acc←shiftΦacc
THEN:rl←extend acc[Lower]              adr1103u write1103 acc
     →ENDIF
ELSE:rl←extend acc[Upper]
ENDIF:adr1103v write1103 rl            LQ;shift
                                       ⴰ Univac 1103A Rotate In MQ
                                       shift←128|adr1103v
                                       mq←shiftΦword read1103 adr1103u
SA;addend;augend;sum;shift             adr1103u write1103 extend mq
ⴰ Univac 1103A Rotate Sum
addend←magni word read1103 adr1103u
augend←digitcompi acc
sum←augend+addend                      SN;od;shift
shift←128|adr1103v                     ⴰ Univac 1103A Rotate Negative
acc←shiftΦdouble digitcompr sum        od←word read1103 adr1103u
                                       shift←128|adr1103v
                                       acc←shiftΦ˜(-double)↑od
```

PROGRAM 14-18   Rotate in the Univac 1103A.

Fixed-Point Arithmetic

Fixed-point operands are in the u-address and v-address locations, which may include the accumulator and MQ. The results are placed in the v-address locations, with several exceptions.

```
a TP Load                    a RS Subtract
a TN Negate                  a ST Subtract From Accumulator
a TM Make Absolute           a MP Multiply
a RA Add                     a MA Multiply Cumulative
a AT Add To Accumulator      a DV Divide
a QA Add Masked By MQ
```

TABLE 14-19   Fixed-point instructions of the Univac 1103A.

Load and Store.   The two-address format is used in TP (originally called Transfer Positive) to give a memory-to-memory Move. The instruction becomes a Load or Store by specifying in the u-address or v-address the accumulator or MQ; if both registers are specified, a register-to-register operation results. Only the lower accumulator can be thus loaded.

```
TP:od                          TM:od
A Univac 1103A Load            A Univac 1103A Load Absolute
od←word read1103 adr1103u       od←word read1103 adr1103u
adr1103v write1103 extend od   adr1103v write1103 extend od[0]≠od


TN:od
A Univac 1103A Load Negative
od←word read1103 adr1103u
adr1103v write1103 extend~od
```

PROGRAM 14-20   Load in the Univac 1103A.

Sign change.   Negate and Make Absolute combine the Move, Load, and Store actions with sign control.

Add and Subtract.   Addition either uses a double-length memory operand by left-extending its sign, or extends the memory operand by high-order zeros

```
RA:ad:addend:augend:sum          QA:ad:addend:augend:sum
A Univac 1103A Add               A Univac 1103A Add Masked By MQ
acc←extend word read1103 adr1103u  ad←word read1103 adr1103u
augend←magni acc                 addend←magni ad∧mq
ad←extend word read1103 adr1103v  augend←digitcompi acc
addend←magni ad                  sum←augend+addend
sum←augend+addend                acc←double digitcompr sum
acc←double zerocompr sum         adr1103v write1103 acc
adr1103u write1103 acc


ST:sb:subtrahend:minuend:difference
A Univac 1103A Subtract From Accumulator
sb←word read1103 adr1103u
subtrahend←magni~extend sb
minuend←magni acc
difference←minuend+subtrahend
acc←double zerocompr difference
adr1103v write1103 acc
```

PROGRAM 14-21   Add and Subtract in the Univac 1103A.

to form a positive quantity. Again, the operands can be from memory, drum, accumulator, or MQ. The resulting sum is placed in the specified memory location (using the u-address!) and in the full accumulator.

Negative zero.   A negative-zero sum results when addend and augend are negative zero. Similarly, a negative-zero difference occurs when the minuend is negative zero and the subtrahend is positive zero. We describe this behavior by using `magni` for the interpretation of the operands and `zerocompr` for the interpretation of the results. The results are the same as for digit complement, except for the negative zero.

Add Masked By MQ adds the result of the And of one operand and the MQ as a positive quantity to the full accumulator; there is no corresponding masked subtraction. Observe that the result location is specified by the u-operand in some cases, and by the v-operand in others.

Multiply and Divide.   The multiplier is placed from its u-location into the MQ. The multiplicand is obtained from the v-location. In regular Multiplication, the product replaces the accumulator content. In Cumulative Multiplication, the product is added to the original accumulator content. When the content has a high-order 1 bit, a possible (but not necessary) overflow is signaled by stopping the computer. It is up to the operator to decide whether an overflow indeed occurred; if not, he can restart the computer. When the v-location specifies the MQ, the content of the u-location is squared.

```
MA;multiplier;multiplicand;augend;result
⌐ Univac 1103A Multiply Cumulative
mq←word read1103 adr1103u
multiplier←digitcompi mq
Oflo report acc[Sign]≠acc[1]
→OUT stop1103
acc←wordφacc
multiplicand←digitcompi word read1103 adr1103v
augend←digitcompi wordφacc
result←augend+multiplicand×multiplier
acc←double digitcompr result


DV;divisor;dividend;quotient;remainder
⌐ Univac 1103A Divide
divisor←digitcompi word read1103 adr1103u
dividend←digitcompi acc
stop←(|dividend)≥(|divisor)×radix*word-1
→OUT stop
remainder←divisor|dividend
quotient←(dividend-remainder)÷divisor
acc←double digitcompr remainder
mq←word digitcompr quotient
adr1103v write1103 extend mq
```

PROGRAM 14-22   Multiply and Divide in the Univac 1103A.

The divisor is obtained from the u-location; the dividend is in the accumulator and is replaced by the remainder. The quotient is stored in the v-location. The remainder is always zero or positive, smaller than the magnitude of the divisor; −22 divided by 7 gives quotient −4, remainder 6.

Floating-Point Arithmetic

Floating-point operations place their result in the MQ and use the accumulator and MQ for intermediate results; the specification of either or both as a v-operand gives erroneous results (here indicated by setting these registers to zero). Fixed-point sign-change operations can be used.

```
a FA F Add              a FD F Divide
a FS F Subtract         a NP F Pack
a FM F Multiply         a UP F Unpack
a FI F Multiply Cumulative  b FR Set F Round
a FP F Multiply Polynomial
Legend: F = Floating-Point.
```

TABLE 14-23   Floating-point instructions of the Univac 1103A.

Floating-point Add and Subtract.   The two addresses of the instruction format specify the operands; the result location is implied to be MQ. When the u-address specifies the MQ, the instruction resembles a classical one-address instruction.

```
FA;addend;augend;sum
a Univac 1103A Floating-Point Add
augend←fl1103i word read1103 adr1103u
acc[]←0
mq[]←0
addend←fl1103i word read1103 adr1103v
sum←augend+addend
mq←fl1103r sum
```

PROGRAM 14-24   Floating-point Add in the Univac 1103A.

Floating-point Multiply and Divide.   Two unusual and powerful operations are designed to be used with Repeat. Multiply Cumulative, when repeated, provides a vector inner product; Multiply Polynomial, when repeated, gives rapid evaluation of a factored polynomial.

```
FI;multiplier;multiplicand;augend;result
a Univac 1103A Floating-Point Multiply Cumulative
F4 write1103 mq
multiplier←fl1103i word read1103 adr1103u
mq[]←0
multiplicand←fl1103i word read1103 adr1103v
augend←fl1103i word read1103 F4
result←augend+multiplicand×multiplier
mq←fl1103r result


FP;addend;multiplier;multiplicand;result
a Univac 1103A Floating-Point Multiply Polynomial
multiplicand←fl1103i mq
mq[]←0
multiplier←fl1103i word read1103 adr1103u
acc[]←0
addend←fl1103i word read1103 adr1103v
result←(multiplicand×multiplier)+addend
mq←fl1103r result
```

PROGRAM 14-25   Floating-point Multiply in the Univac 1103A.

Other floating-point operations.   Pack and Unpack provide facilities for converting between integer and floating-point formats. In both instructions, the u-address refers to the coefficient, and the v-address to the exponent.

```
NP;od                                   UP;od;r1
ᴀ Univac 1103A Floating-Point Pack      ᴀ Univac 1103A Floating-Point Unpack
→ERROR adr1103u=adr1103v                od←word read1103 adr1103u
od←word read1103 adr1103v               r1←wordρ0
mq←word read1103 adr1103u               r1[Exp]←od[Exp]≠od[Coef[0]]
acc[]←0                                 od[Exp]←od[Coef[0]]
mq[Exp]←od[Exp]≠mq[Coef[0]]             adr1103u write1103 extend od
adr1103u write1103 extend mq            adr1103v write1103 extend r1
```

```
FR
ᴀ Univac 1103A Set Floating-point Round
fltruncate←1=fld Control
```

PROGRAM 14-26   Floating-point Pack and Unpack in the Univac 1103A.

Floating-point Compare.   Branch On Equal and Branch On Greater compare fixed-point as well as floating-point operands.

14.1.6

Instruction Sequencing

Linear Sequence

Normal sequence is controlled by the instruction address.

Next instruction.   Incrementing the instruction address is complicated because of the two memory types—core and drum—and because of the embedding of the lower accumulator and the MQ in groups of addresses. Each of three groups of addresses—core memory, MQ and accumulator together, and drum memory—are cyclic. If the highest address in the group is incremented, the result is the lowest address in that group! These requirements are reflected in ifetch1103: When the limit of a memory or a drum group is reached, the corresponding origin is substituted. The accumulator may not be used as an instruction location; such an instruction address causes a stop.

```
cycle1103
ᴀ basic cycle of the Univac 1103A
REPEAT:interrupt1103
    execute ifetch1103
    Invadr report((iadr<memcap,Mq,Acc,Drum)ι1)∈ 1 3
→UNTIL stop1103
```

```
inst←ifetch1103                         yes←stop1103
ᴀ Univac 1103A instruction fetch        ᴀ Univac 1103A stop condition
inst←word read1103 iadr                 yes←v/ind
iadr←iadr+1
iadr←(0,Drum,iadr)[(memcap,Drum+drumcap)ιiadr]
```

PROGRAM 14-27   Basic cycle and instruction fetch of the Univac 1103A.

Unconditional branch.   Branch On Switch includes an unconditional branch.

Completion. Stop is intended as an unconditional end-of-program stop; Stop On Switch is a manually controlled stop, which sets the instruction address to an address where the program can be continued.

```
PS                          MS
ᴀ Univac 1103A Stop      ᴀ Univac 1103A Stop On Switch
   Stop report 1            Stop report(1.stopsw)[4|fld Control]
                            iadr←adr1103v
```

PROGRAM 14-28   Stop in the Univac 1103A.

Decision

A variety of tests and comparisons is available.

Conditional branching.   Branch On Switch reflects the hands-on user supervision commonly used on early machines. Branch On MQ Sign tests the sign of the MQ, then rotates the MQ by one place. Depending upon the value of the sign, a branch is taken either to the u-address or to the v-address. When one of the branch addresses points to the instruction itself, a bit-scan results.

```
EJ;od;comparand                         MJ
ᴀ Univac 1103A Branch On Equal      ᴀ Univac 1103A Branch On Switch
od←double read1103 adr1103u         →If(1.branchsw)[4|fld Control]
→If odᴧ.=acc                        THEN: ᴀ branch
THEN: ᴀ equal                           iadr←adr1103v
    iadr←adr1103v                   ENDIF:
ENDIF:comparand←digitcompi acc
acc←double digitcompr comparand
```

```
TJ;od;comparand;negzero                 ZJ
ᴀ Univac 1103A Branch On Greater    ᴀ Univac 1103A Branch On Zero
od←double read1103 adr1103u         →IFᴠ/acc
comparand←digitcompi acc            THEN: ᴀ non-zero
negzero←ᴧ/acc.~od                       iadr←adr1103u
→If negzeroᴠ(digitcompi od)>comparand   →ENDIF
THEN: ᴀ greater                     ELSE: ᴀ zero
    iadr←adr1103v                       iadr←adr1103v
ENDIF:acc←double digitcompr comparand  ENDIF:
```

```
QJ                                      SJ
ᴀ Univac 1103A Branch On MQ Sign    ᴀ Univac 1103A Branch On Sign
→IF mq[Sign]                        →IF acc[Sign]
THEN: ᴀ minus                       THEN: ᴀ minus
    iadr←adr1103u                       iadr←adr1103u
    →ENDIF                              →ENDIF
ELSE: ᴀ plus                        ELSE: ᴀ plus
    iadr←adr1103v                       iadr←adr1103v
ENDIF:mq←1⌽mq                       ENDIF:
```

PROGRAM 14-29   Conditional Branch in the Univac 1103A.

Branch On Equal and Branch On Greater, when repeated, give efficient table-search operations.

Iteration

Incrementation and termination.   Count And Branch provides an efficient means of closing loops. The instruction reduces the count and branches until the count becomes negative.

```
IJ;count
ค Univac 1103A Count And Branch
count←(digitcompi double read1103 adr1103u)-1
acc←double digitcompr count
→If count≥0
THEN: ค store and branch
    adr1103u write1103 acc
    iadr←adr1103v
ENDIF:
```

PROGRAM 14-30   Count And Branch in the Univac 1103A.

Repeat.   The Repeat is a major feature of the 1103A; it is intended to apply to almost all other instructions. The manual lists, for each instruction, its speed—when executed on its own, and when repeated.

Repeat is a meta-instruction that executes a subject instruction many times without instruction fetch, so operations move at data-fetch–limited rate.

incr1103 shows the incrementing of the addresses of the subject instruction including the cyclic subdivision of storage space. In contrast to the rules applying to instruction fetch, the accumulator and MQ addresses are each cyclic on their own; indeed, there are six cycles for the six accumulator-address groups.

```
RP;cont;incru;incrv;count              value←value incr1103 inc;origin;limit
ค Univac 1103A Repeat                   ค Univac 1103A address increment
cont←fld Control[0]                      origin←0,(Mq+512×ɩ7),Drum
incru←fld Control[1]                     limit←memcap,(Acc+512×ɩ7),Drum+drumcap
incrv←fld Control[2]                     →If inc
count←fld Count                          THEN:value←value+1
memory[F1;Addressv]←inst[Addressv]         value←(origin,value)[limitɩvalue]
ค fetch instruction to be repeated      ENDIF:
inst←ifetch1103
ค Repeat as subject instruction
→ERROR(fld Opcode)=61
ค mark instruction address for branch
iadr←⁻1
→WHILE(contⱽcount≠0)∧iadr=⁻1
    execute inst
    inst[Addressu]←adrsize magnr(fld Addressu) incr1103 incru
    inst[Addressv]←adrsize magnr(fld Addressv) incr1103 incrv
    count←count-1
    →Δ
ENDWHILE:→If(fld Opcode)∈ 34 35
THEN: ค record control and count for TJ and EJ branches
    mq[]←0
    mq[Addressv]←cont,incru,incrv,(ρCount) magnr count
ENDIF:iadr←F1⌈iadr
```

PROGRAM 14-31   Repeat in the Univac 1103A.

The leftmost bit of the control field, when 1, causes the Repeat to continue independently of the count. When the subject instruction is a Branch, the repetition is stopped as soon as a branch succeeds. As a consequence, the

two-way branch instructions ZJ, SJ, and QJ are repeated only once. Branch On Equal and Branch On Greater, however, may be repeated as part of a search operation; their final count is recorded in the MQ. Branch On Switch, when repeated, effectively becomes Wait On Switch.

The content of F1 is used as the next instruction, unless a branch occurs. Since the implementation uses the instruction-address register as a counter during the Repeat operation, its original content is lost. The instruction address is not saved; the programmer must place the address of the next instruction in the v-address of the Repeat instruction, from where the operation places it in location F1.

The manual takes the trouble to describe the action of a repeated Repeat, although such a construction has no advantage over a single Repeat; the location of the subject instruction is derived in a complicated way from the first Repeat instruction. We simplify our description by signaling a repeated Repeat as an error condition.

Delegation

Subroutine Call.   Call is fairly primitive. It merely stores the successor address, then branches. There are no special facilities for state-saving or parameter passing.

```
RJ;return                                IP
ฅ Univac 1103A Call                      ฅ Univac 1103A Supervisor Call
  Invadr report regadr adr1103u            memory[F1;Addressv]←adrsize magnr iadr
  →OUT stop1103                            iadr←F2
  return←word read1103 adr1103u
  return[Addressv]←adrsize magnr iadr
  adr1103u write1103 return
  iadr←adr1103v
```

PROGRAM 14-32   Call and Supervisor Call in the Univac 1103A.

Supervisor Call.   Supervisor Call branches to the fixed address F2. The updated instruction address is placed in location F1 and may be used to find and inspect the 30 bits of parameter that can be placed in a Supervisor Call instruction.

14.1.7

Supervision

Integrity

Policing.   Invalid addresses and operations, and overflows, stop the machine.

Control Switching

There are no control modes, except for the switchable mode governing rounding in floating-point normalization.

Interruption.   The 1103A seems to have been the first commercial machine to have an interruption system [Mersel, 1956]. The system, suggested by

Richard Turner of NASA, provides for an external asynchronous interruption when enabled by a Control instruction, EF. After the interruption system was developed, it was retrofitted to the card reader-punch to signal the appearance of a card row under the brushes or punches.

Interrupt action.   The instruction at location F3 is executed without disturbing the instruction address iadr. If a Supervisor Call instruction is stored at F3, then the instruction address is stored at fixed address F1 and the 1103A takes its next instruction from fixed address F2.

```
interrupt1103
ᴀ interrupt action of 1103A
→If signal
THEN: ᴀ execute instruction at F3
      execute word read1103 F3
      signal←0
ENDIF:
```

PROGRAM 14-33   Interrupt action in the Univac 1103A.

Context switching.   State-saving, interrupt disabling, and so forth are left entirely to the programmer of the interrupting program.

14.1.8

Input/Output

Devices

The principal I/O devices are magnetic tapes. There are also card and paper-tape readers and punches, a console typewriter, and console switches. Usually, cards were read to tape off-line, and tape output was printed off-line.

Direct Input/Output

I/O control is by direct copy logic, like that of the 704. A single 8-bit buffer register reads and writes to byte devices, such as tape, and a single 36-bit buffer is used for cards.

Overlapped Input/Output

Control selects the device and function encoded in the v-location. Read and Write transfer a word or an 8-bit byte to and from storage. Print sends the rightmost byte of the v-location to the typewriter; Punch performs the same action for the paper-tape punch.

```
b ER Read    a PR Print
b EW Write   a EF Control
b PU Punch
```

TABLE 14-34   Input/output instructions of the Univac 1103A.

Read and Write. The choice between byte or word transmission to and from the input and output buffer is determined by the Control field.

```
ER                                    EW
  ⋀ Univac 1103A Read                   ⋀ Univac 1103A Write
  →IF 0=2|fld Control                   →IF 0=2|fld Control
  THEN: ⋀ serial                        THEN: ⋀ serial
        adr1103v write1103(-word)↑ioa        ioa←⁻8↑word read1103 adr1103v
        →ENDIF                                →ENDIF
  ELSE: ⋀ parallel                      ELSE: ⋀ parallel
        adr1103v write1103 iob                iob←word read1103 adr1103v
  ENDIF:                                ENDIF:
```

PROGRAM 14-35   Input/output Read and Write in the Univac 1103A.

14.1.9

Implementation Notes

Drum address interlacing.   The physical interlace of logical addresses 16 K through 32 K−1 on the drum can be manually changed by a plugboard. Consecutive logical words may be physically spaced by 4, 8, 16, 32, or 64. For big data arrays, the spacing can be so selected that a processing loop will be completed just when the next array element becomes available. In practice, this technique was used for repeated production runs by trying various interlaces and settling on the one giving the best overall time.

Subtractor.   The implementation is built around a subtractor, not an adder, so as to yield positive zero in the 1's-complement notation.

Realization.   The 1103A was the first Univac machine using a core memory, rather than an electrostatic memory, as in the 1103.

Speed.   The memory cycle takes 8 μs; addition time is about 50 μs; multiplication, 110 μs; and division, 480 μs.

14.1.10

Bibliography

Univac Corporation, 1958: *The Univac Scientific 1103A Programming Manual.* Form U 1519A (Our defining reference).

Carr, J.W. III [1959b], reprinted in Bell & Newell [1971, 205–8], gives a concise description of the 1103A instruction logic. His description, however, does not include the rules and effects of the embedding of accumulator and MQ.

Borgerson et al. [1978], Mersel [1956], Mullaney [1952], Snyder [1977], Stanga [1967], Tomash and Cohen [1979].

14.1.11

Exercises

14-1 Give the formal description of the rotate instructions SP and SS, assuming consistency with SN and SA, respectively.

14-2 Give the formal description of the fixed-point instructions AT, RS, and MP, assuming consistency with ST, RA, and MA.

14-3 Give the formal description of the floating-point instructions FS, FM, and FD, assuming consistency with the other floating- point instructions.

14-4 The Load operations TP, TN, and TM are described at the representation level. What problem must be overcome to describe them in terms of the values that are represented?

14-5 What is the result of an Exclusive Or (CC) that specifies the accumulator in the v-address?

14-6 Give the results for Extract, where
   a. The u-address specifies the accumulator.
   b. The u-address specifies the MQ, and the v-address specifies the accumulator.
   c. The u-address and the v-address specify the MQ.

14-7 What is the effect of Make Absolute (TM), with the accumulator specified in both the u- and the v-address?

14-8 Give the result for Add Masked By MQ (QA) when the u-address specifies the MQ.

14.2
CDC 6600

14.2.1
Highlights

History

The CDC 6600 is a highly innovative supercomputer, whose system architecture is more radical than its CPU architecture. It is a descendant of the 1103A.

Architect. Seymour Cray was the architect.

Dates. The first shipment was in September 1964.

Noteworthy

Extended core storage.   Although added as an option after the original announcement of the machine, the Extended Core Storage (ECS) represents a remarkable approach to systems operation. It provides a capacity of two megawords (of 60 bits each) and a very fast transfer rate as a result of interleaved operation, so programs can be moved rapidly to and from the extended store. So the extended store is an alternative to program relocation via mapping. Since more than one processor can have access to the extended store, it also is a communication means in multiprocessing.

Lots of working store.   A large and fast working store effectively reduces bit traffic. This fact became apparent in the 1103A; it is a key design characteristic of the 6600; it is exploited even more extensively in the Cray 1. A total of 24 working-store registers of 60 or 18 bits is available; in bits, this is just what the IBM System/360 (1965) with floating-point option provided. In the 6600, logic and arithmetic is between registers only.

Implied addressing.   Loading an address into one of the address registers automatically loads or stores the corresponding operand register. Not only are the data available—so is the address, for further address manipulation.

Short, three-address instructions.   Register–register–register instructions take 15 bits; register–register–memory instructions take 30.

Extrema.   A complete set of extrema for floating-point arithmetic is provided. In comparison to the extrema bit used in the Zuse Z4 (1945) and IBM Stretch (1961) formats, a more efficient notation is obtained in the 6600 by using special exponent values to denote the extrema.

Peripheral processors.   The 6600 showed the right way to do I/O. The CPU, which is specialized for scientific computing, is memory-coupled to 10 peripheral processors (PPUs). These are fully general, small binary computers, as described in Section 14.3. They do all the transfers and device-control operations. One PPU runs the operating system for the whole machine, so

CPU cycles are not invested in operating-system tasks. The console is similarly handled by a PPU.

Polling. The CPU cannot interrupt the PPUs. Most interprocessor signaling is by polling.

Peculiarities

Architecturally, the 6600 is a "dirty" machine—so it is hard to compile efficient code.

Lack of generality. Thirty-bit instructions may not cross word boundaries, and branches are to whole words only, which results in 23 percent of all compiled instructions being No Operation.

Instructions should not be placed near the limit of the valid memory area, since an instruction prefetch may exceed this limit and result in an error condition. This error condition occurs even though a branch may see to it that the actual program does not exceed the memory limit.

Specialized registers. There are three kinds of working store registers. Of these, some are specialized for either loading or storing. This specialization makes allocation hard.

Lack of symmetry. The instruction set is asymmetric with regard to addition and subtraction and the use of the various types of registers.

Signed addresses. Addresses occupy 18 bits, whereas only 17 bits are required for the maximum address capacity. The eighteenth bit serves as a sign bit; address arithmetic and modification are all with signed quantities. Nevertheless, the eighteenth bit is redundant, since any desired addition or subtraction can be accomplished with 17-bit modular arithmetic.

Incomplete fixed-point arithmetic. There is no full-word fixed-point Multiply or Divide. Also, fixed-point overflow is not noted.

Floating-point normalization and rounding. There is no automatic post-normalization in floating point. Rounding is with a preround. There is no guard digit.

Aborted ECS Move. The Move to and from ECS is aborted when an interrupt from the PPU occurs. The interrupted program must reinitiate the Move; that is, the operating system depends on the good will and competence of the problem programmer.

Cooperation of the user. As another example of compulsory user cooperation, the first memory location (the origin location) allocated to a user program must initially be set to all-zeros, in order for error conditions to be recorded properly.

Too few PPUs. There are not enough PPUs; in the 7600, their number was enlarged.

Minimal policing. In spite of the 1103A precedent, the 6600 has only rudimentary policing—for example, there is no invalid-operation detection.

Descendants

Fully compatible processors with a lower performance are the 6400 (1966) and the 6500 (1967). The 6600 design was continued in the CDC 7600 (1969) and Cyber 170 (1970) series. A major design change was made with the CDC STAR100 (1973).

14.2.2

Machine Language

Language Level

Design philosophy.   The language level is fairly close to the implementation; it is designed for assembly language programming.

Unit System

With its 60 bits the 6600 departs radically from the 36-bit word size of the 1103A tradition.

```
format6600                    configure6600
A CDC 6600 information units   A configuration for the CDC 6600
A representation radix         A memory capacity
radix←2                        memcap←radix*17
A information units            A ecs capacity
word←60                        ecscap←radix*21
adrsize←18
ecssize←24
A address capacity
adrcap←(radix*adrsize)-1
```

PROGRAM 14-36   Basic parameters of the CDC 6600.

Configuration.   The CPU and its memory are surrounded by 10 peripheral processors, each with a private memory. A large ECS supplements the main memory. The address size for the ECS is called ecssize.

Spaces

Memory name-space.   The main memory name-space has 2^{17} words. The ECS has 2^{21} words.

Working store.   The CDC 6600 has eight 60-bit *operand* registers (reg), coupled to eight 18-bit *address* registers (adr). There are also eight 18-bit *index* registers (x). Of the eight operand registers, five can be loaded from memory, and two stored into memory.

In the comments of space6600 we give the manufacturer's names in parentheses. In our description, however, we use names that match those in other machines.

Control store.   Besides the instruction address, there are origin and limit registers for memory and extended memory mapping, an exchange address for context switching, an indicator for PPU interruption, a mask to specify the error-exit mode, and a stop bit.

```
space6600                                                         name6600
A CDC 6600 spaces                                                 A CDC 6600 space names
A memory                      A - origin (RA)                     A memory embedding
  memory←?(memcap,word)ρradix   origin←?adrcap                    A - invalid address
A extended storage              ecsorigin←?ecscap                   Invadr←11
  ecs←?(ecscap,word)ρradix    A - limit (FL)                      A - indefinite operand
A working store                 limit←?adrcap                       Indef←10
A - data (X)                    ecslimit←?ecscap                  A - infinite operand
  reg←?(8,word)ρradix         A - exchange address                 Floflo←9
A - indices (B)                 exadr←?adrcap                     A - exit conditions
  x←?(8,adrsize)ρradix        A - exit mode (EM)                    Any← 9 10 11
A - addresses (A)               mask←?3ρradix
  adr←?(8,adrsize)ρradix      A - indicator
A control store                 ind←?radix
A - instruction address (P)   A - stop condition
  iadr←?adrcap                  stop←?radix
```

PROGRAM 14-37   Spaces of the CDC 6600.

Embedding.   Three error conditions are recorded at the memory-origin location, in bit positions shown in `name6600`. The user should initiate this word to all-zeros.

Programming model.   The 6600 CPU is notable not only for the number of register bits, but also for the peculiar coupling of the data registers and the address registers. The programming model also illustrates the restriction of some data registers to being only loaded, and others to being only stored. The third notable feature is the Extended Core Storage, with its own address, origin, and limit registers.

Operand Specification

Number of addresses.   Most instructions have three addresses, of which at least two refer to registers.

Address phrase.   Memory access is with an index plus displacement address; a branch target is specified by a single-address field.

Operation Specification

There is a 6-bit opcode, which sometimes extends to 9 bits.

Mnemonics.   We use the manufacturer's mnemonics only in part, since for arithmetic and logic the manufacturer uses an expression rather than a mnenomic. Furthermore, our mnemonics reflect our space designations: A for address, R for operand, and X for index. We follow CDC, however, in using D for (low-order) double precision, F for floating point, I for (fixed-point) integer, and R for rounded (Program 14-39).

Instruction list.   The 6600 has 73 instructions, including two optional ECS instructions (Table 14-40). There are no supervisory or I/O instructions, since these functions are done by the PPUs.

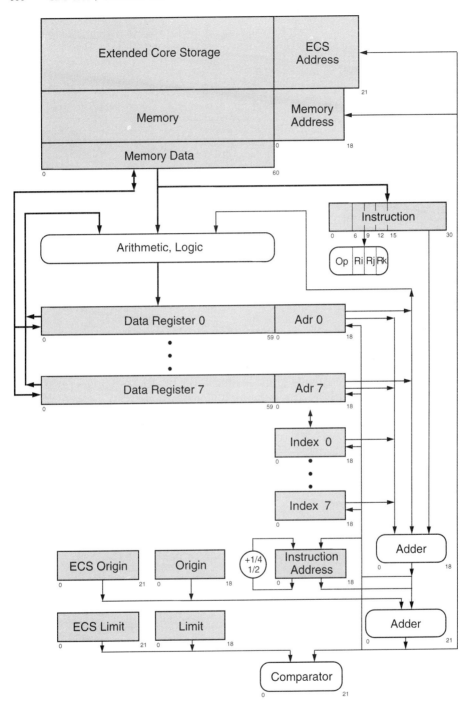

FIGURE 14-38   Programming model for the CDC 6600.

Instruction Structure

Machine-language syntax.   There are three syntactic pattern groups. The basic pattern occupies 15 bits; the other two pattern groups are extended with

a→PS	LR	FRM	→c	b→RJ	c→JP
→b	AR	RRM	→c	REC	c→EQ
→c	LRI	DRM	→c	WEC	c→NE
→b	ARI	MR	RXX		c→GE
→c	NR	FRD	AXX		c→LT
→c	RR	RRD	AXY		c→ADA
→c	UR	NO	XXX		c→XDA
→c	PR	CR	XXY		c→RDA
BR	FRA	→c	→c	b→ZR	c→ADX
BRM	FRS	→c	→c	NZ	c→XDX
BRA	DRA	→c	→c	PL	c→RDX
BRS	DRS	RXA	RXR	NG	c→ADR
BRC	RRA	AXA	AXR	IR	c→XDR
BRN	RRS	AXB	AXS	OR	c→RDR
BRO	IRA	XXA	XXR	DF	
BRE	IRS	XXB	XXS	ID	

PROGRAM 14-39   Operation-code list of the CDC 6600.

a address arithmetic
c ADX Address Plus Disp To Index
c RDX Register Plus Disp To Index
a XXX Index Add
a RXX Add Register To Index
c XDX Add Disp To Index
a AXX Add Address To Index
a XXY Index Subtract
a AXY Subtract Address From Index
  a data handling
a XXA Access W Index Sum
a XXB Access W Index Difference
c XDA Access W Index Plus Disp
a AXA Access W Address Plus Index
a AXB Access W Address Minus Index
c ADA Access W Address Plus Disp
a RXA Access W Register Plus Index
c RDA Access W Register Plus Disp
b REC Read From ECS
b WEC Write To ECS
  a logic and shift
a BRC Not
a BRM And
a BRA Or
a BRS Exclusive Or
a BRE Equality
a BRN And Not
a BRO Or Not
a MR Form Mask
a CR Population Count
a AR Shift Arithmetic Right
a ARI Shift Arithmetic Indirect Right
a LR Rotate Left
a LRI Rotate Indirect Left
  a fixed-point arithmetic
a BR Load
a XXR Load Index Sum
a XXS Load Index Difference
c XDR Load Index Plus Disp
a AXR Load Address Plus Index
a AXS Load Address Minus Index
c ADR Load Address Plus Disp

a IRA Add
a RXR Add Index
c RDR Add Disp
a IRS Subtract
  a floating-point arithmetic
a FRA F Add
a DRA F Add Low-order
a RRA F Add R
a FRS F Subtract
a DRS F Subtract Low-Order
a RRS F Subtract R
a FRM F Multiply
a DRM F Multiply Low-Order
a RRM F Multiply R
a FRD F Divide
a RRD F Divide R
a NR Normalize
a RR Normalize R
a UR Unpack
a PR Pack
  a sequencing
a NO No Operation
a PS Stop
c JP Branch
b ZR Branch On Zero
b NZ Branch On Non-Zero
b PL Branch On Positive
b NG Branch On Negative
c EQ Branch On Equal
c NE Branch On Not Equal
c GE Branch On Greater Or Equal
c LT Branch On Less
b IR Branch On Within Range
b OR Branch On Out Of Range
b DF Branch On Definite
b ID Branch On Indefinite
b RJ Call

Legend: Disp = Displacement; F = Floating-Point; R = Rounded; W = With.

TABLE 14-40   Instruction list of the CDC 6600.

an address field to 30 bits (Program 14-41).

```
                syntax6600
              a Opcode,Ri,Rj,Rk
              b 0 0 0 0 0 1 ,Opb,Rj,Address
              b 0 0 0 0 1 1 ,Opb,Rj,Address
              c 0 0 0 0 1 0 ,Ri,Rj,Address
              c 0 0 0 1 0 0 ,Ri,Rj,Address
              c 0 0 0 1 0 1 ,Ri,Rj,Address
              c 0 0 0 1 1 0 ,Ri,Rj,Address
              c 0 0 0 1 1 1 ,Ri,Rj,Address
              c 1 0 1 0 0 0 ,Ri,Rj,Address
              c 1 0 1 0 0 1 ,Ri,Rj,Address
              c 1 0 1 0 1 0 ,Ri,Rj,Address
              c 1 1 0 0 0 0 ,Ri,Rj,Address
              c 1 1 0 0 0 1 ,Ri,Rj,Address
              c 1 1 0 0 1 0 ,Ri,Rj,Address
              c 1 1 1 0 0 0 ,Ri,Rj,Address
              c 1 1 1 0 0 1 ,Ri,Rj,Address
              c 1 1 1 0 1 0 ,Ri,Rj,Address
```

PROGRAM 14-41   Instruction syntax of the CDC 6600.

Instruction format.   Three instruction formats, one of 15 bits and two of 30 bits, match the syntactic patterns (Program 14-42). Thirty-bit instructions cannot straddle word boundaries.

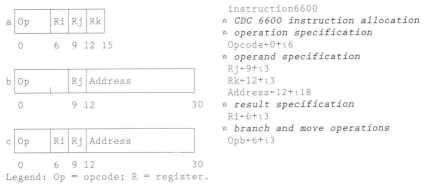

```
instruction6600
A CDC 6600 instruction allocation
A operation specification
Opcode←0+ι6
A operand specification
Rj←9+ι3
Rk←12+ι3
Address←12+ι18
A result specification
Ri←6+ι3
A branch and move operations
Opb←6+ι3
```

PROGRAM 14-42   Instruction allocation in the CDC 6600.

Status format.   Status is brief: There are one indicator, three mask bits, and a stop condition. They are not part of the program status to be switched between tasks.

14.2.3

Addressing

Direct addressing.   Memory addressing is always via an address register. Address registers have 18 bits, even though the address capacity requires only 17 bits; the leftmost bit serves as a sign bit.

Implicit loading and storing.   Loading address registers 1 to 5 with an address automatically loads the corresponding operand register with the addressed value. Similarly, loading of address registers 6 and 7 causes a store of operand registers 6 and 7, respectively. Loading of address register 0 has no corresponding implied action. Register 0, however, is implied in data movement between memory and ECS.

```
    r access6600 address;valid
  ⍝ CDC 6600 memory access
    valid←limit>adrcap|address
    Invadr report6600~valid
    →If(r>0)∧(r<6)∨valid
    THEN:→CASE((~valid),r<6)⍳1
        C0: ⍝ invalid read-address
            reg[r;]←memory[0;]
            →ENDCASE
        C1: ⍝ read from memory
            reg[r;]←memory[map6600 address;]
            →ENDCASE
        C2: ⍝ write into memory
            memory[map6600 address;]←reg[r;]
      ENDCASE:
    ENDIF:adr[r;]←adrsize zerocompr address
```

PROGRAM 14-43   Memory read and write in the CDC 6600.

An invalid address is noted by a limit check and causes a stop if the error mask is set accordingly. An invalid read address causes reading from memory location 0; an invalid write address causes no memory access at all.

access6600 shows that memory access takes place only if the register address is larger than zero and either the memory address is valid or reading is implied (the register address is smaller than six). If memory access takes place, three cases are distinguished: The read address (from registers 1 to 5) is invalid, which causes a read from memory location zero; the read address is valid, resulting in a normal read; and the write address (from registers 6 to 7) is valid, resulting in normal writing at the specified location.

Address Mapping

All memory addresses are augmented by an origin, as shown in map6600, and tested against a limit. The limit check is described as part of access6600.

```
    location←map6600 address
  ⍝ CDC 6600 address mapping
    location←origin+adrcap|address
```

PROGRAM 14-44   Address mapping in the CDC 6600.

Address Modification

Memory access is with an address that may be constructed as the sum of address, index, operand, or displacement values (Program 14-51).

Index Arithmetic

The content of the index registers can be changed by loading, adding, or subtracting the content of other index, address, or operand registers, or of an immediate field. These are all three-address operations.

Index operations.   Index arithmetic uses 18-bit signed digit-complement values, obtained from an index or address register, a displacement, or the 18 low-order bits of an operand register. Index register 0 always has a zero

```
c ADX Address Plus Disp To Index    c XDX Add Disp To Index
c RDX Register Plus Disp To Index   a AXX Add Address To Index
a XXX Index Add                     a XXY Index Subtract
a RXX Add Register To Index         a AXY Subtract Address From Index
Legend: Disp = Displacement.
```

TABLE 14-45   Index arithmetic instructions of CDC 6600.

```
    ADX;displacement;address
  ค CDC 6600 Address Plus Displacement To Index
    displacement←fld Address
    address←magni adr[fld Rj;]
    x[fld Ri;]←adrsize zerocompr address+displacement

    RXX;index;value
  ค CDC 6600 Add Register To Index
    index←magni(0≠fld Rk)∧x[fld Rk;]
    value←magni reg[fld Rj;Adrpart]
    x[fld Ri;]←adrsize zerocompr value+index

    XXY;indexk;indexj
  ค CDC 6600 Index Subtract
    indexk←magni~(0≠fld Rk)∧x[fld Rk;]
    indexj←magni(0≠fld Rj)∧x[fld Rj;]
    x[fld Ri;]←adrsize zerocompr indexj+indexk
```

PROGRAM 14-46   Index arithmetic in the CDC 6600.

value. Address arithmetic, including the generation of negative zeros, is as in fixed-point arithmetic.

Address Level

Indirect addressing.   Indirection is via registers; there is no indirection via memory as a single action.

Immediate addressing.   Immediate addresses are used in address, index, and fixed-point arithmetic.

14.2.4
Data

There is no explicit provision for character strings.

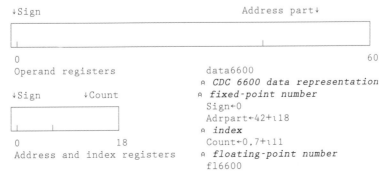

```
↓Sign                              Address part↓
┌─────────────────────────────────────────────────────┐
│                                                       │
└─────────────────────────────────────────────────────┘
0                                                      60
Operand registers                 data6600
                                ค CDC 6600 data representation
↓Sign           ↓Count          ค fixed-point number
┌───────────────────────────────┐  Sign←0
│                               │  Adrpart←42+ι18
└───────────────────────────────┘ ค index
0               18                Count←0,7+ι11
Address and index registers     ค floating-point number
                                  fl6600
```

PROGRAM 14-47   Logic and fixed-point formats in the CDC 6600.

Logical

Logical formats.   Logic is performed in the operand registers with 60-bit vectors.

Fixed-Point Numbers

Notation and allocation.   Fixed-point numbers are represented with 60 or 18 binary digits, using 1's-complement notation. A negative zero occurs in an addition when both operands are negative zero. We describe this occurrence with `magni` and `zerocompr`, as in the 1103A.

Floating-Point Numbers

Closure and normal form.   Infinity and indefinite are separately represented. Negligible is combined with zero. Both normalized and unnormalized operands are allowed. Results are usually unnormalized.

Floating-point format.   The floating-point format has the coefficient sign leftmost, followed by the exponent; the coefficient digits are rightmost. This order is a first requirement for comparing floating-point numbers as though they were fixed-point numbers.

Floating-point ranges.   Arithmetic with extrema makes it desirable to distinguish extreme and normal representation ranges.   The extrema are positive and negative infinity, and indefinite.   The four normal ranges are strictly positive, strictly negative, positive zero, and negative zero.

Prior to an arithmetic operation, the range of the floating-point values is usually determined as shown in `range6600i`. When extrema are encountered, the result is often known without further computation, and an extreme result can be represented as shown in `range6600r`.

Floating-point representation.   The coefficient is an integer and is represented in 1's-complement.   The exponent is represented in 1's-complement with inverted sign—a notation that is not a bias notation because of the two zeros. An exponent field of all-ones, the maximum positive exponent, represents infinity—the coefficient sign further distinguishes positive and negative infinity. An all-zeros exponent, the minimal exponent, represents negligible or zero—again, both signs are possible. A 1 followed by 10 zeros represents an exponent value 0, as does a 0 followed by 10 ones. Since the latter, a negative zero, is never generated, it is used to denote indefinite. The exponent bits are inverted when the coefficient sign is minus. This inversion is required to make the floating-point numbers comparable as fixed-point numbers when the coefficient has complement notation.

Arithmetic with operands in the normal range can give extreme results. If the result exponent is less than or equal to the minimal exponent, underflow arises, and a positive zero is represented.   For a result exponent equal to or exceeding the maximum exponent, a positive or negative infinity is represented, and an overflow is signaled, which stops the processor if the mask bits so indicate (a stopped processor is noted by the operating system on a PPU).

↓Sign

	Exponent	Coefficient	

01   12   60

```
f16600
ⴷ CDC 6600 floating-point number
ⴷ base
base←2
ⴷ exponent allocation
Exp←1+ι11
ⴷ coefficient allocation
Coef←0,12+ι48
ⴷ radix point
point←0
ⴷ extreme exponent
extexp←(radix*0⌊ρ1↓Exp)-1
ⴷ range identifiers
ⴷ - normal range
posnorm←0
negnorm←1
poszero←2
negzero←3
ⴷ - extrema
posinf←4
neginf←5
indef←6
```

```
rep←range6600r r
ⴷ CDC 6600 range representation
rep←wordρ0
→CASE(indef,posinf,neginf,poszero)ιr
C0:  ⴷ indefinite
     rep[Exp]←signinv(ρExp)ρ1
     Indef report6600 1
     →ENDCASE
C1:  ⴷ positive infinity
     rep[Exp]←1
     Floflo report6600 1
     →ENDCASE
C2:  ⴷ negative infinity
     rep[1↑Coef]←1
     Floflo report6600 1
     →ENDCASE
C3:  ⴷ zero
ENDCASE:
```

```
r←range6600i rep;sign;exponent;negzerox
ⴷ CDC 6600 range interpretation
sign←rep[Coef[0]]
exponent←digitcompi signinv rep[Exp]≠sign
negzerox←(exponent=0)∧rep[1↑Exp]=sign
→CASE(negzerox,(exponent=extexp),∧/rep=sign)ι1
C0:  ⴷ indefinite
     r←indef
     →ENDCASE
C1:  ⴷ infinity
     r←(posinf,neginf)[sign]
     →ENDCASE
C2:  ⴷ zero
     r←(poszero,negzero)[sign]
     →ENDCASE
C3:  ⴷ normal range
     r←(posnorm,negnorm)[sign]
ENDCASE:
```

PROGRAM 14-48   Floating-point format in the CDC 6600.

14.2.5

Operations

Data Handling

Data movement.   The 60-bit Operand registers are each loaded or stored implicitly whenever new addresses are put into the corresponding address register.

Memory access is only to and from the operand registers. There is no direct memory access to the address and index registers, and no memory-to-memory data movement.

```
numexp←fl6600i rep;exponent;coefficient;number
⍝ CDC 6600 floating-point interpretation
exponent←digitcompi signinv rep[Exp]≠rep[1↑Coef]
coefficient←digitcompi rep[Coef]
number←coefficient×base*exponent
numexp←number,exponent


rep←fl6600r numexp;exponent;coefficient;xmax;xmin
⍝ CDC 6600 floating-point representation
rep←wordρ0
(¯extexp) normalize numexp,¯extexp
→CASE(exponent≤(¯extexp),extexp-1)⍳1
C0: ⍝ underflow
    rep←range6600r poszero
    →ENDCASE
C1: ⍝ normal range
    rep[Coef]←(ρCoef) digitcompr truncate coefficient
    rep[Exp]←(coefficient<0)≠signinv(ρExp) digitcompr exponent
    →ENDCASE
C2: ⍝ overflow
    rep←range6600r(posinf,neginf)[coefficient<0]
    Floflo report6600 1
ENDCASE:
```

PROGRAM 14-49   Floating-point representation in the CDC 6600.

```
a XXA Access W Index Sum            b REC Read From ECS
a XXB Access W Index Difference     b WEC Write To ECS
c XDA Access W Index Plus Disp
a AXA Access W Address Plus Index
a AXB Access W Address Minus Index
c ADA Access W Address Plus Disp
a RXA Access W Register Plus Index
c RDA Access W Register Plus Disp
Legend: Disp = Displacement; W = With.
```

TABLE 14-50   Memory access instructions of the CDC 6600.

```
XDA;displacement;index
⍝ CDC 6600 Access With Index Plus Displacement
displacement←fld Address
index←magni(0≠fld Rj)∧x[fld Rj;]
(fld Ri) access6600 index+displacement


AXB;index;address
⍝ CDC 6600 Access With Address Minus Index
index←magni˜(0≠fld Rk)∧x[fld Rk;]
address←magni adr[fld Rj;]
(fld Ri) access6600 address+index


RXA;index;value
⍝ CDC 6600 Access With Register Plus Index
index←magni(0≠fld Rk)∧x[fld Rk;]
value←magni reg[fld Rj;Adrpart]
(fld Ri) access6600 value+index
```

PROGRAM 14-51   Load and Store in the CDC 6600.

Block Move to and from ECS.   Reading from, and writing into, Extended Core Storage (ECS) is a block at a time. Any block length may be specified as the sum of an index and a displacement; thus both direct and indirect addressing are possible. The origin addresses of the block in memory and in

extended memory are obtained from address register 0 and operand register 0, respectively.

Large block moves are relatively fast because of interleaved memory operation. This fast block move is a basic means of storage reallocation in the 6600.

```
REC;m;length;address;addressecs;invmem;invecs
ᴀ CDC 6600 Read From ECS
m←mask
Invadr report6600 0.5≠1|iadr WHERE mask←1
length←(digitcompi(0≠fld Rj)∧x[fld Rj;])+fld Address
address←magni adr[0;]
addressecs←magni reg[0;]
invmem←limit≤adrcap|address+length
invecs←limitecs≤ecscap|addressecs+length
Invadr report6600 invmem∨invecs WHERE mask←m
→OUT invmem∨invecs∨0.5≠1|iadr
memory[map6600 address+ιlength;]←ecs[originecs+addressecs+ιlength;]
→OUT ind
iadr←iadr+0.5
```

PROGRAM 14-52   Read from extended memory in the CDC 6600.

The instructions that move to or from ECS must start on a word boundary; otherwise, the instruction is not executed, and a trap to the origin location is always taken (for this purpose the mask is temporarily made 1), where the processor stops. Following a successful move, the next instruction is taken on the word boundary, skipping half a word. An unsuccessful move takes the next instruction in the normal order, executing the right halfword. Thus an incomplete transmission can be detected by a branch instruction placed in the right half of the word containing the move instruction. A transmission to or from ECS is omitted when the addresses are invalid. When a PPU interrupts, as signaled by ind, the transmission is cut short and must be restarted by programming.

Logic

In contrast to the 1103A, the 6600 has quite general logic operations and shift. These operations apply to the 60-bit logical vectors in operand registers.

a BRC	Not	a MR	Form Mask
a BRM	And	a CR	Population Count
a BRA	Or	a AR	Shift Arithmetic Right
a BRS	Exclusive Or	a ARI	Shift Arithmetic Indirect Right
a BRE	Equality	a LR	Rotate Left
a BRN	And Not	a LRI	Rotate Indirect Left
a BRO	Or Not		

TABLE 14-53   Logical and shift instructions of the CDC 6600.

Connectives.   The connectives NOT, AND, OR, EXCLUSIVE OR, EQUALITY, AND NOT, and OR NOT are provided. The last two connectives should be distinguished from NOT AND (NAND) and NOT OR (NOR).

Vector operations.   Form Mask creates a left-aligned string of 1 bits of specified length. Population Count gives the plus-reduction of a logical vector.

```
BRM                                    BRC
A CDC 6600 And                         A CDC 6600 Not
 reg[fld Ri;]←reg[fld Rj;]∧reg[fld Rk;]    reg[fld Ri;]←˜reg[fld Rk;]


BRO
A CDC 6600 Or Not
 reg[fld Ri;]←reg[fld Rj;]∨˜reg[fld Rk;]
```

PROGRAM 14-54   And, Or Not, and Not in the CDC 6600.

```
CR                                     MR
A CDC 6600 Population Count            A CDC 6600 Form Mask
 reg[fld Ri;]←word magnr+/reg[fld Rk;]    reg[fld Ri;]←word↑(fld Rj.Rk)ρ1
```

PROGRAM 14-55   Population Count and Form Mask in the CDC 6600.

Shift.   Arithmetic right shifts and logical rotations are provided. The shift amount is specified either directly in the j and k fields of the instruction, or indirectly via the signed count field of an index register.

```
     ARI;shift
   A CDC 6600 Shift Arithmetic Indirect Right
     shift←digitcompi x[fld Rj;Count]
     →CASE(shift< 0 64)ι1
     C0:  A rotate left
         reg[fld Ri;]←(64|-shift)Φreg[fld Rk;]
         →ENDCASE
     C1:  A arithmetic right shift
         reg[fld Ri;]←word↑(shiftρreg[fld Rk;Sign]),reg[fld Rk;]
         →ENDCASE
     C2:  A excessive right shift
         reg[fld Ri;]←0
     ENDCASE:


     LR;shift
   A CDC 6600 Rotate Left
     shift←fld Rj.Rk
     reg[fld Ri;]←shiftΦreg[fld Ri;]
```

PROGRAM 14-56   Rotate and Arithmetic Shift in the CDC 6600.

In Shift Arithmetic Indirect Right a positive count indicates an arithmetic right shift, and a negative count indicates a left rotate. A positive count exceeding 63 clears the result register to all-zeros, regardless of the operand sign; a negative count uses only the low-order six count bits. In Rotate Indirect Left the count sign has the reverse meaning: A positive count gives the rotate, and a negative count the arithmetic right shift, or the cleared register.

Fixed-Point Arithmetic

Fixed-point arithmetic delivers a 60-bit result in an operand register. Eighteen-bit operands are obtained from index, address, and operand registers, or as a displacement; 60-bit operands may be obtained from the operand registers. There is no fixed-point multiply or divide, but floating-point may be used for this purpose.

Load and Store.   An operand register may be loaded with a sign-extended 18-bit sum of an address, index, or displacement. Load (BR) gives a 60-bit register-to-register move.

```
a BR   Load                        a IRA  Add
a XXR  Load Index Sum              a RXR  Add Index
a XXS  Load Index Difference       c RDR  Add Disp
c XDR  Load Index Plus Disp        a IRS  Subtract
a AXR  Load Address Plus Index
a AXS  Load Address Minus Index
c ADR  Load Address Plus Disp
Legend: Disp = Displacement.
```

TABLE 14-57   Fixed-point instructions of the CDC 6600.

Add and Subtract.   An index, displacement, or operand may be added to
the content of an operand register using 18-bit signed arithmetic (even for the
operand). The result is sign-extended to the full word size. Full-word addition
and subtraction is provided only between operand registers. Subtraction
is only index from index, index from address, and operand from operand.
Thornton [1970] notes the lack of generality; a complete set would require
considerably more operation-code space.

```
AXR;index;address;rl                    BR
A CDC 6600 Load Address Plus Index      A CDC 6600 Load
index←magni(0≠fld Rk)∧x[fld Rk;]          reg[fld Ri;]←reg[fld Rj;]
address←magni adr[fld Rj;]
rl←adrsize zerocompr address+index
reg[fld Ri;]←rl[(word-adrsize)ρ0],rl


RDR;displacement;value;rl
A CDC 6600 Add Displacement
displacement←fld Address
value←magni reg[fld Rj;Adrpart]
rl←adrsize zerocompr value+displacement
reg[fld Ri;]←rl[(word-adrsize)ρ0],rl


IRS;subtrahend;minuend;difference
A CDC 6600 Subtract
subtrahend←magni~reg[fld Rk;]
minuend←magni reg[fld Rj;]
difference←minuend+subtrahend
reg[fld Ri;]←word zerocompr difference
```

PROGRAM 14-58   Fixed-point arithmetic in the CDC 6600.

Negative zero.   Negative-zero results occur when two negative zeros are
added. magni and zeromagnr give the correct result, as for the 1103A.

Compare.   As in the 1103A, comparison is combined with branching.

```
a FRA  F Add                   a FRD  F Divide
a DRA  F Add Low-order         a RRD  F Divide R
a RRA  F Add R                 a NR   Normalize
a FRS  F Subtract              a RR   Normalize R
a DRS  F Subtract Low-Order    a UR   Unpack
a RRS  F Subtract R            a PR   Pack
a FRM  F Multiply
a DRM  F Multiply Low-Order
a RRM  F Multiply R
Legend: F = Floating-Point; R = Rounded.
```

TABLE 14-59   Floating-point instructions of CDC 6600.

Floating-Point Arithmetic

High-order, low-order, and rounded operations are provided. The extrema are recognized and treated according to their nature in the various operations. As a first step, the range of the operands is determined, and is used to find the result range as illustrated by range matrices, such as `rngadd`. `show6600` gives a symbolic display of the result ranges for each combination of the seven operand ranges.

Floating-point Add and Subtract.   The exponent of a normal sum is made equal to the largest exponent of the operands. So the sum may be

```
RRA;r;od1;od2;addend;augend;sum;result
A CDC 6600 Floating-Point Add Rounded
r←rngadd[range6600i reg[fld Rj;];range6600i reg[fld Rk;]]
→IF r<0
THEN: A normal sum
    od2←f16600i reg[fld Rk;]
    od1←f16600i reg[fld Rj;]
    addend←od1 round6600 od2
    augend←od2 round6600 od1                      show6600 rngadd
    sum←augend+addend                       n  n  n  n +ω -ω  i
    result←sum,od1[1]⌈od2[1]                 n  n  n  n +ω -ω  i
    reg[fld Ri;]←f16600r result             n  n  n  n +ω -ω  i
    →ENDIF                                   n  n  n  n +ω -ω  i
ELSE: A extreme sum                         +ω +ω +ω +ω +ω  i  i
    reg[fld Ri;]←range6600r r               -ω -ω -ω -ω  i -ω  i
ENDIF:                                       i  i  i  i  i  i  i
```

```
DRS;r;od1;od2;subtrahend;minuend;difference;high;result
A CDC 6600 Floating-Point Subtract Low-Order
r←rngsub[range6600i reg[fld Rj;];range6600i reg[fld Rk;]]
→IF r<0
THEN: A normal difference
    subtrahend←od2[0] WHERE od2←f16600i reg[fld Rk;]
    minuend←od1[0] WHERE od1←f16600i reg[fld Rj;]
    difference←minuend-subtrahend                 show6600 rngsub
    high←f16600r difference,od1[1]⌈od2[1]    n  n  n  n -ω +ω  i
    result←(difference-high[0]),high[1]-ρ1↓Coef   n  n  n  n -ω +ω  i
    reg[fld Ri;]←f16600r result             n  n  n  n -ω +ω  i
    →ENDIF                                   n  n  n  n -ω +ω  i
ELSE: A extreme difference                  +ω +ω +ω +ω  i +ω  i
    reg[fld Ri;]←range6600r r               -ω -ω -ω -ω -ω  i  i
ENDIF:                                       i  i  i  i  i  i  i
```

```
operand←od2 round6600 od1;larger;normalized;unlikesign
A rounded addition in CDC 6600
larger←od1[1]>od2[1]
normalized←∧/≠/reg[(fld Rj),fld Rk;2↑Coef]
unlikesign←≠/reg[(fld Rj),fld Rk;Sign]
→IF larger∨unlikesign∨normalized
THEN:operand←od1[0]+ 1 ¯1[od1[0]<0]×2*od1[1]-ρ1↓Coef
    →ENDIF
ELSE:operand←od1[0]
ENDIF:
```

Legend: i = indefinite; n = normal action; ω = infinity;
        operands: positive, negative, 0, -0, ω, -ω, i.

PROGRAM 14-60   Floating-point Add and Subtract in the CDC 6600.

unnormalized, even if both operands are normalized.

Rounding is performed by attaching a low-order bit to an operand prior to the operation. The operand with the larger exponent is so extended, or both operands are, if both operands are normalized or have unlike sign. This procedure is, of course, not equivalent to mathematical rounding.

The normalization test in `round6600` tests if the two high-order coefficient bits differ in the j- as well as in the k-register.

```
FRM;r;od1;od2;multiplier;multiplicand;product;result
∩ CDC 6600 Floating-Point Multiply
r←rngmpy[range6600i reg[fld Rj;];range6600i reg[fld Rk;]]
→IF r<0
THEN: ∩ normal product
    od2←fl6600i reg[fld Rk;]                                    show6600 rngmpy
    multiplier←od2[0]                                  n   n   0   0  +ω  -ω   i
    od1←fl6600i reg[fld Rj;]                           n   n   0   0  -ω  +ω   i
    multiplicand←od1[0]                                0   0   0   0   i   i   i
    product←multiplicand×multiplier                   0   0   0   0   i   i   i
    result←product,(ρ1↓Coef)+od1[1] expmpy od2[1]    +ω  -ω   i   i  +ω  -ω   i
    reg[fld Ri;]←fl6600r result                       -ω  +ω   i   i  -ω  +ω   i
    →ENDIF                                             i   i   i   i   i   i   i
ELSE: ∩ extreme product
    reg[fld Ri;]←range6600r r                                   show6600 rngdiv
ENDIF:                                                n   n  +ω  -ω   0   0   i
                                                      n   n  -ω  +ω   0   0   i
                                                      0   0   i   i   0   0   i
exp←exp1 expmpy exp2;normalized                       0   0   i   i   0   0   i
∩ CDC 6600 exponent of product                       +ω  -ω  +ω  -ω   i   i   i
normalized←∧/≠/reg[(fld Rj),fld Rk;2↑Coef]           -ω  +ω  -ω  +ω   i   i   i
exp←(~normalized)↑exp1+exp2                            i   i   i   i   i   i   i
```

Legend: i = indefinite; n = normal action; ω = infinity;
        operands: positive, negative, 0, -0, ω, -ω, i.

PROGRAM 14-61   Floating-point Multiply in the CDC 6600.

```
RR;r;od;rl
∩ CDC 6600 Normalize Rounded
r←range6600i reg[fld Rk;]
→CASE(r<poszero,posinf)ι1
CO: ∩ normal range
    od←fl6600i reg[fld Rk;]
    reg[fld Ri;]←fl6600r od[0]+ 1  1[od[0]<0]×2*od[1]-ρ1↓Coef
    rl←fl6600i reg[fld Ri;]
    x[fld Rj;]←adrsize magnr od[1]-rl[1]
    →ENDCASE
C1: ∩ zero
    reg[fld Ri;]←range6600r poszero
    x[fld Rj;]←adrsize magnr 48
    →ENDCASE
C2: ∩ infinite or indefinite
    reg[fld Ri;]←reg[fld Rk;]
    x[fld Rj;]←adrsize magnr 0
ENDCASE:

UR;exponent;coefficient
∩ CDC 6600 Unpack
exponent←digitcompi signinv reg[fld Rk;Exp]≠reg[fld Rk;Sign]
coefficient←digitcompi reg[fld Rk;Coef]
x[fld Rj;]←adrsize digitcompr exponent
reg[fld Ri;]←word digitcompr coefficient
```

PROGRAM 14-62   Floating-point Normalize and Unpack in the CDC 6600.

Floating-point Multiply and Divide.   When both operands are normalized, the product is also normalized; otherwise, the exponent of the high-order product is the sum of the exponents of the operands plus the coefficient digit-length.   Rounded and low-order multiply are similar to rounded and low-order addition. Low-order multiply can be used for fixed-point operands, provided the product does not exceed 48 bits. Pack and Unpack are convenient in such a case, since the exponent bits are not 0 for integers.

Other floating-point operations.   Normalize gives a correctly normalized result and places the value of the normalizing shift in an index register. In Normalize Rounded an extra low-order bit is attached to the operand prior to normalization.

Pack and Unpack are akin to the 1103A operations with these names; the exponent and coefficient appear as integers in an index and operand register, respectively.

14.2.6

Instruction Sequencing

Linear Sequence

Next instruction.   The basic cycle is simple, in accordance with the architectural design philosophy. The instruction fetch, however, is complex, because 15- and 30-bit instructions are packed in a 60-bit word. The long instructions may not straddle word boundaries in the 6400 and the 6500; in the 6600, such an instruction wraps around within the current 60-bit word, as shown in ifetch6600.

```
cycle6600
ᴀ basic cycle of the CDC 6600            inst←ifetch6600;field
  REPEAT:interrupt6600                   ᴀ CDC 6600 instruction fetch
     execute ifetch6600                  →IF limit>adrcap|iadr
  →UNTIL stop                            THEN: ᴀ valid instruction
                                              field←(word×1|iadr)Φmemory[map6600Liadr;]
                                         →ENDIF
  PS                                     ELSE: ᴀ stop instruction
ᴀ CDC 6600 Stop                               field←15ρ0
  stop←1                                 ENDIF:inst←(word×ilength6600 field)↑field
                                         iadr←iadr+ilength6600 field
  length←ilength6600 inst
ᴀ CDC 6600 instruction length
  length←0.25×1+(fld Opcode)∈(1+ι7).,. 40 48 56 ∘.+ι3

  which report6600 condition
ᴀ CDC 6600 error report
  memory[origin;which]←∨/memory[origin;which],condition
  →If∨/memory[origin;Any]∧mask
  THEN: ᴀ make error stop instruction
     memory[origin;12+ιadrsize]←adrsize magnr⌈iadr
     iadr←origin
  ENDIF:
```

PROGRAM 14-63   Basic cycle and instruction fetch of the CDC 6600.

Completion.   The instruction Stop applies to the CPU only. The supervisor keeps running in a PPU and should notice a stopped CPU (by polling) and take action. So a stop is equivalent to an interruption. The operation code of Stop is all zero, which has program-diagnostic value and makes it easy to construct a Stop when an error occurs.

Error stops are recorded by `report6600`. When the corresponding mask bit is 1, a stop instruction is placed at the origin location, and the instruction address is made zero, hence pointing to that location. Therefore, the next instruction is a Stop at the origin location. The preceding instruction address is also recorded at the origin location. Only the integer part of the instruction address is recorded, however. Moreover, an intervening branch may have occurred, which makes it difficult to trace the offending instruction.

Sequencing instructions.   The 6600 combines testing with branching, which results in many conditional-branch instructions. There are no special iteration provisions; delegation is facilitated by a Branch that stores the instruction address.

```
a NO   No Operation          c NE   Branch On Not Equal
a PS   Stop                   c GE   Branch On Greater Or Equal
c JP   Branch                 c LT   Branch On Less
b ZR   Branch On Zero         b IR   Branch On Within Range
b NZ   Branch On Non-Zero     b OR   Branch On Out Of Range
b PL   Branch On Positive     b DF   Branch On Definite
b NG   Branch On Negative     b ID   Branch On Indefinite
c EQ   Branch On Equal        b RJ   Call
```

TABLE 14-64   Sequencing instructions of the CDC 6600.

Unconditional Branch.   The Unconditional Branch has an indexed target address. All target addresses are subject to memory mapping. The mapping and the limit check for the target address are part of the instruction fetch. An invalid address may result in an error stop. The Unconditional Branch invalidates the instruction cache; a Conditional Branch does not—a fact that programmers quickly notice. Hence Branch On Equal, with both index registers zero, is often used as an Unconditional Branch.

Decision

Conditional branching.   The target of all conditional branches is an absolute address, which cannot be modified. As in the 1103A, comparisons apply to pairs of fixed-point or floating-point numbers. Positive and negative infinity give consistent results. A separate test for indefinite is necessary, since indefinite cannot fit any compare sequence; it requires the comparison result `unordered`, or, as is the case in the 6600, a separate test.

Branch On Zero and Branch On Not-Zero recognize fixed-point positive and negative zero, and hence also floating-point zero, as a zero. Branch On Positive and Branch On Negative test only the sign bit; hence negative zero counts as negative. Branch On Equal and Branch On Not Equal consider positive and negative zero to be unequal. Branch On Greater Or Equal and

```
JP;displacement;index                         ZR
ⱥ CDC 6600 Branch                             ⱥ CDC 6600 Branch On Zero
displacement←digitcompi inst[Address]          →If 0=digitcompi reg[fld Rj;]
index←digitcompi(0≠fld Ri)∧x[fld Ri;]          THEN:iadr←fld Address
iadr←index+displacement                        ENDIF:


IR;r                                          PL
ⱥ CDC 6600 Branch On Within Range             ⱥ CDC 6600 Branch On Positive
r←range6600i reg[fld Rj;]                       →If 0=reg[fld Rj;Sign]
→If˜r∈posinf,neginf                            THEN:iadr←fld Address
THEN:iadr←fld Address                           ENDIF:
ENDIF:


GE;operand;comparand                          ID;r
ⱥ CDC 6600 Branch On Greater Or Equal         ⱥ CDC 6600 Branch On Indefinite
operand←radixcompi(0≠fld Ri)∧x[fld Ri;]         r←range6600i reg[fld Rj;]
comparand←radixcompi(0≠fld Rj)∧x[fld Rj;]       →If r=indef
→If operand≥comparand                           THEN:iadr←fld Address
THEN:iadr←fld Address                            ENDIF:
ENDIF:
```

PROGRAM 14-65   Branch in the CDC 6600.

Branch On Less consider positive zero to be greater than negative zero. The last four comparisons apply to index values.

Iteration

Incrementation and termination.   Incrementation and termination each require a separate instruction. The return branch uses 30 bits.

Delegation

Call.   Call places a return branch instruction at the head of the subroutine, then branches to the next full word in the routine. The user can use the second half of the first word for parameters. At the end of the subroutine, a branch to the return branch at the head of the routine should be made. The return branch is a Branch On Equal (EQ), with operand register 0 specified for both operand and comparand; hence it is an unconditional branch. Thornton comments on the dangers of such self-modifying code: "The reader must simply determine" whether he wishes to take the risk. In any case, he cannot use this instruction simply for a recursive subroutine. Also, he is advised to store no closer than eight words from the current instruction address, since the instruction cache does not test for such a case [Thornton, 1970].


```
RJ;eq
ⱥ CDC 6600 Call
eq←(,3 magnr 0 4 0 0),adrsize magnr⌈iadr
→If limit>fld Address
THEN: ⱥ store Branch on Equal instruction
    memory[map6600 fld Address;ιword÷2]←eq
ENDIF:iadr←1+fld Address
```

PROGRAM 14-66   Call in the CDC 6600.

14.2.7

Supervision

Normally, supervision of the system is performed by a supervisor running on a PPU. There is a hardware option, which we do not describe, to have this supervisor in the CPU.

Concurrency

Several CPUs can have concurrent access to the ECS. The central processor and all peripheral processors are architecturally concurrent. The group of PPUs shares one implementation.

Processor interconnection.   The interconnection of the processors is not visible in the architecture.

Process Interaction

Signaling.   A PPU can switch the program status of the CPU by supplying an exchange address and setting the indicator (ind), which initiates an Exchange Jump. The PPUs can read the CPU's instruction address. Other communication is by shared memory.

Integrity

Protection.   Memory protection is provided by the origin and limit registers; there is no protection within the user's space. There is no need for privileged operations, since there are no supervisory or I/O instructions in the CPU.

Control Switching

Interruption.   For proper synchronization, the testing and resetting of the indicator is implemented as one indivisible action by serializing access to the indicator. Interrupt occurs only prior to an instruction that starts at a word boundary. Since the duration of transmission to and from ECS would give a considerable interrupt latency, these move instructions are aborted when an interruption occurs.

```
interrupt6600
ᴀ CDC 6600 interrupt action
ᴀ serialize indicator
→If ind∧0=1|iadr
THEN:ind←0
   ᴀ end serialization
   exchange exadr
ENDIF: ᴀ end serialization
```

PROGRAM 14-67   Interruption action in the CDC 6600.

Dispatching.   A program is initialized or resumed by an exchange operation that is triggered by a PPU.

State Preservation

Context switching.   The exchange of status specified by the exchange address occurs automatically upon interruption. Registers are block-loaded and block-stored as part of such an exchange.

```
      exchange address;oldpack;newpack
    ⍝ CDC 6600 exchange of context
      oldpack←(16,word)ρ0
      oldpack[ι3;6+ιadrsize]←adrsize magnr iadr,origin,limit
      oldpack[3;9+ι3]←mask
      oldpack[4 5 ;ιecssize]←ecssize magnr ecsorigin,ecslimit
      oldpack[ι8;24+ιadrsize]←x
      oldpack[ι8;42+ιadrsize]←adr
      oldpack[8+ι8;]←reg
      newpack←memory[address+ι16;]
      iadr←magni newpack[0;6+ιadrsize]
      origin←magni newpack[1;6+ιadrsize]
      limit←magni newpack[2;6+ιadrsize]
      mask←newpack[3;9+ι3]
      ecsorigin←magni newpack[4;ιecssize]
      ecslimit←magni newpack[5;ιecssize]
      x←newpack[ι8;24+ιadrsize]
      adr←newpack[ι8;42+ιadrsize]
      reg←newpack[8+ι8;]
      memory[address+ι16;]←oldpack
```

    PROGRAM 14-68   Context switching in the CDC 6600.

Tools of Control

Initial program load.   Initial program loading of the CPU is accomplished by a PPU.

14.2.8
Input/Output

I/O is handled by Peripheral Processors—complete processors that are discussed in Section 14.3.

14.2.9
Implementation Notes

The 6600 has a marvelous implementation, with

- Raw CPU speed
- An instruction cache that traps small loops
- Multiple arithmetic functional units

Concurrent units.   There are 10 independent, concurrently operating, units for the various arithmetic functions. In view of the relative durations and frequencies of addition and multiplication, one floating-point adder and two floating-point multiplication units are used. An ingenious "scoreboard" manages the concurrency among these units.

Speed.   The 6600 has a minor cycle of 100 ns. Floating-point addition takes four of these cycles; floating-point multiplication, 10.

14.2.10
Bibliography

Control Data Corporation, 1969: *Control Data 6400/6500/6600 Computer System Reference Manual.* Publication 60100000. St. Paul, Minnesota (our defining reference).

Thornton, J.E., 1980: "The CDC 6600 Project." *Ann Hist Comput* **2**, 4: 338–48.

Thornton [1970] gives valuable motivation for the design. He covers architecture and implementation in an intermixed manner and omits details, such as the precise interpretation of negative zero.

Casale [1962], Clayton et al. [1964], Thornton [1964].

14.2.11
Exercises

14-9 Give the formal description of the index arithmetic instructions RDX, XXX, XDX, AXX, and AXY from ADX, RXX, and XXY, assuming consistency of design.

14-10 Give the formal description of the memory access instructions XXA, XXB, AXA, ADA, and RDA, assuming consistency with the instructions shown in this section.

14-11 Derive the instruction Store Into Extended Memory (WEC) from REC.

14-12 Give the description of the logical functions and shifts BRA, BRS, BRE, BRN, AR, and LRI from the corresponding instructions shown in this section.

14-13 Give the description of the fixed-point instructions XXR, XXS, XDR, AXS, ADR, IRA, and RXR from BR, AXR, RDR, and IRS.

14-14 Give the description of the floating-point instructions FRA, DRA, FRS, RRS, DRM, RRM, NR, and PR, assuming consistency with the floating-point instructions shown in this section.

14-15 Give the description of the branch instructions NZ, NG, EQ, NE, LT, OR, and DF, assuming consistency with the branch instructions shown in this section.

14-16 How many opcode bits would be required to make register-to-register arithmetic operations completely general?

14-17 Why does the Call instruction generate the instruction EQ and not the Unconditional Branch JP?

14-18 What happens if the X field of the Jump instruction UJN is all-ones?

14-19 Program an arithmetic right shift using the shifting operations provided in the 6600 CPU.

14.3
CDC 6600 PPU

14.3.1
Highlights

History

The architecture of the 6600 PPU is essentially that of the CDC 160, a 12-bit minicomputer. The implementation is wholly new, and is integrated with the 6600 CPU.

Architect. Seymour Cray was the architect.

Dates. The CDC 160 was shipped in 1960; the PPU, as part of the 6600, in 1964.

Noteworthy

The strong constraints of the virtual implementation of the PPU foreshadow, in a way, similar constraints in microprocessors and RISC computers.

Reduced instruction set. Because of the virtual implementation, each instruction should preferably be performed in one cycle; exceptions, such as data transfer, should be simple in nature. There is just one shift. There is no multiplication or division, and there are no aids for programming these operations.

Memory-reflected registers. Sixty-four index registers are located in memory.

Many addressing modes. There are five addressing modes, including immediate, direct, indexed, and indirect.

Virtual implementation. The 10 PPUs are virtual—there is one implementation, which is commutated among the PPUs.

Peculiarities

Lack of generality. The 6-bit operation code is almost completely used, which may explain why there is little symmetry between the connectives or between Add and Subtract. Also, the 6- and 12-bit instruction fields are variously interpreted as signed and unsigned quantities.

Six-bit character. The six-unit size is more apparent in the PPU than in the 6600 CPU. Adherence to the 6-bit byte put the I/O at a disadvantage at a time when ASCII was becoming the standard.

Descendants

The DEC PDP1 was heavily influenced by the CDC 160.

14.3.2

Machine Language

Language Level

Design philosophy.   The shared implementation requires that working and control store for each processor be held to a minimum.

Unit System

The PPU uses the *six* system.

```
 formatΔppu                      configureΔppu
 ⍝ CDC 6600 PPU information units ⍝ configuration for the CDC 6600 PPU
 ⍝ representaton radix            ⍝ memory capacity
  radix←2                         memcap←adrcap
 ⍝ information units             ⍝ io capacity
  word←12                         iocap←12
  accsize←18
  cpuword←60
 ⍝ address capacity
  adrcap←radix*word
 ⍝ maximum number of io devices
  iomax←12
```

PROGRAM 14-69   Basic parameters of the CDC 6600 PPU.

Configuration.   There are 12 independent control units, which are used for communication between a PPU and an I/O device or between PPUs. Any PPU can address any control unit.

Spaces

Memory name-space.   Memory name-space is 4096 words of 12 bits each.

Working store.   The working store consists of the 18-bit accumulator.

Control store.   The control store also is minimal: the instruction address and a stop bit.

Input/output state.   For each I/O device, two status bits signify active/inactive and full/empty. These I/O states are common to all PPUs.

Embedding.   Index registers are embedded in the first 64 memory locations— another means of simplifying the virtual implementation.

Programming model.   The 6600 PPU is clearly a 12-bit minicomputer that has been minimally augmented to handle the 18 bit addresses required for

```
spaceΔppu                              nameΔppu
A CDC 6600 PPU spaces                  A CDC 6600 PPU space names
A memory                               A 64 indices
  memory←?(memcap,word)ρradix           Index←0
A accumulator                          A input/output status
  acc←?accsizeρradix                    Active←0
A control store                         Full←1
A - instruction address
  iadr←?memcap
A - stopped state
  stop←?radix
A input/output
A - device status
  iostate←?(iocap,2)ρradix
```

PROGRAM 14-70   Spaces of the CDC 6600 PPU.

the 6600 main memory. The reader will be interested in comparing it with the much later DEC PDP8 (1965, Figure 15-4). The 6600 PPU programming model is also notable for the paths required for the relative branching. The 64 index registers are embedded in the main memory. They can be added to a displacement in the arithmetic adder to give an effective memory address.

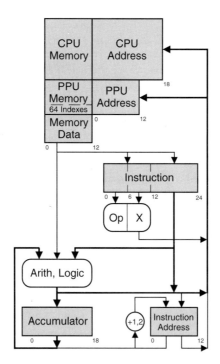

FIGURE 14-71   Programming model for the CDC 6600 PPU.

Operand Specification

Number of addresses.   The PPU is a one-address machine.

Address phrase. The address phrase contains either an index field and a full 12-bit displacement, or an 18-bit direct address that can be used for the CPU memory.

Operation Specification

Mnemonics. We use the instruction mnemonics of the manufacturer. The last letter of a mnemonic identifies the addressing mode: C, long immediate; D, direct; I, indirect; M, modified; and N, short immediate.

a→PSN	→e	LDI	→b	b→LDM	c→CRD	
→d	→e	ADI	→b	ADM	c→CWD	
→d	→e	SBI	→b	SBM	d→LJM	
UJN	→e	LMI	→b	LMM	d→RJM	
ZJN	PSN	STI	→b	STM	d→IAM	
NJN	PSN	RAI	→b	RAM	d→OAM	
PJN	EXN	AOI	→b	AOM	d→FNC	
MJN	RPN	SOI	→b	SOM	e→LDC	
SHN	LDD	→b	IAN	b→→c	e→ADC	
LMN	ADD	→b	→d	CRM	e→LPC	
LPN	SBD	→b	OAN	→c	e→LMC	
SCN	LMD	→b	→d	CWM		
LDN	STD	→b	ACN	AJM		
LCN	RAD	→b	DCN	IJM		
ADN	AOD	→b	FAN	FJM		
SBN	SOD	→b	→d	EJM		

PROGRAM 14-72   Operation-code list of the CDC 6600 PPU.

Instruction Structure

Instruction list. The 64 instructions fully occupy the 6-bit operation code. Three codes, however, are used for No Operation; two of them could be reassigned. Many codes are used to specify the choice of addressing, but they are not always systematically. By far the largest group of operations is that for fixed-point arithmetic.

Machine-language syntax. There are five syntactic pattern groups.

```
    syntaxΔppu
a Opcode.X
b 1 0 1 .Ope.X.D
b 1 1 0 .Ope.X.D
c 1 1 0 0 0 0 .X
c 1 1 0 0 1 0 .X
d 0 0 0 0 0 1 .X.D
d 0 0 0 0 1 0 .X.D
d 1 1 1 0 0 1 .X.D
d 1 1 1 0 1 1 .X.D
d 1 1 1 1 1 1 .X.D
e 0 1 0 0 0 0 .Address
e 0 1 0 0 0 1 .Address
e 0 1 0 0 1 0 .Address
e 0 1 0 0 1 1 .Address
```

PROGRAM 14-73   Instruction syntax of the CDC 6600 PPU.

A	*logic and shift*	b	SOM Decrement
e	LPC And Long	a	SOI Decrement Indirect
a	LPN And Immediate	a	SOD Decrement Index
a	SCN And Not Immediate	A	*sequencing*
b	LMM Exclusive Or	a	PSN No Operation
e	LMC Exclusive Or Long	a	PSN No Operation
a	LMN Exclusive Or Immediate	a	PSN No Operation
a	LMI Exclusive Or Indirect	d	LJM Branch
a	LMD Exclusive Or Index	a	UJN Jump
a	SHN Shift	b	AJM Branch On Active
A	*fixed-point arithmetic*	b	IJM Branch On Inactive
b	LDM Load	b	FJM Branch On Full
e	LDC Load Long	b	EJM Branch On Empty
a	LDN Load Immediate	a	MJN Jump On Negative
a	LDI Load Indirect	a	ZJN Jump On Zero
a	LDD Load Index	a	PJN Jump On Positive
a	LCN Load Complement	a	NJN Jump On Non-Zero
b	STM Store	d	RJM Call
a	STI Store Indirect	A	*supervision*
a	STD Store Index	a	EXN Force Exchange Jump In CPU
b	ADM Add	a	RPN Read CPU Instruction Address
e	ADC Add Long	A	*input/output*
a	ADN Add Immediate	c	CRD Read Word From CPU Memory
a	ADI Add Indirect	b	CRM Read Block From CPU Memory
a	ADD Add Index	c	CWD Write Word Into CPU Memory
b	RAM Add And Replace	b	CWM Write Block Into CPU Memory
a	RAI Add And Replace Indirect	a	IAN Read Word
a	RAD Add And Replace Index	d	IAM Read Block
b	SBM Subtract	a	OAN Write Word
a	SBN Subtract Immediate	d	OAM Write Block
a	SBI Subtract Indirect	a	ACN Activate Device
a	SBD Subtract Index	a	DCN Disconnect Device
b	AOM Increment	a	FAN Control
a	AOI Increment Indirect	d	FNC Control Immediate
a	AOD Increment Index		

PROGRAM 14-74   Instruction list of the CDC 6600 PPU.

Instruction format.   The five syntactic pattern groups give three instruction formats with single- or double-word length.   All instructions have a 6-bit operation code leftmost, followed by an index address, by an index and displacement field, or by a CPU-memory address.

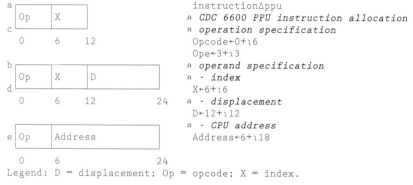

```
                          instructionΔppu
                          A CDC 6600 PPU instruction allocation
                          A operation specification
                          Opcode←0+ι6
                          Ope←3+ι3
                          A operand specification
                          A - index
                          X←6+ι6
                          A - displacement
                          D←12+ι12
                          A - CPU address
                          Address←6+ι18
```

Legend: D = displacement; Op = opcode; X = index.

PROGRAM 14-75   Instruction allocation in the CDC 6600 PPU.

14.3.3

Addressing

Reading and writing is performed with multiple words. There is no address mapping.

Direct addressing.   Since the address size is equal to the word size, regular arithmetic can be used for address calculation. Furthermore, the 18-bit adder size is equal to the CPU address size, which eases the calculation of CPU addresses.

```
               data←size readΔppu address;location
             ⍝ CDC 6600 PPU read from memory
               location←address+ιsize÷word
               data←,memory[memcap|location;]

               address writeΔppu data;location
             ⍝ CDC 6600 PPU write into memory
               location←address+ι(ρ,data)÷word
               memory[memcap|location;]←word wide data
```

PROGRAM 14-76   Memory read and write in the CDC 6600 PPU.

Reading and writing are defined for groups of 12-bit words, as occurs in variable-length moves; in processing, only one word is transferred at a time.

Address Modification

adrΔppu gives index plus displacement address modification.   When the index address is zero, the displacement is the address.   The indices are addressed directly for index arithmetic.

```
address←adrΔppu;index;displacement        address←adrΔppux
⍝ CDC 6600 PPU addressing                 ⍝ CDC 6600 PPU indirect addressing
index←magni(0≠fld X)∧memory[fld X;]       address←Index+magni memory[fld X;]
displacement←fld D
address←index+displacement
```

PROGRAM 14-77   Addressing in the CDC 6600 PPU.

Address Level

Indirect addressing.   adrΔppux gives indirect addressing via an index.

Immediate addressing.   The 6-bit index field and the 18-bit address field can be used immediately.

14.3.4

Data

Character Strings

Character set and size.   The processor assumes 6-bit characters that are processed in pairs.

Logical

Logical formats.   All 18 bits of the accumulator, or the lower 12 bits, or the lower six bits are used.

```
↓Sign        Low↓          ↓Sign                dataΔppu
┌──────────────────┐      ┌──────────────┐      A CDC ppu data allocation
│     Lower        │      │              │      A accumulator
└──────────────────┘      └──────────────┘        Sign←0
0      6          18      0            12       Lower←6+ι12
Accumulator               Memory word           Low←12+ι6
```

PROGRAM 14-78   Logic and fixed-point formats in the CDC 6600 PPU.

Fixed-Point Numbers

Notation and allocation.   Numbers are represented and interpreted either in digit-complement notation or as positive magnitudes. The digit complement produces a negative zero under the same circumstances as for the Univac 1103A or the 6600 CPU and is described using `magni` and `zerocompr`, as discussed for the 1103A.

14.3.5

Operations

Data Handling

Data movement.   There are no operations that move data within a PPU memory. All data movement is between the PPU memory and the CPU memory or I/O.

Logic

Connectives.   The connectives are AND, AND NOT, and EXCLUSIVE OR. This set is a subset of the connectives of the 6600 CPU. AND NOT is called Selective Clear.

```
e LPC And Long              e LMC Exclusive Or Long
a LPN And Immediate         a LMN Exclusive Or Immediate
a SCN And Not Immediate     a LMI Exclusive Or Indirect
b LMM Exclusive Or          a LMD Exclusive Or Index
```

PROGRAM 14-79   Logical connectives of the CDC 6600 PPU.

The addressing modes of the logical connectives are not symmetrically available for the three connectives. We show three examples, the other addressing modes are illustrated by fixed-point arithmetic instructions.

```
LPC                          SCN
A CDC 6600 PPU And Long      A CDC 6600 PPU And Not Immediate
acc←acc∧inst[Address]        acc←acc∧~(-accsize)↑inst[X]


LMI
A CDC 6600 PPU Exclusive Or Indirect
acc←acc≠(-accsize)↑word readΔppu adrΔppux
```

PROGRAM 14-80   AND, AND NOT, and EXCLUSIVE OR in the CDC 6600 PPU.

For each connective, one operand is the accumulator. The other operand is left-extended with zeros to the full accumulator size, if needed, prior to applying the connective. Hence, depending upon the connective, the high-order accumulator bits either are cleared or remain unchanged.

Shift. There is only one Shift instruction; depending on the sign of the shift amount, it gives arithmetic left shift or logical right shift.

```
SHN;shift
 ⍝ CDC 6600 PPU Shift
 shift←digitcompi inst[X]
 →IF shift≥0
 THEN: ⍝ rotate left
    acc←shiftΦacc
    →ENDIF
 ELSE: ⍝ shift logical right
    acc←(-accsize)↑shift↓acc
 ENDIF:
```

PROGRAM 14-81   Shift in the CDC 6600 PPU.

Fixed-Point Arithmetic

Apart from loading and storing, fixed-point arithmetic is limited to addition and subtraction. Six-bit immediate and 12-bit memory operands are taken as positive values.

b	LDM Load	b	RAM	Add And Replace
e	LDC Load Long	a	RAI	Add And Replace Indirect
a	LDN Load Immediate	a	RAD	Add And Replace Index
a	LDI Load Indirect	b	SBM	Subtract
a	LDD Load Index	a	SBN	Subtract Immediate
a	LCN Load Complement	a	SBI	Subtract Indirect
b	STM Store	a	SBD	Subtract Index
a	STI Store Indirect	b	AOM	Increment
a	STD Store Index	a	AOI	Increment Indirect
b	ADM Add	a	AOD	Increment Index
e	ADC Add Long	b	SOM	Decrement
a	ADN Add Immediate	a	SOI	Decrement Indirect
a	ADI Add Indirect	a	SOD	Decrement Index
a	ADD Add Index			

TABLE 14-82   Fixed-point instructions of the CDC 6600 PPU.

Load and Store. Loading from memory resets the upper six bits of the 18-bit accumulator. Load Complement effectively increases the range of the 6-bit immediate value with an extended sign bit; Load Long does not need such an extension.

Add and Subtract. Add And Replace is an Add To Accumulator combined with an Add To Memory; the sum appears in each place with the proper length. Since an immediate short operand and a memory operand are too short to represent a full negative zero, they cannot yield a negative-zero result.

Increment and Decrement. Increment and Decrement are equivalent to Add And Replace with an implied addend of 1 and −1, respectively.

```
LDM                                      LDC
A CDC 6600 PPU Load                      A CDC 6600 PPU Load Long
acc←(-accsize)↑word readΔppu adrΔppu      acc←inst[Address]


LDN                                      STI
A CDC 6600 PPU Load Immediate            A CDC 6600 PPU Store Indirect
acc←(-accsize)↑inst[X]                    adrΔppux writeΔppu acc[Lower]


LDI                                      STD
A CDC 6600 PPU Load Indirect             A CDC 6600 PPU Store Index
acc←(-accsize)↑word readΔppu adrΔppux     (fld X) writeΔppu acc[Lower]


LCN
A CDC 6600 PPU Load Complement
acc←˜(-accsize)↑inst[X]
```

PROGRAM 14-83   Load and Store in the CDC 6600 PPU.

```
ADC;addend;augend;sum                    RAM;addend;augend;sum
A CDC 6600 PPU Add Long                   A CDC 6600 PPU Add And Replace
addend←fld Address                        addend←magni word readΔppu adrΔppu
augend←magni acc                          augend←digitcompi acc
sum←augend+addend                         sum←augend+addend
acc←accsize zerocompr sum                 acc←accsize digitcompr sum
                                          adrΔppu writeΔppu acc[Lower]


ADN;addend;augend;sum
A CDC 6600 PPU Add Immediate             SBI;sb;subtrahend;minuend;difference
addend←fld X                              A CDC 6600 PPU Subtract Indirect
augend←digitcompi acc                     sb←(-accsize)↑word readΔppu adrΔppux
sum←augend+addend                         subtrahend←magni˜sb
acc←accsize digitcompr sum                minuend←magni acc
                                          difference←minuend+subtrahend
                                          acc←accsize zerocompr difference


ADD;addend;augend;sum
A CDC 6600 PPU Add Index
addend←magni word readΔppu fld X
augend←digitcompi acc
sum←augend+addend
acc←accsize digitcompr sum
```

PROGRAM 14-84   Add and Subtract in the CDC 6600 PPU.

```
AOD;count                                SOM;count
A CDC 6600 PPU Increment Index           A CDC 6600 PPU Decrement
count←magni word readΔppu fld X           count←magni word readΔppu adrΔppu
acc←accsize digitcompr count+1            acc←accsize digitcompr count-1
(fld X) writeΔppu acc[Lower]              adrΔppu writeΔppu acc[Lower]
```

PROGRAM 14-85   Increment and Decrement in the CDC 6600 PPU.

Compare.   Following a long-standing tradition, and to minimize status, comparison is combined with branching.

14.3.6

Instruction Sequencing

The basic execution cycle is simple: There is no interrupt. The only complication is the instruction length, which may be one or two words. The length depends, in a complex way, on the operation code.

Sequencing instructions.   Branching and testing are combined, with the

```
cycleΔppu                              inst←ifetchΔppu;field
ᴀ basic cycle of the CDC 6600 PPU      ᴀ CDC 6600 PPU instruction fetch
REPEAT:execute ifetchΔppu              ᴀ instruction words
  →UNTIL stop                            field←,(2×word) readΔppu iadr
                                       ᴀ instruction
                                         inst←(word×ilengthΔppu field)↑field
                                       ᴀ increment instruction address
                                         iadr←adrcap|iadr+(ρinst)÷word

length←ilengthΔppu inst
ᴀ CDC 6600 PPU instruction length
length←1+(fld Opcode)∈1,2,(16+ι4),(40+ι8),49,(51+ι5),57,59,63
```

PROGRAM 14-86   Basic cycle and instruction fetch of the CDC 6600 PPU.

attendant increase of instructions as in the 1103A and the 6600. Apart from the Conditional Branches there are just the No Operation, Unconditional Branch, and Call instructions.

```
a PSN No Operation    b AJM Branch On Active     a MJN Jump On Negative
a PSN No Operation    b IJM Branch On Inactive   a ZJN Jump On Zero
a PSN No Operation    b FJM Branch On Full       a PJN Jump On Positive
d LJM Branch          b EJM Branch On Empty      a NJN Jump On Non-Zero
a UJN Jump                                       d RJM Call
```

TABLE 14-87   Sequencing instructions of the CDC 6600 PPU.

Linear Sequence

Unconditional Branch.   There are an absolute Unconditional Branch and a relative one, a Jump. The relative address is specified immediately in the index field as a signed offset.

Completion.   An Unconditional Jump with zero offset is defined as a Stop. An initial program load is necessary to start the processor again. Normally, when a PPU is idle, it keeps polling by means of a small loop that tests a CPU memory word that is set aside as a message buffer.

Decision

Conditional branching.   The I/O conditions are tested with conditional absolute branches; arithmetic is tested with conditional relative branches.

Branch On Zero or Branch On Not-Zero recognize only positive zero; negative zero is treated as not-zero. In a similar way, the sign tests treat positive zero as positive and negative zero as negative.

The four I/O-status branches specify the device with the index field X and the absolute target address with the displacement field D.

Iteration

Incrementation and termination.   These actions must be programmed; there are no special provisions.

```
    LJM                                UJN
    ⍺ CDC 6600 PPU Branch              ⍺ CDC 6600 PPU Jump
    iadr←adrΔppu                       iadr←iadr+digitcompi inst[X]
                                       stop←0=digitcompi inst[X]



    AJM                                PJN
    ⍺ CDC 6600 PPU Branch On Active    ⍺ CDC 6600 PPU Jump On Positive
    →If iostate[fld X;Active]          →If acc[Sign]=0
    THEN:iadr←fld D                    THEN:iadr←iadr+digitcompi inst[X]
    ENDIF:                             ENDIF:



    FJM                                NJN
    ⍺ CDC 6600 PPU Branch On Full      ⍺ CDC 6600 PPU Jump On Non-Zero
    →If iostate[fld X;Full]            →If∨/acc
    THEN:iadr←fld D                    THEN:iadr←iadr+digitcompi inst[X]
    ENDIF:                             ENDIF:
```

PROGRAM 14-88   Branch in the CDC 6600 PPU.

Delegation

Call.   Call stores a return address one word beyond the head of the subroutine, then branches to the next memory location after that. In contrast to the Call in the 6600 CPU, only an address is stored, not a full instruction; it is assumed that the programmmer places at the head of the subroutine a Branch, whose address is replaced by Call.

```
            RJM;return
            ⍺ CDC 6600 PPU Call
            return←adrΔppu
            (return+1) writeΔppu word magnr iadr
            iadr←return+2
```

PROGRAM 14-89   Call in the CDC 6600 PPU.

State preservation.   Since each PPU performs only one task, there is no need for state preservation.

14.3.7

Supervision

Process Interaction

Signaling.   The PPU forces an exchange jump in the CPU by setting the exchange address and the indicator of the CPU. The exchange address is specified in the PPU accumulator. The signals are sent to the CPU, as described by the `controlΔcpu` function. The PPU can read the instruction address of the CPU with `senseΔcpu`; this information is placed in the PPU accumulator. Further details of these sense-and-control operations, or the read-and-write operations to and from the CPU memory and the I/O devices, are not shown. Their action can be described with shared variables when a CPU and PPU each operate in a workspace of their own.

```
EXN
ᴀ CDC 6600 PPU Force Exchange Jump In CPU
controlΔcpu magni acc
```

```
RPN
ᴀ CDC 6600 PPU Read CPU Instruction Address
acc←accsize magnr senseΔcpu
```

PROGRAM 14-90   Signaling in the CDC 6600 PPU.

Critical section.   The integrity of the interaction between CPU and PPU is ensured by serializing access to the CPU indicator. The implementation of the PPUs as virtual processors ensures that CPU interactions are handled by only one PPU at a given moment.

Control Switching

Interruption.   PPUs are intended to be dedicated to one task. They cannot be interrupted; all interaction with I/O is by polling.

Tools of Control

Initial program load.   Initial program load is from 12 rows of 12 switches, the so-called dead-start program. This program must call upon cards, tapes, or disks for initial loading.

Real-time clock.   The real-time clock can be read as an input device; it runs continuously with a 1 μs cycle, and thus counts up to 4096 in about 4 ms.

14.3.8
Input/Output

Devices

Store.   Mass-storage disk files and magnetic-tape units of (for their time) high capacity are available.

Source and sink.   The program-controlled console consists of two CRTs and an alphanumeric keyboard. A data channel converter allows attaching of the CDC 3600 series card readers and punches, magnetic tape equipment, line printers, and so forth.

Input/Output Processor

A PPU constitutes a fully general programmable I/O processor—a major and clean conceptual advance. I/O instructions deal with CPU memory and with regular I/O devices. Transmission is a word or a block at a time, with 60-bit CPU memory words and 12-bit PPU words.

```
c CRD Read Word From CPU Memory      a IAN Read Word
b CRM Read Block From CPU Memory     d IAM Read Block
c CWD Write Word Into CPU Memory     a OAN Write Word
b CWM Write Block Into CPU Memory    d OAM Write Block
                                     a ACN Activate Device
                                     a DCN Disconnect Device
                                     a FAN Control
                                     d FNC Control Immediate
```

TABLE 14-91   Input/output instructions of the CDC 6600 PPU.

Read and Write. Communication from the CPU memory to the PPU memory, or reverse, is with one or many 60-bit CPU words at a time. In each case, the CPU address is specified by the PPU accumulator. The PPU memory address is given either by the index or the displacement field of the instruction. The length of the block move is given in CPU words by the content of an index.

```
    CRD
A CDC 6600 PPU Read Word From CPU Memory
  (fld X) writeΔppu cpuword readΔcpu magni acc


    CRM
A CDC 6600 PPU Read Block From CPU Memory
  0 writeΔppu word magnr iadr
  (fld D) writeΔppu(cpuword×adrΔppux) readΔcpu magni acc


    CWD
A CDC 6600 PPU Write Word Into CPU Memory
  (magni acc) writeΔcpu cpuword readΔppu fld X


    CWM
A CDC 6600 PPU Write Block Into CPU Memory
  0 writeΔppu word magnr iadr
  (magni acc) writeΔcpu(cpuword×adrΔppux) readΔppu fld D
```

PROGRAM 14-92   Communication with CPU in the CDC 6600 PPU.

Reading and writing from and to the peripheral control unit is done one 12-bit PPU-word at a time, or a block of memory of these words at a time. A single word is transferred to and from the lower 12 bits of the accumulator; block transfer is directly to or from the PPU memory. The control unit is identified by the X field; the block length in words is specified by the accumulator content; the PPU memory address is specified by the D field.

In word transfer, the PPU just waits when the control unit is inactive. In block transfer, the active status of the control unit is tested during transmission, and the operation is terminated when the control unit becomes inactive; during reading, a final zero word is recorded in memory without changing the count in the accumulator prior to termination. The instruction address is temporarily stored in memory location zero, since the implementation uses the instruction address register to hold the memory address during block transfer.

Sense and Control.   A control unit can be activated or deactivated by appropriate instructions. Deactivating an inactive channel or activating an active channel hangs up the PPU. Twelve status bits can be sent to a channel

```
IAM;address;count                        TAN
⍝ CDC 6600 PPU Read Block               ⍝ CDC 6600 PPU Read Word
memory[0;]←word magnr iadr               acc[Lower]←readΔio fld X
address←fld D
REPEAT:→IF iostate[fld X;Active]
   THEN: ⍝ read word and count
      address writeΔppu readΔio fld X
      address←address+1
      count←(digitcompi acc)-1
      acc←accsize digitcompr count
      →ENDIF
   ELSE: ⍝ mark final word with zero
      address writeΔppu wordρ0
ENDIF:→UNTIL(count=0)∨˜iostate[fld X;Active]
iadr←magni memory[0;]
```

```
OAM;address;count                        OAN
⍝ CDC 6600 PPU Write Block              ⍝ CDC 6600 PPU Write Word
memory[0;]←word magnr iadr               (fld X) writeΔio acc[Lower]
address←fld D
REPEAT:→If iostate[fld X;Active]
   THEN: ⍝ write word and count
      (fld X) writeΔio word readΔppu address
      address←address+1
      count←(digitcompi acc)-1
      acc←accsize digitcompr count
ENDIF:→UNTIL(count=0)∨˜iostate[fld X;Active]
iadr←magni memory[0;]
```

PROGRAM 14-93   Input/output Read and Write in the CDC 6600 PPU.

from the low- order accumulator by Control or from the D field by the Control Immediate instruction.

```
ACN                             DCN
⍝ CDC 6600 PPU Activate Device  ⍝ CDC 6600 PPU Disconnect Device
iostate[fld X;Active]←1         iostate[fld X;Active]←0
```

PROGRAM 14-94   Input/output Sense and Control in the CDC 6600 PPU.

14.3.9
Implementation Notes

Each PPU is implemented with a private memory and four registers of 12 to 18 bits, including the accumulator and the instruction address. All other equipment, such as an adder, incrementer, and counter, is shared in a rotating manner, called the *barrel*, among the PPUs. The cycle of the PPUs is 100 ns; one rotation of the barrel is 1 μs, which matches the memory cycle. The choice of 10 PPUs therefore follows from the ratio of these cycles.

14.3.10
Bibliography

Control Data Corporation, 1969: *Control Data 6400/6500/6600 Computer System Reference Manual.* Publication 60100000. St. Paul, Minnesota (our defining reference).

Ibbett and Topham [1989].

14.3.11

Exercises

14-20 Give the description of the logical connectives LPN, LMM, LMC, LMN, and LMD, assuming consistency with the logical and arithmetic instructions shown in this section.

14-21 Give the description of the fixed-point arithmetic instructions LDD, STM, ADM, ADI, RAI, RAD, SBM, SBN, SBD, AOM, AOI, SOI, and SOD, assuming consistency with the arithmetic instructions shown in this section.

14-22 Give the description of the branch instructions IJM, EJM, MJN, and ZJN, assuming consistency with the Branch instructions shown in this section.

14-23 At what points does the PPU deviate from the pure RISC concept?

14-24 Show how to perform a logical NOT and OR with the PPU logical operations.

14-25 How would you perform a logical left shift in the PPU?

14-26 Show that the set of address modes is complete for Load and Store.

14.4
Cray 1*

14.4.1
Highlights

History

Architect.   Seymour Cray was the chief architect.

Dates.   The Cray 1 family of machines consists of three machines: the original Cray 1, the Cray 1/S, and the Cray 1/M. The first installation of a Cray 1 was at the Los Alamos Scientific Laboratories in 1976; all told, 17 machines were installed before the machine went out of production, in 1980. The Cray 1/S was introduced in 1979, and 38 machines were installed before production ended in 1983. The last machine, the Cray 1/M, was introduced in 1982 and taken out of production in 1984; eight were installed.

Noteworthy

Vector registers.   Architecturally the Cray 1 is classified by its designers as a second-generation vector machine, succeeding and learning from the CDC STAR100 [Hintz and Tate, 1972] and the Texas Instruments ASC [Watson, 1972; R.M. Russell, 1978]. Whereas those predecessors are designed to handle long vectors, the Cray 1 aims at efficient processing of short vectors, and a short vector/scalar break-even length. The major conceptual breakthrough of the vector processor is the use of a working store of eight 64-word vector registers. These vector registers markedly reduce the bit traffic, which makes the vector processing inherently more efficient than element-by-element operation. All logic and arithmetic is performed among these vector registers, complemented with eight scalar registers.

Index registers.   Besides the 64-bit vector and scalar registers, there are eight 24-bit index registers—a simplification as compared to the index and address registers of the CDC 6600 (1964).

Buffer registers.   The sets of scalar and the index registers are each supported by a 64-word buffer of appropriate word size. These buffers communicate with memory and serve as a rapid-access temporary store. They do not participate in operations other than moves.

Small instruction set.   Compared to other contemporary vector machines (e.g., the CDC Cyber 205), the Cray 1 has a remarkably lean and simple architecture. A relatively small instruction set (104 codes) uses 16-bit and 32-bit instructions, for high instruction density.

---

*   Preliminary sketch research by Amos Omondi. See also Omondi [1994].

Large memory.   The (for its time) large main memory (8 MB) made a substantial contribution to performance on large jobs that constituted much of the Cray 1's workload.

Sixty-four–bit word with 2's-complement notation.   The 64-bit word with 2's-complement notation is a marked departure from the 60-bit word of the 6600–7600 and the long-standing digit-complement tradition—a clear step toward the classical architecture.

Interruption.   There are indicators that interrupt—another break with the Cray tradition.

Peculiarities

Uniform vectors.   There is no hardware assistance for handling sparse data; a significant omission is the absence of vector gather-and-scatter operations. The latter is corrected in later Cray designs. Long vector transfers from store tend to degrade performance.

Boundary protection.   Address mapping is bounded by two absolute addresses, as in the IBM Stretch (1961), not by an absolute origin and a relative limit, as in the 6600.

Limited extrema.   The extrema Infinity and Negligible are represented by a range of exponent values, as in the Stretch. An underflow result is represented as 0 only when it is less than the lower range limit. An overflow result is always made equal to the lower infinity range boundary and signaled as an exception. There is no indefinite extremum; underflow overrules overflow (just opposite from the Stretch choice).

Rounding.   Floating point normally has truncated results. Multiply, however, offers truncation, rounding, and half-precision rounding.

No division.   Division is not explicitly provided in the operation set; it must be programmed using Approximate Reciprocal and Divide Step.

Weak subroutine Call.   There are no stacking facilities for subroutine calling; the programmer must explicitly organize the use of registers to get the desired effect.

Channels.   In a surprising step backward, the I/O is not via peripheral processors, but via 12 input and 12 output channels.

Descendants

After 9 years, the Cray 2 (1985) was introduced, followed by the Cray X-MP (1985), the Cray Y-MP (1988), the C-90 (1992), and the T90 (1995).

14.4.2

Machine Language

Language Level

Design philosophy.   The machine language is close to the implementation. Although there is considerable implementation concurrency that the programmer does not have to organize, optimum performance requires that he nevertheless consider it.

Unit System

Units   The 64-bit word divides into 16-bit instruction *parcels*. The address length is 24 bits, which is also the word length of index registers. No other subunits are manipulable.

```
initiateΔC1                      formatΔC1
 A initiation of the Cray 1      A Cray 1 information units
formatΔC1                        A representation radix
configureΔC1                       radix←2
spaceΔC1                         A information units
controlΔC1                         parcel←16
dataΔC1                            adrsize←24
                                   word←64
                                 A address capacity
                                   adrcap←radix*22
configureΔC1
A configuration for the Cray 1
A memory capacity
memcap←radix*19
```

PROGRAM 14-95   Basic parameters of the Cray 1.

Configuration.   Main memory capacity is 0.5, 1, 2, 4, or 8 million words.

```
spaceΔC1
A Cray 1 spaces
A memory                          A control store
memory←?(memcap,word)ρradix       A - instruction address (P)
A working store                     iadr←0.25×?4×adrcap
A - vector registers (V)          A - mapping values (BA,LA)
vec←?(8 64 ,word)ρradix             origin←16×?radix*18
A - scalar registers (S)            limit←16×?radix*18
reg←?(8,word)ρradix               A - rounded representation
A - scalar buffer (T)               roundmode←0
sbr←?(64,word)ρradix              A exchange address (XA)
A - index registers (A)             exadr←16×?radix*8
x←?(8,adrsize)ρradix              A - indicators (F)
A - index buffer (B)                ind←?9ρradix
xbr←?(64,adrsize)ρradix           A - error mask (M)
A - vector length (VL)              mask←?5ρradix
vl←?65                            A - stop condition
A - vector mask                     stop←?radix
vm←?wordρradix
```

PROGRAM 14-96   Spaces of the Cray 1.

Spaces

The spaces of the Cray 1 are described with our standard nomenclature. The letters used in the Cray literature are given in the comment lines.

Working store.   Working storage consists of eight 64-element vector registers (vec) with 64 bits per element, eight 64-bit scalar registers (reg), sixty-four 64-bit scalar buffer registers (sbr), eight 24-bit index registers (x), and sixty-four 24-bit index buffer registers (xbr). The vector and scalar registers serve as the sources and destinations for arithmetic and logical operations; the index registers are used to hold addresses for memory references and to hold values for shift counts, for iteration, as well as for I/O channel operations.

The vector length, vl, specifies the length of vector operands and results; its value ranges from 0 up to (and including) 64. A simulation study shows that a maximum vl of 32 would give essentially the same performance.

Each bit of a 64-bit vector mask (vm) corresponds to an element of a vector. The vector mask controls the selection of vector elements in a vector merge operation.

Control store.   The instruction address, iadr, identifies the next instruction location; its resolution is a quarterword parcel, as in the 6600.

origin and limit are used in address mapping; their resolution is a block of 16 words.

The exchange address, exadr, specifies the address of the 16-word exchange package, used for context switching; its resolution is a 16-word block; its extent is the first 4096 words of memory.

The nine indicators (ind) identify interruption sources. The five error-mask bits (mask) select various interrupt modes.

Programming model.   The most notable feature is the stunning amount of register. The diagram can only suggest the actual magnitude of the eight vector registers. It likewise merely summarizes the several independent arithmetic functional units.

Operand Specification

Number of addresses.   The three-address tradition of the 6600 is continued in the Cray 1. Arithmetic and logical operations specify up to three register addresses. Loads and stores specify one register address and one memory address.

Address phrase.   Operand addresses have word resolution. They are formed from an index and a 22-bit displacement. Branch addresses use 24 bits for parcel resolution.

Operation Specification

Mnemonics.   The mnemonics are our own. The manual uses an octal code to refer to instructions. Almost all available operation codes are used.

The instruction list (Table 14-99) is remarkably short for a machine with the vector as a datatype. The combinations scalar to scalar, scalar to vector, and vector to vector are systematically provided. Noticeably absent are vector reduction (such as the plus or times reduction) and the vector search or scan.

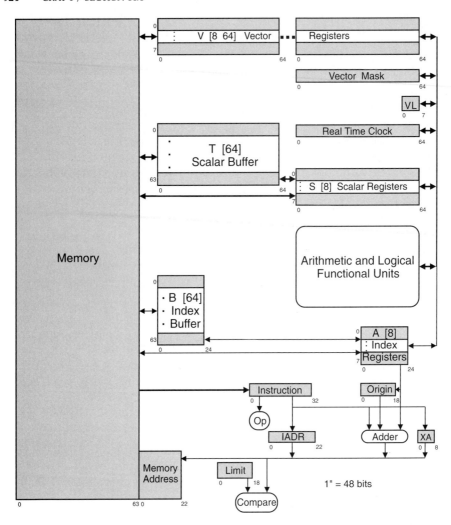

FIGURE 14-97 Programming model for the Cray 1.

a→ERR	→e	a→→e	AD	a→ANDS	MPSF	b→CHS	d→LDA	h→STB
→b	→e	→e	SB	ANDV	MPVF	CHL	STA	h→LDT
ATL	→h	→h	ADF	ORS	MPSH	CHCL	LDS	h→STT
STM	SSA	→h	SBF	ORV	MPVH	ATXA	STS	h→RMSK
EX	→h	AND	MPF	DIFS	MPSR	STTM	e→TA	h→LMSK
→h	→h	DIF	MPH	DIFV	MPVR		e→TCA	h→SLS
→f	PCNT	XOR	MPR	SMV	DSSF		e→ITS	h→SRS
→f	LZR	EQ	DSF	VMV	DSVF		e→ICTS	h→SL
→g	ADA	MSK	RAF	SLV	ADSF	c→ATSP	f→BR	h→SR
→g	SBA	OR	→c	SRV	ADVF	ATS	f→BRR	h→TTS
→g	MPA	→h	TMTS	DLV	SBSF	ATSF	g→BRC	h→STTX
→g	CHNR	→h	MKTS	DRV	SBVF	SM	h→BRB	
→g	→h	→h	→h	ADS	RAVF	SH	h→TSA	
→g	→h	→h	→h	ADV	VTM	S1	h→BTA	
→g	→h	DL	VXTS	SBS	LDV	S2	h→ATB	
→g	→h	DR	STVX	SBV	STV	S4	h→LDB	

PROGRAM 14-98 Operation-code list of the Cray 1.

∩ *address arithmetic*
d LDA   Load Index
e TA   Load Index Immediate
h TSA   Load Index Short
e TCA   Load Index Complement
a SSA   Scalar To Index
h BTA   Index Buffer To Index
h LDB   Load Index Buffer
h ATB   Index To Index Buffer
d STA   Store Index
h STB   Store Index Buffer
a ADA   Index Add
a SBA   Index Subtract
a MPA   Index Multiply
∩ *logic and shift*
a AND   And
a ANDV And Vector
a ANDS And Scalar W Vector
a OR   Or
a ORV   Or Vector
a ORS   Or Scalar W Vector
a DIF   And Not
a DIFV And Not Vector
a DIFS And Scalar W Not Vector
a XOR   Exclusive Or
a EQ   Equal
a MSK   Merge
a LZR   Left-Zero Count
a PCNT Population Count
h SL   Shift Left
h SLS   Shift Left And Save
a DL   Shift Left D
h SR   Shift Right
h SRS   Shift Right And Save
a DR   Shift Right D
a SLV   Shift Left Vector
a DLV   Shift Left D Vector
a SRV   Shift Right Vector
a DRV   Shift Right D Vector
∩ *fixed-point arithmetic*
d LDS   Load
e ITS   Load Immediate
e ICTS Load Complement
a VXTS Vector To Scalar
c ATS   Index To Scalar
c ATSP Index Positive To Scalar
h TTS   Buffer To Scalar
a MKTS Mask To Scalar
a LDV   Load Vector
a STVX Scalar To Vector
a ATL   Index To Length
h LDT   Load Buffer
h STTX Scalar To Buffer
a STM   Set Mask
h LMSK Set Left Mask
h RMSK Set Right Mask
a VTM   Set Mask From Vector

d STS   Store
h STT   Store Buffer
a STV   Store Vector
a VMV   Merge Vector
a SMV   Merge Scalar W Vector
a AD   Add
a ADV   Add Vector
a ADS   Add Scalar To Vector
a SB   Subtract
a SBV   Subtract Vector
a SBS   Subtract Scalar From Vector
∩ *floating-point arithmetic*
c ATSF Index To F Scalar
c SH   F Load Immediate Half
c S1   F Load Immediate One
c S2   F Load Immediate Two
c S4   F Load Immediate Four
c SM   F Load Maximum Integer
a ADF   F Add
a ADVF F Add Vector
a ADSF F Add Scalar To Vector
a SBF   F Subtract
a SBVF F Subtract Vector
a SBSF F Subtract Scalar From Vector
a MPF   F Multiply
a MPR   F Multiply R
a MPH   F Multiply Half R
a MPVF F Multiply Vector
a MPVR F Multiply Vector R
a MPVH F Multiply Vector Half R
a MPSF F Multiply Scalar W Vector
a MPSR F Multiply Scalar W Vector R
a MPSH F Multiply Scalar W Vector Half R
a DSF   F Divide Step
a DSVF F Divide Step Vector
a DSSF F Divide Step Vector By Scalar
a RAF   F Approximate Reciprocal
a RAVF F Approximate Reciprocal Vector
∩ *sequencing*
f BR   Branch
g BRC   Branch Conditional
f BRR   Call
h BRB   Return
∩ *supervision*
a EX   Normal Exit
a ERR   Error Exit
b ATXA Set Exchange Address
a TMTS Load Time
b STTM Set Time
∩ *input/output*
b CHS   Channel Select
b CHL   Channel Limit
a CHNR Channel Number
b CHCL Clear Channel Interrupt

Legend: D = Double; F = Floating-Point; R = Rounded; W = With.

TABLE 14-99   Instruction list of the Cray 1.

Types of control.   Besides the instructions, nine indicators and five masks are used to control the machine operation.

Instruction Structure

Machine language syntax. The three-register pattern and the field extensions to accommodate an address field (Program 14-100) are similar to the 6600 approach. The three pattern groups of the 6600, however, have grown to eight pattern groups.

```
    syntaxΔC1
a 0 0 ,Opcode,Ri,Rj,Rk
a 0 1 ,Opcode,Ri,Rj,Rk
a 1 1 ,Opcode,Ri,Rj,Rk
b 0 0 0 0 0 0 1 ,Opi,Rj,Rk
c 0 1 1 1 0 0 1 ,Ri,Opj,Rk
d 1 0 ,Opc,Rh,Ri,D
e 0 0 1 0 0 0 0 ,Ri,D
e 0 0 1 0 0 0 1 ,Ri,D
e 0 1 0 0 0 0 0 ,Ri,D
e 0 1 0 0 0 0 1 ,Ri,D
f 0 0 0 0 1 1 0 ,Unused,Branch
f 0 0 0 0 1 1 1 ,Unused,Branch
g 0 0 0 1 ,Rh,Unused,Branch
h 0 0 0 0 1 0 1 ,Ri,Count
h 0 0 1 0 0 1 0 ,Ri,Count
h 0 0 1 0 1 0 0 ,Ri,Count
h 0 0 1 0 1 0 1 ,Ri,Count
h 0 0 1 1 1 0 0 ,Ri,Count
h 0 0 1 1 1 0 1 ,Ri,Count
h 0 0 1 1 1 1 0 ,Ri,Count
h 0 0 1 1 1 1 1 ,Ri,Count
h 0 1 0 0 0 1 0 ,Ri,Count
h 0 1 0 0 0 1 1 ,Ri,Count
h 0 1 0 1 0 1 0 ,Ri,Count
h 0 1 0 1 0 1 1 ,Ri,Count
h 0 1 0 1 1 0 0 ,Ri,Count
h 0 1 0 1 1 0 1 ,Ri,Count
h 0 1 1 1 1 0 0 ,Ri,Count
h 0 1 1 1 1 0 1 ,Ri,Count
```

PROGRAM 14-100   Instruction syntax of the Cray 1.

Instruction format. Instructions occupy either one or two 16-bit parcels. A 22-bit displacement is used for data transfer; a 24-bit parcel address is used for branching. The register fields are specialized for operand specification (j and k) or for result (i) specification, but at times the i-location is also used as operand (Program 14-101).

Indicators. The nine indicators are for real-time clock, maintenance attention, floating-point error, operand range error, program range error, memory (parity) error, I/O, and normal and error supervisor call (Program 14-102).

Interruption masks. The five interruption masks specify: interruptible monitor mode, interrupt on correctable memory error, interrupt on uncorrectable memory error, interrupt on floating-point error, and monitor mode. The interruptible monitor mode disables the clock, attention, I/O, and normal call indicators. The monitor mode disables all indicators except the memory errors. These memory errors can be selectively disabled for correctable single-parity errors and for uncorrectable multiple errors.

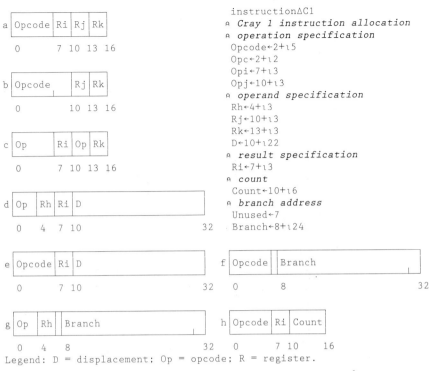

```
                                    instructionΔC1
                                    ⋒ Cray 1 instruction allocation
                                    ⋒ operation specification
                                      Opcode←2+ι5
                                      Opc←2+ι2
                                      Opi←7+ι3
                                      Opj←10+ι3
                                    ⋒ operand specification
                                      Rh←4+ι3
                                      Rj←10+ι3
                                      Rk←13+ι3
                                      D←10+ι22
                                    ⋒ result specification
                                      Ri←7+ι3
                                    ⋒ count
                                      Count←10+ι6
                                    ⋒ branch address
                                      Unused←7
                                      Branch←8+ι24
```

Legend: D = displacement; Op = opcode; R = register.

PROGRAM 14-101   Instruction allocation in the Cray 1.

```
        indicatorΔC1
      ⋒ Cray 1 indicator allocation    ⋒ mask allocation
        Clock←0                          Intmon←0
        Att←1                            Memcorr←1
        Floflo←2                         Flerror←2
        Invadr←3                         Memuncorr←3
        Ifetch←4                         Monitor←4
        Parity←5
        Io←6
        Errorexit←7
        Normalexit←8
```

PROGRAM 14-102   Indicators in the Cray 1.

14.4.3

Addressing

Direct addressing.   Memory addressing is the classical direct addressing—there is no implied memory access as a result of loading an address, as there was in the 6600.

```
    data←readΔC1 address              address writeΔC1 data;location
  ⋒ Cray 1 read from memory          ⋒ Cray 1 write into memory
    data←memory[mapΔC1 address;]        location←mapΔC1 address
                                       →If ̃ind[Invadr]
                                       THEN:memory[location;]←data
                                       ENDIF:
```

PROGRAM 14-103   Memory read and write in the Cray 1.

Address Mapping

All program-generated store addresses are relative to an `origin` and may not exceed the `limit` value. `origin` and `limit` have a resolution of 16 words. `limit` is an absolute address, not an address relative to `origin`, as in the 6600.

```
location←mapΔC1 address
ᴀ Cray 1 address mapping
location←origin+address
Invadr report location≥limit
```

PROGRAM 14-104   Address mapping in the Cray 1.

Address Modification

The direct memory addresses used in loading and storing data and index registers are obtained by adding a displacement to an index, specified by the h-field. When the index address is zero, no index is added.

```
address←adrΔC1;index;displacement
ᴀ Cray 1 addressing
index←radixcompi(0≠fld Rh)∧x[fld Rh;]
displacement←radixcompi inst[D]
address←index+displacement
```

PROGRAM 14-105   Memory addressing in the Cray 1.

Register addressing.   Scalar and index registers zero are interpreted as containing special values when referenced in the h, j, or k fields of an instruction, irrespective of what values they may actually contain. In the h and the j fields, they deliver the value 0; in the k field, the index delivers a low-order 1; the scalar, a high-order 1.

```
index←xj                          index←xk
ᴀ Cray 1 j-index                  ᴀ Cray 1 k-index
index←(0≠fld Rj)∧x[fld Rj;]       →IF 0=fld Rk
                                  THEN:index←(-adrsize)↑1
                                     →ENDIF
                                  ELSE:index←x[fld Rk;]
                                  ENDIF:


data←regj                         data←regk
ᴀ Cray 1 scalar j-operand         ᴀ Cray 1 scalar k-operand
data←(0≠fld Rj)∧reg[fld Rj;]      →IF 0=fld Rk
                                  THEN:data←word↑1
                                     →ENDIF
veci data                         ELSE:data←reg[fld Rk;]
ᴀ Cray 1 vector i-result          ENDIF:
vec[fld Ri;ιvl;]←data


data←vecj                         data←veck
ᴀ Cray 1 vector j-operand         ᴀ Cray 1 vector k-operand
data←vec[fld Rj;ιvl;]             data←vec[fld Rk;ιvl;]
```

PROGRAM 14-106   Register addressing in the Cray 1.

Index Arithmetic

The operations on the indices and on the index buffer transfer indices to and from memory and various working store locations, and perform basic index arithmetic.

d	LDA	Load Index		h	ATB	Index To Index Buffer
e	TA	Load Index Immediate		d	STA	Store Index
h	TSA	Load Index Short		h	STB	Store Index Buffer
e	TCA	Load Index Complement		a	ADA	Index Add
a	SSA	Scalar To Index		a	SBA	Index Subtract
h	BTA	Index Buffer To Index		a	MPA	Index Multiply
h	LDB	Load Index Buffer				

TABLE 14-107   Index arithmetic instructions of the Cray 1.

The indices can be loaded and stored from memory. The short immediate load provides a 6-bit positive index value; the plain immediate load provides a 22-bit positive index value. Immediate complement load supplies a 22-bit negative index value, but it is in digit complement. In contrast to the 6600, the index registers can be loaded and stored directly from and to (the lower 24 bits of) memory.

```
LDA                                 SSA
a Cray 1 Load Index                 a Cray 1 Scalar To Index
x[fld Ri;]←(-adrsize)↑read∆C1 adr∆C1   x[fld Ri;]←(-adrsize)↑regj


TSA                                 ATB
a Cray 1 Load Index Short           a Cray 1 Index To Index Buffer
x[fld Ri;]←(-adrsize)↑inst[Count]   xbr[fld Count;]←x[fld Ri;]


TCA                                 STA
a Cray 1 Load Index Complement      a Cray 1 Store Index
x[fld Ri;]←⁻(-adrsize)↑inst[D]      adr∆C1 write∆C1(-word)↑x[fld Ri;]
```

PROGRAM 14-108   Load and Store Index in the Cray 1.

Index buffer load and store.   The index buffer is loaded and stored a block at a time. The start of the block in the buffer is specified by the i-index. The buffer addressing is circular; buffer location 63 is followed by location 0. The start of the block in memory is specified by index 0. The value of the Count field plus 1 is the block length.

```
STB;location;data
a Cray 1 Store Index Buffer
location←(magni x[fld Ri;])+ι1+fld Count
data←((1+fld Count),-word)↑xbr[64|location;]
((magni x[0;])+ι1+fld Count) write∆C1 data
```

PROGRAM 14-109   Store Index Buffer in the Cray 1.

Index Add and Multiply.   In contrast to the 6600 the Cray 1 has Multiply for indices and for scalars. Add, Subtract, and Multiply are simple and similar to one another; no overflow is noted.

```
MPA;multiplier;multiplicand;product
⋒ Cray 1 Index Multiply
  multiplier←radixcompi xk
  multiplicand←radixcompi xj
  product←multiplicand×multiplier
  x[fld Ri;]←adrsize radixcompr product
```

PROGRAM 14-110   Index Multiply in the Cray 1.

Address Level

Immediate addressing.   Several immediate instructions provide a fast means of loading scalars and indices.

14.4.4
Data

The three main classes of datatypes are logical, fixed-point numbers, and floating-point numbers; each can generally be handled as 64-bit entities or as vectors of such entities.

Logical

Logical formats.   Logical bits are manipulated as 64-bit vectors and as matrices with 64-bit rows.

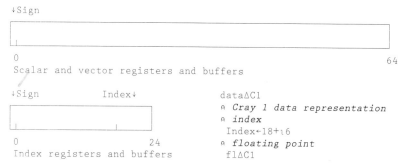

PROGRAM 14-111   Logic and fixed-point formats in the Cray 1.

Fixed-Point Numbers

Notation and allocation.   Fixed-point numbers are represented in 2's-complement and occupy either 24 bits or 64 bits. The 64-bit numbers are manipulated as scalars or as elements of vectors.

Floating-Point Numbers

Closure and normal form.   The exponent range is divided into four quarters. The lowest quarter represents a zero or negligible value; true zero is represented as a string of all zeros. The two middle quarters represent normal negative and positive exponents. The upper quarter represents overflow and acts as infinity. There is no indefinite extremum.

Floating-point format. Floating point numbers have 64 bits. The coefficient is represented with 48 bits in signed magnitude, and the exponent is represented with 15 bits in biased notation. The extreme ranges are recognized by the two high-order exponent bits. This encoding is less efficient than that of the 6600, but the normal range of 14 bits is still larger than the 11 bits of the 6600. Floating-point numbers are comparable as fixed point, but only positive, negative, and zero are used as branch criteria.

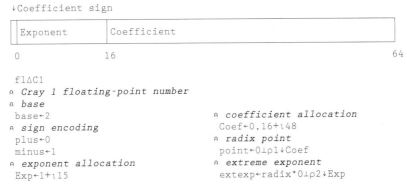

```
↓Coefficient sign
```

Exponent	Coefficient	
0	16	64

```
f1∆C1
A Cray 1 floating-point number
A base
base←2                        A coefficient allocation
A sign encoding                 Coef←0,16+ι48
plus←0                        A radix point
minus←1                         point←0⊥1↓Coef
A exponent allocation         A extreme exponent
Exp←1+ι15                       extexp←radix*0⊥ρ2↓Exp
```

PROGRAM 14-112   Floating-point format in the Cray 1.

Floating-point representation. Extreme operands are not explicitly recognized in floating-point interpretation; the exponent is noted, however, and is used in determining the range of the result.

```
numexp←f1∆C1i rep;exponent;coefficient;number
A Cray 1 floating-point interpretation
exponent←biasi rep[Exp]
coefficient←signmagni rep[Coef]
number←coefficient×base*exponent-point
numexp←number,exponent

rep←f1∆C1r numexp;exponent;coefficient;xmax;xmin;oflo
A Cray 1 floating-point representation
rep←wordρ0
(-2×extexp) normalize 1↑numexp
rep[Coef]←(ρCoef) signmagnr round∆C1 coefficient
rep[Exp]←(ρExp) biasr extexp⊥exponent
oflo←(exponent≥extexp)∨(exponent≥-extexp)∧(1↓numexp)≥extexp
Floflo report oflo∧mask[Flerror]∧~mask[Monitor]

result←round∆C1 number
A Cray 1 rounding
→CASE roundmode
C0: A truncated
    result←truncate number
    →ENDCASE
  C1: A rounded
    result←(×number)×⌊0.75+|number
    →ENDCASE
  C2: A half rounded
    result←(2*19)×(×number)×⌊0.75+|number÷2*19
ENDCASE:
```

PROGRAM 14-113   Floating-point representation in the Cray 1.

A result overflow is represented as an infinity. Infinity is also recorded when one of the operands is infinite, provided that the result is not negligible or zero. This rule shows that negligible has precedence over infinity.

Rounding.   All arithmetic is normally truncated. Multiply can also be specified with a rounded or with a half-precision rounded result.

Floating-point vector representation.   The vector interpretation and representation use the scalar floating-point functions for each vector element. A WHILE (not REPEAT UNTIL) loop is used to describe this repetition; the vector may have length 0, hence no elements (Program 14-114).

```
vector←vflΔCli rep
 ⍝ Cray 1 floating-point vector interpretation
 vector← 0 2 ρ0
 →WHILE 0≠1↑ρrep
    vector←vector,flΔCli rep[0;]
    rep← 1 0 ↓rep
    →Δ
 ENDWHILE:


 rep←vflΔClr vector
 ⍝ Cray 1 floating-point vector representation
 rep←(0,word)ρ0
 →WHILE 0≠1↑ρvector
    rep←rep,flΔClr vector[0;]
    vector← 1 0 ↓vector
    →Δ
 ENDWHILE:
```

PROGRAM 14-114   Floating-point vector representation in the Cray 1.

14.4.5

Operations

We describe, for each datatype, the scalar and the vector operations. In vector operations, the destination vector location must not overlap the source vector locations.

Data Handling

Data movement.   There are no memory-to-memory Move operations. Transfer between memory and a buffer is described as part of index or fixed-point operations. The length of the vector operands is specified by the vector length; it gives the number of adjacent elements (starting at the leftmost element) that participate in the operation.

Logic

Connectives.   The connectives AND, OR, and AND NOT can be applied between 64-bit logical words, between logical matrices with 64-bit rows, or between such a matrix and a vector that is expanded to a matrix; the other connectives apply to 64-bit vectors only.

```
a AND   And                          a LZR   Left-Zero Count
a ANDV  And Vector                   a PCNT  Population Count
a ANDS  And Scalar W Vector          h SL    Shift Left
a OR    Or                           h SLS   Shift Left And Save
a ORV   Or Vector                    a DL    Shift Left D
a ORS   Or Scalar W Vector           h SR    Shift Right
a DIF   And Not                      h SRS   Shift Right And Save
a DIFV  And Not Vector               a DR    Shift Right D
a DIFS  And Scalar W Not Vector      a SLV   Shift Left Vector
a XOR   Exclusive Or                 a DLV   Shift Left D Vector
a EQ    Equal                        a SRV   Shift Right Vector
a MSK   Merge                        a DRV   Shift Right D Vector
Legend: D = Double; W = With.
```

TABLE 14-115   Logical and shift operations of the Cray 1.

```
ANDV                               DIFS
a Cray 1 And Vector                a Cray 1 And Scalar With Not Vector
→OUT(fld Ri)∈(fld Rj),fld Rk       →OUT(fld Ri)=fld Rk
veci vecj∧veck                     veci((vl,word)ρregj)∧~veck


EQ                                 MSK
a Cray 1 Equal                     a Cray 1 Merge
reg[fld Ri;]←regj=regk             reg[fld Ri;]←reg[fld Ri;]∧~regk
                                   reg[fld Ri;]←reg[fld Ri;]∨regj∧regk
```

PROGRAM 14-116   AND, EQUAL, AND-NOT, and MERGE in the Cray 1.

Merge.   Merge strongly resembles the 1103A Extract; it matches on the bit-level the word-level actions of the vector merge. The k-operand serves as a mask that selects the bits either from the j-operand or from the i-operand. The result replaces the i-operand.

Vector operations.   Population Count and Left-Zero Count are only defined for single 64-bit logical vectors.

```
LZR                                PCNT
a Cray 1 Left-Zero Count           a Cray 1 Population Count
x[fld Ri;]←adrsize magnr regjιl    x[fld Ri;]←adrsize magnr+/regj
```

PROGRAM 14-117   Left-Zero and Population Count in the Cray 1.

Shift.   Shifts are logical left and right, apply to scalars and vectors, and are of single and double length; there is no arithmetic shift. The shifted result either replaces the content of the register that is shifted or is placed in register 0, with the operand register remaining unchanged. For single scalar shifts, the shift amount is in the Count field; for double and vector shifts, the shift amount is in the k-register. In single right shift, the complement on 64 of the Count is used (an implementation request?). The scalar double shift uses the concatenation of the i- and j-registers as operand and yields one word. The i- register is shifted left, filling from the j register. For the vector double shift, each vector element is filled from its successor.

```
SR;shift                                    SLS;shift
ᴀ Cray 1 Shift Right                        ᴀ Cray 1 Shift Left And Save
shift←-(64-fld Count)                        shift←fld Count
reg[fld Ri;]←(-word)↑shift↓reg[fld Ri;]     reg[0;]←word↑shift↓reg[fld Ri;]


DL;shift;rl                                 SRV;shift
ᴀ Cray 1 Shift Left Double                  ᴀ Cray 1 Shift Right Vector
shift←magni xk                               →OUT(fld Ri)=fld Rj
rl←word↑shift↓reg[fld Ri;].regj              shift←0.-magni xk
reg[fld Ri;]←rl                              veci(vl.-word)↑shift↓vecj


DLV;shift
ᴀ Cray 1 Shift Left Double Vector
→OUT(fld Ri)=fld Rj
shift←0.magni xk
veci(vl.word)↑shift↓vecj. 1 0 ↓vecj↔0
```

PROGRAM 14-118   Logical Shift in the Cray 1.

Fixed-Point Arithmetic

The choice of scalar and vector dimensions, and of register and buffer locations, gives rise to a variety of Load, Store, and Merge operations. Arithmetic is limited to Add and Subtract, but floating point can be used for fixed-point multiplication. Overflow is not detected during the execution of any of the instructions in this category.

d	LDS	Load	a	STM	Set Mask	
e	ITS	Load Immediate	h	LMSK	Set Left Mask	
e	ICTS	Load Complement	h	RMSK	Set Right Mask	
a	VXTS	Vector To Scalar	a	VTM	Set Mask From Vector	
c	ATS	Index To Scalar	d	STS	Store	
c	ATSP	Index Positive To Scalar	h	STT	Store Buffer	
h	TTS	Buffer To Scalar	a	STV	Store Vector	
a	MKTS	Mask To Scalar	a	VMV	Merge Vector	
a	LDV	Load Vector	a	SMV	Merge Scalar W Vector	
a	STVX	Scalar To Vector	a	AD	Add	
a	ATL	Index To Length	a	ADV	Add Vector	
h	LDT	Load Buffer	a	ADS	Add Scalar To Vector	
h	STTX	Scalar To Buffer	a	SB	Subtract	
			a	SBV	Subtract Vector	
			a	SBS	Subtract Scalar From Vector	

Legend: W = With.

TABLE 14-119   Fixed-point instructions of the Cray 1.

Load and Store.   Transmission is between the scalar or vector registers, and memory or the other working store registers. Registers may be also loaded immediately from the displacement field. Index To Scalar gives sign extension; Index To Scalar Positive has zero extension. Load Vector is designed for scanning arrays with arbitrary stride, thus giving fast scanning of arrays.

Buffer load and store.   The scalar buffer can be loaded, a block of adjacent full words at a time, in a way similar to the loading of the index buffer with indices.

```
LDS                                STS
ค Cray 1 Load                      ค Cray 1 Store
  reg[fld Ri;]←readΔC1 adrΔC1        adrΔC1 writeΔC1 reg[fld Ri;]


ITS                                ATL
ค Cray 1 Load Immediate            ค Cray 1 Index To Length
  reg[fld Ri;]←(-word)↑inst[D]       vl←1+64|(magni xk)-1


VXTS                               STTX
ค Cray 1 Vector To Scalar          ค Cray 1 Scalar To Buffer
  reg[fld Ri;]←vec[fld Rj;fld Rk;]   sbr[fld Count;]←reg[fld Ri;]


LDV;start;incr                     STVX
ค Cray 1 Load Vector               ค Cray 1 Scalar To Vector
  start←magni x[0;]                  vec[fld Ri;magni xk[Index];]←regj
  incr←radixcompi xk
  veci readΔC1 start+incr×ιvl
```

PROGRAM 14-120   Fixed-point Load and Store in the Cray 1.

```
LDT;address;data;location
ค Cray 1 Load Buffer
  address←(magni x[fld Ri;])+ι1+fld Count
  data←readΔC1 address
  location←(magni x[0;])+ι1+fld Count
  sbr[location;]←data
```

PROGRAM 14-121   Store Scalar Buffer in the Cray 1.

Vector merge.   The vector-merge operations use the part of the vector mask that is specified by the vector length. Where the mask is 1, a corresponding word element from the j-operand is selected; where 0, the k-operand is selected; the result is placed in the i-location. Merge Vector merges two vectors; Merge Scalar With Vector replicates the scalar to form a vector of proper dimension in APL fashion; this vector then merges with the vector operand.

```
VMV;mask                           SMV;mask
ค Cray 1 Merge Vector              ค Cray 1 Merge Scalar With Vector
→OUT(fld Ri)∈(fld Rj),fld Rk       →OUT(fld Ri)=fld Rk
  mask←(vl↑vm)∘.=wordρ1              mask←(vl↑vm)∘.=wordρ1
  veci(mask∧vecj)∨(~mask)∧veck      veci(mask∧(vl,word)ρregj)∨(~mask)∧veck
```

PROGRAM 14-122   Fixed-point Merge in the Cray 1.

Mask generation.   The mask used in the merge operations can be created with Set Mask From Vector by inspecting a vector for zero, non-zero, positive, or negative. A mask can also be obtained from a scalar register; in RMSK and LMSK a mask is made with a specified number of right or left 1 bits, in a way similar to Form Mask in the 6600.

Add and Subtract.   Fixed-point Add and Subtract are provided in three forms: scalar with scalar, vector with vector, and scalar extended to vector with vector.

```
VTM                                    STM
ᴀ Cray 1 Set Mask From Vector          ᴀ Cray 1 Set Mask
→CASE 4|fld Rk                         vm←regj
C0:vm←word↑0=radixcompi vecj
   →ENDCASE
C1:vm←word↑0≠radixcompi vecj           RMSK
   →ENDCASE                            ᴀ Cray 1 Set Right Mask
C2:vm←word↑0≤radixcompi vecj           reg[fld Ri;]←(fld Count)≤ιword
   →ENDCASE
C3:vm←word↑0>radixcompi vecj
ENDCASE:
```

PROGRAM 14-123   Form vector mask in the Cray 1.

```
AD;addend;augend;sum                   SBV;subtrahend;minuend;difference
ᴀ Cray 1 Add                           ᴀ Cray 1 Subtract Vector
addend←radixcompi regk                 →OUT(fld Ri)∈(fld Rj),fld Rk
augend←radixcompi regj                 subtrahend←radixcompi veck
sum←augend+addend                      minuend←radixcompi vecj
reg[fld Ri;]←word radixcompr sum       difference←minuend-subtrahend
                                       veci word radixcompr difference


ADS;addend;augend;sum
ᴀ Cray 1 Add Scalar To Vector
→OUT(fld Ri)=fld Rk
addend←radixcompi regj
augend←radixcompi veck
sum←augend+addend
veci word radixcompr sum
```

PROGRAM 14-124   Fixed-point Add and Subtract in the Cray 1.

Compare.   Comparison must be performed by subtraction, after which a sign test can be performed with a Conditional Branch.

Floating-Point Arithmetic

Floating-point arithmetic operations are defined for normalized operands only.   Floating-point operation can use the fixed-point load and store op-

```
c ATSF Index To F Scalar               a DSF  F Divide Step
c SH   F Load Immediate Half           a DSVF F Divide Step Vector
c S1   F Load Immediate One            a DSSF F Divide Step Vector By Scalar
c S2   F Load Immediate Two            a RAF  F Approximate Reciprocal
c S4   F Load Immediate Four           a RAVF F Approximate Reciprocal Vector
c SM   F Load Maximum Integer
a ADF  F Add
a ADVF F Add Vector
a ADSF F Add Scalar To Vector
a SBF  F Subtract
a SBVF F Subtract Vector
a SBSF F Subtract Scalar From Vector
a MPF  F Multiply
a MPR  F Multiply R
a MPH  F Multiply Half R
a MPVF F Multiply Vector
a MPVR F Multiply Vector R
a MPVH F Multiply Vector Half R
a MPSF F Multiply Scalar W Vector
a MPSR F Multiply Scalar W Vector R
a MPSH F Multiply Scalar W Vector Half R
Legend: F = Floating-Point; R = Rounded; W = With.
```

TABLE 14-125   Floating-point instructions of the Cray 1.

erations, as well as the fixed-point sign and zero test.   There is neither single-instruction full-word fixed-point to floating-point conversion, nor any reverse conversion. All dyadic operations are scalar with scalar, vector with vector, and scalar extended to vector with vector.

Floating-point Load.   Index To Floating-Point Scalar gives fixed-point to floating-point conversion of an index value. The values 0.5, 1, 2, and 4 can be loaded as implied immediate values. Load Maximum Integer creates a constant used in programming to make a floating-point number from signed integers whose absolute value occupies less than 47 bits. Subtracting such an integer in fixed point from this constant, then subtracting the difference in floating point, yields a correct normalized result.

```
ATSF
A Cray 1 Index to Floating-Point Scalar
reg[fld Ri;]←flΔClr magni xk


S2
A Cray 1 Floating-Point Load Immediate Two
reg[fld Ri;]←flΔClr 2


SM
A Cray 1 Floating-Point Load Maximum Integer
reg[fld Ri;]←flΔClr 0.75×2*48
```

PROGRAM 14-126   Floating-point Load in the Cray 1.

Floating-point Add and Subtract.   Add and Subtract are straightforward; there is no rounding option. If an operand is an extremum, the result is also an extremum, unless it is negligible. So infinity minus infinity gives negligible instead of indefinite. The Stretch, which also has no indefinite, embodies the other alternative by making the result infinite.

```
ADF;ad;au;sum;exp              ADVF;ad;au;sum;exp
A Cray 1 Floating-Point Add   A Cray 1 Floating-Point Add Vector
ad←flΔCli regk                 →OUT(fld Ri)∈(fld Rj),fld Rk
au←flΔCli regj                 ad←vflΔCli veck
sum←au[0]+ad[0]                au←vflΔCli vecj
exp←au[1]⌈ad[1]                sum←au[;,0]+ad[;,0]
reg[fld Ri;]←flΔClr sum,exp    exp←au[;,1]⌈ad[;,1]
                              veci vflΔClr sum,exp
```

PROGRAM 14-127   Floating-point Add in the Cray 1.

Floating-point Multiply.   Scalar and vector multiplication are with truncated product, rounded product, and rounded half-precision product. The half-precision product has the low-order 24 coefficient bits 0. The result is infinite if there is an overflow, if an operand is infinite, or if the sum of the two operand exponents minus one is infinite. Infinity times zero, however, gives zero.

Fixed-point products.   When a positive fixed-point integer is shifted left some places and is multiplied with another such integer, then a correct 48-bit integer product can be obtained if the two integers jointly are represented with

48 or fewer bits and if the sum of the two shifts is exactly 48. Such a product is inherent in the representation, which allows non-zero coefficients with a maximum-negative exponent (represented as an all-zeros field) and gives an exponent underflow the maximum-negative exponent.

```
MPF;mr;md;product;exp
ᐃ Cray 1 Floating-Point Multiply
mr←flᐃC1i regk
md←flᐃC1i regj
product←md[0]×mr[0]
exp←md[1]⌈mr[1]
reg[fld Ri;]←flᐃC1r product,exp
```

```
MPVR;mr;md;product;roundmode;exp
ᐃ Cray 1 Floating-Point Multiply Vector Rounded
→OUT(fld Ri)∈(fld Rj),fld Rk
mr←vflᐃC1i veck
md←vflᐃC1i vecj
product←md[;,0]×mr[;,0]
exp←md[;,1]⌈mr[;,1]
veci vflᐃC1r product,exp WHERE roundmode←1
```

```
MPSH;mr;md;product;roundmode;exp
ᐃ Cray 1 Floating-Point Multiply Scalar With Vector Half Rounded
→OUT(fld Ri)=fld Rk
mr←flᐃC1i regj
md←vflᐃC1i veck
product←md[;,0]×mr[0]
exp←md[;,1]⌈mr[1]
veci vflᐃC1r product,exp WHERE roundmode←2
```

PROGRAM 14-128   Floating-point Multiply in the Cray 1.

Floating-point Divide.   Division is not available as such, but two powerful means of computing a reciprocal are supplied. Approximate Reciprocal gives a starting value for a Newton-Raphson process, and Divide Step gives the core of the iteration, subtracting the product of the operand and its approximate reciprocal from 2. Approximate Reciprocal assumes without testing that the high-order coefficient bit is 1; its result is accurate to 30 bits and has the low-order 18 bits set at 0. One Divide Step suffices to give a 48-bit correct reciprocal; there is no need for a loop. In fact, another Divide Step spoils the reciprocal. Hence the result of one Divide Step, when multiplied with the dividend, yields the quotient. These operations may take a scalar or a vector of floating-point numbers as their operands.

Other floating-point operations.   There is no instruction specifically for normalization; to normalize a number, the typical method is to add 0.

Floating-point Compare.   As in fixed-point operation, floating-point comparison is achieved by a subtraction followed by a sign or zero test. Since the floating-point representation matches fixed-point representation in its sign and zero representation, the same Conditional Branch can be applied to both representations.

```
DSF;mr;md;quotient;exp
ᴀ Cray 1 Floating-Point Divide Step
mr←flΔC1i regk
md←flΔC1i regj
quotient←2-md[0]×mr[0]
exp←md[1]⌈mr[1]
reg[fld Ri;]←flΔC1r quotient,exp
```

```
RAVF;od1;od;r1
ᴀ Cray 1 Floating-Point Approximate Reciprocal Vector
→OUT(fld Ri)=fld Rj
od1←vecj
od←vflΔC1i od1 WHERE od1[;Coef[1]]←1
r1←(÷od[;,0]),(2×extexp)-od[;,1]
veci(vl,word)↑ 0 ¯18 ↓vflΔC1r r1
```

PROGRAM 14-129   Floating-point division aids in the Cray 1.

14.4.6

Instruction Sequencing

Linear Sequence

Next instruction.   As a major break with the 6600 tradition, double-length instructions may straddle word boundaries. Instruction addresses are subject to address mapping. A violation of the absolute upper limit is signaled by the Ifetch indicator. The instruction length is determined from the first six operation-code bits.

```
cycleΔC1                          inst←ifetchΔC1;pair;length
ᴀ basic cycle of the Cray 1      ᴀ Cray1 instruction fetch
REPEAT:interruptΔC1               pair←,memory[origin+⌊iadr÷⍳2;]
   execute ifetchΔC1              length←ilengthΔC1(word×1|iadr)↓pair
→UNTIL stop                       inst←length↑(word×1|iadr)↓pair
                                  iadr←iadr+length÷word
                                  Ifetch report iadr>limit
length←ilengthΔC1 field;long
ᴀ Cray 1 instruction length
long←2=magni 2↑field
long←long∨1=magni 4↑field
long←long∨(magni 6↑field)∊ 3 8 16
length←word×0.25×1+long
```

PROGRAM 14-130   Basic cycle and instruction fetch of the Cray 1.

Sequencing instructions.   There are only four sequencing instructions: Unconditional Branch, Conditional Branch, Call, and Return.

Unconditional Branch.   Unconditional branching is via an address field or, in the case of Return, via an address contained in an index buffer register. The branch address applies to quarterword instruction parcels—another break with the crude 6600 approach.

Completion.   A wait can be programmed as a branch loop, after a timer has been set.

Decision

Conditional branching.   Conditional branching is on the sign or zero status of index register 0 or scalar register 0. These eight options are specified in the h-field.

```
BR                            yes←condition∆Cl c
∩ Cray 1 Branch               ∩ Cray 1 branch condition
  iadr←0.25×fld Branch          →CASE c
                                CO: ∩ zero index         C4: ∩ zero value
                                    yes←˜∨/x[0;]              yes←˜∨/reg[0;]
BRC                                 →ENDCASE                 →ENDCASE
∩ Cray 1 Branch Conditional     C1: ∩ non-zero index     C5: ∩ non-zero value
  →If condition∆Cl fld Rh           yes←∨/x[0;]              yes←∨/reg[0;]
  THEN:iadr←0.25×fld Branch         →ENDCASE                 →ENDCASE
  ENDIF:                        C2: ∩ positive index     C6: ∩ positive value
                                    yes←˜x[0;0]              yes←˜reg[0;0]
                                    →ENDCASE                 →ENDCASE
                                C3: ∩ negative index     C7: ∩ negative value
                                    yes←x[0;0]               yes←reg[0;0]
                                    →ENDCASE             ENDCASE:
```

PROGRAM 14-131   Branching in the Cray 1.

Iteration

There are no special instructions to aid iteration, except for fairly complete sign tests on the address and scalar registers. An increment test and branch can be accomplished in two 16-bit instructions.

Delegation

Call and Return.   Delegation is accomplished through the use of the Call, which stores the address of the following instruction in index buffer location 0, then changes the contents of the instruction address. The programmer must save the content of location 0 in case of nested calls. Return addresses a specified buffer register to retrieve the return address.

```
BRR                              BRB
∩ Cray 1 Call                    ∩ Cray 1 Return
  xbr[0;]←adrsize magnr 4×iadr     iadr←0.25×magni xbr[fld Count;]
  iadr←0.25×fld Branch
```

PROGRAM 14-132   Call and Return in the Cray 1.

14.4.7

Supervision

Concurrency

Any number of I/O channels may be in concurrent operation with one another and with the central processor.

Integrity

The processor operates either in the monitor or in the user mode, as indicated by the `Monitor` mask bit.

Supervisory instructions.   The supervisory instructions deal with state changing and with the clock.

```
a EX    Normal Exit          a TMTS Load Time
a ERR   Error Exit           b STTM Set Time
b ATXA  Set Exchange Address
```

PROGRAM 14-133   Supervisory instructions of the Cray 1.

Privileged operations.   The instructions Set Exchange Address and Load Time (as well as the I/O instructions) are limited to the monitor mode; in the user mode they are treated as No Operation.

Protection.   Memory is protected by relocation `origin` and `limit` boundary.

Control Switching

Interruption.   Various error conditions are detected and set indicators if the appropriate masks allow. Any indicator that is set causes an interruption. The interrupt action consists of an exchange sequence, as in the 6600.

```
interruptΔC1
 ⍝ Cray 1 interrupt action
 →If∨/ind
 THEN: ⍝ exchange context
    exchange exadr
 ENDIF:
```

PROGRAM 14-134   Interrupt action in the Cray 1.

Dispatching.   A change from monitor to user mode may be initiated by the Normal Exit instruction after setting the exchange address with Set Exchange Address. The `Exit` indicator is not set in the monitor mode.

Humble access.   Normal sequencing may be interrupted by the Normal Exit or Error Exit instructions. Error Exit is intended to signal a programming error, but the instructions as such differ only by the `Normalexit` and `Errorexit` indicators, respectively. Error Exit has operation code all-zeros, which helps in detecting unwanted excursions.

```
 ATXA                              EX
 ⍝ Cray 1 Set Exchange Address    ⍝ Cray 1 Normal Exit
 →OUT˜mask[Monitor]               Normalexit report˜mask[Monitor]
 exadr←16×magni ¯8↑¯4↓xj          exchange exadr
```

PROGRAM 14-135   Dispatch and humble access in the Cray 1.

State Preservation

Context switching.   For status preservation, each program (user or monitor) has an associated *Exchange Package*—a 16-word block of store; this package must always lie within the lower 4 K words of memory. The exchange package contains all the information necessary to begin a new job, restart an old one, or identify causes and types of interruption. Specifically, this information consists of the instruction address, scalar registers, indices, origin, limit, mask, vector length, indicators, and exchange address. Included, but not shown, are implementation bits, which indicate whether a memory error is correctable, plus the store address that produced the error and syndrome bits (which indicate whether 0, 1, 2, or more bits of a memory word are incorrect). For correctable errors, the syndrome bits also identify the bit in error. Finally, the type of read in progress (scalar, vector, instruction fetch, or I/O) at the time of an error is indicated.

```
exchange address;oldpack;newpack
ᴀ Cray 1 exchange of context
oldpack←(16,word)ρ0
oldpack[0;16+ιadrsize]←adrsize magnr iadr
oldpack[1 2 ;18+ι18]←18 magnr(origin,limit)÷16
oldpack[1;39]←1↑mask
oldpack[2;36+ι4]←1↓mask
oldpack[3;16+ι24]←(8 magnr exadr÷16),(7 magnr vl),ind
oldpack[ι8;40+ιadrsize]←x
oldpack[8+ι8;]←reg
newpack←memory[address+ι16;]
iadr←magni newpack[0;16+ιadrsize]
origin←16×magni newpack[1;18+ι18]
limit←16×magni newpack[2;18+ι18]
mask←newpack[1;39],newpack[2;36+ι4]
exadr←16×magni newpack[3;16+ι8]
vl←magni newpack[3;24+ι7]
ind←newpack[3;31+ι9]
x←newpack[ι8;40+ιadrsize]
reg←newpack[8+ι8;]
memory[address+ι16;]←oldpack
```

PROGRAM 14-136   Context switch in the Cray 1.

The vector and buffer registers are not part of the exchange package; these must be switched by program control.

An exchange sequence, then, simply involves using the current exchange address (`exadr`), to locate the exchange package of the program to be started (restarted) and swapping the relevant working and control storage with the package. The contents of the exchange address may be altered with Set Exchange Address in monitor mode. The supervisor must reset the indicators of the swapped-out package; otherwise, another interrupt and exchange occur as soon as the program is swapped back and resumed.

Tools of Control

Real-time clock.   A 64-bit counter is incremented by 1 at the end of each clock period (12.5 ns). Its contents may be set only in monitor mode, but it may be read by the user program. The main use of the clock is to time program execution.

An interrupt interval register and an interrupt countdown register, with five associated instructions, are provided as an option (not shown).

Initial program load.   A minicomputer (the *Maintenance Control Unit*) is attached for maintenance, control, and performance monitoring. The minicomputer also handles initial program load by means of an exchange sequence.

14.4.8

Input/Output

Devices

Store.   Mass storage on the system typically consists of a number of Cray Research disk controllers and disk-storage units (each with a capacity of up to 2424 MB per drive).

Source and sink.   There is no attached source and sink; one or more small computers mediate source–sink traffic.

Channel

In a sharp break with the 6600 tradition, the Cray 1 I/O system consists of 12 input and 12 output channels, each 16 (data) bits wide; each channel has direct access to main memory and transfers data at a rate of up to 160 Mb/second. Any number of channels may be in operation concurrently.

```
b CHS  Channel Select   a CHNR Channel Number
b CHL  Channel Limit    b CHCL Clear Channel Interrupt
```

TABLE 14-137   Input/output instructions of the Cray 1.

I/O control uses a 20-bit channel address register and a 20-bit channel limit register for each I/O channel.

The channels are divided into four channel groups, each of which contains either six input or six output channels. Channel groups are served equally; each group is scanned once every four clock periods to determine whether there are pending I/O requests. A priority system resolves the order of service if there are multiple requests within a channel group.

Peripheral Processor

In contrast to the Cray 1, the Cray 1/S and Cray 1/M allow I/O to be handled by separate processors, in a way comparable with that of the 6600 PPUs.

14.4.9

Implementation Notes

Fast, large memory.   Cray is quoted as saying "Virtual memory is for weenies." He commits a lot of the system budget to a large, fast main memory.

In the Cray 1 this memory is of up to 1 million 64-bit words, at 50 ns cycle time.

Fast clock.   The machine uses fast circuits and achieves, with a 12.5 ns clock, a peak performance of 80 MFlops for unchained operations and 160 MFlops for chained operations.

Fast scalar and vector processing units.   Twelve concurrent scalar and vector functional units are each heavily pipelined.

Chained operation.   In chained operations, two vector units can send their output directly to a third, which gives very short vector startup time and break-even vector length. In theory, a much higher performance is possible by chaining several functional units, but it is easy to see that such a program can hardly do useful work. Chaining conditions are completely detected, and chaining is automatically arranged, by the hardware.

Instruction buffers.   Four instruction buffers, each capable of holding 1024 bits of instructions, enable small loops to be processed entirely out of the buffer. The instruction-scheduling mechanism is similar to, but simpler than, that of the 6600.

Storage organization.   Physical memory is a linear vector of 64-bit words (with 8 parity bits per word) and has a size ranging from 0.25 M to 4 M words, depending on the production model.

There is a mismatch between the memory bandwidth provided and the maximum capability of the processing unit; only one sixth of the (theoretically) necessary bandwidth is provided [Hockney and Jesshope, 1981].

Checking.   In a significant departure from earlier Cray machines, the Cray 1 has extensive parity checking, with single-error correction and double-error detection.

14.4.10
Bibliography

S Series Mainframe Reference Manual HR 0029, 1984 (our defining reference).

The presentations in the literature, written at different periods and using different versions of the *Hardware Reference Manual*, vary slightly in details.

R.M. Russell [1978] (also reprinted in Siewiorek, Bell, and Newell [1982]) and Johnson [1978] are two short overviews written by Cray Research staff.

Baskett and Keller [1977] is an overview of the machine's organization plus a discussion of an evaluation study carried out at the Los Alamos Scientific Laboratory.

Thompson [1986], Ibbett and Topham [1989], and Elzen and MacKenzie [1994] each gives a discussion of the entire line of Crays.

August et al. [1989], Dungworth [1979], Hintz and Tate [1972], Hockney and Jesshope [1981], Karin and Smith [1987], Mangione-Smith [1994], Omondi [1994], R.M. Russell [1978], Watson [1972].

14.4.11
Exercises

14-27 Give the description of the index-arithmetic instructions TA, BTA, LDB, ADA, and SBA, assuming consistency with the indexing instructions shown in this section.

14-28 Give the description of the logical and shift instructions AND, ANDS, OR, ORV, ORS, DIF, DIFV, XOR, SL, SRS, DR, SLV, and DRV, assuming consistency with the logical instructions shown in this section.

14-29 Give the description of the fixed-point arithmetic instructions ICTS, ATS, ATSP, TTS, MKTS, LMSK, STT, STV, ADV, SB, and SBS, assuming consistency with the fixed-point arithmetic instructions shown in this section.

14-30 Give the description of the floating-point arithmetic instructions SH, S1, S4, ADSF, SBF, SBVF, SBSF, MPR, MPH, MPVF, MPVH, MPSF, MPSR, DSVF, DSSF, and RAF, assuming consistency with the floating-point instructions shown in this section.

14-31 How would you program a half-precision division?

14-32 If half of all divisions in naive FORTRAN programs are divisions by constants, and if a hardware divide would take twice as long as a hardware multiply, how long might a reciprocal operation take (relative to multiply time) to yield the same speed as if hardware divide were provided and used for constant divisions?

14-33 Identify four substantial ways in which the Cray 1 is architecturally similar to its ancestor, the 6600.

14-34 Identify four substantial ways in which the Cray 1 is different from the 6600 at the architectural level; for each, speculate about why Cray departed from his previous decision.

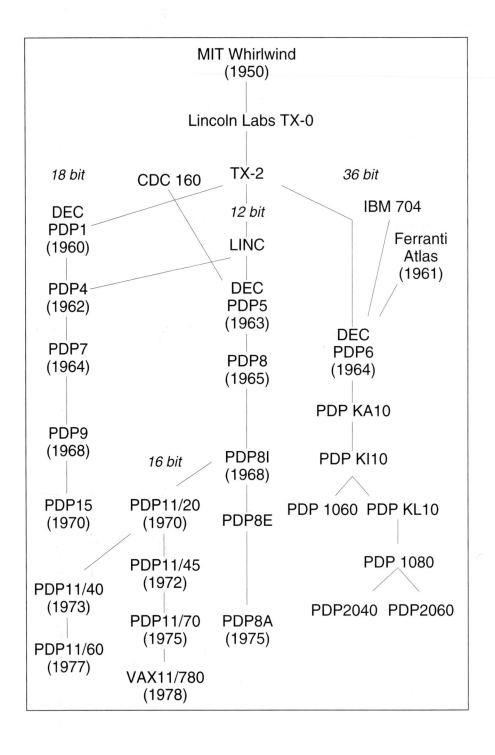

15

Bell House

The Minicomputer Revolution

Three times, technological and market forces have come together to create real computer revolutions:

- The mainframe revolution, starting with the pioneer computer era through the time-shared computer era (1940–1965)
- The minicomputer revolution (1965–1975)
- The microcomputer revolution, including the microprocessor and workstation (1975–1985)

In each case, technological advance has permitted an order-of-magnitude reduction in computer cost. Each time, this cost reduction has not only enlarged existing markets, but has also made whole new *kinds* of uses economical, and vast latent markets have leapt out to meet the advancing technology.

In each case, the suppliers of existing markets have been busy prospering where they were. They have overlooked the new markets until others proved them out and established themselves in them.

What is a minicomputer? Loosely speaking, a *minicomputer* is understood to be any small, cheap binary computer to which I/O devices are easily attached. *Small* and *cheap* are of course relative to the computers of the day. Surprisingly, cheap and easy attachability to electronic devices not made by the computer manufacturer is an essential, not an optional, characteristic.

More carefully and strictly, the term as originally used implied

- A stored-program computer, with all the generality that implies
- A computer optimized for control and sensing, as opposed to numerical computing, character manipulation, or file maintenance
- A simple architecture with a short data word size and short instructions
- A lean, fast parallel implementation of a simplified operation set, usually without floating point, and often even without multiply and divide
- A standard I/O bus with simple attachment of devices
- No concession to ease of programming, which was normally done in assembly language

What is not a minicomputer?   The flavor of the original definition is best conveyed by counterexamples. First, nothing big or costly is a minicomputer—the order-of-magnitude price difference is quintessential.

Second, none of the small, cheap computers that operate (serially) on characters or decimal digits are minicomputers—for example, the IBM 1401, the IBM System/360 Models 20 and 30, the IBM System/3, the IBM System/34: They are a different kind of machine.

Finally, and most subtly, the small cheap scientific computers are not considered to be minicomputers. Such machines—for example, the Librascope LGP30 (1957), the Bendix G20 (1961), the IBM 1620 (1960)—are distinguished primarily by purpose. They are designed for doing arithmetic computations, not for controlling attached instruments. These differences in purpose lead to differences in word length, operation set (a designer of small scientific machines would never even think of omitting multiplication), and I/O attachability.

Architecturally, it is instructive to compare a typical minicomputer to a first-generation scientific computer—the IBM 701 (1953), for instance. The 701 is like a minicomputer in its

- Short (18-bit) instruction
- Short number (18-bit) datatype
- Direct unbuffered I/O
- Small operation set, fairly primitive (33 operations, no floating point)

The 701 is unlike the DEC PDP8 (1965) in having

- A 36-bit number datatype
- Full 36-bit multiply, divide
- A rich I/O complement—drums, magnetic tapes, printer, and so forth

Why minicomputers?   The enabling technology advances were cheap and reliable transistor–diode and transistor–transistor logic, and modest-cost, reliable magnetic-core memories.

The untapped market was for laboratory machines that could control instruments and take and reduce data. Many such computers are integrated into instruments by the instrument manufacturers; many others are tied into laboratory setups by the experimenters themselves.

Architecturally, the minicomputers are descendants of the Whirlwind family of high-speed control computers built at MIT and Lincoln Laboratories in the fifties for air-defense control. Digital Equipment Corporation's designers came from the Whirlwind family laboratories, and the Whirlwind concepts were ideal for the sensing and control needs of laboratory computers.

Who?   Although the CDC 160 (1960) was essentially a 12-bit minicomputer architecture, Digital Equipment Corporation under Ken Olsen popularized the minicomputer [Bell, Mudge, and McNamara, 1978]. After developing a popular set of circuit modules and a few modestly successful pilot models, DEC hit the jackpot with the Programmed Data Processor PDP8 (1965). This computer evolved into a family of related architectures and many implementations.

In 1970, Digital introduced a totally new architectural family of 16-bit minicomputers, the PDP11 [Bell et al., 1970].

Other prominent early minicomputer manufacturers were Data General, whose Nova was widely used as an embedded mini; Hewlett-Packard, whose HP-1000 family evolved with more emphasis on scientific computing and less on control; Interdata (later a part of Perkin-Elmer); Texas Instruments; Varian (later sold to Univac); Scientific Data Systems (later sold to Xerox); and Honeywell.

Of these, only Honeywell had been among the major manufacturers of mainframe computers. Where were the others? Why did they not perceive and meet the new market opportunity? The best explanation is that their very success handicapped them. They justified new products with market forecasts, and market forecasters are adept at predicting growth in known markets only.

A second factor was the tendency to confuse the totally new market for laboratory computers with a recognized latent market for small scientific computers emphasizing floating-point calculations. The established mainframe manufacturers, when they did recognize the minicomputer revolution, tended to respond with small scientific machines.

Evolution. Just as the printer inveigled the vast potentials of computing into the office, so instrument control inveigled it into laboratories. Once scientists had their *own* computers, no matter how simple, they discovered many new uses. Many of these involved scientific computing, so the minicomputer rapidly evolved into a general purpose machine, with full-word numbers, floating-point arithmetic, larger address spaces, and so forth.

Digital, for example, evolved from the 16-bit architecture of the PDP11 family into a 32-bit architecture for the VAX11 family, and thus was born the super-minicomputer. As one would expect, the prefixes cancel, and a VAX looks much like a classical computer. Similar classical computers have come from Data General, Hewlett-Packard, Harris, and so forth.

The other direction of evolution has been downward. Minicomputer manufacturers have moved to make integrated-circuit versions of their machines, thus capitalizing on their large software bases.

15.1
DEC PDP8

15.1.1
Highlights

History

The PDP8 was the first mass-market minicomputer. It was a reimplementation of the PDP5 architecture. It is based upon the Princeton IAS (1952) architecture, originally without multiply and divide.

Architects.   Gordon Bell and Allen Kotok were the architects.

Dates.   The PDP8 was first introduced in 1965. The PDP5, its compatible predecessor, appeared in 1963.

Noteworthy

The PDP8 departs from the IAS design in its addressing, in the specification of the operations, and in the I/O system.

Indirect addressing.   The PDP8 addressing system is very interesting, although not especially clean. Indirect addressing is the principal technique for expanding the tiny 7-bit abbreviated direct address. The target addresses are full 12-bit words.

Auto-indexing.   A direct address may point to one of eight substitutive index registers, called *pointers*. These registers, embedded in main memory, not only give a level of indirection, but also are automatically preincremented by 1 upon each reference.

Memory segmentation.   A very simple paging scheme applies to all direct addresses, allowing them to be relative to the start of memory or the start of the 128-word block ("page") to which the instruction address currently points.

In later models the segmentation system was expanded to allow all addresses to be prefixed with a 3-bit segment prefix so as to enable (awkward) addressing to 2^{15} words.

Expanded operation code.   The three operation-code bits of the basic direct-address format are used for six operations. One code is used for an I/O operation and one operation code is expanded twice to yield another nine operand-less operations and one spare.

Microinstructions.   The expanded operation codes contain various microaction bits, which can be independently used to specify their actions in many combinations. Thus the number of operations proves to be much larger than might be expected from the three opcode bits of the basic format.

Easy device attachment.   It is logically, electrically, and physically easy to attach arbitrary I/O devices to the PDP8. This ease proved very important in vastly enlarging the application range of computers.

Exposed interface.   The interface control and sense lines are exposed to, and operated upon by, the programmer, who can easily write device drivers for new or strange devices.

Direct input/output.   The I/O instruction specifies control bits to the device.

Minimal channel.   The PDP8, although a minicomputer, incorporates a block-transfer channel that operates concurrently with the CPU and signals by interruption, thus providing direct memory access (DMA).

Peculiarities

Microinstructions.   The microinstructions are reminiscent of the STC ZEBRA's, but are less intricate, since they do not deal with the microactions of instruction fetch. Still, the idea is suitable only for handcoding. For a compiler, it is more efficient for the machine architect to encode the set of useful microcode combinations.

No Load.   Instead of providing a Load that clears the previous content of the accumulator, the PDP8 clears it on Store. Load is accomplished by adding into a clear accumulator.

No Subtract.   One loads the subtrahend, changes its sign, then adds the minuend.

Immediate Multiply and Divide.   The multiplier and divisor of the Extended Arithmetic Element are immediate values.

DEC tape.   The PDP8 uses an economical magnetic tape. It uses a clock track to provide block addresses on the tape, so one can replace a block (conventionally 128 words) by an updated block without copying the tape.

15.1.2

Machine Language

Language Level

Design philosophy.   The architecture reflects the implementation. The machine is designed to be coded in assembler language.

Unit System

The unit system is *six*; 6-bit characters are handled in I/O. A machine word of 12 bits is used throughout.

```
initiate8                        format8
A initiation of the DEC PDP8     A DEC PDP8 information units
format8                          A representation radix
configure8                       radix←2
space8                           A information units
name8                            word←12
instruction8                     double←24
data8                            pagesize←2*7
interface8                       A address capacity
                                 adrcap←radix*word


configure8
A configuration for the DEC PDP8
A memory capacity
memcap←radix*word
```

PROGRAM 15-1   Basic parameters of the DEC PDP8.

Configuration.   We give a complete description of an early version of the machine.   The architecture has a 4096 word memory and includes the Extended Arithmetic Element option, which provides, for example, for hardware multiplication and division.

Spaces

Memory name-space.   The name-space is 2^{12} words.

```
space8
A DEC PDP8 spaces
A memory
memory←?(memcap,word)ρradix
A working store
A - accumulator
acc←?wordρradix                  A - interrupt enable
A - carry                        enable←?2ρradix
carry←?radix                     A - stop condition
A - multiplier/quotient          stop←?radix
mq←?wordρradix                   A - manual control
A ˙ step counter                 key←?8ρradix
step←?5ρradix                    switch←?wordρradix
A control store                  A input/output
A - instruction address          A - interface signals
iadr←?adrcap                     interface←?80ρradix
```

PROGRAM 15-2   Spaces of the DEC PDP8.

Working store.   The working store is a 12-bit accumulator with a 1-bit carry (called Link in the DEC literature and the mnemonics). A 12-bit MQ and a 5-bit step counter are added in the Extended Arithmetic Element option.

Control store.   There are an instruction address, a 2-bit interrupt-enable mask, a stop condition, 12 switches, and eight console keys.

Input/output signals.   Some of the 80 signals of the interface between processor and external units are accessible by programming.

Embedding.   Eight (substitutive autoincremented) indexes are embedded in memory; the accumulator and MQ are not. The interrupt routine address and the return address use memory locations 1 and 0, respectively.

```
 name8
A DEC PDP8 space names
A memory names
A - return from interrupt
 Return←0                        A key names
A - interrupt routine           A - manual stop
 Intadr←1                        Stop←5
A - autoincrement indices       A - single cycle
 Index←8+ι8                      Single←7
```

PROGRAM 15-3   Embedding in the DEC PDP8.

Two of the keys of manual control are designated Stop and Single Cycle. We do not describe the other keys.

Programming model.   The model is surprisingly similar to that of the IAS machine, except that the word length is so short.

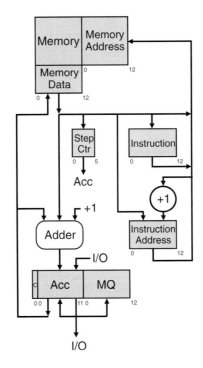

FIGURE 15-4   Programming model for the DEC PDP8.

Operand Specification

Number of addresses.   Instructions have at most one explicit address.

Address phrase.   The 7-bit address is augmented with a page-table bit and an indirect-address bit.

Operation Specification

Mnemonics.   Our mnemonics are mainly derived from the defining reference. The three operations that contain microactions are each identified by one mnemonic. The mnemonics of their micro actions are shown with these operations in Programs 15-18, 15-19, and 15-24.

```
a→AND      b→IOT       SHL
   TAD     c→OP1       ASR
   ISZ     d→OP2       LSR
   DCA     e→EAE      f→ION
   JMS                f→IOF
   JMP
  →b          MUL
  →cde        DIV
              NMI
```

PROGRAM 15-5   Operation-code list of the DEC PDP8.

The operation-code list contains 18 instructions, using six syntactic pattern groups.

Types of control.   There is a minimum of status; there are no indicators or modes.

Instruction list.   The instruction classes of the PDP8 are logic, fixed-point arithmetic, sequencing, supervision, and I/O.

```
  A logic and shift            A sequencing
a AND  And                   a JMP  Branch
e LSR  Shift Logical Right    d OP2  Skip And Stop Actions
e SHL  Shift Arithmetic Left  a ISZ  Increment And Skip On Zero
e ASR  Shift Arithmetic Right a JMS  Call
e NMI  Normalize                A supervision
  A fixed-point arithmetic    f IOF  Disable Interrupt
e EAE  Load Actions           f ION  Enable Interrupt
a DCA  Store And Clear          A input/output
c OP1  Complement Actions     b IOT  Input/Output Transfer
a TAD  Add
e MUL  Multiply
e DIV  Divide
```

TABLE 15-6   Instruction list of the DEC PDP8.

Instruction Structure

Machine-language syntax.   The first and main syntactic pattern reflects the single-address IAS design. Four patterns are used to specify microactions.

```
  syntax8
a Opcode,Indirect,Page,Address
b 1 1 0 ,Device,Iop4,Iop2,Iop1
c 1 1 1 0 ,Cla,Cll,Cma,Cml,Rot,Iac
d 1 1 1 1 ,Cla,Skip,Osr,Hlt,0
e 1 1 1 1 ,Cla,Mqa,Sca,Lmq,Ope,1
f 1 1 0 0 0 0 0 0 0 0 0 1
f 1 1 0 0 0 0 0 0 0 0 1 0
```

PROGRAM 15-7   Instruction syntax of the DEC PDP8.

Instruction format. Four formats correspond to the seven syntactic patterns. The formats contain many 1-bit fields that specify microactions. The three Iop bits specify I/O modes whose meaning depends upon the device that is addressed. Format e is frequently extended with an immediate value that specifies a shift amount or serves as operand.

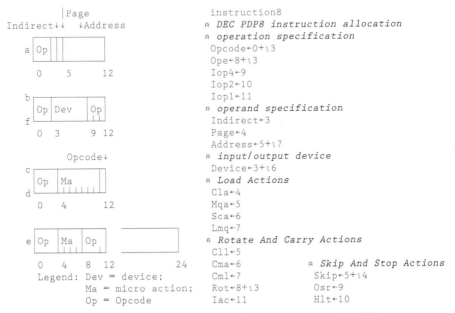

```
                                    instruction8
        |Page                       ↑ DEC PDP8 instruction allocation
Indirect↓↓  ↓Address                ↑ operation specification
                                    Opcode←0+ι3
  a │Op│ │        │                 Ope←8+ι3
                                    Iop4←9
    0     5     12                  Iop2←10
                                    Iop1←11
  b ┌──┬───┬────┐                   ↑ operand specification
    │Op│Dev│ Op │                   Indirect←3
  f └──┴───┴────┘                   Page←4
    0   3     9  12                 Address←5+ι7
                                    ↑ input/output device
          Opcode↓                   Device←3+ι6
  c ┌──┬──────────┐                 ↑ Load Actions
    │Op│Ma        │                 Cla←4
  d └──┴──────────┘                 Mqa←5
    0   4        12                 Sca←6
                                    Lmq←7
  e ┌──┬───┬──┬────────────┐        ↑ Rotate And Carry Actions
    │Op│Ma │Op│            │        Cll←5
    0   4   8  12        24         Cma←6          ↑ Skip And Stop Actions
    Legend: Dev = device;          Cml←7          Skip←5+ι4
            Ma = micro action;     Rot←8+ι3       Osr←9
            Op = Opcode            Iac←11         Hlt←10
```

PROGRAM 15-8   Instruction allocation in the DEC PDP8.

15.1.3

Addressing

The 7 bits of the address field in an instruction are expanded to the 12 address bits that memory requires by address mapping and indirection. There is no additive index modification—only substitutive indexing.

Direct addressing. Reading and writing is always performed one word at a time.

```
data←read8 address              address write8 data
↑ DEC PDP8 read from memory    ↑ DEC PDP8 write into memory
data←memory[address;]           memory[address;]←data
```

PROGRAM 15-9   Memory read and write in the DEC PDP8.

Segmentation

Address mapping Two forms of segmentation are provided to compensate (1) for the small 7-bit direct address, and (2) for the small 4096 memory name-space. In either case, all pages are resident in main memory all the time. The first form of mapping, called *paging*, is shown in Program 15-10. The `Page` bit in the direct address specifies whether the `Address` field is to be prefixed either by a 5-bit zero-page address or by the 5-bit page address of the current instruction address.

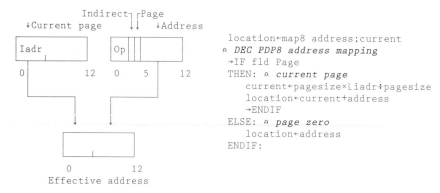

```
                                    location←map8 address;current
                                    ∩ DEC PDP8 address mapping
                                    →IF fld Page
                                    THEN: ∩ current page
                                       current←pagesize×⌊iadr÷pagesize
                                       location←current+address
                                       →ENDIF
                                    ELSE: ∩ page zero
                                       location←address
                                    ENDIF:
```

PROGRAM 15-10   Address mapping in the DEC PDP8.

As an option (not illustrated), a second form of segmentation expands the actual memory capacity up to 2^{15} words. In the extended range, an (embedded) 3-bit register, the Program Field register, furnishes a segment prefix on all instruction effective addresses. Another 3-bit register, the Data Field register, furnishes the segment prefix for all data addresses. This segmentation mapping is applied to the target 12-bit effective addresses generated by indirect addressing.

```
            address←adr8
          ∩ DEC PDP8 addressing
          ∩ paging
            address←map8 fld Address
          ∩ indirection
          →If fld Indirect
            THEN:address←indirect8 address
            ENDIF:
```

PROGRAM 15-11   Addressing in the DEC PDP8.

Address Level

Indirect addressing. Indirect addresses are themselves modified by page-bit mapping. Thus two sets of 128 memory words may be used for indirection. The target of the indirect address is a 12-bit address, which is not modified.

List addressing. Indirect addressing in page zero may target one of the eight index registers at memory locations 8 through 15. These index registers are preincremented before use, and hence give a means of list addressing. There is no corresponding decrement; hence there is no stack addressing.

Immediate addressing. In the Extended Arithmetic Element operation an extra instruction word may be fetched that serves as an immediate operand in multiplication or division. Only thus can a multiplier or divisor be specified.

```
address←indirect8 direct
ᴀ DEC PDP8 indirect address
→IF direct∈Index
THEN: ᴀ preincrement
   address←1+magni memory[direct;]
   memory[direct;]←word magnr address
   →ENDIF
ELSE: ᴀ no increment
   address←magni memory[direct;]
ENDIF:
```

PROGRAM 15-12   Indirect addressing in the DEC PDP8.

15.1.4
Data

Character Strings

Character set and size.   The ASCII character set is used on the I/O devices. No CPU operations depend on the character code, and no CPU provision is made for characters.

Logical

Logical formats.   There is a 12-bit logical-vector datatype. In a logical Or the five bits of the Step Counter correspond to the five low-order bits of the accumulator.

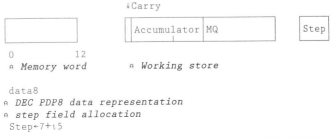

```
data8
ᴀ DEC PDP8 data representation
ᴀ step field allocation
Step←7+ι5
```

PROGRAM 15-13   Data specification in the DEC PDP8.

Fixed-Point Numbers

Notation and allocation.   Fixed-point numbers are 2's-complement 12-bit integers.

15.1.5
Operations

A variety of implied-operand operations are invoked with an operation code and with modifiers, called *microactions* (Program 15-8). These microactions work independently, so that one instruction can specify several operations.

Data Handling

Data movement. All data movement occurs by clears, adds, and stores.

Logic

Connectives. The AND of the accumulator and a memory location is a regular instruction. The OR between the accumulator and the MQ or the Step Counter can be obtained as a microaction (Program 15-18).

```
            AND
          ∩ DEC PDP8 And
            acc←acc∧read8 adr8
```

PROGRAM 15-14   And in the DEC PDP8.

Shift. There is a complete set of shifts of the accumulator and MQ together—arithmetic and logical, left and right—with an immediately specified shift amount. Prior to the shift, the Extended Arithmetic Element microactions can be taken. The shift amount is found by adding 1 to the value of the next instruction word.

```
 SHL                                       ASR;shift
∩ DEC PDP8 Shift Arithmetic Left          ∩ DEC PDP8 Shift Arithmetic Right
∩ micro actions                           ∩ micro actions
 EAE                                        EAE
∩ shift                                    ∩ shift
 shift←1+magni ifetch8                      shift←1+magni ifetch8
 acc←word↑shift↓acc,mq                      mq←word↑word↓(shiftρacc[0]),acc,mq
 mq←word↑shift↓mq                           acc←word↑(shiftρacc[0]),acc
```

PROGRAM 15-15   Arithmetic Shift in the DEC PDP8.

Rotate. A rotate of the accumulator and the carry can be performed as a micro action; the movement is 1 or 2 bits to the left or to the right (Program 15-21).

```
            LSR;shift
          ∩ DEC PDP8 Shift Logical Right
          ∩ micro actions
            EAE
          ∩ shift
            shift←1+magni ifetch8
            mq←(-word)↑(-shift)↓acc,mq
            acc←(-word)↑(-shift)↓acc
```

PROGRAM 15-16   Logical Shift in the DEC PDP8.

Normalize. The contents of the accumulator and MQ are shifted left until the leftmost two bits are different; hence the number is normalized. The corresponding shift amount is recorded in the step counter. The carry is used in the implementation of this instruction and is unpredictable after the operation. The Extended Arithmetic Element microactions may precede the operation.

```
NMI;shift
∩ DEC PDP8 Normalize
∩ micro actions
  EAE
∩ normalization
  shift←¯1+(acc,mq)ι¯acc[0]
  acc←word↑shift↓acc,mq
  mq←word↑shift↓mq
  step←(ρstep) magnr shift
  carry←?radix
```

PROGRAM 15-17   Normalize in the the DEC PDP8.

Fixed-Point Arithmetic

Load and Store.   The Extended Arithmetic Element group of microactions performs four independent Load actions. This group can be invoked as the regular instruction EAE, or as part of the Normalize, Shift, Multiply, and Divide instructions.

The accumulator is cleared by the microaction CLA, or as part of the microaction LMQ that moves the accumulator content to the MQ. Loading then can be done by clearing the accumulator and ORing the MQ or the step counter, all as part of the Extended Arithmetic Element microactions. Clear Accumulator is also part of the Complement microactions and of the Skip And Stop microactions.

```
EAE                              MQA
∩ DEC PDP8 Load Actions          ∩ DEC PDP8 Or MQ
∩ Clear Accumulator              →If fld Mqa
  CLA                            THEN:acc←acc∨mq
∩ Or MQ                          ENDIF:
  MQA
∩ Or Step Counter
  SCA                            SCA
∩ Accumulator To MQ              ∩ DEC PDP8 Or Step Counter
  LMQ                            →If fld Sca
                                 THEN:acc[Step]←acc[Step]∨step
                                 ENDIF:

  CLA
∩ DEC PDP8 Clear Accumulator
  →If fld Cla                    LMQ
  THEN:acc[]←0                   ∩ DEC PDP8 Accumulator To MQ
  ENDIF:                         →If fld Lmq
                                 THEN:mq←acc
                                      acc[]←0
                                 ENDIF:

  DCA
∩ DEC PDP8 Store And Clear
  adr8 write8 acc
  acc[]←0
```

PROGRAM 15-18   Load and Store in the DEC PDP8.

Loading from memory is accomplished by following Clear Accumulator with an Add instruction. Store And Clear (DCA) is a regular instruction that clears the accumulator after storing its contents.

Complement.   The accumulator can be inverted as a microaction of the Complement action group. This inversion gives the 1's complement. Subsequently, the accumulator may be incremented in this same group, such that the 2's-complement is obtained as a combination of these two actions.

```
OP1                                  CML
Ɑ DEC PDP8 Complement Actions        Ɑ DEC PDP8 Complement Carry
Ɑ Clear Accumulator                  →If fld Cml
  CLA                                THEN:carry←˜carry
Ɑ Clear Carry                        ENDIF:
  CLL
Ɑ Complement Accumulator
  CMA                                ROT;shift;rl
Ɑ Complement Carry                   Ɑ DEC PDP8 Rotate Accumulator
  CML                                →If 2≤fld Rot
Ɑ Rotate Accumulator                 THEN:shift←×/inst[Rot]/ ˜1 1 2
  ROT                                     rl←shiftΦcarry,acc
Ɑ Increment Accumulator                  acc←1↓rl
  IAC                                     carry←1↑rl
                                     ENDIF:


  CLL
Ɑ DEC PDP8 Clear Carry               IAC
  →If fld Cll                        Ɑ DEC PDP8 Increment Accumulator
  THEN:carry←0                       →If fld Iac
  ENDIF:                             THEN:acc←word magnr 1+magni acc
                                     ENDIF:


  CMA
Ɑ DEC PDP8 Complement Accumulator
  →If fld Cma
  THEN:acc←˜acc
  ENDIF:
```

PROGRAM 15-19   Complement Actions in the DEC PDP8.

Other actions of the Complement group are complementing the carry, clearing the accumulator, and clearing the carry. The most complicated action of the complement group is the Rotate. The three bits of the rotate field specify in order: right, left, 2/1 bit. In combination with complementing, this action can give ±0.25, ±0.5, ±2 and ±4 times the accumulator content.

Add and Subtract.   A 2's complement Add is provided as an independent instruction; there is no Subtract. Subtraction is accomplished by first complementing the accumulator as the subtrahend, then adding the minuend from memory to it. The carry out of an addition is EXCLUSIVE-ORed with the current carry value, which is convenient for multiple-precision operation. To get the normal carry, the current carry must be reset prior to the instruction.

```
TAD;addend;augend;sum
Ɑ DEC PDP8 Add
addend←radixcompi read8 adr8
augend←radixcompi acc
sum←augend+addend
acc←word radixcompr sum
carry←carry≠word carryfrom augend,addend
```

PROGRAM 15-20   Add in the DEC PDP8.

Multiply and Divide.   The multiplier is an immediate 12-bit value. The product is developed in the accumulator and MQ. The carry is set to 0.

Similarly, the divisor is an immediate value, and the dividend is located in the accumulator and MQ. The remainder is placed in the accumulator; the quotient, in the MQ; the carry is used as a quotient overflow indicator, which includes zero-divisor.

```
MUL;multiplier;multiplicand;product;pd
⋀ DEC PDP8 Multiply
⋀ micro actions
  EAE
⋀ multiplication
  multiplier←radixcompi ifetch8
  multiplicand←radixcompi mq
  product←multiplicand×multiplier
  pd←double radixcompr product
  acc←word↑pd
  mq←word↓pd
  carry←0


DIV;divisor;dividend;quotient;remainder
⋀ DEC PDP8 Divide
⋀ micro actions
  EAE
⋀ division
  divisor←radixcompi ifetch8
  dividend←radixcompi acc,mq
  quotient←truncate dividend÷divisor+divisor=0
  remainder←dividend-quotient×divisor
  acc←word radixcompr remainder
  mq←word radixcompr quotient
  carry←xmax∨xmin∨divisor=0
```

PROGRAM 15-21   Multiply and Divide in the DEC PDP8.

Compare.   Comparison must be accomplished by subtraction—that is, by complementation and addition.

15.1.6

Instruction Sequencing

Linear Sequence

Next instruction.   The next instruction is specified by the instruction address. The basic cycle contains an interrupt facility, but otherwise is straightforward.

```
cycle8                              inst←ifetch8
⋀ basic cycle of the DEC PDP8      ⋀ DEC PDP8 instruction fetch
  REPEAT:interrupt8                   inst←memory[iadr;]
    execute ifetch8                   iadr←adrcap|iadr+1
  →UNTIL stop8


true←stop8
⋀ DEC PDP8 stop condition
  true←key[Stop]∨key[Single]∨stop
```

PROGRAM 15-22   Basic cycle and instruction fetch of the DEC PDP8.

Unconditional branch.   One of the six precious direct-address operation codes is used for an unconditional branch. This branch is the only means, apart from interruption, of changing the page to which the instruction address and its associated data belong.

```
         JMP
       ⋒ DEC PDP8 Branch
         iadr←adr8
```

PROGRAM 15-23   Unconditional Branch in the DEC PDP8.

Completion.   Stop is a microaction that can be combined with a conditional skip, clearing the accumulator, and ORing the accumulator with a set of switches. Manual stopping is achieved with the Stop and Single Cycle keys.

```
    OP2                                 OSR
  ⋒ DEC PDP8 Skip And Stop Actions    ⋒ DEC PDP8 Or Switch
  ⋒ Conditional Skip                    →If fld Osr
    SKIP                                THEN:acc←acc∨switch
  ⋒ Clear Accumulator                   ENDIF:
    CLA
  ⋒ Or Switch
    OSR                                 HLT
  ⋒ Stop                              ⋒ DEC PDP8 Stop
    HLT                                 stop←fld Hlt


    SKIP
  ⋒ DEC PDP8 Conditional Skip
  ⋒ select from sign, zero, carry
    select←∨/inst[Skip[ι3]]∧acc[0],(0=magni acc),carry
  ⋒ skip on true or false
    iadr←iadr+inst[Skip[3]]≠select
```

PROGRAM 15-24   Skip and Stop actions in the DEC PDP8.

Decision

Conditional branching.   The conditional skip microaction causes the machine to skip the next instruction if any of up to three specified conditions (accumulator negative, accumulator zero, carry) is satisfied. This condition may also be inverted.

Iteration

Incrementation and termination.   Increment and Skip On Zero can be used to close a loop based upon a count in memory.

```
       ISZ;dest;count
     ⋒ DEC PDP8 Increment And Skip On Zero
       dest←adr8
       count←1+radixcompi read8 dest
       dest write8 word radixcompr count
       iadr←iadr+count=0
```

PROGRAM 15-25   Increment and Skip in the DEC PDP8.

Delegation

Call and return. Call saves the updated instruction address in the addressed location and then branches to the next location after that. No special provision is made for return, except that indirect addressing can point to the saved address.

```
JMS;dest
ค DEC PDP8 Call
dest←adr8
dest write8 word magnr iadr
iadr←dest+1
```

PROGRAM 15-26   Call in the DEC PDP8.

15.1.7

Supervision

Control Switching

Interruption. The only source of interruption is an external request coming over the interface; no internal interrupt requests are generated. When interruption is enabled, and an external interruption request occurs, the updated instruction address is stored in the return location, memory location 0, and a branch occurs to the interrupt routine, starting at location 1. Further interruption is disabled.

```
interrupt8
ค DEC PDP8 interrupt action
→If interface[Int]∧enable[0]
THEN:interface[Int]←0
     enable[]←0
     Return write8 word magnr iadr
     iadr←Intadr
ENDIF:enable[0]←enable[1]
```

PROGRAM 15-27   Interruption action in the DEC PDP8.

Interruption can be enabled and disabled by programming. IOF disables immediately. ION enables, however, with a delay of one instruction. This intervening instruction may be used for a Branch that returns to the interrupted routine. The 2-bit enable vector describes the one-instruction lag.

```
IOF                            ION
ค DEC PDP8 Disable Interrupt   ค DEC PDP8 Enable Interrupt
enable[]←0                     enable[1]←1
```

PROGRAM 15-28   Interruption enable in the DEC PDP8.

Tools of Control

Initial program load. A wired-in load sequence reads paper tape.

15.1.8

Input/Output

Devices

Store.   The DEC tapes provide block-addressed storage that behaves logically like a disk (but is much slower).

Source and sink.   The source/sink configuration is very complete, with paper tape, magnetic tape, punched cards, printer, communications, and display.

Interface

The I/O interface has a word-wide memory address and word-wide bidirectional data transfer; the device address is 6 bits wide.

```
interface8
⍝ DEC PDP8 interface allocation
Break←0
Cycle←1                          Outputdata←32+ι12
Dataadr←2+ι12                    Datain←44+ι12
Incr←14                          Ioskip←56
Direction←15                     Clear←57
Inputdata←16+ι12                 Int←58
Noincr←28                        Iomod←59+ι3
Breakrequest←29                  Dataout←62+ι12
Control←30+ι2                    Deviceadr←74+ι6
```

PROGRAM 15-29   Interface signals in the DEC PDP8.

Direct Input/Output

The I/O transfer instruction acts directly upon the interface. The meaning of `Iop` depends upon the device. Device zero is the processor, where `Iop` 1 gives `ION`, and `Iop` 2 gives `IOF`.

Read and Write.   Up to 12 bits can be copied at a time to or from an I/O device from or to the accumulator.

Sense and Control.   Sensing and control of devices is via the interface signals `Iomod`.

```
IOT
⍝ DEC PDP8 Input/Output Transfer
interface[Dataout]←acc
interface[Deviceadr]←inst[Device]
interface[Iomod]←inst[Iop4,Iop2,Iop1]
iadr←iadr+interface[Ioskip]
acc←(acc∧˜interface[Clear])∨interface[Datain]
```

PROGRAM 15-30   Input/output transfer in the DEC PDP8.

Channel

A direct memory-access channel provides concurrent block-transfers.

15.1.9

Implementation Notes

Many implementations and realizations have been built.

Performance. With a 1.5 μs cycle, addition requires 3 μs, or 4.5 μs with indirect address. The I/O rate is 8 Mb per second (based on DMA).

Device attachment to the PDP8s is unusually simple, and Digital sells circuit components with which one can readily build controllers for all kinds of devices.

15.1.10

Bibliography

Digital Equipment Corporation, 1965: *PDP-8, A High Speed Digital Computer*. Form 5369 100-6/65. Maynard, MA (our defining reference).

Bell and Newell [1971, Chapter 5] describes the PDP8. So does Siewiorek, Bell, and Newell [1982, Chapter 8]. Each of these books gives a detailed multilayer description of the PDP8; the latter is derived from, but improves on, the earlier.

15.1.11

Exercises

15-1 Multiply the accumulator content with 4, 2, −1, −2, and −4, using the Complement Actions.

15-2 Use the Skip And Halt Actions to skip the next instruction if the accumulator content is smaller than zero, smaller than or equal to zero, or greater than zero.

15-3 Devise a meaningful set of Extended Arithmetic Element actions in which at least CLA and LMQ are used.

15-4 Write a loop of not more than six instructions to perform extended-precision addition.

15-5 Give the instruction sequence that performs a subtraction with the minuend in the accumulator and the subtrahend in memory.

15.2
DEC PDP11

15.2.1
Highlights
History

Architects.   The chief architect was Gordon Bell. The PDP11 is one of the best documented computer designs, in both the rationale for its architecture and the evolution of its implementations.

Dates.   The PDP11 was announced in 1970 [Bell et al., 1970], and the first implementation, the PDP11/20, was shipped that year. We describe the DEC PDP11/45 (1973) with its floating-point feature, but without the memory-management feature.

Family tree.   The PDP11 had 10 implementations in 10 years—probably a record. Mudge observes that a new implementation seems to have been justified whenever realization technology advanced by a factor of 2 [Bell, Mudge, and McNamara, 1978, Chapter 13]. Models 20, 45, and 70 represent upward-compatible architectures.

Noteworthy

Addressing modes.   The most interesting aspect of the PDP11 is the addressing. The PDP11 introduced the concept of addressing modes—rich and general.

Embedding in registers.   The stack pointer and the instruction address are in the general register set. The embedded instruction address can be used ingeniously to give immediate and relative addressing, but only half the addressing modes are meaningful.

Extensible instructions.   Instruction formats may be one, two, or three words long, accommodating zero, one, and two full-length addresses. This arrangement is rather like that of the IBM 1401 (1960).

Extensive status.   The PDP11 has extensive status—a marked difference from the PDP8 (1965).

Stack facilities.   The implied systems stack uses a general register as pointer location; programmed stacks that use a memory location for the pointer are facilitated by the addressing modes and by increment and decrement instructions.

Powerful conversion.   The instruction set includes conversion from floating point to fixed point, from biased exponent notation to 2's complement and reverse, separation of integer and fractional parts of a floating-point number (which aids conversion to decimal), and various size conversions.

Embedded device registers.   I/O device registers are mapped onto main storage name-space.

UNIBUS. A standard interface for I/O devices is used.

Peculiarities

Cramped design.   The basic design did not permit easy extension of function, such as the floating-point option, so inconsistencies arose as the design evolved: The opcode space is crowded; the address modes and the PSW are not readily usable for floating point; fixed-point size is determined by an instruction bit, but floating-point size by a mode bit; Add Carry is supplied instead of Add With Carry; Exclusive Or is defined quite differently from And; there are only 2 bits for addressing the six floating-point registers; and the offsets of relative branches are not uniform in size.

Highly encoded opcodes.   The operations are highly encoded, with up to three levels of extension. The codes are densely packed, leaving little room for growth.

Embedded status.   The basic status word is embedded in main memory. This practice, however, is not followed for the (later designed) floating-point status.

The "backwards byte." If memory is considered a vector of numbered bytes, each word's less-significant byte occurs before its more significant byte. This impropriety still haunts the PDP11's VAX descendants.

Borrow.   In extended precision, the carry out of an addition is recorded in the status word. In subtraction, however, a borrow is recorded as the inverse of the carry produced in the effective addition. This inconsistency is a source of confusion.

Descendants

The DEC VAX11 (1978) is an incompatible extension.

15.2.2
Machine Language

Language Level

Design philosophy.   The machine is designed to be compiler coded. Understandability was given as a design goal in [Bell et al., 1970, Chapter 9], but evaluation in [Bell, Mudge, and McNamara, 1978, Chapter 16], assesses understandability as having "received little attention. The PDP11 was initially a hard machine to understand."

The design is a sophisticated one, based on extensive experience with earlier minicomputers and extensive measurements. Some nine weaknesses in earlier minicomputers were identified and specifically (and intelligently) addressed in the PDP11 design.

Unit System

The unit system is *four* with, as basic information units, the 8-bit byte and the 16-bit word.

```
initiate11                       format11
∩ initiation of the DEC PDP11    ∩ DEC PDP11 information units
format11                         ∩ representation radix
configure11                      radix←2
space11                          ∩ information units
name11                           byte←8
control11                        word←16
                                 long←32
                                 double←64
configure11                      ∩ address capacity
∩ configuration for the DEC PDP11   adrcap←radix*word
∩ memory capacity
memcap←radix*word
```

PROGRAM 15-31   Basic parameters of the DEC PDP11.

Configuration.   We describe the machine with 2^{16} bytes of memory.

Spaces

Memory name-space.   Memory is a vector of bytes, grouped into words. Words consist of 2 bytes and must begin on an even address. Larger entities, such as floating-point words, are considered multiple words and aligned as such.

```
space11                            name11
∩ DEC PDP11 spaces                 ∩ DEC PDP11 space names
∩ memory                           ∩ memory names
memory←?(memcap,byte)ρradix        ∩ - program status
∩ working store                    Psw←memcap-2
∩ - general registers              ∩ - stack limit
reg←?(16,word)ρradix               Slw←memcap-4
∩ - floating-point registers       ∩ - programmed interrupt
flreg←?(6,double)ρradix            Piw←memcap-6
∩ control store                    ∩ - interrupt vector
∩ - indicators                     Intvec←4×ι43
ind←?43ρradix                      ∩ register names
∩ - floating-point status          ∩ - stack pointer
flstatus←?wordρradix               Sp←6
∩ - floating-point exception       ∩ - instruction address
fle←?4ρradix                       Pc←7
∩ - stop and wait                  ∩ - input/output devices
stop←?radix                        name11io
wait←?radix
```

PROGRAM 15-32   Spaces and embedding of the DEC PDP11.

Working store.   Eight register addresses are mapped upon a set of sixteen 16-bit general registers depending upon the system state, as discussed later with Programs 15-42 and 15-43. For the floating-point option, the working store is extended with six 64-bit registers.

Control store.   The control store contains 43 indicators, a stop bit, and a wait bit. The floating-point extension includes 16 status bits and 4 exception code bits. A program status word (PSW) is embedded as the last word of installed memory.

Memory embedding.   Besides the PSW, a stack limit address, a programmed-interrupt word, and the peripheral device registers are mapped onto the high 4 K bytes of memory name-space. The low-order 256 bytes of memory are reserved for trap and interrupt vectors by `limit11` (Program 15-42).

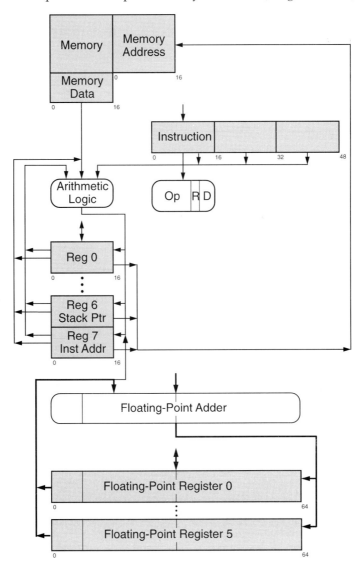

FIGURE 15-33   Programming model for the DEC PDP11.

Register embedding.   The register addresses include an operation-implied stack pointer (Sp), which can contain only even binary numbers (word addresses), and an operation-implied instruction-address register (Pc), similarly constrained.

Programming model.   The floating-point machine, unlike that of the IBM System/360 (1965), has paths carrying data between the two sets of registers. The architecture is unmistakably designed for 16-bit implementations. The to-memory addition and logical operations imply an architecturally invisible second memory data register. Conversely, the long Instruction Register in the architecture can, because of the careful ordering of fetch and use of source and destination operands, be implemented with a one-word register. The programming model does not represent the different order of bytes in memory and registers.

Operand Specification

Number of addresses.   Instructions have zero addresses, one address, or two addresses.

Address phrase.   Each address phrase has 6 bits. It specifies one of eight addressing modes and one of eight directly addressed registers. If a 16-bit address field is needed, the instruction is extended. So instructions may be 1, 2, or 3 words long.

Operation Specification

Mnemonics.   We use DEC's mnemonics. Occasionally we treat a group of instructions as one instruction with modifiers (such as the byte/word modifier). We do not follow DEC in using mnemonics to distinguish floating-point mode-bit settings such that more than one mnemonic applies to one instruction. Finally, we limit our mnemonics to four letters, compressing some floating-point mnemonics.

a→→d	i	i	i	LDCI	JMP	i→SPL	i
MOV	SOB	i	i	LDCF	→ij	j→CLCC	i
CMP	d→→h	d→BPL	e→→h	f→JSR	SWAB	j→SECC	i
BIT	BR	BMI	→h	g→CLR	h→MARK	k→HALT	k→i
BIC	BNE	BHI	MULF	COM	i	WAIT	SETD
BIS	BEQ	BLOS	MODF	INC	i	RTI	SETL
→b	BGE	BVC	ADDF	DEC	SXT	BPT	i
→ce	BLT	BVS	LDF	g→NEG	h→→k	IOT	i
b→ADD	BGT	BCC	SUBF	ADC	LDFS	RSET	i
b→SUB	BLE	BCS	CMPF	SBC	STFS	RTT	i
c→MUL	→f	EMT	STF	TST	STST	i	i
DIV	→f	TRAP	DIVF	g→ROR	h→CLRF	k→CFCC	
ASH	→g	→g	STEX	ROL	TSTF	SETF	
ASHC	→g	→g	STCI	ASR	ABSF	SETI	
XOR	→g	→g	STCF	ASL	NEGF	i	
i	→h	i	LDEX	h→→k	i→RTS	i	

PROGRAM 15-34   Operation-code list of the DEC PDP11.

Instruction list. The rich instruction repertoire covers most instruction classes other than decimal arithmetic. The I/O design is such that it requires no instructions other than moves.

	∩ *data handling*		e	DIVF	F Divide
a	MOV	Move	e	CMPF	F Compare
	∩ *logic and shift*		h	TSTF	F Test
g	CLR	Clear		∩ *sequencing*	
g	COM	Not	k	HALT	Stop
a	BIS	Or	k	WAIT	Wait
c	XOR	Exclusive Or	d	BR	Branch
a	BIC	And Not	h	JMP	Branch Indirect
a	BIT	Bit Test	d	BPL	Branch On Plus
c	ASH	Shift Arithmetic	d	BMI	Branch On Minus
c	ASHC	Shift Arithmetic Long	d	BLT	Branch On Less
g	ASL	Shift Arithmetic Left	d	BLE	Branch On Less Or Equal
g	ASR	Shift Arithmetic Right	d	BEQ	Branch On Equal
g	ROL	Rotate Left	d	BNE	Branch On Not Equal
g	ROR	Rotate Right	d	BGE	Branch On Greater Or Equal
h	SWAB	Swap Byte	d	BGT	Branch On Greater
	∩ *fixed-point arithmetic*		d	BLOS	Branch On Low Or Equal
h	SXT	Extend Sign	d	BHI	Branch On High
g	NEG	Negate	d	BCS	Branch On Carry
g	INC	Increment	d	BCC	Branch On No Carry
g	DEC	Decrement	d	BVS	Branch On Overflow
b	ADD	Add	d	BVC	Branch On No Overflow
g	ADC	Add Carry	c	SOB	Decrement And Branch
b	SUB	Subtract	f	JSR	Call
g	SBC	Subtract Borrow	i	RTS	Return
c	MUL	Multiply	h	MARK	Mark Stack
c	DIV	Divide		∩ *supervision*	
a	CMP	Compare	d	TRAP	Trap
g	TST	Test	d	EMT	Emulator Trap
	∩ *floating-point arithmetic*		k	BPT	Breakpoint Trap
h	CLRF	Clear F	k	IOT	Input/Output Trap
e	LDF	F Load	k	RTI	Return From Interrupt
e	LDCI	F Load From Integer	k	RTT	Return From Trap
e	LDCF	F Load To Or From D	j	CLCC	Clear Condition
e	STF	F Store	j	SECC	Set Condition
e	STCI	F Store To Integer	i	SPL	Set Priority Level
e	STCF	F Store To Or From D	k	SETI	Set Integer Mode
e	LDEX	Load Exponent	k	SETL	Set Long Integer Mode
e	STEX	Store Exponent	k	SETF	Set F Mode
h	NEGF	F Negate	k	SETD	Set F D Mode
h	ABSF	F Make Absolute	h	LDFS	Load F Status
e	ADDF	F Add	h	STFS	Store F Status
e	SUBF	F Subtract	h	STST	Store F Exception Code
e	MULF	F Multiply	k	CFCC	Copy F Condition
e	MODF	F Multiply To Integer	k	RSET	Reset Bus

Legend: D = Double; F = Floating-Point.

TABLE 15-35   Instruction list of the DEC PDP11.

Instruction Structure

Machine-language syntax. The instruction syntax is highly involved; there are 22 patterns and 11 pattern groups, with up to three levels of extension. The first pattern has only 3 opcode bits and is used for five instructions. The remaining three codes (0, 6, 7) are used for multiple levels of extended codes. The one-address and two-address categories have very few spare codes.

```
      syntax11
a Byte,Opcode,Source[M],Source[R],Dest[M],Dest[R]
b 0 1 1 0 ,Source[M],Source[R],Dest[M],Dest[R]
b 1 1 1 0 ,Source[M],Source[R],Dest[M],Dest[R]
c 0 1 1 1 ,Opb,Source[R],Dest[M],Dest[R]
d 0 0 0 0 ,Opf,Offset
d 1 0 0 0 ,Opf,Offset
e 1 1 1 1 ,Opf,Rfl,Dest[M],Dest[R]
f 0 0 0 0 1 0 0 ,Source[R],Dest[M],Dest[R]
g Byte, 0 0 0 1 0 1 0 ,Ops,Dest[M],Dest[R]
g Byte, 0 0 0 1 0 1 1 ,Ops,Dest[M],Dest[R]
g Byte, 0 0 0 1 1 0 0 ,Ops,Dest[M],Dest[R]
h 0 0 0 0 0 0 0 0 ,Ops,Dest[M],Dest[R]
h 0 0 0 0 1 1 0 1 ,Ops,Dest[M],Dest[R]
h 1 1 1 1 0 0 0 0 ,Ops,Dest[M],Dest[R]
h 1 1 1 1 0 0 0 1 ,Ops,Dest[M],Dest[R]
i 0 0 0 0 0 0 0 1 0 0 0 0 ,Dest[R]
i 0 0 0 0 0 0 0 1 0 0 1 1 ,Dest[R]
j 0 0 0 0 0 0 0 1 0 1 0 ,Cadr
j 0 0 0 0 0 0 0 1 0 1 1 ,Cadr
k 0 0 0 0 0 0 0 0 0 0 0 0 ,Ope
k 1 1 1 1 0 0 0 0 0 0 0 0 ,Ope
k 1 1 1 1 0 0 0 0 0 0 0 1 ,Ope
```

PROGRAM 15-36   Instruction syntax of the DEC PDP11.

Instruction format.   The 11 syntactic pattern groups give rise to eight instruction formats.   The fields of the first format are found in various combinations in the later formats, but the floating-point and branch formats d and e deviate from this scheme.   The operation-code bits range all over the 16-bit format, starting at the left with opcode and ending after extension upon extension at the right with ope.

Status format.   There are two status formats—one for the basic machine and another for floating-point status. Of the basic 16-bit PSW, 4 bits are used as conditions: Negative, Zero, Carry, and Overflow. One bit determines the trace mode, in which a trap occurs after each instruction execution. Three bits encode the processor interrupt priority level. Two sets of 2 bits each determine the current and previous operating mode; these encode the Kernel, Supervisor, and User mode. One bit specifies the register set currently being used. Three bits are unused.

Basic status is embedded in memory. We have defined a function stout that reads selected status bits, and a function stin that alters selected bits.

Floating-point status notes the floating-point modes, masks, and error handling; the conditions are the same as those of the basic status, but apply to the floating-point operations. Floating-point status is not embedded, but is placed in a control register. Since branches test only the basic conditions, the floating-point conditions must be moved to the basic conditions for that purpose.

Indicators.   Ten indicators record general interrupt conditions, one of which is used for floating point. The floating-point error code register fle effectively expands the single floating-point error indicator Fle to indicate seven individual error causes. A variable number of indicators is available for the I/O devices (Program 15-80).

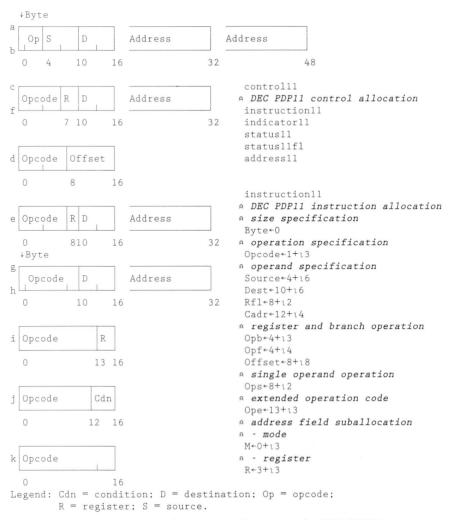

Legend: Cdn = condition; D = destination; Op = opcode;
         R = register; S = source.

PROGRAM 15-37   Instruction allocation in the DEC PDP11.

```
indicator11
ρ DEC PDP11 indicators
ρ program              ρ emulator
Warning←0              Emt←6
Spec←1                 ρ general trap
Invop←2                Trap←7
ρ breakpoint           ρ programmed interrupt
Bpt←3                  Pir←40
ρ input/output         ρ floating-point
Iot←4                  Fle←41
ρ power failure        ρ input/output devices
Powerfail←5            indicator11io
```

PROGRAM 15-38   Indicators of the DEC PDP11.

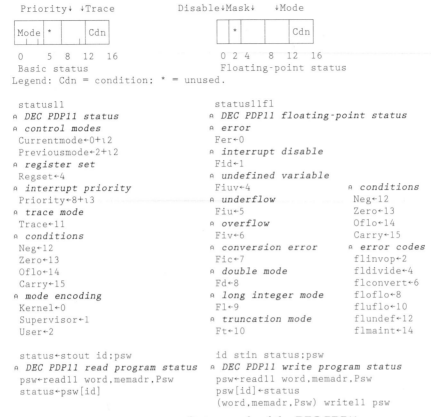

PROGRAM 15-39   Status words of the DEC PDP11.

15.2.3
Addressing

Direct addressing.   The addressing modes specify the data size and data space; hence they strongly affect storage access.   In our description, each address is a three-element vector. The allocation function `address11` indicates that the vector elements represent the data size, data space, and address value, in that order (Program 15-40). Data size (in bits) and address value are integers; data space is a code designating the general registers, the floating-point registers, and memory with the integers 0, 1, and 2, respectively.

Reading and writing differ according to the space involved. For the general registers, the specified number of low-order bits is read from, or replaced in, the addressed register. For the floating-point registers, the proper number of high-order bits is transferred. For memory, as many bytes as the size requires are read or written, starting at the addressed byte.

Backwards byte.   The low-order byte of a data word is placed before the high-order byte of that word in the address space. When the data size is a

```
data←read11 address;size;location          address11
⍝ DEC PDP11 read from store                ⍝ DEC PDP11 address allocation
size←address[Size]                         ⍝ attributes
→CASE address[Space]                        Size←0
CO: ⍝ register                              Space←1
   location←regmap11 address[Value]         Value←2
   data←(-size⌊word)↑reg[location;]        ⍝ space identifiers
   →ENDCASE                                 regadr←0
C1: ⍝ floating-point register               flregadr←1
   data←size↑flreg[6|address[Value];]       memadr←2
   flinvop report11fl address[Value]≥6
   →ENDCASE
C2: ⍝ memory
   location←address[Value]+adrperm11 size
   adrcheck11 location
   data←,memory[memcap|location;]
ENDCASE:


address write11 data;size;location         perm←adrperm11 size;loc
⍝ DEC PDP11 write into store               ⍝ DEC PDP11 address permutation
size←address[Size]                          loc←⍳size⊥byte
→CASE address[Space]                        ⍝ permute even-odd
CO: ⍝ register                              perm←(⍴loc)↑,⌽2 wide loc
   location←regmap11 address[Value]
   reg[location;(-size)↑↑word]←data
   →ENDCASE
C1: ⍝ floating-point register
   flinvop report11fl address[Value]≥6
   →OUT address[Value]≥6
   flreg[address[Value];⍳size]←data
   →ENDCASE
C2: ⍝ memory
   location←address[Value]+adrperm11 size
   adrcheck11 location
   →OUT suppress11
   memory[location;]←byte wide data
ENDCASE:
```

PROGRAM 15-40   Memory read and write in the DEC PDP11.

multiple of words, as in floating point, the interchange of bytes occurs for each word. This permutation of bytes is described in adrperm11 (Program 15-40). As an example the eight bytes of a double floating-point number, when numbered 0 to 7 in high-to-low order, appear in memory in the order 1 0 3 2 5 4 7 6.

Policing. Memory addresses are policed for word alignment and invalid addresses, as described in adrcheck11 (Program 15-72). Writing is suppressed in case of an error.

Address Modification

Address modes. The address modes, shown in adr11 (Program 15-41), are:

- Register: The operand is in the register.
- Register indirect: The register contents address the memory location of the operand.
- Postincrement: The register contents address the memory location of the operand; then, the register is incremented.

- Postincrement indirect: The register contents address a word in memory containing the address of the operand. The register is incremented after the reference.
- Predecrement: The register is first decremented and then used to address the operand.
- Predecrement indirect: The contents of the register are first decremented and then used to address a word in memory containing the address of the operand.
- Index plus displacement: The word following the instruction is added to the contents of the register to form the address of the operand.
- Index plus displacement indirect: The word following the instruction is added to the contents of the register to form the address of a word in memory containing the address of the operand.

For each address mode, a vector indicating the addressed space, the data size, and the address value is constructed. The action of the address mode depends in subtle ways upon the register type. Thus, in floating point, the register mode refers to a floating-point register, but the register-indirect mode uses a fixed-point register. Furthermore, in fixed point the data size is always a word when the stack pointer or instruction address are addressed.

Register addressing.   Register access uses `regin` and `regout`; the eight register addresses are mapped onto the 16 physical registers with `regmap11`.

```
address←size adr11 field;r;step;rf        address←size adr11fl field;r;step;rf
ᴀ DEC PDP11 addressing                    ᴀ DEC PDP11 floating-point address
r←fld field[R]                            r←fld field[R]
step←(size,word)[r∈Sp,Pc]                 step←(size,word)[r=Pc]
→CASE fld field[M]                        →CASE fld field[M]
C0: ᴀ register                            C0: ᴀ register
    address←size,regadr,r                     address←size,flregadr,r
    →ENDCASE                                  →ENDCASE
C1: ᴀ register indirect                    C1: ᴀ register indirect
    rf←magni read11 word,regadr,r             rf←magni read11 word,regadr,r
    address←size,memadr,rf                    address←size,memadr,rf
    →ENDCASE                                  →ENDCASE
C2: ᴀ postincrement                        C2: ᴀ postincrement
    address←size,1↓step incr11 r              address←step incr11 r
    →ENDCASE                                  →ENDCASE
C3: ᴀ postincrement indirect               C3: ᴀ postincrement indirect
    rf←magni read11 word incr11 r             rf←magni read11 word incr11 r
    address←size,memadr,rf                    address←size,memadr,rf
    →ENDCASE                                  →ENDCASE
C4: ᴀ predecrement                         C4: ᴀ predecrement
    address←size,1↓step decr11 r              address←step decr11 r
    →ENDCASE                                  →ENDCASE
C5: ᴀ predecrement indirect                C5: ᴀ predecrement indirect
    rf←magni read11 word decr11 r             rf←magni read11 word decr11 r
    address←size,memadr,rf                    address←size,memadr,rf
    →ENDCASE                                  →ENDCASE
C6: ᴀ index+displacement                   C6: ᴀ index+displacement
    address←size displ11 r                    address←size displ11 r
    →ENDCASE                                  →ENDCASE
C7: ᴀ index+displacement indirect          C7: ᴀ index+displacement indirect
    rf←magni read11 word displ11 r            rf←magni read11 word displ11 r
    address←size,memadr,rf                    address←size,memadr,rf
ENDCASE:                                   ENDCASE:
```

PROGRAM 15-41   Addressing in the DEC PDP11.

```
address←size displl r;index;displacement
⍝ DEC PDP11 index plus displacement
displacement←magni ifetchll
index←magni regout r
address←size,memadr,adrcap|index+displacement
```

```
address←size incrll r;count                address←size decrll r;count
⍝ DEC PDP11 postincrement                   ⍝ DEC PDP11 predecrement
address←size,memadr,magni regout r         count←(magni regout r)-size÷byte
count←address[Value]+size÷byte             Warning report(r=Sp)∧count=limitll
r regin word magnr count                   Spec report(r=Sp)∧count=limitll-16
                                           address←size,memadr,adrcap|count
                                           r regin word magnr address[Value]
```

```
out←limitll
⍝ DEC PDP11 stack limit
→IF Kernel=magni stout Currentmode
THEN: ⍝ kernel limit
   out←magni readll word,memadr,Slw
   →ENDIF
ELSE: ⍝ user and supervisor limit
   out←256
ENDIF:
```

PROGRAM 15-42   Addressing modes in the DEC PDP11.

Registers are often used as even–odd pairs. When pairs of registers are addressed, the first address is normally even; the second address, obtained by oddll, is always odd. An odd first address signifies a single register.

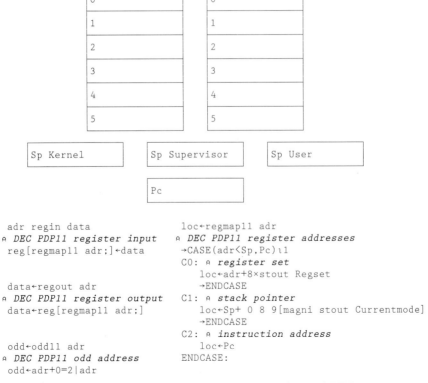

```
adr regin data                     loc←regmapll adr
⍝ DEC PDP11 register input          ⍝ DEC PDP11 register addresses
reg[regmapll adr;]←data            →CASE(adr<Sp,Pc)⍳1
                                   C0: ⍝ register set
                                      loc←adr+8×stout Regset
data←regout adr                       →ENDCASE
⍝ DEC PDP11 register output         C1: ⍝ stack pointer
data←reg[regmapll adr;]                loc←Sp+ 0 8 9[magni stout Currentmode]
                                      →ENDCASE
                                   C2: ⍝ instruction address
odd←oddll adr                         loc←Pc
⍝ DEC PDP11 odd address            ENDCASE:
odd←adr+0=2|adr
```

PROGRAM 15-43   Register mapping in the DEC PDP11.

Register mapping.   Context switching time is reduced by the use of a duplicate set of general registers 0 through 5 and a triplicate set of stack pointers (register 6). There is only one instruction address (register 7), since vector interrupt addresses are immediate. The choice between general register sets is determined by the register-set bit of the PSW; the choice among stack pointers depends upon the current mode code of the PSW being Kernel, Supervisor, or User.

Size specification.   In fixed point the operand size is either a byte or a word. In some instructions this choice is made by the `Byte` bit. In contrast, the floating-point choice between longword and double-word operands is based upon a mode setting.

```
    size←size11                     size←size11fl
  ⋀ DEC PDP11 operand size        ⋀ DEC PDP11 floating-point size
    size←(word,byte)[fld Byte]      size←(long,double)[flstatus[Fd]]
```

PROGRAM 15-44   Operand size in the DEC PDP11.

Index Arithmetic

Index operations.   The use of general purpose registers avoids the need for specific index-arithmetic operations.

List and stack addressing.   Any register can address a list in memory with the postincrement mode. Similarly, a stack in memory can be addressed using both postincrement and predecrement. These modes work properly for all data sizes.

System stack.   The system stack is implied in the interruption action and in status-switching operations. `pop11` and `push11` describe the access to this stack using the stack pointer (`Sp`). The stack grows downward, with the pointer addressing the last-changed word of the stack. The elements of the stack always have word size. A stack is not allowed to grow downward into the reserved memory area—the first 256 words of memory. In the Kernel mode, the lower limit is given by the stack limit `Slw`. When the limit is passed, an indicator is set and an interruption occurs.

```
    data←pop11                      push11 data
  ⋀ DEC PDP11 read from stack     ⋀ DEC PDP11 write onto stack
    data←read11 word incr11 Sp      (word decr11 Sp) write11 data
```

PROGRAM 15-45   System stack access in the DEC PDP11.

Address Level

Indirect addressing.   Indirection is systematically available for the four basic address modes.

Immediate addressing.   The embedding of the instruction address in a general register provides an ingenious means of immediate addressing. When the instruction address register is specified in the postincrement mode, the operand is obtained as an immediate word from the instruction stream, with the instruction address properly updated; when the postincrement indirect mode is used, a directly addressed operand is obtained; similarly, in the index plus displacement mode, a relatively addressed operand is obtained.

15.2.4
Data

Character Strings

Character set and size.   The 8-bit ASCII character set is supported, but it does not affect the architecture.

Character-string formats.   There is no character-string datatype, although the addressing modes make character-by-character processing easy.

Logical

Logical formats.   The same operations apply to byte and word-length Boolean vectors.

Fixed-Point Numbers

Notation and allocation.   Most operations apply to byte and word-length binary 2's-complement integers. Addition and subtraction use word-length operands only. Word allocation in memory is with backwards bytes.

```
  ┌──────────┐       ┌────────────────┐       ┌────────────────┐
  │          │       │ High    Low    │       │ Low     High   │
  └──────────┘       └────────────────┘       └────────────────┘
  0         8         0             16          0             16
  Byte                Register word             Memory word

  signal11NZ r1                signal11NZO r1
  a DEC PDP11 numeric result   a DEC PDP11 arithmetic result
  Neg stin 1↑r1                Neg stin 1↑r1
  Zero stin~v/r1               Zero stin~v/r1
  Oflo stin 0                  Oflo stin xmaxvxmin
```

PROGRAM 15-46   Fixed-point formats in the DEC PDP11.

Fixed-point conditions.   Most logical and arithmetic operations signal negative and zero results; arithmetic results also indicate overflow.

Floating-Point Numbers

Closure and normal form.   Zuse's hidden-bit normalized form is used. Zero is represented with an all-zeros format. When the exponent bits are all-zeros (minimal exponent) and the coefficient sign is minus, the number is considered undefined.

Floating-point format.   The exponent occupies 8 bits. The coefficient has 24 or 56 bits besides the hidden bit.

```
↓Sign
┌─────────────────────────────────────┐  ┌────────────────────────────────┐
│ │Exp  │Coefficient      long│        │  │                         double│
└─────────────────────────────────────┘  └────────────────────────────────┘
0         9                      32                                      64
Legend: Exp = exponent.

fl11 size
A DEC PDP11 floating-point number
A base
base←2                          A coefficient allocation
A sign encoding                   Coef← 0 0 ,9+ιsize-9
plus←0                          A radix point
minus←1                           point←0⊥ρ1↓Coef
A exponent allocation           A extreme exponent
Exp←1+ι8                          extexp←radix*0⊥ρ1↓Exp
```

PROGRAM 15-47   Floating-point format in the DEC PDP11.

Floating-point representation.   The coefficient is represented with signed magnitude and a hidden high-order data bit. The representation uses truncation or rounding, depending upon the truncation-mode bit. The exponent is represented with biased 2's complement.

```
number←fl11i rep;exponent;coefficient;Exp;Coef
A DEC PDP11 floating-point interpretation
fl11ρrep
exponent←biasi rep[Exp]
→IF exponent≠-extexp
THEN: A normalized
   coefficient←signmagni insertbit rep[Coef]
   number←coefficient×base*exponent-point
   →ENDIF
ELSE: A zero or undefined
   number←0
   flundef report11fl flstatus[Fiuv]∧1↑rep[Coef]
ENDIF:

rep←size fl11r number;exponent;coefficient;uflo;Exp;Coef
A DEC PDP11 floating-point representation
fl11 size
(-extexp) normalize number
rep←sizeρ0
→IF flstatus[Ft]
THEN: A truncate
   rep[Coef]←hidebit(ρCoef) signmagnr truncate coefficient
   →ENDIF
ELSE: A round
   rep[Coef]←hidebit(ρCoef) signmagnr round coefficient
ENDIF:rep[Exp]←(ρExp) biasr exponent+xmax
A out of domain
uflo←(exponent≤-extexp)∧number≠0
floflo report11fl xmax∧flstatus[Fiv]
fluflo report11fl uflo∧flstatus[Fiu]
A zero for underflow
rep←rep∧~(uflo∧~flstatus[Fiu])

signal11FNZ rl                    signal11FNZO result
A DEC PDP11 fl numeric result    A DEC PDP11 fl arithmetic result
flstatus[Neg]←rl[1↑Coef]          flstatus[Neg]←result<0
flstatus[Zero]←~∨/rl              flstatus[Zero]←result=0
flstatus[Oflo]←0                  flstatus[Oflo]←xmax
flstatus[Carry]←0                 flstatus[Carry]←0
```

PROGRAM 15-48   Floating-point representation in the DEC PDP11.

Underflow occurs when the exponent is minimal and the number is not zero. In that case, an underflow is signaled when the underflow mask is on. Otherwise, the underflow is equated with a 0 result and represented as all-zeros. Overflow is reported when the overflow mask is on. An undefined operand is reported as an exception when the undefined variable mask bit is on. Exceptional floating-point results set the floating-point error indicator Fle and give an appropriate 4-bit error code by means of reportllfl (Program 15-73).

Floating-point conditions.   The floating-point sign conditions are set according to the representation of the number that is just loaded. The sign and overflow conditions are set for all represented results. The floating-point carry bit is set only in Store To Integer, when the integer range is exceeded.

15.2.5

Operations

Data Handling

Data movement.   The two-address Move operates straightforwardly but with great power, because of the addressing modes. The PDP11 Move may be programmed as though it were a memory-to-memory machine, a general-register machine, or a stack machine, all with one operation. Also, successive elements of a vector may be moved efficiently.

```
MOV:od
ρ DEC PDP11 Move
od←readll sizell adrll Source
(sizell adrll Dest) writell od
signalllNZ od
```

PROGRAM 15-49   Move in the DEC PDP11.

Format and code transformation.   Floating-point Load, Store, and Multiply-To-Integer include type conversions.

Logic

The connectives are NOT, OR, EXCLUSIVE OR, AND NOT, and CLEAR. Bit Test uses an AND to set conditions, but otherwise does not change the data.

g	CLR	Clear	c	XOR	Exclusive Or
g	COM	Not	a	BIC	And Not
a	BIS	Or	a	BIT	Bit Test

TABLE 15-50   Logical connectives of the DEC PDP11.

Connectives.   Most connectives allow all address modes for the operands and result, with a choice between byte and word size. Operands of the Exclusive Or, however, are always a word, with the source operand in a register.

```
        BIT;od1;od2;r1                    COM;dest;r1
      ⋀ DEC PDP11 Bit Test              ⋀ DEC PDP11 Not
        od1←read11 size11 adr11 Source    dest←size11 adr11 Dest
        od2←read11 size11 adr11 Dest      r1←˜read11 dest
        r1←od2∧od1                        dest write11 r1
        signal11NZ r1                     signal11NZ r1


        BIC;dest;od1;od2;r1               XOR;dest;od1;od2;r1
      ⋀ DEC PDP11 And Not               ⋀ DEC PDP11 Exclusive Or
        od1←read11 size11 adr11 Source    od1←regout fld Source[R]
        dest←size11 adr11 Dest            dest←word adr11 Dest
        od2←read11 dest                   od2←read11 dest
        r1←od2∧˜od1                       r1←od2≠od1
        dest write11 r1                   dest write11 r1
        signal11NZ r1                     signal11NZ r1


        CLR;dest
      ⋀ DEC PDP11 Clear
        dest←size11 adr11 Dest
        dest write11 size11ρ0
        signal11NZ 0
```

PROGRAM 15-51   Connectives of the DEC PDP11.

Shift.   There are two types of arithmetic shifts: a shift with signed shift amount and word-sized operands, and a 1-bit shift into carry with explicitly specified shift direction and variable operand size.

```
    c ASH  Shift Arithmetic        g ROL  Rotate Left
    c ASHC Shift Arithmetic Long   g ROR  Rotate Right
    g ASL  Shift Arithmetic Left   h SWAB Swap Byte
    g ASR  Shift Arithmetic Right
```

TABLE 15-52   Shift instructions of the DEC PDP11.

The explicit signed shift amount is obtained with the full set of addressing modes. The last bit that is shifted out is placed in the Carry. The operand to be shifted is always in a register. For the long shift, the operand is in a register extended with its odd neighbor. When the register address is odd, just one register is used, and the shift acts as a rotate.

```
ASH;dest;shift;od;value;result;r1    ASHC;dest;shift;od;value;result;r1
⋀ DEC PDP11 Shift Arithmetic        ⋀ DEC PDP11 Shift Arithmetic Long
dest←byte adr11 Dest                 dest←byte adr11 Dest
shift←radixcompi ˉ6↑read11 dest      shift←radixcompi ˉ6↑read11 dest
od←regout fld Source[R]              od←regout fld Source[R]
value←radixcompi od                  od←od,regout odd11 fld Source[R]
result←value×radix*shift             value←radixcompi od
r1←word radixcompr⌊result            result←value×radix*shift
(fld Source[R]) regin r1             r1←long radixcompr⌊result
Carry stin ˉ1↑shiftΦod,0             (fld Source[R]) regin word↑r1
signal11NZO r1                       (odd11 fld Source[R]) regin word↓r1
                                     Carry stin ˉ1↑shiftΦod,0
                                     signal11NZO r1


ASR;dest;od;r1
⋀ DEC PDP11 Shift Arithmetic Right
dest←size11 adr11 Dest
od←read11 dest
r1←od[0],ˉ1↓od
dest write11 r1
Carry stin ˉ1↑od
signal11NZ r1
Oflo stin(1↑od)≠ˉ1↑od
```

PROGRAM 15-53   Arithmetic Shift in the DEC PDP11.

Rotate.   Rotation is by only 1 bit, through carry, and has explicitly specified direction. A special case is the swapping of high- and low-order bytes in a word, which is equivalent to an 8-bit rotate.

```
ROL;dest;od;rl                 SWAB;dest;od;rl
ª DEC PDP11 Rotate Left        ª DEC PDP11 Swap Byte
dest←size11 adr11 Dest         dest←word adr11 Dest
od←read11 dest                 od←read11 dest
rl←1↓od,stout Carry            rl←byteФod
dest write11 rl                dest write11 rl
Carry stin 1↑od                Carry stin 0
signal11NZ rl                  signal11NZ rl
Oflo stin≠/2↑od
```

PROGRAM 15-54   Rotate in the DEC PDP11.

Fixed-Point Arithmetic

The arithmetic-instruction set is complete, including Increment and Decrement, but not Make Absolute. There is no Multiply or Divide in the earliest low-end versions, such as model 20, but they are standard in Model 45. Conditions are set according to the arithmetic result. Test inspects a number for sign and zero.

```
h SXT   Extend Sign    b SUB   Subtract
g NEG   Negate         g SBC   Subtract Borrow
g INC   Increment      c MUL   Multiply
g DEC   Decrement      c DIV   Divide
b ADD   Add            a CMP   Compare
g ADC   Add Carry      g TST   Test
```

TABLE 15-55   Fixed-point instructions of the DEC PDP11.

Monadic arithmetic.   Negation, Increment, and Decrement have variable operand size. Extend Sign uses the sign condition to make a word. A positive sign yields 0; a negative sign, -1. Increment and Decrement are convenient for counting; they also can be used to program a stack or list with a pointer in memory.

```
INC;dest;count;rl                NEG;dest;operand;rl
ª DEC PDP11 Increment            ª DEC PDP11 Negate
dest←size11 adr11 Dest           dest←size11 adr11 Dest
count←radixcompi read11 dest     operand←radixcompi read11 dest
rl←size11 radixcompr count+1     rl←size11 radixcompr-operand
dest write11 rl                  dest write11 rl
signal11NZO rl                   signal11NZO rl
                                 Carry stin operand≠0

SXT;rl
ª DEC PDP11 Extend Sign
rl←wordρstout Neg
(word adr11 Dest) write11 rl
signal11NZ rl
```

PROGRAM 15-56   Monadic fixed-point arithmetic in the DEC PDP11.

Add and Subtract.   Addition and subtraction have word-size operands and result signaling. Add Carry and Subtract Borrow can be used for extended precision. The dyadic Add With Carry would have been far superior, but the opcode space is too cramped for such a two-address instruction. Furthermore, using Subtract With Carry would have been cleaner than indicating the state of an inverse carry.

```
ADD;dest;ad;addend;augend;sum;rl;cy        SUB;dest;ad;addend;augend;sum;rl;cy
∩ DEC PDP11 Add                            ∩ DEC PDP11 Subtract
ad←read11 word adr11 Source                ad←read11 word adr11 Source
addend←radixcompi ad                       addend←radixcompi~ad
dest←word adr11 Dest                       dest←word adr11 Dest
augend←radixcompi read11 dest              augend←radixcompi read11 dest
sum←augend+addend                          sum←augend+addend+1
rl←word radixcompr sum                     rl←word radixcompr sum
dest write11 rl                            dest write11 rl
signal11NZO rl                             signal11NZO rl
cy←word carryfrom augend,addend            cy←word carryfrom augend,addend,1
Carry stin cy                              Carry stin~cy


ADC;dest;addend;augend;sum;rl;cy           TST;rl
∩ DEC PDP11 Add Carry                      ∩ DEC PDP11 Test
addend←stout Carry                         rl←read11 size11 adr11 Dest
dest←size11 adr11 Dest                     signal11NZ rl
augend←radixcompi read11 dest              Carry stin 0
sum←augend+addend
rl←size11 radixcompr sum
dest write11 rl
signal11NZO rl
cy←size11 carryfrom augend,addend
Carry stin cy
```

PROGRAM 15-57   Add and Subtract in the DEC PDP11.

Multiply and Divide.   Multiply has two word-size operands and the multiplicand in a register. The product is developed in the multiplicand register and its odd neighbor. When the register address is odd, only the low-order product is recorded. The carry condition signals that the product has a significant high-order word.

```
MUL;dest;multiplier;multiplicand;product;rl
∩ DEC PDP11 Multiply
dest←fld Source[R]
multiplier←radixcompi read11 word adr11 Dest
multiplicand←radixcompi reg[dest;]
product←multiplicand×multiplier
rl←long radixcompr product
dest regin word↑rl
(odd11 dest) regin word↓rl
signal11NZ rl
Carry stin∨/rl[0]≠word↑rl
```

PROGRAM 15-58   Multiply in the DEC PDP11.

Division has word-size divisor, quotient, and remainder. The dividend is in an even–odd register pair and is replaced by the quotient and remainder. The addressed register must be even.

Compare.   Compare is equivalent to a subtract with the conditions—including the borrow—properly set, but without recording the difference value. The sign and zero status of a single value can be tested with TST.

```
CMP;addend;augend;sum;r1
ค DEC PDP11 Compare
addend←radixcompi~read11 size11 adr11 Dest
augend←radixcompi read11 size11 adr11 Source
sum←augend+addend+1
r1←size11 radixcompr sum
signal11NZO r1
Carry stin~size11 carryfrom augend,addend,1
```

PROGRAM 15-59   Compare in the DEC PDP11.

Floating-Point Arithmetic

The floating-point option consists of a separate arithmetic unit—with its own registers, modes, masks, and conditions—that can operate concurrently with the basic arithmetic unit. Since the processors maintain the order of the instruction stream in the use of each other's results, the concurrency of the arithmetic units does not show in the architecture; the separate working and control store are clearly visible, however.

```
h CLRF Clear F                 h NEGF F Negate
e LDF  F Load                  h ABSF F Make Absolute
e LDCI F Load From Integer     e ADDF F Add
e LDCF F Load To Or From D     e SUBF F Subtract
e STF  F Store                 e MULF F Multiply
e STCI F Store To Integer      e MODF F Multiply To Integer
e STCF F Store To Or From D    e DIVF F Divide
e LDEX Load Exponent           e CMPF F Compare
e STEX Store Exponent          h TSTF F Test
Legend: D = Double; F = Floating-Point.
```

PROGRAM 15-60   Floating-point instructions of the DEC PDP11.

Because of lack of opcode space, one operand of the dyadic operations is specified by a 2-bit register field in the instruction; thus only four out of the six floating-point registers can be specified. The other operand is specified with the full set of address modes, but the register address must be 0–5 (Program 15-40).

Floating-point Load and Store.   The Move instruction cannot be used to move floating-point numbers, since it does not apply to the floating-point registers and conditions. Hence there are a floating-point Load and Store.

```
LDF;operand
ค DEC PDP11 Floating-Point Load
operand←fl11i read11 size11fl adr11fl Dest
flreg[fld Rfl;ιsize11fl]←size11fl fl11r operand
signal11FNZO operand
```

PROGRAM 15-61   Floating-point Load in the DEC PDP11.

Conversion.   Load From Integer, Store To Integer, and Multiply To Integer give conversion from and to fixed point. Load and Store Exponent move an integer in a fixed-point register to and from the exponent field of a floating-point register.

With the floating-point data size determined by a mode setting, the instructions Load and Store To or From Double are a convenient means to obtain the not-currently-specified size.

```
   LDEX;exp
 ⋒ DEC PDP11 Load Exponent
   exp←radixcompi read11 word adr11 Dest
   flreg[fld Rf1;1+ι8]←8 biasr exp
   signal11FNZ flreg[fld Rf1;ιsize11fl]


   LDCI;size;operand
 ⋒ DEC PDP11 Floating-Point Load From Integer
   size←(word,long)[flstatus[Fl]]
   operand←radixcompi size↑read11 size adr11 Dest
   flreg[fld Rf1;ιsize11fl]←size11fl fl11r operand
   signal11FNZO operand


   STCF;size;operand
 ⋒ DEC PDP11 Floating-Point Store To Or From Double
   size←(double,long)[flstatus[Fd]]
   operand←fl11i flreg[fld Rf1;ιsize11fl]
   (size adr11fl Dest) write11 size fl11r operand
   signal11FNZO operand
```

PROGRAM 15-62   Floating-point conversion in the DEC PDP11.

Floating-point sign control and addition.   Floating-point sign control includes Make Absolute. Addition and subtraction operate straightforwardly upon the interpretation of the operands, then represent the result and set the conditions according to the result value.

```
    ABSF;dest;result
  ⋒ DEC PDP11 Floating-Point Make Absolute
    dest←size11fl adr11fl Dest
    result←|fl11i read11 dest
    dest write11 size11fl fl11r result
    signal11FNZO result


    ADDF;addend;augend;sum
  ⋒ DEC PDP11 Floating-Point Add
    addend←fl11i read11 size11fl adr11fl Dest
    augend←fl11i flreg[fld Rf1;ιsize11fl]
    sum←augend+addend
    flreg[fld Rf1;ιsize11fl]←size11fl fl11r sum
    signal11FNZO sum
```

PROGRAM 15-63   Floating-point Make Absolute and Add in the DEC PDP11.

Floating-point Multiply and Divide.   Multiply To Integer splits the product into an integer part and a fraction part. The integer part is represented in 2's complement in a floating-point register; the fraction is retained in floating point in the corresponding odd-numbered register. When the register address is odd, only the fraction is recorded. The conditions are set according to the total product. This instruction is convenient in converting a number to decimal by repeated multiplication with 10.

Floating-point Compare.   The generally specified operand is subtracted from the register operand and the floating-point conditions are set according to the difference.

```
      MODF;multiplier;multiplicand;product;integer;fraction
    ∩ DEC PDP11 Floating-Point Multiply To Integer
      multiplier←fl11i read11 size11fl adr11fl Dest
      multiplicand←fl11i flreg[fld Rfl;ιsize11fl]
      product←multiplicand×multiplier
      fraction←1|product
      integer←product-fraction
      flreg[odd11 fld Rfl;ιsize11fl]←size11fl radixcompr integer
      flreg[fld Rfl;ιsize11fl]←size11fl fl11r fraction
      signal11FNZO product
```

PROGRAM 15-64   Floating-Point Multiply To Integer in the DEC PDP11.

15.2.6

Instruction Sequencing

Linear Sequence

Next instruction.   The basic cycle is very simple. One word is fetched by `ifetch11`, using basic incrementing. Additional instruction words are fetched as needed by the various addressing modes. Source address phrases, if any, are fetched prior to the destination address phrase.

```
    cycle11                        inst←ifetch11
  ∩ basic cycle of the DEC PDP11  ∩ DEC PDP11 instruction fetch
    REPEAT:interrupt11             inst←read11 word incr11 Pc
        execute ifetch11
    →UNTIL stop
```

PROGRAM 15-65   Basic cycle and instruction fetch of the DEC PDP11.

Sequencing instructions.   Completion, Unconditional Branch, Iteration, and Delegation are each covered by a single appropriate instruction. Decision has by far the largest group of instructions, even though condition setting is separated from condition testing.

```
k HALT  Stop                      d BLOS Branch On Low Or Equal
k WAIT  Wait                      d BHI  Branch On High
d BR    Branch                    d BCS  Branch On Carry
h JMP   Branch Indirect           d BCC  Branch On No Carry
d BPL   Branch On Plus            d BVS  Branch On Overflow
d BMI   Branch On Minus           d BVC  Branch On No Overflow
d BLT   Branch On Less            c SOB  Decrement And Branch
d BLE   Branch On Less Or Equal   f JSR  Call
d BEQ   Branch On Equal           i RTS  Return
d BNE   Branch On Not Equal       h MARK Mark Stack
d BGE   Branch On Greater Or Equal
d BGT   Branch On Greater
```

TABLE 15-66   Sequencing instructions of the DEC PDP11.

Completion.   Both Stop and Wait are provided. Stop is not valid in the user mode.

```
    HALT                              WAIT
  ∩ DEC PDP11 Stop                  ∩ DEC PDP11 Wait
    Invop report Kernel≠magni stout Currentmode   wait←1
    →OUT suppress11
    stop←1
```

PROGRAM 15-67   Completion in the DEC PDP11.

Unconditional branch.   All instructions are single or multiple words, so branch addresses are *word* addresses, and the offsets that are specified in branch instructions are shifted left one place to yield even-byte addresses. Since the next instruction address is in a general register, a move into this register constitutes an indirect unconditional branch. Also, with index plus dispacement a two-word relative branch can be achieved; BR is a one-word relative branch.   JMP can be used for a direct branch.   The register-direct mode is not allowed for this instruction. When an indirect mode is used, the instruction is equivalent to a direct move into the instruction address register.

```
BR;iadr;offset                        JMP;dest
ⁿ DEC PDP11 Branch                    ⁿ DEC PDP11 Branch Indirect
iadr←magni reg[Pc;]                   dest←word adr11 Dest
offset←2×radixcompi inst[Offset]      Invop report dest[Space]=regadr
reg[Pc;]←word magnr iadr+offset       Spec report 1=2|dest[Value]
                                      →OUT suppress11
                                      reg[Pc;]←word magnr dest[Value]
```

PROGRAM 15-68   Unconditional Branch in the DEC PDP11.

Decision

Conditional branching.   The conditions in the PSW are used to separate the branch test from the arithmetic and logical actions. All conditional branches are relative to the next instruction address, using a signed offset that indicates the number of words to be jumped. Fourteen combinations of the fixed-point conditions are used; the floating-point conditions must be moved to the fixed-point conditions before they can be so tested. The tests on Less and on Greater apply to signed quantities; the tests on Low and on High apply to unsigned quantities. The unsigned tests are supplemented by the tests on Carry and No Carry, which give unsigned Low and unsigned High Or Equal, respectively.

```
BLT;iadr;offset                       BLOS;iadr;offset
ⁿ DEC PDP11 Branch On Less            ⁿ DEC PDP11 Branch On Low Or Equal
→If≠/stout Neg,Oflo                   →If∨/stout Zero,Carry
THEN:iadr←magni reg[Pc;]              THEN:iadr←magni reg[Pc;]
   offset←2×radixcompi inst[Offset]      offset←2×radixcompi inst[Offset]
   reg[Pc;]←word magnr iadr+offset       reg[Pc;]←word magnr iadr+offset
ENDIF:                                ENDIF:


BEQ;iadr;offset                       BCS;iadr;offset
ⁿ DEC PDP11 Branch On Equal           ⁿ DEC PDP11 Branch On Carry
→If stout Zero                        →If stout Carry
THEN:iadr←magni reg[Pc;]              THEN:iadr←magni reg[Pc;]
   offset←2×radixcompi inst[Offset]      offset←2×radixcompi inst[Offset]
   reg[Pc;]←word magnr iadr+offset       reg[Pc;]←word magnr iadr+offset
ENDIF:                                ENDIF:
```

PROGRAM 15-69   Conditional Branch in the DEC PDP11.

Iteration

Incrementation and termination.   Decrement And Branch can be used to close a Repeat loop: As long as the count is not 0, a backward jump takes place. The word offset is specified by the unsigned 6-bit destination field, as opposed to a signed 8-bit offset field, used in other branches.

```
SOB;count;iadr
ᴀ DEC PDP11 Decrement And Branch
count←(radixcompi regout fld Source[R])-1
(fld Source[R]) regin word radixcompr count
→If count≠0
THEN:iadr←magni reg[Pc;]
     reg[Pc;]←word magnr iadr-2×fld Dest
ENDIF:
```

PROGRAM 15-70   Decrement And Branch in the DEC PDP11.

Delegation

Call and return.   Call (JSR) pushes the contents of the linkage register specified by R onto the stack and places the next instruction address (the return address) into that register; then, the subroutine address becomes the instruction address. Call allows nesting to any level. It implements a coroutine structure when the linkage register specifies the instruction address register and the stack pointer is used with preincrement indirect addressing as the subroutine address.

Return (RTS) places the return address from the linkage register in the instruction address register and restores the old contents of the linkage register from the stack.

```
JSR;dest                              RTS
ᴀ DEC PDP11 Call                      ᴀ DEC PDP11 Return
ᴀ fetch instruction address          reg[Pc;]←regout fld Dest[R]
dest←word adrll Dest                  (fld Dest[R]) regin popll
ᴀ test address
Invop report dest[Space]=regadr
Spec report 1=2|dest[Value]           MARK;sub
→OUT suppressll                       ᴀ DEC PDP11 Mark Stack
ᴀ push linkage pointer onto stack     sub←(magni regout Sp)+2×fld Dest
pushll regout fld Source[R]           Sp regin word radixcompr sub
ᴀ store instruction address           reg[Pc;]←regout 5
(fld Source[R]) regin reg[Pc;]        5 regin popll
ᴀ new instruction address
reg[Pc;]←word magnr dest[Value]
```

PROGRAM 15-71   Call and Return in the DEC PDP11.

Mark Stack instruction.   The Mark Stack instruction is used to identify parameters placed on the stack in a subroutine call. The instruction is supposed to be placed on the stack, following the parameter list. As part of the standard return, the instruction address is made to point at this stacked instruction. Its destination field specifies the length of the parameter list in the stack and is used to clean out the whole list. The instruction address of the calling routine is obtained from register 5, and the new top value of the stack (a possible return address to a higher level calling routine) replaces the content of register 5.

15.2.7

Supervision

Concurrency

Processor interconnection.   Multiprocessing is obtained by connecting several processors to the central bus.

Integrity

Invalid operation codes and stack overflows cause interruptions. There is no memory protection, but addresses—including the instruction address—are checked against memory capacity and for proper alignment.

Suppression.   Various instructions are suppressed when an invalid specification or mode of operation is encountered. This suppression is controlled by the setting of indicators.

```
adrcheck11 location                    yes←suppress11
⍺ DEC PDP11 address check              ⍺ DEC PDP11 operation suppression
⍺ memory capacity                      yes←v/ind[Spec,Invop]
Spec report location≥memcap
⍺ word allignment
Spec report 0≠(2⌊ρ,location)|⌊/location
```

PROGRAM 15-72   Policing in the DEC PDP11.

Floating-point reports.   The single floating-point indicator Fle must serve many purposes; hence the floating-point error register fle is set to a 4-bit code to indicate the last cause that set the indicator.

```
code report11fl condition
⍺ floating-point error report
→If condition
THEN: ⍺ set indicator and code
   fle←(ρfle) magnr code
   Fle report 1
ENDIF:
```

PROGRAM 15-73   Floating-point error reporting in the DEC PDP11.

Privileged operations.   Supervisory instructions deal with humble access, dispatching, and the setting of machine state. Set Priority Level is the only privileged operation allowed; it is in the Kernel state, and is ignored in other states.

```
d TRAP Trap                        k SETI Set Integer Mode
d EMT  Emulator Trap               k SETL Set Long Integer Mode
k BPT  Breakpoint Trap             k SETF Set F Mode
k IOT  Input/Output Trap           k SETD Set F D Mode
k RTI  Return From Interrupt       h LDFS Load F Status
k RTT  Return From Trap            h STFS Store F Status
j CLCC Clear Condition             h STST Store F Exception Code
j SECC Set Condition               k CFCC Copy F Condition
i SPL  Set Priority Level          k RSET Reset Bus
Legend: D = Double; F = Floating-Point.
```

TABLE 15-74   Supervisory instructions of the DEC PDP11.

Control Switching

Interruption.   The PDP11 was designed especially for real-time control, so rapid response to interrupts was important. Vectored interrupt is used to sort requests quickly; multiple priority levels allow nested interrupts.

The nested interrupt system causes the CPU to accept the highest-priority peripheral device interrupt if it is above the processor's current priority level. The peripheral device transmits the address of the interrupt vector to be used.

Upon a trap or an interrupt, the processor saves the entire 16-bit PSW and the instruction address on the stack. The processor takes the new contents of the instruction address register from the first word of the trap or interrupt vector, and a new PSW from the second word of the vector.

```
interrupt11;who;old;new          progint11;who;nr
⋒ DEC PDP11 interrupt action     ⋒ DEC PDP11 programmed interrupt
progint11                        who←7-(7↑read11 byte,memadr,Piw)ι1
REPEAT: ⋒ search indicators      →If who>magni stout Priority
    who←indι1                    THEN: ⋒ record request number twice
    →If who≠ρind                     nr←byte magnr who×34
    THEN: ⋒ process indicator        (byte,memadr,Piw+1) write11 nr
        ind[who]←0                   Pir report 1
        old←stoutιword           ENDIF:
        push11 old
        push11 reg[Pc;]
        reg[Pc;]←read11 word,memadr,Intvec[who]
        Spec report 1=2|magni reg[Pc;]
        new←read11 word,memadr,2+Intvec[who]
        new[Previousmode]←old[Currentmode]
        (ιword) stin new
        wait←0
ENDIF:→UNTIL¯wait
Bpt report stout Trace
```

PROGRAM 15-75   Interruption action in the DEC PDP11.

The interrupt vectors are in a set of fixed locations for such conditions as power failure, odd addressing errors, stack errors, bus-timeout errors, memory parity errors, reserved instruction use, use of trace mode, and use of trapping instructions.

Trace.   When the `trace` bit in the status word is on, the `Bpt` indicator is set, which causes the processor to interrupt after each instruction. Return From Trap (Program 15-77) ensures that a trace interrupt is taken not immediately upon return, but rather after one subject instruction is executed.

Programmed interrupt.   The programmer can set a bit in the first 7 bits of the programmed interrupt word `Piw`. The 7 bits indicate an interrupt request with priority 7 down to 1. When the system priority is less then the requesting priority, the interrupt is granted. In that case, the level of the interrupt is indicated in bits 0 to 2 and in bits 4 to 6 of the location next to `Piw`, and the `Pir` indicator is set.

Priority.   The processor priority level is programmable in the kernel mode by `SPL`, which sets the priority bits in the PSW. Device-interrupt priority is independent of service-routine priority.

Humble access.   Besides programmed interrupt, the instructions Trap, Emulator Trap, Breakpoint Trap, and Input/Output Trap set an indicator that causes an interruption; the latter initiates a corresponding routine. The instructions are identical except for the routine to which they refer.

```
TRAP                        BPT
a DEC PDP11 Trap           a DEC PDP11 Breakpoint Trap
ind[Trap]←1                 ind[Bpt]←1
```

PROGRAM 15-76   Humble access in the DEC PDP11.

Dispatching.   The two entities (status and instruction address) that are pushed onto the system stack at the moment of interruption are restored by Return From Interrupt (RTI). Return From Trap performs the same actions, but also resets the trap indicator.

```
RTI                               RTT
a DEC PDP11 Return From Interrupt a DEC PDP11 Return From Trap
reg[Pc;]←pop11                    reg[Pc;]←pop11
(ιword) stin pop11                (ιword) stin pop11
                                  ind[Bpt]←0
```

PROGRAM 15-77   Dispatch in the DEC PDP11.

Modes.   The floating-point size modes Fd and Fl are set by four distinct instructions. They concern the choices between long and double floating-point size and between the word or long integer size that is used in floating-to-fixed conversion.

```
CLCC;cnd                          SPL
a DEC PDP11 Clear Condition       a DEC PDP11 Set Priority Level
cnd←inst[Cadr]/Neg,Zero,Oflo,Carry →If Kernel=magni stout Currentmode
cnd stin 0                        THEN:Priority stin inst[Dest[R]]
                                  ENDIF:


SETL                              SETF
a DEC PDP11 Set Long Integer Mode a DEC PDP11 Set Floating-Point Mode
flstatus[Fl]←1                    flstatus[Fd]←0
```

PROGRAM 15-78   Mode control in the DEC PDP11.

Conditions.   Set Condition and Clear Condition set or reset individual conditions. The specific set of conditions is indicated with the bits of the Cadr field in the instruction.

State Preservation

Context switching.   Context-switching operations store and restore floating-point status, conditions, and exceptions; the systems stack is not implicitly used for these entities. Store Floating-Point Exception Code stores the 4-bit floating-point error code at the destination address; when this address points to memory, the content of the floating-point interruption location is stored in the next memory word.

```
   LDFS
 ᴀ DEC PDP11 Load Floating-Point Status
   flstatus←read11 word adr11 Dest


   STFS;dest
 ᴀ DEC PDP11 Store Floating-Point Status
   (word adr11 Dest) write11 flstatus


   STST;fleadr
 ᴀ DEC PDP11 Store Floating-Point Exception Code
   fleadr←read11 word,memadr,Intvec[Fle]
   (long adr11 Dest) write11(-long)↑fle,fleadr


   CFCC
 ᴀ DEC PDP11 Copy Floating-Point Condition
   (Neg,Zero,Oflo,Carry) stin flstatus[Neg,Zero,Oflo,Carry]
```

PROGRAM 15-79   Status switching in the DEC PDP11.

Tools of Control

Timer.   System timers are available as options.

15.2.8

Input/Output

Direct, buffered, and channel I/O can be used.   Device registers and the channel regsiters are mapped onto main storage.

```
   name11io                      indicator11io
 ᴀ DEC PDP11 device addresses  ᴀ DEC PDP11 input/output indicators
   Ttyinw←memcap-142             Ttyin←12
   Ttyoutw←memcap-138            Ttyout←13
   Ptpinw←memcap-150             Ptpin←14
   Ptpoutw←memcap-146            Ptpout←15
   Clockw←memcap-154             Clock←16
   Realtimew←memcap-160          Realtime←17
   Printerw←memcap-178           Printer←32
   Disk256w←memcap-210           Disk256←33
   Disk64w←memcap-242            Disk64←34
   Dectapew←memcap-288           Dectape←35
   Diskcrdw←memcap-256           Diskcrd←36
   Tapew←memcap-176              Tape←37
```

PROGRAM 15-80   Input/output control in the DEC PDP11.

Interfaces

Central bus.   The UNIBUS is a central bus with processor, memory, and peripheral devices attached. The bus is asynchronous and has concurrency of 1. The format of communication is the same for each device on the bus. Each device has assigned priority for bus access in case of contention.

15.2.9

Implementation Notes

Bit-traffic bottleneck.   The asynchronous UNIBUS allows memory systems and devices of varying speeds to be attached without changing bus protocol. The bus, however, is a performance bottleneck, and is not suitable for faster implementations unless cache is used to reduce memory traffic.

Timing.   Byte instructions take equal or more time than word instructions. Instruction times depend upon the addressing mode. Fixed-point addition is minimal: 300 ns and about 2 μs with memory access; multiplication is about 5 μs; division, 9 μs; floating-point addition, 6 μs; multiplication, 8 μs; and division, 9 μs.

15.2.10

Bibliography

Digital Equipment Corporation, 1973: *PDP11/45 Processor Handbook.* Maynard, MA (our defining reference).

Bell, C.G. et al., 1970: "A New Architecture for Minicomputers—The DEC PDP11." *Proc., AFIPS Spring Joint Computer Conf.,* 657–75. Reprinted in Bell, Mudge, and McNamara [1978], Chapter 9.

Bell, C.G. and W.D. Strecker, 1976: "Computer Structures: What Have We Learned from the PDP11?" *Proc., 3rd Annual Symposium on Computer Architecture,* **4**, 4: 1–14.

Bell, C.G. and J.C. Mudge, 1978: "The Evolution of the PDP-11." Bell, Mudge, and McNamara [1978], Chapter 16.

Russell, R.D., 1978: "The PDP-11: A Case Study of How *Not* to Design Condition Codes." *Proc., 5th Annual International Symposium on Computer Architecture,* **6**, 7: 190–94.

Hunt [1980].

15.2.11

Exercises

15-6 List five specific inconsistencies between fixed-point and floating-point arithmetic.

15-7 Show how the instruction MOV can be used to:

    a. Place the content of memory location a in location b

    b. Place a number n in location b

    c. Replace an element of a vector in memory

    d. Replace an element of a vector and move to the next element

    e. Load a register

    f. Store a register

    g. Load or store indirect via memory location a

    h. Move data from one register to another register

    i. Load or store indexed

    j. Load or store indexed indirect

    k. Load or store indirect via a register

    l. Push a literal upon a stack

    m. Push the content of a memory location upon a stack

    n. Pop an element from a stack and place it in memory or a register

    o. Duplicate the top of a stack

    p. Store an item in the place specified by the top of a stack

    q. Pop an item from a stack and push it upon another stack

15-8 Give the PDP11 instruction that changes the size of the number in floating-point register 2. How would you change the size if the number were in register 5?

15-9 Give the description of the logical and shift instructions BIS, ASL, and ROR, assuming consistency with the instructions shown in this section.

15-10 Give the description of the fixed-point instructions DEC, SBC, and DIV, assuming consistency with the fixed-point instructions shown in this section.

15-11 Give the description of the floating-point instructions CLRF, LDCF, STF, STCI, STEX, NEGF, SUBF, MULF, DIVF, CMPF, and TSTF assuming consistency with the instructions shown in this section.

15-12 Give the description of the branch instructions BPL, BMI, BLE, BNE, BGE, BGT, BHI, BVS, BVC, and BCC, assuming consistency with the branch instructions shown in this section.

15-13 Give the description of the supervisory instructions EMT, SECC, SETI, and SETD assuming consistency with the supervisory instructions shown in this section.

15.3
DEC VAX11/780*

15.3.1
Highlights

History

Architects.   The chief architect was William Strecker.

Dates.   The architecture was done from April 1975 to April 1976. The first VAX, a VAX11/780, was shipped early in 1978.

Family tree.   We describe the DEC VAX11/780, abbreviated as VAX780. This incompatible descendant of the DEC PDP11 (1970) was the first of the VAX family, which came to include high-performance, mid-range, and workstation implementations.   It was designed as an architecture proper, intended for family-wide use and several generations of implementations.

The architects set out to design an upward-compatible extension of the PDP11.   The redesign was occasioned by users' outstripping the virtual-address size of the PDP11, and by the continuing drop in real memory costs.

The PDP11 architecture proved too constraining, so a new (*native-mode*) 32-bit architecture was developed, with an explicit PDP11 compatibility mode tightly integrated.

The VAX architecture was carefully based on extensive (published) measurements of PDP11 use patterns and operation frequencies, to give bit efficiency (static and dynamic).

Noteworthy

Open-ended architecture.   The architecture was designed to cover a wide range of implementations and to be extensible—indeed, completely open-ended—with respect to operations, datatypes, and addressing modes. This approach made it possible to specify the natural number of operands for each operation without loss of bit efficiency.

Orthogonal instruction format.   The 1-byte operation code may be followed by a highly variable number of address phrases, each 1 to 10 bytes long.

Careful, limited compatibility with the PDP11.   Strict upward compatibility of PDP11 datatypes and addressing mode (semantics) was preserved in VAX native mode.

Many addressing modes.   VAX has all the PDP11 has, and more.   The addressing modes were matched against high-level language needs for

- Literals

---

* Initial sketch research done by M.K. Smotherman

- Own locals (scalars, arrays)
- Dynamic locals (scalars, arrays)
- Arguments by value (scalars, arrays)
- Arguments by reference (scalars, arrays)
- Globals
- Temporaries

Indexing.   Indexing is a prefix operator, so instruction bits are paid for index specification only when indexing is used. Index values are scaled by the (fixed-length) operand size in address calculation.

Frequency-based design.   PDP11 measurement showed the predominance of short literals, short data and branch displacements, and true indexing, so the VAX architecture emphasizes these. It even includes floating-point literals with short range and precision for common constants.

General register set.   As in the PDP11, the VAX incorporates in the general registers a stack pointer and the next instruction address, to great effect. The same unified set of sixteen 32-bit general registers is used as fixed-point and floating-point accumulators, and as addressing registers, an improvement over the PDP11. Longer quantities are handled in register pairs.

Large name-space   The name-space for virtual memory is 2^{32} bytes. The potential physical name-space is 2^{30} bytes.

Heavy embedding.   All peripheral-device registers are embedded in a system region of the name-space.

Memory management by page, without segmentation.   Segmentation with paging was explicitly rejected in favor of four specific access modes with access controlled at the page level. A capability-based memory-management system, with the ability to page larger (multipage) objects, was considered and rejected.

Large set of datatypes.   The VAX provides the PDP11 datatypes, plus new ones for commercial and number-crunching computing: character strings, one packed and two unpacked decimal types, and extended-range, extended-precision floating point. A logical-vector type addressable at the bit level—reminiscent of the IBM Stretch (1961) and the Burroughs B1700 (1972)—is provided, especially to aid compilers.

Large and rich operation set.   Besides being large because it includes many datatypes, the set is augmented with some interesting new operations, such as insertion and deletion of elements in a queue, or a multiple Branch designed for the Case structure.

Extensive supervisory capabilities.   A process model is designed and supported, with four hierarchical access modes; separate memory allocation for the system-wide kernel, per-process supervisory code, and user code; and a stack pointer for each execution mode to provide proper nesting.

A standard Call.   "Anyone can call anyone" for all languages, calls to the common-language run-time system, and calls to the operating system. Calling state is preserved.

A Procedure Call instruction sets up linked activation records on the stack.

Interruptible instructions.   The interrupt latency of long character-string and decimal operations is shortened by making these instructions interruptible. The interrupted instructions can be resumed because vital address values are preserved in fixed register locations.

Peculiarities

Complex, perhaps rococco.   VAX shows the second-system effect, like the Stretch and the CDC STAR100 (1973) and Cybers. Good ideas seem to be elaborated to excess. There are lots of frills. At times, competing architectural alternatives, such as indirect addressing and a Move Address operation, are both incorporated. The architecture demands a microcoded implementation.

Microprocessor technology limited the amount that could be done on one chip; hence the VAX architecture lost its cost/performance advantage in that technological environment. RISC architecture became popular, even in DEC.

Backward addressing.   Unfortunately, the backward addressing of the numeric data bits, found in the PDP11, is maintained—in a slightly different way—in the VAX 780. Since VAX 780 character strings are addressed in the normal (forward) way, the anomaly is the more obvious.

Borrow.   The PDP11 is also followed by indicating the borrow in a subtraction; hence the carry condition is set in subtraction to the inverse of its setting in addition.

Instruction prefetching.   This implementation technique intrudes into the architecture when instructions are written after prefetch, but before normal fetch.

15.3.2

Machine Language

Language Level

Design philosophy. The VAX is a complex–instruction-set computer (CISC), with many addressing modes and many and elaborate operations. It is designed to be almost exclusively compiler coded.

To give maximum power and efficiency in compiler-generated code, the architects determined to make operations and address phrases entirely orthogonal, and to make operations and datatypes as orthogonal as possible. The VAX architecture is the purest extant in this respect.

The architecture assumes, and is designed to assist, a comprehensive operating system. The DEC VAX/VMS operating system was designed with and for the VAX architecture. VAX also became the most popular vehicle for the industry-standard UNIX operating system.

The architects considered and rejected several alternatives: soft architecture (several language-specific instruction sets implemented on a system-standard microprocessing architecture), stack architecture, and descriptor architecture.

Unit System

Basic information units are the 8-bit byte, 16-bit word, 32-bit longword, and 64-bit quadword. The longword serves a floating-point word and the quadword as a double-length floating-point word.

```
initiate780                            format780
A initiation of the DEC VAX780         A DEC VAX780 information units
format780                              A principal radix
configure780                           radix←2
space780                               A information units
name780                                digit←4
control780                             byte←8
decimal780                             word←16
                                       long←32
                                       quad←64
                                       A address capacity
configure780                           adrcap←radix*long
A configuration for the DEC VAX780     A page size
A memory capacity                      pagesize←radix*9
memcap←radix*long-2
```

PROGRAM 15-81   Basic parameters of the DEC VAX780.

Configuration.   Virtual storage is a linear vector of 2^{32} bytes divided into four regions of equal size. The first two regions are allocated on a per process basis; the upper two quarters are the system region, with the lower quarter used and the upper reserved.

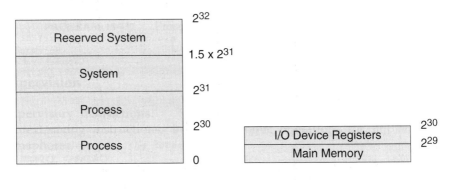

Virtual name-space   Physical name-space

FIGURE 15-82   Name-space configurations in the DEC VAX780.

Peripheral device registers are mapped onto the system region. The lower half of the physical name-space refers to physical memory, and the upper half is reserved for peripheral device registers. System control blocks containing 512 longwords for interrupt vectors are allocated in the system region.

Spaces

Memory.   Memory is a homogeneous vector of bytes; there are no alignment restrictions.

Working store.   There are 16 general registers of 32 bits each. Sixty-four–bit operands are stored in two adjacent registers and are addressed by the even-numbered register.

Control store.   Status is preserved in a 32-bit longword `status` (PSL). User execution mode allows access only to the lower 16-bits, the user PSW. Memory management uses three base registers and three limit registers for memory mapping.   Each of these is page aligned; their low-order 9 bits are 0.   A System Control Block base register points to a block that contains trap and interrupt vectors. A Process Control Block base register points to a block that contains the saved context for a process.

```
  space780                              name780
ค DEC VAX780 spaces                   ค DEC VAX780 space names
ค memory                              ค working store names
  memory←?(memcap,byte)ρradix         ค - argument pointer
ค working store                         Ap←12
ค - general registers                 ค - frame pointer
  reg←?(16,long)ρradix                  Fp←13
ค control store                       ค - stack pointer
ค - stack pointers                      Sp←14
  sp←?(5,long)ρradix                  ค - instruction address
ค - program status                      Pc←15
  status←?longρradix                  ค virtual address spaces
ค - indicators                          Program←0
  ind←?20ρradix                         Control←1
ค - trap code                           System←2
  trap←1+?7
ค - page tables base and length
  origin←4×?3ρmemcap÷4
  limit←?3ρradix*22
ค system control block base
  scb←?memcap
ค process control block base
  pcb←?memcap
ค - addressing depth
  adrdepth←?radix
ค - data type
  fl←0
ค - linear memory access
  interlock←?radix
ค - stop
  stop←?radix
```

PROGRAM 15-83   Spaces and embedding of the DEC VAX780.

The control space also includes 20 indicators, the type of error trapping, the limitation of indirect addressing to one level, the recognition of a floating-point operation in immediate addressing, the linearization of memory access to ensure proper interlocking, and the machine stop.

Register embedding.   Four of the general registers are implied by certain operations: the argument pointer (Ap), used by procedure calls; the frame pointer (Fp), used by procedure calls to point to an activation record on the stack; the stack pointer (Sp); and the instruction address (Pc). There are different stack pointers for the five execution modes, but only one of these is accessible at a time as Sp.

Memory embedding. All the I/O control and device registers are embedded, as are many other things. We do not show these addresses.

Programming model. The most distinctive feature is the variability of the instruction length. The datapath is just that of a register machine.

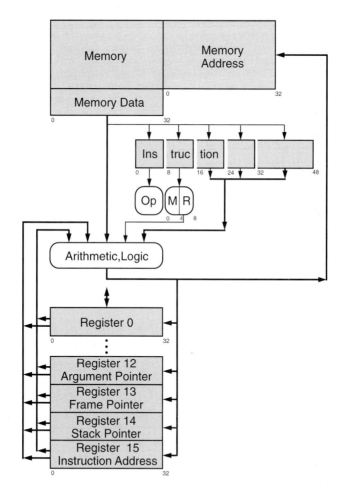

FIGURE 15-84   Programming model for the DEC VAX780.

The architecture lends itself readily to a one-adder implementation, or to one in which address calculation is independent of and concurrent with arithmetic. The programming model does not represent the different order of bytes in memory and registers.

Operand Specification

Number of addresses.   Dyadic operations can be specified with two addresses (the result replaces one of the operands) and with three addresses (one for each of the operands and one for the result).

Any number of address phrases may be used, so that each operation can take exactly as many as it naturally needs. Generally, zero to six address phrases suffice for an instruction; for the Case instructions, however, the number of address phrases that may be required is unlimited.

Address phrase.   An address phrase may be 1 to 10 bytes long to include an indexing prefix and operand specifier, or to include the constants of literal operand specifiers.

Operation Specification

Types of control.   System control is exerted with instructions, status words, and indicators. The 244 instructions use almost all the operation codes.

Mnemonics.   We use the DEC mnemonics. Each VAX780 instruction is represented as a separate function, even though some functions differ only by the lengths of the operands.

a→HALT	ADDP4	ADDF2	ADDD2	ADDB2	ADDW2	ADDL2	BBS
NOP	ADDP6	ADDF3	ADDD3	ADDB3	ADDW3	ADDL3	BBC
REI	SUBP4	SUBF2	SUBD2	SUBB2	SUBW2	SUBL2	BBSS
BPT	SUBP6	SUBF3	SUBD3	SUBB3	SUBW3	SUBL3	BBCS
RET	CVTPT	MULF2	MULD2	MULB2	MULW2	MULL2	BBSC
RSB	MULP	MULF3	MULD3	MULB3	MULW3	MULL3	BBCC
LDPCTX	CVTTP	DIVF2	DIVD2	DIVB2	DIVW2	DIVL2	BBSSI
SVPCTX	DIVP	DIVF3	DIVD3	DIVB3	DIVW3	DIVL3	BBCCI
CVTPS	MOVC3	CVTFB	CVTDB	BISB2	BISW2	BISL2	BLBS
CVTSP	CMPC3	CVTFW	CVTDW	BISB3	BISW3	BISL3	BLBC
INDEX	SCANC	CVTFL	CVTDL	BICB2	BICW2	BICL2	FFS
CRC	SPANC	CVTRFL	CVTRDL	BICB3	BICW3	BICL3	FFC
PROBER	MOVC5	CVTBF	CVTBD	XORB2	XORW2	XORL2	CMPV
PROBEW	CMPC5	CVTWF	CVTWD	XORB3	XORW3	XORL3	CMPZV
INSQUE	MOVTC	CVTLF	CVTLD	MNEGB	MNEGW	MNEGL	EXTV
REMQUE	MOVTUC	ACBF	ACBD	CASEB	CASEW	CASEL	EXTZV
BSBB	BSBW	MOVF	MOVD	MOVB	MOVW	MOVL	INSV
BRB	BRW	CMPF	CMPD	CMPB	CMPW	CMPL	ACBL
BNEQ	CVTWL	MNEGF	MNEGD	MCOMB	MCOMW	MCOML	AOBLSS
BEQL	CVTWB	TSTF	TSTD	BITB	BITW	BITL	AOBLEQ
BGTR	MOVP	EMODF	EMODD	CLRB	CLRW	CLRL	SOBGEQ
BLEQ	CMPP3	POLYF	POLYD	TSTB	TSTW	TSTL	SOBGTR
JSB	CVTPL	CVTFD	CVTDF	INCB	INCW	INCL	CVTLB
JMP	CMPP4	i	i	DECB	DECW	DECL	CVTLW
BGEQ	EDITPC	ADAWI	ASHL	CVTBL	BISPSW	ADWC	ASHP
BLSS	MATCHC	i	ASHQ	CVTBW	BICPSW	SBWC	CVTLP
BGTRU	LOCC	i	EMUL	MOVZBL	POPR	MTPR	CALLG
BLEQU	SKPC	i	EDIV	MOVZBW	PUSHR	MFPR	CALLS
BVC	MOVZWL	i	CLRQ	ROTL	CHMK	MOVPSL	XFC
BVS	ACBW	i	MOVQ	ACBB	CHME	PUSHL	i
BCC	MOVAW	i	MOVAQ	MOVAB	CHMS	MOVAL	i
BCS	PUSHAW	i	PUSHAQ	PUSHAB	CHMU	PUSHAL	i

PROGRAM 15-85   Operation-code list of the DEC VAX780.

⌐ *address arithmetic*
MOVA	Move Address BWLQ
INDEX	Compute Index
POPR	Pop Registers
PUSHL	Push Long
PUSHA	Push Address BWLQ
PUSHR	Push Registers
INSQUE	Insert Into Queue
REMQUE	Remove From Queue

⌐ *data handling*
MOVC	Move(Fitted)Characters
EXTV	Extract Field(Extended)
INSV	Insert Into Field
CMPC	Compare(Fitted)Characters
CMPV	Compare Field(Extended)
LOCC	Locate Character
SKPC	Skip Character
SANC	Scan/Span Characters
MATCHC	Match Characters
EDITPC	Edit
MOVTC	Translate(And Test)

⌐ *logic and shift*
CLR	Clear BWLQ
MCOM	Not BWL
BIS	Or(Replace)BWL
XOR	Exclusive Or(Replace)BWL
BIC	And Not(Replace)BWL
BIT	Bit Test BWL
FF	Rightmost One/Zero
ASH	Shift Arithmetic LQD
ROTL	Rotate Long

⌐ *binary arithmetic*
MOV	Move BWLQ
CVT	Convert BBWWLL To WLLBBW
MOVZWL	Extend BBW To WLL
MNEG	Negate BWL
TST	Test BWL
INC	Increment BWL
DEC	Decrement BWL
ADD	Add(Replace)BWL
ADWC	Add With Carry
SUB	Subtract(Replace)BWL
SBWC	Subtract With Carry
MUL	Multiply(Replace)BWL
EMUL	Multiply Extended
DIV	Divide(Replace)BWL
EDIV	Divide Extended
CMP	Compare BWL

⌐ *decimal arithmetic*
MOVP	Move Decimal
CVT	Convert LDDSDT To DLSDTD
ADDP	Add(Replace)Decimal
SUBP	Subtract(Replace)Decimal
MULP	Multiply Decimal
DIVP	Divide Decimal
CMPP	Compare(Fitted)Decimal

⌐ *floating-point arithmetic*
MOV	Move FD
CVT	Convert FD To DF
CVT	Convert FFFDDD To BWLBWL
CVTRL	Convert FD Rounded To Long
CVT	Convert BWLBWL To FFFDDD
MNEG	Negate FD
TST	Test FD
ADD	Add(Replace)FD
SUB	Subtract(Replace)FD
MUL	Multiply(Replace)FD
EMOD	Multiply Extended FD
POLY	Polynomial FD
DIV	Divide(Replace)FD
CMP	Compare FD

⌐ *sequencing*
NOP	No Operation
HALT	(Breakpoint)Stop
JMP	Branch Absolute
BR	Branch BW
BL	Branch On Less(E)(Unsigned)
BG	Branch On Greater(E)(Unsigned)
BEQL	Branch On Equal
BNEQ	Branch On Not Equal
BV	Branch On(No)Overflow
BC	Branch On(No)Carry
BB	Branch On One/Zero(And Set/Clear)
BLB	Branch On Low One/Zero
CASE	Case BWL
ACB	Branch On Compare BWLFD
AOBL	Branch On Increment Less(E)
SOBG	Branch On Decrement Greater(E)
JSB	Call
BSB	Call BW
CALL	Call Procedure(With Arguments)
RSB	Return
RET	Return From Procedure

⌐ *supervision*
REI	Return From Interrupt
LDPCTX	Load Process Context
SVPCTX	Save Process Context
MOVPSL	Store Status
BICPSW	And Not Status
BISPSW	Or Status
CHMK	Change To Kernel
CHME	Change To Execute
CHMS	Change To Supervisor
CHMU	Change To User
XFC	Extended Function
BBSSI	Branch On One And Set I
BBCCI	Branch On Zero And Clear I
ADAWI	Add Word I
MTPR	Load Internal Register
MFPR	Store Internal Register
PROBE	Test Read/Write Access
CRC	Cyclic Redundancy Check

Legend: B = Byte; D = Decimal/Double; E = Or Equal; F = Floating-point;
I = Interlocked; L = Long; Q = Quad; S = Separate;
T = Trailing; W = Word; () = option; / = alternative.

TABLE 15-86   Compressed instruction list of the DEC VAX780.

Instruction list. The compressed instruction list has one entry for instructions that differ only in one or two parameters; we abbreviate the mnemonics accordingly. We still distinguish, however, binary, decimal, and floating-point operations.

Instruction Structure

Machine-language syntax. The minimal syntax consists of a single byte occupied completely by the 8-bit operation code.

```
syntax780
a Opcode
```

PROGRAM 15-87   Instruction syntax of the DEC VAX780.

Instruction format. There is one format type. A 1-byte opcode is followed by an unrestricted number ($\geq$ 0) of address specifiers. Each address phrase consists of 1 address byte that specifies the addressing mode with a 4-bit field M and the register involved with the 4-bit field R. An immediate field is specified by two mode bits followed by 6 bits of immediate data (Program 15-91).

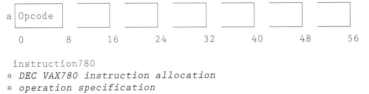

```
instruction780
a DEC VAX780 instruction allocation
a operation specification
Opcode←0+ι8
a operand specification
M←0+ι4
R←4+ι4
Immediate←2+ι6
```

PROGRAM 15-88   Instruction allocation in the DEC VAX780.

Status format. The status format contains
- A PDP11 compatibility mode bit
- An indication that a trace is in process
- An indication that an interruption occurred in the middle of a (long) instruction
- An indication of the use of an interruption stack
- The current mode (kernel, executive, supervisor, user)
- The previous mode
- The interrupt priority level
- Three interrupt-enable masks
- A trace mode indication
- Four conditions

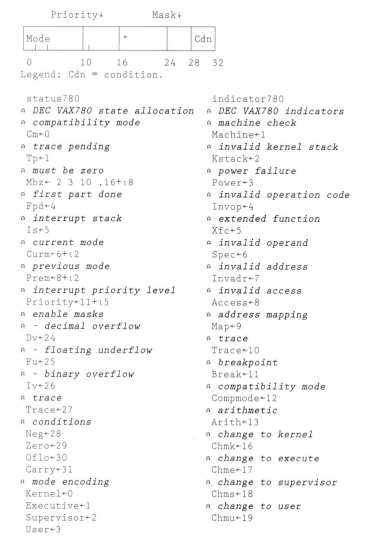

```
    Priority↓              Mask↓

  ┌──────────┬──────┬──────┬──────┬──────┐
  │ Mode     │      │  *   │      │ Cdn  │
  └──────────┴──────┴──────┴──────┴──────┘
  0          10    16      24  28  32
  Legend: Cdn = condition.


  status780                    indicator780
  ⋀ DEC VAX780 state allocation ⋀ DEC VAX780 indicators
  ⋀ compatibility mode         ⋀ machine check
   Cm←0                         Machine←1
  ⋀ trace pending              ⋀ invalid kernel stack
   Tp←1                         Kstack←2
  ⋀ must be zero               ⋀ power failure
   Mbz← 2 3 10 ,16+ι8           Power←3
  ⋀ first part done            ⋀ invalid operation code
   Fpd←4                        Invop←4
  ⋀ interrupt stack            ⋀ extended function
   Is←5                         Xfc←5
  ⋀ current mode               ⋀ invalid operand
   Curm←6+ι2                    Spec←6
  ⋀ previous mode              ⋀ invalid address
   Prem←8+ι2                    Invadr←7
  ⋀ interrupt priority level   ⋀ invalid access
   Priority←11+ι5               Access←8
  ⋀ enable masks               ⋀ address mapping
  ⋀ - decimal overflow          Map←9
   Dv←24                       ⋀ trace
  ⋀ - floating underflow        Trace←10
   Fu←25                       ⋀ breakpoint
  ⋀ - binary overflow           Break←11
   Iv←26                       ⋀ compatibility mode
  ⋀ trace                       Compmode←12
   Trace←27                    ⋀ arithmetic
  ⋀ conditions                  Arith←13
   Neg←28                      ⋀ change to kernel
   Zero←29                      Chmk←16
   Oflo←30                     ⋀ change to execute
   Carry←31                     Chme←17
  ⋀ mode encoding              ⋀ change to supervisor
   Kernel←0                     Chms←18
   Executive←1                 ⋀ change to user
   Supervisor←2                 Chmu←19
   User←3
```

PROGRAM 15-89   Status word and indicators of the DEC VAX780.

Indicators.   Indicators provide policing of invalid operands, addresses, and operations. Also, machine errors, the PDP11 compatibility mode, page access, index range control, and various overflow conditions are indicated.

15.3.3

Addressing

Direct addressing.   Reading and writing apply generally, and—where applicable—orthogonally, to immediate data, registers, and memory. Since numbers of any length are placed backward in memory, in contrast to alphanumeric character strings, two modes of memory reading and writing are distinguished. Writing from (single or multiple) registers is always backward.

This order must be reversed when registers are loaded. The length of character strings is given in bytes; all other sizes are in bits.

Address vector.   The address modes concern the size and space of the data and the address value. These three attributes are passed as a three-element vector to `read780` and `write780`. The allocation of this address vector and the identifiers of the various spaces are given in `address780`.

```
data←read780 address;size;location          address780
⍝ DEC VAX780 read from store               ⍝ DEC VAX780 address allocation
size←address[Size]                          ⍝ attributes
→CASE address[Space]                        Size←0
C0: ⍝ immediate                             Space←1
   →IF f1                                   Value←2
   THEN: ⍝ floating point                  ⍝ space identifiers
      data←size↑ 0 1 0 0 0 0 ,2↓address     immadr←0
      →ENDIF                                regadr←1
   ELSE: ⍝ fixed point                      memadr←2
      data←(-size)↑2↓address                stradr←3
   ENDIF:→ENDCASE                           ⍝ page table allocation
C1: ⍝ register                             ⍝ - valid page
   location←address[Value]+Φı⌈size÷long     Valid←0
   data←(-size)↑,reg[location;]             ⍝ - protection code
   →ENDCASE                                 Prc←1+ı4
C2: ⍝ memory numeric                       ⍝ - modified frame
   location←address[Value]+Φısize÷byte      Mdf←5
   data←,memory[0 map780 location;]         ⍝ - page frame
   →ENDCASE                                 Frame←12+ı20
C3: ⍝ memory character string
   location←address[Value]+ı⌈size
   data←memory[0 map780 location;]
ENDCASE:


address write780 data;size;location
⍝ DEC VAX780 write in store
size←address[Size]
→CASE address[Space]
C0: ⍝ immediate
   Invadr report 1
   →ENDCASE
C1: ⍝ register
   reg[address[Value];(-size⌊long)↑ılong]←(-size⌊long)↑data
   reg[16|address[Value]+1;(size=quad)/ılong]←(-long)↓data
   →ENDCASE
C2: ⍝ memory numeric
   location←1 map780 address[Value]+Φısize÷byte
   →OUT suppress780
   memory[location;]←byte wide data
   →ENDCASE
C3: ⍝ memory character string
   location←1 map780 address[Value]+ı⌈size
   →OUT suppress780
   memory[location;]←data
ENDCASE:
```

PROGRAM 15-90   Memory read and write in the DEC VAX780.

Segmentation

The four regions of the virtual memories can be considered as segments; no segmentation is provided for users.

Address Mapping

The virtual address is translated through page tables to the physical address using 512-byte pages (Program 15-140). The allocation of the 32-bit table entries is shown in `address780` (Program 15-90).

The system-region base register points to a contiguous system-region page table in physical memory. Control- and program-region base registers contain virtual addresses of page tables in the system region. This indirection makes the page tables in virtual memory for control and program regions contiguous and enables these page tables themselves to be paged. Stack pointers for user, supervisor, executive, and kernel modes contain pointers to the control and program regions.

Address Modification

Address modification is specified by 16 addressing modes.

```
 ┌──────────┐   ┌────┬────┬──────┬──────┬───────────────┐
 │ M│ Imm   │   │ M  │ R  │ byte │ word │          long │
 └──────────┘   └────┴────┴──────┴──────┴───────────────┘
 0 2       8    0    4    8      16     24              40
Legend:  Imm = immediate;  M = address mode;  R = register.
```

```
address←adr780 size;inst;index;dp;indirect    s←step780
a DEC VAX780 addressing                       a stepsize in DEC VAX780
inst←ifetch780 byte                           s←(size,long)[9=fld M]
→CASE((fld M)< 4 5 7 8 10)ι1
C0:  a immediate, mode 0 1 2 3
     address←size,immadr,inst[Immediate]
     →ENDCASE
C1:  a index plus address, mode 4
     index←(size÷byte)×magni reg[fld R;]
     Invadr report Pc=fld R
     address←size,memadr,index+disp780
     →ENDCASE
C2:  a register, mode 5 6
     address←size,regadr,fld R
     →ENDCASE
C3:  a predecrement, mode 7
     address←step780 decr780 fld R
     →ENDCASE
C4:  a postincrement, mode 8 9
     address←step780 incr780 fld R
     →ENDCASE
C5:  a index plus displacement, mode 10 11 12 13 14 15
     index←magni reg[fld R;]
     dp←ifetch780(byte,word,long)[((fld M)< 12 14)ι1]
     address←size,memadr,index+radixcompi dp
ENDCASE:→If(fld M)∈ 6 9 11 13 15
THEN:  a indirect, mode 6 9 11 13 15
     indirect←long,address[Space,Value]
     address←size,memadr,magni read780 indirect
ENDIF:
```

PROGRAM 15-91   Addressing in the DEC VAX780.

Index plus displacement.   Modes 10 to 15 obtain an index from a general register and use a byte, word, or long (full address) field in the instruction stream as displacement.   Mode 4 specifies a displacement as an address to which, in turn, all addressing modes and sizes apply, as shown in disp780. This indirect specification may be applied only once and must refer to memory. In this mode the index measures multiples of the data size, not of bytes.

Predecrement and postincrement.   The PDP11 predecrement and postincrement are found in modes 7 to 9. Postincrement can be used indirectly; the increment is then 4 bytes (the address size). The increment and decrement actions incr780 and decr780 are almost identical to the corresponding PDP11 functions.

```
      value←disp780;displacement
    ∩ DEC VAX780 general displacement
      adrdepth←adrdepth+1
      displacement←adr780 word
      value←displacement[Value]
      Invadr report(displacement[Space]≠memadr)∨adrdepth>1
      adrdepth←adrdepth-1
```

```
      address←size incr780 r;count           address←size decr780 r;count
    ∩ DEC VAX780 postincrement             ∩ DEC VAX780 predecrement
      address←size,memadr,magni reg[r;]     count←(magni reg[r;])-size÷byte
      count←address[Value]+size÷byte        address←size,memadr,count
      reg[r;]←long magnr count              reg[r;]←long magnr count
```

PROGRAM 15-92   Addressing modes in the DEC VAX780.

String addressing.   A string is specified by an address and a length. The string address is a regular byte address that points to the leftmost byte of the string; the length indicates the number of contiguous bytes of the string. These two items can be obtained with full-address modification. The string length is a 16-bit integer read from a register or from memory.

```
      address←adr780str;length;value ′      address←adr780dec;length;value
    ∩ DEC VAX780 string addressing        ∩ DEC VAX780 decimal addressing
      length←magni read780 adr780 word      length←0.5×1+magni read780 adr780 word
      value←(adr780 byte)[Value]            value←(adr780 byte)[Value]
      address←length,stradr,value           address←length,stradr,value
```

PROGRAM 15-93   String addressing in the DEC VAX780.

Decimal addressing.   A decimal number is represented as a data string. The length, however, refers to the number of decimal digits, and not to the string length in bytes. All decimal numbers are signed and use half a byte for a sign or a digit. The size parameter that is supplied by the decimal addressing functions gives the number of bytes needed for digits and sign. The actual number of bytes to be addressed depends upon the decimal format that is used.

Address Level

Indirect addressing.   Indirect addressing applies to the register, postincrement, and index-plus-displacement modes. Noticeably absent is an indirect predecrement mode, as in the PDP11.

Immediate addressing.   Immediate data are specified in modes 0 to 3 by an all-zeros 2-bit mode field and a 6-bit immediate field. These six bits are extended either to a binary positive integer or to a positive floating-point value. In the latter case, the leftmost three immediate bits are used as low-order exponent bits, and the rightmost three immediate bits are used as high-order coefficient bits; the sign bit is made 0, and the high-order exponent bit is made 1. This arrangement gives 64 floating-point values that vary from 0.5 up to 128 with increments varying from one sixteenth to eight.

Address Arithmetic

Index operations.   Since the index values reside in general registers, ordinary fixed-point arithmetic can be used to perform operations upon the indices. Some specialized operations, however, are supplied for address generation, system stack access, subrange checking, queue insertion, and queue deletion.

```
a MOVAB  Move Address Byte   a PUSHAB Push Address Byte
a MOVAW  Move Address Word   a PUSHAW Push Address Word
a MOVAL  Move Address Long   a PUSHAL Push Address Long
a MOVAQ  Move Address Quad   a PUSHAQ Push Address Quad
a INDEX  Compute Index       a PUSHR  Push Registers
a POPR   Pop Registers       a INSQUE Insert Into Queue
a PUSHL  Push Long           a REMQUE Remove From Queue
```

TABLE 15-94   Index arithmetic instructions of the DEC VAX780.

Address calculation.   Any specifiable address can be placed in any location. Both specifications may use full mode control. The operation may be for a byte, word, longword, or quadword operand size. Sign and zero value of the results are signaled (Program 15-100).

```
MOVAL;od                              INDEX;sub;low;high;size;index;rl
ꓥ DEC VAX780 Move Address Long        ꓥ DEC VAX780 Compute Index
od←long magnr(adr780 long)[Value]     sub←radixcompi read780 adr780 long
(adr780 long) write780 od             low←radixcompi read780 adr780 long
signal780NZ od                        high←radixcompi read780 adr780 long
                                      size←radixcompi read780 adr780 long
                                      index←radixcompi read780 adr780 long
                                      rl←long radixcompr(index+sub)×size
                                      (adr780 long) write780 rl
                                      Arith report(sub<low)∨sub>high)
                                      signal780NZ rl WHERE trap←7
                                      status[Carry]←0
```

PROGRAM 15-95   Address movement and index computation in the DEC VAX780.

Compute index.   A subscript is added to an index and this sum is multiplied with a size. The subscript is checked for upper and lower bounds. The instruction is intended for arrays of fixed-length elements in languages such as COBOL, FORTRAN, and PL/I. The instruction may be applied repeatedly to each dimension of a higher-order array.

System stack access.   The system stack may be accessed by specifying it explicitly in reading with postincrement mode (pop), or in writing with predecrement (push). These actions are described by the system-stack access functions `pop780` and `push780`, which give implied system stack access. `pop780reg` and `push780reg` pop and push groups of registers, specified by an integer vector of register addresses.

```
data←pop780                              push780 data
A DEC VAX780 read from stack     A DEC VAX780 write onto stack
data←read780 long incr780 Sp      (long decr780 Sp) write780 data


pop780reg who                            push780reg who
A pop selected registers         A push selected registers
→WHILE 0≠ρwho                     →WHILE 0≠ρwho
   reg[1↑who;]←pop780                push780 reg[1↑who;]
   who←1↓who                          who←1↓who
   →∆                                  →∆
ENDWHILE:                        ENDWHILE:
```

PROGRAM 15-96   System stack access in the DEC VAX780.

Stack addressing operations.   A byte, word, or quadword address can be pushed as a long quantity onto the system stack. Push Long pushes a longword onto the system stack. There are no corresponding pop instructions.

A selection from the first 14 registers can be pushed onto, or popped from, the system stack. (Stack pointer and instruction address are excluded.) The desired registers are specified by the first 14 bits of a word-size logical vector.

```
PUSHL;od                                 POPR;who
A DEC VAX780 Push Long           A DEC VAX780 Pop Registers
od←read780 adr780 long           who←15↑Φread780 adr780 word
push780 od                        pop780reg who/ι15
signal780NZ od


PUSHAW;od                                PUSHR;who
A DEC VAX780 Push Address Word   A DEC VAX780 Push Registers
od←long magnr(adr780 word)[Value]  who←15↑Φread780 adr780 word
push780 od                        push780regΦwho/ι15
signal780NZ od
```

PROGRAM 15-97   Stack operations in the DEC VAX780.

Queue insertion and deletion.   Insert Into Queue and Remove From Queue assume a queue that is organized with forward and backward chaining using aligned long-address pairs. The memory actions of each of these operations are atomic (called *interlocked* by DEC) to ensure the integrity of the operation.

15.3.4
Data

Character Strings

Character set and size.   The 8-bit ACSII character set is used. The character encoding is visible in operations that use the 8-bit bytes as logical or numeric strings.

```
INSQUE;entry;pred;succ
ᴀ DEC VAX780 Insert Into Queue
entry←(adr780 long)[Value]
pred←(adr780 long)[Value]
succ←magni read780 long,memadr,pred
Spec report 0≠4|entry,pred,succ
→OUT suppress780
interlock←1
ᴀ entry forward to successor
(long,memadr,entry) write780 long magnr succ
ᴀ predecessor forward to entry
(long,memadr,pred) write780 long magnr entry
ᴀ entry backward to predecessor
(long,memadr,entry+4) write780 long magnr pred
ᴀ successor backward to entry
(long,memadr,succ+4) write780 long magnr entry
interlock←0
status[Neg]←succ<pred
status[Zero]←succ=pred
status[Oflo]←entry=succ
status[Carry]←succ>pred


REMQUE;entry;pred;succ
ᴀ DEC VAX780 Remove From Queue
entry←(adr780 long)[Value]
pred←magni read780 long,memadr,entry+4
succ←magni read780 long,memadr,entry
Spec report 0≠4|entry,pred,succ
→OUT suppress780
interlock←1
ᴀ predecessor forward to successor
(long,memadr,pred) write780 long magnr succ
ᴀ successor backward to predecessor
(long,memadr,succ+4) write780 long magnr pred
(adr780 long) write780 long magnr entry
interlock←0
status[Neg]←succ<pred
status[Zero]←succ=pred
status[Oflo]←entry=succ
status[Carry]←succ>pred
```

PROGRAM 15-98   Queue operations in the DEC VAX780.

Character-string formats.   Eight-bit characters may be used in strings of length 0 to 65535.

Queue.   Two longwords are used for list pointers in a doubly linked list. They contain either relative or absolute 32-bit addresses.

Logical

Logical formats.   Boolean vectors usually have fixed-length byte, word, or longword format.

Variable-length bit vectors are specified by a base (with byte resolution), a start position relative to the base (with bit resolution), and a size in bits. These vectors are processed more slowly than are the fixed-length vectors, since their neighbors must remain unchanged. The vector length is limited to 32 bits. The vector may be located in memory or in working store. When the vector is located in working store, it must start within the addressed register. The backwards byte permeates the definition.

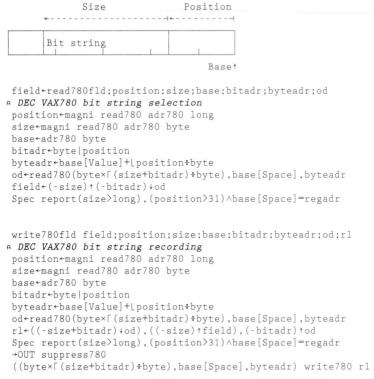

```
field←read780fld;position;size;base;bitadr;byteadr;od
ᴀ DEC VAX780 bit string selection
position←magni read780 adr780 long
size←magni read780 adr780 byte
base←adr780 byte
bitadr←byte|position
byteadr←base[Value]+⌊position÷byte
od←read780(byte×⌈(size+bitadr)÷byte),base[Space],byteadr
field←(-size)↑(-bitadr)↓od
Spec report(size>long),(position>31)∧base[Space]=regadr


write780fld field;position;size;base;bitadr;byteadr;od;r1
ᴀ DEC VAX780 bit string recording
position←magni read780 adr780 long
size←magni read780 adr780 byte
base←adr780 byte
bitadr←byte|position
byteadr←base[Value]+⌊position÷byte
od←read780(byte×⌈(size+bitadr)÷byte),base[Space],byteadr
r1←((-size+bitadr)↓od),((-size)↑field),(-bitadr)↑od
Spec report(size>long),(position>31)∧base[Space]=regadr
→OUT suppress780
((byte×⌈(size+bitadr)÷byte),base[Space],byteadr) write780 r1
```

PROGRAM 15-99   Field access in the DEC VAX780.

Fixed-Point Numbers

Binary notation and allocation.   Byte, word, or longword integers use 2's-complement notation.   The 0-to-32–bit variable-length bit fields can be compared as signed 2's-complement integers or as unsigned binary integers.

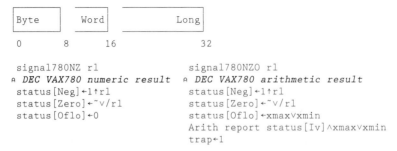

```
signal780NZ r1                  signal780NZO r1
ᴀ DEC VAX780 numeric result     ᴀ DEC VAX780 arithmetic result
status[Neg]←1↑r1                status[Neg]←1↑r1
status[Zero]←˜∨/r1             status[Zero]←˜∨/r1
status[Oflo]←0                 status[Oflo]←xmax∨xmin
                                Arith report status[Iv]∧xmax∨xmin
                                trap←1
```

PROGRAM 15-100   Binary numbers in the DEC VAX780.

Binary overflow.   Binary fixed-point overflow causes an arithmetic interruption when not masked off by the Iv mask bit in the status word. The Arith indicator is also used for overflow or underflow in other representations and for signaling division by 0. The cause of the interruption is indicated by the trap code, which is stacked as part of the interruption action.

Packed decimal.   All decimal arithmetic applies to 0-to-31–digit integers and uses signed-magnitude notation. The packed format has two digits per byte and the sign as the last four bits in the low-order byte. This format is identical to the IBM System/360's packed decimal (1965).

Overflow during representation causes an arithmetic interrupt when the decimal overflow mask Dv in the status word is 1; the trap code 6 identifies the overflow as decimal. The sign and overflow conditions are set in all decimal instructions.

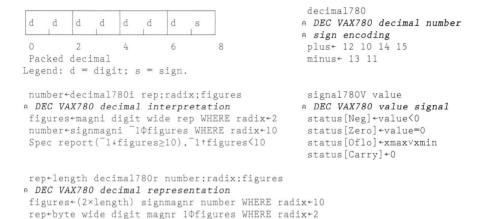

```
 _____          decimal780
| d   d | d   d | d   d | d   s |      ค DEC VAX780 decimal number
|___|___|___|___|___|___|___|___|      ค sign encoding
 0       2       4       6       8     plus← 12 10 14 15
Packed decimal                         minus← 13 11
Legend: d = digit; s = sign.


number←decimal780i rep;radix;figures       signal780V value
ค DEC VAX780 decimal interpretation        ค DEC VAX780 value signal
figures←magni digit wide rep WHERE radix←2 status[Neg]←value<0
number←signmagni ‾1Φfigures WHERE radix←10 status[Zero]←value=0
Spec report(‾1↓figures≥10),‾1↑figures<10   status[Oflo]←xmax∨xmin
                                           status[Carry]←0


rep←length decimal780r number;radix;figures
ค DEC VAX780 decimal representation
figures←(2×length) signmagnr number WHERE radix←10
rep←byte wide digit magnr 1Φfigures WHERE radix←2
Arith report status[Dv]∧xmax∨xmin WHERE trap←6
```

PROGRAM 15-101   Packed decimal number in the DEC VAX780.

Unpacked decimal.   For conversion purposes, there are two unpacked decimal formats, with one digit per byte. The sign either is the first byte (called *leading separate*) or is encoded as a zone in the last byte (called *trailing embedded*). The latter format is similar to the 360's unpacked decimal.

Unpacked decimal digits have the two low-order zone bits 1. In the representation functions, these bits are set by adding 48 to the digit or sign values. Unpacked representation signals overflow in the same manner in packed representation (Program 15-102).

Floating-Point Numbers

Closure and normal form.   Floating point is normalized with hidden bit. There is no gradual underflow.

Floating-point format.   Floating point has either a single-precision longword or a double-precision quadword format. The difference is in the number of coefficient bits.

Floating-point representation.   The floating-point coefficient is represented as a binary fraction with signed-magnitude notation. The exponent is a power

s		z	d	z	d	z	d		z	d	z	d	z	d	s	d

```
0       1       2       3       4    0       1       2       3       4
Decimal with separate leading sign  Decimal with trailing embedded sign
Legend: d = digit; s = sign; z = zone.
```

```
number←decimal780tΔi rep;radix;digits;sign
⍝ DEC VAX780 trailing embedded sign decimal interpretation
digits←magni 0 4 ↓rep WHERE radix←2
sign←magni ¯1 4 ↑rep
Spec report(3≠magni ¯1 ¯4 ↓rep),sign<10
number←signmagni sign,digits WHERE radix←10


rep←length decimal780tΔr number;radix;figures
⍝ DEC VAX780 trailing embedded sign decimal representation
figures←length signmagnr number WHERE radix←10
rep←byte magnr 1↓figures+48 WHERE radix←2
rep[length-2;⍳4]←digit magnr 1↑figures
Arith report status[Dv]∧xmax∨xmin WHERE trap←6


number←decimal780sΔi rep;radix;digits;sign;plus;minus
⍝ DEC VAX780 leading separate sign decimal interpretation
digits←magni 1 4 ↓rep WHERE radix←2
sign←magni 1 8 ↑rep WHERE plus← 43 32 WHERE minus←45
Spec report(3≠magni ¯1 ¯4 ↓rep),~sign∊plus,minus
number←signmagni sign,digits WHERE radix←10


rep←length decimal780sΔr number;radix;figures;plus;minus
⍝ DEC VAX780 leading separate sign decimal representation
plus←43-48 WHERE minus←45-48
figures←length signmagnr number WHERE radix←10
rep←byte magnr figures+48 WHERE radix←2
Arith report status[Dv]∧xmax∨xmin WHERE trap←6
```

PROGRAM 15-102   Unpacked decimal number in the DEC VAX780.

```
↓Sign
```

Exp	Coefficient	Long		Double

```
0       9                       32                          64
Legend: Exp = exponent.
```

```
fl780 size
⍝ DEC VAX780 floating-point number
⍝ base
 base←2
⍝ sign encoding
 plus←0
 minus←1
⍝ exponent allocation
 Exp←1+⍳8
⍝ coefficient allocation
 Coef← 0 0 ,9+⍳size-9
⍝ radix point
 point←0⊥⍴1↓Coef
⍝ extreme exponent
 extexp←radix*0⊥⍴1↓Exp
```

PROGRAM 15-103   Floating-point format in the DEC VAX780.

of 2 and is represented in excess-128 notation. Zero is defined as a positive coefficient sign with 0 exponent. A negative sign with 0 exponent gives a *reserved* operand indication.

Overflow during representation always sets the Arithmetic indicator and causes an interruption. Underflow either gives a 0 result or sets the Arithmetic indicator, depending upon the underflow mask bit in the status word (as in the 360). The trap code gives the cause of the interruption.

```
number←fl780i rep;exponent;coefficient;plus;minus
ᴀ DEC VAX780 floating-point interpretation
fl780ρrep
exponent←biasi rep[Exp]
→IF exponent≠-extexp
THEN: ᴀ normal range
   coefficient←signmagni insertbit rep[Coef]
   number←coefficient×base*exponent-point
   →ENDIF
ELSE: ᴀ zero or reserved
   number←0
   Spec report 1↑rep[Coef]
ENDIF:


rep←size fl780r number;exponent;coefficient;plus;minus;uflo;xmax;xmin
ᴀ DEC VAX780 floating-point representation
fl780 size
(-extexp) normalize number
rep←sizeρ0
rep[Coef]←hidebit(ρCoef) signmagnr round coefficient
rep[Exp]←(ρExp) biasr exponent+xmax
ᴀ out of domain
uflo←(exponent≤-extexp)∧number≠0
Arith report xmax∨status[Fu]∧uflo
trap←(3×xmax)+5×uflo
ᴀ zero for underflow
rep←rep∧˜uflo∧˜status[Fu]
```

PROGRAM 15-104   Floating-point representation in the DEC VAX780.

15.3.5

Operations

Data Handling

Data handling is quite complete, including moves, format and code transformation, search, and comparison operations.

a MOVC3	Move Characters	a LOCC	Locate Character
a MOVC5	Move Fitted Characters	a SKPC	Skip Character
a EXTV	Extract Field	a SCANC	Scan Characters
a EXTZV	Extract Field Extended	a SPANC	Span Characters
a INSV	Insert Into Field	a MATCHC	Match Characters
a CMPC3	Compare Characters	a MOVTC	Translate
a CMPC5	Compare Fitted Characters	a MOVTUC	Translate And Test
a CMPV	Compare Field	a EDITPC	Edit
a CMPZV	Compare Field Extended		

TABLE 15-105   Data-handling instructions of the DEC VAX780.

Interruptible instruction.   Since the length of a character string may be 65535 bytes, the character-handling instructions can become relatively time consuming. Hence they are made interruptible. General registers 0 to 6 are used, as needed, to record the address and length values at the moment of interruption. The First Part Done indicator `Fpd` is set to 1 to indicate that the first part of the instruction—the fetching and interpretation of the instruction bytes—is done. When such an instruction is resumed following an interruption, the register contents are used and further updated.

We describe character-string operations as a single action, which is indeed their architectural property, even when the fields overlap. Furthermore, we note that, after the parameters are obtained, the contents of the first set of registers become unpredictable, since they are used by the implementation. We also show the contents of these registers at the end of the operation, which is part of the architecture. We do not show the action of an interruption halfway through an instruction.

Data movement.   Data movement is performed on a whole character string at once, not one character at a time. It may be specified with or without *fitting*. Move Characters specifies a source and destination address and a single length; the instruction matches the paradigm of Chapter 4. In Move Fitted Character the source and destination field differ in length; the instruction specifies two lengths and a fill character that extends a source field that is shorter than the destination field.

The carry indicates that the source operand is shorter than the destination operand. The negative condition is not useful, since it considers the two lengths as signed values (which they are not).

```
MOVC5;source;dest;fill;od;rl;odleft;odend;rlend;oversize
ρ DEC VAX780 Move Fitted Characters
source←adr780str
fill←read780 adr780 byte               regend780 par
dest←adr780str                         ρ DEC VAX780 parameters in registers
regend780?6ρadrcap                     reg[ιρpar;]←long magnr par
od←read780 source WHERE ind[Fpd]←1
rl←(dest[Size],byte)↑od⊤(dest[Size],byte)ρfill
dest write780 rl
odleft←0⌈source[Size]-dest[Size] WHERE ind[Fpd]←0
odend←source[Value]+source[Size]⌊dest[Size]
rlend←dest[Value]+dest[Size]
regend780 odleft,odend,0,rlend,0,0
oversize←(signed780 source[Size])-signed780 dest[Size]
signal780NZ word radixcompr oversize
status[Carry]←source[Size]<dest[Size]


result←signed780 operand
ρ DEC VAX780 signed interpretation
result←radixcompi word magnr operand
```

PROGRAM 15-106   Move characters in the DEC VAX780.

Format and code transformation.   There is a complete set of conversion operations among datatypes. Conversions between the fixed- and floating-point formats are in the floating-point operation set.

Bit-string operations. Bit strings are extracted according to the specifications shown in Program 15-99. The strings are interpreted either as signed values or as positive values and are converted to a long binary format. Conversely, a binary value may be inserted into a bit string, ignoring any high-order bits.

```
EXTV;operand;rl                 INSV
A DEC VAX780 Extract Field      A DEC VAX780 Insert Into Field
operand←radixcompi read780fld    write780fld read780 adr780 long
rl←long radixcompr operand       status[Neg,Zero,Oflo,Carry]←0
→OUT suppress780
(adr780 long) write780 rl
signal780NZO rl
status[Carry]←0
```

PROGRAM 15-107   Field extraction and insertion in the DEC VAX780.

Character and field comparison. In character-string comparison, the source characters are compared to the destination characters, but do not replace them. Field comparison interprets the source bit-string as a binary number and compares it to a long binary destination operand.

```
CMPC3;source;dest;operand;comparand;match;odleft;odend;cdend
A DEC VAX780 Compare Characters
source←adr780str
dest←source[Size,Space],(adr780 byte)[Value]
regend780?4ρadrcap
operand←radixcompi read780 source WHERE ind[Fpd]←1
comparand←radixcompi read780 dest
match←(operand≠comparand)ι1
odleft←source[Size]-match WHERE ind[Fpd]←0
odend←source[Value]+match
cdend←dest[Value]+match
regend780 odleft,odend,odleft,cdend
signal780NZ byte radixcompr operand[match]-comparand[match]
status[Carry]←~word carryfrom operand[match],-comparand[match]


CMPZV;operand;comparand
A DEC VAX780 Compare Field Extended
operand←magni read780fld
comparand←radixcompi read780 adr780 long
signal780NZ long radixcompr comparand-operand
status[Carry]←comparand<operand
```

PROGRAM 15-108   Character and field comparison in the DEC VAX780.

Data search. Locate Characters notes the first occurrence (left to right) of a given character in a character string. The various result parameters are left in the first four general registers. The zero condition is set when no match is found.

Scan Characters translates a character string by means of a table, then selects from each translated byte the bits that are specified by a mask and denotes the first bit that is 1.

Translation. Translate replaces the bytes of a source character-string by their translation, as obtained from a specified table. When the result string is longer than the source string, the source string is extended with fill characters.

```
        LOCC;char;source;data;match;odleft;odend
      ⍝ DEC VAX780 Locate Character
        char←magni read780 adr780 byte
        source←adr780str
        regend780?2ρadrcap
        data←magni read780 source WHERE ind[Fpd]←1
        match←dataιchar
        odleft←source[Size]-match WHERE ind[Fpd]←0
        odend←source[Value]+match
        regend780 odleft,odend
        status[Neg,Oflo,Carry]←0
        status[Zero]←match=ρdata

        SCANC;source;table;data;mask;match;odleft;odend
      ⍝ DEC VAX780 Scan Characters
        source←adr780str
        table←(adr780 byte)[Value]
        regend780?4ρadrcap
        data←magni read780 source WHERE ind[Fpd]←1
        mask←((ρdata),byte)ρread780 adr780 byte
        match←(∨/mask∧memory[table+data;])ι1
        odleft←source[Size]-match WHERE ind[Fpd]←0
        odend←source[Value]+match
        regend780 odleft,odend,0,table
        status[Neg,Oflo,Carry]←0
        status[Zero]←match=ρdata
```

PROGRAM 15-109   Character string search in the DEC VAX780.

```
   MOVTC;source;fill;table;dest;data;rl;odleft;odend;rlend
 ⍝ DEC VAX780 Translate
   source←adr780str
   fill←read780 adr780 byte
   table←(adr780 byte)[Value]
   dest←adr780str
   regend780?5ρadrcap
   data←magni read780 source WHERE ind[Fpd]←1
   rl←(dest[Size],byte)↑memory[table+data;]⍪(dest[Size],byte)ρfill
   dest write780 rl
   odleft←0⌈source[Size]-dest[Size] WHERE ind[Fpd]←0
   odend←source[Value]+source[Size]⌊dest[Size]
   rlend←dest[Value]+dest[Size]
   regend780 odleft,odend,0,rlend,0
   status[Neg,Oflo,Carry]←0
   status[Zero]←source[Size]<dest[Size]
```

PROGRAM 15-110   Translate in the DEC VAX780.

Edit.   The packed decimal to character-string edit operation resembles the IBM 360 Edit operation.

Logic

The logical operations include the subset of the connectives and the test operations found in the PDP11, as well as a rightmost 0 or 1 test and an all-zeros test. We show the shift and rotate operations as part of the logical operations.

Connectives.   The connectives are with byte, word, and longword operands. The dyadic operations are with three addresses and with two addresses (where the result replaces one operand). Clear, the set-to-0 connective, is also with

a	CLRB	Clear Byte	a	BICB2	And Not Replace Byte
a	CLRW	Clear Word	a	BICB3	And Not Byte
a	CLRL	Clear Long	a	BICW2	And Not Replace Word
a	CLRQ	Clear Quad	a	BICW3	And Not Word
a	MCOMB	Not Byte	a	BICL2	And Not Replace Long
a	MCOMW	Not Word	a	BICL3	And Not Long
a	MCOML	Not Long	a	BITB	Bit Test Byte
a	BISB2	Or Replace Byte	a	BITW	Bit Test Word
a	BISB3	Or Byte	a	BITL	Bit Test Long
a	BISW2	Or Replace Word	a	FFC	Rightmost Zero
a	BISW3	Or Word	a	FFS	Rightmost One
a	BISL2	Or Replace Long	a	ASHL	Shift Arithmetic Long
a	BISL3	Or Long	a	ASHQ	Shift Arithmetic Quad
a	XORB2	Exclusive Or Replace Byte	a	ROTL	Rotate Long
a	XORB3	Exclusive Or Byte			
a	XORW2	Exclusive Or Replace Word			
a	XORW3	Exclusive Or Word			
a	XORL2	Exclusive Or Replace Long			
a	XORL3	Exclusive Or Long			

TABLE 15-111   Logical and shift operations of the DEC VAX780.

a quadword result, which may be used to generate a double-length floating-point value of 0. Bit Test forms the AND of the operands and sets the conditions to indicate an all-zeros result, as in the PDP11.

```
CLRQ                                  MCOML;rl
a DEC VAX780 Clear Quad               a DEC VAX780 Not Long
(adr780 quad) write780 quadρ0         rl←~read780 adr780 long
signal780NZ quadρ0                    (adr780 long) write780 rl
                                      signal780NZ rl


BICB2;od1;dest;od2;rl
a DEC VAX780 And Not Replace Byte     BISW3;od1;od2;rl
od1←read780 adr780 byte               a DEC VAX780 Or Word
dest←adr780 byte                      od1←read780 adr780 word
od2←read780 dest                      od2←read780 adr780 word
rl←od2∧~od1                           rl←od2∨od1
dest write780 rl                      (adr780 word) write780 rl
signal780NZ rl                        signal780NZ rl
```

PROGRAM 15-112   Connectives of the DEC VAX780.

Logical vector operations.   Consistently with the backwards byte, the rightmost—rather than the leftmost—1 or 0 bit is noted.

```
BITW;od1;od2;rl                  FFC;field;match;rl
a DEC VAX780 Bit Test Word       a DEC VAX780 Rightmost Zero
od1←read780 adr780 word          field←read780fld
od2←read780 adr780 word          match←(Φfield)ιl
rl←od1∧od2                       rl←long radixcompr match
signal780NZ rl                   (adr780 long) write780 rl
                                 status[Neg,Oflo,Carry]←0
                                 status[Zero]←match=ρfield
```

PROGRAM 15-113   All-zero test and rightmost-zero count in the DEC VAX780.

Shift.   Binary arithmetic shift applies to long and quad operand lengths. There is no logical right shift.

Rotate.   There is just one Rotate; its operand is a longword; operand and result are always addressed separately.

```
ASHQ;shift;operand;rl
  A DEC VAX780 Shift Arithmetic Quad
  shift←radixcompi read780 adr780 byte
  operand←radixcompi read780 adr780 quad
  rl←quad radixcomprLoperand×radix*shift
  (adr780 quad) write780 rl
  signal780NZO rl
  status[Carry]←0


ROTL;shift;od;rl
  A DEC VAX780 Rotate Long
  shift←radixcompi read780 adr780 byte
  od←read780 adr780 long
  rl←shiftΦod
  (adr780 long) write780 rl
  signal780NZ rl
```

PROGRAM 15-114   Shift and Rotate in the DEC VAX780.

Fixed-Point Arithmetic

Binary arithmetic applies systematically to byte, word, and longword operands; the dyadic operations are all with three and two addresses. The monadic operations include size conversion, negation, increment, decrement, and sign test. Provisions are made for extended-precision operation with longword operands.

a	MOVB	Move Byte	a	ADDB2	Add Replace Byte
a	MOVW	Move Word	a	ADDB3	Add Byte
a	MOVL	Move Long	a	ADDW2	Add Replace Word
a	MOVQ	Move Quad	a	ADDW3	Add Word
a	CVTBW	Convert Byte To Word	a	ADDL2	Add Replace Long
a	CVTBL	Convert Byte To Long	a	ADDL3	Add Long
a	CVTWB	Convert Word To Byte	a	ADWC	Add W Carry
a	CVTWL	Convert Word To Long	a	SUBB2	Subtract Replace Byte
a	CVTLB	Convert Long To Byte	a	SUBB3	Subtract Byte
a	CVTLW	Convert Long To Word	a	SUBW2	Subtract Replace Word
a	MOVZBW	Extend Byte To Word	a	SUBW3	Subtract Word
a	MOVZBL	Extend Byte To Long	a	SUBL2	Subtract Replace Long
a	MOVZWL	Extend Word To Long	a	SUBL3	Subtract Long
a	MNEGB	Negate Byte	a	SBWC	Subtract W Carry
a	MNEGW	Negate Word	a	MULB2	Multiply Replace Byte
a	MNEGL	Negate Long	a	MULB3	Multiply Byte
a	TSTB	Test Byte	a	MULW2	Multiply Replace Word
a	TSTW	Test Word	a	MULW3	Multiply Word
a	TSTL	Test Long	a	MULL2	Multiply Replace Long
a	INCB	Increment Byte	a	MULL3	Multiply Long
a	INCW	Increment Word	a	EMUL	Multiply Extended
a	INCL	Increment Long	a	DIVB2	Divide Replace Byte
a	DECB	Decrement Byte	a	DIVB3	Divide Byte
a	DECW	Decrement Word	a	DIVW2	Divide Replace Word
a	DECL	Decrement Long	a	DIVW3	Divide Word
			a	DIVL2	Divide Replace Long
			a	DIVL3	Divide Long
			a	EDIV	Divide Extended
			a	CMPB	Compare Byte
			a	CMPW	Compare Word
			a	CMPL	Compare Long

Legend: W = With.

TABLE 15-115   Fixed-point instructions of the DEC VAX780.

Load and Store.   Loading and storing are accomplished with the Move operation, where each address can apply either to memory or to a register. A format is extended by supplying extra 0 bits to the left.

```
MOVW;od
  ⋀ DEC VAX780 Move Word
  od←read780 adr780 word
  (adr780 word) write780 od
  signal780NZ od
```

```
MOVZBL;od
  ⋀ DEC VAX780 Extend Byte To Long
  od←(-long)↑read780 adr780 byte
  (adr780 long) write780 od
  signal780NZ od
```

PROGRAM 15-116   Move and Extend in the DEC VAX780.

Size conversion.   All three operand sizes can be converted to the other two as signed quantities. Overflow is signaled, and the result sign is noted.

```
CVTLB;operand;rl
  ⋀ DEC VAX780 Convert Long To Byte
  operand←radixcompi read780 adr780 long
  rl←byte radixcompr operand
  (adr780 byte) write780 rl
  signal780NZO rl
  status[Carry]←0
```

PROGRAM 15-117   Fixed-point size conversion in the DEC VAX780.

Sign control.   The sign can be negated; as in the PDP11, there is no Make Absolute operation.

Increment and decrement.   These operations add and subtract 1 from the operand. The setting of the carry indicator reflects the carry in Increment and the borrow in Decrement, as in the PDP11.

```
MNEGW;operand;rl
  ⋀ DEC VAX780 Negate Word
  operand←radixcompi read780 adr780 word
  rl←word radixcompr-operand
  (adr780 word) write780 rl
  signal780NZO rl
  status[Carry]←⁻status[Zero]
```

```
TSTB;od
  ⋀ DEC VAX780 Test Byte
  od←read780 adr780 byte
  signal780NZ od
  status[Carry]←0
```

```
INCB;dest;count;rl
  ⋀ DEC VAX780 Increment Byte
  dest←adr780 byte
  count←radixcompi read780 dest
  rl←byte radixcompr count+1
  dest write780 rl
  signal780NZO rl
  status[Carry]←count=⁻1
```

```
DECL;dest;count;rl
  ⋀ DEC VAX780 Decrement Long
  dest←adr780 long
  count←radixcompi read780 dest
  rl←long radixcompr count-1
  dest write780 rl
  signal780NZO rl
  status[Carry]←count=0
```

PROGRAM 15-118   Binary monadic arithmetic in the DEC VAX780.

Add and Subtract.   In contrast to the PDP11, the VAX780 has Add With Carry. Zero-result signaling, however, still is for the current partial addition, not for the total extended addition. In subtraction a borrow is noted instead of a carry.

```
ADDW3;addend;augend;sum;rl
⍝ DEC VAX780 Add Word
 addend←radixcompi read780 adr780 word
 augend←radixcompi read780 adr780 word
 sum←augend+addend
 rl←word radixcompr sum
 (adr780 word) write780 rl
 signal780NZO rl
 status[Carry]←word carryfrom augend,addend


SUBL2;dest;addend;augend;sum;rl
⍝ DEC VAX780 Subtract Replace Long
 addend←radixcompi˜read780 adr780 long
 dest←adr780 long
 augend←radixcompi read780 dest
 sum←augend+addend+1
 rl←long radixcompr sum
 dest write780 rl
 signal780NZO rl
 status[Carry]←˜long carryfrom augend,addend,1


SBWC;dest;addend;augend;sum;rl
⍝ DEC VAX780 Subtract With Carry
 addend←radixcompi˜read780 adr780 long
 dest←adr780 long
 augend←radixcompi read780 dest
 sum←augend+addend+˜status[Carry]
 rl←long radixcompr sum
 dest write780 rl
 signal780NZO rl
 status[Carry]←˜long carryfrom augend,addend,˜status[Carry]
```

PROGRAM 15-119   Binary addition and subtraction in the DEC VAX780.

```
MULB2;dest;multiplier;multiplicand;product;pd
⍝ DEC VAX780 Multiply Replace Byte
 multiplier←radixcompi read780 adr780 byte
 dest←adr780 byte
 multiplicand←radixcompi read780 dest
 product←multiplicand×multiplier
 pd←byte radixcompr product
 dest write780 pd
 signal780NZO pd
 status[Carry]←0


DIVW3;divisor;dividend;quotient;qt
⍝ DEC VAX780 Divide Word
 divisor←radixcompi read780 adr780 word
 dividend←radixcompi read780 adr780 word
 →IF divisor=0
 THEN: ⍝ zero divisor
    qt←word radixcompr dividend
    signal780NZ qt
    status[Oflo]←1
    →ENDIF
 ELSE: ⍝ normal division
    quotient←truncate dividend÷divisor
    qt←word radixcompr quotient
    signal780NZO qt
 ENDIF:(adr780 word) write780 qt
 status[Carry]←0
```

PROGRAM 15-120   Binary multiplication and division in the DEC VAX780.

Multiply and Divide. The product of a multiplication is equal to the operand size. Similarly, the divisor, dividend, and quotient all have the same size. There is no remainder. Extended-precision multiply forms a quad-size product from a longword multiplier and multiplicand. Extended-precision divide forms a longword quotient and remainder from a quad-size dividend and longword divisor.

Compare. Comparison sets the condition, including the borrow, as in subtraction. The overflow condition is set to 0.

Decimal Arithmetic

Each decimal operand has its own length and address; the only exceptions are Move Decimal and one of the Compare Decimal instructions; there one length applies to two operands. Decimal operations use some general registers for intermediate results to permit interruptions during the operation and to show final address and length values. The First Part Done indicator indicates when an interruption may occur, as in the data-handling operations.

The carry condition is set to 0 in all decimal operations except Move Decimal, which leaves it undisturbed.

a MOVP	Move Decimal	a ADDP4	Add Replace Decimal
a CVTPL	Convert Decimal To Long	a ADDP6	Add Decimal
a CVTLP	Convert Long To Decimal	a SUBP4	Subtract Replace Decimal
a CVTPS	Convert Decimal To Separate	a SUBP6	Subtract Decimal
a CVTSP	Convert Separate To Decimal	a MULP	Multiply Decimal
a CVTPT	Convert Decimal To Trailing	a DIVP	Divide Decimal
a CVTTP	Convert Trailing To Decimal	a CMPP3	Compare Decimal
a ASHP	Shift Arithmetic Decimal	a CMPP4	Compare Fitted Decimal

TABLE 15-121   Decimal instructions of the DEC VAX780.

Move. The decimal move instruction specifies the length and address of the operand and the address of the result. The operand is not merely moved, but also interpreted: −0 is changed to +0.

```
MOVP;source;dest;number
a DEC VAX780 Move Decimal
source←adr780dec
dest←source[Size,Space],(adr780 byte)[Value]
regend780?4padrcap
number←decimal780i read780 source WHERE ind[Fpd]←1
dest write780 source[Size] decimal780r number
regend780 0,source[Value],0,dest[Value] WHERE ind[Fpd]←0
status[Neg,Zero,Oflo]←(number<0),(number=0),0
```

PROGRAM 15-122   Decimal move in the DEC VAX780.

Conversion. Conversion is between a binary longword and the two types of unpacked decimal. Conversion from the unpacked format with trailing sign uses a table to translate the sign and digit part of the low-order operand byte. This translated byte is then interpreted as the trailing sign and digit representation, and is subsequently converted to the packed format. Similarly, a translation table is used for the low-order byte in the conversion to the unpacked format with trailing sign. Conversion to or from unpacked decimal with separate leading sign uses the corresponding unpacked representation and interpretation functions. The sign byte is not translated.

```
CVTLP;operand;dest
⍝ DEC VAX780 Convert Long To Decimal
operand←radixcompi read780 adr780 long
dest←adr780dec
regend780?4⍴adrcap
dest write780 dest[Size] decimal780r operand WHERE ind[Fpd]←1
regend780 0 0 0 ,dest[Value] WHERE ind[Fpd]←0
signal780V operand

CVTTP;source;table;dest;od;rl;result
⍝ DEC VAX780 Convert Trailing To Decimal
source←adr780str
table←(adr780 byte)[Value]
dest←adr780str
regend780?4⍴adrcap
od←read780 source WHERE ind[Fpd]←1
rl←(¯1 0 ↓od)⍪memory[table+magni ¯1 8 ↑od;]
result←decimal780t∆i rl
dest write780 dest[Size] decimal780r result
regend780 0,source[Value],0,dest[Value] WHERE ind[Fpd]←0
signal780V result
Spec report 32≤dest[Size],source[Size]

CVTPS;source;dest;operand
⍝ DEC VAX780 Convert Decimal To Separate
source←adr780dec
dest[Size]←1+dest[Size] WHERE dest←adr780str
regend780?4⍴adrcap
operand←decimal780i read780 source WHERE ind[Fpd]←1
dest write780 dest[Size] decimal780s∆r operand
regend780 0,source[Value],0,dest[Value] WHERE ind[Fpd]←0
signal780V operand
Spec report 32≤dest[Size],source[Size]
```

PROGRAM 15-123   Decimal conversion in the DEC VAX780.

The unpacked decimal representation is treated as a character string, except that the length applies to the number of digits. Thus, in the leading separate-sign representation, the string length must be increased by 1 to accommodate the sign byte.

Decimal shift.   The shift is arithmetic and allows rounding; the round tolerance is specified by the four low-order bits of a separate byte-sized operand.

```
ASHP;shift;source;round;dest;operand;result
⍝ DEC VAX780 Shift Arithmetic Decimal
shift←radixcompi read780 adr780 byte
source←adr780dec
round←16|magni read780 adr780 byte
dest←adr780dec
regend780?4⍴adrcap
operand←decimal780i read780 source WHERE ind[Fpd]←1
result←(×operand)×⌊(|operand×10*shift)+0.1×round
dest write780 dest[Size] decimal780r result
regend780 0,source[Value],0,dest[Value] WHERE ind[Fpd]←0
signal780V result
```

PROGRAM 15-124   Decimal shift in the DEC VAX780.

Dyadic decimal arithmetic.   The dyadic decimal arithmetic operations follow directly from the packed decimal formats and their length and address specification. Replacing an operand by a result is an option only for addition and subtraction. Division does not preserve a remainder. The quotient is truncated.

```
ADDP6;src1;src2;addend;augend;sum;dest
⍝ DEC VAX780 Add Decimal
src1←adr780dec
src2←adr780dec
dest←adr780dec
regend780?6ρadrcap
addend←decimal780i read780 src1 WHERE ind[Fpd]←1
augend←decimal780i read780 src2
sum←augend+addend
dest write780 dest[Size] decimal780r sum
regend780 0,src1[Value],0,src2[Value],0,dest[Value] WHERE ind[Fpd]←0
signal780V sum


SUBP4;source;dest;subtrahend;minuend;difference
⍝ DEC VAX780 Subtract Replace Decimal
source←adr780dec
dest←adr780dec
regend780?4ρadrcap
subtrahend←decimal780i read780 source WHERE ind[Fpd]←1
minuend←decimal780i read780 dest
difference←minuend-subtrahend
dest write780 dest[Size] decimal780r difference
regend780 0,source[Value],0,dest[Value] WHERE ind[Fpd]←0
signal780V difference
```

PROGRAM 15-125   Decimal addition and subtraction in the DEC VAX780.

Decimal compare.   Comparison sets the conditions according to the result of a subtraction; the difference is not saved.

Floating-Point Arithmetic

All floating-point operations apply to the normal longword format and to the double-length quadword format. These two formats can be converted to and from binary fixed point. The dyadic operations are all specified both with a separately addressed result and with the result replacing one of the operands. The carry condition is always set to 0. Reserved floating-point operands give unpredictable result conditions, but leave the result location unchanged.

Floating-point move.   The floating-point Move is similar to the fixed-point Move; the immediate operand has floating-point operand format.

Floating-point conversion.   Format conversion either extends the coefficient with low-order 0s or rounds the coefficient to fewer bits.
Code conversion from binary fixed point is exact, except that a binary longword is rounded when converted to single-length floating point. Code conversion to binary fixed point is truncated, except that conversion to the longword format can be specified to be rounded. High-order significant bits that are lost in fixed point are signaled as an overflow condition (not as a carry, as in the PDP11).

a	MOVF	Floating-point Move	a	ADDF2	F Add Replace
a	MOVD	Move D	a	ADDF3	F Add
a	CVTFD	Convert F To D	a	ADDD2	Add Replace D
a	CVTDF	Convert D To F	a	ADDD3	Add D
a	CVTFB	Convert F To Byte	a	SUBF2	F Subtract Replace
a	CVTFW	Convert F To Word	a	SUBF3	F Subtract
a	CVTFL	Convert F To Long	a	SUBD2	Subtract Replace D
a	CVTRFL	Convert F R To Long	a	SUBD3	Subtract D
a	CVTDB	Convert D To Byte	a	MULF2	F Multiply Replace
a	CVTDW	Convert D To Word	a	MULF3	F Multiply
a	CVTDL	Convert D To Long	a	MULD2	Multiply Replace D
a	CVTRDL	Convert D R To Long	a	MULD3	Multiply D
a	CVTBF	Convert Byte To F	a	EMODF	F Multiply Extended
a	CVTWF	Convert Word To F	a	EMODD	Multiply Extended D
a	CVTLF	Convert Long To F	a	POLYF	F Polynomial
a	CVTBD	Convert Byte To D	a	POLYD	Polynomial D
a	CVTWD	Convert Word To D	a	DIVF2	F Divide Replace
a	CVTLD	Convert Long To D	a	DIVF3	F Divide
a	MNEGF	F Negate	a	DIVD2	Divide Replace D
a	MNEGD	Negate D	a	DIVD3	Divide D
a	TSTF	F Test	a	CMPF	F Compare
a	TSTD	Test D	a	CMPD	Compare D

Legend: D = Double; F = Floating-Point; R = Rounded.

TABLE 15-126   Floating-point instructions of the DEC VAX780.

```
CVTDF;fl;operand
A DEC VAX780 Convert Double To Floating-Point
operand←fl780i read780 adr780 quad WHERE fl←1
(adr780 long) write780 long fl780r operand
signal780V operand


CVTFL;fl;operand
A DEC VAX780 Convert Floating-Point To Long
operand←fl780i read780 adr780 long WHERE fl←1
(adr780 long) write780 long radixcompr truncate operand
signal780V operand


CVTWD;operand
A DEC VAX780 Convert Word To Double
operand←radixcompi read780 adr780 word
(adr780 quad) write780 quad fl780r operand
signal780V operand
```

PROGRAM 15-127   Floating-point conversion in the DEC VAX780.

Sign control.   Only Negate is provided, as is consistent with the fixed-point instruction set, but it differs from the PDP11 floating point.

Floating-point Add and Subtract.   The eight addition and subtraction instructions follow from the size and addressing options.

```
ADDF2;fl;dest;addend;augend;sum
A DEC VAX780 Floating-Point Add Replace
addend←fl780i read780 adr780 long WHERE fl←1
dest←adr780 long
augend←fl780i read780 dest
sum←augend+addend
dest write780 long fl780r sum
signal780V sum
```

PROGRAM 15-128   Floating-point addition in the DEC VAX780.

Floating-point Multiply and Divide. There are eight normal Multiply and Divide operations and two pairs of special multiplications.

Polynomial evaluation uses a table of floating-point coefficients, similar to that in the Univac 1103A.

Extended-precision multiplication uses an 8-bit low-order multiplier extension to obtain an extended product, which is split into a long fixed-point integer part and a floating-point fraction part!

```
POLYD;fl;argument;degree;table;result
∩ DEC VAX780 Polynomial Double
  argument←fl780i read780 adr780 quad WHERE fl←1
  degree←magni read780 adr780 word WHERE fl←0
  Spec report degree>31
  table←adr780 quad
  result←0 WHERE ind[Fpd]←1
  regend780?6ρadrcap
  REPEAT:result←(argument×result)+fl780i read780 table
    degree←degree-1
    table[Value]←table[Value]+8
  →UNTIL degree=0
  regend780 0 0 0 ,table[Value], 0 0 WHERE ind[Fpd]←0
  reg[0 1 ;]←long wide quad fl780r result
  signal780V result
```

PROGRAM 15-129   Floating-point multiplication in the DEC VAX780.

Floating-point Compare. The floating-point comparisons are similar to the fixed-point operations.

15.3.6

Instruction Sequencing

Linear Sequence

Next instruction. The basic cycle uses an instruction address in register 15, which is incremented during instruction fetch. The operation code of an instruction is fetched with a byte increment. As part of the address modes, larger increments—such as a word or a longword—may be fetched. The execution cycle is classical, except that an interruption within an instruction may occur (not shown).

```
cycle780                           inst←ifetch780 size
∩ basic cycle of the DEC VAX780    ∩ DEC VAX780 instruction fetch
  REPEAT:execute ifetch780 byte      inst←read780 size incr780 Pc
    interrupt780
  →UNTIL stop
```

PROGRAM 15-130   Basic cycle and instruction fetch of the DEC VAX780.

Sequencing instructions. The list of sequencing instructions is relatively lengthy because the complete set of decision and size options is generally made available. Also, many decision types, including the novel Case, are included.

a	NOP	No Operation	a	JSB	Call
a	HALT	Stop	a	BSBB	Call Byte
a	BPT	Breakpoint Stop	a	BSBW	Call Word
a	JMP	Branch Absolute	a	CALLG	Call Procedure
a	BRB	Branch Byte	a	CALLS	Call Procedure W Arguments
a	BRW	Branch Word	a	RSB	Return
a	BLSS	Branch On Less	a	RET	Return From Procedure
a	BLEQ	Branch On Less Or Equal			
a	BEQL	Branch On Equal			
a	BNEQ	Branch On Not Equal			
a	BGEQ	Branch On Greater Or Equal			
a	BGTR	Branch On Greater			
a	BLEQU	Branch On Less Or Equal Unsigned			
a	BGTRU	Branch On Greater Unsigned			
a	BCS	Branch On Carry			
a	BCC	Branch On No Carry			
a	BVS	Branch On Overflow			
a	BVC	Branch On No Overflow			
a	BBS	Branch On One			
a	BBC	Branch On Zero			
a	BBSS	Branch On One And Set			
a	BBCS	Branch On Zero And Set			
a	BBSC	Branch On One And Clear			
a	BBCC	Branch On Zero And Clear			
a	BLBS	Branch On Low One			
a	BLBC	Branch On Low Zero			
a	CASEB	Case Byte			
a	CASEW	Case Word			
a	CASEL	Case Long			
a	ACBB	Branch On Compare Byte			
a	ACBW	Branch On Compare Word			
a	ACBL	Branch On Compare Long			
a	ACBF	Branch On F Compare			
a	ACBD	Branch On Compare D			
a	AOBLSS	Branch On Increment Less			
a	AOBLEQ	Branch On Increment Less Or Equal			
a	SOBGTR	Branch On Decrement Greater			
a	SOBGEQ	Branch On Decrement Greater Or Equal			

Legend: D = Double; F = Floating-Point; W = With.

TABLE 15-131   Sequencing instructions of the DEC VAX780.

```
JMP;iadr                           size jump780 condition;offset;iadr
a DEC VAX780 Branch Absolute       a DEC VAX780 conditional jump
iadr←(adr780 word)[Value]          offset←radixcompi ifetch780 size
reg[Pc;]←long magnr iadr           →If condition
                                   THEN:iadr←magni reg[Pc;]
                                        reg[Pc;]←long magnr iadr+offset
BRW                                ENDIF:
a DEC VAX780 Branch Word
word jump780 1
```

PROGRAM 15-132   Unconditional Branch in the DEC VAX780.

Unconditional branch.   The target address of the absolute branch JMP has the general addressing modes; hence it includes a relative branch. The relative branch (BR) fetches an immediate offset with byte or word length.

Completion.   The HALT instruction stops the processor in the Kernel mode. Otherwise, the invalid operation interruption is taken. The operation code of this instruction is all-zeros, which helps to detect excursions into data areas.

Decision

Conditional branching.   Indicators are used to separate branching test and action. All conditional branches are relative with a byte-size offset. The main group of conditional branches is based upon the conditions as set by a prior signed or unsigned comparison, exactly as in the PDP11.

```
 BEQL                                  BBSS;position;dest;od
a DEC VAX780 Branch On Equal         a DEC VAX780 Branch On One And Set
 byte jump780 status[Zero]             position←magni read780 adr780 long
                                       dest←adr780 byte
                                       dest[Value]←dest[Value]+Lposition÷byte
 BCS                                   od←read780 dest
a DEC VAX780 Branch On Carry           byte jump780 od[byte|-position+1]
 byte jump780 status[Carry]            od[byte|-position+1]←1
                                       dest write780 od

 BLBS;od
a DEC VAX780 Branch On Low One        BVC
 od←read780 adr780 long              a DEC VAX780 Branch On No Overflow
 byte jump780 ¯1↑od                    byte jump780˜status[Oflo]
```

PROGRAM 15-133   Conditional Branch in the DEC VAX780.

Branching may also be on the low-order bit of a longword or on a specified bit of a bit string. In the latter case, the bit may be also set or cleared.

Case.   The multiway branch Case implements a case statement. A selector operand is range-checked and then used as an index for a table of relative branch displacements. The Case falls through if the select value is outside the range specified by a start and end value.

```
 CASEB;select;start;end;case;iadr
a DEC VAX780 Case Byte
 select←magni read780 adr780 byte
 start←magni read780 adr780 byte
 end←magni read780 adr780 byte
 case←select-start
 iadr←magni reg[Pc;]
 →IF case≤end
 THEN:reg[Pc;]←long magnr iadr+2×case
    →ENDIF
 ELSE:reg[Pc;]←long magnr iadr+2×end+1
 ENDIF:
```

PROGRAM 15-134   Case in the DEC VAX780.

Iteration

Incrementation and termination.   Branch On Compare Long implements the For loop. The addend is added to the loop control index, and the new index is compared to the limit. The branch succeeds as long as the index does not exceed the range indicated by the limit and the sign of the addend.

```
ACBL;end;addend;dest;index;rl
∩ DEC VAX780 Branch On Compare Long
end←magni read780 adr780 long
addend←magni read780 adr780 long
dest←adr780 long
index←addend+radixcompi read780 dest
rl←long radixcompr index
dest write780 rl                        SOBGTR;dest;index;rl
→IF addend≥0                            ∩ DEC VAX780 Branch On Decrement Greater
THEN: ∩ increment                       dest←adr780 long
    word jump780 index≤end              index←⁻1+radixcompi read780 dest
    →ENDIF                              byte jump780 index≥0
ELSE: ∩ decrement                       rl←long radixcompr index
    word jump780 index≥end              dest write780 rl
ENDIF:signal780NZO rl                   signal780NZO rl
```

PROGRAM 15-135   Decrement And Branch in the DEC VAX780.

Special cases that add or subtract 1 and compare against 0—such as SOBGTR—require two addresses fewer than does Branch On Compare Long.

Delegation

Subroutine call and return.   The absolute and relative Call operations save only the return address on the stack. Return From Subroutine restores the return address from the stack.

```
JSB;iadr                               BSBW;iadr
∩ DEC VAX780 Call                      ∩ DEC VAX780 Call Word
iadr←(adr780 byte)[Value]              iadr←magni reg[Pc;]
push780 reg[Pc;]                       push780 long magnr iadr+2
reg[Pc;]←long magnr iadr               word jump780 1


RSB
∩ DEC VAX780 Return
reg[Pc;]←pop780
```

PROGRAM 15-136   Subroutine call and return in the DEC VAX780.

Procedure call and return.   Call Procedure With Arguments and Return From Procedure implement procedure calls with linked activation records on stack. The first word of a procedure is the entry mask, which specifies which of the first 12 registers to save on the stack.

CALLS saves those registers along with the argument pointer, frame pointer, instruction address, PSW, the entry mask, and an address for a condition handler routine; then it loads the frame pointer with the contents of the stack pointer and loads the argument pointer with the address of the argument list.

Call Procedure has no arguments on the stack, but is otherwise the same.

Return From Procedure uses the frame pointer to locate the saved state on the stack; loads the stack pointer with the frame pointer; restores the PSW through the argument pointer and those registers that were specified in the entry mask; tests the second mask bit to see whether the argument list was placed on the stack; and, if so, removes it.

```
CALLS;dest;mask;argsp
ค DEC VAX780 Call Procedure With Arguments
ค push argument count
push780 read780 adr780 long
ค fetch procedure mask
dest←adr780 word
mask←read780 dest
Spec report mask[2 3]
ค align stack
argsp←reg[Sp;]
reg[Sp; 30 31]←0
ค create stack frame
push780reg(mask[4+ι12]/Φι12),Pc,Fp,Ap
status[Neg,Zero,Oflo,Carry]←0
push780 argsp[30 31], 1 0 ,mask[4+ι12],status[word+ι11],5ρ0
push780 longρ0
ค set interrupt masks
status[Dv,Iv,Fu]←mask[0 1],0
ค set pointers and instruction address
reg[Fp;]←reg[Sp;]
reg[Ap;]←argsp
reg[Pc;]←long magnr dest[Value]+2


RET;mask
ค DEC VAX780 Return From Procedure
ค restore stack pointer
reg[Sp;]←long magnr 4+magni reg[Fp;]
ค restore registers
mask←pop780
Spec report mask[word+ι8]
pop780reg Ap,Fp,Pc,Φmask[4+ι12]/Φι12
ค restore stack alignment
reg[Sp;]←long magnr(magni reg[Sp;])+magni mask[ι2]
→If mask[2]
THEN: ค eliminate arguments from stack
   reg[Sp;]←long magnr(magni reg[Sp;])+4×magni pop780
ENDIF: ค restore status
status[word+ιword]←mask[word+ιword]
```

PROGRAM 15-137   Procedure call and return in the DEC VAX780.

15.3.7

Supervision

Supervisory instructions.   Supervision is aided by status-switching and context-saving instructions, including atomic operations for implementing semaphores.

```
a REI    Return From Interrupt   a XFC    Extended Function
a LDPCTX Load Process Context     a BBSSI  Branch On One And Set I
a SVPCTX Save Process Context     a BBCCI  Branch On Zero And Clear I
a MOVPSL Store Status             a ADAWI  Add Word I
a BICPSW And Not Status           a MTPR   Load Internal Register
a BISPSW Or Status                a MFPR   Store Internal Register
a CHMK   Change To Kernel         a PROBER Test Read Access
a CHME   Change To Execute        a PROBEW Test Write Access
a CHMS   Change To Supervisor     a CRC    Cyclic Redundancy Check
a CHMU   Change To User
Legend: I = Interlocked.
```

TABLE 15-138   Supervisory instructions of the DEC VAX780.

Concurrency

Processor interconnection.   Multiple processors can be attached to the central UNIBUS.

Process Interaction

Critical section.   Branch On One And Set Interlocked implements a binary semaphore that is tested for 1; Branch On Zero And Clear Interlocked implements the test for 0. Add Word Interlocked may be used to implement an integer semaphore.

```
ADAWI;addend;dest;augend;sum;r1
ค DEC VAX780 Add Word Interlocked
addend←radixcompi read780 adr780 word
dest←adr780 word
Spec report(0≠2|dest[Value])∧dest[Space]=memadr
→OUT suppress780
interlock←1
augend←radixcompi read780 dest
sum←augend+addend
r1←long radixcompr sum
dest write780 r1
interlock←0
signal780NZO r1
status[Carry]←word carryfrom augend,addend
```

PROGRAM 15-139   Interlocking in the DEC VAX780.

Integrity

Overall modes.   A *compatibility* mode executes PDP11 non-privileged instructions. A *native* mode executes VAX instructions. This native mode can operate normally or in a special *interrupt stack* mode, which provides for system-wide context. These modes are specified by the compatibility bit Cm and the interrupt stack bit Is. The interrupt stack mode is used for interrupt handling of the physical I/O. Software operating in this context has full Kernel-mode privileges. The only privileged operation is SPL (Set Priority Level), which is valid only in Kernel mode.

Access modes.   The normal native mode has four *access modes* that determine the privilege level of the currently executing program:
   • Kernel mode, used for operating system kernel operations
   • Executive mode, used for logical I/O
   • Supervisor mode, used for command interpreters
   • User mode, used for user programs
   The access mode is indicated in the status word by the Current mode field; the last preceding access mode is indicated by the Previous mode field.

Page protection.   Memory is protected by paging. Accessibility of a page is based on the execution mode and is specified in the page table.
   The two high-order address bits determine the choice among Program, Control, and System space (reserved system space is not used). Each of these

spaces has its own page table, specified by origin and limit. The page-table argument is formed by adding the appropriate origin to the page part of the address (multiplied by 4 because the table entries occupy 4 bytes). The argument may not exceed the table limit. The page-table entry contains the 20-bit frame address, which is concatenated with the 9-bit byte address to give the physical memory location.

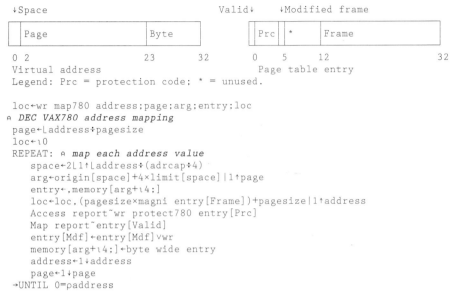

```
loc←wr map780 address;page;arg;entry;loc
ᴀ DEC VAX780 address mapping
page←⌊address÷pagesize
loc←⍳0
REPEAT: ᴀ map each address value
    space←2⊥1↑⌊address÷(adrcap÷4)
    arg←origin[space]+4×limit[space]|1↑page
    entry←,memory[arg+⍳4;]
    loc←loc,(pagesize×magni entry[Frame])+pagesize|1↑address
    Access report˜wr protect780 entry[Prc]
    Map report˜entry[Valid]
    entry[Mdf]←entry[Mdf]∨wr
    memory[arg+⍳4;]←byte wide entry
    address←1↓address
    page←1↓page
→UNTIL 0=ρaddress
```

PROGRAM 15-140   Address mapping in the DEC VAX780.

When a page is not in memory, the operating system should have set the `Valid` bit of the page entry to 0, which causes the `Map` indicator to be turned on when the page is accessed. Upon writing, the modified frame bit `Mdf` is set automatically.

Protection code.   The entry of the page table contains a 4-bit protection code (`Prc`), which specifies read–write, read-only, and no-access to any of the four modes Kernel, Executive, Supervisor, and User. A mode has at least the privileges of the modes that are less important. Code 4 gives all access to all modes, and code 0 no access to any mode; the other cases are determined by inspecting two code bits for reading and the other two code bits for writing (code 1 is unpredictable). A violation of protection sets the `Access` indicator.

```
valid←wr protect780 code
ᴀ DEC VAX780 memory protection
ᴀ read access
valid←(magni status[Curm])≤magni 2↑code
→If wr
THEN: ᴀ write access
    valid←valid∧(magni status[Curm])<magni˜2↓code
ENDIF: ᴀ all or nothing
valid←(4=magni code)∨valid∧0≠magni code
```

PROGRAM 15-141   Protection code in the DEC VAX780.

Probe operations.   Test Read Access and Test Write Access are used by operating system routines to validate memory-access rights of a caller when providing services.

Control Switching

Interruption.   The interrupt system has 31 priority levels. Interrupt service routines use the interrupt-stack mode and operate at the same interrupt priority as the interrupt source. Traps use the kernel mode.

There are five stack pointers: one for the interrupt-stack mode and one each for the four access modes when not operating in the interrupt-stack mode. These distinct stack pointers allow proper nesting in their respective stacks. currentsp780 determines the stack pointer that belongs to a given program status longword status.

```
interrupt780;who;psl                yes←suppress780
Ɐ DEC VAX780 interrupt action      Ɐ DEC VAX780 operation suppression
who←indɩl                           yes←v/ind[Spec,Invadr]
→If who≠pind
THEN:ind[who]←0
  Ɐ switch stack pointers
    psl←status
    sp[currentsp780;]←reg[Sp;]
    status←read780 long,memadr,scb+2+4×who
    reg[Sp;]←sp[currentsp780;]
  Ɐ preserve return values          pointer←currentsp780
    push780 psl                     Ɐ DEC VAX780 current stack pointer
    push780 reg[Pc;]                pointer←(4×status[Is])⌈magni status[Curm]
    push780 long magnr trap
  Ɐ interrupt routine address
    reg[Pc;]←read780 long,memadr,scb+4×who
    Spec report 1=2|magni reg[Pc;]
ENDIF:
```

PROGRAM 15-142   Interruption action in the DEC VAX780.

Upon interrupt, the processor obtains the corresponding status word and changes the stack pointer according to the mode indicated in that status word, then saves the instruction address and the status on the stack, and obtains a new instruction address from the corresponding interrupt vector.

Illegal memory access, floating overflow, and divide by 0 always interrupt; decimal overflow, floating-point underflow, and fixed-point overflow interrupt on the basis of the mask bits in the status word.

Dispatching.   Return From Interrupt restores the status of an interrupted program such that it can resume its actions as if no interrupt had occurred. The instruction address and PSW are obtained from the current stack. The status is tested to ensure that it specifies the proper level of privileges and the proper priority in relation to the dispatching program; also, invalid bit patterns are checked. Subsequently, the stack pointers are interchanged, and the instruction address and status word are restored.

```
REI;iadr;psl
⌐ DEC VAX780 Return From Interrupt
⌐ retrieve return values
iadr←pop780
psl←pop780
⌐ check return status
Spec report(magni psl[Curm])>magni status[Curm]
Spec report psl[Is]∧(~status[Is])∨Kernel≠magni psl[Curm]
Spec report(magni psl[Priority])>magni status[Priority]
Spec report psl[Is]∧0=magni psl[Priority]
Spec report(0≠magni psl[Priority])∧Kernel≠magni psl[Curm]
Spec report(magni psl[Prem])<magni psl[Curm]
Spec report psl[Mbz]
Spec report psl[Cm]∧psl[Fpd.Is.Dv.Fu.Iv]∨User≠magni psl[Curm]
⌐ preserve interrupt stack pointer
sp[currentsp780;]←reg[Sp;]
⌐ set return values
reg[Pc;]←iadr
psl[Tp]←psl[Tp]∨status[Tp]
status←psl
reg[Sp;]←sp[currentsp780;]
```

PROGRAM 15-143   Dispatch in the DEC VAX780.

State Preservation

Context switching.   The Process Control Block is a block of 24 longwords containing copies of the general registers, the four access mode stack pointers, the process status word, the program-and-control–region base registers and limit registers. A process context switch is made by executing Save Process Context, which saves the state into the process control block pointed to by the process control block base (pcb), then loads that base register with the address of a new process control block and subsequently executing Load Process Context.

Humble access.   Mode changes can act as humble accesses to call operating-system service routines. Change to Supervisor, for example, first checks that the current mode is not the interrupt-stack mode; next, the stack pointers are switched. The new stack pointer specifies the supervisor mode unless the current mode has a higher privilege (hence it has a lower-mode code value).

```
CHMS;psl;code
⌐ DEC VAX780 Change To Supervisor
stop←stop∨status[Is]
→OUT stop
⌐ switch stack pointers and push return values
psl←status
sp[currentsp780;]←reg[Sp;]
status[Curm]←2 magnr Supervisor⌊magni status[Curm]
reg[Sp;]←sp[currentsp780;]
code←radixcompi read780 adr780 word
push780 psl
push780 reg[Pc;]
push780 long radixcompr code
⌐ set supervisor values
status[Cm.Tp.Fpd.Dv.Fu.Iv.Trace.Neg.Zero.Oflo.Carry]←0
status[Prem]←psl[Curm]
reg[Pc;]←read780 long.memadr.scb+48
```

PROGRAM 15-144   Humble access in the DEC VAX780.

The return values are pushed onto the new stack, followed by a sign-extended code word that is supplied by the program. Various bits of the new status word are cleared, and the previous mode is noted in the previous mode field. Finally, the new instruction address is obtained from the longword starting at byte 48 of the system control block, outside the control of the current program.

Status changing.   Status bits can be set on and off with Or Status and And Status, respectively. A 16-bit mask is used to change the desired bits. Only the low-order eight bits of the status word may be changed; otherwise, the operation is suppressed.

```
BISPSW;mask
ᴀ DEC VAX780 Or Status
mask←read780 adr780 word
Spec report mask[ι8]
→OUT suppress780
status[16+ι16]←maskvstatus[16+ι16]
```

PROGRAM 15-145   Status changing in the DEC VAX780.

15.3.8
Input/Output

Device registers are mapped onto main storage, but not all instructions can be used with addresses in I/O mapped storage.

Input/Output Operation

Direct, buffered, and channel I/O can be attached.

Interfaces

Bus configuration.   The single central synchronous bus connects processors, memory, and I/O devices. Devices are connected to the bus via buffered UNIBUS and MASSBUS interface adapters, which perform memory mapping. These interfaces allow use of the same peripherals as those for the PDP11.

15.3.9
Implementation Notes

The instruction prefetch buffer is not updated by instruction modification. Therefore, the architecture requires that data written by a program cannot later be interpreted as instructions unless an intervening context switch or Return from Exception or Interruption occurs to clear the buffer.

15.3.10

Bibliography

Aspinall, D.B. and Y.N. Patt, 1985: "Retrofitting the VAX-11/780 Microarchitecture for IEEE Floating Point Arithmetic." *IEEE Transactions on Computers*, **C-34**, 8: 692–708.

Strecker, W., 1978: "VAX11/780: A Virtual Address Extension to the DEC PDP11 Family." Bell, Mudge, and McNamara, [1978], Chapter 17.

Clark and Levy [1982], Clark [1983], Emer and Clark [1984], Hall and Robinson [1991], Levy and Eckhouse [1980], Wiecek [1982].

Our defining references are: Digital Equipment Corporation, 1977: *VAX11/780 Architecture Handbook* and Digital Equipment Corporation, 1978: *VAX11/780 Hardware Handbook*.

15.3.11

Exercises

15-14 What is the advantage of Push Address Word over Move Address Word with the stack pointer specified as register and predecrement specified as mode?

15-15 Give the description of the index arithmetic instructions MOVAB, PUSHL, and PUSHAQ, assuming consistency with the index arithmetic instructions shown in this section.

15-16 Give the description of the data-handling instructions EXTZV, CMPC5, CMPV, SKPC, SPANC, and MATCHC, assuming consistency with the data-handling instructions shown in this section.

15-17 Give the description of the logical and shift instructions CLRB, MCOMW, BISB2, XORL3, BICW3, BITB, FFS, and ASHL, assuming consistency with the logical and shift instructions shown in this section.

15-18 Give the description of the binary instructions MOVQ, CVTWL, MOVZBW, MNEGL, TSTW, INCL, DECW, ADDB2, ADWC, SUBW3, MULL3, DIVB2, and CMPL assuming consistency with the binary instructions shown in this section.

15-19 Give the description of the decimal instructions CVTPL, CVTSP, CVTPT, ADDP4, SUBP6, MULP, DIVP, and CMPP3, assuming consistency with the instructions shown in this section.

15-20 Give the description of the floating-point instructions MOVF, CVTFD, CVTDW, CVTRDL, CVTBF, MNEGF, TSTD, ADDD3, SUBF3, MULF2, POLYF, DIVD2, and CMPF, assuming consistency with the instructions shown in this section.

15-21 Give the description of the branch instructions BRB, BLSS, BNEQ, BGTRU, BGEQ, BCS, BBC, BLBC, CASEL, ACBB, ACBF, AOBLSS, BSBB, and CALLG, assuming consistency with the branch instructions shown in this section.

15-22 Give the description of the supervisory instructions BICPSW, CHME, BBSSI, and BBCCI, assuming consistency with the instructions shown in this section.

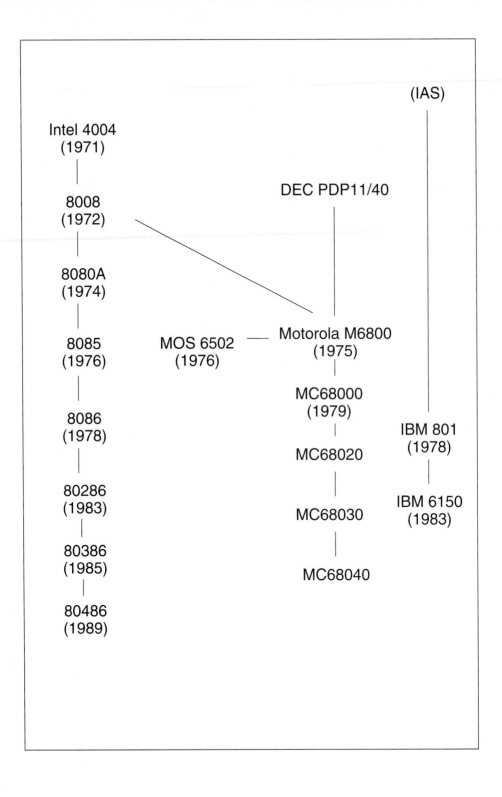

16

Microcomputer House

The Microcomputer Era*

Architecture for Control

As integrated circuitry advanced, it became possible, in 1971, to get a complete, if primitive, CPU on a single chip. The Intel 4004 (1971), with a 4-bit–wide datapath, was originally developed as a generalized substitute for logical control circuitry. It was a forerunner of rather generalized 8-bit microprocessors (the Intel 8008 [1972], 8080 [1974], the Motorola 6800 [1975], and the MOS 6502 [1976]), which have found application by the million, originally as embedded controllers, and later as the CPUs of entire microcomputer systems, most notably those by Apple, IBM and IBM clones, Tandy (Radio Shack), and Amiga.

The 8-bit microprocessors were designed not to be microcomputer CPUs, however, but rather to be controllers. Hence their architectures are determined in part by the limits of the microprocessor technology, in greater measure by the technology of the whole microcomputer system, and most profoundly by the expected mode of application as embedded controllers.

Architecturally, these microprocessors are the clear descendants of the 1960s minicomputers. However, the microprocessors resemble the uncles more than the parents—they are architecturally much more similar to airborne and spaceborne computers than to the ground-based general purpose minis. This resemblance is not, so far as we can determine, because the designers had previous experience with airborne machines, but rather because the application desiderata for microprocessors closely match those of airborne computers. Hence, when the wheel was reinvented, it was again round, with rim and spokes.

---

* Part of this material is from Brooks [1976] and is used by permission of Euromicro.

The Application and Technology Desiderata

Control applications.   Control applications, as opposed to scientific computation and business data processing, have their own set of properties. First,
they typically use much more of the memory space for program than for data.

Fixed programs.   Each copy of a machine is typically dedicated to a single
application, so that it will "always" contain the same program. It does not
run a succession of independently prepared programs, much less does it
multiprogram such a set.

Many replications.   There are many copies of a machine with the same
program.

No backing-store.   The system typically contains no backing-store; hence
program overlay is not practical, and memory cost varies directly with total
program size.

Costly memory.   Memory is available in small increments, so a savings in
program size translates directly into a system cost savings, which is in turn
multiplied by the machine-copy replication. The bit budget translates directly
to cost.

Cross-assembly.   Since programs are infrequently written, cross-assembly is
a viable technique.

Ease of programming.   Ease is not an important factor, since programs are
infrequently written.

Logic substitutes.   Microcomputers were first applied as a substitute for direct
integrated-circuit logic. Hence the users are apt to be professional electrical
engineers and amateur programmers. More important, the microprocessor
most often does what wired logic does—lots of bit tests, Boolean logic,
comparisons, counts. Short data fields (4 to 8 bits) usually suffice, but one
wants many different operations upon them.

Rich function, low cost.   The internal logic—both registers and controls—is
quite cheap. Function is pin-limited, and hence bit-limited—not limited by
the number of logic gates required.

From all of these points it follows that instruction-bit efficiency is the
dominant goal of the architectures.

In all of these respects (except the last), the microcomputer desiderata
are precisely the same as those shaping airborne computers, with the latter
minimizing *weight* rather than *cost*.

Consequent Architectures

We can characterize the microprocessor architecture that emerged in
response to the desiderata listed. Similarities among models from different
manufacturers exceed the differences:

- Eight-bit word length
- Short operation codes, with extended operation codes for less frequent
  functions
- Two-address instructions, with much implication and abbreviation

- Many address-abbreviation techniques:
  - "0-page" 1-byte addresses to the first 256 bytes
  - Immediate operands
  - Relative branches
  - Many addressing modes
  - Index or base registers
  - Register-to-register operations
- Few accumulators, index registers, or base registers, so that very short (1- to 3-bit) addresses suffice for these
- I/O operations often mapped onto regular memory space, via devices being given ordinary addresses
- Stacks for maximum ease of subroutine use, since subroutining is a chief technique for shrinking program size
- No multiplication or division

The Rereturn to the Womb

In what particular ways do the most popular 8-bit microprocessors—the Intel 8008 and 8080, the Motorola 6800, and the MOS 6502—resemble the early IAS, EDSAC-type machines, and, for that matter, the PDP8? Does each wave of computers really retrace the whole sequence of growth, starting with stark simplicity and bare of software?

Let us consider an IBM 701 (1953), a DEC PDP8 (1965), and a Motorola M6800 (1974). Not one is a first of its generation; each is typical:

- Each has direct-programmed I/O, without buffer or channel.
- Each is uniprogrammed—there is no multiprogramming.
- Each represents data with short (18-, 12-, 8-bit) binary words.
- Each has a simple, fixed-point operation set.
- Each addresses a small memory.
- Each is used with minimal software.

Indeed, one perceives the restart most clearly in the software. People did indeed program microcomputers in the late seventies in hex absolute, as in the days of yore! An assembler was a luxury; compilers aroused heated debates.

Sophistications and Surprises

The 8-bit microcomputer is not, however, a 701 or a PDP8 phase-shifted 20 or 10 years. Some of the subsequent evolutions and inventions, wrought so painfully in mainframe architecture, came into minicomputer architecture, and some of those came into microcomputer architecture. Most microcomputer architectures appear to be more heavily influenced by the DEC PDP11 (1970) than by any other predecessor machine.

Addressing modes. The most conspicuous sophistications are the multiple addressing modes, with vigorous exploitation of every address-abbreviation technique. Indexing is provided as a matter of course; so is the stack, with its powerful methods for subroutine control.

Interrupt. Even the more primitive modern microprocessors incorporate program interruption—a quite sophisticated technique.

Address capacity.   The most important sophistication is larger address capacity. The 701 addressed 4 K full words (36 bits). The PDP8 addressed 4 K 12-bit words. The 6800 addresses 64 K 8-bit bytes. The 6800 designers may have, like the others, provided too little address capacity, but at least they started much further along.

Others.   Besides these major sophistications, one sees many smaller ones. All the microprocessors include hardware aids for programmed multiple-precision arithmetic. Several incorporate binary-coded decimal addition and subtraction; others incorporate at least carry-correct for such. Many embody normalization operations to facilitate programmed floating point. Condition code registers to increase branching power are also common.

What are the surprises?

Instruction abbreviation.   The first surprise to us is the degree of success at instruction abbreviation. A static count of the built-in monitor indicates that the 6800 averages 2.0 bytes (or 16 bits) per instruction! Even when the weaker power of the operation set is considered, this efficiency is still excellent.

Classical logic and shift.   A second surprise is that there is little new in bit manipulation. One might have expected the extreme emphasis on control applications to have yielded new operation concepts, but it has not. One sees the same familiar Boolean logic, register shifts and rotations, and bit tests. The only novelty is the carry indicator's participation in accumulator shift. Even that echoes the 701 P,Q bits in a way.

Surprising omissions are the Multiply-Step, Divide-Step primitive operations. These would seem to be easy and useful facilities. Other surprising omissions are aids for character-string moving and for table search.

Evolution to the Classical Computer

The 8-bit micros were indeed effective as control computers. How about more general uses? If the 6800 (1974) was about as powerful as the 701 (1953), why did microcomputers not render all other computers obsolete and unsalable? The reasons are basic—word length, addressing capacity, and, to a lesser extent, speed.

The circuit technology continued to advance, yielding smaller feature sizes and larger chip areas—hence, many more logic and memory elements on a chip. This led to new generations of 16-, 32-, and 64-bit microprocessors. The Intel 8086 (1976) is architecturally a modest upgrade from the 8080, but the implementation is 16 bits wide and much faster. Address space is still a problem. So Intel broke its architecture twice, providing 20-bit addresses in the 80286 (1983) and 32-bit addresses in the 80386 (1985).

In a brilliant technological and business coup, Steve Jobs and Steve Wozniak built a general purpose *personal computer* around the 8-bit 6502 chip. Marketed as the Apple II, it created a whole new computer market for millions of machines.

IBM responded by building a personal computer around the Intel 8080 line of chips.

Motorola took a much riskier gamble, and won, for a while. Early on, it did a major architectural redesign of the M6800, yielding the MC68000 family (1979), and then provided a virtual-memory companion chip. This design recognized that the chip would be used as a system CPU, as well as an embedded controller, so the address size was enlarged to 20 bits, then 24, then 32, and the working store was enlarged to 16 registers of 32 bits each. The MC68000 is a real mainframe computer, architecturally comparable to the IBM 704, the IBM System/360, and the DEC VAX11/780 supermini. Speeds are comparable, as well, with the MC68000 yielding performance about half that of a 780. The *maxi*, *mini*, and *micro* stratification lines for computers are rapidly blurring.

The MC68000 family has been used as the CPU for successful supermicrocomputers by Apple, Sun Microsystems, Apollo, and others. Neither Motorola nor Intel has become a major supplier of computer systems that integrate CPU, memory, and I/O.

Just as the minicomputer revolution caught the prominent mainframe manufacturers prospering and blind to innovation, so the microcomputer revolution caught the minicomputer manufacturers blinded by prosperity. Once aroused, Digital, Data General, Hewlett-Packard, and so forth, have been striving to come from behind. At first, new 32-bit microprocessor architectures came from new vendors—Sun, MIPS, and even IBM. DEC has used MIPS processors in its new workstation line, side by side with VAX-architecture workstations, although it finally developed a competitive microprocessor of its own, the Alpha (1991). So has Hewlett-Packard. Alpha's architecture is designed aiming at a 25 year lifetime and a 1000-fold performance increase, to 400 GIPS.

Bibliography

Brooks [1976], Colwell et al. [1985], Comerford [1992], Sites [1993], Toong and Gupta [1981].

16.1
Intel 8080A*

16.1.1
Highlights
History

Architect.   The chief architect was Frederico Faggin.

Family tree and dates.   The Intel 4004 was designed by M.E. Hoff for calculators only.   It appeared in 1971.   Then Hoff and Feeney did the architecture of the Intel 8008 (1972).   The 8080 appeared in 1974, as did the Zylog Z-80.   The 8080 was quickly displaced by the 8080A, a minor variant.

Descendants.   The 16-bit 8086, with Stephen Morse and Bruce Ravenel as architects, appeared in 1976.   The 8086, widely used in the IBM PC and compatibles, was one of two implementations of a single architecture: the 8086 and the 8088, a 16-bit CPU designed to interface to an 8-bit external bus. This architecture incorporated built-in multiplication and was not upward compatible from the 8080A.

Memory break.   The 80186/80188 implement a modestly extended operation set and include a relocatable I/O control block.   The most notable additions are parameter-passing and state-saving operations for subroutine call and return, and an array-bounds–checking operation.

The 80286 (1983) awkwardly extends the virtual address space to 2^{30} bytes and provides memory management and protection.

The 80386 (1985) extends the architecture to 32 bits.   Architectural innovations in the 80386 include a virtual 8086 mode and a 4 GB maximum memory segment.

The 80486 (1989) is a much faster implementation.

Noteworthy

Eight-bit data, 16-bit addresses.   The Intel 8080A had to fit the chip size of the then-current realization technology.   Its design is representative for 8-bit datapath with 16-bit addresses, and does not yet reflect the move to wider datapaths that larger chip sizes and greater densities allow.

Stacks.   The architecture follows the DEC PDP11 (1970) in investing in a system stack and pointer and in facilities for other stacks in memory with a suitable set of operations.

Complete logic.   The 8080A has a proper set of connectives, but does not have vector operations, such as left-zero or all-ones counts.

Restricted arithmetic.   There is no Multiply or Divide, not even a Multiply Step or Divide Step.   In contrast with the 360 (1965) and the PDP11, there

---

*   Original sketch research by M.K. Smotherman.

is a proper Add With Carry, but not an extended 0 test as in the Motorola MC68000.

Minimal rotate. The 1-bit rotate, left and right, through carry or not, is enough to program any rotate or shift.

Minimal decimal. The decimal correct allows extended 10's-complement addition.

Peculiarities

Few addressing modes. In contrast to the minicomputers and later developments, such as the MC68000, there are no addressing modes. All address calculation is to be programmed.

Backwards bytes. The 16 bits of an address are placed backward in memory, as in the PDP11.

No overflow. There is no provision for detecting the signed overflow on addition or subtraction; hence proper arithmetic for signed integers is not possible, and signed numbers cannot be compared reliably by subtraction.

Irregular indicators. The carry bit is set to 1 in And, and to 0 in the other logical operations. This seems to be dictated by the implementation.

Conditional call. Subroutine jumps and returns may be performed conditionally. These options—accidents of the implementation—are used infrequently and are removed in the 8086.

Minimal interrupt. The interrupting device sends a whole instruction, which can be used to identify the sender.

Enabled status not testable. The enabled status of the interruption system cannot be determined by programming.

16.1.2
Machine Language
Language Level

Design philosophy. The 8080A is designed with the knowledge of what a classical computer should be, but is minimized to fit the severe constraints of the realization. This minimization expresses itself in the 8-bit data width, the minimal Rotate, the Decimal Adjust, the total absence of Multiply and Divide, and the minimal interrupt.

Unit System

The basic information unit is the 8-bit word.

```
initiate8080                          format8080
A initiation of the Intel 8080A       A Intel 8080A information units
format8080                            A representation radix
configure8080                         radix←2
space8080                             A information units
name8080                              digit←4
control8080                           word←8
                                      adrsize←16
                                      A address capacity
configure8080                         adrcap←radix*adrsize
A configuration for the Intel 8080A
A memory capacity
memcap←adrcap
iocap←4
```

PROGRAM 16-1   Basic parameters of the Intel 8080A.

Spaces

Memory name-space.   Memory is a matrix of 64 K 8-bit words. Another 64 K-word separate address space for the stack may be installed. The first 64 bytes are reserved for interrupt service routines.

```
space8080                             name8080
A Intel 8080A spaces                  A Intel 8080A space names
A memory                              A working registers
memory←?(memcap,word)ρradix          A - general register pairs
A working store                       Bc← 0 1
reg←?(10,word)ρradix                  De← 2 3
A control store                       A - memory address
A - instruction address               Hl← 4 5
iadr←?adrcap                          A - status
A - interrupt request                 Psw← 6 7
irq←?radix                           A - conditions
A - interrupt enable                  F←6
enable←?2ρradix                      A - accumulator
A input/output                        A←7
ioport←?(iocap,word)ρradix           A - stack pointer
                                      Sp← 8 9
```

PROGRAM 16-2   Spaces and embedding of the Intel 8080A.

Working store.   The 8-bit accumulator (A) serves as an implied operand and result location for arithmetic and logical operations.

The six 8-bit secondary accumulators (B, C, D, E, H, L) can be considered three register pairs (Bc, De, and Hl); these register pairs contain implied memory addresses for some operations.

Control store.   Five condition bits and a Run status bit are placed in the 8-bit status word (F), which forms a 16-bit processor status word (PSW) with the accumulator.

The interrupt-enable mask is described by a 2-bit vector, as in the DEC PDP8 (1965): one bit is the current enable bit; the other is the enable bit that will become active in the next execution cycle.

Embedding.   The 16-bit stack pointer (Sp) and the 16-bit processor status word (Psw) are embedded in working store.

A maximum of 256 peripheral devices may have their registers mapped onto main-storage name-space.

Programming model.   In the microprocessors, both datapath and addresses are relatively narrow, requiring and enabling a rich bus connectivity among many short registers. As in the IBM 1401 (1960) and other narrow machines, most of the register positions in the model are devoted to addresses—only one byte for data proper.

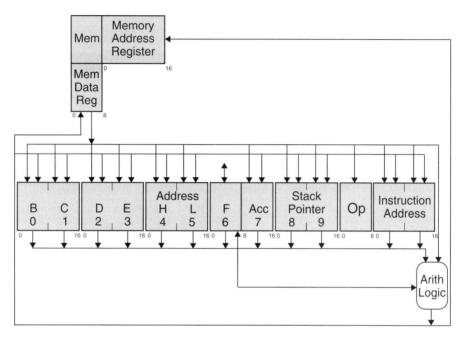

FIGURE 16-3   Programming model for the Intel 8080A.

Operand Specification

Number of addresses.   The Move has two addresses. All other instructions have one or no address. An address applies either to a register or through a register pair to memory.

Operation Specification

Mnemonics.   We use the mnemonics established by Intel. We deviate by splitting LDAX and STAX each in two instructions (LDAB, LDAD and STAB, STAD). Also, we combine each of the Conditional Branch, Call, and Return groups into one instruction.

Instruction list.   The instruction list is asymmetric for address arithmetic, and over-symmetric for sequencing.

a→MOV	ORA	STA	DI	
b→HLT	CMP	LDA	EI	
c→NOP	e→RT	f→RLC	f→ADI	h→LXI
→h	→gh	RRC	ACI	h→INX
→f	JP	RAL	SUI	h→DAD
→h	→f	RAR	SBI	h→DCX
INR	CL	DAA	ANI	h→POP
DCR	→gh	CMA	XRI	h→PUSH
MVI	→f	STC	ORI	
→f	RST	CMC	CPI	
d→ADD	f→STAB	f→JMP	g→RET	
ADC	LDAB			
SUB	STAD	OT	PCHL	
SBB	LDAD	IN	SPHL	
ANA	SHLD	XTHL	g→CALL	
XRA	LHLD	XCHG		

PROGRAM 16-4   Operation-code list in the Intel 8080A.

		address arithmetic	c	INR	Increment
f	LHLD	Load HL	c	DCR	Decrement
h	LXI	Load Pair Immediate	d	ADD	Add
g	SPHL	HL To Stack Pointer	f	ADI	Add Immediate
f	XTHL	Swap Stack With HL	d	ADC	Add With Carry
f	XCHG	Swap DE With HL	f	ACI	Add With Carry Immediate
f	SHLD	Store HL	d	SUB	Subtract
h	INX	Increment Pair	f	SUI	Subtract Immediate
h	DCX	Decrement Pair	d	SBB	Subtract With Borrow
h	DAD	Add Pair To HL	f	SBI	Subtract With Borrow Immediate
h	POP	Pop From Stack	d	CMP	Compare
h	PUSH	Push Onto Stack	f	CPI	Compare Immediate
		data handling			*decimal arithmetic*
a	MOV	Move	f	DAA	Decimal Adjust
c	MVI	Move Immediate			*sequencing*
		logic and shift	c	NOP	No Operation
f	CMA	Not	b	HLT	Stop
f	CMC	Invert Carry	f	JMP	Branch
d	ANA	And	g	PCHL	Branch To HL
f	ANI	And Immediate	e	JP	Branch On Condition
d	ORA	Or	g	CALL	Call
f	ORI	Or Immediate	e	CL	Call On Condition
d	XRA	Exclusive Or	g	RET	Return
f	XRI	Exclusive Or Immediate	e	RT	Return On Condition
f	RLC	Rotate Left			*supervision*
f	RAL	Rotate Left Through Carry	f	DI	Disable Interrupt
f	RRC	Rotate Right	f	EI	Enable Interrupt
f	RAR	Rotate Right Through Carry	e	RST	Restart
		fixed-point arithmetic			*input/output*
f	LDA	Load	f	OT	Output
f	LDAB	Load Via BC	f	IN	Input
f	LDAD	Load Via DE			
f	STC	Set Carry			
f	STA	Store			
f	STAB	Store Via BC			
f	STAD	Store Via DE			

TABLE 16-5   Instruction list of the Intel 8080A.

Instruction Structure

Machine-language syntax.   The first two instruction bits, when 0 1, specify a two-address operation—the addresses apply to registers or indirectly to memory; otherwise, the instruction bits specify a one-address operation, which involves either the source address or the destination address. Apart from these three basic patterns, there are seven zero-address patterns, and seven patterns that specify a register pair rather than a single register.

```
              syntax8080
        a 0 1 ,Dest,Source
        b 0 1 1 1 0 1 1 0
        c 0 0 ,Dest,Ops
        d 1 0 ,Opd,Source
        e 1 1 ,Rp,On,Ops
        f 0 0 ,Opd, 0 1 0
        f 0 0 ,Opd, 1 1 1
        f 1 1 ,Opd, 0 1 1
        f 1 1 ,Opd, 1 1 0
        g 1 1 ,Opr, 1 0 0 1
        g 1 1 ,Opr, 1 1 0 1
        h 0 0 ,Rp, 0 0 0 1
        h 0 0 ,Rp, 0 0 1 1
        h 0 0 ,Rp, 1 0 0 1
        h 0 0 ,Rp, 1 0 1 1
        h 1 1 ,Rp, 0 0 0 1
        h 1 1 ,Rp, 0 1 0 1
```

PROGRAM 16-6   Instruction syntax of the Intel 8080A.

Instruction format.   The 8-bit instructions may be extended with an 8-bit word or a 16-bit address, which gives the fixed lengths of 1, 2, or 3 bytes. Instruction bits are saved by implied addressing of the accumulator and by implied addressing of memory by a register pair.

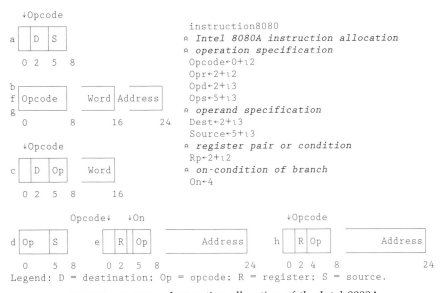

PROGRAM 16-7   Instruction allocation of the Intel 8080A.

Address Specification

Registers and memory are specified by a 3-bit instruction field. Register pairs are specified by a 2-bit instruction field. Memory is either specified by a 16-bit instruction field, or is implied by addresses in register pairs.

Status format.   The five conditions (Zero, Sign, Carry, Auxiliary carry, and Parity) and the Run status bit are combined into a status word in register F; the remaining two bits of the register are always 0. The auxiliary carry, Carry4, is propagated from bit 4 to bit 3. It is used for adjusting sum digits when doing programmed decimal arithmetic.

```
┌─────────────┐                    status8080
│ │ │ │ │ │ │ │ │                  ⋂ Intel 8080A status allocation
└─────────────┘                    ⋂ conditions
 0         8                       Neg←0
Register F                         Zero←1
                                   Carry←7
control8080                        Carry4←3
⋂ Intel 8080A control allocation   Parity←5
  instruction8080                  ⋂ executing state
  status8080                       Run←6
  address8080                      ⋂ permanent zero
                                   reg[F; 2 4]←0
```

PROGRAM 16-8   Status word in the Intel 8080A.

16.1.3

Addressing

Direct addressing.   An address has three attributes: the size of the addressed data, the space that is addressed, and the location within that space. The data size is either an 8-bit word or a 16-bit address. The address space is either the register set or memory.

An address is placed backward in memory, with its low-order word to the left of its high-order word. Hence reading from, or writing into, memory involves a transposition of those words. Such a transposition is not needed when an address is located in a register pair.

Registers are directly addressed with a 3-bit instruction field. Register 6, the status register F, is not directly addressed. Instead, a source or destination address 6 signifies indirect access to memory via the register-pair H1.

```
address←size adr8080 f                  adr←rp8080sp
⋂ Intel 8080A addressing                ⋂ Intel 8080A pair or stack pointer
→IF F≠fld f                             adr←(4 2 ρBc,De,H1,Sp)[fld Rp;]
THEN: ⋂ register
   address←size,regadr,fld f
   →ENDIF                               adr←rp8080ps
ELSE: ⋂ memory                          ⋂ Intel 8080A pair or status
   address←size,memadr,magni,reg[H1;]   adr←(4 2 ρBc,De,H1,Psw)[fld Rp;]
ENDIF:
```

PROGRAM 16-9   Addressing in the Intel 8080A.

```
data←read8080 address;location          address8080
ᴀ Intel 8080A read from storage         ᴀ Intel 8080A address allocation
size←address[Size]                      ᴀ attributes
location←address[Value]+ιsize∔word       Size←0
→IF address[Space]=regadr                Space←1
THEN: ᴀ register                        Value←2
   data←,reg[location;]                 ᴀ space identifiers
   →ENDIF                                regadr←1
ELSE: ᴀ memory                          memadr←2
   data←,memory[memcap|Φlocation;]
ENDIF:


address write8080 data;size;location
ᴀ Intel 8080A write into storage
size←address[Size]
location←address[Value]+ιsize∔word
→IF address[Space]=regadr
THEN: ᴀ register
   reg[location;]←word wide data
   →ENDIF
ELSE: ᴀ memory
   memory[memcap|Φlocation;]←word wide data
ENDIF:
```

PROGRAM 16-10   Memory read and write in the Intel 8080A.

The two bits Rp address one of four pairs; bit combination 1 1 usually addresses the stack pointer (rp8080sp), but exceptionally the PSW (rp8080ps), depending upon the operation. We will note when the PSW participates as a register pair.

Address Modification

The 8080A has no address modification through indexing. Some instructions, however, imply address incrementation and decrementation.

Postincrement and predecrement.   A register pair may be used to access a word-wide or an address-wide stack in memory with postincrement and predecrement.

```
address←size incr8080 r;count;rl    address←size decr8080 r;count;rl
ᴀ Intel 8080A postincrement          ᴀ Intel 8080A predecrement
address←size,memadr,magni,reg[r;]    count←(magni,reg[r;])-size∔word
count←address[Value]+size∔word       address←size,memadr,count
rl←adrsize magnr count               rl←adrsize magnr count
reg[r;]←word wide rl                 reg[r;]←word wide rl
```

PROGRAM 16-11   Postincrement and predecrement in the Intel 8080A.

System stack access.   pop8080 and push8080 describe access to the address-wide system stack through the stack pointer Sp. The system stack grows to lower addresses, with the pointer addressing the top word of the stack (the lowest current stack address).

```
data←pop8080                        push8080 data
ᴀ Intel 8080A read from stack      ᴀ Intel 8080A write onto stack
data←read8080 adrsize incr8080 Sp  (adrsize decr8080 Sp) write8080 data
```

PROGRAM 16-12   System-stack access in the Intel 8080A.

Index Arithmetic

Index arithmetic applies to the 16-bit addresses residing in the four register pairs Bc, De, Hl, and Sp. Hl is generally used to address memory, and Sp to address the stack in memory.

```
f LHLD  Load HL                  h INX   Increment Pair
h LXI   Load Pair Immediate      h DCX   Decrement Pair
g SPHL  HL To Stack Pointer      h DAD   Add Pair To HL
f XTHL  Swap Stack With HL       h POP   Pop From Stack
f XCHG  Swap DE With HL          h PUSH  Push Onto Stack
f SHLD  Store HL
```

TABLE 16-13   Addressing instructions of the Intel 8080A.

Address load and store.   All four register pairs can be loaded immediately. Hl can be swapped with the top of the stack and with the pair De, but not with Bc. The stack pointer can be set from Hl, but cannot be stored as a 16-bit entity.

```
LHLD;address;source                  LXI;data
ᴀ Intel 8080A Load HL               ᴀ Intel 8080A Load Pair Immediate
address←magni ifetch8080 adrsize    data←ifetch8080 adrsize
source←adrsize,memadr,address       reg[rp8080sp;]←word wide data
reg[Hl;]←word wide read8080 source


                                     XCHG
XTHL;data                           ᴀ Intel 8080A Swap DE With HL
ᴀ Intel 8080A Swap Stack With HL     reg[De,Hl;]←reg[Hl,De;]
data←pop8080
push8080 reg[Hl;]
reg[Hl;]←word wide data              SPHL
                                     ᴀ Intel 8080A HL To Stack Pointer
                                     reg[Sp;]←reg[Hl;]
```

PROGRAM 16-14   Address load and store in the Intel 8080A.

Address increment and decrement.   Increment Pair and Decrement Pair update an address in a register pair, or in the stack pointer, by 1. They can be used to address a stack of 8-bit words in memory. These operations are the same as the address postincrement and predecrement, except that the resulting address is not used.

```
INX;temp                            DCX;temp
ᴀ Intel 8080A Increment Pair       ᴀ Intel 8080A Decrement Pair
temp←word incr8080 rp8080sp         temp←word decr8080 rp8080sp
```

PROGRAM 16-15   Address increment and decrement in the Intel 8080A.

Address addition.   Any of the four register pairs (including Hl) can be added as a 16-bit quantity to Hl. This addressing operation is the only one that sets the carry bit, using signal8080C (Program 16-18).

```
DAD;addend;augend;sum
ด Intel 8080A Add Pair To HL
addend←radixcompi.reg[rp8080sp;]
augend←radixcompi.reg[Hl;]
sum←augend+addend
reg[Hl;]←word wide adrsize radixcompr sum
signal8080C augend,addend
```

PROGRAM 16-16   Address addition in the Intel 8080A.

Stack addressing. POP removes an address from the system stack and places it in a register pair; PUSH places an address from a register pair in the system stack. For these operations, the PSW is moved instead of the stack pointer. The change of register F leaves the fixed-zero and Run bits unchanged.

```
POP                              PUSH
ด Intel 8080A Pop From Stack     ด Intel 8080A Push Onto Stack
reg[rp8080ps;]←word wide pop8080   push8080 reg[rp8080ps;]
reg[F; 2 4 6]← 0 0 1
```

PROGRAM 16-17   Stack operations in the Intel 8080A.

Address Level

Immediate addressing.   A separate set of instructions specifies immediate addressing for all dyadic operations.

16.1.4
Data

Character Strings

Character set and size.   The design assumes 8-bit characters; there are no character strings. Nothing in the CPU architecture depends upon the character encoding.

Logical

Logical formats.   Boolean vectors are one 8-bit word long.

Fixed-Point Numbers

Notation and allocation.   Binary radix complement is used for 8-bit integers and 16-bit addresses. Addresses are stored in memory with the high-order and low-order byte switched. Decimal numbers use 4-bit binary coded decimal, with two digits in a byte; only Decimal Adjust uses this format.

In subtraction, a borrow is recorded in the carry indicator; Subtract With Borrow uses the content of that indicator as a borrow. The auxiliary carry notes the carry out of bit 4 into bit 3, as in addition. A Decimal Adjust cannot be used after a subtraction, since it requires a carry, not a borrow. Hence the setting of the auxiliary carry in subtraction serves little purpose.

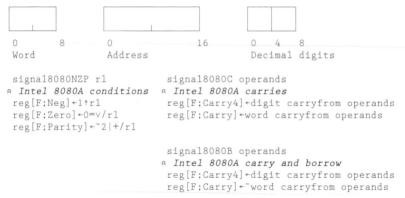

```
0       8      0                    16    0   4   8
Word           Address                    Decimal digits
```

```
signal8080NZP rl                 signal8080C operands
ᴀ Intel 8080A conditions         ᴀ Intel 8080A carries
reg[F;Neg]←1↑rl                   reg[F;Carry4]←digit carryfrom operands
reg[F;Zero]←0=∨/rl                reg[F;Carry]←word carryfrom operands
reg[F;Parity]←~2|+/rl

                                 signal8080B operands
                                 ᴀ Intel 8080A carry and borrow
                                 reg[F;Carry4]←digit carryfrom operands
                                 reg[F;Carry]←~word carryfrom operands
```

PROGRAM 16-18   Data in the Intel 8080A.

16.1.5
Operations

Data Handling

Data handling must be programmed through registers.

Data movement.   The one-word Move is memory to register, register to register, and register to memory. Since the memory address is specified by the content of register pair H1, a memory-to-memory move would accomplish nothing. Instead, this instruction is interpreted as a Stop (syntactic pattern b).

```
MOV;data                         MVI;data
ᴀ Intel 8080A Move               ᴀ Intel 8080A Move Immediate
data←read8080 word adr8080 Source   data←ifetch8080 word
(word adr8080 Dest) write8080 data   (word adr8080 Dest) write8080 data
```

PROGRAM 16-19   Move in the Intel 8080A.

The immediate move is to register or to memory.

Logic

Logical connectives and Rotate apply to 8-bit words in the accumulator.

f	CMA	Not	d	XRA	Exclusive Or
f	CMC	Invert Carry	f	XRI	Exclusive Or Immediate
d	ANA	And	f	RLC	Rotate Left
f	ANI	And Immediate	f	RAL	Rotate Left Through Carry
d	ORA	Or	f	RRC	Rotate Right
f	ORI	Or Immediate	f	RAR	Rotate Right Through Carry

TABLE 16-20   Logical instructions of the Intel 8080A.

Connectives.   The logical connectives instructions are Not, And, Or, and Exclusive Or. The dyadic connectives are with storage operand and with immediate operand. The conditions are set according to the arithmetic meaning of the result, with the carry conditions set to 0. The Immediate And is anomalous in setting the auxiliary carry to 1.

```
CMA                            ORA;od
⋒ Intel 8080A Not              ⋒ Intel 8080A Or
reg[A;]←˜reg[A;]               od←read8080 word adr8080 Source
                               reg[A;]←reg[A;]∨od
                               reg[F;Carry.Carry4]←0
ANI;od                         signal8080NZP reg[A;]
⋒ Intel 8080A And Immediate
od←ifetch8080 word
reg[A;]←reg[A;]∧od
reg[F;Carry.Carry4]← 0 1
signal8080NZP reg[A;]
```

PROGRAM 16-21   Not, And, and Or in the Intel 8080A.

Rotate. Rotation is 1 bit left or right, with or without the carry bit. Carry is the only condition that changes during Rotate. There is no shift, but any 1-bit shift is easily programmed using the carry.

```
   Carry↓

  ┌────┬─┐                    ┌──────┐
  │    │ │                    │      │
  └────┴─┘                    └──────┘

  0        8                  0      8
  F register                  Accumulator
```

```
RLC                            RAR;result
⋒ Intel 8080A Rotate Left      ⋒ Intel 8080A Rotate Right Through Carry
reg[F;Carry]←1↑reg[A;]         result←˜1⌽reg[F;Carry].reg[A;]
reg[A;]←1⌽reg[A;]              reg[F;Carry]←1↑result
                               reg[A;]←1↓result
```

PROGRAM 16-22   Rotate in the Intel 8080A.

Fixed-Point Arithmetic

Most fixed-point operations apply to the 8-bit accumulator. There is proper provision for extended precision, but no provision for multiplication or division.

f	LDA	Load	d ADD	Add
f	LDAB	Load Via BC	f ADI	Add Immediate
f	LDAD	Load Via DE	d ADC	Add With Carry
f	STC	Set Carry	f ACI	Add With Carry Immediate
f	STA	Store	d SUB	Subtract
f	STAB	Store Via BC	f SUI	Subtract Immediate
f	STAD	Store Via DE	d SBB	Subtract With Borrow
c	INR	Increment	f SBI	Subtract With Borrow Immediate
c	DCR	Decrement	d CMP	Compare
			f CPI	Compare Immediate

TABLE 16-23   Fixed-point instructions of the Intel 8080A.

Load and Store. Load and Store apply to the 8-bit accumulator, register A. The address is either direct as a 16-bit instruction extension, or in register pairs Bc or De. A Load or Store with the address in Hl is part of the Move instruction (Program 16-19).

```
LDA;address                              STAD;dest
ค Intel 8080A Load                       ค Intel 8080A Store Via DE
  address←magni ifetch8080 adrsize         dest←word,memadr,magni,reg[De;]
  reg[A;]←read8080 word,memadr,address     dest write8080 reg[A;]


LDAB;source
ค Intel 8080A Load Via BC
  source←word,memadr,magni,reg[Bc;]
  reg[A;]←read8080 source
```

PROGRAM 16-24   Load and Store in the Intel 8080A.

Increment and decrement.   Increment adds an implied 1 to an 8-bit operand in a register or in memory.   The sign, zero, parity, and auxiliary carry conditions are set, but the carry-out of the addition is not disturbed.   Similarly, Decrement subtracts 1 from the operand and sets the same conditions.

```
     INR;dest;count;rl;c                 DCR;dest;count;rl;c
   ค Intel 8080A Increment              ค Intel 8080A Decrement
     dest←word adr8080 Dest               dest←word adr8080 Dest
     count←magni read8080 dest            count←magni read8080 dest
     rl←word magnr count+1                rl←word magnr count-1
     dest write8080 rl                    dest write8080 rl
     c←digit carryfrom count,1            c←digit carryfrom count,¯1
     reg[F;Carry4]←c                      reg[F;Carry4]←c
     signal8080NZP rl                     signal8080NZP rl
```

PROGRAM 16-25   Increment and decrement in the Intel 8080A.

Add and Subtract.   The addend is derived from a register or from memory. All conditions are set.   On addition, a carry out of bit 0 and an auxiliary carry out of bit 4 are noted.   In Add With Carry the regular carry indicator participates in the addition.

```
ADD;ad;addend;augend;sum                 ADC;ad;addend;augend;sum
ค Intel 8080A Add                        ค Intel 8080A Add With Carry
  ad←read8080 word adr8080 Source          ad←read8080 word adr8080 Source
  addend←radixcompi ad                     addend←radixcompi ad
  augend←radixcompi reg[A;]                augend←radixcompi reg[A;]
  sum←augend+addend                        sum←augend+addend+reg[F;Carry]
  reg[A;]←word radixcompr sum              reg[A;]←word radixcompr sum
  signal8080C augend,addend                signal8080C augend,addend,reg[F;Carry]
  signal8080NZP reg[A;]                    signal8080NZP reg[A;]


SBI;addend;augend;sum
ค Intel 8080A Subtract With Borrow Immediate
  addend←radixcompi¯ifetch8080 word
  augend←radixcompi reg[A;]
  sum←augend+addend+¯reg[F;Carry]
  reg[A;]←word radixcompr sum
  signal8080B addend,augend,¯reg[F;Carry]
  signal8080NZP reg[A;]
```

PROGRAM 16-26   Addition in the Intel 8080A.

In subtraction, a borrow is noted in the carry condition; the auxiliary carry records the carry out of bit 4, as in addition.   Subtract With Borrow uses the contents of the carry indicator as a borrow.

Compare.   Comparison is accomplished by subtraction. Hence the indicators are set accordingly—noting a borrow, not a carry.

```
CPI;operand;comparand
ⴲ Intel 8080A Compare Immediate
operand←radixcompi~ifetch8080 word
comparand←radixcompi reg[A;]
signal8080B comparand,operand,1
signal8080NZP word radixcompr comparand+operand+1
```

PROGRAM 16-27   Comparison in the Intel 8080A.

Decimal Arithmetic

Decimal addition.   Pairs of binary-coded-decimal digits can be added. Decimal addition starts with a binary addition. The regular and auxiliary carry of the binary addition show whether the sum of the corresponding decimal digits is 16 or more. Next, Decimal Adjust tests the two sum digits for a value greater than 9. If a digit is greater than 9 (or 16), Decimal Adjust corrects it by adding 6. A carry is recorded when it was 1 prior to the correction or when it is produced in the correction. So extended addition using repeated cycles of ADC followed by DAA is possible.

```
DAA;carry10;addend;augend;sum
ⴲ Intel 8080A Decimal Adjust
carry10←9<magni digit wide reg[A;]
addend←16⊥6×reg[F;Carry,Carry4]∨carry10
augend←radixcompi reg[A;]
sum←augend+addend
reg[A;]←word radixcompr sum
reg[F;Carry,Carry4]←carry10∨reg[F;Carry],0
signal8080NZP reg[A;]
```

PROGRAM 16-28   Decimal Adjust in the Intel 8080A.

Decimal adjust does not apply to subtraction. The 8086 has an instruction DAS, Decimal Adjust For Subtraction.

16.1.6

Instruction Sequencing

The basic instruction cycle fetches a one-word instruction. The instruction execution may fetch subsequent words as immediate data or as addresses.

```
cycle8080                              inst←ifetch8080 size
ⴲ basic cycle of the Intel 8080A   ⴲ Intel 8080A instruction fetch
REPEAT:interrupt8080                   inst←read8080 size,memadr,iadr
   execute ifetch8080 word             iadr←iadr+size÷word
→UNTIL~reg[F;Run]
```

```
HLT
ⴲ Intel 8080A Stop
reg[F;Run]←0
```

PROGRAM 16-29   Basic cycle and instruction fetch of the Intel 8080A.

Sequencing instructions.   The Intel 8080A has decision and delegation. Iteration is aided by increment and decrement operations, but these are not combined with branches.

c	NOP	No Operation	g	CALL	Call
b	HLT	Stop	e	CL	Call On Condition
f	JMP	Branch	g	RET	Return
g	PCHL	Branch To HL	e	RT	Return On Condition
e	JP	Branch On Condition			

TABLE 16-30   Sequencing instructions of the Intel 8080A.

Linear Sequence

Completion.   The 8080A has an explicit Stop instruction.

Unconditional Branch.   The Unconditional Branch is direct, or indirect via register H1.

```
JMP                                PCHL
a Intel 8080A Branch               a Intel 8080A Branch To HL
iadr←magni ifetch8080 adrsize      iadr←magni.reg[Hl;]
```

PROGRAM 16-31   Unconditional Branch in the Intel 8080A.

Decision

Conditional branching.   Decision uses conditions to separate test and action. Each of the Zero, Negative, Carry, and Parity conditions may be used as a criterion for branching or not branching. The same criteria are used in Conditional Call and Return.

```
JP;branch                           true←condition8080;cond
a Intel 8080A Branch On Condition   a Intel 8080A condition test
branch←magni ifetch8080 adrsize     cond←(Zero,Carry,Neg,Parity)[fld Rp]
→If condition8080                   true←reg[F;cond]=fld On
THEN:iadr←branch
ENDIF:
```

PROGRAM 16-32   Conditional Branch in the Intel 8080A.

Delegation

Call and Return.   Processor state-saving uses the system stack in memory. Call and Return save and restore the return address on the stack. PUSH and POP can save and restore the rest of the processor state excluding the interrupt-enable bit. Parameters can be placed upon the stack. Nested calls to any depth are allowed.

```
CALL;branchadr                      RT
a Intel 8080A Call                  a Intel 8080A Return On Condition
branchadr←magni ifetch8080 adrsize  →If condition8080
push8080 adrsize magnr iadr         THEN:iadr←magni pop8080
iadr←branchadr                      ENDIF:
```

PROGRAM 16-33   Call and Return in the Intel 8080A.

16.1.7

Supervision

Concurrency

Processor interconnection. Multiprocessing provisions are made via a central bus.

Process Interaction

Signaling.   Processor interaction must be established via the interruption mechanism.

Integrity

There is no protection, and only one execution mode.

Control Switching

Interruption.   If the interrupt-enable flag is on, and the interrupt request line, `irq`, is made high by an external device, the CPU interrupts after the current instruction is completed. The interrupt-enable bit is then turned off, and the CPU accepts a one-word instruction from the interrupting device via the data bus. The external device is responsible for generating the inserted instruction. About the only reasonable instruction to be executed at interrupt is a Restart, which identifies the device in the 3-bit `Dest` field, as is indicated in `interrupt8080`. The instruction received is executed, and the normal execution cycle is resumed.

```
interrupt8080
ค Intel 8080A interrupt action
→If irq∧enable[0]
THEN: ค execute RST from databus
      execute 1 1 ,(3 magnr who), 1 1 1
      irq←0
      enable[]←0
ENDIF:enable[0]←enable[1]
```

PROGRAM 16-34   Interruption action in the Intel 8080A.

Interrupt handling.   Restart is a special 1-byte jump to subroutine instruction whose 3-bit address refers to the first 64 bytes of memory: `RST N` is equivalent to `CALL 8×N`. Return is used to return from interrupts invoked via Restart as well as returns from subroutines. Enable Interrupt acts after a one-instruction delay. Thus a Return instruction can be executed before the system is enabled and any pending interrupt is taken.

```
RST                             EI
ค Intel 8080A Restart           ค Intel 8080A Enable Interrupt
  push8080 adrsize magnr iadr     enable[1]←1
  iadr←8×fld Dest
```

PROGRAM 16-35   Interrupt-handling operations in the Intel 8080A.

State Preservation

Context switching.   The only state that an interruption saves on the system stack is the instruction address. The instructions PUSH and POP can save and retrieve the status register and the accumulator using the system stack.

Supervisory operations.   Enable and Disable Interrupt and Restart can be used as part of interrupt handling, but no status indicator in the PSW or elsewhere allows testing of the enabled state.

```
f DI    Disable Interrupt   e RST   Restart
f EI    Enable Interrupt
```

TABLE 16-36   Supervisory operations of the Intel 8080A.

16.1.8
Input/Output

Direct Input/Output

The 8080A can communicate with 256 input and output devices. It uses direct control—data are transferred a byte at a time between the accumulator and the outside world. Direct, buffered, and channel I/O can be implemented on special chips. The single central bus allows only concurrency of 1.

Overlapped Input/Output

Read and Write.   Two instructions perform the I/O. Both send the device address on the address lines and receive or send data on the data lines. A status bit is also set to signal that an input or output operation is in progress.

```
OT;port                   IN;port
 ∩ Intel 8080A Output      ∩ Intel 8080A Input
   port←magni ifetch8080 word  port←magni ifetch8080 word
   ioport[port;]←reg[A;]       reg[A;]←ioport[port;]
```

PROGRAM 16-37   Input/output Read and Write in the Intel 8080A.

16.1.9
Implementation Notes

Five thousand transistors are placed in a 0.164 by 0.190-inch silicon chip and consume 1 watt of power.

Computing speed is limited by processor speed, not memory speed. Memory cycles constitute only one-fifth to one-third of the machine's cycles.

The backwards bytes in the address specification resulted from constraints of the serial implementation.

16.1.10
Bibliography

Osborne, A., 1976: *An Introduction to Microcomputers*, vol. 2. Berkeley, CA: Osborne.

Leventhal, L.A., 1978: *8080A/8085 Assembly Language Programming*. Berkeley, CA: Osborne/McGraw-Hill (our defining reference).

Dollhoff, T., 1979: *16-Bit Microprocessor Architecture*. Reston, VA: Reston.

Morse, S.P., B. Ravenel, S. Mazor, and W. Pohlman, 1980: "Intel Microprocessors—8008 to 8086." *Computer*, **13**, 10: 42–60.

Crawford [1986, 1990], Faggin and Hoff [1972], Feeney [1974], Hoff [1970], Morse et al. [1978], Palmer [1980], Rafiquzzaman [1990].

16.1.11
Exercises

16-1 Give the description of SHLD (Store Address), assuming consistency with the instructions shown in this section.

16-2 Give the description of the logical and shift instructions CMC, ANA, ORI, XRA, XRI, RAL, and RRC, assuming consistency with the logical and shift instructions shown in this section.

16-3 Give the description of the fixed-point arithmetic instructions LDAD, STC, STA, STAB, ADI, ACI, SUB, SBB, SUI, and CMP, assuming consistency with the fixed-point arithmetic instructions shown in this section.

16-4 Give the description of the sequencing and supervisory instructions CL and DI, assuming consistency with the sequencing and supervisory instructions shown in this section.

16-5 Give the programs for a 1-bit logical and arithmetic left and right shift.

16.2
Motorola M6800*

16.2.1
Highlights

History

Architect. Not known to us.

Dates. The Motorola M6800 was delivered in 1975.

Noteworthy

As a microprocessor, the M6800 resembles the Intel 8080A (1974) in its 8-bit word, 16-bit address, system stack, programmmed stack operations, logical connectives, lack of logical vector operations, 1-bit rotate through carry, addition and subtraction with extended precision, conditions, branch, call, and return. We note a few differences.

Clean design. The M6800 architecture appears as a consistent new design without traces of an evolutionary development.

Dedicated registers. The M6800 does not group its registers into a register set, but treats them as a disjunct set, with each member dedicated to a special purpose.

Addressing modes. There are several addressing modes, including address-abbreviation techniques.

No backwards byte. The M6800 breaks the DEC PDP11 (1970) tradition of recording low-order and high-order bytes backward in memory.

Rich set of branch conditions. The branch conditions closely resemble the PDP11 conditions by including tests for the results of signed and unsigned arithmetic.

Supervision. Supervisory facilities include a Wait operation, humble access, and proper access to the interrupt-enable control.

Peculiarities

Limited register set. There are only two arithmetic registers (accumulators); all other working store is for address manipulation. The two accumulators are symmetric, except that a few operations apply to only one of them. Also, the register-to-register operations are asymmetric.

Stack access. In a remarkable deviation from the system stack access established by the PDP11 and 8080A, the M6800 uses preincrement and

---

* Original sketch research by M.K. Smotherman.

postdecrement instead of postincrement and predecrement; the stack grows downward, and the stack pointer points to one word beyond (below) the top element of the stack.

Borrow.   Unfortunately, the PDP11 is followed in recording a borrow upon subtraction, instead of a carry. This behavior limits the usefulness of Decimal Adjust.

Descendants

The Motorola M6809 and the MOS Technology 6502 (1976) are the immediate incompatible descendants of the M6800. The Motorola MC68000 family members are the subsequent, even less compatible, descendants.

16.2.2

Machine Language

Language Level

Design philosophy.   As a typical microprocessor the M6800 assumes assembly-level programming. The 16-bit control variables such as the index, stack pointer, and instruction address are restricted to their primary purpose, in contrast to the PDP11 design philosophy. This approach emphasizes the 8-bit data size of the M6800, contrary to the frequent 16-bit functions of the 8080A.

Unit System

The basic information unit is the 8-bit byte; addresses use 16 bits.

```
initiate68                              format68
 ⍝ initiation of the Motorola 6800       ⍝ Motorola 6800 information units
 format68                                ⍝ representation radix
 configure68                             radix←2
 space68                                 ⍝ information units
 name68                                  digit←4
 control68                               word←8
                                         adrsize←16
                                         ⍝ address capacity
 configure68                             adrcap←radix*adrsize
 ⍝ configuration for the Motorola 6800
 ⍝ memory capacity
 memcap←adrcap
```

PROGRAM 16-38   Basic parameters of the Motorola 6800.

Spaces

Memory name-space.   Memory is a linear array of 64 K bytes. The first 256 words are distinguished as a base page, which can be addressed with one word.

The eight highest bytes are reserved for four interrupt-routine addresses. Peripheral device registers are mapped onto the name-space at implementation-dependent locations.

```
space68                              name68
A Motorola 6800 spaces               A Motorola 6800 space names
A memory                             A memory allocation
 memory←?(memcap,word)ρradix         A - interrupt address
A working store                       Intadr←memcap-8
A - accumulators                     A accumulator allocation
 acc←?(2,word)ρradix                  A←0
A - index                             B←1
 index←?adrcap
A - stack pointer
 sp←?adrcap
A control store
A - instruction address
 iadr←?adrcap
A - status word
 status← 1 1 ,?6ρradix
A - indicators
 ind←?4ρradix
A - stop condition
 stop←?radix
```

PROGRAM 16-39   Spaces of the Motorola 6800.

Working store.   The two 8-bit accumulators are called A and B. The index (index) and stack pointer (sp) are each capable of addressing all of memory; each acts as an integer that does not show its encoding as a 16-bit binary magnitude.

Control store.   The 8-bit status word (status) has the two high-order bits fixed as 1; five status bits are used as conditions; four indicators represent interrupt causes; one bit disables interrupts.

Embedding.   The dedicated control values are not embedded in a larger register array or memory. I/O data and control registers are embedded in memory.

Programming model.   The 6800 has fewer addressable registers than the 8080A, but otherwise its model is very similar. Notice how it resembles that of the IBM 1401 (1960), and the IBM System/360 (1965) character model, in that almost all of the registers are used for addresses and other control, and so only two bytes for operands proper.

Operand Specification

Number of addresses.   The M6800 uses one- and two-address instructions. When there are two addresses, one is a 1-bit accumulator address. The stack pointer and index are addressed by operation-code implication.

Address phrase.   The address phrase includes an address-mode designator in the first byte, then 0, 1, or 2 bytes of address.

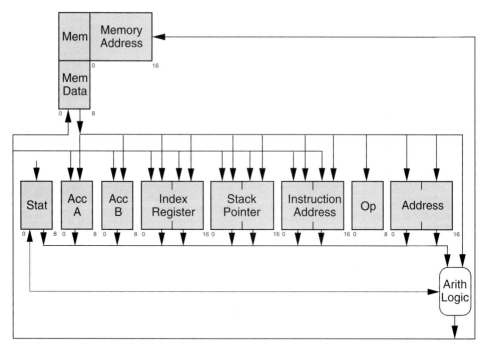

FIGURE 16-40   Programming model for the Motorola 6800.

Operation Specification

Mnemonics. The set of 71 mnemonics is that used by Motorola.

a→		SBA	BRA	TSX	b→NEG	c→SUB	d→CPX
		CBA		INS		CMP	→gh
NOP			BHI	→f		SBC	LDS
			BLS	→f	COM		STS
			BCC	DES	LSR	AND	e→LDX
			BCS	TXS		BIT	STX
TAP	TAB		BNE	→f	ROR	LDA	f→PUL
TPA	TBA		BEQ	→f	ASR	STA	f→PSH
INX			BVC	RTI	ASL	EOR	g→JMP
DEX	DAA		BVS	RTS	ROL	ADC	g→JSR
CLV			BPL		DEC	ORA	h→BSR
SEV	ABA		BMI			ADD	
CLC			BGE		INC	→d	
SEC			BLT		TST	→d	
CLI			BGT	WAI	→g	→de	
SEI			BLE	SWI	CLR	→de	

PROGRAM 16-41   Operation-code list of the Motorola 6800.

Instruction Structure

Instruction list.   The instruction list is typical for a microprocessor; it has rather complete address arithmetic, logic, addition, subtraction, and branching; no long shifts, multiplication, division, or elaborate supervisory operations.

```
       a address arithmetic          b NEG Negate
 e LDX Load Index                     b INC Increment
 d LDS Load Pointer                   b DEC Decrement
 a TSX Pointer To Index               c ADD Add
 a TXS Index To Pointer               a ABA Add Accumulators
 e STX Store Index                    c ADC Add With Carry
 d STS Store Pointer                  c SUB Subtract
 a INX Increment Index                a SBA Subtract Accumulators
 a INS Increment Pointer              c SBC Subtract With Borrow
 a DEX Decrement Index                c CMP Compare
 a DES Decrement Pointer              a CBA Compare Accumulators
 d CPX Compare Index                     a decimal arithmetic
 f PUL Pop                            a DAA Decimal Adjust
 f PSH Push                              a sequencing
       a logic and shift             a NOP No Operation
 b COM Not                            g JMP Branch
 c AND And                            a BRA Jump
 c ORA Or                             a BPL Jump On Plus
 c EOR Exclusive Or                   a BMI Jump On Minus
 b TST Test                           a BLT Jump On Less
 c BIT Bit Test                       a BLE Jump On Less Or Equal
 b CLR Clear                          a BEQ Jump On Equal
 b LSR Shift Logical Right            a BNE Jump On Not Equal
 b ASL Shift Arithmetic Left          a BGE Jump On Greater Or Equal
 b ASR Shift Arithmetic Right         a BGT Jump On Greater
 b ROL Rotate Left                    a BLS Jump On Low Or Equal
 b ROR Rotate Right                   a BHI Jump On High
       a fixed-point arithmetic       a BCS Jump On Carry
 c LDA Load                           a BCC Jump On No Carry
 a TAB Accumulator A To B             a BVS Jump On Overflow
 a TBA Accumulator B To A             a BVC Jump On No Overflow
 a TPA Load Condition                 g JSR Call
 a TAP Set Condition                  h BSR Jump To Subroutine
 a SEV Set Overflow                   a RTS Return
 a SEC Set Carry                         a supervision
 a CLV Reset Overflow                 a RTI Return From Interrupt
 a CLC Reset Carry                    a SEI Disable Interrupt
 c STA Store                          a CLI Enable Interrupt
                                      a WAI Wait
                                      a SWI Programmed Interrupt
```

TABLE 16-42   Instruction list of the Motorola 6800.

Machine-language syntax.   The syntax has a complex operation code with two levels of code extension. The 1-bit accumulator address, 2-bit address mode, and operation code are all packed into one 8-bit word. To make these fields fit, the accumulator address occurs at two places, and the address mode is truncated in a few patterns by requiring its left bit to be 1.

```
          syntax68
   a 0 0 .Opcode
   b 0 1 .M.Opa
   c 1.Acc.M.Opa
   d 1 0 .M. 1 1 .Opb
   e 1 1 .M. 1 1 1 .Opc
   f 0 0 1 1 0 0 1 .A0
   f 0 0 1 1 0 1 1 .A0
   g 0 1 1 .M0. 1 1 1 0
   g 1 0 1 .M0. 1 1 0 1
   h 1 0 0 0 1 1 0 1
```

PROGRAM 16-43   Instruction syntax of the Motorola 6800.

Instruction format.   The basic instruction format occupies one word. The instruction may be extended with 8 or 16 bits for immediate data or for an address.

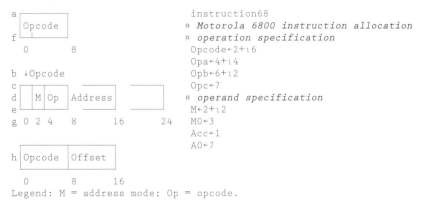

```
a ┌─────────┐                    instruction68
  │ Opcode  │                    ⋒ Motorola 6800 instruction allocation
f └─────────┘                    ⋒ operation specification
  0         8                    Opcode←2+ι6
                                 Opa←4+ι4
b ↓Opcode                        Opb←6+ι2
c ┌──┬──┬────────┬─────┐         Opc←7
d │  │M │Op│Address│    │        ⋒ operand specification
e └──┴──┴────────┴─────┘         M←2+ι2
g 0  2  4  8      16    24       MO←3
                                 Acc←1
                                 AO←7

h ┌────────┬────────┐
  │ Opcode │ Offset │
  └────────┴────────┘
  0        8       16
Legend: M = address mode; Op = opcode.
```

PROGRAM 16-44   Instruction allocation in the Motorola 6800.

Status format.   The status word contains a negative, zero, and overflow condition bit, a high-order carry bit and a carry out of bit 4 into bit 3, the auxiliary or half carry `Carry4`, used for programmed decimal addition, as in the 8080A. The indicators are for system reset, system error, humble access, and I/O.

```
status68                        indicator68
⋒ Motorola 6800 status allocation   ⋒ Motorola 6800 indicator allocation
⋒ conditions                    Reset←3
Neg←4                           Error←2
Zero←5                          Program←1
Oflo←6                          Iot←0
Carry←7
Carry4←2
⋒ interrupt disable
Disable←3
```

PROGRAM 16-45   Status word and indicators in the Motorola 6800.

16.2.3

Addressing

Storage access may be immediate, from or to a register, and from or to memory. These alternatives are specified by the address-space attribute.

Direct addressing.   An address may be truncated to only one word, into the zero page, or two words, into all of memory. The latter is called (idiosyncratically in the 6800) Extended Addressing.

Address Modification

There are two sets of address modes. The normal address mode, which applies to Load, Store, and dyadic operations, allows immediate addressing

```
data←size read68 address;loc          address write68 data;loc
⍝ Motorola 6800 read from store       ⍝ Motorola 6800 write into store
→CASE address[Space]                  →CASE address[Space]
C0: ⍝ immediate                       C0: ⍝ immediate
   data←ifetch68 size                    →ERROR
   →ENDCASE                           C1: ⍝ accumulator
C1: ⍝ accumulator                        acc[address[Value];]←data
   data←acc[address[Value];]             →ENDCASE
   →ENDCASE                           C2: ⍝ memory
C2: ⍝ memory                             loc←address[Value]+ι(ρ,data)÷word
   loc←address[Value]+ιsize÷word         memory[adrcap|loc;]←word wide data
   data←,memory[adrcap|loc;]          ENDCASE:
ENDCASE:
```

PROGRAM 16-46   Storage read and write in the Motorola 6800.

(not for Store) and truncated direct addressing, whereas the alternate address mode, which applies to monadic operations, addresses the two accumulators. Both sets include indexed and full (extended) direct addressing.

```
address←adr68                          address68
⍝ Motorola 6800 addressing            ⍝ Motorola 6800 address allocation
→CASE fld M                           ⍝ attributes
C0: ⍝ immediate                        Space←0
   address←immadr,0                    Value←1
   →ENDCASE                           ⍝ space identifiers
C1: ⍝ truncated                        immadr←0
   address←memadr,magni ifetch68 word  accadr←1
   →ENDCASE                            memadr←2
C2: ⍝ indexed
   address←memadr,index68
   →ENDCASE
C3: ⍝ direct
   address←memadr,magni ifetch68 adrsize
ENDCASE:
```

```
address←adr68a                         address←index68;displacement
⍝ Motorola 6800 alternate addressing  ⍝ Motorola 6800 address modification
→CASE fld M                            displacement←magni ifetch68 word
C0: ⍝ accumulator A                    address←index+displacement
   address←accadr,A
   →ENDCASE
C1: ⍝ accumulator B
   address←accadr,B
   →ENDCASE
C2: ⍝ indexed
   address←memadr,index68
   →ENDCASE
C3: ⍝ direct
   address←memadr,magni ifetch68 adrsize
ENDCASE:
```

PROGRAM 16-47   Addressing in the Motorola 6800.

Address calculation.   Every operation that can take a full memory address can also use the indexed mode. The instruction fetches an extra word from memory—the 8-bit positive displacement—which is added to the full index value to get the effective address.

System stack access.   Stack access is with a preincrement pop and a postdecrement push, which assumes a stack that grows downward and has the stack pointer pointing at a location one word below the top of the stack. This action is clearest for single-word access, with double-word access built from two single actions (which is what the implementation does).

```
data←pop68 size                      push68 data
⋒ Motorola 6800 pop from stack       ⋒ Motorola 6800 push onto stack
sp←sp+1                              (memadr,sp) write68(-word)↑,data
data←word read68 memadr,sp           sp←sp-1
→If size=adrsize                     →If adrsize=ρ,data
THEN:sp←sp+1                         THEN:(memadr,sp) write68 word↑,data
   data←data,word read68 memadr,sp      sp←sp-1
ENDIF:                               ENDIF:
```

PROGRAM 16-48   System stack access in the Motorola 6800.

Pop, Push, Call, Return, Return From Interrupt, and Programmed Interrupt use the stack pointer. Addressing via the stack pointer is not possible in other instructions. Only working and control store can be placed directly on the system stack.

Address arithmetic

The index and the stack pointer can be transferred to each other and each can be loaded, stored, incremented, and decremented. The index can be compared, which is useful in a limit check.

```
e LDX Load Index        a INX Increment Index
d LDS Load Pointer      a INS Increment Pointer
a TSX Pointer To Index  a DEX Decrement Index
a TXS Index To Pointer  a DES Decrement Pointer
e STX Store Index       d CPX Compare Index
d STS Store Pointer     f PUL Pop
                        f PSH Push
```

TABLE 16-49   Address arithmetic instructions of the Motorola 6800.

Address Load and Store.   Index and Pointer Load and Store can be indexed. Pointer To Index increments the value that is placed in the Index; Index to Pointer decrements the value. So the index can be set to the top of the stack, which is 1 more than the current value of the stack pointer. Load Pointer and Store Index set the negative and zero indicators (Program 16-53).

```
LDS;od                               STX;r1
⋒ Motorola 6800 Load Pointer         ⋒ Motorola 6800 Store Index
od←adrsize read68 adr68              r1←adrsize magnr index
sp←magni od                          adr68 write68 r1
signal68NZ od                        signal68NZ r1


TSX                                  TXS
⋒ Motorola 6800 Pointer To Index     ⋒ Motorola 6800 Index To Pointer
index←adrcap|sp+1                     sp←adrcap|index-1
```

PROGRAM 16-50   Address Load and Store in the Motorola 6800.

Address increment and decrement.   Incrementing or decrementing the index sets the 0 condition. The pointer operations set no conditions. The comparison sets the negative, zero, and overflow conditions as for a subtract of the comparand from the index.

```
INX                                    CPX;comparand;r1
ⱥ Motorola 6800 Increment Index        ⱥ Motorola 6800 Compare Index
index←index+1                          comparand←magni adrsize read68 adr68
status[Zero]←index=0                   r1←word magnr index-comparand
                                       signal68NZO r1


DES
ⱥ Motorola 6800 Decrement Pointer
sp←sp-1
```

PROGRAM 16-51   Address Increment, Decrement, Compare in the Motorola 6800.

Stack addressing.   Pop and Push load and place the accumulators from and onto the stack. Programmed stacks can be implemented with Increment and Decrement; these stacks are limited to 256 words. There is no increment or decrement addressing mode.

```
          PUL                      PSH
          ⱥ Motorola 6800 Pop      ⱥ Motorola 6800 Push
          acc[fld A0;]←pop68 word  push68 acc[fld A0;]
```

PROGRAM 16-52   Stack operations in the Motorola 6800.

Address Level

Immediate addressing.   The main address mode can specify an immediate address of 1 or 2 bytes.

Indirect addressing.   There is no separate provision for indirect addressing, although the index or the stack pointer can be loaded and addressed through. This decomposition is like that in the 360.

16.2.4
Data

Character Strings

Character set and size.   The M6800 handles 8-bit characters, but no strings. Nothing in the CPU architecture depends upon character encoding.

Logical

Logical formats.   Boolean vectors have 8-bit word length.

Fixed-Point Numbers

Notation and allocation.   Numeric data are an 8-bit number or a 16-bit address represented as 2's-complement integers. A word is treated as two decimal digits in Decimal Adjust.

In logical operations (and in load and store operations) the negative and zero condition reflect the result; overflow is set to 0. In addition and subtraction, the overflow is set according to the result of the operation; also, a carry or a borrow are set. The half carry applies to addition and is set in that operation only.

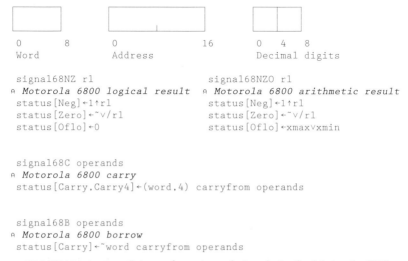

```
0        8   0              16   0   4   8
Word         Address             Decimal digits

signal68NZ r1                    signal68NZO r1
 ∩ Motorola 6800 logical result   ∩ Motorola 6800 arithmetic result
 status[Neg]←1↑r1                  status[Neg]←1↑r1
 status[Zero]←˜∨/r1                status[Zero]←˜∨/r1
 status[Oflo]←0                    status[Oflo]←xmax∨xmin


signal68C operands
 ∩ Motorola 6800 carry
 status[Carry,Carry4]←(word,4) carryfrom operands


signal68B operands
 ∩ Motorola 6800 borrow
 status[Carry]←˜word carryfrom operands
```

PROGRAM 16-53   Integer formats and signals in the Motorola 6800.

16.2.5

Operations

Data Handling

Data handling is performed through the accumulators.

Logic

The M6800 has logical connectives, arithmetic and logical shift, but no logical vector operations. All these apply to 8-bit operands in either accumulator.

```
b COM Not              b CLR Clear
c AND And              b LSR Shift Logical Right
c ORA Or               b ASL Shift Arithmetic Left
c EOR Exclusive Or     b ASR Shift Arithmetic Right
b TST Test             b ROL Rotate Left
c BIT Bit Test         b ROR Rotate Right
```

TABLE 16-54   Logical and shift instructions of the Motorola 6800.

Connectives. The niladic CLEAR, monadic NOT, and dyadic AND, OR, and EX-
CLUSIVE OR are provided. BIT executes an AND without changing the operands;
only the zero and negative conditions are set. TST just tests a word in memory
or in an accumulator for zero or negative.

```
COM;dest;rl                CLR
 ⋒ Motorola 6800 Not        ⋒ Motorola 6800 Clear
 dest←adr68a                adr68a write68 wordρ0
 rl←¯word read68 dest       status[Carry]←0
 dest write68 rl            signal68NZ wordρ0
 status[Carry]←1
 signal68NZ rl
                           TST;rl
                            ⋒ Motorola 6800 Test
                            rl←word read68 adr68a
 AND;od;rl                  signal68NZ rl
 ⋒ Motorola 6800 And
 od←word read68 adr68
 rl←acc[fld Acc;]∧od
 acc[fld Acc;]←rl          BIT;od
 signal68NZ rl              ⋒ Motorola 6800 Bit Test
                            od←word read68 adr68
                            signal68NZ acc[fld Acc;]∧od
```

PROGRAM 16-55   Logical connectives in the Motorola 6800.

Shift. All shifts are by 1 bit, and can be performed either in an accumulator
or in memory. The Carry indicator participates in all shifts, receiving the
high-order bit from left-shifted words and the low-order bit from right-shifted
words.

```
LSR;dest;od;rl                    ROL;dest;od;rl
 ⋒ Motorola 6800 Shift Logical Right   ⋒ Motorola 6800 Rotate Left
 dest←adr68a                       dest←adr68a
 od←word read68 dest               od←word read68 dest
 rl←¯1↓0,od                        rl←1↓od,status[Carry]
 dest write68 rl                   dest write68 rl
 status[Carry]←¯1↑od               status[Carry]←1↑od
 signal68NZ rl                     signal68NZ rl
 status[Oflo]←(1↑rl)≠¯1↑od         status[Oflo]←(1↑rl)≠1↑od
```

```
ASL;dest;od;rl
 ⋒ Motorola 6800 Shift Arithmetic Left
 dest←adr68a
 od←word read68 dest
 rl←1↓od,0
 dest write68 rl
 status[Carry]←1↑od
 signal68NZ rl
 status[Oflo]←(1↑rl)≠1↑od
```

PROGRAM 16-56   Shift and Rotate in the Motorola 6800.

In arithmetic right shift, the sign byte is replicated; in logical right shift, 0
enters on the left. Rotate Left and Right include the Carry in the rotation of
the accumulator or memory word. Conditions are set in all shifts and rotates;
the overflow is set as the exclusive or of the carry and negative sign condition.

Fixed-Point Arithmetic

There is provision for extended precision. There is no Multiply or Divide.

```
c LDA Load                    b NEG Negate
a TAB Accumulator A To B      b INC Increment
a TBA Accumulator B To A      b DEC Decrement
a TPA Load Condition          c ADD Add
a TAP Set Condition           a ABA Add Accumulators
a SEV Set Overflow            c ADC Add With Carry
a SEC Set Carry               c SUB Subtract
a CLV Reset Overflow          a SBA Subtract Accumulators
a CLC Reset Carry             c SBC Subtract With Borrow
c STA Store                   c CMP Compare
                              a CBA Compare Accumulators
```

TABLE 16-57   Fixed-point instructions of the Motorola 6800.

Load and Store.   Either accumulator can be loaded or stored or transferred to the other. Accumulators A and B are symmetric, except that only A can receive and set the status bits. The two high-order status bits are always 1.

```
LDA                              TAB
a Motorola 6800 Load             a Motorola 6800 Accumulator A To B
acc[fld Acc;]←word read68 adr68  acc[B;]←acc[A;]
signal68NZ acc[fld Acc;]         signal68NZ acc[A;]


TPA                              SEV
a Motorola 6800 Load Condition   a Motorola 6800 Set Overflow
acc[A;]←status                   status[Oflo]←1


TAP                              CLC
a Motorola 6800 Set Condition    a Motorola 6800 Reset Carry
status← 1 1 ,2↓acc[A;]           status[Carry]←0


STA
a Motorola 6800 Store
adr68 write68 acc[fld Acc;]
signal68NZ acc[fld Acc;]
```

PROGRAM 16-58   Load and Store in the Motorola 6800.

Sign control.   Negation is equivalent to subtraction from 0. A borrow occurs in all cases except when the operand is 0.

```
NEG;dest;operand;r1
a Motorola 6800 Negate
dest←adr68a
operand←radixcompi word read68 dest
r1←word radixcompr-operand
dest write68 r1
status[Carry]←operand≠0
signal68NZO r1
```

PROGRAM 16-59   Sign control in the Motorola 6800.

Increment and Decrement.   These two instructions change an accumulator with +1 or −1. They set the zero and negative conditions. The carry (or borrow) is not affected, which is convenient when they are used in an iteration count for extended-precision operation.

```
INC;dest;count;rl
ᴀ Motorola 6800 Increment
dest←adr68a
count←magni word read68 dest
rl←word magnr count+1
dest write68 rl
signal68NZO rl
```

PROGRAM 16-60   Increment in the Motorola 6800.

Add and Subtract.   Extended precision is facilitated by Add With Carry and Subtract With Borrow. A borrow is noted as the inverse of the carry that occurs when the complement of the subtrahend is added. The zero test applies only to the last metadigit, not to the metanumber.

```
SUB;addend;augend;sum;sm                    ABA;addend;augend;sum;sm
ᴀ Motorola 6800 Subtract                    ᴀ Motorola 6800 Add Accumulators
addend←radixcompi˜word read68 adr68         addend←radixcompi acc[B;]
augend←radixcompi acc[fld Acc;]             augend←radixcompi acc[A;]
sum←augend+addend+1                          sum←augend+addend
sm←word radixcompr sum                       sm←word radixcompr sum
acc[fld Acc;]←sm                             acc[A;]←sm
signal68B augend,addend,1                    signal68C augend,addend
signal68NZO sm                               signal68NZO sm


ADC;addend;augend;sum;sm
ᴀ Motorola 6800 Add With Carry
addend←radixcompi word read68 adr68
augend←radixcompi acc[fld Acc;]
sum←augend+addend+status[Carry]
sm←word radixcompr sum
acc[fld Acc;]←sm
signal68C augend,addend,status[Carry]
signal68NZO sm
```

PROGRAM 16-61   Add and Subtract in the Motorola 6800.

Compare.   Comparison is equivalent to subtraction without recording the difference. Only the conditions are set. A borrow is noted as in Subtract. Compare accumulators is similarly equivalent to subtracting B from A.

```
CBA;operand;comparand
ᴀ Motorola 6800 Compare Accumulators
operand←radixcompi˜acc[B;]
comparand←radixcompi acc[A;]
rl←word magnr comparand+operand+1
signal68B comparand,operand,1
signal68NZO rl
```

PROGRAM 16-62   Compare in the Motorola 6800.

Decimal Arithmetic

Decimal addition.   A decimal correction can be applied for extended-precision addition as in the 8080A. The operation does not apply to subtraction. The half carry, which is used to correct the low-order digit, is set only in an addition (Program 16-51). This architecture is cleaner than that of the 8080A, which sets its auxiliary carry also in various irrelevant operations.

```
DAA;carry10;addend;augend;sum
ᴀ Motorola 6800 Decimal Adjust
carry10←9<magni digit wide acc[A;]
addend←16⊥6×status[Carry,Carry4]∨carry10
augend←radixcompi acc[A;]
sum←augend+addend
acc[A;]←word radixcompr sum
status[Carry]←carry10[0]∨status[Carry]
signal68NZO acc[A;]
```

PROGRAM 16-63   Decimal Adjust in the Motorola 6800.

16.2.6

Instruction Sequencing

Linear Sequence

Next instruction.   The basic cycle and instruction fetch are classical. One instruction word is fetched prior to execution. An additional word or address may be fetched as part of the instruction execution.

```
cycle68                           inst←ifetch68 size
ᴀ basic cycle of the Motorola 6800  ᴀ Motorola 6800 instruction fetch
REPEAT:interrupt68                inst←size read68 memadr,iadr
   execute ifetch68 word         iadr←adrcap|iadr+size÷word
→UNTIL stop
```

PROGRAM 16-64   Basic cycle and instruction fetch of the Motorola 6800.

Completion.   An external stop signal, such as from a Single Cycle switch, stops the processor. Normal program suspension is by waiting.

Sequencing instructions.   Linear sequence and decision are with Unconditional and Conditional Branches; delegation is with Call and Return. Iteration has no special instructions, but can be programmed with Increment and Decrement.

```
g JMP Branch                      a BLS Jump On Low Or Equal
a BRA Jump                        a BHI Jump On High
a BPL Jump On Plus                a BCS Jump On Carry
a BMI Jump On Minus               a BCC Jump On No Carry
a BLT Jump On Less                a BVS Jump On Overflow
a BLE Jump On Less Or Equal       a BVC Jump On No Overflow
a BEQ Jump On Equal               g JSR Call
a BNE Jump On Not Equal           h BSR Jump To Subroutine
a BGE Jump On Greater Or Equal    a RTS Return
a BGT Jump On Greater
```

TABLE 16-65   Sequencing instructions of the Motorola 6800.

Unconditional Branch.   The target of the Unconditional Branch is either absolute, with the indexed or (full) direct-address options, or relative, with a signed 8-bit offset.

```
JMP                             BRA;offset
ⴻ Motorola 6800 Branch         ⴻ Motorola 6800 Jump
  iadr←adr68[Value]              offset←radixcompi ifetch68 word
                                 iadr←adrcap|iadr+offset
```

PROGRAM 16-66   Unconditional Branch in the Motorola 6800.

Decision

Conditions separate the branch test from the branch action.

Conditional Branch.   All conditional branches are relative with an 8-bit signed offset. The branch condition is either a single condition bit that is on or off, as in the 8080A, or a combination of conditions that indicate the result of a signed or unsigned comparison, as in the PDP11.

```
BLT;offset                           BLS;offset
ⴻ Motorola 6800 Jump On Less        ⴻ Motorola 6800 Jump On Low Or Equal
  offset←radixcompi ifetch68 word     offset←radixcompi ifetch68 word
  →If status[Neg]≠status[Oflo]        →If status[Zero]∨status[Carry]
  THEN:iadr←adrcap|iadr+offset        THEN:iadr←adrcap|iadr+offset
  ENDIF:                              ENDIF:


BNE;offset                           BPL;offset
ⴻ Motorola 6800 Jump On Not Equal   ⴻ Motorola 6800 Jump On Plus
  offset←radixcompi ifetch68 word     offset←radixcompi ifetch68 word
  →If˜status[Zero]                    →If˜status[Neg]
  THEN:iadr←adrcap|iadr+offset        THEN:iadr←adrcap|iadr+offset
  ENDIF:                              ENDIF:


BGT;offset
ⴻ Motorola 6800 Jump Greater
  offset←radixcompi ifetch68 word
  →If˜status[Zero]∨status[Neg]≠status[Oflo]
  THEN:iadr←adrcap|iadr+offset
  ENDIF:
```

PROGRAM 16-67   Conditional Branch in the Motorola 6800.

Delegation

Call and Return.   Call has an absolute target, with the indexed or direct address options, or a relative target with signed offset. The next-instruction address is pushed on the system stack. Return restores the instruction address from the stack.

```
JSR;next                         BSR;offset
ⴻ Motorola 6800 Call            ⴻ Motorola 6800 Jump To Subroutine
  next←adr68[Value]               offset←radixcompi ifetch68 word
  push68 adrsize magnr iadr       push68 adrsize magnr iadr
  iadr←next                       iadr←adrcap|iadr+offset


RTS
ⴻ Motorola 6800 Return
  iadr←magni pop68 adrsize
```

PROGRAM 16-68   Call and Return in the Motorola 6800.

State preservation.   Call and Return save and restore only the return address on stack. Nested calls may be made to any depth.

16.2.7
Supervision

Concurrency

Multiprocessing is obtained by connecting processors to the central bus.

Integrity

There is no memory protection, and no policing of invalid operations or invalid addresses.

Supervisory instructions.   Supervision can use interrupt enabling and disabling, dispatch, wait, and humble access.   The M6800 has only one execution mode; hence there are no privileged operations.

```
a RTI Return From Interrupt  a WAI Wait
a SEI Disable Interrupt      a SWI Programmed Interrupt
a CLI Enable Interrupt
```

TABLE 16-69   Supervisory instructions of the Motorola 6800.

Control Switching

Interruption.   Interruption occurs when an indicator is set; the I/O indicator is the only indicator that can be masked.   The interrupt action turns off the indicator, disables the interruption system, places the system context on the system stack, and changes the instruction address to the corresponding interrupt service address.

```
interrupt68;mask;who                 pushcontext68
a Motorola 6800 interrupt action     a Motorola 6800 preserve context
mask←(~status[Disable]),3ρ1          push68 adrsize magnr iadr
who←(ind∧mask)ι1                     push68 adrsize magnr index
→If who≠ρind                         push68 acc[A;]
THEN:ind[who]←0                      push68 acc[B;]
   status[Disable]←1                 push68 status
   pushcontext68
   iadr←Intadr+2×who
ENDIF:                               popcontext68
                                     a Motorola 6800 restore context
                                     status←pop68 word
RTI                                  acc[B;]←pop68 word
a Motorola 6800 Return From Interrupt acc[A;]←pop68 word
popcontext68                         index←magni pop68 adrsize
                                     iadr←magni pop68 adrsize
```

PROGRAM 16-70   Interruption action in the Motorola 6800.

The four interrupt-service routine addresses in the fixed locations at the end of memory correspond to four interrupt causes: reset or initial program load, unmaskable interrupt, programmed interrupt, and maskable I/O interrupt. Interrupts do not distinguish between interrupt sources in the same group, so the service routine must poll or use added hardware.

State Preservation

Dispatch.   Upon interrupt, the processor saves all the processor state: the status register, the accumulators, the index and the next-instruction address, but not the stack pointer. Return From Interrupt restores the processor state and dispatches the interrupted process.

Humble access.   Programmmed Interrupt saves the state, just as a regular interruption, and branches to the corresponding interrupt address.

```
SWI                                       WAI
⋒ Motorola 6800 Programmed Interrupt      ⋒ Motorola 6800 Wait
Program report 1                          REPEAT: ⋒ wait for interrupt
                                          →UNTIL ind[Iot]
                                          status[Disable]←0
SEI
⋒ Motorola 6800 Disable Interrupt
status[Disable]←1
```

PROGRAM 16-71   Context switching in the Motorola 6800.

16.2.8
Input/Output

Direct Input/Output

Optional attachments provide many combinations of direct, overlapped, and channel I/O concurrency.

16.2.9
Implementation Notes

Extra hardware can provide Interrupt vectoring that addresses an 8-bit buffer with identification of the interrupt source.

16.2.10
Bibliography

Motorola Semiconductor Products, Inc., 1975b: *M6800 Microprocessor Programming Manual*. Austin, TX: Motorola Semiconductor Products (our defining reference).

Motorola Semiconductor Products, Inc., 1975a: *Microprocessor Applications Manual*. Austin, TX: Motorola Semiconductor Products.

Hoff [1972], Osborne [1976].

16.2.11

Exercises

16-6 Give the description of the address arithmetic instructions LDX, STS, INS, and DEX, assuming consistency with the address arithmetic instructions shown in this section.

16-7 Give the description of the logical and shift instructions ORA, EOR, ASR, and ROR, assuming consistency with the logical and shift instructions shown in this section.

16-8 Give the description of the fixed-point arithmetic instructions TBA, SEC, CLV, DEC, ADD, SBA, SBC, and CMP, assuming consistency with the fixed-point arithmetic instructions shown in this section.

16-9 Give the description of the sequencing and supervisory instructions BGE, BEQ, BLE, BHI, BMI, BVS, BVC, BCS, BCC, and CLI, assuming consistency with the sequencing and supervisory instructions shown in this section.

16.3
MOS 6502

16.3.1
Highlights

History

Date.   The MOS Technology 6502 (1976), designed as a logical engine, was incorporated into the Apple II personal computer (as well as the KIM-1 personal-computer kit). The programming support provided for it made it an immensely important CPU, the first machine learned by a generation of computer scientists.

Family tree.   The 6502 is very like the Motorola 6800, so we will discuss it in terms of the differences. It is not nearly so clean as the 6800. The differences between the two machines lie primarily in their spaces and their addressing, not in their operation, sequencing, or I/O.

Noteworthy

Spaces.   Whereas the 6800 has two accumulators and one index register, the 6502 has one accumulator and two index registers.

Instruction set.   The 72 instructions of the 6800 are reduced in the 6502 to 59, mainly by eliminating several branches.

Addressing modes. Whereas the 6800 has an orthogonal set of six addressing modes, the 6502 has 10 far-less-orthogonal modes.

Decimal mode.   A decimal mode bit, when on, makes all Add With Carry and Subtract With Carry operations work as though the operands and results were packed decimal numbers. There is, therefore, no need for the Decimal Adjust instruction and an auxiliary carry. Unfortunately, the 0 condition is not valid in decimal mode.

Indirect addressing.   The 6502 provides two forms of indirect addressing: One uses a modified instruction address indirectly; the other modifies the indirectly obtained address.

Carry, not borrow, set in subtraction.   In contrast to the Subtract With Borrow of the 6800, the Subtract With Carry of the 6502 does not invert the carry-out (and invert it again upon use in the next subtraction), but records the carry as produced by adding the complement of the subtrahend.

Peculiarities

Backwards byte.   All 16-bit fields, including addresses in instructions, have the least significant byte at the lower memory address.

Spaces.   Whereas the 6800 has 16-bit index and the stack pointer addresses, the two indices and the stack pointer in the 6502 are 8 bits each. Moreover, the index and the stack pointer operate modularly in the first and second 256-word memory page, respectively.

Only extended addition.   The instruction set contains only Add With Carry and Subtract With Carry, not the plain Add and Subtract. For the latter, the carry must be set correctly in a prior operation. The initial carry for a set of extended additions must be set to 0, and the initial carry for a set of extended subtractions must be set to 1.

Overflow flag dually used.   The overflow status bit serves both as a regular overflow condition and as an external signal indicator.

Interrupt dually used.   The four interrupt classes of the 6800 are reduced to three in the 6502 by combining the external interrupt with the programmed interrupt. So that the two interrupt causes can be distinguished, the programmed interrupt sets the `Break` status bit to 1; all other interrupts set it to 0.

16.3.2

Machine Language

Unit System

An 8-bit data and 16-bit address size are used, as in the 6800.

Spaces

Memory name-space.   The 6502 has a linear memory of 64 K bytes, with the first 256 bytes distinguished as a base page, which can be addressed with 1 byte, all as in the 6800.

```
    space6502                           format6502
    ⋒ MOS 6502 spaces                   ⋒ MOS 6502 information units
    ⋒ memory                            ⋒ representation radix
    memory←?(memcap,word)ρradix         radix←2
    ⋒ working store                     ⋒ information units
    ⋒ - accumulator                     word←8
    acc←?wordρradix                     adrsize←16
    ⋒ - indices                         page←2*word
    index←?2ρpage                       ⋒ address capacity
    ⋒ - stack pointer                   adrcap←radix*adrsize
    sp←page+?page
    ⋒ control store
    ⋒ - instruction address             name6502
    iadr←?adrcap                        ⋒ MOS 6502 space names
    ⋒ - status word                     ⋒ memory allocation
    status←?wordρradix                  ⋒ - interrupt address
    ⋒ - indicators                      Intadr←memcap-6
    ind←?3ρradix                        ⋒ index allocation
    ⋒ - stop condition                  X←0
    stop←?radix                         Y←1
```

PROGRAM 16-72   Parameters and spaces of the MOS 6502.

The second page of 256 bytes is the only memory accessible by the stack pointer, unlike in the 6800. It is usually reserved for the stack.

Working store.   The working store is quite different from that of the 6800: The 6502 has only one 8-bit accumulator (Acc) but two 8-bit indices (X and Y) and a stack pointer of only 8 bits (sp).

Control store.   There is the usual 16-bit instruction address (iadr) and an 8-bit status word (status), of which only 7 bits are used for conditions and modes.

Embedding.   The high-order six bytes of memory are reserved for three interrupt routine addresses, versus the high-order eight bytes in the 6800.

Peripheral devices are memory-mapped at implementation-dependent addresses, as in the 6800.

Programming model.   Notice that whereas the 6800 has two accumulators and one index register, the 6502 has two indexes and one accumulator. It has a carry bit attached to it, which participates not only in addition, but also in shifting.

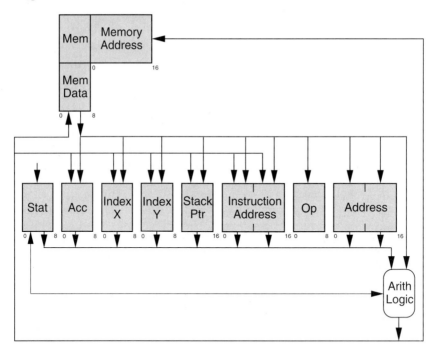

FIGURE 16-73   Programming model for the MOS 6502.

Operand Specification

Number of addresses.   Since there is only one accumulator, its address is implied. Instructions contain no or one memory address and have few fixed lengths: one, two, or three words, as in the 6800.

Address phrase.   As in the 6800, the address phrase consists of some address-mode bits in the first instruction byte, then 0, 1, or 2 bytes of address.

Operation Specification

Mnemonics.   The mnemonics are those used by MOS. They resemble those of the 6800. The immediate operation modes of Load Y, Compare X, and Compare Y are described here as the separate instructions LIY, CIX, and CIY to simplify the instruction syntax.

```
         a→BRK              b→ORA    c→TXA
           PHP      DEY       AND      TXS
           BPL      BCC       EOR      TAX
           CLC      TYA       ADC      TSX
           JSR      LIY       STA      DEX
           PLP      TAY       LDA
           BMI      BCS       CMP      NOP
           SEC      CLV       SBC
           RTI      CIY     b→ASL    d→STY
           PHA      INY       ROL    d→LDY
           BVC      BNE       LSR    e→BIT
           CLI      CLD       ROR    e→CPY
           RTS      CIX       STX    e→CPX
           PLA      INX       LDX    f→JMP
           BVS      BEQ       DEC
           SEI      SED       INC
```

PROGRAM 16-74   Operation-code list of the MOS 6502.

Mode.   The use of the decimal mode alters the radix of the addition and subtraction operations.

Instruction Structure

Instruction list.   The difference with the 6800 is noticeable in that instructions refer to the indices X and Y and no longer need to differentiate between accumulators. Also, several instructions—such as some branches—have been deleted.

Machine-language syntax.   The syntax is quite different from that of the 6800. Although there is no longer an accumulator specification field, a large number of addressing modes have to be squeezed into the format. Orthogonality loses. Not all operations can use all sensible address modes.

```
         syntax6502
     a Opcode, 0 0 0
     b Opb,M, 0 1
     b Opb,M, 1 0
     c 1,Opc, 1 0 1 0
     d 1 0 0 ,M3, 1 0 0
     d 1 0 1 ,M3, 1 0 0
     e 0 0 1 0 ,M4, 1 0 0
     e 1 1 0 0 ,M4, 1 0 0
     e 1 1 1 0 ,M4, 1 0 0
     f 0 1 ,M2, 0 1 1 0 0
```

PROGRAM 16-75   Instruction syntax of the MOS 6502.

```
     ∩ address arithmetic              ∩ fixed-point arithmetic
  b LDX Load X                      b LDA Load
  d LDY Load Y                      a SEC Set Carry
  a LIY Load Y Immediate            a CLC Reset Carry
  c TSX Pointer To X                a CLV Reset Overflow
  c TAX Accumulator To X            a SED Set Decimal
  a TAY Accumulator To Y            a CLD Reset Decimal
  b STX Store X                     b STA Store
  d STY Store Y                     b INC Increment
  c TXS X To Pointer                b DEC Decrement
  c TXA X To Accumulator            b ADC Add With Carry
  a TYA Y To Accumulator            b SBC Subtract With Carry
  a INX Increment X                 b CMP Compare
  a INY Increment Y                    ∩ sequencing
  c DEX Decrement X                 c NOP No Operation
  a DEY Decrement Y                 f JMP Branch
  e CPX Compare X                   a BPL Jump On Plus
  a CIY Compare X Immediate         a BMI Jump On Minus
  e CPY Compare Y                   a BEQ Jump On Equal
  a CIX Compare Y Immediate         a BNE Jump On Not Equal
  a PLA Pop Accumulator             a BCS Jump On Carry
  a PLP Pop Status                  a BCC Jump On No Carry
  a PHA Push Accumulator            a BVS Jump On Overflow
  a PHP Push Status                 a BVC Jump On No Overflow
     ∩ logic and shift              a JSR Call
  b AND And                         a RTS Return
  b ORA Or                             ∩ supervision
  b EOR Exclusive Or                a RTI Return From Interrupt
  e BIT Bit Test                    a SEI Disable Interrupt
  b LSR Shift Logical Right         a CLI Enable Interrupt
  b ASL Shift Arithmetic Left       a BRK Programmed Interrupt
  b ROL Rotate Left
  b ROR Rotate Right
```

TABLE 16-76   Instruction list of the MOS 6502.

Instruction format.   The format is essentially the same as that of the 6800 (Program 16-44), except for the details of allocation of the first byte.

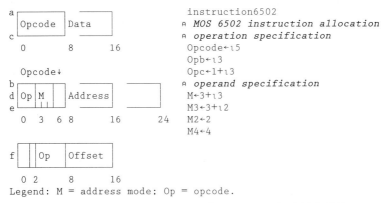

```
instruction6502
∩ MOS 6502 instruction allocation
∩ operation specification
Opcode←ι5
Opb←ι3
Opc←1+ι3
∩ operand specification
M←3+ι3
M3←3+ι2
M2←2
M4←4
```

Legend: M = address mode; Op = opcode.

PROGRAM 16-77   Instruction allocation in the MOS 6502.

Status format.   Five status bits are used as conditions: Carry, Overflow, Sign, Zero, and Break, which is set by Programmed Interrupt. The Oflo condition can be set by external conditions, as well as by program action. One status bit controls the decimal mode; another enables interrupts. The decimal mode eliminates the need for the auxiliary carry condition of the 6800.

```
    status6502                     indicator6502
 ⍝ MOS 6502 status allocation   ⍝ MOS 6502 indicator allocation
 ⍝ conditions                     Reset←2
 Neg←0                            Error←1
 Zero←6                           Int←0
 Oflo←1
 Carry←7
 Break←3
 ⍝ decimal mode
 Decimal←4
 ⍝ interrupt disable
 Disable←5
```

PROGRAM 16-78   Status and indicators in the MOS 6502.

16.3.3

Addressing

Direct addressing.   As in the 6800, 8-bit or 16-bit direct addresses may be used. Data fetch is always an 8-bit word. Addresses read from memory are 8 or 16 bits, with backwards byte addressing.

```
 data←size read6502 address;loc     address write6502 data;size;loc
 ⍝ MOS 6502 read from store        ⍝ MOS 6502 write into store
 →CASE address[Space]               →CASE address[Space]
 C0: ⍝ immediate                    C0: ⍝ immediate
    data←ifetch6502 word                →ERROR
    →ENDCASE                        C1: ⍝ memory
 C1: ⍝ memory                           size←ρ,data
    loc←address[Value]+⍳size÷word       loc←address[Value]+⍳size÷word
    data←,memory[loc;]                  memory[loc;]←word wide data
 ENDCASE:                           ENDCASE:
```

PROGRAM 16-79   Storage read and write in the MOS 6502.

Address Modification

Address calculation.   The addressing modes allow immediate, direct, index plus displacement, and indirect addressing with index X and Y, and 16-bit full address or 8-bit page address. Not all possible combinations are allowed. Nine modes are shown in adr6502, and only a subset of these can be selected in an operation. The first eight modes can be used in eight dyadic and Load operations. Modes 1, 3, 5, and 7 can be used by seven monadic operations, including shifts and rotates. The latter four operations can also operate upon the implied accumulator (not shown as an address mode). The modes are not orthogonal with respect to X and Y; the subsets available for a given instruction are even less orthogonal. Load and Store to and from the index registers themselves allow only indexing by the opposite register, which involves the use of address mode 8.

```
address←adr6502 mode;direct;displacement
⍝ MOS 6502 addressing
→CASE mode
C0: ⍝ X plus page displacement indirect
    displacement←magni ifetch6502 word
    direct←memadr,page|index[X]+displacement
    address←memadr,magni adrsize read6502 direct
    →ENDCASE
C1: ⍝ direct page address                    address6502
    address←memadr,magni ifetch6502 word     ⍝ MOS 6502 address allocation
    →ENDCASE                                 ⍝ attributes
C2: ⍝ immediate                              Space←0
    address←immadr,0                         Value←1
    →ENDCASE                                 ⍝ space identifiers
C3: ⍝ direct address                         immadr←0
    address←memadr,magni ifetch6502 adrsize  memadr←1
    →ENDCASE
C4: ⍝ Y plus indirect displacement
    direct←memadr,magni ifetch6502 word
    displacement←magni adrsize read6502 direct
    address←memadr,adrcap|index[Y]+displacement
    →ENDCASE
C5: ⍝ X plus page displacement
    displacement←magni ifetch6502 word
    address←memadr,page|index[X]+displacement
    →ENDCASE
C6: ⍝ Y plus displacement
    displacement←magni ifetch6502 adrsize
    address←memadr,adrcap|index[Y]+displacement
    →ENDCASE
C7: ⍝ X plus displacement
    displacement←magni ifetch6502 adrsize
    address←memadr,adrcap|index[X]+displacement
    →ENDCASE
C8: ⍝ Y plus page displacement
    displacement←magni ifetch6502 word
    address←memadr,page|index[Y]+displacement
ENDCASE:
```

PROGRAM 16-80   Addressing in the MOS 6502.

Index Arithmetic

The Negative and Zero conditions are set by all index operations except Store. Index comparison sets the Carry as for subtraction.

Index operations.   Increment and Decrement Index operate modulo 256 with no overflow indication—an essential difference from full-address 6800 indexing.

Stack addressing.   As in the 6800, the subroutine and interrupt instructions use the stack, and the accumulator can be pushed and popped. Unlike the 6800, the 6502 can also push and pop the status register. As in the 6800, other instructions cannot address via the stack pointer. The 6502 stack pointer addresses the second page of memory (addresses 256 through 511); increment and decrement are modular in that page (push6502, Program 16-81).

List addressing.   Indirect addressing with postindexing provides quite straightforward manipulation of chained lists.   The list can be scattered throughout the full memory, but the pointer into the list must be kept in the zero page.

Address Level

Indirect addressing. The 6502 has powerful (and costly) indirect addressing, in two modes.

In preindexed indirect addressing, mode 0, the 1-byte content of X is added modulo 256 to the address byte. The 1-byte sum is the effective address to be used indirectly.

In postindexed indirect addressing, mode 4, the 1-byte address specifies (in the zero page) a 2-byte indirect address, which is then indexed by the (1-byte) contents of Index Y.

The eight Load, Store, and dyadic arithmetic, logical, and compare operations admit of either preindexed or postindexed indirect addressing. These instructions need only one word of address, into the zero page.

Immediate addressing.   As in the 6800 and in most microprocessors, immediate addressing is provided. In the 6502, immediate addresses are limited to one word, and the immediate mode can be specified only for the dyadic operations and the Load and Compare operations of the accumulator and the indices.

16.3.4
Data

The logical and and fixed-point arithmetic data have 8-bit size. Binary numbers use radix-complement notation; decimal numbers, two-digit binary coded decimal, as in the 6800.

16.3.5
Operations

The entire set of operations is essentially a subset of that of the 6800, except that the 6502 has X and Y versions of all index-register operations and the 6800 has A and B versions of all accumulator operations. Leventhal provides a table showing the 6800 instruction corresponding to each 6502 instruction [Leventhal, 1979, pp. 3-34 to 3-37].

The semantics of corresponding operations are as similar as one would expect, except for the peculiarities noted earlier.

Logic

All logical operations set the Negative and Zero conditions. The shifts and rotates set the Carry as well.

Connectives. The Not and Test of the 6800 are missing. Bit performs the AND of the operand and the accumulator and sets the Zero condition according to the result. Also, the leftmost two bits of the memory operand are placed in the Negate and Overflow condition.

Shift. The arithmetic right shift of the 6800 is missing; the rotates are identical to the 6800 operations.

Fixed-Point Arithmetic

All arithmetic operations except Store set the Negate and Zero conditions. Compare sets the Carry as well, and Add and Subtract set the Carry and Overflow condition.

Load and Store. Whereas the 6800 allows transfer, addition, subtraction, and comparison between its accumulators, the 6502 has transfer between its one-word index registers and its accumulator.

Add and Subtract. The 6800 provides an Add and Subtract that ignore the previous setting of the Carry. Other 6800-only operations include Clear, Complement, and Negate.

Compare. The carry is set as for subtraction.

Decimal Arithmetic

Decimal Add and Subtract. Set and Clear operations occur in the 6502 for its Decimal mode; the 6800 has a Decimal Adjust operation.

16.3.6

Instruction Sequencing

The 6502 is essentially like the 6800, except for a less complete set of tests.

```
cycle6502                            inst←ifetch6502 size
ᴀ basic cycle of the MOS 6502        ᴀ MOS 6502 instruction fetch
REPEAT:interrupt6502                 inst←size read6502 memadr,iadr
    execute ifetch6502 word          iadr←adrcap|iadr+size÷word
→UNTIL stop


                                     pushcontext6502
interrupt6502;mask;who               ᴀ MOS 6502 preserve context
ᴀ MOS 6502 interrupt action          push6502 adrsize magnr iadr
mask←(~status[Disable]),2ρ1          push6502 status
who←(ind∧mask)ι1
→If who≠ρind
THEN:ind[who]←0                      push6502 data
    status[Disable]←1                ᴀ MOS 6502 push onto stack
    pushcontext6502                  (memadr,sp) write6502 word↑,data
    iadr←Intadr+2×who                sp←page+page|sp-1
ENDIF:                               →If adrsize=ρ,data
                                     THEN:(memadr,sp) write6502 word↓,data
                                         sp←page+page|sp-1
                                     ENDIF:
```

PROGRAM 16-81   Basic cycle and interrupt of the MOS 6502.

Linear Sequence

Next instruction. As in the 6800, the Branch addresses are relative, with a signed 8-bit offset. There are no other relative addresses.

Decision

Conditional branching. Simple indirect addressing applies only to the Jump instruction. The Jump always has a 2-byte address, which may be direct or indirect. Of the 19 sequencing instructions of the 6800 shown in Table 16-65 the six instructions Jump On Less, Less Or Equal, Greate Or Equal, Greater, Low Or Equal, and High are omitted in the 6502. They can be performed by two successive branches.

Delegation

Call and return. The 6502 does have Call and Return as in the 6800, but omits the relative call (BSR). As in the 6800, Call and Return save and restore only the instruction address on the stack.

16.3.7
Supervision

Concurrency

Concurrency is as in the 6800. Integrity—policing, supervisory mode, protection—is also as in the 6800 (i.e., it is non-existent).

Control Switching

Interruption. The 6502 has the same interruption action as the 6800, but it saves less context automatically. Both machines can enable and disable interruptions.

Dispatching. Return From Interrupt restores the saved state as in the 6800.

Humble access. The 6800 as well as the 6502 can cause an intentional interruption. The 6502 shares the external interrupt with programmed interrupt and sets the Break condition upon intentional interruption. The 6800 interrupts to a distinct address, which saves a test.

State Preservation

Context switching. Whereas the 6800 pushes the status, the accumulators, the index, and the instruction address onto the stack, the 6502 pushes only the status and instruction address.

16.3.8
Input/Output

Essentially, the 6502's I/O is the same as that of the 6800.

16.3.9
Bibliography

Leventhal, L.A., 1979: *6502 Assembly Language Programming.* Berkeley, CA: Osborne/McGraw-Hill (our defining reference).

16.3.10
Exercises

16-10 Give the description of the logical and arithmetic instructions AND, ORA, EOR, LDA, STA, ADC, SBC, and CMP, which have address modes 0 through 7, except that STA cannot have mode 2.

16-11 Give the description of the shift and rotate instructions LSR, ASL, ROL, and ROR, which have address modes 1, 3, 5, and 7, but also use the accumulator for mode value 2.

16-12 Give the description of Load Index Y (LDY), which has address modes 1, 3, 5, and 7.

16-13 Give the description of the Increment and Decrement instructions INC and DEC, which have address modes 1, 3, 5, and 7.

16-14 Give the description of the sequencing instructions NOP, BPL, BMI, BEQ, BNE, BCS, BCC, BVS, BVC, JSR, and RTS, which have no address-mode choices, and JMP, which has absolute 16-bit addressing and 16-bit indirect addressing for its modes 0 and 1, respectively.

16-15 Give the description of the supervisory instructions RTI, SEI, CLI, and BRK.

16.4
Motorola MC68000

16.4.1
Highlights

Although its name resembles that of the M6800, the MC68000 is a complete departure from Motorola's first microprocessor. This strategy differs from Intel's, which tried to maintain some degree of compatibility with its 8-bit microprocessors while moving up to 16-bit processors. The MC68000 family is used in various workstations, and most notably in the Apple Macintosh.

History

Architects.   Thomas Gunter, Skip Stritter, and John Zolnowsky.

Dates.   The Motorola MC68000 microprocessor was announced in 1979; the first processor chips were made available in 1980.

Noteworthy

The MC68000 is one of the first 16-bit wordlength designs and represents a definite growth from a microprocessor architecture toward a more complete classical architecture.

Address capacity.   The use of a 16-bit word leads indirectly to a maximum address length of 32 bits. Thus the address registers have 32 bits. Initial addressing capacity was 24 bits, but in successor machines the 32-bit capacity is available.

Operand sizes.   Operand sizes are normally byte, word, and longword. When the shorter lengths are used in data registers, the high-order bits of those registers remain unchanged.

Alignment.   The 16-bit word means that instructions, words, and longwords must be aligned on 16-bit boundaries in memory. The system stack works with words; when bytes are placed on the system stack, they must be grouped in pairs. Bytes of immediate data are extended to words.

Address registers.   In addition to the eight data registers, a separate set of eight addressing registers is user-accessible, as in the Cray designs.

Addressing modes. Twelve addressing modes are provided to give maximum bit efficiency.

No backwards byte.   The 16-bit word size helps the MC68000 to break the miniprocessor and microprocessor tradition of the backwards byte. Nevertheless, bit addressing in a field is right to left.

Rich operation set.   The operation set includes decimal arithmetic, procedure call support, and several instructions (e.g., Link And Allocate, Unlink, Check Against Bound) intended for higher programming languages.

Proper extended precision.   Add With Carry is a dyadic operation that handles the carry correctly and sets the zero indicator according to the extended result.

Extend bit.   The carry serves two purposes: In extended precision, it represents the carry from one metadigit to the next; in unsigned comparison, it indicates that the operand is greater than or equal to the comparand after subtracting the comparand from the operand. When borrows are noted—instead of carries—in negation, subtraction, and comparison, the first statement still holds, and in the second statement "less than" should replace "greater than or equal to." The two purposes conflict when the number of metadigits of extended precision is tested with unsigned comparison. The MC68000 solves this conflict by using an Extend bit for extended precision that is set only for negation, addition, subtraction, and shift, whereas the carry and borrow are changed for almost all data arithmetic operations, including comparison. Address arithmetic does not set any condition, except for address comparison.

Multiprocessing.   Critical-section control with Test And Set and bus contention circuits are intended for multiprocessing.

Supervision.   Supervision is aided by a trace mode, vector interrupt with 256 interrupt locations, humble access, privileged operations, and dual stacks. But there is no timer.

Peculiarities

Complex instruction formats.   The instruction formats are highly complex. Not only are there many syntactic patterns, but the patterns overlap in a complex manner. As an example, the bit configurations of invalid address modes are used for operation-code extension. This procedure is repeated for up to three levels.

Selective address modes.   The many address modes are only selectively available. Often the choice of available modes is obvious; at times, however, only lack of opcode bits seems to be the reason to eliminate modes that would have been useful. Thus extended-precision negation has eight addressing modes, whereas extended-precision addition and subtraction can specify only two modes, which moreover must be the same for both operands.

Lack of orthogonality.   The instruction formats show a decided lack of orthogonality. As a consequence, it is hard to know which options and modes are available for a given operation and how they are specified. Thus NEG has a memory-to-memory mode, but ADD does not.

Borrow.   The PDP11 is followed by noting a borrow, the inverse of a carry, in subtraction and comparison.

Descendants

On top of the MC68000, Motorola created a family of upward and downward compatible architectures. The MC68008 is a reduced version with an 8-bit bus and 1 MB address space. The first major extension, the MC68010, added virtual memory capability; it is capable of suspending and resuming an instruction execution in the midst of an instruction, as opposed to restarting an instruction. The MC68020, upward compatible with the MC68010, has operating-system support for a virtual machine, address space expanded from 16 MB (24 bit) to 4.3 GB (32 bit), and coprocessor support such as for a floating-point coprocessor or paged memory management.

16.4.2

Machine Language

Unit System

The unit system is *four*, which expresses itself in information units of 4, 8, 16, and 32 bits. The 4-bit digit is used in decimal arithmetic.

```
initiate680                          format680
⍝ initiation of the Motorola 68000   ⍝ Motorola 68000 information units
format680                            ⍝ representation radix
configure680                         radix←2
space680                             ⍝ information units
name680                              digit←4
control680                           byte←8
                                     word←16
                                     long←32
configure680                         ⍝ address capacity
⍝ configuration for the Motorola 68000   adrcap←radix*long
⍝ memory capacity
memcap←radix*24
```

PROGRAM 16-82   Basic parameters of the Motorola MC68000.

Configuration.   The choice of memory configuration in our description is arbitrary.

Spaces

Memory name-space.   Memory name-space is linear, with an initial maximum capacity of 16 MB. Words and longwords must be word aligned. Four of these address spaces can be used, one each for the user program, user data, supervisor program, and supervisor data. All writes occur in the data spaces. (The multiple spaces are not shown in our description.)

The low-order 1024 bytes of memory are reserved for 255 interrupt addresses.

Working store.   Eight 32-bit data registers (reg) are used as source and destination registers for operations and as index registers in addressing. Byte-length and word-length operations do not affect high-order bits in the data

```
space680                              name680
 ⍺ Motorola 68000 spaces               ⍺ Motorola 68000 space names
 ⍺ memory                              ⍺ address registers
   memory←?(memcap,byte)⍴radix         ⍺ - stack pointer
 ⍺ working store                         Sp←7
 ⍺ - data registers                    ⍺ - alternate pointer
   reg←?(8,long)⍴radix                    Ap←8
 ⍺ - address registers
   adr←?(9,long)⍴radix
 ⍺ control store
 ⍺ - instruction address
   iadr←?adrcap
 ⍺ - indicators
   ind←?48⍴radix
 ⍺ - program state
   status←?word⍴radix
 ⍺ wait state
   wait←?radix
 ⍺ stopped state
   stop←?radix
```

PROGRAM 16-83   Spaces of the Motorola MC68000.

registers.   Nine 32-bit address registers (`adr`) are used as base-addressing registers and stack pointers. Register 7 is the system stack pointer (`Sp`); register 8 is the alternate stack pointer (`Ap`), which is swapped with the system stack pointer when the processor changes from user mode to supervisor mode or reverse. Results destined for the address registers are sign-extended.

Control store.   There is a 16-bit processor status word (`status`). The user mode has access only to the low-order byte of this word. Forty-eight indicators are used; there is a wait state and a stopped state.

Embedding.   Peripheral device registers are mapped onto the memory address space at implementation-dependent locations.

Programming model.   In this programming model, the light lines indicate datapaths that may be 8, 16, or 32 bits wide, depending upon the operation. The heavy paths always carry address data, which is long. The heavy use of full-length registers shows that this is a fully evolved microprocessor, up to the fullword registers and datapaths that characterized the original IAS proposal. The variable-length instruction makes this programming model reminiscent of the VAX11/780 , the fully evolved version of the minicomputer.

Operand Specification

Number of addresses.   The MC68000 is a two-address machine; the result replaces one of the operands.

Address phrase.   The basic address phrase consists of a 3-bit modifier field followed by a 3-bit register-address field and possibly by word or longword extension fields. The Move operation uses two such phrases (with the modifier and address field interchanged in the first phrase). Usually, however, a basic phrase is used for one operand, and the other operand is specified by just one register field. A separate mode field is then used for size and to-memory specification (Program 16-87).

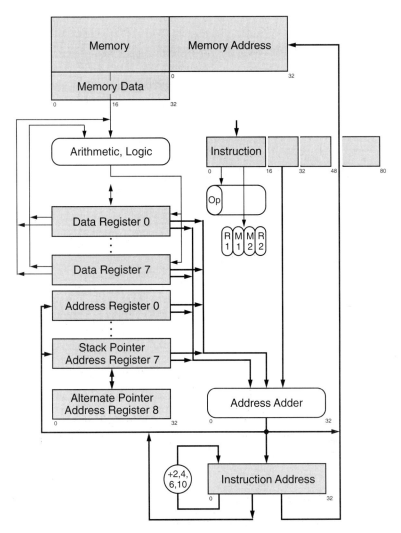

FIGURE 16-84   Programming model for the Motorola MC68000.

a→→bk	b→ORI	c→ORIR	e→TRAPL	g→SUBX	ROXR	BCLRI	o→EXGM
MOVEB	ANDI	ANDIR	TRAPH	g→ADDX	ROR	BSETI	p→CHK
MOVEL	SUBI	i	LINK	h→DIV	j→ASM	m→NBCD	LEA
MOVEW	ADDI	i	UNLK	SUBA	LSM	PEA	q→SUBQ
→bp	→cl	i	MOVTU	i	ROXM	m→MVFRW	q→EOR
ADDQ	EORI	EORIR	MOVFU	CMPA	ROM	MVFRL	r→MOVEP
→v	CMPI	i	→f	MUL	i	m→MVTRW	r→CMPM
→x	→c	i	i	ADDA	i	MVTRL	s→i
OR	b→NEGX	d→MOVFS	f→RESET	i	i	m→JSR	t→SCC
SUB	CLR	i	NOP	i	i	JMP	u→DBCC
OPC10	NEG	MOVTC	STOP	i→ASRI	k→BTST	n→SWAP	v→BCC
CMP	NOT	MOVTS	RTE	LSRI	BCHG	n→EXTW	w→BSR
AND	→dm	i	i	ROXRI	BCLR	n→EXTL	x→MOVEQ
ADD	TST	TAS	RTS	RORI	BSET	o→SBCD	
→hi	→dm	i	TRAPV	ASR	l→BTSTI	o→ABCD	
OPC15	→dem	i	RTR	LSR	BCHGI	o→EXG	

PROGRAM 16-85   Operation-code list in the Motorola MC68000.

Operation Specification

Mnemonics. We mostly follow the mnemonics of Motorola. We deviate when one mnemonic applies to more than one syntactic pattern or when distinct mnemonics are conveniently combined to one operation. Thus the postfixes `to CCR` and `to SR` are combined to the postfix R. MOVE is split in three operations: MOVEB, MOVEW, and MOVEL. TRAP is split in TRAPL and TRAPH. DIVS and DIVH are combined with DIV; similarly, MULS and MULH are combined to MUL.

∩	*address arithmetic*	
h	ADDA	Add Address
h	SUBA	Subtract Address
h	CMPA	Compare Address
p	LEA	Load Effective Address
m	PEA	Push Effective Address
e	LINK	Link And Allocate
e	UNLK	Unlink
∩	*logic and shift*	
k	BSET	Set Bit
l	BSETI	Set Bit Immediate
k	BCLR	Reset Bit
l	BCLRI	Reset Bit Immediate
k	BCHG	Change Bit
l	BCHGI	Change Bit Immediate
k	BTST	Test Bit
l	BTSTI	Test Bit Immediate
b	CLR	Clear
b	NOT	Not
a	AND	And
b	ANDI	And Immediate
a	OR	Or
b	ORI	Or Immediate
q	EOR	Exclusive Or
b	EORI	Exclusive Or Immediate
i	LSR	Shift
i	LSRI	Shift Immediate
i	ASR	Shift Arithmetic
i	ASRI	Shift Arithmetic Immediate
j	LSM	Shift Memory
j	ASM	Shift Memory Arithmetic
i	ROR	Rotate
i	RORI	Rotate Immediate
i	ROXR	Rotate With Carry
i	ROXRI	Rotate With Carry Immediate
j	ROM	Rotate Memory
j	ROXM	Rotate With Carry Memory
n	SWAP	Swap Register Halves
∩	*fixed-point arithmetic*	
a	MOVEB	Move Byte
a	MOVEW	Move Word
a	MOVEL	Move Long
x	MOVEQ	Move Quick
r	MOVEP	Move Peripheral Data
m	MVTRW	Load Multiple Word
m	MVTRL	Load Multiple Long
m	MVFRW	Store Multiple Word
m	MVFRL	Store Multiple Long
o	EXG	Swap Registers
o	EXGM	Swap Mixed Registers
b	TST	Test

n	EXTW	Sign-extend To Word
n	EXTL	Sign-extend To Long
b	NEG	Negate
b	NEGX	Negate With Borrow
a	ADD	Add
b	ADDI	Add Immediate
a	ADDQ	Add Quick
g	ADDX	Add With Carry
a	SUB	Subtract
b	SUBI	Subtract Immediate
q	SUBQ	Subtract Quick
g	SUBX	Subtract With Borrow
h	MUL	Multiply
h	DIV	Divide
a	CMP	Compare
b	CMPI	Compare Immediate
r	CMPM	Compare Memory
p	CHK	Check Against Bound
∩	*decimal arithmetic*	
m	NBCD	Negate Decimal With Borrow
o	ABCD	Add Decimal With Carry
o	SBCD	Subtract Decimal With Borrow
∩	*sequencing*	
f	NOP	No Operation
m	JMP	Branch
v	BCC	Jump On Condition
u	DBCC	Jump On Decrement
m	JSR	Call
w	BSR	Jump To Subroutine
f	RTS	Return
∩	*supervision*	
f	STOP	Wait
d	TAS	Test And Set
e	TRAPL	Trap Low
e	TRAPH	Trap High
f	TRAPV	Trap On Overflow
f	RTE	Return From Interrupt
f	RTR	Return And Restore
e	MOVTU	Set User Pointer
e	MOVFU	Store User Pointer
d	MOVTC	Set Condition
t	SCC	Test Condition
d	MOVTS	Set Status
d	MOVFS	Store Status
c	ANDIR	And Status Immediate
c	ORIR	Or Status Immediate
c	EORIR	Exclusive Or Status Immediate
a	OPC10	Emulator Code 10
a	OPC15	Emulator Code 15
∩	*input/output*	
f	RESET	Reset Devices

TABLE 16-86 Instruction list of the Motorola MC68000.

Invalid operations.   Operation codes and modes are policed and give an invalid-operation exception when encountered in a program. Syntactic pattern s has no valid instructions; it is guaranteed not to be used for future extensions of the instruction set. All other illegal instructions are reserved for future extensions.

Instruction list.   The instruction list resembles the list of a classical computer more than that of a microprocessor. There is a multiple register move, decimal arithmetic, and substantial supervision. Absent still are character-handling operations and floating point.

Instruction Structure

Machine-language syntax.   Pattern a is the basic syntactic pattern, with a 4-bit opcode field and two sets of 3-bit register address and 3-bit addressing mode fields. The pattern allows 16 operation codes, 11 of which are used. The dyadic pattern is changed to a monadic pattern by using the first register and mode bits for opcode bits and in some cases for a size, condition, or 1-bit mode field. A second change of the basic pattern preserves both register fields, but uses one or two mode fields for opcode, size, or 1-bit mode fields. A third major variation eliminates both sets of register and mode fields to obtain a niladic pattern.

```
    syntax680
a  Opcode,R1,M1,M2,R2
b  0 0 0 0 ,Opd,0,Sz,M2,R2
b  0 1 0 0 ,Opd,0,Sz,M2,R2
c  0 0 0 0 ,Opd,0,Sz, 1 1 1 1 0 0
d  0 1 0 0 ,Opd, 0 1 1 ,M2,R2
e  0 1 0 0 1 1 1 0 0 1 ,Opf,R2
f  0 1 0 0 1 1 1 0 0 1 1 1 0 ,Opg        o 1 0 0 1 ,R1, 1 0 0 0 0 ,Rm,R2
g  1 0 0 1 ,R1,1,Sz, 0 0 ,Rm,R2          o 1 1 0 0 ,R1, 1 0 0 0 0 ,Rm,R2
g  1 1 0 1 ,R1,1,Sz, 0 0 ,Rm,R2          o 1 1 0 0 ,R1, 1 0 1 0 0 ,Rm,R2
h  1,Opc,R1,M0, 1 1 ,M2,R2               o 1 1 0 0 ,R1, 1 1 0 0 0 ,Rm,R2
i  1 1 1 0 ,R1,M0,Sz,Opf,R2              p 0 1 0 0 ,R1, 1 1 ,Oph,M2,R2
j  1 1 1 0 ,Opd,M0, 1 1 ,M2,R2           q 0 1 0 1 ,R1,1,Sz,M2,R2
k  0 0 0 0 ,R1,1,Ope,M2,R2               q 1 0 1 1 ,R1,1,Sz,M2,R2
l  0 0 0 0 1 0 0 0 ,Ope,M2,R2            r 0 0 0 0 ,R1,1,Sz, 0 0 1 ,R2
m  0 1 0 0 1 0 0 0 0 ,Oph,M2,R2          r 1 0 1 1 ,R1,1,Sz, 0 0 1 ,R2
m  0 1 0 0 1 0 0 0 1 ,Oph,M2,R2          s 0 1 0 0 1 0 1 0 1 1 1 1 1 1 0 0
m  0 1 0 0 1 1 0 0 1 ,Oph,M2,R2          t 0 1 0 1 ,Cdn, 1 1 ,M2,R2
m  0 1 0 0 1 1 1 0 1 ,Oph,M2,R2          u 0 1 0 1 ,Cdn, 1 1 0 0 1 ,R2
n  0 1 0 0 1 0 0 0 0 1 0 0 0 ,R2         v 0 1 1 0 ,Cdn,D1
n  0 1 0 0 1 0 0 0 1 0 0 0 ,R2           w 0 1 1 0 0 0 0 1 ,D1
n  0 1 0 0 1 0 0 0 1 1 0 0 0 ,R2         x 0 1 1 1 ,R1,0,D1
```

PROGRAM 16-87   Instruction syntax of the Motorola MC68000.

Extended operation code.   Up to three levels of code extension are used (e.g., a to b to e to f). The extensions frequently use unused field or mode codes. Thus the bit size field may specify three lengths: byte, word, and long. One code pattern (usually 1 1) is therefore available to be used as code extension. For instance, pattern q of SUBQ uses the unused M1 modes of pattern a of ADDQ, then pattern t of SCC uses the unused size code 1 1 of SUBQ, and, in turn, pattern u of DBCC uses the unused mode code 0 0 1 in M2 of SCC.

Instruction format.   Instructions have 16-bit word resolution and are placed in memory on word boundaries. The eight instruction formats correspond to the 28 syntactic patterns (Program 16-88). The basic length of all instructions is one word. The source and destination specifications can each extend the instruction format with a word for an index, or with a word or longword for a displacement. Thus the maximum instruction length can be 5 words. In Program 16-88 only the extensions of the first instruction format are shown. All formats except for the last, the x format, can be extended.

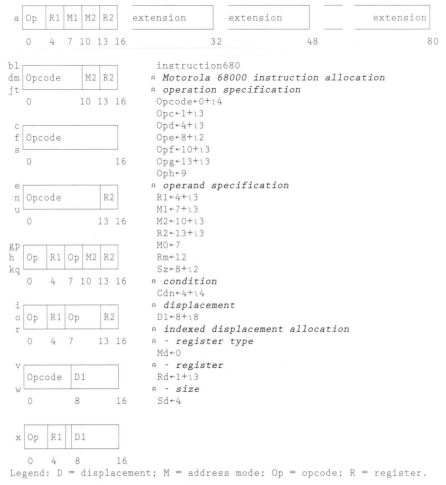

Legend: D = displacement; M = address mode; Op = opcode; R = register.

PROGRAM 16-88   Instruction allocation in the Motorola MC68000.

Status format.   The status word has a supervisory byte, which contains the trace bit, the supervisory mode bit, and the priority level field. The user byte of the status word contains the familiar negative, zero, overflow, and carry conditions, as well as the Extend bit that is used in extended-precision arithmetic. In the user mode, all status can be read, but only the user byte can be changed.

Indicators.   The 48 interrupt indicators include machine malfunction, programming errors, tracing, two emulator codes, eight I/O indicators, and 16 programmed interrupts.

```
↓Mode↓Priority              Trap↓ ↓Emulators

┌──┬─┬──┬──┬─────┐  ┌─┬──────┬──┬─┬──┬────────┬─────────┐
│  │*│* │Cdn│     │  │*│Errors│  │*│* │ In/out │ Program │
└──┴─┴──┴──┴─────┘  └─┴──────┴──┴─┴──┴────────┴─────────┘

0   3 5  8 11   16   0 2     9 12  16      24       32              48
Status              Indicators
Legend: Cdn = condition;  * = unused.
```

```
control680                        indicator680
ᴀ Motorola 68000 control allocation  ᴀ Motorola 68000 indicator allocation
instruction680                    ᴀ machine malfunction
indicator680                      Mach←2
status680                         ᴀ invalid address
address680                        Invadr←3
                                  ᴀ invalid operation code
                                  Invop←4
status680                         ᴀ divide by zero
ᴀ Motorola 68000 program status     Divide←5
ᴀ operating modes                 ᴀ out of bounds
Trace←0                           Bound←6
Supervisor←2                      ᴀ overflow trap
ᴀ priority level                  Oflotrap←7
Priority←5+ι3                      ᴀ privilege violation
ᴀ conditions                      Priv←8
Cond←8+ι8                          ᴀ trace
Extend←11                         Tracetrap←9
Neg←12                            ᴀ emulator codes
Zero←13                           Opc10←10
Oflo←14                           Opc15←11
Carry←15                          ᴀ uninitialized interrupt
                                  Uninit←15
                                  ᴀ input/output
                                  Ioerror←24
                                  Inout←25+ι7
                                  ᴀ programmed trap
                                  Trap←32+ι16
```

PROGRAM 16-89   Status word and indicators in the Motorola MC68000.

16.4.3

Addressing

Direct addressing.   Addresses are defined with size, space, and value attributes. The size may be a byte, word, or longword. The spaces are data registers, address registers, memory, and immediate data. Data registers have a longword length; access with byte or word size affects only the rightmost bits of the registers. Address registers support only word or longword operands, a sign-extended result replaces the entire register content. The order of bytes in memory is the same as the order in registers; there is no backwards byte! Immediate data apply to reading only.

```
data←read680 address;size;loc        address680
A Motorola 68000 read from store     A Motorola 68000 address allocation
size←address[Size]                   A attributes
→CASE address[Space]                  Size←0
C0: A data register                  Space←1
    data←(-size)↑reg[address[Value];]  Value←2
    →ENDCASE                          A space identifiers
C1: A address register               regadr←0
    data←(-size)↑adr[address[Value];]  adradr←1
    →ENDCASE                          memadr←2
C2: A memory                         immadr←3
    loc←address[Value]+ιsize÷byte     A scope identifiers
    data←,memory[adrcap|loc;]          any←0
    adrcheck680 loc                  data←1
    →ENDCASE                          mem←2
C3: A immediate                      control←3
    data←size magnr address[Value]    alter←4
ENDCASE:

address write680 data;size;loc
A Motorola 68000 write into store
size←ρdata
→CASE address[Space]
C0: A data register
    →OUT suppress680
    reg[address[Value];(-size)↑ιlong]←data
    →ENDCASE
C1: A address register
    Invop report size=byte
    →OUT suppress680
    adr[address[Value];]←((long-size)ρdata[0]),data
    →ENDCASE
C2: A memory
    loc←address[Value]+ιsize÷byte
    adrcheck680 loc
    →OUT suppress680
    memory[loc;]←byte wide data
ENDCASE:

adrcheck680 loc
A Motorola 68000 address check
A alignment on even boundary
 Invadr report 0≠(2⌊ρloc)|address[Value]
A check address capacity
 Invadr report loc≥memcap
```

PROGRAM 16-90   Storage read and write in the Motorola MC68000.

Address Modification

The 3-bit mode field can specify eight modes. Mode 7, however, uses the register field to specify another five modes, which gives a total of 12 modes. These modes are

- Direct addressing of a data register or an address register
- Memory addressing via an address register, with or without postincrement or predecrement
- Index plus immediate or indexed displacement
- Direct addressing with a 16-bit truncated address or with a full 32-bit address

```
      address←size adr680 mrs;mode;r;scope;index;displacement
    ⍝ Motorola 68000 addressing
      mode←mrs[0] WHERE r←mrs[1] WHERE scope←2↑2↓mrs
      →CASE 11⌊mode+r×mode=7
   C0: ⍝ data register, mode 0
         address←size,regadr,r
         Invop report scope∈mem,control
         →ENDCASE
   C1: ⍝ address register, mode 1
         address←size,adradr,r
         Invop report scope∈data,mem,control
         →ENDCASE
   C2: ⍝ address register indirect, mode 2
         address←size,memadr,radixcompi adr[r;]
         →ENDCASE
   C3: ⍝ postincrement, mode 3
         address←(size⌈word×r=Sp) incr680 r
         Invop report scope∈control
         →ENDCASE
   C4: ⍝ predecrement, mode 4
         address←(size⌈word×r=Sp) decr680 r
         Invop report scope∈control
         →ENDCASE
   C5: ⍝ index plus displacement, mode 5
         index←radixcompi adr[r;]
         displacement←radixcompi ifetch680 word
         address←size,memadr,index+displacement
         →ENDCASE
   C6: ⍝ index plus indexed displacement, mode 6
         index←radixcompi adr[r;]
         address←size,memadr,index+disp680
         →ENDCASE
   C7: ⍝ absolute truncated, mode 7 0
         address←size,memadr,radixcompi ifetch680 word
         →ENDCASE
   C8: ⍝ absolute, mode 7 1
         address←size,memadr,radixcompi ifetch680 long
         →ENDCASE
   C9: ⍝ relative truncated, mode 7 2
         index←iadr
         displacement←radixcompi ifetch680 word
         address←size,memadr,index+displacement
         Invop report scope∈alter
         →ENDCASE
   C10: ⍝ relative indexed displacement, mode 7 3
         index←iadr
         address←size,memadr,index+disp680
         Invop report scope∈alter
         →ENDCASE
   C11: ⍝ immediate, mode 7 4
         address←size,immadr,magni immediate680 size
         Invop report(r>4)∨scope∈control,alter
      ENDCASE:
```

PROGRAM 16-91   Addressing in the Motorola MC68000.

- Relative addressing with a truncated address or with an indexed displacement
- Immediate addressing

The data size may be a byte, a word, or a longword. When the increment or decrement mode applies to the stack pointer, the pointer maintains word resolution even if the data size is a byte. Relative addressing is always relative to the start of the corresponding extension word. The displacement is always a signed value.

Address mode subsets. Usually only a subset of the 12 addressing modes is allowed in an operation. There are four major scopes:

- The *data* scope excludes the use of address registers (mode 1).
- The *memory* scope excludes both register types (modes 0 and 1).
- The *control* scope, which applies to addresses used for branching or for address computation, is even more restrictive than the memory scope; it also excludes the increment, decrement, and immediate addresses (modes 0, 1, 3, 4, and 11), leaving seven modes.
- The *alter* scope can be combined with the data or the memory scope and excludes, furthermore, addresses that cannot or should not be altered—relative and immediate addresses (modes 9, 10, and 11, where 11 is encoded as 7 4).

For the scope designated *any*, all modes are valid. Violation of the scope restrictions causes an invalid-operation interruption.

```
↓Md ↓Sd

┌──────────────────────┐      value←disp680;inst;size;index;displacement
│Rd│ │*│ │D1│          │      ⋀ Motorola 68000 indexed displacement
└──────────────────────┘      inst←ifetch680 word
0   4  8       16             size←(word,long)[fld Sd]
Index extension               →IF fld Md
Legend: D = displacement;     THEN: ⋀ data register
        Md = register type;       index←radixcompi(-size)↑reg[fld Rd;]
        R = register;             →ENDIF
        Sd = size;            ELSE: ⋀ address register
        * = unused.               index←radixcompi(-size)↑adr[fld Rd;]
                              ENDIF:displacement←radixcompi inst[D1]
                              value←index+displacement

address←size incr680 r;pointer          address←size decr680 r;pointer
⋀ Motorola 68000 postincrement          ⋀ Motorola 68000 predecrement
pointer←magni adr[r;]                    pointer←(magni adr[r;])-size≢byte
address←size,memadr,pointer             address←size,memadr,pointer
adr[r;]←long magnr pointer+size≢byte     adr[r;]←long magnr pointer
```

PROGRAM 16-92   Addressing modes in the Motorola MC68000.

Postincrement and predecrement.   Increment and decrement follow the classical architecture. Any address register can be used as pointer. The indexed displacement uses a separate format which contains an 8-bit signed displacement and specifies which data or address register contains the index.

Source and operand selection.   Several dyadic instructions specify a choice between to-register and to-memory operation with the MO bit. In Program 16-93, source680 and dest680 show that the size is specified by the Size field, as shown in size680; the memory address uses the address modes specified by the M2 and R2 fields, as shown in mode680.

```
source←source680 scope              dest←dest680 scope
ᴀ Motorola 68000 source selection   ᴀ Motorola 68000 destination selection
→IF fld M0                          →IF fld M0
THEN: ᴀ register address            THEN: ᴀ address mode
   source←size680,regadr,fld R1        dest←size680 mode680 scope,alter
   →ENDIF                              →ENDIF
ELSE: ᴀ address mode                ELSE: ᴀ register address
   source←size680 mode680 scope        dest←size680,regadr,fld R1
ENDIF:                              ENDIF:


address←size mode680 scope
ᴀ Motorola 68000 mode address
address←size adr680(fld M2),(fld R2),scope


size←size680                        od←immediate680 size
ᴀ Motorola 68000 data size          ᴀ Motorola 68000 immediate data
size←(byte,word,long)[fld Sz]       od←(-size)↑ifetch680 size⌐word
```

PROGRAM 16-93   Field and size specification in the Motorola MC68000.

Immediate addressing. Immediate data may have byte, word, or longword size. The data follow the first instruction word. Since instructions have word resolution, byte-length immediate data occupy the rightmost byte of a word, the left byte being unused.

System-stack access. The system stack grows from high to low addresses, with the stack pointer pointing at the last item entered in the stack. The use of the stack is always with word or longword—not byte—resolution.

```
data←pop680 size                    push680 data
ᴀ Motorola 68000 read from stack    ᴀ Motorola 68000 write onto stack
data←read680 size incr680 Sp        ((ρdata) decr680 Sp) write680 data
```

PROGRAM 16-94   System-stack access in the Motorola MC68000.

Address Arithmetic

The address arithmetic instructions apply to the address registers and to the user stack. The operand size is either a word or a longword. The result placed in the address registers has always longword size. The instructions do not affect the conditions, except for Compare Address.

```
h ADDA  Add Address         p LEA   Load Effective Address
h SUBA  Subtract Address    m PEA   Push Effective Address
h CMPA  Compare Address     e LINK  Link And Allocate
                            e UNLK  Unlink
```

TABLE 16-95   Address arithmetic instructions of the Motorola MC68000.

Address operations. Compare Address is a subtraction without changing the destination operand, but noting the difference and borrow in the conditions. Load Effective Address places an effective address in an address register; Push Effective address pushes the effective address onto the system stack.

```
ADDA;size;source;addend;augend;sum   CMPA;size;source;addend;augend;sum
⋀ Motorola 68000 Add Address         ⋀ Motorola 68000 Compare Address
size←(word,long)[fld M0]             size←(word,long)[fld M0]
source←size mode680 any              source←size mode680 any
addend←radixcompi read680 source     addend←radixcompi˜read680 source
augend←radixcompi adr[fld R1;]       augend←radixcompi(-size)↑adr[fld R1;]
cum←augend+addend                    sum←augend+addend+1
adr[fld R1;]←long radixcompr sum     size signal680B augend,addend,1
                                     signal680NZO long radixcompr sum


LEA;address
⋀ Motorola 68000 Load Effective Address
address←byte mode680 control
adr[fld R1;]←long magnr address[Value]

PEA;address
⋀ Motorola 68000 Push Effective Address
address←byte mode680 control
push680 long magnr address[Value]
```

PROGRAM 16-96   Address arithmetic in the Motorola MC68000.

Stack and list addressing.   Link And Allocate pushes the contents of the specified address register, the frame pointer, onto the stack, then replaces the content of that register with the updated stack pointer, and adds a (usually negative) displacement to the stack pointer to allocate parameter space on the stack. Unlink restores the stack pointer from the specified address register and restores the previous content of that address register, the frame pointer, from the stack.

```
LINK;addend;augend;sum                   UNLK
⋀ Motorola 68000 Link And Allocate       ⋀ Motorola 68000 Unlink
push680 adr[fld R2;]                      adr[Sp;]←adr[fld R2;]
adr[fld R2;]←adr[Sp;]                     adr[fld R2;]←pop680 long
addend←radixcompi ifetch680 word
augend←radixcompi adr[Sp;]
sum←augend+addend
adr[Sp;]←long radixcompr sum
```

PROGRAM 16-97   Stack operations of the Motorola MC68000.

16.4.4

Data

Character Strings

The MC68000 handles 8-bit characters, but no character strings. The instructions are independent of the character set encoding.

Logical

Logical formats.   The logical formats are the same as the binary fixed-point formats.

Fixed-Point Numbers

Binary notation and allocation.   Binary fixed-point arithmetic uses radix-complement notation and applies to byte-, word-, and longword-length data.

For arithmetic, the common signaling is for negative, zero, and overflow. For addition, the `Carry` bit is set; for subtraction, a borrow is noted in this status bit as the inverse of a carry. The `Extend` bit is used in extended precision and remains unchanged in other operations, such as logical connectives or data movement. Hence the extend bit is set less frequently than the carry bit; when it is set, however, it is always equal to the carry bit. The carry bit makes it possible to compare unsigned integers.

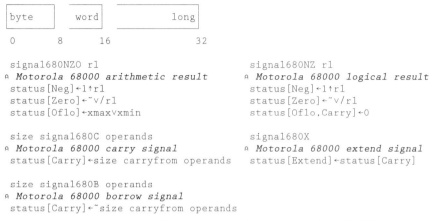

```
signal680NZO rl                          signal680NZ rl
A Motorola 68000 arithmetic result       A Motorola 68000 logical result
status[Neg]←1↑rl                         status[Neg]←1↑rl
status[Zero]←~∨/rl                       status[Zero]←~∨/rl
status[Oflo]←xmax∨xmin                   status[Oflo,Carry]←0

size signal680C operands                 signal680X
A Motorola 68000 carry signal            A Motorola 68000 extend signal
status[Carry]←size carryfrom operands    status[Extend]←status[Carry]

size signal680B operands
A Motorola 68000 borrow signal
status[Carry]←~size carryfrom operands
```

PROGRAM 16-98   Binary number in the Motorola MC68000.

Decimal representation.   Decimal arithmetic applies to bytes only. Two binary coded decimal digits are placed in one byte. Negative and overflow are undefined for decimal arithmetic. Decimal arithmetic is aimed at extended precision; a cumulative zero result is noted in the zero condition.

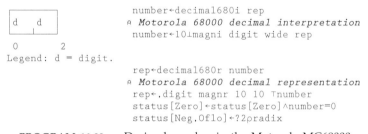

```
                         number←decimal680i rep
                         A Motorola 68000 decimal interpretation
                         number←10⊥magni digit wide rep
     0        2
Legend: d = digit.
                         rep←decimal680r number
                         A Motorola 68000 decimal representation
                         rep←,digit magnr 10 10 ⊤number
                         status[Zero]←status[Zero]∧number=0
                         status[Neg,Oflo]←?2ρradix
```

PROGRAM 16-99   Decimal number in the Motorola MC68000.

16.4.5

Operations

Data Handling

Data movement.   The MC68000 combines Move with Load and Store; we treat it there.

Logic

Logic includes connectives applying to bits and logical vectors, shifts, and rotates. There are no other logical-vector operations. Most shifts and rotates are for any shift amount. All applicable operations may be specified as direct and immediate. Address registers do not participate in logic or shifts.

```
k BSET   Set Bit                      i LSR    Shift
1 BSETI  Set Bit Immediate            i LSRI   Shift Immediate
k BCLR   Reset Bit                    i ASR    Shift Arithmetic
1 BCLRI  Reset Bit Immediate          i ASRI   Shift Arithmetic Immediate
k BCHG   Change Bit                   j LSM    Shift Memory
1 BCHGI  Change Bit Immediate         j ASM    Shift Memory Arithmetic
k BTST   Test Bit                     i ROR    Rotate
1 BTSTI  Test Bit Immediate           i RORI   Rotate Immediate
b CLR    Clear                        i ROXR   Rotate With Carry
b NOT    Not                          i ROXRI  Rotate With Carry Immediate
a AND    And                          j ROM    Rotate Memory
b ANDI   And Immediate                j ROXM   Rotate With Carry Memory
a OR     Or                           n SWAP   Swap Register Halves
b ORI    Or Immediate
q EOR    Exclusive Or
b EORI   Exclusive Or Immediate
```

TABLE 16-100   Logical and shift operations of the Motorola MC68000.

Connectives.   The dyadic connective instructions, such as And, combine data at an effective address with the content of a data register. The result is placed at the effective address in memory or in the register. The immediate operations combine immediate data with destination data.

```
NOT;dest;r1                           CLR;dest
ₐ Motorola 68000 Not                  ₐ Motorola 68000 Clear
dest←size680 mode680 data             dest←size680 mode680 data
r1←~read680 dest                      dest write680 size680ρ0
dest write680 r1                      signal680NZ size680ρ0
signal680NZ r1


AND;dest;od2;od1;r1                   ORI;dest;od2;od1;r1
ₐ Motorola 68000 And                  ₐ Motorola 68000 Or Immediate
od2←read680 source680 data            od2←immediate680 size680
dest←dest680 mem                      dest←size680 mode680 data
od1←read680 dest                      od1←read680 dest
r1←od1∧od2                            r1←od1∨od2
dest write680 r1                      dest write680 r1
signal680NZ r1                        signal680NZ r1


BSETI;size;bitadr;dest;od             BTST;size;bitadr;dest;od
ₐ Motorola 68000 Set Bit Immediate    ₐ Motorola 68000 Test Bit
size←(byte,long)[0=fld M2]            size←(byte,long)[0=fld M2]
bitadr←size|-1+magni ifetch680 word   bitadr←size|-1+magni reg[fld R1;]
dest←size mode680 data                dest←size mode680 data
od←read680 dest                       od←read680 dest
status[Zero]←~od[bitadr]              status[Zero]←~od[bitadr]
od[bitadr]←1
dest write680 od
```

PROGRAM 16-101   Logical connectives in the Motorola MC68000.

Bit operations. Bit operations are monadic: setting to 0, setting to 1, inverting, or testing. The bit is specified by a bit address that refers to the bits in a byte or in a longword. The bits are addressed right to left. The bit address is either the content of a register or an immediate quantity. Only the 0 condition is set.

Shift. The general arithmetic or logical shift occurs in the data specified by R2. Only the rightmost bits of the register participate if the length is a byte or a word. The shift amount may be specified directly (modulo 64) from the R1 register, or immediately from the instruction field R1. The shift direction is specified by an instruction bit. The carry does not participate in the shift; it is set according to the last bit that is shifted out. The extend bit is equal to the carry, except that it is not changed for a 0 shift. Shift Memory has a shift amount of either $+1$ or -1.

```
ASR;shift;loc;od;r1;cx                      LSRI;shift;loc;od;r1;cx
ⱥ Motorola 68000 Shift Arithmetic           ⱥ Motorola 68000 Shift Immediate
shift←64|magni reg[fld R1;]                  shift←fld0 R1
loc←(long-size680)+ιsize680                  loc←(long-size680)+ιsize680
od←reg[fld R2;loc]                           od←reg[fld R2;loc]
→CASE(fld M0)⌈2×shift=0                       →CASE(fld M0)⌈2×shift=0
C0:  ⱥ right shift                           C0:  ⱥ right shift
    r1←size680↑od[shiftρ0],od                    r1←size680↑(shiftρ0),od
    cx←od[size680-shift]                         cx←od[size680-shift]
    →ENDCASE                                      →ENDCASE
C1:  ⱥ left shift                            C1:  ⱥ left shift
    r1←size680↑shift↓od                          r1←size680↑shift↓od
    cx←od[shift-1]                               cx←od[shift-1]
    →ENDCASE                                      →ENDCASE
C2:  ⱥ zero shift                            C2:  ⱥ zero shift
    r1←od                                        r1←od
    cx←0,status[Extend]                          cx←0,status[Extend]
ENDCASE:reg[fld R2;loc]←r1                   ENDCASE:reg[fld R2;loc]←r1
signal680NZ r1                               signal680NZ r1
status[Carry,Extend]←cx                      status[Carry,Extend]←cx
```

PROGRAM 16-102   Shift in the Motorola MC68000.

```
ROXR;shift;loc;od;r1;cx                      ROM;shift;dest;od;r1
ⱥ Motorola 68000 Rotate With Carry           ⱥ Motorola 68000 Rotate Memory
shift←64|magni reg[fld R1;]                  shift← ¯1 1[fld M0]
loc←(long-size680)+ιsize680                  dest←word mode680 mem,alter
od←reg[fld R2;loc],status[Extend]           od←read680 dest
→CASE(fld M0)⌈2×shift=0                       r1←shiftΦod
C0:  ⱥ right rotate                          dest write680 r1
    r1←¯1↓(-shift)Φod                        signal680NZ r1
    cx←2ρ¯1↑(-shift)Φod                      status[Carry,Extend]←2ρshift↑od
    →ENDCASE
C1:  ⱥ left rotate
    r1←¯1↓shiftΦod                           SWAP
    cx←2ρ¯1↑shiftΦod                         ⱥ Motorola 68000 Swap Register Halves
    →ENDCASE                                  reg[fld R2;]←wordΦreg[fld R2;]
C2:  ⱥ zero rotate                          signal680NZ reg[fld R2;]
    r1←¯1↓od
    cx←0,status[Extend]
ENDCASE:reg[fld R2;loc]←r1
signal680NZ r1
status[Carry,Extend]←cx
```

PROGRAM 16-103   Rotate in the Motorola MC68000.

Rotate. Plain Rotate is similar to logical shift; it operates in the rightmost part of a register, is specified by a direct or immediate shift amount and a direction bit, and sets the carry bit according to the last bit shifted out. The extend bit, however, is not set at all. In Rotate With Carry the extend bit extends the operand and is set according to the last bit shifted out of the register, or left unchanged in case of 0 shift amount. Rotate Memory rotates only 1 bit left or 1 bit right; there is no 0 shift—the extend bit participates always.

Swap.   Swap Register Halves interchanges the left and right word of a register. Swap clears the carry bit and does not effect the extend bit. Hence it is not equivalent to Rotate 16 bits.

Fixed-Point Arithmetic

Fixed-point arithmetic is primarily binary and includes provisions for extended precision, immediate, and short immediate (called *quick*) operations. Arithmetic applies to operands in data registers or in memory. The move operations also involve address registers.

a	MOVEB	Move Byte		b	NEGX	Negate With Borrow
a	MOVEW	Move Word		a	ADD	Add
a	MOVEL	Move Long		b	ADDI	Add Immediate
x	MOVEQ	Move Quick		a	ADDQ	Add Quick
r	MOVEP	Move Peripheral Data		g	ADDX	Add With Carry
m	MVTRW	Load Multiple Word		a	SUB	Subtract
m	MVTRL	Load Multiple Long		b	SUBI	Subtract Immediate
m	MVFRW	Store Multiple Word		q	SUBQ	Subtract Quick
m	MVFRL	Store Multiple Long		g	SUBX	Subtract With Borrow
o	EXG	Swap Registers		h	MUL	Multiply
o	EXGM	Swap Mixed Registers		h	DIV	Divide
b	TST	Test		a	CMP	Compare
n	EXTW	Sign-extend To Word		b	CMPI	Compare Immediate
n	EXTL	Sign-extend To Long		r	CMPM	Compare Memory
b	NEG	Negate		p	CHK	Check Against Bound

TABLE 16-104   Binary instructions of the Motorola MC68000.

Load and Store.   Move allows all meaningful address modifications on source and destination data. Move Quick has a sign-extensible 8-bit immediate operand and data-register destination. Swap Registers interchanges the content of either two data registers or two address registers.

Swap Mixed Registers interchanges the content of an address and a data register. Move Peripheral Data packs alternate bytes of memory (which may have been stored unpacked by an I/O transmission) to or from a data register.

Multiple register load and store.   A selection of words or longwords from the data registers and the address registers is moved to or from a set of contiguous memory locations. The register selection is made by an immediate 16-bit mask. Each bit of the mask designates from right to left the data registers 0 through 7, followed by address registers 0 through 7. The address modes are the usual control modes; in Load Multiple, there is also a postincrement mode; in Store Multiple, a predecrement mode. For the predecrement mode, the mask specification must be reversed!

```
MOVEW:od;mdst;dest
ρ Motorola 68000 Move Word
od←read680 word mode680 any
mdst←(fld M1),(fld R1),data,alter
dest←word adr680 mdst
dest write680 od
signal680NZ od


EXG:R12
ρ Motorola 68000 Swap Registers
R12←(fld R1),fld R2
→IF 0=fld M2
THEN: ρ data registers
   reg[R12;]←reg[ΦR12;]
   →ENDIF
ELSE: ρ address registers
   adr[R12;]←adr[ΦR12;]
ENDIF:




MVTRW:mask;source;operand
ρ Motorola 68000 Load Multiple Word
mask←Φifetch680 word
→IF 3=fld M2
THEN: ρ postincrement
   source←(word×+/mask) incr680 fld R2
   →ENDIF
ELSE: ρ control scope
   source←(word×+/mask) mode680 control
ENDIF:operand←radixcompi word wide read680 source
reg[(8↑mask)/ι8;]←long radixcompr(+/8↑mask)↑operand
adr[(8↓mask)/ι8;]←long radixcompr(+/8↑mask)↓operand
```

```
MOVEQ:operand;rl
ρ Motorola 68000 Move Quick
operand←radixcompi inst[D1]
rl←long radixcompr operand
reg[fld R1;]←rl
signal680NZ rl



EXGM:od
ρ Motorola 68000 Swap Mixed Registers
od←adr[fld R2;]
adr[fld R2;]←reg[fld R1;]
reg[fld R1;]←od



MVFRW:mask;dest;od
ρ Motorola 68000 Store Multiple Word
→IF 4=fld M2
THEN: ρ predecrement
   mask←ifetch680 word
   dest←(word×+/mask) decr680 fld R2
   →ENDIF
ELSE: ρ control scope
   mask←Φifetch680 word
   dest←(word×+/mask) mode680 control
ENDIF:od←,mask/(16,-word)↑reg⊤adr
dest write680 od
```

PROGRAM 16-105   Load and Store in the Motorola MC68000.

Sign control.   Negation can be with and without borrow. Sign extension is from a byte to a word, or from a word to a longword. Test reads any alterable location, except the address registers, and sets the negative and zero conditions.

```
NEG:dest;operand;rl
ρ Motorola 68000 Negate
dest←size680 mode680 data,alter
operand←radixcompi read680 dest
rl←size680 radixcompr-operand
dest write680 rl
signal680NZO rl
status[Carry]←operand=0
```

```
TST:od
ρ Motorola 68000 Test
od←read680 size680 mode680 data,alter
signal680NZ od


EXTL
ρ Motorola 68000 Sign-extend To Long
reg[fld R2:ιword]←reg[fld R2;word]
signal680NZ reg[fld R2;]
```

PROGRAM 16-106   Sign control in the Motorola MC68000.

Add and Subtract.   Addition and subtraction are with and without carry or borrow. The short-immediate operations differ from those for Move in two ways. First, the length of the immediate field is only 3 bits and is not sign-extended, but rather is interpreted as a value from 1 to 8. Second, the destination is not restricted to being a register, but under address mode control.

```
ADD;dest;source;addend;augend;sum;sm        ADDQ;dest;addend;augend;sum;sm
ꓥ Motorola 68000 Add                        ꓥ Motorola 68000 Add Quick
source←source680 any                        addend←fld0 R1
addend←radixcompi read680 source            dest←size680 mode680 alter
dest←dest680 mem                            augend←radixcompi read680 dest
augend←radixcompi read680 dest              sum←augend+addend
sum←augend+addend                          sm←size680 radixcompr sum
sm←size680 radixcompr sum                   dest write680 sm
dest write680 sm                            signal680NZO sm
signal680NZO sm                             (ρsm) signal680C addend,augend
(ρsm) signal680C addend,augend              signal680X
signal680X


ADDX;dest;source;addend;augend;sum;sm
ꓥ Motorola 68000 Add With Carry
source←size680 adr680(4×fld Rm),fld R2
addend←radixcompi read680 source
dest←size680 adr680(4×fld Rm),fld R1        SUBI;ad;addend;dest;augend;sum;sm
augend←radixcompi read680 dest              ꓥ Motorola 68000 Subtract Immediate
sum←augend+addend+status[Extend]            ad←˜immediate680 size680
sm←size680 radixcompr sum                   addend←radixcompi ad
dest write680 sm                            dest←size680 mode680 data,alter
→IF sum=0                                   augend←radixcompi read680 dest
THEN: ꓥ zero result                         sum←augend+addend+1
    status[Neg,Oflo]←0                      sm←size680 radixcompr sum
    →ENDIF                                  dest write680 sm
ELSE: ꓥ non-zero result                     signal680NZO sm
    signal680NZO sm                         (ρsm) signal680B addend,augend,1
ENDIF:signal680X
(ρsm) signal680C addend,augend,status[Extend]
```

PROGRAM 16-107   Binary addition in the Motorola MC68000.

Add With Carry is either register to register (mode 0) or predecremented memory to predecremented memory (mode 4). This choice in modes, which occurs also in some other operations, is specified by the instruction bit Rm; no further scope limitation is needed.

Multiply and Divide.   Multiply specifies the word-size operands by an effective address and a data-register address and places the longword product in the data register. Results are signaled as for a move. When the M0 bit is 1, the data are treated as signed; otherwise, they are treated as unsigned.

Divide obtains a longword dividend from a data register, a word-size divisor from the effective address location, and places the word-size remainder and quotient left to right in the register. Sign control and signals are as in Multiply, except that quotient overflow is signaled. A 0 divisor causes a Divide exception.

Compare.   Compare subtracts the effective address operand from the register operand and sets the conditions without recording the difference. Compare

```
CMP;dest;addend;au;augend;sum;sm            CMPM;source;dest;addend;augend;sum;sm
ꓥ Motorola 68000 Compare                    ꓥ Motorola 68000 Compare Memory
dest←size680 mode680 any                    source←size680 adr680 3,fld R2
addend←radixcompi˜read680 dest              addend←radixcompi read680 source
au←(-size680)↑reg[fld R1;]                  dest←size680 adr680 3,fld R1
augend←radixcompi au                        augend←radixcompi read680 dest
sum←augend+addend+1                         sum←augend+addend+1
sm←size680 radixcompr sum                   sm←size680 radixcompr sum
signal680NZO sm                             signal680NZO sm
(ρsm) signal680B addend,augend,1            (ρsm) signal680B addend,augend,1
```

PROGRAM 16-108   Binary comparison in the Motorola MC68000.

Memory is similar, but uses the postincrement mode for both operands. Compare Immediate subtracts immediate data from the alterable effective-address operand.

Boundary check.   Compare Against Bound uses 0 and the value of the effective-address operand as two boundaries. If the register value is outside the bounds, a `Bound` interrupt is signaled, with the negative condition indicating the sign of the value. If the value is within bounds, the negative indicator is unpredictable. The zero, overflow, and carry conditions are always unpredictable.

```
CHK;bound;operand
ᕟ Motorola 68000 Check Against Bound
bound←radixcompi read680 word mode680 data
operand←radixcompi(-word)↑reg[fld R1;]
→IF(operand<0)∨operand>bound
THEN: ᕟ out of bounds
    status[Neg]←operand<0
    Bound report 1
    →ENDIF
ELSE: ᕟ within bounds
    status[Neg]←?radix
ENDIF:status[Zero,Oflo,Carry]←?3ρradix
```

PROGRAM 16-109   Boundary check in the Motorola MC68000.

Decimal Arithmetic

There are three decimal operations, each with unsigned two-digit operands, and with the extend bit participating for extended arithmetic. At the start of a calculation, the extend bit must be cleared. A decimal carry is noted in the carry and extend bits.

m NBCD	Negate Decimal With Borrow	o SBCD	Subtract Decimal With Borrow
o ABCD	Add Decimal With Carry		

TABLE 16-110   Decimal instructions of the Motorola MC68000.

Decimal addition.   Decimal add or subtract are either memory to memory with predecrement mode (mode 4), or register to register (mode 0). The choice between mode 0 and mode 4 is specified by instruction bit Rm. Negate Decimal has full addressing control.

```
ABCD;source;dest;addend;augend;sum
ᕟ Motorola 68000 Add Decimal With Carry
source←byte adr680(4×fld Rm),fld R2
addend←decimal680i read680 source
dest←byte adr680(4×fld Rm),fld R1
augend←decimal680i read680 dest
sum←augend+addend+status[Extend]
dest write680 decimal680r sum
status[Zero]←status[Zero]∧sum=0
status[Carry,Extend]←sum≥100
```

PROGRAM 16-111   Add Decimal in the Motorola MC68000.

16.4.6

Instruction Sequencing

The basic execution cycle of the MC68000 fetches one instruction word. Extensions of the instruction are fetched as needed by the address modes. The stopped state bit is set by persistent hardware failure and is reset by a system reset.

```
cycle680                              inst←ifetch680 size
ⁿ basic cycle of the Motorola 68000  ⁿ Motorola 68000 instruction fetch
 REPEAT:execute ifetch680 word        inst←read680 size,memadr,iadr
    interrupt680                       iadr←iadr+size∻byte
 →UNTIL stop
```

PROGRAM 16-112   Basic cycle and instruction fetch of the Motorola MC68000.

Sequencing instructions.   The sequencing instructions are classical, with provisions for decision, iteration, and delegation.

```
f NOP    No Operation        m JSR    Call
m JMP    Branch              w BSR    Jump To Subroutine
v BCC    Jump On Condition   f RTS    Return
u DBCC   Jump On Decrement
```

TABLE 16-113   Sequencing instructions of the Motorola MC68000.

Linear Sequence

Completion.   Normal completion in the user mode is by humble access.

Unconditional Branch.   The address modes for branches give the address of the next instruction.   Only control modes are allowed, since register addresses, immediate addresses, and the increment and decrement modes are not meaningful. Relative addressing, however, is possible and meaningful.

```
JMP
ⁿ Motorola 68000 Branch
iadr←(word mode680 control)[Value]
```

PROGRAM 16-114   Unconditional Branch in the Motorola MC68000.

Decision

Conditional branching.   Decision uses condition codes to separate the test from the action. Eight condition codes (including *never*) and their inverses can be selected by the 4-bit condition field of the conditional-branch instruction. This set is equivalent to the M6800 and PDP11 conditions.   Moreover, an all-zeros condition field always satisfies the condition; Motorola labels this unconditional branch with a separate instruction mnemonic.   When the condition succeeds, a relative branch is taken. The branch offset is either the signed 8-bit displacement field, or, if this field is 0, a signed 16-bit extension field.   In either case the branch is relative to the word following the first instruction word.

```
BCC;oldadr;offset                          yes←condition680;cz;1;1z;czon;cv
A Motorola 68000 Jump On Condition         A Motorola 68000 condition test
oldadr←iadr                                A low or equal
→IF 0=fld D1                               cz←∨/status[Carry,Zero]
THEN:offset←radixcompi ifetch680 word      A less
  →ENDIF:                                  1←≠/status[Neg,Oflo]
ELSE:offset←radixcompi inst[D1]            A less or equal
ENDIF:iadr←oldadr+offset×condition680      1z←1∨status[Zero]
                                           A carry,zero,overflow,negative
                                           czon←status[Carry,Zero,Oflo,Neg]
                                           A condition vector
                                           cv←0,cz,czon,1,1z
                                           yes←(fld ¯1↑Cdn)=cv[fld ¯1↓Cdn]
```

PROGRAM 16-115   Conditional Branch in the Motorola MC68000.

Iteration

Incrementation and termination.   Jump On Decrement allows iteration. The iteration test is made only when the specified condition is not satisfied. In that case, a count in the specified data register is decremented and a signed offset is added to the instruction address. If the count is 0 prior to decrementing, the branch is not taken.

```
DBCC;oldadr;offset;count
A Motorola 68000 Jump On Decrement
oldadr←iadr
offset←radixcompi ifetch680 word
→If˜condition680
THEN:count←magni reg[fld R2;word+ιword]
    reg[fld R2;word+ιword]←word magnr count-1
    iadr←oldadr+offset×count≠0
ENDIF:
```

PROGRAM 16-116   Decrement and branch in the Motorola MC68000.

Delegation

Call and Return.   Call pushes the instruction address as a return address onto the system stack and branches to an absolute address. Jump To Subroutine similarly pushes the return address, but branches to a relative address with a short or a long offset. Return restores the instruction address by obtaining the return address from the stack. Return And Restore fetches the user byte of the status word from the stack prior to retrieving the return address.

Link and Unlink (Program 16-97) can be used to implement linked activity records on the stack. A Move operation with the predecrement mode can be used to place call-by-value parameters on the stack. Push Effective Address

```
JSR;address                        BSR;oldadr;offset
A Motorola 68000 Call              A Motorola 68000 Jump To Subroutine
address←word mode680 control       oldadr←iadr
push680 long magnr iadr            →IF 0=fld D1
iadr←magni address[Value]          THEN:offset←radixcompi ifetch680 word
                                       →ENDIF:
                                   ELSE:offset←radixcompi inst[D1]
RTS                                ENDIF:push680 long magnr iadr
A Motorola 68000 Return            iadr←oldadr+offset
iadr←magni pop680 long
```

PROGRAM 16-117   Call and Return in the Motorola MC68000.

(Program 16-96) can place the address for call-by-reference parameters on the stack.

16.4.7
Supervision

Concurrency

Processor interconnection.   Multiprocessing is obtained by connecting processors to a central bus.

Integrity

System integrity is ensured by policing and privileged operations.

Protection.   Memory-addressing errors, illegal or unimplemented operations, and divide by zero are policed. Trap On Overflow (Program 16-122) and Check Against Bounds (Program 16-109) are run-time checks that result in an interruption.

Control Switching

Interruption.   When the system is in the `Trace` mode, the `Tracetrap` indicator is turned on prior to the interrupt action to ensure that a trace interruption is noted. The I/O indicators are masked according to the priority level stated in the status word.

There are seven interrupt priority levels. The highest level is not maskable. If, after masking, no indicator is found to be turned on, instruction sequencing is resumed. If the wait condition is turned on, the search is repeated until an I/O indicator turns on. When an interrupt indicator is noted, the status is

```
interrupt680;who;oldstatus;intadr          mask←mask680;prior
ⁿ Motorola 68000 interrupt action         ⁿ Motorola 68000 interrupt mask
ind[Tracetrap]←status[Trace]               prior←magni status[Priority]
REPEAT:who←(ind∧mask680)ι1                 mask←(ρind)ρ1
   →If who≠ρind                            mask[⁻1↓Inout]←prior≤1+ιρ⁻1↓Inout
   THEN:ind[who]←0
        oldstatus←status
        swapsp 1                           swapsp s
        push680 long magnr iadr            ⁿ Motorola 68000 swap stack pointers
        push680 oldstatus                  →If status[Supervisor]≠s
        status[Trace]←wait←0               THEN:adr[Sp,Ap;]←adr[Ap,Sp;]
        priority680 who                        status[Supervisor]←s
        intadr←long,memadr,who×4           ENDIF:
        iadr←magni read680 intadr
        Invadr report 1=2|iadr
        stop←(who=Mach)∧ind[Mach]          priority680 who;prior
ENDIF:→UNTIL˜wait                          ⁿ Motorola 68000 prority adjustment
                                           →If who∊Inout
                                           THEN:prior←1+Inoutιwho
                                               status[Priority]←3 magnr prior
yes←suppress680                            ENDIF:
ⁿ Motorola 68000 operation suppression
yes←∨/ind
```

PROGRAM 16-118   Interruption action in the Motorola MC68000.

preserved and the stack pointers are switched, such that the supervisor pointer becomes the active pointer, and the supervisor state is set.

Then, the processor saves both the instruction address and the status word on the stack, disables the trace and wait modes, and adjusts the priority. A new instruction address is taken from the interrupt vectors. A persistent machine check is noted and sets the `stop` state; otherwise, sequencing is resumed.

Privileged operations.   The supervisory operations deal with process interaction, waiting, humble access, context switching, dispatching, and emulation. Privileged operations are Wait, Return From Interrupt, Move To Status, And Status, Or Status, Exclusive Or Status, Set or Store User Pointer, and the I/O operation Reset Devices.

```
f STOP   Wait                      d MOVTC Set Condition
d TAS    Test And Set              t SCC   Test Condition
e TRAPL  Trap Low                  d MOVTS Set Status
e TRAPH  Trap High                 d MOVFS Store Status
f TRAPV  Trap On Overflow          c ANDIR And Status Immediate
f RTE    Return From Interrupt     c ORIR  Or Status Immediate
f RTR    Return And Restore        c EORIR Exclusive Or Status Immediate
e MOVTU  Set User Pointer          a OPC10 Emulator Code 10
e MOVFU  Store User Pointer        a OPC15 Emulator Code 15
```

TABLE 16-119   Supervisory instructions of the Motorola MC68000.

Emulator codes.   Emulator Code 10 and Emulator Code 15 are set aside for emulation purposes; they each have their own interrupt address.

Critical section.   Test And Set gives critical-section control. The instruction tests a byte, sets the negative and zero indicators, sets the high-order bit of the byte to 1, and then stores the byte, all as one indivisible action.

```
TAS;dest;od
ﬁ Motorola 68000 Test And Set
dest←byte mode680 data,alter
ﬁ start serialization
od←read680 dest
signal680NZ od
dest write680 od WHERE od[0]←1
ﬁ end serialization
```

PROGRAM 16-120   Critical-section control in the Motorola MC68000.

Waiting.   Wait (mnemonic `Stop`) may only be issued in the supervisory state. A new status word is fetched as part of the Wait instruction. The new status must specify the supervisory mode; otherwise, a privileged operation interruption is taken.

```
STOP
ﬁ Motorola 68000 Wait
Priv report˜status[Supervisor]
→OUT suppress680
status←ifetch680 word
Priv report˜status[Supervisor]
wait←1
```

PROGRAM 16-121   Wait in the Motorola MC68000.

Humble access.   Trap Low and Trap High use the 3-bit R2 field to give one of
16 program-controlled interrupts that can be used to call supervisory routines.
Trap On Overflow gives humble access if an overflow has occurred.

```
TRAPL                              TRAPV
A Motorola 68000 Trap Low  A Motorola 68000 Trap On Overflow
Trap[fld R2] report 1          Oflotrap report status[Oflo]
```

PROGRAM 16-122   Humble access in the Motorola MC68000.

Dispatching.   The privileged operation Return From Interrupt restores full
status and the instruction address from the system stack and switches pointers
to restore the user stack pointer.

```
RTE
A Motorola 68000 Return From Interrupt
Priv report~status[Supervisor]
→OUT suppress680
status←pop680 word                RTR
iadr←magni pop680 long            A Motorola 68000 Return And Restore
swapsp 0                            status[Cond]←byte↓pop680 word
                                   iadr←magni pop680 long
```

PROGRAM 16-123   Dispatch in the Motorola MC68000.

State Preservation

Context switching.   In the supervisory state, the user pointer is in the
alternate pointer location. The privileged operations Set User Pointer and
Store User Pointer move the user pointer from and to an address register,
which makes it subject to computation.

All 16 status bits can be read in the user or supervisory mode with Store
Status. The 8 low-order status bits can be set by Set Condition and can be
altered by the byte-size Status Immediate connectives. The full status word
can be changed only by privileged operations, such as Set Status, or by the
word-size Status Immediate connectives. Test Condition stores an all-zeros or
all-ones byte, according to the outcome of the condition that is specified in the
same manner as for the conditional branch condition.

```
MOVFU                              MOVTU
A Motorola 68000 Store User Pointer  A Motorola 68000 Set User Pointer
Priv report~status[Supervisor]     Priv report~status[Supervisor]
→OUT~status[Supervisor]            →OUT~status[Supervisor]
adr[fld R2;]←adr[Ap;]              adr[Ap;]←adr[fld R2;]

MOVFS;dest                         MOVTC;dest
A Motorola 68000 Store Status      A Motorola 68000 Set Condition
dest←word mode680 data,alter       dest←word mode680 data
dest write680 status               status[Cond]←byte↓read680 dest

ANDIR;size;od2;od1;rl              SCC;dest
A Motorola 68000 And Status Immediate  A Motorola 68000 Test Condition
size←(byte,word)[fld 1↓Sz]         dest←byte mode680 data,alter
od2←immediate680 size              dest write680 bytepcondition680
od1←status[(word-size)+ιsize]
rl←od1∧od2
Priv report(size=word)∧~status[Supervisor]
→OUT suppress680
status[(word-size)+ιsize]←rl
```

PROGRAM 16-124   Context switching in the Motorola MC68000.

16.4.8

Input/Output

Direct, buffered, and channel I/O can be attached to the processor.

Read and Write.   Data transmission is controlled by dedicated memory locations.

Sense and Control.   The only specific I/O instruction, Reset Devices, is a privileged operation that activates the reset line of external devices. The processor is not reset.

An interrupting peripheral device provides an 8-bit interrupt vector number.

16.4.9

Implementation Notes

Asynchronous logic with a 4–16 MHz clock frequency is used. Instructions take 3 to 12 clock cycles, which gives operation times from 200 ns to 3 μs. Two levels of microprogramming are used to increase the regularity of the VLSI design.

16.4.10

Bibliography

Motorola Semicondutor Products, Inc., 1982: *MC68000 16-bit Microprocessor User's Manual.* 3rd ed. Austin, TX: Motorola Semiconductor Products (our defining reference).

Stritter and Gunter [1979].

16.4.11

Exercises

16-16 Give the description of the address arithmetic instruction SUBA, assuming consistency with the address arithmetic instructions shown in this section.

16-17 Give the description of the logical and shift instructions BSET, BCLR, BCLRI, BCHG, BCHGI, BTSTI, ANDI, OR, EOR, EORI, LSR, ASRI, LSM, ASM, ROR, RORI, ROXRI, and ROXM, assuming consistency with the logical and shift instructions shown in this section.

16-18 Give the description of the binary arithmetic instructions MOVB, MOVEL, EXTW, NEGX, ADDI, SUB, SUBQ, SUBX, MUL, DIV, and CMPI, assuming consistency with the binary arithmetic instructions shown in this section.

16-19 Give the description of the decimal arithmetic instructions NBCD, and SBCD, assuming consistency with the decimal arithmetic instructions shown in this section.

16-20 Give the description of the supervisory instructions MOVTS, ORIR, EORIR, and TRAPH, assuming consistency with the supervisory instructions shown in this section.

16.5
IBM 6150

16.5.1
Highlights

History

The IBM 6150 is also known as the processing element of Research Processor 3, or RP3-PE, as the processor of the RT Personal Computer, and as the processor of the RS-6000, which adds a floating-point chip.

Architects. John Cocke and George Radin were the architects.

Dates. The original IBM 801 design dates from 1978.

Family tree. The idea of a RISC computer was first presented by John Cocke and George Radin in their design of the IBM 801. The 801 was not marketed as such, but rather was used as a processor within several systems. The 6150 is a descendant of the 801 and reflects several adjustments that are based on this early experience.

Noteworthy

Design philosophy.   RISC computers aim to gain efficiency in two ways. First, they assume an optimizing compiler that uses the machine language as target. Second, they assume a VLSI implementation that has the machine language as source. In a VLSI implementation, costliness expresses itself as space upon the chip. To obtain optimal speed, relatively more space is allocated to the datapath circuits than to the control circuits, so that the instruction set is reduced to instructions that can almost all be performed in one short cycle. The optimizing compiler has the task of constructing more elaborate instructions—such as multiplication or division—from these single-cycle operations. The instruction set is designed such that this compilation can be done efficiently—for instance, with Multiply Step and Divide Step. Whereas, in many computers, the datapath uses something like 40 percent of the circuits (and the control, 60 percent), these figures are reversed for a RISC design.

Thirty-two–bit word. The 6150 is a 32-bit word design. In the implementation a corresponding 32-bit–wide datapath is assumed.

Simple syntax. There are only two instruction lengths (no extensions) and two opcode lengths, both of which are easily distinguished. Field lengths adhere to the 4-bit unit size. The designers use extra instructions instead of modifier fields.

Instruction efficiency. Two-thirds of the instructions use the 16-bit formats. Most of the 32-bit instructions have immediate data, which also improves the bit efficiency of a program. This attention to bit efficiency shows also in details. For instance, since large logical patterns are more frequent than large numbers, the immediate fields for logical instructions are larger than the immediate fields for arithmetic instructions. Within arithmetic, furthermore, the immediate field of Subtract Immediate is shorter than that of Subtract From Immediate.

Reduced function.   The drive toward simple single-cycle operation is recognizable not only in simple operations, but also in simple addressing modes and in full-register operation. These design decisions contrast with the complex addressing modes and partial-register operation of mini- and microprocessors, such as the Motorola MC68000. Another example of reduced function is the definition of alignment or that of an odd–even register address. In the IBM System/360 (1965) these are defined to cause an interrupt when improperly compiled. In the 6150 they are defined such that no error can occur.

Large, well-ordered status.   The control store matches the working store in size and in organization: it has sixteen 32-bit registers.

Two-address operation.   The original 801 design had three-address operation. Three 5-bit register addresses were used in a uniform 32-bit instruction. Bit efficiency, however, has led to 16-bit and 32-bit instructions, a 4-bit register specification, and two-address operation. All these changes represent a return to the classical architecture.

Immediate data.   Almost all dyadic operations can be specified with immediate data. Furthermore, this mode has many variations, such as long and short fields. Also, in addressing, a short 4-bit displacement may be used as well as a long 16-bit displacement.

General purpose registers.   There is no separate set of address registers, and there is no separate address arithmetic.

Register-to-register operation.   All logic and arithmetic takes place between registers. Memory participates only in Load and Store operations.

Multiple Load and Store.   These two operations and the status switching operations are the only actions that involve more than one cycle.

Multiply Step and Divide Step.   These single-cycle operations enable a compiler to program a multiplication and division; they also aid in radix conversion.

Software dependence.   The 6150 does not police restrictions that apply to branching. As another example, interrupt priority levels can be assigned to the status words such that an unending sequence of interrupt actions occurs. In all these cases, the assumption is that the system software is correct and that the compilers will generate only valid programs.

Peculiarities

The design consistently reflects the RISC aims. Only minor peculiarities can be noted.

Partial left-zero count.   The left-zero count applies only to the lower 16-bits of a register; the count starts in the middle of the register.   There is no corresponding operation on the upper 16 register bits.

Deviating address mode.   The address mode for Load Halve Short differs from that for Load Short or Load Byte Short, and from that for Load Halve Signed Short.

Delayed branch.   Perhaps the most conspicuous RISC peculiarity is the delayed branch: A branch that takes place after the instruction that sequentially follows the branch is executed. This impropriety is a time saver for the implementation, but a challenge for the compiler; it is not policed.

Ad hoc solutions.   Some compromises are made to force instructions into the 16-bit format. Bit operations select among the 32 bits in a word with 4 bits from a register field, and one in the opcode. Some branch instructions use a 4-bit field to specify a condition, whereas other branch instructions use another 3-bit field for this purpose. Another example is the return address of Branch And Link that is stored in register 15—the only case of implied register use.

16.5.2
Machine Language

Unit System

The unit system is *four*. The 4-bit field dominates the instruction formats; the data formats are power-of-2 multiples of 4 bits.

```
initiate6150                        format6150
A initiation of the IBM 6150        A IBM 6150 information units
format6150                          A representation radix
configure6150                       radix←2
space6150                           A information units
name6150                            byte←8
control6150                         half←16
data6150                            word←32
                                    A address capacity
                                    adrcap←radix*word

configure6150
A configuration for the IBM 6150
A memory capacity
memcap←adrcap
```

PROGRAM 16-125   Basic parameters of the IBM 6150.

Configuration.   Address capacity is 4 GB. A typical configuration has scores of megabytes of memory.

Spaces

Memory name-space.   Memory is byte addressable. Halfwords are assumed to be aligned on an even byte boundary; words are aligned on a multiple of 4 boundary.

```
space6150                              name6150
ค IBM 6150 spaces                      ค IBM 6150 space names
ค memory                               ค memory
 memory←?(memcap,byte)ρradix           ค - old/new psw
ค working store                         Psw←256
ค - registers                          ค control registers
 reg←?(16,word)ρradix                  ค - timer source
ค control store                         Tsource←6
ค - status                             ค - timer
 status←?(16,word)ρradix                Timer←7
ค - current instruction address        ค - timer control
 oldadr←2×?⌊0.5×memcap                  Tct←8
ค - machine check level                ค - multiplier/quotient
 mclevel←?radix                         Mq←10
ค - program check level                ค - machine and program check
 pclevel←?radix                         Check←11
ค - wait state                         ค - interrupt request
 wait←?radix                            Ireq←12
ค - stopped state                      ค - instruction address
 stop←?radix                            Iadr←13
                                       ค - interrupt status
                                        Int←14
                                       ค - condition
                                        Cond←15
```

PROGRAM 16-126   Spaces of the IBM 6150.

Working store.   There are sixteen 32-bit general purpose registers. All registers are almost equal in their behavior; no register is set aside as a stack pointer. In addressing, however, register 0 acts as an all-zeros index. In one Call instruction, register 15 is implied for the return address.

Control store.   The control store also consists of sixteen 32-bit registers. These registers contain a multiplier-quotient register, which normally is considered working store. Otherwise, the registers contain control information, such as the instruction address, internal and programmed indicators, condition bits, a timer, and its controls. Seven registers are reserved for future use, and in five registers only the lower 16 bits or fewer are used. Each control register exerts its own controlling function and is changed accordingly. The registers are, however, also addressable as a unit.

Besides the status registers, the machine also preserves the address of the current instruction (`oldadr`) and distinguishes interrupt levels for machine errors and program errors, a stopped state, and a wait state.

Embedding.   Control registers are not embedded in memory or working store. Working store is not embedded in memory.

Programming model.   The surprise is that the 6150 is a fully evolved microprocessor; the datapath is no longer narrow, and the programming model looks suprisingly like that of the 360. It looks even more like the current ESA descendant of the 360, with its full 32-bit addresses. Note the provision of the separate MQ register as part of sixteen sparsely populated control registers.

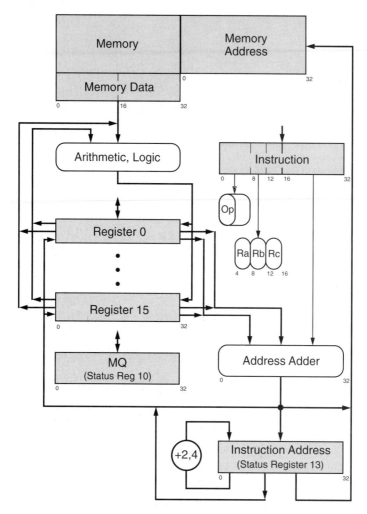

FIGURE 16-127 Programming model for the IBM 6150.

Operand Specification

Number of addresses. Except for loading and storing, the 6150 uses two-address register-to-register operation throughout.

Address phrase. Only one address phrase occurs in an instruction; it consists of one register address and a variety of displacement fields, or of two register-address fields.

Operation Specification

Mnemonics. The mnemonics in our description (Table 16-128) are the 6150 mnemonics, except that we have limited the number of characters to five.

Instruction list. The phrase "Reduced Instruction Set" refers to instruction function (such as single-cycle operation), not to the number of instructions. Rather, the reduced function tends to increase the number of instructions some.

ᴀ *address arithmetic*
a CA16 Address 16-Bit
f CAS   Address Short
c CAU   Address Upper
c CAL   Address Lower
c CAL16 Address Lower 16-Bit

ᴀ *logic and shift*
a CLRBU Clear Bit Upper
a CLRBL Clear Bit Lower
a SETBU Set Bit Upper
a SETBL Set Bit Lower
a MFTB   Move From Test
a MFTIU Move From Test I Upper
a MFTIL Move From Test I Lower
a MTTB   Move To Test
a MTTIU Move To Test I Upper
a MTTIL Move To Test I Lower
a ONEC   Not
a N   And
c NIUZ   And I Upper
c NIUO   And I Upper One-extended
c NILZ   And I Lower
c NILO   And I Lower One-extended
a O   Or
c OIU   Or I Upper
c OIL   Or I Lower
a X   Exclusive Or
c XIU   Exclusive Or I Upper
c XIL   Exclusive Or I Lower
a CLZ   Left-Zero Count
a SL   Shift Left
a SLP   Shift Left Paired
a SLI   Shift Left I
a SLIP   Shift Left I + 16
a SLPI   Shift Left Paired I
a SLPIP Shift Left Paired I + 16
a SR   Shift Right
a SRP   Shift Right Paired
a SRI   Shift Right I
a SRIP   Shift Right I + 16
a SRPI   Shift Right Paired I
a SRPIP Shift Right Paired I + 16
a SAR   Shift Arithmetic Right
a SARI   Shift Arithmetic Right I
a SARIP Shift Arithmetic Right I + 16

ᴀ *fixed-point arithmetic*
c L   Load
d LS   Load Short
c LC   Load Byte
d LCS   Load Byte Short
c LH   Load Half
a LHS   Load Half Short
c LHA   Load Half Signed
d LHAS   Load Half Signed Short
a LIS   Load I Short
c LM   Load Multiple
c ST   Store
d STS   Store Short
c STC   Store Byte
d STCS   Store Byte Short
c STH   Store Half
d STHS   Store Half Short
c STM   Store Multiple

a MC03 Move Low Byte To Byte 0
a MC13 Move Low Byte To Byte 1
a MC23 Move Low Byte To Byte 2
a MC33 Move Low Byte
a MC30 Move Byte 0 To Low Byte
a MC31 Move Byte 1 To Low Byte
a MC32 Move Byte 2 To Low Byte
a EXTS Extend Sign
a TWOC Negate
a ABS   Make Absolute
a INC   Increment
a DEC   Decrement
a A   Add
a AE   Add W Carry
c AI   Add I
a AIS   Add I Short
c AEI   Add W Carry I
a S   Subtract
a SE   Subtract W Carry
a SIS   Subtract I Short
a SF   Subtract From
c SFI   Subtract From I
a M   Multiply Step
a D   Divide Step
a C   Compare
c CI   Compare I
a CIS   Compare I Short
a CL   Compare Unsigned
c CLI   Compare Unsigned I

ᴀ *sequencing*
a BBR   Branch On Condition
a BBRX   Branch D On Condition
a BNBR   Branch On Not Condition
a BNBRX Branch D On Not Condition
e JB   Jump On Condition
b BB   Jump On Condition I
b BBX   Jump D On Condition I
b BNB   Jump On Not Condition I
b BNBX   Jump D On Not Condition I
a BALR   Branch And Link
a BALRX Branch D And Link
g BALA   Branch And Link I
g BALAX Branch D And Link I
b BALI   Jump And Link I
b BALIX Jump D And Link I

ᴀ *supervision*
c TSH   Test And Set Half
a WAIT Wait
c SVC   Supervisor Call
a TLT   Trap On Less
a TGTE Trap On Greater Or Equal
c TI   Trap On Condition I
c LPS   Load Program Status
a MFS   Move From Status
a MTS   Move To Status
a CLRSB Clear Status
a SETSB Set Status

ᴀ *input/output*
c IOR   Read
c IOW   Write

Legend: D = Delayed; I = Immediate; W = With.

TABLE 16-128   Instruction list of the IBM 6150.

The 6150 has 118 instructions. The instruction list has no data handling, and no decimal or floating-point arithmetic. The other classes of instructions are quite complete (except that there is no multiply or divide). The instruction list would have been noticeably shorter if instruction alternatives were specified by modifier bits, instead of separate operation codes.

a→AIS	a→SARI	a→SAR	a→ABS	a→WAIT	b→i	c→SVC	c→LPS	d→→e
INC	SARIP	EXTS	A	AE	i	AI	AEI	STCS
SIS	i	SF	S	SE	i	CAL16	SFI	STHS
DEC	i	CL	O	CA16	i	OIU	CLI	STS
CIS	LIS	C	TWOC	ONEC	i	OIL	CI	LCS
CLRSB	i	MTS	N	CLZ	i	NILZ	NIUZ	LHAS
MFS	i	D	M	i	i	NILO	NIUO	→f
SETSB	i	i	X	i	i	XIL	XIU	LS
CLRBU	SRI	SR	BNBR	i	BNB	CAL	CAU	e→JB
CLRBL	SRIP	SRP	BNBRX	MC03	BNBX	LM	STM	f→CAS
SETBU	SLI	SL	i	MC13	→g	LHA	LH	g→BALA
SETBL	SLIP	SLP	LHS	MC23	→g	IOR	IOW	g→BALAX
MFTIU	SRPI	MFTB	BALR	MC33	BALI	TI	STH	
MFTIL	SRPIP	TGTE	BALRX	MC30	BALIX	L	ST	
MTTIU	SLPI	TLT	BBR	MC31	BB	LC	STC	
MTTIL	SLPIP	MTTB	BBRX	MC32	BBX	TSH	i	

PROGRAM 16-129   Operation-code list of the IBM 6150.

Instruction Structure

Machine-language syntax.   There are seven groups of syntactic patterns, which can be simply parsed by the implementation. The operation-code field occupies 4 bits when the leftmost instruction bit is 0; otherwise, there are 8 opcode bits. The leftmost four operation-code bits determine the instruction length.

```
syntax6150
a 1 0 0 1 ,Opcode,Rb,Rc
a 1 0 1 0 ,Opcode,Rb,Rc
a 1 0 1 1 ,Opcode,Rb,Rc
a 1 1 1 0 ,Opcode,Rb,Rc
a 1 1 1 1 ,Opcode,Rb,Rc
b 1 0 0 0 ,Opcode,Rb,D1
c 1 1 0 0 ,Opcode,Rb,Rc,Ihalf
c 1 1 0 1 ,Opcode,Rb,Rc,Ihalf
d 0,Opi,Imm,Rb,Rc
e 0 0 0 0 ,Imm,Ibyte
f 0 1 1 0 ,Ra,Rb,Rc
g 1 0 0 0 1 0 1 0 ,Address
g 1 0 0 0 1 0 1 1 ,Address
```

PROGRAM 16-130   Instruction syntax of the IBM 6150.

Instruction format.   Instructions are either 16 or 32 bits long. There are no instruction extensions caused by addressing modes. All instruction fields are multiples of 4 bits. Immediate data is 4, 8, or 16 bits. The address displacement is 4, 8, or 24 bits.

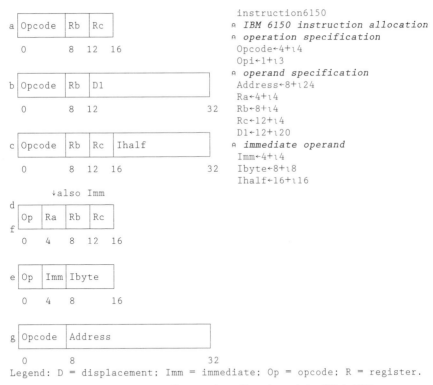

Legend: D = displacement; Imm = immediate; Op = opcode; R = register.

PROGRAM 16-131   Instruction allocation of the IBM 6150.

Status format.   The allocation of the interrupt status bits in the lower half of status register Int is given by status6150 (Program 16-132). These indicators concern: machine status, such as problem versus supervisory state; enabling and priority level of interruptions; memory protection and mapping; error retry and error stopping; and the number of the current working-store array. In the original 6150, this array number is not used, since there is only one working store.

Indicators.   The interruption indicators in the lower half of status register Check concern machine checks (bits 16 through 23), and program checks (bits 24 through 31). There are seven interrupt-request indicators in register Ireq.

Conditions.   The familiar result conditions are placed in the low-order byte of status register Cond. Negative, zero, and positive are distinct and correspond in signed or unsigned comparison with less, equal, and greater. Bit 24 is always 0; it can be used to make a no-operation or unconditional branch. Bit 31, the test bit, is set only by programming.

16.5.3

Addressing

Direct addressing.   The alignment of halfwords and words occurs by ignoring the low-order bit or bits of the address. Memory addressing wraps around

```
control6150                        indicator6150
A IBM 6150 control allocation     A IBM 6150 indicator allocation
instruction6150                   A machine checks
indicator6150                     Machine←16+ι8
condition6150                     Parity←18
status6150                        Timeop←19
timer6150                         Timedata←20
                                  A program checks
                                  Program←24+ι8
                                  Known←24
                                  Unknown←25
                                  Trap←26
status6150                        Priv←27
A interrupt status               Invop←28
A parity error retry enable      Invadr←29
Parenable←19                      Invdata←30
A storage protection
Protect←20
A problem status                 condition6150
Problem←21                        A IBM 6150 condition allocation
A memory mapping                 A result conditions
Map←22                            Neg←25
A interrupt mask                 Zero←26
Mask←23                          Pos←27
A stop mask                      Carry←28
Stop←24                          Oflo←30
A register set number            A test bit
Regset←25+ι3                      Test←31
A priority                       A permanent zero
Priority←29+ι3                    status[Cond;24]←0
```

PROGRAM 16-132   Status word and indicators of the IBM 6150.

at its maximum 2^{32} capacity, independently of the installed configuration. Address mapping and address protection occur in a storage control unit and are specified in the interrupt status control bits. In the absence of address mapping, a 24-bit addressing mode occurs, which checks the high-order eight address bits for 0.

```
data←size read6150 address;location
A IBM 6150 read from memory
address←size align6150 address      address←size align6150 address;grain
location←address+ιsize÷byte         A IBM 6150 memory alignment
data←,memory[memcap|location;]      grain←4⌊size÷byte
                                    address←grain×⌊address÷grain


address write6150 data;location
A IBM 6150 write in memory
address←(ρ,data) align6150 address
location←address+ι(ρ,data)÷byte
memory[memcap|location;]←byte wide data
```

PROGRAM 16-133   Memory read and write in the IBM 6150.

Address Modification

Register addressing.   Function regc shows that an index value specified by the instruction field Rc is defined to be 0 when Rc is 0—a definition found in the 360 and 6600. The twin of a specified register is that register whose address is the same except for the low-order bit. A register and its twin form an even–odd pair of addresses.

```
data←regc                        r←twin field
⍝ IBM 6150 register access       ⍝ IBM 6150 twin register of pair
data←(0≠fld Rc)∧reg[fld Rc:]     r←magni inst[field]≠ 0 0 0 1
```

PROGRAM 16-134   Register addressing in the IBM 6150.

Address calculation.   The six address modes are very much alike—a marked contrast with the mini- and microprocessor address modes. All modes add an address to an index obtained from the register specified by `regc`. In one mode the address is a base specified by `Rb`. In the other modes the addend is a displacement (either a 16-bit field that is sign-extended or unsigned, or a short unsigned 4-bit displacement). The short displacement is shifted 0, 1, or 2 bits to address a byte, halfword, or word, respectively.

```
address←adr6150:index:displacement      address←adr6150b:index:displacement
⍝ IBM 6150 signed address               ⍝ IBM 6150 short byte address
index←magni regc                        index←magni regc
displacement←radixcompi inst[Ihalf]     displacement←fld Imm
address←index+displacement              address←index+displacement

address←adr6150u:index:displacement     address←adr6150h:index:displacement
⍝ IBM 6150 unsigned address             ⍝ IBM 6150 short half-word address
index←magni regc                        index←magni regc
displacement←fld Ihalf                  displacement←2×fld Imm
address←index+displacement              address←index+displacement

address←adr6150x:base:index             address←adr6150w:index:displacement
⍝ IBM 6150 base-index address           ⍝ IBM 6150 short word address
base←magni reg[fld Rb:]                 index←magni regc
index←magni regc                        displacement←4×fld Imm
address←base+index                      address←index+displacement
```

PROGRAM 16-135   Memory addressing in the IBM 6150.

Index Arithmetic

Index operations.   The use of general purpose registers obviates the need for most address or index-arithmetic instructions. The five addressing instructions load an effective address into a register. The two instructions with suffix 16 perform 16-bit address addition; they are intended to simulate 16-bit addressing architectures.

```
a CA16  Address 16-Bit   c CAL    Address Lower
f CAS   Address Short    c CAL16  Address Lower 16-Bit
c CAU   Address Upper
```

TABLE 16-136   Address arithmetic instructions of the IBM 6150.

Load effective address.   Address Lower and Address Short load the effective address obtained from the base-displacement and base-index modification in a register. Address Lower 16-Bit and Address 16-Bit perform the same modification but for a 16-bit adder length, except that in Address 16-Bit register `Rc` is not replaced by 0 when the `Rc` field is 0.

```
CAL                                    CAS
ᴀ IBM 6150 Address Lower               ᴀ IBM 6150 Address Short
  reg[fld Rb:]←word magnr adr6150        reg[fld Ra:]←word magnr adr6150x


CAL16                                  CA16:index:base
ᴀ IBM 6150 Address Lower 16-Bit        ᴀ IBM 6150 Address 16-Bit
  reg[fld Rb:]←word magnr adr6150        index←magni reg[fld Rc:]
  reg[fld Rb:Upper]←regc[Upper]         base←magni reg[fld Rb:]
                                        reg[fld Rb:]←word magnr base+index
                                        reg[fld Rb:Upper]←reg[fld Rc:Upper]

  CAU:index:displacement
ᴀ IBM 6150 Address Upper
  index←magni regc
  displacement←magni word↑inst[Ihalf]
  reg[fld Rb:]←word magnr index+displacement
```

PROGRAM 16-137   Load effective address in the IBM 6150.

Address Upper uses the 16-bit displacement for the high-order part of the address—a function that is not available as an address mode. These specialized instructions seem designed to aid in porting IBM PC (Intel 80x86) programs.

Stack and list addressing.   Postincrement store and predecrement load are typical multicycle operations that must be programmed on a RISC computer.

16.5.4
Data

Character Strings

Character set and size.   The computer assumes an 8-bit character set, but is independent of the character-set encoding. There is no character string datatype, since multiple character strings invariably involve multiple-cycle operations.

Logical

Logical formats.   The logical formats are the same as the numeric formats: byte, halfword, word.

Fixed-Point Numbers

Notation and allocation.   Data may be a byte, halfword, or word during loading and storing. During these operations, an upper and lower halfword and a low-order byte may be specified in the register. The six low-order bits of a register are used to specify a shift amount. Logic and arithmetic are normally a word at a time. Fixed-point data are represented in 2's complement.

Signaling.   Logic, arithmetic, and comparison set the negative (less than), zero (equal to), and positive (greater than) conditions. Arithmetic also sets the overflow and carry conditions. Subtraction sets a carry rather than a borrow.

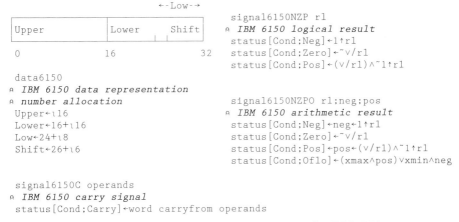

```
      ←-Low-→
┌─────────────┬────────┬───────┐
│             │        │       │
│ Upper       │ Lower  │ Shift │
│             │        │ ┊ ┊   │
└─────────────┴────────┴───────┘

0               16              32

data6150
ℎ IBM 6150 data representation
ℎ number allocation
Upper←ι16
Lower←16+ι16
Low←24+ι8
Shift←26+ι6


signal6150C operands
ℎ IBM 6150 carry signal
status[Cond:Carry]←word carryfrom operands
```

```
signal6150NZP r1
ℎ IBM 6150 logical result
status[Cond:Neg]←1↑r1
status[Cond:Zero]←˜∨/r1
status[Cond:Pos]←(∨/r1)∧˜1↑r1


signal6150NZPO r1;neg;pos
ℎ IBM 6150 arithmetic result
status[Cond:Neg]←neg←1↑r1
status[Cond:Zero]←˜∨/r1
status[Cond:Pos]←pos←(∨/r1)∧˜1↑r1
status[Cond:Oflo]←(xmax∧pos)∨xmin∧neg
```

PROGRAM 16-138   Data representation in the IBM 6150.

16.5.5

Operations

Data Handling

Data movement.   Data movement is performed via Load and Store operations; all data handling must be programmed.

Logic

Logic includes bit operations, connectives, a vector operation, and shifts—there are no rotates. All operations are register to register. For dyadic operations, one operand is normally in the register specified by Rc, or immediate, and the other operand and the result are in the register specified by Rb.

```
a CLRBU Clear Bit Upper           a X     Exclusive Or
a CLRBL Clear Bit Lower           c XIU   Exclusive Or I Upper
a SETBU Set Bit Upper             c XIL   Exclusive Or I Lower
a SETBL Set Bit Lower             a CLZ   Left-Zero Count
a MFTB  Move From Test            a SL    Shift Left
a MFTIU Move From Test I Upper    a SLP   Shift Left Paired
a MFTIL Move From Test I Lower    a SLI   Shift Left I
a MTTB  Move To Test              a SLIP  Shift Left I + 16
a MTTIU Move To Test I Upper      a SLPI  Shift Left Paired I
a MTTIL Move To Test I Lower      a SLPIP Shift Left Paired I + 16
a ONEC  Not                       a SR    Shift Right
a N     And                       a SRP   Shift Right Paired
c NIUZ  And I Upper               a SRI   Shift Right I
c NIUO  And I Upper One-extended  a SRIP  Shift Right I + 16
c NILZ  And I Lower               a SRPI  Shift Right Paired I
c NILO  And I Lower One-extended  a SRPIP Shift Right Paired I + 16
a O     Or                        a SAR   Shift Arithmetic Right
c OIU   Or I Upper                a SARI  Shift Arithmetic Right I
c OIL   Or I Lower                a SARIP Shift Arithmetic Right I + 16
Legend: I = Immediate.
```

TABLE 16-139   Logical and shift instructions of the IBM 6150.

Bit operations.   A selected bit is set to 0 or to 1. Bit selection is by the 4-bit Rc field. The fifth bit that is necessary to select out of 32 bits is supplied by the operation code. Condition bit `Test` can be set from any bit in register Rb, or reverse. The bit specification is the same as for the Set and Clear operations.

```
CLRBU                             MFTB;rl
A IBM 6150 Clear Bit Upper        A IBM 6150 Move From Test
  reg[fld Rb;Upper[fld Rc]]←0       rl←status[Cond;Test]
  signal6150NZP reg[fld Rb;]        reg[fld Rb;32|magni reg[fld Rc;]]←rl

MTTIL;rl
A IBM 6150 Move To Test Immediate Lower
  rl←reg[fld Rb;Lower[fld Rc]]
  status[Cond;Test]←rl
```

PROGRAM 16-140   Bit operations in the IBM 6150.

Connectives.   The classical subset of NOT, AND, OR, and EXCLUSIVE OR is available. Since the immediate instruction formats have at most 16 bits, there is an Immediate Upper and an Immediate Lower operation. For OR and EXCLUSIVE OR, the null element is 0, but for AND the null element is 1. Hence And Immediate is also provided with 1-extension.

```
ONEC;rl                           X;rl
A IBM 6150 Not                    A IBM 6150 Exclusive Or
  rl←~reg[fld Rc;]                  rl←reg[fld Rb;]≠reg[fld Rc;]
  reg[fld Rb;]←rl                  reg[fld Rb;]←rl
  signal6150NZP rl                 signal6150NZP rl

NILZ;rl                           OIU;rl
A IBM 6150 And Immediate Lower    A IBM 6150 Or Immediate Upper
  rl←reg[fld Rc;]∧(-word)↑inst[Ihalf]   rl←reg[fld Rc;]∨word↑inst[Ihalf]
  reg[fld Rb;]←rl                  reg[fld Rb;]←rl
  signal6150NZP rl                 signal6150NZP rl

NIUO;rl
A IBM 6150 And Immediate Upper One-extended
  rl←reg[fld Rc;]∧inst[Ihalf].halfρ1
  reg[fld Rb;]←rl
  signal6150NZP rl
```

PROGRAM 16-141   Connectives in the IBM 6150.

Count Left-Zero.   The number of 0s to the left of the leftmost 1 is determined for the lower 16 bits of the register specified by Rc and placed in the register specified by Rb. There is no corresponding operation for the upper part of the register.

```
CLZ;rl
A IBM 6150 Left-Zero Count
  rl←word magnr reg[fld Rc;Lower]ι1
  reg[fld Rb;]←rl
```

PROGRAM 16-142   Count Left-Zero in the IBM 6150.

Shift.   The normal shift places the result in the operand register specified by Rb. The *paired* shift operations use the twin register of a pair for the result. The shift direction is determined by the opcode. The shift amount is specified either directly in the low-order six bits of the register specified by Rc, or immediately with the 4-bit Rc field and a low-order opcode bit of the paired shift instructions.

```
SRI;shift;rl                          SAR;shift;operand;result;rl
ᵃ IBM 6150 Shift Right Immediate      ᵃ IBM 6150 Shift Arithmetic Right
shift←fld Rc                          shift←magni reg[fld Rc;Shift]
rl←(-word)↑(-shift)↓reg[fld Rb;]      operand←radixcompi reg[fld Rb;]
reg[fld Rb;]←rl                       result←⌊operand×radix*-shift
signal6150NZP rl                      rl←word radixcompr result
                                      reg[fld Rb;]←rl
                                      signal6150NZP rl

SLPIP;shift;rl
ᵃ IBM 6150 Shift Left Paired Immediate + 16
shift←16+fld Rc
rl←word↑shift↓reg[fld Rb;]
reg[twin Rb;]←rl
signal6150NZP rl
```

PROGRAM 16-143   Shift in the IBM 6150.

Fixed-Point Arithmetic

Fixed-point arithmetic is always register to register, with all register bits participating. In dyadic operations one operand may be 16-bit immediate or 4-bit immediate. Load and Store operations may have byte, halfword, and word operands and may even move multiple words to and from a set of registers.

c	L	Load	a	EXTS	Extend Sign
d	LS	Load Short	a	TWOC	Negate
c	LC	Load Byte	a	ABS	Make Absolute
d	LCS	Load Byte Short	a	INC	Increment
c	LH	Load Half	a	DEC	Decrement
a	LHS	Load Half Short	a	A	Add
c	LHA	Load Half Signed	a	AE	Add W Carry
d	LHAS	Load Half Signed Short	c	AI	Add I
a	LIS	Load I Short	a	AIS	Add I Short
c	LM	Load Multiple	c	AEI	Add W Carry I
c	ST	Store	a	S	Subtract
d	STS	Store Short	a	SE	Subtract W Carry
c	STC	Store Byte	a	SIS	Subtract I Short
d	STCS	Store Byte Short	a	SF	Subtract From
c	STH	Store Half	c	SFI	Subtract From I
d	STHS	Store Half Short	a	M	Multiply Step
c	STM	Store Multiple	a	D	Divide Step
a	MC03	Move Low Byte To Byte 0	a	C	Compare
a	MC13	Move Low Byte To Byte 1	c	CI	Compare I
a	MC23	Move Low Byte To Byte 2	a	CIS	Compare I Short
a	MC33	Move Low Byte	a	CL	Compare Unsigned
a	MC30	Move Byte 0 To Low Byte	c	CLI	Compare Unsigned I
a	MC31	Move Byte 1 To Low Byte			
a	MC32	Move Byte 2 To Low Byte			
Legend: I = Immediate; W = With.					

TABLE 16-144   Fixed-point instructions of the IBM 6150.

Load and Store.   Load and Store have their operand or result rightmost in the registers. Load uses zero extension to fill the remainder of the register. For halfwords there is also a Load with sign extension. Addressing is with the signed displacement and index mode, or with the short displacement addressing modes for bytes, halfwords, and words. This regular set of operations is, however, disrupted by Load Half Word, which does not use a standard addressing mode, but just uses the content of register Rc as an address.

Load Immediate Short uses the zero-extended Rc field. It is the only immediate Load, but the Load Address operations can also be used as such.

Byte moves.   A set of moves to and from the low-order register position makes it possible to assemble bytes into words or halfwords from a variety of sources, or to disassemble words to a variety of destinations.

```
LHS;rl
A IBM 6150 Load Half Short
rl←(-word)↑half read6150 magni reg[fld Rc;]
reg[fld Rb;]←rl

LHA;operand
A IBM 6150 Load Half Signed
operand←radixcompi half read6150 adr6150
reg[fld Rb;]←word radixcompr operand

LC;rl                               LIS
A IBM 6150 Load Byte                A IBM 6150 Load Immediate Short
rl←(-word)↑byte read6150 adr6150      reg[fld Rb;]←(-word)↑inst[Rc]
reg[fld Rb;]←rl


                                    MC23;rl
LCS;rl                              A IBM 6150 Move Low Byte To Byte 2
A IBM 6150 Load Byte Short          rl←reg[fld Rc;Low]
rl←(-word)↑byte read6150 adr6150b     reg[fld Rb;(2×byte)+↑byte]←rl
reg[fld Rb;]←rl


                                    STM;rl
ST                                  A IBM 6150 Store Multiple
A IBM 6150 Store                    rl←,reg[((fld Rb)+↑16-fld Rb;]
adr6150 write6150 reg[fld Rb;]        adr6150s write6150 rl
```

PROGRAM 16-145   Load and Store in the IBM 6150.

Load and Store Multiple.   A consecutive set of registers, starting with the register specified by Rb up to and including register 15, can be moved in one operation to or from memory. Load and Store Multiple are the only multiple-cycle instructions apart from some status-switching operations. Their usefulness depends on the compiler's using a strict ordering strategy for the register contents.

Sign control.   Extend Sign takes the low-order 16 bits of register Rc as a signed operand and extends this operand to a 32-bit result. Negate and Make Absolute change the sign of the operand. Since the maximum negative number has no corresponding positive representation, it remains unchanged and an overflow is signaled. The carry is set when a 0 operand is negated.

```
            EXTS;operand
          A IBM 6150 Extend Sign
            operand←radixcompi reg[fld Rc;Lower]
            reg[fld Rb;]←word radixcompr operand
            signal6150NZP reg[fld Rb;]

            TWOC
          A IBM 6150 Negate;operand
            operand←radixcompi reg[fld Rc;]
            reg[fld Rb;]←word radixcompr-operand
            status[Cond;Carry]←operand=0
            signal6150NZPO reg[fld Rb;]
```

PROGRAM 16-146   Sign control in the IBM 6150.

Increment and Decrement.   Increment and Decrement use a 4-bit immediate operand to change the value in register Rb. The conditions are not disturbed, since address modification is the major use.

```
INC;addend;augend;sum
ⱥ IBM 6150 Increment
addend←fld Rc
augend←radixcompi reg[fld Rb;]
sum←augend+addend
reg[fld Rb;]←word radixcompr sum
```

PROGRAM 16-147   Increment in the IBM 6150.

Add and Subtract.   Addition and subtraction are with and without carry and with direct or immediate operand. A carry, or inverse borrow, is noted. In the extended operations, the 0 condition is set, but not cumulatively. In subtraction, the immediate operand may be a short subtrahend or a long minuend.

```
                                  AE;carry;addend;augend;sum
A;addend;augend;sum               ⱥ IBM 6150 Add With Carry
ⱥ IBM 6150 Add                    carry←status[Cond;Carry]
addend←radixcompi reg[fld Rc;]    addend←radixcompi reg[fld Rc;]
augend←radixcompi reg[fld Rb;]    augend←radixcompi reg[fld Rb;]
sum←augend+addend                 sum←augend+addend+carry
reg[fld Rb;]←word radixcompr sum  reg[fld Rb;]←word radixcompr sum
signal6150NZPO reg[fld Rb;]       signal6150NZPO reg[fld Rb;]
signal6150C addend,augend         signal6150C addend,augend,carry


SIS;addend;augend;sum                    SFI;addend;augend;sum
ⱥ IBM 6150 Subtract Immediate Short      ⱥ IBM 6150 Subtract From Immediate
addend←magni˜(-word)↑inst[Rc]            addend←magni˜reg[fld Rc;]
augend←radixcompi reg[fld Rb;]           augend←radixcompi inst[Ihalf]
sum←augend+addend+1                      sum←augend+addend+1
reg[fld Rb;]←word radixcompr sum         reg[fld Rb;]←word radixcompr sum
signal6150NZPO reg[fld Rb;]              signal6150NZPO reg[fld Rb;]
signal6150C addend,augend,1             signal6150C addend,augend,1
```

PROGRAM 16-148   Addition and subtraction in the IBM 6150.

Multiply Step.   The low-order two multiplier bits from the Mq status register multiply the multiplicand in the Rc register, and the product is added to the contents of register Rb. This cumulative product is placed in register Rb and the two high-order bits of Mq, while Mq is shifted 2 bits to the right. This action is a step of the Booth algorithm for multiplying 2 bits at a time [Blaauw, 1976, p. 89].

In Booth's multiply step the two multiplier bits are interpreted as either 0, 1, 2, -1, or -2, depending upon the carry bit. Multiplier bit 31 and the carry bit each add the multiplicand once. Multiplier bit 30 should add twice the multiplicand, but instead it subtracts twice the multiplicand and sets the carry for the next cycle, which is equivalent to adding the multiplicand four times—the net result being the same, except that this device yields the correct sign bit.

In the 6150 the carry bit is set and interpreted inversely from this algorithm. The initial value of the carry must be 1. The normal initial value of Rb is 0. These two initial values can be obtained by subtracting register Rb from itself. When register Rb is not 0, the multiplication is cumulative: The product is added to the initial register value.

```
M;multiplicand;multiplier;augend;product
⍝ IBM 6150 Multiply Step
  multiplicand←radixcompi reg[fld Rc;]
  multiplier←+/(status[Mq; 30 31]/ ¯2 1),~status[Cond;Carry]
  augend←radixcompi reg[fld Rb;]
  product← 0 4 ⊤augend+multiplier×multiplicand
  status[Cond;Carry]←~status[Mq;30]
  reg[fld Rb;]←word radixcompr product[0]
  status[Mq;]←(2 radixcompr product[1]),¯2↓status[Mq;]
```

PROGRAM 16-149   Multiply Step in the IBM 6150.

Divide Step.   Divide Step is based upon the 1-bit non-restoring division
algorithm [Blaauw, 1976, p. 115]. The divisor is assumed to be in register Rc;
the dividend, in register Rb and status register Mq. The quotient digit is set
in the low-order bit of Mq, and the remainder is shifted 1 bit to the left in Rb
and Mq.

The divisor or its complement is subtracted from the dividend, such that
the absolute value of the remainder is smaller than that of the dividend. The
quotient digit is recorded as 1 if the remainder and divisor have the same sign.
The carry is set as the quotient digit. Overflow is indicated if the dividend
and remainder have the same sign after the first cycle and should be tested at
that moment. Remainder correction is called for if, after the last divide step,
remainder and divisor sign differ (as indicated by the carry). The correction
consists of adding the divisor to the remainder without shifting or changing
the quotient.

```
D;divisor;drsign;dividend;ddsign;remainder;rmsign;quotient
⍝ IBM 6150 Divide Step
  divisor←radixcompi reg[fld Rc;]
  drsign←divisor≥0
  dividend←radixcompi reg[fld Rb;],status[Mq;0]
  ddsign←dividend≥0
  remainder←dividend+ 1 ¯1[ddsign=drsign]×divisor
  rmsign←remainder≥0
  reg[fld Rb;]←word radixcompr remainder
  quotient←rmsign=drsign
  status[Mq;]←1↓status[Mq;],quotient
  status[Cond;Oflo]←ddsign=rmsign
  status[Cond;Carry]←drsign=rmsign
```

PROGRAM 16-150   Divide Step in the IBM 6150.

Compare.   Comparison is signed or unsigned, with direct or immediate
comparand. The conditions are set according to the true relation of operand
and comparand (not according to the sign of the result of a comparison).
Hence it is not necessary to note overflow and carry, as it is in the DEC PDP11
(1970). The immediate comparisons have a 16-bit comparand. The Rb field
is not used, since there is no numeric result—one of the rare occurrences of
an unused instruction field. Signed comparison has also a short-immediate
form to compare against zero or a small positive value, such as a tolerance or
increment.

```
CI:operand:comparand                    CL:operand:comparand
ᴀ IBM 6150 Compare Immediate            ᴀ IBM 6150 Compare Unsigned
operand←radixcompi reg[fld Rc:]         operand←magni reg[fld Rb:]
comparand←radixcompi inst[Ihalf]        comparand←magni reg[fld Rc:]
status[Cond:Neg]←operand<comparand      status[Cond:Neg]←operand<comparand
status[Cond:Zero]←operand=comparand     status[Cond:Zero]←operand=comparand
status[Cond:Pos]←operand>comparand      status[Cond:Pos]←operand>comparand


CIS
ᴀ IBM 6150 Compare Immediate Short
operand←radixcompi reg[fld Rb:]
comparand←fld Rc
status[Cond:Neg]←operand<comparand
status[Cond:Zero]←operand=comparand
status[Cond:Pos]←operand>comparand
```

PROGRAM 16-151   Comparison in the IBM 6150.

16.5.6

Instruction Sequencing

Instruction fetch determines the instruction length from the first four instruction bits. The instruction address of the instruction that is executed in this cycle, oldadr, is remembered; it is recorded with the status information of a program check interruption.

```
cycle6150                               inst←ifetch6150:iadr
ᴀ basic cycle of the IBM 6150           ᴀ IBM 6150 instruction fetch
 REPEAT:execute ifetch6150              oldadr←magni status[Iadr:]
    interrupt6150                       inst←half read6150 oldadr
 →UNTIL stop                            iadr←oldadr+2
                                        →If 4=ilength6150
                                        THEN: ᴀ long instruction
 length←ilength6150                        inst←inst.half read6150 iadr
 ᴀ IBM 6150 instruction length            iadr←iadr+2
 length←2×1+(fldɩ4)∈ 8 12 13            ENDIF:status[Iadr:]←word magnr iadr
```

PROGRAM 16-152   Basic cycle and instruction fetch of the IBM 6150.

Sequencing instructions.   There is decision and delegation; there is no iteration. Branches are absolute or relative, with or without delayed branch execution. Branch addresses are interpreted as even, since instructions are aligned on halfword boundaries.

```
a BBR    Branch On Condition            a BALR  Branch And Link
a BBRX   Branch D On Condition          a BALRX Branch D And Link
a BNBR   Branch On Not Condition        g BALA  Branch And Link I
a BNBRX  Branch D On Not Condition      g BALAX Branch D And Link I
e JB     Jump On Condition              b BALI  Jump And Link I
b BB     Jump On Condition I            b BALIX Jump D And Link I
b BBX    Jump D On Condition I
b BNB    Jump On Not Condition I
b BNBX   Jump D On Not Condition I
Legend: D = Delayed; I = Immediate.
```

TABLE 16-153   Sequencing instructions of the IBM 6150.

Linear Sequence

Unconditional Branch.   The conditional branches have the unconditional branches as a subset.

Completion.   There is no Stop instruction. Completion is signaled by `WAIT`, a privileged operation.

Decision

Conditional Branch.   The condition bits occupy the low-order halfword of status word `Cond`. The high-order byte of this halfword is reserved for future use. The branch condition normally applies to all 16 condition bits. In Jump On Condition, however, it applies to the lower eight condition bits. In both cases, all the seven defined conditions are included; either one or nine conditions are reserved for later use. Instruction bits select the condition to be tested and the use of its value, or inverse. These bits differ for Jump On Condition from those for the other branch instructions.

```
BBRX;target
⋒ IBM 6150 Branch Delayed On Condition
→If status[Cond;Lower[fld Rb]]
THEN:target←2×⌊0.5×magni reg[fld Rc;]
    execute ifetch6150
    status[Iadr;]←word magnr target
ENDIF:


JB;iadr;target
⋒ IBM 6150 Jump On Condition
→If status[Cond;Low[fld 1↓Imm]]=fld 1↑Imm
THEN:iadr←magni status[Iadr;]
    target←iadr+2×radixcompi insҩ[Ibyte]
    status[Iadr;]←word magnr target
ENDIF:


BNB;iadr;target
⋒ IBM 6150 Jump On Not Condition Immediate
→If˜status[Cond;Lower[fld Rb]]
THEN:iadr←magni status[Iadr;]
    target←iadr+2×radixcompi inst[D1]
    status[Iadr;]←word magnr target
ENDIF:
```

PROGRAM 16-154   Conditional Branch in the IBM 6150.

The direct branch target is the content of register `Rc`, whose low-order bit is taken as 0. The immediate branch target is used as an (8-bit or 20-bit) halfword offset of a relative address, and therefore is shifted by one.

Delayed execution.   All branches, except Jump On Condition, can be specified with or without delayed execution of the actual branch. The delay of the branch action allows one subsequent instruction to be performed prior to changing the instruction address. The branch address is independent of the subsequent instruction, even if it is relative. The branch and its subsequent instruction form a meta-instruction. Interruption is not allowed within this meta-instruction. The subsequent instruction should not alter the instruction address; a branch or status-switching instruction that can do so is not allowed. This restriction is not policed, however.

The purpose of the delayed branch execution is to gain performance (the subsequent instruction has usually been fetched anyway); the compiler has the task of rearranging the instruction order without changing the meaning of the code.

Delegation

Call and Return.   Call instructions are unconditional. The target address is the content of register Rc, an immediate 24-bit address, or a 20-bit halfword offset of a relative address. In each case the low-order address bit is made 0. The return address is placed in register Rb, or in register 15. The latter case is the only use of a dedicated register. In case of delayed branching, the return address is 4 more than the address following the branch instruction to make space for the extra instruction. A Conditional Branch with format a can be used as a Return instruction.

```
BALA;target                         BALI;iadr;target
a IBM 6150 Branch And Link Immediate  a IBM 6150 Jump And Link Immediate
reg[15;]←status[Iadr;]              reg[fld Rb;]←status[Iadr;]
target←2×⌊0.5×fld Address           iadr←¯4+magni status[Iadr;]
status[Iadr;]←word magnr target     target←iadr+2×radixcompi inst[D1]
                                    status[Iadr;]←word magnr target

BALRX;return;target
a IBM 6150 Branch Delayed And Link
return←4+magni status[Iadr;]
reg[fld Rb;]←word magnr return
target←2×⌊0.5×magni reg[fld Rc;]
execute ifetch6150
status[Iadr;]←word magnr target
```

PROGRAM 16-155   Call in the IBM 6150.

16.5.7

Supervision

Concurrency

Supervisory instructions.   Supervision has instructions for critical-section control, waiting, humble access, dispatching, and status switching. Privileged instructions are Wait, Load Program Status, and Move, Clear, and Set Status (but not if they refer to Mq or Cond).

```
c TSH    Test And Set Half              c LPS    Load Program Status
a WAIT   Wait                           a MFS    Move From Status
c SVC    Supervisor Call                a MTS    Move To Status
a TLT    Trap On Less                   a CLRSB  Clear Status
a TGTE   Trap On Greater Or Equal       a SETSB  Set Status
c TI     Trap On Condition I
Legend: I = Immediate.
```

TABLE 16-156   Supervisory instructions of the IBM 6150.

Process Interaction

Critical section.   Test And Set Half is proposed for critical-section control; it is not yet detailed in our defining document (but see Program 12-94 for an early example).

Control Switching

Interruption.   The interrupt action follows the classical pattern of finding an active masked-on interruption cause, storing the current status, and loading status belonging to the interrupt handler.

```
interrupt6150
A IBM 6150 interrupt action
REPEAT: A test sources
    programcheck6150
    machinecheck6150
    intrequest6150
→UNTIL~wait
```

```
programcheck6150
A IBM 6150 program interrupt
→Ifv/status[Check;Program]
THEN: A program status switch
    status[Iadr;]←word magnr oldadr
    switchstatus6150 Psw+128
ENDIF:
```

```
machinecheck6150;error;mask
A IBM 6150 machine interrupt
error←v/status[Check;Machine]
mask←status[Int;Stop]
→CASE(error,mask)ι0
C0: A no error
    →ENDCASE
C1: A stop on error
    stop←1
    wait←0
    →ENDCASE
C2: A machine status switch
    switchstatus6150 Psw+112
ENDCASE:
```

```
intrequest6150;ind;enable;mask;who
A IBM 6150 interrupt request
ind←status[Check;16+ι7]
enable←~status[Int;Mask]vmclevelvpclevel
mask←(magni status[Int;Priority])≥ι7
who←(enable∧ind∧mask)ι1
→If who≠ρind
THEN: A interrupt request status switch
    switchstatus6150 Psw+16×who
ENDIF:
```

```
which report6150 condition
A IBM 6150 set on condition
→If condition
THEN: A set indicators
    status[Check;Known,which]←1
    stop←pclevelvmclevel
ENDIF:
```

```
yes←suppress6150
A IBM 6150 operation suppression
yes←v/status[Check;Lower]
```

PROGRAM 16-157   Interruption action in the IBM 6150.

Interruption levels and priorities.   Interruptions caused by program check, machine check, and interrupt requests are handled as separate interruption *levels*. A program-check status switch is always taken and gives the address of the instruction that caused the error (using `oldadr`), *not* the address of the instruction following the error. A machine check status interruption is taken only when the stop mask bit is 1; otherwise, the machine stops.

When a program check and machine check each cause a status switch, the machine check occurs last and therefore is resolved first. Interrupt requests are taken only if there is neither a program check nor a machine check, if the interrupt is enabled by the interrupt control `Mask` bit, and if the interrupt priority value is lower than the current priority value of the processor. The interrupt request bits are bits 16 through 22 in the interrupt-request status register and have corresponding priorities 0 through 6. The processor has priority 0 through 7, as noted in the priority bits of the interrupt-control status register. The lower a priority value, the greater the priority.

The program check bits contain a Known bit that is set when the source of the error is known; it is set for all reported conditions. When the source is not known, the Unknown bit is set instead. When a program check occurs while the processor is on the machine-check level or on the program-check level, the machine stops.

Status switch. Program check, machine check, supervisory call, and the seven interrupt request priorities each have a pair of old and new program status locations. The instruction-address word, the interrupt-state halfword, and the condition halfword are stored. The program state that is loaded is the instruction address and the interrupt state; it is deemed unnecessary to load the conditions. Only the defined bits of the halfwords are loaded. The reserved bits of any status word are unpredictable, as indicated by reserve6150.

```
             switchstatus6150 psw
           ⋀ IBM 6150 program status switch
             psw write6150 status[Iadr;]
             (psw+4) write6150 status[Int;Lower]
             (psw+6) write6150 status[Cond;Lower]
             status[Iadr;]←word read6150 psw+8
             status[Int;Lower]←half read6150 psw+12
             reserve6150
             wait←0


             reserve6150
           ⋀ IBM 6150 unpredictable status
             status[(ι16),9;]←?(7,word)ρradix
             status[Tct;(ι25),28]←?26ρradix
             status[Check;ι16]←?16ρradix
             status[Ireq;(ι16),23+ι9]←?25ρradix
             status[Int;(ι19),28]←?20ρradix
             status[Cond;(ι24),29]←?25ρradix
             status[Cond;24]←0
```

PROGRAM 16-158   Status switching action in the IBM 6150.

Wait state. Instruction sequencing is resumed after the search for interruption causes, unless the processor is in the wait state. In that case, the processor continues to test the interrupt causes for an interrupt request with proper priority. Interruptions turn off the wait state. The processor enters the wait state by the privileged instruction Wait.

```
             WAIT
           ⋀ IBM 6150 Wait
             Priv report6150 status[Int;Problem]
             →OUT suppress6150
             wait←1
```

PROGRAM 16-159   Wait in the IBM 6150.

Humble access. Supervisor Call causes a status switch to a block of storage locations reserved for this purpose. A 16-bit code obtained from an unsigned effective address is recorded as part of the saved status.

```
            SVC
            ⍝ IBM 6150 Supervisor Call
            switchstatus6150 Psw+144
            (Psw+158) write6150 half magnr adr6150u
```

PROGRAM 16-160   Humble access in the IBM 6150.

Trap.   The Trap instructions act like conditional supervisor calls. They conditionally set the `Trap` program check bit. The immediate instruction compares the content of Rc with a sign-extended 8-bit immediate field. Any comparison condition can be specified. The direct instructions compare the content of register Rb with the content of register Rc for greater, equal, or less.

```
TI;comparand;operand;lt;eq;gr            TLT
⍝ IBM 6150 Trap On Condition Immediate   ⍝ IBM 6150 Trap On Less
comparand←radixcompi inst[Ihalf]         comparand←magni reg[fld Rc;]
operand←radixcompi reg[fld Rc;]          operand←magni reg[fld Rb;]
lt←operand<comparand                     Trap report6150 operand<comparand
eq←operand=comparand
gr←operand>comparand
Trap report6150 inst[1↓Rb]∨.∧lt,eq,gr
```

PROGRAM 16-161   Conditional Trap in the IBM 6150.

Dispatching.   Load Program Status is a privileged operation that restores the instruction address, interrupt control, and program conditions. If the low-order bit of field Rb is 1, then one instruction will be executed before any interruption is taken. When Load Program Status is given while the system is on the machine-check level, that level is left and the machine-check bits are reset. When the instruction is given on the program-check level, that level is left and the program-check bits are reset. These levels can be left only via this instruction.

```
LPS                                      levelreset6150
⍝ IBM 6150 Load Program Status           ⍝ IBM 6150 check level reset
Priv report6150 status[Int;Problem]      →CASE(mclevel,pclevel)⍳1
→OUT suppress6150                        C0: ⍝ reset machine check
status[Iadr;]←word read6150 adr6150         status[Check;Machine]←0
status[Int;Lower]←half read6150 adr6150+4   mclevel←0
status[Cond;Lower]←half read6150 adr6150+6   →ENDCASE
reserve6150                              C1: ⍝ reset program check
levelreset6150                              status[Check;Program]←0
→If 2|fld Rb                                pclevel←0
THEN:execute ifetch6150                      →ENDCASE
ENDIF:                                   C2: ⍝ normal level
                                         ENDCASE:
```

PROGRAM 16-162   Dispatch in the IBM 6150.

State Preservation

Context switching.   Move From and To Status move a word from and to the status registers; they address the 16-register control store as a regular array with the Rb field. Set Status and Reset Status set or reset a single bit in a low-order status register. Field Rc addresses the particular bit. These instructions are privileged unless they apply to the Mq or the condition bits.

```
MTS
A IBM 6150 Move To Status
Priv report6150 status[Int;Problem]∧~(fld Rb)∈Mq.Cond
→OUT suppress6150
status[fld Rb;]←reg[fld Rc;]
reserve6150

CLRSB
A IBM 6150 Clear Status
Priv report6150 status[Int;Problem]∧~(fld Rb)∈Mq.Cond
→OUT suppress6150
status[fld Rb;Lower[fld Rc]]←0
reserve6150
```

PROGRAM 16-163   Context switching in the IBM 6150.

Tools of Control

Timer.   The value of status register `Timer` is decremented by an external clock. When the value reaches zero, the content of the register is replaced by the content of `Tsource`, and the `Alarm` bit is set in the timer-control register. When the timer enable bit is 1, an interrupt request is entered in the interrupt-request register according to the priority in the timer priority bits. If the `Alarm` bit is still on when another alarm is signaled, the timer overflow bit is set. The timer alarm and overflow bits must be reset by programming.

```
timer6150                            timeraction6150;count;level;set
A IBM 6150 timer allocation          A IBM 6150 timer action
A timer interrupt enable             count←magni status[Timer;]
Tenable←25                           status[Timer;]←word magnr count-1
A timer alarm                        →If count=1
Alarm←26                             THEN: A reset and alarm
A timer alarm overflow                   status[Timer;]←status[Tsource;]
Toflo←27                                 status[Tct;Toflo]←status[Tct;Alarm]
A timer priority                         status[Tct;Alarm]←1
Tprior←29+ι3                             level←6⌊magni status[Tct;Tprior]
                                         set←status[Tct;Tenable]
                                         status[Ireq;level]←status[Ireq;level]∨set
                                     ENDIF:
```

PROGRAM 16-164   Timer control in the IBM 6150.

16.5.8

Input/Output

Any type of device and access method may be connected to the processor, as is the case with most mini- and microprocessors.

Read and Write.   The content of the register specified by `Rb` is transferred to or from the device specified by the low-order 24 bits of the effective address. The eight high-order bits of this address must be 0, otherwise a program check interrupt occurs. The I/O instructions are not privileged as such; each device can test the state of the processor and can decide whether or not to accept or send data in the problem state or to signal a Data Exception interrupt.

```
c IOR    Read
c IOW    Write
```

TABLE 16-165   Input/output instructions of the IBM 6150.

16.5.9

Bibliography

IBM Corporation: *IBM RP3-PE Functional Specification* (undated technical memorandum; our defining reference).

Blaauw [1976], Colwell et al. [1988], Davidson [1986], Diefendorff [1994], Katevenis [1983], Patterson and Ditzel [1980], Patterson and Sequin [1981; 1982], Patterson [1985], Radin [1982], Sites [1993], Stallings [1986a, 1986b].

16.5.10

Exercises

16-21 Give the description of the logical and shift instructions CLRBL, SETBU, SETBL, MFTIU, MFTIL, MTTB, MTTIU, N, NIUZ, NILO, O, OIL, XIU, XIL, SL, SLP, SLI, SLIP, SLPI, SARI, SARIP, SR, SRP, SRIP, SRPI, and SRPIP, assuming consistency with the logical and shift instructions shown in this section.

16-22 Give the description of the binary arithmetic instructions L, LS, LH, LHAS, LM, STS, STC, STCS, STH, STHS, MC03, MC13, MC33, MC30, MC31, MC32, ABS, DEC, AI, AIS, AEI, S, SE, SF, C, and CLI, assuming consistency with the binary arithmetic instructions shown in this section.

16-23 Give the description of the sequencing instructions BBR, BNBR, BNBRX, BB, BBX, BNBX, BALR, BALAX, and BALIX, assuming consistency with the sequencing instructions shown in this section.

16-24 Give the description of the supervisory instructions TGTE, MFS, and SETSB, assuming consistency with the supervisory instructions shown in this section.

16-25 How would you perform decimal addition and subtraction on the IBM 6150?

Appendix A

APL Summary

This appendix summarizes the subset of APL that is used in this book. The summary is given in tables and examples. The text is intended to be a brief introduction to APL. For a discussion of the full language, the reference manual by Pakin [1972], the introduction by Polivka and Pakin [1975] and the dictionary by Iverson [1987] are recommended.

The differences among various extensions of the language do not affect the basic subset used in this text.

Introduction

dog←cat+5 is a simple APL expression. The expression is sufficiently close to common algebraic notation that the reader will guess that 5 is added to the value of cat, and that this sum is called dog. If the value of cat is 7, then the value of dog is 12.

The concepts that this interpretation of dog←cat+5 presupposes are:

1. Evaluation of an expression, such as adding 5 to cat and assigning the name dog to this value
2. Data, such as 5
3. Names, such as the term cat
4. Primitive functions, such as +

Furthermore, the repeated use of this expression with different values for cat makes it desirable to introduce the concept of defined functions.

These concepts are treated in turn.

A.1
Evaluation of an Expression

Expressions are evaluated in APL from right to left, without any operator precedence rule. Thus, 5+7x3-1 is evaluated first as 5+7x2, next as 5+14, and finally as 19. In contrast, algebraic evaluation would give 5+21-1, or 26-1, or 25, and a left-to-right evaluation 12x3-1, or 36-1, or 35. (APL has so many operators, at so many conceptual levels, that a precedence rule becomes too complex to remember and use.)

The order of evaluation may be changed with *parentheses*. An expression within parentheses is evaluated first. Thus, 5+(7x3)-1 is evaluated as 5+21-1, or 5+20, or 25.

A.2

Data

Data may be characters, numbers, or logical values.

Data elements

Characters.   Each of the *characters* of Table A-1 may be used as a data element. Most characters can be entered directly from an APL keyboard. Some characters, the *overstruck characters* are made by striking a key, backspacing, and striking another key.

```
a b c d e f g h i j k l m n o p q r s t u v w x y z ∆ □
A B C D E F G H I J K L M N O P Q R S T U V W X Y Z ∆
0 1 2 3 4 5 6 7 8 9  ̄
ˋ ( ) [ ] ; ˜ ∧ ∨ + - × ÷ * ⊛ ∟ ⌈ | ? < ≤ = ≥ > ≠
ρ , ⊤ ⍳ ⌽ ⊖ ⊗ ⊥ ⊤ ↑ ↓ ∈ ∆ ⍱
/ \ . ∘ ← →
∇ : ⍺
```

TABLE A-1   Subset of APL characters.

The basic subset of APL has no character-string datatype. Vectors of characters are used instead.

Numbers.   *Numbers* are represented in our subset as decimal integers, or decimal fractions, or both. The *minus sign* is attached to the left and is raised to distinguish it from the negation operator. Thus, the result of 7-12 is ̄5.

Logical values.   The logical values *true* and *false* are represented by the integers 1 and 0 respectively. They are treated as a subset of the numbers; APL is not strongly typed.

Arrays

A character, number, or logical value is often an element of an array. In APL, *arrays* have a regular structure, obtained by ordering the elements in groups of equal size. These groups may in turn be ordered in groups. The size of a group is called a *dimension* of the array; the number of times the grouping is repeated is the *rank* of the array; each grouping is called a *coordinate* of the array. The several dimensions of an array make up the *dimension vector*, often shortened to *the dimension*. The dimension of the dimension vector is the rank.

Vector, matrix, scalar.   A single group of elements is called a *vector*. The dimension of the vector is the number of elements in the vector; the rank is 1. Thus, the vector 2 5 4 7 2 1 has one coordinate and dimension 6.

When groups of groups are taken, the array is called a *matrix*. Program A-2 shows an example of a 2 by 5 matrix. The dimension of this matrix is the vector 2 5. The rightmost element of the dimension vector gives the dimension of the lowest-order grouping; the elements to the left represent in turn the higher-order coordinates. The low-order grouping of an array is called a *row*. When a group contains no elements, it is *empty* and its dimension is zero.

Program A-2 also shows an array of rank 3 with dimension vector 2 3 4 and rows with four elements each. The examples shown in this program will be used as operands in subsequent examples.

```
   scalar              vector              matrix                  array
7                 3 8 0 9 ¯5 11        5  2 ¯3  9  1        4    7    3  ¯1
                                      ¯4  0  8 12  2       ¯2   11    0   5
                                                           4    8    9  ¯6

                                                          ¯8    3    9   4
                                                           2  ¯13   20   1
                                                           0   ¯3   ¯7   6
```

PROGRAM A-2   Arrays.

When a datum is only a single element, it is called a *scalar*. Since no grouping takes place, the dimension is empty and the rank is 0. For a vector the dimension vector is a one-element vector, not a scalar.

Representation of arrays.   A numeric array is displayed by placing its numbers, separated by spaces, in the pertinent groupings, as shown in Program A-2. A numeric vector may appear in an expression. Thus, dog←cat+2 5 8 indicates the addition of the vector 2 5 8 to cat.

A character array is represented without space between the elements of a row. Thus, a character vector with the three characters c, a, and t as elements is displayed as cat.

Specification of characters.   The three symbols cat can represent either a three-element character vector or the name of a variable. When such a group of characters appears in an expression, it is always interpreted as a name, as was the case in dog←cat+5. When a character vector appears in an expression, it is enclosed with single quotes. Thus, 'cat' represents a three-element character vector in an expression. When the single quote itself is an element of a character vector, it is specified by two single quotes in succession: 'don''t care' specifies the 10-character vector don't care.

Indexing

Elements of an array can be identified by an *index*, which itself can be an array; vector indices are very common. An index is placed between two *square brackets*, and the values for each coordinate are separated by a *semicolon*. The higher coordinates are placed to the left of the lower. The numbering of the elements is from low to high—that is, from left to right, and from top to bottom. The numbering starts with 0, called *zero origin*, or with 1, the *one origin*. In this text, only zero origin is used. Thus, 2 5 7 8[1] is 5. The element in the third row and the fifth column of a matrix, counting from the top left corner, is specified by [2;4]. The index of the lowest order dimension, the row, specifies the *column* to which each element belongs.

Program A-3 gives further examples using the arrays of Program A-2. In all the APL examples, the first line, which is indented six spaces, gives a specification; the following lines (without indentation) give the result.

```
      vector[5 4 4 1]          matrix[1;3]              array[1;0;3]
11 ‾5 ‾5 8                  12                      4

      vector[]                 matrix[;3]               array[;0;]
3 8 0 9 ‾5 11               9 12                    4  7  3 ‾1
                                                   ‾8  3  9  4
                                 matrix[1;]
                              ‾4 0 8 12 2
```

PROGRAM A-3   Indexing examples.

For each coordinate, as many values as desired may be specified in any order, including repetitions. Thus, 'cat'[1 0 2] gives act, and 'dog'[2 1 1 0] gives good. An index may also be specified by an expression: 2 5 7 8 [3-1] is the same as 2 5 7 8 [2], which gives 7. When the index value for a coordinate is empty, all elements along that coordinate participate. Thus, 2 5 7 8 [] is the same as 2 5 7 8, and matrix[;3] gives all elements of column 3 of matrix.

A.3
Names

Names may identify data, such as cat, or user-defined functions.

Names, or *identifiers,* for data or functions are composed of alphabetic characters; numeric characters; the delta, Δ; and the underscored delta, Δ̲. The first character may not be numeric. No spaces are allowed in a name. cat5 is interpreted as a four-character name, cat 5 as the name cat to the left of the number 5, and 5cat, or 5 cat, as the number 5 to the left of the name cat.

A.4
Primitive Functions

The *primitive functions* of APL are classified as *monadic* (applying to one operand), or *dyadic* (applying to two operands). Primitive functions are represented by a single symbol; the same symbol may be used monadically and dyadically.

Primitive functions can also be classified according to the rank of the operands. The *scalar functions* apply to scalars, and each has a scalar result. They may, however, also be used with compatible arrays in a straightforward element-by-element extension. All other functions are called *mixed-rank functions.*

Logical Scalar Functions

The logical functions of the subset used in this book are the NOT, AND, and OR. These functions are explained by the examples of Programs A-4 and A-5. The symbol ⍝ indicates that all that follows it on the same line is a comment, not part of the executable APL.

NOT.   The NOT gives the inverse of the operand, which must be a logical value. As is true for all functions, the NOT applies to the entire expression to its right, be it a single value, an array, or a more complex expression.

```
        ~ 0 1 ⍝ not
    1 0
```

PROGRAM A-4   NOT.

AND and OR.   These logical functions will be used only with the logical values.

```
    0 0 1 1 ∧ 0 1 0 1 ⍝ and                    0 0 1 1 ∨ 0 1 0 1 ⍝ or
0 0 0 1                                    0 1 1 1
```

PROGRAM A-5   AND and OR.

Arithmetic Scalar Functions

Monadic arithmetic functions.   The APL subset in this book has as monadic scalar arithmetic functions: *negation, signum, reciprocal, absolute value, floor, ceiling,* and *random. Negation* inverts the sign of the operand. Note that the negate and subtract symbol differs from the negative sign symbol, ‾; the latter is not a function, but part of the number representation. The *signum,* or *direction,* is 1 when the operand is positive, ‾1 when negative, and 0 when the operand is zero. *Absolute value* gives the magnitude of the operand. *Floor* gives the greatest integer equal to, or less than, the operand. *Ceiling* gives the smallest integer equal to, or greater than, the operand. The use of floor and ceiling as a pair of functions was introduced by APL, and has been widely adopted. Note the behavior with negative arguments. *Random,* or *roll,* selects randomly one of the non-negative integers smaller than the operand. Program A-6 gives typical results for successive invocations.

```
     - 3.14 0 ‾2.17 ⍝ negation              | 3.14 0 ‾2.17 ⍝ magnitude
‾3.14 0 2.17                             3.14 0 2.17

     × 3.14 0 ‾2.17 ⍝ signum                 ÷ 3.14 ‾2.17 ⍝ reciprocal
1 0 ‾1                                   0.3184713376 ‾0.4608294931

     ⌊ 3.14 0 ‾2.17 ⍝ floor                  ⌈ 3.14 0 ‾2.17 ⍝ ceiling
3 0 ‾3                                   4 0 ‾2

     ? 1 2 5 5 17 ⍝ random                  ? 1 2 5 5 17 ⍝ random
0 1 2 2 3                                0 1 3 4 6
```

PROGRAM A-6   Monadic arithmetic functions.

Dyadic arithmetic functions.   Our subset has as dyadic scalar functions: *add, subtract, multiply, divide, exponentiate, logarithm, minimum, maximum,* and *residue.* Residue is also called *modulus.* Multiply is represented by the symbol ×, as established in mathematics. The symbol for exponentiation is *, not ** as in FORTRAN and other languages. The symbol for logarithm is ⊛.

```
       3 ‾2 + 5 4 ⍝ add                      3 ‾2 - 5 4 ⍝ subtract
    8 2                                    ‾2 ‾6

       3 ‾2 × 5 4 ⍝ multiply                 3 ‾2 ÷ 5 4 ⍝ divide
   15 ‾8                                  0.6 ‾0.5

       3 ‾2 * 5 4 ⍝ power                     3 2 ⊛ 5 16 ⍝ log
  243 16                                 1.464973521 4

       5 ‾2 ⌊ 3 4 ⍝ minimum                   5 ‾2 ⌈ 3 ‾4 ⍝ maximum
    3 ‾2                                   5 ‾2

       3 2 | ‾5 4 ⍝ residue                   3 2 | 5 4 ⍝ modulus
    1 0                                    2 0
```

PROGRAM A-7   Dyadic arithmetic functions.

Relations.   The relations are: *less than, greater than or equal to, less than or equal to, greater than, equal to,* and *unequal to.* When a relation is true, its result is 1; when false, its result is 0. These functions follow closely the established meaning.

```
     1 2 3 < 3 2 1 ⍝ less                 1 2 3 ≥ 3 2 1 ⍝ greater or equal
  1 0 0                                0 1 1

     1 2 3 = 3 2 1 ⍝ equal               1 2 3 ≠ 3 2 1 ⍝ unequal
  0 1 0                                1 0 1

     1 2 3 > 3 2 1 ⍝ greater             1 2 3 ≤ 3 2 1 ⍝ less or equal
  0 0 1                                1 1 0
```

PROGRAM A-8   Relational functions.

Extension to arrays.   The examples show that scalar functions can be used for arrays. The monadic functions are simply applied to each element of an array. Thus, | 5 ‾2 3 gives 5 2 3. For the dyadic functions, the operands must have the same dimension vectors. The function is applied to corresponding elements of both arrays. Thus, 5 8 3 × 2 8 1 gives 10 64 3, a result that differs from classical vector multiplication.

The dyadic functions also allow one operand to be an array and the other a scalar. In that case, the scalar participates as operand with all elements of the array. Thus, 9 2 5 + 2 or 2 + 9 2 5 gives 11 4 7.

Mixed-Rank Functions

In contrast to the scalar functions, the mixed-rank functions are not applied element by element to an array; the dimension of their result depends upon the given function. Except for transposition, they are peculiar to APL; they are handy because the concepts that they embody are *not* peculiar to APL.

Dimension.   The *dimension*, or *size*, represented by the Greek letter rho, ρ, yields the dimension of the operand. The dimension of the dimension is the rank of the operand. Thus, ρ 9 5 2 gives 3 and ρρ 9 5 2 gives 1. Program A-9 gives the example operands of Program A-2 and shows what the dimension operator produces for each. The example also shows that the dimension of a scalar is empty (no printout) and its rank is 0.

```
        scalar           vector              matrix              array
7                     3 8 0 9 ⁻5 11       5   2 ⁻3  9   1       4    7    3   ⁻1
                                          ⁻4   0   8  12   2   ⁻2   11    0    5
                                                                    4    8    9   ⁻6

                                                                   ⁻8    3    9    4
                                                                    2  ⁻13   20    1
                                                                    0   ⁻3   ⁻7    6


        ρscalar          ρvector            ρmatrix              ρarray
            6                2 5              2 3 4


        ρρscalar         ρρvector           ρρmatrix             ρρarray
0           1                 2                  3
```

PROGRAM A-9   Dimension.

Ravel.   The *ravel* is represented by a *comma*. When applied to an array, the ravel yields the vector comprising the elements of the array. Programs A-9 and A-10 show that the elements are taken left to right and low to high order.

```
        ,vector                        ,matrix
3 8 0 9 ⁻5 11                5 2 ⁻3 9 1 ⁻4 0 8 12 2


        ,array
4 7 3 ⁻1 ⁻2 11 0 5 4 8 9 ⁻6 ⁻8 3 9 4 2 ⁻13 20 1 0 ⁻3 ⁻7 6
```

PROGRAM A-10   Ravel.

Index generator.   The *index generator* is represented by the Greek letter iota, ι. The index generator of the integer n yields a vector composed of the n integers 0 through $n - 1$, assuming zero-origin indexing. Thus, ι5 gives 0 1 2 3 4; ι0 gives an empty numeric vector.

```
        ι7                          ι1              ι0
0 1 2 3 4 5 6                        0
```

PROGRAM A-11   Index generator.

Reverse.   The *reverse*, Φ, reverses the order of the elements of each row of an array. Hence Φ 3 5 becomes 5 3. Reversal along the leading, or high-order, axis is specified by ⊖, also known as *upset*. The examples of Program A-2 are used in Program A-12.

```
        Φvector                    Φmatrix                      Φarray                      Θarray
11 ¯5 9 0 8 3               1  9 ¯3  2  5           ¯1   3   7   4          ¯8   3   9   4
                           2 12  8  0 ¯4            5   0  11  ¯2           2 ¯13  20   1
                                                   ¯6   9   8   4           0  ¯3  ¯7   6

                            Θmatrix                4   9   3  ¯8           4   7   3  ¯1
                  ¯4  0  8 12  2                    1  20 ¯13   2          ¯2  11   0   5
                   5  2 ¯3  9  1                    6  ¯7  ¯3   0           4   8   9  ¯6
```

PROGRAM A-12   Reverse.

Transpose.   The *transpose* is represented by the symbol, ⍉. In this text, transposition is applied only to matrices. The rows of a matrix become columns, and the columns become rows.

```
          ⍉vector                              ⍉matrix
   3  8  0  9 ¯5 11                         5 ¯4
                                           2  0
                                          ¯3  8
                                           9 12
                                           1  2
```

PROGRAM A-13   Transpose.

Reshape.   *Reshape*, or *restructure*, is represented by the dyadically used ρ. The reshape gives to the elements of an array—the right operand—the dimension specified by the left operand. When the number of elements in the array is insufficient, they are repeated cyclicly. When only part of the elements of the array are used, the remaining elements are ignored.

```
          9ρ2                               9ρvector
   2 2 2 2 2 2 2 2 2                3  8  0  9 ¯5 11  3 8  0

          2 4 ρ 1 2 4                       2 4 ρmatrix
     1 2 4 1                            5   2 ¯3  9
     2 4 1 2                            1  ¯4  0  8
```

PROGRAM A-14   Reshape.

Catenate.   The *comma* used dyadically represents catenation. The *catenation* of two vectors results in a vector comprising the elements of the right operand placed next to and right of the elements of the left operand. The catenation of two arrays catenates the rows of these arrays, assuming that the other dimensions are compatible.

```
        vector, 12 13                     matrix,[0]2
   3  8  0  9 ¯5 11 12 13            5   2 ¯3  9   1
                                   ¯4   0  8 12.  2
                                    2   2  2  2   2

          matrix,2                         matrix, 1 2 3 4 5
     5   2 ¯3  9  1  2               5   2 ¯3  9  1
    ¯4   0  8 12  2  2              ¯4   0  8 12  2
                                    1   2  3  4  5
```

PROGRAM A-15   Catenate.

When one desires to catenate along other coordinates, one can place the number of the coordinate to the right of the comma between square brackets. Thus, `matrix1,[0]matrix2` gives catenation along dimension zero, which is the column catenation of these two matrices. Instead of `,[0]` the *over*, $\neg$, can be used.

Index of.   The *index of* is represented by the dyadically used *iota*, ι. It is a generalized table lookup that finds the (first) index of each element of the right operand in the left operand, which must be a vector. The result is an index with the same dimension as the right operand. The right operand, and hence the result, may have any dimension.

When the right element is a scalar, the leftmost element of the left operand that is equal to the scalar is found. The index of this element is the result. When no equality is found, the function returns the dimension of the left argument—i.e., the argument is outside the table. Note that 0-origin indexing means that the first position has index 0.

When the right operand is an array, the above process is repeated for each element of the array.   Thus, `'act'ι'cat'` results in `1 0 2`, and `8 5 4 5 ι 5 7` results in `1 4`.

```
        3 5 0 2 3 ι 3 2 0 1 2 3                3 8 12 0 ιιmatrix
     0 3 2 5 3 0                            5 5 5 5 4
                                            5 3 1 2 5
```

PROGRAM A-16   Index of.

Rotate.   *Rotate* uses the same symbol as reverse, but with a left operand. The left operand specifies the number of places that the rows of the right operand are rotated. Positive integers indicate a rotation to the left; negative integers give rotation towards the right. Rotation along other axes uses an axis specification between square brackets, or the upset symbol used for reverse.

```
        2Φvector               ⁻3Φmatrix                1Θmatrix
     0 9 ⁻5 11 3 8          ⁻3  9  1  5  2          ⁻4  0  8 12  2
                             8 12  2 ⁻4  0           5  2 ⁻3  9  1
```

PROGRAM A-17   Rotate.

Decode.   The *decode*, or base value, represented by $\bot$, determines the value of the right operand as interpreted in the number system specified by the left operand. The left operand may be a scalar or vector; the right operand may be any numeric array. For the common case with the left operand a scalar and the right operand a vector, the elements of the right operand are interpreted as the digits of the positional representation with the left operand as radix and are evaluated accordingly. Thus, $2\bot 1\ 1\ 0$ is 6; $3\bot 1\ 1\ 0$ is 12, and $10\bot 1\ 1\ 0$ is 110 (one hundred ten). In Program A-18 the first example converts hours, minutes, seconds to seconds.

```
       24 60 60 ⊥ 1 2 3            10⊥ 2 2 0              10⊥matrix
     3723                         220              46 20 ⁻22 102 12
```

PROGRAM A-18   Decode.

Encode.   The *encode*, or representation, is represented by the symbol ⊤ and is the opposite of the decode. The left argument of the encode represents the radix of the positional representation with which the elements of the right argument are to be represented. When the right operand is a scalar, the result is the vector of the digits of this scalar in the number system specified by the left operand. Thus, 2 2 2 2 ⊤37 gives the four low-order digits of the binary representation of 37—that is, 0 1 0 1. Vector left arguments of ⊥ and ⊤ handle mixed radix systems such as that for hours, minutes, seconds.

```
      2 2 2 2 2 T12                        24 60 60 T10000
     0 1 1 0 0                            2 46 40
```

PROGRAM A-19   Encode.

Replicate.   *Replication* is represented by the dyadically used *slash*, /. The left operand should be a vector of non-negative integers. The right operand should be an array of which the rows have the same dimension as the left operand. For each 0 in the left operand, the corresponding elements in the rows of the right operand are deleted. For a positive integer *n* in the left operand, the corresponding elements in the rows of the right operand are repeated *n* times. When the left argument is a logical vector, the function is sometimes called *selection*, or *compression*.

Thus, 1 0 1 0 1 /'craft' gives cat, and 0 3 1 0 / 0 1 2 3 gives 1 1 1 2.

```
      0 1 0 1 0 1 /vector              2 0 3 0 1 /matrix
    8 9 11                           5  5 ‾3 ‾3 ‾3  1
                                    ‾4 ‾4  8  8  8  2

      1/vector
    3 8 0 9 ‾5 11
```

PROGRAM A-20   Replicate.

Take.   The *take* is represented by the *upward arrow*, ↑. It selects contiguous prefixes or suffixes. The left operand must be a vector whose dimension equals the rank of the right operand. The right operand may be an array. Each element of the left operand determines how many elements along the corresponding coordinate of the right operand are taken. When the element is positive, the first elements are taken; when the element is negative, the last elements are taken. Thus, ‾3↑'fact' gives act, and 2↑ 0 1 2 3 4 gives 0 1.

```
      4↑vector                       ‾9↑vector
    3 8 0 9                        0 0 0 3 8 0 9 ‾5 11

      2 3 ↑matrix                    3 ‾2 ↑matrix
     5  2 ‾3                        9  1
    ‾4  0  8                       12  2
                                    0  0
```

PROGRAM A-21   Take.

When the take specifies more elements than are contained in the right operand, a numeric operand is treated as if extended with 0s, and a character operand with blanks. Thus, ‾6↑ 1 2 3 gives 0 0 0 1 2 3, and 6↑ 1 2 3 gives 1 2 3 0 0 0.

Drop.   *Drop* is the opposite of take. It is represented by a *downward arrow*, ↓, and indicates the number of elements along each coordinate that must be eliminated. Thus, 1↓'fact' gives act, and ‾2↓ 0 1 2 3 4 gives 0 1 2.

```
        4↓vector                          ‾9↓vector
    ‾5 11

        1 3 ↓matrix                       ‾1 ‾2 ↓matrix
    12   2                            5   2 ‾3
```

PROGRAM A-22   Drop.

Membership.   The *membership* function is represented by the Greek letter *epsilon*, ∈. The function determines, for each element of the left operand, whether it occurs in the right operand, and indicates a positive result with 1 and a negative result with 0. Thus, 'factual'∈'cat' gives 0 1 1 1 0 1 0, and 2 5 ∈ 0 1 2 3 2 1 gives 1 0. Membership yields a logical result, whereas index yields a numeric result.

```
        3∈vector                          matrix∈vector
    1                                  0 0 0 1 0
                                       0 1 1 0 0
        vector∈matrix
    0 1 1 1 0 0
```

PROGRAM A-23   Membership.

Sort index.   The *sort index* or *grade up*, ⍋, determines the ascending sorting order of a numeric vector operand. When the grade up is used as an index for the vector, the elements of the vector are delivered in their sorted order.

```
        ⍋vector                           vector[⍋vector]
    4 2 0 1 3 5                        ‾5 0 3 8 9 11
```

PROGRAM A-24   Sort index.

Execute.   The *execute* function, ⍎, executes a character vector operand as an APL expression. Thus, the character string '124' becomes the number 124. The execute does not apply to character arrays of higher dimensions.

```
        ⍎ '3+4'                           ⍎ 'vector'
    7                                  3 8 0 9 ‾5 11
```

PROGRAM A-25   Execute.

Composite Functions

The composite functions are obtained by applying an *operator* to one or two primitive functions. Hence, an operator yields a function of functions. We discuss the slash (/), the backslash (\) and the period (.), which yield the reduction, the scan, the inner product, and the outer product.

Reduction.   The *reduction* operator, the slash, /, has a scalar dyadic operator placed to its left. The reduction is applied monadically to an array. The effect of the operator is the same as if the dyadic operator were placed between the row elements of the array. Thus, each row is reduced to one element, and the rank of the array is reduced by 1. The add reduction, +/, is equivalent to the algebraic summation, Σ. Thus, +/ 5 ¯2 3 gives 6. Similarly, the multiply reduction is equivalent to algebraic repeated multiplication, $\prod$; ×/ 5 ¯2 3 gives ¯30. Program A-26 gives further examples.

```
      +/ 2 ¯5 11                          ×/ 2 ¯5 11
 8                                    ¯110

      L/ 2 ¯5 11                          Γ/ 2 ¯5 11
  ¯5                                  11

      v/ 0 1 1 0                          ^/ 0 1 1 0
 1                                    0
```

PROGRAM A-26   Reduction operator.

Scan.   The *scan* operator, the back slash, \, also has a scalar dyadic operator to its left. The scan replaces each element by the reduction of that element and the elements to its left. The scan is normally not used in description functions; it occurs in decode (Program 9-8).

```
      +\ 2 ¯5 11                          ×\ 2 ¯5 11
 2 ¯3 8                               2 ¯10 ¯110

      L\ 2 ¯5 11                          Γ\ 2 ¯5 11
 2 ¯5 ¯5                              2 2 11

      v\ 0 1 1 0                          ^\ 0 1 1 0
 0 1 1 1                              0 0 0 0
```

PROGRAM A-27   Scan.

Inner product.   The *inner product* is specified by two dyadic scalar functions separated by a *period*, such as ∧.=. The right function, here =, is applied first to the elements of the two operands. Each row of the left operand is combined as a vector with the elements selected along the highest dimension of the right operand. Thus, for two matrices, the rows of the left operand are combined with the columns of the right operand. Each vector result is subsequently reduced by the second function, here ∧, to a single element.

With the two functions + and ×, the classical matrix product is obtained.

```
      3 ¯2 +.× 5 4                        3 ¯2 ×.+ 5 4
 7                                    16

      0 1 4 7 L.Γ 5 3 2 1                 0 1 4 7 Γ.L 5 3 2 1
 3                                    2

      0 1 ∧.= 0 1                         0 1 v.∧ 1 0
 1                                    0
```

TABLE A-28   Inner-product operator.

Outer product. The *outer product* is specified by one dyadic scalar function placed to the right of the symbol ∘ and *period*, such as ∘.+. Each element of the right operand is combined with all elements of the left operand using the scalar function, here +. Therefore, the result has a rank that is the sum of the ranks of the two operands. When the function is times, ×, the classical Cartesian product is obtained.

```
        3 ‾2 ∘.+ 5 4                       3 ‾2 ∘.× 5 4
    8 7                                 15  12
    3 2                               ‾10  ‾8

        2 4 ∘.⌈ 5 3 2 1                   2 4 ∘.⌊ 5 3 2 1
    5 3 2 2                             2 2 2 1
    5 4 4 4                             4 3 2 1

        0 1 ∘.∧ 0 1                       0 1 ∘.∨ 1 0
    0 0                                 1 0
    0 1                                 1 1
```

PROGRAM A-29   Outer-product operator.

Specification

A variable, identified by a name, such as dog, is given a value by the *specification*, or assignment function, the *left-pointing arrow*, ←. The value of the expression to the right of the arrow, including its dimensions, becomes the new value of the variable. Thus, if in dog←cat+5, cat is a 3 by 5 matrix, dog will be a 3 by 5 matrix whose elements are 5 greater than the corresponding elements of cat.

```
            dog WHERE dog← 7 8
    7 8

            dog WHERE dog[0]←9
    9 8

            dog WHERE dog[]←10
    10 10
```

PROGRAM A-30   Specification.

When the variable is an array, part of that variable, as selected by an index, may be assigned a value. Thus, if dog is a 2 by 4 numeric matrix, the center four elements may be made zero by dog[;1 2]←0. (For WHERE see Program 9-28.)

A.5
Defined Functions

One or more expressions may be combined into a *defined function*. A defined function has a name and may specify two, one, or no explicit operands and one or no explicit results. The names of the function, the operands, and the result are given in the function *header*.

Defined functions have the same appearance as the primitive functions of APL. Since they are specified by the user and not by the system, they are called *defined functions*. We call them *functions* for short.

```
out←in1 plus in2                    in1 dogplus in2
⍝ dyadic with explicit result       ⍝ dyadic with implicit result
out←in1+in2                         dog←in1+in2


out←catplus in                      dogcatplus in
⍝ monadic with explicit result      ⍝ monadic with implicit result
out←cat+in                          dog←cat+in


out←catplus5                        dogcatplus5
⍝ nilladic with explicit result     ⍝ nilladic with implicit result
out←cat+5                           dog←cat+5
```

PROGRAM A-31   Forms of defined functions.

Function header.   The first line of a function, the *function header*, gives the form of the function when it is used in an expression. Because of the variations in the number of operands and results, there are six forms of functions, as shown in Program A-31. Program A-32 shows corresponding examples of each of these functions as they appear in an expression.

```
dog←cat plus 5              cat dogplus 5

dog←catplus 5              dogcatplus 5

dog←catplus5               dogcatplus5
```

PROGRAM A-32   Defined functions used in expressions.

The names used in the function header for the operands and the result are valid only within the function; they are *local names*. As the function is used in an expression, the value of an operand in that expression is passed on to the operand of the function. Conversely, the value of the result of the function is made available to the calling expression. Thus, the value of `cat` in the first expression of Program A-32 is passed on to `in1` of the functions `plus`, just as `in2` gets the value 5; the result `out` of `plus` is made available to be assigned to `dog`.

Local variables.   Any variable that is used in a function may be declared to be local; it is valid only within the function and the functions called by it. A variable is made local by placing the variable name after the main part of the header, separated by semicolon. A local variable is distinct from a variable of the same name used outside the function. Program A-33 illustrates the use of a local variable `cat` in the function `doggetcat`.

Global variables.   A variable that is accessible both within and outside a function is called *global*. An example is `dog` in `doggetcat`. In contrast to most languages, implicitly declared variables are global, not local.

Function declaration.   A function is declared by giving the header and preceding it by a downward-pointing delta, the *del*, ∇. Under the header are listed the expressions that form the body of the function. The end of the function declaration is given by a second del with no operand (Program A-33).

```
     ∇  doggetcat;cat              ∇  label←UNTIL condition
[1]     ⍝ chase              [1]     label←(~condition)/REPEAT
[2]     dog←0                      ∇
[3]     REPEAT:cat←?5
[4]        dog←5|dog+1
[5]     →UNTIL dog=cat
     ∇
```

PROGRAM A-33   Example of local variable, label, and branch.

Line numbers.   In displaying functions in this text we normally show neither the initial and final *del*, nor the line numbers that are used in editing.

Branch.   The expressions of a function are evaluated in their numeric order. This order may be changed by a branch. The *branch* is represented by the *right-pointing arrow*, →. The arrow should always be leftmost in an expression. The value to the right of the arrow indicates the number of the expression to be executed next, the *branch target*. Thus, →5 specifies a branch to line 5. An expression to the right of the arrow is evaluated first, and its result is used as the branch target. Thus, →5-3 specifies a branch to line 2.

When there is no line number corresponding to the branch target, the execution of the function terminates and control returns to the caller. This rule includes a branch to 0, which is a standard way of terminating a function.

Conditional branch.   When the branch target is empty, as opposed to 0, the branch is not taken and execution continues with the next expression. Thus, when →test/5 appears on, say, line 12, it results in a branch to line 5 when test is equal to 1; it results in no branch, hence continuation with line 13, when test is equal to 0.

Label.   An expression of a function may be identified by a label. The *label* is a name placed to the left of an expression and separated from the expression by a colon. Thus, the label REPEAT identifies line 3 of doggetcat, as the continuation of the loop. The value of a label is equal to the number of the line on which it appears. Thus, REPEAT has the value 3. A label is a local variable and may be used in an expression. The use of a label as a branch target keeps the target correct when lines are deleted or inserted in the function. (For the function UNTIL see also Program 9-25.)

Comment.   Text that is preceded by a *comment* symbol, ⍝, is not executed. The comment applies to the remainder of the line. doggetcat, line 1, illustrates the use of comments.

User-interface functions.   The various APL implementations give aids for entering, editing, and debugging functions. These are not discussed in this text.

A.6

Idioms

Description Idioms

In this subsection we give some idioms that occur frequently in the machine descriptions.

Space initiation.   In the descriptions the spaces are initiated to arbitrary values; Program A-34 gives the typical expression. The rightmost number (here, 2) is the radix; the left number is the size of the space (here, 16). The space may involve more dimensions such as (regcap,word) for a set of regcap registers, each of length word.

```
          ?16ρ2
 1 1 0 0 1 1 0 0 0 0 1 1 1 1 1 0
```

PROGRAM A-34   Arbitrary binary values.

Index vector.   In the allocation of formats, the fields are indicated by their leftmost position and their length, using the notation of Program A-35. Even the leftmost field of a format is indicated by 0+ιlength.

```
          27+ι10
 27 28 29 30 31 32 33 34 35 36
```

PROGRAM A-35   Integers starting at a given value.

Selection.   At various places a choice among a few alternatives must be specified. In the example of Program A-36, a sign criterion is either 0 or 1 and selects accordingly either 1 or ¯1 from a two-element vector.

```
          1 ¯1 [sign] WHERE sign←?2
       ¯1
```

PROGRAM A-36   Indexing an immediate vector.

Encoded rows.   The encode function of APL extends the rank of an array with a high-order dimension. For a vector, each element is made into a column. Since it is more customary to think of the rows of a matrix as constituting encodings, we introduce a transpose in the encode and the decode expressions, as shown in Program A-37.

```
   2⊥ Q 4 ρ 0 1 1 1 , 0 1 0 1              Q 2 2 2 2 T 7 5
 7 5                                     0 1 1 1
                                         0 1 0 1
```

PROGRAM A-37   Representation of matrix rows.

Ravel.   The ravel is often used as an intermediate function in an expression. Thus, in Program A-38, it is used to obtain the number of elements of a matrix, as an alternative to multiplying the dimensions of the matrix.

```
        ρ,matrix                              ×/ρmatrix
  10                                    10
```

PROGRAM A-38   Number of elements of a matrix.

Change of rank.   A single value can be either a scalar, a one element vector, or indeed a one-element array of any rank. APL consistently recognizes the difference between scalars and vectors in functions such as the encode and decode. At times it may be desirable to change a scalar into a one-element vector, or vice versa. The first action is conveniently accomplished by the ravel. Changing a one-element vector into a scalar can be done by the encode (which reduces the operand rank by 1). The zero-base encode is defined such that it leaves the element value unchanged.

```
        ρρvector                        ρvector
  1                                6

        ρ0⊥ρvector                      0⊥ρvector
                                   6
```

PROGRAM A-39   Converting vector to a scalar.

Any and all.   The frequently occurring concepts *any* and *all* are expressed by the OR-reduction and the AND-reduction. The inner product extends this concept, for instance by an equality test, as illustrated for the vectors in Program A-40. Both operands can be arrays; most frequently they are matrices. Observe that any-unequal is the inverse of all-equal.

```
        0 1 0 0 v.≠ 0 1 0 1          0 1 0 0 ∧.= 0 1 0 1
  1                                  0
```

PROGRAM A-40   Any-unequal versus all-equal.

Making even.   An integer (such as a register address) may be forced to be even by using the floor in combination with halving and doubling, as shown in Program A-41.

```
              2×⌊0.5×vector
        2 8 0 8 ⁻6 10
```

PROGRAM A-41   Force to even.

Fractional part.   The fractional part of a positive number is obtained by taking its value modulo 1. The integer part, of course, is obtained with the floor.

```
        1|12.45 ⍝ fraction          ⌊12.45 ⍝ integer
  0.45                              12
```

PROGRAM A-42   Fractional and integral part of a number.

Digits to characters.   A vector of digits may be changed to a corresponding character vector by indexing.

$$\text{'0123456789'[0 5 3]}$$
$$053$$

PROGRAM A-43   Translating digits to characters.

Characters to digits.   The dyadic iota, which has the nature of a search, may be used to change a character vector into a numeric vector. When the characters represent digits, the decode may subsequently be used to obtain the numeric value of the character vector; or, execute can be used.

$$\text{'0123456789'ι'053'} \qquad\qquad \text{10⊥'0123456789'ι'053'}$$
$$0\ \ 5\ 3 \qquad\qquad\qquad\qquad\qquad 53$$

PROGRAM A-44   Translating characters to digits.

Range search.   The dyadic iota can also be used to determine the range of a value, such as an address or a floating-point exponent. To achieve this the value is compared with a vector of range boundaries, and the comparison result is searched for the first 1 (or 0). n boundaries separate n+1 ranges; the last range is the default case. Such a range search is often used as the selection criterion in a CASE decision.

$$\text{(value< ¯128 0 128)ι1 WHERE value←¯7}$$
$$1$$

$$\text{(value< ¯128 0 128)ι1 WHERE value←200}$$
$$3$$

PROGRAM A-45   Range search.

Sequence of tests.   The criterion of a CASE decision can be a sequence of diverse tests. Thus, a value may be tested for zero, then for being even, then for exceeding a limit, and if none of these are met the value may receive a normal treatment. Again, the dyadic iota may be used to search for a test result that is 1.

$$\text{((value=0),(0=2|value),(value>128))ι1 WHERE value←8}$$
$$1$$

$$\text{((value=0),(0=2|value),(value>128))ι1 WHERE value←37}$$
$$3$$

PROGRAM A-46   Sequence of tests.

All-zero test.   For a Boolean vector, an all-zero test is obtained by taking the NOT of an OR-reduction. For a numeric vector, the AND reduction of each element equated to zero can be used.

$$\text{~∨/ 0 0 0 1 0} \qquad\qquad \text{∧/ 0 2 9 0 2 =0}$$
$$0 \qquad\qquad\qquad\qquad\qquad 0$$

PROGRAM A-47   Test for all-zero.

Parity.   The parity of a Boolean vector is by definition the modulo two arithmetic sum of the elements.

```
2|+/ 1 1 0 1 0
1
```

PROGRAM A-48   Odd parity.

System Functions

A few system functions are occasionally used in a machine description. System functions have the quad, □, as the first character of their name.

Time stamp.   □ts is the *time stamp* in years, months, days, hours, minutes, seconds, and milliseconds.

```
□ts
1989 6 15 13 27 38 193
```

PROGRAM A-49   Time stamp.

State indicator.   The □lc gives the *state indicator vector*. This vector lists the line number of the current expression and the line numbers of all expressions that are calling functions whose execution is suspended. Thus, if function one calls function two on, say, line 12 and if line 3 of two contains □lc, the value of this expression is 3 12.

```
□lc
7 7 2 1 11 11
```

PROGRAM A-50   Line numbers of state indicator.

List of symbols.   Table A-51 gives a list of APL symbols that are described in this section. Next to each symbol, its name and synonyms are listed. When a symbol is used monadically and dyadically, it is listed twice.

A.7
Bibliography

Hoffnagle, G.F., ed., 1991: "Special Issue on APL." *IBM Systems J*, **30**, 4.

Iverson, K.E., 1987: "A Dictionary of APL." *APL Quote Quad*, **18**, 1 (Sep.): 5–40.

Pakin, S., 1972: *APL/360 Reference Manual*.   2nd ed.   Chicago: Science Research Associates.

Polivka, R.P., and S. Pakin, 1975: *APL: The Language and Its Usage*. Englewood Cliffs, N.J.: Prentice-Hall.

Zaks, R., 1978: *A Microprogrammed APL Implementation*. Berkeley: Sybex.

Monadic		Dyadic	
a...z	lower case letters		
A...Z	capital letters		
Δ delta			
Δ	underscored delta		
□ quad	system function name		
0...9	digits		
¯ minus	numeric sign		
' quote	character delimiter		
( )	brackets		
[ ]	index delimiters		
; semicolon	dimension delimiter		
~ not	inverse		
		∧ and	
		∨ or	
		+ plus	add
- minus	negate	- minus	subtract
| stile	absolute	| mod	modulus of
× signum	direction	× times	multiplied by
÷	reciprocal	÷ over	divided by
		* power	to the power
		⊛ log	logarithm of
⌊	floor	⌊	minimum
⌈	ceiling	⌈	maximum
? roll	pseudo random choice		
		< less	is less than
		≤	is less or equal
		= equal	is equal to
		≥	is more or equal
		> greater	is more than
		≠ unequal	is not equal to
ρ rho	dimension	ρ rho	shape
, comma	ravel	, comma	catenate
		⨤ over	high-order catenate
ι iota	index generate	ι iota	index of
Φ phi	reverse	Φ phi	rotate
⊖ theta	high-order reverse	⊖ theta	high-order rotate
⍉	transpose		
		⊥ base	interpret
		⊤	represent
		↑ take	
		↓ drop	
		∈ epsilon	is member of
⍋ gradeup	sort index		
		⍕ pawn	execute
		/ slash	replication
		/ slash	reduction operator
		\ backslash	scan operator
		. period	product operator
∘ jot	outer product		
		← l.arrow	assignment
→ r.arrow	branch		
∇ del	function specifier		
: colon	label specifier		
⍝ *lamp*	comment specifier		

TABLE A-51   Summary of symbols.

Appendix B

Bibliography

Abrams, P.S., 1970: "An APL Machine." *Slac Report* 114. Stanford: Stanford University (February).

Agerwala, T. and J. Cocke, 1987. *High Performance Reduced Instruction Set Processors.* IBM Thomas J. Watson Research Laboratory.

Aiken, H.H., 1937: Proposed calculating machine. Memorandum dated by unknown recipient, published in *IEEE Spectrum*, August 1964; reprinted in Randell (1975), 191–98.

Aiken, H.H. and G.M. Hopper, 1946: "The Automatic Sequence Controlled Calculator." *Electrical Engineering*, **65**, 384–91, 449–54, 522–28.

Aiken, H.H., 1949: "Description of a Relay Calculator, Mark 2." *Annals of the Computation Laboratory XXIV.* Cambridge, MA: Harvard University Press.

Akela, J. and D.P. Siewiorek, 1991: "Modeling and Measurement of the Impact of Input/Output on System Performance." *Comput Archit News*, **19**, 3: 90–399.

Alexander, C., 1964: *Notes on the Synthesis of Form.* Cambridge, MA: Harvard University Press.

Allmark, R.H. and J.R. Lucking, 1962: "Design of an Arithmetic Unit Incorporating a Nesting Store." *Proc., IFIP Congress '62*, 694–98. Reprinted in Bell and Newell [1971], 262–66.

Amdahl, G.M., 1964: "The Structure of System/360, Part III: Processing Unit Design Considerations." *IBM Systems J*, **3**, 2: 144–64.

Amdahl, G.M., G.A. Blaauw, and F.P. Brooks, Jr., 1964: "Architecture of the IBM System/360." *IBM J of Res and Dev*, **8**, 2: 87–101.

Amdahl, G.M., 1967: "Validity of the Single Processor Approach to Achieving Large Scale Computing Capabilities." *Proc., AFIPS Spring Joint Computer Conf.*, **30**: 483–85.

Amdahl, G.M., 1970: "Storage and I/O Parameters and System Potential." *Proc., IEEE Computer Group Conf.*, 371–72.

Amdahl, G.M., 1983: "Architectural Concepts for High-Performance, General Purpose Computers." *Proc., IFIPS Congress*, 369–73.

American National Standards Institute, 1968: *The American National Standards Code for Information Interchange X3.4.* New York.

Anderson, D.W., F.J. Sparacio, and R.M. Tomasulo, 1967: "The IBM System/360 Model 91: Machine Philosophy and Instruction Handling." *IBM J of Res and Dev*, **11**, 1: 8–24.

Anderson, G.A. and E.D. Jensen, 1975: "Computer Interconnection Structures: Taxonomy, Characteristics, and Examples." *Compt Surv*, **7**, 4 (Dec.): 197–213.

Anderson, J.P., 1961: "A Computer for Direct Execution of Algorithmic Languages." *Proc., AFIPS Eastern Joint Computer Conf.*, **20**: 184–93.

Anderson, J.P., S.A. Hoffman, J. Shifman and R.J. Williams, 1962: "D825—A Multiple-Computer System for Command and Control." *Proc., AFIPS Fall Joint Computer Conf.*, **22**: 86–96.

Anderson, S.F., J.G. Earle, R.E. Goldschmidt, and D.M. Powers, 1967: "The IBM System/360 Model 91 Floating-Point Execution Unit." *IBM J of Res and Dev*, **11**, 1: 34–53.

Andrews, M., 1980: *Principles of Firmware Engineering in Microprogram Control*. Potomac, MD: Computer Science Press.

Arden, B.W., B.A. Galler, T.C. O'Brien and F.H. Westerfelt, 1966: "Program and Addressing Structures in a Time-Sharing Environment." *JACM*, **13**, 1: 1–16.

Arvind and R.A. Iannucci, 1983: "A Critique of Multiprocessing von Neumann Style." *Proc., 10th Ann Int Symp on Comp Arch*, 426–35.

Ashenhurst, R.L. and N. Metropolis, 1959: "Unnormalized Floating-Point Arithmetic." *JACM*, **6**: 415–28.

Ashenhurst, R.L., 1962: "The Maniac III Arithmetic System." *Proc., AFIPS Spring Joint Computer Conf.*, **21**: 195–202.

Ashenhurst, R.L., 1971: "Number Representation and Significance Monitoring." In J.R. Rice, ed., *Mathematical Software* (ACM Monograph Series). New York: Academic Press, 67–92.

Aspinall, D.B. and Y.N. Patt, 1985: "Retrofitting the VAX-11/780 Microarchitecture for IEEE Floating Point Arithmetic." *IEEE Trans on Comp*, **C-34**, 8: 692–708.

Astrahan, M.M., B. Housman, J.F. Jacobs, R.P. Mayer, and W.H. Thomas, 1956: "The Logical Design of a Digital Computer for a Large-Scale Real-Time Application." *Proc., AIEE–ACM–IRE 1956 Western Joint Computer Conf.*, **9**: 70–75.

Atanasoff, J.V., 1940: "Computing Machine for the Solution of Large Systems of Linear Algebraic Equations." Report, Iowa State College.

Atkins, D.E. and H.L. Garner, 1973: "Computer Arithmetic: An Introduction and Overview." *IEEE Trans on Comp*, **C-22**, 6: 549–51.

August, M.C. et al., 1989, "Cray X-MP: The Birth of a Supercomputer." *Computer*, **22**, 1 (Jan.): 45–51.

Babbage, C., 1837: "On the Mathematical Powers of the Calculating Engine." In Randell [1975], 7–52.

Babbage, G.H.P., 1910: "Babbage's Analytical Engine." In Randell [1975], 65–70.

Backus, J.W., et. al., 1957: "The FORTRAN Automatic Coding System." *Proc., IRE–AIEE–ACM 1957 Western Joint Computer Conf.*, **11**: 188–98. Reprinted in Rosen [1967], 29–47.

Baer, J.L., 1976: "Multiprocessing Systems." *IEEE Trans on Comp*, **C-25**, 12: 1271–76.

Bagley, J. D., 1976: "Microprogrammable Virtual Machines." *Computer*, **9**, 2 (Feb.): 35–42.

Baker, F.T., 1972: "Chief Programmer Team Management of Production Programming." *IBM Systems J*, **11**, 1: 56–73.

Barbacci, M.R., 1981: "Instruction Set Processor Specifications (ISPS): The Notation and Its Application." *IEEE Trans on Comp*, **C-30**, 1: 24–40.

Barbacci, M.R. and D.P. Siewiorek, 1982: *The Design and Analysis of Instruction Set Processors*. New York: McGraw-Hill.

Barnes, G.H., R.M. Brown, M. Katz, D.J. Kuck, D.L. Slotnick, and R.A. Stokes, 1968: "The ILLIAC IV Computer." *IEEE Trans on Comp*, **C-17**, 8: 746–57.

Barton, R.S., 1961: "A New Approach to the Functional Design of a Digital Computer." *Proc., IRE–AIEE–ACM 1961 Western Joint Computer Conf.*, **19**: 393–96.

Bashe, C.J., L.R. Johnson, J.H. Palmer, and E.E. Pugh, 1986: *IBM's Early Computers*. Cambridge, MA: MIT Press.

Bashkow, T.R., A. Sasson, and A. Kronfeld, 1967: "System Design of a FORTRAN Machine." *IEEE Trans on Comp*, **EC-16**, 4: 485–99.

Baskett, T. and T.W. Keller, 1977: "An Evaluation of the CRAY-1 Computer." In D.J. Kuck, D.H. Lawrie, and A.H. Sameh [1977], 71–84.

Baylis, M.H.J., D.G. Fletcher, and D.J. Howarth, 1968: "Paging Studies Made on the ICT Atlas Computer." *Proc., IFIPS Congress*, 831–37.

Beerstis, V., 1980: "Security and Protection of Data in the IBM System/38." *Proc., 7th Ann Int Symp on Comp Arch, Comput Archit News*, **8**, 3: 245–52.

Belady, L.A., 1966: "A Study of Replacement Algorithms for Virtual Storage Computers." *IBM Systems J*, **5**, 2: 78–101.

Bell, C.G., R. Cady, H. McFarland, B. Delagi, J. O'Laughlin, R. Noonan, and W. Wulf, 1970: "A New Architecture for Minicomputers—The DEC PDP11." *Proc., AFIPS Spring Joint Computer Conf.*, 657–75. Reprinted in Bell, Mudge, and McNamara [1978], Chapter 9.

Bell, C.G. and A. Newell, 1971: *Computer Structures: Readings and Examples*. New York: McGraw-Hill.

Bell, C.G. and W.D. Strecker, 1976: "Computer Structures: What Have We Learned from the PDP11?" *Proc., 3rd Ann Int Symp on Comp Arch, Comput Archit News*, **4**, 4: 1–14. Used in Bell, Mudge, and McNamara [1978], Chapter 16.

Bell, C.G., 1977: private communication.

Bell, C.G., A. Kotok, T.N. Hastings, and R. Hill, 1978: "The Evolution of the DEC System 10." *CACM*, **21**: 44–62.

Bell, C.G. and J.C. Mudge, 1978: "The Evolution of the PDP-11." Bell, Mudge, and McNamara [1978], Chapter 16.

Bell, C.G., J.C. Mudge, and J.E. McNamara, 1978: *Computer Engineering*. Bedford, MA: Digital Press.

Bender, R.R., D.T. Doody, and P.N. Stoughton, 1960: "A Description of the IBM 7074 System." *Proc., IRE–AIEE–ACM 1960 Eastern Joint Computer Conf.*, **18**: 161–71.

Berkling, K.J., 1971: "A Computing Machine Based on Tree Structures." *IEEE Trans on Comp*, **C-20**, 4: 404–18.

Bershad, B.N., D.D. Redell, and J.R. Ellis, 1992: "Fast Mutual Exclusion for Uniprocessors." *Comput Archit News*, **20**, Special: 223–33.

Blaauw, G.A., 1952: *The Application of Selenium Rectifiers as Switching Devices in the Mark IV Calculator*. Ph.D. dissertation, Harvard University, Cambridge, MA.

Blaauw, G.A., 1959: "Indexing and Control-Word Techniques." *IBM J of Res and Dev*, **3**, 3: 288–301.

Blaauw, G.A., 1964: "The Structure of System/360, Part V, Multisystem Organization." *IBM Systems J*, **3**, 2: 181–95.

Blaauw, G.A. and F.P. Brooks, Jr., 1964: "Outline of the Logical Structure of System/360." *IBM Systems J*, **3**, 2: 119–35.

Blaauw, G.A., 1965: "Door de Vingers Zien." Inaugural Address, Technische Hogeschool Twente, Enschede, The Netherlands.

Blaauw, G.A., 1970: "Hardware Requirements for the Fourth Generation." In F. Gruenberger, *Fourth Generation Computers*. Englewood Cliffs, NJ: Prentice-Hall, 155–68.

Blaauw, G.A., 1971: "The Use of APL in Computer Design." In MC-25 Informatica Symposium. *Mathematical Centre Tracts* **37**. Amsterdam: Mathematical Centre.

Blaauw, G.A., 1972: "Computer Architecture." *Electronische Rechenanlagen*, **14**, 4: 154–59.

Blaauw, G.A., 1976: *Digital System Implementation*. Englewood Cliffs, NJ: Prentice-Hall.

Blaauw, G.A. and A.J.W. Duijvestijn, 1980: "The Use of the Inner-Product Operator of APL in Graph Applications." *Proc. of APL 80*. Amsterdam: North-Holland, 3–11.

Blake, R.P., 1977: "Exploring a Stack Architecture." *Computer*, **10**, 5: 30–39.

Blakernay, C.R., L.F. Cudney, and C.R. Eickhorn, 1967: "Design Characteristics of the 9020 System." *IBM Systems J*, **6**, 2: 80–94.

Bloch, E., 1959: "The Enginneering Design of the Stretch Computer." *Proc., IRE–AIEE–ACM 1959 Eastern Joint Computer Conf.*, **16**: 48–58.

Bloch, R.N., 1947: "Mark I Calculator." In *Proceedings of a Symposium on Large-Scale Digital Calculating Machinery*, 7–14 Jan. 1947. Cambridge, MA: Harvard University Press. Reprinted with additional introduction in MIT Press, 1985.

Blosk, R.T., 1960: "The Instruction Unit of the Stretch Computer." *Proc., IRE–AIEE–ACM 1960 Eastern Joint Computer Conf.*, **18**: 299–324.

Bock, R.C., 1963: "An Interrupt Control for the B5000 Data Processor." *Proc., AFIPS Fall Joint Computer Conf.*, **24**: 229–42.

Böhm, C. and A. Jacopini, 1966: "Flow Diagrams, Turing Machines, and Languages with Only Two Formation Rules." *CACM*, **9**, 5: 366–71.

Booth, A.D., 1951: "A Signed Binary Multiplication Technique." *Quarterly J of Applied Mathematics*, **4**, 2: 236–40.

Borgerson, B.R., M.L. Hanson, and P.A. Hartley, 1978: "The Evolution of the Sperry Univac 1100 Series: A History, Analysis, and Projection." *CACM*, **21**, 1 (Jan.): 25–43.

Bose, P. and E.S. Davidson, 1984: "Design of Instruction Set Architectures for Support of High-Level Languages." *Proc., 11th Ann Int Symp on Comp Arch, Comput Archit News*, **12**, 3: 198-207.

Bowden, B.V., ed., 1953: *Faster Than Thought: A Symposium on Digital Computing Machines*. London: Pittman.

Bowker, G. and R. Giordano, eds., 1993: "Special Issue on Computing in Manchester." *IEEE Ann Hist Comput*, **15**, 3: 6–62.

Bradlee, D.G., S.J. Eggers, and R.R. Henry, 1991: "The Effect on RISC Performance of Register Set Size and Structure versus Code Generation Strategy." *Comput Archit News*, **19**, 3: 330–39.

Brent, R.P., 1973: "On the Precision Attainable with Various Floating-Point Number Systems." *IEEE Trans on Comp*, **C-22**, 6: 601–07.

Bromley, A.G., 1982: "Charles Babbage's Analytical Engine, 1838." *IEEE Ann Hist Comput*, **4**, 3: 196–217.

Brooker, R.A., 1959: "Techniques for Dealing with Two-Level Storage." *Computer J*, **2**, 4: 189–94.

Brooker, R.A., 1970: "Influence of High-level Languages on Computer Design." *Proc. IEE*, **117**, 7: 1219–24.

Brooks, F.P., Jr., 1956: *The Analytic Design of Automatic Data Processing Systems*. Ph.D. Dissertation, Harvard University.

Brooks, F.P., Jr., 1957: "Multicase Binary Codes for Nonuniform Character Distributions." *IRE Convention Record*, 63–68.

Brooks, F.P. and D.W. Sweeney, 1957: "Program Interrupt System." U.S. Patent 3,048,332 (August 7, 1962, filed December 9, 1957).

Brooks, F.P., Jr., 1958: "A Program-Controlled Program Interruption System." *Proc., IRE–ACM–AIEE 1957 Eastern Joint Computing Conf.*, **12**: 128–32.

Brooks, F.P., Jr., G.A. Blaauw, and W. Buchholz, 1959: "Processing Data in Bits and Pieces." *Proc., International Conf. on Information Processing '59*, 375–82.

Brooks, F.P., Jr., 1962: "Advanced Computer Organization: Addressing." *Proc., IFIPS Congress '62*, 564.

Brooks, F.P., Jr. and K.E. Iverson, 1963: *Automatic Data Processing*. New York: Wiley.

Brooks, F.P., Jr., 1965: "The Future of Computer Architecture." *Proc., IFIPS Congress '65*, 87–91.

Brooks, F.P., Jr. and K.E. Iverson, 1969: *Automatic Data Processing, System/360 Edition*. New York: Wiley.

Brooks, F.P., Jr., 1975: *The Mythical Man-Month*. Reading, MA: Addison-Wesley. Twentieth-anniversary ed., 1995.

Brooks, F.P., Jr., 1976: "An overview of microprocessor architecture and software." *Euromicro Symposium on Microprocessing and Microprogramming*. Amsterdam: North-Holland Publishing Company, 1-3A.

Brooks, F.P., Jr., I.E. Sutherland, chairs, et al., 1995: *Evolving the High Performance Computing and Communications Initiative to Support the National Information Infrastructure*. Washington, National Academy Press.

Brown, D.T., E.L. Eibsen, and C.A. Thorn, 1972: "Channel and Direct Access Device Architecture." *IBM Systems J*, **11**, 3: 186–99.

Brown, J.L. et al., 1964: "IBM System/360 Engineering." *Proc., AFIPS Fall Joint Computer Conf.*, **26**: 205–32.

Buchholz, W., 1953: "The System Design of the IBM Type 701 Computer." *Proc. IRE*, **41**, 10: 99–104.

Buchholz, W., 1959: "Fingers or Fists (The Choice of Decimal or Binary Representation)." *CACM*, **2**, 12: 3–11.

Buchholz, W., ed., 1962: *Planning a Computer System*. New York: McGraw-Hill.

Buchholz, W., 1981: "The Origin of the Word 'Byte.' " *IEEE Ann Hist Comput*, **3**, 1: 72. Reprinted in **10**, 4 (1989): 340.

Buckle, J.K., 1978: *The ICL 2900 Series*. London: Macmillan.

Burks, A.W., H.H. Goldstine, and J. von Neumann, 1946: "Preliminary Discussion of the Logical Design of an Electronic Computing Instrument." Report to U.S. Army Ordnance Department. Also in A.H. Taub, ed., *Collected Works of John von Neumann*. New York: Macmillan, 1963; **5**: 34–79. Reprinted in Bell and Newell [1971], 92–119.

Burnett, G.J. and E.G. Coffman, 1970: "A Study of Interleaved Memory Systems." *Proc., AFIPS Spring Joint Computer Conf.*, **36**: 467–74.

Burr, W.E., A.H. Coleman, and W.R. Smith, 1977: "Overview of the Military Computer Family Architecture Selection." *Proc., AFIPS National Computer Conf.*, **46**: 131–38.

Burroughs Corporation, 1964: *Burroughs B5500 Reference Manual*. Detroit, MI.

Cajori, F., 1929: *A History of Mathematical Notations*. Chicago: Open Court.

Campbell, S.G., 1962: "Floating-Point Operation." In Buchholz [1962], 92–121.

Campbell, S.G., P.S. Herwitz, and J.H. Pomerene, 1962: "A Nonarithmetical System Extension." In Buchholz [1962], 254–71.

Campbell-Kelly, M., 1980a: "Programming the EDSAC: Early Programming Activity at the University of Cambridge." *IEEE Ann Hist Comput*, **2**, 1: 7–36.

Campbell-Kelly, M., 1980b: "Programming the Mark 1: Early Programming Activity at the University of Manchester." *IEEE Ann Hist Comput*, **2**, 2: 130–68.

Campbell-Kelly, M., 1981: "Programming the Pilot ACE: Early Programming at the National Physical Laboratory." *IEEE Ann Hist Comput*, **3**, 2: 133–62.

Campbell-Kelly, M., 1992a: "The Airy Tape: An Early Chapter in the History of Debugging." *IEEE Ann Hist Comput*, **14**, 4: 16–25.

Campbell-Kelly, M., ed., 1992b: "Computing at the University of Cambridge—Special Issue." *IEEE Ann Hist Comput*, **14**, 4: 8–58.

Campbell-Kelly, M., 1995: "ICL and the Evolution of the British Mainframe." *Computer J*, **38**, 5: 400–12.

Cardelli, L. and P. Wegner, 1985: "On Understanding Types, Data Abstraction, and Polymorphism." *Compt Surv*, **17**, 4: 471–522.

Carlson, C.B., 1963: "The Mechaninization of a Push-Down Stack." *Proc., AFIPS Fall Joint Computer Conf.*, **24**: 243–50.

Carr, J.W., III, 1959a: "Error Analysis in Floating-Point Arithmetic." *CACM*, **2**, 5: 10–15.

Carr, J.W., III, 1959b: "Univac Scientific (1103A) Instruction Logic." In Gamble et al. [1956], **2**: 77–83. Reprinted in Bell and Newell [1971], 205–08.

Carr, J.W. III, 1959c: "IBM 650 Instruction Logic." In Gamble et al. [1956], **2**: 93–98. Reprinted in Bell and Newell [1971], 220–23.

Casale, C.T., 1962: "Planning the CDC 3600." *Proc., AFIPS Fall Joint Computer Conf.*, **22**: 73–85.

Case, R.P., 1970: Personal communication.

Case, R.P. and A. Padegs, 1978: "Architecture of the IBM System/370." *CACM*, **21**, 1: 73–96.

Ceruzzi, P.E., 1981: "The Early Computers of Konrad Zuse, 1935 to 1945." *IEEE Ann Hist Comput*, **3**, 3: 241–62.

Chen, P.M. and D.A. Patterson, 1994: "A New Approach to I/O Performance Evaluation—Self-scaling I/O Benchmarks, Predicted I/O Performance." *ACM Trans Comput Syst*, **12**, 4: 308–39.

Chen, S., 1984: "Large-Scale and High-Speed Multiprocessor System for Scientific Applications." In Hwang [1984], 46–58.

Chen, T.C., 1964: "The Overlap Design of the IBM System/360 Model 92." *Proc., AFIPS Fall Joint Computer Conf.*, **26**: 73–80.

Chen, T.C., 1971: "Parallelism, Pipelining, and Computer Efficiency." *Computer Design*, **11**, 1: 69–74.

Chesley, G.D., 1971: "The Hardware-Implemented High-Level Machine Language for SYMBOL." *Proc., AFIPS Spring Joint Computer Conf.*, **38**: 563–74.

Chinal, J.P., 1972: "Some Comments on Postcorrections for Nonrestoring Division." *IEEE Trans on Comp*, **C-21**, 12: 67–91.

Christiansen, C., L. Kanter, and G.M. Monroe, 1957: "Input/output system." U.S. Patent 3,812,475, filed 1957; issued 1974.

Chu, Y., ed., 1975: *High Level Language Computer Architecture*. New York: Academic Press.

Clark, D.W. and H.M. Levy. 1982: "Measurement and Analysis of Instruction Use in the VAX-11/780." *Proc., 9th Ann Int Symp on Comp Arch, Comput Archit News*, **10**, 3: 9–17.

Clark, D.W., 1983: "Cache Performance in the VAX 11/780." *ACM Trans Comput Syst*, **1**, 1: 24–37.

Clayton, B.B., E.K. Dorf, and R.E. Fagen, 1964: "An Operating System and Programming Systems for the 6600." *Proc., AFIPS Fall Joint Computer Conf.*, **26**: 41–75.

Cocke, J. and H.G. Kolsky, 1959: "The Virtual Memory in the STRETCH Computer." *Proc., IRE–AIEE–ACM Eastern Joint Computer Conf.*, **16**: 82–93.

Cocke, J. and J.T. Schwartz, 1970: *Programming Languages and Their Compilers: Preliminary Notes*. 2nd rev. ed. Courant Institute of Mathematical Sciences.

Codd, E.F., E.S. Lowry, E. McDonough, and C.A. Scalzi, 1959: "Multiprogramming Stretch: Feasibility Considerations." *CACM*, **2**, 11: 13–17.

Cody, W.J., 1973: "Static and Dynamic Numerical Characteristics of Floating-Point Arithmetic." *IEEE Trans on Comp*, **C-22**, 6: 598–601.

Cody, W.J. and H. Kuki, 1973: "A Statistical Study of the Accuracy of Floating-Point Number Systems." *CACM*, **16**, 4: 223–30.

Cohen, D., 1981: "On Holy Wars and a Plea for Peace." *Computer*, **14**, 10: 48–54.

Colwell, R.P., C. Hitchcock, E. Jensen, H. Brinkley-Sprunt, and C. Kollar, 1985: "Computers, Complexity, and Controversy." *Computer*, **18**, 9: 8–19.

Colwell, R.P., E.F. Gehringer, and E.D. Jensen, 1988: "Performance Effects of Architectural Complexity in the Intel 432." *ACM Trans Comput Syst*, **6**, 3: 296–339.

Comerford, R., 1992: "How DEC Developed Alpha." *IEEE Spectrum*, **29**, 7 (July): 26–31.

Compagnie des Machines Bull, undated: *Idée Directrice du Gamma 60*. Reference manual. Paris, France.

Conti, C.J., 1964: "System Aspect: System/360 Model 92." *Proc., AFIPS Fall Joint Computer Conf.*, **26**: 81–95.

Conti, C.J., D.H. Gibson, and S.H. Pitkowsky, 1968: "Structural Aspects of the System/360 Model 85, Part I: General Organization." *IBM Systems J*, **7**, 1: 2–14.

Control Data Corporation, 1969: *Control Data 6400/6500/6600 Computer System Reference Manual*. Publication 60100000. St. Paul, Minnesota.

Conway, M.E., 1968: "How Do Committees Invent?" *Datamation*, **14**, 4: 28–31.

Corbato, F.J., M. Merwin-Daggett, and R.C. Daley, 1962: "An Experimental Time-Sharing System." *Proc., AFIPS Spring Joint Computer Conf.*, **21**: 335–44.

Cornyn, J.J., W.R. Smith, A.H. Coleman, and W.R. Svirsky, 1977: "Life Cost Models for Comparing Computer Family Architectures." *Proc., AFIPS National Computer Conf.*, **46**: 185–200.

Cowart, B.E., R. Rice, and S.F. Lundstrom, 1971: "The Physical Attributes and Testing Aspects of the SYMBOL System." *Proc., AFIPS Spring Joint Computer Conf.*, **38**: 589–600.

Cragon, H.C., 1979: "An Evaluation of Code Space Requirements and Performance of Various Architectures." *Comput Archit News*, **7**, 5: 5–21.

Crawford, J.H., 1986: "Architecture of the Intel 80386." *IEEE Micro*: 154–60.

Crawford, J.H., 1990: "The i486 CPU: Executing Instructions in One Clock Cycle." *IEEE Micro* (Feb.): 27–36.

Cray Research: *S Series Mainframe Reference Manual HR 0029*, 1984. Minnesota: Cray Research.

Croarken, M., 1993: "The Beginnings of the Manchester Computer Phenomenon: People and Influences." *IEEE Ann Hist Comput*, **15**, 3: 9–16.

Dahl, O.J., E.W. Dijkstra, and C.A.R. Hoare, 1972: *Structured Programming*. New York: Academic Press.

Dally, W.J. and J.T. Kajiya, 1985: "An Object Oriented Architecture." *Proc., 12th Ann Int Symp on Comp Arch*, 154–61.

Davidson, E., 1986: "A Broader Range of Possible Answers to the Issues Raised by RISC." *Proc. Spring COMPCON*.

Davies, P.M., 1972: "Readings in Microprogramming." *IBM Systems J*, **11**, 1: 16–40.

Davis, G.M., 1960: "The English Electric KDF9 Computer System." *Computer Bulletin* (December): 119–20.

Davis, N.C. and S.E. Goodman, 1978: "The Soviet Block's Unified System of Computers." *Compt Surv*, **10**, 2: 93–122.

Delesalle, P.D.M.R.M., 1981: "Introduction to a Taxonomy of Computer Architecture." In Workshop on Taxonomy in Computer Architecture, organized by IFIP WG.10.1. *Arbeitsberichte des Instituts für Mathematische Maschinen und Datenverarbeitung (Informatik)*, **14**, 8 (Dec.): 1–17, Erlangen.

Denning, P.J., 1968: "The Working Set Model for Program Behavior." *CACM*, **11**, 5: 323–33.

Denning, P.J., 1970: "Virtual Memory." *Compt Surv*, **2**, 3: 153–89.

Dennis, J.B., 1965: "Segmentation and the Design of Multiprogrammed Computer Systems." *JACM*, **12**, 4: 589–602.

Dennis, J.B. and Van Horn, E.C., 1966: "Programming Semantics for Multiprogrammed Computations." *CACM*, **9**, 3: 143–55.

Dennis, J.B. and D.P. Misunas, 1974: "A Preliminary Architecture for a Basic Data Flow Processor." *Proc., 2nd Ann Int Symp on Comp Arch, Comput Archit News*, **3**, 4: 126–32.

DeRosa, J.A., and H.M. Levy, 1987: "An Evaluation of Branch Architectures." *Proc., 14th Ann Int Symp on Comp Arch, Comput Archit News*, **15**, 2: 10–16.

Descartes, R., 1637: *Discourse on the Method of Rightly Conducting the Reason.* Translator, Laurence J. Lafleur. New York: Macmillan, 1960.

Diefendorff, K., 1994: "History of the Power PC Architecture." *Communications of the ACM*, **37**, 6: 28–33.

Digital Equipment Corporation, 1965: *PDP-8, A High Speed Digital Computer.* Form 5369 100-6/65. Maynard, MA.

Digital Equipment Corporation, 1971a: *PDP11/20, 15, r20 Processor Handbook.* Maynard, MA.

Digital Equipment Corporation, 1971b: *PDP11/45 Processor Handbook.* Maynard, MA.

Digital Equipment Corporation, 1973: *PDP11/45 Processor Handbook.* Maynard, MA.

Digital Equipment Corporation, 1977: *VAX11 Architecture Handbook.* Maynard, MA.

Digital Equipment Corporation, 1978: *VAX11/780 Hardware Handbook.* Maynard, MA.

Dijkstra, E.W., 1965: "Solution of a Problem in Concurrent Programming Control." *CACM*, **8**, 9: 569.

Dijkstra, E.W., 1968: "GOTO Statement Considered Harmful." *CACM*, **11**, 3: 147–48.

Dirac, J., 1963: "Test and Set Operation." Project memorandum, IBM Corporation.

Djordjevic, J., R.N. Ibbett, and F.H. Sumner, 1980a: "Evaluation of Some Proposed Name-Space Architectures Using ISPS." *Proc. IEE*, **127.E.4**: 120–25.

Djordjevic, J., R.N. Ibbett, and M.R. Barbacci, 1980b: "Evaluation of Computer Architecture Using ISPS." *Proc. IEE* **127.E.4**: 126–35.

Dollhoff, T., 1979: *16-Bit Microprocessor Architecture.* Reston, VA: Reston.

Doran, R.W., 1975: "The ICL 2900 Computer Architecture (Compared with the Burroughs B6700)." *Comput Archit News*, **4**, 3: 24.

Dreyfus, P., 1959a: "System Design of the Gamma 60." *Proc., AIEE–ACM–IRE 1958 Western Joint Computer Conf.*, **13**: 130–32.

Dreyfus, P., 1959b: "Programming Design Features of the GAMMA 60 Computer." *Proc., AIEE–ACM–IRE 1958 Eastern Joint Computer Conf.*, **14**: 174–81.

Drummond, M.E., 1973: *Evaluation and Measurement Techniques for Digital Computer Systems.* Englewood Cliffs, NJ: Prentice-Hall.

Dugan, R.J., 1983: "System/370 Extended Architecture: A Program View of the Channel Subsystem." *Proc., 10th Ann Int Symp on Comp Arch*, 270–76.

Dungworth, M., 1979: "The CRAY-1 Computer System." *Infotech State of the Art Report: Supercomputers*, **2**: 51–76.

Dunwell, S.W., 1957: "Design Objectives for the IBM Stretch Computer." *Proc., AIEE–ACM–IRE 1956 Eastern Joint Computer Conf.*, **10**: 20–22.

Eckert, J. P., Jr., J.R. Weiner, H.F. Welsh, and H.F. Mitchell, 1952: "The UNIVAC System." *Review of Electronic Digital Computers, Proc., AIEE–IRE 1951 Joint Computer Conf.*, 6–16.

Eckert, J.P., Jr., 1957: "Univac-Larc, the Next Step in Computer Design." *Proc., AIEE–ACM–IRE 1956 Eastern Joint Computer Conf.*, 16–20.

Eckert, J.P., Jr., J.C. Chu, A.B. Tonik, and W.F. Schmitt, 1959: "Design of Univac-LARC System: I." *Proc., IRE–AIEE–ACM 1959 Eastern Joint Computer Conf.*, **16**: 59–65.

Edwards, D.B.G., A.E. Knowles, and J.V. Woods, 1980: "MU6-G: A New Design to Achieve Mainframe Performance from a Mini-Sized Computer." *Proc., 7th Ann Int Symp on Comp Arch, Comput Archit News*, **8**, 3: 161–67.

EEC-KDF, 1966: *KDF9—Programming Manual*. Publication number 1000168. Kidsgrove, UK: English Electric Computers.

Eickemeyer, R.J., and J.H. Patel, 1987: "Performance Evaluation of Multiple Register Sets." *Proc., 14th Ann Int Symp on Comp Arch, Comput Archit News*, **15**, 2: 264–71.

Eidgenösse Technische Hochschule–Zürich, Institute for Applied Mathematics, 1952: *User Manual Z4* (German). Zürich: Eidgenösse Technische Hochschule.

Elzen, B. and D. Mackenzie, 1991: "The Charismatic Engineer—Seymour Cray and the Development of Supercomputing." *Jaarboek voor de Geschiedenis van Bedrijf en Techniek*, **8**.

Elzen, B. and D. Mackenzie, 1994: "The Social Limits of Speed: the Development and Use of Supercomputers." *IEEE Ann Hist Comput*, **16**, 1: 46–61.

Emer, J.S. and D.W. Clark, 1984: "A Characterization of Processor Performance in the VAX-11/780." *Proc., 11th Ann Int Symp on Comp Arch, Comput Archit News*, **12**, 3: 301–11.

England, E.M., 1975: "Capability Concept, Mechanism, and Structure in System 250." *Revue Française d'Automatique, Informatique et Recherche Operationelle*, **9.B.3**: 47–62.

Enslow, P.H., Jr., 1974: *Multiprocessors and Parallel Processing*. New York: John Wiley.

Ercegovac, M.D., 1973: "Radix-16 Evaluation of Certain Elementary Functions." *IEEE Trans on Comp*, **C-22**, 6: 561–66.

Ershov, A.P., 1980: *The British Lectures*. Philadelphia: Hayden.

Esch, R. and P. Calingaert, 1957: *Univac I, Central Computer Programming*. Cambridge, MA: Harvard University Computation Laboratory.

Evans, B.O., 1986: "System/360: A Retrospective view." *Ann Hist Comput*, **8**, 2: 155–79.

Everett, R.R., 1952: "The Whirlwind I Computer." *Review of Electronic Digital Computers, Proc., AIEE–IRE 1951 Joint Computer Conf.*, 70–75.

Fabry, R.S., 1974: "Capability-Based Addressing." *CACM*, **17**, 7: 403–12.

Faggin, F. and M.E. Hoff, 1972: "Standard Parts and Custom Design Merge in Four-Chip Processor Kit." *Electronics* (April).

Falkoff, A.D., K.E. Iverson, and E.H. Sussenguth, 1964: "A Formal Description of System/360." *IBM Systems J*, **3**, 3: 198–261.

Fatheringham, I., 1961: "Dynamic Storage Allocation in the Atlas Computer Including an Automatic Use of a Backing Store." *CACM*, **4**, 10: 435–36.

Feeney, H., 1974: "A New Microcomputer Family." *WESCON Technical Papers*, **15**, 1.

Fernbach, S., ed., 1986: *Supercomputers: Class VI systems, Hardware, and Software*. Amsterdam: North-Holland.

Ferrari, D., G. Serazzi, and G. Zeigner, 1983: *Measurement and Tuning of Computer Systems*. Englewood Cliffs, NJ: Prentice-Hall.

Feustel, E.A., 1972: "The Rice Research Computer: A Tagged Architecture." *Proc., AFIPS Spring Joint Computer Conf.*, **40**: 369–77.

Feustel, E.A., 1973: "On the Advantages of Tagged Architectures." *IEEE Trans on Comp*, **C-22**, 7: 644–52.

Flynn, M.J., 1966: "Very High-Speed Computing Systems." *Proc. IEEE*, **54**, 12: 1901–09.

Flynn, M.J., 1972a: "Some Computer Organizations and Their Effectiveness." *IEEE Trans on Comp*, **C-21**, 9: 948–60.

Flynn, M.J., 1972b: "Towards More Efficient Computer Organizations." *Proc., AFIPS Spring Joint Computer Conf.*, **40**: 1211–17.

Flynn, M.J., 1974: "Trends and Problems in Computer Organization." *Proc., IFIPS Congress*, 3–10.

Flynn, M.J., 1975: "Microprogramming—Another Look at Internal Computer Control." *Proc. IEEE*, **63**, 11: 1554–67.

Flynn, M.J., 1977: "The Interpretive Interface: Resources and Program Representation in Computer Organization." In D.J. Kuck, D.H. Lawrie, and A.H. Sameh [1977], 41–69.

Flynn, M.J., 1980: "Directions and Issues in Architecture and Language." *Computer*, **13**, 10: 5–22.

Flynn, M.J., J.D. Johnson, and S.P. Wakefield, 1985: "On Instruction Sets and Their Formats." *IEEE Trans on Comp*, **C-34**, 3: 242–54.

Flynn, M.J., 1995: *Computer Architecture: Pipelined and Parallel Processor Design*. Boston: Jones and Bartlett.

Forgie, J.W., 1957: "The Lincoln TX-2 Input–Output System." *Proc., IRE–AIEE–ACM 1957 Western Joint Computer Conf.*, **11**: 156–60.

Frankel, S.P., 1957: "Logical Design of a General-Purpose Computer (LGP-30)." *IRE Transactions on Electronic Computers*, **EC-6**, 1: 5–14.

Frankovich, J.M. and H.P. Peterson, 1957: "A Functional Description of the Lincoln TX-2 Computer." *Proc., IRE–AIEE–ACM 1957 Western Joint Computer Conf.*, **11**: 146–55.

Frizzell, C.E., 1953: "Engineering Design of the IBM Type 701 Computer." *Proc. IRE*: 1275–87.

Fuchs, H. and J. Poulton, 1985: "Parallel Processing in Pixel-Planes, a VLSI Logic-Enhanced Memory for Raster Graphics." *Proc. of ICCD '85, IEEE Conf. on Computer Design*, 193–97.

Fuller, S.H., 1976: "Price/Performance of C.mmp and the PDP-10." *Proc., 3rd Ann Int Symp on Comp Arch, Comput Archit News*, **4**, 4: 195–202.

Fuller, S.H., P. Shaman, D. Lamb, and W.E. Burr, 1977a: "Evaluation of Computer Architectures via Test Programs." *AFIPS National Computer Conf.*, **46**: 147–60.

Fuller, S.H., H.S. Stone, and W.E. Burr, 1977b: "Initial Selection and Screening of CFA Candidate Computer Architectures." *AFIPS National Computer Conf.*, **46**: 139–46.

Fuller, S.H. and W.E. Burr, 1977c: "Measurement and Evaluation of Alternative Computer Architectures." *Computer*, **10**, 10: 24–35.

Gamble, E.M., S. Ramo, and D.E. Wooldridge, eds., 1959: *Handbook of Automation, Computation and Control*. 2 vols. New York: Wiley.

Garner, H.L., 1959: "The Residue Number System." *IRE Transactions on Electronic Computers*, **EC-8**, 6: 140–47.

Garner, H.L., 1965: "Number Systems and Arithmetic." In F.L. Alt, ed., *Advances in Computers*. New York: Academic Press, 131–94.

Garner, H.L., 1976: "A Survey of Some Recent Contributions to Computer Arithmetic." *IEEE Trans on Comp*, **C-25**, 12: 1277–82.

Geerdink, W.J.M., 1975: Master's thesis. Technische Hogeschool Twente, Enschede, The Netherlands.

Gehringer, E.F. and J.L. Keedy, 1985: "Tagged Architecture: How Compelling Are Its Advantages?" *Proc., 12th Ann Int Symp on Comp Arch*, 162–70.

Gehringer, E.F. and R.P. Colwell, 1986: "Fast Object-Oriented Procedure Calls: Lessons from the Intel 432." *Proc., 13th Ann Int Symp on Comp Arch, Comput Archit News*, **14**, 2: 92–102.

Gentleman, W.M. and S.B. Marovich, 1974: "More on Algorithms that Reveal Properties of Floating-Point Arithmetic Units." *CACM*, **17**, 5: 276–77.

Gibson, C.T., 1966: "Time-Sharing with IBM System/360: Model 67." *Proc., AFIPS Spring Joint Computer Conf.*, 61–78.

Gifford, D., A. Spector, R. Case, and A. Padegs, 1987: "Case Study: IBM's System/360–370 Architecture." *CACM*, **30**, 4: 291–307.

Gill, S., 1958: "Parallel Programming." *Computer J*, **1**, 1: 2–10.

Giloi, W.K., 1983: "Towards a Taxonomy of Computer Architecture Based on the Machine Data Type View." *Proc., 10th Ann Int Symp on Comp Arch*, 6–15.

Gogliardi, U.O., 1973: "Report on Software Related Advances in Computer Hardware." *Proc. of a Symposium on the High Cost of Software*. Menlo Park, CA: Stanford Research Institute.

Goldberg, D., 1990: "Computer Arithmetic." In Hennessy and Patterson [1990], Appendix A.

Goldberg, D., 1991: "What Every Computer Scientist Should Know about Floating-Point Arithmetic." *Compt Surv*, **23**, 1: 5–48.

Goldberg, I.B., 1967: "Twenty-Seven Bits Are Not Enough for 8-Digit Accuracy." *CACM*, **10**, 2: 105–06.

Goldstein, M., 1963: "Significance Arithmetic on a Digital Computer." *CACM*, **6**, 3: 111–17.

Gordon, B., 1956: "An Optimizing Program For the IBM 650." *JACM*, **3**, 1: 3–5.

Graham, G.S. and P.J. Denning, 1972: "Protection—Principles and Practice." *Proc., AFIPS Spring Joint Computer Conf.*, **41**, 1: 417–30.

Grau, A.A., 1962: "On a Floating-Point Number Representation for Use with Algorithmic Languages." *CACM*, **5**: 160–61.

Gray, L.H. and J.C. Harrison, 1959: "Normalized Floating-Point Arithmetic with an Index of Significance." *Proc., IRE–AIEE–ACM 1959 Eastern Joint Computing Conf.*, **16**: 244–48.

Greenstadt, J.L., 1957: "The IBM 709 Computer." *New Computers, Reprinted from the Manufacturers' ACM Conf.*, 92–98.

Gregory, Y. and R.M. Reynolds, 1963: "The Solomon Computer." *IEEE Trans on Comp*, **EC-12**, 6: 774–81.

Gries, D., 1978: "Data Types." In D. Gries, ed., *Programming Methodology: A Collection of Aricles by Members of IFIP WG2.3*. New York: Springer-Verlag, 263–68.

Gross, T., 1985: "Floating-Point Arithmetic on a Reduced-Instruction-Set Computer." In *Proc. 7th Symp. on Comp. Arithmetic*, ed. K. Hwang. Washington: IEEE Computer Society Press, 86–92.

Grumette, M., 1958: "IBM 704 Code Nundrums." *CACM*, **1**, 3: 3–13.

Gustafson, J.L., 1988: "Reevaluating Amdahl's Law." *CACM*, **31**, 5 (May): 532–33.

Hall, J.A. and P.T. Robinson, 1991: "Virtualizing the VAX Architecture." *Comput Archit News*, **19**: 380–89.

Hammerstrom, D.W. and E.S. Davidson, 1977: "Information Content of CPU Memory Referencing Behaviour." *Proc., 4th Ann Int Symp on Comp Arch, Comput Archit News*, **5**, 7: 184–92.

Händler, W., 1975: *Lecture Notes in Computer Science 26*. Berlin: Springer, 439–52.

Hansen, E., 1965: "Interval Arithmetic in Matrix Computation." *J SIAM–Numer Anal*, Ser. B, **2**, 2: 308–20.

Hauck, E.A. and B.A. Dent, 1968: "Burroughs B6500/B7500 Stack Mechanism." *Proc., AFIPS Spring Joint Computer Conf.*, **32**: 245–54.

Hayashi, H., A. Hattori, and H. Akimoto, 1983: "ALPHA: A High-Performance LISP Machine Equipped with a New Stack Structure and Garbage Collection System." *Proc., 10th Ann Int Symp on Comp Arch*, 342–48.

Hellerman, H. 1972: *Digital Computer System Principles*. 2nd ed. New York: McGraw-Hill.

Hellerman, H. and H.J. Smith, Jr., 1970: "Throughput Analysis of Some Idealized Input, Output, and Compute Overlap Configurations." *Compt Surv*, **2**, 2: 111–18.

Hennessy, J. and D.A. Patterson, 1990: *Computer Architecture: A Quantitative Approach*. San Mateo, CA: Morgan Kaufmann.

Herwitz, P.S. and J.H. Pomerene, 1960: "The Harvest System." *Proc., IRE–AIEE–ACM 1960 Western Joint Computer Conf.*, **17**: 23–32.

Hintz, R.G. and D.P. Tate, 1972: "Control Data STAR-100 Processor Design." *Proc., Fall COMPCON*, 1–4.

Hockney, R.W. and C.R. Jesshope, 1981: *Parallel Computers*. Bristol, UK: Adam Hilger.

Hoff, M.E., 1970: "Impact of LSI on Future Microcomputers." *IEEE National Convention Digest*, IEEE.

Hoff, M.E., 1972: "The One-Chip CPU—Computer or Component?" *WESCON*.

Hoffnagle, G.F., 1991: "Special Issue on APL." *IBM Systems J*, **30**, 4.

Hord, R.M., 1982: *ILLIAC IV: The First Supercomputer*. Rockville, MD: Computer Science Press.

Houdek, M.E., F.G. Soltis, and R.L. Hoffman, 1981: "IBM System/38 Support for Capability-Based Addressing." *Proc., 8th Ann Int Symp on Comp Arch, Comput Archit News*, **9**, 3: 341–48.

Howarth, D.J., R.B. Payne, and F.H. Sumner, 1961: "The Manchester University Atlas Operating System, Part II: User's Description." *Computer J*, **4**, 3: 226–29.

Huck, J.C. and M.J. Flynn, 1983: "A Comparative Analysis of Computer Architectures." *Proc., IFIPS Congress*, 699–703.

Huffman, D.A., 1952: "A Method for the Construction of Minimum Redundancy Codes." *Proc. IRE*, **40**: 1094–1101.

Hughes, E.S., 1954: "The IBM Magnetic Drum Calculator Type 650—Engineering and Design Considerations." *Proc., AIEE–IRE–ACM 1954 Western Joint Computer Conf.*, 140–54.

Hunt, J.G., 1980: "Interrupts." *Software Practice and Experience*, **10**, 7 (July): 523–30.

Hurd, C.C., ed., 1983: "Special Issue: IBM 701." *Ann Hist Comput*, **5**, 2: 110–219.

Hurd, C.C., ed., 1986: "Special Issue: IBM 650." *Ann Hist Comput*, **8**, 1: 3–88.

Husson, S.S., 1970: *Microprogramming: Principles and Practices.* Englewood Cliffs, NJ: Prentice-Hall.

Hwang, K., 1979: *Computer Arithmetic.* New York: Wiley.

Hwang, K., S.-P. Su, and L.M. Ni, 1981: "Vector Computer Architecture and Processing Techniques." In M.C. Yovits, ed., *Advances in Computers.* New York: Academic Press, 115–97.

Hwang, K., 1984: *Supercomputers: Design and Application.* Silver Spring, MD: IEEE Computer Society Press.

Hwang, K. and F.A. Briggs, 1984: *Computer Architecture and Parallel Processing.* New York: McGraw-Hill.

Ibbett, R.N. and N.P. Topham, 1989: *Architecture of High Performance Computers.* 2 vols. New York: Springer-Verlag.

IBM Corporation, 1953: *Principles of Operation Type 701 and Associated Equipment.* Form 24-6042-2. New York.

IBM Corporation, 1955a: *IBM Electronic Data-Processing Machines Type 704 Manual of Operation.* Form 24-6661-0. New York.

IBM Corporation, 1955b: *Manual of Operation, Type 650 Magnetic Drum Data-Processing Machine.* Form 22-6060-1. New York.

IBM Corporation, 1956: *Programmer's Reference Manual, The FORTRAN Automatic Coding System for the IBM 704 EDPM.* New York.

IBM Corporation, 1959a: *IBM 705 Data Processing System.* Form A22-6506-0. New York.

IBM Corporation, 1959b: *General Information Manual, 1401 Data Processing System.* Form D24-1401-0 9/59. New York.

IBM Corporation, 1961: *Reference Manual, 7030 Data Processing System.* Form A22-6530. White Plains, N.Y.

IBM Corporation, 1964: *Operating System/360, Concepts and Facilities.* Form GC28-6535. New York.

IBM Corporation, undated: *System/370 Extended Architecture Principles of Operation.* Armonk, NY: IBM Corp.

IBM Corporation, 1965: *System/370 Principles of Operation.* Armonk, NY: IBM Corp.

IBM Corporation, 1967: *IBM System/360 Principles of Operation.* Form A22-6821-6. New York.

IBM Corporation, 1988: *System/370 Enterprise Systems Architecture Principles of Operation.* Armonk, NY: IBM Corp.

IBM Corporation: *IBM RP3-PE Functional Specification* (undated technical memorandum).

IEEE, 1987: "IEEE Standard 754-1985 for Binary Floating-Point Arithmetic." *SIGPLAN*, **22**, 2: 9–25.

IEEE Floating-Point Standard, *see* D. Stevenson [1981].

Iliffe, J.K., 1972: *Basic Machine Principles*. 2nd ed. London: Macdonald.

Iliffe, J.K., 1982: *Advanced Computer Design*. Englewood Cliffs, NJ: Prentice-Hall.

Intel Corporation, 1981: *iAPX 432 General Data Processor Architectural Reference Manual*. Santa Clara, CA: Intel Corp.

Iverson, K.E., 1962: *A Programming Language*. New York: Wiley.

Iverson, K.E., 1987: "A Dictionary of APL." *APL Quote Quad*, **18**, 1 (Sep.): 5–40.

Johnson, M., 1982: "Some Requirements for Architectural Support of Software Debugging." *First Symposium on Architectural Support for Programming Languages and Operating Systems, Comput Archit News*, **10**, 2: 140–48.

Johnson, P.M., 1978: "An Introduction to Vector Processing." *Computer Design*, **17**, 2: 89–97.

Joseph, M., 1970: "An Analysis of Paging and Program Behaviour." *Computer J*, **13**, 1: 48–54.

Kain, R.Y., 1996: *Advanced Computer Architecture: A System Design Approach*. Englewood Cliffs, NJ: Prentice-Hall.

Karin, S. and N.P. Smith, 1987: *The Supercomputer Era*. Boston: Harcourt Brace Jovanovich.

Kassel, L., 1959: *George Programming Model*. Report ANL-5995. Argonne National Laboratory.

Katevenis, M., 1983: *Reduced Instruction Set Computer Architectures for VLSI*. Ph.D. Dissertation, University of California, Berkeley. Reprinted by MIT Press, 1985.

Keedy, J.L. 1979: "A Problem With the Test and Set Instruction." *Operating Systems Review*, **13**, 4: 1.

Keedy, J.L., K. Ramamohanarao, and J. Rosenberg, 1979: "On Implementing Semaphores with Sets." *Computer J*, **22**, 2: 146–50.

Keeley, J.F., 1967: "An Application-Oriented Multiprocessing System." *IBM Systems J*, **6**, 2: 78–132.

Kent, J.G., 1977: "Highlights of a Study of Floating-Point Instructions." *IEEE Trans on Comp*, **C-26**, 7: 660–66.

Kilburn, T., 1949a: "The Manchester University Digital Computing Machine." *Report of a Conf. on High Speed Automatic Calculating Machines*, 119–22.

Kilburn, T., 1949b: "The University of Manchester High-Speed Digital Computing Machine." *Nature*, **164**: 684.

Kilburn, T., D.B.G. Edwards, and C.E. Thomas, 1956: "The Manchester University Mark II Digital Computing Machine." *Proc. IEE*, **103.B.2**: 247–68.

Kilburn, T., D.J. Howarth, and R.B. Payne, 1961a: "The Manchester University Atlas Operating System, Part I: Internal Organization." *Computer J*, **4**, 3: 222–25.

Kilburn, T., R.B. Payne, and D.J. Howarth, 1961b: "The Atlas Supervisor." *Proc., AFIPS Eastern Joint Computer Conf.*, **20**: 279–94.

Kilburn, T., D.B.G. Edwards, M.J. Lanigan, and F.H. Sumner, 1962: "One-Level Storage System." *IRE Transactions on Electronic Computers*, **EC-11**, 2: 223–35. Reprinted in Bell and Newell [1971], 276–90.

Kinslow, H.A., 1964: "The Time-Sharing Monitor System." *Proc., AFIPS Fall Joint Computer Conf.*, **26**, 1: 443–54.

Kiseda, J.R., H.E. Petersen, W.C. Seelbach and M. Teig, 1961: "A Magnetic Associative Memory." *IBM J of Res and Dev*, **5**, 2: 106–21.

Knoblock, D.E., D.C. Loughry, and C.A. Vissers, 1975: "Insight Into Interfacing." *IEEE Spectrum*, **12**, 5: 50–57.

Knuth, D.E., 1968: *The Art of Computer Programming*. Reading, MA: Addison-Wesley.

Knuth, D.E. and G.S. Rao, 1975: "Activity in Interleaved Memory." *IEEE Trans on Comp*, **C-24**, 9: 943–44.

Knuth, D.E., 1981: *The Art of Computer Programming*, 3 vols. 2nd edition. Reading, MA: Addison-Wesley.

Kuck, D.J., 1968: "ILLIAC IV Software and Application Programming." *IEEE Trans on Comp*, **C-17**, 8: 758–70.

Kuck, D.J., D.S. Parker, and A.H. Sameh, 1977: "Analysis of Rounding Methods in Floating-Point Arithmetic." *IEEE Trans on Comp*, **C-26**, 7: 643–50.

Kuck, D.J., D.H. Lawrie, and A.H. Sameh, eds., 1977. *High Speed Computer and Algorithm Organization*. New York: Academic Press.

Kuck, D.J., 1978: *The Structure of Computers and Computations*, **1**. New York: Wiley.

Kuki, H. and J. Ascoly, 1971: "FORTRAN Extended-Precision Library." *IBM Systems J*, **10**, 1: 39–61.

Kulish, U., 1977: "Mathematical Foundation of Computer Arithmetic." *IEEE Trans on Comp*, **C-26**, 7: 610–20.

Kung, H.T., 1982: "Why Systolic Architectures?" *Computer*, **15**, 1: 37–46.

Kunkel, S.R. and A.J. Smith, 1986: "Optimal Pipelining in Supercomputers." *Proc., 13th Ann Int Symp on Comp Arch, Comput Archit News*, **14**, 2: 404–11.

Lamport, L., 1987: "A Fast Mutual Exclusion Algorithm." *ACM Trans Comput Syst*, **5**, 1 (Feb.): 1–11.

Lampson, B.W., 1969: "Dynamic Protection Structures." *Proc., AFIPS Fall Joint Computer Conf.*, **35**: 27–38.

Lampson, B.W., 1982: "Fast Procedure Calls." *First Symposium on Architectural Support for Programming Languages and Operating Systems, Comput Archit News*, **10**, 2: 66–76.

Lampson, B.W., G. McDaniel, and S.M. Ornstein, 1984: "An Instruction Fetch Unit for a High-Performance Personal Computer." *IEEE Trans on Comp*, **C-33**, 8: 712–30.

Lavington, S.H., 1975: *A History of Manchester Computers*. Manchester, UK: National Computer Center.

Lavington, S.H., 1977: "Assessing the Power of an Order Code." *Proc., IFIPS Congress*, 477–80.

Lavington, S.H., 1978: "The Manchester Mark I and Atlas: A Historical Perspective." *CACM*, **21**, 1: 4–12.

Lavington, S.H., 1980: *Early British Computers*. Bedford, MA: Digital Press.

Lavington, S.H., 1993: "Manchester Computer Architectures, 1948–1975." *IEEE Ann Hist Comput*, **15**, 3: 44–54.

Leclerc, B., 1990: "From Gamma 2 to Gamma E.T.: The Birth of Electronic Computing at Bull." *IEEE Ann Hist Comput*, **12**, 1: 5–22.

Leventhal, L.A. 1978: *8080A/8085 Assembly Language Programming*. Berkeley, CA: Osborne/McGraw-Hill.

Leventhal, L.A., 1979: *6502 Assembly Language Programming.* Berkeley, CA: Osborne/McGraw-Hill.

Levy, H.M. and R.H. Eckhouse, 1980: *Computer Architecture and Programming, The VAX-11.* Bedford, MA: Digital Press.

Levy, H.M., 1984: *Capability-Based Computer Systems.* Bedford, MA: Digital Press.

Lilja, D.J. and P.L. Bird, eds., 1994: *The Interaction of Compilation Technology and Computer Architecture.* Boston: Kluwer.

Lincoln, N.R., 1977: "It's Really Not As Much Fun Building a Supercomputer As It Is Simply Inventing One." In D.J. Kuck, D.H. Lawrie, and A.H. Sameh [1977], 3–11.

Lindgren, M., 1987: *Glory and Failure: The Difference Engines of Johann Müller, Charles Babbage and George and Edvard Scheutz.* Linköping, Sweden: Linköping Studies in Art and Science. Also Cambridge, MA: MIT Press, 1990.

Lonergan, W. and P. King, 1961: "The Burroughs B-5000." *Datamation* **7**, 5: 28–32. Reprinted in Bell and Newell [1971], 267–73.

Lukasiewicz, J., 1951 *Aristotle's Syllogistic Form from the Standpoint of Modern Formal Logic.* Oxford: Clarendon Press.

Lukoff, H., L.M. Spandorfer, and F.F. Lee, 1959: "Design of the Univac-LARC System: II." *Proc., IRE–AIEE–ACM 1959 Eastern Joint Computer Conf.*, **16**: 66–74.

Lukoff, H., 1979: *From Dits to Bits. A Personal History of the Electronic Computer.* Portland, OR: Robotics Press.

Lunde, A., 1977: "Empirical Evaluation of Some Features of Instruction Set Processor Architectures." *CACM*, **20**, 3: 143–53.

MacDougall, M., 1984: "Instruction-Level Program and Processor Modeling." *Computer*, **17**, 7 14–23.

MacKenzie, C.E., 1980: *Coded Character Sets, History and Development.* Reading, MA: Addison-Wesley.

MacKenzie, D., 1991: "The Influence of Los Alamos and Livermore National Laboratories on the Development of Supercomputing." *Ann Hist Comput*, **13**: 179–201.

Maher, R.J., 1961: "Problems of Storage Allocation in a Multiprocessor Multiprogrammed System." *CACM*, **4**, 10: 421–22.

Malcolm, M.A., 1972: "Algorithms to Reveal Properties of Floating-Point Arithmetic." *CACM*, **15**, 11: 949–51.

Mangione-Smith, B., 1994: "Register Requirements for High Performance Code Scheduling." In Lilja and Bird [1994], 51–86.

Marczynski, R.W., 1980: "The First Seven Years of Polish Digital Computers." *IEEE Ann Hist Comput*, **2**, 1: 37–48.

Mattson, R.L., J. Geisei, D.R. Slutz and I.L. Traiger, 1970: "Evaluation Techniques for Storage Hierarchies." *IBM Systems J* **9**, 2: 78–117.

Matula, D.W., 1967: "In-and-Out Conversions." *CACM*, **11**, 1: 47–50.

Maurer, W.D., 1966: "A Theory of Computer Instructions." *JACM*, **13**, 2: 226–35.

McCarthy, J., 1960: "Recursive Functions of Symbolic Expressions and Their Computation by Machine, Part I." *CACM*, **3** (April): 184–95. Reprinted in Rosen [1967], 455–80.

McCracken, D., 1957: *Digital Computer Programming.* New York: Wiley.

McDaniel, G., 1982: "An Analysis of a Meta Instruction Set using Dynamic Instruction Frequencies." *First Symposium on Architectural Support for Programming Languages and Operating Systems, Comput Archit News*, **10**, 2: 167–76.

McGee, W.C., 1965: "On Dynamic Program Relocation." *IBM Systems J*, **4**, 3: 184–99.

McKeeman, W.M., 1967: "Representation Error for Real Numbers in Binary Computer Arithmetic." *IEEE Trans on Comp*, **EC-16**, 5: 682–83.

Meggitt, J.E., 1962: "Pseudo Divisions and Pseudo Multiplication Processes." *IBM J of Res and Dev*, **6**, 2: 210–26.

Melbourne, A.J. and J.M. Pugmire, 1965: "A Small Computer for Direct Processing of Fortran Statements." *Computer J*, **8**, 4: 24–27.

Mersel, J., 1956: "Program Interrupt on the Univac Scientific Computer." *Proc., AIEE–ACM–IRE 1956 Western Joint Computer Conf.*, **9**: 52–53.

Metropolis, N. and R.L. Ashenhurst, 1958: "Significant Digit Computer Arithmetic." *IRE Transactions on Electronic Computers*, **EC-7** (Dec.): 265–67.

Metropolis, N. and R.L. Ashenhurst, 1963: "Basic Operations in an Unnormalized Arithmetic System." *IEEE Trans on Comp*, **EC-12**: 896–904.

Metropolis, N. and J. Worlton, 1980: "A Trilogy of Errors in the History of Computing." *IEEE Ann Hist Comput*, **2**, 1: 49–59.

Metropolis, N., J. Howlett, and G. Rota, eds., 1980: *A History of Computing in the 20th Century*. New York: Academic Press.

Mills, H., 1971: "Chief Programmer Teams, Principles, Procedures." *IBM Federal Systems Division Report*, FSC 71-5108, Gaithersburg, MD.

Minter, C.R., 1980: *A Processor Design for the Efficient Implementation of APL*. New York: Garland.

Mitchell, C.L. and M.J. Flynn, 1990: "The Effects of Processor Architecture on Instruction Memory Traffic." *ACM Trans Comput Syst*, **8**, 3: 230–50.

Miura, K., 1986: "Supercomputing in Japan." *Proc. of Tenth IFIP Congress*, 557–74.

Moore, R.E., 1966: *Interval Analysis*. Englewood Cliffs, NJ: Prentice Hall.

Moore, B.B., A. Padegs, R. Smith, and W. Buchholz, 1987: "Concepts of the System/370 Vector Architecture." *Proc., 14th Ann Int Symp on Comp Arch, Comput Archit News*, **15**, 2: 282–88.

Morris, D. and R.N. Ibbett, 1979: *The MU5 Computer System*. New York: Springer-Verlag.

Morris, R., 1971: "Tapered Floating-Point. A New Floating-Point Representation." *IEEE Trans on Comp*, **C-20**, 12: 1578–79.

Morse, S.P., W.B. Pohlman, and B.W. Ravenel, 1978: "The Intel 8086 Microprocessor: A 16-Bit Evolution of the 8080." *Computer*, **11**, 6: 18–27.

Morse, S.P., B.W. Ravenel, S. Mazor, and W.B. Pohlman, 1980: "Intel Microprocessors—8008 to 8086." *Computer*, **13**, 10: 42–60.

Motorola Semiconductor Products, Inc., 1975a: *Microprocessor Applications Manual*. Austin, TX: Motorola Semiconductor Products.

Motorola Semiconductor Products, Inc., 1975b: *M6800 Microprocessor Programming Manual*. Austin, TX: Motorola Semiconductor Products.

Motorola Semiconductor Products, Inc., 1982: *MC68000 16-bit Microprocessor User's Manual*. 3rd ed. Austin, TX: Motorola Semiconductor Products.

Myers, G.J., 1977a: "The Case Against Stack-Oriented Instruction Sets." *Comput Archit News*, **6**, 3: 7–10.

Myers, G.J., 1977b: *The Design of Computer Architectures to Enhance Software Reliability.* Ph.D. dissertation, Polytechnic Institute of New York.

Myers, G.J., 1978: *Advances in Computer Architecture.* New York: Wiley.

Myers, G.J., 1982: *Advances in Computer Architecture, Second Edition.* New York: Wiley.

Naur, P., ed., 1963: "Revised Report on the Algorithmic Language ALGOL60." *CACM*, **6**, 1: 1–17. Reprinted in Rosen [1967], 79–117.

Needham, R.M. and W.T. Wilner, 1972: "Protection Systems and Protection Implementations" *Proc., AFIPS Fall Joint Computer Conf.*, **41**, 1: 571–78.

Needham, R.M. and R.D.H. Walker, 1977: "The Cambridge CAP Computer and Its Protection System." *Proc., 6th ACM Symposium on Operating System Principles*, 1–10.

Needham, R.M., 1992: "Later Developments at Cambridge: Titan, CAP, and the Cambridge Ring." *IEEE Ann Hist Comput*, **14**, 4: 57–58.

Nicolau, A. and J.A. Fisher, 1984: "Measuring the Parallelism Available for Very Long Instruction Word Architectures." *IEEE Trans on Comp*, **C-33**, 11: 968–76.

Nievergelt, J. and M.I. Irland, 1970: "Bounce-And-Skip: A Technique for Directing the Flow of Control in Programs." *Computer J*, **13**, 3: 261–62.

Norton, R.L. and J.A. Abraham, 1983: "Adaptive Interpretation as a Means of Exploiting Complex Instruction Sets." *Proc., 11th Ann Int Symp on Comp Arch, Comput Archit News*, **12**, 3: 277–83.

Oblonsky, J.G., 1980: "Antonin Svoboda, 1907–1980." *IEEE Ann Hist Comput*, **2**, 4: 289.

Omondi, A.R., 1994: *Computer Arithmetic Systems: Algorithms, Architecture, and Implementation.* Englewood Cliffs, NJ: Prentice-Hall.

Organick, E.I., 1972: *The Multics System: An Examination of Its Structure.* Cambridge, MA: MIT Press.

Organick, E.I., 1973: *Computer System Organization: The B5700/6700 Series.* New York: Academic Press.

Osborne, A., 1976: *An Introduction to Microcomputers*, vol. 2. Berkeley, CA: Osborne.

Oxford English Dictionary, 1989: Revised edition. Oxford: Clarendon Press.

Padegs, A., 1964: "Channel Design Considerations." *IBM Systems J*, **3**, 2: 165–80.

Padegs, A., 1968: "Structural Aspects of the System/360 Model 85, III Extensions to Floating-Point Architecture." *IBM Systems J*, **7**, 1: 22–29.

Padegs, A., 1981: "System/360 and Beyond." *IBM J of Res and Dev*, **25**, 5 (Sep.): 377-90.

Padegs, A., 1983: "System/370 Extended Architecture: Design Considerations." *IBM J of Res and Dev*, **27**, 3: 198–205.

Padegs, A., B.B. Moore, R.M. Smith, and W. Buchholz, 1988: "The IBM System/370 Vector Architecture: Design Considerations." *IEEE Transaction on Computers*, **37**, 5: 509–20.

Pakin, S., 1972: *APL\360 Reference Manual.* 2nd ed. Chicago: Science Research Associates.

Palmer, J., 1980: "The Intel 8087 Numeric Data Processor." *Proc., 7th Ann Int Symp on Comp Arch, Comput Archit News*, **8**, 3: 174–81.

Parmelee, R.P., T.I. Peterson, C.C. Tillman, and D.J. Hatfield, 1972: "Virtual Storage and Virtual Machine Concepts." *IBM Systems J*, **11**, 2: 99–130.

Padegs, A., 1983: "System/370 Extended Architecture: Design Considerations." *IBM J of Res and Dev*, **27**, 3: 198–205.

Padegs, A., B.B. Moore, R.M. Smith, and W. Buchholz, 1988: "The IBM System/370 Vector Architecture: Design Considerations." *IEEE Transaction on Computers*, **37**, 5: 509–20.

Pakin, S., 1972: *APL\360 Reference Manual.* 2nd ed. Chicago: Science Research Associates.

Palmer, J., 1980: "The Intel 8087 Numeric Data Processor." *Proc., 7th Ann Int Symp on Comp Arch, Comput Archit News*, **8**, 3: 174–81.

Parmelee, R.P., T.I. Peterson, C.C. Tillman, and D.J. Hatfield, 1972: "Virtual Storage and Virtual Machine Concepts." *IBM Systems J*, **11**, 2: 99–130.

Parnas, D.L., 1972: "On the Criteria to Be Used in Decomposing Systems into Models." *Comm. ACM.* **15**, 12: 1053–58.

Patterson, D.A. and D.R. Ditzel, 1980: "The Case for the Reduced Instruction Set Computer." *Comput Archit News*, **8**, 6 (Oct.): 25–33.

Patterson, D.A. and C.H. Sequin, 1981: "RISC I: A Reduced Instruction Set Architecture." *Comput Archit News*, **9**, 3: 443–58.

Patterson, D.A. and C.H. Sequin, 1982: "A VLSI RISC." *Computer*, **15**, 9: 8–21.

Patterson, D.A., 1985: "Reduced Instruction Set Computers." *CACM*, **28**, 1: 8–21.

Pawlak, Z. and A. Wakulicz, 1957: "Use of Expansions with a Negative Basis in the Arithmometer of a Digital Computer." *Bulletin de l'Académie Polonaise des Sciences*, **5**, 3: 232–36.

Pawlak, Z., 1959: "An Electronic Digital Computer Based on the '−2' System." *Bulletin de l'Académie Polonaise des Sciences*, **7**, 12: 713–21.

Phelps, B.E., 1980: "Early Electronic Computer Developments at IBM." *IEEE Ann Hist Comput*, **2**, 3: 253–67.

Phister, M., Jr., 1958: *Logical Design of Digital Computers.* New York: Wiley.

Pickstone, J.V. and G. Bowker, 1993: "The Manchester Heritage." *IEEE Ann Hist Comput*, **15**, 3: 7–8.

Piepho, R.S. and W.S. Wu, 1989: "A Comparison of RISC Architectures." *IEEE Micro*, **9**, 4: 51–62.

Polivka, R.P. and S. Pakin, 1975: *APL: The Language and Its Usage.* Englewood Cliffs, NJ: Prentice-Hall.

Pooch, U.W. and A. Nieder, 1973: "A Survey of Indexing Techniques for Sparse Matrices." *Compt Surv*, **5**, 2: 109–33.

Porter, R.E., 1960: "The RW-400—A New Polymorphic Data System." *Datamation*, **6**, 1: 8–14.

Pugh, E.W., L.R. Johnson, and J.H. Palmer, 1991: *IBM's 360 and Early 370 Systems.* Cambridge, MA: MIT Press.

Pugh, E.W., 1995: *Building IBM: Shaping an Industry and Its Technology.* Cambridge, MA: MIT Press.

Radin, G., 1982: "The 801 Minicomputer." *Comput Archit News*, **10**, 2: 39–47.

Radin, G., 1983: "The 801 Minicomputers." *IBM J of Res and Dev*, **27**, 3: 237–46.

Rafiquzzaman, M., 1990: *Microprocessors and Microcomputer-Based System Design.* Boca Raton, FL: CRC Press.

Ralston, A., 1980. "Random Number Generation on the Ferranti Mark 1." *Ann Hist Comput*, **2**, 3: 270–71.

Randell, B., ed., 1973: *The Origins of Digital Computers—Selected Papers.* Berlin: Springer-Verlag.

Randell, B., ed., 1975: *The Origins of Digital Computers—Selected Papers.* 2nd ed. New York: Springer-Verlag.

Remington Rand Univac, 1958: *The Univac Scientific Computer Model 1103A Programming Manual.* Form U 1519A. Sperry Rand Corporation.

Renwick, W. and A.J. Cole, 1971: *Digital Storage Systems.* London: Chapman and Hall.

Rice, R., 1971: "SYMBOL—A Major departure from Classic Software Dominated by Von Neumann Computing Systems." *Proc., AFIPS Spring Joint Computer Conf.,* **38**: 575–88.

Richards, R.K., 1955: *Arithmetic Operations in Digital Computers.* Princeton, NJ: Van Norstrand.

Rosin, R.F., ed., 1987: "Special Issue: The Burroughs B5000." *Ann Hist Comput*, **9**, 1: 6–93.

Ross, H.D., Jr., 1953: "The Arithmetic Element of the IBM Type 701 Computer." *Proc. IRE* **41**, 10: 1287–94.

Royse, D., 1957: "The IBM 650 RAMAC System Disk Storage Operation." *Proc., IRE–AIEE–ACM 1957 Western Joint Computer Conf.,* **11**: 43–49.

Ruggiero, J.F. and D.A. Corriell, 1969: "An Auxiliary Processing System for Array Calculations." *IBM Systems J*, **8**, 2: 118–35.

Russell, R.D., 1978: "The PDP-11: A Case Study of How *Not* to Design Condition Codes." *Proc., 5th Ann Int Symp on Comp Arch, Comput Archit News*, **6**, 7: 190–94.

Russell, R.M., 1978: "The Cray-1 Computer System." *CACM*, **21**, 1 (Jan.): 63–72. Reprinted in Siewiorek, Bell, and Newell [1982], 743–52.

Saltzer, J.H. and M.D. Schroeder, 1975: "The Protection of Information in Computer Systems." *Proc. IEEE*, **63**, 9: 1278–1308.

Sammet, J.E., 1969: *Programming Languages: History and Fundamentals.* Englewood Cliffs, NJ: Prentice-Hall.

Sammet, J.E., 1976: "Roster of Programming Languages for 1974–1975." *Comm. ACM* **15**, 7: 601–10.

Scalzi, C.A., A.G. Ganey, and R.J. Schmalz, 1989: "Enterprise Systems Architecture/370: An Architecture for Multiple Virtual Space Access and Authorization." *IBM Systems J*, **28**, 1: 15–38.

Schroeder, M.D. and J.H. Saltzer, 1972: "A Hardware Architecture for Implementation Protection Rings." *CACM*, **15**, 3: 157–70.

Schwartz, H.R., 1981: "The Early Years of Computing in Switzerland." *IEEE Ann Hist Comput*, **3**, 2: 241–62.

Seeber, R.R., 1960: "Associative Self-Sorting Memory." *Proc., IRE–AIEE–ACM 1960 Eastern Joint Computer Conf.,* **18**: 179–87.

Shannon, C.E., 1938: "A Symbolic Analysis of Relay and Switching Circuits." *Transactions of the AIEE* **57**: 713–23.

Shannon, C.E. and W. Weaver, 1949: *The Mathematical Theory of Communication.* Urbana, IL: University of Illinois Press.

Siewiorek, D.P., C.G. Bell, and A. Newell, 1982: *Computer Structures: Principles and Examples.* New York: McGraw-Hill.

Sites, R.L., 1978: "An Analysis of the Cray-1 Computer." *Proc., 5th Ann Int Symp on Comp Arch, Comput Archit News*, **6**, 7: 101–06.

Sites, R.L., 1993: "The Alpha AXP Architecture." *CACM*, **36**, 2 (Feb.): 33–44.

Smith, A.J., 1982: "Cache Memories." *Computer Surveys*, **14**, 3: 473–530.

Smith, F.D., 1978: *Models of Multiprocessing for Transaction-Oriented Computer Systems.* Ph.D. Dissertation, University of North Carolina, Chapel Hill.

Smith, R.E., 1989. "A Historical Overview of Computer Architecture." *Ann Hist Comput*, **10**, 4: 277–303.

Smith, W.R. et al., 1971: "SYMBOL—A Large Experimental System Exploring Major Hardware Replacement of Software." *Proc., AFIPS Spring Joint Computer Conf.*, **38**: 601–16.

Sneeringer, J., 1975: *A Dynamic-Type Programming Language That Allows Type Control.* Ph.D. Dissertation, University of North Carolina, Chapel Hill.

Snyder, S.S., 1977: *Influence of U.S. Cryptologic Organizations on the Digital Computer Industry.* No. SRH 003, National Archives.

Speiser, A.P., 1980: "The Relay Calculator Z4." *Ann Hist Comput*, **2**, 3: 242–45.

Speiser, A.P., 1989: Letter to the authors.

Staff of the Computation Laboratory, 1946: "The Manual of Operation of the Automatic Sequence Controlled Calculator." *Annals of the Computation Laboratory of Harvard University*, **1**. Cambridge, MA.: Harvard University Press. Reprinted with additional foreword and introduction as volume 8 of the Charles Babbage Institute Reprint Series. Cambridge, MA: MIT Press, 1985.

Stallings, W., 1986a: "An Annotated Bibliography on Reduced Instruction Set Computers." *Comput Archit News*, **14**, 5:13–19.

Stallings, W., 1986b: *Reduced Instruction Set Computers.* New York: IEEE Computer Society Press.

Stanga, D.C., 1967: "UNIVAC 1108 Multiprocessor System." *Proc., AFIPS Spring Joint Computer Conf.*, **30**: 67–74.

Steel, T.B., ed., 1966: *Formal Language Description Languages for Computer Programming.* Amsterdam: North Holland.

Sterbenz, P.H., 1974: *Floating-Point Computation.* Englewood Cliffs, NJ: Prentice-Hall.

Stern, N., 1981: *from ENIAC to UNIVAC: An Appraisal of the Eckert-Mauchly Computers.* Bedford, MA: Digital Press.

Stevens, L.D., 1952: "Engineering Organization of Input and Output for the IBM 701 Electronic Data Processing Machine." *Proc., AIEE–IRE–ACM Joint Computer Conf.*, **2**: 81–85.

Stevens, W.Y., 1958: *A Study of Decision Operations in Digital Computers.* Unpublished Ph.D. dissertation, Cornell University.

Stevens, W.Y., 1964: "The Structure of System/360: Part II: System Implementations." *IBM Systems J*, **3**, 2: 136–42.

Stevenson, D.A. and W.H. Vermillion, 1968: "Core Storage as a Slave Memory for Disk Storage Devices." In *Proc., IFIP '68*, F86–F91.

Stevenson, D., 1981: "A Proposed Standard for Binary Floating-Point Arithmetic." *Computer*, **14**, 3: 51–62.

Stiefel, E., 1951: Letter to Zuse. Document 017/002 Computer archive GMD, Schloss Birlinghoven, Sankt Augustin, Germany.

Stone, H.S., ed., 1975: *Introduction to Computer Architecture*. Chicago: Science Research Associates.

Stone, H.S., 1987: *High-Performance Computer Architecture*. Reading, MA.: Addison-Wesley.

Strecker, W.D., 1971: "An Analysis of the Instruction Execution Rate in Certain Computing Structures." Ph.D. dissertation, Carnegie-Mellon University.

Strecker, W.D., 1978: "VAX11/780: A Virtual Address Extension to the DEC PDP11 Family." Bell, Mudge, and McNamara, [1978], Chapter 17.

Strecker, W.D., 1983: "Transient Behavior of Cache Memories." *ACM Trans Comput Syst*, **1**, 4: 281–93.

Stritter, E. and T. Gunter, 1979: "A Microprocessor Architecture for a Changing World: The Motorola 68000." *Computer*, **12**, 2: 43–52.

Svigals, J., 1959: "IBM 7070 Data Processing System." *Proc., IRE–AIEE–ACM 1959 Western Joint Computer Conf.*, **15**: 222–31.

Svoboda, A., 1957: "Rational Number System of Residual Classes." *Info Proc Machines*, **5**: 1–29.

Swartzlander, E.E., Jr., 1976: *Computer Design Development: Principal Papers*. Rochelle Park, NJ: Hayden.

Sweeney, D.W., 1965: "An Analysis of Floating-Point Addition." *IBM Systems J*, **4**, 1: 31–41.

Sweet, R., 1982: "Static Analysis of the Mesa Instruction Set." *First Symposium on Architectural Support for Programming Languages and Operating Systems, Comput Archit News*, **10**, 2: 158–66.

Tanenbaum, A., 1978: "Implications of Structured Programming for Machine Architecture." *CACM*, **21**, 3: 237–46.

Thomas, G. and A.G. Necula, 1977: "Multidimensional Array Accessing in the MU5 Computer." *Proc., IFIPS Congress*, 655–59.

Thompson, J.R., 1986: "The CRAY-1, the CRAY-XMP, the CRAY-2 and Beyond: The Supercomputers of Cray Research." In Fernbach [1986], 69–81.

Thornton, J.E., 1964: "Parallel Operation in the Control Data 6600." *Proc., AFIPS Fall Joint Computer Conf.*, **26**: 33–40 (also in Swartzlander [1976], 277–84).

Thornton, J.E., 1970: *Design of a Computer—The CDC 6600*. Glenview, IL: Scott, Foresman.

Thornton, J.E., 1980: "The CDC 6600 Project." *IEEE Ann Hist Comput*, **2**, 4: 338–48.

Thurber, K.J. and L.D. Wald, 1975: "Associative and Parallel Processors." *Compt Surv*, **7**, 4: 215–55.

Thurber, K.J., 1976: *Large Scale Computer Architecture*. Rochelle Park, NJ: Hayden.

Tjaden, G.S. and M.S. Flynn, 1970: "Detection and Parallel Execution of Independent Instructions." *IEEE Trans on Comp*, **C-19**, 10: 889–95.

Tomash, E. and A.A. Cohen, 1979: "The Birth of an ERA: Engineering Research Associates, Inc. 1946–1955." *IEEE Ann Hist Comput*, **1**, 2: 83–97.

Toong, H.D. and A. Gupta, 1981: "An Architectural Comparison of Contemporary 16-bit Microprocessors." *IEEE Micro*, **1**: 26–37.

Tovey, S.D.F., Sir, 1950: "Johann Sebastian Bach." In *Encyclopædia Britannica*, ed. W. Yust. Chicago: Encyclopædia Britannica, **2**: 869–75.

Tucker, S.G., 1967: "Microprogram Control for System/360." *IBM Systems J*, **6**, 4: 222–41.

Tucker, S.G., 1986: "The IBM 3090: An Overview." *IBM Systems J*, **25**, 1: 4–19.

Turn, R., 1974: *Computers of the 1980's*. New York: Columbia University Press.

Univac Corporation, 1958: *The Univac Scientific 1103A Programming Manual*, Form U 1519A.

Univac Corporation, undated: *Univac Scientific Computing System Model 1103A*, Form EL338.

Van Horn, E.C., 1966: "Computer Design for Asynchronously Reproducible Multiprocessing." Technical Report MAC34. Cambridge, MA: MIT Press.

Van der Poel, W.L., 1952: "A Simple Electronic Digital Computer." *Applied Scientific Research*, **B.2**: 367–400.

Van der Poel, W.L., 1956, 1962: *The Logical Principles of Some Simple Computers*. Ph.D. Thesis, University of Amsterdam. Reprinted, The Hague, The Netherlands: Excelsior.

Van der Poel, W.L., 1959: "ZEBRA, A Simple Binary Computer." *Proc. ICIP* (UNESCO, Paris), 361–65. Reprinted in Bell and Newell [1971], 200–04.

Van der Poel, W.L., 1962a: *The Logical Principles of Some Simple Computers*. Amsterdam: Excelsior.

Van der Poel, W.L., 1962b: "Micro-Programming and Trickology." W. Hoffmann, ed., *Digitale Informationswandler*. Braunschweig: Vieweg, 269–311.

Van der Poel, W.L., 1988: "Early Dutch Computer." *Ann Hist Comput*, **10**, 3: 221.

Van der Poel, W.L., 1990, 1992: Letters to the authors.

Vissers, C.A., 1977: *Interface: Definition, Design, and Description of the Relation of Digital System Parts*. Ph.D. Dissertation, Technische Hogeschool Twente, Enschede, The Netherlands.

Von Neumann, J., 1946: See Burks et al. [1946].

Von Neumann, J., 1963: *Design of Computers, Theory of Automata, and Numerical Analysis*. In A.H. Taub, series ed., *Collected Works of John von Neumann*, **5**. New York: Pergamon Press.

Von Neumann, J., 1993: "First Draft of a Report on the EDVAC (with typos corrected and references fixed by Michael D. Godfrey." *IEEE Ann Hist Comput*, **15**, 4: 27–75.

Wadey, W.G., 1960: "Floating-Point Arithmetics." *JACM* **7**, 3: 129–39.

Ware, W.H., ed., 1960: *Soviet Computer Technology—1959*, RM-2541. Santa Monica, CA: The RAND Corp.

Watson, W.J., 1972: "The TI ASC—A Highly Modular and Flexible Super Computer Architecture." *Proc., AFIPS Fall Joint Computer Conf.*, **41**, 1: 221–28.

Weber, H., 1967: "A Microprogrammed Implementation of EULER on the IBM System/360 Model 30." *CACM*, **10**, 9: 549–58.

Weik, M.H., 1961: "A Third Survey of Domestic Electronic Digital Computing Systems." AD-253212 (PB 171265). Ballistic Res. Lab., Aberdeen Proving Ground.

Wheeler, D.J., 1992: "The EDSAC Programming Systems." *IEEE Ann Hist Comput*, **14**, 4: 34–40.

Whitehead, A.N. and B. Russell, 1910–1913: *Principia Mathematica*. Cambridge, UK: Cambridge University Press.

Wiecek, C., 1982: "A Case Study of VAX-11 Instruction Set Usage for Compiler Execution." *Symposium on Architectural Support for Programming Languages and Operating Systems, Comput Archit News*, **10**, 2: 177–84.

Wilkes, M.V., 1949: "Contribution to a Discussion." *Report of a Conf. on High Speed Automatic Calculating Machines* (Cambridge, UK: 22–29 June 1949), 126–28.

Wilkes, M.V. and W. Renwick, 1949a: "The EDSAC." *Report of a Conf. on High Speed Automatic Calculating Machines* (Cambridge, UK: 22–29 June 1949), 9–12. Reprinted in Randell [1973], 389–93.

Wilkes, M.V. and W. Renwick, 1949b: "The EDSAC, An Electronic Calculating Machine." *J of Scientific Instrumentation*, **26**: 385–91.

Wilkes, M.V., 1951: "The Best Way to Design an Automatic Calculating Machine." *Manchester University Computer Inaugural Conf.*, 16–21.

Wilkes, M.V., D.J. Wheeler, and S. Gill, 1951, 1959: *The Preparation of Programs for an Electronic Digital Computer*. Reading, MA: Addison-Wesley.

Wilkes, M.V., 1952: "The EDSAC Computer." *Review of Electronic Computers, Proc., AIEE-IRE Joint Computer Conf.*, 79–83.

Wilkes, M.V. and J.B. Stringer, 1953: "Microprogramming and the Design of the Control Circuits in an Electronic Digital Computer." *Proc., Cambridge Philosophical Society*, **49**, 2: 230–38.

Wilkes, M.V., 1965: "Slave Memories and Dynamic Storage Allocation." *IEEE Transactions on Electronic Computers*, **EC-14**, 2: 270–71.

Wilkes, M.V., 1969: "The Growth and Interest in Microprogramming: A Literature Survey." *Compt Surv*, **1**, 3: 139–45.

Wilkes, M.V., 1972: *Time-Sharing Computer Systems*. 2nd ed. New York: American Elsevier.

Wilkes, M.V., 1982: "Hardware Support for Memory Protection." *First Symposium on Architectural Support for Programming Languages and Operating Systems, Comput Archit News*, **10**, 2: 107–16.

Wilkes, M.V., 1985: *Memoirs of a Computer Pioneer*. Cambridge, MA: MIT Press.

Wilkes, M.V., 1992: "EDSAC 2." *IEEE Ann Hist Comput*, **14**, 4: 49–56.

Wilkinson, J.H., 1963: *Rounding Errors in Algebraic Processes*. Englewood Cliffs, NJ: Prentice-Hall.

Williams, F.C. and T. Kilburn, 1948: "Electronic Digital Computers." *Nature*, **162**: 487.

Williams, F.C. and T. Kilburn, 1952: "The University of Manchester Computing Machine." *Proc., AIEE-IRE Joint Computer Conf.*, 57–61.

Wilner, W.T., 1972: "Design of the Burroughs B1700." *Proc., AFIPS Fall Joint Computer Conf.*, **41**, 1: 489–97.

Wirth, N., 1976: *Algorithms + Data Structures = Programs*. Englewood Cliffs, NJ: Prentice-Hall.

Witt, B.I., 1966: "The Functional Structure of Operating System/360: Job and Task Management." *IBM Systems J*, **5**, 1: 12–29.

Wolczko, M. and I. Williams, 1994: "The Influence of the Object-Oriented Language Model on a Supporting Architecture." In Lilja and Bird [1994], 223–47.

Woods, J.V. and A.T.T. Wheen, 1983: "MU6P: An Advanced Microprocessor Architecture." *Computer J*, **26**, 3: 208–17.

Yang, J.H. and J. Anderson, 1995: "A Fast, Scalable Mutual Exclusion Algorithm." *Distributed Computing*, **9**, 1 (Aug.): 51–60.

Yau, S.S.S. and Y.C. Liu, 1973: "Error Correction in Redundant Residue Number Systems." *IEEE Trans on Comp*, **C-22**, 1: 5–11.

Yohe, J.M., 1973: "Roundings in Floating-Point Arithmetic." *IEEE Trans on Comp*, **C-22**, 6: 577–86.

Yuen, C.K., 1975: "On the Floating-Point Representation of Complex Numbers." *IEEE Transaction on Computers*, **C-24**, 8: 761–66.

Zaks, R., 1978: *A Microprogrammed APL Implementation*. Berkeley: Sybex.

Zemanek, H., 1965: "Alphabets and Codes." *Elektronische Rechenanlagen*, **7**, 5: 239–58.

Zuse, K., 1936: "Method for Automatic Execution of Calculations with the Aid of Computers." In Randell [1975], 159–66.

Zuse, K., 1962: "The Outline of Computer Development from Mechanics to Electronics." Translation reprinted in Randell [1973], 171–86.

Zuse, K., 1980: "Installation of the German Computer Z4 in Zürich in 1950." *IEEE Ann Hist Comput*, **2**, 3: 239–41.

Zuse, K., 1991: "Computerarchitektur aus damaliger und heutiger Sicht" ("A past and present view of computer architecture"), Technical report of a seminar talk (in German with English translation), Abteilung für Informatik, Eidgenössische Technische Hochschule Zürich.

Name Index

Machine Index

Bold denotes a major treatment of a particular machine. Italics indicate figures dedicated to a particular machine. Incidental references to machines, including tables that illustrates several machines, are set in roman. Figure number 0 denotes a frontispiece, as in 14-0.

Subject Index

Boldface designates definition or substantial treatments.